KT-582-291

BROMLEY LIBRARIES

3 0128 02234 0395

ENSER'S FILMED BOOKS AND PLAYS

ENSER'S FILMED BOOKS AND PLAYS

A List of Books and Plays from which Films have been Made,
1928–2001

Compiled by
ELLEN BASKIN

BROMLEY PUBLIC LIBRARIES	
02234039	
Cypher	13.03.04
	£60.00
BECREF	

ASHGATE

© A.G.S. Enser 1968, 1971, 1972, 1975, 1985, 1987
© Ashgate Publishing Limited, 1993, 2003

All rights reserved. No part of this publication may be reproduced, stored in a retrieval system, or transmitted in any form or by any means, electronic, mechanical, photocopying, recording, or otherwise without the prior permission of the publisher.

Published by
Ashgate Publishing Limited
Gower House
Croft Road
Aldershot
Hants GU11 3HR
England

Ashgate Publishing Company
Suite 420
101 Cherry Street
Burlington, VT 05401-4405
USA

British Library Cataloguing in Publication Data

Enser's filmed books and plays : a list of books and plays
    from which films have been made 1928–2001. – 6th ed.
    1.Film adaptations – Bibliography
    I.Baskin, Ellen II.Enser, A.G.S. (Alfred George Sidney), 1915– III.Filmed
    books and plays
    011.3'7

Library of Congress Cataloging-in-Publication Data

Baskin, Ellen.
    Enser's filmed books and plays : a list of books and plays from which
films have been made 1928–2001 / edited by Ellen Baskin. – 6th ed.
        p. cm.
    Rev. ed. of: Filmed books and plays / by A.G.S. Enser. 1987.
    Includes index.
        ISBN 0-7546-0878-6 (alk. paper)
        1. Film adaptations – Bibliography. I. Enser, A. G. S. Filmed books
    and plays. II. Title.

Z5784.M9B385 2002
[PN1997.85]
016.79143'6–dc21

                                                                2002028174

This book is printed on acid-free paper.

ISBN 0 7546 0878 6

Typeset by Manton Typesetters, Louth, Lincolnshire, UK.
Printed and bound in Great Britain by MPG Books Ltd, Bodmin, Cornwall.

CONTENTS

INTRODUCTION
—————— FROM THE COMPILER ——————

Enser's Filmed Books and Plays 1928–2001 remains the only comprehensive printed compendium of motion picture and television adaptations of books and plays. This latest edition includes several thousand new listings, covering the years 1992–2001 and representing live-action and animated feature films and made-for-television serials and miniseries.

An essential reference tool for the serious film buff or literary researcher, *Enser's Filmed Books and Plays* includes films made in the United States, Great Britain, Canada, Australia and non-English-speaking countries. The cross-indexed information makes it easy to trace a particular film, a particular author or, where applicable, the various adaptations of a particular book or play.

Selection criteria established earlier have remained in place in this edition. Any close adaptation of a book or play has been included, but we have excluded titles that were so loosely based on the original as to be unrecognizable. In those instances where a film's release year was different in the US from the UK, the earlier date has been taken, along with the appropriate country of origin. On a number of occasions a filmed version of a stage play was itself based on another work. In such cases, an attempt has been made to include the original source and the stage version.

In this edition, we elected not to include notations for video availability. Virtually all movies released in recent years are ultimately marketed in this format, along with a number of made-for-television titles (especially those produced for cable networks), but general accessibility to older titles often becomes more difficult, as these go 'out of print' in the same way as books. Also, new DVD technology is just now catching up with both contemporary and classic film titles, so an accurate up-to-date listing would have been impossible to compile. A recommended resource for checking video/DVD availability for any film title is the Internet Movie Database (IMDb.com).

For a good portion of the twentieth century, motion picture production was dominated by a small group of powerful studios – names still familiar today, such as Universal, Paramount, MGM, Columbia and Warner Bros. These companies still exist, but they are no longer the only means of film production. Far from it, in fact. Studios still produce feature and made-for-television films – more made for cable than for network broadcast these days – but they also serve in large part as distributors for independently produced projects.

As the major film studios lost their iron-clad grip on production and distribution, the independent film earned new prominence and respect. Independent films, which can range from a very low-budget movie to a multi-million dollar enterprise, may be financed by a number of companies, often from a number of different countries. There are also several independent companies which have achieved distinction on both the big and small screens in recent years, such as Miramax and HBO. Anyone who has been to the movies in recent years can recall seeing a string of company names leading off a film's opening credits (and that doesn't even include the 'a film by' credit often awarded to a director and above-the-title actor and actress listings!). For space considerations, we have listed only one or two production entities for each new title in this edition of *Enser's Filmed Books and Plays*, endeavouring to choose those most recognizable or traceable.

It should also be noted that in a number of instances independent companies – which sometimes were formed to produce a single movie – have ceased to exist by the time this volume has gone to print, so a particular company may be difficult or impossible to trace. This may be especially true for older listings which have been carried over from earlier editions. Again, the internet, via both the Internet Movie Database or a more general search, can be a valuable tool for tracking further information about any individual title.

Enser's Filmed Books and Plays aims to be correct and complete up to December 2001. The publishers would encourage readers to inform us of any missing items, so that they can be incorporated into a future edition. Also welcome would be general comments and suggestions about the structure and content of the book.

Ellen Baskin
Santa Monica

HOW TO USE THIS BOOK

The book is divided into three main sections with additional lists and indexes.

Film Title Index

This listing is the heart of the book, assuming that the reader has the name of a film in mind and wants to find out certain basic facts about it; but more importantly, whether it is based on a book or a play, which they can then read.

The index is arranged alphabetically under the film's title and gives much information about the film and its published source, such as country of origin, the director, distribution or production company, whether the title of the book and film are different, or whether the filmed version is perhaps a musical, a made-for-TV series, or available on video.

Remember that the articles 'The', 'A' or 'An' are not taken as being part of the film's main title, but are placed at the end of the title. Foreign language films are listed most frequently under their English titles.

An example of an entry from the Film Title Index is shown below. The sample entry is repeated at the beginning of the Film Title Index.

Title of film ———	**Kiss Me Kate** ——————— Date of release
Studio name and ——— country of origin	MGM (US) 1953 dir. George Sidney —— **M** ~ Director's name
	MILBERG (US) 1958 dir. George Schaefer
British, etc. title, ——— where applicable	GB title. —— Author and title
	TV(US) ~ of book (if title is
Abbreviations as ——— listed below	**Shakespeare, W.** *Taming of the Shrew, The* different from **P** film title)
Means adapted ——— from a play	**Spewack, S. and Spewack, B.** ——— Author of film **P**

Author Index

This listing is for the use of readers who want to see whether their favourite authors' books have been made into a feature film or a film for television.

The Index is arranged alphabetically by author with a further alphabetical arrangement of each author's works.

An example of an entry from the Author Index appears below. The sample entry is repeated at the beginning of the Author Index.

Author's name —— **Spewack, B. and Spewack, S.** —— Means adapted
Book or play title —— **Kiss Me Kate** from a play
P —— Film title (if
Studio name and —— MGM (US) 1953 dir. George Sidney different)
country of origin **M**
MILBERG (US) 1958 dir. George Schaefer —— Director's name
British, etc. title **TV(US)**
(if different) GB title: —— Date of release
—— Abbreviations as
listed below

Change of Title Index

It happens very often that a new title is given to a book or play when it appears as a film. This index pulls out all those books and plays where this has occurred.

An example of a Change of Title Index entry is shown below. The sample entry is repeated at the beginning of the Change of Title Index.

Book or play title —— **Taming of the Shrew, The**
Author's name —— Shakespeare, W.
Kiss Me Kate —— Film title
Studio name, —— MGM (US) 1953 dir. George Sidney —— Director's name
location and MILBERG (US) 1958 dir. George Schaefer
release date GB title:
British, etc. title
(if different)

In addition to these three main sections there are three supplementary indexes which reflect reader interest in made-for-TV movies, miniseries and serials, musical films and animated films. Each of these indexes is arranged in alphabetical order and the reader can then refer back to the main entry for that film to obtain details of it and its original published source material.

Two lists which give general help to an understanding of the book are included. The *List of Abbreviated Production and Distribution Company Names*, at the end of the book, will be useful for identification purposes. It has proved difficult to keep an exact record of companies within this fast-moving industry, particularly with regard to the production of films made for television or foreign language films, and the companies linked to some of the older films. However, wherever possible the abbreviated name and full name have been supplied. The *List of Country Abbreviations* (overleaf) lists the names of the countries in which films have been made, both in their abbreviated form (as it appears in the main entries) and in full.

COUNTRY ABBREVIATIONS

Alg	Algeria	Jap	Japan
Arg	Argentina	Kor	Korea
Aus	Australia	S. Kor	South Korea
Austria	Austria	Lux	Luxembourg
Bel	Belgium	Mex	Mexico
Bra	Brazil	Neth	Netherlands
Can	Canada	Nor	Norway
China	China	NZ	New Zealand
Col	Colombia	Pan	Panama
Czech	Czechoslovakia	Peru	Peru
Den	Denmark	Phil	Philippines
Eire	Eire	Pol	Poland
Fr	France	Port	Portugal
GB	Great Britain	Rus	Russia
Ger	Germany	SA	South Africa
W. Ger	West Germany	Sp	Spain
Gre	Greece	Swe	Sweden
HK	Hong Kong	Switz	Switzerland
Hun	Hungary	Tai	Taiwan
Ice	Iceland	Tur	Turkey
Ind	India	US	United States of America
Iran	Iran		
Ire	Ireland	USSR	USSR
Israel	Israel	Yugo	Yugoslavia
It	Italy	Zam	Zambia

FILM TITLE INDEX

Title of film ——— **Kiss Me Kate** ————————— Date of release

Studio name and ——— MGM (US) 1953 dir. George Sidney ⌐ Director's name
country of origin **M**
                  MILBERG (US) 1958 dir. George Schaefer

British, etc. title, ——— GB title. ———————————— Author and title
where applicable **TV(US)** of book (if title is
                              different from
Abbreviations as ⌐ **Shakespeare, W.** *Taming of the Shrew, The* film title)
listed below **P**

Means adapted ⌐ **Spewack, S. and Spewack, B.** ————— Author of film
from a play **P**

A = Animated film   **TV** (GB, US, etc.) = Made for British,
Ch = Made for children   American, etc. television
M = Based on a musical   **TVSe** = Made-for-television series or miniseries

Aaron Slick from Punkin Crick
PAR (US) 1952 dir. Claude Binyon
GB title: Marshmallow Moon
Benjamin, W.
P

Abdication, The
WAR (GB) 1974 dir. Anthony Harvey
Wolff, R.
P

Abduction of St. Anne
Q. MARTIN (US) 1975 dir. Harry Falk
TV(US)
McMahon, T. P. *Issue of the Bishop's Blood, The*

Abe Lincoln in Illinois
RKO (US) 1940 dir. John Cromwell
COMPASS (US) 1964
dir. George Schaefer
TV(US)
Sherwood, R. E. *Abe Lincoln of Illinois*
P

Abie's Irish Rose
UA (US) 1952 dir. Edward A. Sutherland
Nichols, A.
P

About Face
WAR (US) 1952 dir. Roy del Ruth
Monks, J. and Finklehoffe, F. F.
Brother Rat
P

About Last Night ...
TRISTAR (US) 1986 dir. Edward Zwick
Mamet, D. *Sexual Perversity in Chicago*
P

About Mrs. Leslie
PAR (US) 1954 dir. Daniel Mann
Delmar, V.

Above Suspicion
MGM (US) 1943 dir. Richard Thorpe
MacInnes, H.

Above us the Waves
GFD (GB) 1955 dir. Ralph Thomas
Warren, C. E. T. and Benson, J.

Absolute Power
COL (US) 1997 dir. Clint Eastwood
Baldacci, D.

Absolute Beginners
VIRGIN (GB) 1985 dir. Julien Temple
MacInnes, C.

Absolute Hell
BBC (GB) 1991 dir. Anthony Page
TV(GB)
Ackland, R. *Pink Room, The*
P

Accent on Youth
PAR (US) 1935 dir. Wesley Ruggles
Raphaelson, S.
P

Acceptable Risk
V Z/SERTNER (US/Can) 2001 dir.
William A. Graham
TV(US/Can)

Cook, R.

Accident
MON (GB) 1967 dir. Joseph Losey

Mosley, N.

Accidental Tourist, The
WAR (US) 1988 dir. Lawrence Kasdan

Tyler, A.

Accompanist, The
STUDIO CANAL+ (Fr) 1992 dir. Claude
Miller

Berberova, N.

Account Rendered
RANK (GB) 1957
dir. Peter Graham Scott

Barrington, P.

Accused, The
PAR (US) 1948 dir. William Dieterle

Truesdell, J. *Be Still My Love*

Accused of Murder
REP (US) 1956 dir. Joe Kane

Burnett, W. R. *Vanity Row*

Aces High
EMI (GB/Fr) 1976 dir. Jack Gold

Sherriff, R. C. *Journey's End*
P

Acorn People, The
NBC ENT (US) 1981
dir. Joan Tewkesbury
TV(US)

Jones, R.

Across 110th Street
UA (US) 1972 dir. Barry Shear

Ferris, W.

Across the Bridge
RANK (GB) 1957 dir. Ken Annakin

Greene, G.

Across Five Aprils
LCA (US) 1990 dir. Kevin Meyer
TV(US)

Hunt, I.

Across the Wide Missouri
MGM (US) 1951 dir. William Wellman

De Voto, B.

Act of Love
PAR TV (US) 1980 dir. Jud Taylor
TV(US)

Mitchell, P.

Act of Love
UA (US) 1954 dir. Anatole Litvak

Hayes, A. *Girl on the Via Flaminia, The*

Act of Murder, An
UN (US) 1948 dir. Michael Gordon

Lothar, E. *Mills of God, The*

Act of Vengeance
LORIMAR (US) 1986
dir. John MacKenzie
TV(US)

Armbrister, T.

Action for Slander
UA (GB) 1938 dir. Tim Whelan

Borden, M.

Action in the North Atlantic
WAR (US) 1943 dir. Lloyd Bacon

Gilpatric, G.

Action of the Tiger
MGM (GB) 1957 dir. Terence Young

Wellard, J.

Act of Will
PORTMAN (GB) 1989 dir. Don Sharp
TVSe(GB)
Bradford, B. T.

Act One
WAR (US) 1963 dir. Dore Schary
Hart, M.

Actor's Revenge, An
DAIEI (Jap) 1963 dir. Kon Ichikawa
Otokichi, M.

Actress, The
MGM (US) 1953 dir. George Cukor
Gordon, R. *Years Ago*
P

Ada
MGM (US) 1961 dir. Daniel Mann
Williams, W. *Ada Dallas*

Adam Bede
BBC (GB) 1991 dir. Giles Foster
TV(GB)
Eliot, G.

Adam had Four Sons
COL (US) 1941 dir. Gregory Ratoff
Bonner, C. *Legacy*

Adding Machine, The
RANK (GB) 1968 dir. Jerome Epstein
Rice, E.
P

Address Unknown
COL (US) 1944
dir. William Cameron Menzies
Taylor, K.

Admirable Crichton, The
COL (GB) 1957 dir. Lewis Gilbert
US title: Paradise Lagoon
COMPASS (US) 1968
dir. George Schaefer
TV(US)
Barrie, Sir J. M.
P

Adolf Hitler—My Part in his Downfall
UA (GB) 1972 dir. Norman Cohen
Milligan, S.

Adorable Julia
ETOILE (Austria/Fr) 1962
dir. Alfred Weidenmann
GB title: Seduction of Julia, The
Maugham, W. S.
P

À Double Tour
PARIS/PANI (Fr/It) 1959
dir. Claude Chabrol
Gegauff, P. *Clé de la Rue Saint Nicolas, La*

Advancement of Learning, An
BBC/A&E (GB) 1996 dir. Maurice
Phillips
TV(GB)
Hill, R.

Advance to the Rear
MGM (US) 1964 dir. George Marshall
Chamberlain, W. *Company of Cowards, The*

Adventure
MGM (US) 1945 dir. Victor Fleming
Davis, C. B. *Anointed, The*

Adventure in Iraq
WAR (US) 1943 dir. D. Ross-Lederman
Archer, W. *Green Goddess, The*
P

Adventure in the Hopfields
ABP (GB) 1954 dir. John Guillermin

Lavin, N. and Thorp, M. *Hop Dog, The*

Adventure Island
PAR (US) 1947 dir. Peter Stewart

Stevenson, R. L. *Ebb Tide*

Adventurers, The
PAR (US) 1970 dir. Lewis Gilbert

Robbins, H.

Adventures of Baron Munchausen, The
COL (GB) 1988 dir. Terry Gilliam

Raspe, R. E. *Twelve Adventures of the Celebrated Baron Munchausen*

Adventures of Bullwhip Griffin, The
DISNEY (US) 1965 dir. James Neilson

Fleischman, S. *By the Great Horn Spoon*

Adventures of Captain Fabian, The
REP (US) 1951 dir. William Marshall

Shannon, R. *Fabulous Ann Medlock*

Adventures of Gerard, The
UA (GB) 1970 dir. Jerzy Skolimowski

Doyle, Sir A. C. *Exploits of Brigadier Gerard, The*

Adventures of Hajji Baba, The
FOX (US) 1954 dir. Don Weis

Morier, J. J. *Adventures of Hajji Baba of Ispahan*

Adventures of Huck Finn, The
DISNEY (US) 1993 dir. Stephen Sommers

Twain, M. *Adventures of Huckleberry Finn, The*

Adventures of Huckleberry Finn, The
MGM (US) 1960 dir. Michael Curtiz
TAFT (US) 1981 dir. Jack B. Hively
TV(US)

Twain, M.

Adventures of Martin Eden, The
COL (US) 1942 dir. Sidney Salkow

London, J. *Martin Eden*

Adventures of Pinocchio, The
NEW LINE (US/GB) 1996 dir. Steve Barron
Ch

Collodi, C.

Adventures of Quentin Durward, The
MGM (GB) 1955 dir. Richard Thorpe
US title: Quentin Durward

Scott, Sir W. *Quentin Durward*

Adventures of Robinson Crusoe, The
UA (Mex/US) 1954 dir. Luis Bunuel

Defoe, D. *Robinson Crusoe*

Adventures of Sherlock Holmes, The
FOX (US) 1939 dir. Alfred Werker
GB title: Sherlock Holmes
GRANADA (GB) 1984 dir. Paul Annett
TVSe(GB)

Doyle, Sir A. C.

Adventures of Tom Sawyer, The
UA (US) 1938 dir. Norman Taurog

Twain, M.

Advise and Consent
COL (US) 1962 dir. Otto Preminger

Drury, A.

Advocate's Devil, The
COL TRISTAR (US) 1997 dir. Jeff
Bleckner
TV(US)
Dershowitz, A.

Aerodrome, The
BBC (GB) 1983 dir. Giles Foster
TV(GB)
Warner, R.

Affair in Mind, An
BBC (GB) 1988 dir. Clive Luke
TV(GB)
Rendell, R.

Affairs of Cellini, The
FOX (US) 1934 dir. Gregory La Cava
Mayer, E. J. *Firebrand*
P

Affliction
LARGO (US) 1997 dir. Paul Schrader
Banks, R.

African Queen, The
ROMULUS (US/GB) 1951
dir. John Huston
Forester, C. S.

After All
DIRECTOR'S CIRCLE (US) 1999 dir.
Helaine Head
TV(US)
Emery, L.

After Dark, My Sweet
AVENUE (US) 1990 dir. James Foley
Thompson, J.

After Julius
YTV (GB) 1979 dir. John Glenister
TV(GB)
Howard, E. J.

Aftermath: A Test of Love
COL (US) 1991 dir. Glenn Jordan
TV (US)
Kinder, G. *Victim: The Other Side of
Murder*

After Office Hours
BI (GB) 1935 dir. Thomas Bentley
van Druten, J. *London Wall*
P

**Aftershock: Earthquake in New
York**
HALLMARK (US) 1999 dir. Mikael
Salomon
TVSe(US)
Scarborough, C.

After the Ball
BL (GB) 1957 dir. Compton Bennett
De Frece, Lady *Recollections of Vesta
Tilly*

After the Harvest
ALBERTA (Can) 2001 dir. Jeremy
Podeswa
TV(Can)
Ostenso, M. *Wild Geese*

After Tomorrow
FOX (US) 1932 dir. Frank Borzage
Golden, J. and Strange, H.
P

Against all Odds
COL (US) 1984 dir. Taylor Hackford
Homes, G. *Build My Gallows High*

Agency
CAROLCO (Can) 1981
dir. George Kaczender
Gottlieb, P.

Age of Consent
COL (Aust) 1969 dir. Michael Powell
Lindsay, N.

Age of Innocence, The
RKO (US) 1934 dir. Philip Moeller
COL (US) 1993 dir. Martin Scorsese

Wharton, E.

Agitator, The
BN (GB) 1944 dir. John Harlow

Riley, W. *Peter Pettinger*

Agnes Browne
OCTOBER (US) 1999 dir. Anjelica Huston

O'Carroll, B.

Agnes of God
COL (US) 1985 dir. Norman Jewison

Pielmeier, J.
P

Agony and the Ecstacy, The
FOX (US) 1965 dir. Carol Reed

Stone, I.

Ah, Wilderness!
MGM (US) 1935 dir. Clarence Brown
M. ALBERG (US) 1959
dir. Robert Mulligan
TV(US)

O'Neill, E.
P

Aimee & Jaguar
SENATOR (Ger) 1997 dir. Max Farberbock

Fischer, E.

Air America
TRISTAR (US) 1990
dir. Roger Spottiswoode

Robbins, C.

Air de Famille, Un
STUDIO CANAL+ (Fr) 1996 dir. Cedric Klapisch

Jaoui, A. and Bacri, J.-P.
P

Airport
UN (US) 1970 dir. George Seaton

Hailey, A.

Airspeed
AIRSPEED (US) 1998 dir. Robert Tinnell
TV(US)

Sands, A.

Air Si Pur, Un
FRANCE 2 (Fr) 1997 dir. Yves Angelo

Hamsun, K. *Last Chapter*

Aisuru
NIKKATSU (Jap) 1997 dir. Kei Kumai

Endo, S. *Woman I Abandoned, The*

Akenfield
ANGLIA (GB) 1975 dir. Peter Hall

Blythe, R.

À La Mode
FRANCE 2 (Fr) 1993 dir. Remy Duchemin

Morgieve, R.

Alamo: 13 Days to Glory, The
FRIES (US) 1987 dir. Burt Kennedy
TV(US)

Tinkle, J. L. *Thirteen Days to Glory: The Seige of the Alamo*

Alan and Naomi
TRITON (US) 1992
dir. Sterling van Wagenen

Levoy, M.

À La Place Du Coeur
STUDIO CANAL+ (Fr) 1998 dir. Robert Guediguian

Baldwin, J. *If Beale Street Could Talk*

Alarmist, The
KEY ENT (US) 1997 dir. Evan Dunsky

Reddin, K. *Life During Wartime*
P

Albert RN
DIAL (GB) 1953 dir. Lewis Gilbert
US title: Break to Freedom

Morgan, G.
P

Albuquerque
PAR (US) 1948 dir. Ray Enright

Short, L.

Alex
NZ FILM (Aust/NZ) 1992 dir. Megan Simpson Huberman

Duder, T.

Alex and the Gypsy
TCF (US) 1976 dir. John Korty

Elkin, S. *Bailbondsman, The*

Alex: The Life of a Child
MANDY (US) 1986
dir. Robert Markowitz
TV (US)

Deford, F.

Alexa
BBC (GB) 1982 dir. Laurence Moody
TVSe(GB)

Newman, A.

Alfie
PAR (GB) 1966 dir. Lewis Gilbert

Naughton, B.
P

Alf's Button Afloat
GAINS (GB) 1938 dir. Marcel Varnel

Darlington, W. A. *Alf's Button*

Algiers
WANGER (US) 1938 dir. John Cromwell

d'Ashelbe, R. *Pépé le Moko*

Alibi
CORONA (GB) 1942
dir. Brian Desmond Hirst

Archard, M.

Alibi Ike
WAR (US) 1935 dir. Ray Enright

Lardner, R.

Alice
HEMDALE (Bel/Pol/GB) 1980
dir. Jerry Gruza

Carroll, L. *Alice's Adventures in Wonderland*

Alice Adams
RKO (US) 1933 dir. George Stevens

Tarkington, B.

Alice in Wonderland
PAR (US) 1933 dir. Norman Z. McLeod
Ch
DISNEY (US) 1951
dir. Clyde Geronomi, Hamilton Luske, Wilfred Jackson
A, Ch
M. EVANS (US) 1955
dir. George Schaefer
Ch, TV(US)
COL TV (US) 1985 dir. Harry Harris
Ch, TV(US)
BBC (GB) 1986 dir. Barry Letts
TVSe(GB)
HALLMARK (US) 1999 dir. Nick Willing
Ch, TV(US)

Carroll, L. *Alice's Adventures in Wonderland*

Alice's Adventures in Wonderland
FOX (GB) 1972 dir. William Sterling
A, Ch

Carroll, L.

Alice Through the Looking Glass
PROJECTOR (GB) 1998 dir. John Henderson
TV(GB)

Carroll, L. *Through the Looking Glass and What Alice Found There*

Aliens in the Family
BBC (GB) 1987 dir. Christine Secombe
TVSe(GB)

Mahy, M.

Alive
COL (US) 1993 dir. Frank Marshall

Read, P. P.

Allan Quatermain and the Lost City of Gold
CANNON (US) 1987 dir. Gary Nelson

Haggard, Sir H. R. *Allan Quatermain*

Alla Rivoluzione Sulle Due Cavalli
PANTER (It) 2001 dir. Maurizio Sciarra

Ferrari, M.

All Creatures Great and Small
EMI (GB) 1974 dir. Claude Whatham

Herriot, J. *If Only They Could Talk; It Shouldn't Happen to a Vet; Lord God Made Them All, The*

Allegheny Uprising
RKO (US) 1939 dir. William A. Seiter
GB title: First Rebel, The

Swanson, N. H. *First Rebel, The*

All Fall Down
MGM (US) 1961
dir. John Frankenheimer

Herlihy, J. L.

All for Mary
RANK (GB) 1955 dir. Wendy Toye

Brooke, H. and Bannerman, K.
P

All Hands on Deck
TCF (US) 1961 dir. Norman Taurog
M

Morris, D. R.

Alligator Named Daisy, An
RANK (GB) 1955 dir. J. Lee Thompson

Terrot, C.

All Men are Enemies
FOX (US) 1934 dir. George Fitzmaurice

Aldington, R.

All Men are Mortal
WAR (GB/Neth) 1995 dir. Até de Jong

De Beauvoir, S.

All My Sons
UI (US) 1948 dir. Irving Reis
BBC (GB) 1990 dir. Jack O'Brien
TV(GB)

Miller, A.
P

All Neat in Black Stockings
WAR (GB) 1968
dir. Christopher Morahan

Gaskell, J.

All of Me
PAR (US) 1934 dir. James Flood

Porter, R. *Chrysalis*
P

All of Me
UN (US) 1984 dir. Carl Reiner

Davis, E. *Me Two*

All or Nothing At All
LWT (GB) 1993 dir. Andrew Grieve
TVSe(GB)

Andrews, G.

All Over the Guy
LIONS GATE (US) 2001 dir. Julie Davis

Bucatinsky, D. *I Know You Are, But What Am I?*
P

All Over the Town
RANK (GB) 1948 dir. Derek Twist

Delderfield, R. F.
P

All Passion Spent
BBC (GB) 1986 dir. Martyn Friend
TVSe(GB)

Sackville-West, V.

All Quiet on the Western Front
UN (US) 1930 dir. Lewis Milestone
M. ARCH (US) 1979 dir. Delbert Mann
TV(US)

Remarque, E. M.

All that Money can Buy
RKO (US) 1941 dir. William Dieterle

Benet, S.V. *Devil and Daniel Webster, The*

All the Brothers were Valiant
MGM (US) 1953 dir. Richard Thorpe

Williams, B. A.

All the Fine Young Cannibals
MGM (US) 1960 dir. Michael Anderson

Marshall, R. *Bixby Girls, The*

All the King's Men
COL (US) 1949 dir. Robert Rossen

Warren, R. P.

All the Little Animals
BRIT SCREEN (GB) 1998 dir. Jeremy Thomas

Hamilton, W.

All the President's Men
WAR (US) 1976 dir. Alan J. Pakula

Woodward, R. and Bernstein, C.

All the Pretty Horses
COL (US) 2000 dir. Billy Bob Thornton

McCarthy, C.

All the Rivers Run
Crawford (Aust) 1983 dir. George Miller, Pino Amenta
TV(Aust)

Cato, N.

All the Way Home
PAR (US) 1963 dir. Alex Segal
PAR (US) 1971 dir. Fred Coe
TV (US)

Agee, J. *Death in the Family, A*

All the Way Up
GRANADA/EMI (GB) 1970
dir. James MacTaggart

Turner, D. *Semi Detached*
P

All This and Heaven Too
WAR (US) 1940 dir. Anatole Litvak

Field, R.

Almost Blue
CECCHI (It) 2000 dir. Alex Infascelli

Lucarelli, C.

Almost Dead
DELTA (US) 1996 dir. Ruben Preuss
TV(US)

Valtos, W. *Resurrection*

Almost Golden: The Jessica Savitch Story
ABC PROD (US) 1995 dir. Peter Werner
TV(US)

Blair, G. *Almost Golden*

Almost Married
FOX (US) 1932
dir. W. Cameron Menzies

Soutar, A. *Devil's Triangle*

Aloha Means Goodbye
UN TV (US) 1974 dir. David Lowell Rich
TV(US)

Hintze, N.

11

Along Came a Spider
FOX TV (US) 1970 dir. Lee H. Katzin
TV(US)
Lee, L. *Sweet Poison*

Along Came a Spider
PAR (US) 2001 dir. Lee Tamahori
Patterson, J.

Along Came Jones
UA (US) 1945 dir. Stuart Heisler
LeMay, A. *Useless Cowboy, The*

Alphabet Murders, The
MGM (GB) 1966 dir. Frank Tashlin
Christie, A. *ABC Murders, The*

Altered States
WAR (US) 1980 dir. Ken Russell
Chayefsky, P.

Altri Uomini
DEAN (It) 1997 dir. Claudio Bonivento
Carlucci, A. and Rossetti, P. *Io il Tabano*

Always in My Heart
WAR (US) 1942 dir. Joe Graham
Bennett D. and White, I. *Fly Away Home*
P

Always Outnumbered
HBO (US) 1998 dir. Michael Apted
TV(US)
Mosley, W. *Always Outnumbered, Always Outgunned*

Amadeus
ORION (US) 1984 dir. Milos Forman
Shaffer, P.
P

Amants, Les
NEF (Fr) 1958 dir. Louis Malle
Vivant, D. *Point de Lendemain*

Amateur, The
FOX (Can) 1982 dir. Charles Jarrot
Littell, R.

Amateur, El
ALEPH (Arg) 2000 dir. Juan Bautista Stagnaro
Dayub, M.

Amateur Gentlemen, The
UA (GB) 1936 dir. Thornton Freeland
Farnol, J.

Amazing Dr. Clitterhouse, The
WAR (US) 1938 dir. Anatole Litvak
Lyndon, B.
P

Amazing Howard Hughes, The
EMI TV (US) 1977
dir. William A. Graham
TVSe(US)
Dietrich, W. and Thomas, B. *Howard: The Amazing Mr. Hughes*

Amazing Mr Blunden, The
HEMDALE (GB) 1972
dir. Lionel Jeffries
Ch
Barber, A. *Ghosts, The*

Amazing Quest of Ernest Bliss, The
KLEMENT (GB) 1936 dir. Alfred Zeisler
US title: Romance & Riches
Oppenheim, E. P. *Amazing Quest of Mr Ernest Bliss, The*

Ambassador, The
CANNON (US) 1984
dir. J. Lee Thompson
Leonard, E. *52 Pick-Up*

Ambush
MGM (US) 1949 dir. Sam Wood
Short, L.

Ambushers, The
COL (US) 1967 dir. Harry Levin
Hamilton, D.

Ambush Murders, The
FRIES (US) 1982
dir. Steven Hilliard Stern
TV(US)
Bradlee, Jr., B.

**Amelia Earhart: The Final
Flight**
AVE PICT (US) 1994 dir. Yves Simoneau
TV(US)
Rich, D. L. *Amelia Earhart: A Biography*

America, America
WAR (US) 1964 dir. Elia Kazan
GB title: Anatolian Smile, The
Kazan, E.

Americana
CROWN (US) 1983 dir. David
Carradine
Robinson, H. M. *Perfect Round, The*

American Buffalo
GOLDWYN (US) 1996 dir. Michael
Corrente
Mamet, D.
P

American Christmas Carol, An
SM-HEM (US) 1979 dir. Eric Till
TV(US)
Dickens, C. *Christmas Carol, A*

American Clock, The
AMBLIN (US) 1993 dir. Bob Clark
TV(US)
Miller, A.
P

American Daughter, An
HEARST (US) 2000 dir. Sheldon Larry
TV(US)
Wasserstein, W.
P

American Dream, An
WAR (US) 1966 dir. Robert Gist
GB title: See You in Hell, Darling
Mailer, N.

American Friend, The
CINEGATE (W. Ger) 1977
dir. Wim Wenders
Highsmith, P. *Ripley's Game*

American Geisha
INTERSCOPE (US) 1986
dir. Lee Philips
TV(US)
Dalby, L. *Geisha*

**American Guerilla in the
Philippines, An**
TCF (US) 1950 dir. Fritz Lang
GB title: I Shall Return
Wolfert, I.

Americanization of Emily, The
MGM (US) 1964 dir. Arthur Hiller
Huie, W. B.

American Psycho
MUSE (US) 2000 dir. Mary Harron
Easton Ellis, B.

American Tragedy, An
PAR (US) 1931 dir. Josef von Sternberg
Dreiser, T.

American Tragedy, An
FOX TV (US) 2000 dir. Lawrence
Schiller
TVSe(US)
Schiller, L. and Willwerth, J. *American
Tragedy: The Uncensored Story of the
Simpson Defense*

Amerika
FILMOVE (Czech) 1994 dir. Vladimir
Michalek
Kafka, F.

Ames Fortes, Les
STUDIO CANAL+ (Fr/Bel) 2001 dir.
Raoul Ruiz

Giono, J.

Amico del Cuore, L'
CECCHI (It) 1999 dir. Vincenzo
Salemme

Salemme, V.
P

Amies de Ma Femme, Les
STUDIO CANAL+ (Fr) 1992 dir. Didier
Van Cauwelaert

Adler, P.

Amityville Horror, The
AIP (US) 1979 dir. Stuart Rosenberg

Anson, J.

Amityville II: The Possession
ORION (US) 1982
dir. Damiano Damiani

Holzer, H. *Murder in Amityville*

Amongst Barbarians
BBC (GB) 1990 dir. Jane Howell
TV(GB)

Wall, M.

Among the Cinders
NEW WORLD (US) 1985
dir. Rolf Haedrich

Shadbolt, M.

Amore, L'
TEVERE (It) 1948
dir. Roberto Rossellini

Cocteau, J.
P

Amore Molesto, L'
LUCKY RED (It) 1995 dir. Mario
Martone

Ferrante, E.

Amorous Adventures of Moll Flanders, The
PAR (GB) 1965 dir. Terence Young

Defoe, D. *Fortunes and Misfortunes of the
Famous Moll Flanders, The*

Amorous Prawn, The
BL (GB) 1962 dir. Anthony Kimmins
US title: Playgirl and the War Minister,
The

Kimmins, A.
P

Amos
BRYNA (US) 1985 dir. Michael Tuchner
TV(US)

West, S.

Amsterdam Affair
LIP/TRIO/GROUP W (GB) 1968
dir. Gerry O'Hara

Freeling, N. *Love in Amsterdam*

Amy and Isabelle
HARPO (US) 2001 dir. Lloyd Kramer
TV(US)

Strout, E.

Amy Fisher: My Story
SPECTACOR/JAFFE (US) 1992 dir.
Bradford May
TVSe(US)

Eftimiades, M.

Anastasia
FOX (GB) 1956 dir. Anatole Litvak
COMPASS (US) 1967
dir. George Schaefer
TV(US)

Maurette, M. and Bolton, G.
P

Anastasia: The Mystery of Anna
TELECOM (US) 1986
dir. Marvin Chomsky
TVSe(US)

Kurth, P. *Anastasia: The Riddle of Anna
Anderson*

Anatomy of a Murder
COL (US) 1959 dir. Otto Preminger
Traver, R.

Anatomy of an Illness
CBS ENT (US) 1984
dir. Richard Heffron
TV(US)
Cousins, N.

And a Nightingale Sang
PORTMAN (GB) 1989 dir. Robert
Knights
TV(GB)
Taylor, C. P.
P

Anderson Tapes, The
COL (US) 1971 dir. Sidney Lumet
Sanders, L.

And I Alone Survived
OSL (US) 1978 dir. William Graham
TV(US)
Elder, L. and Streshinsky, S.

And Never Let Her Go
GREENWALD (US) 2001 dir. Peter
Levin
TVSe(US)
Rule, A. *And Never Let Her Go: Thomas
Capano: The Deadly Seducer*

And Now Miguel
UI (US) 1965 dir. James B. Clark
Krumgold, J.

And Now the Screaming Starts
AMICUS (GB) 1973
dir. Roy Ward Baker
Case, D. *Fengriffen*

And Now Tomorrow
PAR (US) 1944 dir. Irving Pichel
Field, R.

And One Was Wonderful
MGM (US) 1940 dir. Robert Sinclair
Miller, A. D.

Andre
PAR (US) 1994 dir. George Miller
Goodridge, H. and Dietz, L. *Seal Called
Andre, A*

Androcles and the Lion
RKO (US) 1952 dir. Chester Erskine
Shaw, G. B.
P

Andromeda Strain, The
UN (US) 1971 dir. Robert Wise
Crichton, M.

And the Band Played On
HBO (US) 1993 dir. Roger Spottiswoode
TV(US)
Shilts, R.

And the Beat Goes On: The Sonny and Cher Story
L. THOMPSON (US) 1999 dir. David
Burton Morris
TV(US)
Bono, S. *And the Beat Goes On*

... And the Earth Did Not Swallow Him
AM PLAY (US) 1995 dir. Severo Perez
Rivera, T. *... Y No Se Lo Trago La Tierra*

And Then There Were None
ABP (US) 1945 dir. René Clair
GB title: Ten Little Niggers
EMI (GB) 1974 dir. Peter Collinson
Christie, A. *Ten Little Niggers*

And the Sea will Tell
COL (US) 1991 dir. Tommy L. Wallace
TVSe(US)
Bugliosi, V. and Henderson, B. B.

Angel
PAR (US) 1937 dir. Ernest Lubitsch

Lengyel, M.
P

Angela's Ashes
UN (US/Ire) 1999 dir. Alan Parker

McCourt, F.

Angel at My Table, An
FINE LINE (Aust) 1991
dir. Jane Campion

Frame, J.

Angel Baby
ALLIED (US) 1960 dir. Paul Wendkos

Barber, E. O. *Jenny Angel*

Angel City
FAC-NEW (US) 1980 dir. Philip Leacock
TV(US)

Smith, P.

Angel Dusted
NRW (US) 1981 dir. Dick Lowry
TV(US)

Etons, U.

Angele
INTERAMA (Fr) 1934
dir. Marcel Pagnol

Giono, J.

Angel from Texas, An
WAR (US) 1940 dir. Ray Enright

Kaufman, G. S. *Butter and Egg Man, The*

Angel Heart
TRISTAR (US) 1987 dir. Alan Parker

Hjortsberg, W. *Falling Angel*

Angelique
FRANCOS (Fr/W. Ger/It) 1964
dir. Bernard Borderie

Golon, S.

Angel Levine, The
UA (US) 1970 dir. Jan Kadar

Malamud, B.

Angels and Insects
GOLDWYN (GB) 1995 dir. Philip Haas

Byatt, A. S. *Morpho Eugenia*

Angel Who Pawned Her Harp, The
BL (GB) 1954 dir. Alan Bromly

Terrot, C.

Angel with the Trumpet, The
BL (GB) 1949 dir. Anthony Bushell

Lothar, E.

Angie
HOLLYWOOD (US) 1994 dir. Martha Coolidge

Wing, A. *Angie, I Says*

Anglo-Saxon Attitudes
EUSTON (GB) 1992 dir. Diarmuid Lawrence
TVSe(GB)

Wilson, A.

Angry Harvest
CCC (Ger) 1986 dir. Agnieszka Holland

Field, H. and Mierzenski, S.

Angry Hills, The
MGM (GB) 1959 dir. Robert Aldrich

Uris, L.

Animal Crackers
PAR (US) 1930 dir. Victor Heerman

Ryskind, M. and Kaufman, G. S.
P

Animal Factory
FRANCHISE (US) 2000 dir. Steve Buscemi

Bunker, E.

Animal Farm

ABP (GB) 1955 dir. John Halas, Joy
Batchelor
HALLMARK (US) 1999 dir. John
Stephenson
TV(US)
A

Orwell, G.

Animal Kingdom, The

RKO (US) 1932 dir. Edward H. Griffith
GB title: Woman in His House, The

Barry, P.
P

Anita no Perd el Tren

CANAL+ ESPANA (Sp) 2001 dir.
Ventura Pons

Baulenas, L.-A. *Bones Obres*

Anna and the King of Siam

FOX (US) 1946 dir. John Cromwell

Landon, M.

Annabelle's Affairs

FOX (US) 1931 dir. Alfred Werker

Kummer, C. *Good Gracious Annabelle*
P

Anna Christie

MGM (US) 1930 dir. Clarence Brown

O'Neill, E.
P

Anna Karenina

MGM (US) 1935 dir. Clarence Brown
BL (GB) 1947 dir. Julien Duvivier
BBC (GB) 1977 dir. Basil Coleman
TVSe(GB)
RASTAR (US) 1985 dir. Simon Langton
TV(GB/US)
CHANNEL 4/WGBH (GB/US) 2000
dir. David Blair
TVSe(GB/US)
WAR (US) 1997 dir. Bernard Rose

Tolstoy, L.

Anna Lucasta

COL UA (US) 1949 dir. Irving Rapper
UA (US) 1958 dir. Arnold Laven

Yordan, P.
P

Anna of the Five Towns

BBC (GB) 1985 dir. Martyn Friend
TVSe(GB)

Bennett, A.

Année des Meduses, L'

AT (Fr) 1987 dir. Christopher Frank

Frank, C.

Anne Frank

TOUCHSTONE (US) 2001 dir. Robert
Dornhelm
TVSe(US)

Muller, M. *Anne Frank: The Biography*

Anne of Avonlea

BBC (GB) 1975 dir. Joan Croft
TVSe(GB)

Montgomery, L. M.

Anne of Green Gables

RKO (US) 1934 dir. George Nicholls
BBC (GB) 1972 dir. Joan Craft
TVSe(GB)
SULLIVAN (Can) 1985 dir. Kevin
Sullivan
TVSe(Can)

Montgomery, L. M.

Anne of the Thousand Days

UN (GB) 1969 dir. Charles Jarrot

Anderson, M.
P

Anne of Windy Poplars

RKO (US) 1940 dir. Jack Hively

Montgomery, L. M. *Anne of Windy
Willows*

Annie
COL (US) 1982 dir. John Huston
M

Meehan, T.
P

Annie Get Your Gun
MGM (US) 1950 dir. George Sidney
M

Fields, H. and Fields, D.
P

Annie's Coming Out
ENT (Aust) 1984 dir. Gil Brealey
US title: Test of Love, A

Crossley, R.

Anniversary, The
WAR (GB) 1968 dir. Roy Ward Baker

MacIlwraith, W.
P

Ann Vickers
RKO (US) 1933 dir. John Cromwell

Lewis, S.

Another Country
GOLDCREST (GB) 1984 dir. Marek Kanievska

Mitchell, J.
P

Another Day in Paradise
TRIMARK (US) 1998 dir. Larry Clark

Little, E.

Another Language
MGM (US) 1933 dir. Edward H. Griffith

Franken, R.
P

Another Man's Poison
EROS (GB) 1951 dir. Irving Rapper

Sands, L. *Deadlock*
P

Another Part of the Forest
UN (US) 1948 dir. Michael Gordon

Hellman, L. F.
P

Another Shore
EAL (GB) 1948 dir. Charles Crichton

Reddin, K.

Another Time, Another Place
PAR (GB) 1958 dir. Lewis Allen

Coffee, L. *Weep No More*

Another Time, Another Place
CINEGATE (GB) 1983
dir. Michael Radford

Kesson, J.

Another Woman
ALLIANCE (Can) 1994 dir. Alan Smythe
TV(Can)

Dalton, M.

Another Woman's Husband
HEARST (US) 2000 dir. Noel Nosseck
TV(US)

Tuttle Villegas, A. and Hugo, L.
Swimming Lessons

Anthony Adverse
WAR (US) 1936 dir. Mervyn LeRoy

Allen, H.

Antony and Cleopatra
RANK (GB) 1972 dir. Charlton Heston
ITV (GB) 1974 dir. Trevor Nunn, Jon Scoffield
TV(GB)

Shakespeare, W.
P

Any Number Can Play
MGM (US) 1949 dir. Mervyn LeRoy

Heth, E. H.

Anything Can Happen
PAR (US) 1952 dir. George Seaton
M

Papashvily, G. and Papashvily, H.

Anything Goes
PAR (US) 1936 dir. Lewis Milestone
M
PAR (US) 1956 dir. Robert Lewis
M

Bolton, G., Wodehouse, P. G., Lindsay, H. and Crouse, R.
P

Anything to Survive
SABAN/SCHERICK (US) 1990
dir. Zale Dalen
TV(US)

Wortman, E. *Almost Too Late*

Any Wednesday
WAR (US) 1966 dir. Robert Ellis Miller
GB title: Bachelor Girl Apartment

Resnik, M.
P

Anywhere But Here
FOX (US) 1999 dir. Wayne Wang

Simpson, M.

Anzio
PAN (It) 1968 dir. Edward Dmytryk
GB title: Battle for Anzio, The

Thomas, W. V.

Apache
UA (US) 1954 dir. Robert Aldrich

Wellman, P. I. *Bronco Apache*

Ape, The
MON (US) 1940 dir. William Nigh

Shirk, A.
P

Ape and Essence
BBC (GB) 1966 dir. David Benedictus
TV(GB)

Huxley, A.

Apocalypse Watch, The
RHI (US) 1997 dir. Kevin Connor
TVSe(US)

Ludlum, R.

Apollo 13
UN (US) 1995 dir. Ron Howard

Lovell, Jr., J. A. and Kluger, J. *Lost Moon*

Appaloosa, The
UN (US) 1968 dir. Sidney J. Furie
GB title: Southwest to Sonora

MacLeod, R.

Apple Dumpling Gang, The
DISNEY (US) 1974 dir. Norman Tokar
Ch

Bickham, J. M.

Appointment with Death
CANNON (US) 1989
dir. Michael Winner

Christie, A.

Appointment with Venus
GFD (GB) 1951 dir. Ralph Thomas
US title: Island Rescue

Tickell, J.

Apprenticeship of Duddy Kravitz, The
RANK (Can) 1974 dir. Ted Kotcheff

Richler, M.

Après-Midi d'un Tortionnaire, L'
YMC (Fr) 2001 dir. Lucian Pintilie

Jela, D.

April Love
TCF (US) 1957 dir. Henry Levin

Chamberlain, G. A.

April Morning
GOLDWYN TV (US) 1988
dir. Delbert Mann
TV(US)
Fast, H.

Apt Pupil
TRISTAR (US) 1998 dir. Bryan Singer
King, S.

Arabesque
UN (US) 1966 dir. Stanley Donen
Votler, G. *Cipher, The*

Arch of Triumph
UA (US) 1948 dir. Lewis Milestone
HTV (GB) 1984 dir. Waris Hussein
TV(GB)
Remarque, E. M.

Are Husbands Necessary?
PAR (US) 1942 dir. Norman Taurog
Rorick, I. S. *Mr and Mrs Cugat*

Aren't Men Beasts!
AB (GB) 1937 dir. Graham Cutts
Sylvaine, V.
P

Aren't We All?
PAR (GB) 1932
dir. Harry Lachman, Rudolf Maté
Lonsdale, F.
P

Are You In The House Alone?
FRIES PROD (US) 1978
dir. Walter Grauman
TV(US)
Peck, R. H.

Are You With It?
UN (US) 1948 dir. Jack Hively
M
Perrin, S. and Balzer, G.
P

Argent, L'
EOS (Switz/Fr) 1983
dir. Robert Bresson
Tolstoy, L. *False Note, The*

Ariana
UN TV (US) 1989 dir. Paul Krasny
TV(US)
Raab, S.

Arizona
COL (US) 1940 dir. Wesley Ruggles
Kelland, C. B.

Arms And The Man
WARDOUR (GB) 1932 dir. Cecil Lewis
ARGENT (GB) 1982
TV(GB)
Shaw, G. B.
P

Around the World in Eighty Days
UA (US) 1956 dir. Michael Anderson, Kevin McClory
HARMONY (US) 1989
dir. Buzz Kulik
TVSe(US)
Verne, J.

Arrangement, The
WAR (US) 1969 dir. Elia Kazan
Kazan, E.

Arrowhead
PAR (US) 1953
dir. Charles Marquis Warren
Burnett, W. R. *Adobe Walls*

Arrow in the Dust
ABP (US) 1954 dir. Lesley Selander
Foreman, L. L. *Road to San Jacinto*

Arrowsmith
UA (US) 1931 dir. John Ford
Lewis, S.

Arsène Lupin
MGM (US) 1932 dir. Jack Conway
LeBlanc. M. and de Croisset, F.
P

Arsenic and Old Lace
WAR (US) 1944 dir. Frank Capra
COMPASS (US) 1962
dir. George Schaefer
TV(US)
Kesselring, J. O.
P

Art (delicat) de la Seduction, L'
BLUE DAHLIA (Fr) 2001 dir. Richard
Berry
Aubert, J.-M. *Kurtz*

Artists in Crime
BBC (GB) 1990 dir. Silvio Narizzano
TV(GB)
Marsh, N.

Art of Crime, The
UN TV (US) 1975 dir. Richard Irving
TV(US)
Smith, M. *Gypsy in Amber*

Arturo's Island
MGM (It) 1962 dir. Damiano Damiani
Morante, E.

Ashanti
COL (Switz) 1979 dir. Richard Fleischer
Vasquez-Figueroa, A. *Ebano*

Ashenden
BBC (GB) 1992 dir. Christopher
Morahan
TVSe(GB)
Maugham, W. S.

Ashes and Diamonds
POLSKI (Pol) 1958 dir. Andrzej Wajda
Andrzejewski, J.

Ashes of Time
SCHOLAR (HK) 1994 dir. Kar-Wai
Wong
Cha, L. *Eagle Shooting Heroes, The*

As Husbands Go
FOX (US) 1934 dir. Hamilton McFadden
Crothers, R.
P

As Is
BRANDMAN (US) 1986
dir. Michael Lindsay-Hogg
TV(US)
Hoffman, W. H.
P

Ask Any Girl
MGM (US) 1959 dir. Charles Walters
Wolfe, W.

As Long As They're Happy
GFD (GB) 1955 dir. J. Lee Thompson
Sylvaine, V.
P

Aspen
UN TV (US) 1977 dir. Douglas Heyes
TVSe(US)
Hirschfeld, B.

Aspern
CONN (Port) 1981
dir. Eduardo de Gregorion
James, H. *Aspern Papers, The*

Asphalt Jungle, The
MGM (US) 1950 dir. John Huston
Burnett, W. R.

Assassination Bureau, The
PAR (GB) 1969 dir. Basil Dearden
London, J. and Fish, R.

Assault
RANK (GB) 1971 dir. Sidney Hayers
Young, K. *Ravine, The*

Assault, The
CANNON (Neth) 1986
dir. Fons Rademakers
Mulisch, H.

Assault and Matrimony
NBC (US) 1987 dir. James Frawley
TV(US)
Anderson, J.

Assault at West Point
MOSAIC (US) 1994 dir. Harry Moses
TV(US)
Marszalek, J. F. *Court-Martial of Johnson Whittaker, The*

Assault on a Queen
PAR (US) 1966 dir. Jack Donohue
Finney, J.

Assignment in Brittany
MGM (US) 1943 dir. Jack Conway
MacInnes, H.

Assignment 'K'
COL (GB) 1968 dir. Val Guest
Howard, H.

Assignment Paris
COL (US) 1952 dir. Robert Parrish
Gallico, P. *Trial by Terror*

Assisi Underground, The
CANNON (GB) 1985
dir. Alexander Ramati
Ramati, A.

Assistant, The
MIRACLE PICT (Can/GB) 1997 dir.
Daniel Petrie
Malamud, B.

Associate, The
HOLLYWOOD (US) 1996 dir. Daniel
Petrie
Prieto, J. *Socio, El*

As Summers Die
TELEPIC (US) 1986
dir. Jean-Claude Tramont
TV(US)
Groom, W.

As the Earth Turns
WAR (US) 1934 dir. Alfred E. Green
Carroll, G.

Astonished Heart, The
GFD (GB) 1949 dir. Terence Fisher,
Anthony Darnborough
Coward, N.
P

As You Desire Me
MGM (US) 1932
dir. George Fitzmaurice
Pirandello, L.
P

As You Like It
FOX (GB) 1936 dir. Paul Czinner
SANDS (GB) 1992 dir. Christine Edzard
Shakespeare, W.
P

At Bertram's Hotel
BBC (GB) 1986 dir. Mary McMurray
TV(GB)
Christie, A.

Atlantic
BI (GB) 1929 dir. E. A. Dupont
Raymond, E. *Berg, The*
P

Atlantide
STUDIO CANAL+ (Fr/It) 1992 dir. Bob
Swain
Benoit, P.

Atlantis, The Lost Continent
MGM (US) 1961 dir. George Pal
Hargreaves, Sir G.
P

At Mother's Request
VISTA (US) 1987 dir. Michael Tuchner
TVSe(US)

Coleman, J.

At Play in the Fields of the Lord
UN (US) 1991 dir. Hector Babenco

Matthiessen, P.

Atrocity Exhibition, The
THE BUSINESS (US) 1999 dir. Jonathan Weiss

Ballard, J. G.

Attack
UA (US) 1956 dir. Robert Aldrich

Brooks, N. *Fragile Fox*
P

Attack on Fear
TOM (US) 1984 dir. Mel Damski
TV(US)

Mitchell, D., Mitchell, C. and Ofshe, R. *Light on Synanon, The*

Attack on Terror: The FBI Versus The Ku Klux Klan
WAR TV (US) 1975
dir. Marvin Chomsky
TVSe(US)

Whitehead, D. *Attack on Terror: The FBI Against The Ku Klux Klan in Mississippi*

Attempt to Kill
AA (GB) 1961 dir. Royston Murray

Wallace, E. *Lone House Mystery, The*

At the Earth's Core
BL (GB) 1976 dir. Kevin Connor

Burroughs, E. R.

At the End of the Day: The Sue Rodriguez Story
AMW (Can) 1999 dir. Sheldon Larry
TV(Can)

Rodriguez, S. and Hobbs Birnie, L. *Uncommon Will: The Death and Life of Sue Rodriguez*

At the Midnight Hour
ALLIANCE (Can) 1995 dir. Charles Jarrott
TV(Can)

Scott, A.

At the Villa Rose
AB (GB) 1939 dir. Walter Summers
US title: House of Mystery

Mason, A. E. W.

Attica
ABC (US) 1980 dir. Marvin J. Chomsky
TV(US)

Wicker, T. *Time to Die, A*

Attic, The: The Hiding of Anne Frank
TELECOM/YTV (US/GB) 1988
dir. John Erman
TV(GB/US)

Gies, M. and Gold, A. L. *Anne Frank Remembered: The Story of the Woman Who Helped to Hide the Frank Family*

At War with the Army
PAR (US) 1951 dir. Hal Walker

Allardice, J.
P

Audition
OMEGA (Jap) 1999 dir. Akashi Miike

Murakami, R.

Audrey Rose
UA (US) 1977 dir. Robert Wise

De Felitta, F.

August
GOLDWYN (US) 1996 dir. Anthony
Hopkins
Mitchell, J.
P

Chekhov, A. *Uncle Vanya*
P

Aunt Clara
BL (GB) 1954 dir. Anthony Kimmins
Streatfeild, N.

Auntie Mame
WAR (US) 1958 dir. Morton da Costa
Dennis, P.

Austeria
POLSKI (Pol) 1988
dir. Jerzy Kawaterowicz
Stryzkowski, J.

**Autobiography of Miss Jane
Pittman, The**
TOM (US) 1974 dir. John Korty
TV(US)
Gaines, E. J.

Auto da Compadecida, O
GLOBO (Bra) 2000 dir. Guel Arraes
Suassuna, A.
P

Autumn Crocus
BI (GB) 1934 dir. Basil Dearden
Anthony, C. L.
P

Autumn Shroud, An
BBC/A&E (GB) 1996 dir. Richard
Standeven
TV(GB)
Hill, R. *April Shroud, An*

Avalanche Express
FOX (Eire) 1979 dir. Mark Robson
Forbes, C.

Avanti!
UA (US) 1972 dir. Billy Wilder
Taylor, S.
P

Avengers, The
REP (US) 1950 dir. John Auer
Beach, R. E. *Don Careless*

Avenging Angel, The
CURTIS LOWE (US) 1995 dir. Craig R.
Baxley
TV(US)
Stewart, G.

L'Aveu
CORONA (Fr) 1970 dir. Costa-Gavras
London, A. and London, L. *On Trial*

Aviator, The
MGM/UA (US) 1985 dir. George Miller
Gann, E. K.

Awake to Danger
NBC (US) 1995 dir. Michael Tuchner
TV(US)
Nixon, J. L. *Other Side of Dark, The*

Awakening, The
EMI (GB) 1980 dir. Mike Newell
Stoker, B. *Jewel of the Seven Stars, The*

Awakening, The
ALLIANCE (Can) 1995 dir. George
Bloomfield
TV(Can)
Coughlin, P.

Awakening Land, The
WAR TV (US) 1978 dir. Boris Sagal
TVSe(US)
Richter, C.

Awakenings
COL (US) 1990 dir. Penny Marshall
Sacks, O.

Away All Boats
UI (US) 1956 dir. Joseph Pevney

Dodson, K.

Awfully Big Adventure, An
BRIT SCREEN (GB) 1995 dir. Mike Newell

Bainbridge, B.

Awful Truth, The
COL (US) 1937 dir. Leo McCarey

Richman, A.
P

Baba
BEIJING (China) 2000 dir. Shou Wang
Wang, S. *I Am Your Dad*

Babar: King of the Elephants
NELVANA (Can/Fr) 1999 dir. Raymond Jafelice
A, Ch
de Brunhoff, J.

Babbit
WAR (US) 1934 dir. William Keighley
Lewis, S.

Babe
MGM TV (US) 1975 dir. Buzz Kulik
TV(US)
Zaharias, B. D. and Paxton, H. *This Life I've Led: My Autobiography*

Babe
UN (Aust) 1995 dir. Chris Noonan
A, Ch
King-Smith, D. *Babe, the Gallant Pig* (US); *The Sheep-Pig* (GB)

Babe Ruth
LYTTLE (US) 1991 dir. Mark Tinker
TV(US)
Cramer, R. W. *Babe: The Legend Comes to Life*
Wagenheim, K. *Babe Ruth, His Life and Legend*

Babette's Feast
DAN FI (Den) 1987 dir. Gabriel Axel
Blixen, K. aka Dinesen, I.

Baby
TNT (US) 2000 dir. Robert Allan Ackerman
TV(US)
MacLachlan, P.

Baby and the Battleship, The
BL (GB) 1956 dir. Jay Lewis
Thorne, A.

Baby Dance, The
EGG (US) 1998 dir. Jane Anderson
TV(US)
Anderson, J.
P

Baby Doll
WAR (US) 1956 dir. Elia Kazan
Williams, T.
P

Baby Love
AVCO (GB) 1969 dir. Alistair Reid
Christian, T. C.

Baby-Sitters Club, The
COL (US) 1995 dir. Melanie Mayron
Martin, A. M.

Baby, The Rain Must Fall
COL (US) 1965 dir. Robert Mulligan
Foote, H. *Travelling Lady, The*
P

Bachelor, The
NEW LINE (US) 1999 dir. Gary Sinyor
Megrue, R. C. *Seven Chances*
P

Bachelor Flat
TCF (US) 1961 dir. Frank Tashlin

Grossman, B.
P

Bachelor in Paradise
MGM (US) 1961 dir. Jack Arnold

Caspary, V.

Bachelor Party, The
UA (US) 1957 dir. Delbert Mann

Chayefsky, P.
P

Back from the Dead
FOX (US) 1957
dir. Charles Marquis Warren

Turney, C. *Other One, The*

Background
ABP (GB) 1953 dir. Daniel Birt
US title: Edge of Divorce

Chetham-Strode, W.
P

Background to Danger
WAR (US) 1943 dir. Raoul Walsh

Ambler, E. *Uncommon Danger*

Back Home
DISNEY (US) 1990 dir. Piers Haggard
TV(US)

Magorian, M.

Backstairs at the White House
FRIENDLY (US) 1979
dir. Michael O'Herlihy
TVSe(US)

Parks, L. R. *My Thirty Years Backstairs at the White House*

Back Street
UN (US) 1932 dir. John M. Stahl
UN (US) 1941 dir. Robert Stevenson
UN (US) 1961 dir. David Miller

Hurst, F.

Back to God's Country
UN (US) 1953 dir. Joseph Pevney

Curwood, J. O.

Bad As I Wanna Be: The Dennis Rodman Story
COL TRISTAR (US) 1998 dir. Jean De Segonzac
TV(US)

Rodman, D. and Keown, T. *Bad As I Wanna Be*

Bad City Blues
SHOWCASE (US) 1999 dir. Michael Stevens

Willocks, T.

Bad Day at Black Rock
MGM (US) 1954 dir. John Sturges

Breslin, H. *Bad Time at Honda*

Bad for Each Other
COL (US) 1954 dir. Irving Rapper

McCoy, H.

Bad Little Angel
MGM (US) 1939 dir. William Thiele

Turnbull, M. *Looking After Sandy*

Bad Man, The
MGM (US) 1940 dir. Richard Thorpe
GB title: Two Gun Cupid

Brown, P. E.
P

Bad Manners
DAVIS (US) 1997 dir. Jonathan Kaufer

Gilman, D. *Ghost in the Machine*
P

Bad Medicine
TCF (US) 1985 dir. Harvey Miller

Horowitz, S. *Calling Dr. Horowitz*

Bad Men of Tombstone
ABP (US) 1949 dir. Kurt Neumann

Monaghan, J. *Last of the Badmen*

Bad Moon
MORGAN CREEK (US) 1996 dir. Eric Red

Smith, W. *Thor*

Bad Ronald
LORIMAR (US) 1974 dir. Buzz Kulik
TV(US)

Vance, J. H.

Badge of the Assassin
BLATT/SINGER (US) 1985
dir. Mel Damski
TV(US)

Tannenbaum, R. K. and Rosenberg, P.

Bad Seed, The
WAR (US) 1956 dir. Mervyn LeRoy
WAR (US) 1985 dir. Paul Wendkos
TV(US)

March, W.

Bahama Passage
PAR (US) 1941 dir. Edward H. Griffith

Hayes, N. *Dildo Cay*

Bailame el Agua
PLOT (Sp) 2000 dir. Josecho San Mateo

Valdes, D.

Baise-moi
STUDIO CANAL+ (Fr) 2000 dir. Coralie Trinh Thi, Virginie Despentes

Despentes, V.

Bait, The
ABC (US) 1973 dir. Leonard Horn
TV(US)

Uhnak, D.

Baja Oklahoma
HBO (US) 1988 dir. Bobby Roth
TV(US)

Jenkins, D.

Balalaika
MGM (US) 1939 dir. Reinhold Schunzel

Maschwitz, E.
P

Balcony, The
BL (US) 1963 dir. Joseph Strick

Genet, J.
P

Balia, La
RAI (It) 1999 dir. Marco Bellocchio

Pirandello, L. *Nanny, The*

Ballad of Gregorio Cortez, The
EMBASSY (US) 1983
dir. Robert M. Young

Parades, A. *With a Pistol in His Hand*

Ballad of Lucy Whipple, The
C. ANDERSON (US) 2001 dir. Jeremy Paul Kagan
TV(US)

Cushman, K.

Ballad of Narayama
ROEI (Jap) 1983 dir. Shohei Imamura

Fukazawa, S.

Ballad of the Sad Café, The
MI/HOBO (US/GB)
1991 dir. Simon Callow

McCullers, C.

Albee, E.
P

Ballet Shoes
BBC (GB) 1975 dir. Timothy Combe
TVSe(GB)

Streatfeild, N.

Balloon Farm
DISNEY (US) 1999 dir. William Dear
TV(US)
Ch

Nolen, J. *Harvey Potter's Balloon Farm*

Ballroom of Romance, The
BBC (GB) 1980 dir. Patrick O'Connor
TV(GB)
Trevor, W.

Bambi
DISNEY (US) 1942 dir. David Hand
A, Ch
Salten, F.

Banana Ridge
ABP (GB) 1941 dir. Walter C. Mycroft
Travers, B.
P

Bande à Part
ANOUCHKA/ORSAY (Fr) 1964
dir. Jean-Luc Godard
Hitchens, D. and Hitchens, B. *Fool's Gold*

Bandit of Sherwood Forest, The
COL (US) 1946
dir. George Sherman, Henry Levin
Castleton, P. A. *Son of Robin Hood*

Band of Angels
WAR (US) 1957 dir. Raoul Walsh
Warren, R. P.

Band of Brothers
DREAMWORKS (US/GB) 2001 dir.
David Franken, Tom Hanks, David
Leland, Richard Loncraine, David
Nutter, Phil Alden Robinson, Mikael
Salomon, Tony To
TVSe(US/GB)
Ambrose, S. E. *Band of Brothers, A: E Company 506th Regiment, 101st Airborne From Normandy to Hitler's Nest*

Bang the Drum Slowly
PAR (US) 1973 dir. John Hancock
Harris, M.

Banjo on my Knee
TCF (US) 1936 dir. John Cromwell
Hamilton, H.

Bank Shot, The
UA (US) 1974 dir. Gower Champion
Westlake, D. E.

Barabbas
COL (It) 1962 dir. Richard Fleischer
Lagerkvist, P.

Barbara
PER HOLST (Den) 1997 dir. Nils
Malmros
Jacobsen, J.-F.

Barbarella
PAR (Fr/It) 1967 dir. Roger Vadim
Forest, J.-C.

Barbarian, The
MGM (US) 1933 dir. Sam Wood
GB title: Night in Cairo, A
Selwyn, E.
P

Barbarians at the Gate
COL/HBO (US) 1993 dir. Glenn Jordan
TV(US)
Burrough, B. and Helyar, J. *Barbarians at the Gate: The Fall of RJR Nabisco*

Barchester Chronicles, The
BBC (GB) 1982 dir. David Giles
TVSe(GB)
Trollope, A. *Barchester Towers; Warden, The*

Bare Essence
WAR TV (US) 1982 dir. Walter
Grauman
TVSe(US)
Rich, M.

Barefoot in Athens
COMPASS (US) 1966
dir. George Schaefer
TV(US)
Anderson, M.
P

Barefoot in the Park
PAR (US) 1967 dir. Gene Saks
Simon, N.
P

Barefoot Mailman, The
COL (US) 1951 dir. Earl McEvoy
Pratt, T.

Bar Girls
ORION (US) 1994 dir. Marita Giovanni
Hoffman, L.
P

Barjo
CENTRE EURO (Fr) 1992 dir. Jerome
Boivin
Dick, P. K. *Confessions of a Crap Artist*

Barnabo of the Mountains
NAUTILUS (It/Fr) 1994 dir. Mario
Brenta
Buzzati, D.

Baroness and the Butler, The
FOX (US) 1938 dir. Walter Lang
Bus-Fekete, L. *Lady Has a Heart, A*
P

Baron Munchhausen
CESK (Czech) 1962 dir. Karel Zeman
Burger, G.

Barretts of Wimpole Street, The
MGM (US) 1934 dir. Sidney Franklin
MGM (US) 1956 dir. Sidney Franklin
Besier, R.
P

Barry Lyndon
WAR/HAWK (GB) 1975
dir. Stanley Kubrick
Thackeray, W. M.

Bas-Fonds, Les
ALB (Fr) 1936 dir. Jean Renoir
Gorky, M.
P

Basil
SHOWCAREER (GB) 1998 dir. Radha
Bharadwaj
Collins, W.

Basketball Diaries, The
NEW LINE (US) 1995 dir. Scott Kalvert
Carroll, J.

Bastard, The
UN TV (US) 1978 dir. Lee Katzin
TVSe(US)
Jakes, J.

Bastard Out of Carolina
SHOWTIMEWORKS (US) 1996 dir.
Anjelica Huston
TV(US)
Allison, D.

Bat, The
ALLIED (US) 1959 dir. Crane Wilbur
Rinehart, M. R.
P

Bates Motel
UN TV (US) 1987 dir. Richard Rothstein
TV(US)
Bloch, R. *Psycho*

Battle, The
GAU (Fr) 1934 dir. Nicolas Farkas
Farrere, C.

Battle Cry
WAR (US) 1954 dir. Raoul Walsh
Uris, L.

Battlefield Earth
FRANCHISE (US) 2000 dir. Roger
Christian
Hubbard, L. R.

Battle of Britain
UA (GB) 1969 dir. Guy Hamilton

Wood, D. and Dempster, D. *Narrow Margin, The*

Battle of the River Plate, The
RANK (GB) 1956 dir. Michael Powell, Emeric Pressburger
US title: Pursuit of the Graf Spee

Powell, M. *Graf Spee*

Battle of the Sexes, The
PROM (GB) 1960 dir. Charles Crichton

Thurber, J. *Catbird Seat, The*

Battle of the V1
MAY-SEW (GB) 1958 dir. Vernon Sewell
US title: Unseen Heroes

Newman, B.

Battle of Villa Fiorita, The
WAR (GB) 1964 dir. Delmer Daves
US title: Affair at the Villa Morita

Godden, R.

Battle Royale
TOEI (Jap) 2000 dir. Kinji Fukasaku

Takami, K.

BAT 21
TRISTAR (US) 1988 dir. Peter Markle

Angerson, W. C.

Bat Whispers, The
UA (US) 1930 dir. Roland West

Rinehart, M. R. *Bat, The*
P

Bawdy Adventures of Tom Jones, The
UN (GB) 1976 dir. Cliff Owen
M

Fielding, H. *History of Tom Jones, A Foundling, The*

Baxter!
EMI (GB) 1972 dir. Lionel Jeffries
Ch

Platt, K. *Boy Who Could Make Himself Disappear, The*

Beach, The
FOX (US) 2000 dir. Danny Boyle

Garland, A.

Beachcomber, The
GFD (GB) 1954 dir. Muriel Box

Maugham, W. S. *Vessel of Wrath*

Beaches
TOUCHSTONE (US) 1988 dir. Garry Marshall

Dart, I. R.

Beachhead
UA (US) 1954 dir. Stuart Heisler

Hubler, R. G. *I've Got Mine*

Beans of Egypt, Maine, The
AM PLAY (US) 1994 dir. Jennifer Warren

Chute, C.

Bear, The
TRISTAR (Fr) 1989
dir. Jean-Jacques Annaud

Curwood, J. O. *Grizzly King, The*

Bear Island
COL (Can/GB) 1979 dir. Don Sharp

MacLean, A.

Bears and I, The
DISNEY (US) 1974
dir. Bernard McEveety
Ch

Leslie, R. F.

Beast, The
COL (US) 1988 dir. Kevin Reynolds

Mastrosimone, W. *Nanawatai*
P

Beast, The
M. R. JOYCE (US) 1996 dir. Jeff
Bleckner
TVSe(US)
Benchley, P.

Beast From 20,000 Fathoms, The
WAR (US) 1953 dir. Eugene Lourie
Bradbury, R. *Foghorn, The*

Beast with Five Fingers, The
WAR (US) 1946 dir. Robert Florey
Harvey, W. F.

Beast Within, The
MGM/UA (US) 1982 dir. Philippe Mora
Levy, E.

Beat the Devil
ROMULUS (GB) 1953 dir. John Huston
Helvick, J.

Beau Brummell
MGM (GB) 1954 dir. Curtis Bernhardt
Fitch, C.
P

Beau Geste
PAR (US) 1939 dir. William A. Wellman
UI (US) 1966 dir. Douglas Heyes
BBC (GB) 1982 dir. Douglas Camfield
TVSe(GB)
Wren, P. C.

Beau Ideal
RKO (US) 1931 dir. Herbert Brenon
Wren, P. C.

Beauty
GRAND (US) 1998 dir. Jerry London
TV(US)
Wilson, S.

Beau James
PAR (US) 1957 dir. Melville Shavelson
Fowler, G.

Beautiful Thing
CHANNEL 4 FILMS (GB) 1996 dir.
Hettie MacDonald
Harvey, J.

Beautiful Mind, A
IMAGINE ENT (US) 2001 dir. Ron
Howard
Nasar, S. *Beautiful Mind, A: A Biography
of John Forbes Nash, Jr.*

Beauty and the Beast
LOPERT (Fr) 1947 dir. Jean Cocteau
PALM (US) 1976 dir. Fielder Cook
TV(US)
CANNON (US) 1987
dir. Eugene Marner
DISNEY (US) 1991
dir. Gary Trousdale, Kirk Wise
A, Ch, M
de Villeneuve, Mme.

Beauty for Sale
MGM (US) 1933
dir. Richard Boleslawski
Baldwin, F. *Beauty*

Because They're Young
COL (US) 1960 dir. Paul Wendkos
Farris, J. *Harrison High*

Beck
FILMCASE (Neth/Bel) 1993 dir. Jacob
Bijl
Sjowall, M. and Wahloo, P. *Locked
Room, The*

Becket
PAR (GB) 1963 dir. Peter Glenville
Anouilh, J.
P

Becky Sharp
RKO (US) 1935 dir. Rouben Mamoulian
Thackeray, W. M. *Vanity Fair*

Bedelia
GFD (GB) 1946 dir. Lance Comfort
Caspary, V.

Bedford Incident, The
COL (GB) 1965 dir. James B. Harris
Rascovich, M.

Bedknobs and Broomsticks
DISNEY (US) 1971
dir. Robert Stevenson
Ch
Norton, M. *Bed-Knob and Broomstick*

Bed of Lies
WOLPER TV(US) 1992
dir. William A. Graham
Salerno, S. *Deadly Blessing*

Bedroom Window, The
DELAUR (US) 1987 dir. Curtis Hanson
Holden, A. *Witness, The*

Bed Sitting Room, The
UA (GB) 1969 dir. Richard Lester
Milligan, S. and Antrobus, J.
P

Bedtime Story, A
PAR (US) 1933 dir. Norman Taurog
Horniman, R. *Bellamy the Magnificent*

Beecham
YTV (GB) 1990 dir. Vernon Lawrence
TV(GB)
Brahms, C. and Sherrin, N.

Before and After
HOLLYWOOD (US) 1996 dir. Barbet Schroeder
Brown, R.

Before He Wakes
CBS (US) 1998 dir. Michael Scott
TV(US)
Bledsoe, J.

Before Winter Comes
COL (GB) 1968 dir. J. Lee Thompson
Keefe, F. L. *Interpreter, The*

Before Women Had Wings
HARPO (US) 1997 dir. Lloyd Kramer
TV(US)
Fowler, C.

Beg!
ARTS MAGIC (GB) 1994 dir. Robert Golden
Lily, P. and Glass, D.
P

Beggarman, Thief
UN TV (US) 1979 dir. Lawrence Doheny
TVSe(US)
Shaw, I.

Beggars of Life
PAR (US) 1928 dir. William Wellman
Tully, J.

Beggar's Opera, The
BL (GB) 1952 dir. Peter Brook
M
Gay, J.
P

Beggar's Opera, The
BARRANDOV (Czech) 1991
dir. Jiri Menzel
Gay, J.
P
Havel, V.
P

Beginning and the End, The
ALAMEDA (Mex) 1993 dir. Arturo Ripstein
Mahfouz, N.

Beguiled, The
UN (US) 1971 dir. Don Siegel
Cullinan, T. *Bedeviled, The*

Behaving Badly
CHANNEL 4 (GB) 1989 dir. David
Tucker
TVSe(GB)
Heath, C.

Behind that Curtain
FOX (US) 1929 dir. Irving Cummings
Biggers, E. D.

Behind the Headlines
RANK (GB) 1956 dir. Charles Saunders
Chapman, R.

Behind the Mask
BL (GB) 1958 dir. Brian Desmond Hurst
Wilson, J. R. *Pack, The*

Behind the Rising Sun
RKO (US) 1943 dir. Edward Dmytryk
Young, J. R.

Behind the Sun
VIDEO (Bra/Fr) 2001 dir. Walter Salles
Kadare, I. *Broken April*

Behold a Pale Horse
COL (US) 1964 dir. Fred Zinnemann
Pressburger, E. *Killing a Mouse on Sunday*

Behold my Wife
PAR (US) 1934 dir. Mitchell Leisen
Parker, G. *Translation of a Savage, The*

Being at Home With Claude
NFB (Can) 1992 dir. Jean Beaudin
Dubois, R. D.
P

Being There
LORIMAR (US) 1979 dir. Hal Ashby
Kosinski, J.

Bejewelled
DISNEY CH (US/GB) 1991
dir. Terry Marcel
TV(GB/US)
Babson, M. *Bejewelled Death*

Bel Ami
BBC (GB) 1971 dir. John Davies
TVSe(GB)
de Maupassant, G.

Believers, The
ORION (US) 1987 dir. John Schlesinger
Conde, N. *Religion, The*

Bell, The
BBC (GB) 1982 dir. Barry Davis
TV(GB)
Murdoch, I.

Belladonna
OLY (GB) 1934 dir. Robert Milton
Hichens, R.

Bella Mafia
KONIGSBERG (US) 1997 dir. David
Greene
TV(US)
LaPlante, L.

Bell'Antonio, Il
CINA (It/Fr) 1960 dir. Piero Piccioni
Brancati, V.

Bell, Book and Candle
COL (US) 1958 dir. Richard Quine
van Druten, J.
P

Belle de Jour
CURZON (Fr/It) 1967 dir. Luis Bunuel
Kessel, J.

Belle Noiseuse, La
FRANCE 3 (Fr) 1991 dir. Jacques
Rivette
de Balzac, H.

Belle of New York, The
MGM (US) 1952 dir. Charles Walters
M
McLellan, C. M. S. and Morton, H.
P

Bell for Adano, A
FOX (US) 1945 dir. Henry King
Hayward (US) 1967 dir. Mel Ferber
TV(US)
Hersey, J.

Bell Jar, The
AVCO (US) 1979 dir. Larry Peerce
Plath, S.

Bellman and True
HANDMADE (GB) 1987
dir. Richard Loncraine
Lowden, D.

Bells are Ringing
MGM (US) 1960 dir. Vincente Minnelli
M
Comden, B. and Green, A.
P

Belles on Their Toes
FOX (US) 1952 dir. Henry Levin
Gilbreth, Jr., F. B. and Carey, E.

Belly Fruit
STANDARD (US) 1999 dir. Kerri Green
Blinkoff, S., Bernhard, M., Borrus J. and Green K.
P

Bellyful
STUDIO CANAL+ (Fr) 2000 dir. Melvin Van Peebles
Van Peebles, M.

Beloved
TOUCHSTONE (US) 1998 dir. Jonathan Demme
Morrison, T.

Beloved Bachelor, The
PAR (US) 1931 dir. Lloyd Corrigan
Peple, E. H.
P

Beloved/Friend
CANAL+ ESPANA (Sp) 1999 dir. Ventura Pons
Benet I. and Jornet, J. M. *Testament*

Beloved Infidel
FOX (US) 1959 dir. Henry King
Graham, S. and Frank, G.

Beloved Vagabond, The
COL (GB) 1936 dir. Curtis Bernhardt
Locke, W. J.

Below the Belt
ATLANTIC (US) 1982
dir. Robert Fowler
Drexler, R. *To Smithereens*

Belstone Fox, The
RANK (GB) 1973 dir. James Hill
Rook, D. *Ballad of the Belstone Fox, The*

Bend of the River
UI (US) 1952 dir. Anthony Mann
GB title: Where the River Bends
Gulick, W. *Bend of the Snake*

Bengal Brigade
UI (US) 1954 dir. Laslo Benedek
GB title: Bengal Rifles
Hunter, H. *Bengal Tiger*

Ben Hur
MGM (US) 1926 dir. Fred Niblo
MGM (US) 1959 dir. William Wyler
Wallace, L.

Bent
CHANNEL 4 FILMS (GB) 1997 dir. Sean Mathias
Sherman, M.
P

Benvenuta
NI (Bel/Fr) 1982 dir. André Delvaux
Lilar, S. *Confession Anonyme, La*

Bequest to the Nation
UN (GB) 1973 dir. James Cellan Jones
Rattigan, T.
P

Berkeley Square
FOX (US) 1933 dir. Frank Lloyd
MILBERG (US) 1959
dir. George Schaefer
TV(US)
Balderston, J. L.
P

Berlin Affair, The
CANNON (It/Ger) 1985
dir. Liliana Cavani
Tanizaki, J. *Buddhist Cross, The*

Berlin Alexanderplatz
TELECUL/CH 4 (Fr/GB) 1985
dir. Rainer Werner Fassbinder
TVSe(Fr/GB)
Doblin, A.

Berlin, Tunnel 21
FILMWAYS (US) 1981
dir. Richard Michaels
TV(US)
Lindquist, D.

Bernardine
FOX (US) 1957 dir. Henry Levin
Chase, M.
P

Best Actress
E! (US) 2000 dir. Harvey Frost
TV(US)
Kane, J.

Best Defense
PAR (US) 1984 dir. Willard Huyck
Grossbach, R. *Easy and Hard Ways Out*

Best Foot Forward
MGM (US) 1943 dir. Edward Buzzell
M
Holmes, J. C.
P

Best Friends for Life
HALLMARK (US) 1998 dir. Michael
Switzer
TV(US)
Hearon, S. *Life Estates*

Best Little Girl in the World, The
SPELLING (US) 1981
dir. Sam O'Steen
TV(US)
Levenkron, S.

Best Little Whorehouse in Texas
UN (US) 1982 dir. Colin Higgins
M
King, L. L. and Masterson, P.
P

Best Man, The
UA (US) 1964 dir. Franklin Schaffner
Vidal, G.
P

Best Man Wins, The
COL (US) 1934 dir. Erle C. Kenton
Kohn, B. G.

Best of Everything, The
FOX (US) 1959 dir. Jean Negulesco
Jaffe, R.

Best of Friends, The
LONDON (GB) 1994 dir. Alvin Rakoff
TV(GB)
Whitemore, H.

Best Place To Be, The
R. HUNTER (US) 1979 dir. David Miller
TVSe(US)
van Slyke, H.

Best Years of Our Lives, The
GOLDWYN (US) 1946
dir. William Wyler
Kantor, M. *Glory for Me*

Bête Humaine, La
PARIS (Fr) 1938 dir. Jean Renoir
Zola, E.

Betrayal
METRO (US) 1974 dir. Gordon Hessler
TV(US)
Disney, D. M. *Only Couples Need Apply*

Betrayal
EMI TV (US) 1978 dir. Paul Wendkos
TV(US)
Freeman, L. and Roy, J.

Betrayal
VIRGIN (GB) 1982 dir. David Jones
Pinter, H.
P

Betrayal from the East
RKO (US) 1945 dir. William Berke
Hynd, A.

Betrayal of Trust
COS-MEU (US) 1994 dir. George
Kaczender
US(TV)
Noel, B. and Watterson, K. *You Must be
Dreaming*

Betrayed by Love
E. J. SCHERICK (US) 1994 dir. John
Power
TV(US)
Jones, A. *FBI Killer, The*

Betsy, The
UA (US) 1978 dir. Daniel Petrie
Robbins, H.

Better Living
GOLDHEART (US) 1998 dir. Max
Meyer
Walker, G. F.
P

Betty
MK2 (Fr) 1992 dir. Claude Chabrol
Simenon, G.

Betty Blue
GAU (Fr) 1986 dir. Jean-Jacques Beineix
Dijan, P. *372 Le Matin*

Betty Fisher et Autres Histoires
STUDIO CANAL+ (Fr/Can) 2001 dir.
Claude Miller
Rendell, R. *Tree of Hands, The*

Betty Ford Story, The
WAR TV (US) 1987 dir. David Greene
TV(US)
Ford, B. and Chase, C. *Times Of My Life,
The*

Between Friends
HBO (US) 1983 dir. Lou Antonio
List, S. *Nobody Makes Me Cry*

Between Heaven and Hell
FOX (US) 1956 dir. Richard Fleischer
Gwaltney, F. I. *Day the Century Ended,
The*

Between Two Women
J. AVNET (US) 1986 dir. Jon Avnet
TV(US)
Martin, G. *Living Arrows*

Between Two Worlds
WAR (US) 1944 dir. Edward A. Blatt
Vane, S. *Outward Bound*
P

Between Us Girls
UN (US) 1942 dir. Henry Koster

Gignoux, R. *Le Fruit Vert*
P

Beulah Land
COL TV (US) 1980 dir. Virgil Vogel,
Harry Falk
TVSe(US)

Coleman, L.

Beware My Lovely
RKO (US) 1952 dir. Harry Horner

Dineli, M. *Man, The*
P

Beware of Pity
TC (GB) 1946 dir. Maurice Elvey

Zweig, S.

Beyond Bedlam
METRODOME (GB) 1993 dir. Vadim
Jean

Knight, H. A.

Beyond Mombasa
COL (GB) 1955 dir. George Marshall

Eastwood, J. *Mark of the Leopard*

Beyond Obsession
WAR (US) 1994 dir. David Greene
TV(US)

Hammer, R.

Beyond Reasonable Doubt
J&M (NZ) 1980 dir. John Laing

Yallop, D.

Beyond Suspicion
VZ/SERTNER (US) 1993 dir. William A.
Graham
TV(US)

Bakos, S. C. *Appointment for Murder*

Beyond the Curtain
RANK (GB) 1960 dir. Compton Bennett

Wallis, A. J. and Blair, C. E. *Thunder
Above*

Beyond the Forest
WAR (US) 1949 dir. King Vidor

Engstrandt, S. D.

Beyond Therapy
NEW WORLD (US) 1987
dir. Robert Altman

Durang, C.
P

Beyond the Reef
UN (US) 1981 dir. Frank C. Clark

Richer, C. *Tikoyo and his Shark*

Beyond this Place
REN (GB) 1959 dir. Jack Cardiff

Cronin, A. J.

B.F.'s Daughter
MGM (US) 1948 dir. Robert Z. Leonard

Marquand, J. P.

Bhowani Junction
MGM (GB) 1955 dir. George Cukor

Masters, J.

Bicentennial Man
COL (US) 1999 dir. Chris Columbus

Asimov, I. and Silverberg, R. *Positronic
Man, The*

Bicycle Thief, The
MGM (It) 1949 dir. Vittorio de Sica

Bartolini, L.

Big and Hairy
NEW CITY (US) 1998 dir. Philip Spink
TV(US)

Daly, B.

Big Bear
TELEFILM (Can) 1999 dir. Gil Cardinal
TVSe(Can)
Weibe, R. *Temptations of Big Bear, The*

Big Boodle, The
UA (US) 1957 dir. Richard Wilson
GB title: Night in Havana
Sylvester, R.

Big Bounce, The
WAR (US) 1969 dir. Alex March
Leonard, E.

Big Broadcast, The
PAR (US) 1932 dir. Frank Tuttle
Manley, W. F. *Wild Waves*

Big City, The
R. D. BANSAL (Ind) 1963
dir. Satyajit Ray
Mitra, N. M.

Big Clock, The
PAR (US) 1947 dir. John Farrow
Fearing, K.

Big Country, The
UA (US) 1958 dir. William Wyler
Hamilton, D.

Big Fella
FORTUNE (GB) 1937 dir. J. E. Wills
McKay, C. *Banjo*

Big Fisherman, The
CENT (US) 1959 dir. Frank Borzage
Douglas, L. C.

Big Fix, The
UN (US) 1978 dir. Jeremy Paul Kagan
Simon, R. L.

Big Hand for the Little Lady, A
WAR (US) 1966 dir. Fielder Cook
GB title: Big Deal at Dodge City
Carroll, S.
P

Big Heat, The
COL (US) 1953 dir. Fritz Lang
McGivern, W. P.

Big Heist, The
ALLIANCE/A&E (US/Can) 2001 dir.
Robert Markowitz
TV(US/Can)
Volkman, E. and Cummings, J. *Heist, The: How a Gang Stole $8,000,000 at Kennedy Airport and Lived to Regret It*

Big Kahuna, The
FRANCHISE (US) 1999 dir. John
Swanbeck
Rueff, R. *Hospitality Suite*
P

Big Knife, The
UA (US) 1955 dir. Robert Aldrich
Odets, C.
P

Big Land, The
WAR (US) 1957 dir. Gordon Douglas
GB title: Stampeded
Gruber, F. *Buffalo Grass*

Big Man, The
PALACE (GB) 1990 dir. David Leland
McIlvanney, W.

Big Night, The
UA (US) 1951 dir. Joseph Losey
Ellin, S. *Dreadful Summit*

Big Pond, The
PAR (US) 1930 dir. Hobart Henley
Middleton, G. and Thomas, A. E.
P

Big Red
DISNEY (US) 1962 dir. Norman Tokar
A, Ch
Kjelgaard, J. A.

Big Sky, The
RKO (US) 1952 dir. Howard Hawks
Guthrie, Jr, A. B.

Big Sleep, The
WAR (US) 1946 dir. Howard Hawks
ITC (GB) 1977 dir. Michael Winner
Chandler, R.

Big Street, The
RKO (US) 1942 dir. Irving Reis
Runyon, D. *Little Pinks*

Big Town, The
COL (US) 1987 dir. Ben Bolt
Howard, C. *Arm, The*

Bilingual Lover, The
ATRIUM (Sp/It) 1993 dir. Vicente Aranda
Marse, J.

Billie
UA (US) 1965 dir. Don Weis
Alexander, R. *Time Out for Ginger*
P

Billionaire Boys Club, The
ITC (US) 1987 dir. Marvin Chomsky
TVSe(US)
Horton, S.

Billion Dollar Brain
UA (GB) 1967 dir. Ken Russell
Deighton, L.

Bill of Divorcement, A
RKO (US) 1932 dir. George Cukor
RKO (US) 1940 dir. John Farrow
GB title: Never to Love
Dane, C.
P

Billy Bathgate
TOUCHSTONE (US) 1991 dir. Robert Benton
Doctorow, E. L.

Billy Budd
AAL (GB) 1962 dir. Peter Ustinov
Melville, H.

Billy Liar
WAR (GB) 1963 dir. John Schlesinger
Waterhouse, K.

Billy: Portrait of a Street Kid
CARLINER (US) 1977
dir. Steven Gethers
TV(US)
Downs, R. C. S. *Peoples*

Billy the Kid
MGM (US) 1930 dir. King Vidor
MGM (US) 1941 dir. David Millar
Burns, W. N. *Saga of Billy the Kid, The*

Biloxi Blues
UN (US) 1988 dir. Mike Nichols
Simon, N.
P

Bingo
BBC (GB) 1990 dir. Don Taylor
TV(GB)
Bond, E.

Bingo Long Travelling All-Stars and Motor Kings, The
UN (US) 1976 dir. John Badham
Brashler, W.

Biography (of a Bachelor Girl)
MGM (US) 1935 dir. Edward H. Griffith
Behrman, S. N. *Biography*
P

Bionic Ever After?
GALLANT (US) 1994 dir. Steve Stafford
TV(US)
Caidin, M. *Cyborg*

Birch Interval
GAMMA III (US) 1976
dir. Delbert Mann
Crawford, J.

Birdcage, The
MGM (US) 1996 dir. Mike Nichols
Poiret, J. *Cage Aux Folles, La*
P

Birdman of Alcatraz
UA (US) 1961 dir. John Frankenheimer
Gaddis, T. E.

Birds, The
UN (US) 1963 dir. Alfred Hitchcock
Du Maurier, D.

Birds Fall Down, The
BBC (GB) 1978 dir. John Glenister
TVSe(GB)
West, R.

Birdy
TRISTAR (US) 1984 dir. Alan Parker
Wharton, W.

Birthday Party, The
CINERAMA (GB) 1968
dir. William Friedkin
BBC (GB) 1988 dir. Kenneth Ives
TV(GB)
Pinter, H.
P

Bishop Misbehaves, The
MGM (US) 1935 dir. E. A. Dupont
GB title: Bishop's Misadventures, The
Jackson, F.
P

Bishop Murder Case, The
MGM (US) 1930 dir. Nick Grinde,
David Burton
van Dine, S. S.

Bishop's Wife, The
RKO (US) 1947 dir. Henry Koster
Nathan, R. *In Barley Fields*

Bitch, The
BW (GB) 1979 dir. Gerry O'Hara
Collins, J.

Bitter Harvest
RANK (GB) 1963
dir. Peter Graham Scott
Hamilton, P. *Street Has a Thousand Eyes, The*

Bitter Harvest
FRIES (US) 1981 dir. Roger Young
TV(US)
Halbert, F. and Halbert, S.

Bitter Moon
COL (Fr/GB) 1992 dir. Roman Polanski
Bruckner, P. *Lunes de Fiel*

Bitter Sweet
UA (GB) 1933 dir. Herbert Wilcox
MGM (US) 1940 dir. W. S. Van Dyke
M
Coward, N.
P

Bitter Tea of General Yen, The
COL (US) 1932 dir. Frank Capra
Stone, Mrs G.

Black Aces
UN (US) 1937 dir. Buck Jones
Payne, S.

Black and Blue
EVOLVE (US) 1999 dir. Paul Shapiro
TV(US)
Quindlen, A.

Black Angel
UN (US) 1946 dir. Roy William Neill
Woolrich, C.

Black Arrow
COL (US) 1948 dir. Gordon Douglas
GB title: Black Arrow Strikes, The
SOUTHERN TV (GB) 1972
TVSe(GB)
TOWER (US) 1985 dir. John Hough
TV(US/GB)
Stevenson, R. L.

Blackbeard's Ghost
DISNEY (US) 1968
dir. Robert Stevenson
Ch
Stahl, B.

Black Beauty
FOX (US) 1946 dir. Max Nosseck
TIGON (GB) 1971 dir. James Hill
UN (US) 1978 dir. Daniel Haller
Ch, TVSe(US)
WAR (US/GB) 1994 dir. Caroline
Thompson
Sewell, A.

Blackboard Jungle, The
MGM (US) 1955 dir. Richard Brooks
Hunter, E.

Black Camel
FOX (US) 1931
dir. Hamilton MacFadden
Biggers, E. D.

Black Candle, The
TYNE-TEES (GB) 1991
dir. Roy Battersby
TV(GB)
Cookson, C.

Black Cauldron, The
DISNEY (US) 1985 dir. Ted Berman,
Richard Rich
A, Ch
Alexander, L. *Chronicles of Prydain, The*

Black Eye
WAR (US) 1974 dir. Jack Arnold
Jacks, J. *Murder on the Wild Side*

Black Fox
RHI (US) 1995 dir. Steven H. Stern
TV(US)
Braun, M.

Black Fury
WAR (US) 1935 dir. Michael Curtiz
Irving, H. R. *Bohunk*
P

Black Hawk Down
COL (US) 2001 dir. Ridley Scott
Bowden, M. *Black Hawk Down: A Story of Modern War*

Blackheath Poisonings, The
CENTRAL (GB) 1992 dir. Stuart Orme
TVSe(GB)
Symons, J.

Black Jack
ENT (GB) 1979 dir. Kenneth Loach
Garfield, L.

Black Joy
WINCAST/WEST ONE (GB) 1977
dir. Anthony Simmons
Ali, J. *Dark Days and Light Nights*
P

Black Light
MH FILMS (GB) 1994 dir. Med Hondo
Daeninckx, D. *Lumière Noire*

Black Limelight
ABPC (GB) 1938 dir. Paul Stein
Sherry, G.
P

Black Magic
UA (US) 1949 dir. Gregory Ratoff
Dumas, A. *Memoirs of a Physician*

Blackmail
BI (GB) 1929 dir. Alfred Hitchcock
Bennett, C.
P

Blackmailed
GFD (US) 1950 dir. Marc Allegret
Myers, E. *Mrs Christopher*

Black Marble, The
AVCO (US) 1980
dir. Harold Becker
Wambaugh, J.

Black Market Baby
BRUT (US) 1977 dir. Robert Day
GB title: Don't Steal My Baby
TV(US)
Christman, E. *Nice Italian Girl, A*

Black Narcissus
ARC (GB) 1946 dir. Michael Powell
Godden, R.

Black Rain
ART EYE (Jap) 1988
dir. Shohei Imamura
Ibuse, M.

Black River
FOX TV (US) 2001 dir. Jeff Bleckner
TV(US)
Koontz, D.

Black Robe
ALLIANCE (Can/Aust) 1991
dir. Bruce Beresford
Moore, B.

Black Rose, The
FOX (US) 1950 dir. Henry Hathaway
Costain, T. B.

Black Shield of Falworth, The
UI (US) 1954 dir. Rudolph Maté
Pyle, H. *Men of Iron*

Black Stallion, The
UA (US) 1979 dir. Carroll Ballard
Ch
Farley, W.

Black Stallion Returns, The
MGM (US) 1983 dir. Robert Dalva
Ch
Farley, W.

Black Sunday
PAR (US) 1977 dir. John Frankenheimer
Harris, T.

Black Swan, The
FOX (US) 1942 dir. Henry King
Sabatini, R.

Black Tower, The
ANGLIA (GB) 1985 dir. Ronald Humble
TVSe(GB)
James, P. D.

Black Tulip, The
CINERAMA (Fr) 1963
dir. Christian-Jaque
BBC (GB) 1970 dir. Derek Martinus
TVSe(GB)
Dumas, A.

Black Velvet Gown, The
TYNE-TEES (GB) 1991
dir. Norman Stone
TV(GB)
Cookson, C.

Black Widow
FOX (US) 1954 dir. Nunnally Johnson
Quentin, P. *Fatal Woman*

Black Widow Murders: The Blanche Tayor Moore Story
LORIMAR (US) 1993 dir. Alan Metzger
TV(US)
Schutze, J. *Preacher's Girl*

Black Windmill, The
PAR (GB) 1974 dir. Don Siegel

Egleton, C. *Seven Days to a Killing*

Blade Runner
WAR (US) 1982 dir. Ridley Scott

Dick, P. K. *Do Androids Dream of Electric Sheep?*

Blanche
TELEPRESSE (Fr) 1971
dir. Walerian Borowczyk

Slowacki, J. *Mazepa*

Blanche Fury
CIN (GB) 1948 dir. Marc Allégret

Shearing, J.

Blank Page, The
COVERT (US) 1997 dir. Adam Langer

Langer, A.
P

Blaue, Der
BR (Ger) 1994 dir. Lienhard Wawrzyn

Wawrzyn, L.

Blaze
TOUCHSTONE (US) 1989
dir. Ron Shelton

Starr, B. and Perry, H. *Blaze Starr: My Life as Told to Huey Perry*

Blaze of Noon
PAR (US) 1947 dir. John Farrow

Gann, E. K.

Bleak House
BBC (GB) 1985 dir. Ross Devenish
TVSe(GB)

Dickens, C.

Blessed Event
WAR (US) 1932 dir. Roy del Ruth

Seff, M. and Wilson, F.
P

Bless the Beasts and Children
COL (US) 1971 dir. Stanley Kramer

Swarthout, G.

Bless the Child
PAR (US/Ger) 2000 dir. Chuck Russell

Spellman, C. C.

Blind Alley
COL (US) 1939 dir. Charles Vidor

Warwick, J.
P

Blind Ambition
TIME-LIFE (US) 1979
dir. George Schaefer
TVSe(US)

Dean, J.

Dean, M. *Mo: A Woman's View of Watergate*

Blind Date
RANK (GB) 1959 dir. Joseph Losey
US title: Chance Meeting

Howard, L.

Blinded by the Light
TIME-LIFE (US) 1980
dir. John A. Alonzo
TV(US)

Brancato, R. F.

Blind Faith
NBC (US) 1990 dir. Paul Wendkos
TVSe(US)

McGinniss, J.

Blindfold
UI (US) 1965 dir. Philip Dunne

Fetcher, L.

Blind Goddess, The
FOX (GB) 1947 dir. Harold French

Hastings, Sir P.
P

Blind Man's Buff
GEMINI (Port/Fr) 1994 dir. Manoel de Oliveira
Monteiro, P.
P

Bliss
NSW (Aust) 1984 dir. Ray Lawrence
Carey, P.

Blithe Spirit
CIN (GB) 1945 dir. David Lean
COMPASS (US) 1966
dir. George Schaefer
TV(US)
Coward, N.
P

Blockhouse, The
GALACTUS (GB) 1973 dir. Clive Rees
Clebert, J. P. *Blockhaus, Le*

Blonde
GREENWALD (US/Can/Aust) 2001
dir. Joyce Chopra
TVSe(US/Can/Aust)
Oates, J. C.

Blondes for Danger
WILCOX (GB) 1938 dir. Jack Raymond
Price, E. *Red for Danger*

Blood Alley
WAR (US) 1955 dir. William Wellman
Fleischman, A. S.

Blood and Orchids
LORIMAR (US) 1986 dir. Jerry Thorpe
TVSe(US)
Katkov, N.

Blood and Sand
FOX (US) 1941 dir. Rouben Mamoulian
Ibanez, V. B.

Bloodbrothers
WAR (US) 1978 dir. Robert Mulligan
Price, R.

Blood from the Mummy's Tomb
MGM-EMI (GB) 1971 dir. Seth Holt
Stoker, B. *Jewel of the Seven Stars, The*

Bloodhounds of Broadway
FOX (US) 1952 dir. Harmon Jones
COL (US) 1989 dir. Howard Brookner
Runyon, D.

Blood Hunt
BBC (GB) 1986 dir. Peter Barber-Fleming
TV(GB)
Gunn, N.

Bloodline
PAR (US) 1979 dir. Terence Young
Sheldon, S.

Blood of Others, The
HBO PREM (Can/Fr) 1984
dir. Claude Chabrol
TV(Can/Fr)
De Beauvoir, S.

Blood on the Moon
RKO (US) 1948 dir. Robert Wise
Short, L. *Gunman's Choice*

Blood Oranges, The
KARDANA (US) 1998 dir. Philip Haas
Hawkes, J.

Blood Red Roses
CHANNEL 4 (GB) 1987
TVSe(GB)
McGrath, J.

Blood Relatives
FILMCORD (Can/Fr) 1981
dir. Claude Chabrol
McBain, E.

Blood Rights
BBC (GB) 1991 dir. Leslie Manning
TVSe(GB)

Phillips, M.

Blood Sport
DLT (US) 1989 dir. Harvey Hart
TV(US)

Francis, D.

Blood Wedding
LIBRA (Sp) 1981 dir. Carlos Saura

Lorca, F. G.
P

Blott on the Landscape
BBC (GB) 1985 dir. Roger Bamford
TVSe(GB)

Sharpe, T.

Blow
NEW LINE (US) 2001 dir. Ted Demme

Porter, B.

Blue and the Gray, The
COL TV (US) 1982
dir. Andrew McLaglen
TVSe(US)

Catton, B.

Blue Angel, The
PAR (Ger) 1930 dir. Josef von Sternberg
FOX (US) 1959 dir. Edward Dmytryk

Mann, H. *Professor Unrath*

Bluebeard's Eighth Wife
PAR (US) 1938 dir. Ernst Lubitsch

Savoir, A.
P

Bluebell
BBC (GB) 1986 dir. Moira Armstrong
TVSe(GB)

Perry, G.

Blue Bird, The
FOX (US) 1940 dir. Walter Lane
FOX (US/Rus) 1976 dir. George Cukor

Maeterlinck, M.
P

Blue Blood
MIQ (GB) 1973 dir. Andrew Sinclair

Thynne, A. *Carry Cot, The*

Blue City
PAR (US) 1986 dir. Michelle Manning

Macdonald, R.

Blue Denim
TCF (US) 1959 dir. Philip Dunne
GB title: Blue Jeans

Herlihy, J. L. and Noble, W.
P

Blue Fin
S. AUST (Aust) 1978 dir. Carl Schultz

Thiele, C.

Bluegrass
LAN (US) 1988 dir. Simon Wincer
TVSe(US)

Deal, B.

Blue Knight, The
LORIMAR (US) 1973 dir. Robert Butler
TVSe(US)

Wambaugh, J.

Blue Lagoon, The
GFD (GB) 1949 dir. Frank Launder
COL (US) 1980 dir. Randal Kleiser

Stacpoole, H. D.

Blue Max, The
FOX (US) 1966 dir. John Guillermin

Hunter, J. D.

Blue Moon
COL TRISTAR (US) 1999 dir. Ron
Lagomarsino
TV(US)
Rice, L.

Blue River
HALLMARK (US) 1995 dir. Larry
Elikann
TV(US)
Canin, E.

Blue Rodeo
WAR (US) 1996 dir. Peter Werner
TV(US)
Mapson, J.

Blues in the Night
WAR (US) 1941 dir. Anatole Litvak
Gilbert, E. *Hot Nocturne*
P

Blush
BEIJING (China) 1994 dir. Shaohong Li
Tong, S.

B. Monkey
MIRAMAX (GB/It) 1998 dir. Michael
Radford
Davies, A.

Boat, The
COL (Ger) 1981 dir. Wolfgang Petersen
Buchheim, L.-G.

Bobby Deerfield
WAR (US) 1977 dir. Sydney Pollack
Remarque, E. M. *Heaven has no
Favourites*

Bobo, The
WAR (US) 1978 dir. Robert Parrish
Cole, B. *Olimpia*

Bodies, Rest and Motion
FINE LINE (US) 1993 dir. Michael
Steinberg
Hedden, R.
P

Body, The
COMPASS (Ger/US) 2000 dir. Jonas
McCord
Sapir, R. B.

Body and Soul
CARLTON (GB) 1993 dir. Moira
Armstrong
TVSe(GB)
Bernstein, M.

Body in the Library, The
BBC (GB) 1984 dir. George Gallaccio
TV(GB)
Christie, A.

Body Parts
PAR (US) 1991 dir. Eric Red
Boileau, P and Narcejac, T. *Choice Cuts*

Body Snatcher, The
RKO (US) 1945 dir. Robert Wise
Stevenson, R. L.

Body Snatchers
WAR (US) 1993 dir. Abel Ferrara
Finney, J. *Invasion of the Body Snatchers*

Boeing-Boeing
PAR (US) 1965 dir. John Rich
Camoletti, M.
P

Boesman & Lena
PATHE (Fr/SA) 2000 dir. John Berry
Fugard, A.
P

Bofors Gun, The
RANK (GB) 1968 dir. Jack Gold

McGrath, J. *Events Whilst Guarding the Bofors Gun*
P

Bogie
FRIES (US) 1980 dir. Vincent Sherman
TV(US)

Hyams, J.

Bohème, La
NEW YORKER/ERATO (Fr/It) 1989 dir. Leo Conencini
M

Puccini, G.

Bohemian Life
FILMS A2/PYRAMIDE (Fr) 1992 dir. Aki Kaurismaki

Murger, H. *Scènes de la Vie Bohème*

Boiling Point
HEXAGON (US) 1993 dir. James B. Harris

Petievich, G. *Money Men*

Bojangles
MGM TV (US) 2001 dir. Joseph Sargent
TV(US)

Haskins, J. and Mitgang, N. R. *Mr. Bojangles—The Biography of Bill Robinson*

Bollywood
SONI-KAHN (Ind) 1994 dir. B. J. Kahn
M

Tharoor, S. *Show Business*

Bomb, The
CHANNEL 4 (Ger) 1987 dir. H. C. Gorlitz

Molin, L.

Bombay Mail
UN (US) 1933 dir. Edwin L. Martin

Blochman, L. G.

Bombshell
MGM (US) 1933 dir. Victor Fleming
GB title: Blonde Bombshell

Franke, C. and Crane, M.
P

Bonanno: A Godfather's Story
PAULSON (US) 1999 dir. Michael Poulette
TVSe(US)

Bonanno, J. and Lalli, S. *Man of Honor, A*

Bonanno, B. *Bound by Honor*

Bone Collector, The
COL (US) 1999 dir. Phillip Noyce

Deaver, J.

Bones and Silence
BBC/A&E (GB) 1998 dir. Maurice Phillips
TV(GB)

Hill, R.

Bonfire of the Vanities, The
WAR (US) 1990 dir. Brian De Palma

Wolfe, T.

Bongwater
ALLIANCE IND (US) 1998 dir. Richard Sears

Hornburg, M.

Bonjour Tristesse
COL (GB) 1957 dir. Otto Preminger

Sagan, F.

Bonne Soupe, La
BELSTAR (Fr/It) 1963 dir. Robert Thomas

Marceau, F.
P

Bon Voyage
DISNEY (US) 1962 dir. James Neilson

Hayes, M. and Hayes, J. A.

Bon Voyage
BBC (GB) 1985 dir. Mike Vardy
TV(GB)
Coward, N.

Boom!
UI (GB) 1968 dir. Joseph Losey
Williams, T. *Milk Train Doesn't Stop Here Anymore, The*
P

Boost, The
HEMDALE (US) 1988
dir. Harold Becker
Stein, B. *Ludes*

Bopha!
TAUBMAN (US) 1993 dir. Morgan Freeman
Mtwa, P.
P

Bordertown
WAR (US) 1934 dir. Archie Mayo
Graham, C.

Born Again,
AVCO (US) 1978 dir. Irving Rapper
Colson, C.

Born Free
COL (GB) 1965 dir. James Hill
Adamson, J.

Born on the Fourth of July
UN (US) 1989 dir. Oliver Stone
Kovic, R.

Born Reckless
FOX (US) 1930 dir. John Ford
Clarke, D. H. *Louis Beretti*

Born to be Bad
RKO (US) 1950 dir. Nicholas Ray
Parrish, A. *All Kneeling*

Born to be Sold
SAMUELS (US) 1981
dir. Burt Brinckerhoff
TV(US)
McTaggart, L. *Baby Brokers, The*

Born to Kill
RKO (US) 1947 dir. Robert Wise
GB title: Lady of Deceit
Gunn, J. E. *Deadlier than the Male*

Born Too Soon
REP (US) 1993 dir. Noel Nosseck
TV(US)
Mehren, E.

Born Yesterday
COL (US) 1950 dir. George Cukor
MILBERG (US) 1956 dir. Garson Kanin
TV(US)
HOLLYWOOD (US) 1993 dir. Luis Mandoki
Kanin, G.
P

Borrowers, The
FOX TV (US) 1973 dir. Walter C. Miller
Ch, TV(US)
WORKING TITLE TV/TNT (US/GB) 1992 dir. John Henderson
Ch, TVSe(US/GB)
POLYGRAM (US/GB) 1997 dir. Peter Hewitt
Norton, M. *Borrowers, The; Borrowers Afield, The; Borrowers Afloat, The; Borrowers Aloft, The*

Borstal Boy
BRIT SCREEN (GB/Ire) 2000 dir. Peter Sheridan
Behan, B.

Bossa Nova
COL (Bra/US) 2000 dir. Bruno Barreto
Sant'Anna, S. *Miss Simpson*

Boss of Bosses
BLEECKER (US) 1999 dir. Dwight H. Little
TV(US)

O'Brien, J. F., Kurins, A. and Shames, L. *Boss of Bosses—The Fall of the Godfather: The FBI and Paul Castellano*

Bostonians, The
RANK (GB) 1984 dir. James Ivory

James, H.

Boston Strangler, The
FOX (US) 1968 dir. Richard Fleischer

Frank, G.

Botany Bay
PAR (US) 1952 dir. John Farrow

Nordhoff, C. B. and Hall, J. N.

Bottom of the Bottle, The
TCF (US) 1956 dir. Henry Hathaway
GB title: Beyond the River

Simenon, G.

Boudu Sauvé des Eaux
M. SIMON (Fr) 1932 dir. Jean Renoir

Fauchois, R.
P

Bought
WAR (US) 1931 dir. Archie Mayo

Henry, H. *Jackdaws Strut*

Bound for Glory
UA (US) 1976 dir. Hal Ashby

Guthrie, W.

Bounty, The
ORION (GB) 1984 dir. Roger Donaldson

Hough, R. *Captain Bligh and Mr Christian*

Bouquet of Barbed Wire
LWT (GB) 1976 dir. Tony Wharmby
TVSe(GB)

Newman, A.

Bourne Identity, The
WAR TV (US) 1988 dir. Roger Young
TVSe(US)

Ludlum, R.

Boxer and Death, The
PRAHA (Czech/Ger) 1962 dir. Peter Solan

Hen, J.

Box of Delights, The
BBC (GB) 1984 dir. Renny Rye
Ch, TVSe(GB)

Masefield, J.

Boycott
N. TWAIN (US) 2001 dir. Clark Johnson
TV(US)

Burns, S. *Daybreak of Freedom*

Boyd's Shop
RANK (GB) 1960 dir. Henry Cass

Ervine, St. J. G.
P

Boy Friend, The
MGM (GB) 1971 dir. Ken Russell
M

Wilson, S.
P

Boy in the Bush, The
CHANNEL 4 (GB) 1984
dir. Rob Stewart
TVSe(GB)

Lawrence, D. H. and Skinner, M. L.

Boy Meets Girl
WAR (US) 1938 dir. Lloyd Bacon

Spewack, B. and Spewack, S.
P

Boy on a Dolphin, The
FOX (US) 1957 dir. Jean Negulesco

Divine, D.

Boys, The
ARENAFILM (Aust) 1999 dir. Rowan Woods

Graham, G.
P

Boys from Brazil, The
ITC (US/GB) 1978
dir. Franklin Shaffner

Levin, I.

Boys from Syracuse, The
UN (US) 1940 dir. E. A. Sutherland
M

Abbott, G.

Shakespeare, W. *Comedy of Errors, The*
P

Boys in Brown
GFD (GB) 1949 dir. Montgomery Tully

Beckwith R.
P

Boys in the Band, The
WAR (US) 1970 dir. William Friedkin

Crowley, M.
P

Boys Next Door, The
HALLMARK (US) 1996 dir. John Erman
TV(US)

Griffin, T.
P

Boy who Drank Too Much, The
MTM (US) 1980 dir. Jerrold Freedman
TV(US)

Greene, S.

Bramble Bush
WAR (US) 1960 dir. Daniel Petrie

Mergendahl, C.

Branded
PAR (US) 1950 dir. Rudolph Maté

Evans, E.

Brandy for the Parson
MGM (GB) 1952 dir. John Eldridge

Household, G.

Branwen
TELLESYN (GB) 1994 dir. Ceri Sherlock

Miles, G.
P

Brasher Doubloon, The
FOX (US) 1946 dir. John Brahm
GB title: High Window, The

Chandler, R. *High Window, The*

Brass Bottle, The
RANK (US) 1964 dir. Harry Keller

Anstey, F.

Brass Target
UN (US) 1978 dir. John Hough

Nolan, F. *Algonquin Project, The*

Brat Farrar
PHILCO (US) 1950 dir. Gordon Duff
TV(US)
BBC (GB) 1986 dir. Leonard Lewis
TVSe(GB)

Tey, J.

Bravados, The
FOX (US) 1958 dir. Henry King

O'Rourke, F.

Brave, The
MAJ (US) 1997 dir. Johnny Depp

McDonald, G.

Brave Bulls, The
COL (US) 1951 dir. Robert Rossen

Lea, T.

Brave Little Toaster, The
HYP (US) 1989 dir. Jerry Rees
A, Ch

Disch, T. M.

Brave Little Toaster Goes to Mars, The
HYP (US) 1999 dir. Robert C. Ramirez
A, Ch, TV(US)

Disch, T. M.

Brave New World
UN (US) 1980 dir. D. B. Brinckerhoff
TV(US)
USA NETWORK (US) 1998 dir. Leslie
Libman, Larry Williams
TV(US)

Huxley, A.

Bravo Two Zero
MIRAMAX (SA) 2001 dir. Tom Clegg

McNab, A.

Bread or Blood
BBC (GB) 1981 dir. Peter Smith
TVSe(GB)

Hudson, W. H. *Shepherd's Life, A*

Breaker Morant
S. AUST (Aust) 1980
dir. Bruce Beresford

Ross, K.
P

Breakfast at Tiffany's
PAR (US) 1961 dir. Blake Edwards

Capote, T.

Breakfast of Champions
SUMMIT (US) 1999 dir. Alan Rudolph

Vonnegut, Jr. K.

Breakheart Pass
UA (US) 1975 dir. Tom Gries

MacLean, A.

Breaking Point, The
WAR (US) 1950 dir. Michael Curtiz

Hemingway, E. *To Have and Have Not*

Breaking Point, The
BUTCHER (GB) 1961
dir. Lance Comfort

Meynell, L.

Breaking the Surface: The Greg Louganis Story
GREEN-EPSTEIN (US) 1997 dir. Steven
H. Stern
TV(US)

Louganis, G. and Marcus, E.

Breaking Up
WAR (US) 1997 dir. Robert Greenwald

Cristofer, M.
P

Break in the Circle
EXC (GB) 1955 dir. Val Guest

Loraine, P.

Break in the Sun
BBC (GB) 1981 dir. Roger Singleton-
Turner
TVSe(GB)

Ashley, B.

Breakout
COL (US) 1975 dir. Tom Gries

Asinof, E., Hinckle, W. and Turner, W.
Ten-Second Jailbreak, The

Break Out
CFTF (GB) 1983 dir. Frank Godwin
US title: Breakout
Ch

Gillham, B. *Place to Hide, A*

Break the News
GFD (GB) 1938 dir. Rene Clair

de Gouriadec, L. *Mort en fuite, La*

Breath of French Air, A
YTV (GB) 1991 dir. Robert Tronson
TV(GB)

Bates, H. E.

Breath of Scandal, A
PAR (US) 1960 dir. Michael Curtiz, Mario Russo

Molnar, F. *Olympia*
P

Breathing Lessons
SIGNBOARD HILL (US) 1994 dir. John Erman
TV(US)

Tyler, A.

Brewster's Millions
BRITISH & DOMINION (GB) 1935 dir. Thornton Freeland
UA (US) 1945 dir. Allan Dwan
UN (US) 1985 dir. Walter Hill

McCutcheon, G. B.

Brian's Song
COL TV (US) 1971 dir. Buzz Kulik
TV(US)
COL TRISTAR (US) 2001 dir. John Gray
TV(US)

Sayers, G. and Silverman, A. *I am Third*

Bridal Path, The
BL (GB) 1959 dir. Frank Launder

Tranter, N.

Brides are Like That
WAR (US) 1936 dir. William McGann

Conners, B. *Applesauce*
P

Bride in Black, The
NEW WORLD (US) 1990 dir. James Goldstone
TV(US)

Woolrich, C.

Bride of Re-Animator
WILDSTREET (US) 1991 dir. Brian Yuzna

Lovecraft, H. P. *Herbert West—The Re-Animator*

Bride Wore Black, The
UA (Fr/It) 1967 dir. François Truffaut
Irish, W.

Bride Wore Red, The
MGM (US) 1937 dir. Dorothy Arzner

Molnar, F. *Girl from Trieste, The*
P

Brideshead Revisited
GRANADA (GB) 1981 dir. Charles Sturridge
TVSe(GB)

Waugh, E.

Bridge, The
FONO (W. Ger) 1959 dir. Bernhard Wicki

Gregor, M.

Bridge, The
CHANNEL 4 (GB) 1992 dir. Sydney Macartney

Hemingway, M.

Bridge at Remagen, The
UA (US) 1969 dir. John Guillermin

Hechler, K.

Bridge in the Jungle, The
UA (US/Mex) 1970 dir. Pancho Kohner

Traven, B.

Bridge of San Luis Rey, The
UA (US) 1944 dir. Rowland V. Lee

Wilder, T.

Bridge on the River Kwai, The
COL (GB) 1957 dir. David Lean

Boulle, P.

Bridges at Toko-Ri, The
PAR (US) 1954 dir. Mark Robson

Michener, J. A.

Bridges of Madison County, The
WAR (US) 1995 dir. Clint Eastwood
Waller, R. J.

Bridget Jones's Diary
WORKING TITLE (GB) 2001 dir.
Sharon Maguire
Fielding, H.

Bridge Too Far, A
UA (GB/US) 1977
dir. Richard Attenborough
Ryan, C.

Bridge to the Sun
MGM (Fr/US) 1961 dir. Etienne Périer
Terasaki, G.

Brief Encounter
CIN (GB) 1945 dir. David Lean
ITC (US) 1974 dir. Alan Bridges
TV(US)
Coward, N. *Still Life*
P

Brigadoon
MGM (US) 1954 dir. Vincente Minnelli
M
Lerner, A. J. and Loewe, F.
P

Bright Leaf
WAR (US) 1950 dir. Michael Curtiz
Fitz-Simons, F.

Bright Lights, Big City
MGM/UA (US) 1988 dir. James Bridges
McInerney, J.

Brighton Beach Memoirs
UN (US) 1986 dir. Gene Saks
Simon, N.
P

Brighton Rock
AB (GB) 1947 dir. John Boulting
US title: Young Scarface
Greene, G.

Bright Shining Lie, A
HBO (US) 1998 dir. Terry George
TV(US)
Sheehan, N. *Bright Shining Lie, A: John Paul Vann and America in Vietnam*

Bright Victory
UI (US) 1951 dir. Mark Robson
GB title: Lights Out
Kendrick, B. H. and Allen, W. H.

Brilliant Lies
BAYSIDE (Aust) 1996 dir. Richard Franklin
Williamson, D.
P

Brimstone and Treacle
NAMARA (GB) 1982
dir. Richard Loncraine
Potter, D.
P

Bringing Out the Dead
PAR (US) 1999 dir. Martin Scorsese
Connelly, J.

Britannia Mews
TCF (GB) 1948 dir. Jean Negulescu
US title: Forbidden Street, The
Sharp, M.

British Agent
WAR (US) 1934 dir. Michael Curtiz
Lockhart, Sir R. H. B. *Memoirs of a British Agent*

British Intelligence
WAR (US) 1940 dir. Terry Morse
GB title: Enemy Agent
Kelly, A. P.
P

Broadway
UN (US) 1942 dir. W. A. Seiter
Dunning, P. and Abbott, G.
P

Broadway Bound
ABC PROD (US) 1992 dir. Paul Bogart
TV(US)
Simon, N.
P

Broken Arrow
FOX (US) 1950 dir. Delmer Daves
Arnold, E. *Blood Brother*

Broken Cord, The
UN TV (US) 1992 dir. Ken Olin
TV(US)
Dorris, M.

Broken Lullaby
PAR (US) 1931 dir. Ernst Lubitsch
Rostand, M. *Homme que J'ai tué, L'*
P

Broken Lullaby
ALLIANCE (Can) 1994 dir. Michael Kennedy
TV(Can)
Pace, L.

Broken Promise
EMI TV (US) 1981 dir. Don Taylor
TV(US)
Hayes, K. and Lazzarino, A.

Broken Trust
FONDA (US) 1995 dir. Geoffrey Sax
TV(US)
Wood, W. P. *Court of Honor*

Broken Vows
HALMI (US) 1987 dir. Jud Taylor
TV(US)
Davis, D. S. *Where the Dark Streets Go*

Bronx Tale, A
TRIBECA (US) 1993 dir. Robert De Niro
Palminteri, C.
P

Brotherhood of Murder
SHOWTIME (US) 1999 dir. Martin Bell
TV(US)
Martinez, T. and Guinther, J.

Brotherhood of the Rose
NBC (US) 1989 dir. Marvin Chomsky
TVSe(US)
Morrell, D.

Brotherly Love
CBS (US) 1985 dir. Jeff Bleckner
TV(US)
Blankenship, W. D.

Brother Of Sleep
BA FILMPROD (Ger) 1995 dir. Joseph Vilsmaier
Schneider, R. *Schlafes Bruder*

Brother Orchid
WAR (US) 1940 dir. Lloyd Bacon
Connell, R. E.

Brother Rat
FOX (US) 1938 dir. William Keighley
Monks, J. and Finklehoffe, F. R.
P

Brothers, The
GFD (GB) 1947 dir. David MacDonald
Strong, L. A. G.

Brothers in Law
BL (GB) 1957 dir. Ray Boulting
Cecil, H.

Brothers in Trouble
RENEGADE (GB) 1995 dir. Udayan Prasad
Hussein, A. *Return Journey*

Brothers Karamazov, The
MGM (US) 1957 dir. Richard Brooks
MOSFILM (USSR) 1968 dir. Ivan Pyriev
Dostoevsky, F.

Brother's Kiss, A
OVERSEAS (US) 1996 dir. Seth Zvi
Rosenfeld
Rosenfeld, S. Z.
P

Brothers Rico, The
COL (US) 1957 dir. Phil Karlson
Simenon, G.

Brother's Tale, A
GRANADA (GB) 1983 dir. Les Chatfield
TVSe(GB)
Barstow, S.

Broth of a Boy
E. DALTON (Eire) 1958
dir. George Pollack
Leonard, H. *Big Birthday, The*
P

Browning Version, The
GFD (GB) 1951 dir. Anthony Asquith
P. MAIN (GB) 1994 dir. Mike Figgis
Rattigan, T.
P

Brown on 'Resolution'
GB (GB) 1935 dir. Walter Forde
US title: Born for Glory
Forester, C. S.

Brown's Requiem
J&T (US) 1998 dir. Jason Freeland
Ellroy, J.

Brute, La
CAPRICORNE (Fr) 1987 dir. Claude
Guillemot
des Cars, G.

Buccaneer, The
PAR (US) 1937 dir. Cecil B. De Mille
PAR (US) 1958 dir. Anthony Quinn
Saxon, L. *LaFitte the Pirate*

Buccaneers, The
BBC (GB) 1995 dir. Philip Saville
TVSe(GB)
Wharton, E.

Bud and Lou
BANNER (US) 1978
dir. Robert C. Thompson
TV(US)
Thomas, B.

Buddha of Suburbia, The
BBC (GB) 1993 dir. Roger Michell
TVSe(GB)
Kureishi, H.

Buddies
TOHO/SHOCHIKU (Jap) 1990
dir. Yasuo Furuhata
Mukoda, K.

Buddy
COL (US) 1997 dir. Caroline Thompson
Lintz, G. *Animals Are My Hobby*

Buddy Buddy
MGM (US) 1981 dir. Billy Wilder
Veber, F.
P

Buffalo Bill and the Indians
UA (US) 1976 dir. Robert Altman
Kopit, A. *Indians*
P

Buffalo Girls
TRILOGY (US) 1995 dir. Charles Haid
TVSe(US)
McMurtry, L.

Bug
PAR (US) 1975 dir. Jeannot Szwarc
Page, T. *Hephaestus Plague, The*

Bugles in the Afternoon
WAR (US) 1952 dir. Roy Rowland
Haycox, E.

Bulldog Drummond
GOLDWYN (US) 1929
dir. F. Richard Jones
McNeile, H. C. *Sapper*

Bullitt
WAR (US) 1968 dir. Peter Yates
Pike, R. L. *Mute Witness*

Bully
STUDIO CANAL+ (Fr/GB) 2000 dir.
Larry Clark
Schutze, J. *Bully: A True Story of High School Revenge*

Bumblebee Flies Anyway, The
SHOOTING GALLERY (US) 2000 dir.
Martin Duffy
TV(US)
Cormier, R.

Bump in the Night
RHI (US) 1991 dir. Karen Arthur
TV(US)
Holland, I.

Bunker, The
TIME-LIFE (US) 1981
dir. George Schaefer
TV(US)
O'Donnell, J. P.

Bunker Bean
RKO (US) 1936
dir. William Hamilton, Edward Kelly
Wilson, H. L.

Bunny Lake is Missing
COL (GB) 1965 dir. Otto Preminger
Piper, E.

Burden of Proof, The
ABC PROD (US) 1992
dir. Mike Robe
TVSe(US)
Turow, S.

Burglar, The
COL (US) 1957 dir. Paul Wendkos
Goodis, D.

Burglar
WAR (US) 1987 dir. Hugh Wilson
Block, L.

Burglars, The
COL (Fr/It) 1971 dir. Henri Verneuill
Goodis, D. *Burglar, The*

Buried Alive
AIRTIME (GB) 1983
TVSe(GB)
Bennett, A.

Burmese Harp, The
NIKKATSU (Jap) 1956
dir. Kon Ichikawa
Takeyama, M.

Burn 'em up O'Connor
MGM (US) 1938
dir. Edward Sedgwick
Campbell, Sir M. *Salute to the Gods*

Burning Bed, The
TA (US) 1984 dir. Robert Greenwald
TV(US)
McNulty, F.

Burning Bridges
LORIMAR TV (US) 1990
dir. Sheldon Larry
TV(US)
Miller, I.

Burning Glass, The
ATV (GB) 1956 dir. Cyril Coke
TV(GB)
ATV (GB) 1960 dir. David Boisseau

Morgan, C.

Burning Hills, The
WAR (US) 1956 dir. Stuart Heisler
GB title: Apache Territory

L'Amour, L.

Burning Season, The
HBO (US) 1994 dir. John
Frankenheimer
TV(US)

Revkin, A.

Cowell, A. *Decade of Destruction*

Burning Secret
VESTRON (GB/Ger) 1988
dir. Andrew Birkin

Zweig, S. *Brennendes Geheimnis*

Burnt Money
MANDARIN (Arg/Fr) 2000 dir.
Marcelo Pineyro

Piglia, R. *Plata Quemada*

Burnt Offerings
UA (US) 1976 dir. Dan Curtis

Marasco, R.

Business Affair, A
STUDIO CANAL+ (GB/Fr) 1994 dir.
Charlotte Brandstorm

Skelton, B. *Tears Before Bedtime; Weep
No More*

Busman's Honeymoon
MGM (GB) 1940 dir. Arthur Woods
US title: Haunted Honeymoon

Sayers, D. L.

Bus Stop
FOX (US) 1956 dir. Joshua Logan

Inge, W.
P

Busy Body, The
PAR (US) 1967 dir. William Castle

Westlake, D. E.

Butcher, The
FREEWAY (It) 1998 dir. Aurelia
Grimaldi

Reyes, A.

Butcher Boy, The
WAR (Ire/US) 1997 dir. Neil Jordan

McCabe, P.

Butley
SEVEN KINGS (GB/US) 1973
dir. Harold Pinter

Gray, S.
P

But Not For Me
PAR (US) 1959 dir. Walter Lang

Raphaelson, S. *Accent on Youth*
P

Butterbox Babies
SULLIVAN ENT (Can) 1995 dir. Don
McBrearty
TV(Can)

Cahill, B.

Buttercup Chain, The
COL (GB) 1969 dir. Robert Ellis Miller

Elliot, J.

Butterfield 8
MGM (US) 1960 dir. Daniel Mann

O'Hara, J.

Butterflies are Free
COL (US) 1972 dir. Milton Katselas

Gershe, L.
P

Butterfly
J&M (US) 1982 dir. Matt Cimber

Cain, J. M.

But the Flesh is Weak
MGM (US) 1932 dir. Jack Conway

Novello, I. *Truth Game, The*
P

Bwana
AURUM (Sp) 1996 dir. Imanol Uribe

del Moral, I. *Mirada del Hombre, La*
P

By Candlelight
UN (US) 1933 dir. James Whale

Geyer, S.
P

By Dawn's Early Light
HBO (US) 1990 dir. Jack Sholder
TV(US)

Prochnau, W. *Trinity's Child*

Bye Bye Birdie
COL (US) 1963 dir. George Sidney
COL (US) 1995 dir. Gene Saks
M

Stewart, M.
P

Bye Bye Braverman
WAR (US) 1968 dir. Sidney Lumet

Markfield, W. *To an Early Grave*

By Love Possessed
UA (US) 1961 dir. John Sturges

Cozzens, J. G.

By the Light of the Silvery Moon
WAR (US) 1953 dir. David Butler

Tarkington, B. *Penrod*

C

Cabaret
CINERAMA (US) 1972 dir. Bob Fosse
M

van Druten, J. *I am a Camera*
P

Cabin in the Cotton
WAR (US) 1932 dir. Michael Curtiz
Knoll, H. H.

Cabin in the Sky
MGM (US) 1943 dir. Vincente Minnelli
M

Root, L.
P

Cactus Flower
COL (US) 1969 dir. Gene Saks
Burrows, A.
P

Caddie
HEMDALE (Aust) 1976
dir. Donald Crombie
Brink, C. R. *Caddie Woodlawn*

Cadence
NEW LINE (US) 1990 dir. Martin Sheen
Weaver, G. *Count a Lonely Cadence*

Caesar and Cleopatra
RANK (GB) 1945 dir. Gabriel Pascal
TALENT (US) 1976
dir. James Cellan Jones
TV(US)

Shaw, G. B.
P

Cage Aux Folles, La
UA (Fr/It) 1978 dir. Edouard Molinaro
Poiret, J.
P

Cahier Volé, La
PROVIDENCE (Fr) 1992 dir. Christine
Lipinska
Deforges, R.

Caine Mutiny, The
COL (US) 1954 dir. Edward Dmytryk
Wouk, H.

Caine Mutiny Court-Martial, The
MALTESE (US) 1988
dir. Robert Altman
TV(US)

Wouk, H.
P

Cairo
MGM (GB) 1963 dir. Wolf Rilla
Burnett, W. R. *Asphalt Jungle, The*

Cakes and Ale
BBC (GB) 1974 dir. Bill Hays
TVSe(GB)

Maugham, W. S.

Cal
WAR (GB) 1984 dir. Pat O'Connor
MacLaverty, B.

Caleb Williams
TYNE-TEES (GB) 1983 dir. Herbert
Wise
TVSe(GB)

Godwin, W. *Adventures of Caleb
Williams (Or Things As They Are),
The*

Calendar, The
GFD (GB) 1948 dir. Arthur Crabtree

Wallace, E.

Calendar Girl, Cop, Killer? The Bambi Bembenek Story
VZ SERTNER (US) 1992 dir. Jerry
London
TV(US)

Greenya, J.

California Gold Rush
TAFT (US) 1981 dir. Jack Hively
TV(US)

Harte, B. *Luck of Roaring Camp, The;
Outcasts of Poker Flat, The*

California Suite
COL (US) 1975 dir. Herbert Ross

Simon, N.
P

Callan
EMI (GB) 1974 dir. Don Sharp

Mitchell, J. *Red File for Callan, A*

Call Her Savage
PAR (US) 1932 dir. John Francis Dillon

Thayer, T.

Calling Philco Vance
WAR (US) 1939 dir. William Clemens

van Dine, S. S. *Kennel Murder Case, The*

Call it a Day
WAR (US) 1937 dir. Archie Mayo

Smith, D.
P

Call me Anna
FINNEGAN (US) 1990
dir. Gilbert Cates
TV(US)

Duke, P. and Turan, K. *My Name is
Anna: The Autobiography of Patty Duke*

Call me Madam
TCF (US) 1953 dir. Walter Lang
M

Lindsay, H. and Crouse, R.
P

Call of the Wild
UA (US) 1935 dir. William Wellman
MASSFILMS (GB/Fr/It/Ger) 1972
dir. Ken Annakin
FRIES (US) 1976 dir. Jerry Jameson
TV(US)
RHI (US) 1993 dir. Michael Toshiyuki
Uno
TV(US)

London, J.

Call of the Wild: Dog of the Yukon
KING GREENLIGHT (Can) 1996 dir.
Peter Svatek
TV(Can)

London, J. *Call of the Wild*

Calm at Sunset
HALLMARK (US) 1996 dir. Daniel
Petrie
TV(US)

Watkins, P. *Calm at Sunset, Calm at
Dawn*

Came a Hot Friday
ORION (NZ) 1985 dir. Ian Mune

Morrieson, R. H.

Camelot
WAR (US) 1967 dir. Joshua Logan
M

Lerner, A. J. and Loewe, F.
P

White, T. H. *Once and Future King, The*

Camerons, The
BBC (GB) 1979 dir. Peter Moffatt
TVSe(GB)
Crichton, R.

Cameron's Closet
SVS (US) 1989 dir. Armand Mastroianni
Brandner, G.

Camille
MGM (US) 1936 dir. George Cukor
ROSEMONT (US/GB) 1984
dir. Desmond Davis
TV(GB/US)
Dumas, A. fils *Dame aux Camélias, La*

Camille Claudel
GAU BR (Fr) 1989 dir. Bruno Nuytten
Paris, R.-M.

Camomile Lawn, The
CHANNEL 4 (GB) 1992 dir. Peter Hall
TVSe(GB)
Wesley, M.

Campbell's Kingdom
RANK (GB) 1957 dir. Ralph Thomas
Innes, H.

Campus, Der
CONSTANTIN (Ger) 1998 dir. Sonke
Wortmann
Schwanitz, D.

Can Can
TCF (US) 1960 dir. Walter Lang
M
Burrows, A.
P

Cancel My Reservation
MGM-EMI (US) 1972 dir. Paul Bogart
L'Amour, L. *Broken Gun, The*

Candleshoe
DISNEY (GB) 1977 dir. Norman Tokar
Innes, M. *Christmas at Candleshoe*

Candy
CINERAMA (US) 1968
dir. Christian Marquand
Southern, T. and Hoffenberg, M.

Cannery Row
MGM (US) 1982 dir. David S. Ward
Steinbeck, J.

Can of Worms
DISNEY (US) 1999 dir. Paul Schneider
TV(US)
Mackel, K.

Canone Inverso
CECCHI (It) 2000 dir. Ricky Tognazzi
Maurensig, P.

Canterbury Tales, The
UA (It/Fr) 1972 dir. Pier Paolo Pasolini
Chaucer, G.

Canterville Ghost, The
MGM (US) 1943 dir. Jules Dassin
HTV (GB/US) 1986 dir. Paul Bogart
TV(GB/US)
SIGNBOARD HILL (US) 1996 dir.
Sydney Macartney
TV(US)
Wilde, O.

Canyon Passage
UN (US) 1946 dir. Jacques Tourneur
Haycox, E.

Cape Fear
UI (US) 1962 dir. J. Lee Thompson
UN (US) 1991 dir. Martin Scorsese
MacDonald, J. D. *Executioners, The*

Caper of the Golden Bulls, The
EMBASSY (US) 1966 dir. Russel Rouse
GB title: Carnival of Thieves
McGivern, W. P.

Captain Apache
BENMAR (US/Sp) 1971
dir. Alexander Singer

Whitman, S. E.

Captain Blood
WAR (US) 1935 dir. Michael Curtiz

Sabatini, R.

Captain Boycott
INDIVIDUAL (GB) 1947
dir. Frank Launder

Rooney, P.

Captain Brassbound's Conversion
COMPASS (US) 1960
dir. George Schaefer
TV(US)

Shaw, G. B.
P

Captain Carey USA
PAR (US) 1950 dir. Mitchell Leisen
GB title: After Midnight

Albrand, M. *Dishonoured*

Captain Caution
UA (US) 1940 dir. Richard Wallace

Roberts, K.

Captain Conan
STUDIO CANAL+ (Fr) 1996 dir.
Bertrand Tavernier

Vercel, R.

Captain Corelli's Mandolin
WORKING TITLE (GB/Fr) 2001 dir.
John Madden

de Bernières, L. *Corelli's Mandolin*

Captain from Castille
FOX (US) 1947 dir. Henry King

Shellabarger, S.

Captain Horatio Hornblower, R. N.
WAR (GB) 1951 dir. Raoul Walsh

Forester, C. S. *Captain Hornblower, R. N.*

Captain is a Lady, The
MGM (US) 1940 dir. Robert Sinclair

Crothers, R. *Old Lady 31*
P

Captain January
FOX (US) 1936 dir. David Butler
Ch

Richards, L. E.

Captain Lightfoot
UI (US) 1955 dir. Douglas Sirk

Burnett, W. R.

Captain Newman, M.D.
UI (US) 1963 dir. David Miller

Rosten, L.

Captain Pirate
COL (US) 1952 dir. Ralph Murphy
GB title: Captain Blood, Fugitive

Sabatini, R. *Captain Blood Returns*

Captains and the Kings
UN TV (US) 1976 dir. Douglas Heyes,
Allen Reisner
TVSe(US)

Caldwell, T.

Captains Courageous
MGM (US/GB) 1937
dir. Victor Fleming
ROSEMONT (US) 1977
dir. Harvey Hart
TV(GB/US)
HALLMARK (US) 1996 dir. Michael
Anderson
TV(US)

Kipling, R.

Captain's Doll, The
BBC (GB) 1982 dir. Claude Whatham
TV(GB)
Lawrence, D. H.

Captain's Table, The
RANK (GB) 1958 dir. Jack Lee
Gordon, R.

Captive, The
STUDIO CANAL+ (Fr) 2000 dir.
Chantal Akerman
Proust, M. *À La Recherche du Temps Perdu*

Captive in the Land, A
GLORIA/GORKY (US/USSR) 1991
dir. John Berry
Aldridge, J.

Capture of Grizzly Adams, The
TAFT (US) 1982 dir. Don Kessler
TV(US)
Sellier, Jr., C. E.

Caravan
BL (GB) 1946 dir. Arthur Crabtree
Smith, Lady E.

Caravans
BORDEAUX (US/Iran) 1978
dir. James Fargo
Michener, J. A.

Caravan to Vaccares
RANK (GB/Fr) 1974
dir. Geoffrey Reeve
MacLean, A.

Card, The
GFD (GB) 1952 dir. Ronald Neame
US title: Promoter, The
Bennett, A.

Cardinal, The
COL (US) 1963 dir. Otto Preminger
Robinson, H. M.

Career
PAR (US) 1959 dir. Joseph Anthony
Lee, J.
P

Career
RKO (US) 1939 dir. Leigh Jason
Stong, P. D.

Careful, He Might Hear You
SYME (Aust) 1983 dir. Carl Schultz
Elliott, S. *Signs of Life*

Care of Time, The
ANGLIA (GB) 1990 dir. John Howard
Davies
TV(GB)
Ambler, E.

Caresses
TVE (Sp) 1997 dir. Ventura Pons
Belbel, S.
P

Caretaker, The
BL (GB) 1963 dir. Clive Donner
US title: Guest, The
Pinter, H.
P

Caretakers, The
UA (US) 1963 dir. Hall Bartlett
GB title: Borderlines
Telfer, D.

Carey Treatment, The
MGM (US) 1972 dir. Blake Edwards
Hudson, J. *Case of Need, A*

Caribbean Mystery, A
WAR (US) 1983 dir. Robert Lewis
TV(US)
BBC (GB) 1988 dir. Christopher Pettit
TV(GB)
Christie, A.

Carlito's Way
UN (US) 1993 dir. Brian De Palma

Torres, E. *Carlito's Way; After Hours*

Carmen
TRIUMPH (Fr) 1984 dir. Francesco Rosi

Merimée, P.
Bizet, G.

Carnival
RANK (GB) 1946 dir. Stanley Haynes

MacKenzie, Sir C.

Carnosaur
NEW HORIZON (US) 1993 dir. Adam Simon

Knight, H. A.

Carolina
FOX (US) 1934 dir. Henry King
GB title: House of Connelly

Green, P. *House of Connelly, The*
P

Carolina Skeletons
KUSHNER-LOCKE (US) 1991 dir. John Erman
TV (US)

Stout, D.

Caroline?
B&E (US) 1990 dir. Joseph Sargent
TV(US)

Konigsburg, E. L. *Father's Arcane Daughter*

Caroline Chérie
GAU (Fr) 1951 dir. Richard Pottier

Saint-Laurent, C.

Carousel
TCF (US) 1956 dir. Henry King
M

Molnar, F. *Liliom*
P

Carpetbaggers, The
PAR (US) 1964 dir. Edward Dmytryk

Robbins, H.

Carrie
PAR (US) 1952 dir. William Wyler

Dreiser, T. *Sister Carrie*

Carrie
UA (US) 1976 dir. Brian De Palma

King, S.

Carried Away
FINE LINE (US) 1996 dir. Bruno Barreto

Harrison, J. *Farmer*

Carriers
ROSEMONT (US) 1998 dir. Alan Metzger
TV(US)

Lynch, P.

Carrie's War
BBC (GB) 1974 dir. Paul Stone
TVSe(GB)

Bawden, N.

Carrington
FREEWAY (GB/Fr) 1995 dir. Christopher Hampton

Holroyd, M. *Lytton Strachey: A Biography*

Carrington, V. C.
BL (GB) 1954 dir. Anthony Asquith
US title: Court Martial

Christie, D. and Christie, C.
P

Carry on, Admiral
REN (GB) 1957 dir. Val Guest

Hay, I. and Hall, S. K. *Off the Record*
P

Carry on Sergeant
AAM (GB) 1958 dir. Gerald Thomas

Delderfield, R. F. *Bull Boys, The*
P

Carve Her Name with Pride
RANK (GB) 1958 dir. Lewis Gilbert

Minney, R. J.

Casablanca
WAR (US) 1943 dir. Michael Curtiz

Burnett, M. and Alison, J. *Everybody Comes to Rick's*
P

Casanova Brown
INTERNATIONAL (US) 1944 dir. Sam Wood

Dell, F. *Bachelor Father*
P

Case Against Mrs Ames, The
PAR (US) 1936 dir. William A. Seiter

Roche, A. S.

Case of Deadly Force, A
TELECOM (US) 1986
dir. Michael Miller
TV(US)

O'Donnell, Jr., L. *Deadly Force: The Story of how a Badge can become a License to Kill*

Case of Sergeant Grischa, The
RKO (US) 1930 dir. Herbert Brenon

Zweig, A.

Case of the Black Cat, The
WAR (US) 1936 dir. William McGann

Gardner, E. S. *Case of the Caretaker's Cat, The*

Case of the Curious Bride, The
WAR (US) 1935 dir. Michael Curtiz

Gardner, E. S.

Case of the Frightened Lady, The
BL (GB) 1940 dir. George King
US title: Frightened Lady, The

Wallace, E.

Case of the Hillside Stranglers, The
FRIES (US) 1989 dir. Steven Gethers
TV(US)

O'Brien, D. *Two of a Kind: The Hillside Stranglers*

Case of the Howling Dog, The
WAR (US) 1934 dir. Alan Crosland

Gardner, E. S.

Case of the Lucky Legs, The
WAR (US) 1935 dir. Archie Mayo

Gardner, E. S.

Case of the Stuttering Bishop, The
WAR (US) 1937 dir. William Clemens

Gardner, E. S.

Case of the Velvet Claws, The
WAR (US) 1936 dir. William Clemens

Gardner, E. S.

Cash McCall
WAR (US) 1960 dir. Joseph Pevney

Hawley, C.

Cash on Demand
COL (GB) 1963 dir. Quentin Lawrence

Gillies, J.
P

Casino Murder Case, The
MGM (US) 1935 dir. Edwin Marin

van Dine, S. S.

Casino
UN (US) 1995 dir. Martin Scorsese

Pileggi, N.

Casino Royale
COL (GB) 1967 dir. John Huston
Fleming, I.

Cass Timberlane
MGM (US) 1947 dir. George Sidney
Lewis, S.

Cast a Dark Shadow
EROS (GB) 1955 dir. Lewis Gilbert
Green, J. *Murder Mistaken*
P

Cast a Giant Shadow
UA (US) 1966 dir. Melville Shavelson
Berkman, T.

Cast a Long Shadow
UA (US) 1959 dir. Thomas Carr
Overholser, W. D.

Castaway
VIRGIN (GB) 1986 dir. Nicolas Roeg
Irvine, L.

Castle, The
BR (Ger) 1997 dir. Michael Haneke
Kafka, F.

Castle in the Air
ABP (GB) 1952 dir. Henry Cass
Melville, A.
P

Castle Keep
COL (US) 1969 dir. Sydney Pollack
Eastlake, W.

Castle of Adventure
TVS (GB) 1990
Ch, TV(GB)
Blyton, E.

Casual Sex?
UN (US) 1988 dir. Genevieve Robert
Goldman, W. *Casual Sex*
P

Casualties of War
COL (US) 1989 dir. Brian De Palma
Lang, D.

Casualty of War, A
BLAIR (US) 1990 dir. Tom Clegg
TV(GB/US)
Forsyth, F.

Catacombs
BL (GB) 1964 dir. Gordon Hessler
US title: Woman Who Wouldn't Die, The
Bennett, J.

Cat and Mouse
EROS (GB) 1958 dir. Paul Rotha
Halliday, M.

Cat and the Canary, The
PAR (US) 1939 dir. Elliot Nugent
GALA (GB) 1978 dir. Radley Metzger
Willard, J.
P

Cat Ballou
COL (US) 1965 dir. Eliot Silverstein
Chanslor, R. *Ballad of Cat Ballou, The*

Cat Chaser
VESTRON (US) 1989 dir. Abel Ferrara
Leonard, E.

Catch me a Spy
RANK (GB) 1971 dir. Dick Clement
Marton, G. and Meray, T.

Catch-22
PAR (US) 1970 dir. Mike Nichols
Heller, J.

Cat Creeps, The
UN (US) 1930 dir. Rupert Julian
Willard, J. *Cat and the Canary, The*
P

Catered Affair, The
MGM (US) 1956 dir. Richard Brooks
Chayefsky, P.
P

Cater Street Hangman, The
YTV/A&E (GB/US) 1998 dir. Sarah Hellings
TV(GB/US)
Perry, A.

Catherine the Great
KORDA (GB) 1934 dir. Paul Czinner
Lengyel, M. *Czarina, The*
P

Catholics
GLAZIER (US) 1973 dir. Jack Gold
TV(US)
Moore, B.

Cadow
MGM (GB) 1971 dir. Sam Wanamaker
L'Amour, L.

Cat on a Hot Tin Roof
MGM (US) 1958 dir. Richard Brooks
GRANADA (GB) 1976
dir. Robert Moore
TV(GB/US)
Williams, T.
P

Cattle Annie and Little Britches
UN (US) 1981 dir. Lamont Johnson
Ward, R.

Caught
MGM (US) 1948 dir. Max Ophuls
Block, L. *Wild Calendar*

Caught
CINEHAUS (US) 1996 dir. Robert M. Young
Pomerantz, E. *Into It*

Cause Celebre
ANGLIA (GB) 1988 dir. John Gorrie
TV(GB)
Rattigan, T.
P

Cavalcade
FOX (US) 1932 dir. Frank Lloyd
Coward, N.
P

Caveman's Valentine, The
UN (US) 2001 dir. Kasi Lemmons
Green, G. D.

Caviar Rouge, Le
GALAXY (Fr/Switz) 1988
dir. Robert Hossein
Hossein, R. and Dard, F.

Cazalets, The
BBC (GB) 2001 dir. Suri Krishnamma
TVSe(GB)
Howard, E. J. *Light Years, The; Marking Time*

Cease Fire
CINEWORLD (US) 1985
dir. David Nutter
Fernandez, G. *Vietnam Trilogy*
P

Ceiling Zero
WAR (US) 1935 dir. Howard Hawks
Wead, F.
P

Cela S'Appelle L'Aurore
MARCEAU/LAE (Fr/It) 1955
dir. Luis Bunuel
Robles, E.

Celebration Family
VZ/SAMUELS (US) 1987 dir. Robert Day
TV(US)
Nason, D. and Etchison, B.

Celebrity
NBC (US) 1984 dir. Paul Wendkos
TVSe(US)
Thompson, T.

Celeste
PEL (W. Ger) 1981 dir. Percy Adlon
Albaret, C. *Monsieur Proust*

Celestina, La
LOLAFILMS (Sp) 1996 dir. Gerardo Vera
de Rojas, R.

Cell 2455, Death Row
COL (US) 1955 dir. Fred F. Sears
Chessman, C.

Cement Garden, The
LAURENTIC (Fr/Ger/GB) 1993 dir. Andrew Birkin
McEwan, I.

Cemetery Club, The
TOUCHSTONE (US) 1993 dir. Bill Duke
Menchell, I.
P

Centennial
UN TV (US) 1979 dir. Virgil Vogel, Paul Krasny, Harry Falk, Bernard McEveety
TVSe(US)
Michener, J. A.

Centennial Summer
FOX (GB) 1946 dir. Otto Preminger
Idell, A. E.

Ceremonie, La
FRANCE 3 (Fr) 1995 dir. Claude Chabrol
Rendell, R. *Judgment in Stone, A*

Ceremony, The
UA (US/Sp) 1963 dir. Laurence Harvey
Grendel, F.

Certain Smile, A.
FOX (US) 1958 dir. Jean Negulesco
Sagan, F.

Cervantes
PRISMA (Sp/It/Fr) 1968 dir. Vincent Sherman
Frank, B.

C'est La Vie
FRANCE 3 (Fr) 2001 dir. Jean-Pierre Ameris
de Hennezel, M. and Bottaro, C. *Mort Intime, La*

Chad Hanna
FOX (US) 1940 dir. Henry King
Edmonds, W. D.

Chalk Garden, The
RANK (GB) 1963 dir. Ronald Neame
Bagnold, E.

Challenge to Lassie
MGM (US) 1949 dir. Richard Thorpe
Atkinson, E. *Greyfriar's Bobby*

Chamade, La
ARIANE (Fr) 1969 dir. Alain Cavalier
US title: Heartkeeper, The
Sagan, F.

Chamber, The
UN (US) 1996 dir. James Foley
Grisham, J.

Chambermaid on the Titanic, The
FRANCE 2 (Fr) 1997 dir. J. J. Bigas Luna

Decoin, D. *Femme de Chambre du Titanic, La*

Chambre des Officiers, La
FRANCE 2 (Fr) 2001 dir. François Dupeyron

Dugain, M.

Champion
UA (US) 1949 dir. Mark Robson

Lardner, R.

Champions
EMBASSY (GB) 1983 dir. John Irvin

Champion, B. and Powell, J.
Champion's Story: A Great Human Triumph

Champion's Fight, A
NBC STUDIOS (US) 1998 dir. James A. Contner
TV(US)

McDaniel, L. *Don't Die My Love*

Chance to Sit Down, A
BBC (GB) 1981 dir. Paul Ciappessoni
TVSe(GB)

Daneman, M.

Chanel Solitaire
GARDENIA (Fr/GB) 1981
dir. George Kaczender

Dulay, C.

Change of Place, A
ALLIANCE (Can) 1994 dir. Donna Deitch
TV(Can)

Sinclair, T.

Changes
NBC (US) 1991 dir. Charles Jarrot
TV(US)

Steel, D.

Changes, The
BBC (GB) 1975 dir. John Prowse
Ch, TVSe(GB)

Dickinson, P.

Chant of Jimmie Blacksmith, The
FOX (Aust) 1979 dir. Fred Schepisi

Keneally, T.

Chapman Report, The
WAR (US) 1962 dir. George Cukor

Wallace, I.

Chapter Two
COL (US) 1979 dir. Robert Moore

Simon, N.
P

Character
ALMERICA (Bel/Neth) 1997 dir. Mike van Diem

Bordewijk, F. *Karakter*

Charley and the Angel
DISNEY (US) 1974
dir. Vincent McEveety

Stanton, W. *Golden Evenings of Summer, The*

Charley Moon
BL (GB) 1956 dir. Guy Hamilton

Arkell, R.

Charley's Aunt
FOX (US) 1941 dir. Archie Mayo
GB title: Charley's American Aunt

Thomas, B.
P

Charley Varrick
UN (US) 1973 dir. Don Siegel

Reese, J. *Looters, The*

Charlie Chan Carries On
FOX (US) 1931 dir. Hamilton McFadden

Biggers, E. D.

Charlie Muffin
EUSTON (GB) 1979 dir. Jack Gold
Freemantle, B. *Charlie, M*

Charlotte Gray
CHANNEL 4 FILMS (GB/Aust/Ger)
2001 dir. Gillian Armstrong
Faulks, S.

Charlotte's Web
SCOTIA-BARBER (US) 1972
dir. Charles A. Nichols
A, Ch
White, E. B.

Charly
CINERAMA (US) 1968
dir. Ralph Nelson
Keyes, D. *Flowers for Algernon*

Charters and Caldicott
BBC (GB) 1985 dir. Julian Amyes
TVSe(GB)
Bingham, S.

Chase, The
NERO (US) 1947 dir. Arthur Ripley
Woolrich, C. *Black Path of Fear, The*

Chase, The
COL (US) 1966 dir. Arthur Penn
Foote, H.

Chasing Yesterday
RKO (US) 1935 dir. George Nicholls, Jr.
France, A. *Crime of Sylvester Bonnard, The*

Cheaper by the Dozen
FOX (US) 1950 dir. Walter Lang
Gilbreth, Jr., F. B. and Carey, E. G.

Cheating Cheaters
UN (US) 1934 dir. Richard Thorpe
Marcin, M.
P

Checkers
FOX (US) 1937
dir. H. Bruce Humberstone
Young, R. J.
P

Cheers for Miss Bishop
PAR (US) 1941 dir. Tay Garnett
Aldrich, Mrs B. *Miss Bishop*

Cheetah
DISNEY (US) 1989 dir. Jeff Blyth
Ch
Caillou, A. *Cheetahs, The*

Cheri
BBC (GB) 1973 dir. Claude Whatham
TVSe(GB)
Colette

Chernobyl: The Final Warning
CAROLCO (US/USSR) 1991
dir. Anthony Page
TV(US/USSR)
Gale, R. P. and Hauser, T. *Final Warning: The Legacy of Chernobyl*

Cherry Picker, The
FOX-RANK (GB) 1974 dir. Peter Curran
Phillips, M. *Pick up Sticks*

Cherry Orchard, The
MELANDA (Gre/Fr) 1999 dir. Michael Cacoyannis
Chekhov, A.
P

Chessgame
GRANADA (GB) 1983 dir. William Brayne, Ken Grieve, Roger Tucker
TVSe(GB)
Price, A. *Labyrinth Makers, The; Alamut Ambush, The; Colonel Butler's Wolf*

Cheyenne Autumn
WAR (US) 1964 dir. John Ford
Sandoz, M.

Chicago Cab
CASTLE HILL (US) dir. Mary Cybulski, John Tintori
Kern, W. *Hellcab*
P

Chicken Chronicles, The
AVCO (US) 1977 dir. Francis Simon
Diamond, P.

Chicken Every Sunday
FOX (US) 1948 dir. George Seaton
Taylor, R.

Chicken-Wagon Family
FOX (US) 1939 dir. Herbert I. Leeds
Benefield, B.

Chienne, La
BRAU (Fr) 1931 dir. Jean Renoir
de la Fouchardière, G.

Chiefs
HIGHGATE (US) 1983
dir. Jerry London
TVSe(US)
Woods, S.

Child in the House
EROS (GB) 1956 dir. C. Baker Endfield
McNeill, J.

Child is Born, A
WAR (US) 1939 dir. Lloyd Bacon
Axelson, Mrs M. M.
P

Child is Missing, A
MOORE-WEISS (US) 1995 dir. John Power
TV(US)
Stout, D. *Dog Hermit, The*

Child of Darkness, Child of Light
WIL COURT (US) 1991
dir. Marina Sargenti
TV(US)
Patterson, J. *Virgin*

Children Are Watching Us, The
MAGLI (It) 1942 dir. Vittorio de Sica
Viola, C. G. *Prico*

Children of a Lesser God
PAR (US) 1986 dir. Randa Haines
Medoff, M.
P

Children of Dynmouth, The
BBC (GB) 1987 dir. Peter Hammond
TV(GB)
Trevor, W.

Children of Green Knowe, The
BBC (GB) 1986 dir. Colin Cant
TVSe(GB)
Boston, L. M.

Children of Hiroshima
KEL (Jap) 1952 dir. Kaneto Shindo
Osada, A.

Children of My Heart
TAPESTRY (Can) 2001 dir. Keith Ross Leckie
TV(Can)
Roy, G.

Children of Sanchez, The
HALL BARTLETT (US/Mex) 1978
dir. Hall Bartlett
Lewis, O.

Children of the Corn
NEW WORLD (US) 1984
dir. Fritz Kiersch
King, S.

Children of the Dust
KONIGSBERG (US) 1995 dir. David Greene
TVSe(US)

Carlile, C.

Children of the New Forest, The
BBC (GB) 1977 dir. John Frankau
TVSe(GB)
BBC (GB) 1998 dir. Andrew Morgan
TVSe (GB)

Marryat, Captain F.

Children of the North
BBC (GB) 1991 dir. David Drury
TVSe(GB)

Power, M. S.

Children's Hour, The
UA (US) 1961 dir. William Wyler
GB title: Loudest Whispers, The

Hellman, L. F.
P

Children's Midsummer Night's Dream, A
SANDS (GB) 2001 dir. Christine Edzard
Ch

Shakespeare, W. *Midsummer Night's Dream, A*
P

Child's Play
PAR (US) 1972 dir. Sidney Lumet

Marasco, R.
P

Child's Play
BBC/A&E (GB) 1998 dir. David Wheatley
TV(GB)

Hill, R.

Child Star: The Shirley Temple Story
DISNEY (US/Aust) 2001 dir. Nadia Tass

Temple Black, S. *Child Star*

Chilly Scenes of Winter (*also known as* Head Over Heels)
UA (US) 1979 dir. Joan Micklin Silver
Beattie, A.

Chiltern Hundreds, The
TC (GB) 1949 dir. John Paddy Carstairs

Home, W. D.
P

Chimera
ANGLIA (GB) 1991 dir. Nicholas Gillott
TV(GB)

Gallagher, S.

China
PAR (US) 1943 dir. John Farrow

Forbes, R. *Fourth Brother, The*

China Cry
PENLAND (US) 1990 dir. James E. Collier

Lam, N. and Burke, I.

China Seas
MGM (US) 1935 dir. Tay Garnett

Garstin, C.

China Sky
RKO (US) 1945 dir. Ray Enright

Buck, P.

Chinese Coffee
SHOOTING GALLERY (US) 2000 dir. Al Pacino

Lewis, I.
P

Chinese Ghost Story II
GORDON (China) 1990
dir. Ching Siu-Tung
Ling, P. S. *Strange Tales of Liao Zhai*

Chisholms, The
LAN (US) 1979 dir. Mel Stuart
TVSe(US)
Hunter, E.

Chitty, Chitty Bang Bang
UA (GB) 1968 dir. Ken Hughes
Ch
Fleming, I.

Chloe
DENTSU (Jap) 2001 dir. Go Riju
Vian, B. *Ecume des Jours, L'*

Chocky
THAMES (GB) 1984 dir. Chris Hodson
Ch, TVSe(GB)
Wyndham, J.

Chocolat
MIRAMAX (GB/US) 2000 dir. Lasse
Hallstrom
Harris, J.

Chocolate Soldier, The
MGM (US) 1941 dir. Roy del Ruth
M
Molnar, F. *Guardsman, The*
P

Chocolate War, The
MCEG (US) 1988 dir. Keith Gordon
Cormier, R.

Choir, The
BBC (GB) 1995 dir. Ferdinand Fairfax
TVSe(GB)
Trollope, J.

Choirboys, The
LORIMAR (US) 1977 dir. Robert
Aldrich
Wambaugh, J.

Chopper
AFFC (Aust) 2000 dir. Andrew Dominik
Read, M. B. *From the Inside*

Chorus Line, A
COL (US) 1985
dir. Richard Attenborough
M
Dante, N., Kirkwood, J. and Hamlisch, M.
P

Chorus of Disapproval, A
HOBO (GB) 1989 dir. Michael Winner
Ayckbourn, A.
P

Chosen, The
CONTEM (US) 1981
dir. Jeremy Paul Kagan
Potok, C.

Choses de la Vie, Les
LIRA/FIDA (Fr/It) 1969
dir. Claude Sautet
Guimard, P.

Christabel
BBC (GB) 1988 dir. Adrian Shergold
TVSe(GB)
Bielenberg, C. *Past is Myself, The*

Christiane F
FOX (Ger) 1981 dir. Ulrich Edel
Hermann, K. and Rieck, H.

Christine
COL (US) 1983 dir. John Carpenter
King, S.

Christine Jorgensen Story, The
UA (US) 1970 dir. Irving Rapper

Jorgensen, C.

Christmas Box, The
BPG (US) 1995 dir. Marcus Cole
TV(US)

Evans, R. P.

Christmas Carol, A
MGM (US) 1938 dir. Edwin L. Marin
ENT PAR (US)
1984 dir. Clive Donner
TV(US)
HALLMARK (US) 1999 dir. David Jones
TV(US)

Dickens, C.

Christmas Carol: The Movie
CHANNEL 4 FILMS (GB/Ger) 2001 dir. Jimmy T. Murakami

Dickens, C. *Christmas Carol, A*

Christmas Festival, A
COMPASS (US) 1959
dir. Albert McCleery
TV(US)

Bemelmans, L. *Borrowed Christmas, A*

Christmas Holiday
UN (US) 1944 dir. Robert Siodmak

Maugham, W. S.

Christmas Romance, A
JAFFE/BRAUNSTEIN (US) 1994 dir. Sheldon Larry
TV(US)

Davis, M.

Christmas Secret, The
CBS TV (US) 2000 dir. Ian Barry
TV(US)

Sullivan, R., Wolfe, G. and Porter, J. *Flight of the Reindeer*

Christmas Story, A
MGM/UA (US) 1983 dir. Bob Clark

Shepherd, J. *In God We Trust, All Others Pay Cash*

Christmas to Remember, A
ENGLUND (US) 1978
dir. George Englund
TV(US)

Swarthout, G. *Melodeon, The*

Christmas Tree, The
FOX (Fr/It) 1969 dir. Terence Young

Bataille, M.

Christmas Tree, The
DISNEY TELEFILMS (US) 1996 dir. Sally Field
TV(US)

Salamon, J. and Weber, J.

Christmas Wish, The
POLSON (US) 1998 dir. Ian Barry
TV(US)

Siddoway, R.

Christopher Bean
MGM (US) 1933 dir. Sam Wood

Howard, S. *Late Christopher Bean, The* P

Christopher Strong
RKO (US) 1933 dir. Dorothy Arzner

Frankau, G.

Christ Stopped At Eboli
ART EYE (It/Fr) 1979
dir. Francesco Rosi

Levi, C.

Christy
PAX TV (US) 2000 dir. Chuck Bowman
TV(US)

Marshall, C.

Christy: Choices of the Heart
CANAN (US) 2001 dir. George
Kaczender, Don McBrearty
TVSe(US)

Marshall, C. *Christy*

Chronicle of a Death Foretold
ITAL/MEDIA (It/Fr) 1987
dir. Francesco Rosi

Marquez, G. G.

Chronicles of Narnia, The
BBC (GB) 1989 dir. Marilyn Fox, Alex
Kirby
TVSe(GB)

Lewis, C. S. *Lion, The Witch and the
Wardrobe, The; Prince Caspian; Voyage of
the Dawn Treader, The; Silver Chair, The*

Chu Chin Chow
GAU (GB) 1934 dir. Walter Forde
M

Asche, O. and Norton, F.
P

Chuka
PAR (US) 1967 dir. Gordon Douglas

Jessup, R.

Chunuk Bair
AVALON (NZ) 1992 dir. Dale G.
Bradley

Shadbolt, M.
P

Ciao, Professore
CECCHI (It) 1992 dir. Lina Wertmuller

D'Orta, M. *Io Speriamo Che Me Lo Cavo*

Cider House Rules, The
MIRAMAX (US) 1999 dir. Lasse
Hallstrom

Irving, J.

Cielo Cade, Il
RAI (It) 2000 dir. Andrea Frazzi,
Antonio Frazzi

Mazzetti, L.

Cimarron
RKO (US) 1930 dir. Wesley Ruggles
MGM (US) 1960 dir. Anthony Mann

Ferber, E.

Cincinnati Kid, The
MGM (US) 1965 dir. Norman Jewison

Jessup, R.

Cinderella Liberty
FOX (US) 1974 dir. Mark Rydell

Ponicsan, D.

Cinder Path, The
TYNE TEES (GB) 1994 dir. Simon
Langton
TVSe(GB)

Cookson, C.

Circle of Children, A
FOX (US) 1977 dir. Don Taylor
TV(US)

MacCracken, M.

Circle of Deceit
BIOSKOP/ARTEMIS (Fr/W. Ger)
1981 dir. Volker Schlondorff

Born, N.

Circle of Deception
FOX (GB) 1960 dir. Jack Lee

Waugh, A. *Guy Renton, A London Story*

Circle of Friends
RANK (Ire/GB) 1995 dir. Pat O'Connor

Binchy, M.

Circle of Two
BORDEAUX (Can) 1980
dir. Jules Dassin

Baird, M. T. *Lesson in Love, A*

Circumstances Unknown
WIL COURT (US) 1995 dir. Robert
Lewis
TV(US)

Heckler, J.

Circus Queen Murder
COL (US) 1933 dir. Roy William Neill
Abbot, A. *Murder of the Circus Queen, The*

Citadel, The
MGM (GB) 1938 dir. King Vidor
BBC (GB) 1983 dir. Peter Jefferies
TVSe(GB)
Cronin, A. J.

Citizen Cohn
HBO (US) 1992 dir. Frank Pierson
TV(US)
Von Hoffman, N.

Citizen X
HBO (US) 1995 dir. Chris Gerolmo
TV(US)
Cullen, R. *Killer Department, The*

City Across The River
UI (US) 1949 dir. Maxwell Shane
Shulman, I. *Amboy Dukes, The*

City and the Dogs, The
INCA (Peru) 1985
dir. Francisco J. Lombardi
Llosa, M. V.

City Boy
ACCENT ENT (Can) 1994 dir. John Kent Harrison
TV(Can)
Porter, G. S. *Freckles*

City for Conquest
WAR (US) 1940 dir. Anatole Litvak
Kandel, A.

City of Joy
TRISTAR (US) 1992 dir. Roland Joffe
LaPierre, D.

City Streets
PAR (US) 1931 dir. Rouben Mamoulian
Boothe, E. *Ladies of the Mob*

Ciudad de los Prodigios, La
FRANCE 3 (Fr/Port/Sp) 1999 dir. Mario Camus
Mendoza, E.

Civil Action, A
PAR (US) 1998 dir. Steven Zaillian
Harr, J.

Claim, The
BBC (GB/Fr) 2000 dir. Michael Winterbottom
Hardy, T. *Mayor of Casterbridge, The*

Clair de Femme
GAU (Fr/It/Ger) 1979 dir. Costa-Gavras
Gary, R.

Clairvoyant, The
GB (GB) 1935 dir. Maurice Elvey
Lothar, E.

Clandestine Marriage, The
BRIT SCREEN (GB) 1999 dir. Christopher Miles
Coleman, G. and Garrick, D.
P

Clan of the Cave Bear, The
WAR (US) 1986 dir. Michael Chapman
Auel, J. M.

Clara's Heart
WB (US) 1988 dir. Robert Mulligan
Olshan, J.

Clarissa
BBC (GB) 1991 dir. Robert Bierman
TVSe(GB)
Richardson, S.

Clash by Night
RKO (US) 1952 dir. Fritz Lang
Odets, C.
P

Classe de Neige, La
STUDIO CANAL+ (Fr) 1998 dir. Claude Miller
US title: Class Trip
Carrere, E.

Class Enemy
SFB (Ger) 1984 dir. Peter Stein
Williams, N.
P

Classified Love
CBS ENT (US) 1986 dir. Don Taylor
TV(US)
Foxman, S.

Class of Miss MacMichael, The
GALA (GB) 1978 dir. Silvio Narizzano
Hutson, S. *Eff Off*

Class Relations
ART EYE (Ger/Fr) 1983
dir. Jean Marie Straub, Daniele Huillet
Kafka, F. *Amerika*

Claudelle Inglish
WAR (US) 1961 dir. Gordon Douglas
GB title: Young and Eager
Caldwell, E.

Claudia
FOX (US) 1943 dir. Edmund Goulding
Franken, R.

Claudia and David
FOX (US) 1946 dir. Walter Lang
Franken, R.

Clayhanger
ATV (GB) 1976 dir. John Davies, David Reid
TVSe(GB)
Bennett, A.

Clear and Present Danger
PAR (US) 1994 dir. Phillip Noyce
Clancy, T.

Clearcut
TELEFILM (Can) 1991
dir. Richard Bugajski
Kelly, M. T. *Dream Like Mine, A*

Cleopatra
FOX (US) 1963
dir. Joseph L. Manciewicz
Franzero, C. M. *Life and Times of Cleopatra, The*

Cleopatra
HALLMARK (US) 1999 dir. Franc Roddam
TVSe(US)
George, M. *Memoirs of Cleopatra, The*

Client, The
WAR (US) 1994 dir. Joel Schumacher
Grisham, J.

Climax, The
UN (US) 1944 dir George Waggner
Cochran, E.
P

Clive of India
FOX (US) 1935 dir. Richard Boleslawski
Lipscombe, W. P. and Minney, R. J.
P

Clochemerle
BLUE RIBBON (Fr) 1948
dir. Pierre Chénal
BBC (GB) 1972 dir. Spencer Chapman
TVSe(GB)
Chevallier, G.

Clockers
40 ACRES (US) 1995 dir. Spike Lee
Price, R.

Clockwork Orange, A
WAR (GB) 1971 dir. Stanley Kubrick
Burgess, A.

Cloning of Joanna May, The
GRANADA (GB) 1992 dir. Philip Saville
TVSe(GB)
Weldon, F.

Closely Watched Trains
CESK (Czech) 1966 dir. Jiri Menzel
Hrabal, B.

Closer, The
ION (US) 1990 dir. Dimitri Logothetis
Larusso, II, L. *Wheelbarrow Closers*
P

Clothes in the Wardrobe, The
BBC (GB) 1992 dir. Waris Hussein
TV(GB)
Ellis, A. T.

Cloud Howe
BBC (GB) 1982 dir. Tom Cotter
TVSe(GB)
Gibbon, L. G.

Clouds of Witness
BBC (GB) 1972 dir. Hugh David
TVSe(GB)
Sayers, D. L.

Cloud Waltzing
AVV/YTV (US/GB) 1987
dir. Gordon Flemyng
TV(GB/US)
Gates, T.

Clover
RHI (US) 1997 dir. Jud Taylor
TV(US)
Sanders, D.

Clubbable Woman, A
BBC (GB) 1996 dir. Ross Devenish
TV(GB)
Hill, R.

Cluny Brown
FOX (US) 1946 dir. Ernst Lubitsch
Sharp, M.

Coal Miner's Daughter
UN (US) 1980 dir. Michael Apted
Lynn, L. and Vecsey, G.

Cobb
WAR (US) 1994 dir. Ron Shelton
Stump, A. *Cobb: A Biography*

Cobra
WAR (US) 1986 dir. G. P. Cosmatos
Gosling, P. *Fair Game*

Cobweb, The
MGM (US) 1955 dir. Vincente Minnelli
Gibson, W.

Coca-Cola Kid, The
CINECOM (Aust) 1985
dir. Dusan Makevejev
Moorhouse, F. *Americans, Baby, The; Electrical Experience, The*

Cocaine and Blue Eyes
COL TV (US) 1983
dir. E.W. Swackhamer
TV(US)
Zackel, F.

Cockeyed Miracle, The
MGM (US) 1946 dir. S. Sylvan Simon
Seaton, G.
P

Cockfighter
EMI (US) 1974 dir. Monte Hellman
Willeford, C.

Cocktail
TOUCHSTONE (US) 1988
dir. Roger Donaldson
Gould, H.

Cocoon
FOX (US) 1985 dir. Ron Howard
Saperstein, D.

Code Name: Emerald
MGM/UA (US) 1985
dir. Jonathan Sanger
Bass, R. *Emerald Illusion, The*

Codename: Kyril
INCITO/HTV (US/GB) 1988
dir. Ian Sharp
TV(GB/US)
Trenhaile, J. *Man Called Kyril, A*

Code of the Woosters
CENTRAL (GB) 1991 dir. Simon
Langton
TV(GB)
Wodehouse, P. G.

Coffee, Tea or Me?
CBS ENT (US) 1983
dir. Norman Panama
TV(US)
Baker, T. and Jones, R.

Coiffeur Pour Dames
HOCHE (Fr) 1952 dir. Jean Boyer
GB title: Artist with Ladies, An
Armont, P. and Gerbidon, M.
P

Cold Comfort Farm
BBC (GB) 1971 dir. Peter Hammond
TV(GB)
BBC (GB) 1995 dir. John Schlesinger
TV(GB)
Gibbons, S.

Colder Kind of Death, A
CTV (Can) 2001 dir. Brad Turner
TV(Can)
Bowen, G.

Cold Heart of a Killer, The
HAMDON (US) 1996 dir. Paul
Schneider
TV(US)
Henry, S. *Murder on the Iditarod Trail*

Cold Heaven
HEMDALE (US) 1992 dir. Nicolas Roeg
Moore, B.

Colditz Story, The
BL (GB) 1954 dir. Guy Hamilton
Reid, R. P.

Cold Moon
GAU (Fr) 1991 dir. Luc Besson, Andrée
Martinez
Bukowski, C. *Copulating Mermaid of
Venice; Trouble with the Battery*

Cold River
PACIFIC (US) 1982 dir. Fred G. Sullivan
Judson, W.

Cold Room, The
HBO PREM (US) 1984
dir. James Dearden
TV(US)
Caine, J.

Cold Sassy Tree
TNT (US) 1989 dir. Joan Tewkesbury
TV(US)
Burns, O. A.

Cold Sweat
CORONA/FAIRFILM (It/Fr) 1974
dir. Terence Young
Matheson, R. *Ride the Nightmare*

Cold Turkey
UA (US) 1970 dir. Norman Lear
Rau, M. and Rau, N. *I'm Giving Them
Up For Good*

Cold Wind in August
UA (US) 1961 dir. Alexander Singer
Wohl, B.

Collector, The
BL (US) 1965 dir. William Wyler
Fowles, J.

Colonel Chabert, Le
CCFC (Fr) 1943 dir. Réne Le Hénaff
STUDIO CANAL+ (Fr) 1994 dir. Yves Angelo
de Balzac, H.

Colonel Effingham's Raid
FOX (US) 1945 dir. Irving Pichel
GB title: Man of the Hour
Fleming, B.

Color of Money, The
DISNEY (US) 1986 dir. Martin Scorsese
Tevis, W.

Color Purple, The
WAR (US) 1986 dir. Steven Spielberg
Walker, A.

Coma
MGM (US) 1978 dir. Michael Crichton
Cook, R.

Comancheros, The
FOX (US) 1961 dir. Michael Curtiz
Wellman, P. I.

Comanche Territory
TORNASOL (Sp/Fr) 1997 dir. Gerardo Herrero
Perez-Reverte, A. *Territorio Comanche*

Come and Get It
UA (US) 1936
dir. Howard Hawks, William Wyler
Ferber, E.

Come and See
MOSFILM (USSR) 1985
dir. Elem Klimov
Adamovich, A. *Story of Khatyn, The*

Comeback, The
CBS ENT (US) 1989
dir. Jerrold Freedman
TV(US)
Epstein, S. *Eye of the Beholder*

Come Back Charleston Blue
WAR (US) 1972 dir. Mark Warren
Himes, C. *Heat's On, The*

Come Back, Little Sheba
PAR (US) 1952 dir. Daniel Mann
GRANADA (US) 1977
dir. Silvio Narizzano
TV(GB/US)
Inge, W.
P

Come Back to the Five and Dime, Jimmy Dean, Jimmy Dean
SANDCASTLE (US) 1982
dir. Robert Altman
Graczyk, E.
P

Come Blow Your Horn
PAR (US) 1963 dir. Bud Yorkin
Simon, N.
P

Comedians, The
MGM (US/Fr) 1967 dir. Peter Glenville
Greene, G.

Comedie de L'innocence
STUDIO CANAL+ (Fr) 2000 dir. Raoul Ruiz
Bontempelli, M. *Boy With Two Mothers, The*

Comedy Man, The
BL (GB) 1964 dir. Alvin Rakoff

Hayes, D.

Come Fill the Cup
WAR (US) 1951 dir. Gordon Douglas

Ware, H.

Come Fly with Me
MGM (US) 1963 dir. Henry Levin

Glemser, B. *Girl on a Wing*

Come Home Charlie and Face Them
LWT (GB) 1990 dir. Roger Bamford
TVSe(GB)

Delderfield, R. F.

Come in Spinner
BBC (GB) 1991 dir. Ray Marchand
TV(GB)

Cusack, D.

Comfort of Strangers, The
SOVEREIGN (US/It) 1990
dir. Paul Schrader

McEwan, I.

Coming Out of the Ice
KONIGSBERG (US) 1982
dir. Waris Hussein
TV(US)

Herman, V.

Command, The
WAR (US) 1954 dir. David Butler

Bellah, J. W.

Command Decision
MGM (US) 1948 dir. Sam Wood

Haines, W. W.

Commissar
GORKY (USSR) 1988
dir. Alexander Askoldov

Grossman, V. *City of Bardish, A*

Commissioner, The
NEW ERA VISION (US/GB) 1998 dir.
George Sluizer

Johnson, S.

Commitments
ARABESQUE FILMS (US) 2001 dir.
Carol Mayes
TV(US)

Green, C.

Commitments, The
Fox (GB/US) 1991 dir. Alan Parker

Doyle, R.

Common Ground
LORIMAR TV (US) 1990
dir. Michael Newell
TVSe(US)

Lukas, J. A.

Common Touch, The
BN (GB) 1941 dir. John Baxter

Ayres, H.

Communion
NEW LINE (US) 1989
dir. Philippe Mora

Streiber, W.

Company Limited
CHILRANGALI (Ind) 1971
dir. Satyajit Ray

Shankar

Company of Wolves, The
PALACE (GB) 1984 dir. Neil Jordan

Carter, A.

Complicity
CARLTON FILMS (GB) 2000 dir. Gavin
Millar

Banks, I.

Compromising Positions
PAR (US) 1985 dir. Frank Perry

Isaacs, S.

Compulsion
FOX (US) 1959 dir. Richard Fleischer
Levin, M.

Conagher
IMAGINE TV (US) 1991
dir. Reynaldo Villalobos
TV(US)
L'Amour, L.

Conceiving Ada
HOTWIRE (Ger/US) 1997 dir. Lynn
Hershman-Leeson
Toole, B. A. *Ada, the Enchantress of*
Numbers, A Selections from the Letters of
Lord Byron's Daughter and Her
Description of the First Computer

Condemned
UA (US) 1929 dir. Wesley Ruggles
Niles, B. *Condemned to Devil's Island*

Condemned of Altona, The
FOX (Fr/It) 1962 dir. Vittorio di Sica
Sartre, J.-P.
P

Condominium
UN TV (US) 1980 dir. Sidney Hayers
TVSe(US)
MacDonald, J. D.

Condorman
DISNEY (US) 1981 dir. Charles Jarrot
Sheckley, R. *Game of X, The*

Conduct Unbecoming
BL (GB) 1975 dir. Michael Anderson
England, B.
P

Cone of Silence
BL (GB) 1960 dir. Charles Frend
US title: Trouble in the Sky
Beatty, D.

Confession, The
EL DORADO (US) 1999 dir. David
Hugh Jones
Yurick, S. *Fertig*

Confessional
GRANADA (GB) 1989
dir. Gordon Flemyng
TVSe(GB)
Higgins, J.

Confessions from a Holiday Camp
COL (GB) 1977 dir. Norman Cohen
Lea, T.

Confessions of a Driving Instructor
COL (GB) 1976 dir. Norman Cohen
Lea, T.

Confessions of a Pop Performer
COL (GB) 1975 dir. Norman Cohen
Lea, T.

Confessions of a Window Cleaner
COL (GB) 1974 dir. Val Guest
Lea, T.

Confessions of Felix Krull, The
FILMAUFBAU (Ger) 1958
dir. Kurt Hoffman
Mann, T.

Confidential Agent
WAR (US) 1945 dir. Herman Shumlin
Greene, G.

Confidentially Yours
IS (Fr) 1984 dir. François Truffaut
Williams, C. *Long Saturday Night, The*

Conflict of Wings
BL (GB) 1953 dir. John Eldridge
US title: Fuss Over Feathers
Sharp, D.

Conformist, The
CURZON (It/Fr/W. Ger) 1969
dir. Bernardo Bertolucci

Moravia, A.

Congo
PAR (US) 1995 dir. Frank Marshall

Crichton, M.

Connecticut Yankee, A
FOX (US) 1931 dir. David Butler

Twain, M. *Connecticut Yankee in King Arthur's Court, A*

Connecticut Yankee in King Arthur's Court, A
PAR (US) 1948 dir. Tay Garnett
GB title: Yankee in King Arthur's Court, A
M
CONSOL (US) 1989 dir. Mel Damski
TV(US)
Twain, M.

Connection, The
CONT (US) 1961 dir. Shirley Clarke

Gelber, J.
P

Connecting Rooms
TELSTAR (GB) 1969
dir. Franklin Gollings

Hart, M. *Cellist, The*
P

Conquering Horde
PAR (US) 1931 dir. Edward Sloman

Hough, E. *North of 36*

Conquest
MGM (US) 1937 dir. Clarence Brown
GB title: Marie Walewska

Jerome, H.
P

Conquest of Space
PAR (US) 1955 dir. Byron Haskin

Bonestell, C. and Ley, W.
P

Conrack
FOX (US) 1974 dir. Martin Ritt

Conroy, P. *Water is Wide, The*

Consenting Adult
STARGER (US) 1985 dir. Gilbert Cates
TV(US)

Hobson, L. Z.

Consider Your Verdict
CHARTER (GB) 1938 dir. Roy Boulting

Housman, L.
P

Conspiracy of Silence
CBC (Can) 1991 dir. Francis
Mankiewicz
TVSe(Can)

Priest, L.

Conspiracy of Terror
LORIMAR (US) 1975
dir. John Llewellyn Moxey
TV(US)

Delman, D.

Conspirator
MGM (GB) 1949 dir. Victor Saville

Slater, H.

Conspirators, The
WAR (US) 1944 dir. Jean Negulesco

Prokosch, F. *City of Shadows*

Constant Nymph, The
GAU (GB) 1933 dir. Basil Dean
WAR (US) 1943 dir. Edmund Goulding

Kennedy, M.

Consultant, The
BBC (GB) 1983 dir. Cyril Coke
TVSe(GB)
McNeil, J.

Consuming Passions
GOLDWYN (GB) 1988 dir. Giles Foster
Palin, M. and Jones, T. *Secrets*
P

Contact
WAR (US) 1997 dir. Robert Zemeckis
Sagan, C.

Contract on Cherry Street
COL TV (US) 1977
dir. William A. Grahan
TV(US)
Rosenberg, P.

Convicted
COL (US) 1950 dir. Henry Levin
Flavin, M. *One Way Out*
P

Convicts
STERLING (US) 1991 dir. Peter
Masterson
Foote, H.
P

Convicts Four
ALLIED (US) 1962 dir. Millard
Kaufman
GB title: Reprieve
Resko, J. *Reprieve*

Cool Breeze
MGM (US) 1972 dir. Barry Pollack
Burnett, W. R. *Asphalt Jungle, The*

Cool, Dry Place, A
FOX (US) 1999 dir. John N. Smith
Jaffe, M. G. *Dance Real Slow*

Cooler Climate, A
PAR (US) 1999 dir. Susan Seidelman
TV(US)
Collier, Z.

Cool Hand Luke
WAR (US) 1967 dir. Stuart Rosenberg
Pearce, D.

Cool World, The
WISEMAN (US) 1963
dir. Shirley Clarke
Miller, W.

Cop
ATLANTIC (US) 1988
dir. James B. Harris
Ellroy, J. *Blood on the Moon*

Cormorant, The
BBC (GB) 1993 dir. Peter Markham
TV(GB)
Gregory, S.

Corn is Green, The
WAR (US) 1945 dir. Irving Rapper
M. EVANS (US) 1956
dir. George Schaefer
TV(US)
WAR (US) 1979 dir. George Cukor
TV(US)
Williams, E.
P

Coroner Creek
COL (US) 1948 dir. Ray Enright
Short, L.

Corpse Came C.O.D., The
COL (US) 1947 dir. Henry Levin
Starr, J.

Corridor of Mirrors
GFD (GB) 1948 dir. Terence Young
Massie, C.

Corrupt
NEW LINE (It) 1983 dir. Robert Faenza

Fleetwood, H. *Order of Death, The*

Corsican Brothers, The
UA (US) 1942 dir. Gregory Ratoff
ROSEMONT (US) 1985 dir. Ian Sharp
TV(US)

Dumas, A. *Deux Frères*

Cosi
MIRAMAX (Aust) 1996 dir. Mark Joffe

Nowra, L.
P

Cottage to Let
GFD (GB) 1941 dir. Anthony Asquith
US title: Bombsight Stolen

Kerr, G.
P

Cotton Comes to Harlem
UA (US) 1969 dir. Ossie Davis

Himes, C.

Couch Trip, The
ORION (US) 1988 dir. Michael Ritchie

Kolb, K.

Counsellor at Law
UN (US) 1933 dir. William Wyler

Rice, E.
P

Counsel's Opinion
KORDA (GB) 1933 dir. Allan Dwan

Wakefield, G.
P

Counterattack
COL (US) 1945 dir. Zoltan Korda
GB title: One Against Seven

Stevenson, J. and Stevenson, P.
P

Counterfeit Traitor, The
PAR (US) 1962 dir. George Seaton

Klein, A.

Counterpoint
UI (US) 1968 dir. Ralph Nelson

Sillitoe, A. *General, The*

Count of Monte Cristo, The
UA (US) 1934 dir. Rowland V. Lee
ROSEMONT (GB) 1975
dir. David Greene
TV(GB)
(Fr/GB) 1987 dir. Denys de la Patellière
TV(Fr/GB)
CITE (Fr) 1998 dir. Josee Dayan
TVSe(Fr)
TOUCHSTONE (US) 2002 dir. Kevin
Reynolds

Dumas, A.

Country Dance
MGM (GB) 1969 dir. J. Lee Thompson

Kennaway, J. *Household Ghosts*

Country Diary of an Edwardian Lady, The
CENTRAL (GB) 1984 dir. Dirk
Campbell
TVSe(GB)

Holden, E.

Country Girl, The
PAR (US) 1954 dir. George Seaton
PAR (US) 1974 dir. Paul Bogart
TV(US)

Odets, C.
P

Country Girls, The
LF (GB) 1983
dir. Desmond Davis

O'Brien, E.

Country Life
MIRAMAX (Aust) 1994 dir. Michael
Blakemore

Chekhov, A. *Uncle Vanya*
P

Count Your Blessings
MGM (US) 1959 dir. Jean Negulesco

Mitford, N. *Blessing, The*

Coup de Torchon
FT (Fr) 1981 dir. Bertrand Tavernier
GB title: Clean Slate

Thompson, J. *POP: 1280*

Courage of Kavik, the Wolf Dog, The
PANTHEON (US) 1980 dir. Peter Carter
TV(US)

Morey, W. *Kavik the Wolf Dog*

Court Martial of George Amstrong Custer, The
HALLMARK (US) 1977
dir. Glenn Jordan
TV(US)

Jones, D. C.

Courtneys of Curzon Street, The
BL (GB) 1947 dir. Herbert Wilcox
US title: Courtney Affair, The

Tranter, F.

Courtship of Eddie's Father, The
MGM (US) 1963 dir. Vincente Minnelli

Toby, M.

Cousin Bette
BBC (GB) 1971 dir. Gareth Davies
TVSe(GB)
FOX (GB/US) 1998 dir. Des McAnuff

de Balzac, H.

Cousin Phillis
BBC (GB) 1982 dir. Mike Healey
TVSe(GB)

Gaskell, E.

Covenant with Death, A
WAR (US) 1966 dir. Lamont Johnson

Becker, S.

Cover Her Face
ANGLIA (GB) 1985 dir. John Davies
TVSe(GB)

James, P. D.

Cowboy
COL (US) 1957 dir. Delmer Daves

Harris, F. *On the Trail: My Reminiscences as a Cowboy*

Cowboys, The
WAR (US) 1972 dir. Mark Rydell

Jennings, W. D.

Cow Country
ABP (US) 1953 dir. Lesley Selander

Bishop, C. *Shadow Range*

Coyote
MOLECULE (Fr/Can) 1992 dir. Richard Ciupka

Michaud, M.

Crabe Tambour, Le
AMLF (Fr) 1977
dir. Pierre Schoendoerffer

Schoendoerffer, P.

Cracker Factory, The
EMI (US) 1979 dir. Burt Brinckerhoff
TV(US)

Rebeta-Burditt, J.

Crack in the Mirror
FOX (US) 1960 dir. Richard Fleischer

Haedrich, M.

Cradle Song, The
M. EVANS (US) 1956
dir. George Schaefer
TV(US)
COMPASS (US) 1960
dir. George Schaefer
TV(US)

Sierra, G. M.
P

Cradle will Fall, The
P&G (US) 1983
dir. John Llewellyn Moxey
TV(US)
Clark, M. H.

Craig's Wife
COL (US) 1936 dir. Dorothy Arzner
Kelly, G.
P

Cranford
BBC (GB) 1972 dir. Hugh David
TVSe(GB)
Gaskell, E.

Crash
FRIES (US) 1978 dir. Barry Shear
TV(US)
Elder, R. and Elder, S.

Crash
ALLIANCE (Can/Fr/GB) 1996 dir.
David Cronenberg
Ballard, J. G.

Crawlspace
TITUS (US) 1972 dir. Joan Newland
TV(US)
Lieberman, H.

Craze
EMI (GB) 1973 dir. Freddie Francis
Seymour, H. *Infernal Idol*

Crazy
CONSTANTIN (Ger) 2000 dir. Hans-
Christian Schmid
Lebert, B.

Crazy in Alabama
TRISTAR (US) 1999 dir. Antonio
Banderas
Childress, M.

Crazy in Love
OHYLMEYER (US) 1992 dir. Martha
Coolidge
TV(US)
Rice, L.

Creator
UN (US) 1985 dir. Ivan Passer
Leven, J.

Creature
MGM TV (US) 1998 dir. Stuart Gillard
TVSe(US)
Benchley, P. *White Shark*

Crime and Punishment
COL (US) 1935 dir. Josef von Sternberg
GAU (Fr) 1935 dir. Pierre Chenal
AA (US) 1958 dir. Denis Sanders
BBC (GB) 1979 dir. Michael Darlow
TVSe(GB)
HALLMARK (US) 1998 dir. Joseph
Sargent
TV(US)
Dostoevsky, F. M.

Crime + Punishment in Suburbia
KILLER (US) 2000 dir. Rob Schmidt
Dostoevsky, F. *Crime and Punishment*

Crime by Night
WAR (US) 1944 dir. William Clemens
Homes, G. *Forty Whacks*

Crime in the Streets
AA (US) 1956 dir. Don Siegel
Rose, R.
P

Crime of the Century
HBO (US) 1996 dir. Mark Rydell
TV(US)
Kennedy, L. *Airman and the Carpenter,
The*

Crimes of the Heart
DELAUR (US) 1986
dir. Bruce Beresford
Henley, B.
P

Criminal Behavior
PRESTON FISCHER (US) 1992 dir.
Michael Miller
TV(US)
Macdonald, R. *Ferguson Affair, The*

Crimson Circle, The
NEW ERA (GB) 1929 dir. Fred Zelnick
WAINRIGHT (GB) 1936
dir. Reginald Denham
Wallace, E.

Crimson Rivers, The
STUDIO CANAL+ (Fr) 2000 dir.
Mathieu Kassavitz
Grange, J.-C. *Rivieres Pourpres*

Crisis at Central High
TIME-LIFE (US) 1981
dir. Lamont Johnson
TV(US)
Huckaby, E. P.

Criss Cross
UI (US) 1949 dir. Robert Siodmak
Tracy, D.

CrissCross
MGM (US) 1992 dir. Chris Menges
Sommer, S.

Critical Care
VILLAGE ROADSHOW (Aust/US)
1997 dir. Sidney Lumet
Dooling, R.

Critical List, The
MTM INC (US) 1978 dir. Lou Antonio
TVSe(US)
Goldberg, Dr. M.

Critic's Choice
WAR (US) 1963 dir. Don Weis
Levin, I.
P

Crocodile Tears
ARIZTICAL (US) 1997 dir. Ann Coppel
Sod, T. *Satan and Simon DeSoto*
P

Crooked Road, The
GALA (GB/Yugo) 1964 dir. Don
Chaffey
West, M. L. *Big Story, The*

Crooked Hearts, The
LORIMAR (US) 1972 dir. Jay Sandrich
TV(US)
Watson, C. *Miss Lonelyhearts 4122*

Cross and the Switchblade, The
FOX (US) 1970 dir. Don Murray
Wilkerson, D.

Cross Country
NEW WORLD (Can) 1983
dir. Paul Lynch
Kastle, H.

Cross Creek
UN (US) 1983 dir. Martin Ritt
Rawlings, M. K.

Crossfire
RKO (US) 1947 dir. Edward Dmytryk
Brooks, R. *Brick Foxhole, The*

Crossfire Trail
TNT (US) 2001 dir. Simon Wincer
TV(US)
L'Amour, L.

Crossing, The
A&E/COL TRISTAR (US) 2000 dir.
Robert Harmon
TV(US)
Fast, H.

Crossing Delancey
WAR (US) 1988 dir. Joan Micklin Silver
Sandier, S.
P

Crossings
SPELLING (US) 1986
dir. Karen Arthur
TVSe(US)
Steel, D.

Crossing to Freedom
TELECOM/GRANADA (GB/US) 1990
dir. Norman Stone
TV(GB/US)
Shute, N. *Pied Piper, The*

Crossmaheart
LEX (GB) 1998 dir. Henry Herbert
Bateman, C. *Cycle of Violence*

Cross of Iron
AVCO (GB/Ger) 1977
dir. Sam Peckinpah
Henrich, W.

Crosswinds
PAR (US) 1951 dir. Lewis R. Foster
Burtis, T. *New Guinea Gold*

Crouching Beast, The
OLY (GB) 1935 dir. Victor Hanbury
Williams, V. *Clubfoot*

Crouching Tiger, Hidden Dragon
SONY (China/US) 2000 dir. Ang Lee
Wang, D.-L.

Crowded Sky, The
WAR (US) 1960 dir. Joseph Pevney
Searls, H.

Crown Matrimonial
TALENT (US) 1974 dir. Alan Bridges
TV(US)
Ryton, R.
P

Crucible, The
FOX (US) 1996 dir. Nicholas Hytner
Miller, A.
P

Crucifer of Blood, The
AGAMEMNON (US) 1991
dir. Fraser Heston
TV(US)
Doyle, Sir A. C.
Giovanni, P.
P

Cruel Doubt
NBC (US) 1992 dir. Yves Simoneau
TVSe(US)
McGinniss, J.

Cruel Passion
TARGET (GB) 1977 dir. Chris Boger
De Sade, Marquis *Justine*

Cruel Sea, The
GFD (GB) 1952 dir. Charles Frend
Monsarrat, N.

Cruel Train
BBC (GB) 1995 dir. Malcolm McKay
TV(GB)
Zola, E. *Bête Humaine, La*

Cruising
LORIMAR (US) 1980
dir. William Friedkin
Walker, G.

Crusoe
ISLAND (US) 1989 dir. Caleb Deschanel
Defoe, D. *Robinson Crusoe*

Cry for Happy
COL (US) 1961 dir. George Marshall
Campbell, G.

Cry for Love, A
FRIES/SACKS (US) 1980
dir. Paul Wendkos
TV(US)
Robinson, J. S. *Bedtime Story*

Cry for the Strangers
MGM (US) 1982 dir. Peter Medak
TV(US)
Saul, J.

Cry Freedom
UN (GB) 1987
dir. Richard Attenborough
Woods, D. *Biko*

Cry from the Streets, A
EROS (GB) 1958 dir. Lewis Gilbert
Coxhead, E. *Friend in Need, The*

Cry Havoc
MGM (US) 1943 dir. Richard Thorpe
Kenward, A. R. *Proof Thru' the Night*
P

Crying Child, The
IRISH (US) 1996 dir. Robert Michael
Lewis
TV(US)
Michaels, B.

Cry in the Dark, A
CANNON (US) 1988 dir. Fred Schepisi
Bryson, J. *Evil Angels*

Cry in the Night, A
WAR (US) 1956 dir. Frank Tuttle
Masterson, W. *All Through the Night*

Cry in the Night, A
TELESCENE (Can/Fr) 1993 dir. Robin
Spry
TV(Can/Fr)
Clark, M. H.

Cry in the Wild, A
CONCORDE (US) 1990
dir. Mark Griffiths
Paulsen, G. *Hatchet*

Cry of Battle
WAR (US) 1964 dir. Irving Lerner
Appel, B. *Fortress in the Rice*

Cry of the City
FOX (US) 1948 dir. Robert Siodmak
Helseth, H. E. *Chair for Martin Rome,
The*

Cry of the Innocent
NBC ENT (US) 1980
dir. Michael O'Herlihy
Forsyth, F. *In No Comebacks*

Cry, The Beloved Country
BL (GB) 1951 dir. Zoltan Korda
MIRAMAX (US/SA) 1995 dir. Darrell
Roodt
Paton, A.

Cry Tough
UA (US) 1959 dir. Paul Stanley
Shulman, I. *Children of the Dark*

Cry Wolf
WAR (US) 1947 dir. Peter Godfrey
Carleton, Mrs M. C.

Cuckoo in the Nest, A
GB (GB) 1938 dir. Tom Walls
Travers, B.
P

Cuckoo Sister, The
BBC (GB) 1986 dir. Marilyn Fox
TVSe(GB)

Alcock, V.

Cuisine et Dependances
STUDIO CANAL+ (Fr) 1993 dir.
Philippe Muyl

Jaoui, A. and Bacri, J.-P
P

Cujo
WAR (US) 1982 dir. Lewis Teague

King, S.

Cultivating Charlie
GMS (US) 1993 dir. Alex Georges

Voltaire *Candide*

Cupid & Cate
HALLMARK (US) 2000 dir. Brent
Shields
TV(US)

Bartolomeo, C. *Cupid and Diana*

Curacao
SHOWTIME (US) 1993 dir. Carl Schultz
TV(US)

Buchanan, J. D. *Prince of Malta, The*

Cure for Love, The
BL (GB) 1949 dir. Robert Donat

Greenwood, W.
P

Curse of Frankenstein, The
WAR (GB) 1957 dir. Terence Fisher

Shelley, M. W. *Frankenstein*

Curse of the Starving Class
SHOWTIME (US) 1995 dir. Michael
McClary
TV(US)

Shepard, S.
P

Curse of the Werewolf, The
RANK (GB) 1961 dir. Terence Fisher

Endore, G. *Werewolf of Paris, The*

Curtain Up
GFD (GB) 1952 dir. Ralph Smart

King, P. *On Monday Next*
P

Custard Boys, The
FOREST HALL (GB) 1979
dir. Colin Finbow

Rae, J.

Custody of the Heart
HEARST (US) 2000 dir. David Jones
TV(US)

Delinsky, B. *Woman's Place, A*

Cutter and Bone
UA (US) 1981 dir. Ivan Passer
GB title: Cutter's Way

Thornburg, N.

Cynara
GOLDWYN (US) 1933 dir. King Vidor

Harwood, H. M.
P

Cyrano de Bergerac
UA (US) 1950 dir. Michael Gordon
COMPASS (US) 1962
dir. George Schaefer
TV(US)
UGC (Fr) 1990 dir. Jean-Paul
Rappeneau

Rostand, E.
P

D

Da
FILM DALLAS (US) 1988
dir. Matt Clarke
Leonard, H.
P

Dad
UN (US) 1989 dir. Gary D. Goldberg
Wharton, W.

Daddy
NBC (US) 1991 dir. Michael Miller
Steel, D.

Daddy Long Legs
FOX (US) 1931 dir. Alfred Santell
FOX (US) 1955 dir. Jean Negulesco
M
Webster, J.

Daddy's Dyin' ... Who's Got the Will?
MGM/UA (US) 1990 dir. Jack Fisk
Shores, D.
P

Dain Curse, The
POLL (US) 1978 dir. E. W. Swackhamer
TVSe(US)
Hammett, D.

Daisy Kenyon
FOX (US) 1947 dir. Otto Preminger
Janeway, Mrs E.

Daisy Miller
PAR (US) 1974 dir. Peter Bogdanovich
James, H.

Dalva
GOLDSMITH (US) 1996 dir. Ken
Cameron
TV(US)
Harrison, J.

Damage
CHANNEL 4 FILMS (Fr/GB) 1992 dir.
Louis Malle
Hart, J.

Dam Busters, The
ABP (GB) 1954 dir. Michael Anderson
Brickhill, P.

Damnation Alley
FOX (US) 1977 dir. Jack Smight
Zalazny, R.

Damned, The
BL (GB) 1961 dir. Joseph Losey
US title: These Are The Damned
Lawrence, H. L. *Children of the Light, The*

Damned Don't Cry, The
WAR (US) 1950 dir. Vincent Sherman
Walker, G. *Case History*

Damn Yankees
WAR (US) 1958 dir. George Abbott,
Stanley Donen
GB title: What Lola Wants
M
Adler, R. and Ross, J.
P
Wallop, D. *Year the Yankees Lost the Pennant, The*

Damsel in Distress, A
RKO (US) 1937 dir. George Stevens
M
Wodehouse, P. G.

Dance Hall
FOX (US) 1941 dir. Irving Pichel
Burnett, W. R.

Dance Me Outside
YORKTOWN (Can) 1994 dir. Bruce McDonald
Kinsella, W. P.

Dance of Death, The
PAR (GB) 1968 dir. David Giles
Strindberg, A.
P

Dance of the Dwarfs
DOVE (Phil/US) 1982 dir. Gus Trikonis
Household, G.

Dance Pretty Lady
BI (GB) 1932 dir. Anthony Asquith
Mackenzie, Sir C. *Carnival*

Dances with Wolves
ORION (US) 1990 dir. Kevin Costner
Blake, M.

Dancing at Lughnasa
CAPITOL (Ire/GB/US) 1998 dir. Pat O'Connor
Friel, B.
P

Dancing in the Dark
FOX (US) 1949 dir. Irving Reis
Kaufman, G. S., Dietz, H. and Schwarz, A. *Bandwagon, The*
P

Dancing in the Dark
CBC (Can) 1986 dir. Leon Marr
Barfoot, J.

Dancing Lady
MGM (US) 1933 dir. Robert Z. Leonard
M
Bellah, J. W.

Dancing Years, The
ABPC (GB) 1949 dir. Harold French
ATV (GB) 1976
TV(GB)
Novello, I.

Dandy in Aspic, A
COL (GB) 1968 dir. Anthony Mann
Marlowe, D.

Danger Ahead
MON (GB) 1940 dir. Ralph Staub
Erskine, L. Y. *Renfrew's Long Trail*

Dangerous Beauty
NEW REGENCY (US) 1998 dir. Marshall Herskovitz
Rosenthal, M. *Honest Courtesan, The*

Dangerous Company
FINNEGAN (US) 1982 dir. Lamont Johnson
TV(US)
Johnson, R. and McCormick, M. *Too Dangerous To Be at Large*

Dangerous Corner
RKO (US) 1934 dir. Phil Rosen
Priestley, J. B.
P

Dangerous Davies – The Last Detective
INNER CIRCLE (GB) 1980 dir. Val Guest
Thomas, L.

Dangerous Days of Kiowa Jones, The
MGM (US) 1966 dir. Alex March
TV(US)
Adams, C.

Dangerous Evidence: The Lori Jackson Story
HEARST (US) 1999 dir. Sturla Gunnarsson
TV(US)

Cohen, E. A. and Shapiro, M. J. *Dangerous Evidence*

Dangerous Exile
RANK (GB) 1957
dir. Brian Desmond Hurst
Wilkins, V. *King Reluctant, A*

Dangerous Journey
CHANNEL 4 (GB) 1985
TVSe (GB)
Bunyan, J. *Pilgrim's Progress, The*

Dangerous Liaisons
WAR (US) 1988 dir. Stephen Frears
de Laclos, P. *Liaisons Dangereuses, Les*
Hampton, C. *Liaisons Dangereuses, Les*
P

Dangerous Minds
HOLLYWOOD (US) 1995 dir. John N. Smith
Johnson, L. *My Posse Don't Do Homework*

Dangerous to Know
PAR (US) 1938 dir. Robert Florey
Wallace, E. *On The Spot*
P

Dangerous Woman, A
AMBLIN (US) 1993 dir. Stephen Gyllenhaal
Morris, M. M.

Danger Route
UA (GB) 1967 dir. Seth Holt
York, A. *Eliminator, The*

Danger Signal
WAR (US) 1945 dir. Robert Florey
Bottome, P.

Danger Within
BL (GB) 1958 dir. Don Chaffey
US title: Breakout
Gilbert, M. *Death in Captivity*

Daniel
PAR (GB) 1983 dir. Sidney Lumet
Doctorow, E. L. *Book of Daniel, The*

Daniel Deronda
BBC (GB) 1970 dir. Joan Croft
TVSe(GB)
Eliot, G.

Danny Jones
CINERAMA (GB) 1972
dir. Jules Bricken
Collier, J. L. *Fires of Youth*

Danny the Champion of the World
COL (GB) 1989 dir. Gavin Millar
Ch
Dahl, R.

Danton
GAU/TF1 (Fr/Pol) 1982
dir. Andrzej Wajda
Przybyszewska, S. *Danton Affair, The*
P

Darby's Rangers
WAR (US) 1957 dir. William Wellman
GB title: Young Invaders, The
Altieri, Major J.

Dark-Adapted Eye, The
BBC (GB) 1995 dir. Tim Fywell
TVSe(GB)
Rendell, R.

Dark Angel, The
GOLDWYN (US) 1935
dir. Sidney Franklin
Bolton, G.
P

Dark Angel, The
BBC (GB) 1989 dir. Peter Hammond
TVSe(GB)
Le Fanu, S. *Uncle Silas*

Dark at the Top of the Stairs, The
WAR (US) 1960 dir. Delbert Mann
Inge, W. M.
P

Dark Command
REP (US) 1940 dir. Raoul Walsh
Burnett, W. R.

Darker than Amber
FOX (US) 1970 dir. Robert Clouse
MacDonald, J. D.

Dark Eyes
EXCELSIOR (It) 1987
dir. Nikita Mikhalkov
Chekhov, A. *Stories*

Dark Half, The
ORION (US) 1993 dir. George A. Romero
King, S.

Dark Holiday
ORION TV (US) 1989 dir. Lou Antonio
TV(US)
LePere, G. *Never Pass This Way Again*

Dark Journey
LF GBN (US) 1937
dir. Victor Saville
Biro, L.
P

Darkness Falls
LIONS GATE (GB) 1998 dir. Gerry Lively
Crisp, N. J.
P

Dark Night
GOODYEAR (Tai/HK) 1986
dir. Fred Tan
Li-Eng, S.

Dark Passage
WAR (US) 1947 dir. Delmer Daves
Goodis, D.

Dark Secret of Harvest Home, The
UN TV (US) 1978 dir. Leo Penn
TVSe(US)
Tryon, T. *Harvest Home*

Dark Tower, The
WAR (GB) 1943 dir. John Harlow
Woolcott, A. and Kaufman, G. S.
P

Dark Victory
WAR (US) 1939 dir. Edmund Goulding
UN (US) 1976 dir. Robert Butler
TV(US)
Brewer, G. E. and Bloch, B.
P

Dark Waters
UA (US) 1944 dir. André de Toth
Cockrell, F. M. and Cockrell, M.

Dark Wind, The
SEVEN ARTS (US) 1991 dir. Errol Morris
Hillerman, T.

Darling Buds of May, The
YTV (GB) 1991 dir. Robert Tronson
TV(GB)
Bates, H. E.

Darling, How Could You
PAR (US) 1951 dir. Mitchell Leisen
GB title: Rendezvous
Barrie, Sir J. M. *Alice Sit-by-the-Fire*
P

Darlings of the Gods
THAMES (GB) 1991
dir. Catherine Millar
TVSe(GB)

O'Connor, G.

Daughter of the Dragon
PAR (US) 1931 dir. Lloyd Corrigan

Rohmer, S. *Daughter of Fu Manchu*

Daughter of the Mind
FOX (US) 1969 dir. Walter Grauman
TV(US)

Gallico, P. *Hand of Mary Constable, The*

Daughters Courageous
WAR (US) 1939 dir. Michael Curtiz

Bennett, D. *Fly Away Home*
P

David
KINO (W. Ger) 1982 dir. Peter Lilienthal

Konig, J.

David
ITC (US) 1988 dir. John Erman
TV(US)

Rothenberg, M. and White, M.

David and Lisa
BL (US) 1963 dir. Frank Perry
HARPO (US) 1998 dir. Lloyd Kramer
TV(US)

Rubin, T. I. *Lisa and David*

David Copperfield
MGM (US) 1935 dir. George Cukor
OMNIBUS (GB) 1970
dir. Delbert Mann
TV(GB)
BBC (GB) 1974 dir. Joan Craft
TVSe(GB)
BBC (GB) 1986 dir. Barry Letts
TVSe(GB)
BBC (GB) 2000 dir. Simon Curtis
TVSe(GB)
HALLMARK (US) 2000 dir. Peter
Medak
TVSe(US)

Dickens, C.

David's Mother
HEARST (US) 1994 dir. Robert Allan
Ackerman
TV(US)

Randall, B.
P

Dawning, The
TVS (GB) 1988 dir. Robert Knights
TVSe(GB)

Johnston, J. *Old Jest, The*

Daybreak
GFD (GB) 1946 dir. Compton Bennett

Hoffe, M.

Daybreak
HBO SHOW (US) 1993 dir. Steven
Tolkin
TV(US)

Browne, A. *Beirut*
P

Daydream Believers: The Monkees Story
PEBBLEHUT (US) 2000 dir. Neil
Fearnley
TV(US)

Bronson, H. *Hey Hey We're the Monkees*

Day in the Death of Joe Egg, A
COL (GB) 1971 dir. Peter Medak

Nichols, P.
P

Day Lincoln Was Shot, The
GREENWALD (US) 1998 dir. John Gray
TV(US)

Bishop, J.

Day of the Dog
BANON (Aust) 1993 dir. James
Ricketson

Weller, A.

Day of the Dolphin, The
AVCO (US) 1973 dir. Mike Nichols

Merle, R.

Day of the Jackal, The
UN (Fr/GB) 1973 dir. Fred Zinnemann
Forsyth, F.

Day of the Locust, The
PAR (US) 1975 dir. John Schlesinger
West, N.

Day of the Outlaw, The
UA (US) 1958 dir. André de Toth
Wells, L. E.

Day of the Triffids, The
RANK (GB) 1962 dir. Steve Sekely
BBC (GB) 1981 dir. Ken Hannam
TVSe (GB)
Wyndham, J.

Day One
SPELLING (US) 1989
dir. Joseph Sargent
TV(US)
Wyden, P. *Day One: Before Hiroshima and After*

Day the Bubble Burst, The
FOX (US) 1982 dir. Joseph Hardy
TV(US)
Thomas, G. and Witts, M. M.

Day the Loving Stopped, The
MONASH-ZEIT (US) 1981
dir. Delbert Mann
TV(US)
List, J. A.

Day They Robbed the Bank of England, The
MGM (GB) 1959 dir. John Guillermin
Brophy, J.

Day to Remember, A
GFD (GB) 1953 dir. Ralph Thomas
Tickell, J. *Hand and the Flower, The*

Dazzle
MULTIMEDIA PROD (US) 1995 dir. Richard Colla
TVSe(US)
Krantz, J.

D-Day the Sixth of June
FOX (US) 1956 dir. Henry Koster
Shapiro, L. *Sixth of June, The*

Dead, The
VESTRON (US) 1987 dir. John Huston
Joyce, J.

Dead Babies
OVERSEAS (US) 2001 dir. William Marsh
Amis, M.

Dead by Sunset
TRISTAR TV (US) 1995 dir. Karen Arthur
TVSe(US)
Rule, A.

Dead Calm
WAR (Aust) 1989 dir. Phillip Noyce
Williams, C.

Dead Cert
UA (GB) 1974 dir. Tony Richardson
Francis, D.

Dead End
UA (US) 1937 dir. William Wyler
Kingsley, S.
P

Deadfall
FOX (GB) 1968 dir. Bryan Forbes
Cory, D.

Deadheads
BBC/A&E (GB) 1997 dir. Edward Bennett
TV(GB)
Hill, R.

Dead Husbands
WIL COURT (US) 1998 dir. Paul
Shapiro
TV(US)
Randall, B. *Last Man on the List, The*

Dead in the Water
K. BRIGHT/MTE (US) 1991 dir. Bill
Condon
TV(US)
Whittington, H. *Web of Murder*

Deadline at Dawn
RKO (US) 1946 dir. Harold Clurman
Irish, W.

Deadly Affair, The
COL (GB) 1966 dir. Sidney Lumet
Le Carré, J. *Call for the Dead*

Deadly Appearances
SHAFTESBURY (Can) 2000 dir. George
Bloomfield
TV(Can)
Bowen, G.

Deadly Companions, The
WAR (US) 1961 dir. Sam Peckinpah
Fleischman, A. S. *Yellowleg*

Deadly Duo
UA (US) 1962 dir. Reginald LeBorg
Jessup, R.

Deadly Eyes
WAR (US) 1983 dir. Robert Clouse
Herbert, J.

Deadly Family Secrets
FILERMAN (US) 1995 dir. Richard T.
Heffron
TV(US)
Coen, F. *Vinegar Hill*

Deadly Friend
WAR (US) 1986 dir. Wes Craven
Henstell, D. *Friend*

Deadly Harvest
CBS ENT (US) 1972
dir. Michael O'Herlihy
TV(US)
Household, G. *Watcher in the Shadows*

Deadly Hunt, The
FOUR STAR (US) 1971
dir. John Newland
TV(US)
Stadley, P. *Autumn of a Hunter*

Deadly Intentions
GREEN-EPSTEIN (US) 1985
dir. Noel Black
TVSe(US)
Stevens, W. R.

Deadly is the Female
UA (US) 1949 dir. Joseph Lewis
Kantor, M. *Gun Crazy*

Deadly Love
POWER (US) 1995 dir. Jorge Montesi
TV(US)
Gottlieb, S. *Love Bite*

Deadly Medicine
MULTIMEDIA Ent/KRANTZ (US) 1991
dir. Richard A. Colla
TV(US)
Reed, R. and Moore, K.

Deadly Record
AA (GB) 1959 dir. Lawrence
Huntington
Hooke, N. W.

Deadly Relations
WIL COURT (US) 1993 dir. Bill Condon
TV(US)
Donohue, C. and Hall, S. *Deadly
Relations: A True Story of Murder in a
Suburban Family*

Deadly Silence, A
GREENWALD (US) 1989
dir. John Patterson
TV(US)
Kleiman, D.

Deadly Trap, The
NG (Fr/It) 1971
dir. René Clément
Cavanaugh, A. *Children are Gone, The*

Deadly Vision, A
HILL-FIELDS (US) 1997 dir. Bill Norton
TV(US)
Greenburg, D. *Love Kills*

Deadly Whispers
HILL-FIELDS (US) 1995 dir. Bill Norton
TV(US)
Schwarz, T.

Dead Man's Island
PAPAZIAN-HIRSCH (US) 1996 dir. Peter Hunt
TV(US)
Hart, C.

Dead Man's Walk
HALLMARK (US) 1996 dir. Yves Simoneau
TVSe(US)
McMurtry, L.

Dead Man Walking
POLYGRAM (US/GB) 1995 dir. Tim Robbins
Prejean, Sister H.

Dead Men Tell No Tales
ALL (GB) 1938 dir. David MacDonald
Beeding, F. *Norwich Victims, The*

Dead Men Tell No Tales
FOX (US) 1971 dir. Walter Grauman
TV(US)
Roos, K. *To Save His Life*

Dead Man's Folly
WAR (US) 1986 dir. Clive Donner
TV(US)
Christie, A.

Dead of Jericho, The
CENTRAL (GB) 1989
dir. Edward Bennett
TV(GB)
Dexter, C.

Dead on the Money
INDIEPROD (US) 1991
dir. Mark Cullingham
TV(US)
Ingalls, R. *End of Tragedy, The*

Dead Ringers
FOX (Can) 1988 dir. David Cronenberg
Wood, B. and Geasland, J. *Twins*

Dead Silence
HBO (US) 1996 dir. Daniel Petrie, Jr.
TV(US)
Deaver, J. *Maiden's Grave, A*

Dead Solid Perfect
HBO (US) 1988 dir. Bobby Roth
TV(US)
Jenkins, D.

Dead Zone, The
PAR (US) 1983 dir. David Cronenberg
King, S.

Dealing: or The Berkeley-to-Boston-Forty-Brick-Lost-Bag-Blues
WAR (US) 1972 dir. Paul Williams
Douglas, M.

Dear Brigitte
FOX (US) 1965 dir. Henry Koster
Haase, J. *Erasmus with Freckles*

Dear Heart
WAR (US) 1964 dir. Delbert Mann
Mosel, T.

Dear Inspector
ARIANE/MONDEX (Fr) 1977
dir. Philippe de Broca
Rouland, J.-P. and Olivier, C. *Tendre Poulet*

Dear John
SANDREW (Swe) 1964
dir. Lars Magnus Lindgren
Lansburg, O.

Dear Mr Prohack
GFD (GB) 1949 dir. Thornton Freeland
Bennett, A. *Mr Prohack*

Dear Murderer
GFD (GB) 1947 dir. Arthur Crabtree
Clowes, St. J. L.
P

Dear Octopus
GFD (GB) 1943 dir. Harold French
US title: Randolph Family, The
Smith, D.
P

Dear Ruth
PAR (US) 1947 dir. William D. Russell
Krasna, N.
P

Death and the Maiden
FINE LINE (US/GB) 1994 dir. Roman Polanski
Dorfman, A.
P

Death at Broadcasting House
PHOENIX (GB) 1934
dir. Reginald Denham
Gielgud, V. H.

Death Benefit
CHRIS/ROSE (US) 1996 dir. Mark Piznarski
TV(US)
Heilbroner, D.

Death Be Not Proud
WESTFALL (US) 1975 dir. Donald Wrye
TV(US)
Gunther, J.

Death Dreams
D. CLARK (US) 1991 dir. Martin Donovan
TV(US)
Katz, W.

Death in California, A
LORIMAR (US) 1985 dir. Delbert Mann
TVSe(US)
Barthel, J.

Death in Canaan, A
WAR (US) 1978 dir. Tony Richardson
TV(US)
Barthel, J.

Death in Venice
WAR (It) 1971 dir. Luchino Visconti
Mann, T.

Death is Part of the Process
BBC (GB) 1986 dir. Bill Hays
TV(GB)
Bernstein, H.

Death of a Gunfighter
UI (US) 1969 dir. Robert Totten, Don Siegel
Patten, L. B.

Death of an Expert Witness
ANGLIA (GB) 1983 dir. Herbert Wise
TVSe(GB)
James, P. D.

Death of a Salesman
COL (US) 1951 dir. Laslo Benedek
PUNCH (US) 1985
dir. Volker Schlondorff
TV(US)
Miller, A.
P

Death of a Schoolboy
NEUE STUDIO (Austria) 1991
dir. Peter Patzak
Konig, H.

Death of Innocence, A
CARLINER (US) 1971
dir. Paul Wendkos
TV(US)
Popkin, Z.

Death of Me Yet, The
SPELLING (US) 1971
dir. John Llewellyn Moxey
TV(US)
Masterson, W.

Death of Richie, The
H. JAFFE (US) 1977 dir. Paul Wendkos
TV(US)
Thompson, T.

Death of the Heart, The
GRANADA (GB) 1985 dir. Peter
Hammond
TV(GB)
Bowen, E.

Death on the Nile
EMI (GB) 1978 dir. John Guillermin
Christie, A.

Death Sentence
SPEL-GOLD (US) 1974
dir. E.W. Swackhamer
TV(US)
Roman, E. *After the Trial*

Death Stalk
D. WOLPER (US) 1975 dir. Robert Day
TV(US)
Chastain, T.

Death Takes a Holiday
PAR (US) 1934 dir. Mitchell Leisen
UN TV (US) 1971 dir. Robert Butler
TV(US)
Anderson, M. and Casella, A.
P

Death Train
YTV (GB) 1993 dir. David S. Jackson
TV(GB)
MacLean, A.

Deathtrap
WAR (US) 1982 dir. Sidney Lumet
Levin, I.
P

Deathwatch
CONTEM (Fr/Ger) 1979
dir. Bertrand Tavernier
Compton, D. *Unsleeping Eye, The*

Death Wish
CANNON (US) 1974
dir. Michael Winner
Garfield, B.

Decadence
VENDETTA (GB/Ger) 1993 dir. Steven
Berkoff
Berkoff, S.
P

Decameron, The
UA (It/Fr/W. Ger) 1970
dir. Pier Paolo Pasolini
Boccaccio, G.

Decameron Nights
EROS (GB) 1952 dir. Hugo Fregonese
Boccaccio, G. *Decameron, The*

Deceit
BBC (GB) 2000 dir. Stuart Orme
TV(GB)
Francis, C.

Deceivers, The
MI (GB/Ind) 1988
dir. Nicholas Meyer
Masters, J.

Deception
WAR (US) 1946 dir. Irving Rapper
Verneuil, L. *Jealousy*
P

Deceptions
COL (US) 1985 dir. Robert Chenault
TVSe(US)
Michael, J.

Decision Before Dawn
FOX (US) 1951 dir. Anatole Litvak
Howe, G. L. *Call it Treason*

Decision of Christopher Blake, The
WAR (US) 1948 dir. Peter Godfrey
Hart, M. *Christopher Blake*
P

Decline and Fall ... of a Birdwatcher
FOX (GB) 1968 dir. John Karsh
Waugh, E. *Decline and Fall*

Decoration Day
M. REES (US) 1990
dir. Robert Markowitz
TV(US)
Corrington, J. W.

Deep, The
COL-WAR (US) 1977 dir. Peter Yates
Benchley, P.

Deep Blue Sea, The
FOX (GB) 1955 dir. Anatole Litvak
Rattigan, T.
P

Deep End, The
FOX (US) 2001 dir. Scott McGehee, David Siegel
Holding, E. S. *Blank Wall, The*

Deep End of the Ocean, The
COL (US) 1999 dir. Ulu Grosbard
Mitchard, J.

Deep in my Heart
MGM (US) 1954 dir. Stanley Donen
M
Arnold, E.

Deep Six, The
WAR (US) 1958 dir. Rudolph Maté
Dibner, M.

Deep Valley
WAR (US) 1947 dir. Jean Negulesco
Totheroh, D.

Deep Waters
FOX (US) 1948 dir. Henry King
Moore, R. *Spoonhandle*

Deerslayer, The
FOX (US) 1957 dir. Kurt Neumann
SCHICK SUNN (US) 1978
dir. Dick Friedenberg
TV(US)
Cooper, J. F.

Defector, The
PECF (Fr/W. Ger) 1966 dir. Raoul Levy
Thomas, P. *Spy, The*

Degree of Guilt
JAFFE/BRAUNSTEIN (US) 1995 dir.
Mike Robe
TVSe(US)

Patterson, R. N. *Degree of Guilt; Eyes of a Child*

Déjà Vu
CANNON (GB) 1985
dir. Anthony Richmond

Meldal-Johnson, T. *Always*

De la Calle
TIEMPE (Mex) 2001 dir. Gerardo Tort

Davila, J. G.
P

Delavine Affair, The
MON (GB) 1954 dir. Douglas Pierce

Chapman, R. *Winter Wears a Shroud*

Deliberate Intent
FOX TV (US) 2000 dir. Andy Wolk
TV(US)

Smolla, R. A. *Deliberate Intent: A Lawyer Tells the Story of Murder by the Book*

Deliberate Stranger, The
LORIMAR (US) 1986
dir. Marvin Chomsky
TVSe(US)

Larsen, R. W. *Bundy: The Deliberate Stranger*

Delicate Balance, A
SEVEN KEYS (US) 1975
dir. Tony Richardson

Albee, E.
P

Delinquents, The
VILLAGE ROADSHOW (Aust) 1990
dir. Chris Thomson

Rohan, C.

Delitto Impossibile, Un
HERA (It) 2001 dir. Antonello Grimaldi

Mannuzzu, S. *Procedura*

Deliverance
WAR (US) 1973 dir. John Boorman

Dickey, J.

Dellamorte Dellamore
DARC (It/Fr/Ger) 1994 dir. Michele Soavi

Sclavi, T.

Delta of Venus
NEW LINE (US) 1995 dir. Zalman King

Nin, A.

Deluge, The
POLSKI (Pol) 1974 dir. Jerzy Hoffman

Sienkiewicz, H.

Demasiado Amor
COLIFILMS (Fr/Sp) 2001 dir. Ernesto Rimoch

Sefchovich, S.

Demon in My View, A
VIDMARK (Ger) 1992 dir. Petra Haffter

Rendell, R.

Demon Seed
MGM (US) 1977 dir. Donald Cammell

Koontz, D.

Dempsey
FRIES (US) 1983 dir. Gus Trikonis
TV(US)

Dempsey, J. and Dempsey, B. P.

Den Demokratiske Terroristen
FILMFONDS (Ger/Swe) 1992 dir. Per Berglund

Guillou, J.

Denti
CECCHI (It) 2000 dir. Gabriele
Salvatores
Starnone, D.

Dentist in the Chair
REN (GB) 1960 dir. Don Chaffey
Finch, M.

Dernier Tournant, Le
LUX (Fr) 1939 dir. Pierre Chenal
Cain, J. M. *Postman Always Rings Twice,*
The

Desert Fox, The
FOX (US) 1951 dir. Henry Hathaway
GB title: Rommel, Desert Fox
Young, D. *Rommel, The Desert Fox*

Desert Fury
PAR (US) 1947 dir. Lewis Allen
Stewart, R. *Desert Town*

Desert Gold
PAR (US) 1936 dir. James Hogan
Grey, Z.

Desert Hearts
MGM (US) 1986 dir. Donna Deitch
Rule, J. *Desert of the Heart*

Desert Pursuit
ABP (US) 1952 dir. George Blair
Perkins, K. *Desert Voices*

Desert Sands
UA (US) 1955 dir. Lesley Selander
Robb, J. *Punitive Action*

Desert Song
WAR (US) 1943 dir. Robert Florey
M
WAR (US) 1953
dir. Bruce Humberstone
M
Harbach, O., Schwab, L. and Mandel, F.
P

Designated Mourner, The
BBC (GB) 1997 dir. David Hare
Shawn, W.
P

Design for Living
PAR (US) 1933 dir. Ernst Lubitsch
Coward, N.
P

Desire
PAR (US) 1936 dir. Frank Borzage
Szekely, H. and Stemmple, R. A.
P

Desire
FRANCE 2 (Fr) 1995 dir. Bernard Murat
Guitry, S.
P

Desirée
FOX (US) 1954 dir. Henry Koster
Selinko, A.

Desire in the Dust
TCF (US) 1960 dir. William F. Claxton
Whittington, H.

Desire Me
MGM (US) 1947 dir. George Cukor
Frank, L. *Carl and Anna*

Desire Under the Elms
PAR (US) 1958 dir. Delbert Mann
O'Neill, E.
P

Desk Set, The
TCF (US) 1957 dir. Walter Lang
GB title: His Other Woman
Marchant, W.
P

Despair
GALA (Ger) 1978
dir. Rainer Werner Fassbinder
Nabokov, V.

Desperate Characters
ITC (US) 1971 dir. Frank D. Gilroy
Fox, P.

Desperate Hours, The
PAR (US) 1955 dir. William Wyler
MGM (US) 1990 dir. Michael Cimino
Hayes, J.

Desperate Man, The
AA (GB) 1959 dir. Peter Maxwell
Somers, P. *Beginner's Luck*

Desperate Moment
GFD (GB) 1953 dir. Compton Bennett
Albrand, M.

Desperate Ones, The
AIP (Sp/US) 1968
dir. Alexander Ramati
Ramati, A. *Beyond the Mountains*

Desperate Search
MGM (US) 1952 dir. Joseph Lewis
Mayse, A.

Desperate Voyage
WIZAN (US) 1980
dir. Michael O'Herlihy
TV(US)
Kytle, R. *Last Voyage of the Valhalla*

Destination Tokyo
WAR (US) 1943 dir. Delmer Daves
Fisher, S. G.

Destiny of a Spy
UN TV (US) 1969 dir. Boris Sagal
TV(US)
Blackburn, W. J. *Gaunt Women, The*

Destry
UI (US) 1954 dir. George Marshall
Brand, M. *Destry Rides Again*

Destry Rides Again
UN (US) 1939 dir. George Marshall
Brand, M.

Detective, The
FOX (US) 1968 dir. Gordon Douglas
Thorp, R.

Detective, The
BBC (GB) 1985 dir. Don Leaver
TVSe(GB)
Ferris, P.

Detective Story
PAR (US) 1951 dir. William Wyler
Kingsley, S.
P

Det Forsomte Forar
REGNER (Den) 1993 dir. Peter Schroder
Scherfig, H.

Detour
PRC (US) 1946 dir. Edgar G. Ulmer
ENGLEWOOD (US) 1992. dir. Wade
Williams
Goldsmith, M. M.

Devarim
AGAV (Israel) 1995 dir. Amos Gitai
Shabtai, Y. *Past Continuous*

Devices and Desires
ANGLIA (GB) 1991 dir. John Davies
TVSe(GB)
James, P. D.

Devil and the Nun, The
KADR (Pol) 1960
dir. Jerzy Kawalerowicz
Iwaszkiewicz, J.

Devil at 4 O'Clock, The
COL (US) 1961 dir. Mervyn LeRoy
Catto, M.

Devil Commands, The
COL (US) 1941 dir. Edward Dmytryk
Sloane, W. *Edge of Running Water, The*

Devil Dogs of the Air
WAR (US) 1935 dir. Lloyd Bacon
Saunders, J. M.

Devil Doll, The
MGM (US) 1936 dir. Tod Browning
Merritt, A. *Burn, Witch, Burn*

Devil in a Blue Dress
TRISTAR (US) 1995 dir. Carl Franklin
Mosley, W.

Devil in the Flesh
TRANS (Fr) 1947
dir. Claude Autant-Lara
ORION (It/Fr) 1987
dir. Marco Bellocchio
Radiguet, R.

Devil is a Woman, The
PAR (US) 1935 dir. Josef von Sternberg
Louys, P. *Femme et le Pantin, La*

Devil Makes Three, The
MGM (US) 1952 dir. Andrew Marton
Bachmann, L. *Kiss of Death*

Devil Never Sleeps, The
FOX (GB) 1962 dir. Leo McCarey
Buck, P.

Devil Rides Out, The
ABP (GB) 1971 dir. Terence Fisher
US title: Devil's Bride, The
Wheatley, D.

Devils, The
WAR (GB) 1971 dir. Ken Russell
Huxley, A. *Devils of Loudon, The*

Devil's Advocate, The
RANK (Ger) 1977 dir. Guy Green
West, M. L.

Devil's Advocate, The
WAR (US) 1997 dir. Taylor Hackford
Neiderman, A.

Devil's Arithmetic, The
PUNCH 21 (US) 1999 dir. Donna Deitch
TV(US)
Yolen, J.

Devil's Brigade, The
UA (US) 1968 dir. Andrew V.
MacLaglen
Adleman, R. H. and Walton, G.

Devil's Daffodil, The
BL (GB) 1962 dir. Akos Rathonyi
Wallace, E. *Daffodil Mystery, The*

Devil's Disciple, The
M. EVANS (US) 1955
dir. George Schaefer
TV(US)
UA (GB) 1959 dir. Guy Hamilton
Shaw, G. B.
P

Devil's General, The
RYAL (W. Ger) 1955 dir. Helmut
Kautner
Zuckmayer, C.
P

Devil's Island
TRISTAR (Sp) 1994 dir. Juan Piquer
Simon
Nulberry, V.

Devlin
VIACOM PICT (US) 1992 dir. Rick
Rosenthal
TV(US)
Thorp, R.

Devotion
RKO (US) 1931 dir. Robert Milton
Wynne, P. *Little Flat in the Temple, A*

Diabolique
WAR (US) 1996 dir. Jeremiah C.
Chechik
Boileau, P. and Narcejac, T. *Celle qui n'etait pas*

Diaboliques, Les
FILMSONOR (Fr) 1954
dir. Henri-Georges Clouzot
Boileau, P. and Narcejac, T. *Celle qui n'etait pas*

Dial 'M' for Murder
WAR (US) 1954 dir. Alfred Hitchcock
MILBERG (US) 1958
dir. George Schaefer
TIME-LIFE (US) 1981
dir. Boris Sagal
TV(US)
Knott, F.
P

Diamond Girl
ALLIANCE (Can) 1998 dir. Timothy
Bond
TV(Can)
Palmer, D.

Diamond Head
COL (US) 1962 dir. Guy Green
Gilman, P.

Diamond Horseshoe
FOX (US) 1945 dir. George Seaton
Nicholson, K. *Barker, The*
P

Diamond Jim
UN (US) 1935 dir. A. Edward
Sutherland
Morell, P.

Diamond of Jeru, The
USA NETWORK (US/Aust) 2001 dir.
Ian Barry, Dick Lowry
TV(US/Aust)
L'Amour, L.

Diamonds are Forever
UA (GB) 1971 dir. Guy Hamilton
Fleming, I.

Diamond Trap, The
COL TV (US) 1988 dir. Don Taylor
TV(US)
Minahan, J. *Great Diamond Robbery, The*

Diana
BBC (GB) 1983 dir. David Tucker
TVSe(GB)
Delderfield, R. F. *There was a Fair Maid Dwelling; The Unjust Skies*

Diana: Her True Story
M. POLL (US) 1993 dir. Kevin Connor
TV(US)
Morton, A.

Diary of a Chambermaid, The
BOGEAUS (US) 1946
dir. Jean Renoir
Mirbeau, O.

Diary of a City Priest
ITVS (US) 2000 dir. Eugene Martin
McNamee, Father J.

Diary of a Country Priest, The
GGT (Fr) 1950 dir. Robert Bresson
Bernanos, G.

Diary of a Hit Man
VI (US) 1992 dir. Roy London
Pressman, K. *Insider's Price*
P

Diary of a Mad Housewife
UI (US) 1970 dir. Frank Perry
Kaufman, S.

Diary of Anne Frank, The
FOX (US) 1959 dir. George Stevens
FOX (US) 1980 dir. Boris Sagal
TV(US)
BBC (GB) 1987 dir. Gareth Davies
TVSe(GB)

Frank, A. *Anne Frank: The Diary of a Young Girl*

Diary of Major Thompson, The
GALA (Fr) 1955 dir. Preston Sturges
US title: French They are a Funny Race, The

Daninos, P. *Notebooks of Major Thompson, The*

Dick Turpin
STOLL-STAFFORD (GB) 1933
dir. Victor Hanbury, John Stafford

Ainsworth, H. *Rookwood*

Died in the Wool
ITV (GB) 1978 dir. Brian McDuffie
TVSe(GB)

Marsh, N.

Die Hard
FOX (US) 1988 dir. John McTiernan

Thorp, R.

Die Hard 2
FOX (US) 1990 dir. Renny Harlin

Wager, W. *58 Minutes*

Die, Monster, Die!
AIP (US/GB) 1965 dir. Daniel Haller

Lovecraft, H. P. *Color Out of Space, The*

Dieu à Besoin des Hommes
TRANS (Fr) 1950 dir. Jean Delannoy

Quefflec, H. *Recteur de l'Ile de Sein, Un*

Digby – The Biggest Dog in the World
RANK (GB) 1973 dir. Joseph McGrath
Ch

Key, T.

Diggstown
MGM (US) 1992 dir. Michael Ritchie

Wise, L. *Diggstown Ringers, The*

Dimenticare Palermo
PENTA (It/Fr) 1990 dir. Francesco Rosi

Charles-Roux, E.

Dinner at Eight
MGM (US) 1933 dir. George Cukor
TNT (US) 1989 dir. Ron Lagomarsino
TV(US)

Kaufman, G. S. and Ferber, E.
P

Dinner Game, The
GAU (Fr) 1998 dir. Francis Veber

Veber, F. *Diner de Cons, Le*
P

Dinner With Friends
HBO FILMS (US) 2001 dir. Norman Jewison
TV(US)

Margulies, D.
P

Dinosaur Hunter, The
IMP (Can) 2000 dir. Rick Stevenson

Conrad, P. *My Daniel*

Diplomatic Courier
FOX (US) 1952 dir. Henry Hathaway

Cheyney, P. *Sinister Errand*

Dirty Dingus Magee
MGM (US) 1970 dir. Burt Kennedy

Markson, D. *Ballad of Dingus Magee, The*

Dirty Dozen, The
MGM (US) 1967 dir. Robert Aldrich

Nathanson, E. M.

Dirty Mary, Crazy Larry
FOX (US) 1974 dir. John Hough

Unekis, R. *Chase, The*

Dirty Tricks
FILMPLAN (Can) 1980 dir. Alvin Rakoff

Gifford, T. *Glendower Legacy, The*

Dirty Weekend
SCIMITAR (GB) 1993 dir. Michael Winner

Zahavi, H.

Dirty Work
GAU (GB) 1934 dir. Tom Walls

Travers, B.
P

Disappearance, The
CINEGATE (GB/Can) 1977 dir. Stuart Cooper

Marlowe, D. *Echos of Celandine*

Disappearance of Finbar, The
VICTORIA (Ire/Swe/GB) 1996 dir. Sue Clayton

Lombard, C. *Disappearance of Rory Brophy, The*

Disappearance of Garcia Lorca, The
STUDIO CANAL+ (Fr/Sp/US) 1997 dir. Marcos Zurinaga

Gibson, I. *Assassination of Federico Garcia Lorca, The; Federico Garcia Lorca: A Life*

Disappearing Acts
HBO (US) 2000 dir. Gina Prince-Bythewood
TV(US)

McMillan, T.

Disaster in Time
WILDSTREET (US) 1992 dir. David N. Twohy
TV(US)

Kuttner, H. and Moore, C. L. *Vintage Seasons*

Discarnates, The
SHOCHIKU (Jap) 1989 dir. Nobuhiko Obayashi

Yamada, T.

Disclosure
WAR (US) 1994 dir. Barry Levinson

Crichton, M.

Disco Pigs
TEMPLE (Ire) 2001 dir. Kirsten Sheridan

Walsh, E.
P

Dishonoured Lady
MARS (US) 1947 dir. Robert Stevenson

Sheldon, E. and Barnes, M. A.
P

Disputed Passage
PAR (US) 1939 dir. Frank Borzage

Douglas, L. C.

Disraeli
WAR (US) 1929 dir. Alfred E. Green

Parker, L. N.
P

Distant Trumpet, A
WAR (US) 1964 dir. Raoul Walsh

Horgan, P.

Dites-Lui Que Je L'Aime
ART EYE (Fr) 1977 dir. Claude Miller
GB title: This Sweet Sickness
US title: Tell Her I Love Her

Highsmith, P.

Ditchdiggers, Daughters, The
MTM (US) 1997 dir. Johnny Jensen
TV(US)

Thorton, Y. and Coudert, J.

Diva
GALAXIE (Fr) 1981
dir. Jean-Jacques Beineix
Delacorta

Divided We Fall
BIOSCOP (Czech) 2000 dir. Jan Hrebejk
Jarchovsky, P.

Divine Poursuite, La
STUDIO CANAL+ (Fr) 1997 dir. Michel
Deville
Westlake, D. E. *Dancing Aztec*

Diviners, The
ATLANTIS (Can) 1993 dir. Anne
Wheeler
TV(Can)
Laurence, M.

Divorcee, The
MGM (US) 1930 dir. Robert Z. Leonard
Parrott, U. *Ex-Wife*

Divorce of Lady X, The
LONDON (GB) 1938 dir. Tim Whelan
Wakefield, G. *Counsel's Opinion*
P

Divorcing Jack
SCALA (GB) 1998 dir. David Caffrey
Bateman, C.

Doc Hollywood
WAR (US) 1991
dir. Michael Caton-Jones
Shulman, N. B. *What? ... Dead Again?*

Doc Savage—Man of Bronze
WAR (US) 1975 dir. Michael Anderson
Robeson, K.

Dock Brief, The
MGM (GB) 1962 dir. James Hill
US title: Trial & Error
Mortimer, J.
P

Doctor, The
TOUCHSTONE (US) 1991 dir. Randa
Haines
Rosenbaum, E. *Taste of my Own
Medicine, A*

Doctor and the Girl, The
MGM (US) 1949 dir. Curtis Bernhardt
van der Meersch, M. *Bodies and Souls*

Doctor Dolittle
FOX (US) 1967 dir. Richard Fleischer
Ch, M
Lofting, H.

Doctor Faustus
COL (GB) 1967 dir. Richard Burton,
Neville Coghill
Marlowe, C. *Tragical History of Doctor
Faustus*
P

Doctor Fisher of Geneva
BBC (GB) 1984
dir. Michael Lindsay-Hogg
TV(GB)
Greene, G.

Doctor in the House
GFD (GB) 1954 dir. Ralph Thomas
Gordon, R.

Doctor in the Village
NFM (Neth) 1958 dir. Fons Rademakers
Coolen, A.

Doctor's Dilemma, The
MGM (GB) 1958 dir. Anthony Asquith
Shaw, G. B.
P

Doctor's Wives
COL (US) 1971 dir. George Schaefer
Slaughter, F. G.

Doctor, You've got to be Kidding
MGM (US) 1967 dir. Peter Tewkesbury
Mahan, P. W.

Doctor Zhivago
MGM (US) 1965 dir. David Lean
Pasternak, B.

Dodson's Journey
CBS TV (US) 2001 dir. Gregg Champion
TV(US)
Dodson, J. *Faithful Travelers: A Father, A Daughter, A Fly-Fishing Journey of the Heart*

Dodsworth
UA (US) 1936 dir. William Wyler
Lewis, S.

Dog of Flanders, A
RKO (US) 1935 dir. Edward Sloman
FOX (US) 1959 dir. James B. Clark
WOODBRIDGE (Bel/US) 1999 dir. Kevin Brodie
Ouida

Dogs of War, The
UA (GB) 1980 dir. John Irvin
Forsyth, F.

Doing Life
PHOENIX (US) 1986
dir. Gene Reynolds
TV(US)
Bello, S.

Doktor Faustus
SAFIR (Ger) 1982 dir. Franz Seitz
Mann, T.

Dolce Far Niente
EURIMAGES (Bel/Fr) 1999 dir. Nae Caranfil
Vitoux, F. *Comedie de Terracina, Le*

Dollhouse Murders, The
AMIS (US) 1994 dir. Dianne Haak
TV(US)
Wright, B. R.

Dollmaker, The
IPC (US) 1984 dir. Daniel Petrie
TV(US)
Arnow, A.

Doll's House, A
COMPASS (US) 1959
dir. George Schaefer
TV(US)
BL (GB) 1973 dir. Patrick Garland
BBC (GB) 1992 dir. David Thacker
TV(GB)
Ibsen, H.
P

Dolores Claiborne
COL (US) 1995 dir. Taylor Hackford
King, S.

Dombey and Son
BBC (GB) 1983 dir. Rodney Bennett
TVSe(GB)
Dickens, C.

Domenica
RAI (It) 2001 dir. Wilma Labate
Marse, J.

Dominant Sex, The
AB (GB) 1937 dir. Herbert Brenon
Egan, M.
P

Dominique
GRAND PRIZE (GB) 1978
dir. Michael Anderson
Lawlor, H. *What Beckoning Ghost*

Domino Principle, The
ITC (US) 1977 dir. Stanley Kramer
Kennedy, A.

Dona Flor and her Two Husbands
FD (Bra) 1977 dir. Bruno Barretto

Amado, J.

Dona Herlinda and her Son
CLASA (Mex) 1986 dir. J. H. Hermosillo

Paez, J. L.

Donato and Daughter
MULTIMEDIA (US) 1993 dir. Rod Holcomb
TV(US)

Early, J.

Don Camillo's Last Round
RIZZOLI (It) 1955
dir. Carmine Guareschi

Guareschi, G.

Don Chicago
BN (GB) 1945 dir. Maclean Rogers

Roberts, C. E. B.

Don is Dead, The
UN (US) 1973 dir. Richard Fleischer

Albert, M. H.

Don Juan
FRANCE 3 (Fr) 1998 dir. Jacques Weber

Moliere, J. B.
P

Don King: Only in America
HBO (US) dir. John Herzfeld
TV(US)

Newfield, J. *Only in America: The Life and Crimes of Don King*

Donnie Brasco
TRISTAR (US) 1997 dir. Mike Newell

Pistone, J. *Donnie Brasco: My Undercover Life in the Mafia*

Donor Unknown
CITADEL ENT (US) 1995 dir. John Harrison
TV(US)

Mooney, W. H. *Corazon*

Do Not Disturb
FOX (US) 1965 dir. Ralph Levy

Fairchild, W.
P

Do Not Fold, Spindle or Mutilate
LEE RICH (US) 1971 dir. Ted Post
TV(US)

Disney, D. M.

Donovan's Brain
UA (US) 1953 dir. Felix Feist

Siodmak, C.

Don Quixote
VANDOR (Fr) 1933 dir. G. W. Pabst
LENFILM (USSR) 1957
dir. Grigori Kozintsev
EUSTON (GB) 1985
TV(GB)
HALLMARK (US) 2000 dir. Peter Yates
TV(US)

Cervantes, M. de

Don's Party
DOUBLE HEAD (Aust) 1976
dir. Bruce Beresford

Williamson, D.

Don't Bother to Knock
FOX (US) 1952 dir. Roy Ward Baker

Armstrong, C. *Mischief*

Don't Bother to Knock
WAR (GB) 1961 dir. Cyril Frankel
US title: Why Bother to Knock

Hanley, C. *Love From Everybody*

Don't Drink the Water
AVCO (US) 1969
dir. Howard Morris
MAGNOLIA (US) 1994 dir. Woody Allen
TV(US)
Allen, W.
P

Don't Go Near the Water
MGM (US) 1957 dir. Charles Walters
Brinkley, W.

Don't Just Lie There, Say Something
RANK (GB) 1973 dir. Bob Kellet
Pertwee, M.
P

Don't Just Stand There
UN (US) 1967 dir. Ron Winston
Williams, C. *Wrong Venus, The*

Don't Look Back
TBA (US) 1981 dir. Richard Colla
TV(US)
Paige, L. and Lipman, D. *Maybe I'll Pitch Forever*

Don't Look Behind You
FOX FAMILY (US) 1999 dir. David Winning
TV(US)
Duncan, L.

Don't Look Now
BL (GB) 1973 dir. Nicolas Roeg
Du Maurier, D.

Don't Make Waves
MGM (US) 1967 dir. Alexander Mackendrick
Wallach, I. *Muscle Beach*

Don't Raise the Bridge, Lower the River
BL (GB) 1967 dir. Jerry Paris
Wilk, M.

Don't Say a Word
FOX (US) 2001 dir. Gary Fleder
Klavan, A.

Don't Tell Her It's Me
HEMDALE (US) 1990
dir. Malcolm Mowbray
Bird, S. *Boyfriend School, The*

Don't Touch My Daughter
PATCHETT-KAUFMAN (US) 1991 dir. John Pasquin
TV(US)
Dorner, M. *Nightmare*

Door in the Wall, The
ABP (GB) 1956 dir. Glenn H. Alvey, Jr.
Wells, H. G.

Dorian Gray
AIP (It/Ger) 1970
dir. Massimo Dallamano
Wilde, O. *Picture of Dorian Gray, The*

Dormez, Je Le Veux
CDP (Fr) 1997 dir. Irene Jouannet
Minier, M. *Hypnotisme à la Portée de Tous, L'*

Double Bang
NEW CITY (US) 2001 dir. Heywood Gould
Gould, H.

Double Confession
ABP (GB) 1950 dir. Ken Annakin
Garden, J. *All on a Summer's Day*

Double Indemnity
PAR (US) 1944 dir. Billy Wilder
UN (US) 1973 dir. Jack Smight
TV(US)
Cain, J. M.

Double Man, The
WAR (GB) 1967 dir. Franklin Schaffner
Maxfield, H. S. *Legacy of a Spy*

Double Negative
QUADRANT (Can) 1980
dir. George Bloomfield
Macdonald, R. *Three Roads, The*

Double Standard
FRIES (US) 1988 dir. Louis Rudolph
TV (US)
Ellison, J. W.

Doubletake
TITUS (US) 1985 dir. Jud Taylor
TVSe(US)
Bayer, W. *Switch*

Double Take
TOUCHSTONE (US) 2001 dir. George
Gallo
Greene, G. *Across the Bridge*

Double Wedding
MGM (US) 1937 dir. Richard Thorpe
Molnar, F. *Great Love*
P

Doubting Thomas
FOX (US) 1935 dir. David Butler
Kelly, G. *Torch Bearers, The*
P

Doughgirls, The
WAR (US) 1944 dir. James V. Kern
Fields, J.
P

Dove, The
EMI (US) 1974 dir. Charles Jarrot
Graham, R. L. and Gill, D.

Down and Out in Beverly Hills
TOUCHSTONE (US) 1986 dir. Paul
Mazursky
Fauchois, R. *Boudu Sauvé des Eaux*
P

Downhill Racer
PAR (US) 1969 dir. Michael Ritchie
Hall, O. *Downhill Racers*

Down the Long Hills
DISNEY CH (US) 1986
dir. Burt Kennedy
TV(US)
L'Amour, L.

Down 3 Dark Streets
UA (US) 1954 dir. Arnold Laven
Gordon, M. and Gordon, G. *Case File F.B.I.*

Down Will Come Baby
HEARST (US) 1999 dir. Gregory
Goodell
TV(US)
Murphy, G.

Do You Like Women?
FRANCORITZ (Fr/It) 1964
dir. Jean Leon
Bardawil, G.

Dracula
UN (US) 1931 dir. Tod Browning
UI (GB) 1958 dir. Terence Fisher
US title: House of Dracula
EMI (It) 1973 dir. Paul Morrissey
UN (US) 1974 dir. Dan Curtis
TV (US)
AM ZOETROPE (US) 1992 dir. Francis
Ford Coppola
Stoker, B.

Dracula
CIC (GB) 1979 dir. John Badham
Stoker B.
Balderston, J. and Deane, H.
P

Dracula's Daughter
UN (US) 1936 dir. Lambert Hillyer
Stoker, B. *Dracula's Guest*

Dragon Seed
MGM (US) 1944 dir. Jack Conway

Buck, P.

Dragon: The Bruce Lee Story
UN (US) 1993 dir. Rob Cohen

Cadwell, L. L. *Bruce Lee: The Man Only I Knew*

Dragonwyck
FOX (US) 1946
dir. Joseph L. Mankiewicz

Seton, A.

Dramatic School
MGM (US) 1938 dir. Robert B. Sinclair, Jr.

Szekely, H. *School of Drama*
P

Dr. Akagi
TOEI (Jap) 1998 dir. Shohei Imamura

Sakaguchi, A. *Doctor Liver*

Dr. Bull
FOX (US) 1933 dir. John Ford

Cozzens, J. G. *Last Adam, The*

Dr. Cook's Garden
PAR TV (US) 1971 dir. Ted Post
TV(US)

Levin, I.
P

Dreamer of Oz, The: The L. Frank Baum Story
ADAM (US) 1990 dir. Jack Bender
TV(US)

Hearn, M. P.

Dream Girl
PAR (US) 1947 dir. Mitchell Leisen
M. EVANS (US) 1955
dir. George Schaefer
TV(US)

Rice, E.
P

Dreaming Lips
TRAFALGAR (GB) 1936
dir. Paul Czinner, Lee Garmes

Bernstein, H.
P

Dream Merchants, The
COL TV (US) 1980
dir. Vincent Sherman
TVSe(US)

Robbins, H.

Dream of Kings, A
WAR (US) 1969 dir. Daniel Mann

Petrakis, H. M.

Dreams Lost, Dreams Found
ATLANTIC/YTV (US/GB) 1987
dir. Willi Patterson
TV(GB/US)

Wallace, P.

Dreams of Innocence
BELFILMS (Israel) 1993 dir. Dina Zvi-Riklis

Matalon, R. *Tale which Begins with a Funeral of a Snake, A*

Dream West
SCHICK SUNN (US) 1986
dir. Dick Lowry
TVSe(US)

Nevin, D.

Dresser, The
COL (GB) 1983 dir. Peter Yates

Harwood, R.
P

Dress Gray
WAR TV (US) 1986 dir. Glenn Jordan
TVSe(US)

Truscott IV, L. K.

Dressmaker, The
FILM 4 (GB) 1988 dir. Jim O'Brien

Bainbridge, B.

Drive, He Said
COL (US) 1970 dir. Jack Nicholson
Larner, J.

Drive Me Crazy
FOX (US) 1999 dir. John Schultz
Strasser, T. *How I Created My Perfect Prom Date*

Driving Miss Daisy
WAR (US) 1989 dir. Bruce Beresford
Uhry, A.
P

Dr Jekyll and Mr Hyde
PAR (US) 1931 dir. Rouben Mamoulian
MGM (US) 1941 dir. Victor Fleming
BBC (GB) 1980 dir. Alastair Reid
TV(GB)
TELESCENE FG (Can/Aust) 1999 dir. Colin Budds
TV(Can/Aust)
Stevenson, R. L.

Dr No
UA (GB) 1962 dir. Terence Young
Fleming, I.

Drop Dead Darling
SEVEN ARTS (GB) 1966
dir. Ken Hughes
US title: Arrivederci Baby
Deming, R. *Careful Man, The*

Drowning Pool, The
WAR (US) 1975 dir. Stuart Rosenberg
Macdonald, R.

Dr. Socrates
WAR (US) 1935 dir. William Dieterle
Burnett, W. R.

Dr Strangelove; Or How I Learned to Stop Worrying and Love the Bomb
COL (GB) 1963 dir. Stanley Kubrick
George, P. *Red Alert*

Dr Syn
GAU (GB) 1937 dir. Roy William Neill
Thorndike, R. *Christopher Syn*

Dr. Syn, Alias the Scarecrow
DISNEY (US) 1962 dir. James Neilson
Thorndike, R. *Christopher Syn*

Drugstore Cowboy
AVENUE (US) 1989 dir. Gus van Sant
Fogle, J.

Drug Wars: The Camarena Story
ZZY (US) 1990 dir. Brian Gibson
TVSe(US)
Shannon, E. *Desperados: Latin Drug Lords, US Lawmen and the War America Can't Win*

Drug Wars: The Cocaine Cartel
ZZY (US) 1992 dir. Paul Krasny
TVSe(US)
Shannon, E. *Desperados: Latin Drug Lords, US Lawmen and the War America Can't Win*

Drum
PAR (US) 1976 dir. Steve Carver
Onstott, K.

Drum, The
UA (GB) 1938 dir. Zoltan Korda
US title: Drums
Mason, A. E. W.

Drums Along the Mohawk
FOX (US) 1939 dir. John Ford
Edmonds, W. D.

Drums in the Deep South
RKO (GB) 1952
dir. William Cameron Menzies
Noble, H. *Woman with a Sword*

Drums of Fu Manchu
REP (US) 1940 dir. William Witney, John English
Rohmer, S.

Drunks
BMG (US) 1996 dir. Peter Cohn
TV(US)
Lennon, G. *Blackout*
P

Dr. X
WAR (US) 1932 dir. Michael Curtiz
Comstock, H. W.
P

Dry Rot
BL (GB) 1956 dir. Maurice Elvey
Chapman, J.
P

Dry White Season, A
MGM (US) 1989 dir. Euzhan Palcy
Brink, A.

Dubarry was a Lady
MGM (US) 1943 dir. Roy del Ruth
M
Fields, H.
P

Dublin Nightmare
RANK (GB) 1957 dir. John Pomeroy
Loraine, P.

Duel at Diablo
UA (US) 1966 dir. Ralph Nelson
Albert, M. H. *Apache Rising*

Duel in the Sun
MGM (US) 1946 dir. King Vidor
Busch, N.

Duel of Hearts
TNT (US/GB) 1992 dir. John Hough
TV(US/GB)
Cartland, B.

Duellists, The
CIC (GB) 1977 dir. Ridley Scott
Conrad, J. *Point of Honour, The*

Duet for One
CANNON (GB) 1987
dir. Andrei Konchalovsky
Kempinski, T.
P

Duffy of San Quentin
WAR (US) 1954 dir. Walter Doniger
Duffy, C. T. and Jennings, D. *San Quentin Story, The*

Dulcima
EMI (GB) 1971 dir. Frank Nesbitt
Bates, H. E.

Dulcy
MGM (US) 1940 dir. S. Sylvan Simon
Kaufman, G. S. and Connelly, M.
P

Dumbo
DISNEY (US) 1941 dir. Ben Sharpsteen
A, Ch
Aberson, H. and Pearl, H. *Dumbo, the Flying Elephant*

Dummy
WAR TV (US) 1979 dir. Frank Perry
TV(US)
Tidyman, E.

Dune
UN (US) 1984 dir. David Lynch
NEW AMSTERDAM (US/Can) dir. John Harrison
TVSe(US/Can)
Herbert, F.

Dunkirk
MGM (GB) 1958 dir. Leslie Norman
Trevor, E. *Big Pick-Up, The*

Dunwich Horror, The
AIP (US) 1970
dir. Daniel Haller

Lovecraft, H. P. *Shuttered Room, The*

Duped Till Doomsday
DEFA (Ger) 1957 dir. Kurt Jung-Alsen

Fuhmann, F. *Kamaraden*

Durango
HALLMARK (US) 1999 dir. Brent Shields
TV(US)

Keane, J. B.

Dust
DASKA (Bel/Fr) 1985
dir. Marion Hansel

Coetzee, J. M. *In the Heart of the Country*

Dusty Ermine
TWICKENHAM (GB) 1938
dir. Bernard Vorhaus

Grant, N.
P

Dwelling Place, The
TYNE TEES (GB) 1994 dir. Gavin Millar
TVSe(GB)

Cookson, C.

Dying Young
TCF (US) 1991 dir. Joel Schumacher

Leimbach, M.

Dynasty
PARADINE TV (US) 1976
dir. Lee Philips
TV(US)

Michener, J. A.

Each Dawn I Die
WAR (US) 1939 dir. William Keighley

Odlum, J.

Eagle has Landed, The
ITC (GB) 1976 dir. John Sturges

Higgins, J.

Eagle of the Ninth
BBC (GB) 1977 dir. Michael Simpson
TVSe(GB)

Sutcliff, R.

Eagle Shooting Heroes, The: Dong Cheng Xi Jiu
JET TONE (HK) 1994 dir. Jeffrey Lau

Cha, L.

Earl of Chicago
MGM (US) 1940 dir. Richard Thorpe

Williams, B.

Early Life of Stephen Hind, The
BBC (GB) 1974 dir. Timothy Combe
TVSe(GB)

Jameson, S.

Earthly Possessions
RASTAR (US) 1999 dir. James Lapine
TV(US)

Tyler, A.

Earth v. The Flying Saucers
COL (US) 1956 dir. Fred F. Sears

Keyhoe, D. E. *Flying Saucers from Outer Space*

Easiest Way, The
MGM (US) 1931 dir. Jack Conway

Walter, E.
P

East is East
CHANNEL 4 FILMS (GB) 1999 dir. Damian O'Donnell

Khan-Din, A.
P

East Lynne
FOX (US) 1931 dir. Frank Lloyd

Wood, Mrs. H.

East of Eden
WAR (US) 1954 dir. Elia Kazan
NEUFELD (US) 1980
dir. Harvey Hart
TVSe(US)

Steinbeck, J.

East of Piccadilly
ABPC (GB) 1940 dir. Harold Huth

Beckles, G.

East of Sumatra
UI (US) 1953 dir. Budd Boetticher

L'Amour, L.

East Side, West Side
MGM (US) 1949 dir. Mervyn LeRoy

Davenport, M.

Easy Come, Easy Go
PAR (US) 1947 dir. John Farrow

McNulty, J. L. *Third Avenue, New York*

Easy Living
PAR (US) 1937 dir. Mitchell Leisen
Caspary, V.

Easy Money
GFD (GB) 1948 dir. Bernard Knowles
Ridley, A.
P

Easy to Love
WAR (US) 1933 dir. William Keighley
Buchanan, T.
P

Eat a Bowl of Tea
COL (US) 1989 dir. Wayne Wang
Chu, L.

Ebbie
CRESCENT (US) 1995 dir. George
Kaczender
TV(US)
Dickens, C. *Christmas Carol, A*

Ebb Tide
PAR (US) 1937 dir. James Hogan
Stevenson, R. L. and Osbourne, L. *Ebb-Tide, The*

Ebb-Tide, The
GRANADA/A&E (GB) 1998 dir.
Nicholas Renton
TV(GB)
Stevenson, R. L. and Osbourne, L.

Ebony Tower, The
GRANADA (GB) 1984
dir. Robert Knights
TV(GB)
Fowles, J.

Echo of Thunder, The
HALLMARK (US) 1998 dir. Simon
Wincer
TV(US)
Hathorn, L. *Thunderwith*

Echoes
WORKING TITLE (GB) 1988 dir.
Barbara Rennie
TVSe(GB)
Binchy, M.

Echoes in the Darkness
NEW WORLD TV (US) 1987
dir. Glenn Jordan
TVSe(US)
Wambaugh, J.

Echo of Barbara
RANK (GB) 1961 dir. Sidney Hayers
Burke, J.

Eclipse
GALA (GB) 1976 dir. Simon Perry
Wolaston, N.

Eddie and the Cruisers
EMBASSY (US) 1983
dir. Martin Davidson
Kluge, P. F.

Eddie Macon's Run
UN (US) 1983 dir. Jeff Kane
McLendon, J.

Eden
CINEVIA (Fr/Israel) 2001 dir. Amos
Gitai
Miller, A. *Homely Girl*

Edge of Darkness
WAR (US) 1943 dir. Lewis Milestone
Woods, W. H.

Edge of Doom
RKO (US) 1950 dir. Mark Robson
GB title: Stronger than Fear
Brady, L.

Edge of Fury
UA (US) 1958 dir. Robert Gurney, Irving
Lerner
Coates, R. M. *Wisteria Cottage*

121

Edge of the City
MGM (US) 1957 dir. Martin Ritt
GB title: Man is Ten Feet Tall, A
Arthur, R. A.
P

Edipo Alcalde
IMCINE (Mex/Sp) 1996 dir. Jorge Ali
Triana
Sophocles *Oedipus the King*
P

Edith's Diary
ZDF (W. Ger) 1986
dir. Hans W. Geissendoerfer
Highsmith, P.

**Ed McBain's 87th Precinct:
Lightning**
HEARST (1995) dir. Bruce Paltrow
TV(US)
McBain, E. *Lightning*

Ed McBain's 87th Precinct: Ice
HEARST (1996) dir. Bradford May
TV(US)
McBain, E. *Ice*

Education of Little Tree, The
ALLIED FILMS (Can) 1997 dir. Richard
Friedenberg
Carter, F.

Educating Rita
RANK (GB) 1983 dir. Lewis Gilbert
Russell, W.
P

Edward & Mrs. Simpson
THAMES (GB) 1978 dir. Waris Hussein
TVSe(GB)
Donaldson, F. *Edward VIII*

Edward, My Son
MGM (GB) 1949 dir. George Cukor
Morley, R. and Langley, N.
P

Edward II
WORKING TITLE (GB) 1991
dir. Derek Jarman
Marlowe, C.
P

Ed Wood
TOUCHSTONE (US) 1994 dir. Tim
Burton
Grey, R. *Nightmare of Ecstasy*

Eel, The
KSS (Jap) 1997 dir. Shohei Imamura
Yoshimura, A. *Sparkles in the Darkness*

**Effect of Gamma Rays on Man-
in-the-Moon Marigolds,The**
FOX-RANK (US) 1972 dir. Paul
Newman
Zindel, P.
P

Egg and I, The
UN (US) 1947 dir. Chester Erskine
Macdonald, B.

Egyptian, The
FOX (US) 1954 dir. Michael Curtiz
Waltari, M.

Eiger Sanction, The
UN (US) 1975 dir. Clint Eastwood
Trevanian

Eighteen Springs
MANDARIN (China) 1997 dir. Ann Hui
Chang, E.

800 Leagues Down the Amazon
IGUANA (US/Peru) 1993 dir. Luis
Llosa
Verne, J.

Eight Iron Men
COL (US) 1952 dir. Edward Dmytryk
Brown, H. *Sound of Hunting, A*
P

Eight Men Out
ORION (US) 1988 dir. John Sayles
Asinof, E.

8 Million Ways to Die
TRISTAR (US) 1986 dir. Hal Ashby
Block, L. *Stab in the Dark*

84 Charing Cross Road
COL (US/GB) 1987 dir. David Jones
Hanff, H.

83 Hours 'Til Dawn
CONSOL (US) 1990 dir. Donald Wrye
TV(US)
Mackle, B. and Miller, G.

80,000 Suspects
RANK (GB) 1963 dir. Val Guest
Trevor, E. *Pillars of Midnight, The*

E1
NACIONAL (Mex) 1952
dir. Luis Bunuel
Pinto, M. *Pensamientos*

El Dorado
PAR (US) 1966 dir. Howard Hawks
Brown, H. *Stars in their Courses, The*

Eleanor and Franklin
TALENT (US) 1976 dir. Daniel Petrie
TVSe(US)
Lash, J. P.

Eleanor and Franklin: The White House Years
TALENT (US) 1977 dir. Daniel Petrie
TV(US)
Lash, J. P. *Eleanor and Franklin*

Eleanor Marx
BBC (GB) 1977 dir. Jane Howell
TVSe(GB)
Tsuzuki, C. *Life of Eleanor Marx 1855–1899, The: A Socialist Tragedy*

Election
PAR (US) 1999 dir. Alexander Payne
Perrotta, T.

Electra
UA (Gre) 1962
dir. Michael Cacoyannis
Sophocles
P

Electric Vendetta, The
YTV/A&E (GB) 2001 dir. Peter Smith
TV(GB)
Graham, C.

Eleni
WAR (US) 1985 dir. Peter Yates
Gage, N.

Elephant Boy
UA (GB) 1937 dir. Robert Flaherty, Zoltan Korda
Kipling, R. *Toomai of the Elephants*

Elephant Man, The
PAR (GB) 1980 dir. David Lynch
Treves, Sir F. *Elephant Man and Other Reminiscences, The*

Elephant Master, The
STUDIO CANAL+ (Fr) 1995 dir. Patrick Grandperret
Guillot, R.

Elephant Walk
PAR (US) 1954 dir. William Dieterle
Standish, R.

11 Harrowhouse
FOX (GB) 1974 dir. Aram Avakian
Browne, G. A.

Elidor
BBC (GB) 1995 dir. John Reardon
TVSe(GB)
Garner, A.

Elizabeth the Queen
COMPASS (US) 1968
dir. George Schaefer
TV(US)

Anderson, M.
P

Ellen Foster
HALLMARK (US) 1997 dir. John Erman
TV(US)

Gibbons, K.

Ellery Queen: Don't Look Behind You
UN TV (US) 1971 dir. Barry Shear
TV(US)

Queen, E. *Cat of Many Tales*

Ellery Queen: Too Many Suspects
UN TV (US) 1975 dir. David Greene
TV(US)

Queen, E. *Fourth Side of the Triangle, The*

Ellis Island
TELEPIC (US) 1984 dir. Jerry London
TVSe(US)

Stewart, F. M.

Elmer Gantry
UA (US) 1960 dir. Richard Brooks

Lewis, S.

Elusive Pimpernel, The
BL (GB) 1950 dir. Michael Powell

Orczy, Baroness E.

Elvis and Me
NEW WORLD TV (US) 1988
dir. Larry Peerce
TVSe(US)

Presley, P. and Harman, S.

Embassy
HEMDALE (GB) 1972
dir. Gordon Hessler

Coulter, S.

Emigrants, The
SVENSK (Swe) 1970 dir. Jan Troell

Moberg, V.

Emil and the Detectives
UFA (Ger) 1931 dir. Gerhard Lamprecht
DISNEY (US) 1964
dir. Peter Tewkesbury
Ch

Kastner, E.

Emlyn's Moon
HTV (GB) 1990 dir. Pennant Roberts
Ch, TVSe(GB)

Nimmo, J.

Emma
BBC (GB) 1972 dir. John Glenister
TVSe(GB)
MIRAMAX (GB/US) 1996 dir. Douglas McGrath
A&E/MERIDIAN (GB) 1997 dir. Diarmuid Lawrence
TV(GB)

Austen, J.

Emma: Queen of the South Seas
FRIES (US) 1988 dir. Bryan Forbes
TVSe(US)

Dutton, G. *Queen Emma of the South Seas*

Emmanuelle
SF (Fr) 1975 dir. Just Jacklin

Arsan, E.

Emperor Jones, The
UA (US) 1933 dir. Dudley Murphy

O'Neill, E.
P

Emperor's Candlesticks, The
MGM (US) 1937
dir. George Fitzmaurice

Orczy, Baroness E.

Emperor's New Clothes, The
CANNON (US) 1987 dir. David Irving
Ch
Andersen, H. C.

Empire of Passion
PARIS/OSHIMA (Jap) 1980
dir. Magisa Oshima
Nakamura, I.

Empire of the Ants
AIP (US) 1977 dir. Bert I. Gordon
Wells, H. G. *Valley of the Ants, The*

Empire of the Sun
WAR (US) 1987 dir. Steven Spielberg
Ballard, J. G.

Employee's Entrance
WAR (US) 1933 dir. Roy del Ruth
Boehm, D.
P

Empty Canvas, The
CC (It/Fr) 1964 dir. Damiano Damiani
Moravia, A.

Empty Saddles
UN (US) 1937 dir. Les Selander
Wilson, C.

En Cas de Malheur
UCIL (Fr/It) 1958
dir. Claude Autant-Lara
Simenon, G.

Enchanted April
RKO (US) 1935 dir. Harry Beaumont
BBC (GB) 1992 dir. Mike Newell
von Arnim, E. *Enchanted April, The*

Enchanted Castle, The
BBC (GB) 1979 dir. Dorothea Brooking
TVSe(GB)
Nesbit, E.

Enchanted Cottage, The
RKO (US) 1945 dir. John Cromwell
Pinero, Sir A. W.
P

Enchanted Island
WAR (US) 1958 dir. Allan Dwan
Melville, H. *Typee*

Enchantment
RKO (US) 1948 dir. Irving Reis
Godden, R. *Fugue in Time, A*

Encore
GFD (GB) 1951 dir. Harold French, Pat
Jackson, Anthony Pellissier
Maugham, W. S. *Ant and the
Grasshopper, The; Winter Cruise; Gigolo
and Gigolette*

Ending Up
THAMES (GB) 1989 dir. Peter Sasdy
TV(GB)
Amis, K.

Endless Game, The
TELSO (GB) 1990 dir. Bryan Forbes
TV(GB)
Forbes, B.

Endless Love
UN (US) 1981 dir. Franco Zeffirelli
Spencer, S.

Endless Night
BL (GB) 1971 dir. Sidney Gilliat
Christie, A.

End of August, The
QUARTET (US) 1981 dir. Bob Graham
Chopin, K. *Awakening, The*

End of the Affair, The
COL (GB) 1954 dir. Edward Dmytryk
COL (GB/US) 1999 dir. Neil Jordan
Greene, G.

End of the Game
TCF (US/Ger) 1976
dir. Maximilian Schell
Durrenmatt, F. *Judge and his Hangman,*
The
P

End of the River, The
GFD (GB) 1947 dir. Derek Twist
Holdridge, D. *Death of a Common Man*

End of the Road
ALLIED (US) 1970 dir. Aram Avakian
Barth, J.

Enemies, A Love Story
FOX (US) 1989 dir. Paul Mazursky
Singer, I. B.

Enemy, The
PROMARK (US/GB) 2001 dir. Tom
Kinninmont
Bagley, D.

Enemy Below, The
FOX (US) 1957 dir. Dick Powell
Rayner, D. A. *Escort*

Enemy Mine
FOX (US) 1986 dir. Wolfgang Petersen
Longyear, B.

Enemy of the People, An
ENT (US) 1978 dir. George Schaefer
Ibsen, H.
P

Enemy Within, The
HBO (US) 1994 Jonathan Darby
TV(US)
Knebel, F. and Bailey II, C. W.

Enfant Lion, L'
STUDIO CANAL+ (Fr) 1993 dir. Patrick
Grandperret
Guillot, R. *Sirga la Lionne*

Enfant Noir, L'
RHEA (Fr) 1995 dir. Laurent Chevallier
Laye, C.

Enfants du Marais, Les
UCG/IMAGES (Fr) 1999 dir. Jean
Becker
Montforez, G.

Enfants Terribles, Les
MELVILLE (Fr) 1950
dir. Jean-Pierre Melville
Cocteau, J.

England Made Me
HEMDALE (GB) 1972 dir. Peter Duffell
Greene, G.

English, August
TROPIC (Ind) 1994 dir. Dev Benegal
Chatterjee, U.

English Patient, The
MIRAMAX (US) 1996 dir. Anthony
Minghella
Ondaatje, M.

Enigma
EMBASSY (GB/Fr) 1983
dir. Jeannot Szwarc
Barak, M.

Enigma
JAGGED (GB) 2001 dir. Michael Apted
Harris, R.

Ennui, L'
GEMINI (Fr) 1998 dir. Cedric Kahn
Moravia, A. *Noia, La*

Enola Gay
VIACOM (US) 1980
dir. David Lowell Rich
TV(US)
Thomas, G. and Witts, M. M.

Ensign Pulver
WAR (US) 1964 dir. Joshua Logan
Logan, J. and Heggen, T. *Mister Roberts*
P

Entangled
TELEFILM (Can/Fr) 1993 dir. Max
Fischer
Boileau, P. and Narcejac, T. *Veufs, Les*

Entente Cordiale
FLORA (Fr) 1939 dir. Marcel l'Herbier
Maurois, A. *Edward VII and his Times*

Enter Laughing
COL (US) 1967 dir. Carl Reiner
Reiner, C.
P

Entertainer, The
BL (GB) 1960 dir. Tony Richardson
RSO (US) 1976 dir. Donald Wrye
TV(US)
Osborne, J.
P

Entertaining Mr. Sloane
PAR (GB) 1969 dir. Douglas Hickox
Orton, J.
P

Entity, The
FOX (US) 1982 dir. Sidney J. Furie
De Felitta, F.

Entre Las Piernas
AURUM (Fr/Sp) 1999 dir. Manuel
Gomez Pereira
Oristrell, J.

Equus
UA (GB) 1977 dir. Sidney Lumet
Shaffer, P.
P

Eric
LORIMAR (US) 1975
dir. James Goldstone
TV(US)
Lund, D.

Ernesto
CLESI (It) 1978 dir. Salvatore Samperi
Saba, U.

Eroica
KADR (Pol) 1957 dir. Andrzej Munk
Stawinski, J. S.

Escanaba in da Moonlight
PURPLE ROSE (US) 2001 dir. Jeff
Daniels
Daniels, J.
P

Escapade
EROS (GB) 1955 dir. Philip Leacock
MacDougall, R.
P

Escapade in Florence
DISNEY (US) 1962 dir. Steve Previn
Ch
Fenton, E. *Golden Doors, The*

Escape
RKO (GB) 1930 dir. Basil Dean
FOX (US) 1948
dir. Joseph L. Mankiewicz
Galsworthy, J.
P

Escape
MGM (US) 1940 dir. Mervyn LeRoy
Vance, E.

Escape
H. JAFFE (US) 1980
dir. Robert Michael Lewis
TV(US)
Worker, D. and Worker, B.

Escape Artist, The
ORION (US) 1982 dir. Caleb Deschanel
Wagoner, D.

Escape from Alcatraz
PAR (US) 1979 dir. Don Siegel
Bruce, J. C.

Escape from Sobibor
ZENITH (US) 1987 dir. Jack Gold
TV(US)
Rashke, R.

Escape from Zahrein
PAR (US) 1962 dir. Ronald Neame
Barrett, M. *Appointments in Zahrein*

Escape: Human Cargo
SHOWTIME (US) 1998 dir. Simon
Wincer
TV(US)
McDonald, J. and Burleson, C. *Flight From Dhahran*

Escape in the Desert
WAR (US) 1945 dir. Edward A. Blatt
Sherwood, R. E. *Petrified Forest, The*
P

Escape Me Never
UA (GB) 1935 dir. Paul Czinner
WAR (US) 1947 dir. Peter Godfrey
Kennedy, M.
P

Escape to Witch Mountain
DISNEY (US) 1974 dir. John Hough
DISNEY FAMILY (US) 1995 dir. Peter
Rader
Ch, TV(US)
Key, A.

Espionage
MGM (US) 1937 dir. Kurt Neumann
Hackett, W.
P

Esther Waters
WESSEX (GB) 1948 dir. Jan Dalrymple
BBC (GB) 1977 dir. Jane Howell
TVSe(GB)
Moore, G.

État Sauvage, L'
FILMS 1966 (Fr) 1990 dir. Francis Girod
Conchon, G.

Ethan Frome
AM PLAY (US) 1993 dir. John Madden
Wharton, E.

Étoile du Nord, L'
UA (Fr) 1982
dir. Pierre Granier-Deferre
Simenon, G. *Locataire, La*

Eureka!
MGM/UA (GB/US) 1982
dir. Nicolas Roeg
Leasor, J. *Who Killed Sir Harry Oakes?*

Eureka Street
BBC (GB) 1999 dir. Adrien Shergold
TV(GB)
Wilson, R. M.

Europeans, The
GB (GB) 1979 dir. James Ivory
James, H.

Eve
GALA (Fr/It) 1963 dir. Joseph Losey
Chase, J. H.

Evelyn Prentice
MGM (US) 1934 dir. William K. Howard
Woodward, W. E.

Even Cowgirls Get the Blues
NEW LINE (US) 1994 dir. Gus Van Sant
Robbins, T.

Evening in Byzantium
UN TV (US) 1978 dir. Jerry London
TVSe(US)
Shaw, I.

Evening Star, The
RYSHER (US) 1996 dir. Robert Harling
McMurtry, L.

Evensong
GAU (GB) 1934 dir. Victor Saville
Nichols, B.
P

Eve of St. Mark, The
FOX (US) 1944 dir. John M. Stahl
Anderson, M.
P

Evergreen
GAU (GB) 1934 dir. Victor Saville
M
Levy, B. W.
P

Evergreen
METRO (US) 1985 dir. Fielder Cook
TVSe(US)
Plain, B.

Everlasting Secret Family, The
FGH (Aust) 1989 dir. Michael Thornhill
Moorhouse, F. *Everlasting Secret Family and Other Secrets, The*

Everybody's All-American
WAR (US) 1988 dir. Taylor Hackford
Deford, F.

Every Little Crook and Nanny
MGM (US) 1972 dir. Cy Howard
Hunter, E.

Every Morning of the World
BAC (Fr) 1992 dir. Alan Corneau
Quignard, P.

Everything is Thunder
GB (GB) 1936 dir. Milton Rosmer
Hardy, J. B.

Everything to Gain
ADELSON (US) 1996 dir. Michael L. Miller
TV(US)
Bradford, B. T.

Everything You Ever Wanted to Know about Sex but were Afraid to Ask
UA (US) 1972 dir. Woody Allen
Reuben, D.

Every Woman's Dream
KUSHNER-LOCKE (US) 1996 dir. Steven Schachter
TV(US)
Kingsbury, K. *Deadly Pretender*

Evidence of Blood
MGM TV (US) 1998 dir. Andrew Mondshein
TV(US)
Cook, T. H.

Evil That Men Do, The
TRISTAR (US) 1984
dir. J. Lee Thompson
Hill, R. L.

Evil Under the Sun
UN (GB) 1982 dir. Guy Hamilton
Christie, A.

Evita Peron
ZEPHYR (US) 1981
dir. Marvin Chomsky
TVSe(US)
Barnes, J. *Evita: First Lady*
Fraser, N. *Eva Peron*

Evolution's Child
FOXTAIL (US) 1999 dir. Jeffrey Reiner
TV(US)
Booth, M. *Toys of Glass*

Ex, The
LIONS GATE (US/Can) 1996 dir. Mark L. Lester
Lutz, J.

Excalibur
ORION (US) 1981 dir. John Boorman
Malory, Sir T. *Morte d'Arthur, La*

Excellent Cadavers
HBO (US) 1999 dir. Ricky Tognazzi
TV(US)
Stille, A.

Execution, The
COMWORLD (US) 1985
dir. Paul Wendkos
TV(US)
Crawford, O.

Execution of Justice
PARA TV (US) 1999 dir. Leon Ichaso
TV(US)
Mann, E.
P

Execution of Private Slovik, The
UN TV (US) 1974 dir. Lamont Johnson
TV(US)
Huie, W. B.

Executioner's Song, The
FCI (US) 1982 dir. Lawrence Schiller
TVSe(US)
Mailer, N.

Executive Suite
MGM (US) 1954 dir. Robert Wise
Hawley, C.

Ex-Flame
TIFFANY (US) 1930 dir. Victor Halperin
Wood, Mrs H. *East Lynne*

Exile, The
UN (US) 1948 dir. Max Ophuls
Hamilton, C. *His Majesty the King*

Exile
ILLUMINATION (Aust) 1994 dir. Paul Cox
Watson, E. L. G. *Priest Island*

Exit Lines
BBC/A&E (GB) 1997 dir. Ross Devenish
TV(GB)
Hill, R.

Exit to Eden
SAVOY (US) 1994 dir. Garry Marshall
Rice, A.

Exit Wounds
WAR (US) 2001 dir. Andrzej Bartkowiak
Westermann, J.

Exodus
UA (US) 1960 dir. Otto Preminger
Uris, L.

Exorcist, The
WAR (US) 1973 dir. William Friedkin
Blatty, W. P.

Exorcist III, The
TCP (US) 1990 dir. William Peter Blatty
Blatty, W. P. *Legion*

Experiment, Das
FANES (Ger) 2001 dir. Oliver Hirschbiegel
Giordano, M. *Black Box*

Experiment in Terror
COL (US) 1962 dir. Blake Edwards
GB title: The Grip of Fear

Gordon, M. and Gordon, G. *Operation Terror*

Experiment Perilous
RKO (US) 1944 dir. Jacques Tourneur

Carpenter, M.

Exposure
MIRAMAX (Bra) 1991 dir. Walter Salles, Jr.

Fonseca, R.

Expresso Bongo
BL (GB) 1959 dir. Val Guest
M

Mankowitz, W.

Extension du Domaine de la Lutte
STUDIO CANAL+ (Fr) 1999 dir. Philippe Harel

Houellebecq, M.

Extraordinary Seaman, The
MGM (US) 1969
dir. John Frankenheimer

Rock, P.

Extreme Measure
COL (US) 1996 dir. Michael Apted

Palmer, M.

Extremities
ATLANTIC (US) 1986
dir. Robert M. Young

Mastrosimone, W.
P

Eye for an Eye, An
UGC (Fr/It) 1956 dir. André Cayatte

Katcha, V.

Eye for an Eye
PAR (US) 1996 dir. John Schlesinger

Holzer, E.

Eyeless in Gaza
BBC (GB) 1971 dir. James Cellan Jones
TVSe(GB)

Huxley, A.

Eye of God
CYCLONE (US) 1997 dir. Tim Blake Nelson

Nelson, T. B.
P

Eye of the Beholder
FILMLINE (GB/Can/US) 1999 dir. Stephan Elliott

Behm, M.

Eye of the Devil
MGM (GB) 1967 dir. J. Lee Thompson

Loraine, P. *Day of the Arrow*

Eye of the Needle
UA (GB) 1981 dir. Richard Marquand

Follett, K.

Eyes in the Night
MGM (US) 1942 dir. Fred Zinnemann

Kendrick, B. H. *Odour of Violets*

Eyes Wide Shut
WAR (GB/US) 1999 dir. Stanley Kubrick

Schnitzler, A. *Traumnovelle*

Eyes Without A Face
CH ELYSEE (Fr/It) 1959
dir. George Franju

Redon, J.

Eyewitness
MGM (GB) 1970 dir. John Hough
US title: Sudden Terror

Hebden, M. *Eye-witness*

Fabian
UA (Ger) 1982 dir. Wolf Gremm
Kastner, E.

Fabian of the Yard
EROS (GB) 1954
dir. Edward Thommen, Anthony
Beauchamp
Fabian, R.

Face at the Window
PENNANT (GB) 1939 dir. George King
Warren, F. B.
P

Face Behind the Mask, The
COL (US) 1941 dir. Robert Florey
O'Connell, T.
P

Face in the Crowd, A
WAR (US) 1957 dir. Elia Kazan
Schulberg, B. W. *Your Arkansas Traveller*

Face in the Night
GN (GB) 1956 dir. Lance Comfort
Graeme, B. *Suspense*

Face of Fear, The
Q. MARTIN (US) 1971
dir. George McCowan
TV(US)
Cunningham, E. V. *Sally*

Face of Fear, The
WAR TV (US) 1990 dir. Farhad Mann
TV(US)
Koontz, D.

Face on the Milk Carton, The
FAMILY (US) 1995 dir. Waris Hussein
TV(US)
Cooney, C. B. *Face on the Milk Carton, The*
Cooney, C. B. *Whatever Happened to Janie?*

Faces in the Dark
RANK (GB) 1960 dir. David Eady
Boileau, P. and Narcejac, T.

Face to Die For, A
KONIGSBERG (US) 1996 dir. Jack Bender
TV(US)
Werlin, M. and Werlin, M.

Face to Face
RKO (US) 1952
dir. John Brahm, Bretaigne Windust
Crane, S. *Bride Comes to Yellow Sky, The*
Conrad, J. *Secret Sharer, The*

Fahrenheit 451
UI (GB) 1966 dir. François Truffaut
Bradbury, R.

Fail Safe
COL (US) 1963 dir. Sidney Lumet
WAR (US) 2000 dir. Stephen Frears
TV(US)
Burdick, E. and Wheeler, H.

Fair Game
WAR (US) 1995 dir. Andrew Sipes
Gosling, P.

Fair Stood the Wind For France
BBC (GB) 1980 dir. Martyn Friend
TVSe(GB)
Bates, H. E.

Fair Wind to Java
REP (US) 1952 dir. Joseph Kane
Roark, G.

Faithful
MIRAMAX (US) 1996 dir. Paul Mazursky
Palminteri, C.
P

Faithful Unto Death
YTV/A&E (GB) 1998 dir. Baz Taylor
TV(GB)
Graham, C.

Faithless
MGM (US) 1932 dir. Harry Beaumont
Cram, M. *Tinfoil*

Falcon and the Snowman, The
ORION (US) 1985 dir. John Schlesinger
Lindsey, R.

Fall, The
ARG SONO (Arg) 1958 dir. Leopoldo Torre Nilsson
Guido, B.

Fallen Angel
FOX (US) 1945 dir. Otto Preminger
Holland, M.

Fallen Idol, The
FOX (GB) 1948 dir. Carol Reed
US title: Lost Illusion, The
Greene, G. *Basement Room, The*

Fallen Sparrow, The
RKO (US) 1943 dir. Richard Wallace
Hughes, D. B.

Fall From Grace
RYSHER (US) 1994 dir. Waris Hussein
TVSe(US)
Collins, L.

Falling for a Dancer
BBC (GB) 1998 dir. Richard Standeven
TVSe(GB)
Purcell, D.

Falling for You
BBS (US) 1995 dir. Eric Till
TV(US)
Giannunzio, M. *Last Tag*
P

Falling From the Sky! Flight 174
HILL-FIELDS (US/Can) 1995 dir. Jorge Montesi
TV(US/Can)
Hoffer, W. and Hoffer, M. *Freefall*

Fall Into Darkness
PATCHETT-KAUFMAN (US) 1996 dir. Mark Sobel
TV(US)
Pike, C.

Fall of the House of Usher, The
TAFT (US) 1982 dir. James Conway
TV(US)
Poe, E. A.

False Arrest
GIL/HILL (US) 1991 dir. Bill L. Norton
TVSe(US)
Lukezic, J. and Schwarz, T. *False Arrest: The Joyce Lukezic Story*

False Witness
NEW WORLD TV (US) 1989 dir. Arthur Allan Seidelman
TV(US)
Uhnak, D.

Fame is the Name of the Game
UN TV (US) 1966 dir. Stuart Rosenberg
TV(US)

Thayer, T. *One Woman*

Fame is the Spur
TC (GB) 1947 dir. Roy Boulting
BBC (GB) 1982 dir. David Giles
TVSe(GB)

Spring, H.

Family, The
PUBLIC (Jap) 1974
dir. Karei Naru Ichikozo

Yamazaki, T.

Family Affair, A
MGM (US) 1937 dir. George B. Seitz

Rouverol, A. *Skidding*
P

Family Album
NBC (US) 1994 dir. Jack Bender
TVSe(US)

Steel, D.

Family Blessings
DOVE ENT (US/Can) 1996 dir. Nina
Foch, Deborah Raffin
TV(US/Can)

Spencer, L.

Family Business
EUROPEAN (Fr) 1987 dir. Costa-
Gavras

Ryck, F.

Family Business
TRISTAR (US) 1989 dir. Sidney Lumet

Patrick, V.

Family Divided, A
CITADEL ENT (US) 1995 dir. Donald
Wrye
TV(US)

Wall, J. H. *Mother Love*

Family Game, The
TOHO (Jap) 1983
dir. Yoshimitsu Morita

Honma, Y.

Family Honeymoon
UN (US) 1948 dir. Claude Binyon

Croy, H.

Family Life
EMI (GB) 1971 dir. Ken Loach

Mercer, D. *In Two Minds*
P

Family Man, The
TIME-LIFE (US) 1979 dir. Glenn Jordan
TV(US)

Gallagher, T. *Monogamist, The*

Family Nobody Wanted, The
UN TV (US) 1975 dir. Ralph Senensky
TV(US)

Doss, H.

Family of Spies
KING PHOENIX (US) 1990 dir. Stephen
Gyllenhaal
TVSe(US)

Early, P. *Family of Spies, A: Inside the
John Walker Spy Ring*

Blum, H. *I Pledge Allegiance … The True
Story of an American Spy Family*

Family of Strangers, A
ALLIANCE (US) 1993 dir. Sheldon
Larry
TV(US)

Hulse, J. *Jody*

Family Pictures
HEARST (US) 1993 dir. Philip Saville
TVSe(US)

Miller, S.

Family Plot
UN (US) 1976 dir. Alfred Hitchcock

Canning, V. *Rainbird Pattern, The*

Family Rico, The
CBS (US) 1972 dir. Paul Wendkos
TV(US)
Simenon, G. *Brothers Rico, The*

Family Torn Apart, A
HALMI (US) 1993 dir. Craig Baxley
TV(US)
Walker, L. *Sudden Fury*

Family Way, The
BL (GB) 1966 dir. Roy Boulting
Naughton, B. *All in Good Time*
P

Fan, The
FOX (US) 1949 dir. Otto Preminger
GB title: Lady Windemere's Fan
Wilde, O. *Lady Windemere's Fan*
P

Fan, The
PAR (US) 1981 dir. Edward Bianchi
Randall, B.

Fan, The
TRISTAR (US) 1996 dir. Tony Scott
Abrahams, P.

Fanatic
COL (GB) 1965 dir. Silvio Narizzano
US title: Die! Die! My Darling
Blaisdell, A. *Nightmare*

Fancy Pants
PAR (US) 1950 dir. George Marshall
Wilson, H. L. *Ruggles of Red Gap*

Fanfan
STUDIO CANAL+ (Fr) 1993 dir.
Alexandre Jardin
Jardin, A.

Fanny
WAR (US) 1960 dir. Joshua Logan
Behrman, S. N. and Logan, J.
P

Fanny by Gaslight
GFD (GB) 1944 dir. Anthony Asquith
US title: Man of Evil
BBC (GB) 1981 dir. Peter Jefferies
TVSe(GB)
Sadleir, M.

Fanny Hill
GALA (Ger) 1965 dir. Russ Meyer
BW (GB) 1983 dir. Gerry O'Hare
Cleland, J.

Fantasist, The
BLUE DOLPHIN (Ire) 1987
dir. Robin Hardy
McGinley, P. *Goosefoot*

Fantasticks, The
COMPASS (US) 1964
dir. George Schaefer
M, TV(US)
Jones, T. and Schmidt, H.
P

Farewell My Concubine
BEIJING (China) 1993 dir. Kaige Chen
Lee, L.

Farewell, My Lovely
RKO (US) 1944 dir. Edward Dmytryk
AVCO (US) 1975 dir. Dick Richards
Chandler, R.

Farewell to Agnes
MUNCHEN (Ger) 1994 dir. Michael
Gwisdek
Loffler, H. *Silence Under the Sea, The*

Farewell to Arms, A
PAR (US) 1932 dir. Frank Borzage
FOX (US) 1957 dir. Charles Vidor
Hemingway, E.

Farewell to Manzanar
UN TV (US) 1976 dir. John Korty
TV(US)
Wakatsuki, J. and Houston, J. D.

Farewell to the King
ORION (US) 1989 dir. John Milius

Schoendoerffer, P.

Far from the Madding Crowd
WAR (GB) 1967 dir. John Schlesinger
GRANADA (GB) 1998 dir. Nicholas Renton
TVSe(GB)

Hardy, T.

Far Horizons, The
PAR (US) 1955 dir. Rudolph Maté

Emmons, D. G. *Sacajawea of the Shoshones*

Farmer Takes a Wife, The
FOX (US) 1935 dir. Victor Fleming
FOX (US) 1953 dir. Henry Levin
M

Edmonds, W. D. *Rome Haul*

Farmer's Wife, The
AB (GB) 1940 dir. Norman Lee

Phillpotts, E.
P

Far Off Place, A
DISNEY (US) 1993 dir. Mikael Salomon

Van Der Post, Sir L. *Far Off Place, A; Story Like The Wind, A*

Far Pavilions, The
GOLDCREST (GB) 1983 dir. Peter Duffell
TVSe(GB)

Kaye, M. M.

Fast and Loose
GFD (GB) 1954 dir. Gordon Parry

Travers, B. *Cuckoo in the Nest, A*
P

Fast Times at Ridgemont High
UN (US) 1982 dir. Amy Heckerling

Crowe, C.

Fast-Walking
PICKMAN (US) 1982
dir. James B. Harris

Brawley, E. *Rap, The*

Fatal Inversion, A
BBC (GB) 1992 dir. Tim Fywell
TVSe(GB)

Rendell, R.

Fatal Vision
NBC ENT (US) 1984 dir. David Greene
TVSe(US

McGinniss, J.

Fat City
COL (US) 1972 dir. John Huston

Gardner, L.

Fate is the Hunter
FOX (US) 1964 dir. Ralph Nelson

Gann, E. K.

Father, The
BBC (GB) 1985 dir. Kenneth Ives
TV(GB)

Strindberg, A.
P

Father Brown
COL (GB) 1954 dir. Robert Hamer

Chesterton, G. K. *Blue Cross, The*

Father Brown, Detective
PAR (US) 1935 dir. Edward Sedgwick
ATV (GB) 1974 dir. Robert Tronson
TVSe(GB)

Chesterton, G. K. *Wisdom of Father Brown, The*

Father Figure
TIME-LIFE (US) 1980 dir. Jerry London
TV(US)

Peck, R.

Fatherland
HBO (US) 1994 dir. Christopher Menaul
TV(US)
Harris, R.

Father of the Bride
MGM (US) 1950 dir. Vincente Minnelli
DISNEY (US) 1991 dir. Charles Shyer
Streeter, E.

Fathers and Sons
BBC (GB) 1971 dir. Paddy Russell
TVSe(GB)
Turgenev, I.

Father's Doing Fine
ABP (GB) 1952 dir. Henry Cass
Langley, N. *Little Lambs Eat Ivy*
P

Father Sergius
MOSFILM (USSR) 1978
dir. Igor Talankin
Tolstoy, L.

Father was a Fullback
FOX (US) 1949 dir. John M. Stahl
Goldsmith, C.
P

Fathom
FOX (GB) 1967 dir. Leslie Martinson
Forrester, L. *Girl Called Fathom, A*

Fausse Suivante, La
STUDIO CANAL+ (Fr) 2000 dir. Benoit
Jacquot
Marivaux
P

Faust
CNC/BBC (Czech/GB/Fr) 1994 dir.
Ernst Gossner, Jan Svankmajer
Goethe, J. W.
Marlowe, C.
P
Grabbe, C. D.

Favorite Son
NBC (US) 1988 dir. Jeff Bleckner
TVSe(US)
Sohmer, S.

FBI Story, The
WAR (US) 1959 dir. Mervyn LeRoy
Whitehead, D.

FDR – The Last Year
TITUS (US) 1980
dir. Anthony Page
TV(US)
Bishop, J. *FDR's Last Year*

Fear and Loathing in Las Vegas
UN (US) 1998 dir. Terry Gilliam
Thompson, H. S.

Fear is the Key
EMI (GB) 1972 dir. Michael Tuchner
MacLean, A.

Fearless
WAR (US) 1993 dir. Peter Weir
Yglesias, R.

Fearmakers, The
PACEMAKER (US) 1958
dir. Jacques Tourneur
Teilhet, D.

Fear on Trial
LAN (US) 1975 dir. Lamont Johnson
TV(US)
Faulk, J. H.

Feast of All Saints, The
SHOWTIME (US) 2001 dir. Peter Medak
TVSe(US)
Rice, A.

Feast of July
MI (GB) 1995 dir. Christopher Menaul
Bates, H. E.

Federal Hill
TRIMARK (US) 1993 dir. Michael
Corrente
Corrente, M.
P

Fedora
MAINLINE (Ger/Fr) 1978
dir. Billy Wilder
Tryon, T. *Crowned Heads*

Feet of the Snake, The
WELLER/MYERS (GB) 1985
TV(GB)
Chubin, B.

Felicia's Journey
ALLIANCE (Can/GB) 1999 dir. Atom
Egoyan
Trevor, W.

Felidae
FONTANA (Ger) 1994 dir. Michael
Schaack
Pirincci, A.

Fellini Satyricon
UA (It) 1969 dir. Federico Fellini
Petronius *Satyricon*

Female Perversions
TRANSATLANTIC (US/Ger) 1996 dir.
Susan Streitfeld
Kaplan, L. J. *Female Perversions: The
Temptations of Emma Bovary*

Feminine Touch, The
RANK (GB) 1956 dir. Pat Jackson
Russell, S. M. *Lamp is Heavy, A*

Femme du Boulanger, La
PAGNOL (Fr) 1938 dir. Marcel Pagnol
Giono, J. *Jean le Bleu*

Fencing Master, The
ALTUBE (Sp) 1992 dir. Pedro Olea
Perez-Reverte, A.

Ferry to Hong Kong
RANK (GB) 1959 dir. Lewis Gilbert
Catto, M.

F. Est un Salaud
ARENA (Fr/Swe) 1997 dir. Marcel
Gisler
Frank, M.

Feud, The
CASTLE HILL (US) 1990 dir. Bill D'Elia
Berger, T.

Feu Follet, Le
ARCO (Fr/It) 1963 dir. Louis Malle
La Rochhelle, P. D.

Fever in the Blood, A
WAR (US) 1960 dir. Vincent Sherman
Pearson, W.

Few Days in Weasel Creek, A
WAR TV (US) 1981 dir. Dick Lowry
TV(US)
Brent, J.

Few Days With Me, A
GALAXY (Fr) 1989 dir. Claude Sautet
Josselin, J. F.

Few Good Men, A
CASTLE ROCK (US) 1992 dir. Rob
Reiner
Sorkin, A.
P

Fiancée, The
DEFA (Ger) 1984 dir. Gunter Reisch,
Gunther Rucker
Lippold, E. *House with the Heavy Doors,
The*

Fidelité, La
STUDIO CANAL+ (Fr) 2000 dir.
Andrzej Zulawski
de la Fayette, Mme. *Princesse de Cleves,
La*

Fiddler on the Roof
UA (US) 1971 dir. Norman Jewison
M

Stein, J.
P

Field, The
AVENUE (GB) 1990 dir. Jim Sheridan

Keane, J. B.
P

Field of Dreams
UN (US) 1989 dir. Phil A. Robinson

Kinsella, W. P. *Shoeless Joe*

Fiercest Heart, The
FOX (US) 1961 dir. George Sherman

Cloete, S.

Fifteen Streets, The
TYNE-TEES (GB) 1991
dir. David Wheatley
TV(GB)

Cookson, C.

Fifth Missile, The
MGM/UA TV (US) 1986
dir. Larry Peerce
TV(US)

Scortia, T. N. and Robinson, R. M.
Gold Crew, The

Fifth Musketeer, The
SASCH WIEN (Austria) 1978
dir. Ken Annakin

Dumas, A. *Man in the Iron Mask, The*

52 Pick-Up
CANNON (US) 1986
dir. John Frankenheimer

Leonard, E.

Fight Club
FOX (US) 1999 dir. David Fincher

Palahniuk, C.

Fighter, The
UA (US) 1952 dir. Herbert Fine

London, J. *Mexican, The*

Fighting Back
MTM (US) 1980 dir. Robert Lieberman
TV(US)

Bleier, R. and O'Neil, T.

Fighting Caravans
PAR (US) 1931 dir. Otto Brower, David
Burton

Grey, Z.

Fighting Guardsman, The
COL (US) 1945 dir. Henry Levin

Dumas, A. *Companions of Jehu, The*

Fighting O'Flynn, The
UN (US) 1949 dir. Arthur Pierson

McCarthy, J. H.

Fighting Prince of Donegal, The
DISNEY (GB) 1966
dir. Michael 0'Herlihy

Reilly, R. T. *Red Hugh, Prince of Donegal*

Figures in a Landscape
CINECREST (GB) 1970
dir. Joseph Losey

England, B.

File on Devlin, The
COMPASS (US) 1969
dir. George Schaefer
TV(US)

Gaskin, C.

Final Cut, The
BBC (GB) 1995 dir. Mike Vardy
TVSe(GB)

Dobbs, M.

Final Days, The
SAMUELS (US) 1989
dir. Richard Pearce
TV(US)
Woodward, B. and Bernstein, C.

Final Descent
COL TRISTAR (US) 1997 dir. Mike Robe
TV(US)
Davis, R. P. *Glass Cockpit, The*

Final Jeopardy
SANITSKY (US) 2001 dir. Nick Gomez
TV(US)
Fairstein, L.

Finally, Sunday
FILMS A2 (Fr) 1983
dir. François Truffaut
Williams, C. *Long Saturday Night, The*

Final Notice
SHARMHILL (US) 1989
dir. Steven Hilliard Stern
TV(US)
Valin, J.

Final Option, The
MGM/UA (GB) 1983 dir. Ian Sharp
Markstein, G. *Tiptoe Boys, The*

Final Programme, The
MGM-EMI (GB) 1973 dir. Robert Fuest
US title: Last Days of Man on Earth,
The
Moorcock, M.

Final Verdict, The
TURNER (US) 1991 dir. Jack Fisk
TV(US)
St. John, A. R. *Final Verdict*

Finders Keepers
RANK (US) 1984 dir. Richard Lester
Dennis, C. *Next-to-Last Train Ride, The*

Finding Buck McHenry
LIN OLIVER (US) 2000 dir. Charles
Burnett
TV(US)
Slote, A.

Finding the Way Home
MGM/UA TV (US) 1991
dir. Rob Holcomb
TV(US)
Small, G. R. *Mittelmann's Hardware*

Fine Madness, A
WAR (US) 1966 dir. Irvin Kershner
Baker, E.

Fine Romance, A
PC (It) 1992 dir. Gene Saks
Billetdoux, F. *Tchin-Tchin*
P

Fine Things
NBC (US) 1990 dir. Tom Moore
TV(US)
Steel, D.

Finian's Rainbow
WAR (US) 1968 dir. Francis Ford
Coppola
M
Harburg, E. Y. and Saidy, F.
P

Finn and Hattie
PAR (US) 1930 dir. Norman Taurog,
Norman McLeod
Stewart, D. O. *Mr and Mrs Haddock
Abroad*

Fire and Ice
ARABESQUE FILMS (US) 2001 dir.
Bryan Goeres
TV(US)
Fredd, C.

Fire and Rain
WIL COURT (US) 1989
dir. Jerry Jameson
TV(US)
Chandler, J. G.

Fire Down Below
COL (GB) 1957 dir. Robert Parrish
Catto, M.

Firefox
WAR (US) 1982 dir. Clint Eastwood
Thomas, C.

Fire in the Sky
PAR (US) 1993 dir. Robert Lieberman
Walton, T. *Walton Experience, The*

Fire on the Mountain
CARSON (US) 1981 dir. Donald Wrye
TV(US)
Abbey, E.

Fire Over England
UA (GB) 1937 dir. William K. Howard
Mason, A. E. W.

Fire Sale
FOX (US) 1977 dir. Alan Arkin
Klane, R.

Fires on the Plain
DAIEI (JAP) 1959 dir. Kon Ichikawa
O-Oka, S.

Firestarter
UN (US) 1984 dir. Mark L. Lester
King, S.

Firing Squad, The
ATLANTIS (Can/Fr) 1991 dir. Michel
Andrieu
TV(Can/Fr)
McDougall, C. *Execution*

Firm, The
PAR (US) 1993 dir. Sydney Pollack
Grisham, J.

First Among Equals
ITV (GB) 1986 dir. John Gorrie, Sarah
Harding, Brian Mills
TVSe(GB)
Archer, J.

First Blood
ORION (US) 1982 dir. Ted Kotcheff
Morell, D.

First Born
BBC (GB) 1988 dir. Philip Saville
TVSe(GB)
Duffy, M. *Gor Saga, The*

First Comes Courage
COL (US) 1943 dir. Dorothy Arzner
Arnold, E. *Commandos, The*

First Deadly Sin, The
CIC (US) 1980 dir. Brian G. Hutton
Sanders, L.

First Gentleman, The
COL (GB) 1948 dir. Alberto Cavalcanti
US title: Affairs of a Rogue
Ginsbury, N.
P

First Great Train Robbery, The
UA (GB) 1978 dir. Michael Crichton
Crichton, M. *Great Train Robbery, The*

First Lady
WAR (US) 1937 dir. Stanley Logan
Kaufman, G. S. and Dayton, K.
P

First Legion, The
UA (US) 1951 dir. Douglas Sirk
Lavery, E.
P

First Men in the Moon
COL (GB) 1963 dir. Nathan Juran
Wells, H. G.

First Monday in October
PAR (US) 1981 dir. Ronald Neame
Lawrence, J. and Lee, R. E.
P

First Name: Carmen
IS (Fr) 1984 dir. Jean-Luc Godard
Merimée, P. *Carmen*

First Wives Club, The
PAR (US) 1996 dir. Hugh Wilson
Goldsmith, O.

First Year, The
FOX (US) 1932 dir. William K. Howard
Craven, F.
P

First You Cry
MTM (US) 1978 dir. George Schaefer
TV(US)
Rollin, B.

Fitzwilly
UA (US) 1967 dir. Delbert Mann
GB title: Fitzwilly Strikes Back
Tyler, P. *Garden of Cucumbers, A*

Five Against the House
COL (US) 1955 dir. Phil Karlson
Finney, J.

Five and Ten
MGM (US) 1931 dir. Robert Z. Leonard
GB title: Daughter of Luxury
Hurst, F.

Five Boys from Barska Street
POLSKI (Pol) 1953 dir. Aleksander Ford
Kozniewski, K.

Five Branded Women
PAR (It/US) 1960 dir. Martin Ritt
Pirro, U.

Five Card Stud
PAR (US) 1968 dir. Henry Hathaway
Gaulden, R.

Five Children And It
BBC (GB) 1991 dir. Marilyn Fox
Ch, TVSe(GB)
Nesbit, E.

Five Days One Summer
WAR (US) 1982 dir. Fred Zinnemann
Boyle, K. *Maiden Maiden*

Five Finger Exercise
COL (US) 1962 dir. Delbert Mann
Shaffer, P.
P

Five Fingers
FOX (US) 1952
dir. Joseph L. Mankiewicz
Moyzisch, L. C. *Operation Cicero*

Five Graves to Cairo
PAR (US) 1943 dir. Billy Wilder
Biro, L.
P

Five Have A Mystery to Solve
CFF (GB) 1964 dir. Ernest Morris
Ch
Blyton, E.

Five Little Peppers and How They Grew
COL (US) 1939 dir. Charles Barton
Sidley, M.

Five of Me, The
FARREN (US) 1981 dir. Paul Wendkos
TV(US)
Hawksworth, H. and Schwarz, T.

Five on a Treasure Island
BI (GB) 1957 dir. Gerald Landau
Ch
Blyton, E.

Five Red Herrings
BBC (GB) 1975 dir. Robert Tronson
TVSe(GB)
Sayers, D. L.

Five Star Final
WAR (US) 1931 dir. Mervyn LeRoy
Weitzenkorn, L.
P

Five Steps to Danger
UA (US) 1956 dir. Henry S. Kesler
Hamilton, D.

Five Weeks in a Balloon
FOX (US) 1962 dir. Irwin Allen
Verne, J.

Fixer, The
MGM (US) 1969
dir. John Frankenheimer
Malamud, B.

Fixing Frank
MAXIMUM (US) 2001 dir. Michael
Selditch
Hanes, K.
P

Flambards
YTV (GB) 1979 dir. Lawrence Gordon
Clark, Peter Duffell,
Michael Ferguson, Leonard Lewis
TVSe(GB)
Peyton, K. M.

Flame and the Flesh, The
MGM (US) 1954 dir. Richard Brooks
Bailly, A.

Flame in the Streets
RANK (GB) 1961 dir. Roy Baker
Willis, T. *Hot Summer Night*
P

Flame is Love, The
NBC ENT (US) 1979
dir. Michael O'Herlihy
TV(US)
Cartland, B.

Flame Trees of Thika, The
THAMES (GB) 1981 dir. Roy Ward
Baker
TVSe(GB)
Huxley, E.

Flamingo Rising, The
HALLMARK (US) 2001 dir. Martha
Coolidge
TV(US)
Baker, L.

Flamingo Road
WAR (US) 1949 dir. Michael Curtiz
Wilder, R.

Flaming Star
FOX (US) 1960 dir. Don Siegel
Huffaker, C. *Flaming Lance*

Flap
WAR (US) 1970 dir. Carol Reed
GB title: Last Warrior, The
Huffaker, C. *Nobody Loves a Drunken
Indian*

Flashpoint
TRISTAR (US) 1984
dir. William Tannen
La Fontaine, G.

Flash the Sheepdog
CFF (US) 1967 dir. Laurence Henson
Ch
Fidler, K.

Flaxfield, The
COURIER (Bel/Neth) 1983
dir. Jan Gruyaert
Streuvels, S.

Flea in Her Ear, A
FOX (US/Fr) 1968 dir. Jacques Charon
Feydeau, G.
P

Flesh and Blood
BL (GB) 1951 dir. Anthony Kimmins
Bridie, J. *Sleeping Clergyman, A*
P

Flesh and Blood
PAR TV (US) 1979 dir. Jud Taylor
TVSe(US)
Hamill, P.

Flesh and Fantasy
UN (US) 1943 dir. Julien Duvivier
Wilde, O. *Lord Arthur Savile's Crime*

Fleshburn
CROWN (US) 1984 dir. George Gage
Garfield, B. *Fear in a Handful of Dust*

Fletch
UIP (US) 1985 dir. Michael Ritchie
McDonald, G.

Flight from Ashiya
UA (US/Jap) 1963
dir. Michael Anderson
Arnold, E.

Flight from Destiny
WAR (US) 1941 dir. Vincent Sherman
Berkeley, A.
P

Flight of the Doves
COL (US) 1971 dir. Ralph Nelson
Macken, W.

Flight of the Eagle
SUMMIT (Swe) 1983 dir. Jan Troell
Sundman, P.O.

Flight of the Heron, The
BBC (GB) 1976 dir. Alastair Reid
TVSe(GB)
Broster, D. K.

Flight of the Intruder
PAR (US) 1991 dir. John Milius
Coonts, S.

Flight of the Phoenix, The
FOX (US) 1965 dir. Robert Aldrich
Trevor, E.

Flim-Flam Man, The
FOX (US) 1967 dir. Irvin Kershner
Owen, G. *Ballad of the Flim-Flam Man, The*

Floating Away
PEG (US) 1998 dir. John Badham
TV(US)
Sandlin, T. *Sorrow Floats*

Floating Dutchman, The
AA (GB) 1953 dir. Vernon Sewell
Bentley, N.

Floods of Fear
RANK (GB) 1958 dir. Charles Crichton
Hawkins, J. and Hawkins, W.

Florentine, The
BCB (US) 1999 dir. Nick Stagliano
Gray, D. and McCarty-Baker, A.
P

Florentine Dagger, The
WAR (US) 1935 dir. Robert Florey
Hecht, B.

Florian
MGM (US) 1940 dir. Edwin L. Marin
Salten, F.

Flotsam and Jetsam
BBC (GB) 1970 dir. Claude Whatham
TV(GB)
Maugham, W. S.

Flower Drum Song
UI (US) 1961 dir. Henry Koster
M
Lee, C. Y.

Flowers for Algernon
CITADEL (US) 2000 dir. Jeff Bleckner
TV(US)
Keyes, D.

Flowers in the Attic
NEW WORLD (US) 1987
dir. Jeffrey Bloom
Andrews, V. C.

Flowing
EAST-WEST (Jap) 1956 dir. Mikio
Naruse
Koda, A.

Fluke
MGM (US) 1995 dir. Carlo Carlei
Herbert, J.

Fly, The
FOX (US) 1958 dir. Kurt Neumann
FOX (US) 1986 dir. David Cronenberg
Langelaan, G.

Fly Away Peter
GFD (GB) 1948 dir. Charles Saunders
Dearsley, A. P.
P

Flying Down to Rio
RKO (US) 1933 dir. Thornton Freeland
Caldwell, A.
P

Focus
PAR (US) 2001 dir. Neal Slavin
Miller, A.

Fog Over Frisco
WAR (US) 1934 dir. William Dieterle
Dyer, G.

Folies Bergère
FOX (US) 1935 dir. Roy del Ruth
GB title: Man from the Folies Bergère,
The
P
Lothar, R. and Adler, H. *Red Cat, The*

Follow Me
UN (GB) 1972 dir. Carol Reed
US title: Public Eye, The
Shaffer, P. *Public Eye, The*
P

Follow Me Boys!
DISNEY (US) 1966 dir. Norman Tokar
Kantor, M. *God and My Country*

Follow that Dream
UA (US) 1962 dir. Gordon Douglas
Powell, R. *Pioneer Go Home*

Follow that Horse!
WAR (GB) 1959 dir. Alan Bromly
Mason, H. *Photo Finish*

Follow the Fleet
RKO (US) 1936 dir. Mark Sandrich
M
Osborne, H. and Scott, A. *Shore Leave*
P

Follow the River
SIGNBOARD HILL (US) 1995 dir.
Martin Davidson
TV(US)
Thom, J. A.

Follow the Stars Home
HALLMARK (US) 2001 dir. Dick Lowry
TV(US)
Rice, L.

Follow Your Heart
NBC (US) 1990 dir. Noel Nosseck
TV(US)
Everett, P. *Walk Me to the Distance*

Follow Your Heart
GMT (Fr/Ger/It) 1996 dir. Cristina Comencini
Tamaro, S. *Va' Dove ti Porta il Cuore*

Folly to be Wise
BL (GB) 1952 dir. Frank Launden
Bridie, J. *It Depends What You Mean*
P

Fontane Effi Briest
TANGO (W. Ger) 1974
dir. Rainer Werner Fassbinder
Fontane, T.

Fool for Love
CANNON (US) 1985 dir. Robert Altman
Shepard, S.
P

Fools for Scandal
WAR (US) 1938 dir. Mervyn LeRoy
Hamilton, N., Casey, R. and Shute, J. *Return Engagement*
P

Fools of Fortune
PALACE (GB) 1990 dir. Pat O'Connor
Trevor, W.

Fools Parade
COL (US) 1971 dir. Andrew V. McLaglen
GB title: Dynamite Man from Glory Jail
Grubb, D. *Fools Paradise*

Fools Rush In
RANK (GB) 1949
dir. John Paddy Carstairs
Horne, K.
P

Footsteps in the Dark
WAR (US) 1941 dir. Lloyd Bacon
Fodor, L. *Blondie White*
P

Footsteps in the Fog
COL (GB) 1955 dir. Arthur Lubin
Jacobs, W. W. *Interruption, The*

For a Lost Soldier
SIGMA (Neth) 1992 dir. Roeland Kerbosch
van Dantzig, R.

For Better, For Worse
ABP (GB) 1954 dir. J. Lee Thompson
Watkyn, A.
P

Forbidden
ENT (GB/Ger) 1984 dir. Anthony Page
TV(GB)
Gross, L. *Last Jews in Berlin, The*

Forbidden Fruit
CAMEO-POLY (Fr) 1952
dir. Henri Verneuil
Simenon, G. *Act of Passion*

Forbidden Territory
GAU (GB) 1934 dir. Phil Rosen
Wheatley, D.

Forbidden Valley
UN (US) 1938 dir. Wyndham Gittens
Hardy, S.

Forbin Project, The
UN (US) 1970 dir. Joseph Sargent
GB title: Colossus, the Forbin Project
Jones, D. F. *Colossus*

Force of Evil
MGM (US) 1948 dir. Abraham Polonsky
Wolfert, I. *Tucker's People*

Force 10 from Navarone
COL (GB) 1978 dir. Guy Hamilton
MacLean, A.

Ford: The Man and the Machine
LANTANA (US) 1987 dir. Allan Eastman
TVSe(US)
Lacey, R.

Foreign Affairs
INTERSCOPE (US) 1993 dir. Jim O'Brien
TV(US)
Lurie, A.

Foreign Body
ORION (GB) 1986 dir. Ronald Neame
Mann, R.

Foreign Correspondent
UA (US) 1940 dir. Alfred Hitchcock
Sheean, V. *Personal History*

Foreign Exchange
ABC (US) 1970 dir. Roy Baker
TV(US)
Sangster, J.

Foreign Student
BERL (Fr/GB/US) 1994 dir. Eva Sereny
Labro, P.

Forever
EMI (US) 1978 dir. John Korty
TV(US)
Blume, J.

Forever Amber
FOX (US) 1947 dir. Otto Preminger
Winsor, K.

Forever Female
PAR (US) 1953 dir. Irving Rapper
Barrie, Sir J. M. *Rosalind*
P

Forget-Me-Not Murders, The
SPELLING TV (US) 1994 dir. Robert Iscove
TV(US)
Bayer, W. *Wallflower*

Forgotten Story, The
HTV (GB) 1983 dir. John Jacobs
TV(GB)
Graham, W.

For Heaven's Sake
FOX (US) 1950 dir. George Seaton
Segall, H.
P

Forlorn River
PAR (US) 1937 dir. Charles Barton
Grey, Z.

For Love Alone
WARRANTY (Aust) 1986 dir. Stephen Wallace
Stead, C.

For Love Alone
RHI (US) 1996 dir. Michael Lindsay-Hogg
TV(US)
Trump, I.

For Love of the Game
UN (US) 1999 dir. Sam Raimi
Shaara, M.

Formula, The
MGM (US) 1980 dir. John G. Avildsen
Shagan, S.

Forrest Gump
PAR (US) 1994 dir. Robert Zemeckis
Groom, W.

Forsaking All Others
MGM (US) 1934 dir. W. S. Van Dyke

Roberts, E. B. and Cavett, F. M.
P

Forsyte Saga, The
BBC (GB) 1967 dir. David Giles, James Cellan Jones
TVSe(GB)

Galsworthy, J.

Fort Apache
RKO (US) 1948 dir. John Ford

Bellah, J. W. *Massacre*

For Them That Trespass
ABP (GB) 1949 dir. Alberto Cavalcanti

Raymond, E.

For the Term of his Natural Life
FILMO (Aust) 1985 dir. Rob Stewart
TVSe(Aust)

Clarke, M.

For Those I Loved
GALA (Can/Fr) 1983 dir. Robert Enrico
BBC (GB) 1991 dir. Robert R. Enrico
TV(GB)

Gray, M. and Gallo, M.

Fortress
HBO PREM (US) 1985
dir. Arch Nicholson
TV(US)

Lord, G.

Fortunate Pilgrim, The
NBC (US) 1988 dir. Stuart Cooper
TVSe(US)

Puzo, M.

Fortune and Men's Eyes
MGM (US/Can) 1971 dir. Harvey Hart

Herbert, J.
P

Fortune is a Woman
COL (GB) 1956 dir. Sidney Gilliatt
US title: She Played with Fire

Graham, W.

Fortunes and Misfortunes of Moll Flanders, The
GRANADA (GB) 1996 dir. David Attwood
TVSe(GB)

Defoe, D. *Fortunes and Misfortunes of the Famous Moll Flanders, The*

Fortunes of Captain Blood, The
COL (US) 1950 dir. Gordon Douglas

Sabatini, R.

Fortunes of Nigel, The
BBC (GB) 1974 dir. Peter Cregeen
TVSe(GB)

Scott, Sir W.

Fortunes of War
BBC (GB) 1987 dir. James Cellan Jones
TVSe(GB)

Manning, O. *Balkan Trilogy, The*; *Levant Trilogy, The*

Forty Carats
COL (US) 1973 dir. Milton Katselas

Barillet, P. and Gredy, J.-P.
P

Forty Days of Musa Dagh
HIGH INV (US/Tur) 1987
dir. Sarky Mouradia

Werfel, F.

Forty-Second Street
WAR (US) 1933 dir. Lloyd Bacon
M

Ropes, B.

For Whom the Bell Tolls
PAR (US) 1943 dir. Sam Wood

Hemingway, E.

Foster and Laurie
FRIES (US) 1975
dir. John Llewellyn Moxey
TV(US)
Silverman, A.

Fountain, The
RKO (US) 1934 dir. John Cromwell
Morgan, C.

Fountainhead, The
WAR (US) 1949 dir. King Vidor
Rand, A.

Four Daughters
WAR (US) 1938 dir. Michael Curtiz
Hurst, F. *Sister Act*

Four Days in September
COL (US/Bra) 1997 dir. Bruno Barreto
Gabeira, F. *O Que I Isso, Companheiro?*

Four Days Wonder
UN (US) 1936 dir. Sidney Salkow
Milne, A. A.

Four Faces West
UA (US) 1948 dir. Alfred E. Green
Rhodes, E. M. *Paso Por Aqui*

Four Feathers, The
PAR (US) 1929 dir. Lothar Mendes
UA (GB) 1939 dir. Zoltan Korda
ROSEMONT (GB) 1978 dir. Don Sharp
TV(GB)
Mason, A. E. W.

Four Frightened People
PAR (US) 1934 dir. Cecil B. de Mille
Robertson, E. A.

Four Horsemen of the Apocalypse, The
MGM (US) 1961 dir. Vincente Minnelli
Blasco-Ibanez, V.

Four Hours to Kill
PAR (US) 1935 dir. Mitchell Leisen
Krasna, N. *Small Miracle*
P

Four Just Men, The
EAL (GB) 1939 dir. Walter Forde
US title: Secret Four, The
Wallace, E.

Four Men and a Prayer
FOX (US) 1938 dir. John Ford
Garth, D.

Four Musketeers, The
FOX-RANK (Pan/Sp) 1974
dir. Richard Lester
Dumas, A. *Three Musketeers, The*

Four-Poster, The
COL (GB) 1952 dir. Irving Reis
de Hartog, J.
P

Four-Sided Triangle
HAMMER (GB) 1952
dir. Terence Fisher
Temple, W. F.

Fourth Angel, The
RAFFORD (Can/GB) 2001 dir. John Irwin
Hunter, R.

Fourth Man, The
VER NED (Neth) 1984
dir. Paul Verhoeven
Reve, G.

Fourth Protocol, The
RANK (GB) 1987
dir. John MacKenzie
Forsyth, F.

Fourth War, The
CANNON (US) 1990
dir. John Frankenheimer
Peters, S.

Fox, The
WAR (US/Can) 1967 dir. Mark Rydell
Lawrence, D. H.

Fox and the Hound, The
DISNEY (US) 1981 dir. Art Stevens
A, Ch
Mannix, D.

Foxes of Harrow, The
FOX (US) 1947 dir. John M. Stahl
Yerby, F.

Foxfire
UI (US) 1955 dir. Joseph Pevney
Seton, A.

Foxfire
M. REES (US) 1987 dir. Jod Taylor
TV(US)
Cooper, S. and Cronyn, H.
P

Foxfire
RYSHER (US) 1996 dir. Annette
Haywood-Carter
Oates, J. C.

Foxhole in Cairo
BL (GB) 1960 dir. John Llewellyn Moxey
Mosley L. *Cat and the Mice, The*

Fragment of Fear
COL (GB) 1969 dir. Richard C. Sarafian
Bingham, J.

Framed
PAR (US) 1975 dir. Phil Karlson
Powers, A. and Misenheimer, M.

Francesca e Nunziata
MEDIATRADE (It) 2001 dir. Lina
Wertmuller
Natale, M. O.

Franchise Affair, The
ABP (GB) 1951
dir. Lawrence Huntington
BBC (GB) 1988 dir. Leonard Lewis
TVSe(GB)
Tey, J.

Francis
UI (US) 1949 dir. Arthur Lubin
Stern, D.

Francis Gary Powers: The True Story of the U-2 Spy Incident
FRIES (US) 1976 dir. Delbert Mann
TV(US)
Powers, F. G. and Gentry, C. *Operation Overflight*

Frankenstein
UN (US) 1931 dir. James Whale
CURTIS (US) 1973
dir. Glenn Jordan
TV(US)
D. WICKES (US) 1993 dir. David Wickes
TV(US)
TRISTAR (US/GB) 1994 dir. Kenneth
Branagh
Shelley, M. W.

Frankenstein: The True Story
UN TV (US) 1973 dir. Jack Smight
TVSe(US)
Shelley, M. W. *Frankenstein*

Frankenstein Unbound
TCF (US) 1990 dir. Roger Corman
Aldiss, B.

Frankie and Johnny
PAR (US) 1991 dir. Garry Marshall
McNally, T. *Frankie and Johnny in the Clair de Lune*
P

Frankie's House
ANGLIA FILMS (GB/Aust) 1992 dir.
Peter Fisk
TVSe(GB/Aust)
Page, T. *Page After Page*

Frankie Starlight
FINE LINE (Fr/Ire) 1995 dir. Michael
Lindsay-Hogg
Raymo, C. *Dork of Cork, The*

Fraulein
FOX (US) 1957 dir. Henry Koster
McGovern, J.

Freaks
MGM (US) 1932 dir. Tod Browning
Robbins, T. *Spurs*

Freaky Friday
DISNEY (US) 1976 dir. Gary Nelson
DISNEY FAMILY (US) 1995 dir. Melanie
Mayron
Ch, TV(US)
Rodgers, M.

Freckles
RKO (US) 1935 dir. Edward Killy
FOX (US) 1960 dir. Harry Spalding
Porter, G. S.

Freedom Fighter
COL TV (US/GB) 1987
dir. Desmond Davis
TV(GB/US)
Galante, P. *Berlin Wall, The*

Freedom Road
BRAUN (US) 1980 dir. Jan Kadar
TVSe(US)
Fast, H.

Free Frenchman, The
CENTRAL (GB) 1989 dir. Jim Goddard
TVSe(GB)
Read, P. P.

Freejack
WAR (US) 1992 dir. Geoff Murphy
Sheckley, R. *Immortality, Inc.*

Free Soul, A
MGM (US) 1931 dir. Clarence Brown
St. John, A. R.

Freeway
NEW WORLD (US) 1988
dir. Francis Delia
Barkley, D.

French Atlantic Affair, The
MGM TV (US) 1979 dir. Douglas Heyes
TVSe(US)
Lehman, E.

French Connection, The
FOX (US) 1971 dir. William Friedkin
Moore, R.

French Leave
AB (GB) 1930 dir. Jack Raymond
Berkeley, R.
P

**French Lieutenant's Woman,
The**
UA (GB) 1981 dir. Karel Reisz
Fowles, J.

Frenchman's Creek
PAR (US) 1944 dir. Mitchell Leisen
Du Maurier, D.

French Mistress, A
BL (GB) 1960 dir. Roy Boulting
Monro, R.
P

French Silk
VZ/SERTNER (US) 1994 dir. Noel
Nosseck
TV(US)
Brown, S.

French Without Tears
PAR (GB) 1939 dir. Anthony Asquith

Rattigan, T.
P

Frenzy
RANK (GB) 1971 dir. Alfred Hitchcock

La Bern, A. J. *Goodbye Piccadilly, Farewell Leicester Square*

Fresh Bait
FRANCE 2 (Fr) 1995 dir. Bertrand Tavernier

Sportes, M.

Fresh Horses
WEINTRAUB (US) 1988
dir. David Anspaugh

Ketron, L.
P

Frieda
EAL (GB) 1947 dir. Basil Dearden

Millar, R.
P

Fried Green Tomatoes
UN (US) 1991 dir. Jon Avnet

Flagg, F. *Fried Green Tomatoes at the Whistle Stop Cafe*

Friendly Fire
M. ARCH (US) 1979 dir. David Greene
TV(US)

Bryan, C. D. B.

Friendly Persuasion
MGM (US) 1956 dir. William Wyler
AA (US) 1975 dir. Joseph Sargent
TV(US)

West, J.

Friend or Foe
CFF (GB) 1982 dir. John Krish
Ch

Morpurgo, M.

Friends and Lovers
RKO (US) 1931 dir. Victor Schertzinger

Dekobra, M. *Sphinx has Spoken, The*

Friendship in Vienna, A
DISNEY CH (US) 1988
dir. Arthur Allan Seidelman
TV(US)

Orgel, D. *Devil in Vienna, The*

Friendships, Secrets and Lies
WAR TV (US) 1979
dir. Ann Zane Shanks, Marlena Laird
TV(US)

Deal, B. H. *Walls Came Tumbling Down, The*

Friends of Eddie Coyle, The
PAR (US) 1973 dir. Peter Yates

Higgins, G. V.

Frightened Lady, The
BL (GB) 1932 dir. T. Hayes Hunter

Wallace, E. *Case of the Frightened Lady, The*

Fringe Dwellers, The
OZFILMS (Aust) 1986
dir. Bruce Beresford

Gare, N.

Frisk
STRAND (US) 1995 dir. Todd Verow

Cooper, D.

Frog, The
WILCOX (GB) 1937 dir. Jack Raymond

Wallace, E. *Fellowship of the Frog, The*

From Beyond
EMPIRE (US) 1986 dir. Stuart Gordon

Lovecraft, H. P.

From Beyond the Grave
EMI (GB) 1973 dir. Kevin Connor

Chetwynd-Hayes, R. *Elemental, The; Gate Crasher, The; Act of Kindness, An; Door, The*

From Here to Eternity
COL (US) 1953 dir. Fred Zinnemann
COL (US) 1979 dir. Buzz Kulik
TVSe(US)

Jones, J.

From Noon Till Three
UA (US) 1976 dir. Frank D. Gilroy

Gilroy, F. D.

From Russia With Love
UA (GB) 1963 dir. Terence Young

Fleming, I.

From the Dead of Night
PHOENIX (US) 1989 dir. Paul Wendkos
TVSe(US)

Brandner, G. *Walkers*

From the Earth to the Moon
WAR (US) 1958 dir. Byron Haskin

Verne, J.

From the Earth to the Moon
HBO (US) 1998 dir. Tom Hanks, David Frankel, Lili Fini Zanuck, Graham Yost, Frank Marshall, Jon Turtletaub, Gary Fleder, David Carson, Sally Field, Jonathan Mostow
TVSe(US)

Chaikin, A. *Man on the Moon, A*

From the Files of Joseph Wambaugh: A Jury of One
TRISTAR TV (US) 1992 dir. Alan Metzger
TV(US)

Wambaugh, J.

From the Mixed-Up Files of Mrs. Basil E. Frankweiler
ROSEMONT (US) 1995 dir. Marcus Cole
TV(US)

Konigsburg, E. L.

From the Terrace
FOX (US) 1960 dir. Mark Robson

O'Hara, J.

From This Day Forward
RKO (US) 1946 dir. John Berry

Bell, T. *All Brides are Beautiful*

Frontiera, La
CORRIDORI (It) 1996 dir. Franco Giraldi

Vegliani, F.

Frontier Marshall
FOX (US) 1933 dir. Lew Seiler
FOX (US) 1939 dir. Allan Dwan

Lake, S. *Wyatt Earp, Frontier Marshall*

Front Page, The
UA (US) 1931 dir. Lewis Miles
U-I (US) 1974 dir. Billy Wilder

Hecht, B. and MacArthur, C.
P

Front Page Story
BL (GB) 1953 dir. Gordon Parry

Gaines, R. *Final Night*

Frost in May
BBC (GB) 1982 dir. Ronald Wilson
TVSe(GB)

White, A. *Frost in May; Lost Traveller, The; Sugar House, The; Beyond the Glass*

Fruits of Passion
ARGOS (Fr/Jap) 1982 dir. Shuji Terayama

Réage, P. *Return to the Château*

Fuga, La
TELEFE (Arg) 2001 dir. Eduardo
Mignogna
Mignogna, E.

Fugitive, The
RKO (US) 1947 dir. John Ford
Greene, G. *Power and the Glory, The*

Fugitive Among Us
ABC PROD (US) 1992 dir. Michael
Toshiyuki Uno
TV(US)
Cochran, M. *And Deliver Us From Evil*

Fugitive Kind, The
UA (US) 1960 dir. Sidney Lumet
Williams, T. *Orpheus Descending*
P

**Fugitive Nights: Danger in the
Desert**
TRISTAR TV (US) 1993 dir. Gary
Nelson
TV(US)
Wambaugh, J.

Fulfillment of Mary Gray, The
INDIAN NECK (US) 1989
dir. Piers Haggard
TV(US)
Spencer, L. *Fulfillment, The*

Full Blast
ASKA (Can) 1999 dir. Rodrique Jean
Pitre, M. *Ennemi Que Je Connais, L'*

Full Circle
PAR (GB/Can) 1976
dir. Richard Loncraine
Straub, P. *Julia*

Full Circle
NBC (US) 1996 dir. Bethany Rooney
TV(US)
Steel, D.

Full Fathom Fire
CONCORDE (US) 1990
dir. Carl Franklin
Davis, B.

Full Metal Jacket
WB (US) 1987 dir. Stanley Kubrick
Hasford, G. *Short Timers, The*

Full of Life
COL (US) 1956 dir. Richard Quine
Fante, J.

Full Treatment, The
COL (GB) 1960 dir. Val Guest
US title: Stop Me Before I Kill
Thorn, R. S.

Fun
GREYCAT (Can) 1994 dir. Rafal
Zielinsky
Bosley, J.
P

Funeral in Berlin
PAR (GB) 1966 dir. Guy Hamilton
Deighton, L. *Berlin Memorandum, The*

Funny Dirty Little War
CINEVISTA (Sp) 1986
dir. Hector Olivera
Sorino, O.

Funny Farm
WAR (US) 1988 dir. George Roy Hill
Cronley, J.

Funny Girl
COL (US) 1968 dir. William Wyler
M
Lennart, I.
P

Funny Thing Happened on the Way to the Forum, A
UA (GB) 1966 dir. Richard Lester
Shevelove, B. and Gelbart, L.
P

Furies, The
PAR (US) 1950 dir. Anthony Mann
Busch, N.

Further Tales of the City
SHOWTIME (US/Can) 2001 dir. Pierre Gang
TVSe(US/Can)
Maupin, A.

Fury, The
FOX (US) 1978 dir. Brian De Palma
Farris, J.

Futai no Kisetsu
BONOBO (Jap) 2000 dir. Ryuichi Hiroki
Dan, O.

Fuzz
UA (US) 1972 dir. Richard A. Colla
McBain, E.

Fuzzy Pink Nightgown, The
UA (US) 1957 dir. Norman Taurog
Tate, S.

Gabriela
MGM/UA (Port) 1984
dir. Bruno Barreto

Amado, J. *Gabriela, Clove and Cinnamon*

Gabriel Over the White House
MGM (US) 1933 dir. Gregory LaCava

Tweed, T. F. *Rinehard*

Gaby
MGM (US) 1956 dir. Curtis Bernhardt

Sherwood, R. E. *Waterloo Bridge*
P

Gadgetman
HALLMARK (US/GB) 1996 dir. Jim
Goddard
TV(US/GB)

Blackman, M. *Operation Gadgetman*

Gaily, Gaily
UA (US) 1969 dir. Norman Jewison
GB title: Chicago, Chicago

Hecht, B.

Galileo
CINEVISION (GB) 1975
dir. Joseph Losey

Brecht, B.
P

Gallowglass
BBC (GB) 1993 dir. Tim Fywell
TVSe(GB)

Rendell, R.

Gambit
UI (US) 1966 dir. Ronald Neame

Lane, K.

Gambler, The
LENFILM (USSR) 1982 dir. Alexei
Batalov
BBC (GB) 1968 dir. Michael Ferguson
TVSe(GB)

Dostoevsky, F.

Gambling Man, The
TYNE-TEES (GB) 1995 dir. Norman
Stone
TVSe(GB)

Cookson, C.

Game for Vultures
NEW LINE (GB) 1979 dir. James Fargo

Hartmann, N. M.

Game is Over, The
COL (Fr/It) 1967 dir. Roger Vadim

Zola, E. *Kill, The*

Games, The
FOX (GB) 1969 dir. Michael Winner

Atkinson, H.

Game, Set and Match
GRANADA (GB) 1987 dir. Ken Grieve,
Patrick Lau
TVSe(GB)

Deighton, L. *Berlin Game; Mexico Set,
London Match*

Games Mother Never Taught You
CBS ENT (US) 1982 dir. Lee Philips
TV(US)

Harragan, B. L.

Ganashatru
ELECTRIC (Ind) 1989 dir. Satyajit Ray

Ibsen, H. *Enemy of the People, An*
P

Gangster No. 1
BRIT SCREEN (GB) 2000 dir. Paul McGuigan

Mellis, L. and Scinto, D.
P

Gang That Couldn't Shoot Straight, The
MGM (US) 1971
dir. James Goldstone

Breslin, J.

Garden of Allah, The
UA (US) 1936 dir. Richard Boleslawski

Hichens, R.

Garden of the Finzi-Continis, The
DOCUMENTO (It/Ger) 1970
dir. Vittorio de Sica

Bassani, G.

Gardens of Stone
TRISTAR (US) 1987
dir. Francis Ford Coppola

Proffitt, N.

Gas, Food and Lodging
IRS (US) 1992 dir. Allison Anders

Peck, R. *Don't Look and It Won't Hurt*

Gaslight
BN (GB) 1939 dir. Thorold Dickinson
US title: Angel Street
MGM (US) 1944 dir. George Cukor
GB title: Murder in Thornton Square, The

Hamilton, P. *Angel Street*
P

Gate of Hell
DAIEI (Jap) 1953
dir. Teinosuke Kinugasa

Kikuchi, K.

Gathering of Old Men, A
CONSOL (US) 1987
dir. Volker Schlondorff
TV(US)

Gaines, E. J.

Gathering Storm, The
BBC (GB/US) 1974 dir. Herbert Wise
TV(GB/US)

Churchill, Sir W.

Gaudi Afternoon
LOLAFILMS (Sp) 2001 dir. Susan Seidelman

Wilson, B.

Gaudy Night
BBC (GB) 1987 dir. Michael Simpson
TVSe(GB)

Sayers, D. L.

Gaunt Stranger, The
NORTHWOOD (GB) 1938
dir. Walter Forde
US title: Phantom Strikes, The

Wallace, E. *Ringer, The*

Gawain and the Green Knight
THAMES (GB) 1990 dir. J. M. Phillips
TV(GB)

Anon. *Sir Gawain and the Green Knight*

Gay Sisters, The
WAR (US) 1942 dir. Irving Rapper
Longstreet, S.

Gazebo, The
MGM (US) 1959 dir. George Marshall
Coppel, A.

Gemini Man
UN TV (US) 1976 dir. Alan J. Levi
TV(US)
Wells, H. G. *Invisible Man, The*

General, The
J&M (Ire/GB) 1998 dir. John Boorman
Williams, P. *General, The: Godfather of Crime*

General Crack
WAR (US) 1930 dir. Alan Crosland
Preedy, G.

General Died at Dawn, The
PAR (US) 1936 dir. Lewis Milestone
Booth, C. G.

General's Daughter, The
PAR (US/Ger) 1999 dir. Simon West
DeMille, N.

Generation
POLSKI (Pol) 1954 dir. Andrzej Wajda
Czeszko, B.

Generation
AVCO (US) 1969 dir. George Schaefer
GB title: Time for Giving, A
Goodhart, W.
P

Genghis Cohn
BBC/A&E (GB) 1994 dir. Elijah Moshinsky
TV(GB)
Gary, R. *Dance of Genghis Cohn, The*

Gentle Annie
MGM (US) 1944 dir. Andrew Marton
Kantor, M.

Gentle Giant, The
PAR (US) 1967 dir. James Neilson
Ch
Morley, W. *Gentle Ben*

Gentle Gunman, The
GFD (GB) 1952 dir. Basil Dearden
MacDougall, R.
P

Gentleman Jim
WAR (US) 1942 dir. Raoul Walsh
Corbett, J. J. *Roar of the Crowd, The*

Gentleman's Agreement
FOX (US) 1947 dir. Elia Kazan
Hobson, L. Z.

Gentlemen Marry Brunettes
UA (US) 1955 dir. Richard Sale
Loos, A. *But Gentlemen Marry Brunettes*

Gentlemen Prefer Blondes
FOX (US) 1953 dir. Howard Hawks
Loos, A.

Geordie
BL (GB) 1955 dir. Frank Launder
US title: Wee Geordie
Walker, D.

George and Margaret
WAR (GB) 1940 dir. George King
Savory, G.
P

George Wallace
TNT (US) 1997 dir. John Frankenheimer
TVSe(US)
Frady, M. *Wallace*

George Washington
MGM TV (US) 1984 dir. Buzz Kulik
TVSe(US)
Flexner, J. T.

George Washington II: The Forging of a Nation
MGM/UA TV (US) 1986 dir. William A. Graham
TVSe(US)
Flexner, J. T.

George Washington Slept Here
WAR (US) 1942 dir. William Keighley
Kaufman, G. S. and Hart, M.
P

Georgy Girl
COL (GB) 1966 dir. Silvio Narizzano
Forster, M.

Germinal
BBC (GB) 1970 dir. John Davies
TVSe(GB)
STUDIO CANAL+ (Fr/Bel) 1993 dir. Claude Berri
Zola, E.

Gertrud
PATHE (Den) 1966 dir. C. T. Dreyer
Soderberg, H.
P

Gervaise
CLCC (Fr) 1956 dir. René Clément
Zola, E. *Assommoir, L'*

Getaway, The
CINERAMA (US) 1972
dir. Sam Peckinpah
UN (US) 1994 dir. Roger Donaldson
Thompson, J.

Get Carter
MGM (GB) 1971 dir. Mike Hodges
WAR (US) 2000 dir. Stephen T. Kay
Lewis, T. *Jack's Return Home*

Get Christy Love!
WOLPER (US) 1974 dir.
William A. Graham
TV(US)
Uhnak, D. *Ledger, The*

Get Off My Foot
WAR (GB) 1935 dir. William Beaudine
Paulton, E. *Money by Wire*
P

Get Real
BRIT SCREEN (GB) 1998 dir. Simon Shore
Wilde, P. *What's Wrong With Angry?*
P

Get Shorty
MGM (US) 1995 dir. Barry Sonnenfeld
Leonard, E.

Getting it Right
MEDUSA (US) 1989 dir. Randal Kleiser
Howard, E. J.

Getting of Wisdom, The
TEDDERWICK (Aust) 1979
dir. Bruce Beresford
Richardson, H. H.

Getting Out
RHI (US) 1994 dir. John Korty
TV(US)
Norman, M.
P

Getting Straight
COL (US) 1970 dir. Richard Rush
Kolb, K.

Getting Up and Going Home
POLONE/HEARST (US) 1992 dir.
Steven Schachter
TV(US)
Anderson, R.

Get to the Heart: The Barbara Mandrell Story

MANDALAY (US) 1997 dir. Jerry London
TV(US)

Mandrell, B. *Get to the Heart: My Story*

Gettysburg

TURNER (US) 1993 dir. Ronald F. Maxwell

Shaara, M. *Killer Angels, The*

Get Your Stuff

PEOPLES (US) 2000 dir. Max Mitchell

Mitchell, M.
P

Ghost and Mrs Muir, The

FOX (US) 1947
dir. Joseph L. Mankiewicz

Dick, R. A.

Ghost Breakers, The

PAR (US) 1940 dir. George Marshall

Dickey, P.
P

Ghost in Monte Carlo, A

GRADE (GB) 1990 dir. John Hough
TV(GB)

Cartland, B.

Ghost of Flight 401, The

PAR TV (US) 1978
dir. Steven Hilliard Stern
TV(US)

Fuller, J. G.

Ghosts

BBC (GB) 1986 dir. Elijah Moshinsky
TV(GB)

Ibsen, H.
P

Ghosts of Berkeley Square, The

BN (GB) 1947 dir. Vernon Sewell

Brahms, C. and Simon, S. J. *No Nightingales*

Ghosts of Mississippi

COL (US) 1996 dir. Rob Reiner

Evers, M. and Peters, B. *For Us The Living*

Ghost Story

UN (US) 1981 dir. John Irvin

Straub, P.

Ghost Train, The

GFD (GB) 1931 dir. Walter Forde
GFD (GB) 1941 dir. Walter Forde

Ridley, A.
P

Ghoul, The

GAU (GB) 1933 dir. T. Hayes Hunter

King, F.

Giant

WAR (US) 1956 dir. George Stevens

Ferber, E.

Gideon's Day

COL (GB) 1958 dir. John Ford
US title: Gideon of Scotland Yard

Creasey, J.

Gideon's Trumpet

WORLDVISION (US) 1980
dir. Robert Collins
TV(US)

Lewis, A.

Gidget

COL (US) 1959 dir. Paul Wendkos

Kohner, F.

Gidget Grows Up

COL TV (US) 1969 dir. James Sheldon
TV(US)

Kohner, F. *Gidget Goes to New York*

Gift, The
GOLDWYN (Fr) 1983 dir. Michel Lang
Valme and Terzolli *Bankers Also Have Souls*
P

Gift, The
PAR TV (US) 1979 dir. Don Taylor
TV(US)
Hamill, P.

Gift, The
BBC (GB) 1990 dir. Marc Evans, Red Saunders
TVSe(GB)
Dickinson, P.

Gift of Love, The
M. REES (US) 1994 dir. Paul Bogart
TV(US)
Freeman, J. *Set For Life*

Gift of Love, The: A Christmas Story
TELECOM (US) 1983
dir. Delbert Mann
TV(US)
Aldrich, B. S. *Silent Stars Go By, The*

Gigi
CODO (Fr) 1948 dir. Jacqueline Audry
MGM (US) 1958 dir. Vincente Minnelli
M
Colette

Ginger Tree, The
BBC (GB) 1989 dir. Anthony Garner
TVSe(GB)
Wynd, O.

Girl
KUSHNER-LOCKE (US) 1999 dir. Jonathan Kahn
Nelson, B.

Girl, The
METHOD (Fr) 2000 dir. Sande Zeig
Wittig, M.

Girl/Boy
HEMDALE (GB) 1971 dir. Bob Kellett
Percival, D. *Girlfriend*
P

Girl Called Hatter Fox, The
EMI (US) 1977 dir. George Schaefer
TV (US)
Harris, M. *Hatter Fox*

Girl Crazy
MGM (US) 1943 dir. Norman Taurog
M
Bolton, G. and McGowan, J.
P

Girl from Hunan, The
CHINA (China) 1986 dir. Xie Fei, U Lan
Congwen, S. *Xiao, Xiao*

Girl from Petrovka, The
UN (US) 1974 dir. Robert Ellis Miller
Feifer, G.

Girl from Tenth Avenue, The
WAR (US) 1935 dir. Alfred E. Green
GB title: Men on her Mind
Davies, H. H.
P

Girl He Left Behind, The
WAR (US) 1956 dir. David Butler
Hargrove, M.

Girl Hunters, The
FOX (GB) 1963 dir. Roy Rowland
Spillane, M.

Girl in a Swing, The
J&M (GB/US) 1989 dir. Gordon Hessler
Adams, R.

Girl, Interrupted
COL (US) 1999 dir. James Mangold
Kaysen, S.

Girl in the Cadillac
OVERSEAS (US) 1995 dir. Lucas Platt
Cain, J. M. *Enchanted Isle, The*

Girl in the Headlines, The
BL (GB) 1963 dir. Michael Truman
US title: Model Murder Case, The
Payne, L. *Nose on my Face, The*

Girl in the News, The
FOX (GB) 1940 dir. Carol Reed
Vickers, R.

Girl in White, The
MGM (US) 1952 dir. John Sturges
GB title: So Bright the Flame
Barringer, E. D. *Bowery to Bellevue*

Girl Must Live, A
UN (GB) 1939 dir. Carol Reed
Bonett, E.

Girl Named Sooner, A
FOX TV (US) 1975 dir. Delbert Mann
TV(US)
Clauser, S.

Girl Named Tamiko, A
PAR (US) 1962 dir. John Sturges
Kirkbride, R.

Girl of the Limberlost, A
MON (US) 1934 dir. Christy Cabanne
FREEDOM (US) 1990
dir. Burt Brinckerhoff
TV(US)
Porter, G. S.

Girl of the Night
WAR (US) 1960 dir. Joseph Cates
Greenwald, H. *Call Girl, The*

Girl on the Boat, The
UA (GB) 1962 dir. Henry Kaplan
Wodehouse, P. G.

Girl on a Motorcycle
BL (GB/Fr) 1968 dir. Jack Cardiff
US title: Naked Under Leather
de Mandiargues, A. P. *Motocyclette, La*

Girls, Les
MGM (US) 1957 dir. George Cukor
M
Caspary, V.

Girls of Huntington House, The
LORIMAR (US) 1973 dir. Alf Kjellin
TV(US)
Elfman, B.

Girls of Pleasure Island, The
PAR (US) 1953
dir. E. Hugh Herbert, Alvin Ganzer
Maier, W. *Pleasure Island*

Girls of Slender Means, The
BBC (GB) 1975 dir. Moira Armstrong
TVSe(GB)
Spark, M.

Girl, The Gold Watch and Everything, The
PAR TV (US) 1980 dir. William Wiard
TV(US)
MacDonald, J. D.

Girl who Couldn't Quit, The
MON (GB) 1950 dir. Norman Lee
Marks, L.
P

Girl Who Had Everything, The
MGM (US) 1953 dir. Richard Thorpe
St. John, A. R.

Girl With Green Eyes
UA (GB) 1964 dir. Desmond Davis
O'Brien, E. *Lonely Girl, The*

Girl with the Red Hair, The
UA (Neth) 1983 dir. Ben Verbong
DeVries, T.

Give me a Sailor
PAR (US) 1938 dir. Elliott Nugent
Nichols, A.
P

Give Me Your Heart
WAR (US) 1936 dir. Archie Mayo
GB title: Sweet Aloes
Mallory, J. *Sweet Aloes*
P

Give Us the Moon
GFD (GB) 1944 dir. Val Guest
Brahms, C. and Simon, S. J. *Elephant is White, The*

Give Us This Day
GFD (GB) 1949 dir. Edward Dmytryk
US title: Salt to the Devil
Di Donata, P. *Christ in Concrete*

Glad Tidings
EROS (GB) 1953 dir. Wolf Rilla
Delderfield, R. F.
P

Glamorous Night
ABP (GB) 1937
dir. Brian Desmond Hurst
M
Novello, I.
P

Glassblower's Children, The
EURIMAGES (Swe) 1998 dir. Anders Gronkos
Gripe, M.

Glass Cell, The
SOLARIS (Ger) 1981 dir. Hans C. Geissendoerfer
Highsmith, P.

Glass Full of Snow, A
CIN IT (It) 1988 dir. Florestano Vancini
Rossi, N.

Glass House, The
TOM (US) 1972 dir. Tom Gries
TV(US)
Capote, T. and Cooper, W.

Glass Key, The
PAR (US) 1935 dir. Frank Tuttle
PAR (US) 1942 dir. Stuart Heisler
Hammett, D.

Glass Menagerie, The
WAR (US) 1950 dir. Irving Rapper
TALENT (US) 1973
dir. Anthony Harvey
TV(US)
CINEPLEX (US) 1987 dir. Paul Newman
Williams, T.
P

Glass Virgin, The
TYNE-TEES (GB) 1995 dir. Sarah Hellings
TVSe(GB)
Cookson, C.

Glengarry Glen Ross
NEW LINE (US) 1992 dir. James Foley
Mamet, D.
P

Glimpse of Hell, A
FOX TV (US/Can) 2001 dir. Mikael Salomon
TV(US/Can)
Thompson, C. *Glimpse of Hell, A: Explosion on the USS Iowa and Its Cover-Up*

Glitter Dome, The
HBO (US) 1984 dir. Stuart Margolin
TV(US)
Wambaugh, J.

Glitz
LORIMAR (US) 1988 dir. Sandor Stern
TV(US)
Leonard, E.

Glory
TRISTAR (US) 1989 dir. Edward Zwick
Burehard, P. *One Gallant Rush*
Kirstein, L. *Lay this Laurel*

Glory Boys, The
YTV (GB) 1984 dir. Michael Ferguson
TV(GB)
Seymour, G.

Glory Enough for All
THAMES (GB) 1989 dir. Eric Till
TV(GB)
Bliss, M. *Discovery of Insulin, The; Banting: A Biography*

Glory Guys
UA (US) 1965 dir. Arnold Laven
Birney, H. *Dice of God, The*

Gnome-Mobile, The
DISNEY (US) 1967
dir. Robert Stevenson
Ch
Sinclair, U.

Go-Between, The
EMI (GB) 1970 dir. Joseph Losey
Hartley, L. P.

Goddess of Love, The
NEW WORLD TV (US) 1988
dir. James Drake
TV(US)
Anstey, F. *Tinted Venus*

Godfather, The
PAR (US) 1972
dir. Francis Ford Coppola
Puzo, M.

Godfather Part II, The
PAR (US) 1974
dir. Francis Ford Coppola
Puzo, M. *Godfather, The*

God is My Co-Pilot
WAR (US) 1945 dir. Robert Florey
Scott, R. L.

God Said, Ha!
MIRAMAX (US) 1998 dir. Julia Sweeney
Sweeney, J.
P

Gods and Monsters
LIONS GATE (US/GB) 1998 dir. Bill Condon
Bram, C. *Father of Frankenstein*

God's Country and the Woman
WAR (US) 1936 dir. William Keighley
Curwood, J. O.

Godsend, The
CANNON (US) 1980
dir. Gabrielle Beaumont
Taylor, B.

God's Little Acre
UA (US) 1958 dir. Anthony Mann
Caldwell, E.

Godspell
COL (US) 1973 dir. David Greene
M
Tebelak, J. M.
P

Goggle Eyes
BBC (GB) 1993 dir. Carol Wiseman
TVSe(GB)
Fine, A.

Going All the Way
POLYGRAM (US) 1997 dir. Mark Pellington
Wakefield, D.

Going Bananas
CANNON (US) 1988 dir. Boaz Davidson
Borenstein, T. *Kofiko*

Gold
HEMDALE (GB) 1974 dir. Peter Hunt
Smith, W. *Gold Mine*

Gold Coast
PAR (US) 1997 dir. Peter Weller
TV(US)
Leonard, E.

Gold Diggers of Broadway
WAR (US) 1939 dir. Roy del Ruth
Hopwood, A. *Gold Diggers, The*
P

Golden Arrow
WAR (US) 1936 dir. Alfred E. Green
Arlen, M.
P

Golden Bowl, The
BBC (GB) 1972 dir. James Cellan Jones
TVSe(GB)
MI (GB/US) 1999 dir. James Ivory
James, H.

Golden Boy
COL (US) 1939 dir. Rouben Mamoulian
Odets, C.
P

Golden Ear-Rings
PAR (US) 1947 dir. Mitchell Leisen
Foldes, Y.

Goldeneye
ANGLIA (GB) 1990 dir. Don Boyd
TV(GB)
Pearson, J. *Life of Ian Fleming, The*

Goldengirl
AVCO (US) 1979 dir. Joseph Sargent
Lear, P.

Golden Hawk, The
COL (US) 1952 dir. Sidney Salkow
Yerby, F.

Golden Head, The
CINERAMA (US/Hun) 1965
dir. Richard Thorpe
Pilkington, R. *Nepomuk of the River*

Golden Rendezvous
RANK (US) 1977 dir. Ashley Lazarus
MacLean, A.

Goldenrod
TALENT (US) 1977 dir. Harvey Hart
TV(US)
Harker, H.

Golden Salamander, The
GFD (GB) 1949 dir. Ronald Neame
Canning, V.

Golden Seal, The
GOLDWYN (US) 1983 dir. Frank
Zuniga
Marshall, J. V. *River Ran out of Eden, A*

Golden Spiders, The
JAFFE/BRAUNSTEIN (US) 2000 dir.
Bill Duke
TV(US)
Stout, R.

Goldfinger
UA (GB) 1964 dir. Guy Hamilton
Fleming, I.

Gold for the Caesars
MGM (US) 1964 dir. Andre de Toth
Seward, F. A.

Gold in the Streets
FERNDALE (GB/Ire) 1997 dir.
Elizabeth Gill
Noble, J. *Away Alone*
P

Gold of the Seven Saints
WAR (US) 1961 dir. Gordon Douglas

Frazee, S. *Desert Guns*

Go Naked in the World
MGM (US) 1960
dir. Ronald MacDougall

Chamales, T.

Gone du Chaaba, Le
ORLY (Fr) 1998 dir. Christophe Ruggia

Begag, A.

Gone in the Night
HILL-FIELDS (US) 1996 dir. Bill Norton
TVSe(US)

Protess, D. and Warden, R.

Gone to Earth
BL (GB) 1950
dir. Michael Powell, Emeril Pressburger
US title: Wild Heart, The

Webb, M.

Gone with the Wind
MGM (US) 1939 dir. Victor Fleming

Mitchell, M.

Good Baby, A
KARDANA (US) 1998 dir. Katherine
Dieckmann
TV(US)

Rooke, L.

Good Behaviour
BBC (GB) 1983 dir. Bill Hays
TVSe(GB)

Keane, M.

Goodbye Again
UA (US) 1961 dir. Anatole Litvak

Sagan, F. *Aimez-vous Brahms?*

Goodbye Charlie
FOX (US) 1964 dir. Vincente Minnelli

Axelrod, G.
P

Goodbye Columbus
PAR (US) 1969 dir. Larry Peerce

Roth, P.

Goodbye Gemini
CINDERAMA (GB) 1970 dir. Alan
Gibson

Hall, J. *Ask Agamemnon*

Goodbye, Miss 4th of July
FINNEGAN/PINCHUK (US) 1988
dir. George Miller
TV(US)

Janus, C. G. *Miss 4th of July, Goodbye*

Goodbye Mr Chips
MGM (GB) 1939 dir. Sam Wood
BBC (GB) 1984 dir. Gareth Davies
TVSe(GB)

Hilton, J.

Goodbye Mr Chips
MGM (GB) 1969 dir. Herbert Ross
M

Hilton, J. and Burnham, B.
P

Goodbye, My Fancy
WAR (US) 1951 dir. Vincent Sherman

Kanin, F.
P

Goodbye, My Lady
WAR (US) 1956 dir. William Wellman

Street, J. H.

Goodbye People, The
EMBASSY (US) 1984 dir. Herb Gardner

Gardner, H.
P

Good Companions, The
GAU (GB) 1932 dir. Victor Saville
ABP (GB) 1956 dir. J. Lee Thompson
YTV (GB) 1980 dir. Bill Hays, Leonard
Lewis
TVSe(GB)

Priestley, J. B.

Good Cops, Bad Cops
KUSHNER-LOCKE (US) 1990 dir. Paul Wendkos
TV(US)

Clemente, G. W and Stevens, K. *Cops are Robbers, The*

Good Earth, The
MGM (US) 1937 dir. Sidney Franklin
Buck, P.

Good Fairy, The
UN (US) 1935 dir. William Wyler
HALLMARK (US) 1956
dir. George Schaefer
TV(US)
Molnar, F.
P

Good Father, The
FILM 4 (GB) 1986 dir. Mike Newell
Prince, P.

Goodfellas
WAR (US) 1990 dir. Martin Scorsese
Pileggi, N. *Wiseguy: Life in A Mafia Family*

Good Man in Africa, A
CAPITOL (US) 1994 dir. Bruce Beresford
Boyd, W.

Good Morning, Miss Dove
FOX (US) 1955 dir. Henry Koster
Patton, F. G.

Good Mother, The
TOUCHSTONE (US) 1988 dir. Leonard Nimoy
Miller, S.

Good Neighbour Sam
COL (US) 1964 dir. David Swift
Finney, J.

Good Old Boy
DISNEY CH (US) 1988 dir. Tom G. Robertson
TV(US)

Morris, W. *Good Old Boy: A Delta Summer*

Good Old Boys, The
E. J. SCHERICK (US) 1995 dir. Tommy Lee Jones
TV(US)
Kelton, E.

Good Old Soak
MGM (US) 1937 dir. J. Walter Ruben
Marquis, D. *Old Soak, The*
P

Good Soldier, The
GRANADA (GB) 1981 dir. Kevin Billington
TV(GB)
Madox Ford, F.

Good-Time Girl
GFD (GB) 1948 dir. David MacDonald
La Bern, A. J. *Night Darkens the Streets*

Gor
CANNON (US) 1989 dir. Fritz Kiersch
Norman, J. *Tarnsman of Gor*

Gore Vidal's Lincoln
FINNEGAN/PINCHUK (US) 1988
dir. Lamont Johnson
TVSe(US)
Vidal, G. *Lincoln*

Gorgeous Hussy, The
MGM (US) 1936 dir. Clarence Brown
Adams, S. H.

Gorilla, The
FOX (US) 1939 dir. Allan Dwan
Spence, R.
P

Gorillas in the Mist
WAR/UN (US) 1988 dir. Michael Apted
Fossey, D.

Gorky Park
ORION (GB) 1983 dir. Michael Apted
Smith, M. C.

Gormenghast
BBC/WGBH (GB) 2000 dir. Andy
Wilson
TVSe(GB)
Peake, M.

Go Tell It On The Mountain
PRICE (US) 1985 dir. Stan Latham
TV(US)
Baldwin, J.

Go Toward the Light
CORAPEAKE (US) 1988 dir. Mike Robe
TV(US)
Polson, B.

Gotti
LUCCHESI (US) 1996 dir. Robert
Harmon
TV(US)
Capeci, J. and Mustain, G. *Gotti: Rise
and Fall*

Goupi Mains Rouges
MINERVA (Fr) 1943
dir. Jacques Becker
US title: It Happened at the Inn
Very, P.

Go West Young Man
PAR (US) 1936 dir. Henry Hathaway
Riley, L. *Personal Appearance*
P

Grace & Glorie
HALLMARK (US) 1998 dir. Arthur
Allan Seidelman
TV(US)
Ziegler, T.
P

Gracie Allen Murder Case, The
PAR (US) 1939 dir. Alfred E. Green
van Dine, S. S.

Graduate, The
UA (US) 1967 dir. Mike Nichols
Webb, C.

Grambling's White Tiger
INTERPLAN (US) 1981
dir. Georg Stanford Brown
TV(US)
Behrenberg, B. *My Little Brother is
Coming Tomorrow*

Grand Avenue
WILDWOOD (US) 1996 dir. Dave
Sackman
TV(US)
Sarris, G.

Grand Canary
FOX (US) 1934 dir. Irving Cummings
Cronin, A. J.

Grand Central Murder
MGM (US) 1942 dir. S. Sylvan Simon
McVeigh, S.

Grand Hotel
MGM (US) 1932 dir. Edmund Goulding
Baum, V.

Grand Isle
TURNER (US) 1992 dir. Mary Lambert
TV(US)
Chopin, K. *Awakening, The*

Grand National Night
REN (GB) 1953 dir. Bob McNaught
US title: Wicked Wife, The
Christie, D. and Christie, C.
P

Grand Slam
WAR (US) 1933 dir. William Dieterle
Herts, B. R.

Grapes of Wrath, The
FOX (US) 1940 dir. John Ford
Steinbeck, J.

Grass Harp, The
FINE LINE (US) 1995 dir. Charles
Matthau
Capote, T.

Grasshopper, The
NGL (US) 1969 dir. Jerry Paris
McShane, M. *Passing of Evil, The*

**Grass is Always Greener over
the Septic Tank, The**
J. HAMILTON (US) 1978
dir. Robert Day
TV(US)
Bombeck, E.

Grass is Greener, The
UI (GB) 1960 dir. Stanley Donen
Williams, H. and Williams, M.
P

Grass is Singing, The
MAINLINE (Zam/Swe) 1981
dir. Michael Raeburn
Lessing, D.

Grass Roots
JBS (US) 1992
dir. Jerry London
TVSe(US)
Woods, S.

**Grave Secrets: The Legacy of
Hilltop Drive**
HEARST (US) 1992 dir. John Patterson
TV(US)
Williams, B., Williams, J. and
Shoemaker, J. B. *Black Hope Horror, The:
The True Story of a Haunting*

Graveyard Shift
PAR (US) 1990 dir. Ralph S. Singleton
King, S.

Gray Lady Down
UN (US) 1978 dir. David Greene
Lavallee, D. *Event One Thousand*

Grease
PAR (US) 1978 dir. Randal Kleiser
M
Jacobs, J. and Casey, W.
P

Great Balls of Fire
ORION (US) 1989 dir. Jim McBride
Lewis, M.

Great Bank Robbery, The
WAR (US) 1969 dir. Hy Averback
O'Rourke, F.

Great Catherine
WAR (GB) 1968 dir. Gordon Flemyng
Shaw, G. B.
P

Great Day
RKO (GB) 1945 dir. Lance Comfort
Storm, L.

Great Day in the Morning
RKO (US) 1955 dir. Jacques Tourneur
Andrew, R. H.

Great Escape, The
UA (US) 1963 dir. John Sturges
Brickhill, P.

Greatest, The
COL-WAR (US/GB) 1977 dir. Tom
Gries
Ali, M.

Greatest Gift, The
UN TV (US) 1974 dir. Boris Sagal
TV(US)
Farris, J. *Ramey*

Greatest Store in the World, The
BBC (GB) 1999 dir. Jane Prowse
TV(GB)
Shearer, A.

Greatest Story Ever Told, The
UA (US) 1965 dir. George Stevens
Oursler, F.

Greatest Thing That Almost Never Happened, The
FRIES (US) 1977 dir. Gilbert Moses
TV(US)
Robertson, D.

Great Expectations
UN (US) 1934 dir. Stuart Walker
RANK/CIN (GB) 1946
dir. David Lean
SCOTIA-BARBER/ITC (GB) 1974
dir. Joseph Hardy
TV(GB/US)
BBC (GB) 1981 dir. Julian Amyes
TVSe(GB)
PRIMETIME/HTV (GB/US) 1991
dir. Kevin Connor
TVSe(GB/US)
FOX (US) 1998 dir. Alfonso Cuaron
Dickens, C.

Great Game, The
ADELPHI (GB) 1952 dir. Maurice Elvey
Thomas, B. *Shooting Star*
P

Great Gatsby, The
PAR (US) 1949 dir. Elliot Nugent
PAR (US) 1974 dir. Jack Clayton
A&E/BBC (US/GB) 2001 dir. Robert Markowitz
TV(US/GB)
Fitzgerald, F. S.

Great Impersonation, The
UN (US) 1935 dir. Alan Crosland
UN (US) 1942 dir. John Rawlins
Oppenheim, E. P.

Great Imposter, The
UI (US) 1961 dir. Robert Mulligan
Crichton, R.

Great Jasper, The
RKO (US) 1933 dir. J. Walter Ruben
Oursler, F.

Great Lie, The
WAR (US) 1941 dir. Edmund Goulding
Banks, P. *January Heights*

Great Man, The
UI (US) 1956 dir. Jose Ferrer
Morgan, A.

Great Man's Whiskers, The
UN TV (US) 1973 dir. Philip Leacock
TV(US)
Scott, A.
P

Great Meadow, The
MGM (US) 1931 dir. Charles Brabin
Roberts, E. M.

Great Moment, The
PAR (US) 1944. dir. Preston Sturges
Fulop-Miller, R. *Triumph*

Great Mom Swap, The
SIGNBOARD HILL (US) 1995 dir. Jonathan Prince
TV(US)
Haynes, B.

Great Mouse Detective, The
DISNEY (US) 1986
dir. Burny Mattinson
A, Ch
Titus, E. *Basil of Baker Street*

Great Mr. Handel, The
RANK (GB) 1942 dir. Norman Walker
Peach, L. D.

Great Santini, The
ORION (US) 1979 dir. Lewis John Carlino
Conroy, P.

Great Sinner, The
MGM (US) 1949 dir. Robert Siodmak
Dostoevsky, F. *Great Gambler*

Great White Hope, The
FOX (US) 1970 dir. Martin Ritt
Sackler, H.
P

Greeks Had a Word for Them, The
UA (US) 1932 dir. Lowell Sherman
Atkins, Z.
P

Green Berets, The
WAR (US) 1968
dir. John Wayne, Ray Kellogg
Moore, R.

Green Dolphin Street
MGM (US) 1947 dir. Victor Saville
Goudge, E.

Green Fingers
BN (GB) 1946 dir. John Harlow
Arundel, E. *Persistent Warrior, The*

Green for Danger
INDIVIDUAL (GB) 1946
dir. Sidney Gilliat
Brand, C.

Greengage Summer, The
RANK (GB) 1961 dir. Lewis Gilbert
US title: Loss of Innocence
Godden, R.

Green Goddess, The
WAR (US) 1930 dir. Alfred E. Green
Archer, W.
P

Green Grass of Wyoming
FOX (US) 1949 dir. Louis King
O'Hara, M.

Green Grow the Rushes
BL (GB) 1951 dir. Derek Twist
Clewes, H.

Green Helmet, The
MGM (GB) 1960 dir. Michael Forlong
Cleary, J.

Green Ice
ITC (GB) 1981 dir. Ernest Day
Browne, G. A.

Green Light, The
WAR (US) 1937 dir. Frank Borzage
Douglas, L. C.

Green Man, The
BL (GB) 1956 dir. Robert Day
Launder, F. and Gilliat, S. *Meet a Body*
P

Green Man, The
BBC (GB) 1990 dir. Elijah Moshinsky
TVSe(GB)
Amis, K.

Green Mansions
MGM (US) 1959 dir. Mel Ferrer
Hudson, W. H.

Green Mile, The
WAR (US) 1999 dir. Frank Darabont
King, S.

Green Pastures, The
WAR (US) 1936
dir. William Keighley, Marc Connelly
MILBERG (US) 1957
dir. George Schaefer
TV(US)
Connelly, M.
P

Green Scarf, The
BL (GB) 1954
dir. George More O'Ferrall
des Cars, G. *Brute, The*

Green Years, The
MGM (US) 1946 dir. Victor Saville
Cronin, A. J.

Grey Granite
BBC (GB) 1983 dir. Tom Cotter
TVSe(GB)
Gibbon, L. G.

Greystoke: The Legend of Tarzan, Lord of the Apes
WAR (GB) 1984 dir. Hugh Hudson
Burroughs, E. R. *Tarzan of the Apes*

Grifters, The
MIRAMAX (US) 1990
dir. Stephen Frears
Thompson, J.

Gripsholm
BABELSBERG (Ger) 2000 dir. Xavier Koller
Tucholsky, K. *Schloss Gripsholm*

Grissom Gang, The
CINERAMA (US) 1971
dir. Robert Aldrich
Chase, J. H. *No Orchids for Miss Blandish*

Grosse Bagarozy, Der
CONSTANTIN (Ger) 1999 dir. Bernd Eichinger
Krausser, H.

Gross Misconduct
CBC (Can) 1993 dir. Atom Egoyan
TV(Can)
O'Malley, M.

Grot, De
LIVING (Neth) 2001 dir. Martin Koolhoven
Krabbe, T.

Grotesque, The
J&M ENT (GB) 1995 dir. John-Paul Davidson
McGrath, P.

Groundstar Conspiracy, The
UN (US) 1972 dir. Lamont Johnson
Davies, L. P. *Alien, The*

Group, The
UA (US) 1966 dir. Sidney Lumet
McCarthy, M.

Growing Up Brady
PAR TV (US) 2000 dir. Richard Colla
TV(US)
Williams, B. and Kreski, C. *Growing Up Brady ... I Was a Teenage Greg*

Guadalcanal Diary
FOX (US) 1943 dir. Lewis Seiler
Tregaskis, R. W.

Guardian, The
UN (US) 1990 dir. William Friedkin
Greenburg, D. *Nanny, The*

Guardian Angel, The
SANDREW (Swe) 1990
dir. Suzanne Osten
Huch, R. *Der Letste Sommer*

Guardsman, The
MGM (US) 1931 dir. Sidney Franklin
Molnar, F.
P

Guess Who's Sleeping in my Bed?
ABC (US) 1973 dir. Theodore J. Flicker
TV(US)
Chais, P. H. *Six Weeks in August*

Guest in the House
UA (US) 1944 dir. John Brahm

Wilde, H. and Eunson, D.
P

Guide for the Married Man, The
FOX (US) 1967 dir. Gene Kelly

Tarloff, F.

Guilt is my Shadow
ABP (GB) 1950 dir. Roy Kellino

Curtis, P. *You're Best Alone*

Guilty?
GN (GB) 1956 dir. Edmund Greville

Gilbert, M. *Death has Deep Roots*

Guilty
J&M ENT (GB/US) 2000 dir. Anthony Waller

Burke, S.

Guilty as Hell
PAR (US) 1932 dir. Erle C. Kenton

Rubin, D. *Riddle Me This*
P

Guilty Thing Surprised, A
TVS (GB) 1988 dir. Mary McMurray
TVSe(GB)

Rendell, R.

Guinea Pig, The
PILGRIM-PATHE (GB) 1948
dir. Roy Boulting
US title: Outsider, The

Strode, W. S.
P

Guinevere
LIFETIME (US) 1994 dir. Jud Taylor
TV(US)

Woolley, P.

Gulliver's Travels
PAR (US) 1939 dir. Dave Fleischer
EMI (GB) 1976 dir. Peter Hunt
A
HALLMARK (US/GB) dir. Charles Sturridge
TVSe(US/GB)

Swift, J.

Gun and the Pulpit, The
CINETV (US) 1974 dir. Daniel Petrie
TV(US)

Ehrlich, J.

Gunfighters
COL (US) 1947 dir. George Waggner

Grey, Z. *Twin Sombreros*

Gun Fury
COL (US) 1953 dir. Raoul Walsh

Granger, K. R. G. *Ten Against Caesar*

Gun Glory
MGM (US) 1957 dir. Roy Rowland

Yordan, P. *Man of the West*

Gun Runners, The
UA (US) 1958 dir. Don Siegel

Hemingway, E. *To Have and Have Not*

Guns at Batasi
FOX (GB) 1964 dir. John Guillermin

Holles, R. *Siege of Battersea, The*

Gunsmoke
UN (US) 1953 dir. Nathan Juran

Fox, N. A. *Roughshod*

Guns of Darkness
WAR (GB) 1962 dir. Anthony Asquith

Clifford, F. *Act of Mercy*

Guns of Diablo
MGM (US) 1964 dir. Boris Sagal

Taylor, R. L. *Travels of Jaimie McPheeters, The*

Guns of Navarone, The
COL (GB) 1961 dir. J. Lee Thompson

MacLean, A.

Guns of the Timberland
WAR (US) 1960 dir. Robert D. Webb

L'Amour, L.

Guts and Glory: The Oliver North Story
PAPAZIAN-HIRSCH (US) 1989
dir. Mike Robe
TVSe(US)

Bradlee, Jr., B. *Guts and Glory: The Rise and Fall of Oliver North*

Guyana Tragedy: The Story of Jim Jones
KONIGSBERG (US) 1980
dir. William A. Graham
TVSe(US)

Krause, C. A. *Guyana Massacre: The Eyewitness Account*

Guy Named Joe, A
MGM (US) 1943 dir. Victor Fleming

Cairn, J.

Guys and Dolls
MGM (US) 1955
dir. Joseph L. Mankiewicz
M

Runyon, D. *Idyll of Miss Sarah Brown, The*

Burrows, A., Loesser, F. and Swerling, J.
P

Gymkata
MGM/UA (US) 1985 dir. Robert Clouse

Moore, D. T.

Gypsy
WAR (US) 1962 dir. Mervyn LeRoy
RHI (US) 1993 dir. Emile Ardolino
TV(US)
M

Lee, G. R.

Laurents, A., Sondheim, S. and Styne, J.
P

Gypsy and the Gentleman, The
RANK (GB) 1957 dir. Joseph Losey

Hooke, N. W. *Darkness I Leave You*

Gypsy Moths, The
MGM (US) 1969
dir. John Frankenheimer

Drought, J.

H

Habitation of Dragons, The
AMBLIN (US) 1992 dir. Michael
Lindsay-Hogg
TV(US)
Foote, H.
P

Hail Hazana
STILLMAN (Sp) 1978
dir. Jose Maria Guttierez
de Soto, J. M. V. *Infierno y la Brisa, El*

Hail, Hero!
CIN CEN (US) 1969 dir. David Miller
Weston, J.

Hair
UA (US) 1979 dir. Milos Forman
M
MacDermot, G., Ragni, G. and Rado, J.
P

Hairy Ape, The
UA (US) 1944 dir. Alfred Santell
O'Neill, E.
P

Hakuchi
TEZUKA (Jap) 1999 dir. Makoto Tezuka
Sakaguchi, A.

Half a Sixpence
PAR (GB) 1967 dir. George Sidney
M
Cross, B.
P
Wells, H. G. *Kipps*

Half Moon Street
RKO (US) 1986 dir. Bob Swaim
Theroux, P.

Halfway House, The
EAL (GB) 1944 dir. Basil Dearden
Ogden, D.
P

Hallelujah Trail, The
UA (US) 1965 dir. John Sturges
Gulick, B.

Hamilton
TV4SWE (Swe/Nor) 1998 dir. Harald
Zwart
Guillou, J. *Ingen Mans Land; Enda
Segern, Den*

Hamlet
TC (GB) 1948 dir. Laurence Olivier
M. EVANS (US) 1953 dir. Albert
McCleery
TV(US)
CLASSIC (USSR) 1964
dir. Grigori Kozintsev
COL (GB) 1969 dir. Tony Richardson
ATV/UN (GB/US) 1970 dir. Peter
Wood
TV(GB/US)
WAR/GUILD (US/GB) 1990
dir. Franco Zeffirelli
COL (GB) 1996 dir. Kenneth Branagh
MIRAMAX (US) 2000 dir. Michael
Almereyda
HALLMARK (US) 2000 dir. Campbell
Scott, Eric Simonson
TV(US)
Shakespeare, W.
P

Hammerhead
COL (GB) 1968 dir. David Miller
Mayo, J.

Hammer the Toff
BUTCHER (GB) 1952
dir. Maclean Rogers
Creasey, J.

Hammett
WAR (US) 1982 dir. Wim Wenders
Gores, J.

Hamsun
NORDISK (Ger/Nor/Den) 1996 dir. Jan Troell
Hansen, T. *Processen mod Hamsun*
Hamsun, M. *Regnbuen*

Hand, The
ORION/WAR (US) 1981
dir. Oliver Stone
Brandel, M. *Lizard's Tail, The*

Handful of Dust, A
NEW LINE (GB) 1988
dir. Charles Sturridge
Waugh, E.

Handmaid's Tale, The
CINECOM (US) 1990
dir. Volker Schlondorff
Atwood, M.

Hands of a Stranger
TAFT (US) 1987 dir. Larry Elikann
TV(US)
Daley, R.

Hands of Cormac Joyce, The
CRAWFORD (US) 1972
dir. Fielder Cook
TV(US)
Wibberley, L.

Handy Andy
FOX (US) 1934 dir. David Butler
Beach, L. *Merry Andrew*
P

Hangar 18
SCHICK SUNN (US) 1980
dir. James L. Conway
Weverka, R. and Sellier, Jr., C.

Hanged Man, The
UN (US) 1964 dir. Don Siegel
TV(US)
Hughes, D. B. *Ride the Pink Horse*

Hanging Tree, The
WAR (US) 1958 dir. Delmer Daves
Johnson, D. M.

Hanging Up
COL (US) 2000 dir. Diane Keaton
Ephron, D.

Hangover Square
FOX (US) 1945 dir. John Brahm
Hamilton, P.

Hannah
BBC (GB) 1980 dir. Peter Jefferies
TVSe(GB)
Young, E. H. *Miss Mole*

Hanna's War
CANNON (US) 1988
dir. Menahem Golan
Senesh, H. *Diaries of Hannah Senesh, The*
Palgi, Y. *Great Wind Cometh, A*

Hannibal
MGM (US/GB) 2001 dir. Ridley Scott
Harris, T.

Hans Brinker, or the Silver Skates
MILBERG (US) 1957 dir. Sidney Lumet
TV(US)
Dodge, M. M.

Hansel and Gretel
CANNON (US) 1987 dir. Len Talan
Ch
Grimm, J. L. K. and Grimm, W. K.

Happiest Days of Your Life, The
BL (GB) 1950 dir. Frank Launder
Dighton, J.
P

Happiest Millionaire, The
DISNEY (US) 1967 dir. Norman Tokar
M
Biddle, C. D. and Crichton, K.
P

Happiness of Three Women, The
ADELPHI (GB) 1954 dir. Maurice Elvey
Evans, E. *Wishing Well*
P

Happy Anniversary
UA (US) 1959 dir. David Miller
Fields, J. and Chodorov, J. *Anniversary Waltz*
P

Happy Birthday, Gemini
UA (US) 1980 dir. Richard Benner
Innaurato, A. *Gemini*
P

Happy Birthday Shakespeare
BBC (GB) 2000 dir. Nick Hurran
TV(GB)
Wallington, M.

Happy Birthday, Turke!
SENATOR (Ger) 1992
dir. Dorris Dorrie
Arjourni, J.

Happy Birthday, Wanda Jane
COL (US) 1971 dir. Mark Robson
Vonnegut, K.
P

Happy Family, The
APEX (GB) 1952 dir. Muriel Box
US title: Mr. Lord Says No
Hutton, M. G.
P

Happy Hooker, The
SCOTIA-BARBER (US) 1975
dir. Nicholas Sgarro
Hollander, X.

Happy is the Bride
BL (GB) 1957 dir. Roy Boulting
McCracken, E. *Quiet Wedding*
P

Happy Land
FOX (US) 1943 dir. Irving Pichel
Kantor, M.

Happy Thieves, The
UA (US) 1962 dir. George Marshall
Condon, R. *Oldest Confession, The*

Happy Time, The
COL (US) 1952 dir. Richard Fleischer
Fontaine, R. L.
Taylor, S. A.
P

Hardball
PAR (US) 2001 dir. Brian Robbins
Coyle, D. *Hardball: A Season in the Projects*

Hard Core Logo
MIRAMAX (Can) 1996 dir. Bruce McDonald
Turner, M.

Harder They Fall
COL (US) 1956 dir. Mark Robson
Schulberg, B. W.

Hard, Fast and Beautiful
RKO (US) 1951 dir. Ida Lupino
Tunis, J. R.

Hard Steel
GFD (GB) 1942 dir. Norman Walker

Dataller, R. *Steel Saraband*

Hard Times
GRANADA (GB) 1977 dir. John Irvin
TVSe(GB)
BBC (GB) 1994 dir. Peter Barnes
TV(GB)

Dickens, C.

Hard To Forget
ALLIANCE (Can) 1998 dir. Victor Sarin
TV(Can)

Crowe, E. *So Hard to Forget*

Hard Travelling
NEW WORLD (US) 1986
dir. Dan Bessie

Bessie, A. *Bread and a Stone*

Harlow
PAR (US) 1965 dir. Gordon Douglas

Shulman, I.

Harmful Intent
ROSEMONT (US) 1993 dir. John
Patterson
TV(US)

Cook, R.

Harnessing Peacocks
MERIDIAN (GB) 1993 dir. James Cellan
Jones
TV(GB)

Wesley, M.

Harper
WAR (US) 1966 dir. Jack Smight
GB title: Moving Target, The

Macdonald, R. *Moving Target, The*

Harrad Experiment, The
CINERAMA (US) 1973 dir. Ted Post

Rimmer, R. H.

Harriet Craig
COL (US) 1950 dir. Vincent Sherman

Kelly, G. *Craig's Wife*
P

Harriet the Spy
PAR (US) 1996 dir. Bronwen Hughes

Fitzhugh, L.

Harry and Son
ORION (US) 1984 dir. Paul Newman

DeCapite, R. *Lost King, A*

Harry Black and the Tiger
FOX (GB) 1958 dir. Hugo Fregonese
US title: Harry Black

Walker, D.

Harry Potter and the Philosopher's Stone
WAR (US) 2001 dir. Chris Columbus
US title: Harry Potter and the Sorcerer's
Stone

Rowling, J. K.

Harry's Game
YTV (GB) 1982
dir. Lawrence Gordon Clark
TVSe(GB)

Seymour, G.

Harvest
PAGNOL (Fr) 1937
dir. Marcel Pagnol

Giono, J.

Harvey
UN (US) 1950 dir. Henry Koster
TALENT (US)
1972 dir. Fielder Cook
TV(US)
HALLMARK (US) 1999 dir. George
Schaefer
TV(US)

Chase, M.
P

Hasen no Marisu
FGP (Jap) 2000 dir. Satoshi Isaka

Nozawa, H.

Hasty Heart, The
ABP (GB) 1949 dir. Vincent Sherman

Patrick, J.
P

Hatful of Rain, A
FOX (US) 1957 dir. Fred Zinnemann

Gazzo, M. V.
P

Hatter's Castle
PAR (GB) 1941 dir. Lance Comfort

Cronin, A. J.

Haunted, The
FOX TV (US) 1991 dir. Robert Mandel
TV(US)

Curran, R.

Haunted
OCTOBER (US/GB) 1995 dir. Lewis Gilbert

Herbert, J.

Haunted Palace, The
AIP (US) 1963
dir. Roger Corman

Lovecraft, H. P. *Case of Charles Dexter Ward, The*

Haunted Summer
CANNON (US) 1988 dir. Ivan Passer

Edwards, A.

Haunting, The
MGM (GB) 1963 dir. Robert Wise
DREAMWORKS (US) 1999 dir. Jan de Bont

Jackson, S. *Haunting of Hill House, The*

Haunting of Helen Walker, The
ROSEMONT (US) 1995 dir. Tom McLoughlin
TV(US)

James, H. *Turn of the Screw, The*

Haunting of Morella, The
CONCORDE (US) 1990
dir. Jim Wynorski

Poe, E. A.

Hauser's Memory
UN (US) 1970 dir. Boris Sagal
TV(US)

Siodmak, C.

Have His Carcase
BBC (GB) 1987 dir. Christopher Hodson
TVSe(GB)

Sayers, D. L.

Haven
ALLIANCE (US/Can) 2001 dir. John Gray
TVSe(US/Can)

Gruber, R. *Haven: The Dramatic Story of 1,000 World War II Refugees and How They Came to America*

Have You Seen My Son?
MGM TV (US) 1996 dir. Paul Schneider
TV(US)

Olsen, J.

Having Our Say: The Delany Sisters' First 100 Years
COL TRISTAR (US) 1999 dir. Lynne Littman
TV(US)

Delany, S. L., Delany, A. E. and Hearth, A. H. *Having Our Say*

Having Wonderful Crime
RKO (US) 1945 dir. Eddie Sutherland

Rice, C.

Having Wonderful Time
RKO (US) 1938 dir. Alfred Santell

Kober, A.
P

Hawaii
UA (US) 1966 dir. George Roy Hill

Michener, J. A.

Hawk, The
SCREEN (GB) 1993 dir. David Hayman

Ransley, P.

Hawkeye, The Pathfinder
BBC (GB) 1973 dir. David Maloney
TVSe(GB)

Cooper, J. F. *Pathfinder, The*

Haywire
WAR (US) 1980 dir. Michael Tuchner
TV(US)

Hayward, B.

Hazard
PAR (US) 1948 dir. George Marshall

Chanslor, R.

Hazard of Hearts, A
MGM (GB) 1987 dir. John Hough
TV(GB)

Cartland, B.

Head On
GT SCOTT (Aust) 1998 dir. Ana Kokkinos

Tsiolkas, C. *Loaded*

Heads or Tails
CASTLE HILL (Fr) 1983
dir. Robert Enrico

Harris, A. *Follow the Widower*

Heart Beat
WAR (US) 1979 dir. John Byrum

Cassady, C.

Heartbeat
NBC (US) 1993 dir. Michael Miller
TV(US)

Steel, D.

Heartbreak Kid, The
FOX (US) 1972 dir. Elaine May

Friedman, B. J. *Change of Plan, A*

Heartburn
PAR (US) 1986 dir. Mike Nichols

Ephron, N.

Heart is a Lonely Hunter, The
WAR (US) 1968 dir. Robert Ellis Miller

McCullers, C.

Heartless
DANIA (It) 1995 dir. Umberto Marino

Marino, U.
P

Heart of a Child
RANK (GB) 1958 dir. Clive Donner

Bottome, P.

Heart of Darkness
TURNER (US) 1994 dir. Nicolas Roeg
TV(US)

Conrad, J.

Heart of Dixie
ORION (US) 1989 dir. Martin Davidson

Siddons, A. R. *Heartbreak Hotel*

Heart of New York
WAR (US) 1932 dir. Mervyn LeRoy

Freedman, D. *Mendel Inc.*
P

Heart of the Matter
BL (GB) 1953
dir. George More O'Ferrall

Greene, G.

Heart of the Sun
MAK (Can) 1998 dir. Francis Damberger
Lambert, B. *Jennie's Story*
P

Hearts in Atlantis
CASTLE ROCK (US) 2001 dir. Scott Hicks
King, S.

Heartsounds
EMBASSY (US) 1984 dir. Glenn Jordan
TV(US)
Lear, M. W.

Heat
NEW CENTURY (US) 1987 dir. Dick Richards
Goldman, W.

Heat and Dust
UN/ENT (GB) 1983 dir. James Ivory
Jhabvala, R. P.

Heat Lightning
WAR (US) 1934 dir. Mervyn LeRoy
Abbott, G. and Abrams, L.
P

Heat of the Day, The
GRANADA (GB) 1989 dir. Christopher Morahan
TV(GB)
Bowen, E.

Heaven
MIRAMAX (US) 1999 dir. Scott Reynolds
Taylor, C.

Heaven and Earth
WAR (US) 1993 dir. Oliver Stone
Wurts, J. *When Heaven and Earth Changed Places*
Hayslip, J. and Hayslip, L. *Child of War, Woman of Peace*

Heaven and Hell: North and South, Part III
ABC PROD (US) 1994 dir. Larry Peerce
TVSe(US)
Jakes, J. *Heaven and Hell*

Heaven Can Wait
FOX (US) 1943 dir. Ernst Lubitsch
Bus-Fekete, L. *Birthday*
P

Heaven Can Wait
PAR (US) 1978 dir. Warren Beatty, Buck Henry
Segall, H. *Halfway to Heaven*
P

Heaven Fell That Night
IENA (Fr/It) 1958 dir. Roger Vadim
Vidalie, A.

Heaven is a Playground
NEW LINE (US) 1991 dir. Randall Fried
Telander, R.

Heaven Knows, Mr. Allison
FOX (US) 1957 dir. John Huston
Shaw, C.

Heaven's Prisoners
NEW LINE (US) 1996 dir. Phil Joanou
Burke, J. L.

Hedda
SCOTIA-BARBER (GB) 1977 dir. Trevor Nunn
Ibsen, H. *Hedda Gabler*
P

Hedda Gabler
BBC (GB) 1993 dir. Deborah Warner
TV(GB)
Ibsen, H.
P

He Died With a Felafel in His Hand
VILLAGE ROADSHOW (Aust/It) 2001
dir. Richard Lowenstein
Birmingham, J.

Heidi
FOX (US) 1937 dir. Allan Dwan
NBC (US) 1968 dir. Delbert Mann
TV(US)
BBC (GB) 1974
dir. June Wyndham-Davies
TVSe(GB)
DISNEY CH (US) 1993 dir. Michael
Rhodes
TVSe(US)
Ch

Spyri, J.

Heidi Chronicles, The
TNT (US) 1995 dir. Paul Bogart
TV(US)

Wasserstein, W.
P

Heidi's Song
HANNA-BARBERA (US) 1982
dir. Robert Taylor
A

Spyri, J. *Heidi*

Heiress, The
PAR (US) 1949 dir. William Wyler
James, H. *Washington Square*

Helden
SOKAL/GOLDBAUM (Ger) 1959
dir. Franz Peter Wirth
Shaw, G. B. *Arms and the Man*
P

Helen Keller—The Miracle Continues
FOX TV (US) 1984 dir. Alan Gibson
TV(US)

Lash, J. P. *Helen and Teacher*

Helimadoe
KF (Czech) 1994 dir. Jaromil Jires
Havlicek, J.

Hell Below
MGM (US) 1933 dir. Jack Conway
Ellsberg, E. *Pigboats*

Hell Below Zero
COL (GB) 1954 dir. Mark Robson
Innes, H. *White South, The*

Hellcats of the Navy
COL (US) 1957 dir. Nathan Juran
Lockwood, C. A. and Adamson, H. C.
Hellcats of the Sea

Heller in Pink Tights
PAR (US) 1960 dir. George Cukor
L'Amour, L. *Heller With A Gun*

Hell Hath No Fury
BAR-GENE (US) 1991
dir. Thomas J. Wright
TV(US)
Battin, B. W. *Smithereens*

Hell is a City
WAR (GB) 1959 dir. Val Guest
Procter, M.

Hell is Empty
RANK (Czech/GB) 1967
dir. John Ainsworth, Bernard Knowles
Straker, J. F.

Hell is Sold Out
EROS (GB) 1951 dir. Michael Anderson
Dekobra, M.

Hello Dolly!
FOX (US) 1969 dir. Gene Kelly
M

Stewart, M. and Herman, J.
P

Wilder, T. *Matchmaker, The*
P

Hell on Frisco Bay
WAR (US) 1955 dir. Frank Tuttle
McGivern, W. P. *Darkest Hour*

Hello Sister
FOX (US) 1933 dir. Erich von Stroheim
Powell, D.

Hellraiser
CINEMARQUE (GB) 1987
dir. Clive Barker
Barker, C. *Hellbound Heart, The*

Hell's Heroes
UN (US) 1930 dir. William Wyler
Kyne, P. B. *Three Godfathers, The*

Hell Without Limits
AZTECA (Mex) 1978
dir. Arturo Ripstein
Donoso, J.

Helter Skelter
LORIMAR (US) 1976 dir. Tom Gries
TVSe(US)
Bugliosi, V. and Gentry, C.

Hemingway
WILSON (US) 1988 dir. Bernhard Sinkel
TVSe(US)
Baker, C. *Ernest Hemingway: A Life Story*

Henry and June
UN (US) 1990 dir. Philip Kaufman
Nin, A.

Henry V
TC (GB) 1944 dir. Laurence Olivier
RENAISSANCE (GB) 1989
dir. Kenneth Branagh
Shakespeare, W.
P

Henry's Leg
TVS (GB) 1990 dir. Michael Kerrigan
TVSe(GB)
Pilling, A.

He Ran All The Way
UA (US) 1951 dir. John Berry
Ross, S.

Her Cardboard Lover
MGM (US) 1942 dir. George Cukor
Deval, J.
P

Here Comes Mr. Jordan
COL (US) 1941 dir. Alexander Hall
Segall, H. *Halfway to Heaven*
P

Here Come the Littles
ATLANTIC (US) 1985
dir. Bernard Deyries
A, Ch
Peterson, J.

Here we go Round the Mulberry Bush
UA (GB) 1967 dir. Clive Donner
Davies, H.

Her I Naerheden
NORDISK (Den) 2000 dir. Kaspar Rostrup
Christensen, M.

Hero Ain't Nothing But a Sandwich, A
NEW WORLD (US) 1977
dir. Ralph Nelson
Childress, A.

Hero and the Terror
CANNON (US) 1988
dir. William Tanner
Blodgett, M.

Heroines
NTV-PROFIT (Fr) 1997 dir. Gerard Krawczyk
Daeninckx, D. *Playback*

Heroes, The
TVS FILMS (Aust) 1990
dir. Donald Crombie
TV(Aust)
McKie, R.

Heroes of the Telemark
RANK (GB) 1965 dir Anthony Mann
Drummond, J. D. *But for These Men*

Her Own Rules
ADELSON (US) 1998 dir. Bobby Roth
TV(US)
Bradford, B. T.

Herr Puntila and his Servant Matti
BAUERFILM (Austria) 1955
dir. Alberto Cavalcanti
Brecht, B.
P

Her Sister's Secret
PRC (US) 1946 dir. Edgar G. Ulmer
Kaus, G. *Dark Angel*

Her Twelve Men
MGM (US) 1954 dir. Robert Z. Leonard
Baker, L.

He Stayed for Breakfast
COL (US) 1940 dir. Alexander Hall
Duran, M. *Liberté Provisoire*
P

Hester Street
CONN (US) 1975
dir. Joan Micklin Silver
Cahen, A. *Yekl*

He Who Must Die
KASSLER (Fr/It) 1957 dir. Jules Dassin
Kazantzakis, N. *Greek Passion, The*

Hey, I'm Alive!
FRIES (US) 1975 dir. Lawrence Schiller
TV(US)
Klaben, H. and Day, B.

Hidden Blessings
ARABESQUE FILMS (US) 2000 dir.
Timothy Folsome
TV(US)
Thomas, J.

Hidden Fears
KEY (US) 1993 dir. Jean Bodon
Kaminsky, S. *Exercise in Terror*

Hidden Homicide
RANK (US) 1959 dir. Tony Young
Capon, P. *Murder at Shinglestrand*

Hideaway
TRISTAR (US) 1995 dir. Brett Leonard
Koontz, D.

Hideaways, The
UA (US) 1973 dir. Fielder Cook
Konigsburg, E. L. *From the Mixed-up Files of Mrs Basil E. Frankweiler*

Hide in Plain Sight
UA (US) 1980 dir. James Caan
Waller, L.

Hideous Kinky
BBC (GB/Fr) 1998 dir. Gillies
MacKinnon
Freud, E.

Hiding Place, The
WORLD WIDE (US) 1974
dir. James F. Collier
Boom, C. T.

High and Low
TOHO (Jap) 1963 dir. Akira Kurosawa
McBain, E. *King's Ransom, The*

High and the Mighty, The
WAR (US) 1954 dir. William Wellman
Gann, E. K.

High Barbaree
MGM (US) 1947 dir. Jack Conway
Nordhoff, C. B. and Hall, J. N.

High Bright Sun, The
RANK (GB) 1965 dir. Ralph Thomas
US title: McGuire Go Home
Black, I. S.

High Command, The
ABFD (GB) 1936 dir. Thorold Dickinson
Strueby, K. *General Goes Too Far, The*

High Crusade, The
CENTROPOLIS (Ger) 1994 dir. Klaus
Knoesel, Holger Neuhauser
Anderson, P.

Higher and Higher
RKO (US) 1943 dir. Tim Whelan
M
Hurlbut, G. and Logan, J.
P

High Fidelity
TOUCHSTONE (GB/US) 2000 dir.
Stephen Frears
Hornby, N.

High Noon
UA (US) 1952 dir. Fred Zinnemann
Cunningham, J. M. *Tin Star, The*

High Pressure
WAR (US) 1932 dir. Mervyn LeRoy
Kandel, A. *Hot Money*
P

High Price of Passion, The
TAFT (US) 1986 dir. Larry Elikann
TV(US)
Glitman, R. M. *Ruling Passion, The*

High Road to China
WAR (US) 1983 dir. Brian G. Hutton
Cleary, J.

High Sierra
WAR (US) 1941 dir. Raoul Walsh
Burnett, W. R.

High Society
MGM (US) 1956 dir. Charles Walters
M
Barry, P. *Philadelphia Story, The*
P

High Wind in Jamaica, A
FOX (GB) 1965
dir. Alexander Mackendrick
Hughes, R.

Hilary and Jackie
BRIT SCREEN (GB) 1998 dir. Anand
Tucker
DuPre, H. and DuPre, P. *Genius in the
Family, A*

Hilda Crane
FOX (US) 1956 dir. Philip Dunne
Raphaelson, S.
P

Hill, The
MGM (GB) 1965 dir. Sidney Lumet
Rigby, R. and Allen, R. S.
P

Hill in Korea, A
BL (GB) 1956 dir. Julian Aymes
US title: Hell in Korea
Catto, M.

Hill of the Red Fox, The
BBC (GB) 1975 dir. Bob McIntosh
TVSe(GB)
McLean, A. C.

Hills of Heaven, The
BBC (GB) 1978 dir. Eric Davidson
TVSe(GB)
Farrimond, J.

Hi-Lo Country, The
POLYGRAM (GB/US) 1998 dir. Stephen Frears
Evans, M.

Hindenburg, The
UN (US) 1975 dir. Robert Wise
Mooney, M. M.

Hindle Wakes
GB (GB) 1931 dir. Victor Saville
MON (GB) 1952 dir. Arthur Crabtree
Houghton, S.
P

Hip Hopera: Carmen
NEW LINE TV (US) 2001 dir. Robert Townsend
M, TV(US)
Merimée, P. *Carmen*

Hireling, The
COL (GB) 1973 dir. Alan Bridges
Hartley, L. P.

His Double Life
PAR (US) 1933 dir. Arthur Hopkins
Bennett, A. *Buried Alive*

His Excellency
GFD (GB) 1951 dir. Robert Hamer
Christie, D. and Christie, P.
P

His Girl Friday
COL (US) 1940 dir. Howard Hawks
Hecht, B. and MacArthur, C. *Front Page, The*
P

His Glorious Night
MGM (US) 1929 dir. Lionel Barrymore
GB title: Breath of Scandal
Molnar, F. *Olympia*
P

His Majesty O'Keefe
WAR (GB) 1954 dir. Byron Haskin
Kingman, L. and Green, G.

History
SACIS (It) 1988 dir. Luigi Comencina
Morante, E.

History Man, The
BBC (GB) 1981 dir. Robert Knights
TVSe(GB)
Bradbury, M.

History of Mr. Polly, The
GFD (GB) 1949 dir. Anthony Pelissier
BBC (GB) 1980 dir. Lovett Bickford
TVSe(GB)
Wells, H. G.

His Woman
PAR (US) 1931 dir. Edward Sloman
Collins, D. *Sentimentalists, The*

Hitch-Hiker's Guide to the Galaxy, The
BBC (GB) 1981 dir. Alan Bell
TVSe(GB)
Adams, D.

Hitler: A Career
GTO (Ger) 1987
dir. Christian Herrendoerfer, Joachim C. Fest
Fest, J.

Hitler's Children
RKO (US) 1943 dir. Edward Dmytryk
Ziemer, G. *Education for Death*

Hitler's Daughter
WIL COURT (US) 1990
dir. James A. Contner
TV(US)
Benford, T.

Hit Me
CASTLE HILL (US) 1996 dir. Steven
Shainberg
Thompson, J. *Swell Looking Babe, A*

Hit the Deck
MGM (US) 1955 dir. Roy Rowland
M
Fields, H.
P
Osborne, H. *Shore Leave*

H.M. Pulham, Esq
MGM (US) 1940 dir. King Vidor
Marquand, J. P.

H.M.S. Defiant
COL (GB) 1962 dir. Lewis Gilbert
US title: Damn the Defiant
Tilsley, F. *Mutiny*

Hobson's Choice
BL (GB) 1931 dir. Thomas Bentley
BL (GB) 1953 dir. David Lean
CBS ENT (US) 1983 dir. Gilbert Cates
TV(US)
Brighouse, H.
P

Hoffman
ABP (GB) 1970 dir. Alvin Rackoff
Gebler, E. *Shall I Eat You Now?*
P

Hoffman's Hunger
KASSENDER (Neth) 1993 dir. Leon
DeWinter
DeWinter, L.

Holcroft Covenant, The
UN (GB) 1985 dir. John Frankenheimer
Ludlum, R.

Hold Back The Dawn
PAR (US) 1941 dir. Mitchell Leisen
Frings, Mrs. K.

Hold Back The Night
ABP (US) 1956 dir. Allan Dwan
Frank, P.

Holding On
LWT (GB) 1977 dir. Raymond Menmuir,
Gerry Mill
TVSe(GB)
Jones, M.

Hold the Dream
TAFT (GB) 1986 dir. Don Sharp
TVSe(GB)
Bradford, B. T.

Hole, The
PLAY ART (Fr/It) 1959
dir. Jacques Becker
Giovanni, J.

Hole, The
PATHE (GB) 2001 dir. Nick Hamm
Burt, G. *After the Hole*

Hole in the Head, A
UA (US) 1959 dir. Frank Capra
Schulman, A.
P

Hole in the Wall, The
BBC (GB) 1972 dir. Joan Craft
TVSe(GB)
Hammond, P. J.

Holiday
PATHE (US) 1930
dir. Edward H. Griffith
COL (US) 1938 dir. George Cukor
GB title: Free to Live
Barry, P.
P

Holiday Heart
MGM TV (US) 2000 dir. Robert
Townsend
TV(US)
West, C. L.
P

Holiday in Your Heart
VZ/SERTNER (US) 1997 dir. Michael
Switzer
TV(US)
Carter, T. and Rimes, L.

Holiday to Remember, A
JAFFE/BRAUNSTEIN (US) 1995 dir.
Jud Taylor
TV(US)
Creighton, K. *Christmas Love, A*

Hollow Triumph
EL (US) 1948 dir. Steve Sekely
Forbes, M.

Holly and the Ivy, The
BL (GB) 1952
dir. George More O'Ferrall
Browne, W.
P

Hollywood Wives
WAR (US) 1985 dir. Robert Day
TVSe(US)
Collins, J.

Holy Innocents, The
GANESH (Sp) 1985 dir. Mario Camus
Delibes, M.

Holy Matrimony
PAR (US) 1943 dir. John Stahl
Bennett, A. *Buried Alive*

Homage
SKYLINE (US) 1995 dir. Ross Kagan
Marks
Medoff, M. *Homage That Follows, The*
P

Hombre
FOX (US) 1967 dir. Martin Ritt
Leonard, E.

Home and the World, The
NFC (Ind) 1985 dir. Satyajit Ray
Tagore, R.

Home at Seven
BL (GB) 1952 dir. Ralph Richardson
US title: Murder on Monday
Sherriff, R. C.
P

Home Before Dark
WAR (US) 1958 dir. Mervyn LeRoy
Bassing, E.

Homecoming
HALLMARK (US) 1996 dir. Mark Jean
TV(US)
Voight, C.

Homecoming, The
SEVEN KEYS (GB) 1973 dir. Peter Hall
Pinter, H.
P

Homecoming, The—A Christmas Story
LORIMAR (US) 1974 dir. Fielder Cook
TV(US)
Hamner, Jr., E.

Home Fires Burning
M. REES (US) 1989 dir. Glenn Jordan
TV(US)
Inman, R.

Home from the Hill
MGM (US) 1959 dir. Vincente Minnelli
Humphrey, W.

Home in Indiana
TCF (US) 1944 dir. Henry Hathaway
Chamberlain, G. A. *Phantom Filly, The*

Home of the Brave
UA (US) 1949 dir. Mark Robson

Laurents, A.
P

Home Song
DOVE ENT (US) 1996 dir. Nancy
Malone
TV(US)

Spencer, L.

Home Sweet Homicide
FOX (US) 1946 dir. Lloyd Bacon

Rice, C.

Home to Stay
TIME-LIFE (US) 1978
dir. Delbert Mann
TV(US)

Majerus, J. *Grandpa and Frank*

**Homeward Bound: The
Incredible Journey**
DISNEY (US) 1993 dir. Duwayne
Dunham
Ch

Burnford, S. *Incredible Journey, The*

Homme au Chapeau Rond, L'
ALCINA (Fr) 1946 dir. Pierre Billon

Dostoevsky, F. *Eternal Husband, The*

Homme de Nulle Part, L'
CG (Fr) 1987 dir. Pierre Chenal

Pirandello, L.

Hondo
WAR (US) 1953 dir. John Farrow

L'Amour, L.

Honey
PAR (US) 1930 dir. Wesley Ruggles

Miller, A. D. and Thomas, A. E. *Come
out of the Kitchen*
P

Honeymoon for Three
WAR (US) 1941 dir. Lloyd Bacon

Scott, A. and Haight, G. *Goodbye Again*
P

Honeymoon Machine, The
MGM (US) 1961 dir. Richard Thorpe

Semple, L. *Golden Fleecing, The*
P

Honeymoon with a Stranger
TCF (US) 1969 dir. John Peyser
TV(US)

Thomas, R. *Piège pour un Homme Seul*
P

Honey Pot, The
UA (US) 1966 dir. Joseph L. Mankiewicz

Sterling, T. *Evil of the Day, The*

Honey Siege, The
HTV (GB) 1987 dir. John Jacobs
Ch, TVSe(GB)

Buhet, G.

Honkytonk Man
WAR (US) 1982 dir. Clint Eastwood

Carlile, C.

Honor Thy Father
METRO (US) 1973 dir. Paul Wendkos
TVSe(US)

Talese, G.

**Honor Thy Father and
Mother—The True Story of the
Menendez Brothers**
SABAN ENT (US) dir. Paul Schneider
TV(US)

Soble, R. and Johnson, J. *Blood Brothers*

Honor Thy Mother
POV (US) 1992 dir. David Greene
TV(US)

Bledsoe, J. *Blood Games*

Honorary Consul, The
PAR (GB) 1983 dir. John Mackenzie
US title: Beyond the Limit
Greene, G.

Hook, The
MGM (US) 1962 dir. George Seaton
Katcham, V. *Hameçon, The*

Hopalong Cassidy
PAR (US) 1935 dir. Howard Bretherton
Mulford, C. E.

Hopscotch
AVCO (US) 1980 dir. Ronald Neame
Garfield, B.

Horatio Hornblower
A&E/PICTURE PALACE (GB) 1999 dir. Andrew Grieve
TVSe(GB)
A&E/PICTURE PALACE (GB) 2001 dir. Andrew Grieve
TVSe(GB)
Forester, C. S. *Mr. Midshipman Hornblower; Lieutenant Hornblower*

Horizontal Lieutenant, The
MGM (US) 1962 dir. Richard Thorpe
Cotler, G. *Bottletop Affair, The*

Horse in the Grey Flannel Suit, The
DISNEY (US) 1968 dir. Norman Tokar
Ch
Hatch, E. *Year of the Horse, The*

Horseman on the Roof, The
STUDIO CANAL+ (Fr) 1995 dir. Jean-Paul Rappeneau
Giono, J. *Hussard Sur le Toit, Le*

Horseman Riding By, A
BBC (GB) 1978 dir. Paul Ciappessoni, Philip Dudley, Alan Grint
TVSe(GB)
Delderfield, R. F.

Horsemen, The
COL (US) 1970
dir. John Frankenheimer
Kessel, J.

Horse of Pride, The
FF (Fr) 1980
dir. Claude Chabrol
Helias, P.-J.

Horse's Mouth, The
UA (GB) 1958 dir. Ronald Neame
Cary, J.

Horse Soldiers, The
UA (US) 1959 dir. John Ford
Sinclair, H.

Horse Whisperer, The
TOUCHSTONE (US) 1998 dir. Robert Redford
Evans, N.

Horse Without a Head, The
DISNEY (GB) 1963 dir. Don Chaffey
Ch
Berna, P. *Hundred Million Frames, A*

Hors La Vie
BAC (Fr/It/Bel) 1991
dir. Maroun Bagdadi
Auque, R. and Forestier, P.

Hostage
SKOURAS (US) 1992 dir. Robert Young
Allbeury, T. *No Place to Hide*

Hostage Heart, The
MGM (US) 1977 dir. Bernard McEverty
TV(US)
Green, G.

Hostages
PAR (US) 1943 dir. Frank Tuttle
Heym, S.

Hostile Witness
UA (GB) 1968 dir. Ray Milland
Roffey, J.
P

Hotel
WAR (US) 1967 dir. Richard Quine
Hailey, A.

Hotel Berlin
WAR (US) 1945 dir. Peter Godfrey
Baum, V. *Berlin Hotel*

Hotel du Lac
BBC (GB) 1986 dir. Giles Foster
TV(GB)
Brookner, A.

Hotel Imperial
PAR (US) 1939 dir. Robert Florey
Biro, L.
P

Hotel New Hampshire, The
ORION (US) 1984 dir. Tony Richardson
Irving, J.

Hotel Paradiso
MGM (US) 1966 dir. Peter Glenville
Feydeau, G. and Desvallieres, M.
P

Hotel Reserve
RKO (GB) 1944 dir. Victor Hanbury
Ambler, E. *Epitaph for a Spy*

Hotel Shanghai
DURNIOK (Aust) 1997 dir. Peter Patzak
Baum, V.

Hotel Sorrento
HORIZON (Aust/GB) 1995 dir. Richard Franklin
Rayson, H.
P

Hot Enough for June
RANK (GB) 1963 dir. Ralph Thomas
Davidson, L. *Night Before Wenceslas, The*

Hot Rock, The
TCF (US) 1972 dir. Peter Yates
GB title: How to Steal a Diamond in Four Uneasy Lessons
Westlake, D. E.

Hot Spell
PAR (US) 1958 dir. Daniel Mann
Coleman, L. *Next of Kin*
P

Hot Spot, The
ORION (US) 1990 dir. Dennis Hopper
Williams, C. *Hell Hath no Fury*

Houdini
PAR (US) 1953 dir. George Marshall
Kellock, H.

Hound-Dog Man
FOX (US) 1959 dir. Don Siegel
Gipson, F. B. *Circles Round the Wagon*

Hound of the Baskervilles, The
ID (GB) 1932 dir. V. G. Gundrey
FOX (US) 1939 dir. Sidney Lawfield
UA (GB) 1959 dir. Terence Fisher
UN (US) 1972 dir. Barry Crane
TV(US)
HEMDALE (GB) 1977
dir. Paul Morrissey
BBC (GB) 1982 dir. Peter Duguid
TVSe(GB)
EMBASSY (GB) 1983
dir. Douglas Hickox
MUSE ENT (Can) 2000 dir. Rodney Gibbons
TV(Can)
Doyle, Sir A. C.

Hour Before the Dawn, The
PAR (US) 1944 dir. Frank Tuttle
Maugham, W. S.

191

Hour of the Star, The
RAIZ (Bra) 1987 dir. Suzana Amaral
Lispector, C.

Hour of Thirteen, The
MGM (GB) 1952 dir. Harold French
MacDonald, P. *X vs Rex*

House
HOUSEHOLD (Can) 1995 dir. Laurie
Lynd
MacIvor, D.
P

House by the River
REP (US) 1950 dir. Fritz Lang
Herbert, Sir A. P.

House Divided, A
UN (US) 1932 dir. William Wyler
Edens, O. *Heart & Hand*

House Divided, A
AVNET/KERNER (US) 2000 dir. John
Kent Harrison
TV(US)
Leslie, K. A. *Woman of Color, Daughter of Privilege: Amanda Dickson*

Household Saints
FINE LINE (US) 1993 dir. Nancy Savoca
Prose, F.

House in Marsh Road, The
GN (GB) 1960 dir. Montgomery Tully
Meynell, L.
P

House in the Square, The
FOX (GB) 1951 dir. Roy Baker
US title: I'll Never Forget You
Balderston, J. L. *Berkeley Square*
P

House is not a Home, A
PAR (US) 1964 dir. Russell Rouse
Adler, P.

Housekeeper's Daughter, The
UA (US) 1939 dir. Hal Roach
Clarke, D. H.

Housekeeping
COL (US) 1987 dir. Bill Forsyth
Robinson, M.

Houseman's Tale, A
BBC (GB) 1987 dir. Alastair Reid
TVSe(GB)
Douglas, C.

Housemaster
ABPC (GB) 1938 dir. Herbert Brenon
Hay, I. *Bachelor Born*
P

House of a Thousand Candles, The
REP (US) 1936 dir. Arthur Lubin
Nicolson, M.

House of Bernarda Alba, The
GALA (Sp) 1990 dir. Mario Camus
CHANNEL 4 (GB) 1992
dir. Nuria Espert, Stuart Burge
TV(GB)
Lorca, F. G.
P

House of Cards
UN (US) 1968 dir. John Guillerman
Ellin, S.

House of Cards
BBC (GB) 1991 dir. Paul Seed
TVSe(GB)
Dobbs, M.

House of Fear
UN (US) 1945 dir. Roy William Neill
Doyle, Sir A. C. *Adventure of the Five Orange Pips*

House of God, The
UA (US) 1984 dir. Donald Wrye
Shem, S.

House of Mirth, The
PBS (US) 1981 dir. Adrian Hall
TV(US)
CHANNEL 4 FILMS (GB/US) 2000 dir.
Terence Davies
Wharton, E.

House of Numbers
MGM (US) 1957 dir. Russell Rouse
Finney, J.

House of Rothschild, The
FOX (US) 1934 dir. Alfred Werker
Hembert, G.
P

House of Secrets
RANK (GB) 1956 dir. Guy Green
US title: Triple Deception
Noel, S.

House of Secrets
MULTIMEDIA (US) 1993 dir. Mimi
Leder
TV(US)
Boileau, P. and Narcejac, T. *Celle qui n'etait Plus*

House of Strangers
FOX (US) 1949
dir. Joseph L. Mankiewicz
Weidman, J.

House of the Angel, The
ARG SONO (Arg) 1957
dir. Leopoldo Torre Nilsson
Guido, B.

House of the Arrow, The
AB (GB) 1930 dir. Leslie Hiscott
AB (GB) 1940 dir. Harold French
ABP (GB) 1953 dir. Michael Anderson
Mason, A. E. W.

House of the Long Shadows, The
CANNON (GB) 1983 dir. Pete Walker
Biggers, E. D. *Seven Keys to Baldpate*

House of the Seven Gables
UN (US) 1940 dir. Joe May
Hawthorne, N.

House of the Seven Hawks, The
MGM (GB) 1959 dir. Richard Thorpe
Canning, V. *House of the Seven Flies, The*

House of the Spirits, The
COSTADO (Den/Ger/US) 1993 dir.
Bille August
Allende, I.

House of Usher, The
AIP (US) 1960 dir. Roger Corman
GB title: Fall of the House of Usher, The
21st CENTURY (US) 1988
dir. Alan Birkinshaw
Poe, E. A. *Fall of the House of Usher, The*

House of Yes, The
BANDEIRA (US) 1997 dir. Mark S.
Waters
MacLeod, W.
P

House on Garibaldi Street, The
ITC (US) 1979 dir. Peter Collinson
TV(US)
Harel, I.

House on Telegraph Hill, The
FOX (US) 1951 dir. Robert Wise
Lyon, D. *Tentacles*

House That Would Not Die, The
SPELLING (US) 1980 dir. John
Llewellyn Moxey
TV(US)
Michaels, B. *Ammie, Come Home*

Howards End
MI (GB) 1992
dir. James Ivory
Forster, E. M.

Howards of Virginia, The
COL (US) 1940 dir. Frank Lloyd
GB title: Tree of Liberty, The
Page, E. *Tree of Liberty, The*

How Awful About Allan
SPELLING (US) 1970
dir. Curtis Harrington
TV(US)
Farrell, H.

How Do I Love Thee?
ABC (US) 1970 dir. Michael Gordon
De Vries, P. *Let Me Count the Ways*

How Green Was My Valley
FOX (US) 1941 dir. John Ford
BBC (GB) 1975 dir. Donald Wilson
TVSe(GB)
Llewellyn, R.

How He Lied to Her Husband
BI (GB) 1931 dir. Cecil Lewis
Shaw, G. B.
P

How I Won the War
UA (GB) 1967 dir. Richard Lester
Ryan, P.

Howling, The
AVCO (US) 1981 dir. Joe Dante
Brandner, G.

Howling III
SQUARE (Aust) 1987 dir. Philippe
Mora
Brandner, G.

Howling in the Woods, A
UN (US) 1971 dir. Daniel Petrie
TV(US)
Johnston, V.

How Stella Got Her Groove Back
FOX (US) 1998 dir. Kevin Rodney
Sullivan
McMillan, T.

How Sweet It Is
WAR (US) 1968 dir. Jerry Paris
Resnik, M. *Girl in the Turquoise Bikini, The*

How to be Miserable and Enjoy It
ATRIUM (SP) 1994 dir. Enrique Urbizu
Rico-Godoy, C.

How to Make an American Quilt
UN (US) 1995 dir. Jocelyn Moorhouse
Otto, W.

How to Make Love to a Negro Without Getting Tired
ANGELIKA (Fr) 1990
dir. Jacques Benoit
Laferrière, D. *Comment faire l'amour avec un nègre sans se fatiguer*

How to Succeed in Business Without Really Trying
UA (US) 1967 dir. David Swift
M
Mead, S., Burrows, A., Weinstock, J., Gilbert, W. and Loesser, F.
P

HS (hors service)
PARADIS (Bel/Fr) 2001 dir. Jean-Paul
Lilienfeld
Gagnol, A. *M'sieur; Lumieres du Frigo, Les*

Huck and the King of Hearts
TRIMARK (US) 1994 dir. Michael Keusch

Twain, M. *Adventures of Huckleberry Finn, The*

Huckleberry Finn
PAR (US) 1931 dir. Norman Taurog
MGM (US) 1939 dir. Richard Thorpe
UA (US) 1974 dir. J. Lee Thompson
M
ABC (US) 1975 dir. Robert Totten
TV(US)

Twain, M. *Adventures of Huckleberry Finn, The*

Hucksters, The
MGM (US) 1947 dir. Jack Conway

Wakeman, F.

Hud
PAR (US) 1963 dir. Martin Ritt

McMurtry, L. *Horseman, Pass By*

Huey P. Newton Story, A
40 ACRES (US) 2001 dir. Spike Lee
TV(US)

Smith, R. G.
P

Huis Clos
MARCEAU (Fr) 1954
dir. Jacqueline Audry

Sartre, J.-P.
P

Human Comedy, The
MGM (US) 1943 dir. Clarence Brown

Saroyan, W.

Human Desire
COL (US) 1954 dir. Fritz Lang

Zola, E. *Bête Humaine, La*

Human Factor, The
RANK (GB) 1979 dir. Otto Preminger

Greene, G.

Humoresque
WAR (US) 1946 dir. Jean Negulesco

Hurst, F.

Hunchback, The
ALLIANCE (US) 1997 dir. Peter Medak
TV(US)

Hugo, V. *Hunchback of Notre Dame, The*

Hunchback of Notre Dame, The
RKO (US) 1939 dir. William Dieterle
RANK (Fr/It) 1956 dir. Jean Delannoy
BBC (GB) 1977 dir. Alan Cooke
TV(GB)
COL (US/GB) 1982
dir. Michael Tuchner
TV(GB/US)
DISNEY (US) 1996 dir. Gary Trousdale, Kirk Wise
A, Ch, M

Hugo, V.

Hungarians
IFEX (Hun) 1981 dir. Zoltan Fabri

Balazs, J.

Hunger
MKT ST (US) 2001 dir. Maria Giese

Hamsun, K.

Hunger, The
MGM/UA (US) 1983 dir. Tony Scott

Strieber, W.

Hungry Bachelors Club, The
REGENT ENT (US) 1999 dir. Gregory Ruzzin

Myers, L. S.

Hungry Hill
TC (GB) 1947 dir. Brian Desmond Hurst

Du Maurier, D.

Hunter, The
PAR (US) 1980 dir. Buzz Kulik

Keane, C.

Hunters, The
FOX (US) 1958 dir. Dick Powell
Salter, J.

Hunter's Blood
CONCORDE (US) 1987
dir. Robert C. Hughes
Cunningham, J.

Hunt for Red October, The
PAR (US) 1990 dir. John McTiernan
Clancy, T.

Hunt For the Unicorn Killer, The
REGENCY TV (US) 1999 dir. William A. Graham
TVSe(US)
Levy, S. *Unicorn's Secret, The*

Huntingtower
BBC (GB) 1978 dir. Bob Hird
TVSe(GB)
Buchan, J.

Huntress, The
OFFLINE (US) 2000 dir. Jeffrey Reiner
TV(US)
Keane, C.

Hurlyburly
FINE LINE (US) 1998 dir. Anthony Drazan
Rabe, D.
P

Hurricane, The
UA (US) 1937 dir. John Ford
ITC (US) 1979 dir. Jan Troell
Nordhoff, C. B. and Hall, J. N.

Hurricane
METRO (US) 1974 dir. Jerry Jameson
TV(US)
Anderson, W. C. *Hurricane Hunters*

Hurricane, The
UN (US) 1999 dir. Norman Jewison
Carter, R. *Sixteenth Round, The*
Chaiton, S. and Swinton, T. *Lazarus and the Hurricane*

Hurry Sundown
PAR (US) 1967 dir. Otto Preminger
Gilden, K. B.

Husband's Holiday
PAR (US) 1931 dir. Robert Milton
Pascal, E. *Marriage Bed, The*

Hustler, The
FOX (US) 1961 dir. Robert Rossen
Tevis, W.

Hygiene de L'Assassin
TSF (Fr) 1999 dir. François Ruggieri
Nothomb, A. *Librement Trahi*

I

I am a Camera
BI (GB) 1955 dir. Henry Cornelius
van Druten, J.
P

I am a Cat
TOHO (Jap) 1982 dir. Kenichi Kawa
Natsume, S.

I am a Fugitive from a Chain Gang
WAR (US) 1932 dir. Mervyn LeRoy
Burns, R. E.

I am the Cheese
ALMI (US) 1983 dir. Robert Jiras
Cormier, R.

I Believe in You
EAL (GB) 1952 dir. Basil Dearden
Stokes, S. *Court Circular*

I Can Get It For You Wholesale
FOX (US) 1951 dir. Michael Gordon
GB title: This is My Affair
Weidman, J.

Ice Cold in Alex
ABP (GB) 1958 dir. J. Lee Thompson
US title: Desert Attack
Landon, C.

Ice House
UPFRONT/CACTUS (US) 1989
dir. Eagle Pennell
Brinkman, B. *Ice House Heat Waves*
P

Iceman Cometh, The
AFT (US) 1973 dir. John Frankenheimer
O'Neill, E.
P

Ice Palace
WAR (US) 1960 dir. Vincent Sherman
Ferber, E.

Ice Station Zebra
MGM (US) 1968 dir. John Sturges
MacLean, A.

Ice Storm, The
FOX (US) 1997 dir. Ang Lee
Moody, R.

I, Claudius
BBC (GB) 1976 dir. Herbert Wise
TVSe(GB)
Graves, R.

I Confess
WAR (US) 1953 dir. Alfred Hitchcock
Anthelme, P.
P

I'd Climb the Highest Mountain
FOX (US) 1951 dir. Henry King
Harris, C.

Ideal Husband, An
BL (GB) 1948 dir. Alexander Korda
BBC (GB) 1999 dir. Rudolph Cartier
TV(GB)
MIRAMAX (GB/US) 1999 dir. Oliver Parker

Wilde, O.
P

I Died a Thousand Times
WAR (US) 1955 dir. Stuart Heisler

Burnett, W. R. *High Sierra*

Idiot's Delight
MGM (US) 1939 dir. Clarence Brown

Sherwood, R. E.
P

Idle on Parade
COL (GB) 1959 dir. John Gilling

Camp, W.

I Don't Give a Damn
ROLL (Israel) 1988
dir. Shmuel Imberman

Ben Amitz, D.

If …
PAR (GB) 1968 dir. Lindsay Anderson

Sherwin, D. and Howlett, J. *Crusaders*

If a Man Answers
UN (US) 1962 dir. Henry Levin

Wolfe, W.

If I Were Free
RKO (US) 1933 dir. Elliot Nugent

van Druten, J. *Behold We Live*
P

If I Were King
PAR (US) 1938 dir. Frank Lloyd

McCarthy, J. H.

If Tomorrow Comes
CBS ENT (US) 1986 dir. Jerry London
TVSe(US)

Sheldon, S.

If Winter Comes
MGM (US) 1948 dir. Victor Saville

Hutchinson, A. S. M.

If You Could See What I Can Hear
SCHICK SUNN (US) 1982 dir. Eric Till

Sullivan, T. and Gill, D.

I Hate Actors!
GALAXY (Fr) 1988
dir. Gerald Krawczyk

Hecht, B.

I Heard the Owl Call My Name
TOM (US) 1973
dir. Daryl Duke
TV(US)

Craven, M.

Ike
ABC (US) 1979 dir. Melville Shavelson, Boris Sagal
TVSe(US)

Morgan, K. S. *Past Forgetting*

I Killed The Count
GN (GB) 1939 dir. Fred Zelnik

Coppel, A.
P

I Know What You Did Last Summer
COL (US) 1997 dir. Jim Gillespie

Duncan, L.

I Know Why the Caged Bird Sings
TOM (US) 1979
dir. Fielder Cook
TV(US)

Angelou, M.

I Lived With You
GB (GB) 1933 dir. Maurice Elvey
Novello, I.
P

I'll Be Seeing You
SELZNICK (US) 1944
dir. William Dieterle
Martin, C.

I'll Cry Tomorrow
MGM (US) 1955 dir. Daniel Mann
Roth, L. and Frank, G.

Illegal Traffic
PAR (US) 1938 dir. Louis King
Hoover, J. E. *Persons in Hiding*

I'll Get You For This
BL (GB) 1950 dir. Joseph M. Newman
US title: Lucky Nick Cain
Chase, J. H. *High Stakes*

Ill Met By Moonlight
RANK (GB) 1956 dir. Michael Powell,
Emeric Pressburger
US title: Night Ambush
Moss, W. S.

I'll Take Manhattan
KRANTZ (US) 1987
dir. Douglas Hickox, Richard Michaels
TVSe(US)
Krantz, J.

illtown
SHOOTING GALLERY (US) 1996 dir.
Nick Gomez
Williams, T. *Cocaine Kids, The*

Illuminata
OVERSEAS (US/Sp) 1998 dir. John
Turturro
Cole, B.
P

Illusions
PRISM ENT (US) 1992 dir. Victor Kulle
TV(US)
Colley, P. *I'll Be Back Before Midnight*
P

Illustrated Man, The
WAR (US) 1969 dir. Jack Smight
Bradbury, R.

Illustrious Corpses
PEA/LAA (It) 1976 dir. Francesco Rosi
Sciascia, L. *Context, The*

Ilona Comes With the Rain
CARACOL (Col/It/Sp) 1996 dir. Sergio
Cabrera
Mutis, A.

I Loved You Wednesday
TCF (US) 1933 dir. Henry King, William
Cameron Menzies
Ricardei, M. and Dubois, W.
P

I Love Trouble
COL (US) 1948 dir. S. Sylvan Simon
Huggins, R. *Double Take, The*

I Love You, I Love You Not
STUDIO CANAL+ (Fr/Ger/GB) 1997
dir. Billy Hopkins
Kesselman, W.
P

I'm All Right, Jack
BL (GB) 1959 dir. John Boulting
Hackney, A. *Private Life*

Imaginary Crimes
MORGAN CREEK (US) 1994 dir.
Anthony Drazan
Ballantyne, S.

Imaginary Friends
THAMES (GB) 1987 dir. Peter Sasdy
TVSe(GB)
Lurie, A.

I Married a Doctor
WAR (US) 1936 dir. Archie Mayo
Lewis, S. *Main Street*

I Married an Angel
MGM (US) 1942 dir. W. S. Van Dyke
M
Janos, V.
P

I Married A Shadow
IS (Fr) 1983 dir. Robin Davis
Irish, W. *I Married A Dead Man*

I Married a Witch
UA (US) 1942 dir. René Clair
Smith, T. *Passionate Witch, The*

I'm Dancing as Fast as I Can
PAR (US) 1982 dir. Jack Hofsiss
Gordon, B.

I'm Dangerous Tonight
MCA TV (US) 1990 dir. Tobe Hooper
TV(US)
Woolrich, C.

I Met My Love Again
WANGER (US) 1937 dir. Joshua Logan,
Arthur Ripley
Corliss, A. *Summer Lightning*

I'm From Missouri
PAR (US) 1939 dir. Theodore Reed
Croy, H. *Sixteen Hands*

Imitation General
MGM (US) 1958 dir. George Marshall
Chamberlain, W. *Trumpets of Company K*

Imitation of Life
UN (US) 1934 dir. John Stahl
UN (US) 1959 dir. Douglas Sirk
Hurst, F. *Anatomy of Me*

I'm Losing You
LIONS GATE (US) 1999 dir. Bruce
Wagner
Wagner, B.

Immigrants, The
UN (US) 1978 dir. Alan J. Levi
TVSe(US)
Fast, H.

Immortal Sergeant, The
FOX (US) 1943 dir. John Stahl
Brophy, J.

Immortal Story
ORTF (Fr) 1968 dir. Orson Welles
Blixen, K.

I'm Not Rappaport
GRAMERCY (US) 1996 dir. Herb
Gardner
Gardner, H.
P

Impatient Maiden
UN (US) 1932 dir. James Whale
Clarke, D. H. *Impatient Virgin, The*

Implicated
COL TRISTAR (US) 1998 dir. Irving
Belatche
Wyka, F. *Wishful Thinking*

Importance of Being Earnest, The
RANK/GFD (GB) 1952
dir. Anthony Asquith
BBC (GB) 1986 dir. Stuart Burge
TV(GB)
ELEC CON (US) 1992 dir. Kurt Baker
MIRAMAX (GB/US) 2002 dir. Oliver
Parker
Wilde, O.
P

Impossible Years, The
MGM (US) 1968 dir. Michael Gordon

Fisher, B. and Marx, A.
P

Impostors, The
STUDIO CANAL+ (Fr) 1994 dir.
Frederic Blum

Gary, R. *Tête Coupable, La*

In a Child's Name
NEW WORLD (US) 1991 dir. Tom
McLoughlin
TVSe(US)

Maas, P.

Inadmissible Evidence
PAR (GB) 1968 dir. Anthony Page

Osborne, J.
P

In All Innocence
STUDIO CANAL+ (Fr) 1998 dir. Pierre
Jolivet

Simenon, G. *En Cas de Malheur*

In a Lonely Place
COL (US) 1950 dir. Nicholas Ray

Hughes, D. B.

In a Shallow Grave
SKOURAS (US) 1988
dir. Kenneth Bowser

Purdy, J.

In Broad Daylight
NEW WORLD (US) 1991
dir. James Steven Sadwith
TV(US)

MacLean, H.

In Celebration
SEVEN KEYS (GB) 1974
dir. Lindsay Anderson

Storey, D.
P

Incense for the Damned
GN (GB) 1970
dir. Robert Hartford-Davis

Raven, S. *Doctors Wear Scarlet*

Incident in San Francisco
ABC TV (US) 1971 dir. Don Medford
TV(US)

Brown, J. E. *Incident at 125th Street*

Incognito
DIRECTORS' CIRCLE (US) 1999 dir.
Julie Dash
TV(US)

Ray, F.

In Cold Blood
COL (US) 1967 dir. Richard Brooks
HALLMARK (US) 1996 dir. Jonathan
Kaplan
TVSe(US)

Capote, T.

Inconnu Dans La Maison, L'
STUDIO CANAL+ (Fr) 1992 dir.
Georges Lautner

Simenon, G.

Inconvenient Woman, An
ABC (US) 1991 dir. Larry Elikann
TVSe(US)

Dunne, D.

In Country
WAR (US) 1989 dir. Norman Jewison

Mason, B. A.

Incredible Journey, The
DISNEY (US) 1963 dir. Fletcher Markle
A, Ch

Burnford, S.

Incredible Mr. Limpet, The
WAR (US) 1964 dir. Arthur Lubin
A

Pratt, T.

Incredible Shrinking Man, The
UN (US) 1957 dir. Jack Arnold

Matheson, R. *Shrinking Man, The*

Incubus, The
NEW REALM (Can) 1982
dir. John Hough

Russell, R.

In Custody
MI (GB/Ind) 1994 dir. Ismail Merchant

Desai, A.

Indecent Obsession, An
PBL (Aust) 1985 dir. Lex Marinos

McCullough, C.

Indecent Proposal
PAR (US) 1993 dir. Adrian Lyne

Englehard, J.

Indian in the Cupboard, The
COL (US) 1995 dir. Frank Oz
Ch

Banks, L. R.

Indict and Convict
UN TV (US) 1974 dir. Boris Sagal
TV(US)

Davidson, B.

Indiscreet
WAR (GB) 1958 dir. Stanley Donen
REP (US) 1988
dir. Richard Michaels
TV(US)

Krasna, N. *Kind Sir*
P

In Dreams
DREAMWORKS (US) 1999 dir. Neil Jordan

Wood, B. *Doll's Eyes*

I Never Promised You a Rose Garden
NEW WORLD (US) 1977
dir. Anthony Page

Greenberg, J.

I Never Sang for my Father
COL (US) 1970 dir. Gilbert Cates

Anderson, R. W.
P

Infamous Life, An
LC/CINEMAX (It/Fr/Ger) 1990
dir. Giacomo Battiato

Cellini, B.

Infidelity
ATRIUM (Sp) 1995 dir. Enrique Urbizu

Rico-Godoy, C.

Infiltrator, The
HBO SHOW (US) 1995 dir. Jud Taylor
TV(US)

Svoray, Y. and Taylor, N. *In Hitler's Shadow: An Israeli's Amazing Journey Inside Germany's Neo-Nazi Movement*

Infinity
OVERSEAS (US) 1996 dir. Matthew Broderick

Feynman, R. *Surely You're Joking, Mr Feynman; What Do You Care What Other People Think*

Informant, The
SHOWTIME (US) 1998 dir. Jim McBride
TV(US)

Seymour, G. *Field of Blood*

Informer, The
RKO (US) 1935 dir. John Ford

O'Flaherty, L.

Informers, The
RANK (GB) 1963 dir. Ken Annakin
US title: Underworld Informers

Warner, D. *Death of a Snout*

Ingenue Libertine, L'
CODO (Fr) 1950 dir. Jacqueline Audry
Colette

In Harm's Way
PAR (US) 1965 dir. Otto Preminger
Bassett, J. *Harm's Way*

Inheritance
GRANADA (GB) 1967
TV(GB)
Bentley, P.

Inheritance, The
ALLIANCE (US) 1997 dir. Bobby Roth
TV(US)
Alcott, L. M.

Inherit the Wind
UA (US) 1960 dir. Stanley Kramer
COMPASS (US) 1965
dir. George Schaefer
TV(US)
VINCENT (US) 1988 dir. David Greene
TV(US)
MGM TV (US) 1999 dir. Daniel Petrie
TV(US)
Lawrence, J. and Lee, R. E.
P

In Love and War
FOX (US) 1958 dir. Philip Dunne
Myrer, A. *Big War, The*

In Love and War
TA (US) 1987 dir. Paul Aaron
TV(US)
Stockdale, J. and Stockdale, S.

In Love and War
HALLMARK (US) 2001 dir. John Kent
Harrison
TV(US)
Newby, E. *Love and War in the Apennines*

In Love and War
NEW LINE (US) 1996 dir. Richard
Attenborough
Villard, H. S. and Nagel, J. *Hemingway in Love and War*

In Love With an Older Woman
FRIES (US) 1982 dir. Jack Bender
TV(US)
Kaufelt, D. *Six Months With an Older Woman*

In Name Only
RKO (US) 1939 dir. John Cromwell
Brewer, B. *Memory of Love*

Innocent, The
MIRAMAX (GB/Ger) 1993 dir. John
Schlesinger
McEwan, I.

Innocent Bystanders
SCOTIA-BARBER (GB) 1972
dir. Peter Collinson
Munro, J.

Innocent Sinners
RANK (US) 1957 dir. Philip Leacock
Godden, R. *Episode of Sparrows, An*

Innocents, The
FOX (GB) 1961 dir. Jack Clayton
James, H. *Turn of the Screw, The*

Innocents with Dirty Hands
FOX-RANK (Fr/It/Ger) 1975
dir. Claude Chabrol
Neely, R.

Innocent Victims
KUSHNER-LOCKE (US) 1996 dir.
Gilbert Cates
TV(US)
Whisnant, S.

Inn of the Sixth Happiness, The
FOX (GB) 1958 dir. Mark Robson

Burgess, A. *Small Woman, The*

Inochi No Umi
YEE-HA (Jap) 2000 dir. Susumi Fukuhara

Hahakigi, H.

In Old Chicago
FOX (US) 1937 dir. Henry King

Busch, N. *We the O'Leary's*

In Person
RKO (US) 1935 dir. William A. Seiter

Adams, S. H.

In Praise of Older Women
ASTRAL (Can) 1977
dir. George Kaczender
CANAL+ ESPANA (Sp) 1997 dir. Manuel Lombadero

Vizinczey, S.

Inquest
CHARTER (GB) 1939 dir. Roy Boulting

Barringer, M.
P

Inquisitor, The
GALA (Fr) 1981 dir. Claude Miller

Wainwright, J. *Brainwash*

In Search of the Castaways
DISNEY (GB) 1961 dir. Robert Stevenson
Ch

Verne, J. *Captain Grant's Children*

Inside Daisy Clover
WAR (US) 1965 dir. Robert Mulligan

Lambert, G.

Inside Moves
BARBER (US) 1980 dir. Richard Donner

Walton, T.

Inside the Third Reich
ABC (US) 1982 dir. Marvin J. Chomsky
TVSe(US)

Speer, A.

Inspector, The
FOX (GB) 1962 dir. Philip Dunne
US title: Lisa

de Hartog, J.

Inspector Calls, An
BL (GB) 1959 dir. Guy Hamilton
BBC (GB) 1982 dir. Michael Simpson
TVSe(GB)

Priestley, J. B.
P

Inspector General, The
WAR (US) 1949 dir. Henry Koster

Gogol, N. V.
P

Instinct
TOUCHSTONE (US) 1999 dir. Jon Turteltaub

Quinn, D. *Ishmael*

Institute Benjamenta
IMAGE (GB) 1995 dir. Stephen Quay, Timothy Quay

Walser, R. *Jakob von Gunten*

Insurance Man, The
BBC (GB) 1986 dir. Richard Eyre
TV(GB)

Bennett, A.
P

Intensity
TRISTAR (US) 1997 dir. Yves Simoneau
TVSe(US)

Koontz, D.

Intent to Kill
FOX (GB) 1958 dir. Jack Cardiff

Bryan, M.

International Airport
SPELLING (US) 1985
dir. Charles Dubin, Don Chaffey
TV(US)
Bailey, A. *Airport*

Internecine Project, The
MACLEAN (GB) 1974 dir. Ken Hughes
Elkind, M.

Interns, The
COL (US) 1962 dir. David Swift
Frede, R.

Interpol
COL (GB) 1957 dir. John Gilling
US title: Pickup Alley
Forrest, A. J.

Intersection
PAR (US) 1994 dir. Mark Rydell
Guimard, P. *Choses de la Vie, Les*

Interview With the Vampire
GEFFEN (US) 1994 dir. Neil Jordan
Rice, A.

**In the Best of Families:
Marriage, Pride and Madness**
AMBROCO (US) 1994 dir. Jeff Bleckner
TVSe(US)
Bledsoe, J. *Bitter Blood*

In the Cool of the Day
MGM (US) 1962 dir. Robert Stevens
Ertz, S.

In the Deep Woods
GOLCHAN/HILL (US) 1992 dir.
Charles Correll
TV(US)
Conde, N. *In the Deep of the Woods*

In the Doghouse
RANK (GB) 1961 dir. Darcy Conyers
Duncan, A. *It's a Vet's Life*

In the Frame
DLT (US) 1989 dir. Wigbert Wicker
TV(US)
Francis, D.

In the French Style
COL (US/Fr) 1963 dir. Robert Parrish
Shaw, I.

In the Good Old Summertime
MGM (US) 1949 dir. Robert Z. Leonard
M
Laszlo, N. *Parfumerie*
P

In the Heat of the Night
UA (US) 1967 dir. Norman Jewison
Ball, J.

In the Lake of the Woods
HALLMARK (US) 1996 dir. Carl
Schenkel
TV(US)
O'Brien, T.

**In the Line of Duty: Manhunt
in the Dakotas**
PATCHETT-KAUFMAN (US) 1991 dir.
Dick Lowry
TV(US)
Corcoran, J. *Bitter Harvest: Murder in the
Heartland*

In the Name of the People
CBS (US) 2000 dir. Peter Levin
TV(US)
Boland, T.
P

In the Secret State
BBC (GB) 1985 dir. Christopher
Morahan
TV(GB)
McCrum, R.

In the Shadows, Someone's Watching
SABAN ENT (US) 1993 dir. Richard Friedman
TV(US)

Kelman, J. *Someone's Watching*

In the Time of the Butterflies
SHOWTIME (US) 2001 dir. Mariano Barroso
TV(US)

Alvarez, J.

In the Wake of a Stranger
BUTCHER (GB) 1959 dir. David Eady

Black, I. S.

In the Winter Dark
RB (Aust) 1998 dir. James Boyle

Winton, T.

In this House of Brede
TOM (US) 1975
dir. George Schaefer
TV(US)
CHANNEL 4 (GB) 1984
TV(GB)

Godden, R.

In This Our Life
WAR (US) 1942 dir. John Huston

Glasgow, E.

Intimacy
FRANCE 2 (Fr/GB) 2000 dir. Patrice Chereau

Kureishi, H.

Intimate Betrayal
DIRECTORS' CIRCLE (US) 1999 dir. Diane Wynter
TV(US)

Hill, D.

Into the Blue
CARLTON (GB) 1997 dir. Jack Gold
TV(GB)

Goddard, R.

Into Thin Air: Death on Everest
COL TRISTAR (US) 1997 dir. Robert Markowitz
TV(US)

Krakauer, J. *Into Thin Air*

Introducing Dorothy Dandridge
ESPARZA (US) 1999 dir. Martha Coolidge
TV(US)

Mills, E. *Dorothy Dandridge*

Intruder, The
BL (GB) 1953 dir. Guy Hamilton

Maugham, R. *Line on Ginger*

Intruder, The
FILMGROUP (US) 1961
dir. Roger Corman
GB title: Stranger, The

Beaumont, C.

Intruder, The
GRANADA (GB) 1972 dir. Peter Caldwell
TVSe(GB)

Townsend, J. R.

Intruder, The
WIC (Can/GB) 1999 dir. David Bailey

Leimas, B.

Intruder in the Dust
MGM (US) 1949 dir. Clarence Brown

Faulkner, W.

Intruders
CBS ENT (US) 1992 dir. Dan Curtis
TVSe(US)

Hopkins, B.

Inugami
ASMIK (Jap) 2001 dir. Masato Harada

Bando, M.

Invasion of Privacy, An
EMBASSY TV (US) 1983
dir. Mel Damski
TV(US)

Taylor, J. *Asking for It*

Invasion of the Body Snatchers, The
ALLIED (US) 1956 dir. Don Siegel
UA (US) 1978 dir. Philip Kaufman
Finney, J. *Body Snatchers, The*

Investigation
QUARTET (Fr) 1978 dir. Etienne Perier
Laborde, J. *Lesser of Two Evils, The*

Investigation, The: Inside a Terrorist Bombing
GRANADA (US/GB) 1990 dir. Mike Beckham
TV(GB/US)

Mullin, C. *Error of Judgment: The Birmingham Bombings*

Invincible Six, The
MOULIN ROUGE (US/Iran) 1970
dir. Jean Negulesco
Barrett, M. *Heroes of Yucca, The*

Invisible Circus, The
FINELINE (US) 2001 dir. Adam Brooks
Egan, J.

Invisible Man, The
UN (US) 1933 dir. James Whale
UN (US) 1975 dir. Robert Michael Lewis
BBC (GB) 1984 dir. Brian Lighthill
TVSe(GB)

Wells, H. G.

Invisible Stripes
WAR (US) 1939 dir. Lloyd Bacon
Lawes, L. E.

Invitation au Voyage
TRIUMPH (Fr) 1983
dir. Peter Del Monte
Barry, J. *Moi, Ma Soeur*

I Ought to be in Pictures
TCF (US) 1982 dir. Herbert Ross
Simon, N.
P

I Passed for White
WAR (US) 1960 dir. Fred M. Wilcox
Bradley, M. H.

Ipcress File, The
RANK (GB) 1965 dir. Sidney J. Furie
Deighton, L.

Iphighenia
UA (Gre) 1978
dir. Michael Cacoyannis
Euripides
P

I Remember Mama
RKO (US) 1948 dir. George Stevens
van Druten, J.
P

Irene
RKO (US) 1940 dir. Herbert Wilcox
Montgomery, J. H.
P

Irezumi: The Spirit of Tattoo
DAIEI (Jap) 1983
dir. Yoichi Takabayashi
Akae, B.

Iris
MIRAMAX (GB/US) 2001 dir. Richard Eyre
Bayley, J. *Iris, a Memoir of Iris Murdoch; Elegy for Iris*

Irishman, The
S. AUST (Aust) 1978
dir. Donald Crombie

O'Connor, E.

Irish RM, The
CHANNEL 4 (GB) 1982 dir. Roy Ward
Baker, Robert Chetwyn
TVSe(GB)

Somerville, E. and Ross, M.

Iron Curtain
FOX (US) 1948 dir. William Wellman

Gouzenko, I. *This was my Choice*

Iron Duke, The
GAU BR (GB) 1935 dir. Victor Saville

Harwood, H. M.
P

Iron Man
UN (US) 1931 dir. Tod Browning
UI (US) 1951 dir. Joseph Pevney

Burnett, W. R.

Iron Mistress, The
WAR (US) 1952 dir. Gordon Douglas

Wellman, P. I.

Ironweed
TRISTAR (US) 1987
dir. Hector Babenco

Kennedy, W.

Iron Maze
TRANS-TOKYO (US/Jap) 1991
dir. Hiroaki Yoshida

Kutagawa, R. A. *In the Grove*

Isadora
UI (GB) 1969 dir. Karel Reisz
US title: Loves of Isadora, The

Duncan, I. *My Life*

Stokes, S. *Isadora Duncan, An Intimate Portrait*

I Saw What You Did
UN (US) 1965 dir. William Castle
UN (US) 1988 dir. Fred Walton
TV(US)

Curtiss, U.

I Sent a Letter to My Love
ATLANTIC (Fr) 1981
dir. Moshe Mizrahi

Rubens, B.

Ishi: The Last of his Tribe
LEWIS (US) 1978
dir. Robert Ellis Miller
TV(US)

Quinn, T. K. *Ishi in Two Worlds*

Island, The
UN (US) 1980 dir. Michael Ritchie

Benchley, P.

Island at the Top of the World, The
DISNEY (US) 1974
dir. Robert Stevenson

Cameron, I. *Lost Ones, The*

Island in the Sky
WAR (US) 1953 dir. William Wellman

Gann, E. K.

Island in the Sun
FOX (GB) 1957 dir. Robert Rossen

Waugh, A.

Island of Dr. Moreau, The
AIP (US) 1977 dir. Don Taylor
NEW LINE (US) 1996 dir. John
Frankenheimer

Wells, H. G.

Island of Lost Souls
PAR (US) 1932 dir. Erle C. Kenton

Wells, H. G. *Island of Dr Moreau, The*

Island of the Blue Dolphins
UN (US) 1964 dir. James B. Clark
O'Dell, S.

Island on Bird Street, The
APRIL (GB/Den) 1997 dir. Soren
Kragh-Jacobsen
Orlev, U.

Islands in the Stream
PAR (US) 1977 dir. Franklin Schaffner
Hemingway, E.

Isn't it Romantic?
PAR (US) 1948 dir. Norman Z. McLeod
Nolan, J. *Gather Rosebuds*

Is Paris Burning?
PAR (Fr/US) 1965 dir. René Clément
Collins, L. and Lapierre, D.

I Start Counting
UA (GB) 1969 dir. David Greene
Lindop, A. E.

**Is Your Honeymoon Really
Necessary?**
ADELPHI (GB) 1953 dir. Maurice Elvey
Tidmarsh, E. V.
P

It
LORIMAR (US) 1989
dir. Tommy Lee Wallace
TVSe(US)
King, S.

I Take This Woman
PAR (US) 1931 dir. Marion Gering
Rinehart, M. R. *Lost Ecstasy*

It All Came True
WAR (US) 1940 dir. Lewis Seiler
Bromfield, L. *Better Than Life*

It Always Rains on Sundays
EAL (GB) 1947 dir. Robert Hamer
La Bern, A. J.

I Thank A Fool
MGM (GB) 1962 dir. Robert Stevens
Lindop, A. E.

It Happened One Christmas
UN TV (US) 1977 dir. Donald Wrye
TV(US)
Stern, P. V. D. *Greatest Gift, The*

It Happened One Night
COL (US) 1934 dir. Frank Capra
Adams, S. H. *Night Bus*

It Happens Every Thursday
UN (US) 1953 dir. Joseph Pevney
McIlvaine, J.

I, The Jury
UA (US) 1953 dir. Harry Essex
FOX (US) 1982 dir. Richard T. Heffron
Spillane, M.

It Pays to Advertise
PAR (US) 1931 dir. Frank Tuttle
Hackett, W.
P

It Runs in the Family
MGM (US) 1994 dir. Bob Clark
Shepherd, J. *In God We Trust, All Others
Pay Cash; Wanda Hickey's Night of Golden
Memories and Other Disasters*

It's Always Something
UN TV (US) 1990 dir. Richard Compton
TV(US)
Raab, S.

It's Good to be Alive
METRO (US) 1974 dir. Michael Landon
TV(US)
Campanella, R.

It Shouldn't Happen to a Vet
EMI (GB) 1976 dir. Eric Till

Herriot, J. *All Things Bright and Beautiful*

It's Never too Late
ABP (GB) 1956 dir. Michael McCarthy

Douglas, F.
P

It's the Rage
MUTUAL (US) 1999 dir. James D. Stern
TV(US)

Reddin, K. *All the Rage*
P

It's Tough to be Famous
IN (US) 1932 dir. Alfred E. Green

McCall, M. *Goldfish Bowl, The*

It was an Accident
PATHE (GB) 2000 dir. Metin Huseyin

Cameron, J.

Ivanhoe
MGM (GB) 1952 dir. Richard Thorpe
BBC (GB) 1970 dir. David Maloney
TVSe(GB)
COL (US/GB) 1982
dir. Douglas Canfield
TV(GB/US)
BBC/A&E (GB) 1997 dir. Stuart Orme
TVSe(GB)

Scott, Sir W.

I've Been Waiting For You
NBC (US) 1998 dir. Christopher Leitch
TV(US)

Duncan, L. *Gallows Hill*

Ivy
UI (US) 1947 dir. Sam Wood

Lowndes, M. B. *Story of Ivy*

I Wake up Screaming
FOX (US) 1941
dir. H. Bruce Humberstone
GB title: Hot Spot

Fisher, S.

I Walk Alone
PAR (US) 1947 dir. Byron Haskin

Reeves, T. *Beggars are Coming to Town*
P

I Walk the Line
COL (US) 1970
dir. John Frankenheimer

Jones, M. *Exile, An*

I Want What I Want
CINERAMA (GB) 1972 dir. John Dexter

Brown, G.

I Was a Spy
GAU (GB) 1933 dir. Victor Saville

McKenna, M.

I Was Monty's Double
ABP (GB) 1958 dir. John Guillermin
US title: Hell, Heaven and Hoboken

James, M. E. C.

I Went to the Dance
BRAZOS (US) 1989 dir. Leon Blank,
Chris Strachwitz

Savoy, A. A.

Jack Bull, The
NEW CRIME (US) 1999 dir. John Badham
TV(US)

von Kleist, H. *Michael Kohlhaas*

Jackie Brown
MIRAMAX (US) 1997 dir. Quentin Tarantino

Leonard, E. *Rum Punch*

Jackie, Ethel, Joan: Women of Camelot
JUST SINGER (US) 2000 dir. Larry Shaw
TVSe(US)

Taraborrelli, J. R.

Jackknife
CINEPLEX (US) 1989 dir. David Jones

Metcalfe, S. *Strange Snow*
P

Jack of all Trades
GAINS (GB) 1936 dir. Jack Hubert, Robert Stevenson

Vulpuis, P. *Youth at the Helm*
P

Jack the Bear
FOX (US) 1993 dir. Marshall Herskovitz

McCall, D.

Jacobo Timerman: Prisoner Without a Name, Cell Without a Number
CHRYS-YELL (US) 1983
dir. Linda Yellen
TV(US)

Timerman, J. *Prisoner Without a Name, Cell Without a Number*

Jadviga Parnaja
MAFILM (Hun) 2000 dir. Krisztina Deak

Zavada, P.

Jake Lassiter: Justice on the Bayou
CANNELL (US) 1995 dir. Peter Markle
TV(US)

Levine, P. *To Speak For the Dead*

Jake Spanner, Private Eye
FENADY (US) 1989 dir. Lee H. Katzin
TV(US)

Morse, L. A. *Old Dick, The*

Jake's Women
RHI (US) 1996 dir. Glenn Jordan
TV(US)

Simon, N.
P

Jakob the Liar
TRISTAR (US/Fr) 1999 dir. Peter Kassovitz

Becker, J. *Jakob der Lugner*

Jails, Hospitals and Hip Hip
ARTHOUSE (US) 2000 dir. Mark Benjamin, Danny Hoch

Hoch, D.
P

Jalna
RKO (US) 1935 dir. John Cromwell

de la Roche, M.

Jamaica Inn
PAR (GB) 1939 dir. Alfred Hitchcock
HTV (GB) 1983
dir. Lawrence Gordon Clark
TV(GB)

Du Maurier, D.

Jamaica Run
PAR (US) 1953 dir. Lewis R. Foster

Murray, M.

James and the Giant Peach
DISNEY (US) 1996 dir. Henry Selick
Ch

Dahl, R.

James at 15
FOX TV (US) 1977 dir. Joseph Hardy
TV(US)

Wakefield, D.

Jane Doe
CASTLE HILL (US) 1996 dir. Paul Peditto

Peditto, P.
P

Jane Eyre
MON (US) 1934 dir. Christy Cabanne
FOX (US) 1943 dir. Robert Stevenson
OMNIBUS (GB) 1971
dir. Delbert Mann
BBC (GB) 1973 dir. Joan Craft
TVSe(GB)
BBC (GB) 1984 dir. Julian Amyes
TV(GB)
MIRAMAX (Fr/It/GB) 1996 dir. Franco Zeffirelli

Bronte, C.

Jane's House
SPELLING TV (US) 1994 dir. Glenn Jordan
TV(US)

Smith, R. K.

Janie
WAR (US) 1944 dir. Michael Curtiz

Bentham, J. and Williams, H. V.
P

Jassy
GFD (GB) 1947 dir. Bernard Knowles

Lofts, N.

Java Head
ATP (GB) 1934 dir. J. Walter Ruben

Hergesheimer, J.

Jaws
UN (US) 1975 dir. Steven Spielberg

Benchley, P.

Jaya Ganga
NFDC (Fr/Ind) 1996 dir. Vijay Singh

Singh, V.

Jayne Mansfield Story, The
LAN (US) 1980 dir. Dick Lowry
TV(US)

Saxton, M. *Jayne Mansfield and the American Fifties*

Jazz Singer, The
WAR (US) 1953 dir. Michael Curtiz
EMI (US) 1980 dir. Richard Fleischer

Raphaelson, S. *Day of Atonement*
P

Jean de Florette
ORION (Fr) 1987 dir. Claude Berri

Pagnol, M.

Jeannie
TANSA (GB) 1941 dir. Harold French
US title: Girl in Distress
Stuart, A.
P

J. Edgar Hoover
RLC (US) 1987 dir. Robert Collins
TV(US)
Sullivan, W. G. and Brown, W. S. *My 30 Years in Hoover's FBI*

Jeffrey
ORION (US) 1995 dir. Christopher Ashley
Rudnick, P.
P

Jekyll & Hyde
KING PHOENIX (US/GB) 1990 dir. David Wickes
TV(GB/US)
Stevenson, R. L. *Dr. Jekyll and Mr. Hyde*

Jennie Gerhardt
PAR (US) 1933 dir. Marion Gering
Dreiser, T.

Jennie Project, The
H. ROACH (US) 2001 dir. Gary Nadeau
TV(US)
Preston, D. *Jennie*

Jennifer on my Mind
UA (US) 1971 dir. Noel Black
Simon, R. L. *Heir*

Jenny's War
HTV (US/GB) 1985 dir. Steven Gethers
Ch, TVSe(GB/US)
Stoneley, J.

Jeremiah Johnson
WAR (US) 1972 dir. Sidney Pollack
Fisher, V.

Jerry and Tom
LIONS GATE (US) 1998 dir. Saul Rubinek
Cleveland, R.
P

Jerusalem
NORDISK (Swe/Den/Nor) 1996 dir. Bille August
Lagerlof, S.

Jessica
UA (Fr/It) 1961 dir. Jean Negulesco
Sandstrom, F. *Midwife of Pont Clery, The*

Jesus Christ Superstar
UN (US) 1973 dir. Norman Jewison
M
Webber, A. L. and Rice, T.
P

Jesus' Son
ALLIANCE (Can/US) 1999 dir. Alison Maclean
Johnson, D.

Jeux Interdits
R. DORFMANN (Fr) 1952 dir. René Clément
Boyer, F.

Jewel
ALLIANCE (Can/GB/US) 2001 dir. Paul Shapiro
TV(Can/GB/US)
Lott, B.

Jewel in the Crown, The
GRANADA (GB) 1984 dir. Jim O'Brien, Christopher Morahan
TVSe(GB)
Scott, P. *Raj Quartet, The*

Jewel Robbery
WAR (US) 1932 dir. William Dieterle
Fodor, L.
P

Jewels
NBC (US) 1992 dir. Roger Young
TVSe(US)
Steel, D.

Jew Süss
GAU (GB) 1934 dir. Lothar Mendes
US title: Power
TERRA (Ger) 1940 dir. Veit Harlan
Feutchwangler, L.

Jezebel
WAR (US) 1938 dir. William Wyler
Davis, D.
P

JFK
WAR (US) 1991 dir. Oliver Stone
Garrison, J. *On the Trail of the Assassins: My Investigation and Prosecution of the Murder of President Kennedy*
Marrs, J. *Crossfire: The Plot that Killed Kennedy*

JFK: Reckless Youth
HEARST (US) 1993 dir. Harry Winer
TVSe(US)
Hamilton, N.

Jigsaw
BL (GB) 1962 dir. Val Guest
Waugh, H. *Sleep Long My Love*

Jigsaw Man, The
J&M (GB) 1984
dir. Terence Young
Bennett, D.

Jimmy the Kid
NEW WORLD (US) 1982
dir. Gary Nelson
Westlake, D. E.

Jitters
ABC PICT (US) 1997 dir. Bob Saget
TV(US)
Rentschler, L. A.

Joan of Arc
RKO (US) 1948 dir. Victor Fleming
Anderson, M. *Joan of Lorraine*
P

Joe and the Gladiator
BBC (GB) 1971 dir. Anna Home
TVSe(GB)
Cookson, C.

Joey Boy
BL (GB) 1965 dir. Frank Launder
Chapman, E.

John and Mary
FOX (US) 1969 dir. Peter Yates
Jones, M.

John and the Missus
CINEMA (Can) 1987
dir. Gordon Pinsent
Pinsent, G.

John Halifax, Gentleman
BBC (GB) 1974 dir. Tristan de Vere Cole
TVSe(GB)
Craik, D.

John Loves Mary
WAR (US) 1948 dir. David Butler
Krasna, N.
P

John Macnab
BBC (GB) 1976 dir. Donald McWhinnie
TVSe(GB)
Buchan, J.

Johnny Angel
RKO (US) 1945 dir. Edwin L. Marin
Booth, C. G. *Mr. Angel Comes Aboard*

Johnny Belinda
WAR (US) 1948 dir. Jean Negulesco
MILBERG (US) 1958
dir. George Schaefer
TV(US)
LORIMAR (US) 1982 dir. Anthony Page
TV(US)
Harris, E.
P

Johnny Come Lately
CAGNEY (US) 1943
dir. William K. Howard
GB title: Johnny Vagabond
Bromfield, L. *McLeod's Folly*

Johnny Cool
UA (US) 1963 dir. William Asher
McPartland, J. *Kingdom of Johnny Cool, The*

Johnny Got His Gun
CINEMATION (US) 1971
dir. Dalton Trumbo
Trumbo, D.

Johnny Guitar
REP (US) 1953 dir. Nicholas Ray
Chanslor, R.

Johnny Handsome
TRISTAR (US) 1989 dir. Walter Hill
Godey, J. *Three Worlds of Johnny Handsome, The*

Johnny One-Eye
UA (US) 1950 dir. Robert Florey
Runyon, D.

Johnny on the Spot
FANCEY (GB) 1954
dir. Maclean Rogers
Cronin, M. *Paid in Full*

Johnny's Girl
SIGNBOARD HILL (US) 1995 dir. John
Kent Harrison
TV(US)
Rich, K.

Johnny Tremain
DISNEY (US) 1957
dir. Robert Stevenson
Ch
Forbes, E.

Johnny, We Hardly Knew Ye
TALENT (US) 1977 dir. Gilbert Cates
TV(US)
O'Donnell, K. P, Powers, D. F. and
McCarthy, J.

Joker is Wild, The
PAR (US) 1957 dir. Charles Vidor
Cohn, A.

Jolies Choses, Les
M6 (Fr) 2001 dir. Gilles Paquet-Brenner
Despentes, V.

Jolly Bad Fellow, A
BL (GB) 1964 dir. Robert Hamer
Vulliamy, C. E. *Don Among the Dead Men*

Jonah Who Lived in the Whale
FOCUS (Fr/It) 1993 dir. Roberto Faenza
Obersku, J. *Kinderjahren*

Jonathan Livingstone Seagull
PAR (US) 1973 dir. Hill Bartlett
Bach, R.

Joni
WORLD WIDE (US) 1980
dir. James F. Collier
Eareckson, J.

Jory
AVCO (US) 1973 dir. Jorge Fons
Bass, M. R.

Josepha
TRIUMPH (Fr) 1982
dir. Christopher Frank
Frank, C.

Joseph Andrews
UA (GB) 1977 dir. Tony Richardson
Fielding, H.

Joshua Then and Now
TCF (Can) 1985 dir. Ted Kotcheff
Richler, M.

Journey
HALLMARK (US) 1995 dir. Tom
McLoughlin
TV(US)
MacLachlan, P.

Journey for Margaret
MGM (US) 1942 dir. W. S. Van Dyke
White, W. L.

Journey into Fear
RKO (US) 1942
dir. Norman Foster, Orson Welles
Ambler, E.

Journey of August King, The
MIRAMAX (US) 1995 dir. John Duigan
Ehle, J.

Journey's End
TIFFANY (GB/US) 1930
dir. James Whale
Sherriff, R. C.
P

Journey to Shiloh
UI (US) 1966 dir. William Hale
Henry, W.

Journey to the Centre of the Earth
FOX (US) 1959 dir. Henry Levin
CANNON (US) 1989
dir. Rusty Lemorande
HIGH (US) 1993 dir. William Dear
TV(US)
HALLMARK (US) 1999 dir. George
Miller
TVSe(US)
Verne, J.

Joy
UGC (Can/Fr) 1983 dir. Serge Bergon
Laurey, J.

Joy in the Morning
MGM (US) 1965 dir. Alex Segal
Smith, B.

Joy Luck Club, The
HOLLYWOOD (US) 1993 dir. Wayne
Wang
Tan A.

Juarez
WAR (US) 1939 dir. William Dieterle
Harding, B. *Phantom Crown, The*

Jubal
COL (US) 1956 dir. Delmer Daves
Wellman, P. I. *Jubal Troop*

Jubilee Trail
REP (US) 1954 dir. Joseph Kane
Bristow, G.

Jude
BBC (GB) 1996 dir. Michael
Winterbottom
Hardy, T. *Jude the Obscure*

Jude the Obscure
BBC (GB) 1971 dir. Hugh David
TVSe(GB)
Hardy, T.

Judge, The
NBC (US) 2001 dir. Mick Garris
TV(US)
Martini, S.

Judge Dee and the Monastery Murders
ABC (US) 1974 dir. Jeremy Paul Kagan
TV(US)
Van Gulik, R. *Haunted Monastery, The*

Judge Horton and the Scottsboro Boys
TOM (US) 1976 dir. Fielder Cook
TV(US)
Carter, D. T. *Scottsboro: A Tragedy of the American South*

Judgment at Nuremberg
UA (US) 1961 dir. Stanley Kramer
Mann, A.
P

Judgment in Berlin
NEW LINE (US) 1988 dir. Leo Penn
Stern, H. J.

Judgement in Stone, A
SCHULZ (Can) 1987 dir. Ousama Rawi
US title: The Housekeeper
Rendell, R.

Juggler, The
COL (US) 1953 dir. Edward Dmytryk
Blankfort, M.

Jules et Jim
SEDIF (Fr) 1962 dir. François Truffaut
Roche, H.-P.

Julia
FOX (US) 1977 dir. Fred Zinnemann
Hellman, L. F. *Pentimento*

Julia Misbehaves
MGM (US) 1948 dir. Jack Conway
Sharp, M. *Nutmeg Tree, The*

Juliane
PER HOLST (Den) 1999 dir. Hans Kristensen
Aamund, J. *Klinkevals*

Julian Po
CYPRESS (US) 1997 dir. Alan Wade
Scepanovic, B. *Mort de Monsieur Golouja, La*

Julie Johnson
SHOOTING GALLERY (US) 2001 dir. Bob Gosse
Hammond, W.
P

Julius Caesar
MGM (US) 1953
dir. Joseph L. Mankiewicz
MGM (GB) 1969 dir. Stuart Burge
Shakespeare, W.
P

Juloratoriet
SANDREWS (Den/Nor/Swe) 1996 dir. Kjell-Ake Andersson
Tunstrom, G.

Jumanji
INTERSCOPE (US) 1995 dir. Joe Johnston
Van Allsburg, C.

Jumping the Queue
BBC (GB) 1989 dir. Clade Whatham
TVSe(GB)
Wesley, M.

Jungle Book, The
KORDA (US) 1942 dir. Zoltan Korda, André de Toth
DISNEY (US) 1967
dir. Wolfgang Reitherman
A, Ch, M
DISNEY (US) 1994 dir. Stephen Sommers
Ch
Kipling, R.

Junior Miss
FOX (US) 1945 dir. George Seaton
Benson, S.

Juno and the Paycock
BI (GB) 1930 dir. Alfred Hitchcock
O'Casey, S.
P

Jupiter's Darling
MGM (US) 1954 dir. George Sidney
Sherwood, R. E. *Road to Rome, The*
P

Jurassic Park
UN (US) 1993 dir. Steven Spielberg
Crichton, M.

Juror, The
COL (US) 1996 dir. Brian Gibson
Green, G. D.

Just Another Secret
BLAIR (US/GB) 1989
dir. Lawrence Gordon Clark
TV(GB/US)
Forsyth, F.

Just Ask for Diamond
FOX (GB) 1988 dir. Stephen Bayly
US title: Diamond's Edge
Horowitz, A. *Falcon's Malteser, The*

Just Cause
WAR (US) 1995 dir. Arne Glimcher
Katzenbach, J.

Just for You
PAR (US) 1952 dir. Elliot Nugent
Benet, S. V. *Famous*

Justine
FOX (US) 1969 dir. George Cukor
Durrell, L. *Alexandria Quartet, The*

Justinien Trouvé
SOLO (Fr) 1993 dir. Christian Fechner
Folco, M. *Dieu et Nous Seuls Pouvons*

Justiz
BR (Ger) 1993 dir. Hans W.
Geissendorfer
Duerrenmatt, F.

Just Like a Woman
BRIT SCREEN (GB) 1992 dir.
Christopher Monger
Monica, J. *Geraldine, For the Love of a Transvestite*

Just My Imagination
LORIMAR TV (US) 1992 dir. Jonathan
Sanger
TV(US)
Gingher, M. *Bobby Rex's Greatest Hit*

Just Tell Me What You Want
WAR (US) 1980 dir. Sidney Lumet
Allen, J. P.

Just William
AB (GB) 1939 dir. Graham Cutts
Crompton, R.

K

K2
MIRAMAX (US) 1992 dir. Franc
Roddam
Myers, P.
P

Kaleidoscope
NBC (US) 1990 dir. Jud Taylor
TV(US)
Steel, D.

Kamikaze '89
TELECUL (Ger) 1983 dir. Wolf Gremm
Wahloo, P. *Murder on the 31st Floor*

Kamilla and the Thief
PENELOPE (Nor/GB) 1988
dir. Grete Salamonsen
Vinje, K.

Kanal
POLSKI (Pol) 1956 dir. Andrzej Wajda
Stawinski, J. *Kloakerne*

Kane and Abel
EMBASSY (US) 1985 dir. Buzz Kulik
TVSe(US)
Archer, J.

Kangaroo
WORLD FILM (Aust) 1986
dir. Tim Burstall
Lawrence, D. H.

Kate Plus Ten
WAINWRIGHT (GB) 1938
dir. Reginald Denham
Wallace, E.

Kattbreven
CO FILM AB (Swe) 2001 dir. Christina
Olofson
Johansson, E.

Katy
BBC (GB) 1976 dir. Julia Smith
TVSe(GB)
Coolidge, S. *What Katy Did; What Katy
Did at School*

Kazan
COL (US) 1949 dir. Will Jason
Curwood, J. O.

Kean
BBC (GB) 1978 dir. James Cellan Jones
TV(GB)
Sartre, J.-P.
P

Keep, The
PAR (GB) 1983 dir. Michael Mann
Wilson, F. P.

Keeper of the Bees
MON (US) 1935 dir. Christy Cabanne
Porter, G. S.

Keeper of the City
VIACOM (US) 1992 dir. Bobby Roth
TV(US)
Di Pego, G.

Keeper of the Flame
MGM (US) 1942 dir. George Cukor
Wylie, I. A. R.

Keepers of Youth
POWERS (GB) 1931
dir. Thomas Bentley
Ridley, A.
P

Keeping Secrets
FINNEGAN/PINCHUCK (US) 1991
dir. John Korty
TV(US)
Somers, S.

Keeping the Promise
ATLANTIS (US) 1997 dir. Sheldon
Larry
TV(US)
Speare, E. G. *Sign of the Beaver, The*

Keep the Aspidistra Flying
OVERSEAS (GB) 1997 dir. Robert
Bierman
US title: Merry War, A
Orwell, G.

Keep the Change
TISCH (US) 1992 dir. Andy Tennant
TV(US)
McGuane, T.

Keep Your Seats Please
ATP (GB) 1936 dir. Monty Banks
Ilf, E. and Petrov, E. *Twelve Chairs, The*
P

Kennedys of Massachusetts, The
ORION TV (US) 1990
dir. Lamont Johnson
TVSe(US)
Goodwin, D. K. *Fitzgeralds and the Kennedys, The*

Kennel Murder Case, The
WAR (US) 1933 dir. Michael Curtiz
van Dine, S. S.

Kent State
INTERPLAN (US) 1981
dir. James Goldstone
TV(US)
Michener, J. A. *Kent State: What Happened and Why*

Kentuckian, The
UA (US) 1955 dir. Burt Lancaster
Holt, F. *Gabriel Horn, The*

Kentucky
FOX (US) 1938 dir. David Butler
Foote, J. T. *Look of Eagles, The*

Kermesse Heroique, La
TOBIS (Fr) 1935 dir. Jacques Feyder
Spaak, C.

Kes
UA (GB) 1969 dir. Ken Loach
Hines, B. *Kestrel for a Knave, A*

Key, The
WAR (US) 1934 dir. Michael Curtiz
Gore-Brown, R.
P

Key, The
COL (GB) 1958 dir. Carol Reed
de Hartog, J. *Stella*

Key, The
ENT (It) 1983 dir. Giovanni Tinto Brass
Tanizaki, J.

Key Exchange
FOX (US) 1985 dir. Barnet Kellman
Wade, K.
P

Key Largo
WAR (US) 1948 dir. John Huston
Anderson, M.
P

Keys of the Kingdom, The
FOX (US) 1944 dir. John M. Stahl
Cronin, A. J.

Keys to Tulsa
POLYGRAM (US) 1997 dir. Leslie Grief
Berkey, B. F.

Key to Rebecca, The
TAFT (US) 1985 dir. David Hemmings
TVSe(US)
Follett, K.

Khartoum
UA (GB) 1966 dir. Basil Dearden
Caillou, A.

Kid for Two Farthings, A
LF (GB) 1955 dir. Carol Reed
Mankowitz, W.

Kid Galahad
WAR (US) 1937 dir. Michael Curtiz
UA (US) 1962 dir. Phil Karlson
M
Wallace, F.

Kidnapped
FOX (US) 1938 dir. Alfred L. Werker
DISNEY (GB) 1959
dir. Robert Stevenson
RANK (GB) 1971 dir. Delbert Mann
HTV (GB) 1979 dir. Jean Pierre Decourt,
Bob Fuest
TVSe(GB)
HALLMARK (US) 1995 dir. Ivan Passer
TVSe(US)
Ch
Stevenson, R. L.

Kidnapping of the President, The
CROWN (US) 1980
dir. George Mendelink
Templeton, C.

Killdozer
UN TV (US) 1974 dir. Jerry London
TV(US)
Sturgeon, T.

Killer: A Journal of Murder
IXTLAN (US) 1996 dir. Tim Metcalfe
Gaddis, T. E.

Killer Elite, The
UA (US) 1975 dir. Sam Peckinpah
Rostand, R.

Killers, The
UN (US) 1946 dir. Robert Siodmak
UN (US) 1964 dir. Don Siegel
Hemingway, E.

Killers of Kilimanjaro, The
COL (GB) 1959 dir. Richard Thorpe
Hunter, J. A. and Mannix, D. P. *Tales of the African Frontier*

Killing, The
UA (US) 1956 dir. Stanley Kubrick
White, L. *Clean Break*

Killing Affair, A
HEMDALE (US) 1988
dir. David Saperstein
Houston, R. *Monday, Tuesday, Wednesday*

Killing Dad
PALACE (US) 1989 dir. Michael Austin
Quinn, A. *Berg*

Killing in a Small Town
INDIEPROD (US) 1990
dir. Stephen Gyllenhaal
TV(US)
Bloom, J. and Atkinson, J. *Evidence of Love*

Killing Kindness, A
BBC/A&E (GB) 1997 dir. Edward Bennett
TV(GB)

Hill, R.

Killing Mr. Griffin
NBC STUDIOS (US) 1997 dir. Jack Bender
TV(US)

Duncan, L.

Killing of Sister George, The
CINERAMA (US) 1967
dir. Robert Aldrich

Marcus, F.
P

Killings at Badger's Drift, The
YTV/A&E (GB) 1997 dir. Jeremy Silberston
TV(GB)

Graham, C.

Kill Off, The
CABRIOLET (US) 1990
dir. Maggie Greenwald

Thompson, J.

Kim
MGM (US) 1950 dir. Victor Saville
LF (GB) 1984 dir. John Davies
TVSe(GB)

Kipling, R.

Kind Hearts and Coronets
EAL (GB) 1949 dir. Robert Hamer

Horniman, R. *Noblesse Oblige*

Kind Lady
MGM (US) 1935 dir. George B. Seitz
MGM (US) 1951 dir. John Sturges

Chodorov, E.
P

Kind of Alaska, A
CENTRAL (GB) 1984 dir. Kenneth Ives
TV(GB)

Pinter, H.
P

Kind of Loving, A
AA (GB) 1962 dir. John Schlesinger
GRANADA (GB) 1982 dir. Oliver Horsburgh, Gerry Mill, Jeremy Summers
TVSe(GB)

Barstow, S.

Barstow, S. *Watchers on the Shore, The; Rigid True End, The*
(TVSe only)

King and Country
WAR (GB) 1964 dir. Joseph Losey

Hodson, J. L. *Return to the Woods*

Wilson, J. *Hamp*
P

King and I, The
FOX (US) 1956 dir. Walter Lang
M

Landon, M. *Anna and the King of Siam*

Rodgers, R. and Hammerstein II, O.
P

King Creole
PAR (US) 1958 dir. Michael Curtiz

Robbins, H. *Stone for Danny Fisher, A*

King David
PAR (US/GB) 1985
dir. Bruce Beresford

Bible *Samuel I & II; Chronicles I; Psalms of David*

Kingdom Come
FOX (US) 2001 dir. Doug McHenry

Bottrell, D. D. and Jones, J. *Dearly Departed*
P

King in Shadow
BL (Ger) 1961 dir. Harold Braun
Neumann, R. *Queen's Favourite, The*

King Lear
COL (Den/GB) 1970 dir. Peter Brook
GRANADA (GB) 1983
dir. Michael Elliott
TV(GB)
CANNON (US) 1988
dir. Jean-Luc Godard
Shakespeare, W.
P

King of the Damned
GAU (BG) 1935 dir. Walter Forde
Chancellor, J.
P

King of Grizzlies
DISNEY (US) 1970 dir. Ron Kelly
Seton, E. T. *Biography of a Grizzly, The*

King of the Gypsies
PAR (US) 1978 dir. Frank Pierson
Maas, P.

King of the Khyber Rifles
FOX (US) 1954 dir. Henry King
Mundy, T.

King, Queen, Knave
WOLPER (US/Ger) 1972
dir. Jerzy Skolimowski
Nabokov, V.

King Ralph
UN (US) 1991 dir. David S. Ward
Williams, E. *Headlong*

King Rat
COL (US) 1965 dir. Bryan Forbes
Clavell, J.

King Richard and the Crusaders
WAR (US) 1954 dir. David Butler
Scott, Sir W. *Talisman, The*

King Richard II
M. EVANS (US) 1954
dir. George Schaefer
TV(US)
Shakespeare, W.
P

Kings Go Forth
UA (US) 1958 dir. Delmer Daves
Brown, J. D.

King Solomon's Mines
GB (GB) 1937 dir. Robert Stevenson
MGM (US) 1950 dir. Compton Bennett
CANNON (US) 1985
dir. J. Lee Thompson
Haggard, Sir H. R.

King Solomon's Treasure
BARBER ROSE (Can/GB) 1979
dir. Alvin Rakoff
Haggard, Sir H. R. *Alan Quatermain*

King's Row
WAR (US) 1941 dir. Sam Wood
Bellamann, H.

King's Royal
BBC (GB) 1982 dir. Andrew Morgan,
David Reynolds
TVSe(GB)
Quigley, J.

King's Whore, The
J&M (GB) 1990 dir. Axel Corti
Tournier, J. *Jeanne de Luynes, Comtesse de Verne*

Kinoerzaehler, Der
BIOSKOPFILM (Ger) 1993 dir.
Bernhard Sinkel
Hofmann, G.

Kipps
FOX (GB) 1941 dir. Carol Reed
US title: Remarkable Mr Kipps, The
GRANADA (GB) 1960 dir. Stuart
Latham
TVSe(GB)
Wells, H. G.

Kismet
WAR (US) 1930 dir. John Francis Dillon
MGM (US) 1944 dir. William Dieterle
MGM (US) 1955 dir. Vincente Minnelli
M
Knoblock, E.
P

Kiss and Tell
COL (US) 1945 dir. Richard Wallace
Herbert, F. H.
P

Kiss Before Dying, A
UA (US) 1956 dir. Gerd Oswald
UN (US) 1991 dir. James Dearden
Levin, I.

Kissinger and Nixon
PARAGON (US) 1995 dir. Daniel Petrie
TV(US)
Isaacson, W. *Kissinger: A Biography*

Kissing Jessica Stein
FOX (US) 2001 dir. Charles Herman-Wurmfeld
Juergensen, H. and Westfeldt, J.
Lipschtick
P

Kiss Me Deadly
UA (US) 1955 dir. Robert Aldrich
Spillane, M.

Kiss Me Kate
MGM (US) 1953 dir. George Sidney
M
MILBERG (US) 1958 dir. George
Schaefer
TV(US)
Shakespeare, W. *Taming of the Shrew, The*
P
Spewack, S. and Spewack, B.
P

Kiss Me Stupid
UA (US) 1964 dir. Billy Wilder
Bonacci, A. *Oro della Fantasia, L'*
P

Kiss of a Killer
ABC PROD (US) 1993 dir. Larry
Elikann
TV(US)
Yorke, M. *Point of Murder, The*

Kiss of Fire
UN (US) 1955 dir. Joseph M. Newman
Lauritzen, J. *Rose and the Flame, The*

Kiss of the Spider Woman
ISLAND (US/Bra) 1985
dir. Hector Babenco
Puig, M.

Kiss the Blood Off My Hands
UN (US) 1948 dir. Norman Foster
GB title: Blood on my Hands
Butler, G.

Kiss the Boys Goodbye
PAR (US) 1941 dir. Victor Schertzinger
Boothe, C.
P

Kiss the Girls
PAR (US) 1997 dir. Gary Fleder
Patterson, J.

Kiss Them for Me
FOX (US) 1957 dir. Stanley Donen
Wakeman, F. *Shore Leave*

Kiss Tomorrow Goodbye
WAR (US) 1950 dir. Gordon Douglas
McCoy, H.

Kitchen, The
BL (GB) 1961 dir. James Hill
Wesker, A.
P

Kitchen
HARVEST CROWN (HK/Jap) 1996 dir. Ho Yim
Yoshimoto, B.

Kitty
PAR (US) 1945 dir. Mitchell Leisen
Marshall, Mrs. R.

Kitty Foyle
RKO (US) 1940 dir. Sam Wood
Morley, C. D.

Klansman, The
PAR (US) 1974 dir. Terence Young
Huie, W. B.

Klinkevals
NORDISK (Den) 1999 dir. Hans Kristensen
Aamund, J.

Knack, The
UA (GB) 1965 dir. Richard Lester
Jellicoe, A.
P

Knave of Hearts
ABP (GB) 1954 dir. René Clément
US title: Lover Boy
Hemon, L. *M. Ripois and his Nemesis*

Knickerbocker Holiday
UN (US) 1944 dir. Harry Joe Brown
Irving, W. *Father Knickerbocker's History of New York*

Knight in Camelot, A
ROSEMONT (US) 1998 dir. Roger Young
TV(US)
Twain, M. *Connecticut Yankee in King Arthur's Court, A*

Knights of the Round Table
MGM (GB) 1954 dir. Richard Thorpe
Malory, Sir T. *Morte d'Arthur, La*

Knights of the Troubled Order
STUDIO (Pol) 1960
dir. Aleksander Ford
Sienkiewicz, H.

Knight Without Armour
UA (GB) 1937 dir. Jacques Feyder
Hilton, J.

Knockback
BBC (GB) 1985
TV(GB)
Adams, P. and Cooklin, S.

Knock on Any Door
COL (US) 1949 dir. Nicholas Ray
Motley, W.

Knots
CINEGATE (GB) 1975
dir. David I. Munro
Laing, R. D.

Kojak: The Belarus File
UN TV (US) 1985 dir. Robert Markowitz
TV(US)
Loftus, J. *Belarus Secret, The*

Kojak: The Price of Justice
MCA/UN (US) 1987 dir. Alan Metzger
TV(US)
Uhnak, D. *Investigation, The*

Korei
DAIEI STUDIOS (Jap) 2000 dir. Kiyoshi Kurosawa
TV(Jap)
McShane, M. *Séance on a Wet Afternoon*

Kotch
CINERAMA (US) 1971
dir. Jack Lemmon
Topkins, K.

K-PAX
UN (US) 2001 dir. Iain Softley
Brewer, G.

Kramer vs Kramer
COL (US) 1979 dir. Robert Benton
Corman, A.

Kremlin Letter, The
FOX (US) 1970 dir. John Huston
Behn, N.

Kreutzer Sonata, The
FOR (Fr) 1938 dir. Charles Guichard
MOSFILM (USSR) 1987
dir. Mikhail Schweitzer and Sofiya Milkina
Tolstoy, L.

Krippendorf's Tribe
TOUCHSTONE (US) 1998 dir. Todd Holland
Parkin, F.

Kristin Lavransdatter
NORSK (Nor/Swe/Ger) 1995 dir. Liv Ullman
Undset, S.

Kurosufaia
TOHO (Jap) 2000 dir. Shusake Kaneko
Miyabe, M. H.

Laberinto Griego, El
IMPALA (Sp) 1992 dir. Rafael Alcazar

Montalban, M. V.

Laburnum Grove
ABP (GB) 1936 dir. Carol Reed

Priestley, J. B.
P

Lace
LORIMAR (US) 1984 dir. Billy Hale
TVSe(US)

Conran, S.

Lacemaker, The
FRANCE 3 (Fr/It/Ger) 1977
dir. Claude Goretta

Laine, P.

L.A. Confidential
WAR (US) 1997 dir. Curtis Hanson

Ellroy, J.

Laddie
RKO (US) 1935 dir. George Stevens

Porter, G. S.

Ladies and the Champ
DISNEY (US) 2001 dir. Jeff Berry

Hendryx, S. *Last of Jane Austen, The*
P

Ladies Club, The
NEW LINE (US) 1986 dir. A. K. Allen

Black, B. and Bishop, C. *Sisterhood*

Ladies in Love
FOX (US) 1936 dir. Edward H. Griffith

Bus-Fekete, L.
P

Ladies in Retirement
COL (US) 1941 dir. Charles Vidor

Percy, E. and Denham, R.
P

Lady Against the Odds
MGM/UA (US) 1992 dir. Bradford May
TV(US)

Stout, R. *Hand in the Glove*

Lady and the Highwayman, The
GRADE (GB) 1989 dir. John Hough
TV(GB)

Cartland, B. *Cupid Rides Phillion*

Lady and the Monster, The
REP (US) 1944 dir. George Sherman
GB title: Lady and the Doctor, The

Siodmak, C. *Donovan's Brain*

Lady and the Tramp
DISNEY (US) 1955 dir. Hamilton Luske
A, Ch

Greene, W.

Lady Boss
VZ/SERTNER (US) 1992 dir. Charles Jarrott
TVSe(US)

Collins, J.

Lady Chatterley
BBC (GB) 1992 dir. Ken Russell
TVSe(GB)
Lawrence, D. H.

Lady Chatterley's Lover
COL (Fr) 1956 dir. Marc Allégret
CANNON (GB/Fr) 1981
dir. Just Jaeckin
Lawrence, D. H.

Lady Eve, The
PAR (US) 1941 dir. Preston Sturges
Hoffe, M.
P

Lady for a Day
COL (US) 1933 dir. Frank Capra
Runyon, D. *Madame la Gimp*

Lady Forgets, The
HILL (US) 1989 dir. Bradford May
TV(US)
Woolrich, C. *Black Curtain, The*

Lady from Shanghai, The
COL (US) 1948 dir. Orson Welles
King, S. *If I Die Before I Wake*

Lady in Cement
FOX (US) 1968 dir. Gordon Douglas
Albert, M. H.

Lady in the Car with Glasses and a Gun, The
COL (Fr/US) 1969 dir. Anatole Litvak
Japrisot, S.

Lady in the Dark, The
PAR (US) 1944 dir. Mitchell Leisen
Hart, M.
P

Lady in the Lake
MGM (US) 1946
dir. Robert Montgomery
Chandler, R.

Lady in the Morgue
UN (US) 1938 dir. Otis Garrett
GB title: Case of the Missing Blonde, The
Latimer, J.

Lady Killer
WAR (US) 1933 dir. Roy del Ruth
Shaffer, R. K. *Finger Man, The*

Lady L
MGM (Fr/It/US) 1965
dir. Peter Ustinov
Gary, R.

Lady Mislaid, A
ABP (GB) 1958 dir. David Macdonald
Horne, K.
P

Lady of Burlesque
STROMBERG (US) 1943
dir. William Wellman
GB title: Striptease Lady
Lee, G. R. *G-String Murders, The*

Lady of Scandal
MGM (US) 1930 dir. Sidney Franklin
Lonsdale, F. *High Road, The*
P

Lady of the Camellias, The
BBC (GB) 1976 dir. Robert Knights
TVSe(GB)
Dumas fils, A.

Lady of the House
METRO (US) 1978 dir. Ralph Norton,
Vincent Sherman
TV(US)
Stanford, S.

Lady on a Train
UN (US) 1945 dir. Charles David
Charteris, L.

Lady Possessed
REP (US) 1952 dir. William Spier, Roy Kellino

Kellino, P. *Del Palma*

Lady Sings the Blues
PAR (US) 1972 dir. Sidney J. Furie

Holiday, B.

Lady Surrenders, A
UN (US) 1930 dir. John Stahl

Erskine, J. *Sincerity*

Lady to Love, A
MGM (US) 1930 dir. Victor Seastrom

Howard, S. *They Knew What They Wanted*
P

Lady Vanishes, The
MGM (GB) 1938 dir. Alfred Hitchcock
RANK (GB) 1979 dir. Anthony Page

White, E. L. *Wheel Spins, The*

Lady who Wades in the Sea, The
PRESIDENT (Fr) 1991
dir. Laurent Heynemann

Dard, F.

Lady with a Lamp, The
BL (GB) 1951 dir. Herbert Wilcox

Berkeley, R.
P

Laguna Heat
WESTON (US) 1987 dir. Simon Langton
TV(US)

Parker, T. J.

Lair of the White Worm, The
VESTRON (GB) 1988 dir. Ken Russell

Stoker, B.

Lakeboat
PANORAMA ENT. (US/Can) 2000 dir. Joe Mantegna

Mamet, D.
P

Lamarca
MORENA (Bra) 1994 dir. Sergio Rezende

Miranda, E. J. O. *Lamarca Guerilla Captain*

Lamb
CANNON (GB) 1985 dir. Colin Gregg

MacLaverty, B.

Lamp Still Burns, The
TC (GB) 1943 dir. Maurice Elvey

Dickens, M. *One Pair of Feet*

Lancer Spy
FOX (US) 1937 dir. Gregory Ratoff

McKenna, M.

Landfall
AB (GB) 1949 dir. Ken Annakin

Shute, N.

Land Girls
CHANNEL 4 FILMS (GB) 1998 dir. David Leland

Huth, A.

Landlord, The
UA (US) 1970 dir. Hal Ashby

Hunter, K.

Land of Faraway, The
NORD/GORKY (Swe/USSR/Nor) 1988 dir. Vladimir Grammatikov

Lindgren, A. *Mio, My Son*

Landslide
GOLDWYN (US) 1992 dir. Jean-Claude Lord

Bagley, D.

Land that Time Forgot, The
BL (GB) 1974 dir. Kevin Connor
Burroughs, E. R.

Langoliers, The
LAUREL-KING (US) 1995 dir. Tom Holland
TVSe(US)
King, S.

Lanigan's Rabbi
UN TV (US) 1976 dir. Lou Antonio
TV(US)
Kemelman, H. *Friday the Rabbi Slept Late*

Lansky
HBO (US) 1999 dir. John McNaughton
TV(US)
Dan, U., Eisenberg, D. and Landau, E. *Meyer Lansky: Mogul of the Mob*

Lantana
LIONS GATE (Aust) 2000 dir. Ray Lawrence
Bovell, A. *Speaking in Tongues*
P

Lantern Hill
DISNEY (US) 1990 dir. Kevin Sullivan
TV(US)
Montgomery, L. M. *Jane of Lantern Hill*

Lapse of Memory
MAX (Can/Fr) 1992 dir. Patrick Dewolf
Cormier, R. *I Am the Cheese*

Larceny Inc.
WAR (US) 1942 dir. Lloyd Bacon
Perelman, L. and Perelman, S. J. *Night Before Christmas, The*
P

Lark, The
MILBERG (US) 1957
dir. George Schaefer
TV(US)
Anouilh, J.
P

Larry
TOM (US) 1974 dir. William A. Graham
TV(US)
McQueen, Dr. R. *Larry: Case History of a Mistake*

Lash, The
IN (US) 1930 dir. Frank Lloyd
Bartlett, L. V. S. *Adios*

Lassie Come Home
MGM (US) 1943 dir. Fred M. Wilcox
Knight, E. M.

Last Angry Man, The
COL (US) 1959 dir. Daniel Mann
COL (US) 1974 dir. Jerrold Freedman
TV(US)
Green, G.

Last Chance, The
MGM (Switz) 1945
dir. Leopold Lindtberg
Schweizer, R.

Last Contract, The
EURIMAGES (Nor/Swe) 1998 dir. Kjell Sundvall
Grow, J. W.

Last Convertible, The
UN TV (US) 1979 dir. Sidney Hayers, Jo Swerling, Jr., Gus Trikonis
TVSe(US)
Myrer, A.

Last Crop, The
CHANNEL 4 (GB) 1991
dir. Stephen Clayton
TV(GB)
Jolley, E.

Last Dance, The
POLSON (US) 2000 dir. Kevin Dowling
TV(US)
Cope, T. F. *Shift, The*

Last Days of Patton, The
ENT PAR (US) 1986 dir. Delbert Mann
TV(US)
Farago, L.

Last Days of Pompeii, The
RKO (US) 1935 dir. Merian C. Cooper,
Ernest Schoedsack
COL (US) 1984 dir. Peter Hunt
TVSe(US)
Lytton, 1st Baron

Last Debate, The
SHOWTIME (US) 2000 dir. John
Badham
TV(US)
Lehrer, J.

Last Detail, The
COL (US) 1973 dir. Hal Ashby
Ponicsan, D.

Last Don, The
KON-SAN (US) 1997 dir. Graeme
Clifford
TVSe(US)
Puzo, M.

Last Embrace
UA (US) 1979 dir. Jonathan Demme
Bloom, M. T. *13th Man, The*

Last Emperor, The
NKL (China) 1988 dir. Li Han Hsiang
Li Shu Xian *Pu Yi and I; Pu Yi's Later
Life; Pu Yi's Former Life*

Last Exit to Brooklyn
GUILD (Ger) 1989 dir. Ulrich Edel
Selby, Jr., H.

Last Flight, The
WAR (US) 1931 dir. William Dieterle
Saunders, J. M. *Single Lady*

Last Giraffe, The
WESTFALL (US) 1979
dir. Jack Couffer
TV(US)
Leslie-Melville, J. and Leslie-Melville,
B. *Raising Daisy Rothschild*

Last Good Time, The
GOLDWYN (US) 1994 dir. Bob Balaban
Bausch, R.

Last Grenade, The
CINERAMA (GB) 1969
dir. Gordon Flemyng
Sherlock, J. *Ordeal of Major Grigsby, The*

Last Hard Man, The
FOX (US) 1976
dir. Andrew V. McLaglen
Garfield, B. *Gun Down*

Last Hit, The
MTE UNIVERSAL (US) 1993 dir. Jan
Egelson
TV(US)
Ruell, P. *Long Kill, The*

Last Hunt, The
MGM (US) 1956 dir. Richard Brooks
Lott, M.

Last Hurrah, The
COL (US) 1958 dir. John Ford
COL (US) 1977 dir. Vincent Sherman
TV(US)
O'Connor, E.

Last Innocent Man, The
HBO (US) 1987 dir. Roger Spottiswoode
TV(US)
Margolin, P. M.

Last Man on Earth, The
AIP (US/It) 1964 dir. Sidney Salkow

Matheson, R. *I Am Legend*

Last Man to Hang?, The
COL (GB) 1956 dir. Terence Fisher

Bullett, G. *Jury, The*

Last of Mrs Cheyney, The
MGM (US) 1929 dir. Sidney Franklin
MGM (US) 1937
dir. Richard Boleslawski

Lonsdale, F.
P

Last of Philip Banter, The
CINEVISITA (Sp) 1988
dir. Herve Hachuel

Franklin, J.

Last of the Belles
TITUS (US) 1974 dir. George Schlatter
TV(US)

Fitzgerald, F. S.

Last of the High Kings
PARALLEL (Ire/UK) 1996 dir. David
Keating

MacAnna, F.

Last of the Mohicans, The
UA (US) 1936 dir. George B. Seitz
BBC (GB) 1971 dir. David Maloney
TVSe(GB)
SCHICK SUNN (US) 1977
dir. James L. Conway
MORGAN CREEK (US) 1992 dir.
Michael Mann
TV(US)

Cooper, J. F.

Last of the Redmen
COL (US) 1947 dir. George Sherman

Cooper, J. F. *Last of the Mohicans, The*

Last of the Red Hot Lovers
PAR (US) 1972 dir. Gene Saks

Simon, N.
P

Last Orders
SCALA (GB/Ger) 2001 dir. Fred
Schepisi

Swift, G.

Last Page, The
EXCL (GB) 1952 dir. Terence Fisher

Chase, J. H.
P

Last Picture Show, The
COL (US) 1971 dir. Peter Bogdanovich

McMurtry, L.

Last Place on Earth, The
CENTRAL (GB) 1985
dir. Ferdinand Fairfax
TVSe(GB)

Huntford, R. *Scott and Amundsen*

Last Prostitute, The
BBK (US) 1991 dir. Lou Antonio
TV(US)

Borden, W. *Last Prostitute who took Pride
in her Work, The*
P

Last Safari, The
PAR (GB) 1967 dir. Henry Hathaway

Hanley, G. *Gilligan's Last Elephant*

Last Seance, The
GRANADA (GB) 1987 dir. June
Wyndham-Davies
TV(GB)

Christie, A. *Hound of Hell, The*

Last Seen Wearing
CENTRAL (GB) 1989
dir. Edward Bennett
TV(GB)

Dexter, C.

Last September, The
BRIT SCREEN (GB/Fr/Ire) 1999 dir.
Deborah Warner
Bowen, E.

Last Shot you Hear, The
FOX (GB) 1970 dir. Gordon Hessler
Fairchild, W. *Sound of Murder, The*
P

Last Stand at Saber River
TURNER/BRANDMAN (US) 1997 dir.
Dick Lowry
TV(US)
Leonard, E.

Last Summer
FOX (US) 1969 dir. Frank Perry
Hunter, E.

Last Sunset, The
UI (US) 1961 dir. Robert Aldrich
Rigsby, H. *Showdown at Crazy Horse*

Last Temptation of Christ, The
UN (US) 1988 dir. Martin Scorsese
Kazantzakis, N.

Last Time I Saw Paris, The
MGM (US) 1954 dir. Richard Brooks
Fitzgerald, F. S. *Babylon Revisited*

Last To Go, The
INTERSCOPE (US) 1991
dir. John Erman
TV(US)
Cooper, R. R.

Last Tycoon, The
PAR (US) 1976 dir. Elia Kazan
Fitzgerald, F. S.

Last Unicorn, The
SCHICK SUNN (US) 1982
dir. Jules Bass, Arthur Rankin, Jr.
A
Beagle, P. S.

Last Valley, The
CINERAMA (GB) 1970
dir. James Clavell
Pick, J. B.

Last Warning, The
UN (US) 1938 dir. Albert S. Rogell
Latimer, J. *Dead Don't Care, The*

Last Wish
GROSS/BAR (US) 1992 dir. Jeff
Bleckner
TV(US)
Rollin, B.

Last Yellow, The
SCALA (GB) 1999 dir. Julian Farino
Tucker, P.
P

Late Call
BBC (GB) 1975 dir. Philip Dudley
TVSe(GB)
Wilson, A.

Late Edwina Black, The
GFD (GB) 1951 dir. Maurice Elvey
Dinner, W. and Morum, W.
P

Late George Apley, The
FOX (US) 1946
dir. Joseph L. Mankiewicz
Marquand, J. P. *Within the Tides*

Late Great Planet Earth, The
ENT (US) 1979 dir. Robert Amram
Lindsay, H. and Carlson, C. C.

Late Shift, The
HBO (US) 1996 dir. Betty Thomas
TV(US)
Carter, B.

Latin Boys Go To Hell
STRAND (US) 1997 dir. Ela Troyano
Salas, A.

Laughing Anne
REP (GB) 1953 dir. Herbert Wilcox
Conrad, J. *Within the Tides*

Laughing Boy
MGM (US) 1934 dir. W. S. Van Dyke
LaFarge, O.

Laughing Policeman, The
TCF (US) 1973 dir. Stuart Rosenberg
GB title: Investigation of Murder, An
Sjowall, M. and Wahloo, P.

Laughter in the Dark
UA (GB/Fr) 1969 dir. Tony Richardson
Nabokov, V.

Laughter on the 23rd Floor
SHOWTIME (US) 2000 dir. Richard
Benjamin
TV(US)
Simon, N.
P

Laura
FOX (US) 1944 dir. Otto Preminger
Caspary, V.

Lavoura Arcaica
VIDEO (Bra) 2001 dir. Luiz Fernando
Carvalho
Nassar, R.

Law and Disorder
BL (GB) 1957 dir. Charles Crichton
Roberts, D. *Smuggler's Circuit*

Law and Order
UN (US) 1932 dir. Edward L. Cahn
Burnett, W. R. *Saint Johnson*

Law and Order
PAR (US) 1976 dir. Marvin J. Chomsky
TV(US)
Uhnak, D.

Law and the Lady, The
MGM (US) 1951 dir. Edwin H. Knopf
Lonsdale, F. *Last of Mrs. Cheyney, The*
P

L.A. Without a Map
EUROAM (Fr/GB) 1999 dir. Mika
Kaurismaki
Rayner, R.

Lawless Street, A
COL (US) 1955 dir. Joseph H. Lewis
Ward, B. *Marshal of Medicine Bend, The*

Law of Enclosures, The
ALLIANCE (Can) 2000 dir. John
Greyson
Peck, D.

Law of the Tropics
WAR (US) 1941 dir. Ray Enright
Hobart, A. T. *Oil for the Lamps of China*

Lawrence of Arabia
COL/BL (GB/US) 1962 dir. David Lean
Lawrence, T. E. *Seven Pillars of Wisdom*

Laxdale Hall
ABP (GB) 1952 dir. John Eldridge
US title: Scotch on the Rocks
Linklater, E.

League of Frightened Men, The
COL (US) 1937 dir. Alfred E. Green
Stout, R.

League of Gentlemen, The
RANK (GB) 1960 dir. Basil Dearden
Boland, J.

Learning Tree, The
WAR (US) 1969 dir. Gordon Parks
Parks, G.

Lease of Life
EAL (GB) 1954 dir. Charles Frend
Baker, F.

Leather Boys, The
BL (GB) 1963 dir. Sidney J. Furie
George, E.

Leathernecking
RKO (US) 1930 dir. Edward Cline
GB title: Present Arms
M
Fields, H., Rodgers, R. and Hart, L.
Present Arms
P

Leave Her to Heaven
FOX (US) 1945 dir. John M. Stahl
Williams, B. A.

Leaving Las Vegas
LUMIERE (US) 1995 dir. Mike Figgis
O'Brien, J.

Lectrice, La
ORION (Fr) 1989 dir. Michel Deville
Jean, R.

Left Hand of God, The
FOX (US) 1955 dir. Edward Dmytryk
Barrett, W. E.

Left Luggage
GREYSTONE (Bel/Neth/US) 1997 dir.
Jeroen Krabbe
Friedman, C. *Shovel and the Loom, The*

Legacy, A
BBC (GB) 1975 dir. Derek Martinus
TVSe(GB)
Bedford, S.

**Legacy of Sin: The William Coit
Story**
CITADEL ENT (US) 1995 dir. Steven
Schachter
TV(US)
Singular, S. *Charmed to Death*

Legally Blond
MGM (US) 2001 dir. Robert Luketic
Brown, A.

Legend of Bagger Vance, The
FOX (US) 2000 dir. Robert Redford
Pressfield, S.

Legend of Hell House, The
FOX (GB) 1973 dir. John Hough
Matheson, R. *Hell House*

Legend of Lobo, The
DISNEY (US) 1962 dir. James Algar
Ch
Seton, E. T. *Biography of a Grizzly and
Other Animal Stories, The*

Legend of Sleepy Hollow, The
SCHICK SUNN (US) 1980
dir. Henning Schellerup
TV(US)
Irving, W.

Legend of Suram Fortress, The
GRUZIA (USSR) 1985
dir. Sergei Paradjanov
Chonkadze, D.

Legend of the Holy Drinker
ART EYE (It) 1989 dir. Ermanno Olnu
Roth, J.

Legend of the Lost Tomb
TRINITY (US) 1996 dir. Jonathan
Winfrey
TV(US)
Meyers, W. D. *Tales of a Dead King*

Legend of the Mummy
UNAPIX (US) 1997 dir. Jeffrey Obrow
Stoker, B. *Jewel of the Seven Stars, The*

Legend of Walks Far Woman, The
EMI (US) 1982 dir. Mel Damski
TV(US)
Stuart, C. *Walks Far Woman*

Legends of the Fall
TRISTAR (US) 1994 dir. Edward Zwick
Harrison, J.

Lek
RCV (Neth) 2000 dir. Jean van de Velde
van Daalen, J. *Sans Rancune*

Lemon Drop Kid, The
PAR (US) 1951 dir. Sidney Lanfield
Runyon, D.

Lena: My 100 Children
GREENWALD (US) 1987 dir. Ed Sherin
TV(US)
Kuchler-Silberman, L. *One Hundred Children*

Lenny
UA (US) 1974 dir. Bob Fosse
Barry, J.
P

Leona Helmsley: The Queen of Mean
FRIES (US) 1990 dir. Richard Michaels
TV(US)
Pierson, R. *Queen of Mean, The*

Léon Morin, Priest
ROME-PARIS (Fr/It) 1961
dir. Jean-Pierre Melville
Beck, B.

Leontyne
LEONTYNE/ITV (GB) 1990
dir. Richard Goodwin
TV(GB)
Goodwin, R.

Leopard, The
FOX (US/It) 1963 dir. Luchino Visconti
de Lampedusa, G.

Leopard in the Snow
ANGLO-CAN (GB/Can) 1977
dir. Gerry O'Hara
Mather, A.

Leopard Man, The
RKO (US) 1943 dir. Jacques Tourneur
Woolrich, C. *Black Alibi*

Leo und Claire
ODEON (Ger) 2001 dir. Joseph Vilsmaier
Kohn, C. *Jude und das Madchen, Der*

Les Misérables
UA (US) 1935 dir. Richard Boleslawski
FOX (US) 1952 dir. Lewis Milestone
ITC (GB) 1978 dir. Glenn Jordan
TRISTAR (US/GB/Ger) 1998 dir. Bille August
DD/FOX FAMILY (Fr/US) 2000 dir. Josee Dayan
TVSe(Fr/US)
Hugo, V.

Lesson Before Dying, A
HBO (US) 1999 dir. Joseph Sargent
TV(US)
Gaines, E. J.

Less than Zero
FOX (US) 1987 dir. Marek Kanievska
Ellis, B. E.

Let It Ride
PAR (US) 1989 dir. Joe Pytka
Cronley, J. *Good Vibes*

Let Me Call You Sweetheart
GROSSO-JACOB (US) 1997 dir. Bill Corcoran
TV(US)
Clark, M. H.

Let No Man Write My Epitaph
COL (US) 1960 dir. Philip Leacock
Motley, W.

Let's Be Happy
ABP (GB) 1957 dir. Henry Levin
M
Stuart, A. *Jeannie*
P

Let's Do It Again
COL (US) 1953 dir. Alexander Hall
M
Richman, A. *Not so Long Ago*
P

Let's Face It
PAR (US) 1943 dir. Sidney Lanfield
Mitchell, N. and Medcraft, R. *Cradle Snatchers*
P

Let's Kill Uncle
UI (US) 1966 dir. William Castle
O'Grady, R.

Let the People Sing
BN (GB) 1942 dir. John Baxter
Priestley, J. B.

Letter, The
PAR (US) 1929 dir. Jean de Limur
WAR (US) 1940 dir. William Wyler
WAR (US) 1982 dir. John Erman
TV(US)
Maugham, W. S.
P

Letter from an Unknown Woman
UI (US) 1948 dir. Max Ophuls
Zweig, S.

Letters from the Park
RTVE (Cuba) 1988
dir. Tomas Guttierez Alea
Marquez, G. G. *Love in the Time of Cholera*

Letter to Three Wives, A
FOX (US) 1948
dir. Joseph L. Mankiewicz
FOX (US) 1985 dir. Larry Elikann
TV(US)
Klempner, J. *Letter to Five Wives*

Letting Go
ITC (US) 1985 dir. Jack Bender
TV(US)
Wanderer, Dr. Z. and Cabot, T.

Letty Lynton
MGM (US) 1932 dir. Clarence Brown
Lowndes, M. B.

Liaisons Dangereuses, Les
MARCEAU (Fr) 1959 dir. Roger Vadim
de Laclos, P.

Libel
MGM (GB) 1959 dir. Anthony Asquith
Wooll, E.
P

Liberation of Lord Byron Jones, The
COL (US) 1970 dir. William Wyler
Ford, J. H.

Libertine, Le
STUDIO CANAL+ (Fr) 2000 dir.
Gabriel Aghion
Schmitt, E.-E.
P

Lie, The
SELVAGGIA (It) 1985
dir. Giovanni Soldati
Moravia, A. *Attention, L'*

Liebelei
ELITE (Fr) 1932 dir. Max Ophuls
Schnitzler, A.
P

Lie Down With Lions
HANNIBAL (US) 1994 dir. Jim
Goddard
TV(US)
Follett, K.

Lies My Father Told Me
COL (Can) 1975 dir. Jan Kadar
Allan, N.

Lies of the Twins
MCA TV (US) 1991 dir. Tim Hunter
TV(US)
Oates, J. C.

Life
ROUGH TRADE (Aust) 1996 dir.
Lawrence Johnston
Brumpton, J. *Containment*
P

Life and Adventures of Nicholas Nickleby, The
PRIMETIME (GB) 1984
dir. Jim Goddard
TVSe(GB)
COMPANY TV (GB) 2001 dir. Stephen
Whittaker
TV(GB)
Dickens, C. *Nicholas Nickleby*

Life and Extraordinary Adventures of Private Ivan Chonkin, The
PORTOBELLO (Czech/GB/Fr) 1995
dir. Jiri Menzel
Voinovich, V.

Life and Loves of a She-Devil, The
BBC (GB) 1986 dir. Philip Saville
TVSe(GB)
Weldon, F.

Life and Times of Henry Pratt, The
GRANADA (GB) 1992 dir. Adrian
Shergold
TVSe(GB)
Nobbs, D.

Life Begins
WAR (US) 1932 dir. James Flood
GB title: Dream of Life
Axelson, M. M.
P

Life Begins at Eight Thirty
FOX (US) 1942 dir. Irving Pichel
GB title: Light of Heart, The
Williams, E. *Light of Heart, The*
P

Lifeforce
CANNON (US) 1985 dir. Tobe Hooper
Wilson, C. *Space Vampires*

Lifeforce Experiment, The
FILMLINE (UK/Can) 1994 dir. Piers
Haggard
TV(UK/Can)
Du Maurier, D. *Breakthrough, The*

Life for Ruth
RANK (GB) 1962 dir. Basil Dearden
US title: Condemned to Life
Green, J.
P

Life in the Theatre, A
BEACON (US) 1993 dir. Gregory
Mosher
TV(US)
Mamet, D.
P

Lifeline
USA NETWORK (US) 1996 dir. Fred
Gerber
TV(US)
Hopkins, R. *Cross Currents*

Life of Jimmy Dolan, The
WAR (US) 1933 dir. Archie Mayo
GB title: Kid's Last Fight, The
Millhauser, B. and Dix, B. M.
P

Life of Stuff, The
PRAIRIE (GB) 1997 dir. Simon Donald
Donald, S.
P

Life on a String
PBC (Ger/GB/China) 1991
dir. Chen Kaige
Tiesheng, S.

Life with Father
WAR (US) 1947 dir. Michael Curtiz
Day, C.
Lindsay, H. and Crouse, R.
P

Life with Judy Garland: Me and My Shadows
ALLIANCE (US/Can) 2001 dir. Robert Allan Ackerman
TVSe(US/Can)
Luft, L. *Me and My Shadows: A Memoir*

Lift to the Scaffold
NEF (Fr) 1957 dir. Louis Malle
Calef, N.

Light at the Edge of the World, The
MGM (US/Sp) 1971
dir. Kevin Billington
Verne, J. *Lighthouse at the End of the World*

Light in the Forest, The
DISNEY (US) 1958
dir. Herschel Daugherty
Richter, C.

Light in the Piazza, The
MGM (GB) 1962 dir. Guy Green
Spencer, E.

Lightnin'
FOX (US) 1930 dir. Henry King
Bacon, F. and Smith, W.
P

Lightning Strikes Twice
WAR (US) 1951 dir. King Vidor
Echard, M. *Dark Fantastic*

Lightship, The
WAR (US) 1985 dir. Jerzy Skolimowski
Lenz, S. *Das Feuerschiff*

Light That Failed, The
PAR (US) 1939 dir. William Wellman
Kipling, R.

Light up the Sky
BL (GB) 1960 dir. Lewis Gilbert
Storey, R. *Touch it Light*
P

Light Years
MIRAMAX (Fr) 1988 dir. René Laloux
A
Andrevan, J.-P. *Robots Against Gandahar*

Light Years Away
NEW YORKER (Fr) 1932
dir. Alain Tanner
Odier, D. *Voie Sauvage, La*

Like a Bride
IMCINE (Mex) 1993 dir. Guita Schyfter
Nissan, R.

Like Mom, Like Me
CBS ENT (US) 1978
dir. Michael Pressman
TV(US)
Schwartz, S. *Like Mother Like Me*

Like Mother, Like Son: The Strange Story of Sante and Kenny Kimes
CBS TV (US) 2001 dir. Arthur Allan Seidelman
TV(US)
Havill, A. *Mother, the Son and the Socialite, The*

Like Normal People
FOX TV (US) 1979 dir. Harvey Hart
TV(US)
Meyers, R.

Like Water For Chocolate
CINEVISTA (Mex) 1992 dir. Alfonso Arau
Esquivel, L.

L'il Abner
PAR (US) 1959 dir. Melvin Frank
M
Mercer, J., dePaul, G., Panama, N. and Frank, M.
P

Lilacs in The Spring
REP (GB) 1954 dir. Herbert Wilcox
US title: Let's Make Up
Purcell, H. *Glorious Days, The*
P

Lili
MGM (US) 1952 dir. Charles Walters
Gallico, P.

Lilian's Story
MOVIECO (Aust) 1996 dir. Jerzy Domaradzki
Grenville, K.

Lilies
ALLIANCE (Can) 1996 dir. John Greyson
Bouchard, M. M. *Feuillets ou la Répétition d'un Drame Romantique, Les*
P

Lili Marleen
ROXY (Ger) 1980 dir. Rainer Werner Fassbinder
Anderson, L. *Sky has Many Colours, The*

Lilies of the Field, The
UA (US) 1963 dir. Ralph Nelson
Barrett, W. E.

Liliom
FOX (US) 1930 dir. Frank Borzage
Molnar, F.
P

Lilith
COL (US) 1964 dir. Robert Rossen
Salamanca, J. R.

Lily Dale
HALLMARK (US) 1996 dir. Peter Masterson
TV(US)
Foote, H.
P

Limbo
UN (US) 1972 dir. Mark Robson
Silver, J.

Limbo Connection, The
THAMES (GB) 1983 dir. Robert Tronson
TVSe(GB)
Quinn, D.

Limbo Line, The
MONARCH (GB) 1968 dir. Samuel Gallen
Canning, V.

Limited Edition
FRANCE 3 (Fr) 1996 dir. Bernard Rapp
Fiechter, J.-J. *Tiré a Part*

Linda
UN TV (US) 1973 dir. Jack Smight
TV(US)
WIL COURT (US) 1993 dir. Nathaniel
Gutman
TV(US)
MacDonald, J. D.

Linda McCartney Story, The
COL TRISTAR (US) 2000 dir. Armand
Mastroianni
TV(US)
Fields, D. *Linda McCartney: A Portrait*

Lion, The
FOX (GB) 1962 dir. Jack Cardiff
Kessel, J.

Lionheart
CFF (GB) 1968 dir. Michael Forlong
Fullerton, A.

Lion is in the Streets, A
WAR (US) 1953 dir. Raoul Walsh
Langley, A. L.

Lion in Winter, The
AVCO (GB) 1968 dir. Anthony Harvey
Goldman, J.
P

Lion, the Witch and the Wardrobe, The
ITV (US/GB) 1978 dir. Bill Melendez
A, Ch, TV(GB/US)
Lewis, C. S.

Liquidator, The
MGM (GB) 1965 dir. Jack Cardiff
Gardner, J.

Lisa
STUDIO CANAL+ (Fr) 2001 dir. Pierre
Grimblat
Cauvin, P. *Theatre Dans la Nuit*

Lisa, Bright and Dark
BANNER (US) 1973 dir. Jeannot Szwarc
Neufeld, J.

Lisbon Story, The
BN (GB) 1946 dir. Paul Stein
M
Purcell, H. and Parr-Davies, H.
P

List of Adrian Messenger, The
UI (US) 1963 dir. John Huston
MacDonald, P.

Little Apocalypse, The
K.G. (Fr) 1993 dir. Costa-Gavras
Konwicki, T.

Little Ark, The
FOX (US) 1971 dir. James B. Clark
de Hartog, J.

Little Big Man
CIN CEN (US) 1970 dir. Arthur Penn
Berger, T.

Little Blond Death
VER NED (Neth) 1994 dir. Jean van de
Velde
Buch, B. *Kleine Blonde Dood, De*

Little Boy Lost
PAR (US) 1953 dir. George Seaton
Laski, M.

Little Caesar
WAR (US) 1930 dir. Mervyn LeRoy
Burnett, W. R.

Little Colonel
FOX (US) 1935 dir. David Butler
Johnson, A. F.

Little Dorrit
CANNON (GB) 1988
dir. Christine Edzard

Dickens, C.

Little Drummer Girl, The
WAR (US) 1984 dir. George Roy Hill

Le Carré, J.

Little Farm, The
GRANADA (GB) 1973 dir. Silvio
Narizzano
TV(GB)

Bates, H. E.

Little Foxes, The
RKO (US) 1941 dir. William Wyler
MILBERG (US) 1956
dir. George Schaefer
TV(US)

Hellman, L. F.
P

Little Game, A
UN TV (US) 1971 dir. Paul Wendkos
TV(US)

Farrington, F.

Little Girl Fly Away
LONGBOW (US) 1998 dir. Peter Levin
TV(US)

Stone, G.

Little Girls in Pretty Boxes
ABC PROD (US) 1997 dir. Christopher
Leitch
TV(US)

Ryan, J.

Little Girl Who Lives Down The Lane, The
RANK (US/Fr/Can) 1976
dir. Nicolas Gessner

Koenig, L.

Little Gloria ... Happy at Last
METRO (US) 1983 dir. Waris Hussein
TVSe(US)

Goldsmith, B.

Little House on the Prairie
NBC ENT (US) 1974
dir. Michael Landon
TV(US)

Wilder, L. I.

Little Hut, The
MGM (US) 1957 dir. Mark Robson

Roussin, A. and Mitford, N.
P

Little Kidnappers, The
DISNEY CH (US) 1990 dir. Don Shebib
Ch, TV(US)

Paterson, N. *Kidnappers, The*

Little Lord Fauntleroy
UA (US) 1936 dir. John Cromwell
BBC (GB) 1976 dir. Paul Annett
TVSe(GB)
ROSEMONT (GB) 1980 dir. Jack Gold
TV(GB)
BBC (GB) 1995 dir. Andrew Morgan
TVSe(GB)

Burnett, F. H.

Little Man, What Now?
UN (US) 1934 dir. Frank Borzage

Fallada, H.

Little Match Girl, The
NBC (US) 1987
dir. Michael Lindsay-Hogg
Ch, TV(US)

Andersen, H. C.

Little Men
RKO (US) 1935 dir. Philip Rosen
TELEFILM (Can) 1998 dir. Rodney
Gibbons

Alcott, L. M.

Little Mermaid, The
DISNEY (US) 1989 dir. John Masker,
Ron Clements
A, Ch

Andersen, H. C.

Little Minister, The
RKO (US) 1934 dir. Richard Wallace

Barrie, Sir J. M.
P

Little Miss Marker
PAR (US) 1934 dir. Alexander Hall
GB title: Girl in Pawn, The
UN (US) 1980 dir. Walter Bernstein

Runyon, D.

Little Murders
FOX (US) 1971 dir. Alan Arkin

Feiffer, J.
P

Little Nellie Kelly
MGM (US) 1940 dir. Norman Taurog
M

Cohan, G. M.
P

Little Night Music, A
S&T (Austria/Ger) 1977
dir. Harold Prince
M

Wheeler, H. and Sondheim, S.
P

Little Odessa
FINE LINE (US) 1994 dir. James Gray

Koenig, J.

Little Old New York
FOX (US) 1940 dir. Henry King

Young, R. J.
P

Little Prince, The
PAR (US) 1974 dir. Stanley Donen
M

Saint-Exupery, A. de

Little Princess, The
FOX (US) 1939 dir. Walter Lang
BBC (GB) 1973 dir. Derek Martinus
TVSe(GB)
LWT (GB) 1987 dir. Carol Wiseman
TVSe(GB)
WAR (US) 1995 dir. Alfonso Cuaron

Burnett, F. H.

Little Riders, The
DISNEY CH (US) 1996 dir. Kevin
Connor
TV(US)

Shemin, M.

Little Romance, A
WAR (US) 1979 dir. George Roy Hill

Cauvin, P. *Blind Love*

Little Shepherd of Kingdom Come, The
FOX (US) 1961
dir. Andrew V. McLaglen

Fox, J.

Little Shop of Horrors
WAR (US) 1986 dir. Frank Oz
M

Ashman, H. and Menken, A.
P

Little Sir Nicholas
BBC (GB) 1989 dir. Andrew Morgan
TVSe(GB)

Jones, C. A.

Littlest Angel, The
OSTERMAN (US) 1969
dir. Walter C. Miller
TV(US)

Tazewell, C.

Littlest Rebel, The
FOX (US) 1935 dir. David Butler

Peple, E.
P

Little Voice
SCALA (GB) 1998 dir. Mark Herman

Cartwright, J. *Rise and Fall of Little Voice, The*
P

Little Women
RKO (US) 1933 dir. George Cukor
MGM (US) 1948 dir. Mervyn LeRoy
BBC (GB) 1970 dir. Paddy Russell
TVSe(GB)
UN (US) 1978 dir. David Lowell Rich
TVSe(US)
COL (US) 1994 dir. Gillian Armstrong

Alcott, L. M.

Little World of Don Camillo, The
LF (Fr/It) 1952 dir. Julien Duvivier

Guareschi, G.

Live Again, Die Again
UN TV (US) 1974 dir. Richard Colla
TV(US)

Sale, D. *Come to Mother*

Live and Let Die
UA (GB) 1973 dir. Guy Hamilton

Fleming, I.

Live Flesh
FRANCE 3 (Fr/Sp) 1997 dir. Pedro Almodovar

Rendell, R.

Live Now, Pay Later
REGAL (GB) 1962 dir. Jay Lewis

Lindsay, J. *All on the Never-Never*

Lives of a Bengal Lancer
PAR (US) 1935 dir. Henry Hathaway

Brown, F. Y. *Bengal Lancer*

Living Daylights, The
MGM (GB) 1987 dir. John Glen

Fleming, I.

Living Free
COL (GB) 1972 dir. Jack Couffer

Adamson, J.

Living Proof: The Hank Williams, Jr. Story
TELECOM (US) 1983 dir. Dick Lowry
TV(US)

Williams, Jr., H. and Bane, M. *Living Proof*

Lizzie
MGM (US) 1957 dir. Hugo Haas

Jackson, S. *Bird's Nest, The*

Lloyd's of London
FOX (US) 1936 dir. Henry King

Kenyon, C.

Lock up your Daughters
COL (GB) 1969 dir. Peter Coe

Miles, B.
P

Lodger, The
TWICKENHAM (GB) 1932
dir. Maurice Elvey
US title: Phantom Fiend, The
FOX (US) 1944 dir. John Brahm

Lowndes, M. B.

Logan's Run
MGM (US) 1976 dir. Michael Anderson

Nolan, W. and Johnson, G.

Lola Montes
GAMMA (Fr/Ger) 1955
dir. Max Ophuls

Saint-Laurent, C.

Lolita
MGM (GB) 1962 dir. Stanley Kubrick
PATHE (US/Fr) 1997 dir. Adrian Lyne

Nabokov, V.

Lolly Madonna XXX
MGM (US) 1973 dir. Richard C. Sarafian
GB title: Lolly-Madonna War, The
Grafton, S.

London Belongs to Me
UN (GB) 1948 dir. Sydney Gilliatt
US title: Dulcimer Street
THAMES (GB) 1977
dir. Raymond Menmuir, Bill Hays
TVSe(GB)
Collins, N.

London by Night
MGM (US) 1937 dir. William Thiele
Scott, W. *Umbrella Man, The*
P

London Embassy, The
THAMES (GB) 1988 dir. David Giles,
Ronald Wilson
TVSe(GB)
Theroux, P.

London Nobody Knows, The
BL (GB) 1969 dir. Norman Cohen
Fletcher, G.

London Suite
HALLMARK (US) 1996 dir. Jay
Sandrich
TV(US)
Simon, N.
P

Loneliness of the Crocodile, The
OLGA (Ger) 2000 dir. Jobst Oetzmann
Kurbjuweit, D. *Einsamkeit der Krokodile, Die*

Loneliness of the Long Distance Runner, The
BL (GB) 1962 dir. Tony Richardson
Sillitoe, A.

Lonely are the Brave
UI (US) 1962 dir. David Miller
Abbey, E. *Brave Cowboy*

Lonely Guy, The
UN (US) 1984 dir. Arthur Hiller
Friedman, B. J. *Lonely Guy's Book of Life, The*

Lonely Hearts
TOHO (Jap) 1982 dir. Kon Ichikawa
McBain, E. *Lady, Lady, I Did It!*

Lonelyhearts
UA (US) 1958 dir. Vincent J. Donehue
West, N. *Miss Lonelyhearts*

Lonely Lady, The
UN (US) 1982 dir. Peter Sasdy
Robbins, H.

Lonely Passion of Judith Hearne, The
ISLAND/HANDMADE (GB) 1987
dir. Jack Clayton
Moore, B.

Lonely Profession, The
UN TV (US) 1979 dir. Douglas Heyes
TV(US)
Heyes, D. *Twelfth of Never, The*

Lonesome Dove
MOTOWN (US) 1989 dir. Simon Wincer
TVSe (US)
McMurtry, L.

Lone Wolf Returns, The
COL (US) 1936
dir. Roy William McNeill
Vance, L. J.

Long and the Short and the Tall, The
WAR (GB) 1960 dir. Leslie Norman
US title: Jungle Fighters

Hall, W.
P

Long Day's Dying, The
PAR (GB) 1968 dir. Peter Collinson

White, A.

Long Day's Journey into Night
FOX (US) 1962 dir. Sidney Lumet
RHOMBUS (Can) 1996 dir. David
Wellington

O'Neill, E.
P

Longest Day, The
FOX (US) 1962 dir. Ken Annakin,
Andrew Marton, Bernhard Wicki

Ryan, C.

Long Goodbye, The
UA (US) 1973 dir. Robert Altman

Chandler, R.

Long Gray Line, The
COL (US) 1955 dir. John Ford

Maher, M. and Campion, N. R.
*Bringing up the Brass: My 55 Years at
West Point*

Long Haul, The
COL (GB) 1957 dir. Ken Hughes

Mills, M.

Long, Hot Summer, The
FOX (US) 1958 dir. Martin Ritt
L. HILL (US) 1985 dir. Stuart Cooper
TVSe(US)

Faulkner, W. *Hamlet, The*

Longitude
GRANADA/A&E (GB) 2000 dir.
Charles Sturridge
TVSe(GB)

Sobel, D.

Long, Long Trailer, The
MGM (US) 1954 dir. Vincente Minnelli

Twiss, C.

Long Lost Father
RICO (US) 1934
dir. Ernest B. Schoedsack

Stern, G. B.

Long Memory, The
GFD (GB) 1953 dir. Robert Hamer

Clewes, H.

Long Road Home
ROSEMONT (US) 1991 dir. John Korty

Taylor, R. B.

Long Ships, The
BL (GB/Yugo) 1963 dir. Jack Cardiff

Bengtsson, F.

Long Summer of George Adams, The
WAR TV (US) 1982 dir. Stuart Margolin
TV(US)

Hill, W.

Long Voyage Home, The
UA (US) 1940 dir. John Ford

O'Neill, E.
P

Long Wait, The
UA (US) 1954 dir. Victor Saville

Spillane, M.

Look at it this Way
BBC (GB) 1992 dir. Gavin Millar
TVSe(GB)

Cartwright, J.

Look Back in Anger
ABP (GB) 1959 dir. Tony Richardson

Osborne, J.
P

Looking for Alibrandi
BEYOND DIST. (Aust) 2000 dir. Kate Woods

Marchetta, M.

Looking for Clancy
BBC (GB) 1975 dir. Bill Hays
TVSe(GB)

Mulally, F.

Looking for Miracles
DISNEY (US/Can) 1989
dir. Kevin Sullivan

Hotchner, A. E.

Looking for Mr Goodbar
PAR (US) 1987 dir. Richard Brooks

Rossner, J.

Looking for Richard
FOX (US) 1996 dir. Al Pacino

Shakespeare, W. *Richard III*
P

Looking Forward
MGM (US) 1933 dir. Clarence Brown

Anthony, C. L. *Service*
P

Looking Glass War, The
COL (GB) 1969 dir. Frank R. Pierson

Le Carré, J.

Loophole
BW (GB) 1981 dir. John Quested

Pollock, R.

Loose Change
UN TV (US) 1978 dir. Jules Irving
TVSe(US)

Davidson, S.

Loot
BL (GB) 1970 dir. Silvio Narizzano

Orton, J.
P

Lord Camber's Ladies
BI (GB) 1932 dir. Benn W. Levy

Vachell, H. A. *Case of Lady Camber, The*
P

Lord Edgware Dies
TWICKENHAM (GB) 1934
dir. Henry Edwards
BBC (GB) 2000 dir. Brian Farnham
TV(GB)

Christie, A.

Lord Jim
COL (GB) 1964 dir. Richard Brooks

Conrad, J.

Lord Love A Duck
UA (US) 1966 dir. George Axelrod

Hine, A.

Lord of the Flies
BL (GB) 1963 dir. Peter Brooke
COL/PALACE (GB/US) 1990
dir. Harry Hook

Golding, W.

Lord of the Rings, The
UA (US) 1978 dir. Ralph Bakshi
A

Tolkien, J. R. R. *Fellowship of the Ring, The; Two Towers, The*

Lord of the Rings, The: The Fellowship of the Ring
NEW LINE (NZ/US) 2001 dir. Peter Jackson

Tolkien, J. R. R.

Lords of Discipline, The
PAR (US) 1983 dir. Franc Roddam

Conroy, P.

Lorna Doone
ATP (GB) 1934 dir. Basil Dean
COL (US) 1951 dir. Phil Karlson
BBC (GB) 1976 dir. Barry Letts
TVSe(GB)
THAMES (GB) 1990 dir. Alistair Grieve
TV(GB)
BBC/A&E (GB/US) 2000 dir. Mike
Barker
TV(GB/US)

Blackmore, R. D.

Loser Takes All
BL (GB) 1956 dir. Ken Annakin

Greene, G.

Losing Isaiah
PAR (US) 1995 dir. Stephen Gyllenhaal

Margolis, S. J.

Loss of Innocence, A
KONIGSBERG (US) 1996 dir. Graeme
Clifford
TV(US)

Sorensen, V. *On This Star*

Lost and Delirious
LIONS GATE (Can) 2001 dir. Lea Pool

Swan, S. *Wives of Bath, The*

Lost Child, The
HALLMARK (US) 2000 dir. Karen
Arthur
TV(US)

Melanson, Y. and Safran, C. *Looking for
Lost Bird: A Jewish Woman discovers her
Navajo Roots*

Lost Command
COL (US) 1966 dir. Mark Robson

Larteguy, J. *Centurions, The*

Lost Continent, The
WAR (GB) 1968 dir. Michael Carreras

Wheatley, D. *Uncharted Seas*

Lost Empire, The
HALLMARK (US/Ger) 2001 dir. Peter
MacDonald
TVSe(US/Ger)

Cheng-en, W. *Journey to the West*

Lost Empires
GRANADA (GB) 1985 dir. Alan Grint
TVSe(GB)

Priestley, J. B.

Lost Honor of Kathryn Beck, The
COMWORLD (US) 1984
dir. Simon Langton
TV(US)

Boll, H. *Lost Honor of Katharina Blum,
The*

Lost Horizon
COL (US) 1937 dir. Frank Capra
COL (US) 1972 dir. Charles Jarrot
M

Hilton, J.

Lost in the Barrens
CBC (US/Can) 1991 dir. Michael Scott
TV(Can/US)

Mowat, F.

Lost in the Barrens II: The Curse of the Viking Grave
ATLANTIS (Can) 1992 dir. Michael J. F.
Scott
TV(Can)

Mowat, F. *Curse of the Viking Grave*

Lost in the Pershing Point Hotel
NORTHERN (US) 2001 dir. Julia Jay
Pierrepont III

Jordan, L.
P

Lost in Yonkers
COL (US) 1993 dir. Martha Coolidge

Simon, N.
P

Lost Lady, A
WAR (US) 1934 dir. Alfred E. Green
Cather, W.

Lost Language of the Cranes, The
BBC (GB) 1991 dir. Nigel Finch
TV(GB)
Leavitt, D.

Lost Man, The
UN (US) 1969 dir. Robert Alan Arthur
Green, F. L.

Lost Moment, The
UN (US) 1947 dir. Martin Gabel
James, H. *Aspern Papers, The*

Lost Patrol
RKO (US) 1934 dir. John Ford
MacDonald, P. *Patrol*

Lost People, The
GFD (GB) 1949 dir. Bernard Knowles
Boland, B. *Cockpit*
P

Lost Weekend, The
PAR (US) 1945 dir. Billy Wilder
Jackson, C.

Lost World, The
FOX (US) 1960 dir. Irwin Allen
Doyle, Sir A. C.

Lost World, The: Jurassic Park
UN (US) 1997 dir. Steven Spielberg
Crichton, M. *Lost World, The*

Louisiana
CINEMAX (US) 1984
dir. Philippe de Broca
TVSe(US)
Denuzière, M. *Louisiane; Fausse-Rivière*

Louisiana Purchase
PAR (US) 1941 dir. Irving Cummings
M
Ryskind, M.
P

Love Affair, A: The Eleanor and Lou Gehrig Story
FRIES (US) 1978 dir. Fielder Cook
TV(US)
Gehrig, E. and Durso, J. *My Luke and I*

Love Always
CINEWEST (US) 1997 dir. Jude Pauline Eberhard
Baker, S. *Finding Signs*

Love Among the Artists
GRANADA (GB) 1979 dir. Howard Baker, Marc Miller
TVSe(GB)
Shaw, G. B.

Love and Betrayal: The Mia Farrow Story
FOX CIRCLE (US) 1995 dir. Karen Arthur
TVSe(US)
Groteke, K. and Rosen, M. *Mia & Woody: Love and Betrayal*
Epstein, E. Z. and Morella, J. *Mia: The Life of Mia Farrow*

Love and Death on Long Island
BRIT SCREEN (Can/GB) 1997 dir. Richard Kwietniowski
Adair, G.

Love and Hate: A Marriage Made in Hell
CBC/BBC (US/Can/GB) 1991 dir. Francis Mankiewicz
TVSe(US/Can/GB)
Siggins, M. *Canadian Tragedy, A*

Love and Human Remains
TELEFILM (Can) 1993 dir. Denys Arcand

Fraser, B. *Unidentified Human Remains and the True Nature of Love*
P

Love and Mr. Lewisham
BBC (GB) 1972 dir. Christopher Barry
TVSe(GB)

Wells, H. G.

Love and Murder
SHAFTESBURY (Can) 2000 dir. George Bloomfield
TV(Can)

Bowen, G. *Murder at the Mendel*

Love and Rage
SCHLEMMER (Ger/Ire) 1999 dir. Cathal Black

Carney, J. *Playboy and the Yellow Lady, The*

Love Ban, The
BL (GB) 1973 dir. Ralph Thomas

Laffan, K. *It's a 2 ft 6 inch above the Ground World*
P

Love Before Breakfast
UN (US) 1936 dir. Walter Lang

Baldwin, F. *Spinster Dinner*

Love Bites
STUDIO CANAL+ (Fr) 2001 dir. Antoine de Caunes

Benacquista, T. *Morsures de l'aube, Les*

Loved One, The
MGM (US) 1965 dir. Tony Richardson

Waugh, E.

Love for Lydia
LWT (GB) 1977 dir. John Glenister, Piers Haggard, Christopher Hodson, Simon Langton, Michael Simpson, Tony Wharmby
TVSe(GB)

Bates, H. E.

Love from a Stranger
UA (GB) 1937 dir. Rowland V. Lee
EL (US) 1947 dir. Richard Whorf
GB title: Stranger Walked In, A

Vosper, F.
P

Love, Hate, Love
SPELLING (US) 1971 dir. George McCowan
TV(US)

Kaufman, L. *Color of Green*

Love, Honor & Obey: The Last Mafia Marriage
CBS ENT (US) 1993 dir. John Patterson
TVSe(US)

Bonnano, R. *Mafia Marriage*

Love in a Cold Climate
THAMES (GB) 1980 dir. Donald McWhinnie
TVSe(GB)
BBC (GB) 2001 dir. Tom Hooper
TVSe(GB)

Mitford, N. *Love in a Cold Climate; Pursuit of Love, The*

Love in Another Town
ADELSON (US) 1997 dir. Lorraine Senna
TV(US)

Bradford, B. T.

Love in Germany, A
TRIUMPH (Ger) 1984 dir. Andrzej Wajda

Hochhuth, R. *Eine Liebe in Deutschland*

Love in the Afternoon
AA (US) 1957 dir. Billy Wilder
Arianet, C.

Love is a Ball
UA (US) 1963 dir. David Swift
GB title: All This and Money Too
Hardy, L. *Grand Duke and Mr. Pimm, The*

Love is a Many Splendoured Thing
FOX (US) 1955 dir. Henry King
Han Suyin *Many Splendoured Thing, A*

Love is Never Silent
M. REES (US) 1985 dir. Joseph Sargent
TV(US)
Greenberg, J. *In This Sign*

Lovejoy
BBC (GB) 1990 dir. Ken Hannam, David Reynolds
TV(GB)
Gash, J.

Love Leads the Way
DISNEY CH (US) 1984
dir. Delbert Mann
TV(US)
Frank, M. and Clark, B. *First Lady of the Seeing Eye*

Love Letter, The
DREAMWORKS (US) 1999 dir. Peter Chan
Schine, C.

Love Letters
PAR (US) 1945 dir. William Dieterle
Massie, C. *Pity My Simplicity*

Love Letters
MARSTAR (US) 1999 dir. Stanley Donen
TV(US)
Gurney, A. R.
P

Love Letters of a Star
UN (US) 1936 dir. Lewis R. Foster
King, R. *Case of the Constant God, The*

Lovely to Look At
MGM (US) 1952 dir. Mervyn LeRoy
M
Miller, A. D. *Gowns by Roberta*

Love Machine, The
COL (US) 1971 dir. Jack Haley, Jr.
Susann, J.

Love Me Tonight
PAR (US) 1932 dir. Rouben Mamoulian
M
Marchand, L. and Armont, P. *Tailor in the Château*
P

Love Nest
FOX (US) 1951 dir. Joseph Newman
Corbett, S.

Love on a Branch Line
BBC (GB) 1994 dir. Martyn Friend
TVSe(GB)
Hadfield, J.

Love on the Dole
BL (GB) 1941 dir. John Baxter
Greenwood, W.

Love Parade, The
PAR (US) 1929 dir. Ernst Lubitsch
M
Xaurof, L. and Chancel, J. *Prince Consort, The*
P

Lover, The
ITV (GB) 1963 dir. Joan Kemp-Welch
TV(GB)
Pinter, H.
P

Lover, The
FILMS A2 (Fr/GB) 1992 dir. Jean-Jacques Annaud
Duras, M.

Lovers of Lisbon, The
EGC (Fr) 1954 dir. Henri Verneuil
Kessel, J.

Lover's Prayer
OVERSEAS (US/GB) 2001 dir. Reverge Anselmo
Turgenev, I. *First Love*
Chekhov, A. *Peasant Women, The*

Love She Sought, The
ORION TV (US) 1990
dir. Joseph Sargent
TV(US)
Hassler, J. *Green Journey*

Love's Labour's Lost
MIRAMAX (GB/Fr) 2000 dir. Kenneth Branagh
M
Shakespeare, W.
P

Loves Music, Loves to Dance
ALLTIME (US) 2001 dir. Mario Azzopardi
TV(US)
Clark, M. H.

Loves of Carmen, The
COL (US) 1948 dir. Charles Vidor
Merimée, P. *Carmen*

Loves of Joanna Godden, The
GFD (GB) 1947 dir. Charles Frend
Smith, S. K. *Joanna Godden*

Love Story
GFD (GB) 1944 dir. Leslie Arliss
US title: Lady Surrenders, A
Drawbell, J. W. *Love and Forget*

Love Story
PAR (US) 1970 dir. Arthur Hiller
Segal, E.

Love Streams
CANNON (US) 1984
dir. John Cassavetes
Allan, T.
P

Love Under Fire
FOX (US) 1937 dir. George Marshall
Hackett, W.
P

Love! Valour! Compassion!
FINE LINE (US) 1997 dir. Joe Mantello
McNally, T.
P

Love Walked In
TRIUMPH (Arg/US) 1997 dir. Juan José Campanella
Feinmann, J. P. *Ni el Tiro del Final*

Love with a Perfect Stranger
ATLANTIC/YTV (US/GB) 1998
dir. Desmond Davis
TV(GB/US)
Wallace, P.

Lovey: A Circle of Children, Part II
TIME-LIFE (US) 1978 dir. Jud Taylor
TV(US)
MacCracken, M. *Lovey, A Very Special Child*

Loving
COL (US) 1970 dir. Irvin Kershner
Ryan, J. M. *Brook Wilson Ltd*

Loving
SAMSON (GB) 1995 dir. Diarmuid Lawrence
TV(GB)
Green, H.

Loving Couples
SANDREW (Swe) 1964
dir. Mai Zetterling

von Krusenstjerna, A. *Froknarna von Pahlen*

Loving Evangeline
CTV (Can) 1998 dir. Timothy Bond
TV(Can)

Howard, L.

Loving Walter
FF (GB) 1986 dir. Stephen Frears

Cook, D. *Winter Doves*

Lovin' Molly
GALA (US) 1974. dir. Sidney Lumet

McMurtry, L. *Leaving Cheyenne*

Loyalties
AUT (GB) 1933 dir. Basil Dean

Galsworthy, J.
P

L-Shaped Room, The
BL (GB) 1962 dir. Bryan Forbes

Banks, L. R.

Lucia
LEX (GB) 1999 dir. Don Boyd

Scott, Sir W. *Bride of Lammermoor, The*

Lucie Aubrac
CNC (Fr) 1997 dir. Claude Berri

Aubrac, L. *Outwitting the Gestapo*

Luck of Ginger Coffey, The
BL (Can/US) 1964 dir. Irvin Kershner

Moore, B.

Luck of the Irish, The
FOX (US) 1948 dir. Henry Koster

Jones, G. P and Jones, C. B. *There was a Little Man*

Lucky/Chances
NBC (US) 1990 dir. Buzz Kulik
TVSe(US)

Collins, J. *Lucky; Chances*

Lucky Jim
BL (GB) 1957 dir. John Boulting

Amis, K.

Lucky Stiff, The
UA (US) 1948 dir. Lewis R. Foster

Rice, C.

Lucy Gallant
PAR (US) 1955 dir. Robert Parrish

Cousins, M. *Life of Lucy Gallant, The*

Luminous Motion
GOOD MACHINE (US) 1998 dir. Bette Gordon

Bradfield, S. *History of Luminous Motion, The*

Lunatic, The
ISLAND PICT (Fr) 1992
dir. Lol Creme

Winkler, A. C.

Lust for Gold
COL (US) 1949 dir. S. Sylvan Simon

Storm, B. *Thunder God's Gold*

Lust for Life
MGM (US) 1956 dir. Vincente Minnelli

Stone, I.

Luther
SEVEN KEYS (GB) 1973 dir. Guy Green

Osborne, J.
P

Luv
COL (US) 1967 dir. Clive Donner

Schisgal, M.
P

Luxury Liner
PAR (US) 1933 dir. Lothar Mendes

Kaus, G.

Luzhin Defence, The
FRANCE 2 (Fr/GB) 2000 dir. Marleen Gorris

Nabokov, V. *Defence, The*

Lydia Bailey
FOX (US) 1952 dir. Jean Negulesco

Roberts, K.

M. Butterfly
GEFFEN (US) 1993 dir. David
Cronenberg

Hwang, D. H.
P

McCabe and Mrs. Miller
WAR (US) 1971 dir. Robert Altman

Naughton, E. *McCabe*

Macabre
ABP (US) 1958 dir. William Castle

Durant, T. *Marble Forest*

MacArthur's Children
ORION (Jap) 1985
dir. Masahiro Shinoda

Alcu, Y.

Macbeth
REP (US) 1948 dir. Orson Welles
M. EVANS (US) 1954
dir. George Schaefer
TV(US)
COMPASS (US) 1960
dir. George Schaefer
TV(US)
COL-WAR (GB) 1971
dir. Roman Polanski
CROMWELL (GB) 1997 dir. Jeremy
Freeston

Shakespeare, W.
P

McGuffin, The
BBC (GB) 1986 dir. Colin Bucksey
TV(GB)

Bowen, J.

Machine, The
FRANCE 2 (Fr) 1994 dir. François
Dupeyron

Belletto, R.

Machine Gunners, The
BBC (GB) 1983 dir. Colin Cant
TVSe(GB)

Westall, R.

Mackenna's Gold
COL (US) 1969 dir. J. Lee Thompson

Henry, W.

McKenzie Break, The
UA (GB) 1970 dir. Lamont Johnson

Shelley, S.

Mackintosh Man, The
COL-WAR (GB) 1973 dir. John Huston

Bagley, D. *Freedom Trap, The*

Macomber Affair, The
UA (US) 1947 dir. Zoltan Korda

Hemingway, E. *Short Happy Life of*
Francis Macomber, The

Mack the Knife
21st CENTURY (US) 1989
dir. Menahem Golan
M

Brecht, B. and Weill, K. *Threepenny*
Opera, The
P

McVicar
BW (GB) 1980 dir. Tom Clegg
McVicar, J. *McVicar, by Himself*
P

Madame Bovary
MGM (US) 1949 dir. Vincente Minnelli
BBC (GB) 1975 dir. Rodney Bennett
TVSe(GB)
GOLDWYN (Fr) 1991
dir. Claude Chabrol
Flaubert, G.

Madame Butterfly
PAR (US) 1932 dir. Marion Gering
Belasco, D. and Long, J. L.
P

Madame Curie
MGM (US) 1943 dir. Mervyn LeRoy
Curie, E.

Madame Curie
BBC (GB) 1984
TV(GB)
Reid, R.

Madame De
FRANCO-LF (Fr/It) 1953
dir. Max Ophuls
US title: Earrings of Madame De, The
de Vilmorin, L.

Madame Sans-Gene
FOX (Fr/It/Sp) 1962
dir. Christian-Jaque
US/GB title: Madame
Sardou, V.
P

Madame Sousatzka
UN (GB) 1988 dir. John Schlesinger
Rubens, B.

Madame X
MGM (US) 1929 dir. John Barrymore
MGM (US) 1937
dir. James K. McGuiness
UN (US) 1965 dir. David Lowell Rich
UN (US) 1981 dir. Robert Ellis Miller
TV(US)
Bisson, A.
P

Madam Kitty
FOX (It/Fr/Ger) 1977
dir. Giovanni Tinto Brass
Norden, P.

Mad Cows
CAPITOL (GB) 1999 dir. Sara Sugarman
Lette, K.

Mad Death, The
BBC (GB) 1983 dir. Robert Young
TVSe(GB)
Slater, N.

Mad Genius, The
WAR (US) 1931 dir. Michael Curtiz
Brown, M. *Idol, The*
P

Madhouse
EMI (GB) 1974 dir. Jim Clark
Hall, A. *Devilday-Madhouse*

Madigan
UI (US) 1968 dir. Don Siegel
Dougherty, R. *Commissioner, The*

Madison Avenue
FOX (US) 1962 dir. Bruce Humberstone
Kirk, J. *Build-up Boys, The*

Mad Love
MGM (US) 1935 dir. Karl Freund
GB title: Hands of Orlac, The
Renard, M. *Hands of Orlac, The*

Madness of King George, The
CHANNEL 4 FILMS (GB) 1994 dir.
Nicholas Hytner

Bennett, A. *Madness of George III, The*
P

Madness of the Heart
TC (GB) 1949 dir. Charles Bennett

Sandstrom, F.

Madonna: Innocence Lost
JAFFE/BRAUNSTEIN (US) 1994 dir.
Bradford May
TV(US)

Andersen, C. *Madonna: Unauthorized*

Madonna of the Seven Moons
GFD (GB) 1944 dir. Arthur Crabtree

Lawrence, M.

Mad Room, The
COL (US) 1969 dir. Bernard Girard

Denham, R. and Percy, E. *Ladies in Retirement*
P

Madwoman of Chaillot, The
WAR (GB) 1969 dir. Bryan Forbes

Girardoux, J.
P

Mafia Princess
GROUP W (US) 1986 dir. Robert Collins
TV(US)

Giancana, A. and Renner, T. C.
P

Magic
FOX (US) 1978
dir. Richard Attenborough

Goldman, W.

Magic Bow, The
GFD (GB) 1946 dir. Bernard Knowles

Komroff, M.

Magic Box, The
BL (GB) 1951 dir. John Boulting

Allister, R. *Friese-Greene*

Magic Christian, The
COMM (GB) 1969 dir. Joseph McGrath

Southern, T.

Magic Fire
REP (US) 1956 dir. William Dieterle

Harding, B.

Magic Flute, The
SWE TV (Swe) 1974
dir. Ingmar Bergman
M, TV(Swe)

Mozart, W. A.

Magician of Lublin, The
RANK (Israel/Ger) 1979
dir. Menahem Golan

Singer, I. B.

Magic Mountain, The
SEITZ (Ger/Fr/It) 1982
dir. Hans Geissendoerfer

Mann, T.

Magic Moments
ATLANTIC/YTV (GB/US)
dir. Lawrence Gordon Clarke
TV(GB/US)

Roberts, N. *This Magic Moment*

Magic Toyshop, The
GRANADA (GB) 1987
dir. David Wheatley
TV(GB)

Carter, A.

Magnificent Ambersons, The
RKO (US) 1942 dir. Orson Welles

Tarkington, B.

Magnificent Obsession
UN (US) 1935 dir. John M. Stahl
UI (US) 1954 dir. Douglas Sirk
Douglas, L. C.

Magnificent Yankee, The
MGM (US) 1950 dir. John Sturges
COMPASS (US) 1965
dir. George Schaefer
TV(US)
Lavery, E.
P

Magus, The
FOX (GB) 1968 dir. Guy Green
Fowles, J.

Mahabharata, The
CHANNEL 4 (GB) 1990
dir. Peter Brook
Carrière, J.-P.
P

Maidens' Trip
BBC (GB) 1977 dir. Moira Armstrong
TVSe(GB)
Smith, E.

Maids, The
ELY LANDAU (GB) 1974
dir. Christopher Miles
Genet, J.
P

Maigret Sets a Trap
JOLLY (Fr) 1957 dir. Jean Delannoy
Simenon, G.

Mains Sales, Les
RIVERS (Fr) 1951 dir. Fernand Rivers
Sartre, J.-P.
P

Major Barbara
PASCAL (GB) 1941 dir. Gabriel Pascal
Shaw, G. B.
P

Majority of One, A
WAR (US) 1961 dir. Mervyn LeRoy
Spiegelgass, L.
P

Make Haste to Live
REP (US) 1954 dir. William A. Seiter
Gordon, M. and Gordon, G.

Make me an Offer
BL (GB) 1954 dir. Cyril Frankel
Mankowitz, W.

Make me a Star
PAR (US) 1932 dir. William Beaudine
Wilson, H. L. *Merton of the Movies*

Make Mine Mink
RANK (GB) 1960 dir. Robert Asher
Coke, P. *Breath of Spring*
P

Make Way for a Lady
RKO (US) 1936 dir. David Burton
Jordan, E. G. *Daddy and I*

Make Way for Tomorrow
PAR (US) 1937 dir. Leo McCarey
Lawrence, J. *Years Are So Long, The*

Making It
FOX (US) 1971 dir. John Erman
Leigh, J. *What Can You Do?*

Makioka Sisters, The
R5/S8 (Jap) 1985 dir. Kon Ichikawa
Tanizaki, J.

Malachi's Cove
PENRITH (GB) 1973
dir. Henry Herbert
US title: Seaweed Children, The
Trollope, A.

Maladie de Sachs, La
STUDIO CANAL+ (Fr) 1999 dir.
Michael Deville
Winckler, M.

Malarek
SVS/TELESCENE (Can) 1989
dir. Roger Cardinal
Malarek, V. *Hey, Malarek*

Malcolm X
40 ACRES (US) 1992 dir. Spike Lee
Haley, A. and Malcolm X *Autobiography of Malcolm X, The*

Male Animal, The
WAR (US) 1942 dir. Elliot Nugent
Thurber, J. and Nugent, E.
P

Malibu
COL (US) 1983 dir. E. W. Swackhamer
TVSe(US)
Murray, W.

Malice Aforethought
BBC (GB) 1979 dir. Cyril Coke
TVSe(GB)
Iles, F.

Malice in Wonderland
ITC (US) 1985 dir. Gus Trikonis
TV(US)
Eells, G. *Hedda and Louella*

Mallens, The
GRANADA (GB) 1979 dir. Richard
Martin, Mary McMurray, Brian Mills
TVSe(GB)
Cookson, C. *Mallen Streak, The*

Malone
ORION (US) 1987 dir. Harley Kokliss
Wingate, W. *Shotgun*

Maltese Falcon, The
WAR (US) 1941 dir. John Huston
Hammett, D.

Mama Flora's Family
AVNET/KERNER (US) 1998 dir. Peter
Werner
TVSe(US)
Haley, A.

Mambo Kings, The
WAR (US) 1992 dir. Arne Glimcher
Hijeulo, O. *Mambo Kings Play Songs of Love, The*

Mame
WAR (US) 1974 dir. Gene Saks
M
Dennis, P. *Auntie Mame*
Lawrence, J., Lee, R. E. and Herman, J.
P

Man, The
PAR (US) 1972 dir. Joseph Sargent
Wallace, I.

Man About the House, A
LF (GB) 1947 dir. Leslie Arliss
Young, F. B. and Perry, J.
P

Man About Town
FOX (US) 1932 dir. John Francis Dillon
Clift, D.

Man and Superman
MILBERG (US) 1956
dir. George Schaefer
TV(US)
Shaw, G. B.
P

Man at the Carlton Tower
AA (GB) 1961 dir. Robert Tronson
Wallace, E. *Man At The Carlton*

Man Called Horse, A
CIN CEN (US) 1970
dir. Elliot Silverstein
Johnson, D. M.

Man Called Intrepid, A
LORIMAR (GB) 1979 dir. Peter Carter
TVSe(GB)
Stevenson, W.

Man Called Noon, The
SCOTIA-BARBER (GB/Sp/It)
1973 dir. Peter Collinson
L'Amour, L.

Man Called Peter, A
FOX (US) 1955 dir. Henry Koster
Marshall, C.

Manchurian Candidate, The
UA (US) 1962 dir. John Frankenheimer
Condon, R.

Man Could Get Killed, A
UN (US) 1966 dir. Ronald Neame
Walker, D. E. *Diamonds are Danger*

Mandingo
PAR (US) 1975 dir. Richard Fleischer
Onstott, K.

Mandy
GFD (GB) 1952
dir. Alexander Mackendrick
US title: Crash of Silence, The
Lewis, H. *Day is Ours, This*

Maneaters are Loose!
MONA BBC (GB) 1984
dir. Timothy Galfos
TV(GB)
Willis, T. *Man-eater*

Man for all Seasons, A
COL (GB) 1966 dir. Fred Zinnemann
AGAMEMNON (US) 1988
dir. Charlton Heston
TV(US)
Bolt, R.
P

Man from Bitter Ridge, The
UN (US) 1955 dir. Jack Arnold
Raine, W. M. *Rawhide Justice*

Man from Dakota, The
MGM (US) 1940 dir. Leslie Fenton
GB title: Arouse and Beware
Kantor, M. *Arouse and Beware*

Man Hunt
FOX (US) 1941 dir. Fritz Lang
Household, G. *Rogue Male*

Manhunt for Claude Dallas
LONDON (US) 1986 dir. Jerry London
TV(US)
Long, J. *Outlaw: The True Story of Claude Dallas*

Manhunter, The
UN (US) 1976 dir. Don Taylor
TV(US)
Miller, W.

Manhunter
CANNON (US) 1986 dir. Michael Mann
Harris, T. *Red Dragon*

Manifesto
CANNON (Yugo) 1988
dir. Dusan Makajevev
Zola, E. *For a Night of Love*

Man I Married, The
TCF (US) 1940 dir. Irving Pichel
Shisgall, O. *Swastika*

Man in Grey, The
GFD (GB) 1943 dir. Leslie Arliss

Smith, Lady E.

Man in Half-Moon Street, The
PAR (US) 1944 dir. Ralph Murphy

Lyndon, B.
P

Man in Possession, The
MGM (US) 1931 dir. Sam Wood

Harwood, H. M.
P

Man Inside, The
COL (GB) 1958 dir. John Gilling

Graber, M. E.

Man in the Attic, The
FOX (US) 1953 dir. Hugo Fregonese

Lowndes, M. B. *Lodger, The*

Man in the Attic, The
ATLANTIS (US) 1995 dir. Graeme Campbell
TV(US)

Winski, N. *Sex and the Criminal Mind*

Man in the Brown Suit, The
WAR TV (US) 1989 dir. Alan Grint
TV(US)

Christie, A.

Man in the Grey Flannel Suit, The
FOX (US) 1956 dir. Nunnally Johnson

Wilson, S.

Man in the Iron Mask, The
UA (US) 1939 dir. James Whale
ITC (US/GB) 1976 dir. Mike Newell
TV(GB/US)
UA (US/GB) 1998 dir. Randall Wallace
INVISIBLE (US) 1998 dir. William Richert

Dumas, A.

Man in the Middle
FOX (GB) 1963 dir. Guy Hamilton

Fast, H. *Winston Affair, The*

Man in the Mirror, The
WARDOUR (GB) 1936
dir. Maurice Elvey

Garrett, W.

Man in the Net, The
UA (US) 1958 dir. Michael Curtiz

Quentin, P.

Man in the Road, The
GN (GB) 1956 dir. Lance Comfort

Armstrong, A. *He was Found in the Road*

Manitou
ENT (US) 1978 dir. William Girdler

Masterton, G.

Mannen pa Balkogen
NORDISK (Swe/Ger) 1993 dir. Daniel Alfredson

Sjowall, M. and Wahloo, P.

Man of Affairs
GAU (GB) 1937 dir. Herbert Mason
US title: His Lordship

Grant, N. *Nelson Touch, The*
P

Man of La Mancha
UA (US) 1972 dir. Arthur Hiller
M

Wasserman, D.

Cervantes, M. de *Don Quixote*
P

Man of Straw
BBC (GB) 1972 dir. Herbert Wise
TVSe(GB)

Mann, H.

Man of the West
UA (US) 1958 dir. Anthony Mann

Brown, W. C. *Border Jumpers, The*

Man on a String

COL (US) 1960 dir. André de Toth
GB title: Confessions of a Counterspy

Morros, B. *My Ten Years as a Counter-Spy*

Man on Fire

TRISTAR (It/Fr) 1987
dir. Elie Chouraqui

Quinnell, A. J.

Manon of the Spring

ORION (Fr) 1987 dir. Claude Berri

Pagnol, M. *Eau des Collines, L'*

Man on the Eiffel Tower, The

BL (US) 1948 dir. Burgess Meredith

Simenon, G. *Battle of Nerves, A*

Man on the Roof, The

SVENSK (Swe) 1976
dir. Bo Widenberg

Sjowall, M. and Wahloo, M.
Abominable Man, The

Manor, The

FALCON (Czech) 1999 dir. Ken Berris

Nigro, D. *Ravenscroft*
P

Manproof

MGM (US) 1937 dir. Richard Thorpe

Lea, F. H. *Four Marys, The*

Man's Castle

COL (US) 1933 dir. Frank Borzage

Hazard, L.
P

Mansfield Park

BBC (GB) 1983 dir. David Giles
TVSe(GB)
MIRAMAX (GB) 1999 dir. Patricia
Rozema

Austen, J.

Manslaughter

PAR (US) 1930 dir. George Abbott

Miller, A. D.

Man to Remember, A

RKO (US) 1938 dir. Garson Kanin

Haviland-Taylor, K. *Failure*

Mantrap

PAR (US) 1961 dir. Edmond O'Brien

Macdonald, J. D. *Taint of the Tiger*

Manuela

BL (GB) 1957 dir. Guy Hamilton
US title: Stowaway Girl

Woods, W.

Man Who Broke 1,000 Chains, The

JOURNEY (US) 1987 dir. Daniel Mann
TV(US)

Burns, V. G.

Man Who Came Back, The

FOX (US) 1930 dir. Raoul Walsh

Goodman, J. E.
P

Man Who Came to Dinner, The

WAR (US) 1941 dir. William Keighley
UN (US) 1972 dir. Buzz Kulik
TV(US)

Kaufman, G. S. and Hart, M.
P

Man Who Captured Eichmann, The

MARGULIES (US) 1996 dir. William A.
Graham
TV(US)

Malkin, P. Z. and Stein, H. *Eichmann in My Hands*

Man Who Could Cheat Death, The
PAR (GB) 1959 dir. Terence Fisher
Lyndon, B. *Man in Half-Moon Street, The*
P

Man Who Could Work Miracles, The
UA (GB) 1936 dir. Lothar Mendes
Wells, H. G.

Man Who Fell to Earth, The
BL (GB) 1976 dir. Nicholas Roeg
MGM/UA (US) 1987 dir. Robert J. Roth
TV(US)
Tevis, W.

Man Who Had Power over Women, The
AVCO (GB) 1970 dir. John Krish
Williams, G.

Man Who Knew Too Little, The
WAR (US) 1997 dir. Jon Amiel
Farrar, R. *Watch That Man*

Man Who Lived at The Ritz, The
HG (US) 1988 dir. Desmond Davis
TVSe(US)
Hotchner, A. E.

Man Who Loved Cat Dancing, The
MGM (US) 1973 dir. Richard Sarafian
Durham, M.

Man Who Loved Redheads, The
BL (GB) 1954 dir. Harold French
Rattigan, T. *Who is Sylvia?*
P

Man Who Mistook His Wife for a Hat, The
CHANNEL 4 (GB) 1988
dir. Christopher Rawlence
TV(GB)
Sacks, O.

Man Who Never Was, The
FOX (GB) 1955 dir. Ronald Neame
Montague, E. E. S.

Man Who Played God, The
WAR (US) 1932 dir. John G. Adolfi
GB title: Silent Voice, The
Goodman, J. E. *Silent Voice, The*
P

Man Who Understood Women
FOX (US) 1959 dir. Nunnally Johnson
Gary, R. *Colours of the Day, The*

Man Who Watched Trains Go By, The
EROS (GB) 1952 dir. Harold French
Simenon, G.

Man Who Would Be King, The
COL (US) 1975 dir. John Huston
Kipling, R.

Man with a Gun
NORTHWOOD (Can) 1995 dir. David Wyles
Rae, H. C. *Shroud Society, The*

Man with Bogart's Face, The
FOX (US) 1980 dir. Robert Day
Fenady, A. J.

Man Within, The
GFD (GB) 1947 dir. Bernard Knowles
US title: Smugglers, The
Greene, G.

Man with my Face, The
UA (US) 1951 dir. Edward J. Montague
Taylor, S. W.

Man Without a Country, The
ROSEMONT (US) 1973
dir. Delbert Mann
TV(US)
Hale, E. E.

Man Without a Face, The
ICON (US) 1993 dir. Mel Gibson
Holland, I.

Man Without a Star, The
UI (US) 1955 dir. King Vidor
Linford, D.

Man with the Golden Arm, The
UA (US) 1955 dir. Otto Preminger
Algren, N.

Man with the Golden Gun, The
UA (GB) 1974 dir. Guy Hamilton
Fleming, I.

Man with the Twisted Lip, The
GN (GB) 1951 dir. Richard M. Grey
Doyle, Sir A. C.

Man with Three Coffins, The
MWL (S. Kor) 1987 dir. Chang Ho Lee
Lee, J. *Wanderer Never Sleeps, Even on the Road, A*

Man with Two Faces, The
WAR (US) 1934 dir. Archie Mayo
Kaufman, G. S. and Woollcott, A. *Dark Tower, The*
P

Man, Woman and Child
PAR (US) 1983 dir. Dick Richards
Segal, E.

Map of the World, A
OVERSEAS (US) 1999 dir. Scott Elliott
Hamilton, J.

Mapp and Lucia
CHANNEL 4 (GB) 1985
dir. Donald McWhinnie
TVSe(GB)
Benson, E. F.
P

Maracaibo
PAR (US) 1958 dir. Cornel Wilde
Silliphant, S.

Marathon Man
PAR (US) 1976 dir. John Schlesinger
Goldman, W.

Marat/Sade
UA (GB) 1966 dir. Peter Brook
Weiss, P.
P

Marauders, The
MGM (US) 1955 dir. Gerald Mayer
Marcus, A.

Marcus-Nelson Murders, The
UN TV (US) 1973 dir. Joseph Sargent
TV(US)
Raab, S. *Justice in the Back Room*

Margaret Bourke-White
TNT (US) 1989 dir. Lawrence Schiller
TV(US)
Goldberg, V.

Margin for Error
FOX (US) 1943 dir. Otto Preminger
Boothe, C.
P

Maria Chapdelaine
SNC (Fr) 1934 dir. Julien Duvivier
ASTRAL (Can/Fr) 1983 dir. Gilles Carle
Hemon, L.

Marianna Ucria
CECCHI (It/Fr) 1997 dir. Roberto
Faenza
Mariani, D.

Marie
MGM/UA (US) 1985
dir. Roger Donaldson
Maas, P. *Marie: A True Story*

Marie Antoinette
MGM (US) 1938 dir. W. S. Van Dyke
Zweig, S.

Marilyn: The Untold Story
SCHILLER (US) 1980 dir. Jack Arnold
TVSe(US)
Mailer, N. *Marilyn*

Marius
PAR (Fr) 1931 dir. Alexander Korda
Pagnol, M.
P

Marjorie Morningstar
WAR (US) 1958 dir. Irving Rapper
Wouk, H.

Mark, The
FOX (GB) 1961 dir. Guy Green
Israel, C. E.

Mark, I Love You
AUBREY (US) 1980
dir. Gonna Hellstrom
TV(US)
Painter, H. W.

Mark of Cain, The
TC (GB) 1948 dir. Brian Desmond Hurst
Shearing, J. *Airing in a Closed Carriage*

Mark of the Renegade
UI (US) 1951 dir. Hugo Fregonese
FOX (US) 1974 dir. Don McDougall
TV(US)
McCulley, J. *Curse of Capistrano, The*

Mark of Zorro, The
FOX (US) 1940 dir. Rouben Mamoulian
McCulley, J. *Curse of Capistrano, The*

Marksman, The
BBC (GB) 1987 dir. Tom Clegg
TVSe(GB)
Rae, H. C.

Mark Twain & Me
CHILMARK (US/Can) dir. Daniel
Petrie
TV(US/Can)
Quick, D. *Enchantment: A Little Girl's
Friendship with Mark Twain*

Markus Og Diana
NORSK (Nor) 1997 dir. Svein
Scharffenberg
Hagerup, K.

Marlowe
MGM (US) 1969 dir. Paul Bogart
Chandler, R. *Little Sister, The*

Marnie
UI (US) 1964 dir. Alfred Hitchcock
Graham, W.

Marooned
COL (US) 1969 dir. John Sturges
Caidin, M.

Marriage Fool, The
GROSS/BAR (US) 1998 dir. Charles
Matthau
TV(US)
Vetere, R.
P

Marriage is a Private Affair
MGM (US) 1944 dir. Robert Z. Leonard
Kelly, J.

Marriage of a Young Stockbroker, The
FOX (US) 1971 dir. Laurence Turman

Webb, C.

Marriage of Convenience, A
CATFISH (US) 1998 dir. James Keach
TV(US)

Bockoven, G.

Marriage of Figaro, The
BBC (GB) 1990 dir. D. Bailey
M, TV(GB)

Beaumarchais, P. A. C. de
P

Mozart, W. A.

Marriage Playground, The
PAR (US) 1929 dir. Lothar Mendes

Wharton, E. *Children, The*

Married Man, A
LWT (GB) 1985 dir. Charles Jarrott
TVSe(GB)

Read, P. P.

Marry the Girl
WAR (US) 1937 dir. William McGann

Hope, E.

Martian Chronicles, The
NBC ENT (US/GB) 1980
dir. Michael Anderson
TVSe(GB/US)

Bradbury, R.

Martians Go Home
TAURUS (US) 1990 dir. David Odell

Brown, F.

Martin Chuzzlewit
BBC (GB) 1994 dir. Pedr James
TVSe(GB)

Dickens, C.

Marty
COL (US) 1955 dir. Delbert Mann

Chayefsky, P.
P

Marvin and Tige
CASTLE HILL (US) 1985
dir. Eric Weston

Glass, F.

Marvin's Room
TRIBECA (US) 1996 dir. Jerry Zaks

McPherson, S.
P

Mary & Tim
HALLMARK (US) 1996 dir. Glenn
Jordan
TV(US)

McCullough, C. *Tim*

Mary, Mary
WAR (US) 1963 dir. Mervyn LeRoy

Kerr, J.
P

Mary of Scotland
RKO (US) 1936 dir. John Ford

Anderson, M.
P

Mary Poppins
DISNEY (US) 1964
dir. Robert Stevenson
Ch, M

Travers, P. L.

Mary Reilly
TRISTAR (US) 1996 dir. Stephen Frears

Martin, V.

Mary Silliman's War
CITADEL FILMS (Can) 1994 dir.
Stephen Surjik
TV(Can)

Buel, J. D. and Buel, Jr., R. *Way of Duty,
The*

Masada
UN TV (US) 1981 dir. Boris Sagal
GB title: Antagonists, The
TVSe(US)
Gann, E. K. *Antagonists, The*

Mas Alla del Jardin
LOLAFILMS (Sp) 1997 dir. Pedro Olea
Gala, A.

Maschenka
CLASART (GB) 1987
dir. John Goldschmidt
TVSe(GB)
Nabokov, V.

M*A*S*H
FOX (US) 1970 dir. Robert Altman
TVSe(US)
Hooker, R.

Mask of Dimitrios, The
WAR (US) 1944 dir. Jean Negulesco
Ambler, E.

Mask of Fu Manchu
MGM (US) 1932 dir. Charles Brabin,
Charles Vidor
Rohmer, S.

Masque of the Red Death, The
AA (GB) 1964 dir. Roger Corman
CONCORDE (US) 1989
dir. Larry Brand
Poe, E. A.

Masquerade
UA (GB) 1965 dir. Basil Dearden
Canning, V. *Castle Minerva*

Masquerade
ARABESQUE (US) 2000 dir. Roy
Campanella II
TV(US)
Hill, D.

Masquerader, The
GOLDWYN (US) 1933
dir. Richard Wallace
Thurston, K. C.

Massacre in Rome
GN (Fr/It) 1973
dir. George Pan Cosmatos
Katz, R. *Death in Rome*

Mass Appeal
UN (US) 1984 dir. Glenn Jordan
Davis, B. C.
P

Mastergate
SHOWTIME (US) 1992 dir. Michael
Engler
TV(US)
Gelbart, L.
P

Master of Ballantrae, The
WAR (US) 1953 dir. William Keighley
BBC (GB) 1975 dir. Fiona Cumming
TVSe(GB)
COL (US/GB) 1983 dir. Douglas Hickox
TVSe(GB/US)
Stevenson, R. L.

Master of Bankdam
ALL (GB) 1947 dir. Walter Forde
Armstrong, T. *Crowthers of Bankdam,
The*

Master of the Game
ROSEMONT (US/GB) 1984
dir. Kevin Connor, Harvey Hart
TVSe(GB/US)
Sheldon, S.

Master of the Moor
ITV (GB) 1994 dir. Marc Evans
TVSe(GB)
Rendell, R.

Master of the World
AA (US) 1961 dir. William Witney
Verne, J.

Matchmaker, The
PAR (US) 1958 dir. Joseph Anthony
Wilder, T.
P

Matilda
AIP (US) 1978 dir. Daniel Mann
Gallico, P.

Matilda
TRISTAR (US) 1996 dir. Danny DeVito
Ch
Dahl, R.

Mating Game, The
MGM (US) 1959 dir. George Marshall
Bates, H. E. *Darling Buds of May, The*

Matroni et Moi
MAX (Can) 1999 dir. Jean-Philippe
Duval
Martin, A.
P

Matter of Taste, A
STUDIO CANAL+ (Fr) 1999 dir.
Bernard Rapp
Balland, P. *Affaires de Gout*

Matter of Time, A
AIP (US/It) 1976 dir. Vincente Minnelli
Druon, M. *Film of Memory, The*

Matters of the Heart
MCA TV (US) 1990 dir. Michael Rhodes
TV(US)
Wersba, B. *Country of the Heart, The*

Matt Helm
COL TV (US) 1975 dir. Buzz Kulik
TV(US)
Hamilton, D.

Maurice
MI (GB) 1987 dir. James Ivory
Forster, E. M.

Mauvais Genres
STUDIO CANAL+ (Fr/Bel) 2001 dir.
Francis Girod
Aubert, B. *Transfixions*

Maverick Queen, The
REP (US) 1956 dir. Joe Kane
Grey, Z.

Max et Jeremie
TF1 (Fr) 1992 dir. Claire Devers
White, T. *Max Trueblood and the Jersey
Desperado*

Max and Helen
TNT (US) 1990 dir. Philip Saville
TV(US)
Wiesenthal, S. *Max and Helen: A
Remarkable True Love Story*

Maxie
ORION (US) 1985 dir. Paul Aaron
Finney, J. *Marion's Wall*

Maybe Baby
BBC (GB) 2000 dir. Ben Elton
Elton, B. *Inconceivable*

Mayday at 40,000 Feet
WAR (US) 1976 dir. Robert Butler
TV(US)
Ferguson, A. *Jet Stream*

Mayerling
NERO (Fr) 1935 dir. Anatole Litvak
WAR (Fr/GB) 1968 dir. Terence Young
Anet, C.

Mayor of Casterbridge, The
BBC (GB) 1978 dir. David Giles
TVSe(GB)
Hardy, T.

May We Borrow Your Husband?
ITV (GB) 1986 dir. Bob Mahoney
TV(GB)
Greene, G.

Mazes and Monsters
P&G (US) 1982
dir. Steven Hilliard Stern
TV(US)
Jaffe, R.

Me and Him
NC/COL (Ger) 1989 dir. Doris Dorrie
Moravia, A. *Io e Lui*

Me and The Colonel
COL (US) 1958 dir. Peter Glenville
Werfel, F. *Jacobowsky and the Colonel*
P

Me and the Girls
BBC (GB) 1985 dir. Jack Gold
TV(GB)
Coward, N.

Meanest Man in the World, The
FOX (US) 1943 dir. Sidney Lanfield
Cohan, G. M.
P

Mean Season, The
ORION (US) 1985 dir. Philip Borsos
Katzenbach, J. *In the Heat of the Summer*

Mecanique des Femmes, La
CNC (Fr) 2000 dir. Jerome de Missolz
Calaferte, L.

Medal for the General, A
BN (GB) 1944 dir. Maurice Elvey
Ronald, J.

Medea
JANUS (It/Fr/Ger) 1970
dir. Pier Paolo Pasolini
Euripides
P

Medusa's Child
COL TRISTAR (US) 1997 dir. Larry Shaw
TVSe(US)
Nance, J. J.

Medusa Touch, The
ITC (GB/Fr) 1978 dir. Jack Gold
Van Greenaway, P.

Meetings with Remarkable Men
ENT (GB) 1979 dir. Peter Brook
Gurdjieff, G. I.

Meet Joe Black
UN (US) 1998 dir. Martin Brest
Casella, A. *Death Takes a Holiday*
P

Meet Me at the Fair
UN (US) 1952 dir. Douglas Sirk
Markey, G. *Great Companions, The*

Meet Me in St Louis
MGM (US) 1944 dir. Vincente Minnelli
M
Benson, Mrs. S.

Meet Me Tonight
GFD (GB) 1952 dir. Anthony Pelissier
Coward, N. *Red Peppers; Fumed Oak; Ways & Means*
P

Meet Mr Callaghan
EROS (GB) 1954 dir. Charles Saunders
Cheyney, P. *Urgent Hangman, The*

Meet Mr Lucifer
GFD (GB) 1953 dir. Anthony Pelissier
Ridley, A. *Beggar My Neighbour*
P

Meet Nero Wolfe
COL (US) 1936 dir. Herbert Biberman
Stout, R. *Fer de Lance*

Mélo
MK2 (Fr) 1986 dir. Alain Resnais
Bernstein, H.
P

Melody Lingers On, The
IN (US) 1935 dir. David Burton
Brentano, L.

Member of the Wedding, The
COL (US) 1952 dir. Fred Zinnemann
HALLMARK (US) 1997 dir. Fielder Cook
TV(US)
McCullers, C.

Memed my Hawk
EMI (GB) 1984 dir. Peter Ustinov
Kemal, Y.

Memento Mori
BBC (GB) 1992 dir. Jack Clayton
TV(GB)
Spark, M.

Memoirs of a French Whore
AIDART (Fr) 1982 dir. Daniel Duval
Cordelier, J. *Life, The*

Memoirs of an Invisible Man
WAR (US) 1992
dir. John Carpenter
Saint, H. F.

Memoirs of a Survivor
EMI (GB) 1981 dir. David Gladwell
Lessing, D.

Memorias Postumas
SUPERFILMES (Bra/Port) 2001 dir. Andre Klotzel
de Assis, M. *Posthumous Memories of Bras Cubas*

Memories of Midnight
DOVE AUDIO (US) 1991 dir. Gary Nelson
TVSe(US)
Sheldon, S.

Memories of Prison
REGINA (Port) 1989
dir. Nelson Pereira Dos Santos
Ramos, G.

Memories Never Die
UN TV (US) 1982 dir. Sandor Stern
TV(US)
Sherburne, Z. *Stranger in the House*

Memory of Eva Ryker, The
IRWIN ALLEN (US) 1980
dir. Walter Grauman
TV(US)
Stanwood, D. A.

Memory Run
MERIDIAN ENT (US) 1995 dir. Allan A. Goldstein
Stine, H. *Season of the Witch*

Memphis
PROPAGANDA (US) 1992
dir. Yves Simoneau
TV(US)
Foote, S. *September, September*

Men
SHONDEROSA (US) 1997 dir. Zoe Clarke-Williams
Diehl, M.

Menace, The
COL (US) 1932 dir. Roy William Neill
Wallace, E. *Feathered Serpent*

Menace on the Mountain
DISNEY (US) 1970
dir. Vincent McEveety
Hancock, M. A.

Men Are Like That
PAR (US) 1930 dir. Frank Tuttle
Kelly, G. *Show-off, The*
P

Men are Such Fools
WAR (US) 1938 dir. Busby Berkeley
Baldwin, F.

Men in her Life
COL (US) 1941 dir. Gregory Ratoff
Smith, Lady E. *Ballerina*

Men in War
UA (US) 1957 dir. Anthony Mann
Praag, V.V. *Combat*

Men in White
MGM (US) 1934
dir. Richard Boleslawsky
Kingsley, S.
P

Men of Tomorrow
PAR (GB) 1932 dir. Leontine Sagan
Gibbs, A. H. *Young Apollo*
P

Mensaka
TORNASOL (Sp) 1998 dir. Salvador
Garcia Ruiz
Manas, J. A.

Men's Club, The
ATLANTIC (US) 1986 dir. Peter Medak
Michaels, L.

Men's Room, The
BBC (GB) 1991 dir. Antonia Bird
TVSe(GB)
Oakley, A.

Menu for Murder
VZ/SERTNER (US) 1990
dir. Larry Peerce
TV(US)
Wolzien, V.

Mephisto
MAFILM (Hun) 1981 dir. Istvan Szabo
Mann, K.

Mephisto Waltz, The
FOX (US) 1971 dir. Paul Wendkos
Stewart, F.

Mercenaries, The
MGM (GB) 1968 dir. Jack Cardiff
US title: Dark of the Sun
Smith, W. *Dark of the Sun*

Merchant of Venice, The
ATV (GB) 1974 dir. Jonathan Miller
TV(GB)
Shakespeare, W.
P

Merci Pour le Chocolat
STUDIO CANAL+ (Fr) 2000 dir. Claude
Chabrol
Armstrong, C. *Chocolate Cobweb, The*

Mercury Rising
UN (US) 1998 dir. Harold Becker
Pearson, R. D. *Simple Simon*

Mercy
FRANCHISE (US) 2000 dir. Damian
Harris
Lindsey, D. L.

Mermaids
ORION (US) 1990
dir. Richard Benjamin
Dann, P.

Merrill's Marauders
WAR (US) 1962 dir. Samuel Fuller
Ogburn, C. *Marauders, The*

Merry Christmas, Mr. Lawrence
UN (GB) 1983 dir. Nagisa Oshima

Van Der Post, Sir L. *Seed and the Sower The*

Merry Widow, The
MGM (US) 1934 dir. Ernst Lubitsch
M
MGM (US) 1952 dir. Curtis Bernhardt
M

Lehar, F., Leon, V. and Stein, L.

Merton of the Movies
MGM (US) 1947 dir. Robert Alton

Wilson, H. L.

Message From 'Nam
NBC (US) 1993 dir. Paul Wendkos
TV(US)

Steel, D.

Message in a Bottle
WAR (US) 1999 dir. Luis Mandoki

Sparks, N.

Message to Garcia, A
FOX (US) 1936 dir. George Marshall

Hubbard, E. and Rowan, A. S.

Messenger of Death
CANNON (US) 1988
dir. J. Lee Thompson

Burns, R. *Avenging Angels, The*

Metroland
BBC (GB/Fr) 1997 dir. Philip Saville

Barnes, J.

Mexican Hayride
UN (US) 1948 dir. Charles Barton

Fields, H. and Fields, D.
P

Miami Blues
ORION (US) 1990 dir. George Armitage

Willeford, C.

Michael and Mary
UN (GB) 1931 dir. Victor Saville

Milne, A. A.
P

Michael Jordan: An American Hero
FOX FAMILY (US) 1999 dir. Alan Metzger
TV(US)

Naughton, J. *Taking to the Air: The Rise of Michael Jordan*

Michael Kohlhaas
COL (Ger) 1980 dir. Volker Schlondorff

von Kleist, H.

Midaq Alley
ALAMEDA (Mex) 1995 dir. Jorge Fons

Mahfouz, N.

Middlemarch
BBC (GB) 1994 dir. Anthony Page
TVSe(GB)

Eliot, G.

Middle of the Night
COL (US) 1959 dir. Delbert Mann

Chayefsky, P.
P

Middleton's Changeling
HIGH TIMES (GB) 1998 dir. Marcus Thompson

Middleton, T. and Rowley, W. *Changeling, The*
P

Middle Watch
BI (GB) 1930 dir. Norman Walker
AB (GB) 1940 dir. Thomas Bentley

Hay, I. and Hall, S. K.
P

Midnight Blue
DIRECTORS' CIRCLE (US) 2000 dir. Bobby Mardis
TV(US)
Jackson, M.

Midnight Clear, A
A&M (US) 1992 dir. Keith Gordon
Wharton, W.

Midnight Cowboy
UA (US) 1969 dir. John Schlesinger
Herlihy, J. L.

Midnight Edition
SHAPIRO GLICKENHAUS (US) 1994 dir. Howard Libov
Postell, C. *Escape of My Dead Man*

Midnight Episode
COL (GB) 1950 dir. Gordon Parry
Simenon, G. *Monsieur La Souris*

Midnight Express
COL (GB) 1978 dir. Alan Parker
Hayes, B. and Hoffer, W.

Midnight in the Garden of Good and Evil
WAR (US) 1997 dir. Clint Eastwood
Berendt, J.

Midnight Lace
UN (US) 1960 dir. David Miller
UN TV (US) 1981 dir. Ivan Nagy
TV(US)
Green, L. *Mathilda Shouted Fire*
P

Midnight Man
SHOWTIME (US) 1995 dir. Lawrence Gordon Clark
TV(US)
Higgins, J.

Midnight Man, The
UN (US) 1974 dir. Roland Kibbee
Anthony, D. *Midnight Lady and the Mourning Man*

Midshipmaid, The
GB (GB) 1932 dir. Albert de Courville
Hay, I. and Hall, S. K.
P

Midshipman Easy
ATP (GB) 1935 dir. Carol Reed
US title: Men of the Sea
Marryat, F. *Mr. Midshipman Easy*

Midsummer Night's Dream, A
WAR (US) 1935 dir. Max Reinhardt
ITV (GB) 1964 dir. Joan Kemp-Welch
TV(GB)
COL (US) 1967 dir. Dan Eriksen
EAGLE (GB) 1968 dir. Peter Hall
MAINLINE (GB/Sp) 1985 dir. Celestino Corrado
CAPITOL (GB) 1996 dir. Adrian Noble
FOX (GB) 1999 dir. Michael Hoffman
Shakespeare, W.
P

Midwives
C. ANDERSON (US) 2001 dir. Glenn Jordan
TV(US)
Bohjalian, C.

Mighty, The
MIRAMAX (US) 1998 dir. Peter Chelsom
Philbrick, R. *Freak the Mighty*

Mighty Barnum, The
FOX (US) 1934 dir. Walter Lang
Fowler, G. and Meredyth, B.
P

Mighty Quinn, The
MGM (US) 1989 dir. Carl Schenkel
Carr, A. H. Z. *Finding Maubee*

Mikado, The
UN (GB) 1939 dir. Victor Scheitzinger
M
Gilbert, Sir W. S. and Sullivan, Sir A.
P

Milagro Beanfield War, The
UN (US) 1988 dir. Robert Redford
Nichols, J.

Mildred Pierce
WAR (US) 1945 dir. Michael Curtiz
Cain, J. M.

Millenium
FOX (US) 1989 dir. Michael Anderson
Varley, J. *Air Raid*

Millionairess, The
FOX (GB) 1960 dir. Anthony Asquith
Shaw, G. B.
P

Million Dollar Face, The
NEPHI-HAMNER (US) 1981
dir. Michael O'Herlihy
TV(US)
Wyse, L. *Kiss, Inc.*

Million Pound Note, The
GFD (GB) 1954 dir. Ronald Neame
US title: Man with a Million
Twain, M.

Mill on the Floss, The
STANDARD (GB) 1937 dir. Tim Whelan
BBC (GB) 1978 dir. Ronald Wilson
TVSe(GB)
Eliot, G.

Mill on the Po, The
LUX (It) 1949 dir. Alberto Lattuardo
Bacchelli, R.

Min and Bill
MGM (US) 1930 dir. George Hill
Moon, L. *Dark Star*

Minazuki
NIKKATSU (Jap) 1999 dir. Rokuro
Mochizuki
Hanamura, M.

Mind of Mr. Reeder, The
RAYMOND (GB) 1936
dir. Jack Raymond
Wallace, E. *Mind of Mr J. G. Reeder, The*

Mind of Mr. Soames, The
COL (GB) 1970 dir. Alan Cooke
Maine, C. E.

Mind Prey
ABC (US) 1999 dir. D. J. Caruso
TV(US)
Sandford, J.

Mind Reader, The
WAR (US) 1933 dir. Roy del Ruth
Cosby, V.

Mind to Murder, A
ANGLIA (GB) 1996 dir. Gareth Davies
TV(GB)
James, P. D.

Mindwalk
ATLAS (US) 1991 dir. Bernt Capra
Capra, F. *Turning Point, The*

Mine Own Executioner
BI (GB) 1947 dir. Anthony Kimmins
Balchin, N.

Ministry of Fear
PAR (US) 1944 dir. Fritz Lang
Greene, G.

Miniszter Felrelep, A
INTERCOM (Hun) 1997 dir. Andras
Kern, Robert Koltai
Cooney, R. *Out of Order*
P

Minotaur
CINEMA PARDES (US) 1997 dir. Jonathan Tammuz

Tammuz, B.

Minus Man, The
SHOOTING GALLERY (US) 1999 dir. Hampton Fancher

McCreary, L.

Miracle, The
WAR (US) 1959 dir. Irving Rapper

Vollmoeller, K.
P

Miracle Child
WHITE (US) 1993 dir. Michael Pressman
TV(US)

Pendergraft, P.

Miracle in Milan
PDS (It) 1951 dir. Vittorio de Sica

Zavattini, C. *Toto il Buono*

Miracle in the Rain
WAR (US) 1956 dir. Rudolph Maté

Hecht, B.

Miracle in the Wilderness
TNT (US) 1991 dir. Kevin James Dobson
TV(US)

Gallico, P.

Miracle Man, The
PAR (US) 1932 dir. Norman Z. McLeod

Packard, F. L.
P

Miracle of the Bells
PAR (US) 1948 dir. Irving Rapper

Janney, R.

Miracle of the White Stallions, The
DISNEY (US) 1963 dir. Arthur Hiller
GB title: Flight of the White Stallions, The

Podhajsky, A. *Dancing White Horses of Vienna, The*

Miracle on the 17th Green, The
BLATT (US) 1999 dir. Michael Switzer
TV(US)

Patterson, J. and de Jonge, P.

Miracle on 34th Street
FOX (US) 1947 dir. George Seaton
GB title: Big Heart, The
TCF (US) 1973 dir. Fielder Cook
TV(US)

Davies, V.

Miracles for Sale
MGM (US) 1939 dir. Tod Browning

Rawson, C. *Death in a Top Hat*

Miracle Woman, The
COL (US) 1932 dir. Frank Capra

Riskin, R. and Meehan, J. *Bless You Sister*
P

Miracle Worker, The
UA (US) 1962 dir. Arthur Penn
KATZ-GALLIN (US) 1979
dir. Paul Aaron
TV(US)
DISNEY (US) 2000 dir. Nadia Tass
TV(US)

Gibson, W.
P

Mirage
UI (US) 1965 dir. Edward Dmytryk

Ericson, W.

Mirage, Le
MOLECULE (Can/Fr) 1992 dir. Jean-Claude Guiguet

Mann, T.

Miranda
GFD (GB) 1947 dir. Ken Annakin

Blackmore, P.
P

Mirror Crack'd, The
EMI (GB) 1980 dir. Guy Hamilton

Christie, A. *Mirror Crack'd from Side to Side, The*

Mirrors
L. HILL (US) 1985 dir. Harry Winer
TV(US)

Lipton, J.

Misadventures of Margaret, The
GRANADA (GB/Fr/US) 1998 dir. Brian Skeet

Schine, C. *Rameau's Niece*

Misadventures of Mr. Wilt, The
GOLDWYN (US) 1990
dir. Michael Tuchner

Sharpe, T. *Wilt*

Misbegotten
AM WORLD (US) dir. Mark L. Lester

Berman, J. G.

Misery
COL (US) 1990 dir. Rob Reiner

King, S.

Misery Harbour
UIP (Can/Den) 1999 dir. Nils Gaup

Sandemose, A. *Sailor Goes Ashore, A*

Misfit Brigade, The
TRANSWORLD (US) 1988
dir. Gordon Hessler

Hassel, S. *Wheels of Terror*

Mishima
WAR (US) 1985 dir. Paul Schrader

Mishima, Y. *Runaway Horses; Temple of the Golden Pavilion*

Miss Evers' Boys
HBO (US) 1997 dir. Joseph Sargent
TV(US)

Feldshuh, D.
P

Miss Firecracker
CORSAIR (US) 1989
dir. Thomas Schlamme

Henley, B. *Miss Firecracker Contest*
P

Missing
UN (US) 1982 dir. Costa-Gavras

Hauser, T. *Execution of Charles Horman, The*

Missing Pieces
TTC (US) 1983 dir. Mike Hodges
TV(US)

Alexander, K. *Private Investigation, A*

Missing Pieces
HALMARK (US) 2000 dir. Richard Kletter
TV(US)

Hansen, R. *Atticus*

Mission of Danger
MGM (US) 1959 dir. George Waggner, Jacques Tourneur

Roberts, K. *Northwest Passage*

Mission to Moscow
WAR (US) 1943 dir. Michael Curtiz

Davies, J. E.

Miss Julie
LF (Swe) 1950 dir. Alf Sjoberg
TIGON (GB) 1972
dir. Robin Phillips, John Glenister
MOONSTONE (US) 1999 dir. Mike Figgis

Strindberg, J. A.
P

Miss Morison's Ghosts
ANGLIA (GB) 1983 dir. John Bruce
TV(GB)

Morison, E. and Lamont, F. *Adventure, The*

Miss Nobody
ZESPOL (Pol) 1997 dir. Andrzej Wajda
Tryzna, T. *Panna Nikt*

Miss Rose White
LORIMAR TV (US) 1992 dir. Joseph Sargent
TV(US)

Lebow, B. *Shayna Maidel, A*
P

Miss Sadie Thompson
COL (US) 1953 dir. Curtis Bernhardt

Maugham, W. S. *Rain*

Miss Susie Slagle's
PAR (US) 1946 dir. John Berry

Tucker, A.

Mister Buddwing
MGM (US) 1966 dir. Delbert Mann
GB title: Woman Without a Face

Hunter, E. *Buddwing*

Misterioso
BBC (GB) 1991 dir. John Glenister
TV(GB)

Plater, A.

Mistero Buffo
BBC (GB) 1990 dir. Don Coutts
TV(GB)

Fo, D.
P

Mister Quilp
EMI (GB) 1975 dir. Elliot Scott

Dickens, C. *Old Curiosity Shop, The*

Mister Roberts
WAR (US) 1955 dir. John Ford, Mervyn LeRoy

Heggen, T.

Mistral's Daughter
KRANTZ (Fr/Lux/US) 1986
dir. David Hickox, Kevin Connor
TVSe(Fr/Lux/US)

Krantz, J.

Mistress Pamela
MGM-EMI (GB) 1973
dir. Jim O'Connolly

Richardson, S. *Pamela*

Mists of Avalon, The
TNT (US) 2001 dir. Uli Edel
TVSe(US)

Zimmer Bradley, M.

Misty
FOX (US) 1961 dir. James B. Clark

Henry, M. *Misty of Chincoteague*

Misunderstood
MGM/UA (US) 1984
dir. Jerry Schatzberg

Montgomery, F.

Mixed Blessings
NBC (US) 1995 dir. Bethany Rooney
TV(US)

Steel, D.

Mix me a Person
BL (GB) 1962 dir. Leslie Norman

Story, J. T.

Moby Dick
WAR (US) 1930 dir. Lloyd Bacon
WAR (GB) 1956 dir. John Huston
USA PICTURES (US/GB/Aust) 1998
dir. Franc Roddam
TVSe(US/GB/Aust)

Melville, H.

Model Behavior
DISNEY (US) 2000 dir. Mark Rosman

Levin, M. *Janine and Alex, Alex and Janine*

Moderato Cantabile
R. J. LEVY (Fr/It) 1960 dir. Peter Brook

Duras, M.

Modern Hero, A
WAR (US) 1934 dir. G. W. Pabst

Bromfield, L.

Mog
LWT (GB) 1985 dir. Nic Phillips
TVSe(GB)

Tinniswood, P.

Mogambo
MGM (US) 1953 dir. John Ford

Collison, W. *Farewell to Women*
P

Mojo
BBC (GB) 1997 dir. Jez Butterworth

Butterworth, J.
P

Moll Flanders
MGM (US) 1996 dir. Pen Densham
BBC (GB) 1975 dir. Donald McWhinnie
TVSe(GB)

Defoe, D. *Fortunes and Misfortunes of the Famous Moll Flanders, The*

Molly Maguires, The
PAR (US) 1970 dir. Martin Ritt

Lewis, A. H. *Lament for Molly Maguires*

Moment in Time, A
BBC (GB) 1979 dir. Renny Rye
TVSe(GB)

Bates, H. E.

Moment of Danger
ABP (GB) 1960 dir. Laslo Benedek

MacKenzie, D.

Mom for Christmas, A
DISNEY (US) 1990 dir. George Miller
TV(US)

Dillon, B. *Mom by Magic, A*

Mommie Dearest
PAR (US) 1981 dir. Frank Perry

Crawford, C.

Momo
CECCHI (It) 2001 dir. Enzo D'Alo

Ende, M.

Mom, the Wolfman, and Me
TIME-LIFE (US) 1980
dir. Edmond A. Levy
TV(US)

Klein, N.

Monday After the Miracle
CBS (US) 1998 dir. Daniel Petrie
TV(US)

Gibson, W.
P

Moneychangers, The
PAR TV (US) 1976 dir. Boris Sagal
TVSe(US)

Hailey, A.

Money from Home
PAR (US) 1953 dir. George Marshall

Runyon, D.

Money, Power, Murder
CBS ENT (US) 1989 dir. Lee Philips
TV(US)

Lupica, M. *Dead Air*

Money Trap, The
MGM (US) 1966 dir. Burt Kennedy

White, L.

Mongo's Back in Town
CBS ENT (US) 1971
dir. Marvin J. Chomsky
TV(US)
Johnson, E. R.

Monja Alferez, La
GOYA (Sp) 1992 dir. Javier Aguirre
de Erauso, C. *Memorias*
De Qunicey, T. *Spanish Military Nun, The*

Monk Dawson
DEWARR (GB) 1997 dir. Tom Waller
Read, P. P.

Monkey Grip
PAV (Aust) 1982 dir. Ken Cameron
Garner, H.

Monkey House
ATLANTIS (US) 1991 dir. Paul Shapiro, Gilbert Shilton, Allan King
TV(US)
Vonnegut, K. *Next Door; Euphio Question, The; All the King's Men*

Monkey in Winter, A
CIPRA (Fr) 1962 dir. Henri Verneuil
Blondin, A.

Monkey on my Back
UA (US) 1957 dir. André de Toth
Brown, W.

Monkeys, Go Home!
DISNEY (US) 1967
dir. Andrew V. McLaglen
Wilkinson, G. R. *Monkeys, The*

Monkey Shines
ORION (US) 1988
dir. George A. Romero
Stewart, M.

Monocled Mutineer, The
BBC (GB) 1986 dir. Jim O'Brien
TVSe(GB)
Allison, W. and Fairley, J.

Mon Père ... Il m'a Sauvé la Vie
STUDIO CANAL+ (Fr) 2001 dir. Jose Giovanni
Giovanni, J. *Secret Gardens in My Father's Heart, The*

Monsieur Beaucaire
PAR (US) 1946 dir. George Marshall
Tarkington, B.

Monsieur Hire
ORION (Fr) 1989 dir. Patrice Leconte
Simenon, G. *Fiançailles de M. Hire, Les*

Monsignor
FOX (US) 1982 dir. Frank Perry
Leger, J. A. *Monsignore*

Monster Mash: The Movie
PRISM (US) 1995 dir. Joel Cohen, Alec Sokolow
Allman, S. and Pickett, B. *I'm Sorry the Bridge is Out, You'll Have to Spend the Night*
P

Monte Carlo
PAR (US) 1930 dir. Ernst Lubitsch
Tarkington, B. *Monsieur Beaucaire*

Monte Carlo
HIGHGATE (US) 1986
dir. Anthony Page
TVSe(US)
Sheppard, S.

Monte Walsh
CIN CEN (US) 1970
dir. William A. Fraker
Schaefer, J.

Month by the Lake, A
MIRAMAX (GB/US) 1995 dir. John Irvin

Bates, H. E.

Month in the Country, A
EUSTON (GB) 1987 dir. Pat O'Connor

Carr, J. L.

Month in the Country, A
ITV (GB) 1955 dir. Robert Hamer
TV(GB)
BBC (GB) 1955 dir. Bill Hays
TV(GB)
PAR (US) 1985 dir. Quentin Lawrence

Turgenev, A.
P

Moon and Sixpence, The
UA (US) 1942 dir. Albert Lewin

Maugham, W. S.

Mooncussers, The
DISNEY (US) 1971 dir. James Neilson

Vinton, I. *Flying Ebony*

Moondial
BBC (GB) 1988 dir. Colin Cant
Ch, TVSe(GB)

Cresswell, H.

Moonfleet
MGM (US) 1955 dir. Fritz Lang
BBC (GB) 1984 dir. Colin Cant
TVSe(GB)

Faulkner, J. M.

Moon is Blue, The
UA (US) 1953 dir. Otto Preminger

Herbert, F. H.
P

Moon is Down, The
FOX (US) 1943 dir. Irving Pichel

Steinbeck, J.

Moonlight and Valentino
POLYGRAM (US) 1995 dir. David Anspaugh

Simon, E.
P

Moonlight Becomes You
GROSSO-JACOB (US) 1998 dir. Bill Corcoran
TV(US)

Clark, M. H.

Moon of the Wolf
FILMWAYS (US) 1972 dir. Daniel Petrie
TV(US)

Whitten, L. H.

Moonraker
UA (GB) 1979 dir. Lewis Gilbert

Fleming, I.

Moonraker, The
ABP (GB) 1958 dir. David MacDonald

Watkyn, A.
P

Moonshine War, The
MGM (US) 1970 dir. Richard Quine

Leonard, E.

Moon's Our Home, The
PAR (US) 1936 dir. William A. Seiter

Baldwin, F.

Moon-Spinners, The
DISNEY (GB) 1964 dir. James Neilson

Stewart, M.

Moonstone, The
BBC (GB) 1972 dir. Paddy Russell
TVSe(GB)

Collins, W.

Moontide
FOX (US) 1942 dir. Archie Mayo

Robertson, W.

Morals of Marcus, The
GB (GB) 1935 dir. Miles Mander

Locke, W. J. *Morals of Marcus Ordeyne, The*

More Tales of the City
WORKING TITLE/SHOWTIME (US/GB) 1998 dir. Pierre Gang
TVSe(US/GB)

Maupin, A.

Morgan—A Suitable Case for Treatment
BL (GB) 1966 dir. Karel Reisz

Mercer, D.
P

Morning After, The
WOLPER (US) 1974
dir. Richard T. Heffron
TV(US)

Weiner, J. B.

Morning Departure
GFD (GB) 1950 dir. Roy Baker
US title: Operation Disaster

Woollard, K.
P

Morning Glory
RKO (US) 1933 dir. Lowell Sherman

Akins, Z.
P

Morning Glory
DOVE (US) 1993 dir. Steven Hilliard Stern
TV(US)

Spencer, L.

Morocco
PAR (US) 1930 dir. Josef von Sternberg

Vigny, B. *Amy Jolly*
P

Mortal Fear
VZ/SERTNER (US) 1994 dir. Larry Shaw
TV(US)

Cook, R.

Mortal Storm, The
MGM (US) 1940 dir. Frank Borzage

Bottome, P.

Moscow Nights
LF (GB) 1935 dir. Anthony Asquith

Benoit, P.

Mosquito Coast, The
WAR (US) 1986 dir. Peter Weir

Theroux, P.

Most Dangerous Man in the World, The
RANK (GB) 1969 dir. J. Lee Thompson
US title: Chairman, The

Kennedy, J. R. *Chairman, The*

Mother Carey's Chickens
RKO (US) 1938 dir. Rowland V. Lee

Wiggin, K. D.

Mother Courage
ITV (GB) 1959
TV(GB)

Brecht, B.
P

Mother Didn't Tell Me
FOX (US) 1950 dir. Claude Binyon

Bard, M. *Doctor Wears Three Faces, The*

Mother Love
BBC (GB) 1989 dir. Simon Langton
TVSe(GB)

Taylor, D.

Mother, May I Sleep With Danger?
TRISTAR (US) 1996 dir. Jorge Montesi
TV(US)
Jacobs, C. R.

Mother Night
FINE LINE (US) 1996 dir. Keith Gordon
Vonnegut, K.

Mothers and Daughters
PALAMA (Can) 1992 dir. Larry Kent
Ravel A. *Mother Variations*
P

Mother's Boys
MIRAMAX (US) 1994 dir. Yves Simoneau
Taylor, B.

Mother's Gift, A
RHI (US) 1995 dir. Jerry London
TV(US)
Aldrich, B. S. *Lantern in Her Hand, A*

Mother's Revenge, A
MARTINES (US) 1993 dir. Armand Mastroianni
TV(US)
Speight, R. *Desperate Justice*

Mothertime
BBC (GB) 1997 dir. Matthew Jacobs
TV(GB)
White, G.

Mother Wore Tights
FOX (US) 1947 dir. Walter Lang
Young, M.

Moulin Rouge
FOX (US) 1934 dir. Sidney Lanfield
de Bri, L.
P

Moulin Rouge
UA (GB) 1952 dir. John Huston
La Mure, P.

Mountain, The
PAR (US) 1956 dir. Edward Dmytryk
Troyat, H.

Mountain Road, The
COL (US) 1960 dir. Delbert Mann
White, T. H.

Mountains of the Moon
TRISTAR (US) 1990 dir. Bob Rafaelson
Harrison, W. *Burton and Speke*

Mourning Becomes Electra
RKO (US) 1947 dir. Dudley Nichols
O'Neill, E.
P

Mouse and the Child, The
SANRIO (US) 1978 dir. Fred Wolf, Chuck Swenson
GB title: Extraordinary Adventures of the Mouse and the Child, The
A, Ch
Hoban, R.

Mouse and the Woman, The
FACELIFT (GB) 1981 dir. Karl Francis
Thomas, D.

Mouse that Roared, The
COL (GB) 1959 dir. Jack Arnold
Wibberley, L.

Move
FOX (US) 1970 dir. Stuart Rosenberg
Lieber, J.

Moving
HERALD ACE (Jap) 1993 dir. Shinji Soomai
Tanaka, H.

Moving Finger, The
BBC (GB) 1984 dir. Roy Boulting
TV(GB)
Christie, A.

Moving of Sophia Myles, The
PEARSON TV (Can/US) 2000 dir.
Michael Switzer
TV(Can/US)
MacNicholas, J. *Moving of Lilla Barton, The*
P

Moving Targets
ACADEMY (Aust) 1987
dir. Chris Langman
Leopold, K. *When we Ran*

Moviola: The Scarlett O'Hara Wars
WAR TV (US) 1980 dir. John Erman
TV(US)
Kanin, G. *Moviola*

Moviola: The Silent Lovers
WAR TV (US) 1980 dir. John Erman
TV(US)
Kanin, G. *Moviola*

Moviola: This Year's Blonde
WAR TV (US) 1980 dir. John Erman
TV(US)
Kanin, G. *Moviola*

Mr. and Mrs. Bo Jo Jones
FOX TV (US) 1971 dir. Robert Day
TV(US)
Head, A.

Mr. and Mrs. Bridge
MIRAMAX (US) 1990 dir. James Ivory
Connell, E. S. *Mr Bridge; Mrs. Bridge*

Mr. and Mrs. Edgehill
BBC (GB) 1985 dir. Gavin Millar
TV(GB)
Coward, N.

Mr. and Mrs. North
MGM (US) 1941 dir. Robert B. Sinclair
Davis, O.
P

Mr. Belvedere Rings the Bell
FOX (US) 1951 dir. Henry Koster
McEnroe, R. E. *Silver Whistle, The*
P

Mr. Blandings Builds his Dream House
RKO (US) 1948 dir. H. C. Potter
Hodgins, E.

Mr. Deeds Goes to Town
COL (US) 1936 dir. Frank Capra
Kelland, C. B. *Opera Hat*

Mr. Denning Drives North
BL (GB) 1951 dir. Anthony Kimmins
Coppel, A.

Mr. Emmanuel
TC (GB) 1944 dir. Harold French
Golding, L.

Mr. Forbush and the Penguins
BL (GB) 1971 dir. Roy Boulting, Arne Sacksdorff
Billing, G.

Mr. Johnson
AVENUE (Aust) 1990
dir. Bruce Beresford
Carey, J.

Mr. Hobbs takes a Vacation
FOX (US) 1962 dir. Henry Koster
Streeter, E. *Hobbs' Vacation*

Mr. Moses
UA (GB) 1965 dir. Ronald Neame
Catto, M. *Mister Moses*

Mr. Murder
PATCHETT-KAUFMAN (US) 1999 dir.
Dick Lowry
TVSe(US)
Koontz, D.

Mr. North
GOLDWYN (US) 1988
dir. Danny Huston
Wilder, T. *Theophilus North*

Mr. Peabody and the Mermaid
UN (US) 1948 dir. Irving Pichel
Jones, G. P. and Jones, C. B. *Peabody's Mermaid*

Mr. Perrin and Mr. Traill
TC (GB) 1948 dir. Lawrence
Huntington
Walpole, H.

Mr. Pye
CHANNEL 4 (GB) 1986 dir. Michael
Darlow
TVSe(GB)
Peake, M.

Mr. Right
BBC (GB) 1983 dir. Peter Smith
TVSe(GB)
Dale, C. *Spring of Love, A*

Mr. Rock 'n' Roll: The Alan Freed Story
VZ/SERTNER (US) 1999 dir. Andy
Wolk
TV(US)
Jackson, J. A. *Big Beat Heat: Alan Freed and the Early Years of Rock & Roll*

Mr. Skeffington
WAR (US) 1944 dir. Vincent Sherman
von Arnim, E.

Mr. Smith Goes To Washington
COL (US) 1939 dir. Frank Capra
Foster, L. R. *Gentleman From Montana, The*

Mr. Topaze
FOX (GB) 1961 dir. Peter Sellers
US title: I Like Money
Pagnol, M. *Topaze*
P

Mr. Wakefield's Crusade
BBC (GB) 1992 dir. Angela Pope
TVSe(GB)
Rubens, B.

Mr. Winkle Goes to War
COL (US) 1944 dir. Alfred E. Green
GB title: Arms and the Woman
Pratt, T.

Mr. Write
STAR PARTNERS (US) 1994 dir. Charlie
Loventhal
Morris, H. J.
P

Mr. Wroe's Virgins
BBC (GB) 1993 dir. Danny Boyle
TVSe(GB)
Rogers, J.

Mrs. 'arris Goes to Paris
ACCENT (US) 1992 dir. Anthony Shaw
TV(US)
Gallico, P.

Mrs. Capper's Birthday
BBC (GB) 1985 dir. Mike Ockrent
TV(GB)
Coward, N.

Mrs. Dalloway
BBC (GB) 1997 dir. Marleen Gorris
Woolf, V.

Mrs. Doubtfire
FOX (US) 1993 dir. Chris Columbus
Fine, A. *Alias Madame Doubtfire*

Mrs. Gibbons' Boys
BL (GB) 1962 dir. Max Varnel

Glickman, W. and Stein, J.
P

Mrs. Mike
UA (US) 1950 dir. Louis King

Freedman, B. and Freedman, N.

Mrs. Miniver
MGM (US) 1942 dir. William Wyler

Struther, J.

Mrs. Munck
VIACOM PICT (US) 1996 dir. Diane Ladd
TV(US)

Leffland, E.

Mrs. Parkington
MGM (US) 1944 dir. Tay Garnett

Bromfield, L.

Mrs. Pollifax—Spy
UA (US) 1971 dir. Leslie Martinson

Gilman, D. *Unexpected Mrs. Pollifax, The*

Mrs. Pym of Scotland Yard
GN (GB) 1939 dir. Fred Elles

Morland, N.

Mrs. Wiggs of the Cabbage Patch
PAR (US) 1934 dir. Norman Taurog
PAR (US) 1942 dir. Ralph Murphy

Rice, A. H. and Flexner, A. C.

Mrs. Winterbourne
TRISTAR (US) 1996 dir. Richard Benjamin

Woolrich, C. *I Married a Dead Man*

Much Ado About Nothing
GOLDWYN (GB/US) 1993 dir. Kenneth Branagh

Shakespeare, W.
P

Mudlark, The
FOX (GB) 1950 dir. Jean Negulesco

Bonnet, T.

Muggable Mary: Street Cop
CBS ENT (US) 1982 dir. Sandor Stern
TV(US)

Glatzle, M. and Fiore, E. *Muggable Mary*

Muhammad Ali: King of the World
LIONS GATE (US) 2000 dir. John Sacret Young
TV(US)

Remnick, D. *King of the World*

Mujer Bajo la Lluvia, Una
ATRIUM (Sp) 1992 dir. Gerardo Vera
US title: Woman in the Rain, A

Neville E. *Vida en un Hilo, La*
P

Murder
BI (GB) 1930 dir. Alfred Hitchcock

Dane, C. and Simpson, H. *Enter, Sir John*

Murder at the Gallop
MGM (GB) 1963 dir. George Pollock

Christie, A. *After the Funeral*

Murder at the Vicarage
BBC (GB) 1986 dir. Julian Amyes
TV(GB)

Christie, A.

Murder at 75 Birch
NICKI (US) 1999 dir. Michael Scott
TV(US)

Pienciak, R. T. *Murder at 75 Birch Street*

Murder by the Book
ORION TV (US) 1987 dir. Mel Damski
TV(US)

Arrighi, M. *Alter Ego*

Murder by Proxy
EXCL (GB) 1955 dir. Terence Fisher
US title: Blackout
Nielson, H.

Murder C.O.D.
KUSHNER-LOCKE (US) 1990
dir. Alan Metzger
TV(US)
Paulsen, G. *Kill Fee*

Murderer's Row
BL (US) 1966 dir. Henry Levin
Hamilton, D.

Murder Goes to College
PAR (US) 1937 dir. Charles Reisner
Steele, K.

Murder, Inc.
FOX (US) 1960 dir. Burt Balaban, Stuart
Rosenberg
Turkus, B. and Feder, S.

Murder in Coweta County
TELECOM (US) 1983 dir. Gary Nelson
TV(US)
Barnes, M. A.

Murder in Eden
BBC (GB) 1991 dir. Nicholas Renton
TVSe(GB)
McGinley, P. *Bogmail*

Murder in Mind
CBS (US) 1997 dir. Robert Iscove
TV(US)
Cooney, M.
P

Murder in Texas
D. CLARK (US) 1981 dir. Billy Hale
TVSe(US)
Kurth, A. *Prescription: Murder*

Murder in the Cathedral
FILM TRADERS (GB) 1951
dir. George Hoellering
Eliot, T. S.
P

Murder in the Family
FOX (GB) 1938 dir. Al Parker
Ronald, J.

Murder in Three Acts
WAR TV (US) 1986 dir. Gary Nelson
TV(US)
Christie, A.

Murder in Trinidad
FOX (US) 1934 dir. Louis King
Vandercook, J. W.

Murder is Announced, A
BBC (GB) 1985 dir. George Gallaccio
TV(GB)
BBC (GB) 1987 dir. David Giles
TVSe(GB)
Christie, A.

Murder is Easy
WAR (US) 1982 dir. Claude Whatham
TV(US)
Christie, A.

Murder Most Easy
BBC (GB) 1977 dir. Ronald Wilson
TVSe(GB)
Watson, C. *Flaxborough Chronicles, The*

Murder Most Foul
MGM (GB) 1964 dir. George Pollock
Christie, A. *Mrs. McGinty's Dead*

Murder Most Likely
ALLIANCE (Can) 1999 dir. Alex
Chapple
TV(Can)
Harris, M. *Judas Kiss, The: The
Undercover Life of Paul Kelly*

Murder Must Advertise
BBC (GB) 1973 dir. Rodney Bennett
TVSe(GB)
Sayers, D. L.

Murder, My Sweet
RKO (US) 1944 dir. Edward Dmytryk
Chandler, R. *Farewell, My Lovely*

Murder of a Moderate Man
BBC (GB/It) 1985 dir. Robert Tronson
TVSe(GB)
Howlett, J.

Murder of Dr. Harrigan
WAR (US) 1936 dir. Frank McDonald
Eberhart, M. G. *From this Dark Stairway*

Murder of Innocence
HEARST (US) 1993 dir. Tom McLoughlin
TV(US)
Kaplan, J., Papajohn, G. and Zorn, E.

Murder of Quality, A
THAMES (GB) 1991 dir. Gavin Millar
TV(GB)
Le Carré, J.

Murder of Roger Ackroyd, The
BBC (GB) 2000 dir. Andrew Grieve
TV(GB)
Christie, A.

Murder on Shadow Mountain, A
VZ/SERTNER (US) 1999 dir. Dick Lowry
TV(US)
Taylor, J. D. and Bross, D. G.

Murder on the Orient Express
EMI (GB) 1974 dir. Sidney Lumet
BLATT (US) 2001 dir. Cark Schenkel
TV(US)
Christie, A.

Murderous Maids
STUDIO CANAL+ (Fr) 2000 dir. Jean-Pierre Denis
Houdyer, P. *Affaire Papin, L'*

Murder Reported
COL (GB) 1957 dir. Charles Saunders
Chapman, R. *Murder for the Million*

Murder She Said
MGM (GB) 1961 dir. George Pollock
Christie, A. *4.50 from Paddington*

Murders in the Rue Morgue
UN (US) 1932 dir. Robert Florey
AIP (US) 1971 dir. Gordon Hessler
HALMI (US/GB) 1986 dir. Jeannot Szwarc
TV(GB/US)
Poe, E. A.

Murder with Mirrors
WAR (US) 1985 dir. Dick Lowry
TV(US)
Christie, A. *They do it with Mirrors*

Murder Without Crime
ABP (GB) 1950 dir. J. Lee Thompson
Thompson, J. L. *Double Error*
P

Murder Without Motive: The Edmund Perry Story
L. HILL TV (US) 1992 dir. Kevin Hooks
TV(US)
Anson, R. A. *Best Intentions: The Education and Killing of Edmund Perry*

Murphy's Romance
COL (US) 1985 dir. Martin Ritt
Schott, M.

Murphy's War
PAR (GB) 1971 dir. Peter Yates
Catto, M.

Muses Orphelines, Les
LYLA (Can) 2000 dir. Robert Favreau
Bouchard, M. M.
P

Mushroom Picker, The
BBC (GB) 1993 dir. Andy Wilson
TVSe(GB)
Zinik, Z.

Music in the Air
FOX (US) 1934 dir. Joe May
M
Hammerstein II, O. and Kern, J.
P

Music Lovers, The
UA (GB) 1970 dir. Ken Russell
Bowen, C. D. and von Meek, B. *Beloved Friend*

Music Man, The
WAR (US) 1962 dir. Morton da Costa
M
Willson, M.

Music of Chance, The
IRS MEDIA (US) 1993 dir. Philip Haas
Auster, P.

Musketeer, The
MIRAMAX (US/Ger) 2001 dir. Peter Hyams
Dumas, A. *Three Musketeers, The*

Mutiny on the Bounty
MGM (US) 1935 dir. Frank Lloyd
MGM (US) 1962 dir. Lewis Milestone
Nordhoff, C. B. and Hall, J. N.

Mutiny of the Elsinore
ARGYLE (GB) 1937 dir. Roy Lockwood
London, J.

My Antonia
GIDEON (US) 1995 dir. Joseph Sargent
TV(US)
Cather, W.

My Breast
HEARST (US) 1994 dir. Betty Thomas
TV(US)
Wadler, J.

My Brilliant Career
GUO (Aust) 1979 dir. Gillian Armstrong
Franklin, M.

My Brother Jonathan
AB (GB) 1947 dir. Harold French
BBC (GB) 1985 dir. Anthony Garner
TVSe(GB)
Young, F. B.

My Brother's Wife
ADAM (US) 1989 dir. Jack Bender
TV(US)
Gurney, A. R. *Middle Ages, The*
P

My Cousin Rachel
FOX (US) 1952 dir. Henry Koster
BBC (GB) 1983 dir. Brian Farnham
TVSe(GB)
Du Maurier, D.

My Darling Clementine
FOX (US) 1946 dir. John Ford
Lake, S. *Wyatt Earp, Frontier Marshal*

My Daughter Joy
BL (GB) 1950 dir. Gregory Ratoff
US title: Operation X
Nemirowsky, I. *David Golder*

My Death is a Mockery
ADELPHI (GB) 1952 dir. Tony Young
Baber, D.

My Dog Skip
WAR (US) 2000 dir. Jay Russell
Morris, W.

My Fair Lady
WAR (US) 1964 dir. George Cukor
M
Shaw, G. B. *Pygmalion*
P

My Family and Other Animals
BBC (GB) 1987 dir. Peter Barber-Fleming
TVSe(GB)
Wood, C.

My Father, My Son
WEINTRAUB (US) 1988
dir. Jeff Bleckner
TV(US)
Zumwalt, Jr., Admiral, E. and Zumwalt III, E. R.

My Father's Glory
GAU (Fr) 1991 dir. Yves Robert
Pagnol, M. *Gloire de Mon Père, La*

My Father's House
FILMWAYS (US) 1975 dir. Alex Segal
TV(US)
Kunhardt, Jr., P.

My Father's House
GRANADA (GB) 1981 dir. Alan Grint
TVSe(GB)
Conlon, K.

My Father's Shadow: The Sam Sheppard Story
JAFFE/BRAUNSTEIN (US) 1998 dir. Peter Levin
TV(US)
Sheppard, S. R. and Cooper, C. L. *Mockery of Justice: The True Story of the Sheppard Murder Case*

My First Forty Years
TRISTAR/COL (It) 1989
dir. Carlo Vanzina
di Meana, M. R.

My Forbidden Past
RKO (US) 1951 dir. Robert Stevenson
Banks, P. *Carriage Entrance*

My Friend Flicka
FOX (US) 1943 dir. Harold Schuster
O'Hara, M.

My Friend Ivan Lapshin
LENFILM (USSR) 1986
dir. Alexei Cherman
Cherman, Y.

My Friend Joe
PORTMAN ENT (Ger/Ire/GB) 1996
dir. Chris Bould
Pohl, P. *Janne, Min Van*

My Friend Walter
GOLDHIL (US/GB) 1993 dir. Gavin Millar
Ch, TV(US/GB)
Morpurgo, M.

My Gal Sal
FOX (US) 1942 dir. Irving Cummings
Dreiser, T. *My Brother Paul*

My Girl Tisa
IN (US) 1948 dir. Elliott Nugent
Prumbs, L. S. and Smith, S. B.
P

My Gun is Quick
UA (US) 1957 dir. George A. White
Spillane, M.

My Husband's Secret Life
USA NETWORK (US) 1998 dir. Graeme Clifford
TV(US)
Flaherty, J. *Tin Wife*

289

My Kidnapper, My Love
EMI (US) 1980 dir. Sam Wanamaker
TV(US)
Saul, O. *Dark Side of Love, The*

My Left Foot
PALACE (GB) 1989 dir. Jim Sheridan
Brown, C.

My Life as a Dog
SVENSK (Swe) 1984
dir. Lasse Hallstrom
Jonsson, R.

My Life So Far
MIRAMAX (GB) 1999 dir. Hugh
Hudson
Forman, Sir D. *Son of Adam*

My Louisiana Sky
HYP PICTURES (US) 2001 dir. Adam
Arkin
TV(US)
Willis Holt, K.

My Lover, My Son
MGM (US/GB) 1970 dir. John Newland
Grierson, E. *Reputation for a Song*

My Mother's Castle
GAU (Fr) 1991 dir. Yves Robert
Pagnol, M. *Château de ma Mère, Le*

My Mother's Courage
BBS FILMS (Ger/Ire) 1995 dir. Michael
Verhoeven
Tabori, G.

My Mother's Early Lovers
OFF THE GRID (US) 1998 dir. Nora
Jacobson
Smith, S.

My Mother's Ghost
FOX FAMILY (Can) 1997 dir. Elise
Swerhone
TV(Can)
Buffie, M.

My Name is Julia Ross
COL (US) 1945 dir. Joseph H. Lewis
Gilbert, A. *Woman in Red, The*

My Old Man
CBS ENT (US) 1979 dir. John Erman
TV(US)
Hemingway, E.

My Own Country
SHOWTIME (US) 1998 dir. Mira Nair
TV(US)
Verghese, A.

My Own True Love
PAR (US) 1948 dir. Compton Bennett
Foldes, Y. *Make You a Fine Wife*

Myra Breckenridge
FOX (US) 1970 dir. Mike Sarne
Vidal, G.

My Reputation
WAR (US) 1946 dir. Curtis Bernhardt
Jaynes, C. *Instruct my Sorrows*

My Side of the Mountain
PAR (US/Can) 1969 dir. James B. Clark
George, J.

My Sister and I
GFD (GB) 1948 dir. Harold Huth
Bonett, E. *High Pavement*

My Sister Eileen
COL (US) 1942 dir. Alexander Hall
McKenney, R.

My Sister Eileen
COL (US) 1955 dir. Richard Quine
M

Fields, J. and Chodorov, J.
P

My Six Convicts
COL (US) 1952 dir. Hugo Fregonese
Wilson, D. P.

My Son, My Son
UA (US) 1940 dir. Charles Vidor
BBC (GB) 1979 dir. Peter Cregeen
TVSe(GB)

Spring, H.

My Sons
OTANI (Jap) 1992 dir. Yoji Yamada
Shiina, M.

Mysterious Affair at Styles
LWT (GB) 1990 dir. Roy Devenish
TV(GB)

Christie, A.

Mysterious Dr. Fu Manchu
PAR (US) 1929 dir. Rowland V. Lee
Rohmer, S.

Mysterious Island
COL (GB) 1962 dir. Cy Endfield
Verne, J.

Mystery Liner
MON (US) 1934 dir. William Nigh
Wallace, E. *Ghost of John Holling, The*

Mystery of Edwin Drood, The
UN (US) 1935 dir. Stuart Walker
FIRST STANDARD (GB) 1993 dir.
Timothy Forder
Dickens, C.

Mystery of Marie Roget, The
UN (US) 1942 dir. Phil Rosen
Poe, E. A.

Mystery of Mr. X, The
MGM (US) 1934 dir. Edgar Selwyn
MacDonald, P. *X vs. Rex*

Mystery of the Wax Museum
WAR (US) 1933 dir. Michael Curtiz
Belden, C. S.
P

Mystic Masseur
MI (Ind) 2001 dir. Ismail Merchant
Naipaul, V. S.

Mystic Warrior, The
WAR (US) 1984 dir. Richard T. Heffron
TVSe(US)

Hill, R. B. *Hanta Yo*

My Sweet Charlie
UN TV (US) 1970 dir. Lamont Johnson
TV(US)

Westheimer, D.
P

**My Wicked, Wicked Ways ...
The Legend of Errol Flynn**
CBS ENT (US) 1985 dir. Don Taylor
TV(US)

Flynn, E.

My Wife's Family
GB (GB) 1931 dir. Monty Banks
ABPC (GB) 1941 dir. Walter C. Mycroft
ABP (GB) 1956 dir. Gilbert Gunn

Duprez, F., Stephens, H. and Linton,
H. B.
P

Nadie Conoce a Nadie
DMVB (Sp) 1999 dir. Mateo Gil
Bonilla, J.

Naked and the Dead, The
RKO (US) 1958 dir. Raoul Walsh
Mailer, N.

Naked Civil Servant, The
THAMES (GB) 1975 dir. Jack Gold
TV(GB)
Crisp, Q.

Naked Country, The
FILMWAYS (Aust) 1984
dir. Tim Burstall
West, M. L.

Naked Edge, The
UA (GB) 1961 dir. Michael Anderson
Ehrlich, M. *First Train to Babylon*

Naked Eye, The
LOLAFILMS (Sp) 1998 dir. Vicente
Aranda
Delgado, F. G.

Naked Face, The
CANNON (US) 1984 dir. Bryan Forbes
Sheldon, S.

Naked Hours, The
COMPTON (It) 1964 dir. Marco Vicario
Moravia, A. *Appointment at the Beach*

Naked in the Sun
ALLIED (US) 1957 dir. R. John Hugh
Slaughter, F. G. *Warrior, The*

Naked Jungle, The
PAR (US) 1954 dir. Byron Haskin
Stephenson, C. *Leiningen Versus the
Ants*

Naked Lunch
FOX (US) 1991 dir. David Cronenberg
Burroughs, W.

Naked Runner, The
WAR (GB) 1967 dir. Sidney J. Furie
Clifford, F.

Name of the Rose, The
FOX (US/Ger/It/Fr) 1987
dir. Jean-Jacques Annaud
Eco, U.

Nana
MGM (US) 1934 dir. Dorothy Arzner
GB title: Lady of the Boulevards
GALA (Fr/It) 1955 dir. Christian Jacque
MINERVA (Swe) 1971 dir. Mac Ahlberg
CANNON (It) 1982 dir. Dan Wolman
Zola, E.

Nancy Steele is Missing
FOX (US) 1937 dir. George Marshall
Coe, C. F.

Nanny, The
WAR (GB) 1965 dir. Seth Holt
Piper, E.

Narrow Corner
WAR (US) 1933 dir. Alfred E. Green
Maugham, W. S.

Narrowing Circle, The
EROS (GB) 1955 dir. Charles Saunders
Symons, J.

Nastasja
HIT (Pol) 1994 dir. Andrzej Wajda
Dostoevsky, F. *Idiot, The*

Nasty Habits
SCOTIA-BARBER (GB) 1976
dir. Michael Lindsay-Hogg
US title: Abbess, The
Spark, M. *Abbess of Crewe, The*

Nasty Neighbours
FIRST HAND (GB) 1999 dir. Debbie
Isitt
Isitt, D.
P

National Health, The
COL (GB) 1973 dir. Jack Gold
Nichols, P.
P

National Velvet
MGM (US) 1944 dir. Clarence Brown
Bagnold, E.

Native Son
CLASSIC (Arg) 1951 dir. Pierre Chenal
CINECOM (US) 1986
dir. Jerrold Freedman
Wright, R.

Natural, The
TRISTAR (US) 1984 dir. Barry Levinson
Malamud, B. .

Nature of the Beast, The
FILM 4 (GB) 1988 dir. Franco Rosso
Howker, J.

Nazarin
BAR PON (Mex) 1958 dir. Luis Bunuel
Galdos, B. P.

Néa
NEW REALM (Fr/Ger) 1976
dir. Nelly Kaplan
US/GB title: Young Emanuelle
Arsan, E.

Nearly a Nasty Accident
BL (GB) 1961 dir. Don Chaffey
Stringer, D. *Touch Wood*
P

Nearly Man, The
GRANADA (GB) 1974 dir. John Irvin,
Alan Grint
TVSe(GB)
Hopcraft, A.
P

Necessity
B&E (US) 1988 dir. Michael Miller
TV(US)
Garfield, B.

Necronomicon
NEW LINE (US) 1994 dir. Christophe
Gans, Shusuke Kaneko, Brian Yuzna
Lovecraft, H. P.

Needful Things
COL (US) 1993 dir. Fraser Clarke
Heston
King, S.

Negatives
CRISPIN (GB) 1968 dir. Peter Medak
Everett, P.

Neighbors
COL (US) 1981 dir. John G. Avildsen
Berger, T.

Neither the Sea Nor the Sand
TIGON (GB) 1972 dir. Fred Burnley

Honeycombe, G.

Nell
FOX (US) 1994 dir. Michael Apted

Handley, M. *Idioglossia*
P

Nemesis
BBC (GB) 1986 dir. David Tucker
TV(GB)

Christie, A.

Nemici D'Infanzia
RAI (It) 1995 dir. Luigi Magni

Magni, L.

Neon Bible, The
CHANNEL 4 FILMS (GB/Sp) 1995 dir. Terence Davies

Toole, J. K.

Nero
INTERSOUND (It) 1992 dir. Giancarlo Soldi

Sclavi, T.

Nero Wolfe
PAR TV (US) 1979 dir. Frank D. Gilroy
TV(US)

Stout, R. *Doorbell Rang, The*

Nest, The
CONCORDE (US) 1988
dir. Terence Winkless

Cantor, E.

Nest of Gentry
CORINTH (USSR) 1970
dir. Andrei Konchalovski

Turgenev, I. *House of the Gentle Folk*

Net, The
GFD (GB) 1953 dir. Anthony Asquith

Pudney, J.

Never a Dull Moment
RKO (US) 1950 dir. George Marshall

Swift, K. *Who Could Ask For Anything More*

Never a Dull Moment
DISNEY (US) 1967 dir. Jerry Paris

Godey, J.

Never Come Back
BBC (GB) 1990 dir. Joe Waters
TVSe(GB)

Mair, J.

Never Cry Wolf
DISNEY (US) 1983 dir. Carroll Ballard

Mowat, F.

Neverending Story, The
WAR (Ger/GB) 1984
dir. Wolfgang Petersen
Ch

Ende, M.

Neverending Story II, The: The Next Chapter
WAR (Ger) 1989 dir. George Miller
Ch

Ende, M. *Neverending Story, The*

Never Let Me Go
MGM (GB) 1953 dir. Delmer Daves

Bax, R. *Came the Dawn*

Never Love a Stranger
ABP (US) 1958 dir. Robert Stevens

Robbins, H.

Never Say Goodbye
UN (US) 1955 dir. Jerry Hopper

Pirandello, L. *Come Prima Meglio di Prima*
P

Never so Few
MGM (US) 1959 dir. John Sturges

Chamales, T.

Never Steal Anything Small
UN (US) 1958 dir. Charles Lederer
Mamoulian, R. and Anderson, M.
Devil's Hornpipe, The
P

Never Take No for an Answer
INDEPENDENT (GB) 1951
dir. Maurice Cloche, Ralph Smart
Gallico, P. *Small Miracle, The*

Never Tell Me Never
GOLDEN SQUARE (Aust) 1998 dir.
David Elfick
TV(Aust)
Shepherd, J.

Never the Twain Shall Meet
MGM (US) 1931 dir. W. S. Van Dyke
Kyne, P. B.

Never Too Late
WAR (US) 1965 dir. Bud Yorkin
Long, S. A.
P

**New Adventures of Pippi
Longstocking, The**
COL (US) 1988 dir. Ken Annakin
Ch
Lindgren, A.

**New Adventures of Spin &
Marty, The: Suspect Behavior**
DISNEY (US) 2000 dir. Rusty Cundieff
Ch, TV(US)
Zindel, P. *Undertaker's Gone Bananas,
The*

New Centurions, The
COL (US) 1972 dir. Richard Fleischer
GB title: Precinct 45: Los Angeles Police
Wambaugh, J.

New Leaf, A
PAR (US) 1970 dir. Elaine May
Ritchie, J. *Green Heart, The*

New Morals for Old
MGM (US) 1932 dir. Charles Brabin
van Druten, J. *After All*
P

New Road, The
BBC (GB) 1973 dir. Moira Armstrong
TVSe(GB)
Munro, N.

News From the Good Lord
CNC (Fr) 1996 dir. Didier LePecheur
LePecheur, D.

**New Swiss Family Robinson,
The**
TOTAL (US) 1999 dir. Stewart Raffill
TV(US)
Wyss, J. D. *Swiss Family Robinson*

Newton Boys, The
FOX (US) 1998 dir. Richard Linklater
Stanush, C. *Newton Boys, The: Portrait of
an Outlaw Gang*

New York Cop
STP (US) 1995 dir. Toru Murakawa
Ueno, J. *New York Undercover Cop*

Nice Girl Like Me, A
AVCO (GB) 1969 dir. Desmond Davis
Piper, A. *Marry at Leisure*

Nice Guys Sleep Alone
LUNACY (US) 1999 dir. Stu Pollard
Feirstein, B. *Nice Guys Sleep Alone:
Dating in the Difficult Eighties*

Nice Work
BBC (GB) 1989 dir. Christopher Menaul
TVSe(GB)
Lodge, D.

Nicholas and Alexandra
COL (GB) 1971 dir. Franklin Schaffner
Massie, R. K.

Nicholas Nickleby
EAL (GB) 1947 dir. Alberto Cavalcanti
BBC (GB) 1977 dir. Christopher Barry
TVSe(GB)
Dickens, C.

Nico and Dani
MESSIDOR (Sp) 2000 dir. Cesc Gay
Sanchez, J. *Krampack*
P

Night After Night
PAR (US) 1932 dir. Archie Mayo
Bromfield, L. *Single Night*

Night and the City
FOX (GB) 1950 dir. Jules Dassin
TRIBECA (US) 1992 dir. Irwin Winkler
Kersh, G.

Night and the Moment, The
CECCHI (It/Fr) 1994 dir. Anna Maria
Tato
de Jolyot Crebillon, C.-P. *Nuit et le
Moment, La*
P

Nightbreaker
TNT (US) 1989 dir. Peter Markle
TV(US)
Rosenberg, H. *Atomic Soldiers*

Nightbreed
FOX (US) 1990 dir. Clive Barker
Barker, C. *Cabal*

Night Club Scandal
PAR (US) 1937 dir. Ralph Murphy
Rubin, D. *Riddle Me This*
P

Nightcomers, The
AVCO (GB) 1972
dir. Michael Winner
James, H. *Turn of the Screw, The*

Night Comes too Soon
BUTCHER (GB) 1948 dir. Denis
Kavanagh
Lytton, B. *Haunted and the Haunters, The*
P

Night Digger, The
MGM (GB) 1971 dir. Alistair Reid
Cowley, J. *Nest in a Falling Tree*

Nightfall
COL (US) 1956 dir. Jacques Tourneur
Goodis, D.

Nightfall
CONCORDE (US) 1988 dir. Paul
Mayersburg
CONCORDE (US) 2000 dir. Tim Clark,
Gwyneth Gibby
Asimov, I.

Night Falls on Manhattan
PAR (US) 1997 dir. Sidney Lumet
Daley, R. *Tainted Evidence*

Night Flier
NEW LINE (It/US) 1997 dir. Mark
Pavia
King, S.

Nightflyers
NEW CENTURY (US) 1987
dir. T. C. Blake
Martin, G. R. R.

Night Games
GALA (Swe) 1966 dir. Mai Zetterling
Zetterling, M.

Night Has a Thousand Eyes
PAR (US) 1948 dir. John Farrow
Woolrich, C.

Night Has Eyes, The
PATHE (GB) 1942 dir. Leslie Arliss
Kennington, A.

Night in Paradise, A
UN (US) 1946 dir. Arthur Lubin

Hellman, G. S. *Peacock's Feather*

Night in the Life of Jimmy Reardon, A
FOX (US) 1988 dir. William Richert

Richert, W. *Aren't You Even Gonna Kiss Me Goodbye*

Nightjohn
HALLMARK (US) 1996 dir. Charles Burnett
TV(US)

Paulsen, G.

Night Larry Kramer Kissed Me, The
MONTROSE (US) 2000 dir. Tim Kirkman

Drake, D.
P

Night Life of the Gods, The
UN (US) 1935 dir. Lowell Sherman

Smith, T.

Nightmare
UN (US) 1942 dir. Tim Whelan

MacDonald, P. *Escape*

Nightmare
UA (US) 1956 dir. Maxwell Shane

Woolrich, C.

Nightmare Alley
FOX (GB) 1947 dir. Edmund Goulding

Gresham, W.

Nightmare Man, The
BBC (US) 1981 dir. Douglas Camfield
TVSe(GB)

Wiltshire, D. *Child of Vodyanoi*

Nightmare Street
LONGBOW (US) 1998 dir. Colin Bucksey
TV(US)

Tabor, M.

Nightmare Years, The
CONSOL (US) 1989 dir. Anthony Page
TV(US)

Shirer, W.

'Night, Mother
UN (US) 1986 dir. Tom Moore

Norman, M.
P

Night Must Fall
MGM (US) 1937 dir. Richard Thorpe
MGM (GB) 1964 dir. Karel Reisz

Williams, E.
P

Night Nurse
WAR (US) 1931 dir. William Wellman

Macy, D.

Night of January 16th, The
PAR (US) 1941 dir. William Clements

Rand, A.
P

Night of Courage
TITUS (US) 1987 dir. Elliot Silverstein
TV(US)

Williams, B. *In This Fallen City*
P

Night of the Big Heat
PLANET (GB) 1967 dir. Terence Fisher

Lymington, J.

Night of the Demon
COL (GB) 1957 dir. Jacques Tourneur

James, M. R. *Casting the Runes*

Night of the Eagle
IA (GB) 1961 dir. Sidney Hayers
US title: Burn, Witch, Burn
Leiber, F. *Conjure Wife*

Night of the Following Day, The
UN (US) 1969 dir. Hubert Cornfield
White, L. *Snatchers, The*

Night of the Fox
DOVE/ITC (US/GB) 1990
dir. Charles Jarrot
TVSe(GB/US)
Higgins, J.

Night of the Generals, The
COL/BL (GB) 1966 dir. Anatole Litvak
Hirst, H. H.

Night of the Hunter, The
UA (US) 1955 dir. Charles Laughton
KON/SAN (US) 1991
dir. David Greene
TV(US)
Grubb, D.

Night of the Iguana, The
MGM (US) 1964 dir. John Huston
Williams, T.
P

Night of the Juggler
COL (US) 1980 dir. Robert Butler
McGivern, W. P.

Night of the Lepus
MGM (US) 1972 dir. William F. Claxton
Braddon, R. *Year of the Angry Rabbit, The*

Night of the Running Man
AM WORLD (US) 1995 dir. Mark L. Lester
Wells, L.

Night of the Twisters, The
MTM (US) 1996 dir. Tim Bond
TV(US)
Ruckman, I.

Night Ride Home
HALLMARK (US) 1999 dir. Glenn Jordan
TV(US)
Esstman, B.

Nights Below Station Street
CBC (Can) 1998 dir. Norma Bailey
TV(Can)
Richards, D. A.

Night Slaves
B. CROSBY (US) 1970 dir. Ted Post
TV(US)
Sohl, J.

Night They Raided Minsky's, The
UA (US) 1968 dir. William Friedkin
GB title: Night They Invented Striptease, The
Barber, R.

Night to Remember, A
RANK (GB) 1957 dir. Roy Ward Baker
Lord, W.

Nightscream
VZ/SERTNER (US) 1997 dir. Noel Nosseck
TV(US)
Sprecht, R. *Soul of Betty Fairchild, The*

Night Sins
SCRIPPS HOWARD (US) 1997 dir. Robert Allan Ackerman
TVSe(US)
Hoag, T.

Night Train to Munich
TCF (GB) 1940 dir. Carol Reed
Wellesley, G. *Report on a Fugitive*

Night unto Night
WAR (US) 1949 dir. Don Siegel
Wylie, P.

Night was our Friend
MONARCH (GB) 1951
dir. Michael Anderson
Pertwee, M.
P

Night Watch
AVCO (GB) 1973 dir. Brian G. Hutton
Fletcher, L.
P

Night Watch
BL (US/GB) 1995 dir. David S. Jackson
TV(US/GB)
MacLean, A.

Nightwing
COL (Neth) 1975 dir. Arthur Miller
Smith, M. C.

Night Without Stars
GFD (GB) 1951 dir. Anthony Pelissier
Graham, W.

Nijinsky
PAR (US) 1980 dir. Herbert Ross
Nijinsky, R.

Nikki, Wild Dog of the North
DISNEY (US) 1961 dir. Jack Couffer
Curwood, J. O. *Nomads of the North*

9½ Weeks
MGM/UA (US) 1986 dir. Adrian Lyne
McNeill, E.

Nine Girls
COL (US) 1944 dir. Leigh Jason
Pettit, W. H.
P

Nine Hours to Rama
FOX (GB) 1962 dir. Mark Robson
Wolpert, S.

Nine Lives
NORDS (Nor) 1959 dir. Arne Skouen
Howarth, D. *We Die Alone*

Nine Tailors, The
BBC (GB) 1974 dir. Raymond Menmuir
TVSe(GB)
Sayers, D. L.

1915
BBC (GB/Aust) 1983
dir. Chris Thomson
TVSe (Aust/GB)
McDonald, R.

1984
ABP (GB) 1956 dir. Michael Anderson
BBC (GB) 1965
dir. Christopher Morahan
TV(GB)
BBC (GB) 1984 dir. Rudolph Cartier
TV(GB)
VIRGIN (GB) 1984 dir. Michael Radford
Orwell, G.

92 in the Shade
UA (US) 1975 dir. Thomas McGuane
McGuane, T.

Ninfa Plebea
EUROLUX (It) 1996 dir. Lina
Wertmuller
Rea, D.

Ninth Configuration, The
LORIMAR (US) 1980
dir. William P. Blatty
Blatty, W. P.

Ninth Gate, The
STUDIO CANAL+ (Fr/Sp/US) 1999
dir. Roman Polanski
Perez-Reverte, A. *Club Dumas, The*

Ninth Guest, The
COL (US) 1934 dir. Roy William Neill
Bristow, G.

Ninth Street
HODCARRIER (US) 1999 dir. Tim
Rebman, Kevin Willmott
Willmott, K.
P

No Blade of Grass
MGM (GB) 1970 dir. Cornel Wilde
Christopher, J. *Death of Grass*

Noble House
DELAUR (US) 1988 dir. Gary Nelson
TVSe(US)
Clavell, J.

Nobody Lives Forever
O'HARA-HORO (US) 1998 dir. Paul
Wendkos
TV(US)
Buchanan, E.

Nobody Runs Forever
RANK (GB) 1968 dir. Ralph Thomas
US title: High Commissioner, The
Cleary, J. *High Commissioner, The*

Nobody's Fool
PAR (US) 1994 dir. Robert Benton
Russo, R.

Nobody's Perfect
UN (US) 1978 dir. Alan Rafkin
Bosworth, A. R. *Crows of Edwina Hill,
The*

Nobody's Perfekt
COL (US) 1981 dir. Peter Bonerz
Kenrick, T. *Two for the Price of One*

No Down Payment
FOX (US) 1957 dir. Martin Ritt
McPartland, J.

No Escape
PATHE (GB) 1936 dir. Norman Lee
Goodchild, G. and Witty, F. *No Exit*
P

No Escape
COL (US) 1994 dir. Martin Campbell
Herley, R. *Penal Colony, The*

Nogne Traer, De
NORSK (Den) 1992 dir. Morten
Henriksen
Skou-Hansen, T.

No Greater Love
NBC (US) 1996 dir. Richard T. Heffron
TV(US)
Steel, D.

No Hands on the Clock
PAR (US) 1941 dir. Frank McDonald
Homes, G.

No Highway
FOX (GB) 1951 dir. Henry Koster
US title: No Highway in the Sky
Shute, N.

Noh Mask Murders
TOEI (Jap) 1991 dir. Kon Ichikawa
Uchida, Y.

Noises Off
TOUCHSTONE (US) 1992 dir. Peter
Bogdanovich
Frayn, M.
P

No Kidding
AA (GB) 1960 dir. Gerald Thomas
US title: Beware of Children
Anderson, V. *Beware of Children*

No Life King
NEW CENTURY (Jap) 1991
dir. Jun Ichikawa
Ito, S.

No Love for Johnnie
RANK (GB) 1960 dir. Ralph Thomas
Fienburgh, W.

No More Ladies
MGM (US) 1935
dir. Edward H. Griffith, George Cukor
Thomas, A. E.
P

No, My Darling Daughter
RANK (GB) 1961 dir. Ralph Thomas
Brooke, H. and Bannerman, K. *Handful of Tansy, A*
P

None but the Lonely Heart
RKO (US) 1944 dir. Clifford Odets
Llewellyn, R.

No No Nanette
WAR (US) 1930 dir. Clarence Badger
M
RKO (US) 1940 dir. Herbert Wilcox
M
Harbach, O. and Mandel, F.
P

Non Stop New York
GFD (GB) 1937 dir. Robert Stevenson
Attiwill, K. *Sky Steward*

No One Writes to the Colonel
TORNASOL (Sp) 1999 dir. Arturo Ripstein
Marquez, G. G.

No Orchids for Miss Blandish
ALL (GB) 1948 dir. St. John L. Clowes
Chase, J. H.

Noose
ABPC (GB) 1948
dir. Edmond T. Greville
Llewellyn, R.
P

No Place for Jennifer
ABP (GB) 1949 dir. Henry Cass
Hambledon, P. *No Difference to Me*

No Resting Place
ABP (GB) 1951 dir. Paul Rother
Niall, I.

Norman, Is That You?
MGM (US) 1976 dir. George Schlatter
Clark, R. and Bobrick, S.
P

No Room at the Inn
BN (GB) 1948 dir. Dan Birt
Temple, J.
P

No Room for the Groom
UI (US) 1952 dir. Douglas Sirk
Teilhet, D. L. *My True Love*

North
COL (US) 1994 dir. Rob Reiner
Zweibel, A.

Northanger Abbey
BBC (GB) 1987 dir. Giles Foster
TV(GB)
Austen, J.

North and South
BBC (GB) 1975 dir. Rodney Bennett
TVSe(GB)
Gaskell, E.

North and South
WAR (US) 1985 dir. Richard T. Heffron
TVSe(US)
Jakes, J.

North and South, Book II
WAR TV (US) 1986 dir. Kevin Connor
TVSe(US)
Jakes, J. *Love and War*

North Avenue Irregulars, The
DISNEY (US) 1978 dir. Bruce Bilson
GB title: Hill's Angels
Hill, Rev. A. F.

North Dallas Forty
PAR (US) 1979 dir. Ted Kotcheff
Gent, P.

Nor the Moon by Night
RANK (GB) 1958 dir. Ken Annakin
US title: Elephant Gun
Packer, J.

Northern Lights
ALLIANCE (US/Can) 1997 dir. Linda Yellen
TV(US/Can)
Hoffman, J.

Northern Passage
GAU TV (Fr/Can) 1994 dir. Arnaud Selignac
TV(Fr/Can)
Curwood, J. O. *Baree, Son of Kazan*

North Sea Hijack
CIC (GB) 1980 dir. Andrew V. McLaglen
US title: Ffolkes
Davies, J. *Esther, Ruth and Jennifer*

North Shore Fish
SHOWTIMEWORKS (US) 1997 dir. Steve Zuckerman
TV(US)
Horovitz, I.
P

North Star
WAR (Fr/It/GB) 1996 dir. Nils Gaup
Henry, W.

North to Alaska
FOX (US) 1960 dir. Henry Hathaway
Fodor, L. *Birthday Gift*
P

Northwest Mounted Police
PAR (US) 1940 dir. Cecil B. De Mille
Fetherstonhaugh, R. C. *Royal Canadian Mounted Police*

Northwest Passage
MGM (US) 1940 dir. King Vidor
Roberts, K.

No Sad Songs for Me
COL (US) 1950 dir. Rudolph Maté
Southard, R.

No Sex Please — We're British
COL (GB) 1973 dir. Cliff Owen
Marriott, A. and Foot, A.
P

Nostromo
BBC (GB) 1997 dir. Alastair Reid
TVSe(GB)
Conrad, J.

Not a Penny More, Not a Penny Less
BBC (GB) 1990 dir. Clive Donner
TVSe(GB)
Archer, J.

Not as a Stranger
UA (US) 1955 dir. Stanley Kramer
Thompson, M.

Notes From Underground
RENEGADE (US) 1995 dir. Gary Walkow
Dostoevsky, F.

Nothin' But The Truth
PAR (US) 1941 dir. Elliott Nugent
Isham, F. S.

Nothing but the Night
FOX-RANK (GB) 1972 dir. Peter Sasdy
Blackburn, J.

Nothing Lasts Forever
GERBER/ITC (US) 1995 dir. Jack
Bender
TVSe(US)
Sheldon, S.

Nothing Personal
BRIT SCREEN (GB/Ire) 1995 dir.
Thaddeus O'Sullivan
Mornin, D. *All Our Fault*

Nothing Sacred
SELZNICK (US) 1937
dir. William Wellman
Street, J. H. *Letter to the Editor*

**Nothing Too Good For a
Cowboy**
ALLIANCE (Can) 1999 dir. Kari
Skogland
TV(Can)
Hobson, Jr.. R. P.

No Time for Breakfast
BOURLA (Fr) 1980
dir. Jean-Louis Bertucelli
Loriot, N. *Cri, Un*

No Time for Comedy
WAR (US) 1940 dir. William Keighley
Behrman, S. N.
P

No Time for Sergeants
WAR (US) 1958 dir. Mervyn LeRoy
Hyman, M.

Not My Kid
FINNEGAN (US) 1985
dir. Michael Tuchner
TV(US)
Polson, B.

Not Now Darling
MGM (GB) 1973 dir. Ray Cooney, David
Croft
Cooney, R.
P

Not Quite Jerusalem
RANK (GB) 1985 dir. Lewis Gilbert
Kember, P.
P

No Trees in the Street
ABP (US) 1958 dir. J. Lee Thompson
Willis, T.
P

Not Without My Daughter
MGM (US) 1991 dir. Brian Gilbert
Mahmoody, B. and Hoffer, W.

Now and Forever
ABP (GB) 1955 dir. Mario Zampi
Delderfield, R. F. *Orchard Walls, The*
P

No Way Out
ORION (US) 1987 dir. Roger Donaldson
Fearing, K. *Big Clock, The*

No Way to Treat a Lady
PAR (US) 1968 dir. Jack Smight
Goldman, W.

Now Barrabas was a Robber
WAR (GB) 1949 dir. Gordon Parry
Home, W. D. *Now Barrabas*

Nowhere to Go
EAL (GB) 1958 dir. Seth Holt
Mackenzie, D.

Nowhere to Run
MTM (US) 1978 dir. Richard Lang
TV(US)
Einstein, C. *Blackjack Hijack, The*

Now, Voyager
WAR (US) 1942 dir. Irving Rapper
Prouty, O.

Number Seventeen
BIP (GB) 1932 dir. Alfred Hitchcock

Farjeon, J. J.
P

Nun's Story, The
WAR (US) 1959 dir. Fred Zinnemann

Hulme, K.

Nuremberg
ALLIANCE (US/Can) 2000 dir. Yves Simoneau
TVSe(US/Can)

Persico, J. E. *Nuremberg: Infamy on Trial*

Nurse
HALMI (US) 1980
dir. David Lowell Rich
TV(US)

Anderson, P.

Nurse Edith Cavell
RKO (US) 1939 dir. Herbert Wilcox

Berkeley, R. *Dawn*

Nursemaid Who Disappeared, The
WAR (GB) 1939 dir. Arthur Woods

MacDonald, P.

Nurse on Wheels
WAR (GB) 1963 dir. Gerald Thomas

Jones, J. *Nurse is a Neighbour*

Nurse's Secret, The
WAR (US) 1941 dir. Noel M. Smith

Rinehart, M. R. *Miss Pinkerton*

Nutcracker
ATLANTIC (US) 1986 dir. Carroll Ballard
M

Hoffman, E. T. A.

Nutcracker: Money, Madness and Murder
WAR TV (US) 1987
dir. Paul Bogart
TVSe(US)

Alexander, S. *Nutcracker: Money, Madness, Murder: A Family Album*

Nutcracker Prince, The
WAR (US) 1990 dir. Paul Schibli
A

Hoffman, E. T. A. *Nutcracker and the Mouseking, The*

Nuts
WAR (US) 1987 dir. Martin Ritt

Topor, T.
P

O

O
LIONS GATE (US) 2001 dir. Tim Blake Nelson
Shakespeare, W. *Othello*
P

Oak, The
STUDIO CANAL+ (Fr) 1992 dir. Lucian Pintilie
Baiesu, O. *Bylanta*

Object of My Affection, The
FOX (US) 1998 dir. Nicholas Hytner
McCauley, S.

Oblomov
MOSFILM (USSR) 1981 dir. Nikita Milchalkov
Goncharov, I.

Obsession
GFD (GB) 1949 dir. Edward Dmytryk
US title: Hidden Room, The
Coppel, A. *Man About a Dog, A*
P

Occasional Hell, An
GREENLIGHT (US) 1996 dir. Salome Breziner
TV(US)
Silvis, R.

Occupe-toi d'Amélie
LUX (Fr) 1949 dir. Claude Autant-Lara
Feydeau, G.
P

October Man, The
GFD (GB) 1947 dir. Roy Baker
Ambler, E.

Odd Man Out
TC (GB) 1947 dir. Carol Reed
US title: Gang War
Green, F. L.

Odd Couple, The
PAR (US) 1968 dir. Gene Saks
Simon, N.
P

Odd Couple, The: Together Again
PAR TV (US) 1993 dir. Robert Klane
TV(US)
Simon, N.
P

Odds Against Tomorrow
UA (US) 1959 dir. Robert Wise
McGivern, W. P.

Odessa File, The
COL (GB) 1974 dir. Ronald Neame
Forsyth, F.

Odette
BL (GB) 1950 dir. Herbert Wilcox
Tickell, J.

Oedipus the King
UI (GB) 1968 dir. Philip Saville
Sophocles
P

Oedipus Rex
HORIZON (It) 1947
dir. Pier Paolo Pasolini

Sophocles *Oedipus the King*
P

Offence, The
UA (GB) 1972 dir. Sidney Lumet

Hopkins, J. *This Story of Yours*
P

Off to Philadelphia in the Morning
BBC (GB) 1978 dir. Julian Williams
TVSe(GB)

Jones, J.

Of Human Bondage
RKO (US) 1934 dir. John Cromwell
WAR (US) 1946 dir. Edmund Goulding
MGM (GB) 1964 dir. Henry Hathaway

Maugham, W. S.

Of Human Hearts
MGM (US) 1938 dir. Clarence Brown

Morrow, H. *Benefits Forgot*

Of Love and Shadows
MIRAMAX (Arg/Sp) 1994 dir. Betty Kaplan

Allende, I.

Of Mice and Men
UA (US) 1939 dir. Lewis Milestone
METROMEDIA (US) 1981
dir. Reza Badiyi
TV(US)
MGM (US) 1992 dir. Gary Sinese

Steinbeck, J.

Of Unknown Origin
WAR (Can) 1983
dir. George P. Cosmatos

Parker, C. G. *Visitor, The*

Ogre, The
STUDIO CANAL+ (Fr/Ger) 1996 dir. Volker Schlondorff

Tourner, M. *Roi Des Aulnes, Le*

Oh Dad, Poor Dad ... Mama's Hung You In The Closet and I'm Feeling So Sad
PAR (US) 1966 dir. Richard Quine

Kopit, A.
P

Oh! God!
WAR (US) 1977 dir. Carl Reiner

Corman, A.

Oh! Men! Oh! Women!
FOX (US) 1957 dir. Nunnally Johnson

Chodorov, E.
P

Oh! What a Lovely War
PAR (GB) 1969
dir. Richard Attenborough

Chilton, C. and Littlewood, J. *Long, Long Trail, The*
P

Oil for the Lamps of China
WAR (US) 1935 dir. Mervyn LeRoy

Hobart, A. T.

Oklahoma!
MAGNA (US) 1955 dir. Fred Zinnemann
M

Riggs, L. *Green Grow the Lilacs*
P

Rodgers, R. and Hammerstein II, O.
P

Old Acquaintance
WAR (US) 1943 dir. Vincent Sherman

van Druten, J.
P

Old Curiosity Shop, The
BIP (GB) 1934 dir. Thomas Bentley
BBC (GB) 1979 dir. Julian Amyes
TVSe(GB)
RHI (US) 1995 dir. Kevin Connor
TVSe(US)

Dickens, C.

Old Dark House, The
UN (US) 1932 dir. James Whale
BL (GB) 1963 dir. William Castle

Priestley, J. B. *Benighted*

Old Devils, The
BBC (GB) 1992 dir. Tristram Powell
TVSe(GB)

Amis, K.

Old English
WAR (US) 1930 dir. Alfred E. Green

Galsworthy, J.
P

Oldest Living Confederate Widow Tells All
RHI (US) 1994 dir. Ken Cameron
TVSe(US)

Gurganus, A.

Old Gringo
COL (US) 1989 dir. Luis Puenzo

Fuentes, C. *Gringo Viejo*

Old Maid, The
WAR (US) 1939 dir. Edmund Goulding

Wharton, E.

Atkins, Z.
P

Old Man and the Sea, The
WAR (US) 1958 dir. John Sturges
STORKE (US) 1990
dir. Jud Taylor
TV(US)

Hemingway, E.

Old Man Who Read Love Stories, The
KINO VISION (Fr/Aust/Neth) 2001
dir. Rolf de Heer

Sepulveda, L.

Old Men at the Zoo, The
BBC (GB) 1982 dir. Stuart Burge
TVSe(GB)

Wilson, A.

Old Settler, The
KCET (US) 2001 dir. Debbie Allen
TV(US)

Redwood, J. H.
P

Old Times
BBC (GB) 1991 dir. Simon Curtis
TV(GB)

Pinter, H.
P

Old Yeller
DISNEY (US) 1957
dir. Robert Stevenson

Gipson, F. B.

Oleanna
GOLDWYN (US) 1994 dir. David
Mamet

Mamet, D.
P

Oliver!
COL (GB) 1968 dir. Carol Reed
M

Dickens, C. *Oliver Twist*

Oliver's Story
PAR (US) 1978 dir. John Korty

Segal, E.

Oliver Twist
CINEGUILD (GB) 1948 dir. David Lean
TRIDENT (US/GB) 1982
dir. Clive Donner
TV(US/GB)
BBC (GB) 1985 dir. Gareth Davies
TVSe(GB)
DISNEY (US) 1997 dir. Tony Bill
TV(US)

Dickens, C.

Olivia
FDF (Fr) 1950 dir. Jacqueline Audry
'Olivia'

Omega Man, The
WAR (US) 1971 dir. Boris Sagal

Matheson, R. *I Am Legend*

On a Clear Day You Can See Forever
PAR (US) 1970 dir. Vincente Minnelli
M

Lerner, A. J.
P

On Approval
FOX (GB) 1944 dir. Clive Brook

Lonsdale, F.
P

On Beulah Height
BBC/A&E (GB) 1999 dir. Maurice Phillips
TV(GB)

Hill, R.

On Borrowed Time
MGM (US) 1939 dir. Harold S. Bucquet
MILBERG (US) 1957
dir. George Schaefer
TV(US)

Watkins, L. E.

Once a Crook
FOX (GB) 1941 dir. Herbert Mason

Price, E. and Attiwill, K.
P

Once a Jolly Swagman
WESSEX (GB) 1948 dir. Jack Lee
US title: Maniacs on Wheels

Slater, M.

Once an Eagle
UN TV (US) 1977 dir. E. W. Swackhamer, Richard Michaels
TVSe(US)

Myrer, A.

Once in a Lifetime
UN (US) 1933 dir. Russell Mack

Kaufman, G. S. and Hart, M.
P

Once in a Lifetime
NBC (US) 1994 dir. Michael Miller
TV(US)

Steel, D.

Once in the Life
SHOOTING GALLERY (US) 2000 dir. Laurence Fishburne

Fishburne, L. *Riff Raff*
P

Once is not Enough
PAR (US) 1975 dir. Guy Green

Susann, J.

Once More My Darling
UI (US) 1949 dir. Robert Montgomery

Carson, R. *Come Be My Love*

Once More, With Feeling
COL (GB) 1960 dir. Stanley Donen

Kurnitz, H.
P

Once Upon a Time in America
WAR (US) 1984 dir. Sergio Leone

Aaronson, D. *Hoods, The*

Once Upon a Time … When We Were Colored
BET (US) 1995 dir. Tim Reid
Taulbert, C. L.

Once Were Warriors
FINE LINE (NZ) 1994 dir. Lee Tamahori
Duff, A.

Once You Meet a Stranger
WAR (US) 1996 dir. Tommy Lee Wallace
TV(US)
Highsmith, P. *Strangers on a Train*

On Dangerous Ground
RKO (US) 1951 dir. Nicholas Ray
Butler, G.

On Dangerous Ground
TELESCENE PROD (Can/GB) 1996 dir. Lawrence Gordon Clark
TV(Can/GB)
Higgins, J.

One Brief Summer
FOX (GB) 1969 dir. John MacKenzie
Tierney, H. *Valkyrie's Armour*
P

One Day in the Life of Ivan Denizovich
CINERAMA (GB) 1971
dir. Caspar Wrede
Solzhenitsyn, A.

One Deadly Summer
SNC (Fr) 1983 dir. Jean Becker
Japrisot, S.

One Desire
UI (US) 1955 dir. Jerry Hopper
Richter, C. *Tracy Cromwell*

One-Eyed Jacks
PAR (US) 1961 dir. Marlon Brando
Neider, C. *Authentic Death of Hendry Jones, The*

One Flew Over the Cuckoo's Nest
UA (US) 1975 dir. Milos Forman
Kesey, K.

One Foot in Heaven
WAR (US) 1941 dir. Irving Rapper
Spence, H.

One Game, The
CENTRAL (GB) 1988 dir. Mike Vardy
TVSe(GB)
Benet, T.

Onegin
CANWEST (GB) 1999 dir. Martha Fiennes
Pushkin, A. *Eugene Onegin*

One Hour With You
PAR (US) 1932 dir. George Cukor, Ernst Lubitsch
M
Schmidt, L. *Only a Dream*
P

One Hundred and One Dalmatians
DISNEY (US) 1961
dir. Wolfgang Reitherman, Clyde Geronimi, Hamilton Luske
A, Ch
Smith, D. *Hundred and One Dalmations, The*

101 Dalmations
DISNEY (US) 1996 dir. Stephen Herek
Ch
Smith, D. *Hundred and One Dalmations, The*

101 Reykjavik
FILMHUSET (Ice/Den) 2000 dir. Baltasar Kormakur
Helgason, H.

102 Dalmations
DISNEY (US) 2000 dir. Kevin Lima
Ch
Smith, D. *Hundred and One Dalmations, The*

100 Rifles
FOX (US) 1969 dir. Tom Gries
MaeLeod, R. *Californio, The*

One in a Million: The Ron LeFlore Story
EMI (US) 1978 dir. William A. Graham
TV(US)
LeFlore, R. and Hawkins, J. *Breakout*

One is a Lonely Number
MGM (US) 1972 dir. Mel Stuart
Morris, R.

One Man's Way
UA (US) 1964 dir. Denis Sanders
Gordon, A. *Minister to Millions*

One More River
UN (US) 1934 dir. James Whale
GB title: Over the River
Galsworthy, J. *Over the River*

One More Spring
FOX (US) 1935 dir. Henry King
Nathan, R.

One More Tomorrow
WAR (US) 1946 dir. Peter Godfrey
Barry, P. *Animal Kingdom, The*
P

One New York Night
MGM (US) 1935 dir. Jack Conway
GB title: Trunk Mystery, The
Carpenter E. C.
P

One Night in Lisbon
PAR (US) 1941 dir. Edward H. Griffith
van Druten, J. *There's Always Juliet*
P

One of my Wives is Missing
SPEL-GOLD (US) 1976
dir. Glenn Jordan
Thomas, R. *Trap for a Single Man*
P

One of our Dinosaurs is Missing
DISNEY (US) 1975
dir. Robert Stevenson
Ch
Forrest, D. *Great Dinosaur Robbery, The*

One of Those Things
RANK (Den) 1971 dir. Erik Balling
Bodelsen, A. *Hit, and Run, Run, Run*

One Police Plaza
CBS ENT (US) 1986 dir. Jerry Jameson
TV(US)
Caunitz, W. J.

One Shoe Makes it Murder
LORIMAR TV (US) 1982
dir. William Hale
TV(US)
Bercovici, E. *So Little Cause for Caroline*

One Special Moment
ARABESQUE FILMS (US) 2001 dir.
Nelson George
TV(US)
Jackson, B.

One Special Night
GREEN/EPSTEIN (US) 1999 dir. Roger Young
TV(US)
Hartman, J. *Winter Visitor, A*
P

One Special Victory
NBC (US) 1991 dir. Stuart Cooper
TV(US)

Jones, R. *B-Ball: The Team That Never Lost a Game*

One Sunday Afternoon
PAR (US) 1933 dir. Stephen Roberts
WAR (US) 1948 dir. Raoul Walsh

Hagan, J.
P

One That Got Away, The
RANK (GB) 1957 dir. Roy Baker

Burt, K. and Leasor, J.

One Third of a Nation
PAR (US) 1939 dir. Dudley Murphy

Arent, A.
P

One Touch of Venus
UN (US) 1948 dir. William A. Seiter

Perelman, S. J. and Nash, O.
P

One Tough Cop
PATRIOT (US) 1998 dir. Bruno Barreto

Dietl, B. and Gross, K. *One Tough Cop: The Bo Dietl Story*

One True Thing
UN (US) 1998 dir. Carl Franklin

Quindlen, A.

One, Two, Three
UA (US) 1961 dir. Billy Wilder

Molnar, F.
P

One Way Pendulum
UA (GB) 1964 dir. Peter Yates

Simpson, N. F.
P

One-Way Ticket
COL (US) 1935 dir. Herbert Biberman

Turner, E.

One Wild Oat
EROS (GB) 1951 dir. Charles Saunders

Sylvaine, V.
P

On Friday at 11
BL (Ger/Fr/It) 1961 dir. Alvin Rakoff

Chase, J. H. *World In My Pocket, The*

On Golden Pond
UN (US) 1981 dir. Mark Rydell
CBS TV (US) 2001 dir. Ernest Thompson
TV(US)

Thompson, E.
P

On Guard!
STUDIO CANAL+ (Fr) 1997 dir. Philippe de Broca

Feval, P. *Bossu, Le*

On Her Majesty's Secret Service
UA (GB) 1969 dir. Peter Hunt

Fleming, I.

Onion Field, The
AVCO (US) 1979 dir. Harold Becker

Wambaugh, J.

Onionhead
WAR (US) 1958 dir. Norman Taurog

Hill, W.

Only Game in Town, The
FOX (US) 1969 dir. George Stevens

Gilroy, F. D.
P

Only Love
HALLMARK (US) 1998 dir. John Erman
TV(US)

Segal, E.

Only One Survived
CBS ENT (US) 1990 dir. Folco Quilici
TV(US)
Quilici, F. *Danger Adrift*

Only the Valiant
WAR (US) 1950 dir. Gordon Douglas
Warren, C. M.

Only Thrill, The
MOONSTONE (US) 1997 dir. Peter
Masterson
Ketron, L. *Hitching Post, The*
P

Only Two Can Play
BL (GB) 1961 dir. Sidney Gilliat
Amis, K. *That Uncertain Feeling*

Only When I Larf
PAR (GB) 1968 dir. Basil Dearden
Deighton, L.

Only When I Laugh
COL (US) 1981 dir. Glenn Jordan
GB title: It Only Hurts When I Laugh
Simon, N. *Gingerbread Lady, The*
P

On Moonlight Bay
WAR (US) 1951 dir. Roy del Ruth
M
Tarkington, B. *Penrod*

On the Beach
UA (US) 1959 dir. Stanley Kramer
SHOWTIME (US/Aust) 2000 dir.
Russell Mulcahy
TV(US/Aust)
Shute, N.

On the Black Hill
CHANNEL 4 (GB) 1989
dir. Andrew Grieve
TV(GB)
Chatwin, B.

On the Edge
SCREEN ENT (Israel) 1994 dir. Amnon
Rubinstein
Kenaz, Y.

On the Fiddle
AA (GB) 1961 dir. Cyril Frankel
US title: Operation Snafu
Delderfield, R. F. *Stop at a Winner*

On the Night of the Fire
GFD (GB) 1939
dir. Brian Desmond Hurst
US title: Fugitive, The
Green, F. L.

On The Run
CFF (GB) 1969 dir. Pat Jackson
Ch
Bawden, N.

On the Waterfront
COL (US) 1954 dir. Elia Kazan
Schulberg, B. W.

On Valentine's Day
ANGELIKA (US) 1986 dir. Ken
Harrison
Foote, H. *Valentine's Day*
P

On Wings of Eagles
TAFT (US) 1986
dir. Andrew V. McLaglen
TVSe(US)
Follett, K.

On Your Toes
WAR (US) 1939 dir. Ray Enright
Abbott, G.
P

Open Admissions
VIACOM (US) 1988 dir. Gus Trikonis
TV(US)
Lauro, S.
P

Opening Night
ITV (GB) 1978 dir. Brian McDuffie
TV(GB)
Marsh, N.

Opera do Malandro
AUSTRA/TFl (Bra/Fr) 1986
dir. Ruy Guerra
Buarque, C.
P

Operation Amsterdam
RANK (GB) 1958
dir. Michael McCarthy
Walker, D. E. *Adventure in Diamonds*

Operation Daybreak
WAR (US) 1975 dir. Lewis Gilbert
Burgess, A. *Seven Men at Daybreak*

Operation Julie
TYNE-TEES (GB) 1985 dir. Bob
Mahoney
TVSe(GB)
Pratt, C. and Lee, D.

Operation Mad Ball
COL (US) 1957 dir. Richard Quine
Carter, A.
P

O Pioneers!
LORIMAR (US) 1992 dir. Glenn Jordan
TV(US)
Cather, W.

Opposite Sex, The
MGM (US) 1956 dir. David Miller
Boothe, C. *Women, The*
P

Optimists of Nine Elms, The
SCOTIA-BARBER (GB) 1973
dir. Anthony Simmons
Simmons, A.

Oranges are not the only Fruit
A&E/BBC (US/GB) 1990
dir. Beeban Kidron
TVSe(GB/US)
Winterson, J.

Orchid House, The
BBC (GB) 1991 dir. Harold Ove
TV(GB)
Allfrey, P. S.

Ordeal by Innocence
CANNON (GB) 1985
dir. Desmond Davis
Christie, A.

Ordeal in the Arctic
ALLIANCE (US) 1993 dir. Mark Sobel
TV(US)
Lee, R. M. *Death and Deliverance*

Orders are Orders
BL (GB) 1954 dir. David Paltenghi
Hay, I. and Armstrong, A. *Orders is Orders*
P

Orders is Orders
GAU (GB) 1933 dir. Walter Forde
Hay, I. and Armstrong, A.
P

Ordinary Hero, An
INSTITUTO LUCE (It) 1995 dir. Michele
Placido
Stajano, C.

Ordinary Magic
FILMWORKS (Can) 1993 dir. Giles
Walker
Bosse, M.

Ordinary People
PAR (US) 1980 dir. Robert Redford
Guest, J.

Oregon Passage
ABP (US) 1958 dir. Paul Landres
Shirreffs, G. D. *Trails End*

Orient Express
FOX (US) 1934 dir. Paul Martin
Greene, G. *Stamboul Train*

Original Sin
ANGLIA (GB) 1996 dir. Andrew Grieve
TVSe(GB)
James, P. D.

Original Sin
MGM (US/Fr) 2001 dir. Michael
Cristofer
Woolrich, C. *Waltz Into Darkness*

Orlando
BRIT SCREEN (GB) 1992 dir. Sally
Potter
Woolf, V.

Orphans
LORIMAR (US) 1987 dir. Alan J. Pakula
Kessler, L.
P

Orphée
A. PAULVÉÉ (Fr) 1949
dir. Jean Cocteau
Cocteau, J.
P

Orpheus Descending
NED (US) 1990 dir. Peter Hall
TV(US)
Williams, T.
P

Oscar
TOUCHSTONE (US) 1991 dir. John
Landis
Magnier, C.
P

Oscar, The
PAR (US) 1966 dir. Russel Rouse
Sale, R.

Oscar and Lucinda
FOX (Aust/US) 1997 dir. Gillian
Armstrong
Carey, P.

Osterman Weekend, The
FOX (US) 1983 dir. Sam Peckinpah
Ludlum, R.

Otello
CANNON (It) 1986 dir. Franco Zeffirelli
M
Verdi, G.

Othello
MERCURY (US/Fr) 1951
dir. Orson Welles
EAGLE (GB) 1965 dir. Stuart Burge
COL (US/GB) 1995 dir. Oliver Parker
Shakespeare, W.
P

Othello, the Black Commando
EUROCINE (Sp/Fr) 1982 dir. Max H.
Boulois
Shakespeare, W. *Othello*
P

Other, The
FOX (US) 1972 dir. Robert Mulligan
Tryon, T.

Other Halves
OVINGHAM (GB) 1985 dir. John Laing
McCauley, S.

Other Man, The
UN TV (US) 1970 dir. Richard Colla
TV(US)
Lynn, M. *Mrs. Maitland's Affair*

Other Me, The
H. ROACH (US) 2000 dir. Manny Coto
TV(US)
Ryan, M. C. *Me Two*

Other Mother, The
O'HARA-HORO (US) 1995 dir. Bethany
Rooney
TV(US)
Shaefer, C.

Other People's Money
WAR (US) 1991 dir. Norman Jewison
Sterner, J.
P

Other Side of Midnight, The
FOX (US) 1977 dir. Charles Jarrott
Sheldon, S.

Other Side of Paradise, The
CENTRAL (GB) 1992 dir. Renny Rye
TVSe(GB)
Barber, N.

Other Side of Sunday, The
NRK DRAMA (Nor) 1996 dir. Berit
Nesheim
Nortvedt, R. *Sondagsengler*

Other Side of the Mountain, The
UN (US) 1975 dir. Larry Peerce
GB title: Window to the Sky, A
Valens, E. G. *Long Way Up, A*

Other Voices, Other Rooms
GOLDEN EYE (US) 1995 dir. David
Rocksavage
Capote, T.

Other Women's Children
LIFETIME TV (US) 1993 dir. Anne
Wheeler
TV(US)
Klass, P.

Otley
COL (GB) 1968 dir. Dick Clement
Waddell, M.

Otro Barrio, El
TORNASOL (Sp) 2000 dir. Salvador
Garcia Ruiz
Lindo, E.

Our Betters
RKO (US) 1933 dir. George Cukor
Maugham, W. S.
P

Our Guys: Outrage in Glen Rigde
GREENWALD (US) 1999 dir. Guy
Ferland
TV(US)
Lefkowitz, B. *Our Guys*

Our Hearts Were Young and Gay
PAR (US) 1944 dir. Lewis Allen
Skinner, C. O. and Kimbrough, E.

Our John Willie
BBC (GB) 1980 dir. Marilyn Fox
TVSe(GB)
Cookson, C.

Our Lady of the Assassins
STUDIO CANAL+ (Fr) 2000 dir. Barbet
Schroeder
Vallejo, F. *Virgin de Los Sicarios, La*

Our Man in Havana
COL (GB) 1959 dir. Carol Reed
Greene, G.

Our Marriage
PASSAGE (Fr) 1985 dir. Valeria
Sarimento
Tellado, C. *Mi Bodo Contigo*

Our Mother's House
MGM (GB) 1967 dir. Jack Clayton
Gloag, J.

Our Mutual Friend
BBC (GB) 1976 dir. Peter Hammond
TVSe(GB)
BBC (GB) 1998 dir. Julian Farino
TVSe(GB)
Dickens, C.

Our Town
UA (US) 1940 dir. Sam Wood
Wilder, T.
P

Our Vines Have Tender Grapes
MGM (US) 1945 dir. Roy Rowland
Martin, G. V. *For Our Vines Have Tender Grapes*

Our Wife
COL (US) 1941 dir. John M. Stahl
Mearson, L. *Lillian Day*
P

Outback
NIT (Aust) 1970 dir. Ted Kotcheff
Cook, K. *Wake in Fright*

Outcast Lady
MGM (US) 1934 dir. Robert Z. Leonard
GB title: Woman of the World, A
Arlen, M. *Green Hat, The*

Outcast of the Islands, An
LF (GB) 1951 dir. Carol Reed
Conrad, J.

Outcasts of Poker Flat, The
RKO (US) 1937 dir. Christy Cabanne
FOX (US) 1952 dir. Joseph M. Newman
Harte, B.

Outfit, The
MGM (US) 1973 dir. John Flynn
Stark, R.

Outlaw!
HERA (It) 1999 dir. Enzo Monteleone
Fantazzini, H.

Outlaw Josey Wales, The
WAR (US) 1976 dir. Clint Eastwood
Carter, F. *Gone to Texas*

Out of Africa
UN (US) 1985 dir. Sydney Pollack
Dinesen, I.
Thurman, J. *Isak Dinesen*

Out of Sight
JERSEY (US) 1998 dir. Steven Soderbergh
Leonard, E.

Out of the Darkness
CFF (GB) 1985 dir. John Krish
Ch
Hoyland, J. *Ivy Garland, The*

Out of the Fog
WAR (US) 1941 dir. Anatole Litvak
Shaw, I. *Gentle People, The*
P

Out of the Past
RKO (US) 1947 dir. Jacques Tourneur
GB title: Build My Gallows High
Homes, G. *Build My Gallows High*

Out of the Shadows
KUSHNER-LOCKE/YTV (US/GB) 1988 dir. Willi Patterson
TV(GB/US)
Davidson, A.

Out on a Limb
ABC (US) 1987 dir. Robert Butler
TVSe(US)
MacLaine, S.

Outrage!
COL TV (US) 1986 dir. Walter Grauman
TV(US)

Denker, H.

Outside Providence
MIRAMAX (US) 1999 dir. Michael
Corrente

Farrelly, P.

Outsider, The
MGM (GB) 1931 dir. Harry Lachtman
ABPC (GB) 1939 dir. Paul Stein

Brandon, D.
P

Outsider, The
PAR (US) 1980 dir. Tony Luraschi

Leinster, C. *Heritage of Michael Flaherty, The*

Outsiders, The
WAR (US) 1983
dir. Francis Ford Coppola

Hinton, S. E.

Outward Bound
WAR (US) 1930 dir. Robert Milton

Vane, S.
P

Overboard
FAC-NEW (US) 1978 dir. John Newland
TV(US)

Searls, H.

Over the Hill
VILLAGE ROADSHOW (Aust) 1992
dir. George Miller

Taylor, G. *Alone in the Australian Wilderness*

Over 21
COL (US) 1945 dir. Alexander Hall

Gordon, R.
P

Owd Bob
BG (GB) 1938 dir. Robert Stevenson
US title: To the Victor
EVEREST (Can/GB) 1998 dir. Rodney
Gibbons

Olivant, A.

Owl and the Pussycat, The
COL (US) 1970 dir. Herbert Ross

Manhoff, B.
P

Ox-Bow Incident, The
FOX (US) 1943 dir. William Wellman
US title: Strange Incident

Van Tilburg Clark, W.

Oxbridge Blues
BBC (GB) 1984 dir. James Cellan Jones
TVSe(GB)

Raphael, F.

P

Pacific Destiny
BL (GB) 1956 dir. Wolf Rilla

Grimble, Sir A. *Pattern of Islands*

Pack, The
WAR (US) 1977 dir. Robert Clouse

Fisher, D.

Pack of Lies
HALMI (US) 1987 dir. Anthony Page
TV(US)

Whitemore, H.
P

Pad (And How to Use It), The
UI (US) 1966 dir. Brian C. Hutton

Shaffer, P. *Private Ear, The*
P

Paddy
FOX (Ireland) 1969 dir. Daniel Haller

Dunne, L. *Goodbye to the Hill*

Paddy
ARTE FRANCE (Fr) 1999 dir. Gerard
Mordillat

Thomas, H. *John Perkins*

Paddy the Next Best Thing
FOX (US) 1933 dir. Harry Lachman

Page, G.
P

Padre Padrone
RAI (It) 1977 dir. Paolo Taviani, Vittorio
Taviani

Ledda, G.

Paganini Strikes Again
CFF (GB) 1973 dir. Gordon Gilbert
Ch

Lee, B.

Page Miss Glory
PAR (US) 1935 dir. Mervyn LeRoy

Schrank, J. and Dunning, P.
P

Paid
MGM (US) 1930 dir. Sam Wood
GB title: Within the Law

Veiller, B. *Within the Law*
P

Paint Cans
SALTER ST (Can) 1994 dir. Paul
Donovan

Donovan, P.

Painted Veil, The
MGM (US) 1934
dir. Richard Boleslawski

Maugham, W. S.

Paint Your Wagon
PAR (US) 1969 dir. Joshua Logan
M

Lerner, A. J. and Loewe, F.
P

Pair of Briefs
RANK (GB) 1961 dir. Ralph Thomas

Brooke, H. and Bannerman, K. *How
Say You?*
P

Pajama Game, The
WAR (US) 1957 dir. Stanley Donen
M
Bissell, R. P. *7½ Cents*

Pale Horse, The
ANGLIA/A&E (GB) 1997 dir. Charles
Beeson
TV(GB)
Christie, A.

Pal Joey
COL (US) 1957 dir. George Sidney
M
O'Hara, J.

Pallisers, The
BBC (GB) 1974 dir. Hugh David, Ronald
Wilson
TVSe(GB)
Trollope, A. *Can You Forgive Her?*;
Phineas Finn The Irish Member; *Eustace
Diamonds, The*; *Phineas Redux*; *Prime
Minister, The*; *Duke's Children, The*

Palmes de M. Schutz, Les
STUDIO CANAL+ (Fr) 1997 dir. Claude
Pinoteau
Fenwick, J.-N.
P

Palmetto
COL (Ger/US) 1997 dir. Volker
Schlondorff
Chase, J. H. *Just Another Sucker*

Palomino
NBC (US) 1991 dir. Michael Miller
TV(US)
Steel, D.

Pan
NORDISK (Nor/Den/Ger) 1995 dir.
Henning Carlsen
Hamsun, K.

Pandora's Clock
NBC ENT (US) 1996 dir. Eric Laneuville
TVSe(US)
Nance, J. J.

Panic in Needle Park, The
FOX (US) 1971 dir. Jerry Schatzberg
Mills, J.

Pantaleon y Las Visitadoras
TORNASOL (Peru) 1999 dir. Francisco
J. Lombardi
Llosa, M. V.

Panther
POLYGRAM (US/GB) 1995 dir. Mario
Van Peebles
Van Peebles, M. *Blowing in the Wind*

Papa's Angels
CBS TV (US) 2000 dir. Dwight H. Little
TV(US)
Paxton, C. W. and Carden. G. *Papa's
Angels: A Christmas Story*

Papa's Delicate Condition
PAR (US) 1963 dir. George Marshall
Griffith, C.

Paper Chase, The
FOX (US) 1973 dir. James Bridges
Osborn, J. J.

Paperhouse
VESTRON (GB) 1988 dir. Bernard Rose
Storr, C. *Marianne Dreams*

Paper Moon
PAR (US) 1973 dir. Peter Bogdanovich
Brown, J. D. *Addie Pray*

Paper Orchid
COL (GB) 1949 dir. Roy Baker
La Bern, A. J.

Papillon
COL (US) 1973 dir. Franklin Schaffner

Charrière, H.

Paradine Case, The
SELZNICK (US) 1947
dir. Alfred Hitchcock

Hichens, R.

Paradise for Three
MGM (US) 1938 dir. Edward Buzzell

Kastner, E. *Three Men in the Snow*

Paradise Postponed
THAMES (GB) 1986 dir. Alvin Rakoff
TVSe(GB)

Mortimer, J.

Parallax View, The
PAR (US) 1974 dir. Alan J. Pakula

Singer, L.

Parents Terribles, Les
SIRIUS (Fr) 1948 dir. Jean Cocteau

Cocteau, J.
P

Parent Trap, The
DISNEY (US) 1961 dir. David Swift
DISNEY (US) 1998 dir. Nancy Myers
Ch

Kastner, E. *Lottie and Lisa*

Paris Blues
UA (US) 1961 dir. Martin Ritt

Flender, H.

Paris, France
ALLIANCE (Can) 1993 dir. Jerry
Ciccoritti

Walmsley, T.

Paris in Spring
PAR (US) 1935 dir. Lewis Milestone

Taylor, D.
P

Paris Interlude
MGM (US) 1934 dir. Edwin L. Marin

Perelman, S. J. and Perelman, L. *All Good Americans*

Paris Trout
VIACOM (US) 1991
dir. Stephen Gyllenhaal
TV(US)

Dexter, P.

Paris Underground
UA (US) 1945 dir. Gregory Ratoff
GB title: Madame Pimpernel

Shiber, E.

Park is Mine, The
HBO (Can/US) 1985
dir. Steven Hilliard Stern
TV(US)

Peters, S.

Parnell
MGM (US) 1937 dir. John M. Stahl

Schauffler, E.
P

Parole di Mio Padre, Le
RAI (Fr/It) 2001 dir. Francesca
Comencini

Svevo, I. *Conscience of Zeno, The*

Parrish
WAR (US) 1961 dir. Delmer Daves

Savage, M.

Parson of Panamint, The
PAR (US) 1941 dir. William McGann

Kyne, P. B.

Partigiano Johnny, Il
FANDANGO (It) 2000 dir. Guido
Chiesa

Fenoglio, B.

Partners in Crime
AA (GB) 1961 dir. Peter Duffell
Wallace, E. *Man Who Knew, The*

Pascali's Island
AVENUE (GB) 1988 dir. James Dearden
Unsworth, B. *Idol Hunter, The*

Passage, The
HEMDALE (GB) 1978
dir. J. Lee Thompson
Nicolaysen, B. *Perilous Passage, The*

Passage à L'acte
ARENA (Fr) 1996 dir. Francis Girod
Gattegno, J.-P. *Neutralité Malveillante*

Passage from Hong Kong
WAR (US) 1941 dir. D. Ross Lederman
Biggers, E. D. *Agony Column*

Passage Home
GFD (GB) 1955 dir. Roy Baker
Armstrong, R.

Passage to India, A
COL-EMI (GB) 1984 dir. David Lean
Forster, E. M.

Passenger
KADR (Pol) 1963 dir. Andrzej Munk
Posmysz-Piasecka, Z.
P

Passengers, The
COL-WAR (Fr) 1977 dir. Serge LeRoy
Dwyer, K. R. *Shattered*

Passing of the Third Floor Back, The
GB (GB) 1935 dir. Berthold Viertel
Jerome, J. K.
P

Passion
BEYOND (Aust) 1999 dir. Peter Duncan
George, R. *Percy and Rose*
P
Bird, J. *Percy Grainger*

Passionate Friends, The
CIN (GB) 1949 dir. David Lean
GB title: One Woman's Story
Wells, H. G.

Passionate Summer, The
RANK (US) 1958 dir. Rudolph Cartier
Mason, R. *Shadow and the Peak, The*

Passion Flower
MGM (US) 1930 dir. William de Mille
Norris, K.

Passion in the Desert
FINE LINE (US) 1997 dir. Lavinia Currier
de Balzac, H.

Passion of Ayn Rand, The
PEG (US) 1999 dir. Christopher Menaul
TV(US)
Branden, B.

Passion's Way
HEARST (US) 1999 dir. Robert Allan Ackerman
TV(US)
Wharton, E. *Reef, The*

Passport to Treason
EROS (GB) 1956 dir. Robert S. Baker
O'Brine, M.

Password is Courage, The
MGM (GB) 1962 dir. Andrew L. Stone
Castle, J.

Pastor Hall
UA (GB) 1940 dir. Roy Boulting
Toller, E.
P

Past the Bleachers
SIGNBOARD HILL (US) 1995 dir.
Michael Switzer
TV(US)
Bohjalian, C. A.

Patch Adams
BLUE WOLF (US) 1998 dir. Tom
Shadyac
Adams, H. D. and Mylander, M.
*Gesundheit, Good Health is a Laughing
Matter*

Patch of Blue, A
MGM (US) 1965 dir. Guy Green
Kata, E. *Be Ready With Bells and Drums*

Pather Panchali
SAT RAY (Ind) 1955 dir. Satyajit Ray
Bannerjee, B. B.

Pathfinder, The
HALLMARK (US) 1996 dir. Donald
Shebib
TV(US)
Cooper, J. F.

Paths of Glory
UA (US) 1957 dir. Stanley Kubrick
Cobb, H.

Patricia Neal Story, The
SCHILLER (US) 1981
dir. Antony Harvey, Anthony Page
TV(US)
Farrell, B. *Pat & Roald*

Patriot Games
PAR (US) 1992 dir. Phillip Noyce
Clancy, T.

Patriots, The
COMPASS (US) 1963
dir. George Schaefer
TV(US)
Kingsley, S.
P

Patron Saint of Liars, The
PATCHETT-KAUFMAN
(US) 1998 dir. Stephen Gyllenhaal
TV(US)
Patchett, A.

Patterns
UA (US) 1956 dir. Fielder Cook
GB title: Patterns of Power
Serling, R.
P

Patton
FOX (US) 1970 dir. Franklin Schaffner
GB title: Patton: Lust for Glory
Farago, L. *Patton: Ordeal & Triumph*

Patty Hearst
ATLANTIC (US) 1988
dir. Paul Schrader
Hearst, P. *Every Secret Thing*

Pavilion of Women
BEIJING (China/US) 2001 dir. Ho Yim
Buck, P. S.

Pawnbroker, The
PAR (US) 1964 dir. Sidney Lumet
Wallant, E. L.

Payback
PAR (US) 1999 dir. Brian Helgeland
Westlake, D. E. *Hunter, The*

Pay it Forward
WAR (US) 2000 dir. Mimi Leder
Ryan Hyde, C.

Payment Deferred
MGM (US) 1932 dir. Lothar Mendel
Dell, J.
P

Payoff
VIACOM (US) 1991 dir. Stuart Cooper
TV(US)
Owen, R. T.

Payroll
AA (GB) 1960 dir. Sidney Hayers
Bickerton, D.

Peaches
STONERIDGE (Ire) 2000 dir. Nick
Grosso
Grosso, N.
P

Peacock Spring
BBC (GB) 1995 dir. Christopher
Morahan
TV(GB)
Godden, R.

Pearl, The
RKO (US/Mex) 1948
dir. Emilio Fernandez
Steinbeck, J.

Pearl of Death, The
UN (US) 1944 dir. Roy William Neill
Doyle, Sir A. C. *Six Napoleons, The*

Peck's Bad Boy
FOX (US) 1934 dir. Edward Cline
Peck, G. W.

Peeper
FOX (US) 1975 dir. Peter Hyams
Laumer, K. *Deadfall*

Peg of Old Drury
WILCOX (GB) 1935 dir. Herbert Wilcox
Reade, C. and Taylor, T. *Masks and Faces*
P

Peg O' My Heart
MGM (US) 1933 dir. Robert Z. Leonard
Manners, J. H.
P

Pelican Brief, The
WAR (US) 1993 dir. Alan J. Pakula
Grisham, J.

Pelle the Conqueror
CURZON (Den/Swe) 1988
dir. Bille August
Nexo, M. A.

Penelope
MGM (US) 1966 dir. Arthur Hiller
Cunningham, E. V.

Penguin Pool Murder, The
RKO (US) 1932 dir. George Marshall
Palmer, S.

Penmarric
BBC (GB) 1979 dir. Derek Martinus,
Tina Wakerell
TVSe(GB)
Howatch, S.

Penn of Pennsylvania
BN (GB) 1941 dir. Lance Comfort
US title: Courageous Mr. Penn, The
Vulliamy, C. E. *William Penn*

Pentagon Wars, The
JERSEY (US) 1998 dir. Richard
Benjamin
TV(US)
Burton, J. G.

Penthouse, The
PAR (GB) 1967 dir. Peter Collinson
Forbes, J. S. *Meter Man, The*
P

Penthouse, The
GREEN-WHITE (US) 1989
dir. David Greene
TV(US)
Trevor, E.

People, The
METRO (US) 1972 dir. John Korty
US(TV)
Henderson, Z. *Pilgrimage*

People Against O'Hara, The
MGM (US) 1951 dir. John Sturges
Lipsky, E.

People Like Us
ITC (US) 1990 dir. Billy Hale
TVSe(US)
Dunne, D.

People That Time Forgot, The
BW (GB) 1977 dir. Kevin Connor
Burroughs, E. R.

People Will Talk
FOX (US) 1951
dir. Joseph L. Mankiewicz
Goetz, C. *Dr. Praetorius*
P

Pépé le Moko
PARIS (Fr) 1936 dir. Julian Duvivier
d'Ashelbe, R.

Peppermint Pig, The
BBC (GB) 1977 dir. Paul Stone
TVSe(GB)
Bawden, N.

Percy
MGM-EMI (GB) 1971
dir. Ralph Thomas
Hitchcock, R.

Perdita Durango
LOLAFILMS (Mex/US/Sp) 1997 dir.
Alex de la Iglesia
Gifford, B. *59 Degrees and Raining: The Story of Perdita Durango*

Pereira Declares
KG (Port/It) 1995 dir. Roberto Faenza
Tabucci, A. *Sostiene Pereira*

Perez Family, The
GOLDWYN (US) 1995 dir. Mira Nair
Bell, C.

Perfect Alibi, The
RKO (GB) 1931 dir. Basil Dean
Milne, A. A.
P

Perfect Alibi
RYSHER (US) 1995 dir. Kevin Meyer
Frick, R. M. *Where's My Mommy Now?*

Perfect Hero, A
LWT (GB) 1991 dir. James Cellan Jones
TVSe(GB)
Matthew, C.

Perfect Marriage, The
PAR (US) 1946 dir. Lewis Allen
Raphaelson, S.
P

Perfect Murder, A
WAR (US) 1998 dir. Andrew Davis
Knott, F. *Dial M For Murder*
P

Perfect Murder, The
MI (Ind) 1990 dir. Zafar Hai
Keating, H. R. F.

Perfect Murder, The
NORSK (Nor) 1993 dir. Eva Isaksen
Kjaerstad, J. *Homo Falsus*

Perfect Murder, Perfect Town
FOX TV (US) 2000 dir. Kris
Kristofferson
TVSe(US)
Schiller, L.

Perfect Spy, A
BBC (GB) 1987 dir. Peter Smith
TVSe(GB)
Le Carré, J.

Perfect Storm, The
WAR (US) 1999 dir. Wolfgang Petersen
Junger, S. *Perfect Storm, The: A True Story of Men Against the Sea*

Perfect Stranger, A
NBC (US) 1994 dir. Michael Miller
TV(US)
Steel, D.

Perfect Strangers
WAR (US) 1950 dir. Bretaigne Windust
GB title: Too Dangerous to Love
Hecht, B. and MacArthur, C. *Ladies and Gentlemen*
P

Perfect Tribute, The
P&G (US) 1991 dir. Jack Bender
TV(US)
Andrews, M. R.

Perfect Woman, The
GFD (GB) 1949 dir. Bernard Knowles
Geoffrey, W. and Mitchell, B.
P

Peril
TRIUMPH (Fr) 1985 dir. Michel DeVille
Belletto, R. *Sur la Terre Comme au Ciel*

Peril at End House
LWT (GB) 1991 dir. Renny Rye
TV(GB)
Christie, A.

Perilous Journey, A
REP (US) 1953 dir. R. G. Springsteen
Roe, V. *Golden Tide, The*

Period of Adjustment
MGM (US) 1962 dir. George Roy Hill
Williams, T.
P

Permanent Midnight
JD (US) 1998 dir. David Veloz
Stahl, J.

Perri
DISNEY (US) 1957 dir. Ralph Wright
Ch
Salten, F.

Personal Affair
RANK (GB) 1953 dir. Anthony Pelissier
Storm, L.
P

Personal Property
MGM (US) 1937 dir. W. S. Van Dyke
GB title: Man in Possession, The
Harwood, H. M. *Man in Possession, The*
P

Persons in Hiding
PAR (US) 1939 dir. Louis King
Hoover, J. E.

Persuasion
GRANADA (GB) 1971
dir. Howard Baker
TVSe(GB)
BBC/SONY (GB/US) 1995 dir. Roger Michell
Austen, J.

Petain
FRANCE 2 (Fr) 1992 dir. Jean Marboeuf
Ferro, M.

Pete 'n Tillie
UN (US) 1972 dir. Martin Ritt
De Vries, P. *Witch's Milk*

Peter Ibbetson
PAR (US) 1935 dir. Henry Hathaway
Du Maurier, G.

Peter Lundy and the Medicine Hat Stallion
FRIENDLY (US) 1977
dir. Michael O'Herlihy
TV(US)
Henry, M. *San Domingo, The Medicine Hat Stallion*

Peter Pan
DISNEY (US) 1953 dir. Ben Sharpsteen
A
NBC (US) 1955 dir. Michael Kidd
M, TV(US)
ATV (GB) 1976 dir. Dwight Hemion
TV(GB)

Barrie, Sir J. M., Comden, B., Green, A., and Leigh, C. (1955 only)
P

Peter the Great
NBC ENT (US) 1986
dir. Marvin J. Chomsky, Lawrence Schiller
TVSe(US)

Massie, R. K.

Peterville Diamond, The
WAR (GB) 1942 dir. Walter Forde

Fodor, L. *Jewel Robbery*
P

Petit Con
GOLDWYN (Fr) 1985
dir. Gerard Lauzier

Lauzier, G. *Souvenirs d'un jeune Homme*

Petite Sirène, La
WA (Fr) 1984 dir. Roger Andrieux

Dangerfield, Y.

Petrified Forest, The
WAR (US) 1936 dir. Archie Mayo

Sherwood, R. E.
P

Pet Sematary
PAR (US) 1989 dir. Mary Lambert

King, S.

Petticoat Fever
MGM (US) 1936
dir. George Fitzmaurice

Reed, M.
P

Petulia
WAR (US) 1968 dir. Richard Lester

Haase, J. *Me and the Arch Kook Petulia*

Peyton Place
FOX (US) 1957 dir. Mark Robson

Metalious, G.

Phantom Lady
UN (US) 1944 dir. Robert Siodmak

Irish, W.

Phantom of the Opera, The
UN (US) 1943 dir. Arthur Lubin
UI (GB) 1962 dir. Terence Fisher
HALMI (US) 1983
dir. Robert Markowitz
TV(US)
21ST CENTURY (US) 1989 dir. Dwight H. Little
SABAN/SCHERICK (US/Fr) 1990 dir. Tony Richardson
TV(US/Fr)
RETEITALIA (It) 1999 dir. Dario Argento

Leroux, G.

Phantom of the Rue Morgue
WAR (US) 1954 dir. Roy del Ruth

Poe, E. A. *Murders in the Rue Morgue*

Phantoms
MIRAMAX (US) 1998 dir. Joe Chappelle

Koontz, D.

Phantom Tollbooth, The
MGM (US) 1969 dir. Chuck Jones
A

Juster, N.

Pharmacist, The
SENATOR (Ger) 1997 dir. Rainer Kaufmann

Noll, I.

Philadelphia Experiment, The
NEW WORLD (US) 1984
dir. Stewart Raffill
Moore, W. I. and Berlitz, C.

Philadelphia Story, The
MGM (US) 1940 dir. George Cukor
Barry, P.
P

Phoenix and the Carpet, The
BBC (GB) 1976 dir. Clive Doig
TVSe(GB)
Nesbit, E.

Photographing Fairies
BRIT SCREEN (GB) 1997 dir. Nick
Willing
Szilagyi, S.

Physical Assault
TITAN (US) 1973
dir. William M. Bushnell
Kolpacoff, V. *Prisoners of Quai Dong,
The*

Piaf—The Early Years
FOX (Fr) 1982 dir. Guy Casaril
Berteaut, S. *Piaf*

Pianist, The
ASKA (Can) 1992 dir. Claude Gagnon
Ireland, A. *Certain Mr. Takahasi, A*

Pianiste, La
MK2 (Fr) 2001 dir. Michael Haneke
Jelinek, E.

Piano for Mrs. Cimino, A
EMI (US) 1982 dir. George Schaefer
TV(US)
Oliphant, R.

Piano Lesson, The
HALLMARK (US) 1995 dir. Lloyd
Richards
TV(US)
Wilson, A.
P

Piano Player, The
STUDIO HAMBURG (Ger) 1999 dir.
Rolf Schubel
Barkow, N. *Song of Gloomy Sunday, The*

Piccadilly Jim
MGM (US) 1936 dir. Robert Z. Leonard
Wodehouse, P. G.

Pickwick Papers, The
REN (GB) 1952 dir. Noel Langley
BBC (GB) 1985 dir. Brian Lighthill
TVSe(GB)
Dickens, C.

Picnic
COL (US) 1955 dir. Joshua Logan
COL TRISTAR (US) 2000 dir. Ivan
Passer
TV(US)
Inge, W.
P

Picnic at Hanging Rock
AFC (Aust) 1975 dir. Peter Weir
Lindsay, J.

Picture of Dorian Gray, The
MGM (US) 1945 dir. Albert Lewin
CURTIS (US) 1973 dir. Glenn Jordan
TV(US)
Wilde, O.

Piece of Cake
LWT (GB) 1988 dir. Ian Toynton
TVSe(GB)
Robinson, D.

Pieces of Dreams
UA (US) 1970 dir. Daniel Haller
Barrett, W. E. *Wine and the Music, The*

Pied Piper, The
SAG (GB) 1971 dir. Jacques Demy
Browning, R.

Pied Piper, The
FOX (US) 1942 dir. Irving Pichel
Shute, N.

Pigeon That Took Rome, The
PAR (US) 1962 dir. Melville Shavelson
Downes, D. *Easter Dinner, The*

Pilgrimage
FOX (US) 1933 dir. John Ford
Wylie, I. A. R.

Pillow to Post
WAR (US) 1945 dir. Vincent Sherman
Kohn, R. S. *Pillar to Post*
P

Pilot, The
SUMMIT (Can) 1981
dir. Cliff Robertson
Davis, R. P.

Pimpernel Smith
BN (GB) 1941 dir. Leslie Howard
Orczy, Baroness E. *Scarlet Pimpernel, The*

Pinch of Snuff, A
YTV (GB) 1994 dir. Sandy Johnson
TVSe(GB)
Hill, R.

Pink Jungle, The
UI (US) 1968 dir. Delbert Mann
Williams, A. *Snake Water*

Pink String and Sealing Wax
EAL (GB) 1945 dir. Robert Hamer
Pertwee, R.
P

Pinky
FOX (US) 1949 dir. Elia Kazan
Sumner, C. R. *Quality*

Pinocchio
DISNEY (US) 1940 dir. Ben Sharpsteen
A, Ch
CANTO (US) 1968 dir. Sid Smith
TV(US)
BBC (GB) 1978 dir. Barry Letts
Ch, TVSe(GB)
Collodi, C.

Pin To See the Peepshow, A
BBC (GB) 1973 dir. Raymond Menmuir
TVSe(GB)
Jesse, F. T.

Pippi Longstocking
TELEFILM (Can/Ger/Swe) 1997 dir.
Bill Giggie, Michael Schaack, Clive A.
Smith
A, Ch
Lindgren, A.

Pirate, The
MGM (US) 1948 dir. Vincente Minnelli
M
Behrman, S. N.
P

Pirate, The
WAR TV (US) 1978
dir. Ken Annakin
TVSe(US)
Robbins, H.

Pirate Movie, The
FOX (Aust) 1982 dir. Ken Annakin
Sullivan, Sir A. and Gilbert, Sir W.
Pirates of Penzance, The
P

Pirates of Penzance, The
UN (GB) 1982 dir. Wilford Leach
M
Sullivan, Sir A. and Gilbert, Sir W.
P

Pirates of Silicon Valley
TNT (US) 1999 dir. Martyn Burke
TV(US)

Freiberger, P. and Swaine, M. *Fire in the Valley*

Pit and the Pendulum, The
AA (US) 1961 dir. Roger Corman
FULL MOON (US) 1991
dir. Stuart Gordon

Poe, E. A.

Pitfall
UA (US) 1948 dir. André de Toth

Dratler, J.

Pit of Darkness
BUTCHER (GB) 1961
dir. Lance Comfort

McCutcheon, H. *To Dusty Death*

Pixote
UNIFILM (Port) 1981
dir. Hector Babenco

Lonzeiro, J. *Injancia dos Martos*

Place in the Sun, A
PAR (US) 1951 dir. George Stevens

Dreiser, T. *American Tragedy, An*

Place of One's Own, A
GFD (GB) 1945 dir. Bernard Knowles

Sitwell, Sir O.

Place To Go, A
BL (GB) 1963 dir. Basil Dearden

Fisher, M. *Bethnal Green*

Plague, The
ARABA (Fr/Arg) 1992 dir. Luis Puenzo

Camus, A.

Plague Dogs, The
NEPENTHE (GB) 1982
dir. Martin Rosen
A

Adams, R. G.

Plainsman, The
PAR (US) 1937 dir. Cecil B. De Mille

Wilstach, F. *Wild Bill Hickok*

Planet of Junior Brown, The
SHOWTIME (US) 1999 dir. Clement
Virgo
TV(US)

Hamilton, V.

Planet of the Apes
FOX (US) 1968 dir. Franklin Schaffner
FOX (US) 2001 dir. Tim Burton

Boulle, P. *Monkey Planet*

Platoon Leader
CANNON (US) 1988 dir. Aaron Norris

McDonough, J. R.

Playboy of the Western World, The
FOUR PROVINCES (GB) 1962
dir. Brian Desmond Hurst

Synge, J. M.
P

Player, The
AVE PICT (US) 1992 dir. Robert Altman

Tolkin, M.

Playground, The
JERAND (US) 1965 dir. Richard Hilliard

Sulzberger, C. *My Brother Death*

Playing Mona Lisa
BUBBLE FACTORY (US) 2000 dir.
Matthew Huffman

Freedman, M.
P

Playing for Time
SYZYGY (US) 1980 dir. Daniel Mann
TV(US)

Fenelon, F.

Playing With Fire
ARABESQUE (US) 2000 dir. Roy
Campanella II
TV(US)
Mayhew, D.

Play it Again, Sam
PAR (US) 1972 dir. Herbert Ross
Allen, W.
P

Play it as it Lays
UN (US) 1972 dir. Frank Perry
Didion, J.

Plaza Suite
PAR (US) 1971 dir. Arthur Hiller
PAR (US) 1987 dir. Roger Beatty
TV(US)
Simon, N.
P

Please Don't Eat the Daisies
MGM (US) 1960 dir. Charles Walters
Kerr, J.

Please Turn Over
AA (GB) 1959 dir. Gerald Thomas
Thomas, B. *Book of the Month*
P

Pleasure of his Company, The
PAR (US) 1961 dir. George Seaton
Taylor, S. and Skinner, C. O.
P

Pleasures
COL TV (US) 1986 dir. Sharron Miller
Barbach, L.

Pleasure Seekers, The
FOX (US) 1964 dir. Jean Negulesco
Secondari, J. H. *Coins in the Fountain*

Pledge, The
WAR (US) 2001 dir. Sean Penn
Duerrenmatt, F. *Versprechen, Das*

Plenilunio
CANAL+ ESPANA (Sp/Fr) 2000 dir.
Imanol Uribe
Munoz Molina, A.

Plenty
FOX (US) 1985 dir. Fred Schepisi
Hare, D.
P

Pleure pas Germaine
RTBF (Bel/Sp/Fr) 2000 dir. Alain de
Halleux
Jasmin, C.

Plough and the Stars, The
RKO (US) 1936 dir. John Ford
O'Casey, S.
P

Plunder
WILCOX (GB) 1931 dir. Tom Walls
Travers, B.
P

Plunder of the Sun
WAR (US) 1953 dir. John Farrow
Dodge, D.

Plymouth Adventure, The
MGM (US) 1952 dir. Clarence Brown
Gebler, E.

Pocketful of Miracles
UA (US) 1961 dir. Frank Capra
Runyon, D. *Madame la Gimp*

Pocketful of Rye, A
BBC (GB) 1985 dir. Guy Slater
TV(GB)
Christie, A.

Pocket Money
FIRST (US) 1972 dir. Stuart Rosenberg
Brown, J. P. S. *Jim Kane*

Poet's Pub
AQUILA (GB) 1949
dir. Frederick Wilson
Linklater, E.

Point Blank
MGM (US) 1967 dir. John Boorman
Stark, R.

Point Counter Point
BBC (GB) 1968 dir. Rex Tucker
TVSe(GB)
Huxley, A.

Point Last Seen
ALEXANDER/ENRIGHT (US) 1998
dir. Elodie Keene
TV(US)
Nyala, H.

Point Man, The
CAROUSEL (GB/Fr) 2001 dir. John
Glen
TV(GB/Fr)
Hartov, S. *Heat of Ramadan, The*

Poison Pen
AB (GB) 1939 dir. Paul Stein
Llewellyn, R.
P

Pola X
STUDIO CANAL+ (Fr/Ger) 1999 dir.
Leos Carax
Melville, H. *Pierre, or, The Ambiguities*

Poldark
BBC (GB) 1975 dir. Paul Annett,
Christopher Barry, Kenneth Ives
TVSe(GB)
Graham, W. R. *Poldark; Demelza; Jeremy
Poldark; Warleggan*

Polly
DISNEY (US) 1989 dir. Debbie Allen
Ch, TV(US)
Porter, E. H. *Pollyanna*

Pollyanna
DISNEY (US) 1960 dir. David Swift
Ch
BBC (GB) 1973 dir. June Wyndham-
Davies
TVSe(GB)
Porter, E. H.

Ponder Heart, The
PBS (US) 2001 dir. Martha Coolidge
TV(US)
Welty, E.

Poodle Springs
HBO (US) 1998 dir. Bob Rafelson
TV(US)
Parker, R. B. and Chandler, R.

Poof Point, The
H. ROACH (US) 2001 dir. Neal Israel
TV(US)
Weiss, E. and Friedman, M.

Poor Cow
WAR (GB) 1967 dir. Ken Loach
Dunn, N.

Poor Little Rich Girl: The Barbara Hutton Story
ITC (US) 1987 dir. Charles Jarrot
TVSe(US)
Heymann, C. D. *Poor Little Rich Girl*

Pope of Greenwich Village, The
MGM/UA (US) 1984
dir. Stuart Rosenberg
Patrick, V.

Poppy
PAR (US) 1936
dir. A. Edward Sutherland
Donnelly, D.
P

Porgy and Bess
GOLDWYN (US) 1959
dir. Otto Preminger
M

Gershwin, G., Gershwin, I. and Heyward, D.
P

Heyward, D. and Heyward, D. *Porgy*
P

Pork Chop Hill
UA (US) 1959 dir. Lewis Milestone

Marshall, S. L. A.

Port Afrique
COL (GB) 1956 dir. Rudolph Maté

Dyer, B. V.

Porte des Lilas
FILMSONOR (Fr/It) 1957
dir. René Clair

Fallet, R. *Grande Ceinture, La*

Porterhouse Blue
CHANNEL 4 (GB) 1987 dir. Robert Knights
TVSe(GB)

Sharpe, T.

Portia on Trial
REP (US) 1937 dir. George Nicholls, Jr.

Baldwin, F.

Portnoy's Complaint
WAR (US) 1972 dir. Ernest Lehman

Roth, P.

Portrait, The
GREENWALD (US) 1993 dir. Arthur Penn
TV(US)

Howe, T. *Painting Churches*
P

Portrait of a Lady, The
POLYGRAM (US/GB) 1996 dir. Jane Campion

James, H.

Portrait of a Marriage
BBC (GB) 1990 dir. Stephen Whittaker
TVSe(GB)

Nicolson, N.

Portrait of Clare
ABP (GB) 1950 dir. Lance Comfort

Young, F. B.

Portrait of Jennie
SELZNICK (US) 1948
dir. William Dieterle
GB title: Jennie

Nathan, R.

Portrait of the Artist as a Young Man
ULYSSES (GB) 1977 dir. Joseph Strick

Joyce, J.

Poseidon Adventure, The
FOX (US) 1972 dir. Ronald Neame

Gallico, P.

Possessed
MGM (US) 1931 dir. Clarence Brown

Selwyn, E. *Mirage, The*
P

Possessed
WAR (US) 1947 dir. Curtis Bernhardt

Weiman, R. *One Man's Secret*

Possessed
SHOWTIME (US) 2000 dir. Steven E. de Souza
TV(US)

Allen, T. B. *Possessed: The True Story of an Exorcism*

Possessed, The
BBC (GB) 1969 dir. Naomi Capon
TVSe(GB)
Dostoevsky, F.

Possession of Joel Delaney, The
SCOTIA-BARBER (US) 1971
dir. Waris Hussein
Stewart, R.

Possible Worlds
ALLIANCE (Can) 2000 dir. Robert
Lepage
Mighton, J.
P

Postcards from America
CHANNEL 4 FILMS (GB/US) 1994 dir.
Steve McLean
Wojnarowicz, D. *Close to the Knives;
Memories That Smell Like Gasoline*

Postcards from the Edge
COL (US) 1990 dir. Mike Nichols
Fisher, C.

Postino, Il
CECCHI (It) 1994 dir. Michael Radford
Skarmeta, A. *Burning Patience*

Postman, The
WAR (US) 1997 dir. Kevin Costner
Brin, D.

**Postman Always Rings Twice,
The**
MGM (US) 1946 dir. Tay Garnett
PAR (US) 1981 dir. Bob Rafaelson
Cain, J. M.

Power, The
MGM (US) 1968 dir. Byron Hoskin
Robinson, F.

Power and the Prize, The
MGM (US) 1956 dir. Henry Koster
Swiggett, H.

Power of One, The
VILLAGE ROADSHOW (Aust/Fr/US)
1992 dir. John G. Avildsen
Courtenay, B.

Pow Wow Highway
WAR (US) 1989 dir. Jonathan Wacks
Seals, D.

Practical Magic
WAR (US) 1998 dir. Griffin Dunne
Hoffman, A.

Praise
EMCEE (Aust) 1998 dir. John Curran
McGahan, A.

Prayer for the Dying, A
GOLDWYN (GB) 1987 dir. Mike
Hodges
Higgins, J.

Prayer in the Dark, A
WIL COURT (US) 1997 dir. Jerry
Ciccoritti
TV(US)
Ellin, S. *Stronghold*

Pray For Us
FRANCE 3 (Fr) 1994 dir. Jean-Pierre
Vergne
Duroy, L.

Praying Mantis
PORTMAN (GB) 1984 dir. Jack Gold
TVSe(GB)
Monteilhet, H. *Mantes Religieuses, Les*

Precious Bane
BBC (GB) 1989 dir. Christopher Menaul
TV(GB)
Webb, M.

Precious Victims
LAUREL (US) 1993 dir. Peter Levin
TV(US)
Weber, D. W. and Bosworth, Jr., C.

Prediction, The
MOSFILM (Rus/Fr) 1994 dir. Eldar Ryazanov
Ryazanov, E.

Prelude to a Kiss
FOX (US) 1992 dir. Norman Rene
Lucas, C.
P

Prelude to Fame
GFD (GB) 1950 dir. Fergus McDonell
Huxley, A. *Young Archimedes*

Premature Burial, The
AA (US) 1962 dir. Roger Corman
Poe, E. A.

Prescription: Murder
UN (US) 1968 dir. Richard Irving
TV(US)
Levinson, R. and Link, W.
P

Presenting Lily Mars
MGM (US) 1943 dir. Norman Taurog
M
Tarkington, B.

President's Child, The
LAUREN (US) 1992 dir. Sam Pillsbury
TV(US)
Weldon, F.

President's Lady, The
FOX (US) 1953 dir. Henry Levin
Stone, I. *Immortal Wife*

President's Mistress, The
KINGS ROAD (US) 1978
dir. John Llewellyn Moxey
TV(US)
Anderson, P.

President's Plane is Missing, The
ABC (US) 1973 dir. Daryl Duke
TV(US)
Serling, R. J.

Press for Time
RANK (GB) 1966 dir. Robert Asher
McGill, A. *Yea, Yea, Yea*

Pressure Point
UA (US) 1962 dir. Hubert Cornfield
Lindner, R. *Fifty Minute Hour, The*

Prestige
RKO (US) 1932 dir. Tay Garnett
Hervey, H. *Lips of Steel*

Presumed Innocent
WAR (US) 1990 dir. Alan J. Pakula
Turow, S.

Pretty Maids All In A Row
MGM (US) 1971 dir. Roger Vadim
Pollini, F.

Pretty Poison
FOX (US) 1968 dir. Noel Black
WESTGATE (US) 1996 dir. David Burton Morris
TV(US)
Geller, S. *She Let Him Continue*

Pretty Polly
RANK (GB) 1967 dir. Guy Green
US title: Matter of Innocence, A
Coward, N. *Pretty Polly Barlow*

Price, The
TALENT (US) 1971 dir. Fielder Cook
TV(US)
Miller, A.
P

Price, The
CHANNEL 4 (GB) 1985 dir. Peter Smith
TVSe(GB)
Ransley, P.

Price of Glory
NEW LINE (US) 2000 dir. Carlos Avila
Berger, P.

Price of Heaven, The
KONIGSBERG (US) 1997 dir. Peter
Bogdanovich
TV(US)
Gurganus, A. *Blessed Assurance: A Moral Tale*

Price of Silence, The
GN (GB) 1959 dir. Montgomery Tully
Meynell, L. *One Step From Murder*

Price She Paid, The
WI (US) 1992 dir. Fred Walton
TV(US)
Wilmot, C.
P

Prick up your Ears
ZENITH (GB) 1986 dir. Stephen Frears
Lahr, J.

Pride and Extreme Prejudice
USA NETWORK (US) 1990 dir. Ian
Sharp
TV(US)
Forsyth, F.

Pride and Prejudice
MGM (US) 1940 dir. Robert Z. Leonard
BBC (GB) 1980 dir. Cyril Coke
TVSe(GB)
BBC/A&E (GB) 1995 dir. Simon
Langton
TVSe(GB)
Austen, J.

Pride and the Passion, The
UA (US) 1957 dir. Stanley Kramer
Forester, C. S. *Gun, The*

Pride of the Marines
WAR (US) 1945 dir. Delmer Daves
GB title: Forever in Love
Butterfield, R. P. *Al Schmid, Marine*

Priest of Love
ENT (GB) 1981 dir. Christopher Miles
Moore, H. T.

Primary Colors
UN (US) 1998 dir. Mike Nichols
Klein, J.

Prime of Miss Jean Brodie, The
FOX (GB) 1969 dir. Ronald Neame
STV (GB) 1978 dir. John Bruce, Mark
Cullingham, Christopher Hodson, Tina
Wakerell
TVSe(GB)
Spark, M.

Prime Target
MGM/UA (US) 1989 dir. Robert Collins
TV(US)
O'Donnell, L. *No Business Being a Cop*

Primrose Path, The
RKO (US) 1940 dir. Gregory La Cava
Lincoln, V. *February Hill*

Prince and the Pauper, The
WAR (US) 1937 dir. William Keighley
DISNEY (US) 1961 dir. Don Chaffey
TV(US)
BBC (GB) 1976 dir. Barry Letts
TVSe(GB)
WAR (PAN) 1977 dir. Richard Fleischer
US title: Crossed Swords
HALLMARK (US) 2000 dir. Giles Foster
TV(US)
Twain, M.

Prince and the Showgirl, The
WAR (GB) 1957 dir. Laurence Olivier
Rattigan, T. *Sleeping Prince, The*
P

Prince For a Day
NBC (US) 1995 dir. Corey Blechman
TV(US)
Twain, M. *Prince and the Pauper, The*

Prince of Central Park, The
LORIMAR (US) 1977 dir. Harvey Hart
TV(US)
SEAGAL/NASSO (US) 1999 dir. John
Leekley
Rhodes, E.

Prince of Foxes
FOX (US) 1949 dir. Henry King
Shellabarger, S.

Prince of Homburg, The
PBS (US) 1997 dir. Kirk Browning
TV(US)
von Kleist, H. *Prinz Friedrich von
Homburg*
P

Prince of Jutland
MIRAMAX (Neth/GB) 1994 dir. Gabriel
Axel
Grammaticus, S. *Denmark Chronicle*

Prince of Players
FOX (US) 1954 dir. Philip Dunne
Ruggles, E.

Prince of the City
ORION (US) 1981 dir. Sidney Lumet
Daley, R.

Prince of Tides, The
COL (US) 1991 dir. Barbra Streisand
Conroy, P.

Princess Bride, The
FOX (US) 1987 dir. Rob Reiner
Goldman, W.

Princess Comes Across, The
PAR (US) 1936 dir. William K. Howard
Rogger, L. L.

Princess Daisy
NBC ENT (US) 1984 dir. Waris Hussein
TVSe(US)
Krantz, J.

Princess Diaries, The
DISNEY (US) 2001 dir. Garry Marhsall
Cabot, M.

Princess in Love
KUSHNER-LOCKE (US) dir. David
Greene
TV(US)
Pasternak, A.

Prince Who Was a Thief, The
UN (US) 1951 dir. Rudolph Maté
Dreiser, T.

Prisoner, The
COL (GB) 1955 dir. Peter Glenville
Boland, B.
P

Prisoner of Second Avenue, The
WAR (US) 1975 dir. Melvin Frank
Simon, N.
P

Prisoner of Zenda
UA (US) 1937 dir. John Cromwell
MGM (US) 1952 dir. Richard Thorpe
UN (US) 1979 dir. Richard Quine
BBC (GB) 1984 dir. Leonard Lewis
TVSe(GB)
Hope, A.

Prisoner of Zenda, Inc.
SHOWTIMEWORKS (US) 1996 dir.
Stefan Scaini
TV(US)
Hope, A.

Private Affair, A
ARABESQUE (US) 2000 dir. Michael
Toshiyuki Uno
TV(US)
Hill, D.

Private Affairs of Bel Ami, The
UA (US) 1947 dir. Albert Lewin
de Maupassant, G. *Bel Ami*

Private Angelo
ABP (GB) 1949 dir. Peter Ustinov
Linklater, E.

Private Battle, A
P&G (US) 1980
dir. Robert Michael Lewis
TV(US)
Ryan, C. and Ryan, K. M.

Private Lessons
J. FARLEY (US) 1981 dir. Alan Myerson
Greenburg, D. *Philly*

Private Life of Don Juan, The
LF (GB) 1934
dir. Alexander Korda
Bataille, H.
P

Private Lives
MGM (US) 1931 dir. Sidney Franklin
Coward, N.
P

Private Lives of Elizabeth and Essex, The
WAR (US) 1939 dir. Michael Curtiz
Anderson, M. *Elizabeth the Queen*
P

Privates on Parade
HANDMADE (GB) 1982
dir. Michael Blakemore
Nichols, P.
P

Private's Progress, A
BL (GB) 1956 dir. John Boulting
Hackney, A.

Private Worlds
PAR (US) 1935 dir. Gregory La Cava
Bottome, P.

Prize, The
MGM (US) 1963 dir. Mark Robson
Wallace, I.

Prize of Gold, A
COL (GB) 1955 dir. Mark Robson
Catto, M.

Prize of Peril, The
UGC (Fr/Yugo) 1983 dir. Yves Boisset
Sheckley, R.

Prizzi's Honor
FOX (US) 1985 dir. John Huston
Condon, R.

Prof, Le
STUDIO CANAL+ (Fr) 2000 dir.
Alexandre Jardin
Jardin, A. *Petit Sauvage, Le*

Professionals, The
COL (US) 1966 dir. Richard Brooks
O'Rourke, F. *Mule for the Marquesa, A*

Project X
PAR (US) 1968 dir. William Castle
Davies, L. P.

Prometheus: The Life of Balzac
BBC (GB) 1975 dir. Joan Craft
TVSe(GB)
Maurois, A.

Promise, A
KT (Jap) 1987 dir. Yoshishige Yoshida
Sae, S. *Rojuko Kazoku*

Promise, The
COMM (GB) 1969 dir. Michael Hayes
Arbuzov, A.
P

Promise at Dawn
AVCO (US/Fr) 1970 dir. Jules Dassin
Gary, R. *Promisse de l'aube, La*
Taylor, S. *First Love*
P

Promised a Miracle
REP (US) 1988 dir. Stephen Gyllenhaal
TV(US)
Parker, L. and Tanner, D. *We Let Our Son Die*

Promise the Moon
CBC (Can) 1997 dir. Ken Jubenvill
TV(Can)
Platt, R. B.

Promise to Keep, A
WAR TV (US) 1990 dir. Rod Holcomb
TV(US)
Yarmolinsky, J. *Angels Without Wings*

Pronto
SHOWTIMEWORKS (US) 1996 dir. Jim McBride
TV(US)
Leonard, E.

Prospero's Books
FILM 4 (GB/Fr) 1991
dir. Peter Greenaway
Shakespeare, W. *Tempest, The*
P

Proteus
METRODOME (GB) 1996 dir. Bob Keen
Knight, H. A. *Slimer*

Proud and Profane, The
PAR (US) 1956 dir. George Seaton
Crockett, L. H. *Magnificent Devils*

Proud Ones, The
FOX (US) 1956 dir. Robert D. Webb
Athanas, V.

Prudence and the Pill
FOX (GB) 1968 dir. Fielder Cook
Mills, H.
P

Psyche 59
BL (GB) 1964 dir. Alexander Singer
de Ligneris, F. *Psyche 63*

Psycho
UN (US) 1960 dir. Alfred Hitchcock
UN (US) 1998 dir. Gus Van Sant
Bloch, R.

Psycho Beach Party
STRAND (US) 2000 dir. Robert Lee King
Busch, C.
P

PT 109
WAR (US) 1963 dir. Leslie H. Martinson
Donovan, R. J. *PT109—John F. Kennedy in World War II*

Public Defender
RKO (US) 1931 dir. J. Walter Ruben
Goodschild, G. *Splendid Crime, The*

Puenktchen und Anton
BAVARIA (Ger) 1999 dir. Caroline Link
Kaestner, E.

Puerto Escondido
PENRAFILM (It) 1992 dir. Gabriele Salvatores
Cacucci, P.

Pumping Iron
CINEMA 51 (US) 1977
dir. George Butler
Gaines, C. and Butler, G.

Pumping Iron II
BLUE DOLPHIN (US) 1984
dir. George Butler

Gaines, C. and Butler, G. *Pumping Iron II: The Unprecedented Woman*

Pumpkin Eater, The
BL (GB) 1964 dir. Jack Clayton

Mortimer, P.

Punk and the Princess, The
M2 (GB) 1993 dir. Michael Sarne

Sams, G. *Punk, The*

Puppet Masters, The
HOLLYWOOD (US) 1994 dir. Stuart Orme

Heinlein, R. A.

Puppet on a Chain
SCOTIA-BARBER (GB) 1970
dir. Geoffrey Reeve, Don Sharp

MacLean, A.

Purely Belter
CHANNEL 4 FILMS (GB) 2000 dir. Mark Herman

Tulloch, J. *Season Ticket, The*

Purple Mask, The
UN (US) 1955 dir. Bruce Humberstone

Orczy, Baroness E. *Scarlet Pimpernel, The*

Purple Noon
HILLCREST (Fr) 1960
dir. René Clément

Highsmith, P. *Talented Mr. Ripley, The*

Purple Plain, The
GFD (GB) 1954 dir. Robert Parrish

Bates, H. E.

Pursuit of D. B. Cooper, The
UN (US) 1981 dir. Roger Spottiswoode

Reed, J. D. *Free Fall*

Pursuit
ABC (US) 1972 dir. Michael Crichton
TV(US)

Crichton, M. *Binary*

Pursuit of Happiness, The
PAR (US) 1934 dir. Alexander Hall

Langner, L. and Marshall, A.
P

Pursuit of Happiness, The
COL (US) 1971 dir. Robert Mulligan

Rogers, T.

Pushover
COL (US) 1954 dir. Richard Quine

Ballinger, W. *Rafferty*

Walsh, T. *Night Watch, The*

Pygmalion
MGM (GB) 1938 dir. Anthony Asquith
COMPASS (US) 1963
dir. George Schaefer
TV(US)

Shaw, G. B.
P

Q&A
TRISTAR (US) 1990 dir. Sidney Lumet
Torres, E.

QB VII
COL (US) 1974 dir. Tom Gries
TVSe(US)
Uris, L.

Quai Des Brumes
RAB (Fr) 1938 dir. Marcel Carné
MacOrlan, P.

Quai des Orfèvres
MAJ (Fr) 1947
dir. Henri-Georges Clouzot
Steeman, S.-A. *Legitime Defense*

Quality Street
RKO (US) 1937 dir. George Stevens
Barrie, Sir J. M.
P

Quare Fellow, The
BL (GB) 1962 dir. Arthur Dreifuss
Behan, B.
P

Quarry, The
WANDA (Fr/Bel/Sp) 1998 dir. Marion
Hansel
Galgut, D.

Quartet
NEW WORLD (GB/Fr) 1981
dir. James Ivory
Rhys, J.

Quartet
GFD (GB) 1948
dir. Ralph Smart, Harold French,
Arthur Crabtree, Ken Annakin
Maugham, W. S. *Facts of Life, The; Alien
Corn, The; Kite, The; Colonel's Lady, The*

Queen Bee
COL (US) 1955 dir. Ronald MacDougall
Lee, E.

Queenie
NEW WORLD (US) 1987
dir. Larry Peerce
TVSe(US)
Korda, M.

Queen Margot
STUDIO CANAL+ (Fr) 1994 dir. Patrice
Chereau
Dumas, A.

Queen of Spades, The
AB (GB) 1949 dir. Thorold Dickinson
Pushkin, A.

Queen of the Mob
PAR (US) 1940 dir. James Hogan
Hoover, J. E. *Persons in Hiding*

Querelle
TRIUMPH (Fr/Ger) 1983
dir. Rainer Werner Fassbinder
Genet, J. *Querelle de Brest*

Quest for Camelot
WAR (US) 1998 dir. Frederik Du Chau
A, Ch, M

Chapman, V. *King's Damsel, The*

Question of Attribution, A
BBC (GB) 1992 dir. John Schlesinger
TV(GB)

Bennett, A.
P

Question of Honor, A
EMI (US) 1982 dir. Jud Taylor
TV(US)

Grosso, S. and Rosenberg, P. *Point Blank*

Quest for Fire
FOX (Can/Fr) 1982
dir. Jean-Jacques Annaaud

Rosny, J. H.

Quick and the Dead, The
HBO (US) 1987 dir. Robert Day
TV(US)

L'Amour, L.

Quick, Before it Melts
MGM (US) 1964 dir. Delbert Mann

Benjamin, P.

Quick Change
WAR (US) 1990 dir. Howard Franklin,
Bill Murray

Cronley, J.

Quiet American, The
UA (US) 1957 dir. Joseph L. Mankiewicz

Greene, G.

Quiet as a Nun
THAMES (GB) 1982 dir. Moira
Armstrong
TVSe(GB)

Fraser, A.

Quiet Conspiracy, A
ANGLIA (GB) 1989 dir. John Gorrie
TVSe(GB)

Ambler, E.

Quiet Days in Clichy
MIRACLE (Den) 1970
dir. Jens Jorgen Thorsen

Miller, H.

Quiet Duel, The
DAIEI (Jap) 1983 dir. Akira Kurosawa

Kikuta, K.
P

Quiet Earth, The
YEL (NZ) 1985 dir. Greg Murphy
TV(NZ)

Madison, C.

Quiet Flows the Don
GORKI (USSR) 1958
dir. Sergei Gerasimov

Sholokhov, M. *And Quiet Flows the Don*

Quiet Killer
SABAN/SCHERICK (US) 1992 dir.
Sheldon Larry
TV(US)

Cravens, G. and Marr, J. S. *Black Death, The*

Quiet Man, The
REP (US) 1952 dir. John Ford

Walsh, M. *Green Rushes*

Quiet Wedding
PAR (GB) 1941 dir. Anthony Asquith

McCracken, E.
P

Quiet Weekend
AB (GB) 1946 dir. Harold French

McCracken, E.
P

Quiller Memorandum, The
RANK (GB) 1966 dir. Michael Anderson

Trevor, E.

Quills
FOX (US/Ger) 2000 dir. Philip Kaufman

Wright, D.
P

Quiz Show
HOLLYWOOD (US) 1994 dir. Robert Redford

Goodwin, R. *Remembering America: A Voice From the Sixties*

Quo Vadis
MGM (US) 1951 dir. Mervyn LeRoy
RAI (It) 1985 dir. Franco Rossi
TVSe(It)

Sienkiewicz, H.

R2PC: Road to Park City
PHAEDRA (US) 1999 dir. Bret Stern

Stern, B. *How to Shoot a Feature Under $10,000 and Not Go to Jail*

Rabbit, Run
WAR (US) 1970 dir. Jack Smight

Updike, J.

Racers, The
FOX (US) 1955 dir. Henry Hathaway
GB title: Such Men are Dangerous

Ruesch, H. *Racer, The*

Race to Freedom: The Underground Railroad
XENON (Can) 1994 dir. Don McBrearty
TV(Can)

Smucker, B. *Underground to Canada*

Rachel and the Stranger
RKO (US) 1948 dir. Norman Foster

Fast, H. *Rachel*

Rachel Papers, The
UA (GB) 1989 dir. Damian Harris

Amis, M.

Rachel, Rachel
WAR (US) 1968 dir. Paul Newman

Laurence, M. *Jest of God, A*

Racket, The
RKO (US) 1951 dir. John Cromwell

Cormack, B.
P

Radiance
ECLIPSE (Aust) 1998 dir. Rachel Perkins

Mowra, L.
P

Raffles
UA (US) 1939 dir. Sam Wood

Hornung, E. W. *Raffles the Amateur Cracksman*

Rage in Harlem, A
MIRAMAX (US) 1991 dir. Bill Duke

Himes, C.

Rage in Heaven
MGM (US) 1941 dir. W. S. Van Dyke

Hilton, J. *Dawn of Reckoning*

Rage of Angels
NBC (US) 1983 dir. Buzz Kulik
TVSe(US)

Sheldon, S.

Rage to Live, A
UA (US) 1965 dir. Walter Grauman

O'Hara, J.

Raging Bull
UA (US) 1980 dir. Martin Scorsese

La Motta, J.

Raging Calm, A
GRANADA (GB) 1974 dir. June Howson, Gerry Mill
TVSe(GB)

Barstow, S.

Raging Moon, The
MGM (GB) 1970 dir. Bryan Forbes
Marshall, P.

Raging Tide, The
UI (US) 1951 dir. George Sherman
Gann, E. K. *Fiddler's Green*

Ragman's Daughter, The
FOX (GB) 1972 dir. Harold Becker
Sillitoe, A.

Ragtime
PAR (US) 1981 dir. Milos Forman
Doctorow, E. L.

Railway Children, The
BBC (GB) 1968 dir. Julia Smith
TVSe(GB)
MGM (GB) 1970 dir. Lionel Jeffries
Ch
CARLTON TV (GB) 2000 dir. Catherine Morshead
Ch, TV(GB)
Nesbit, E.

Railway Station Man, The
TNT/BBC (US/GB) 1992 dir. Michael Whyte
TV(US/GB)
Johnston, J.

Rain
UA (US) 1932 dir. Lewis Milestone
Maugham, W. S.
P

Rain
NZ FILMS (NZ/US) 2001 dir. Christine Jeffs
Gunn, K.

Rainbow, The
BBC (GB) 1988 dir. Stuart Burge
TVSe(GB)
VESTRON (GB) 1989 dir. Ken Russell
Lawrence, D. H.

Rainbow
TEN-FOUR (US) 1978 dir. Jackie Cooper
TV(US)
Finch, C.

Rainbow Drive
VIACOM (US) 1990 dir. Bobby Roth
TV(US)
Thorpe, R.

Rainmaker, The
PAR (US) 1956 dir. Joseph Anthony
Nash, N. R.
P

Rainmaker, The
AM ZOETROPE (US) 1997 dir. Francis Ford Coppola
Grisham, J.

Rains Came, The
FOX (US) 1939 dir. Clarence Brown
Bromfield, L.

Rains of Ranchipur, The
FOX (US) 1955 dir. Jean Negulesco
Bromfield, L. *Rains Came, The*

Raintree County
MGM (US) 1957 dir. Edward Dmytryk
Lockridge, R.

Raise the Red Lantern
ORION (China) 1991 dir. Zhang Yimov
Tong, S. *Wives and Concubines*

Raise the Titanic
ITC (US) 1980 dir. Jerry Jameson
Cussler, C.

Raising a Riot
BL (GB) 1955 dir. Wendy Toye
Toombs, A.

Raisin in the Sun, A
COL (US) 1961 dir. Daniel Petrie
Hansberry, L.
P

Rally Round the Flag, Boys
FOX (US) 1958 dir. Leo McCarey
Shulman, M.

Rambling Rose
NEW LINE (US) 1991
dir. Martha Coolidge
Willingham, C.

Ramona
FOX (US) 1936 dir. Henry King
Jackson, H. M.

Rampage
WAR (US) 1963 dir. Philip Carlson
Caillou, A.

Ramrod
UA (US) 1947 dir. André de Toth
Short, L.

Ran
NIPPON HERALD (Jap) 1985 dir. Akira Kurosawa
Shakespeare, W. *King Lear*
P

Random Harvest
MGM (US) 1942 dir. Mervyn LeRoy
Hilton, J.

Random Hearts
COL (US) 1999 dir. Sydney Pollack
Adler, W.

Range of Motion
HEARST (US) 2000 dir. Donald Wrye
TV(US)
Berg, E.

Rape, The
MIRACLE (Bel/Neth) 1973
dir. Fons Rademakers
Freeling, N. *Because of the Cats*

Rapture
FOX (US/Fr) 1965 dir. John Guillermin
Hastings, P. *Rapture in my Rags*

Rapture
TRISTAR (US) 1993 dir. Timothy Bond
TV(US)
Tessier, T.

Rare Birds
LIONS GATE (Can) 2001 dir. Sturla Gunnarsson
Riche, E.

Rascal
DISNEY (US) 1969 dir. Norman Tokar
Ch
North, S. *Rascal, a Memoir of a Better Era*

Rat, The
RKO (GB) 1937 dir. Jack Raymond
Novello, I. and Collier, C.
P

Rated X
BERG/MARCIL (US) 2000 dir. Emilio Estevez
TV(US)
McCumder, D. *X-Rated: The Mitchell Brothers, a True Story of Sex, Money and Death*

Rat Race, The
PAR (US) 1960 dir. Robert Mulligan
Kanin, G.
P

Rat's Tale, A
MONTY (US) 1998 dir. Michael F. Huse
A, Ch
Seidler, T.

Rattled
GT FALLS (US) 1996 dir. Tony Randel
TV(US)
Gilmore, J. *Rattlers*

Rattle of a Simple Man
WAR (GB) 1964 dir. Muriel Box
Dyer, C.
P

Razones de Mis Amigos, Las
TORNASOL (Sp) 2000 dir. Gerardo Herrero
Gopegui, B. *Conquista del Aire, La*

Razorback
WAR (Aust) 1984 dir. Russell Mulcahy
Brennan, P.

Razor's Edge, The
FOX (US) 1946 dir. Edmund Goulding
COL (US) 1984 dir. John Byrum
Maugham, W. S.

Reach for Glory
GALA (GB) 1962 dir. Philip Leacock
Rae, J. *Custard Boys, The*

Reach for the Sky
COL (GB) 1956 dir. Lewis Gilbert
Brickhill, P.

Reaching for the Sun
PAR (US) 1941 dir. William Wellman
Smitter, W. *F.O.B. Detroit*

Real Charlotte, The
YTV (GB) 1991 dir. Timothy Barry
TVSe(GB)
Somerville, E. and Ross, M.

Real Glory, The
UA (US) 1939 dir. Henry Hathaway
Clifford, C. L.

Re-Animator
EMPIRE (US) 1985 dir. Stuart Gordon
Lovecraft, H. P. *Herbert West—The Re-Animator*

Reap the Wild Wind
PAR (US) 1942 dir. Cecil B. De Mille
Strabel, T.

Rearview Mirror
SCHICK SUNN (US) 1984 dir. Lou Antonio
TV(US)
Cooney, C. B.

Rear Window
PAR (US) 1954 dir. Alfred Hitchcock
Woolrich, C.

Reason for Living: The Jill Ireland Story
TEN-FOUR (US) 1991
dir. Michael Rhodes
TV(US)
Ireland, J. *Life Lines*

Rebecca
UA (US) 1940 dir. Alfred Hitchcock
BBC (GB) 1979 dir. Simon Langton
TVSe(GB)
CARLTON TV (GB) 1997 dir. Jim O'Brien
TVSe(GB)
Du Maurier, D.

Rebecca of Sunnybrook Farm
FOX (US) 1932 dir. Alfred Santell
FOX (US) 1938 dir. Allan Dwan
BBC (GB) 1978 dir. Rodney Bennett
TVSe(GB)
Wiggin, K. D.

Rebel
MIRACLE (Aust) 1986
dir. Michael Jenkins
Herbert, B. *No Names . . . No Pack Drills*
P

Rebels, The
UN TV (US) 1979 dir. Russ Mayberry
TVSe(US)
Jakes, J.

Recalled to Life
BBC/A&E (GB) 1999 dir. Suri
Krishnamma
TV(GB)
Hill, R.

Reckless
GOLDWYN (US) 1995 dir. Norman
Rene
Lucas, C.
P

Reckless Moment, The
COL (US) 1949 dir. Max Ophuls
Holding, E. S. *Blank Wall, The*

Reckoning, The
COL (GB) 1969 dir. Jack Gold
Hall, P. *Harp That Once, The*

Rector's Wife, The
CHANNEL 4 (GB) 1994 dir. Giles Foster
TVSe(GB)
Trollope, J.

Red Alert
PAR (US) 1977 dir. William Hale
TV(US)
King, H. *Paradigm Red*

Red and the Black, The
TELFRANCE (Fr/It) 1997 dir. Jean-
Daniel Verhaeghe
TVSe(Fr/It)
Stendahl, M. H. B. *Rouge et le Noir, Le*

Red Badge of Courage, The
MGM (US) 1951 dir. John Huston
M. ARCH (US) 1981 dir. Don Taylor
TV(US)
Crane, S.

Redbeard
TOHO (Jap) 1965 dir. Akira Kurosawa
Yamamoto

Red Beret, The
COL (GB) 1953 dir. Terence Young
US title: Paratrooper
Saunders, H. St. G.

Red Canyon
UN (US) 1949 dir. George Sherman
Grey, Z. *Wildfire*

Red Danube, The
MGM (US) 1949 dir. George Sidney
Marshall, B. *Vespers in Vienna*

Red Dust
MGM (US) 1932 dir. Victor Fleming
Collison, W. *Farewell to Women*
P

Red Earth, White Earth
VIACOM (US) 1989 dir. David Greene
TV(US)
Weaver, W.

**Red Firecracker, Green
Firecracker**
BEIJING SALON (China) 1994 dir. Ping
He
Jicai, F.

Red Headed Woman
MGM (US) 1932 dir. Jack Conway
Brush, K.

Red House, The
UA (US) 1947 dir. Delmer Daves
Chamberlain, G. A.

Red-Light Sting, The
UN TV (US) 1984 dir. Rod Holcomb
TV(US)
Post, H. *Whorehouse Sting, The*

Red Pony, The
BL (US) 1949 dir. Lewis Milestone
UN (US) 1973 dir. Robert Totten
TV(US)
Steinbeck, J.

Red Riding Hood
CANNON (US) 1987 dir. Adam Brooks
Ch
Grimm, J. L. K. and Grimm, W. K.

Red River
UA (US) 1948 dir. Howard Hawks
Chase, B. *Chisolm Trail, The*

Red Rose, White Rose
GOLDEN FLARE (HK) 1994 dir.
Stanley Kwan
Chang Rehyer, E. *Golden Horse*

Red Sky at Morning
UN (US) 1971 dir. James Goldstone
Bradford, R.

Red Wagon
BIP (GB) 1935 dir. Paul Stein
Smith, Lady E.

Redwood Curtain
HALLMARK (US) 1995 dir. John Korty
TV(US)
Wilson, L.
P

Reflection of Fear
COL (US) 1973 dir. William A. Fraker
Forbes, S. *Go to thy Deathbed*

Reflections in a Golden Eye
WAR (US) 1967 dir. John Huston
McCullers, C.

Reflections of Murder
ABC (US) 1974 dir. John Badham
TV(US)
Boileau, P. and Narcejac, T. *Celle qui n'etait Plus*

Regeneration
BBC (GB/Can) 1997 dir. Gillies
MacKinnon
Barker, P.

Reilly, Ace of Spies
EUSTON (GB) 1983 dir. Jim Goddard
TVSe(GB)
Lockhart, R. B.

Reincarnation of Peter Proud, The
AVCO (US) 1975 dir. J. Lee Thompson
Ehrlich, M.

Reivers, The
WAR (US) 1969 dir. Mark Rydell
Faulkner, W.

Relative Values
OVERSEAS (GB) 1999 dir. Eric Styles
Coward, N.
P

Relentless
CBS ENT (US) 1977 dir. Lee H. Katzin
TV(US)
Garfield, B.

Relic, The
BBC (GB/US) 1997 dir. Peter Hyams
Preston, D. and Child, L.

Reluctant Debutante, The
MGM (US) 1958 dir. Vincente Minnelli
Home, W. D.
P

Reluctant Heroes
ABP (GB) 1951 dir. Jack Raymond
Morris, C.
P

Reluctant Widow, The
GFD (GB) 1950 dir. Bernard Knowles
Heyer, G.

Remains of the Day, The
COL (GB/US) 1993 dir. James Ivory
Ishiguro, K.

Remains to be Seen
MGM (US) 1953 dir. Don Weis
Lindsay, H. and Crouse, R.
P

Remarkable Mr. Pennypacker, The
FOX (US) 1958 dir. Henry Levin
O'Brian, L.
P

Remember
NBC (US) 1993 dir. John Herzfeld
TVSe(US)
Bradford, B. T.

Remember Last Night?
UN (US) 1936 dir. James Whale
Hobhouse, A. *Hangover Murders, The*

Remember Me
HALLMARK (US) 1995 dir. Michael Switzer
TV(US)
Clark, M. H.

Remembrance
NBC (US) 1996 dir. Bethany Rooney
TV(US)
Steel, D.

Remo Williams: The Adventure Begins
ORION (US) 1985 dir. Guy Hamilton
Murphy, W. and Sapir, R. *Destroyer, The*

Rendezvous
MGM (US) 1935 dir. William K. Howard
Yardley, H. O. *American Black Chamber, The*

Rendezvous
DIRECTORS' CIRCLE (US) 1999 dir. Roy Campanella II
TV(US)
Anderson, B.

Renegades
FOX (US) 1930 dir. Victor Fleming
Armandy, A.

Replacing Dad
THOMPSON (US) 1999 dir. Joyce Chopra
TV(US)
Mickle, S. F.

Report to the Commissioner
UA (US) 1975 dir. Milton Katselas
GB title: Operation Undercover
Mills, J.

Reprisal
COL (US) 1956 dir. George Sherman
Gordon, A.

Requiem
GEMINI (Fr) 1998 dir. Alain Tanner
Tabucchi, A.

Requeim for a Dream
ARTISAN (US) 2000 dir. Darren Aronofsky
Selby, Jr., H.

Requiem for a Heavyweight
COL (US) 1962 dir. Ralph Nelson
GB title: Blood Money
Serling, R.
P

Rescuers: Stories of Courage
SHOWTIME (US) 1997 dir. Peter Bogdanovich, Tim Hunter, Lynne Littman, Tony Bill
TVSe(US)
Drucker, M. and Block, G. *Rescuers: Portraits of Moral Courage in the Holocaust*

Rescuers, The
DISNEY (US) 1977
dir. Wolfgang Reitherman
A, Ch
Sharp, M. *Rescuers, The; Miss Bianca*

Respectable Prostitute, The
MARCEAU (Fr) 1952
dir. Marcel Pagliero, Charles Brabant
Sartre, J.-P.
P

Restoration
MIRAMAX (US/Arg) 1995 dir. Michael
Hoffman
Tremaine, R.

Resurrected, The
SCOTTI (US) 1992 dir. Dan O'Bannon
Lovecraft, H. P. *Case of Charles Dexter Ward, The*

Resurrection
UN (US) 1931 dir. Edwin Carewe
BBC (GB) 1968 dir. David Giles
TVSe(GB)
Tolstoy, L.

Resurrection Man
POLYGRAM (GB) 1997 dir. Marc Evans
McNamee, E.

Retour de Casanova, Le
STUDIO CANAL+ (Fr) 1992 dir.
Edouard Niermans
Schnitzler, A. *Casanovas Heimfahrt*

Return From the Ashes
UA (US) 1965 dir. J. Lee Thompson
Monteilhet, H.

Return from the River Kwai
RANK (GB) 1987
dir. Andrew V. McLaglen
Blair, J. and Blair, C.

Return of Don Camillo, The
MIRACLE (Fr/It) 1953
dir. Julien Duvivier
Guareschi, G. *Don Camillo and the Prodigal Son*

Return of Peter Grimm, The
RKO (US) 1935 dir. George Nicholls
Belasco, D.
P

Return of Sherlock Holmes
GRANADA (GB) 1988 dir. Michael Cox
TV(GB)
Doyle, Sir A. C.

Return of the Antelope, The
GRANADA (GB) 1985 dir. Eugene
Ferguson
Ch, TVSe(GB)
Hall, W.

Return of the Big Cat
DISNEY (US) 1974 dir. Tom Leetch
Dietz, L. *Year of the Big Cat, The*

Return of the Borrowers, The
WORKING TITLE/TNT (GB) 1996 dir.
John Henderson
Ch, TVSe(US)
Norton, M.

Return of the Native, The
SIGNBOARD HILL (US) 1994 dir. Jack
Gold
TV(US)
Hardy, T.

Return of the Soldier, The
BW (GB) 1983 dir. Alan Bridges
West, R.

Return to Algiers
STUDIO CANAL+ (Fr) 2000 dir.
Alexandre Arcady
Bonnell, R. *Grand Vacance*

Return to Earth
KH (US) 1976 dir. Jud Taylor
TV(US)
Aldrin, Jr., E. and Warga, W.

Return to Oz
DISNEY (US) 1985 dir. Walter Murch
Baum, L. F. *Marvellous Land of Oz, The;*
Ozma of Oz

Return to Paradise
UA (US) 1953 dir. Mark Robson
Michener, J. A.

Return to Peyton Place
FOX (US) 1960 dir. Jose Ferrer
Metalious, G.

Return to the Blue Lagoon
COL (US) 1991 dir. William A. Graham
Stacpoole, H. D. *Garden of God, The*

Reuben, Reuben
FOX (US) 1983 dir. Robert Ellis Miller
De Vries, P.

Reunion
RANK (US/Fr/Ger) 1989
dir. Jerry Schatzberg
Uhlman, F.

Reunion
RHI (US) 1994 dir. Lee Grant
TV(US)
Sexton, L. G. *Points of Light*

Reunion in Vienna
MGM (US) 1933 dir. Sidney Franklin
Sherwood, R. E.
P

Revenge
CARLINER (US) 1971 dir. Jud Taylor
TV(US)
Davis, E.

Revenge
COL (US) 1990 dir. Tony Scott
Harrison, J.

Revenger's Comedies, The
BBC (GB/Fr) 1998 dir. Malcolm
Mowbray
Ayckbourn, A.
P

Reversal of Fortune
WAR (US) 1990 dir. Barbet Schroeder
Dershowitz, A.

Revolt of Mamie Stover, The
FOX (US) 1956 dir. Raoul Walsh
Huie, W. B.

Revolutionary, The
UA (US) 1970 dir. Paul Williams
Koningsberger, H.

Reward, The
FOX (US) 1965 dir. Serge Bourgignon
Barrett, M.

Rhapsody
MGM (US) 1954 dir. Charles Vidor
Richardson, H. H. *Maurice Guest*

Rhapsody
DIRECTORS' CIRCLE (US) 2000 dir.
Jeffrey W. Byrd
TV(US)
Mason, F.

Rhapsody in August
ORION (Jap) 1991 dir. Akira Kurosawa
Murata, K. *Nabe-No-Kake*

Rhineman Exchange, The
UN TV (US) 1977 dir. Burt Kennedy
TVSe(US)
Ludlum, R.

Rhodes of Africa
GAU BRI (GB) 1936
dir. Berthold Viertes
US title: Rhodes

Millin, S. G. *Rhodes*

Rhubarb
PAR (US) 1951 dir. Allan Lubin

Smith, H. A.

Ribelle, La
RETEITALIA (It) 1993 dir. Aurelio
Grimaldi

Grimaldi, A. *Storia di Enza, La*

Rich and Famous
MGM (US) 1981 dir. George Cukor

van Druten, J. *Old Acquaintance*
P

Rich and Strange
BIP (GB) 1931 dir. Alfred Hitchcock
US title: East of Shanghai

Collins, D.

Richard's Things
SOUTHERN (GB) 1980
dir. Anthony Harvey

Raphael, F.

Richard III
BL (GB) 1955 dir. Laurence Olivier
BRIT SCREEN (GB) dir. Richard
Loncraine

Shakespeare, W.
P

Rich Are Always With Us, The
WAR (US) 1932 dir. Alfred E. Green

Pettit, E.

Rich in Love
MGM (US) 1993 dir. Bruce Beresford

Humphreys, J.

Rich Man, Poor Girl
MGM (US) 1938 dir. Reinbold Schunzel

Ellis, E. *White Collars*
P

Rich Man, Poor Man
UN (US) 1976 dir. David Greene, Boris
Sagal
TVSe(US)

Shaw, I.

Rich Man's Folly
PAR (US) 1931 dir. John Cromwell

Dickens, C. *Dombey and Son*

Rich Men, Single Women
SPELLING (US) 1990
dir. Elliot Silverstein
TV(US)

Beck, P. and Massman, P.

Richest Man in the World, The: The Story of Aristotle Onassis
KON-SAN (US) 1988 dir. Waris Hussein
TVSe(US)

Evans, P. *Ari: The Life and Time of Aristotle Onassis*

Ricky Nelson: Original Teen Idol
VH1 (US) 1999 dir. Sturla Gunnarsson
TV(US)

Selvin, J. *Ricky Nelson—Idol For a Generation*

Ricochet River
DEEGEE (US) 1998 dir. Deborah Del
Prete

Cody, R.

Riddle of the Sands, The
RANK (GB) 1979 dir. Tony Maylam

Childers, E.

Ride a Wild Pony
DISNEY (Aust) 1976 dir. Don Chaffey

Aldridge, J. *Sporting Proposition, A*

Ride Beyond Vengeance
COL (US) 1966 dir. Bernard McEveety
Dewlen, A. *Night of the Tiger, The*

Riders of the Purple Sage
FOX (US) 1931
dir. Hamilton MacFadden
FOX (US) 1941 dir. James Tinling
ROSEMONT (US) dir. Charles Haid
TV(US)
Grey, Z.

Ride the High Wind
BUTCHER (SA) 1966
dir. David Millin
Harding, G. *North of Bushman's Rock*

Ride the Pink Horse
UI (US) 1947 dir. Robert Montgomery
Hughes, D. B.

Ride With the Devil
UN (US) 1999 dir. Ang Lee
Woodrell, D. *Woe To Live On*

Riding High
PAR (US) 1943 dir. George Marshall
GB title: Melody Inn
Montgomery, J. *Ready Money*
P

Riding in Cars With Boys
COL (US) 2001 dir. Penny Marshall
Donofrio, B.

Rififi
PATHS (Fr) 1955 dir. Jules Dassin
Le Breton, A. *Monsieur Rififi*

Right Approach, The
FOX (US) 1961 dir. David Butler
Kanin, G.
P

Right Hand Man, The
UAA (Aust) 1987 dir. Di Drew
Peyton, K. M.

Right of Way
HBO PREM (US) 1983
dir. George Schaefer
TV(US)
Lee, R.
P

Right Stuff, The
WAR (US) 1983 dir. Philip Kaufman
Wolfe, T.

Right to Live, The
WAR (US) 1935 dir. William Keighley
GB title: Sacred Flame, The
Maugham, W. S. *Sacred Flame, The*
P

Right to Love, The
PAR (US) 1930 dir. Richard Wallace
Glaspell, S. *Brook Adams*

Ring, The
UA (US) 1952 dir. Kurt Neumann
Shulman, I. *Cry Tough*

Ring, The
NBC (US) 1996 dir. Armand
Mastroianni
TV(US)
Steel, D.

Ringer, The
REGENT (GB) 1952 dir. Guy Hamilton
Wallace, E.

Ring of Bright Water
RANK (GB) 1968 dir. Jack Couffer
Maxwell, G.

Ringu
OMEGA (Jap) 1998 dir. Hideo Nakata,
Chisiri Takigawa
Suzuki, K.

Rio Conchos
FOX (US) 1964 dir. Gordon Douglas
Huffaker, C. *Guns of Rio Conchos*

Riot
PAR (US) 1968 dir. Buzz Kulik
Elli, F.

Rise and Shine
FOX (US) 1941 dir. Allan Dwan
Thurber, J. *My Life and Hard Times*

Rise & Walk: The Dennis Byrd Story
FOX WEST (US) 1994 dir. Michael Dinner
TV(US)
Byrd, D. and D'Orso, M. *Rise & Walk: The Trial & Triumph of Dennis Byrd*

Rising of the Moon, The
WAR (Ire) 1957 dir. John Ford
Gregory, Lady I. A.
McHugh, M. J. *Minute's Wait, A*
O'Connor, F. *Majesty of the Law, The*

Rising Son
FOX (US) 1993 dir. Philip Kaufman
Crichton, M.

Rita Hayworth: The Love Goddess
SUSSKIND (US) 1983 dir. James Goldstone
TV(US)
Kobal, J. *Rita Hayworth: The Time, the Place, and the Woman*

Rita, Sue and Bob Too
ORION (GB) 1987 dir. Alan Clarke
Dunbar, A.
P

Ritual
GOTHAM (US) 1999 dir. Stanley Bennett Clay
Clay, S. B.
P

Ritz, The
WAR (US) 1976 dir. Richard Lester
McNally, T.
P

Ritz, The
BBC (GB) 1978 dir. John Godber, Martin Shardlow
TVSe(GB)
Godber, J. *Bouncers*
P

Rivalry, The
DEFARIA (US) 1975 dir. Fielder Cook
TV(US)
Corwin, N.
P

River, The
UA (Ind) 1951 dir. Jean Renoir
Godden, R.

River Lady
UI (US) 1948 dir. George Sherman
Branch, H.

River of Death
CANNON (US) 1988 dir. Steve Carver
MacLean, A.

River Red
CASTLE HILL (US) 1997 dir. Eric Drilling
Drilling, E.
P

River's End
WAR (US) 1930 dir. Michael Curtiz
Curwood, J. O.

Road Back, The
UN (US) 1937 dir. James Whale
Remarque, E. M.

Road Home, The
COL (China) 1999 dir. Yimou Zhang
Bao, S. *Remembrance*

Road House
GAU (GB) 1934 dir. Maurice Elvey
Hackett, W.
P

Road to Mecca, The
VIDEOVISION (US) 1992
dir. Athol Fugard
TV(US)
Fugard, A.
P

Road to Wellville, The
COL (US) 1994 dir. Alan Parker
Boyle, T. C.

Road Show
H. ROACH (US) 1941
dir. Gordon Douglas
Hatch, E.

Roads to Freedom, The
BBC (GB) 1970 dir. James Cellan Jones
TVSe(GB)
Sartre, J.-P. *Age of Reason, The; Reprieve, The; Iron in the Soul*

Road to Singapore
WAR (US) 1931 dir. Alfred E. Green
Pertwee, R. *Heat Wave*
P

Robert Kennedy and his Times
COL (US) 1985 dir. Marvin J. Chomsky
TVSe(US)
Schlesinger, Jr., A. M.

Robbery Under Arms
RANK (GB) 1957 dir. Jack Lee
Boldrewood, R.

Robe, The
FOX (US) 1953 dir. Henry Koster
Douglas, L. C.

Roberta
RKO (US) 1935 dir. William A. Seiter
M
Miller, A. D. *Gowns by Roberta*

Roberto Succo
STUDIO CANAL+ (Fr) 2001 dir. Cedric Kahn
Froment, P. *Je te tue: Histoire Vraie de Roberto Succo*

Robert Rylands' Last Journey
BUXTON (Sp/GB) 1996 dir. Gracia Querejeta
Marias, J. *All Souls*

Robinson Crusoe
BBC (GB) 1974 dir. James MacTaggart
TV(GB)
MIRAMAX (UK/Gre) 1996 dir. Rod Hardy, George Miller
Defoe, D.

Rob Roy
BBC (GB) 1977 dir. Bob Hird
TVSe(GB)
Scott, Sir W.

Rockabye
PEREGRINE (US) 1986
dir. Richard Michael
TV(US)
Koenig, L.

Rockabye
RADIO (US) 1932 dir. George Cukor
Bronder, L.
P

Rockets Galore
RANK (GB) 1958 dir. Michael Ralph
US title: Mad Little Island
Mackenzie, Sir C.

Rockets in the Dunes
RANK (GB) 1960
dir. William Hammond
Ch

Lamplugh, L.

Rock Hudson
KON-SAN (US) 1990 dir. John Nicolella
TV(US)

Gates, P. *My Husband, Rock Hudson*

Rocking Horse Winner, The
TC (GB) 1949 dir. Anthony Pelissier

Lawrence, D. H.

Rocky O'Rourke
BBC (GB) 1976 dir. John Prowse
TVSe(GB)

Sherry, S. *Liverpool Cats, The*

Rogue Cop
MGM (US) 1954 dir. Roy Rowland

McGivern, W. P.

Rogue Trader
GRANADA (GB) 1999 dir. James
Dearden
TV(GB)

Leeson, N. and Whitley, E. *Rogue Trader: How I Brought Down Barings Bank and Shook the Financial World*

Roi Danse, Le
FRANCE 2 (Bel/Fr) 2000 dir. Gerard
Corbiau

Beaussant, P. *Lully ou le Musicien du Soleil*

Romance
MGM (US) 1930 dir. Clarence Brown

Sheldon, E.
P

Romance of a Horse Thief
ALLIED (Yugo) 1971
dir. Abraham Polonsky

Opatashu, D.

Romance of Rosy Ridge, The
MGM (US) 1947 dir. Roy Rowland

Kantor, M.

Roman de Lulu, Le
LAMBERT (Fr) 2001 dir. Pierre-Olivier
Scotto

Decca, D.
P

Romanoff and Juliet
UN (US) 1961 dir. Peter Ustinov

Ustinov, P.
P

Roman Spring of Mrs. Stone, The
WAR (GB/US) 1961 dir. José Quintero

Williams, T.

Romantic Comedy
MGM/UA (US) 1983 dir. Arthur Hiller

Slade, B.
P

Romantic Englishwoman, The
DIAL (GB) 1975 dir. Joseph Losey

Wiseman, T.

Romeo and Juliet
MGM (US) 1936 dir. George Cukor
GFD (GB) 1954 dir. Renato Castellani
PAR (GB) 1968 dir. Franco Zeffirelli
FOX (US) 1996 dir. Baz Lurhmann

Shakespeare, W.
P

Romy and Michele's High School Reunion
TOUCHSTONE (US) 1997 dir. David
Mirkin

Schiff, R. *Ladies Room, The*
P

Ronde, La
S. GARDINE (Fr) 1950 dir. Max Ophuls
INTEROPA (Fr) 1964 dir. Roger Vadim
Schnitzler, A.
P

Rookery Nook
MGM (GB) 1930 dir. Tom Walls
Travers, B.
P

Room at the Top
BI (GB) 1958 dir. Jack Clayton
Braine, J.

Room for One More
WAR (US) 1952 dir. Norman Taurog
Rose, A. P.

Room Service
RKO (US) 1938 dir. William A. Seiter
Murray, J. and Boretz, A.
P

Room Upstairs, The
M. REES (US) 1987 dir. Stuart Margolin
TV(US)
Levinson, N.

Room With a View, A
GOLD (GB) 1985 dir. James Ivory
Forster, E. M.

Rooney
RANK (GB) 1958 dir. George Pollock
Cookson, C.

Roosters
AM PLAY (US) 1993 dir. Robert M. Young
Sanchez-Scott, M.
P

Roots
WOLPER (US) 1977
dir. David Greene, Marvin J. Chomsky, John Erman, Gilbert Moses
TVSe(US)
Haley, A.

Roots of Heaven, The
FOX (US) 1958 dir. John Huston
Gary, R.

Roots: The Next Generation
WAR TV (US) 1979 dir. John Erman, Charles Dubin, Georg Stanford Brown, Lloyd Richards
TVSe(US)
Haley, A.

Rope
WAR (US) 1948 dir. Alfred Hitchcock
Hamilton, P.
P

Rosa e Cornelia
FILMTRE (It) 2000 dir. Giorgio Treves
Binosi, R.
P

Rosalie
MGM (US) 1937 dir. W. S. Van Dyke
M
McGuire, W. A. and Bolton, G.
P

Rosary Murders, The
NEW LINE (US) 1987 dir. Fred Walton
Kienzle, W. X.

Rose and the Jackal, The
WHITE (US) 1990 dir. Jack Gold
TV(US)
Leech, M. *Reveille in Washington*

Roseanna McCoy
RKO (US) 1949 dir. Irving Reis
Hannum, A.

Rosebud

UA (US) 1975 dir. Otto Preminger

Hemingway, J. and Bonnecarrere, P.

Rose Hill

HALLMARK (US) 1997 dir. Christopher Cain
TV(US)

Garwood, J. *For the Roses*

Rose Marie

MGM (US) 1936 dir. W. S. Van Dyke
MGM (US) 1954 dir. Mervyn LeRoy
M

Harbach, O. and Hammerstein, II, O.
P

Rosemary's Baby

PAR (US) 1968 dir. Roman Polanski

Levin, I.

Rosencrantz and Guildenstern are Dead

HOBO/CINECOM (US/GB) 1991 dir. Tom Stoppard

Stoppard, T.
P

Roses are for the Rich

PHOENIX (US) 1987 dir. Michael Miller
TVSe(US)

Lawson, J.

Rose Tattoo, The

PAR (US) 1955 dir. Daniel Mann

Williams, T.
P

Rosie

UN (US) 1967 dir. David Lowell Rich

Gordon, R.
P

Rosie: The Rosemary Clooney Story

FRIES (US) 1982 dir. Jackie Cooper
TV(US)

Clooney, R. and Strait, R. *This For Remembrance*

Rosie Dixon-Night Nurse

COL (GB) 1978 dir. Justin Cartwright

Dixon, R. *Confessions of a Night Nurse*

Roswell

SHOWTIMEWORKS (US) 1994 dir. Jeremy Kagan
TV(US)

Randle, K. D. and Schmitt, D. R. *UFO Crash at Roswell*

Rouge

ICA (HK) 1988 dir. Stanley Kwan

Pik-Wah, L.

Rouge et le Noir, Le

FRANCO-LF (Fr/It) 1954 dir. Claude Autant-Lara

Stendahl, M. H. B.

Rough and the Smooth, The

MGM (GB) 1959 dir. Robert Siodmak
US title: Portrait of a Sinner

Maugham, R.

Rough Cut

PAR (US) 1980 dir. Don Siegel

Lambert, D. *Touch the Lion's Paw*

Roughly Speaking

WAR (US) 1945 dir. Michael Curtiz

Pierson, L. R.

Rough Magic

RPC (GB/US) 1995 dir. Clare Peploe

Chase, J. H. *Miss Shumley Waves a Wand*

Rough Night in Jericho

UN (US) 1967 dir. Arnold Laven

Albert, M. H. *Man in Black, The*

Rough Shoot
UA (GB) 1952 dir. Robert Parrish
US title: Shoot First
Household, G.

Rounders, The
MGM (US) 1965 dir. Burt Kennedy
Evans, M.

Roxanne
COL (US) 1987 dir. Fred Schepisi
Rostand, E. *Cyrano de Bergerac*
P

Roxanne: The Prize Pulitzer
QINTEX (US) 1989 dir. Richard Colla
TV(US)
Pulitzer, R.

Roxie Hart
FOX (US) 1942 dir. William A. Wellman
Watkins, M. *Chicago*
P

Royal Bed, The
RKO (US) 1931 dir. Lowell Sherman
Sherwood, R. E. *Queen's Husband, The*
P

Royal Family of Broadway, The
PAR (US) 1930 dir. George Cukor
GB title: Theatre Royal
Kaufman, G. S. and Ferber, E. *Royal Family, The*
P

Royal Flash
FOX RANK (GB) 1975
dir. Richard Lester
Fraser, G. M.

Royal Hunt of the Sun, The
RANK (GB) 1969 dir. Irving Lerner
Shaffer, P.
P

Royal Scandal, A
FOX (US) 1945 dir. Otto Preminger
GB title: Czarina
Biro, L. and Lengyel, M.
P

Ruby
POLYGRAM (US) 1992 dir. John MacKenzie
Davis, S. *Love Field*
P

Ruby Ridge: An American Tragedy
SCHERICK (US) 1996 dir. Roger Young
TVSe(US)
Walter, J. *Every Knee Shall Bow*

Ruby Ring, The
HALLMARK (US) 1997 dir. Harley Cokeliss
TV(US)
MacGrory, Y. *Secret of the Ruby Ring*

Ruby's Bucket of Blood
SHOWTIME (US) 2001 dir. Peter Werner
TV(US)
Hebert, J.
P

Ruddigore
GALA (GB) 1967 dir. Joy Batchelor
A, M
Gilbert, Sir W. S. and Sullivan, Sir A.
P

Rudy, The Racing Pig
ROYAL (Ger) 1995 dir. Peter Timm
Timm, U. *Rennschwein Rudi Russel*

Rue du Retrait
JML (Fr) 2001 dir. René Féret
Lessing, D. *Diary of a Good Neighbour, The*

Ruggles of Red Gap
PAR (US) 1935 dir. Leo McCarey
Wilson, H. L.

Ruling Passion
BBC/A&E (GB) 1997 dir. Gareth Davies
TV(GB)
Hill, R.

Ruling Class, The
KEEP (GB) 1971 dir. Peter Medak
Barnes, P.
P

Rumble Fish
UN (US) 1983 dir. Francis Ford Coppola
Hinton, S. E.

Rumble on the Docks
COL (US) 1956 dir. Fred Sears
Paley, F.

Rumor of Angels, A
MPCA (US) 2000 dir. Peter O'Fallon
Boylan, G. D. *Thy Son Liveth, Messages from a Soldier to His Mother*

Rumor of War, A
FRIES (US) 1980 dir. Richard T. Heffron
TVSe(US)
Caputo, P.

Rumpelstiltskin
CANNON (US) 1987 dir. David Irving
Ch
Grimm, J. L. K. and Grimm, W. K.

Runaway
HALLMARK (US) 2000 dir. Brandon Thomas
TV(US)
Kay, T.

Runaway Father
HEARST (US) 1991 dir. John Nicolella
Rashke, R.

Runaways, The
LORIMAR (US) 1974 dir. Harry Harris
TV(US)
Canning, V.

Runaway Summer, The
BBC (GB) 1971 dir. Mary Ridge
TVSe(GB)
Bawden, N.

Run, Cougar, Run
DISNEY (US) 1972
dir. Michael Dmytryk
Murphy, R. *Mountain Lion, The*

Runestone, The
HY (US) 1992
dir. Willard Carroll
Rogers, M. E.

Runner Stumbles, The
SIMON (US) 1979 dir. Stanley Kramer
Stitt, M.
P

Running Against Time
FINNEGAN-PINCHUK (US) 1990 dir. Bruce Seth Green
TV(US)
Shapiro, S. *Time to Remember, A*

Running Blind
BBC (GB) 1979 dir. William Brayne
TVSe(GB)
Bagley, D.

Running Man, The
COL (GB) 1963 dir. Carol Reed
Smith, S. *Ballad of the Running Man, The*

Running Man, The
TRISTAR (US) 1987
dir. Paul Michael Glaser
Bachman, R.

Running Out of Time
ARIANE (Sp) 1994 dir. Imanol Uribe
Madrid, J.

Running Scared
PAR (GB) 1972 dir. David Hemmings
McDonald, G.

Run of the Country, The
COL (Ire/US) 1995 dir. Peter Yates
Connaughton, S.

Run Silent, Run Deep
UA (US) 1958 dir. Robert Wise
Beach, E. L.

Run the Wild Fields
SHOWTIME (US) 2000 dir. Paul A.
Kaufman
TV(US)
Vaccaro, R. *And the Home of the Brave*
P

Run Wild, Run Free
COL (GB) 1989 dir. Richard C. Sarafian
Rook, D. *White Colt, The*

Rusar I Hans Famn
GOTAFILM (Swe) 1996 dir. Lennart
Hjulstrom
Gronin, Y. *Karleks Pris*

Rush
MGM (US) 1991 dir. Lili Fini Zanuck
Wozencraft, K.

Russia House, The
MGM (US) 1990 dir. Fred Schepisi
Le Carré, J.

Russian Roulette
ITC (US) 1975 dir. Lou Lombardo
Ardies, T. *Kosygin is Coming*

Russians are Coming, The,
Russians are Coming, The
UA (US) 1966 dir. Norman Jewison
Benchley, N. *Off-Islanders, The*

Russian Singer, The
NORDISK (Den) 1994 dir. Morten
Arnfred
Davidsen, L.

Russicum
TRISTAR/CECCHI (It) 1989
dir. Pasquale Squitieri
Russo, E. *Martedì del Diavolo, Il*

Russkij Bunt
GLOBUS (Rus/Fr) 2000 dir. Aleksandr
Proshkin
Pushkin, A. *Captain's Daughter, The;*
History of Pugachev, A

Ruthless
EL (US) 1948 dir. Edgar G. Ulmer
Stoddart, D. *Prelude to Night*

Sabotage
GB (GB) 1936 dir. Alfred Hitchcock
US title: Woman Alone, A
Conrad, J. *Secret Agent, The*

Saboteur, The
FOX (US) 1965 dir. Bernhard Wicki
Jeorg, W.

Sabrina
PAR (US) 1954 dir. Billy Wilder
GB title: Sabrina Fair
PAR (US) 1995 dir. Sydney Pollack
Taylor, S. *Sabrina Fair*
P

Sacketts, The
SHALAKO (US) 1979 dir. Robert Totten
TVSe(US)
L'Amour, L. *Sackett; Daybreakers, The*

Sacred Flame, The
WAR (US) 1929 dir. Archie Mayo
Maugham, W. S.
P

Sacred Night, The
FRANCE 3 (Fr) 1993 dir. Nicolas Klotz
Ben Jelloun, T. *Nuit Sacrée, La; Enfant Des Sables, L'*

Sacrifice
LIONS GATE (US) 2000 dir. Mark L. Lester
TV(US)
Smith, M.

Sacrifice of Youth
ART EYE (China) 1986
dir. Zhang Luanxin
Manling, Z. *There was that Beautiful Place*

Sade
STUDIO CANAL+ (Fr) 2000 dir. Jacques Benoit
Bramly, S. *Terror in the Bedroom*

Safe Passage
NEW LINE (US) 1994 dir. Robert Allan Ackerman
Bache, E.

Sail a Crooked Ship
COL (US) 1961 dir. Irving Brecher
Benchley, N.

Sailor Beware!
BL (GB) 1956 dir. Gordon Parry
US title: Panic in the Parlor
King, P. and Cary, F. L.
P

Sailor from Gibraltar, The
WOODFALL (GB) 1967
dir. Tony Richardson
Duras, M.

Sailor's Return, The
ARIEL (GB) 1978 dir. Jack Gold
Garnett, D.

Sailor Takes a Wife, The
MGM (US) 1945 dir. Richard Whorf
Erskine, C.
P

Sailor Who Fell From Grace With the Sea, The
FOX RANK (GB) 1976
dir. Lewis John Carlino
Mishima, Y. *Gogo no Eiko*

Saimin
TOHO (Jap) 1999 dir. Masayuki Ochiai
Matsuoka, K.

Saint-Cyr
STUDIO CANAL+ (Fr/Bel) 2000 dir.
Patricia Mazuy
Dangerfield, Y. *Maison d'Esther, La*

Saint in New York
RKO (US) 1938 dir. Ben Holmes
Charteris, L.

St. Ives
WAR (US) 1976 dir. J. Lee Thompson
Bleeck, O. *Procane Chronicle, The*

St. Ives
BBC (GB) 1998 dir. Harry Hook
Stevenson, R. L.

Saint Jack
NEW WORLD (US) 1979
dir. Peter Bogdanovich
Theroux, P.

Saint Joan
UA (GB) 1957 dir. Otto Preminger
COMPASS (US) 1967
dir. George Schaefer
TV(US)
Shaw, G. B.
P

Saint Maybe
HALLMARK (US) 1998 dir. Michael
Pressman
TV(US)
Tyler, A.

St. Pauli Nacht
HAGER MOSS (Ger) 1999 dir.
Sonke Wortmann
Goehre, F.

Salamander, The
ITC (It/GB/US) 1981 dir. Peter Zinner
West, M.

Salem's Lot
WAR (US) 1979 dir. Tobe Hooper
TVSe(US)
King, S.

Sally
WAR (US) 1930 dir. John Francis Dillon
M
Bolton, G., Kern, J. and Grey, C.
P

Sally in our Alley
ABP (GB) 1931 dir. Maurice Elvey
McEvoy, C. *Likes of 'er, The*

Salome
CANNON (Fr/It) 1987
dir. Claude d'Anna
Wilde, O.
P

Salome's Last Dance
VESTRON (GB) 1988 dir. Ken Russell
Wilde, O. *Salome*
P

Saloon Bar
EAL (GB) 1940 dir. Walter Forde
Harvey, F.
P

Salt on Our Skin
VCL (Ger/Can/Fr) 1992 dir. Andrew
Birkin
Groult, B. *Vaisseaux de Coeur, Les*

Saltwater
ART EYE (Ire) 1999 dir. Conor
McPherson
McPherson, C. *This Lime Tree Bower*

Salute John Citizen
BN (GB) 1942 dir. Maurice Elvey
Greenwood, R. *Mr. Bunting at War*

Salute the Toff
BUTCHER (GB) 1952
dir. Maclean Rogers
Creasey, J.

Salzburg Connection, The
FOX (US) 1972 dir. Lee H. Katzin
MacInnes, H.

Same Time, Next Year
UN (US) 1978
dir. Robert Mulligan
Slade, B.
P

Samia
STUDIO CANAL+ (Fr) 2000 dir.
Philippe Faucon
Nini, S. *Ils disent que je suis une beurette*

Sammy Going South
BL (GB) 1963
dir. Alexander Mackendrick
US title: Boy Ten Feet Tall, A
Canaway, W. H.

Samson and Delilah
COMWORLD (US) 1984 dir. Lee Philips
TV(US)
Linklater, E. *Husband of Delilah*

San Antone
REP (US) 1952 dir. Joe Kane
Carroll, C. *Golden Herd*

Sanctuary
FOX (US) 1960 dir. Tony Richardson
Faulkner, W.

Sanctuary
CBS TV (US) 2001 dir. Katt Shea
TV(US)
Roberts, N.

Sanctuary of Fear
M. ARCH (US) 1979
dir. John Llewellyn Moxey
TV(US)
Chesterton, G. K. *Father Brown,
Detective*

Sanders of the River
UA (GB) 1935 dir. Zoltan Korda
US title: Bosambo
Wallace, E.

Sand Pebbles, The
FOX (US) 1966 dir. Robert Wise
McKenna, R.

Sands of the Kalahari
PAR (GB) 1965 dir. Cy Endfield
Mulvihill, W.

Sands of Time, The
WAR TV (US) 1992 dir. Gary Nelson
TV(US)
Sheldon, S.

Sandy Bottom Orchestra, The
SHOWTIME (US) 2000 dir. Bradley
Wigor
TV(US)
Keillor, G. and Nilsson, J. L.

San Francisco Story, The
WAR (US) 1952 dir. Robert Parrish
Summers, R. A. *Vigilante*

Sangaree
PAR (US) 1953 dir. Edward Ludwig
Slaughter, F. G.

Santa and Pete
POLSON (US) 1999 dir. Duwayne Dunham
TV(US)
Moore, C. and Johnson, P.

Santa Fe
COL (US) 1951 dir. Irving Pichel
Marshall, J. L.

Sara
FARABI CINEMA (Iran) 1994 dir. Dariush Mehrjui
Ibsen, H. *Doll's House, A*
P

Saraband for Dead Lovers
EL (GB) 1949 dir. Basil Dearden
Simpson, H.

Saracen Blade, The
COL (US) 1954 dir. William Castle
Yerby, F.

Sarafina!
HOLLYWOOD (SA/US) 1992 dir. Darrell Roodt
Ngema, M.
P

Sarah and Son
PAR (US) 1930 dir. Dorothy Arzner
Shea, T.

Sarah, Plain and Tall
SELF (US) 1991 dir. Glenn Jordan
TV(US)
MacLachlan, P.

Saratoga Trunk
WAR (US) 1945 dir. Sam Wood
Ferber, E.

Satan Bug, The
UA (US) 1965 dir. John Sturges
Stuart, I.

Satan Met a Lady
WAR (US) 1936 dir. William Dieterle
Hammett, D. *Maltese Falcon, The*

Saturday Island
RKO (GB) 1951 dir. Stuart Heisler
US title: Island of Desire
Brooke, H.

Saturday Night and Sunday Morning
BL (GB) 1960 dir. Karel Reisz
Sillitoe, A.

Saturday's Children
WAR (US) 1940 dir. Vincent Sherman
Anderson, M.
P

Saturday's Hero
COL (US) 1950 dir. David Miller
GB title: Idols in the Dust
Lampell, M. *Hero, The*

Saturnin
JUPITER (Czech) 1994 dir. Jiri Vercak
Jirotka, Z.

Sauve-Moi
STUDIO CANAL+ (Fr) 2000 dir. Christian Vincent
Montserrat, R. and Montserrat, R. *Ne crie pas*

Savage, The
PAR (US) 1952 dir. George Marshall
Foreman, L. L. *Don Desperado*

Savage Innocents, The
RANK (Fr/It/GB) 1960 dir. Nicholas Ray
Ruesch, H. *Top of the World*

Savage Messiah
MGM-EMI (GB) 1972 dir. Ken Russell
Ede, H. S.

Savage Nights
STUDIO CANAL+ (Fr/It) 1992 dir.
Cyril Collard
Collard, C. *Nuits Fauves, Les*

Savages
SPEL-GOLD (US) 1974 dir. Lee Katzin
TV(US)
White, R. *Death Watch*

Savage Sam
DISNEY (US) 1963 dir. Norman Tokar
Gipson, F. B.

Savage Wilderness
COL. (US) 1956 dir. Anthony Mann
GB title: The Last Frontier
Emery, R. *Gilded Rooster, The*

Saved by the Light
FOUR POINT (US) 1995 dir. Lewis
Teague
TV(US)
Brinkley, D. and Perry, P.

Saving Grace
EMBASSY (US) 1986
dir. Robert M. Young
Gittelson, C.

Saxon Charm, The
UI (US) 1948 dir. Claude Binyon
Wakeman, F.

Sayonara
WAR (US) 1957 dir. Joshua Logan
Michener, J. A.

Scam
VIACOM (US) 1993 dir. John Flynn
TV(US)
Smith, C. *Ladystinger*

Scandalous John
DISNEY (US) 1971 dir. Robert Butler
Gardner, R. M.

Scandal Sheet
COL (US) 1952 dir. Phil Karlson
GB title: Dark Page, The
Fuller, S.

Scapegoat, The
MGM (GB) 1959 dir. Robert Hamer
Du Maurier, D.

Scaramouche
MGM (US) 1952 dir. George Sidney
Sabatini, R.

Scarecrow
OASIS (NZ) 1981 dir. Sam Pillsbury
Morrieson, R. H.

Scarface
UA (US) 1932 dir. Howard Hawks
Traili, A.

Scarlet and the Black, The
ITC (It/US) 1983 dir. Jerry London
TVSe(It/US)
Gallagher, J. P. *Scarlet Pimpernel of the Vatican, The*

Scarlet and the Black, The
BBC (GB) 1993 dir. Ben Bolt
TVSe(GB)
Stendahl, M. H. B. *Rouge et le Noir, Le*

Scarlet Dawn
WAR (US) 1932 dir. William Dieterle
McCall, M. *Revolt*

Scarlet Letter, The
MAJ (US) 1934 dir. Robert G. Rignola
PBS (US) 1979 dir. Rick Hauser
TVSe(US)
CINERGI (US) 1995 dir. Roland Joffe
Hawthorne, N.

Scarlet Pimpernel, The
UA (GB) 1934 dir. Harold Young
LF (US/GB) 1982
dir. Clive Donner
TVSe(GB/US)
BBC/A&E (GB) 1999 dir. Patrick Lau
TVSe(GB)

Orczy, Baroness E.

Scarlet Street
UN (US) 1945 dir. Fritz Lang
de la Fouchardière, G. *Chienne, La*
P

Scarlett
RHI (US) 1994 dir. John Erman
TVSe(US)

Ripley, A.

Scattergood Baines
RKO (US) 1941 dir. Christy Cabanne
Kelland, C. B.

Scent of a Woman
UN (US) 1992 dir. Martin Brest
Arpino, G. *Buio e il Miele, Il*

Schindler's List
UN (US) 1993 dir. Steven Spielberg
Keneally, T. *Schindler's Ark*

School for Scoundrels
WAR (GB) 1960 dir. Robert Namer
Potter, S. *Gamesmanship, Oneupmanship, Lifemanship*

School of Flesh, The
ORSANS (Fr) 1998 dir. Benoit Jacquot
Michima, Y. *Nikutai no Gakko*

Scold's Bridle, The
BBC (GB) 1998 dir. David Thacker
TV(GB)

Walters, M.

Scoop
BBC (GB) 1972 dir. Roger Murray-Leach
TVSe(GB)
LWT (GB) 1987 dir. Gavin Millar
TV(GB)

Waugh, E.

Scorn
KINETIC (Can) 2000 dir. Sturla Gunnarsson
TV(Can)

Hobbs Birnie, L. *Such a Good Boy*

Scorpio Letters, The
MGM (US) 1967 dir. Richard Thorpe

Canning, V.

Scotch on the Rocks
BBC (GB) 1973 dir. Bob Hird
TVSe(GB)

Hurd, D. and Osmond, A.

Scotland Yard
FOX (US) 1941 dir. Norman Foster

Clift, D.
P

Scream and Scream Again
AIP (GB) 1969 dir. Gordon Hessler

Saxon, P. *Disorientated Man, The*

Screaming Mimi
COL (US) 1958 dir. Gerd Oswald

Brown, F.

Screaming Woman, The
UN TV (US) 1972 dir. Jack Smight
TV(US)

Bradbury, R.

Scrooge
PAR (GB) 1935 dir. Henry Edwards
REN (GB) 1951
dir. Brian Desmond Hurst
FOX (GB) 1970 dir. Ronald Neame
M

Dickens, C. *Christmas Carol, A*

Scrooged
PAR (US) 1988 dir. Richard Donner
Dickens, C. *Christmas Carol, A*

Scruples
WAR (US) 1980 dir. Alan J. Levi
TVSe(US)
Krantz, J.

Scudda Hoo! Scudda Hay!
FOX (US) 1948 dir. F. Hugh Herbert
GB title: Summer Lightning
Chamberlain, G. A.

Scuola, La
CECCHI (It) 1995 dir. Daniele Luchetti
Starnone, D.

Sea Chase, The
WAR (US) 1955 dir. John Farrow
Geer, A.

Seagull, The
WAR (GB) 1969 dir. Sidney Lumet
Chekhov, A.
P

Seagulls over Sorrento
MGM (GB) 1954 dir. John Boulting,
Roy Boulting
US title: Crest of the Wave
Hastings, H.
P

Sea Hawk, The
WAR (US) 1940 dir. Michael Curtiz
Sabatini, R.

Sealed Verdict
PAR (US) 1948 dir. Lewis Allen
Shapiro, L.

Seal Morning
ITV (GB) 1986 dir. Jim Goddard
TV(GB)
Farre, R.

Seance on a Wet Afternoon
RANK (GB) 1964 dir. Bryan Forbes
McShane, M.

Sea of Grass, The
MGM (US) 1947 dir. Elia Kazan
Richter, C.

Search and Destroy
OCTOBER (US) 1995 dir. David Salle
Korder, H.
P

Searchers, The
WAR (US) 1956 dir. John Ford
LeMay, A.

Search for Bridey Murphy, The
PAR (US) 1956 dir. Noel Langley
Bernstein, M.

Search for Beauty
PAR (US) 1934 dir. Erle C. Kenton
Gray, S. E. and Milton, P. R.
P

Searching for Bobby Fischer
MIRAGE (US) 1993 dir. Steven Zaillian
Waitzkin, F.

Searching Wind, The
PAR (US) 1946 dir. William Dieterle
Hellman, L. F.
P

Sea Shall Not Have Them, The
EROS (GB) 1954 dir. Lewis Gilbert
Harris, J.

Season for Miracles, A
HALLMARK (US) 1999 dir. Michael
Pressman
TV(US)
Pappano, M.

Season in Purgatory, A
D. BROWN (US) 1996 dir. David
Greene
TVSe(US)
Dunne, D.

Seasons of Love
SULLIVAN ENT (US) 1999 dir. Daniel
Petrie
TVSe(US)
Dell. G. *Earth Abideth, The*

Sea-Wife
FOX (GB) 1957 dir. Bob McNaught
Scott, J. M. *Sea Wyf and Biscuit*

Sea Wolf, The
FOX (US) 1930 dir. Alfred Santell
WAR (US) 1941 dir. Michael Curtiz
PRIMEDIA (US) 1993 dir. Michael
Anderson
TV(US)
CONCORDE (US) 1997 dir. Gary T.
McDonald
London, J.

Sea Wolves, The
RANK (GB/US/Switz) 1980
dir. Andrew McLaglen
Leasor, J. *Boarding Party*

Sebastian
NORDISK (Nor/Swe) 1996 dir. Svend
Wam
Knutsen, P. *Svart Cayal*

Second Best
REGENCY (GB/US) 1994 dir. Chris
Menges
Cook, D.

Second Jungle Book, The— Mowgli and Baloo
TRISTAR (US) 1997 dir. Duncan
McLachlan
Ch
Kipling, R. *Jungle Book, The*

Second Mrs. Tanqueray, The
VANDYKE (GB) 1952 dir. Dallas Bower
Pinero, Sir A. W.
P

Seconds
PAR (US) 1966 dir. John Frankenheimer
Ely, D.

Second Serve
LORIMAR (US) 1986 dir. Anthony Page
TV(US)
Richards, R. and Ames, J. *Renee
Richards Story, The: The Second Serve*

Second Sight: A Love Story
TTC (US) 1984 dir. John Korty
TV(US)
Hocken, S. *Emma and I*

Second Time Around, The
FOX (US) 1961 dir. Vincent Sherman
Roberts, R. E. *Star in the West*

Secret Adversary, The
LWT (GB) 1986 dir. Tony Wharmby
TV(GB)
Christie, A.

Secret Affair, A
ADELSON (US) 1999 dir. Bobby Roth
TV(US)
Bradford, B. T.

Secret Agent
GAU BR (GB) 1936 dir. Alfred
Hitchcock
Maugham, W. S. *Ashenden*

Secret Agent, The
BBC (GB) 1992 dir. David Drury
TVSe(GB)
FOX (US) 1996 dir. Christopher
Hampton
Conrad, J.

Secret Beyond the Door, The
UI (US) 1948 dir. Fritz Lang
King, R.

Secret Bride, The
WAR (US) 1935 dir. William Dieterle
GB title: Concealment
Ide, L. *Concealment*
P

Secret Cutting
USA NETWORKS (US) 2000 dir. Norma
Bailey
TV(US)
Levenkron, S. *Luckiest Girl in the World,
The*

Secret Diary of Adrian Mole, Aged 13¾, The
THAMES (GB) 1985 dir. Peter Sasdy
TVSe(GB)
Townsend, S.

Secret Garden, The
MGM (US) 1949 dir. Fred M. Wilcox
Ch
BBC (GB) 1975 dir. Katrina Murray
TVSe(GB)
ROSEMONT (US) 1987 dir. Alan Grint
Ch, TV(US)
WAR (US/GB) 1993 dir. Agnieszka
Holland
Burnett, F. H.

Secret Life of Algernon, The
MARANO (Can/GB) 1997 dir. Charles
Jarrot
Greenan, R. H. *Secret Life of Algernon
Pendleton, The*

Secret Life of John Chapman, The
JOZAK (US) 1976 dir. David Lowell
Rich
TV(US)
Coleman, J. R. *Blue Collar Journal*

Secret Life of Walter Mitty, The
RKO (US) 1947 dir. Norman Z. Macleod
Thurber, J.

Secret of Giving
JAFFE/BRAUNSTEIN (US) 1999 dir.
Sam Pillsbury
TV(US)
Curtis, J. *Christmas in Calico*

Secret of N.I.M.H., The
MGM/UA (US) 1982 dir. Don Bluth
A, Ch
O'Brien, R. C. *Mrs Frisby and the Rats of
N.I.M.H.*

Secret of Roah Inish, The
JONES (US) 1994 dir. John Sayles
Fry, R. K. *Secret of Ron Mor Skerry, The*

Secret of Santa Vittoria, The
UA (US) 1969 dir. Stanley Kramer
Crichton, R.

Secret of Stamboul, The
GENERAL (GB) 1936 dir. Andrew
Marton
Wheatley, D. *Eunuch of Stamboul, The*

Secret of St. Ives, The
COL (US) 1949 dir. Phil Rosen
Stevenson, R. L. *St. Ives*

Secret Path, The
GREENWALD (US) 1999 dir. Bruce
Pittman
TV(US)
Evans, R. M. *Childhood's Thief*

Secret Places
RANK (GB) 1983 dir. Zelda Barron
Elliott, J.

Secret Rapture, The
BRIT SCREEN (GB) 1993 dir. Howard Davies
Hare, D.
P

Secrets
NBC (US) 1992 dir. Peter H. Hunt
TV(US)
Steel, D.

Secrets
RHI (US) 1995 dir. Jud Taylor
TV(US)
Esstman, B. *Other Anna, The*

Secret Servant, The
BBC (GB) 1985 dir. Alastair Reid
TVSe(GB)
Lyall, G.

Secret Ways, The
RANK (US) 1961 dir. Phil Karlson
MacLean, A. *Last Frontier*

Secret Weapons
ITC (US) 1985 dir. Don Taylor
TV(US)
Lewis, D. *Sexpionage: The Exploitation of Sex by Soviet Intelligence*

Secret World of Polly Flint
CENTRAL (GB) 1987 dir. David Cobham
Ch, TVSe(GB)
Cresswell, H.

Seduced by Evil
WIL COURT (US) 1994 dir. Tony Wharmby
TV(US)
Wolcott, J.A. *Brujo*

Seduction in Travis County, A
NEW WORLD (US) 1991 dir. George Kaczender
TV(US)
Meins, J. *Murder in Little Rock*

Seduction of Miss Leona, The
SCHERICK (US) 1980 dir. Joseph Hardy
TV(US)
Gundy, E. *Bliss*

Seed
UN (US) 1931 dir. John Stahl
Norris, C. G.

See Here, Private Hargrove
MGM (US) 1944 dir. Wesley Ruggles
Hargrove, M.

See How They Fall
FRANCE 3 (Fr) 1994 dir. Jacques Audiard
White, T. *Triangle*

See How They Run
BL (GB) 1955 dir. Leslie Arliss
CHANNEL 4 (GB) 1984 dir. Les Chatfield, Ray Cooney
TV(GB)
King, P.
P

See How They Run
UN TV (US) 1964 dir. David Lowell Rich
TV(US)
Blankfort, M. *Widow Makers, The*

See Jane Run
HEARST (US) 1995 dir. John Patterson
TV(US)
Fielding, J.

Seekers, The
UN TV (US) 1979 dir. Sidney Hayers
TVSe(US)
Jakes, J.

Seizure: The Story of Kathy Morris
JOZAK (US) 1980 dir. Gerald Isenberg
TV(US)
Mee, Jr., C. L. *Seizure*

Self-Made Hero, A
LUMIERE (Fr) 1996 dir. Jacques
Audiard
Deniau, J.-F.

Selling Hitler
BBC (GB) 1991 dir. Alastair Reid
TVSe(GB)
Harris, R.

Selma, Lord, Selma
DISNEY (US) 1999 dir. Charles Burnett
TV(US)
Webb, S., West, R. and Sikora, F.

Semi-Tough
UA (US) 1977 dir. Michael Ritchie
Jenkins, D.

Send Me No Flowers
UN (US) 1964 dir. Norman Jewison
Barrasch, N. and Moore, C.
P

Sensation
BIP (GB) 1936
dir. Brian Desmond Hurst
Dean, B. and Munro, G. *Murder Gang*
P

Sense and Sensibility
BBC (GB) 1971 dir. David Giles
TVSe(GB)
BBC (GB) 1981 dir. Rodney Bennett
TVSe(GB)
COL (GB/US) 1995 dir. Ang Lee
Austen, J.

Sense of Guilt, A
BBC (GB) 1990 dir. Bruce MacDonald
TVSe(GB)
Newman, A.

Sensitive, Passionate Man, A
FAC-NEW (US) 1977 dir. John Newland
TV(US)
Mahoney, B.

Sentimental Destinies
STUDIO CANAL+ (Fr) 2000 dir. Olivier
Assayas
Chardonne, J.

Sentimental Education
BBC (GB) 1970 dir. David Maloney
TVSe(GB)
Flaubert, G.

Sentinel, The
UN (US) 1977 dir. Michael Winner
Konvitz, J.

Senyora, La
ICA (Sp) 1987 dir. Jordi Cadenar
Mus, A.

Separate Peace, A
PAR (US) 1972 dir. Larry Peerce
Knowles, J.

Separate Tables
UA (US) 1958 dir. Delbert Mann
Rattigan, T.
P

Separation, La
STUDIO CANAL+ (Fr) 1994 dir.
Christian Vincent
Franck, D.

September
HALLMARK/BSKYB (UK/Ger) 1996
dir. Colin Bucksey
TV(UK/Ger)
Pilcher, R.

Sequoia
MGM (US) 1935 dir. Chester Lyons
Hoyt, V. J. *Malibu, A Nature Story*

Serenade
WAR (US) 1956 dir. Anthony Mann
Cain, J. M.

Sergeant, The
WAR (US) 1968 dir. John Flynn
Murphy, D.

Serial
PAR (US) 1980 dir. Bill Persky
McFadden, C.

Serie Noire
GAU (Fr) 1979 dir. Alain Corneau
Thompson, J. *One Hell of a Woman*

Serious Charge
EROS (GB) 1959 dir. Terence Young
King, P.
P

Serpent, The
LA BOETIE (Fr/It/Ger) 1974
dir. Henri Verneuil
Nord, P.

Serpent Son, The
BBC (GB) 1979 dir. Bill Hays
TVSe(GB)
Aeschylus *Oresteia Trilogy, The*

Serpico
PAR (US) 1973 dir. Sidney Lumet
Maas, P.

Servant, The
WAR (GB) 1963 dir. Joseph Losey
Maugham, R.

Servant's Entrance
FOX (US) 1934 dir. Frank Lloyd
Boo, S.

Servants of Twilight, The
TRIMARK (US) 1991 dir. Jeffrey Obrow
TV(US)
Koontz, D. *Twilight*

Service of all the Dead
CENTRAL (GB) 1989
dir. Edward Bennett
TV(GB)
Dexter, C.

Settlement, The
CINETEL (US) 1999 dir. Mark Steilen
Toffler, L. *Death Benefits*
P

Set Up, The
MGM/SHOWTIME (US) 1995 dir.
Strathford Hamilton
TV(US)
Chase, J. H. *My Laugh Comes Last*

Seven Alone
HEMDALE (US) 1974 dir. Earl Bellamy
Morrow, H. *On to Oregon*

Seven Brides for Seven Brothers
MGM (US) 1954 dir. Stanley Donen
M
Benet, S. V. *Sobbin' Women, The*

Seven Cities of Gold
FOX (US) 1955 dir. Robert D. Webb
Ziegler, I. G. *Nine Days of Father Serra*

Seven Days in May
PAR (US) 1964 dir. John Frankenheimer
Knebel, F. and Bailey, II, C. W.

Seven Days' Leave
PAR (US) 1930 dir. Richard Wallace
GB title: Medals
Barrie, Sir J. M. *Old Lady Shows Her Medals, The*
P

Seven Faces of Dr. Lao, The
MGM (US) 1964 dir. George Pal

Finney, C. G.

Seven in Darkness
PAR TV (US) 1969 dir. Michael Caffey
TV(US)

Bishop, L. *Against Heaven's Hand*

Seven Keys to Baldpate
RKO (US) 1930 dir. Reginald Parker
RKO (US) 1935 dir. William Hamilton
RKO (US) 1947 dir. Lew Landers

Biggers, E. D.

Seven Minutes, The
FOX (US) 1971 dir. Russ Meyer

Wallace, I.

Seven Percent Solution, The
UN (US) 1976 dir. Herbert Ross

Meyer, N.

Seven Sinners
GAU (GB) 1937 dir. Albert de Courville
US title: Doomed Cargo

Ridley, A. and Merivale, B. *Wrecker,
The*
P

Seventeen
PAR (US) 1940 dir. Louis King

Tarkington, B.

1776
COL (US) 1972 dir. Peter Hunt
M

Stone, P.
P

Seventh Avenue
UN TV (US) 1977 dir. Richard Irving,
Russ Mayberry
TVSe(US)

Bogner, N.

Seventh Cross, The
MGM (US) 1944 dir. Fred Zinnemann

Seghers, A.

7th Dawn, The
UA (GB) 1964 dir. Lewis Gilbert

Keon, M. *Durian Tree, The*

Seventh Heaven
FOX (US) 1937 dir. Henry King

Strong, A.
P

Seven Thieves
FOX (US) 1960 dir. Henry Hathaway

Catto, M. *Lions at the Kill*

Seventh Sin, The
MGM (US) 1957 dir. Ronald Neame

Maugham, W. S. *Painted Veil, The*

Seven Thunders
RANK (GB) 1957 dir. Hugo Fregonese
US title: Beasts of Marseilles, The

Croft-Cooke, R.

Seven Years in Tibet
TRISTAR (US/Arg) 1997 dir. Jean-
Jacques Annaud

Harrer, H.

79 Park Avenue
UN (US) 1977 dir. Paul Wendkos
TVSe(US)

Robbins, H.

Seven Ways from Sundown
UI (US) 1960 dir. Harry Keller

Huffaker, C.

Seven Year Itch, The
FOX (US) 1955 dir. Billy Wilder

Axelrod, G.
P

Severed Head, A
COL (GB) 1970 dir. Dick Clement

Murdoch, I.

Sex and the Other Man
RIVER ONE (US) 1995 dir. Karl Slovin

Weitz, P. *Captive*
P

Sex and the Single Girl
WAR (US) 1964 dir. Richard Quine

Brown, H. G.

Sex and the Single Parent
TIME-LIFE (US) 1979
dir. Jackie Cooper
TV(US)

Adams, J.

Sex Symbol, The
COL (US) 1974 dir. David Lowell Rich
TV(US)

Bessie, A. *Symbol, The*

S.F.W.
POLYGRAM (US) 1994 dir. Jefery Levy

Wellman, A.

Shabby Tiger
GRANADA TV (GB) 1977 dir. Baz
Taylor
TVSe(GB)

Spring, H.

Shadow Box, The
SHADOW BOX (US) 1980
dir. Paul Newman
TV(US)

Cristofer, M.
P

Shadowhunter
REP (US) 1993 dir. J. S. Cardone
TV(US)

Winski, N.

Shadowlands
BBC (Neth/GB) 1985
dir. Norman Stone
TV(GB)

Straub, P.

Shadowlands
PRICE ENT (GB) 1993 dir. Richard
Attenborough

Nicholson, W.
P

Shadow of a Doubt
SCRIPPS HOWARD (US) 1995 dir.
Brian Dennehy
TV(US)

Coughlin, W. J.

Shadow of Angels
ALB/ARTCO (Ger) 1983
dir. Daniel Schmid

Fassbinder, R. W.
P

Shadow of China
NEW LINE (US/Jap) 1991
dir. Mitsuo Yanagimachi

Nishiki, M. *Snake Head*

Shadow of Obsession
SABAN ENT (US) 1994 dir. Kevin
Connor
TV(US)

Beck, K. K. *Unwanted Attentions*

Shadow of the Wolf
STUDIO CANAL+ (Fr/Can) 1992 dir.
Jacques Dorfmann, Pierre Magny

Theriault, Y. *Agaguk*

Shadow Over Elveron
UN TV (US) 1968 dir. James Goldstone
TV(US)

Kingsley, M.

Shadow Riders, The
COL TV (US) 1982
dir. Andrew V. McLaglen
TV(US)

L'Amour, L.

Shadow Zone: The Undead Express
SHOWTIME (US) 1996 dir. Stephen
Williams
TV(US)

Black, J. R.

Shaft
MGM (US) 1971 dir. Gordon Parks
PAR (US/Ger) 2000 dir. John Singleton

Tidyman, E.

Shaggy Dog, The
DISNEY (US) 1959 dir. Charles Barton
Ch

Salten, F. *Hound of Florence, The*

Shake Hands with the Devil
UA (Ire) 1959 dir. Michael Anderson

Conner, R.

Shalako
WAR (GB) 1968 dir. Edward Dmytryk

L'Amour, L.

Shane
PAR (US) 1953 dir. George Stevens

Schaefer, J.

Shanghai Gesture, The
IN (US) 1941 dir. Josef von Sternberg

Colton, J.
P

Shanghai Surprise
MGM (US) 1986 dir. Jim Goddard

Kenrick, T. *Faraday's Flowers*

Shanghai Triad
SHANGHAI (China) 1995 dir. Yimou
Zhang

Ziao, L.

Shangri-La
COMPASS (US) 1960
dir. George Schaefer
TV(US)

Hilton, J. *Lost Horizon*

Shape of Things to Come, The
BARBER DANN (Can) 1979
dir. George McGowan

Wells, H. G.

Share Out, The
AA (GB) 1962 dir. Gerald Glaister

Wallace, E. *Jack O'Judgement*

Sharky's Machine
WAR (US) 1981 dir. Burt Reynolds

Diehl, W.

Sharpe's Battle
PICTURE PALACE (GB) 1995 dir. Tom
Clegg
TV(GB)

Cornwell, B.

Sharpe's Company
PICTURE PALACE (GB) 1994 dir. Tom
Clegg
TV(GB)

Cornwell, B.

Sharpe's Eagle
PICTURE PALACE (GB) 1993 dir. Tom
Clegg
TV(GB)

Cornwell, B.

Sharpe's Enemy
PICTURE PALACE (GB) 1994 dir. Tom
Clegg
TV(GB)

Cornwell, B.

Sharpe's Gold
PICTURE PALACE (GB) 1995 dir. Tom Clegg
TV(GB)

Cornwell, B.

Sharpe's Honour
PICTURE PALACE (GB) 1994 dir. Tom Clegg
TV(GB)

Cornwell, B.

Sharpe's Regiment
CELTIC/PICTURE PALACE (GB) 1996 dir. Tom Clegg
TV(GB)

Cornwell, B.

Sharpe's Revenge
PICTURE PALACE (GB) 1997 dir. Tom Clegg
TV(GB)

Cornwell, B.

Sharpe's Rifles
PICTURE PALACE (GB) 1993 dir. Tom Clegg
TV(GB)

Cornwell, B.

Sharpe's Siege
CELTIC/PICTURE PALACE (GB) 1996 dir. Tom Clegg
TV(GB)

Cornwell, B.

Sharpe's Sword
PICTURE PALACE (GB) 1995 dir. Tom Clegg
TV(GB)

Cornwell, B.

Sharpe's Waterloo
PICTURE PALACE (GB) 1997 dir. Tom Clegg
TV(GB)

Cornwell, B.

Shattered
MGM-PATHE (US) 1991 dir. Wolfgang Petersen

Neely, R.

Shattered Dreams
CAROLCO (US) 1990 dir. Robert Iscove
TV(US)

Fedders, C. and Elliot, L.

Shattered Vows
RIVER CITY (US) 1984 dir. Jack Bender
TV(US)

Wong, Dr. M. G. *Nun: A Memoir*

Shawshank Redemption, The
COL (US) 1994 dir. Frank Darabont

King, S. *Rita Hayworth and the Shawshank Redemption*

She
RKO (US) 1935 dir. Irving Pichel
WAR (GB) 1965 dir. Robert Day
CONT (It) 1985 dir. Avi Nesher

Haggard, Sir H. R.

She-Devil
ORION (US) 1989 dir. Susan Seidelman

Weldon, F. *Life and Loves of a She-Devil, The*

She Didn't Say No!
ABP (GB) 1958 dir. Cyril Frankel

Troy, U. *We Are Seven*

She Done Him Wrong
PAR (US) 1933 dir. Lowell Sherman

West, M. *Diamond Lil*
P

She Fell Among Thieves
BBC (GB) 1979 dir. Clive Donner
TV(GB)

Yates, D.

She Lives
ABC (US) 1973 dir. Stuart Hagmann
TV(US)
Neimark, P.

Shell Seekers, The
M. REES (US) 1989 dir. Waris Hussein
TV(US)
Pilcher, R.

She Loves Me Not
PAR (US) 1934 dir. Elliott Nugent
Lindsay, H.
P

Sheltering Sky, The
WAR (US) 1990
dir. Bernardo Bertolucci
Bowles, P.

Shepherd of the Hills, The
PAR (US) 1941 dir. Henry Hathaway
Wright, H. B.

Sherlock Holmes and the Voice of Terror
UN (US) 1942 dir. John Rawlins
Doyle, Sir A. C. *His Last Bow*

She Shall Have Murder
BL (GB) 1950 dir. Daniel Birt
Ames, D.

She's Working Her Way Through College
WAR (US) 1952
dir. Bruce Humberstone
Thurber, J. and Nugent, E. *Male Animal, The*
P

Shiki-Jitsu
STUDIO KAJINO (Jap) 2000 dir. Hideaki Anno
Fujitani, A. *Touhimu*

Shiloh
UTOPIA (US) 1996 dir. Dale Rosenbloom
Reynolds Naylor, P.

Shiloh 2: Shiloh Season
WAR (US/GB) 1999 dir. Sandy Tung
Reynolds Naylor, P.

Shimmer
AM PLAY (US) 1995 dir. John Hanson
TV(US)
O'Keefe, J.
P

Shining, The
WAR (GB) 1980 dir. Stanley Kubrick
WAR (US) 1997 dir. Mick Garris
TVSe(US)
King, S.

Shining Hour, The
MGM (US) 1938 dir. Frank Borzage
Winter, K.
P

Shining Season, A
COL TV (US) 1979 dir. Stuart Margolin
TV(US)
Buchanan, W.

Shining Through
FOX (US) 1992 dir. David Selzer
Isaacs, S.

Shining Victory
WAR (US) 1941 dir. Irving Rapper
Cronin, A. J. *Jupiter Laughs*
P

Shi No Toge
SHOCHIKU (Jap) 1990 dir. Kohei Oguri
Shimao, T.

Shipbuilders, The
BN (GB) 1944 dir. John Baxter
Blake, G.

Ship of Fools
COL (US) 1965 dir. Stanley Kramer
Porter, K. A.

Shipping News, The
COL (US) 2001 dir. Lasse Hallstrom
Proulx, E. A.

Ship That Died of Shame, The
RANK (GB) 1955 dir. Basil Dearden
Monsarrat, N.

Shiralee, The
MGM (GB) 1957 dir. Leslie Norman
AUS (Aust) 1987 dir. Greg Ogilvie
TV(Aust)
Niland, D'A.

Shirley Valentine
PAR (GB) 1989 dir. Lewis Gilbert
Russell, W.
P

Shock to the System, A
MEDUSA (US) 1990 dir. Jan Egleson
Brett, S.

Shock Trauma
TELECOM (Can) 1982 dir. Eric Till
TV(Can)
Franklin, J. and Doelp, A.

Shock Treatment
WAR (US) 1964 dir. Denis Sanders
Van Atta, W.

Shoes of the Fisherman, The
MGM (US) 1968 dir. Michael Anderson
West, M. L.

Shogun
PAR (Jap/US) 1981 dir. Jerry London
TVSe(Jap/US)
Clavell, J.

Shootdown
L. HILL (US) 1988
dir. Michael Pressman
TV(US)
Johnson, R. W.

Shooter
PAR TV (US) 1988 dir. Gary Nelson
TV(US)
Kennerly, D. H.

Shooting Party, The
MOSFILM (USSR) 1981
dir. Emil Loteanu
Chekhov, A.

Shooting Party, The
REEVE (GB) 1984 dir. Alan Bridges
Colegate, I.

Shootist, The
PAR (US) 1976 dir. Don Siegel
Swarthout, G.

Shootout
UN (US) 1971 dir. Henry Hathaway
James, W. *Lone Cowboy: My Life Story*

Shoot the Piano Player
PLEIADE (Fr) 1960
dir. François Truffaut
Goodis, D. *Down There*

Shop Around the Corner, The
MGM (US) 1940 dir. Ernst Lubitsch
Laszlo, N. *Parfumerie*
P

Shop at Sly Corner, The
BL (GB) 1946 dir. George King
US title: Code of Scotland Yard
Percy, E.
P

Shopworn Angel
MGM (US) 1938 dir. H. C. Potter

Burnet, D. *Private Pettigrew's Girl*
P

Short Cut to Hell
PAR (US) 1957 dir. James Cagney

Greene, G. *Gun For Sale, A*

Shot, The
B&W (US) 1994 dir. Dan Bell

Bell, D.
P

Shot in the Heart
HBO (US) 2001 dir. Agnieszka Holland
TV(US)

Gilmore, M.

Shout at the Devil
HEMDALE (GB) 1976 dir. Peter Hunt

Smith, W.

Show Boat
UN (US) 1936 dir. James Whale
MGM (US) 1951 dir. George Sidney
M

Ferber, E.

Kern, J. and Hammerstein II, O.
P

Showdown at Abilene
UN (US) 1956 dir. Charles Haas

Young, C. U. *Gun Shy*

Show-Off, The
MGM (US) 1934 dir. Charles Riesner

Kelly, G.
P

Show of Force, A
PAR (US) 1990 dir. Bruno Barreto

Nelson, A. *Murder Under Two Flags*

Shrike, The
UI (US) 1955 dir. José Ferrer

Kramm, J.
P

Shroud for a Nightingale
YTV (GB) 1984 dir. John Gorrie
TVSe(GB)

James, P. D.

Shuttered Room, The
WAR (GB) 1967 dir. David Greene

Lovecraft, H. P.

Shuttlecock
KM (Fr/GB) 1992 dir. Andrew Piddington

Swift, G.

Siao Yu
CENTRAL MOTION (Tai) 1995 dir. Sylvia Chang

Yan, G.

Sicilia!
ALIA (It/Fr) 1999 dir. Daniele Huillet, Jean-Marie Straub

Vittorini, E. *Conversation in Sicily*

Sicilian, The
FOX (It/US) 1987 dir. Michael Cimino

Puzo, M.

Siddhartha
LOTUS (US) 1972 dir. Conrad Rooks

Hesse, H.

Sidelong Glances of a Pigeon Kicker, The
MGM (US) 1970 dir. John Dexter

Boyer, D.

Siesta
LORIMAR (US) 1987 dir. Mary Lambert

Chaplin, P.

Sign of Four, The
WW (GB) 1932 dir. Rowland V. Lee
EMBASSY (GB) 1983
dir. Desmond Davis
GRANADA (GB) 1988 dir. Michael Cox
TV(GB)
MUSE ENT (US) 2001 dir. Rodney
Gibbons
TV(US)

Doyle, Sir A. C.

Sign of the Cross, The
PAR (US) 1932 dir. Cecil B. De Mille

Barrett, W.
P

Sign of the Ram, The
COL (US) 1948 dir. John Sturges

Ferguson, M.

Signpost to Murder
MGM (US) 1964 dir. George Englund

Doyle, M.
P

Silas Marner
BBC (GB) 1985 dir. Giles Foster
TV(GB)

Eliot, G.

Silence of Adultery, The
HEARST (US) 1995 dir. Steven H. Stern
TV(US)

Weil, B. E. and Winter, R. *Adultery, The Forgivable Sin*

Silence of the Lambs, The
ORION (US) 1991 dir. Jonathan Demme

Harris, T.

Silence of the North
UN (Can) 1981 dir. Allan Winton King

Fredrickson, O. and East, B.

Silencers, The
COL (US) 1966 dir. Phil Karlson

Hamilton, D.

Silent Cries
YTV/TRISTAR TV (GB) 1993 dir.
Anthony Page
TV(GB)

Brooks, J. Y. *Guests of the Emperor*

Silent Dust
ABP (GB) 1947 dir. Lance Comfort

Pertwee, R. and Pertwee, M. *Paragon, The*
P

Silent Enemy, The
ROMULUS (GB) 1958
dir. William Fairchild

Pugh, M. *Commander Crabb*

Silent Night, Lonely Night
UN TV (US) 1969 dir. Daniel Petrie
TV(US)

Anderson, R.
P

Silent Partner
RESCUED (Aust) 2000 dir. Alkinos
Tsilimidos

Keene, D.
P

Silent Partner, The
CAROLCO (Can) 1978 dir. Daryl Duke

Bodelsen, A. *Think of a Number*

Silent World of Nicholas Quinn
CENTRAL (GB) 1989
dir. Edward Bennett

Dexter, C.

Silk Hope
POLSON (US) 1999 dir. Kevin Dowling
TV(US)

Naumoff, L.

Silk Stockings
MGM (US) 1957
dir. Rouben Mamoulian
M

Kaufman, G. S., McGrath, L. and
Burrows, A.
P

Silver Bears
EMI (GB) 1978 dir. Ivan Passer
Erdman, P.

Silver Bullet
PAR (US) 1985 dir. Daniel Attias
King, S. *Cycle of the Werewolf*

Silver Chair, The
BBC (GB) 1990 dir. Alex Kirby
Ch, TVSe(GB)
Lewis, C. S. *Prince Caspian and The
Silver Chair*

Silver Chalice, The
WAR (US) 1954 dir. Victor Saville
Costain, T. B.

Silver Darlings, The
ALL (GB) 1947 dir. Clarence Elder,
Clifford Evans
Gunn, N. M.

**Silver Stallion King of the Wild
Brumbies, The**
FILM VICTORIA (Aust) 1993 dir. John
Tatoulis
Mitchell, E. *Silver Brumby, The*

Silver Sword, The
BBC (GB) 1971 dir. Joan Craft
TVSe(GB)
Serraillier, I.

Simon and Laura
RANK (GB) 1955 dir. Muriel Box
Melville, A.
P

Simon Birch
HOLLYWOOD (US) 1998 dir. Mark
Steven Johnson
Irving, J. *Prayer for Owen Meany, A*

Simpatico
FINE LINE (US/GB) 1999 dir. Matthew
Warchus
Shepard, S.
P

Simple Justice
NEW IMAGES (US) 1993 dir. Helaine
Head
TV(US)
Kluger, R.

Simple Plan, A
PAR (US/GB/Fr) 1998 dir. Sam Raimi
Smith, S.

Since You Went Away
UA (US) 1944 dir. John Cromwell
Wilder, M. B.

Sinful Davey
UA (GB) 1969 dir. John Huston
Haggart, D. *Life of David Haggart, The*

Sinful Life, A
NEW LINE (US) 1989
dir. William Schreiner
Graham, M. *Just Like the Pom Pom Girls*
P

Singer Not the Song, The
RANK (GB) 1960 dir. Roy Baker
Lindop, A. E.

Single White Female
COL (US) 1992 dir. Barbet Schroeder
Lutz, J. *SWF Seeks Same*

Sink the Bismarck
FOX (GB) 1960 dir. Lewis Gilbert
Forester, C. S. *Hunting the Bismarck*

Sinner's Holiday
WAR (US) 1930 dir. John G. Adolfi
Baumer, M. *Penny Arcade*
P

Sinner Take All
MGM (US) 1937 dir. Errol Taggart
Chambers, W. *Murder of a Wanton*

Sin of Madelon Claudet
MGM (US) 1931 dir. Edgar Selwyn
Knoblock, E. *Lullaby, The*
P

Sins
NEW WORLD (US) 1986
dir. Douglas Hickox
TVSe(US)
Gould, J.

Sins of Dorian Gray, The
RANKIN-BASS (US) 1983
dir. Tony Maylam
TV(US)
Wilde, O. *Picture of Dorian Gray, The*

Sins of Rachel Cade, The
WAR (US) 1960 dir. Gordon Douglas
Mercer, C. *Rachel Cade*

Sins of the Mother
CORAPEAKE (US) 1991
dir. John Patterson
TV(US)
Olsen, J. *Son*

Sirocco
COL (US) 1951 dir. Curtis Bernhardt
Kessel, J. *Coup de Grâce*

Sister Kenny
RKO (US) 1946 dir. Dudley Nichols
Kenny, E. and Ostenso, M. *And They Shall Walk*

Sister Mary Explains It All
TENNANT/STAMBLER (US) 2001 dir.
Marshall Brickman
TV(US)
Durang, C. *Sister Mary Ignatius Explains It All For You*
P

Sister My Sister
BRIT SCREEN (GB/US) 1994 dir.
Nancy Meckler
Kesselman, W. *My Sister in This House*
P

Sisters, The
WAR (US) 1938 dir. Anatole Litvak
Brinig, M.

Sisters and Other Strangers
FOX (US) 1997 dir. Roger Young
TV(US)
Parker, B. J. *Suspicion of Innocence*

Sitter, The
FNM (US) 1991 dir. Rick Berger
TV(US)
Armstrong, C. *Mischief*

Sitting Pretty
FOX (US) 1948 dir. Walter Lang
Davenport, G. *Belvedere*

Sitting Target
MGM (GB) 1972 dir. Douglas Hickox
Henderson, L.

Situation Hopeless But Not Serious
PAR (US) 1965 dir. Gottfried Reinhardt
Shaw, R. *Hiding Place, The*

Six Against the Rock
GAYLORD (US) 1987 dir. Paul Wendkos
TV(US)
Howard, C.

Six Bridges to Cross
UN (US) 1955 dir. Joseph Pevney

Dinneen, J. F. *They Stole $2.5 Million and Got Away with It*

Six Degrees of Separation
MGM (US) 1993 dir. Fred Schepisi

Guare, J.
P

633 Squadron
UA (GB) 1964 dir. Walter Grauman

Smith, F. E.

Six Million Dollar Man, The
UN TV (US) 1973 dir. Richard Irving
TV(US)

Caidin, M. *Cyborg*

Six-Pack
CHRYSALIDE (Fr) 2000 dir. Alain Berberian

Oppel, J.-H.

Sixten
SVENSK (Swe) 1994 dir. Catti Edfeldt

Stark, U.

Sixth Happiness, The
DREAMFACTORY (GB) 1997 dir. Waris Hussein

Kanga, F. *Trying to Grow*

Six Ways to Sunday
SCOUT (US) 1997 dir. Adam Bernstein

Perry, C. *Portrait of a Young Man Drowning*

Six Weeks
UN (US) 1982 dir. Tony Bill

Stewart, F. M.

Skeezer
M. ARCH (US) 1982 dir. Peter H. Hunt
TV(US)

Yates, E. *Skeezer: Dog With a Mission*

Skin Game, The
BI (GB) 1931 dir. Alfred Hitchcock

Galsworthy, J.
P

Skin of our Teeth, The
GRANADA TV (GB) 1959
TV(GB)

Wilder, T.
P

Skipped Parts
TRIMARK (US) 2001 dir. Tamra Davis

Sandlin, T.

Skyjacked
MGM (US) 1972 dir. John Guillermin

Harper, D. *Hijacked*

Skylark
PAR (US) 1941 dir. Mark Sandrich

Raphaelson, S.
P

Skyscraper Souls
MGM (US) 1932 dir. Edgar Selwyn

Baldwin, F. *Skyscraper*

Sky's on Fire, The
ALL AM TV (US) 1998 dir. Dan Lerner
TV(US)

Tobias, M. *Fatal Exposure*

Slab Boys, The
SKREBA (GB) 1997 dir. John Byrne

Byrne, J.
P

Slapstick of Another Kind
LORIMAR (US) 1984 dir. Steven Paul

Vonnegut, K. *Slapstick*

Slate, Wyn and Me
HEMDALE (Aust) 1987
dir. Don McLennan

Savage, G. *Slate Wyn and Blanche McBride*

Slattery's Hurricane
FOX (US) 1949 dir. André de Toth
Wouk, H.

Slaughterhouse Five
UN (US) 1972 dir. George Roy Hill
Vonnegut, K.

Slaughter on 10th Avenue
UI (US) 1957 dir. Arnold Laven
Keating, W. J. and Carter, R. *Man Who Rocked the Boat, The*

Slave Ship
FOX (US) 1937 dir. Tay Garnett
King, G. S.

Slaves of New York
TRISTAR (US) 1989 dir. James Ivory
Janowitz, T.

Slayground
UN/EMI (GB) 1983 dir. Terry Bedford
Stark, R.

Sleep, Baby, Sleep
CITADEL ENT (US) 1995 dir. Armand Mastroianni
TV(US)
Auerbach, J.

Sleepers
POLYGRAM (US) 1996 dir. Barry Levinson
Carcaterra, L.

Sleeping Beauty
DISNEY (US) 1959 dir. Clyde Geronomi
A, Ch
CANNON (US) 1987 dir. David Irving
Ch
Perrault, C.

Sleeping Car Murders, The
PECF (Fr) 1965 dir. Costa-Gavras
Japrisot, S.

Sleeping Tiger, The
INSIGNIA (GB) 1954 dir. Joseph Losey
Moiseiwitsch, M.

Sleeping with the Devil
NBC (US) 1997 dir. William A. Graham
TV(US)
Finstad, S.

Sleeping with the Enemy
FOX (US) 1991 dir. Joseph Ruben
Price, N.

Sleep my Love
UA (US) 1948 dir. Douglas Sirk
Rosten, L.

Sleep Room, The
CBC (Can) 1998 dir. Anne Wheeler
TV(Can)
Collins, A. *In the Sleep Room: The Story of the CIA Brainwashing Experiments in Canada*

Sleepwalker Killing
COS-MEU (US) 1997 dir. John Cosgrove
TV(US)
Callwood, J. *Sleepwalker, The*

Sleuth
FOX (GB) 1972
dir. Joseph L. Mankiewicz
Shaffer, A.
P

Slight Case of Murder, A
WAR (US) 1938 dir. Lloyd Bacon
Runyon, D. and Lindsay, H.
P

Slight Case of Murder, A
TNT (US) 1999 dir. Steven Schachter
TV(US)
Westlake, D. E. *Travesty, A*

Slightly Honourable
UA (US) 1940 dir. Tay Garnett

Presnell, F. G. *Send Another Coffin*

Slightly Scarlet
RKO (US) 1956 dir. Allan Dwan

Cain, J. A.

Slingshot, The
NORDISK (Den/Swe) 1993 dir. Ake Sandgren

Schutt, R. *Kadisbellan*

Slipping Down Life, A
DVC (US) 1999 dir. Toni Kalem

Tyler, A.

Slow Burn
UN TV (US) 1986
dir. Matthew Chapman
TV(US)

Lyons, A. *Castles Burning*

Slugs, The Movie
NEW WORLD (Sp) 1988 dir. J. P. Simon

Hutson, S.

Small Back Room, The
LF (GB) 1949 dir. Michael Powell, Emeric Pressburger
US title: Hour of Glory

Balchin, N.

Small Killing, A
MOTOWN (US) 1981
dir. Steven Hilliard Stern
TV(US)

Barth, R. *Rag Bag Clan, The*

Small Miracle, The
LAN (US) 1983 dir. Jeannot Szwarc
TV(US)

Gallico, P.

Small Sacrifices
FRIES (US) 1989 dir. David Greene
TVSe(US)

Rule, A.

Small Town Girl
MGM (US) 1936
dir. William A. Wellmen

Williams, B. A.

Small Vices
JAFFE/BRAUNSTEIN (US) 1999 dir. Robert Markowitz
TV(US)

Parker, R. B.

Small Voice, The
BL (GB) 1948 dir. Fergus McDonell
US title: Hideout

Westerby, R.

Small World
GRANADA (GB) 1988 dir. Robert Chetwyn
TVSe(GB)

Lodge, D.

Smash-up on Interstate 5
FILMWAYS (US) 1976
dir. John Llewellyn Moxey
TV(US)

Trevor, E. *Expressway*

Smell of the Night, The
SORPASSO (It) 1998 dir. Claudio Caligari

Sacchettoni, D. *Notti di Arancia Meccanica, Le*

Smiley
FOX (GB) 1955 dir. Anthony Kimmins

Raymond, M.

Smiley's People
BBC (GB) 1982 dir. Simon Langton
TVSe(GB)

Le Carré, J.

Smilin' Through
MGM (US) 1932 dir. Sidney Franklin
MGM (US) 1941 dir. Frank Borzage

Cowl, J. and Murfin, J.
P

Smilla's Sense of Snow
NORDISK (Den/Ger/Swe) 1997 dir.
Bille August

Hoeg, P. *Miss Smilla's Feeling for Snow*

Smoke
DISNEY (US) 1970
dir. Vincent McEveety

Corbin, W.

Smokescreen
BBC (GB) 1994 dir. Giancarlo Gemin
TVSe(GB)

McCutcheon, E.

Smoking/No Smoking
ARENA (Fr) 1993 dir. Alain Resnais

Ayckbourn, A. *Intimate Exchanges*
P

Smoky
FOX (US) 1946 dir. Louis King

James, W.

Smooth Talk
NEPENTHE (US) 1985
dir. Joyce Chopra

Oates, J. C. *Where are you Going, Where have you Been?*

Smugglers, The
UN TV (US) 1968 dir. Norman Lloyd
TV(US)

Hely, E.

Snafu
COL (US) 1945 dir. Jack Moss
GB title: Welcome Home

Solomon, L. and Buchman, H.
P

Snake Pit, The
FOX (US) 1948 dir. Anatole Litvak

Ward, M. J.

Snapper, The
BBC (GB) 1993 dir. Stephen Frears
TV(GB)

Doyle, R.

Snowball Express
DISNEY (US) 1972 dir. Norman Tokar

O'Rear, F. and O'Rear, J. *Château Bon Vivant*

Snowbound
RKO (GB) 1948 dir. David MacDonald

Innes, H. *Lonely Skier, The*

Snow Falling on Cedars
UN (US) 1999 dir. Scott Hicks

Guterson, D.

Snow Goose, The
UN/BBC (US/GB) 1971
dir. Patrick Garland
TV(US/GB)

Gallico, P.

Snow in August
TAURUS 7 (US/Can) 2001 dir. Richard Friedenberg
TV(US/Can)

Hamill, P.

Snows of Kilimanjaro, The
FOX (US) 1952 dir. Henry King

Hemingway, E.

Snow Treasure
TIGON (US) 1968 dir. Irving Jacoby

McSwigan, M. *All Aboard for Freedom*

Snow White
CANNON (US) 1987 dir. Michael Berz
Ch

Grimm, J. L. K. and Grimm, W. K.

Snow White and the Seven Dwarfs
DISNEY (US) 1937 dir. David Hand
A, Ch

Grimm, J. L. K. and Grimm, W. K.

So Big
WAR (US) 1932 dir. William Wellman
WAR (US) 1953 dir. Robert Wise

Ferber, E.

Society Doctor
MGM (US) 1935 dir. George B. Seitz
GB title: After Eight Hours

Reeves, J. *Harbor, The*

So Dear to My Heart
DISNEY (US) 1948 dir. Harold Schuster

North, S.

So Ends Our Night
UA (US) 1941 dir. John Cromwell

Remarque, E. M. *Flotsam*

So Evil My Love
PAR (GB) 1948 dir. Lewis Allen

Shearing, J. *For Her to See*

Sofie
NORSK (Den/Nor/Swe) 1992 dir. Liv
Ullman

Nathansens, H. *Mendel Philipsen and Sons*

Sofies Verden
NFK (Nor) 1999 dir. Eric Gustavson

Gaarder, J. *Sophie's World: A Novel About the History of Philosophy*

So Goes My Love
UN (US) 1946 dir. Frank Ryan
GB title: Genius in the Family, A

Maxim, H. P. *Genius in the Family, A*

Solar Crisis
SHOCHIKU (Jap) 1990
dir. Richard C. Sarafian

Kawata, T.

Soldier and the Lady, The
RKO (US) 1937 dir. George Nicholls, Jr.
GB title: Michael Strogoff

Verne, J. *Michael Strogoff*

Soldier Blue
AVCO (US) 1970 dir. Ralph Nelson

Olsen, T. V. *Arrow in the Sun*

Soldier in the Rain
WAR (US) 1963 dir. Ralph Nelson

Goldman, W.

Soldier of Fortune
FOX (US) 1955 dir. Edward Dmytryk

Gann, E. K.

Soldier's Daughter Never Cries, A
MI (Fr/GB/US) 1998 dir. James Ivory

Jones, K.

Soldier's Story, A
COL (US) 1984 dir. Norman Jewison

Fuller, C. *Soldier's Play, A*
P

Soldiers Three
MGM (US) 1951 dir. Tay Garnett

Kipling, R.

Sole Survivor
COL TRISTAR (US/Can) 2000 dir.
Mikael Salomon
TVSe(US/Can)

Koontz, D.

Solid Gold Cadillac, The
COL (US) 1956 dir. Richard Quine

Teichman, H. and Kaufman, G. S.
P

Solitaire Man, The
MGM (US) 1933 dir. Jack Conway
Spewack, B. and Spewack, S.
P

Solitary Child, The
BL (GB) 1958 dir. Gerald Thomas
Bawden, N.

Solo
TRIUMPH (US/Mex) 1996 dir. Noberto
Barba
Mason, R. *Weapon*

Solomon and Sheba
UA (US) 1959 dir. King Vidor
Wilbur, C.

So Long at the Fair
GFD (GB) 1950 dir. Terence Fisher
Thorne, A.

Somebody Up There Likes Me
MGM (US) 1956 dir. Robert Wise
Graziano, R.

Sombrero
MGM (US) 1953 dir. Norman Foster
Niggli, J. *Mexican Village*

Some Came Running
MGM (US) 1959 dir. Vincente Minnelli
Jones, J.

Some Kind of Hero
PAR (US) 1981 dir. Michael Pressman
Kirkwood, J.

Some Kind of Miracle
LORIMAR (US) 1979
dir. Jerrold Freedman
TV(US)
Willis, M. P. and Willis, J. *But There are Always Miracles*

Some Lie and Some Die
TVS (GB) 1990 dir. Neil Zeiger
TVSe(GB)
Rendell, R.

Someone at the Door
BIP (GB) 1936 dir. Herbert Brenon
Christie, D. and Christie, C.
P

Someone Like You
FOX (US) 2001 dir. Tony Goldwyn
Zigman, L. *Animal Husbandry*

Something Borrowed, Something Blue
CBS (US) 1997 dir. Gwen Arner
TV(US)
Karr, J.

Something for Everyone
NG (US) 1970 dir. Harold Prince
GB title: Black Flowers for the Bride
Kressing, H. *Cook, The*

Something in Disguise
THAMES (GB) 1982 dir. Moira Armstrong
TVSe(GB)
Howard, E. J.

Something of Value
MGM (US) 1957 dir. Richard Brooks
Ruark, R.

Something to Hide
AVCO (GB) 1973 dir. Alastair Reid
Monsarrat, N.

Something Wicked This Way Comes
DISNEY (US) 1983 dir. Jack Clayton
Ch
Bradbury, R.

Something Wild
UA (US) 1961 dir. Jack Garfein
Karmel, A. *Mary Ann*

Sometimes a Great Notion
UN (US) 1974 dir. Paul Newman
GB title: Never Give an Inch
Kesey, K.

Sometimes They Come Back
DELAUR (US) 1991
dir. Tom McLaughlin
TV(US)
King, S.

Some Voices
DRAGON (GB) 2000 dir. Simon Cellan
Jones
Penhall, J.
P

Somewhere in Time
UN (US) 1980 dir. Jeannot Szwarc
Matheson, R. *Bid Time Return*

Son de Mar
LOLAFILMS (Sp) 2001 dir. J. J. Bigas
Luna
Vicent, M.

Song for Martin, A
MOONLIGHT (Den/Ger) 2001 dir. Bille
August
Isaksson, U. *Boken om E*

Song of Bernadette, The
FOX (US) 1943 dir. Henry King
Werfel, F.

Song of Songs
PAR (US) 1933 dir. Rouben Mamoulian
Sheldon, E.
P

Song of Songs, The
BBC (GB) 1973 dir. Peter Wood
TVSe(GB)
Sudermann, H.

Song of the Siren
TALISMA (Israel) 1994 dir. Eitan Fuchs
Linur, I.

Songs in Ordinary Time
COL TRISTAR (US) 2000 dir. Rob
Holcomb
TV(US)
Morris, M. M.

Song Spinner, The
SHOWTIME (US/Can) 1995 dir. Randy
Bradshaw
TV(US/Can)
LeBel, P.

Song to Remember, A
COL (US) 1944 dir. Charles Vidor
Leslie, D. *Polonaise*

Son of Bukunin, The
MEDUSA (It) 1998 dir. Gianfranco
Cabiddu
Atzeni, S.

Son of Fury
TCF (US) 1942 dir. John Cromwell
Marshall, E. *Benjamin Blake*

Son of the Morning Star
REP (US) 1991 dir. Mike Robe
TVSe(US)
Connell, E. S. *Son of the Morningstar:
Custer and the Little Big Horn*

Son-Rise: A Miracle of Love
FILMWAYS (US) 1979 dir. Glenn Jordan
TV(US)
Kaufman, B. N. *Son-Rise*

Sons and Lovers
FOX (GB) 1960 dir. Jack Cardiff
BBC (GB) 1981 dir. Stuart Burge
TVSe(GB)

Lawrence, D. H.

Sophia and Constance
BBC (GB) 1988 dir. Rodney Allison,
Hugh David
TVSe(GB)

Bennett, A. *Old Wives' Tale, The*

Sophia Loren—Her Own Story
EMI (US) 1980 dir. Mel Stuart
TV(US)

Hotchner, A. E. *Sophia Living and Loving: Her Own Story*

Sophie's Choice
UN/ITC (US) 1982 dir. Alan J. Pakula

Styron, W.

Sophisticated Gents, The
D. WILSON (US) 1981 dir. Harry Falk
TVSe(US)

Williams, J. A. *Junior Bachelor Society, The*

Sorcerer
UN (US) 1977 dir. William Friedkin
GB title: Wages of Fear

Arnaud, G. *Wages of Fear, The*

Sordid Lives
DAVIS (US) 2000 dir. Del Shores

Shores, D.
P

So Red the Rose
PAR (US) 1935 dir. King Vidor

Young, S.

Sorekara
TOEI (Jap) 1987 dir. Yoshimitsu Morita

Natsume, S.

Sorrell and Son
UA (GB) 1933 dir. Jack Raymond
YTV (GB) 1984 dir. Derek Bennett
TVSe(GB)

Deeping, W.

Sorry, Wrong Number
PAR (US) 1948 dir. Anatole Litvak
WIL COURT (US) 1989
dir. Tony Wharmby
TV(US)

Fletcher, L.
P

Soseiji
TOHO (Jap) 1999 dir. Shinya
Tsukamoto

Rampo, E.

So This is Love
WAR (US) 1953 dir. Gordon Douglas
GB title: Grace Moore Story, The

Moore, G. *You're Only Human Once*

So this is New York
UA (US) 1948 dir. Richard Fleischer

Lardner, R. *Big Town, The*

Soul Collector, The
HEARST (US) 1999 dir. Michael M.
Scott
TV(US)

Kane, K. *Pocketful of Paradise, A*

Soul of a Painter
SHANGHAI (China) 1994 dir. Shuqin
Huang

Nan, S.

Sound and the Fury, The
FOX (US) 1959 dir. Martin Ritt

Faulkner, W.

Sounder
FOX (US) 1972 dir. Martin Ritt

Armstrong, W. H.

Sound of Music, The
FOX (US) 1965 dir. Robert Wise
M

Lindsay, H. and Crouse, R.
P

Trapp, M. A. *Story of the Trapp Family Singers, The*

Sound of One Hand Clapping, The
S. AUST (Aust) 1998 dir. Richard Flanagan

Flanagan, R.

Sounds from the Mountains
CORINTH (Jap) 1980 dir. Mikio Naruse

Kawabata, Y.

Soursweet
CIC (GB) 1988 dir. Mike Newell

Mo, T.

South Central
MONUMENT (US) 1992 dir. Steven Anderson

Bakeer, D. *Crips*

Southern Cross
G. REEVES (GB) 1983
TV(GB)

Coleman, T.

Southerner, The
UA (US) 1945 dir. Jean Renoir

Perry, G. S. *Hold Autumn in your Hands*

Southern Star, The
COL (GB/Fr) 1969 dir. Sidney Hayers

Verne, J. *Southern Star Mystery, The*

South Pacific
TODD AO (US) 1958 dir. Joshua Logan
M

TOUCHSTONE (US) 2001 dir. Richard Pearce
M, TV(US)

Michener, J. P. *Tales from the South Pacific*

Rodgers, R., Hammerstein II, O., Logan, J. and Osborn, P.
P

South Riding
UA (GB) 1938 dir. Victor Saville
YTV (GB) 1974 dir. James Ormerod, Alastair Reid
TVSe(GB)

Holtby, W.

South Sea Woman
WAR (US) 1953 dir. Arthur Lubin

Rankin, W. M.

Souvenir
CIC (GB) 1987 dir. Geoffrey Reeve

Hughes, D. *Pork Butcher, The*

So Well Remembered
RKO (GB) 1947 dir. Edward Dmytryk

Hilton, J.

Soylent Green
MGM (US) 1973 dir. Richard Fleischer

Harrison, H. *Make Room, Make Room!*

Space
PAR (US) 1985 dir. Joseph Sargent, Lee Phillips
TVSe(US)

Michener, J. A.

Spaceman and King Arthur, The
DISNEY (GB) 1979 dir. Russ Mayberry
US title: Unidentified Flying Oddball

Twain, M. *Connecticut Yankee in King Arthur's Court, A*

Spanish Gardener, The
RANK (GB) 1956 dir. Philip Leacock
Cronin, A. J.

Spare the Rod
BL (GB) 1961 dir. Leslie Norman
Croft, M.

Sparkling Cyanide
WAR (US) 1983 dir. Robert Lewis
TV(US)
Christie, A.

Sparrows Can't Sing
WAR (GB) 1962 dir. Joan Littlewood
Lewis, S. *Sparrers Can't Sing*
P

Spartacus
UN (US) 1960 dir. Stanley Kubrick
Fast, H.

Spasms
PDC (Can) 1984 dir. William Fruet
Maryk, M. and Monahan, B. *Death Bite*

Speak Easily
MGM (US) 1932 dir. Edward Sedgwick
Kelland, C. B. *Footlights*

Spearfield's Daughter
FILMLINE (US) 1986
dir. Gilbert Shelton
TVSe(US)
Cleary, J.

Speedy Death
BBC/WGBH (GB/US) 1998 dir. Audrey
Cooke
TV(GB/US)
Mitchell, G.

Spellbound
PYRAMID (GB) 1940 dir. John Harlow
US title: Spell of Amy Nugent, The
Benson, R. *Necromancers, The*

Spellbound
UA (US) 1945 dir. Alfred Hitchcock
Beeding, F. *House of Dr. Edwards, The*

Spencer's Mountain
WAR (US) 1963 dir. Delmer Daves
Hamner, E.

Spenser: A Savage Place
WAR (US) 1995 dir. Joseph L. Scanlan
TV(US)
Parker, R. B. *Savage Place, A*

Sphere
PUNCH (US) 1997 dir. Barry Levinson
Crichton, M.

Sphinx
WAR (US) 1981
dir. Franklin D. Schaffner
Cook, R.

Spider's Stratagem, The
RED FILM (It) 1970
dir. Bernardo Bertolucci
Borges, J. L. *Theme of the Traitor and the Hero, The*

Spider's Web, The
UA (GB) 1960 dir. Godfrey Grayson
BBC (GB) 1982 dir. Basil Coleman
TV(GB)
Christie, A.
P

Spikes Gang, The
UA (US) 1974 dir. Richard Fleischer
Tippette, G. *Bank Robber, The*

Spiral Road, The
UI (US) 1962 dir. Robert Mulligan
de Hartog, J.

Spiral Staircase, The
RKO (US) 1946 dir. Robert Siodmak
WAR (GB) 1975 dir. Peter Collinson
SABAN (US) 2000 dir. James Head

White, E. L. *Some Must Watch*

Spirit is Willing, The
PAR (US) 1967 dir. William Castle

Benchley, N. *Visitors, The*

Spirit Lost
BET (US) 1997 dir. Neema Barnette

Thayer, N.

Spirit of St. Louis, The
WAR (US) 1957 dir. Billy Wilder

Lindbergh, C. A. *We*

Spirit Rider
CREDO (Can) 1994 dir. Michael J. F. Scott
TV(Can)

Collura, M. L. *Winners*

Spitfire
RKO (US) 1934 dir. John Cromwell

Vollmer, L. *Trigger*
P

Splendor
GOLDWYN (US) 1935 dir. Elliott Nugent

Crothers, R.
P

Split, The
MGM (US) 1968 dir. Gordon Flemyng

Stark, R. *Seventh, The*

Spoilers, The
PAR (US) 1930 dir. Edward Carew
UN (US) 1942 dir. Ray Enright
UN (US) 1955 dir. Jesse Hibbs

Beach, R.

Spoils of Poynton, The
BBC (GB) 1970 dir. Peter Sasdy
TVSe(GB)

James, H.

Spoils of War
EVOLUTION (US) 1994 dir. Richard Lowry
TV(US)

Weller, M.
P

Sporting Club, The
AVCO (US) 1971 dir. Larry Peerce

McGuane, T.

Sport of Kings, The
GAINS (GB) 1931 dir. Victor Saville

Hay, I.
P

Spring, The
NBC STUDIOS (US) 2000 dir. David S. Jackson
TV(US)

Irving, C.

Spring and Port Wine
AA (GB) 1970 dir. Peter Hammond

Naughton, B.
P

Spring in Park Lane
BL (GB) 1948 dir. Herbert Wilcox

Thomas, A. E. and Miller, A. D. *Come Out of the Kitchen*
P

Spring Meeting
ABPC (GB) 1940 dir. Walter C. Mycroft

Farrell, M. J. and Perry, J.
P

Spy
WIL COURT (US) 1989 dir. Philip E Messina
TV(US)

Garbo, N.

Spy at Evening, A
BBC (GB) 1981 dir. Ben Rea
TVSe(GB)

James, D.

Spy Hunt
UN (US) 1950 dir. George Sherman
GB title: Panther's Moon

Canning, V. *Panther's Moon*

Spy in Black, The
COL (GB) 1939 dir. Michael Powell
US title: U-Boat 29

Clouston, J. S.

Spy Killer, The
ABC (US) 1969 dir. Roy Baker
TV(US)

Sangster, J. *Private I*

Spy of Napoleon
TWICKENHAM (GB) 1936
dir. Maurice Elvey

Orczy, Baroness E.

Spyship
BBC (GB) 1983 dir. Michael Custance
TVSe(GB)

Haynes, B. and Keene, T.

Spy Story
GALA (GB) 1976 dir. Lindsay Shonteff

Deighton, L.

Spy Who Came in From the Cold, The
PAR (GB) 1966 dir. Martin Ritt

Le Carré, J.

Spy Who Loved Me, The
UA (GB) 1977 dir. Lewis Gilbert

Fleming, I.

Square Dance
ISLAND (US) 1987 dir. Daniel Petrie

Hines, A.

Square Ring, The
GFD (GB) 1953 dir. Basil Dearden

Peterson, R.
P

Squaw Man, The
MGM (US) 1931 dir. Cecil B. De Mille
GB title: White Man, The

Royle, E. M.
P

Squeaker, The
GAU BR (GB) 1937
dir. William K. Howard
US title: Murder on Diamond Row

Wallace, E.

Squeeze, The
WAR (GB) 1977 dir. Michael Apted

Craig, D.

Stagecoach
UA (US) 1939 dir. John Ford
FOX (US) 1966 dir. Gordon Douglas
HERITAGE (US) 1986 dir. Ted Post
TV(US)

Haycox, E. *Stage to Lordsburg*

Stage Door
RKO (US) 1937 dir. Gregory La Cava

Kaufman, G. S. and Ferber, E.
P

Stage Fright
WAR (GB) 1950 dir. Alfred Hitchcock

Jepson, S. *Man Running*

Stage Struck
RKO (US) 1957 dir. Sidney Lumet

Akins, Z.
P

Staircase
FOX (US/Fr) 1969 dir. Stanley Donen

Dyer, C.
P

Staircase C
FILMS 7 (Fr) 1985
dir. Jean-Charles Tacchella
Murail, E.

Stalag 17
PAR (US) 1953 dir. Billy Wilder
Bevan, D. and Trzcinski, E.
P

Stalker
MOSFILM (USSR) 1979 dir. Andrei
Tarkovsky
Strugatsky, B. and Strugatsky, A.
Picnic by the Roadside

Stalking Moon, The
WAR (US) 1968 dir. Robert Mulligan
Olsen, T. V.

Stalky & Co.
BBC (GB) 1982 dir. Rodney Bennett
TVSe(GB)
Kipling, R.

Stallion Road
WAR (US) 1947 dir. James V. Kern
Longstreet, S.

Stand, The
LAUREL ENT (US) 1994 dir. Mick
Garris
TVSe(US)
King, S.

Stand by Me
COL (US) 1986 dir. Rob Reiner
King, S. *Body, The*

Stand by Your Man
GUBER-PETERS (US) 1981
dir. Jerry Jameson
TV(US)
Wynette, T. and Dew, J.

Stand up Virgin Soldiers
WAR (GB) 1977 dir. Norman Cohen
Thomas, L.

Stanley and Iris
MGM (US) 1990 dir. Martin Ritt
Barker, P. *Union Street*

Stanley and the Women
CENTRAL (GB) 1991 dir. David Tucker
TVSe(GB)
Amis, K.

Star
SCHOOLFIELD (US) 1993 dir. Michael
Miller
TV(US)
Steel, D.

Star 80
WAR (US) 1983 dir. Bob Fosse
Carpenter, T. *Death of a Playmate*

Stark
BBC (GB) 1993 dir. Nadia Tass
TVSe(GB)
Elton, B.

Starlight Hotel
REP (NZ) 1988 dir. Sam Pillsbury
Miller, G. H. *Dream Monger, The*

Star Quality
BBC (GB) 1985 dir. Alan Dosser
TVSe(GB)
Coward, N.

Starry Sky, A
RIOFILMES (Bra) 1996 dir. Tata Amaral
Bonassi, F.

Stars and Bars
COL (US) 1988 dir. Pat O'Connor
Boyd, W.

Starship Troopers
TOUCHSTONE (US) 1997 dir. Paul
Verhoeven
Heinlein, R. A.

Stars in My Crown
MGM (US) 1950 dir. Jacques Tourneur
Brown, J. D.

Stars Look Down, The
GN (GB) 1939 dir. Carol Reed
GRANADA (GB) 1974 dir. Roland Joffe,
Alan Grint, Howard Baker
TVSe(GB)
Cronin, A. J.

Star Spangled Girl, The
PAR (US) 1971 dir. Jerry Paris
Simon, N.
P

Starting Over
PAR (US) 1979 dir. Alan J. Pakula
Wakefield, D.

State Fair
FOX (US) 1933 dir. Henry King
FOX (US) 1945 dir. Walter Lang
M
FOX (US) 1962 dir. José Ferrer
M
Stong, P. D.

State of the Union
MGM (US) 1948 dir. Frank Capra
GB title: World and His Wife, The
Lindsay, H. and Crouse, R.
P

State Secret, The
BL (GB) 1950 dir. Sidney Gilliat
US title: Great Manhunt, The
Huggins, R. *Appointment with Fear*

Stationmaster's Wife, The
TELECUL (Ger) 1983
dir. Rainer Werner Fassbinder
Graf, O. M.

Station West
RKO (US) 1948 dir. Sidney Lanfield
Short, L.

Stay Away, Joe
MGM (US) 1968 dir. Peter Tewkesbury
Cushman, D.

Stay Hungry
UA (US) 1976 dir. Bob Rafaelson
Gaines, C.

Staying On
GRANADA (GB) 1980
dir. Silvio Narizzano, Waris Hussein
TV(GB)
Scott, P.

Stay With Me Till Morning
YTV (GB) 1981 dir. David Reynolds
TVSe(GB)
Braine, J.

Stealing Heaven
FILM DALLAS (GB/Yugo) 1989
dir. Clive Donner
Meade, M.

Steal This Movie
GREENLIGHT (US) 2000 dir. Robert
Greenwald
Hoffman, A. and Hoffman, A. *To
America with Love: Letters From the
Underground*
Jeser, M. *Abbie Hoffman: American Rebel*

Steamboat Round the Bend
FOX (US) 1935 dir. John Ford
Burman, B. L.

Steaming
NEW WORLD (GB) 1985
dir. Joseph Losey
Dunn, N.
P

Steel Magnolias
TRISTAR (US) 1989 dir. Herbert Ross
Harling, R.
P

Stella
TOUCHSTONE (US) 1990 dir. John
Erman
Prouty, O. *Stella Dallas*

Stella Dallas
UA (US) 1937 dir. King Vidor
Prouty, O.

Stepford Wives, The
CONTEM (US) 1975 dir. Bryan Forbes
Levin, I.

Step Lively
RKO (US) 1944 dir. Tim Whelan
Murray, J. and Boretz, A. *Room Service*
P

Steppenwolf
CONTEM (US) 1974 dir. Fred Haines
Hesse, H.

Stepping Out
PAR (US) 1991 dir. Lewis Gilbert
Harris, R.
P

Stepsister From Planet Weird
VILLAGE ROADSHOW (US) 2000 dir.
Steve Boyum
TV(US)
Lantz, F. L.

Sterile Cuckoo, The
PAR (US) 1969 dir. Alan J. Pakula
GB title: Pookie
Nicholson, J.

Stevie
FIRST (US/(GB) 1978
dir. Robert Enders
Whitemore, H.
P

Stick
UN (US) 1985 dir. Burt Reynolds
Leonard, E.

Stiletto
AVCO (US) 1969 dir. Bernard Kowalski
Robbins, H.

Stillwatch
INTERSCOPE (US) 1987
dir. Rod Holcomb
TV(US)
Clark, M. H.

Stir of Echoes
ARTISAN (US) 1999 dir. David Koepp
Matheson, R.

Stolen Airliner, The
BL (GB) 1955 dir. Don Sharp
Ch
Pudney, J. *Thursday Adventure*

Stolen Life, A
PAR (GB) 1939 dir. Paul Czinner
WAR (US) 1946 dir. Curtis Bernhardt
Benes, K. J.

Stone Fox
TAFT (US) 1987 dir. Harvey Hart
TV(US)
Gardiner, J. R.

Stone Killer, The
COL (US) 1973 dir. Michael Winner
Gardner, J. *Complete State of Death, A*

Stones for Ibarra
TITUS (US) 1988 dir. Jack Gold
TV(US)
Doerr, H.

Stonewall
BBC (GB) 1995 dir. Nigel Finch
Duberman, M.

Stopover Tokyo
FOX (US) 1957 dir. Richard L. Breen
Marquand, J. P.

Stop, You're Killing Me
WAR (US) 1952 dir. Roy del Ruth
Runyon, D. and Lindsay, H. *Slight Case of Murder, A*
P

Storm and Sorrow
HEARST (US) 1990 dir. Richard Colla
TV(US)
Craig, R. *Storm and Sorrow in the High High Pamirs*

Storm Fear
UA (US) 1955 dir. Cornel Wilde
Seeley, C.

Storm in a Teacup
LF (GB) 1937 dir. Ian Dalrymple, Victor Saville
Frank, B. *Sturm in Wasserglass*
P

Storm over the Nile
GFD (GB) 1955 dir. Terence Young
Mason, A. E. W. *Four Feathers, The*

Story of Dr. Wassell, The
PAR (US) 1944 dir. Cecil B. De Mille
Hilton, J.

Story of Esther Costello, The
COL (GB) 1957 dir. David Miller
US title: Golden Virgin, The
Monsarrat, N.

Story of G.I. Joe, The
UA (US) 1945 dir. William A. Wellman
Pyle, E. T.

Story of Gilbert and Sullivan, The
BL (GB) 1953 dir. Sidney Gilliatt
Baily, L. *Gilbert and Sullivan and Their World*

Story of Mankind, The
WAR (US) 1957 dir. Irwin Allen
Van Loon, H. W.

Story of O, The
NEW REALM (Fr) 1975 dir. Just Jaeckin
Réage, P.

Story of Qiu Ju, The
SIL-METROPOLE (China) 1992 dir. Yimou Zhang
Chen, Y. B. *Wan Family's Lawsuit, The*

Story of Temple Drake, The
PAR (US) 1933 dir. Stephen Roberts
Faulkner, W. *Sanctuary*

Story of the Beach Boys, The: Summer Dreams
L. HILL (USTV) 1990 dir. Michael Switzer
TV(US)
Gaines, S. *Heroes and Villains: The True Story of the Beach Boys*

Story of the Treasure Seekers, The
BBC (GB) 1982 dir. Roger Singleton-Turner
TVSe(GB)
Nesbit, E.

Story of Women
NEW YORKER (Fr) 1989 dir. Claude Chabrol
Szpiner, F. *Affaire de Femmes, Une*

Storyville
DAVIS (US) 1992 dir. Mark Frost
Galbally, F. and Macklin, R. *Juryman*

Stowaway to the Moon
FOX (US) 1975
dir. Andrew V. McLaglen
TV(US)
Shelton, W. R. *Stowaway to the Moon: The Camelot Odyssey*

Straight from the Heart
TELESCENE (Fr) 1990 dir. Lea Pool
Navarre, Y. *Kurwenal*

Straight, Place and Show
FOX (US) 1938 dir. David Butler
GB title: They're Off
Runyon, D. and Caesar, I.
P

Straight Time
WAR (US) 1978 dir. Ulu Grosbard
Bunker, E. *No Beast so Fierce*

Strange Affair, The
PAR (GB) 1968 dir. David Greene
Toms, B.

Strange Affair of Adelaide Harris, The
BBC (GB) 1979 dir. Paul Stone
TVSe(GB)
Garfield, L.

Strange Affair of Uncle Harry, The
UN (US) 1945 dir. Robert Siodmak
Job, T. *Uncle Harry*
P

Strange Boarders
GB (GB) 1938 dir. Herbert Mason
Oppenheim, E. P. *Strange Boarders of Paradise Crescent, The*

Strange Cargo
MGM (US) 1940
dir. Joseph L. Mankiewicz
Sale, R. *Not Too Narrow, Not Too Deep*

Strange Door, The
UI (US) 1951 dir. Joseph Pevney
Stevenson, R. L. *Sire of Maletroit's Door, The*

Strange Interlude
MGM (US) 1932 dir. Robert Z. Leonard
GB title: Strange Interval
HTV (GB) 1988 dir. Herbert Wise
TVSe(GB)
O'Neill, E.
P

Strange Intruder
ABP (US) 1956 dir. Irving Rapper
Fowler, H. M. *Shades Will Not Vanish*

Strange Justice
PAR (US) 1999 dir. Ernest Dickerson
TV(US)
Mayer, J. and Abramson, J.

Strange One, The
COL (US) 1957 dir. Jack Garfein
GB title: End as a Man
Willingham, C. *End as a Man*

Stranger, The
PAR (Fr/It) 1967 dir. Luchino Visconti
Camus, A.

Stranger Came Home, The
EXCL (GB) 1954 dir. Terence Fisher
US title: Unholy Four, The
Sanders, G. *Stranger at Home*

Stranger in my Arms, A
UI (US) 1958 dir. Helmut Kautner
Wilder, R. *And Ride a Tiger*

Stranger in my Bed
TAFT (US) 1987 dir. Larry Elikann
TV(US)
Stater, B. and Leighton, F. S.

Stranger in our House
INTERPLAN (US) 1978 dir. Wes Craven
TV(US)
Duncan, L. *Summer of Fear*

Stranger in the House
JARFID (GB) 1967 dir. Pierre Rouve
Simenon, G. *Strangers in the House*

Stranger in the Kingdom, A
KINGDOM (US) 1998 dir. Jay Craven
Mosher, H. F.

Stranger in the Mirror, A
SPELLING TV (US) 1993 dir. Charles Jarrot
TV(US)
Sheldon, S.

Stranger in Town
EROS (GB) 1957 dir. George Pollock
Chittenden, F. *Uninvited, The*

Stranger in Town, A
AVE PICT (US) 1995 dir. Peter Levin
TV(US)
Marcus, R. T. *Higher Laws*
P

Stranger is Watching, A
MGM/UA (US) 1982
dir. Sean Cunningham
Clark, M. H.

Strangers and Brothers
BBC (GB) 1984 dir. Jeremy Summers, Ronald Wilson
TVSe(GB)
Snow, C. P.

Strangers in Love
PAR (US) 1932 dir. Lothar Mendes
Locke, W. J. *Shorn Lamb, The*

Strangers in 7a, The
PALOMAR (US) 1972 dir. Paul Wendkos
TV(US)
Farrington, F.

Strangers May Kiss
MGM (US) 1931
dir. George Fitzmaurice
Parrott, U.

Strangers on a Train
WAR (US) 1951 dir. Alfred Hitchcock
Highsmith, P.

Strangers Return
MGM (US) 1933 dir. King Vidor
Stong, P. D.

Strangers When We Meet
COL (US) 1959 dir. Richard Quine
Hunter, E.

Strange Woman, The
UA (US) 1946 dir. Edgar G. Ulmer
Williams, B. A.

Strange World of Planet X, The
EROS (GB) 1958 dir. Gilbert Gunn
US title: Cosmic Monsters
Ray, R.

Strangler's Wood
YTV/A&E (GB) 1999 dir. Jeremy Silberston
TV(GB)
Graham, C.

Strawberry Blonde, The
WAR (US) 1941 dir. Raoul Walsh
Hagan, J. *One Sunday Afternoon*
P

Strawberry Roan
BN (GB) 1944 dir. Maurice Elvey
Street, A. G.

Strawberry Statement, The
MGM (US) 1970 dir. Stuart Hagmann
Kunen, J. S.

Straw Dogs
CINERAMA (GB) 1971
dir. Sam Peckinpah
Williams, G. M. *Siege at Trencher's Farm, The*

Streamers
UA (US) 1983 dir. Robert Altman
Rabe, D.
P

Streetcar Named Desire, A
WAR (US) 1951 dir. Elia Kazan
PSO (US) 1984 dir. John Erman
TV(US)
CBS (US) 1995 dir. Glenn Jordan
TV(US)
Williams, T.
P

Street of Chance
PAR (US) 1942 dir. Jack Hively
Woolrich, C. *Black Curtain, The*

Street of Dreams
PHOENIX (US) 1988
dir. William A. Graham
TV(US)
Harris, T. *Good Night and Good Bye*

Street Scene
UA (US) 1931 dir. King Vidor
Rice, E.
P

Streets of Laredo
RHI (US) 1995 dir. Joseph Sargent
TVSe(US)
McMurtry, L.

Streets of San Francisco, The
WAR TV (US) 1972 dir. Walter
Grauman
TV(US)
Weston, C. *Poor, Poor Ophelia*

Strictly Dishonourable
UN (US) 1931 dir. John Stahl
MGM (US) 1951 dir. Norman Panama,
Melvin Frank
Sturges, P.
P

Strike It Rich
BRIT SCREEN (GB) 1990
dir. James Scott
Greene, G. *Loser Takes All*

Strike Me Pink
UA (US) 1936 dir. Norman Taurog
Kelland, C. B. *Dreamland*

Striptease
CASTLE ROCK (US) 1996 dir. Andrew
Bergman
Hiassen, C. *Strip Tease*

Stripper, The
FOX (US) 1963 dir. Franklin Schaffner
GB title: Woman of Summer
Inge, W. *Loss of Roses, A*
P

Stroker Ace
UN/WAR (US) 1983 dir. Hal Needham
Neely, W. *Stand on It*

Strong Medicine
TELEPIC (US) 1986 dir. Guy Green
TVSe(US)
Halley, A.

Strong Poison
BBC (GB) 1987 dir. Christopher Hodson
TVSe(GB)
Sayers, D. L.

Stuart Little
COL (US) 1999 dir. Rob Minkoff
Ch
White, E. B.

Stuart Saves His Family
PAR (US) 1995 dir. Harold Ramis
Franken, A.

Stud, The
BW (GB) 1978 dir. Quentin Masters
Collins, J.

Stud Farm, The
HUN (Hun) 1978 dir. Andras Kovacs
Gall, I.

Student Prince, The
MGM (US) 1954 dir. Richard Thorpe
M
Romberg, S.
Meyer-Foerster, W. *Old Heidelburg*
P

Studs Lonigan
UA (US) 1960 dir. Irving Lerner
LORIMAR (US) 1979
dir. James Goldstone
TVSe(US)
Farrell, J. T. *Young Manhood of Studs Lonigan, The*

Study in Scarlet, The
WW (US) 1933 dir. Edward L. Marin
Doyle, Sir A. C.

Study in Terror, A
COMPTON-TEKLI (GB) 1965
dir. James Hill
Queen, E.

Stunt Man, The
FOX (US) 1980 dir. Richard Rush
Brodeur, P.

Subject was Roses, The
MGM (US) 1968 dir. Ulu Grosbard
Gilroy, F. D.
P

Submarine Patrol
FOX (US) 1938 dir. John Ford
Milholland, R.

Submerged
NBC (US) 2001 dir. James Keach
TV(US)
Maas, P. *Terrible Hours, The*

Substance of Fire, The
MIRAMAX (US) 1996 dir. Daniel J. Sullivan
Baitz, J. R.
P

Subterraneans, The
MGM (US) 1960
dir. Ronald MacDougall
Kerouac, J.

subUrbia
CASTLE ROCK (US) 1996 dir. Richard Linklater
Bogosian, E.
P

Such a Long Journey
FILMWORKS (GB/Can) 1998 dir. Sturla Gunnarsson
Mistry, R.

Such Good Friends
PAR (US) 1972 dir. Otto Preminger
Gould, L.

Sudden Fear
RKO (US) 1952 dir. David Miller
Sherry, E.

Suddenly, Last Summer
COL (GB) 1959
dir. Joseph I. Mankiewicz
Williams, T.
P

Sudie & Simpson
HEARST (US) 1990
dir. Joan Tewkesbury
TV(US)
Carter, S. F. *Sudie*

Sugar Cane Alley
ORION (Fr) 1984 dir. Euzhan Palcy
Zobel, J. *Rue Cases Negres, La*

Sugar Factory, The
IMAGINE (Aust) 1998 dir. Robert Carter
Carter, R.

Sugarfoot
WAR (US) 1951 dir. Edward L. Marin
Kelland, C. B.

Sugartime
HBO (US) 1995 dir. John N. Smith
TV(US)
Roemer, Jr., W. F. *Roemer: Man Against the Mob*

Suicide Club, The
ANGELIKA (US) 1988 dir. James Bruce
Stevenson, R. L.

Suicide's Wife, The
FAC-NEW (US) 1979 dir. John Newland
TV(US)
Madden, D.

Summer and Smoke
PAR (US) 1961 dir. Peter Glenville
Williams, T.
P

Summer Camp Nightmare
CONCORDE (US) 1987
dir. Bert C. Dragin
Butler, W. *Butterfly Revolution, The*

Summer Girl
LORIMAR (US) 1983
dir. Robert Michael Lewis
TV(US)
Crane, C.

Summer Heat
ATLANTIC (US) 1987
dir. Michie Gleason
Shivers, L. *Here to get my Baby out of Jail*

Summer Holiday
MGM (US) 1948
dir. Rouben Mamoulian
M
O'Neill, E. G. *Ah Wilderness!*
P

Summer Lightning
CHANNEL 4 (GB) 1984 dir. Paul Joyce
TV(GB)
Turgenev, I. *First Love*

Summer Magic
DISNEY (US) 1963 dir. James Neilson
Wiggin, K. D. *Mother Carey's Chickens*

Summer My Father Grew Up, The
SHAPIRO (US) 1991
dir. Michael Tuchner
TV(US)
Jennings, S. *Tooth of the Lion*
P

Summer of Fear
INTERPLAN (US) 1978 dir. Wes Craven
Duncan, L.

Summer of Fear
M. ROBE (US) 1996 dir. Mike Robe
TV(US)
Murphy, G. *Simon Says*

Summer of My German Soldier
HIGHGATE (US) 1978
dir. Michael Tuchner
TV(US)
Greene, B.

Summer of the Seventeenth Doll, The
UA (US/Aust) 1959 dir. Leslie Norman
Lawler, R.
P

Summer Place, A
WAR (US) 1959 dir. Delmer Daves
Wilson, S.

Summer's Lease
BBC (GB) 1989 dir. Martyn Friend
TVSe(GB)
Mortimer, J.

Summer Storm
UA (US) 1944 dir. Douglas Sirk
Chekhov, A. *Shooting Party, The*

Summer Story, A
ITC/ATLANTIC (GB) 1988
dir. Piers Haggard
Galsworthy, J. *Apple Tree, The*

Summertime
UA (US) 1955 dir. David Lean
GB title: Summer Madness
Laurents, A. *Time of the Cuckoo, The*
P

Summertree
WAR (US) 1971 dir. Anthony Newley
Cowen, R.
P

Summer with Monika
SVENSK (Swe) 1952
dir. Ingmar Bergman
Anders, P.

Sum of Us, The
SOUTHERN STAR (Aust) 1994 dir.
Geoff Burton, Kevin Dowling
Stevens, D.
P

Sun also Rises, The
FOX (US) 1957 dir. Henry King
FOX (US) 1984 dir. James Goldstone
TVSe(US)
Hemingway, E.

Sunburn
HEMDALE (GB/US) 1979
dir. Richard C. Sarafian
Ellin, S. *Bind, The*

Sun Child
YTV (GB) 1988 dir. Lawrence Gordon
Clark
TV(GB)
Huth, A.

Sunday in New York
MGM (US) 1963 dir. Peter Tewkesbury
Krasna, N.
P

Sunday in the Country, A
MGM/UA (Fr) 1984
dir. Bertrand Tavernier
Bost, P. *Monsieur L'Admiral va Bientôt Mourir*

Sundays and Cybèle
TERRA (Fr) 1962 dir. Serge Bourgignon
Echasseriaux, B.

Sundown
UA (US) 1941 dir. Henry Hathaway
Lyndon, B.

Sundowners, The
WAR (GB/Aust) 1960
dir. Fred Zinnemann
Cleary, J.

Sunrise at Campobello
WAR (US) 1960 dir. Vincent J. Donehue
Schary, D.
P

Sunset Gang, The
AM PLAY (US) 1991 dir. Calvin Skaggs,
Tony Drazan
TVSe(US)
Adler, W.

Sunset Song
BBC (GB) 1971 dir. Moira Armstrong
TVSe(GB)
Gibbon, L. G.

Sunshine Boys, The
MGM (US) 1975 dir. Herbert Ross
HALLMARK (US) 1997 dir. John Erman
TV(US)
Simon, N.
P

Sun Shines Bright, The
REP (US) 1953 dir. John Ford
Cobb, I. S. *Sun Shines Bright, The; Mob From Massac, The; Lord Provides, The*

Super Cops, The
MGM (US) 1974 dir. Gordon Parks
Whittemore, L. H.

Super-Wife, The
CONSTANTIN (Ger) 1996 dir. Sonke
Wortmann
Lind, H.

Supper, The
FRANCE 2 (Fr) 1993 dir. Edouard
Molinaro
Brisville, J.-C. *Souper, Le*
P

Surprise Package
COL (GB) 1960 dir. Stanley Donen
Buchwald, A. *Gift From the Boys, A*

Surrender-Hell
AA (US) 1959 dir. John Barnwell
Harkins, P. *Blackburn's Headhunters*

Survive
STIGWOOD (Mex) 1976
dir. Rene Cardona
Blair, C.

Survive the Savage Sea
VZ/SERTNER (US) 1992 dir. Kevin
James Dobson
TV(US)
Robertson, D.

Surviving Picasso
WAR (US) 1996 dir. James Ivory
Stassinopoulos, A. H. *Picasso: Creator and Destroyer*

Survivor, The
HEMDALE (Aust) 1981
dir. David Hemmings
Herbert, J.

Susana
PLEXUS (Sp) 1951 dir. Luis Bunuel
Reachi, M.

Susan and God
MGM (US) 1940 dir. George Cukor
GB title: Gay Mrs. Trexel, The
Crothers, R.
P

Susan Lenox, Her Fall and Rise
MGM (US) 1931 dir. Robert Z. Leonard
GB title: Rise of Helga, The
Graham, D.

Susan Slade
WAR (US) 1962 dir. Delmer Daves
Hume, D. *Sin of Susan Slade, The*

Suspect
BL (GB) 1960 dir. Roy Boulting
Balchin, N. *Sort of Traitor, A*

Suspect, The
UN (US) 1944 dir. Robert Siodmak

Ronald, J. *This Way Out*

Suspicion
RKO (US) 1941 dir. Alfred Hitchcock

Iles, F. *Before the Fact*

Suspicious River
BEYOND (Can) 2000 dir. Lynne
Stopkewich

Kasischke, L.

Suzy
MGM (US) 1936
dir. George Fitzmaurice

Gorman, H.

Svengali
WAR (US) 1931 dir. Archie Mayo
REN (GB) 1954 dir. William Alwyn
HALMI (US) 1983 dir. Anthony Harvey
TV(US)

Du Maurier, G. *Trilby*

Swallows and Amazons
EMI (GB) 1974 dir. Claude Whatham
Ch

Ransome, A.

Swallows and Amazons Forever!
BBC (GB) 1984 dir. Andrew Morgan
TVSe(GB)

Ransome, A. *Coot Club; Big Six, The*

Swamp Water
FOX (US) 1941 dir. Jean Renoir
GB title: Man Who Came Back, The

Bell, V.

Swan, The
MGM (US) 1956 dir. Charles Vidor

Molnar, F.
P

Swann
NORSTAR (Can/GB) 1996 dir. Anna
Benson Gyles

Shields, C.

Swann in Love
GAU (Fr) 1984 dir. Volker Schlondorff

Proust, M. *Du côté de chez Swann*

Swarm, The
WAR (US) 1978 dir. Irwin Allen

Herzog, A.

Sweeney Todd
THAMES (GB) 1982 dir. Reginald
Collin
TV(GB)

Dibdin-Pitt, G. *Sweeny Todd, the Demon
Barber of Fleet Street*
P

Sweeney Todd, the Demon Barber of Fleet Street
KING (GB) 1936 dir. George King

Dibdin-Pitt, G.
P

Sweet Bird of Youth
MGM (US) 1962 dir. Richard Brooks
KUSHNER-LOCK (US) 1989
dir. Nicolas Roeg
TV(US)

Williams, T.
P

Sweet Charity
UN (US) 1969 dir. Robert Fosse
M

Simon, N., Fields, D. and Coleman, C.
P

Sweet Country
CINEMA (US) 1987
dir. Michael Cacoyannis

Richards, C.

Sweet Hereafter, The
ALLIANCE (Can) 1997 dir. Atom Egoyan
Banks, R.

Sweet Hostage
BRUT (US) 1975 dir. Lee Phillips
TV(US)
Benchley, N. *Welcome to Xanadu*

Sweet Love, Bitter
FILM 2 (US) 1967 dir. Herbert Danska
Williams, J. *Night Song*

Sweet Ride, The
FOX (US) 1968 dir. Harvey Hart
Murray, W.

Sweet William
ITC (GB) 1980 dir. Claude Whatham
Bainbridge, B.

Swimmer, The
COL (US) 1968 dir. Frank Perry, Sidney Pollack
Cheever, J.

Swing High, Swing Low
PAR (US) 1937 dir. Mitchell Leisen
Walters, G. M. and Hopkins, A. *Burlesque*
P

Swiss Family Robinson
RKO (US) 1940 dir. Edward Ludwig
DISNEY (GB) 1960 dir. Ken Annakin
FOX (US) 1975 dir. Harry Harris
TV(US)
Wyss, J. D.

Switching Channels
TRISTAR (US) 1988 dir. Ted Kotcheff
Hecht, B. and MacArthur, C. *Front Page, The*
P

Sword and the Rose, The
DISNEY (GB) 1953 dir. Ken Annakin
Major, C. *When Knighthood was in Flower*

Sword in the Stone, The
DISNEY (US) 1963
dir. Wolfgang Reitherman
A, Ch
White, T. H. *Once and Future King, The*

Sword of Gideon
HBO (US/Can) 1986
dir. Michael Anderson
TV(US/Can)
Jones, G. *Vengeance*

Sworn to Silence
BLATT/SINGER (US) 1987
dir. Peter Levin
TV(US)
Alibrandi, T. and Armani, F. H. *Privileged Information*

Sybil
LORIMAR (US) 1976 dir. Daniel Petrie
TVSe(US)
Schreiber, F. R.

Sylvia
PAR (US) 1965 dir. Gordon Douglas
Cunningham, E. V.

Sylvia
ENT (NZ) 1985 dir. Michael Firth
Ashton-Warner, S. *Teacher, I Passed This Way*

Sylvia and the Ghost
ECRAN (Fr) 1944
dir. Claude Autant-Lara
Adam, A.
P

Sylvia Scarlett
RKO (US) 1935 dir. George Cukor
Mackenzie, Sir C.

Symphonie Pastorale, La

GIBE (Fr) 1946 dir. Jean Delannoy

Gide, A.

Symphony of Six Million

RKO (US) 1932 dir. Gregory LaCava
GB title: Melody of Life

Hurst, F.

Taboo
IMAGICA (Jap/Fr) 1999 dir. Nagisa Oshima

Shiba, R. *With a Lock of Hair Over His Forehead; Revolt of the Mountain, The; Chronicles of the Shinsengumi*

Taffin
MGM/UA (GB) 1988
dir. Francis Megahy

Mallett, L.

Taggart
UI (US) 1965 dir. R. G. Springsteen

L'Amour L.

Tagget
MCA TV (US) 1991 dir. Richard T. Heffron
TV(US)

Greenfield, I. A.

Tailor of Panama, The
COL (US/Ire) 2001 dir. John Boorman

Le Carré, J.

Tai-Pan
ORION (US) 1986 dir. Daryl Duke

Clavell, J.

Take, The
COL (US) 1974
dir. Robert Hartford-Davis

Newman, G. F. *Sir, You Bastard*

Take, The
MCA TV (US) 1990 dir. Leon Ichaso
TV(US)

Izzi, E.

Take a Giant Step
UA (US) 1959 dir. Philip Leacock

Peterson, L. S.
P

Take a Girl Like You
COL (GB) 1969 dir. Jonathan Miller
BBC/WGBH (GB) 2000 dir. Nick Hurran
TV(GB)

Amis, K.

Take Care of My Little Girl
FOX (US) 1951 dir. Jean Negulesco

Goodin, P.

Takedown
DIMENSION (US) 2000 dir. Joe Chappelle

Shimomura, T. and Markoff, J.

Take Her, She's Mine
MGM (US) 1963 dir. Henry Koster

Ephron, P. and Ephron, H.
P

Take Me Home: The John Denver Story
GRANADA (US) 2000 dir. Jerry London
TV(US)

Denver, J. and Tobier, A. *Take Me Home*

Take Me Home Again
VZ/SERTNER (US) 1994 dir. Tom
McLaughlin
TV(US)
Herrin, L. *Lies Boys Tell, The*

Take My Life
EL (GB) 1947 dir. Ronald Neame
Graham, W. and Taylor, V.

Taking of Pelham 123, The
UA (US) 1974 dir. Joseph Sargent
MGM TV (US) 1998 dir. Felix E. Alcara
TV(US)
Godey, J.

Talented Mr. Ripley, The
MIRAMAX (US) 1999 dir. Anthony
Minghella
Highsmith, P.

Tale of Little Pig Robinson, The
TVS (GB) 1990 dir. Alan Bridges
TVSe(GB)
Potter, B.

Tale of Two Cities, A
MGM (US) 1935 dir. Jack Conway
RANK (GB) 1958 dir. Ralph Thomas
ROSEMONT (US/GB) 1980
dir. Jim Goddard
TV(GB/US)
BBC (GB) 1980 dir. Michael E. Briant
TVSe(GB)
GRANADA (GB) 1989 dir. Philippe
Monnier
TVSe(GB)
Dickens, C.

Tales from the Darkside: the Movie
PAR (US) 1990 dir. John Harrison
Doyle, Sir A. C. *Lot 27a*
King, S. *Cat From Hell*

Tales from the Vienna Woods
CINEMA 5 (Austria/Ger) 1981
dir. Maximilian Schell
von Horvath, O.
P

Tales of Hoffman, The
BL (GB) 1951 dir. Michael Powell,
Emeric Pressburger
M
Offenbach, J.

Tales of Ordinary Madness
GINIS (It) 1981 dir. Marco Ferri
Bukowski, C. *Erections, Ejaculations,
Exhibitions and Tales of Ordinary Madness*

Tales of Terror
WAR (US) 1962 dir. Roger Corman
Poe, E. A. *Morella; Black Cat, The; Facts
of the Case of Dr. Valdemar, The*

Tales of the City
AM PLAY/CHANNEL 4 FILMS (US/
GB) 1994 dir. Alastair Reid
TVSe(US/GB)
Maupin, A.

Talisman, The
BBC (GB) 1980 dir. Richard Bramall
TVSe(GB)
Scott, Sir W.

Talk About a Stranger
MGM (US) 1952 dir. David Bradley
Armstrong, C.

Talking Walls
NEW WORLD (US) 1987
dir. Stephen Verona
McGrady, M. *Motel Tapes, The*

Talk of Angels
POLARIS (US) 1998 dir. Nick Hamm
O'Brien, K. *Mary Lavelle*

Talk Radio
UN (US) 1988 dir. Oliver Stone

Bogosian, E.
P

Singular, S. *Talked to Death: The Life and Murder of Alan Berg*
P

Tall Headlines, The
GN (GB) 1952 dir. Terence Young

Lindop, A. E.

Tall Man Riding
WAR (US) 1955 dir. Lesley Selander

Fox, N. A.

Tall Men, The
FOX (US) 1955 dir. Raoul Walsh

Fisher, C.

Tall Story
WAR (US) 1960 dir. Joshua Logan

Nemerov, H. *Homecoming Game, The*

Talvisota
FINN (Fin) 1989 dir. Pekka Parikka

Tuuri, A.

Tamahine
WAR (GB) 1963 dir. Philip Leacock

Niklaus, T.

Tamango
SNEG (Fr) 1958 dir. John Berry

Merimée, P.

Tamarind Seed, The
SCOTIA-BARBER (GB) 1974
dir. Blake Edwards

Anthony, E.

Taming of the Shrew, The
M. EVANS (US) 1956
dir. George Schaefer
TV(US)
COL (US) 1967 dir. Franco Zeffirelli

Shakespeare, W.
P

Tammy and the Bachelor
UN (US) 1957 dir. Joseph Pevney
GB title: Tammy

Sumner, C. R.

Tangerine Bear, The
ARTISAN (US) 2000 dir. Bert Ring
A, Ch

Paraskevas, M. and Paraskevas, M.

Tape
IFC (US) 2001 dir. Richard Linklater

Belber, S.
P

Tap Roots
UI (US) 1948 dir. George Marshall

Street, J. H.

Taps
FOX (US) 1981 dir. Harold Becker

Freeman, D. *Father Sky*

Taras Bulba
UA (US) 1962 dir. J. Lee Thompson

Gogol, N. V.

Target
CREATIVE (Ind) 1995 dir. Sandip Ray

Ray, P. *Manushar Juddha*

Tarka the Otter
RANK (GB) 1979 dir. David Cobham

Williamson, H.

Tarnished Angels, The
UI (US) 1957 dir. Douglas Sirk

Faulkner, W. *Pylon*

Tarzan
DISNEY (US) 1999 dir. Chris Buck,
Kevin Lima
A, Ch
Burroughs, E. R. *Tarzan of the Apes*

Tarzan, The Ape Man
MGM (US) 1932 dir. W. S. Van Dyke
Burroughs, E. R. *Tarzan of the Apes*

Taste for Death, A
YTV (GB) 1987 dir. John Davies
TVSe(GB)
James, P. D.

Taste of Excitement, A
MONARCH (GB) 1969 dir. Don Sharp
Healey, B. *Waiting for a Tiger*

Taste of Honey, A
BRYANSTON (GB) 1961
dir. Tony Richardson
Delaney, S.
P

Taxi!
WAR (US) 1931 dir. Roy del Ruth
Nicholson, K. *Blind Spot, The*
P

T Bone N Weasel
TNT (US) 1992 dir. Lewis Teague
TV(US)
Klein, J.
P

Tea and Sympathy
MGM (US) 1956 dir. Vincente Minnelli
Anderson, R.
P

Teahouse of the August Moon, The
MGM (US) 1956 dir. Daniel Mann
COMPASS (US) 1962
dir. George Schaefer
TV(US)
Sneider, V.
Patrick, J.
P

Tea in the Harem
M&R (Fr) 1986
dir. Mehdi Charef
Charef, M. *Thé au harem d'Archi Ahmen, Le*

Teamster Boss: The Jackie Presser Story
HBO (US) 1992 dir. Alastair Reid
TV(US)
Neff, J. *Mobbed Up*

Tears in the Rain
ATLANTIC/BL (US/GB) 1988
dir. Don Sharpe
TV(GB/US)
Wallace, P.

Tecumseh: The Last Warrior
AM ZOETROPE (US) 1995 dir. Larry Elikann
TV(US)
Thom, J. A. *Panther in the Sky*

Teenage Rebel
FOX (US) 1956 dir. Edmund Goulding
Sommer, E.
P

Telefon
MGM (US) 1977 dir. Don Siegel
Wager, W.

Telegraphist, The
NORSK (Den/Nor) 1993 dir. Erik Gustavson
Hamsun, K. *Dreamers*

Tell England
CAPITOL (GB) 1931
dir. Anthony Asquith, Gerald Barkas
US title: Battle of Gallipoli, The
Raymond, E.

Tell Me a Riddle
FILMWAYS (US) 1980 dir. Lee Grant
Olsen, T.

Tell Me My Name
TALENT (US) 1977 dir. Delbert Mann
TV(US)
Carter, M.

Tell Me No Secrets
AVE PICT (US) 1997 dir. Bobby Roth
TV(US)
Fielding, J.

Tell Me That You Love Me, Junie Moon
PAR (US) 1970 dir. Otto Preminger
Kellogg, M.

Tell-Tale Heart, The
ADELPHI (GB) 1953 dir. J. B. Williams
ABP (GB) 1960 dir. Ernest Morris
Poe, E. A.

Tell them Willie Boy is Here
UN (US) 1969 dir. Abraham Polonsky
Lawton, H. *Willie Boy*

Tempest
PAR (It/Fr) 1958
dir. Alberto Lattuada
Pushkin, A. *Captain's Daughter, The*

Tempest, The
COMPASS (US) 1960
dir. George Schaefer
TV(US)
MAINLINE (GB) 1980
dir. Derek Jarman
NBC STUDIOS (US) 1998 dir. Jack Bender
TV(US)
Shakespeare, W.
P

Temptation
UN (US) 1935 dir. Irving Pichel
Hichens, R. *Bella Donna*

Temptation Harbour
AB (GB) 1947 dir. Lance Comfort
Simenon, G. *Newhaven-Dieppe*

Temptation of Eileen Hughes, The
BBC (GB) 1988 dir. Trevor Powell
TV(GB)
Moore, B.

Temptations, The
DE PASSE (US) 1998 dir. Allan Arkush
TVSe(US)
Williams, O. and Romanowski, P.

Tenant, The
PAR (Fr) 1976 dir. Roman Polanski
Topor, R.

Ten Days Wonder
HEMDALE (Fr) 1971
dir. Claude Chabrol
Queen, E.

Tenderfoot, The
DISNEY (US) 1964 dir. Byron Paul
Tevis, J. H. *Arizona in the 50's*

Tender is the Night
FOX (US) 1962 dir. Henry King
BBC/SHOWTIME (US/GB) 1985
dir. Robert Knights
TVSe(US/GB)
Fitzgerald, F. S.

Tender Trap, The
MGM (US) 1955 dir. Charles Walters
Shulman, M. and Smith, R. P.
P

Tendre Ennemie
WORLD (Fr) 1938 dir. Max Ophuls
Antoine, W. P. *Ennemie, L'*
P

Ten Little Indians
ABP (GB) 1965 dir. George Pollock
CANNON (US) 1989
dir. Alan Birkinshaw
Christie, A. *Ten Little Niggers*

Ten Million Dollar Getaway, The
WIL COURT (US) 1991
dir. James A. Contner
TV(US)
Feiden, D.

Ten Minute Alibi
BL (GB) 1935 dir. Bernard Vorhaus
Armstrong, A.
P

Tennessee's Partner
RKO (US) 1955 dir. Allan Dwan
Harte, B.

Ten North Frederick
FOX (US) 1958 dir. Philip Dunne
O'Hara, J.

10 Rillington Place
COL (GB) 1970 dir. Richard Fleischer
Kennedy, L.

Ten Seconds to Hell
UA (US) 1959 dir. Robert Aldrich
Bachmann, L. *Phoenix, The*

Tension at Table Rock
RKO (US) 1956
dir. Charles Marquis Warren
Gruber, G. *Bitter Sage*

10 Things I Hate About You
TOUCHSTONE (US) 1999 dir. Gil
Junger
Shakespeare, W. *Taming of the Shrew, The*
P

10.30 p.m. Summer
UA (US/Sp) 1966 dir. Jules Dassin
Duras, M. *10.30 p.m. on a Summer Night*

Tenth Man, The
ROSEMONT (US/GB) 1988
dir. Jack Gold
TV(GB/US)
Greene, G.

Tenth Month, The
HAMILTON (US) 1979
dir. Joan Tewkesbury
TV(US)
Hobson, L. Z.

Term of Trial
WAR (GB) 1962 dir. Peter Glenville
Barlow, J.

Terms of Endearment
PAR (US) 1983 dir. James L. Brooks
McMurtry, L.

Terrible Beauty, A
UA (GB) 1960 dir. Tay Garnett
Roth, A.

Terronauts, The
EMBASSY (GB) 1967
dir. Montgomery Tully
Leinster, M. *Wailing Asteroid, The*

Terror, The
ALL (GB) 1938 dir. Richard Bird
Wallace, E.

Terror in the Shadows
HEARST (US) 1995 dir. William A.
Graham
TV(US)
Allegretto, M. *Night of Reunion*

Terror in the Sky
PAR TV (US) 1971
dir. Bernard L. Kowalski
TV(US)
Hailey, A. and Castle, J. *Runway Zero-Eight*

Terror on Highway 91
CBS (US) 1989 dir. Jerry Jameson
TV(US)
Sellers, S. *Terror on Highway 59*

Tess
COL (Fr/GB) 1981 dir. Roman Polanski
Hardy, T. *Tess of the d'Urbervilles*

Tess of the d'Urbervilles
LWT/A&E (GB) 1998 dir. Ian Sharp
TVSe(GB)
Hardy, T.

Tess of the Storm Country
FOX (US) 1932 dir. Alfred Santell
FOX (US) 1961 dir. Paul Guilfoyle
White, G. M.

Testament
PAR (US) 1983 dir. Lynne Littman
Amen, C. *Last Testament, The*

Testament of Youth
BBC (GB) 1979 dir. Moira Armstrong
TVSe(GB)
Brittain, V.

Testimone a Rischio
MEDIASET (It) 1997 dir. Pasqualte
Pozzessere
Calderoni, P. *Avventura di un Uomo Tranquillo, L'*

Testimony of Two Men
UN TV (US) 1977 dir. Leo Penn, Larry
Yust
TVSe(US)
Caldwell, T.

Tex
DISNEY (US) 1982 dir. Tim Hunter
Hinton, S. E.

Texas
SPELLING TV (US) 1995 dir. Richard
Long
TVSe(US)
Michener, J.

Texas Justice
CBS TV (US) 1995 dir. Dick Lawry
TV(US)
Cartwright, G. *Blood Will Tell*

Texasville
COL (US) 1990 dir. Peter Bogdanovich
McMurtry, L.

Thanks for the Memory
PAR (US) 1938 dir. George Archainbaud
Goodrich, F. and Hackett, A. *Up Pops the Devil*
P

Thanksgiving Promise, The
DISNEY (US) 1986 dir. Beau Bridges
TV(US)

Yorgason, B. and Yorgason, B. *Chester, I Love You*

Thank You, Jeeves
FOX (US) 1936
dir. Arthur Greville Collins

Wodehouse, P. G.

Thank You Mr. Moto
FOX (US) 1937 dir. Norman Foster

Marquand, J. P.

Thark
GB (GB) 1932 dir. Tom Walls

Travers, B.
P

That Certain Feeling
PAR (US) 1956 dir. Norman Panama, Melvin Frank

Kerr, J. and Brooke, E. *King of Hearts*
P

That Championship Season
CANNON (US) 1982 dir. Jason Miller
MGM (US) 1999 dir. Paul Sorvino
TV(US)

Miller, J.
P

That Cold Day in the Park
COMM (Can) 1969 dir. Robert Altman

Miles, R.

That Dangerous Age
LF (GB) 1948 dir. Gregory Ratoff
US title: If This Be Sin

Kennedy, M. and Surgutchoff, I. *Autumn*
P

That Darn Cat!
DISNEY (US) 1965
dir. Robert Stevenson
DISNEY (US) 1997 dir. Bob Spiers

Gordon, M. and Gordon, G. *Undercover Cat*

That Eye, The Sky
WORKING TITLE (Aust) 1994 dir. John Ruane

Winton, T.

That Forsyte Woman
MGM (US) 1949 dir. Compton Bennett
GB title: Forsyte Saga, The

Galsworthy, J. *Man of Property, A*

That Hagen Girl
WAR (US) 1947 dir. Peter Godfrey

Kniepple, E.

That Lady
FOX (GB) 1955 dir. Terence Young

O'Brien, K.

That Night
REGENCY (Fr/US) 1993 dir. Craig Bolotin

McDermott, A.

That Obscure Object of Desire
GALAXIE (Fr/Sp) 1978 dir. Luis Bunuel

Louys, P. *Femme et le Pantin, La*

That Was Then ... This is Now
PAR (US) 1985 dir. Christopher Cain

Hinton, S. E.

That Woman Opposite
MON (GB) 1957 dir. Compton Bennett

Carr, J. D. *Emperor's Snuffbox, The*

Theorem
AETOS (It) 1968 dir. Pier Paolo Pasolini

Pasolini, P. P.

There Are No Children Here
HARPO (US) 1993 dir. Anita Addison
TV(US)
Kotlowitz, A.

There Goes the Bride
ENT (GB) 1980 dir. Terence Marcel
Cooney, R.
P

There Must be a Pony
COL TV (US) 1986 dir. Joseph Sargent
TV(US)
Kirkwood, J.

There's a Girl in my Soup
COL (GB) 1970 dir. Roy Boulting
Frisby, T.
P

There's Always Tomorrow
MGM (US) 1934 dir. Edward Sloman
UN (US) 1956 dir. Douglas Sirk
Parrot, U.

Thérèse
GALA (Fr) 1964 dir. Georges Franju
Mauriac, F. *Thérèse Desqueyroux*

Therese Raquin
BBC (GB) 1980 dir. Simon Langton
TVSe(GB)
Zola, E.

There Shall Be No Night
MILBERG (US) 1956
dir. George Schaefer
TV(US)
Sherwood, R. E.
P

There Was a Little Boy
LORIMAR TV (US) 1993 dir. Mimi
Leder
TV(US)
Jacobs, C. R.

These Thousand Hills
FOX (US) 1958 dir. Richard Fleischer
Guthrie, Jr., A. B.

These Three
UA (US) 1936 dir. William Wyler
Hellman, L. F. *Children's Hour, The*
P

They Call it Murder
FOX (US) 1971 dir. Walter Grauman
TV(US)
Gardner, E. S. *D.A. Draws a Circle, The*

They Came to a City
EAL (GB) 1944 dir. Basil Dearden
Priestley, J. B.
P

They Came to Cordura
COL (US) 1959 dir. Robert Rossen
Swarthout, G.

They Drive by Night
WAR (GB) 1938 dir. Arthur Woods
Curtis, J.

They Drive by Night
WAR (US) 1940 dir. Raoul Walsh
GB title: Road to Frisco, The
Bezzerides, A. I. *Long Haul*

They Gave Him a Gun
MGM (US) 1937 dir. W. S. Van Dyke
Cowen, W. J.

They Knew Mr. Knight
GFD (GB) 1945 dir. Norman Walker
Whipple, D.

They Knew What They Wanted
RKO (US) 1940 dir. Garson Kanin
Howard, S.
P

They Live
UN (US) 1988 dir. John Carpenter
Nelson, R. *Eight O'Clock in the Morning*

They Made Me a Fugitive
WAR (GB) 1947 dir. Alberto Cavalcanti
US title: I Became a Criminal
Budd, J. *Convict has Escaped, A*

They Met in the Dark
RANK (GB) 1943 dir. Karel Lamac
Gilbert, A. *Vanishing Corpse, The*

They Might be Giants
UN (US) 1972 dir. Anthony Harvey
Goldman, J.
P

They're a Weird Mob
RANK (GB) 1966 dir. Michael Powell
Culotta, N.

They Shoot Horses, Don't They?
CINERAMA (US) 1969
dir. Sydney Pollack
McCoy, H.

They've Taken Our Children: The Chowchilla Kidnapping
L. HILL (US) 1993 dir. Vern Gillum
TV(US)
Baugh, J. W. and Morgan, J. *Why Have They Taken Our Children?*

They Were Expendable
MGM (US) 1945 dir. John Ford
White, W. L.

They Were Sisters
GFD (GB) 1945 dir. Arthur Crabtree
Whipple, D.

They Won't Forget
WAR (US) 1937 dir. Mervyn LeRoy
Greene, W. *Death in the Deep South*

Thick as Thieves
OCTOBER (US) 1999 dir. Scott Sanders
Quinn, P.

Thicker Than Blood
TNT PICT (US) 1998 dir. Richard Pearce
TV(US)
Cain, B. *Stand-Up Tragedy*
P

Thicker Than Water
BBC (GB) 1994 dir. Marc Evans
TV(GB)
Jones, D.

Thief
UA (US) 1981 dir. Michael Mann
GB title: Violent Street
Hohimer F. *Home Invaders, The*

Thief Who Came to Dinner, The
WAR (US) 1973 dir. Bud Yorkin
Smith, T. L.

Thieves' Highway
FOX (US) 1949 dir. Jules Dassin
Bezzerides, A. I. *Thieves' Market*

Thieves Like Us
UA (US) 1974 dir. Robert Altman
Anderson, E.

Thin Air
JAFFE/BRAUNSTEIN (US) 2000 dir. Robert Mandel
TV(US)
Parker, R. B.

Thing, The
RKO (US) 1951 dir. Christian Nyby
GB title: Thing from Another World, The
UN (US) 1982 dir. John Carpenter
Campbell, J. W. *Who Goes There?*

Things to Come
UA (GB) 1936
dir. William Cameron Menzies
Wells, H. G. *Shape of Things to Come,
The*

Thin Man, The
MGM (US) 1934 dir. W. S. Van Dyke
Hammett, D.

Thinner
PAR (US) 1996 dir. Tom Holland
King, S.

Thin Red Line, The
PLANET (US) 1964 dir. Andrew Marton
FOX (US) 1998 dir. Terrence Malick
Jones, J.

Third Day, The
WAR (US) 1965 dir. Jack Smight
Hayes, J.

Third Degree Burn
HBO (US) 1989 dir. Roger Spottiswoode
TV(US)
Margolin, P. M.

Third Man, The
GFD (GB) 1949 dir. Carol Reed
Greene, G.

Third Man on the Mountain
DISNEY (GB) 1959 dir. Ken Annakin
Ch
Ullman, J. R. *Banner in the Sky*

Third Miracle, The
AM ZOETROPE (US) 1999 dir.
Agnieszka Holland
Vetere, R.

Third Party Risk
EXCL (GB) 1955 dir. Daniel Birt
Bentley, N.

Third Twin, The
JAFFE/BRAUNSTEIN (US) 1997 dir.
Tom McLoughlin
TV(US)
Follett, K.

Third Voice, The
FOX (US) 1959 dir. Hubert Cornfield
Williams, C. *All the Way*

Thirteen at Dinner
WAR (US) 1985 dir. Lou Antonio
TV(US)
Christie, A. *Lord Edgware Dies*

Thirteen Days
NEW LINE (US) 2000 dir. Roger
Donaldson
May, E. R. and Zelikow, P. D. *Kennedy
Tapes, The: Inside the White House During
the Cuban Missile Crisis*

Thirteenth Floor, The
CENTROPOLIS (US/Ger) 1999 dir.
Josef Rusnak
Galouye, D. *Simulacron 3*

13th Warrior, The
TOUCHSTONE (US) 1999 dir. John
McTiernan
Crichton, M. *Eaters of the Dead*

13 West Street
COL (US) 1962 dir. Philip Leacock
Brackett, L. *Tiger Amongst Us, The*

Thirty Day Princess
PAR (US) 1934 dir. Marion Gering
Kelland, C. B.

38: Vienna Before the Fall
SATEL/ALMARO (Ger) 1988
dir. Wolfgang Gluck
Torberg, F. *Auch das war Wein*

Thirty-Nine Steps, The
GB (GB) 1935 dir. Alfred Hitchcock
RANK (GB) 1959 dir. Ralph Thomas
RANK (GB) 1978 dir. Don Sharp

Buchan, J.

Thirty Seconds Over Tokyo
MGM (US) 1944 dir. Mervyn LeRoy

Lawson, T. and Considine, R.

This Above All
FOX (US) 1942 dir. Anatole Litvak

Knight, E. M.

This Angry Age
DELAUR (It) 1957 dir. René Clément

Duras, M. *Barrage contre le Pacifique, Un*

This Earth is Mine
UI (US) 1959 dir. Henry King

Hobart, A. T. *Cup and the Sword, The*

This Gun for Hire
PAR (US) 1942 dir. Frank Tuttle
BBK (US) 1991 dir. Lou Antonio
TV(US)

Greene, G. *Gun for Sale, A*

This Happy Breed
TC (GB) 1944 dir. David Lean

Coward, N.
P

This Happy Feeling
UN (US) 1958 dir. Blake Edwards

Herbert, F. H. *For Love or Money*
P

This Island Earth
UI (US) 1955 dir. Joseph Newman

Jones, R. F.

This is My Life
FOX (US) 1992 dir. Nora Ephron

Wolitzer, M. *This is Your Life*

This is My Street
WAR (GB) 1963 dir. Sidney Hayers

Maynard, N.

This is the Life
UN (US) 1943 dir. Felix Feist
M

Wray, R. and Lewis, S. *Angela is 22*
P

This Love of Ours
UI (US) 1945 dir. William Deiterle

Pirandello, L. *Come Prima Meglio di Prima*
P

This Man is Dangerous
RIALTO (GB) 1941
dir. Lawrence Huntington

Hume, D. *They Called Him Death*

This Man is Mine
RKO (US) 1934 dir. John Cromwell

Morrison, A. *Love Flies in the Window*
P

This Man is Mine
COL (GB) 1946 dir. Marcel Varnel

Beckwith, R. *Soldier for Christmas, A*

This Man Must Die
AA (Fr) 1970 dir. Claude Chabrol

Blake, N.

This Matter of Marriage
ALLIANCE (Can) dir. Brad Turner
TV(Can)

Macomber, D.

This Property is Condemned
PAR (US) 1966 dir. Sydney Pollack

Williams, T.
P

This Side of Heaven
MGM (US) 1934 dir. William K. Howard
Paradis, M.

This Sporting Life
RANK (GB) 1963 dir. Lindsay Anderson
Storey, D.

This Was a Woman
FOX (GB) 1948 dir. Tim Whelan
Morgan, J.
P

This Woman is Mine
UN (US) 1941 dir. Frank Lloyd
Gabriel, G. W. *I, James Lewis*

Thorn Birds, The
WAR (US) 1979 dir. Daryl Duke
TVSe(US)
McCullough, C.

Thorn Birds, The: The Missing Years
WOLPER (US) 1996 dir. Kevin James Dobson
TVSe(US)
McCullough, C. *Thorn Birds, The*

Those Calloways
DISNEY (US) 1964 dir. Norman Tokar
Annixter, P. *Swift Water*

Those Kids from Town
BN (GB) 1941 dir. Lance Comfort
Arlington, A. *These, Our Strangers*

Those Were the Days
BIP (GB) 1934 dir. Thomas Bentley
Pinero, Sir A. W. *Magistrate, The*
P

Thousand Acres, A
TOUCHSTONE (US) 1997 dir. Jocelyn Moorhouse
Smiley, J.

Thousand Clowns, A
UA (US) 1965 dir. Fred Coe
Gardner, H.
P

Thousand Pieces of Gold
AM PLAY (US) 1990 dir. Nancy Kelly
McCunn, R. L.

1,000 Plane Raid, The
UA (GB) 1969 dir. Boris Sagal
Barker, R. *Thousand Plan, The*

Three
UA (GB) 1969 dir. James Salter
Shaw, I. *Then There Were Three*

Three Blind Mice
VIACOM (US) 2001 dir. Christopher Leitch
TV(US)
Hunter, E.

Three Came Home
FOX (US) 1950 dir. Jean Negulesco
Keith, A.

Three Coins in the Fountain
FOX (US) 1954 dir. Jean Negulesco
Secondari, J. *Coins in the Fountain*

Three Comrades
MGM (US) 1938 dir. Frank Borzage
Remarque, E. M.

Three Cornered Moon
PAR (US) 1933 dir. Elliott Nugent
Tonkonogy, G.
P

Three Days of the Condor
PAR (US) 1975 dir. Sydney Pollack
Grady, J. *Six Days of the Condor*

Three Faces East
WAR (US) 1930 dir. Roy del Ruth
Kelly, A. P.
P

Three Faces of Eve, The
FOX (US) 1957 dir. Nunnally Johnson
Thigpen, C. H. and Cleckley, H. M.

3 for Bedroom C
INT (US) 1952 dir. Milton H. Bren
Lieberson, G.

Three for the Show
COL (US) 1955 dir. H. C. Potter
M
Maugham, W. S. *Home and Beauty*
P

Three Godfathers, The
MGM (US) 1936
dir. Richard Boleslawski
MGM (US) 1948 dir. John Ford
Kyne, P. B.

Three in the Attic
WAR (US) 1968 dir. Richard Wilson
Yafa, S. *Paxton Quigley's had the Course*

Three in the Cellar
AIP (US) 1970 dir. Theodore J. Flicker
Hall, A. *Late Boy Wonder, The*

Three Into Two Won't Go
UI (GB) 1969 dir. Peter Hall
Newman, A.

Three is a Family
UA (US) 1944 dir. Edward Ludwig
Ephron, P. and Ephron, H.
P

Three Lives of Thomasina, The
DISNEY (GB) 1963 dir. Don Chaffey
Ch
Gallico, P. *Thomasina*

Three Men in a Boat
BL (GB) 1956 dir. Ken Annakin
Jerome, J. K.

Three Men on a Horse
WAR (US) 1936 dir. Mervyn LeRoy
Hudson, J. C. and Abbott, G.
P

Three Musketeers, The
RKO (US) 1935 dir. Rowland V. Lee
FOX (US) 1939 dir. Allan Dwan
GB title: Singing Musketeer, The
MGM (US) 1948 dir. George Sidney
FOX-RANK (Pan) 1973
dir. Richard Lester
DISNEY (US/GB) 1993 dir. Stephen
Herek
Dumas, A.

Three on a Date
ABC (US) 1978 dir. Bill Bixby
TV(US)
Buffington, S.

Three on a Spree
UA (GB) 1961 dir. Sidney J. Furie
McCutcheon, G. B. *Brewster's Millions*

Three Sailors and a Girl
WAR (US) 1953 dir. Roy del Ruth
M
Kaufman, G. S. *Butter and Egg Man, The*
P

Three Sisters
BL (GB) 1970 dir. Laurence Olivier
Chekhov, A.
P

Threesome
CBS ENT (US) 1984 dir. Lou Antonio
TV(US)
Gold, H. *Salt*

Three Stooges, The
ICON (US) 2000 dir. James Frawley
TV(US)

Fleming, M. *From Amalgamated Morons to American Icons: The Three Stooges*

Three Strange Lives
FF (Swe) 1980
dir. Ingmar Bergman
Tengroth, B.

Three Weird Sisters, The
BN (GB) 1948 dir. Dan Birt
Armstrong, C. *Case of the Three Weird Sisters, The*

Three Wise Fools
MGM (US) 1946 dir. Edward Buzzell
Strong, A.
P

Three Wishes for Jamie
COL TV (US) 1987
dir. Robert William Young
TV(US)
O'Neal, C.

Three Worlds of Gulliver, The
COL (US/Sp) 1959 dir. Jack Sher
Swift, J. *Gulliver's Travels*

Thrill
NBC STUDIOS (US) 1996 dir. Sam Pillsbury
TV(US)
Byrne, R.

Thumb Tripping
AVCO (US) 1972 dir. Quentin Masters
Mitchell, D.

Thunderball
UA (GB) 1965 dir. Terence Young
Fleming, I.

Thunderhead, Son of Flicka
FOX (US) 1945 dir. Louis King
O'Hara, M.

Thunder in the East
PAR (US) 1951 dir. Charles Vidor
Moorehead, A. *Rage of the Vulture*

Thunder in the Night
FOX (US) 1935 dir. George Archainbaud
Fodor, L. *Woman Lies, A*
P

Thunder on the Hill
UI (US) 1951 dir. Douglas Sirk
GB title: Bonaventure
Hastings, C. *Bonaventure*
P

Thunder Rock
MGM (GB) 1942 dir. Roy Boulting
Ardrey, R.
P

Thursday's Child
ABPC (GB) 1942 dir. Rodney Ackland
Macardle, D.

Thursday's Child
BBC (GB) 1972 dir. Antony Thorpe
TVSe(GB)
Streatfeild, N.

Thursday's Child
VIACOM (US) 1983 dir. David Lowell Rich
TV(US)
Poole, V.

Tiara Tahiti
RANK (GB) 1962
dir. William T Kotcheff
Cotterell, G.

Ticket to Heaven
UA (US) 1981 dir. R. L. Thomas
Freed, J. *Moonwebs*

Tied Up
FRANCHISE (US) 2000 dir. Anthony
Hickox
Lindsay, F.

Tieta do Agreste
COL (Bra/GB) 1996 dir. Carlos Diegnes
Amado, J.

Tiger by the Tail
EROS (GB) 1955 dir. John Gilling
Mair, J. *Never Come Back*

Tiger in the Smoke
RANK (GB) 1956 dir. Roy Baker
Allingham, M.

Tiger Makes Out, The
COL (US) 1967 dir. Arthur Hiller
Schisgal, M. *Tiger, The*
P

Tigers Don't Cry
RANK (SA) 1978
dir. Peter Collinson
Burmeister, J. *Running Scared*

Tiger's Tale, A
ATLANTIC (US) 1988
dir. Peter Douglas
Hannay, A. *Love and Other Natural
Disasters*

Tiger Walks, A
DISNEY (US) 1964 dir. Norman Tokar
Niall, I.

Tiger Woods Story, The
SHOWTIME (US) 1998 dir. LeVar
Burton
TV(US)
Strege, J. *Tiger*

Tight Spot
COL (US) 1955 dir. Phil Karlson
Kantor, L. *Dead Pigeon*
P

Till Death Us Do Part
SABAN/SCHERICK 1992
dir. Yves Simoneau
TV(US)
Bugliosi, V.

Till the End of Time
RKO (US) 1946 dir. Edward Dmytryk
Busch, N. *They Dream of Home*

Till We Meet Again
PAR (US) 1944 dir. Frank Borzage
Maury, A.
P

Till We Meet Again
KRANTZ/YTV (US/GB) 1989
dir. Charles Jarrot
TVSe(GB/US)
Krantz, J.

Timberjack
REP (US) 1954 dir. Joe Kane
Cushman, D. *Ripper from Rawhide*

Time After Time
WAR (US) 1979 dir. Nicholas Meyer
Alexander, K. and Hayes, S.

Time at the Top
HALLMARK (US) 1999 dir. Jimmy
Kaufman
TV(US)
Ormandroyd, E.

Time for Killing, A
COL (US) 1967 dir. Phil Karlson
GB title: Long Ride Home, The
Wolford, N. and Wolford, S. *Southern
Blade*

Time Gentlemen, Please!
ABP (GB) 1952 dir. Lewis Gilbert
Minney, R. J. *Nothing to Lose*

425

Time Limit
UA (US) 1967 dir. Karl Malden
Denker, H. and Berkey, R.
P

Time Machine, The
MGM (US) 1960 dir. George Pal
SCHICK SUNN (US) 1978
dir. Henning Schellerup
TV(US)
Wells, H. G.

Time of Her Time, The
HARDWORK (US) 1997 dir. Francis
Delia
Mailer, N.

Time of Indifference
CONT (It/Fr) 1965
dir. Francesco Maselli
Moravia, A.

Time of Your Life, The
UA (US) 1948 dir. H. C. Potter
Saroyan, W.
P

Time Out of Mind
UN (US) 1947 dir. Robert Siodmak
Field, R.

Timepiece
SIGNBOARD HILL (US) dir. Marcus
Cole
TV(US)
Evans, R. P.

Time Regained
STUDIO CANAL+ (Fr/It/Port) 1999
dir. Raoul Ruiz
Proust, M. À la Recherche du Temps Perdu

Time Remembered
COMPASS (US) 1961
dir. George Schaefer
TV(US)
Anouilh, J.
P

Timestalkers
FRIES (US) 1987 dir. Michael Schultz
TV(US)
Brown, R. Tintype, The

Time to Dance, A
BBC (GB) 1992 dir. Melvyn Bragg
TVSe(GB)
Bragg, M.

Time to Kill, A
WAR (US) 1996 dir. Joel Schumacher
Grisham, J.

Time to Live, A
ITC (US) 1985 dir. Rick Wallace
TV(US)
Weisman, M.-L. Intensive Care

**Time to Love and a Time to Die,
A**
U-I (US) 1958 dir. Douglas Sirk
Remarque, E. M.

Time Without Pity
HARLEQUIN (GB) 1957
dir. Joseph Losey
Williams, E. Someone Waiting
P

Tin Drum, The
UA (Ger/Fr) 1979
dir. Volker Schlöndorff
Grass, G.

Tinker, Tailor, Soldier, Spy
BBC (GB) 1979 dir. John Irvin
TVSe(GB)
Le Carré, J.

Tinseltown
GOLDWYN (US) 1998 dir. Tony
Spiridakis
Spiridakis, T. and Bitterman, S. Self
Storage
P

Tinta Roja
TORNASOL (Sp) 2000 dir. Francisco J. Lombardi

Fuguet, A.

Tip on a Dead Jockey
MGM (US) 1957 dir. Richard Thorpe
GB title: Time for Action

Shaw, I.

Tirano Banderas
ION (Sp) 1993 dir. Jose Luis Garcia Sanchez

Del Valle-Inclan, R.

Tish
MGM (US) 1942 dir. S. Sylvan Simon

Rinehart, M. R. *Tish Marches On*

Titanic Town
BRIT SCREEN (Ire/GB) 1998 dir. Roger Michell

Costello, M.

Titmuss Regained
ANGLIA (GB) 1991 dir. Martyn Friend
TVSe(GB)

Mortimer, J.

Titus
OVERSEAS (US/It) 1999 dir. Julie Taymor

Shakespeare, W. *Titus Andronicus*
P

Tobacco Road
FOX (US) 1941 dir. John Ford

Caldwell, E.

Kirkland, J.
P

Toby Tyler
DISNEY (US) 1959 dir. Charles Barton
Ch

Kaler, J. O.

To Be the Best
GEMMY (US/GB) 1992 dir. Tony Wharmby
TVSe(US/GB)

Bradford, B. T.

To Catch a King
GAYLORD (US) 1984 dir. Clive Donner
TV(US)

Patterson, H.

To Catch a Thief
PAR (US) 1955 dir. Alfred Hitchcock

Dodge, D.

To Dance With the White Dog
P. CLIFFORD (US) 1993 dir. Glenn Jordan
TV(US)

Kay, T.

Today We Live
MGM (US) 1933 dir. Howard Hawks

Faulkner, W. *Turnabout*

To Die For
COL (US/GB) 1995 dir. Gus Van Sant

Maynard, J.

To Dorothy, A Son
BL (GB) 1954 dir. Muriel Box
US title: Cash on Delivery

MacDougall, R.
P

To Find a Man
COL (US) 1971 dir. Buzz Kulik

Wilson, S. J.

To Gillian on her 37th Birthday
RASTAR (US) 1996 dir. Michael Pressman

Brady, M.
P

To Have and Have Not
WAR (US) 1944 dir. Howard Hawks
Hemingway, E.

To Have and to Hold
LWT (GB) 1986 dir. John Bruce
TVSe(GB)
Moggach, D.

To Heal a Nation
ORION TV (US) 1988
dir. Michael Pressman
TV(US)
Scruggs, J. C. and Swerdlow, J. L.

To Hell and Back
UI (US) 1955 dir. Jesse Hibbs
Murphy, A.

To Kill A Cop
COL TV (US) 1978 dir. Gary Nelson
TVSe(US)
Daley, R.

To Kill a Mockingbird
UI (US) 1962 dir. Robert Mulligan
Lee, H.

Tokyo Decadence
NORTHERN (Jap) 1992 dir. Ryu
Murakami
Murakami, R. *Topaz*

To Live and Die in L.A.
MGM/UA (US) 1985
dir. William Friedkin
Petievich, G.

Tom and Huck
DISNEY (US) 1995 dir. Peter Hewitt
Ch
Twain, M. *Adventures of Tom Sawyer, The*

Tom & Viv
BRIT SCREEN (GB/US) 1994 dir. Brian
Gilbert
Hastings, M.
P

Tomb of Ligeia, The
AIP (GB) 1964 dir. Roger Corman
Poe, E. A.

Tom Brown's Schooldays
RKO (US) 1940 dir. Robert Stevenson
REN (GB) 1951 dir. Gordon Parry
BBC (GB) 1971 dir. Gareth Davies
TVSe(GB)
Hughes, T.

Tom Horn
WAR (US) 1980 dir. William Wiard
Horn, T. *Life of Tom Horn, Government
Scout & Interpreter*

Tom Jones
UA (GB) 1963 dir. Tony Richardson
BBC/A&E (GB) 1997 dir. Metin
Huseyin
TVSe(GB)
Fielding, H. *History of Tom Jones, A
Foundling, The*

Tommyknockers, The
KON/SAN (US) 1993 dir. John Power
TVSe(US)
King, S.

Tomorrow and Tomorrow
PAR (US) 1932 dir. Richard Wallace
Barry, P.
P

Tomorrow is Forever
RKO (US) 1946 dir. Irving Pichel
Bristow, G.

Tomorrow the World
UA (US) 1944 dir. Leslie Fenton

D'Usseau, A. and Gow, J. *Deep are the Roots*
P

Tom Sawyer
UA (US) 1973 dir. Don Taylor
M
UN (US) 1973 dir. James Neilson
TV(US)
STONE CANYON (US) 2000 dir. Phil Mendez, Paul Sabella
A, M

Twain, M. *Adventures of Tom Sawyer, The*

Tom's Midnight Garden
BBC (GB) 1974 dir. Myles Land
TVSe(GB)
BBC (GB) 1989 dir. Christine Secombe
TVSe(GB)
HYP (GB) 1999 dir. Willard Carroll

Pearce, P.

Tom Thumb
MGM (GB) 1958 dir. George Pal

Grimm, J. L. K. and Grimm, W. K.

Tonight at 8.30
BBC (GB) 1991 dir. Joan Collins, Paul Annett
TV(GB)

Coward, N.
P

Tonight is Ours
PAR (US) 1933 dir. Stuart Walker

Coward, N. *Queen was in the Parlour, The*
P

Tonight or Never
GOLDWYN (US) 1931
dir. Mervyn LeRoy

Hatvany, L.
P

Tonight We Sing
FOX (US) 1953 dir. Mitchell Leisen
M

Hurok, S. and Goode, R. *Impressario*

Tonka
DISNEY (US) 1958 dir. Lewis R. Foster

Appel, D. *Comanche*

Tony Draws a Horse
GFD (GB) 1950
dir. John Paddy Carstairs

Storm, L.
P

Tony Rome
FOX (US) 1967 dir. Gordon Douglas

Albert, M. H. *Miami Mayhem*

Too Far to Go
ZOETROPE (US) 1982 dir. Fielder Cook

Updike, J.

Too Good to be True
NEWLAND-RAYNOR (US) 1988
dir. Christian I. Nyby II
TV(US)

Williams, B. A. *Leave Her to Heaven*

Too Many Husbands
COL (US) 1940 dir. Wesley Ruggles
GB title: My Two Husbands

Maugham, W. S. *Home and Beauty*
P

Too Much, Too Soon
WAR (US) 1958 dir. Art Napoleon

Barrymore, D. and Frank, G.

Too Rich: The Secret Life of Doris Duke
VZ/SERTNER (US) 1999 dir. John Erman
TVSe(US)

Mansfield, S. *Richest Girl in the World, The*

Duke, P. and Thomas, J. *Too Rich*

Too Young to Go
RANK (GB) 1959 dir. Muriel Box
Shelley, E. *Pick Up Girl*
P

Topaz
UI (US) 1969 dir. Alfred Hitchcock
Uris, L.

Topaze
RKO (US) 1933
dir. Harry d'Abbabie d'Arrast
Pagnol, M.
P

Topkapi
UA (US) 1964 dir. Jules Dassin
Ambler, E. *Light of Day, The*

To Play the King
BBC (GB) 1993 dir. Paul Seed
TVSe(GB)
Dobbs, M.

Topper
MGM (US) 1937
dir. Norman Z. MacLeod
PAPAZIAN (US) 1979
dir. Charles S. Dubin
TV(US)
Smith, T. *Jovial Ghosts, The*

Top Secret Affair
WAR (US) 1957 dir. H. C. Potter
GB title: Their Secret Affair
Marquand, J. P. *Melville Goodwin, USA*

To Race the Wind
GRAUMAN (US) 1980
dir. Walter Grauman
TV(US)
Krents, H.

Torch Song
MULTIMEDIA (US) 1993 dir. Michael
Miller
TV(US)
Krantz, J.

Torch Song Trilogy
NEW LINE (US) 1988 dir. Paul Bogart
Fierstein, H.
P

Torn Apart
CASTLE HILL (US) 1990
dir. Jack Fisher
Zeldis, C. *Forbidden Love, A*

Torrents of Spring
MILLIMETER (US) 1990
dir. Jerzy Skolimowski
Turgenev, I.

Tortilla Flat
MGM (US) 1942 dir. Victor Fleming
Steinbeck, J.

To Save the Children
WESTCOM (US) 1994 dir. Steven
Hilliard Stern
TV(US)
Wixom, H. and Wixom, J. *When Angels Intervene*

To Serve Them All My Days
BBC (GB) 1980 dir. Ronald Wilson
TVSe(GB)
Delderfield, R. F.

To Sir, With Love
COL (GB) 1966 dir. James Clavell
Braithwaite, E. R.

Total Eclipse
PORTMAN (GB/Fr) 1995 dir.
Agnieszka Holland
Hampton, C.
P

Total Loss
MAJADE (Neth) 2000 dir. Dana
Nechushtan
Woudstra, K.

Total Recall
CAROLCO (US) 1990
dir. Paul Verhoeven

Dick, P. K. *We can Remember it for you Wholesale*

To the Devil, a Daughter
EMI (GB/Ger) 1976 dir. Peter Sykes

Wheatley, D.

To the Lighthouse
BBC (GB) 1983 dir. Colin Gregg
TV(GB)

Woolf, V.

Touch
INITIAL (US) 1997 dir. Paul Schrader

Leonard, E.

Touched By a Killer
WI (Can) 2001 dir. Gilbert M. Shilton
TV(Can)

Vetere, R. *Rage of the Blue Moon*
P

Touched by Love
COL (US) 1980 dir. Gus Trikonis

Canada, L. *To Elvis with Love*

Touch of Evil
UN (US) 1958 dir. Orson Welles

Masterson, W. *Badge of Evil*

Touch of Hope, A
NBC (US) 1999 dir. Craig R. Baxley
TV(US)

Kraft, D. and Kraft, R.

Touch of Larceny, A
PAR (GB) 1959 dir. Guy Hamilton

Garve, A. *Megstone Plot, The*

Touch of Love, A
BL (GB) 1969 dir. Waris Hussein
US title: Thank You All Very Much

Drabble, M. *Millstone, The*

Tough Guys Don't Dance
CANNON (US) 1987
dir. Norman Mailer

Mailer, N.

Tourist
FOX (US) 1980 dir. Jeremy Summers
TV(US)

Green, G.

Toutes les Nuits
TPS CINEMA (Fr) 2001 dir. Eugene Green

Flaubert, G. *Première Education Sentimentale, La*

Toutes Peines Confondues
FRANCE 3 (Fr) 1992 dir. Michael Deville

Coburn, A. *Sweetheart*

Tovarich
WAR (US) 1937 dir. Anatole Litvak

Deval, J.
P

Towering Inferno, The
COL-WAR (US) 1975
dir. John Gullermin, Irwin Allen

Stern, R. M. *Tower, The*

Scortia, T. N. and Robinson, R. M. *Glass Inferno, The*

Town like Alice, A
RANK (GB) 1956 dir. Jack Lee
US title: Rape of Malaya, The
AFC (Aust) 1981 dir. David Stevens
TVSe(Aust)

Shute, N.

Town Tamer
PAR (US) 1965 dir. Lesley Selander

Gruber, F.

Town Torn Apart, A
PARAGON (US) 1992 dir. Daniel Petrie
TV(US)

Kammeraad-Campbell, S. *Doc—The Story of Dennis Littky and His Fight for a Better School*

Town Without Pity
UA (US/Switz) 1961
dir. Gottfried Reinhardt

Gregor, M. *Verdict, The*

Toys in the Attic
UA (US) 1963 dir. George Roy Hill

Hellman, L. F.
P

Toy Soldiers
TRISTAR (US) 1991 dir. Daniel Petrie, Jr.

Kennedy, W. P.

Track of the Cat
WAR (US) 1954 dir. William A. Wellman

Van Tilburg Clark, W.

Tracks of Glory: The Major Taylor Story
BARRON (Aust) 1992 dir. Marcus Cole
TVSe(Aust)

Fitzpatrick, J. *Major Taylor Down Under*

Trader Horn
MGM (US) 1931 dir. W. S. Van Dyke
MGM (US) 1973 dir. Reza Badiyi

Lewis, E.

Trading Mom
FOX (US) 1994 dir. Tia Brelis

Brelis, N. *Mummy Market, The*

Trail of the Lonesome Pine, The
PAR (US) 1936 dir. Henry Hathaway

Fox, Jr., J.

Trainspotting
CHANNEL 4 FILMS (GB) 1996 dir. Danny Boyle

Welsh, I.

Traitor's Gate
COL (GB) 1965 dir. Freddie Francis

Wallace, E.

Transplant
TIME-LIFE (US) 1979
dir. William A. Graham
TV(US)

Dossick, P.

Trapeze
UA (US) 1956 dir. Carol Reed

Catto, M. *Killing Frost, The*

Trapped in Silence
READER'S DIG (US) 1986
dir. Michael Tuchner
TV(US)

Hayden, T. *Murphy's Boy*

Traps
FILMOPOLIS (Aust) 1994 dir. Pauline Chan

Grenville, K. *Dreamhouse*

Traveller in Time, A
BBC (GB) 1978 dir. Dorothea Brooking
TVSe(GB)

Uttley, A.

Travellers by Night
TVS (GB) 1985
Ch, TVSe(GB)

Alcock, V.

Traveller's Joy
GFD (GB) 1949 dir. Ralph Thomas

Macrae, A.
P

Travelling North
VIEW PIC (Aust) 1986 dir. Carl Schultz
Williamson, D.
P

Travels with my Aunt
MGM (US) 1972 dir. George Cukor
Greene, G.

Travis McGee
HAJENO (US) 1983
dir. Andrew V. McLaglen
TV(US)
MacDonald, J. D. *Empty Copper Sea, The*

Treacherous Beauties
ALLIANCE (Can) 1994 dir. Charles
Jarrott
TV(Can)
Emerson, C.

Tread Softly Stranger
ALDERDALE (GB) 1958
dir. Gordon Parry
Popplewell, J.
P

Treasure Hunt
BL (GB) 1952 dir. John Paddy Carstairs
Farrell, M. J. and Perry, J.
P

Treasure Island
MGM (US) 1934 dir. Victor Fleming
DISNEY (GB) 1950 dir. Byron Haskin
MGM-EMI (GB/Fr/Ger) 1971
dir. John Hough
BBC (GB) 1977 dir. Michael E. Briant
TVSe(GB)
AGAMEMNON (US) 1990
dir. Fraser Heston
TV(US)
Stevenson, R. L.

Treasure of Lost Canyon, The
UI (US) 1952 dir. Ted Tetzlaff
Stevenson, R. L. *Treasure of Franchard*

Treasure of Matecumbe
DISNEY (US) 1976
dir. Vincent McEveety
Taylor, R. L. *Journey to Matecumbe, A*

Treasure of the Golden Condor
FOX (US) 1953 dir. Delmer Daves
Marshall, E. *Jewel of Mahabar*

Treasure of the Sierra Madre, The
WAR (US) 1948 dir. John Huston
Traven, B.

Tree Grows in Brooklyn, A
FOX (US) 1945 dir. Elia Kazan
FOX (US) 1974 dir. Joseph Hardy
TV(US)
Smith, B.

Tree of Hands
GRANADA (GB) 1988 dir. Giles Foster
Rendell, R.

Trent's Last Case
BL (GB) 1952 dir. Herbert Wilcox
Bentley, E. C.

Trenvia a la Malvarrosa
LOLAFILMS (Sp) 1996 dir. Jose Luis
Garcia Sanchez
Vincent, M.

Trespasser, The
C. GREGG (GB) 1981 dir. Colin Gregg
Lawrence, D. H.

Trial
MGM (US) 1955 dir. Mark Robson
Mankiewicz, D. M.

Trial, The
BL (Fr/It/Ger) 1963 dir. Orson Welles
BBC (GB) 1993 dir. David Hugh Jones
Kafka, F.

Trial: The Price of Passion
TRISTAR TV (US) 1992 dir. Paul Wendkos
TVSe(US)
Irving, C. *Trial*

Trial of Vivienne Ware, The
FOX (US) 1932 dir. William K. Howard
Ellis, K. M.

Trial on the Road/Checkpoint
LENFILM (USSR) 1971
dir. Alexei German
German, Y.

Trials of Oscar Wilde, The
EROS (GB) 1960 dir. Ken Hughes
US title: Man with the Green Carnation, The
Hyde, H. M.

Tribute
FOX (Can) 1980 dir. Bob Clark
Slade, B.
P

Trick of the Eye
SIGNBOARD HILL (US) 1994 dir. Ed Kaplan
TV(US)
Hitchcock, J. S.

Trio
GFD (GB) 1950
dir. Ken Annakin, Harold French
Maugham, W. S. *Verge, The*; *Mr Knowall*; *Sanitorium*

Triple Cross
AA (GB) 1967 dir. Terence Young
Owen, F. *Eddie Chapman Story, The*

Triple Echo
HEMDALE (GB) 1972
dir. Michael Apted
Bates, H. E.

Tripods, The
BBC (GB/US/Aust) 1981
dir. Graham Theakston, Christopher Barry
TVSe(GB/US/Aust)
Christopher, J. *White Mountains, The*

Trip to Bountiful, The
ISLAND (US) 1985 dir. Peter Masterson
Foote, H.
P

Triumph of Love, The
PAR (GB/It) 2001 dir. Clare Peploe
Marivaux
P

Triumph of Sherlock Holmes, The
TWICKENHAM (GB) 1935
dir. Leslie Hiscott
Doyle, Sir A. C. *Valley of Fear, The*

Trojan Women, The
CINERAMA (US) 1971
dir. Michael Cacoyannis
Euripides
P

Tromeo and Juliet
TROMA (US) 1996 dir. Lloyd Kaufman
Shakespeare, W. *Romeo and Juliet*
P

Tropic
ATV (GB) 1979 dir. Matthew Robinson
TVSe(GB)
Thomas, L. *Tropic of Ruislip, The*

Tropic of Cancer
PAR (US) 1970 dir. Joseph Strick
Miller, H.

Tropic Zone
PAR (US) 1952 dir. Lewis R. Foster
Gill, T. *Gentlemen of the Jungle*

Trottie True
TC (GB) 1949 dir. Brian Desmond Hurst
US title: Gay Lady, The
Brahms, C. and Simon, S. J.

Trouble for Two
MGM (US) 1936 dir. J. Walter Rubin
GB title: Suicide Club, The
Stevenson, R. L. *Suicide Club, The*

Trouble in Paradise
PAR (US) 1932 dir. Ernst Lubitsch
Aladar, L. *Honest Finder, The*

Trouble in the Glen
REP (GB) 1954 dir. Herbert Wilcox
Walsh, M.

Troubles
LWT (GB) 1988
dir. Christopher Morahan
TVSe(GB)
Farrell, J. G.

Trouble with Angels, The
COL (US) 1966 dir. Ida Lupino
Trahey, J. *Life with Mother Superior*

Trouble With Girls, The
MGM (US) 1969 dir. Peter Tewkesbury
Keene, D. and Babcock, D. *Chautauqua*

Trouble with Harry, The
PAR (US) 1955 dir. Alfred Hitchcock
Story, J. T.

Trouble With Spies, The
HBO (US) 1987 dir. Burt Kennedy
Lovell, M. *Apple Pie in the Sky*

Trout, The
TRIUMPH (Fr) 1982 dir. Joseph Losey
Vailland, R. *Truite, La*

Truce, The
DAZU (It/Fr/Ger) 1997 dir. Francesco
Rosi
Levi, P.

True as a Turtle
RANK (GB) 1957 dir. Wendy Toye
Coates, J.

True Blue
CHANNEL 4 FILMS (GB) 1996 dir.
Ferdinand Fairfax
Topolski, D. and Robinson, P.

True Confession
PAR (US) 1937 dir. Wesley Ruggles
Verneuil, L. and Berr, G. *Mon Crime*
P

True Confessions
UA (US) 1981 dir. Ulu Grosbard
Dunne, J. G.

True Crime
ZANUCK (US) 1999 dir. Clint
Eastwood
Klavan, A.

True Grit
PAR (US) 1969 dir. Henry Hathaway
Portis, C.

True Women
HALLMARK (US) 1997 dir. Karen
Arthur
TVSe(US)
Windle, J. W.

Truman
SPRING CREEK (US) 1995 dir. Frank
Pierson
TV(US)
McCullough, D.

Truth About Spring, The
UI (GB) 1964 dir. Richard Thorpe
deVere Stacpoole, H. D.

435

Try and Get Me
UA (US) 1951 dir. Cyril Endfield
GB title: Sound of Fury, The
Pagano, J. *Condemned, The*

Tu Que Harias Por Amor
FANDANGO (Sp/It) 2000 dir. Carlos
Saura Medrano
Casariego, M. *Chico que imitaba a
Roberto Carlos, El*

Tuesdays With Morrie
HARPO (US) 1999 dir. Mick Jackson
TV(US)
Albom, M.

Tumult
ATHENA (Den) 1970
dir. Hans Abramson
Allen, J. *Nu*

Tune in Tomorrow …
CINECOM (US) 1990 dir. Jon Amiel
Llosa, M. V. *Aunt Julia and the
Scriptwriter*

Tunes of Glory
UA (GB) 1960 dir. Ronald Neame
Kennaway, J.

Tunnel, The
GAU (GB) 1935 dir. Maurice Elvey
US title: Transatlantic Tunnel
Kellerman, B.

Tunnel of Love, The
MGM (US) 1958 dir. Gene Kelly
De Vries, P.

Turkish Passion
LOLAFILMS (Sp) 1994 dir. Vicente
Aranda
Gala, A.

Turnabout
UA (US) 1940 dir. Hal Roach
Smith, T.

Turn Back the Clock
NBC (US) 1989 dir. Larry Elikann
TV(US)
O'Farrell, W.

Turning, The
PHAEDRA (US) 1992 dir. L. A. Puopolo
Ceraso, C. *Home Fires Burning*
P

**Turning Point of Jim Malloy,
The**
COL TV (US) 1975 dir. Frank D. Gilroy
TV(US)
O'Hara, J. *Doctor's Son, The*

Turn of the Screw
CURTIS (US) 1974 dir. Dan Curtis
TVSe(US)
UNITED (GB) 1999 dir. Ben Bolt
TV(GB)
James, H.

Turn of the Tide
BN (GB) 1935 dir. Norman Walker
Walmsley, L. *Three Fevers*

Turn the Key Softly
GFD (GB) 1953 dir. Jack Lee
Brophy, J.

Turtle Beach
VILLAGE ROADSHOW (Aust) 1992
dir. Stephen Wallace
D'Alpuget, B.

Turtle Diary
RANK (GB) 1985 dir. John Irvin
Hoban, R.

Tuttles of Tahiti, The
RKO (US) 1942 dir. Charles Vidor
Nordhoff, C. B. and Hall, J. N. *No More
Gas*

TV Dante, A: The Inferno Cantos
CHANNEL 4 (GB) 1990
dir. Tom Phillips, Peter Greenaway
TV(GB)

Dante Alighieri *Divina Commedia, La*

Twelfth Night
MILBERG (US) 1957 dir. David Greene
TV(US)
RENAISSANCE (GB) 1996 dir. Trevor Nunn

Shakespeare, W.
P

Twelve Angry Men
UA (US) 1957 dir. Sidney Lumet

Rose, R.
P

Twelve Chairs, The
UMC (US) 1970 dir. Mel Brooks

Ilf, E. and Petrov, E.
P

Twelve O'Clock High
FOX (US) 1949 dir. Henry King

Lay, B. and Bartlett, S.

Twentieth Century
COL (US) 1934 dir. Howard Hawks

Millholland, C. B. *Napoleon of Broadway*
P

Twenty-Four Hours of a Woman's Life
ABPC (GB) 1952 dir. Victor Saville
US title: Affair in Monte Carlo

Zweig, S.

29 Acacia Avenue
COL (GB) 1945 dir. Henry Cass
US title: Facts of Love, The

Constanduros, M. and Constanduros, D. *Acacia Avenue*
P

Twenty-One Days
LF (GB) 1937 dir. Basil Dean

Galsworthy, J. *First and the Last, The*
P

21 Hours at Munich
FILMWAYS (US) 1976
dir. William A. Graham
TV(US)

Groussard, S. *Blood of Israel, The*

Twenty Plus Two
AA (US) 1962 dir. Joseph M. Newman

Gruber, F.

27th Day
COL (US) 1957 dir. William Asher

Mantley, J. *Joseph*

20,000 Leagues Under the Sea
DISNEY (US) 1954
dir. Richard Fleischer
HALLMARK (US) 1997 dir. Michael Anderson
TV(US)
VILLAGE ROADSHOW (US) dir. Rod Hardy
TVSe(US)

Verne, J.

20,000 Years in Sing Sing
WAR (US) 1932 dir. Michael Curtiz

Lawes, L. E.

Twenty-Three Paces to Baker Street
FOX (US) 1956 dir. Henry Hathaway

MacDonald, P.

Twice Round the Daffodils
AA (GB) 1962 dir. Gerald Thomas

Cargill, P. and Beale, J. *Ring for Catty*
P

Twice Shy
DLT (US) 1989 dir. Deirdre Friel
TV(US)

Francis, D.

Twilight for the Gods
UN (US) 1958 dir. Joseph Pevney

Gann, E. K.

Twilight: Los Angeles
OFFLINE (US) 2000 dir. Marc Levin

Smith, A. D.
P

Twilight of Honor
MGM (US) 1963 dir. Boris Sagal
GB title: Charge is Murder, The

Dewlen, A.

Twilight of the Golds, The
HALLMARK (US) 1996 dir. Ross Marks
TV(US)

Tolins, J.
P

Twilight's Last Gleaming
HEMDALE (US/Ger) 1977
dir. Robert Aldrich

Wager, W. *Viper Three*

Twinkle, Twinkle, 'Killer' Kane
UFD (US) 1980 dir. William Peter Blatty

Blatty, W. P.

Twisted Obsession
IVE (US) 1990 dir. Fernando Trueba

Frank, C. *Dream of the Mad Monkey, The*

Twister
VESTRON (US) 1990
dir. Michael Almereyda

Robison, M. *Oh!*

Twist of Fate
COL TV/HTV (US/GB) 1989
dir. Ian Sharp
TVSe(GB/US)

Fish, R. L. *Pursuit*

Twist of Sand, A
UA (GB) 1968 dir. Don Chaffey

Jenkins, G.

Two Against the World
WAR (US) 1936 dir. William McGann
GB title: Case of Mrs. Pembroke, The

Weitzenkorn, L. *Five-Star Final*
P

Two Came Back
VZ/SERTNER (US) 1997 dir. Dick Lowry
TV(US)

Scaling-Kiley, D. and Noona, M.
Albatross

Two Crimes
CUEVANO (Mex) 1994 dir. Roberto Sneider

Ibarguangoitia, J.

Two Deaths
BRIT SCREEN (GB) 1995 dir. Nicolas Roeg

Dubyns, S. *Two Deaths of Senora Puccini, The*

Two-Faced Woman
MGM (US) 1941 dir. George Cuker

Fulda, L.
P

Two Faces of Dr. Jekyll, The
HAMMER (GB) 1960
dir. Terence Fisher
US title: House of Fright

Stevenson, R. L. *Dr. Jekyll and Mr. Hyde*

Two for the Seesaw
UA (US) 1962 dir. Robert Wise

Gibson, W.
P

Two Gentlemen Sharing
PAR (GB) 1969 dir. Ted Kotcheff

Leslie, D. S.

Two in the Dark
RKO (US) 1936 dir. Ben Stoloff

Burgess, G.

Two Kinds of Love
CBS (US) 1983 dir. Jack Bender
TV(US)
Mann, P. *There are Two Kinds of Terrible*

Two Kinds of Women
PAR (US) 1932 dir. William C. de Mille
Sherwood, R. E. *This is New York*
P

Two Left Feet
BL (GB) 1963 dir. Roy Baker
Leslie, D. S. *In My Solitude*

Two-Letter Alibi
BL (GB) 1962 dir. Robert Lynn
Garve, A. *Death and the Sky Above*

Two Loves
MGM (US) 1961 dir. Charles Walters
GB title: Spinster, The
Ashton-Warner, S. *Spinster*

Two Minute Warning
UN (US) 1976 dir. Larry Peerce
La Fontaine, G.

Two Mrs. Carrolls, The
WAR (US) 1947 dir. Peter Godfrey
Vale, M.
P

Two Mrs. Grenvilles, The
LORIMAR (US) 1989 dir. John Erman
TVSe(US)
Dunne, D.

Two Much
POLYGRAM (Sp/US) 1995 dir.
Fernando Trueba
Westlake, D. E.

Two Rode Together
COL (US) 1961 dir. John Ford
Cooke, W. E.

Two Seconds
WAR (US) 1932 dir. Mervyn LeRoy
Lester, E.

Two Small Bodies
ZETA FILM (Ger) 1993 dir. Beth B.
Bell, N.
P

2001, A Space Odyssey
MGM (GB) 1968 dir. Stanley Kubrick
Clarke, A. C. *Sentinel, The*

2010
MGM (US) 1984 dir. Peter Hyams
Clarke, A. C.

Two to Tango
CONCORDE (US/Arg) 1989
dir. Hector Olivera
Feinman, J. P. *Last Days of the Victim*

Two Weeks in Another Town
MGM (US) 1962 dir. Vincente Minnelli
Shaw, I.

Two Women
CHAMPION (It/Fr) 1960
dir. Vittorio de Sica
BBC (GB)1973 dir. Gareth Davies
TVSe(GB)
Moravia, A.

Two Worlds of Jennie Logan, The
FRIES (US) 1979 dir. Frank DeFelitta
TV(US)
Williams, D. *Second Sight*

Two Years Before the Mast
PAR (US) 1946 dir. John Farrow
Dana, R. H.

U

UFO Incident, The
UN TV (US) 1975 dir. Richard Colla
TV(US)
Fuller, J. G. *Interrupted Journey, The*

Ugly American, The
UI (US) 1962 dir. George England
Lederer, W. J. and Burdick, E. L.

Ugly Dachshund, The
DISNEY (US) 1965 dir. Norman Tokar
Stern, G. B.

Ultimate Imposter, The
UN TV (US) 1979 dir. Paul Stanley
TV(US)
Zacha, Sr., W. T. *Capricorn Man, The*

Ulysses
ARCHWAY (It) 1954
dir. Mario Camerini
Homer *Odyssey, The*

Ulysses
BL (GB) 1967 dir. Joseph Strick
Joyce, J.

Unbearable Lightness of Being, The
ORION (US) 1988 dir. Philip Kaufman
Kundera, M.

Unchained
WAR (US) 1955 dir. Hall Bartlett
Scudder, K. J. *Prisoners are People*

Uncle Silas
TC (GB) 1947 dir. Charles Frank
US title: Inheritance, The
Le Fanu, S.

Uncle Tom's Cabin
TAFT (US) 1989 dir. Stan Lathan
TV(US)
Stowe, H. B.

Unconquered
PAR (US) 1947 dir. Cecil B. De Mille
Swanson, N. H.

Uncovered
CIBY 2000 (Sp/GB) 1994 dir. Jim
McBride
Perez-Reverte, A. *Table de Flandes, La*

Underbelly
BBC (GB) 1992 dir. Nicholas Renton
TVSe(GB)
Kippax, F.

Under Capricorn
WAR (GB) 1949 dir. Alfred Hitchcock
S. AUST (Aust) 1983
dir. Rod Hardy
Simpson, H.

Undercover with the KKK
COL TV (US) 1979 dir. Barry Shear
TV(US)
Rowe, Jr., G. T. *My Years with the KKK*

Underground Man, The
PAR TV (US) 1974 dir. Paul Wendkos
TV(US)
Macdonald, R.

Under Heaven
BANNER ENT (US) 1998 dir. Meg
Richman
James, H. *Wings of the Dove, The*

Under Milk Wood
RANK (GB) 1971 dir. Andrew Sinclair
Thomas, D.
P

Under My Skin
FOX (US) 1950 dir. Jean Negulesco
Hemingway, E. *My Old Man*

Underneath
POPULIST (US) 1995 dir. Steven
Soderbergh
Tracy, D. *Criss Cross*

Under New Management
BUTCHER (GB) 1946
dir. John E. Blakeley
Jacob, N.

Under Satan's Sun
ERATO (Fr) 1987 dir. Maurice Pialat
Bernanos, G.

Under Suspicion
LIONS GATE (US/Fr) 2000 dir. Stephen
Hopkins
Wainwright, J. *Brainwash*

Under the Domim Tree
HSA (Israel) 1995 dir. Eli Cohen
Almagor, G. *Etz Hadomim Tafus*

Undertow
CAPSTONE (US) 1991
dir. Thomas Mazziotti
Bell, N. *Raw Youth*
P

Under the Red Robe
FOX (GB) 1937 dir. Victor Sjostrom
Weyman, S.

Under the Volcano
UN (US) 1984 dir. John Huston
Lowry, M.

Under Two Flags
FOX (US) 1936 dir. Frank Lloyd
Ouida

Under World
BBC/A&E (GB) 1998 dir. Edward
Bennett
TV(GB)
Hill, R.

Undue Influence
HALLMARK (US) 1996 dir. Bruce
Pittman
TVSe(US)
Martini, S.

Undying Monster, The
FOX (US) 1943 dir. John Brahm
GB title: Hammond Mystery, The
Kerrvish, J. D.

Uneasy Terms
BN (GB) 1948 dir. Vernon Sewell
Cheyney, P.

Unexpected Mrs. Pollifax, The
WORLD 2000 (US) 1999 dir. Anthony
Shaw
TV(US)
Gilman, D. *Palm for Mrs. Pollifax, A*

Unexpected Uncle
RKO (US) 1941 dir. Peter Godfrey
Hatch, E.

Unfaithful, The
WAR (US) 1947 dir. Vincent Sherman
Maugham, W. S. *Letter, The*
P

Unfinished Piece for Player Piano, An
MOSFILM (USSR) 1977
dir. Nikita Mikhalkov
Chekhov, A. *Platonov*
P

Unforgiven, The
UA (US) 1960 dir. John Huston
LeMay, A. *Siege at Dancing Bird, The*

Unguarded Hour, The
MGM (US) 1936 dir. Sam Wood
Fodor, L.
P

Unholy Matrimony
TAFT (US) 1988 dir. Jerrold Freedman
TV(US)
Dillman, J.

Uninvited
MEDIASET (US/It) 1999 dir. Carlo
Gabriel Nero
Berman, J. G. *Uninvited: He Followed a Dark Path to Obsession*

Uninvited, The
PAR (US) 1944 dir. Lewis Allen
Macardle, D. *Uneasy Freehold*

Union Station
PAR (US) 1950 dir. Rudolph Maté
Walsh, T. *Nightmare in Manhattan*

Unkindness of Ravens, An
TVS (GB) 1988 dir. John Gorrie
TV(GB)
Rendell, R.

Unnatural Causes
ANGLIA (GB) 1994 dir. John Davies
TV(GB)
James, P. D.

Unofficial Rose, An
BBC (GB) 1974 dir. Basil Coleman
TVSe(GB)
Murdoch, I.

Unpleasantness at the Bellona Club, The
BBC (GB) 1973 dir. Ronald Wilson
TVSe(GB)
Sayers, D. L.

Unseen, The
PAR (US) 1945 dir. Lewis Allen
White, E. L. *Her Heart in Her Throat*

Unsinkable Molly Brown, The
MGM (US) 1964 dir. Charles Walters
M
Morris, R. and Willson, M.
P

Unspeakable Acts
LAN (US) 1990 dir. Linda Otto
TV(US)
Hollingsworth, J.

Unstrung Heroes
HOLLYWOOD (US) 1995 dir. Diane
Keaton
Lidz, F.

Unsuitable Job for a Woman, An
BOYD (GB) 1982 dir. Christopher Petit
James, P. D.

Unsuspected, The
WAR (US) 1947 dir. Michael Curtiz
Armstrong, C.

Untamed
PAR (US) 1940 dir. George Archainbaud
Lewis, S. *Mantrap*

Untamed
FOX (US) 1955 dir. Henry King
Moray, H.

Untamed Love
HEARST (US) 1994 dir. Paul Aaron
TV(US)
Hayden T. *One Child*

Until They Sail
MGM (US) 1957 dir. Robert Wise
Michener, J. A. *Return to Paradise*

Up At the Villa
UN (US/GB) 2000 dir. Philip Haas
Maugham, W. S.

Up From the Beach
FOX (US) 1965 dir. Robert Parrish
Barr, G. *Epitaph for an Enemy*

Up 'n' Under
TOUCHDOWN (GB) 1998 dir. John Godber
Godber, J.
P

Up Periscope
WAR (US) 1959 dir. Gordon Douglas
White, R.

Upstairs and Downstairs
RANK (GB) 1959 dir. Ralph Thomas
Thorn, R. S.

Up the Down Staircase
WAR (US) 1967 dir. Robert Mulligan
Kaufman, B.

Up the Garden Path
GRANADA (GB) 1990 dir. David Askey
TVSe(GB)
Limb, S.

Up the Junction
PAR (GB) 1967 dir. Peter Collinson
Dunn, N.

Up the Sandbox
WAR (US) 1973 dir. Irwin Kershner
Roiphe, A. R.

Urbania
COMMOTION (US) 1999 dir. Jon Shear
Reitz, D. *Urban Folk Tales*
P

Used People
LARGO (US) 1992 dir. Beeban Kidron
Graff, T. *Grandmother Plays, The*
P

Users, The
SPELLING (US) 1978
dir. Joseph Hardy
TV(US)
Haber, J.

U-Turn
PHOENIX PICT (US) 1997 dir. Oliver Stone
Ridley, J.

Utz
BBC (GB/It/Ger) 1992
dir. George Sluizer
Chatwin, B.

Vacation in Hell
METROPOLIS (It) 1997 dir. Tonina
Valerii

Paladini, F. *Bangkwang*

Vagabond King, The
PAR (US) 1956 dir. Michael Curtiz
M

McCarthy, J. H.

Friml, R., Post, W. H. and Hooker, B.
P

Valachi Papers, The
CIN INT (Fr/It) 1972
dir. Terence Young

Maas, P.

Valdez is Coming
UA (US) 1971 dir. Edwin Sherin

Leonard, E.

Valentina
OFELIA (Sp) 1983
dir. Antonio José Betancor

Sender, R. J. *Days of Dawn*

Valentine
WAR (US) 2001 dir. Jamie Blanks

Savage, T.

Valentino
UA (GB) 1977 dir. Ken Russell

Steiger, B. and Mank, C.

Valentino Returns
VIDMARK/SKOURAS (US) 1989
dir. Paul Hoffman

Gardner, L. *Christ has Returned to Earth
and Preaches Here Nightly*

Valiant is the Word for Carrie
RKO (US) 1936 dir. Wesley Ruggles

Benefield, B.

Valley of Abraham, The
GEMINI (Fr/Port) 1993 dir. Manoel de
Oliveira

Bessa-Luis, A. *Vale Abraao*

Valley of Decision, The
MGM (US) 1945 dir. Tay Garnett

Davenport, M.

Valley of Song
ABPC (GB) 1953 dir. Gilbert Gunn

Morgan, C. *Choir Practice*
P

Valley of the Dolls
FOX (US) 1967 dir. Mark Robson

Susann, J.

Valley of the Dolls 1981
FOX TV (US) 1981 dir. Walter Grauman
TVSe(US)

Susann, J. *Valley of the Dolls*

Valley of the Giants
WAR (US) 1938 dir. William Keighley

Kyne, P. B.

Valley of the Sun
RKO (US) 1942 dir. George Marshall
Kelland, C. B.

Valmont
ORION (GB) 1989 dir. Milos Forman
de Laclos, P. *Liaisons dangéreuses, Les*

Value for Money
RANK (GB) 1955 dir. Ken Annakin
Boothroyd, D.

Vampire Hunter D: Bloodlust
FILMLINK (Jap/US) 2000 dir. Yoshiaki Kawajiri
Kikuchi, H. *D—Demon Deathchase*

Vampire$
LARGO (US) 1998 dir. John Carpenter
Steakley, J.

Van, The
BBC (GB) 1996 dir. Stephen Frears
Doyle, R.

Vanessa, Her Love Story
MGM (US) 1935 dir. William K. Howard
Walpole, H.

Vanished
UN (US) 1971 dir. Buzz Kulik
TVSe(US)
Knebel, F.

Vanished
NBC (US) 1995 dir. George Kaczender
TV(US)
Steel, D.

Vanishing, The
INGRID (Swe) 1990 dir. George Sluizer
FOX (US) 1993 dir. George Sluizer
Krabbe, T. *Golden Egg, The*

Vanishing Act
LEVINSON-LINK (US) 1986
dir. David Greene
TV(US)
Thomas, R. *Piège pour un homme seul*
P

Vanishing American, The
PAR (US) 1925 dir. George B. Seitz
Grey, Z.

Vanishing Virginian, The
MGM (US) 1941 dir. Frank Borzage
Williams, Mrs. R. *Father was a Handful*

Vanity Dies Hard
ITV (GB) 1995 dir. Alan Grint
TVSe(GB)
Rendell, R.

Vanity Fair
HOL (US) 1932 dir. Chester M. Franklin
BBC (GB) 1967 dir. David Giles
TVSe(GB)
BBC (GB) 1987 dir. Diarmuid Lawrence, Michael Owen Morris
TVSe(GB)
BBC/A&E (GB) 1999 dir. Marc Munden
TVSe(GB)
Thackeray, W. M.

Vanquished, The
PAR (US) 1953 dir. Edward Ludwig
Brown, K.

Vanya on 42nd Street
CHANNEL 4 FILMS (GB/US) 1994 dir. Louis Malle
Chekhov, A. *Uncle Vanya*
P

Vassa
IFEX (USSR) 1983 dir. Gleb Panfilov
Gorky, M.
P

Veille Canaille
FRANCE 3 (Fr) 1992 dir. Gerard Jourd'hui

Brown, F. *His Name Was Death*

Velocity of Gary, The
CINEVILLE (US) 1999 dir. Dan Ireland

Still, J.
P

Vendetta
RKO (US) 1950 dir. Mel Ferrer

Merimée, P. *Columba*

Vendetta
RAI (Swe) 1995 dir. Mikael Hafstrom

Guillou, J.

Vendetta
HBO (US) 1999 dir. Nicholas Meyer
TV(US)

Gambino, R.

Vendetta: Secrets of a Mafia Bride
TRIBUNE (US) 1991
dir. Stuart Margolin
TVSe(US)

Modignani, S. C. *Donna D'Onore*

Vendetta II: The New Mafia
FILMLINE (US) 1993 dir. Ralph L. Thomas
TVSe(US)

Modignani, S. C. *Woman of Honor*

Venetian Affair, The
MGM (US) 1966 dir. Jerry Thorpe

MacInnes, H.

Venetian Bird
GFD (GB) 1952 dir. Ralph Thomas
US title: Assassin, The

Canning, V.

Vengeance
BL (GB/Ger) 1962 dir. Freddie Francis

Siodmak, C. *Donovan's Brain*

Vengeance is Mine
KINO (Jap) 1979 dir. Shohei Imamura

Saki, R.

Vengeance Valley
MGM (US) 1951 dir. Richard Thorpe

Short, L.

Venom
PAR (GB) 1982 dir. Piers Haggard

Scholefield, A.

Venus in Furs
COMM (GB/It/Ger) 1970
dir. Jess Franco
K FILMS (Neth) 1994 dir. Victor Nieuwenhuijs, Maarte Seyferth

von Sacher-Masoch, L. *Venus im Pelz*

Verdict, The
WAR (US) 1946 dir. Don Siegel

Zangwill, I. *Big Bow Mystery, The*

Verdict
CCC (Fr/It) 1974 dir. André Cayatte

Coupon, H.

Verdict, The
FOX (US) 1982 dir. Sidney Lumet

Reed, B.

Veronico Cruz
BFI (Arg/GB) 1988 dir. Miguel Pereira

Ramos, F.

Vertigo
PAR (US) 1958 dir. Alfred Hitchcock

Boileau, P. and Narcejac, T. *Living and the Dead, The*

Very British Coup, A
SKREBA (GB) 1988 dir. Mick Jackson
TVSe(GB)
Mullin, C.

Very Missing Person, A
UN TV (US) 1972 dir. Russ Mayberry
TV(US)
Palmer, S. and Flora, F. *Hildegarde Withers Makes the Scene*

Very Moral Night, A
HUNG (Hun) 1977 dir. Karoly Makk
Hunyady, S. *House with the Red Light, The*

Vessel of Wrath
PAR (GB) 1938 dir. Erich Pommer
US title: Beachcomber, The
Maugham, W. S.

Vice Squad
UA (US) 1953 dir. Arnold Laven
GB title: Girl in Room 17, The
White, L. T. *Harness Bull*

Vice Versa
TC (GB) 1948 dir. Peter Ustinov
Anstey, F.

Vicki
FOX (US) 1953 dir. Harry Horner
Fisher, S. *I Wake Up Screaming*

Victoria Regina
COMPASS (US) 1961
dir. George Schaefer
TV(US)
Housman, L.
P

Victoria the Great
RKO (GB) 1937 dir. Herbert Wilcox
Housman, L. *Victoria Regina*
P

Victors, The
BL (GB) 1963 dir. Carl Foreman
Baron, A. *Human Kind, The*

Victor's Big Score
MUSHIKUKI (US) 1992 dir. Brian Anthony
Hill, J.

Victory
PAR (US) 1940 dir. John Cromwell
BRIT SCREEN (GB/Fr) 1997 dir. Mark Peploe
Conrad, J.

Vie de Bohème, La
FILMS A2 (Fr) 1992 dir. Aki Kaurismaki
Murger, H. *Scènes de la Vie de Bohème*

Vie Fantome, La
MAXFILMS (Can) 1992 dir. Jacques Leduc
Sallenave, D.

View from Pompey's Head, The
FOX (US) 1955 dir. Philip Donne
GB title: Secret Interlude
Basso, H.

View from the Bridge, A
TRANS (Fr) 1961 dir. Sidney Lumet
Miller, A.
P

Vig
LIONS GATE (US) 1998 dir. Graham Theakston
TV(US)
Hapenny, P.
P

Vigil in the Night
RKO (US) 1940 dir. George Stevens
Cronin, A. J.

Vigo—Passion For Life
NITRATE (US) 1998 dir. Julien Temple
Ward, C. *Love's a Revolution*
P
Salles Gomes, P. E. *Jean Vigo*

Vikings, The
UA (US) 1958 dir. Richard Fleischer
Marshall, E. *Viking, The*

Village of the Damned
MGM (GB) 1960 dir. Wolf Rilla
UN (US) 1995 dir. John Carpenter
Wyndham, J. *Midwich Cuckoos, The*

Village Tale, A
RKO (US) 1935 dir. John Cromwell
Strong, P.

Villain
EMI (GB) 1971 dir. Michael Tuchner
Barlow, J. *Burden of Proof, The*

Villette
BBC (GB) 1970 dir. Moira Armstrong
TVSe(GB)
Bronte, C.

Vintage, The
MGM (US) 1957 dir. Jeffrey Hayden
Keir, U.

Violators, The
RKO (US) 1957 dir. John Newland
Beckhardt, I. and Brown, W.

Violence at Noon
KINO (Jap) 1966 dir. Nagisa Oshima
Takeoa, T.

Violent Enemy, The
MONARCH (GB) 1969 dir. Don Sharp
Marlowe, H. *Candle for the Dead, A*

Violent Men, The
COL (US) 1955 dir. Rudolph Maté
GB title: Rough Company
Hamilton, D.

Violent Saturday
FOX (US) 1955 dir. Richard Fleischer
Heath, W. L.

Virgin and the Gypsy, The
LONDON SCR (GB) 1970
dir. Christopher Miles
Lawrence, D. H.

Virginian, The
PAR (US) 1929 dir. Victor Fleming
PAR (US) 1946 dir. Stuart Gilmore
WAR (US) 2000 dir. Bill Pullman
TV(US)
Wister, O.

Virgin Island
BL (GB) 1958 dir. Pat Jackson
White, R. *Our Virgin Island*

Virgin Soldiers, The
COL (GB) 1969 dir. John Dexter
Thomas, L.

Virgin Suicides, The
AM ZOETROPE (US) 1999 dir. Sofia
Coppola
Eugenides, J.

Virgin Witch
TIGON (GB) 1970 dir. Ray Austin
Vogel, K.

Virtual Obsession
VZ/SERTNER (US) 1998 dir. Mick
Garris
TV(US)
James. P. *Host*

Virtual Sexuality
TRISTAR (GB) 1999 dir. Nick Hurran
Rayban, C.

Virtuoso
BBC (GB) 1988 dir. Tony Smith
TV(GB)
Ogden, B.

Virus
VZ/SERTNER (US) 1995 dir. Armand
Mastroianni
TV(US)
Cook, R.

Visas and Virtue
CEDAR GROVE (US) 1997 dir. Chris
Tashima
Toyama, T.
P

Vision Quest
WAR (US) 1985 dir. Harold Becker
Davis, T.

Visit, The
FOX (US) 1964 dir. Bernhard Wicki
Durrenmatt, F.
P

Visit, The
URBANWORLD (US) 2000 dir. Jordan
Walker-Pearlman
Russell, K.
P

Visitors
BBC (GB) 1987 dir. Piers Haggard
TV(GB)
Potter, D. *Sufficient Carbohydrate*
P

Visitors, The
BBC (GB) 1972 dir. Donald Wilson
TVSe(GB)
McMinnies, M.

Visit to a Small Planet
PAR (US) 1960 dir. Norman Taurog
Vidal, G.
P

Viva San Isidro!
CECCHI (It) 1995 dir. Dante Cappelletti
Cacucci, P. *San Isidro Futbol*

Viva Zapata!
FOX (US) 1952 dir. Elia Kazan
Pinchon, E. *Zapata the Unconquerable*

Vivero Letter, The
PROMARK (US) 1999 dir. H. Gordon
Boos
Bagley, D. *Story of the Vivero Letter, The*

V. I. Warshawski
HOLLYWOOD (US) 1991
dir. Jeff Kanew
Paretsky, S.

Voce Delle Lune, La
PENTA (It) 1990 dir. Federico Fellini
Cavazzini, E. *Poem of the Lunatics, The*

Voice From the Grave
COS-MEU (US) 1996 dir. David S.
Jackson
TV(US)
Mercado, C.

Voice of Bugle Ann, The
MGM (US) 1936 dir. Richard Thorpe
Kantor, M.

Voice of the Heart
PORTMAN (GB) 1989
dir. Tony Wharmby
TVSe(GB)
Bradford, B. T.

Voice of the Turtle
WAR (US) 1947 dir. Irving Rapper
van Druten, J.
P

Voices, The
BBC (GB) 1965 dir. Dennis Vance
TV(GB)
Crane, R. *Hero's Walk*

Voices
HEMDALE (GB) 1973
dir. Kevin Billington
Lortz, R. *Children of the Night*
P

Voices From a Locked Room
SONY (US/GB) 1995 dir. Malcolm
Clarke
Stuart, M. A. *Double Jeopardy*

Voices Within: The Lives of Truddi Chase
NEW WORLD TV (US) 1990
dir. Lamont Johnson
TVSe(US)
Chase, T. *When Rabbit Howls*

Volaverunt
COLIFILMS (Fr/Sp) 1999 dir. J. J. Bigas
Luna
Larreta, A.

Voleur de Vie
FRANCE 3 (Fr) 1997 dir. Yves Angelo
Sigurdardottir, S.

Volpone
SIRITZKY (Fr) 1947
dir. Maurice Tourneur
Jonson, B.
P

Voltaire
WAR (US) 1933 dir. John Adolfi
Gibbs, G. and Dudley, E. L.

Von Ryan's Express
FOX (US) 1965 dir. Mark Robson
Westheimer, D.

Vow to Cherish, A
WORLDWIDE PICT (US) 1999 dir. John
Schmidt
TVSe(US)
Raney, D.

Voyage of the Damned
ITC (GB) 1976 dir. Stuart Rosenberg
Thomas, G. and Witts, M. M.

Voyage of the Unicorn
HALLMARK (US) 2000 dir. Philip
Spink
TVSe(US)
Christensen, J. C. *Voyage of the Basset,
The*

Vulkan, Der
MACT (Ger/Fr) 1999 dir. Ottokar
Runze
Mann, K.

Vulture, The
YOSHA (Israel) 1981 dir. Yaky Yosba
Kaniuk, Y. *Last Jew, The*

Waco
PAR (US) 1966 dir. R. G. Springsteen
Sanford, H. and Lamb, M. *Emporia*

Wag the Dog
NEW LINE (US) 1997 dir. Barry
Levinson
Beinhart, L. *American Hero*

Wages of Fear
FDF (Fr/It) 1953
dir. Henri-Georges Clouzot
Arnaud, G.

Waiting Game, The
ALLIANCE (Can) 1998 dir. Victor Sarin
TV(Can)
Krentz, J. A.

Waiting to Exhale
FOX (US) 1995 dir. Forest Whitaker
McMillan, T.

Wait til the Sun Shines Nellie
FOX (US) 1952 dir. Henry King
Reyher, F.

Wait Until Dark
WAR (US) 1967 dir. Terence Young
Knott, F.
P

Wake Me When It's Over
FOX (US) 1960 dir. Mervyn LeRoy
Singer, H.

Wake of the Red Witch
REP (US) 1948 dir. Edward Ludwig
Roark, G.

Wake up and Live
FOX (US) 1937 dir. Sidney Lanfield
Brande, D.

Waking the Dead
POLYGRAM (US) 1999 dir. Keith
Gordon
Spencer, S.

Walkabout
FOX (Aust) 1971 dir. Nicholas Roeg
Marshall, J. V.

Walking Across Egypt
MITCHUM (US) 2001 dir. Arthur Allan
Seidelman
TV(US)
Edgerton, C.

Walking Shadow
A&E (US) 2001 dir. Po-Chih Leong
TV(US)
Parker, R. B.

Walking Stick, The
MGM (GB) 1970 dir. Eric Till
Graham, W.

Walking Through the Fire
TIME-LIFE (US) 1979 dir. Robert Day
TV(US)
Lee, L.

Walk in the Spring Rain, A
COL (US) 1969 dir. Guy Green
Maddux, R.

Walk in the Sun, A
FOX (US) 1945 dir. Lewis Milestone
Brown, H. P. M.

Walk on the Wild Side, A
COL (US) 1962 dir. Edward Dmytryk
Algren, N.

Walk with Love and Death, A
FOX (US) 1969 dir. John Huston
Koningsberger, H.

Wall, The
TIME-LIFE (US) 1982
dir. Robert Markowitz
Hersey, J.

Wallenberg: A Hero's Story
PAR (US) 1985 dir. Lamont Johnson
TVSe(US)
Werbell, F. and Clarke, T. *Lost Hero: The
Mystery of Raoul Wallenberg*

Wall of Noise
WAR (US) 1963 dir. Richard Wilson
Stein, D. M.

Walls of Jericho, The
FOX (US) 1948 dir. John M. Stahl
Wellman, P. I.

Waltzes from Vienna
GFD (GB) 1933 dir. Alfred Hitchcock
US title: Strauss's Great Waltz
Bolton, G.
P

Waltz of the Toreadors
RANK (GB) 1962 dir. John Guillermin
Anouilh, J.
P

Wanderers, The
ORION (US) 1979 dir. Philip Kaufman
Price, R.

Wandering Jew, The
OLY (GB) 1933 dir. Maurice Elvey
Thurston, E. T.
P

Wandering Soul Murders, The
CTV (Can) 2001 dir. Brad Turner
TV(Can)
Bowen, G.

War and Love
CANNON (US/Israel) 1985
dir. Moshe Mizrahi
Eisner, J. P. *Survivor, The*

War and Peace
PAR (US/It) 1956 dir. King Vidor
MOSFILM (Rus) 1967
dir. Sergei Bondarchuk
BBC (GB) 1972 dir. John Davies
TVSe(GB)
Tolstoy, L.

War and Remembrance
LWT (US/GB) 1989 dir. Dan Curtis
TVSe(US/GB)
Wouk, H.

War at Home, The
TOUCHSTONE (US) 1996 dir. Emilio
Estevez
Duff, J. *Homefront*
P

War Between the Tates, The
TALENT (US) 1977 dir. Lee Philips
TV(US)
Lurie, A.

Ware Case, The
EAL (GB) 1938 dir. Robert Stevenson
Bancroft, G. P.
P

War in the Highlands
ARENA (Fr/Swe) 1998 dir. Francis Reusser

Ramuz, C.-F. *Guerre dans le Haut-Pays, La*

Warlock
FOX (US) 1959 dir. Edward Dmytryk

Hall, O.

War Lord, The
UN (US) 1965 dir. Franklin Schaffner

Stevens, L. *Lovers, The*
P

War Lover, The
COL (GB) 1962 dir. Philip Leacock

Hersey, J.

Warm Water Under a Red Bridge
BAP (Jap/Fr) 2001 dir. Shohei Imamura

Henmi, Y.

Warn London
BL (GB) 1934 dir. T. Hayes Hunter

Clift, D.

Warning Shot
PAR (US) 1966 dir. Buzz Kulik

Masterson, W. *711—Officer Needs Help*

Warn That Man
AB (GB) 1942 dir. Laurence Huntington

Sylvaine, V.
P

Warning to Wantons
AQUILA (GB) 1949
dir. Donald B. Wilson

Mitchell, M.

War of the Buttons, The
ENIGMA (Jap/GB/Fr) 1994 dir. John Roberts

Pergaud, L. *Guerre des Boutons, La*

War of the Roses, The
FOX (US) 1989 dir. Danny DeVito

Adler, W.

War of the Worlds
PAR (US) 1953 dir. Byron Haskin

Wells, H. G.

War Requiem
BBC (GB) 1989 dir. Derek Jarman
TV(GB)

Britten, B.

Warrior Spirit
CINEVIDEO (Can) 1994 dir. René Manzor
TV(Can)

Curwood, J. O.

War Wagon, The
UI (US) 1967 dir. Burt Kennedy

Huffaker, C. *Badman*

War Zone, The
CHANNEL 4 FILMS (GB) 1999 dir. Tim Roth

Stuart, A.

Washington: Behind Closed Doors
PAR (US) 1977 dir. Gary Nelson
TVSe(US)

Ehrlichman, J. *Company, The*

Washington Masquerade
MGM (US) 1932 dir. Charles Brabin
GB title: Mad Masquerade

Bernstein, H. *Claw, The*
P

Washington Square
HOLLYWOOD (US) 1997 dir. Agnieszka Holland

James, H.

Watcher in the Woods
DISNEY (US) 1980 dir. John Hough
Randall, F. E.

Watchers
UN (US) 1988 dir. Jon Hess
Koontz, D.

Watchers Reborn
CONCORDE (US) 1998 dir. John Carl
Buechler
Koontz, D. *Watchers*

Watch House, The
BBC (GB) 1988 dir. Ian Keill
TVSe(GB)
Westall, R.

Watch it Sailor!
COL (GB) 1961 dir. Wolf Rilla
Cary, F. L. and King, P.
P

Watch on the Rhine
WAR (US) 1943 dir. Herman Shumlin
Hellman, L. F.
P

Water Babies, The
PA (GB/Pol) 1978 dir. Lionel Jeffries
A
Kingsley, C.

Water Drops on Burning Rocks
STUDIO IMAGES 6 (Fr) 2000 dir.
François Ozon
Fassbinder, R. W. *Tropfen auf Heisse*
Steine
P

Water Engine, The
TNT/AMBLIN (US)
1992 dir. Steven Schachter
TV(US)
Mamet, D.
P

Waterfall, The
BBC (GB) 1980 dir. Peter Duffell
TVSe(GB)
Drabble, M.

Waterfront
GFD (GB) 1950 dir. Michael Anderson
US title: Waterfront Women
Brophy, J.

Water Gypsies, The
SDC (GB) 1932 dir. Maurice Elvey
Herbert, Sir A. P.

Waterland
CHANNEL 4 (GB) 1992 dir. Stephen
Gyllenhaal
Swift, G.

Waterloo Bridge
UN (US) 1931 dir. James Whale
MGM (US) 1940 dir. Mervyn LeRoy
Sherwood, R. E.
P

Watership Down
CIC (GB) 1978 dir. Martin Rosen
A, Ch
Adams, R.

Watusi
MGM (US) 1959 dir. Kurt Neumann
Haggard, Sir H. R. *King Solomon's*
Mines

Way for a Sailor
MGM (US) 1930 dir. Sam Wood
Wetjen, A. R.

Way of a Gaucho
FOX (US) 1952 dir. Jacques Tourneur
Childs, H. *Gaucho*

Way to the Gold, The
FOX (US) 1957 dir. Robert D. Webb
Steele, W. D.

Wayward Bus, The
FOX (US) 1957 dir. Victor Vicas
Steinbeck, J.

Way West, The
UA (US) 1967 dir. Andrew V. McLaglen
Guthrie, Jr., A. B.

Way We Live Now, The
BBC (GB) 2001 dir. David Yates
TVSe(GB)
Trollope, A.

Way We Were, The
COL (US) 1973 dir. Sydney Pollack
Laurents, A.

W.C. Fields and Me
UN (US) 1976 dir. Arthur Hiller
Monti, C. and Rice, C.

Weak and the Wicked, The
APB (GB) 1953 dir. J. Lee Thompson
Henry, J. *Who Lie in Gaol*

Weak at Denise
GUERILLA (GB) 1999 dir. Julian Nott
Williams, G.

Weaker Sex, The
TC (GB) 1948 dir. Roy Baker
McCracken, E. *No Medals*
P

We Are Not Alone
WAR (US) 1939 dir. Edmund Goulding
Hilton, J.

Weather in the Streets, The
BBC (GB) 1984 dir. Gavin Millar
TV(GB)
Lehman, R.

Wedding, The
TYNE-TEES (GB) 1984
dir. Gordon Flemyng
TV(GB)
Pritchett, V. S.

Wedding, The
HARPO (US) 1998 dir. Charles Burnett
TVSe(US)
West, D.

Wednesday Woman, The
CBP (US) 2000 dir. Christopher Leitch
TV(US)
Davidson, M. *Thursday Woman, The*

Weekend, The
GRANADA (GB/US) 2000 dir. Brian
Skeet
Cameron, P.

Weekend at Dunkirk
FOX (Fr/It) 1964 dir. Henri Verneuil
Merle, R. *Weekend à Zuydcoote*

Weekend at the Waldorf
MGM (US) 1945 dir. Robert Z. Leonard
M
Baum, V. *Grand Hotel*

Weep No More My Lady
STUDIO CANAL+/RYSHER
(US/Fr) 1992 dir. Michael Andrieu
TV(US/Fr)
Clark, M. H.

Wee Willie Winkie
FOX (US) 1937 dir. John Ford
Kipling, R.

Weight of Water
STUDIO CANAL+ (Fr/US) 2000 dir.
Kathryn Bigelow
Shreve, A.

Weir of Hermiston
BBC (GB) 1973 dir. Tina Wakerell
TVSe(GB)

Stevenson, R. L.

Weiser
EURIMAGES (Pol) 2001 dir. Wojciech
Marczewski

Huelle, P. *Weiser Dawidek*

We Joined the Navy
WAR (GB) 1962 dir. Wendy Toye

Winton, J.

Welcome Back, Mr. McDonald
TOHO (Jap) 1998 dir. Koki Mitani

Mitani, K. *Radio no Jikan*
P

Welcome to Hard Times
MGM (US) 1967 dir. Burt Kennedy
GB title: Killer on a Horse

Doctorow, E. L.

Welcome to Sarajevo
CHANNEL 4 FILMS (GB/US) 1997 dir.
Michael Winterbottom

Nicholson, M. *Natasha's Story*

Welcome to the Club
COL (US) 1970 dir. Walter Shenson

Wood, C. B.

Welcome to Woop Woop
SCALA (Aust/GB) 1997 dir. Stephan
Elliott

Kennedy, D. *Dead Heart, The*

We Live Again
UA (US) 1934 dir. Rouben Mamoulian

Tolstoy, L. *Resurrection*

Well, The
NSW (Aust) 1997 dir. Samantha Lang

Jolley, E.

Went the Day Well?
EAL (GB) 1942 dir. Alberto Cavalcanti
US title: Forty-Eight Hours

Greene, G.

We of the Never Never
AP (Aust) 1982 dir. Igor Auzins

Gunn, A.

Werckmeister Harmoniak
BABELSBERG (Ger/It/Fr) 2000 dir.
Agnes Hranitzki, Bela Tarr

Krasznahorkai, L. *Melancholy of
Resistance, The*

We're No Angels
PAR (US) 1955 dir. Michael Curtiz
PAR (US) 1989 dir. Neil Jordan

Husson, A. *My Three Angels*
P

We're Not Dressing
PAR (US) 1934 dir. Norman Taurog

Barrie, Sir J. M. *Admirable Crichton, The*
P

Western Union
FOX (US) 1941 dir. Fritz Lang

Grey, Z.

West Eleven
WAR (GB) 1963 dir. Michael Winner

Del Rivo, L. *Furnished Room, The*

Westing Game, The
SHOWTIMEWORKS (US) 1997 dir.
Terence H. Winkless
TV(US)

Raskin, E.

West of the Pecos
RKO (US) 1934 dir. Phil Rosen
RKO (US) 1945 dir. Edward Killy

Grey, Z.

West Side Story
UA (US) 1961
dir. Robert Wise, Jerome Robbins
M

Laurents, A., Sondheim, S. and Bernstein, L.
P

West Side Waltz, The
VZ/SERTNER (US) 1995 dir. Ernest Thompson
TV(US)

Thompson, E.
P

Westward Passage
RKO (US) 1932 dir. Robert Milton

Barnes, M. A.

We, The Accused
BBC (GB) 1980 dir. Richard Stroud
TVSe(GB)

Raymond, E.

We the Living
SCALERA (It) 1942
dir. Goffredo Allessandrini

Rand, A.

We Think the World of You
CINECOM (GB) 1988 dir. Colin Gregg

Ackerley, J. R.

Wet Parade, The
MGM (US) 1932 dir. Victor Fleming

Sinclair, U.

We Were Dancing
MGM (GB) 1942 dir. Robert Z. Leonard

Coward, N. *Tonight at 8.30*
P

We Were Strangers
COL (US) 1949 dir. John Huston

Sylvester, R. *Rough Sketch*

We Were the Mulvaneys
VZ/SERTNER (US) 2002 dir. Peter Werner
TV(US)

Oates, J. C.

Whale for the Killing, A
PLAYBOY (US) 1981
dir. Richard T. Heffron
TV(US)

Mowat, F.

Whale Music
ALLIANCE (Can) 1994 dir. Richard J. Lewis

Quarrington, P.

Whales of August, The
ALIVE (US) 1987 dir. Lindsay Anderson

Barry, D.
P

What a Life
PAR (US) 1939 dir. Theodore Reed

Goldsmith, C.
P

What Became of Jack and Jill?
FOX (GB) 1971 dir. Bill Rain

Moody, L. *Ruthless Ones, The*

What Becomes of the Broken Hearted?
POLYGRAM (NZ) 1999 dir. Ian Mune

Duff, A.

What Dreams May Come
POLYGRAM (US) 1998 dir. Vincent Ward

Matheson, R.

Whatever Happened to Aunt Alice?
PALOMAR (US) 1969 dir. Lee H. Katzin

Curtiss, U. *Forbidden Garden, The*

What Ever Happened to Baby Jane?

WAR (US) 1962 dir. Robert Aldrich
SPECTACOR (US) 1991
dir. David Greene
TV(US)

Farrell, H. *Baby Jane*

What Every Woman Knows

MGM (US) 1934 dir. Gregory La Cava

Barrie, Sir J. M.
P

What Girls Learn

SHOWTIME (US) 2001 dir. Lee Rose
TV(US)

Cook, K.

What Happened Was ...

GOOD MACHINE (US) 1993 dir. Tom
Noonan

Noonan, T.
P

What Love Sees

ROSEMONT (US) 1996 dir. Michael
Switzer
TV(US)

Vreeland, S.

What Mad Pursuit

BBC (GB) 1985 dir. Tony Smith
TV(GB)

Coward, N.

What Price Glory?

FOX (US) 1952 dir. John Ford

Anderson, M. and Stallings, L.
P

What's a Nice Girl Like You ...?

UN TV (US) 1971 dir. Jerry Paris
TV(US)

Cunningham, E. V. *Shirley*

What's Eating Gilbert Grape

PAR (US) 1993 dir. Lasse Hallstrom

Hedges, P.

What's Love Got to Do With It?

TOUCHSTONE (US) 1993 dir. Brian
Gibson

Turner, T. and Loder, K. *I, Tina*

What's the Worst That Could Happen?

MGM (US) 2001 dir. Sam Weisman

Westlake, D. E.

What the Deaf Man Heard

HALLMARK (US) 1997 dir. John Kent
Harrison
TV(US)

Gearino, G. D. *What the Deaf-Mute Heard*

Wheeler-Dealers

MGM (US) 1963 dir. Arthur Hiller
GB title: Separate Beds

Goodman, G. J. W. *Wheeler-Dealers, The*

Wheels

UN TV (US) 1978 dir. Jerry London
TVSe(US)

Hailey, A.

When Eight Bells Toll

RANK (GB) 1971 dir. Etienne Perier

MacLean, A.

When Good Ghouls Go Bad

FOX (Aust/US) 2001 dir. Patrick Read
Johnson
TV(Aust/US)

Stine, R. L.

When Hell was in Session

AUBREY-HAMNER (US) 1979 dir. Paul
Krasny
TV(US)

Denton, Jr., J. A. and Brandt, E.

When Ladies Meet

MGM (US) 1933 dir. Harry Beaumont
MGM (US) 1941 dir. Robert Z. Leonard

Crothers, R.
P

When Love Kills: The Seduction of John Hearn
ALEXANDER-ENRIGHT (US) 1993 dir. Larry Elikann
TVSe(US)

Green, B. *Soldier of Fortune Murders, The*

When Michael Calls
FOX (US) 1972 dir. Philip Lcacock
TV(US)

Farris, J.

When my Baby Smiles at Me
FOX (US) 1948 dir. Walter Lang

Walters, G. M. and Hopkins, A. *Burlesque*
P

When Secrets Kill
SCRIPPS HOWARD (US) 1997 dir. Colin Bucksey
TV(US)

MacDonald, P. *Mother's Day*

When the Bough Breaks
TAFT (US) 1986 dir. Waris Hussein
TV(US)

Kellerman, J.

When the Boys Meet the Girls
MGM (US) 1965 dir. Alvin Ganzer

Bolton, G. and McGowan, J. *Girl Crazy*
P

When the Dark Man Calls
WIL COURT (US) 1995 dir. Nathaniel Gutman
TV(US)

Kaminsky, S.

When the Green Woods Laugh
YTV (GB) 1991 dir. Robert Tronson
TV(GB)

Bates, H. E.

When the Legends Die
FOX (US) 1972 dir. Stuart Millar

Borland, H.

When the Light Comes
ADDED (Ger/Neth) 1999 dir. Stijn Coninx

van der Laan, H. *Waar Blijft Het Licht*

When the Whales Came
FOX (GB) 1989 dir. Clive Rees

Morpurgo, M. *Why Whales Came*

When the Wind Blows
MELTDOWN (GB) 1987 dir. J. T. Murakami
A

Briggs, R.

When Time Ran Out
WAR (US) 1980 dir. James Goldstone

Thomas, G. and Witts, M. M. *Day the World Ended, The*

When Tomorrow Comes
UN (US) 1939 dir. John M. Stahl

Cain, J. A.

When we are Married
BN (GB) 1943 dir. Lance Comfort

Priestley, J. B.
P

When Worlds Collide
PAR (US) 1951 dir. Rudolph Maté

Balmer, E. and Wylie, P.

Where are the Children?
COL (US) 1986 dir. Bruce Malmuth

Clark, M. H.

Where Does it Hurt?
HEMDALE (US) 1971 dir. Rod Amateau

Amateau, R. and Robinson, B. *Operator, The*

Where Eagles Dare
MGM (GB) 1969 dir. Brian G. Hutton

MacLean, A.

Where Love has Gone
PAR (US) 1964 dir. Edward Dmytryk

Robbins, H.

Where Pigeons Go To Die
WORLD (US) 1990 dir. Michael Landon
TV(US)

Campbell, R. W.

Where's Charley?
WAR (US) 1952 dir. David Butler

Thomas, B. *Charley's Aunt*
P

Where Sinners Meet
RKO (US) 1934 dir. J. Walter Ruben

Milne, A. A. *Dover Road, The*
P

Where's Poppa?
UA (US) 1970 dir. Carl Reiner

Klane, R.

Where the Boys Are
MGM (US) 1960 dir. Henry Levin
ITC (US) 1980 dir. Hy Averback

Swarthout, G.

Where the Heart Is
FOX (US) 2000 dir. Matt Williams

Letts, B.

Where the Hot Wind Blows
MGM (Fr/It) 1958 dir. Jules Dassin

Vailland, R.

Where the Lilies Bloom
UA (US) 1974 dir. William A. Graham

Cleaver, V. and Cleaver, B.

Where the Red Fern Grows
EMI (US) 1974 dir. Norman Tokar

Rawls, W.

Where the Rivers Flow North
CALEDONIA (US) 1993 dir. Jay Craven

Mosher, H. F.

Where There's A Will
EROS (GB) 1955 dir. Vernon Sewell

Delderfield, R. F.
P

Where the River Runs Black
MGM (US) 1986 dir. Christopher Cain

Kendall, D. *Lazaro*

Where the Sidewalk Ends
FOX (US) 1960 dir. Otto Preminger

Stuart, W. L. *Night Cry*

Where the Spies Are
MGM (GB) 1965 dir. Val Guest

Leasor, J. *Passport to Oblivion*

Where Were You When the Lights Went Out?
MGM (US) 1968 dir. Hy Averback

Magnier, C.
P

While I Live
DRYHURST (GB) 1947 dir. John Harlow

Bell, R. *This Same Garden*
P

While My Pretty One Sleeps
GROSSO-JACOB (US) 1997 dir. Jorge Montesi
TV(US)

Clark, M. H.

While the City Sleeps
RKO (US) 1956 dir. Fritz Lang

Einstein, C. *Bloody Spur, The*

While the Patient Slept
IN (US) 1935 dir. Ray Enright

Eberhart, M. G.

While the Sun Shines
ABP (GB) 1947 dir. Anthony Asquith
Rattigan, T.
P

Whipping Boy, The
COL TV (US/GB) 1994 dir. Sydney
Macartney
TV(US/GB)
Fleischman, A. S.

Whirlpool
FOX (US) 1949 dir. Otto Preminger
Endore, G. *Methinks the Lady*

Whisky Galore
EAL (GB) 1948
dir. Alexander MacKendrick
US title: Tight Little Island
Mackenzie, Sir C.

Whisperers, The
UA (GB) 1966 dir. Bryan Forbes
Nicolson, R. *Mrs. Ross*

Whispering Smith
PAR (US) 1948 dir. Leslie Fenton
Spearman, F. H.

Whistle Blower, The
HEMDALE (GB) 1987
dir. Simon Langton
Hale, J.

Whistle Down the Wind
RANK (GB) 1961 dir. Bryan Forbes
Bell, M. H.

Whistle Stop
UA (US) 1946 dir. Leonide Moguy
Wolff, M. M.

Whistling in the Dark
MGM (US) 1941 dir. S. Sylvan Simon
Gross, L. and Carpenter, E. C.
P

White Banners
WAR (US) 1938 dir. Edmund Goulding
Douglas, L. C.

White Buffalo, The
EMI (US) 1977 dir. J. Lee Thompson
Sale, R.

White Cargo
BI (GB) 1930 dir. J. D. Williams, A. W.
Barnes
MGM (US) 1942 dir. Richard Thorpe
Gordon, L.
P

White Cockatoo
WAR (US) 1935 dir. Alan Crosland
Eberhart, M. G.

White Corridors
GFD (GB) 1951 dir. Pat Jackson
Ashton, H. *Yeoman's Hospital*

White Dawn, The
PAR (US) 1974 dir. Philip Kaufman
Houston, J.

White Dog
PAR (US) 1982 dir. Samuel Fuller
Gary, R.

White Fang
FOX (US) 1936 dir. David Butler
FOX (It/Sp/Fr) 1974 dir. Lucio Fulci
DISNEY (US) 1991 dir. Randal Kleiser
London, J.

**White Hot: The Mysterious
Murder of Thelma Todd**
NEWFELD-KEATING (US) 1991
dir. Paul Wendkos
TV(US)
Edmonds, A. *Hot Toddy*

White Hunter, Black Heart
WAR (US) 1990 dir. Clint Eastwood
Viertel, P.

White Lie
MCA TV (US) 1991 dir. Bill Condon
TV(US)

Charters, S. *Louisiana Black*

White Mischief
BBC/COL (GB) 1988
dir. Michael Radford

Fox, J.

White of the Eye
CANNON (GB) 1987
dir. Donald Cammell

Tracy, M. *Mrs. White*

White Palace
UN (US) 1990 dir. Luis Mandoki

Savan, G.

White Peak Farm
BBC (GB) 1988 dir. Andrew Morgan
Ch, TVSe(GB)

Doherty, B.

White Raven, The
HERMES (US) 1998 dir. Andrew
Stevens
TV(US)

Blodgett, M.

White River Kid, The
NEW CITY (US) 1999 dir. Arne
Glimcher

Ryan, J. F. *Little Brothers of St. Mortimer, The*

White Sister
MGM (US) 1933 dir. Victor Fleming

Crawford, E. M. and Hackett, W.
P

White Tower, The
RKO (US) 1950 dir. Ted Tetzlaff

Ullman, J. R.

White Trash
BAKER (US) 1992 dir. Fred Baker

Baker, F.
P

White Unicorn, The
GFD (GB) 1947 dir. Bernard Knowles
US title: Bad Sister

Sandstrom, F. *Milk White Unicorn, The*

White Witch Doctor
FOX (US) 1953 dir. Henry Hathaway

Stinetorf, L. A.

Who?
BL (GB) 1974 dir. Jack Gold
US title: Man Without a Face

Budrys, A.

Who Framed Roger Rabbit?
TOUCHSTONE (US) 1988 dir. Robert
Zemeckis
A, Ch

Wolf, G. K. *Who Censored Roger Rabbit?*

Who Goes There?
BL (GB) 1952 dir. Anthony Kimmins
US title: Passionate Sentry, The

Dighton, J.
P

Who has Seen the Wind
CIN WORLD (Can) 1980 dir.
Allan King

Mitchell, W. O.

Who is Julia?
CBS ENT (US) 1986
dir. Walter Grauman
TV(US)

Harris, B. S.

Who is Killing the Great Chefs of Europe?
WAR (US) 1978 dir. Ted Kotcheff
GB title: Too Many Chefs

Lyons, N. and Lyons, I. *Someone is Killing the Great Chefs of Europe*

Who Killed the Cat?
GN (GB) 1966 dir. Montgomery Tully
Ridley, A. and Borer, M. *Tabitha*
P

Whole Town's Talking, The
COL (US) 1935 dir. John Ford
GB title: Passport to Fame
Burnett, W. R.

Whole Truth, The
COL (GB) 1958 dir. John Guillermin
Mackie, P.
P

Who'll Save Our Children?
TIME-LIFE (US) 1978
dir. George Schaefer
TV(US)
Maddox, R. *Orchard Children, The*

Who'll Stop the Rain?
UA (US) 1978 dir. Karel Reisz
GB title: Dog Soldiers
Stone, R. *Dog Soldiers*

Whore
TRIMARK (GB) 1991 dir. Ken Russell
Hines, D. *Bondage*
P

Who's Afraid of Virginia Woolf?
WAR (US) 1966 dir. Mike Nichols
Albee, E.
P

Whose Baby?
7 NETWORK-CRAWFORDS (Aust)
1990 dir. Ian Barry
TVSe(Aust)
Duck, C. and Thomas, M.

Whose Life is it Anyway?
MGM (US) 1981 John Badham
Clark, B.
P

Who's Got the Action?
PAR (US) 1963 dir. Daniel Mann
Rose, A. *Four Horse Players are Missing*

Who, Sir? Me, Sir?
BBC (GB) 1986 dir. Colin Cant
TVSe(GB)
Peyton, K. M.

Who Was That Lady?
COL (US) 1960 dir. George Sidney
Krasna, N. *Who Was That Lady I Saw You With?*
P

Why Didn't They Ask Evans?
LWT (GB) 1980 dir. John Davies, Tony Wharmby
TVSe(GB)
Christie, A.

Why Me?
LORIMAR (US) 1984 dir. Fielder Cook
TV(US)
Harmon, L. M.

Why Me?
TRIUMPH (US) 1990
dir. Gene Quintano
Westlake, D. E.

Why Not Stay for Breakfast?
ENT (GB) 1979 dir. Terence Martel
Stone, G. and Cooney, R.
P

Why Shoot the Teacher?
QUARTET (Can) 1976
dir. Silvio Narizzano
Braithwaite, M.

Why Would I Lie?
UA (US) 1980 dir. Larry Peerce
Hodges, H. *Fabricator, The*

Wicked Lady, The
GFD (GB) 1946 dir. Leslie Arliss
CANNON (GB) 1983
dir. Michael Winner

King-Hall, M. *Life and Death of the Wicked Lady Skelton, The*

Wicked Woman, A
MGM (US) 1934 dir. Charles Brabin

Austin, A.

Wide-Eyed and Legless
BBC (GB) 1993 dir. Richard Loncraine
TV(GB)

Longden, D. *Diana's Story; Lost for Words*

Wide Sargasso Sea
LAUGH KOOK (Aust) 1993 dir. John Duigan

Rhys, J.

Widow
LORIMAR (US) 1976
dir. J. Lee Thompson
TV(US)

Caine, L.

Wife, The
ARTISTIC (US) 1995 dir. Tom Noonan

Noonan, T. *Wifey*
P

Wife Vs. Secretary
MGM (US) 1936 dir. Clarence Brown

Baldwin, F.

Wilby Conspiracy, The
UA (GB) 1975 dir. Ralph Nelson

Driscoll, P.

Wild Affair, The
BL (GB) 1965 dir. John Irish

Sansom, W. *Last Hours of Sandra Lee, The*

Wild and the Willing, The
RANK (GB) 1962 dir. Ralph Thomas
US title: Young and Willing

Dobie, L. and Sloman, R. *Tinker, The*
P

Wild at Heart
GOLDWYN (US) 1990 dir. David Lynch

Gifford, B.

Wild Bill
UA (US) 1995 dir. Walter Hill

Babe, T. *Fathers and Sons*
P

Dexter, P. *Deadwood*

Wild Card
DAVIS (US) 1992 dir. Mel Damski
TV(US)

Thackrey, Jr., T. *Preacher*

Wild Country, The
DISNEY (US) 1971 dir. Robert Totten

Moody, R. *Little Britches*

Wild Duck, The
ORION (GB) 1983 dir. Henri Safran

Ibsen, H.
P

Wildflower
HEARST (US) 1991 dir. Diane Keaton
TV(US)

Flanigan, S. *Alice*

Wild Games
INTEGRAL (Bel/Ger/Fr) 1997 dir. Benoit Lamy

Blanc, H.-F. *Combat de Fauves au Crepuscule*

Wild Geese, The
RANK (GB) 1978
dir. Andrew V. McLaglen

Carney, D.

Wild Geese II
UN (GB) 1985 dir. Peter Hunt
Carney, D. *Square Circle, The*

Wild Geese Calling
FOX (US) 1991 dir. John Brahm
White, S. E.

Wild Harvest
GN (US) 1961 dir. Jerry Baerwitz
Longstreet, S.

Wild in the Country
FOX (US) 1961 dir. Philip Dunne
Salamanca, J. R. *Lost Country, The*

Wild Justice
LEE LIGHTING (GB) 1993 dir. Tony
Wharmby
TVSe(GB)
Smith, W.

Wild Man of Borneo, The
MGM (US) 1941 dir. Robert B. Sinclair
Mankiewicz, H. J. and Connelly, M.
P

Wild River
FOX (US) 1960 dir. Elia Kazan
Deal, B. *Dunbar's Cove*
Huie, W. B. *Mud on the Streets*

Wild Times
METRO (US) 1980
dir. Richard Compton
TVSe(US)
Garfield, B.

Wild Women
SPELLING (US) 1970 dir. Don Taylor
TV(US)
Forte, V. *Trailmakers, The*

Will Any Gentleman
ABP (GB) 1953 dir. Michael Anderson
Sylvaine, V.
P

Willard
CINERAMA (US) 1971 dir. Daniel
Mann
Gilbert, S. *Ratman's Notebook*

Will: G. Gordon Liddy
SHAYNE (US) 1982
dir. Robert Lieberman
TV(US)
Liddy, G. G. *Will*

Will of Their Own, A
WAR (US) 1998 dir. Karen Arthur
TVSe(US)
Shreve, S. R. *Daughters of the New World*

Will Success Spoil Rock Hunter?
FOX (US) 1957 dir. Frank Tashlin
GB title: Oh! For a Man!
Axelrod, G.
P

Will There Really Be A Morning?
ORION (US) 1983 dir. Fielder Cook
TV(US)
Farmer, F.

Willy Wonka and the Chocolate Factory
PAR (US) 1971 dir. Mel Stuart
Ch
Dahl, R. *Charlie and the Chocolate Factory*

Wilt
RANK (GB) 1989 dir. Michael Tuchner
Sharpe, T.

Wimbledon Prisoner, The
BBC (GB) 1994 dir. Robert Young
TVSe(GB)
Williams, N.

Winchell
HBO (US) 1998 dir. Paul Mazursky
TV(US)

Klurfeld, H. *Walter Winchell: His Life and Times*

Wind Cannot Read, The
RANK (GB) 1958 dir. Ralph Thomas

Mason, R.

Wind in the Willows, The
ALLIED FILMMAKERS (GB) 1995 dir. Terry Jones
Ch

Grahame, K.

Windmills of the Gods
ITC (US) 1988 dir. Lee Philips
TVSe(US)

Sheldon, S.

Windom's Way
RANK (GB) 1957 dir. Ronald Neame

Ullman, J. R.

Winds of Jarrah, The
FILMCORP (Aust) 1983
dir. Mark Egerton

Dingwall, J. *House in the Timberwoods, The*

Winds of War, The
PAR (US) 1983 dir. Dan Curtis
TVSe(US)

Wouk, H.

Windwalker
PACIFIC (US) 1981 dir. Keith Merrill

Yorgason, B.

Winged Victory
FOX (US) 1944 dir. George Cukor

Hart, M.
P

Wings of the Dove, The
MIRAMAX (GB/US) 1997 dir. Iain Softley

James, H.

Winner, The
VILLAGE ROADSHOW (US) 1997 dir. Alex Cox

Riss, W. *Darker Purpose, A*
P

Winnie
NBC (US) 1988 dir. John Korty
TV(US)

Bolnick, J. P. *Winnie: My Life in the Institution*

Winnie the Pooh and the Honey Tree
DISNEY (US) 1965
dir. Wolfgang Reitherman
A, Ch

Milne, A. A. *Winnie the Pooh*

Winslow Boy, The
IS (GB) 1945 dir. Anthony Asquith
SONY (US) 1999 dir. David Mamet

Rattigan, T.
P

Winstanley
OTHER (GB) 1977
dir. Kevin Brownlow, Andrew Mollo

Caute, D. *Comrade Jacob*

Winston Churchill—The Wilderness Years
SOUTHERN TV (GB) 1981 dir. Ferdinand Fairfax
TVSe(GB)

Gilbert, M.

Winter in Lisbon, The
JET (Sp) 1990 dir. Jose Antonio Zorrilla

Molina, A. M.

Winter Guest, The
CHANNEL 4 FILMS (GB) 1997 dir.
Alan Rickman
MacDonald, S.
P

Winter Kills
AVCO (US) 1979 dir. William Richert
Condon, R.

Winter Meeting
WAR (US) 1948 dir. Bretaigne Windust
Vance, E.

Winter of our Discontent, The
LORIMAR (US) 1983 dir. Waris Hussein
TV(US)
Steinbeck, J.

Winter People
COL (US) 1989 dir. Ted Kotcheff
Ehle, J.

Winterset
RKO (US) 1936 dir. Alfred Santell
COMPASS (US) 1959
dir. George Schaefer
TV(US)
Anderson, M.
P

Winter Sleepers
PALLADIO (Ger) 1997 dir. Tom Tykwer
Pyszora, A.-F. *Expense of the Spirit*

Winter's Tale, The
WAR (GB) 1968 dir. Frank Dunlop
Shakespeare, W.
P

Winter Tan, A
TELEFILM (Can) 1987 dir. Louise Clark
Holder, M. *Give Sorrow Words*

Wired
TAURUS (US) 1989 dir. Larry Peerce
Woodward, B.

Wise Blood
NEWLINE (US) 1980 dir. John Huston
O'Connor, F.

Wit
HBO FILMS (US) 2001 dir. Mike
Nichols
TV(US)
Edson, M.
P

Witches, The
HAMMER (GB) 1966 dir. Cyril Frankel
US title: Devil's Own, The
Curtis, P. *Devil's Own, The*

Witches, The
WAR (US) 1990 dir. Nicolas Roeg
Dahl, R.

Witches of Eastwick, The
WAR (US) 1987 dir. George Miller
Updike, J.

Witches of Salem, The
FDF (Fr/Ger) 1957
dir. Raymond Rouleau
Miller, A. *Crucible, The*
P

Witchfinder General
TIGON (GB) 1968 dir. Michael Reeves
Bassett, R.

Witching Hour, The
PAR (US) 1934 dir. Henry Hathaway
Thomas, A. E.
P

Witch's Daughter, The
BBC (GB) 1971 dir. David Maloney
TVSe(GB)
HALLMARK (GB) 1996 dir. Alan
Macmillan
TV(GB)
Bawden, N.

With Closed Eyes
PARADIS (It/Fr/Sp) 1994 dir.
Francesca Archibugi
Tozzi, F.

Within the Law
MGM (US) 1939 dir. Gustav Machaty
Veiller, B.
P

Without Apparent Motive
VALORIA (Fr) 1971 dir. Philippe Labro
McBain, E. *Ten Plus One*

Without a Trace
FOX (US) 1983 dir. Stanley R. Jaffe
Gutcheon, B. *Still Missing*

Without Love
MGM (US) 1945 dir. Harold S. Bucquet
Barry, P.
P

Without Reservations
RKO (US) 1946 dir. Mervyn LeRoy
Allen, J. and Livingston, M. *Thanks God, I'll Take it From Here*

Without Warning: The James Brady Story
HBO (US) 1991
dir. Michael Toshiyuki Uno
TV(US)
Dickenson, M. *Thumbs Up: The Life and Courageous Comeback of White House Press Secretary Jim Brady*

Witness for the Prosecution
UA (US) 1957 dir. Billy Wilder
UA TV (US) 1982 dir. Alan Gibson
TV(US)
Christie, A.
P

Wives and Daughters
BBC (GB) 1971 dir. Hugh David
TVSe(GB)
Gaskell, E.

Wives and Lovers
PAR (US) 1963 dir. John Rich
Allen, J. P. *First Wife, The*
P

Wiz, The
DISNEY (US) 1978 dir. Sidney Lumet
M
Brown, W.
P
Baum, L. F. *Wonderful Wizard of Oz, The*
P

Wizard of Loneliness
SKOURAS (US) 1988 dir. Jenny Bowen
Nichols, J.

Wizard of Oz, The
MGM (US) 1939 dir. Victor Fleming
M
Baum, L. F. *Wonderful Wizard of 0z, The*

Wolfen
WAR (US) 1981 dir. Michael Wadleigh
Strieber, W.

Wolf Larsen
ABP (US) 1958 dir. Harman Jones
London, J. *Sea Wolf, The*

Wolf to the Slaughter
TVS (GB) 1988 dir. John Gorrie
TVSe(GB)
Rendell, R.

Wolves of Kromer, The
FIRST RUN (US) 1998 dir. Will Gould
Lambert, C.
P

Wolves of Willoughby Chase, The
ZENITH (GB) 1988 dir. Stuart Orme
Aiken, J.

Woman Called Moses, A
H. JAFFE (US) 1978 dir. Paul Wendkos
TVSe(US)
Heidish, M.

Woman Chaser, The
DEFINITIVE (US) 1999 dir. Robinson Devor
Willeford, C.

Woman from the Provinces, A
OKO (Pol) 1987 dir. Andrzej Baranski
Sieminski, W.

Woman I Love, The
RKO (US) 1937 dir. Anatole Litvak
GB title: Woman Between, The
Kessel, J. *Equippage, L'*

Woman in a Dressing Gown
GODWIN (GB) 1957
dir. J. Lee Thompson
Willis, T.
P

Woman in Black, The
CENTRAL FILMS (GB) 1989 dir. Herbert Wise
TV(GB)
Hill, S.

Woman in the Hall, The
GFD (GB) 1947 dir. Jack Lee
Stern, G. B.

Woman in the Window, The
RKO (US) 1944 dir. Fritz Lang
Wallis, J. H. *Once Off Guard*

Woman in White, The
WAR (US) 1948 dir. Peter Godfrey
BBC (GB) 1982 dir. John Bruce
TVSe(GB)
Collins, W.

Woman Named Jackie, A
L. PERSKY (US) 1991 dir. Larry Peerce
TVSe(US)
Heymann, C. D.

Woman Obsessed
FOX (US) 1959 dir. Henry Hathaway
Mantley, J. *Snow Birch, The*

Woman of Independent Means, A
FOGWOOD (US) 1995 dir. Robert Greenwald
TVSe(US)
Hailey, E. F.

Woman of Rome
MINERVA (lt) 1954 dir. Luigi Zampa
Moravia, A.

Woman of Straw
UA (GB) 1964 dir. Basil Dearden
Arley, C.

Woman of Substance, A
OPT (US) 1984 dir. Don Sharp
TVSe(US)
Bradford, B. T.

Woman of the Dunes, The
CONTEM (Jap) 1964
dir. Hiroshi Teshigahara
Abé, K. *Woman in the Dunes*

Woman on the Beach, The
RKO (US) 1947 dir. Jean Renoir
Wilson, M. *None so Blind*

Woman on the Run: The Lawrencia Bembenek Story
NBC (US) 1993 dir. Sandor Stern
TVSe(US)
Bembenek, L. *Woman on Trial, A*

Woman Rebels, A
RKO (US) 1936 dir. Mark Sandrich
Syrett, N. *Portrait of a Rebel*

Woman's Angle, A
ABP (GB) 1952 dir. Leslie Arliss

Feiner, R. *Three Cups of Coffee*

Woman's Face, A
MGM (US) 1941 dir. George Cukor

de Croisset, F. *Il était une fois*
P

Woman's Guide to Adultery, A
CARLTON (GB) 1993 dir. David
Hayman
TVSe(GB)

Clewlow, C.

Woman's Secret, A
RKO (US) 1949 dir. Nicholas Ray

Baum, V. *Mortgage on Life*

Woman's Vengeance, A
UN (US) 1947 dir. Zolta Korder

Huxley, A. *Gioconda Smile, The*
P

Woman Wanted
MOTION (Can/US) 1999 dir. Kiefer
Sutherland

Glass, J. M.

Woman Who Loved Elvis, The
GROSS/BAR (US) 1993 dir. Bill Bixby
TV(US)

Kalpakian, L. *Graced Land*

Woman With No Name, The
ABP (GB) 1950 dir. Ladislas Vajda

Charles, T. *Happy Now I Go*

Women, The
MGM (US) 1939 dir. George Cukor

Boothe, C.
P

Women in Love
UA (GB) 1969 dir. Ken Russell

Lawrence, D. H.

Women in White
UN TV (US) 1979 dir. Jerry London
TVSe(US)

Slaughter, F. G.

Women of Brewster Place, The
PHOENIX (US) 1989 dir. Donna Deitch
TVSe(US)

Naylor, G.

Women of Twilight
ROMULUS (GB) 1952
dir. Gordon Parry
US title: Twilight Women

Rayman, S.
P

Women's Room, The
WAR (US) 1980 dir. Glenn Jordan
TVSe(US)

French, M.

Women Talking Dirty
ROCKET (US) 1999 dir. Corky Giedroyc

Dewar, I.

Wonder Bar
WAR (US) 1934 dir. Lloyd Bacon
M

Herczeg, G., Farkas, K. and Katscher, R.
P

Wonder Boy
STUDIO CANAL+ (Fr) 1994 dir. Paul
Vecchiali

Leroy, F.

Wonder Boys
PAR (US) 2000 dir. Curtis Hanson

Chabon, M.

Wonderful Country, The
UA (US) 1959 dir. Robert Parrish

Lea, T.

Wonderful Ice Cream Suit, The
DISNEY (US) 1998 dir. Stuart Gordon
Bradbury, R. *Magic White Suit, The*
P

Wonderful World of the Brothers Grimm, The
MGM (US) 1962 dir. Henry Levin, George Pal
Ch
Grimm, J. L. K. and Grimm, W. K. *Dancing Princess, The; Cobbler & the Elves, The; Singing Bone, The*
Gerstner, H. *Die Bruder Grimm*

Wood Beyond, The
BBC/A&E (GB) 1998 dir. Edward Bennett
TV(GB)
Hill, R.

Wooden Horse, The
BL (GB) 1950 dir. Jack Lee
Williams, E.

Wooden Man's Bride, The
LONG SHONG (Tai) 1994 dir. Jia Pingau
Pingau, J.

Woodlanders, The
BBC (GB) 1970 dir. John Davies
TVSe(GB)
CHANNEL 4 FILMS (GB) 1997 dir. Phil Agland
Hardy, T.

Woodstock
BBC (GB) 1973 dir. David Maloney
TVSe(GB)
Scott, Sir W.

Woof
CENTRAL (GB) 1990 dir. David Cobham
Ch, TVSe(GB)
Ahlberg, A.

Word, The
FRIES (US) 1978 dir. Richard Lang
TVSe(US)
Wallace, I.

Words Upon the Window Pane
PEMBRIDGE (Ire) 1994 dir. Mary McGuckian
Yeats, W. B.
P

Working Man, The
WAR (US) 1933 dir. John Adolf
Franklin, E.

Work is a Four Letter Word
UI (GB) 1968 dir. Peter Hall
Livings, H. *Eh?*
P

World According to Garp, The
WAR (US) 1982 dir. George Roy Hill
Irving, J.

World in His Arms, The
UN (US) 1952 dir. Raoul Walsh
Beach, R.

World is Full of Married Men, The
NEW REALM (GB) 1979 dir. Robert Young
Collins, J.

World of Henry Orient, The
UA (US) 1964 dir. George Roy Hill
Johnson, N.

World of Suzie Wong, The
PAR (GB) 1960 dir. Richard Quine
Mason, R.

Worlds Apart
SCANLON (Israel) 1980 dir. Barbara Noble
Kollek, A. *Don't Ask Me If I Love*

World, The Flesh and the Devil, The
MGM (US) 1959
dir. Ronald MacDougall

Shiel, M. P. *Purple Cloud, The*

Worm's Eye View
ABP (GB) 1951 dir. Jack Raymond

Delderfield, R. F.
P

Worth Winning
FOX (US) 1989 dir. Will Mackenzie

Lewandowski, D.

Woundings
MUSE (GB) 1998 dir. Roberta Hanley

Noon, J.
P

Wrath of God, The
MGM (US) 1972 dir. Ralph Nelson

Graham, J.

Wreath of Roses, A
GRANADA (GB) 1987) dir. John
Madden
TV(GB)

Taylor, E.

Wrecking Crew, The
COL (US) 1968 dir. Phil Karlson

Hamilton, D.

Wreck of the Mary Deare, The
MGM (US) 1959 dir. Michael Anderson

Innes, H.

Written in Blood
YTV/A&E (GB) 1998 dir. Jeremy
Silberston
TV(GB)

Graham. C.

Written on the Wind
UN (US) 1956 dir. Douglas Sirk

Wilder, R.

Wrong Box, The
COL (GB) 1966 dir. Bryan Forbes

Stevenson, R. L. and Osbourne, L.

Wrong is Right
COL (US) 1982 dir. Richard Brooks
GB title: Man with the Deadly Lens,
The

McCarry, C. *Deadly Angels, The*

WUSA
PAR (US) 1970 dir. Stuart Rosenberg

Stone, R. *Hall of Mirrors*

Wuthering Heights
UA (US) 1939 dir. William Wyler
BBC (GB) 1978 dir. Peter Hammond
TVSe(GB)
MGM-EMI (GB) 1970 dir. Robert Fuest
PLEXUS (Sp) 1983 dir. Luis Bunuel
PAR (GB/US) 1992 dir. Peter
Kosminsky

Bronte, E.

Wynne and Penkovsky
BBC (GB/US) 1985 dir. Paul Seed
TVSe(GB/US)

Wynne, G. *Man from Moscow, A*

Xiu Xiu: The Sent-Down Girl
GOOD MACHINE (China/HK) 1998
dir. Joan Chen

Yan, G. *Tian Yu*

Yangtse Incident
BL (GB) 1957 dir. Michael Anderson
US title: Battle Hell

Earl, L.

Yankee Pasha
UI (US) 1954 dir. Joseph Pevney

Marshall, E.

Yank in Ermine, A
MON (GB) 1955 dir. Gordon Parry

Carstairs, J. P. *Solid! Said the Earl*

Year in Provence, A
BBC/A&E (GB) 1993 dir. David Tucker
TVSe(GB)

Mayle, P.

Yearling, The
MGM (US) 1946 dir. Clarence Brown
RHI (US) dir. Rod Hardy
TV(US)

Rawlings, M. K.

Year of Living Dangerously, The
MGM/UA (Aust) 1982 dir. Peter Weir

Koch, C. J.

Year of the Dragon
MGM/UA (US) 1985
dir. Michael Cimino

Daley, R.

Year of the Gun
TRIUMPH (US) 1991
dir. John Frankenheimer

Mewshaw, M.

Years Between, The
FOX (GB) 1946 dir. Compton Bennett

Du Maurier, D.
P

Yellow Canary, The
FOX (US) 1963 dir. Buzz Kulik

Masterson, W. *Evil Come, Evil Go*

Yellow Earth
GUANGXI (China) 1985 dir. Chen
Kaige
Ke Lan *Echo in the Valley*

Yellow Jack
MGM (US) 1938 dir. George B. Seitz
Howard, S.
P

Yellow Sands
AB (GB) 1938 dir. Herbert Brenon
Phillpotts, E. and Phillpotts, A.
P

Yellowstone Kelly
WAR (US) 1959 dir. Gordon Douglas
Fisher, C.

Yellowthread Street
YTV (GB) 1990 dir. Ronald Graham
TVSe(GB)
Marshall, W.

Yellow Ticket, The
FOX (US) 1931 dir. Raoul Walsh
GB title: Yellow Passport, The
Morton, M.
P

Yen Family, The
FUJI (Jap) 1990 dir. Yojiro Takita
Tani, T. *Kimura Family, The*

Yentl
MGM/UA (US) 1983
dir. Barbra Streisand
M
Singer, I. B. *Yentl, the Yeshiva Boy*

Yerma
ARTIMAGEN (Sp) 1998 dir. Pilar
Tavora
Garcia Lorca, F.

Yes, Giorgio
MGM/UA (US) 1982 dir. Franklin
Schaffner
Piper, A.

Yes, My Darling Daughter
WAR (US) 1939 dir. William Keighley
Reed, M.
P

Yesterday's Child
PAR TV (US) 1977 dir. Corey Allen, Bob
Rosenbaum
TV(US)
Disney, D. M. *Night of Clear Choice*

Yesterday's Children
COS/MEU (US) 2000 dir. Marcus Cole
TV(US)
Cockell, J.

Yield to the Night
ABP (GB) 1956 dir. J. Lee Thompson
US title: Blonde Sinner
Henry, J.

Yixizhuoma
BEIJING (China) 2000 dir. Fei Xie
Zhaxidawa *Ming*

**You Can't Get Away with
Murder**
WAR (US) 1939 dir. Lewis Seiler
Lawes, L. and Finn, J. *Chalked Out*
P

You Can't Go Home Again
CBS ENT (US) 1979 dir. Ralph Nelson
TV(US)
Wolfe, T.

You Can Thank Me Later
CINEQUEST (Can) 1998 dir. Shimon
Dotan
Safdie, O. *Hyper-Allergenic*
P

You Can't See Round Corners
UI (Aust) 1969 dir. David Cahill
Cleary, J.

You Can't Take it With You
COL (US) 1938 dir. Frank Capra
Kaufman, G. S. and Hart, M.
P

You'll Like My Mother
UN (US) 1972 dir. Lamont Johnson
Hintze, N. A.

You'll Never See Me Again
UN (US) 1973 dir. Jeannot Szwarc
TV(US)
Woolrich, C.

Young and Innocent
GFD (GB) 1937 dir. Alfred Hitchcock
US title: Girl was Young, A
Tey, J. *Shilling for Candles, A*

Young and Willing
UA (US) 1942 dir. Edward H. Griffith
Swann, F. *Out of the Frying Pan*
P

Young at Heart
WAR (US) 1954 dir. Gordon Douglas
Hurst, F.

Young Bess
MGM (US) 1953 dir. George Sidney
Irwin, M.

Young Billy Young
UA (US) 1969 dir. Burt Kennedy
Henry, W. *Who Rides with Wyatt?*

Youngblood Hawke
WAR (US) 1963 dir. Delmer Daves
Wouk, H.

Young Cassidy
MGM (GB) 1964
dir. Jack Cardiff, John Ford
O'Casey, S. *Mirror in my House*

Young Dr. Kildare
MGM (US) 1938 dir. Harold S. Bucquet
Brand, M.

Young Doctors, The
UA (US) 1961 dir. Phil Karlson
Hailey, A. *Final Diagnosis, The*

Youngest Profession, The
MGM (US) 1943 dir. Edward Buzzell
Day, L.

Young in Heart, The
SELZNICK (US) 1938
dir. Richard Wallace
Wylie, I. A. R. *Gay Banditti, The*

Young Ivanhoe
FILMLINE (Can/Fr) 1995 dir. Ralph L. Thomas
TV(Can/Fr)
Scott, Sir W. *Ivanhoe*

Young Joe, the Forgotten Kennedy
ABC (US) 1977 dir. Richard T. Heffron
TV(US)
Searls, H. *Lost Prince, The: Young Joe, The Forgotten Kennedy*

Young Lions, The
FOX (US) 1958 dir. Edward Dmytryk
Shaw, I.

Young Lovers, The
MGM (US) 1964 dir. Samuel Goldwyn, Jr.
Halevy, J.

Young Man with a Horn
WAR (US) 1950 dir. Michael Curtiz
GB title: Young Man of Music
Baker, D.

Young Philadelphians, The
WAR (US) 1959 dir. Vincent Sherman
GB title: City Jungle, The
Powell, R. *Philadelphian, The*

Young Pioneers
ABC (US) 1976 dir. Michael O'Herlihy
TV(US)
Lane, R. W.

Young Savages, The
UA (US) 1960 dir. John Frankenheimer
Hunter, E. *Matter of Conviction, A*

Young Visitors, The
CHANNEL 4 (GB) 1984 dir. James Hill
Ashford, D.

Young Warriors
UN (US) 1966 dir. John Peyser
Matheson, R. *Beardless Warriors*

Young Widow, The
UA (US) 1946 dir. Edwin L. Marin
Cushman, C. F.

Young Winston
COL-WAR (GB) 1972
dir. Richard Attenborough
Churchill, Sir W. S. *My Early Life*

Young Wives' Tale
ABP (GB) 1951 dir. Henry Cass
Jeans, R.
P

Young Woodley
BI (GB) 1929 dir. Thomas Bentley
van Druten, J.
P

You Only Live Twice
UA (GB) 1966 dir. Lewis Gilbert
Fleming, I.

You're a Big Boy Now
WAR (US) 1967
dir. Francis Ford Coppola
Benedictus, D.

You're Only Young Twice
ABP (GB) 1952 dir. Terry Gilbert
Bridie, J. *What Say They*
P

Your Money or Your Wife
BRENTWOOD (US) 1972
dir. Allen Reisner
TV(US)
Craig, J. *If You Want to See Your Wife Again*

Your Name Poisons My Dreams
CDP(Sp) 1996 dir. Pilar Miro
Leguina, J. *Tu Nombre Envenena Mis Suenos*

Your Ticket is No Longer Valid
CAROLCO (Can) 1980
dir. George Kaczender
Gary, R.

You've Got Mail
WAR (US) 1998 dir. Nora Ephron
Laszlo, N. *Parfumerie*
P

Yvonne's Perfume
ZOULOU (Fr) 1994 dir. Patrice Leconte
Modiano, P. *Villa Triste*

Z
WAR (Fr/Alg) 1968 dir. Costa-Gavras
Vassilikos, V.

Zandy's Bride
WAR (US) 1974 dir. Jan Troell
Loss, L. B. *Stranger, The*

Zappa
IS (Den) 1984 dir. Bille August
Reuter, B.

Zarak
COL (GB) 1956 dir. Terence Young
Bevan, A. C. *Story of Zarak Khan, The*

Zaza
PAR (US) 1938 dir. George Cukor
Berton, P. and Simon, C.
P

Zastrozzi
CHANNEL 4 (GB) 1986 dir. David G.
Hopkins
TVSe(GB)
Shelley, P. B.

Zazie Dans le Métro
CONN (Fr) 1960
dir. Louis Malle
Queneau, R.

Zebre, Le
LAMBART (Fr) 1992 dir. Jean Poiret
Jardin, A.

Zenon: Girl of the 21st Century
DISNEY (US) 1999 dir. Kenneth
Johnson
TV(US)
Sadler, M. and Bollen, R.

Zero Kelvin
NORSK (Nor/Swe) 1995 dir. Hans
Petter Moland
Tutein, P. *Larsen*

Zooman
SHOWTIMEWORKS (US) 1995 dir.
Leon Ichaso
TV(US)
Fuller, C. *Zooman and the Sign*
P

Zoo 2000
BBC (GB) 1984
TV(GB)
Chertas, J.

Zoot Suit
UN (US) 1982 dir. Luis Valdez
Valdez, L.
P

Zorba and Lucky
CECCHI (It) 1998 dir. Elzo D'Alo
A, Ch
Sepulveda, L. *Story of a Seagull and the Cat who Taught her to Fly*

Zorba the Greek
FOX (GB) 1964 dir. Michael Cacoyannis
Kazantzakis, N.

Zoya

NBC (US) 1995 dir. Richard Colla
TVSe(US)
Steel, D.

Zwart Meteoor, De

SIGMA (Neth) 2001 dir. Guido Pieters
Egbers, T.

AUTHOR INDEX

Author's name ——— **Spewack, B. and Spewack, S.**
Book or play title ——— **Kiss Me Kate**
P ——— Means adapted from a play
Studio name and ——— MGM (US) 1953 dir. George Sidney ——— Film title (if different)
country of origin **M**
MILBERG (US) 1958 dir. George Schaefer ——— Director's name
British, etc. title ——— **TV(US)**
(if different) GB title: ——— Date of release
——— Abbreviations as listed below

A = Animated film
Ch = Made for children
M = Based on a musical

TV (GB, US, etc.) = Made for British, American, etc. television
TVSe = Made-for-television series or miniseries

Aamund, J.
Klinkevals

Juliane
PER HOLST (Den) 1999 dir. Hans
Kristensen

Aamund, J.
Klinkevals

NORDISK (Den) 1999 dir. Hans
Kristensen

Aaronson, D.
Hoods, The

Once Upon a Time in America
WAR (US) 1984 dir. Sergio Leone

Abbey, E.
Brave Cowboy

Lonely are the Brave
UI (US) 1962 dir. David Miller

Abbey, E.
Fire on the Mountain

CARSON (US) 1981 dir. Donald Wrye
TV(US)

Abbot, A.
Murder of the Circus Queen, The

Circus Queen Murder
COL (US) 1933 dir. Roy William Neill

Abbott, G.
Boys from Syracuse, The

UN (US) 1940 dir. E. A. Sutherland
M

Abbott, G.
On Your Toes

P
WAR (US) 1939 dir. Ray Enright

Abbott, G. and Abrams, L.
Heat Lightning

P
WAR (US) 1934 dir. Mervyn LeRoy

Abé, K.
Woman in the Dunes

Woman of the Dunes, The
CONTEM (Jap) 1964
dir. Hiroshi Teshigahara

Aberson, H. and Pearl, H.
Dumbo, the Flying Elephant

Dumbo
DISNEY (US) 1941 dir. Ben Sharpsteen
A, Ch

Abrahams, P.
Fan, The

TRISTAR (US) 1996 dir. Tony Scott

Ackerley, J. R.
We Think the World of You

CINECOM (GB) 1988 dir. Colin Gregg

Ackland, R.
Pink Room, The

P
Absolute Hell
BBC (GB) 1991 dir. Anthony Page
TV(GB)

Adair, G.
Love and Death on Long Island
BRIT SCREEN (Can/GB) 1997 dir.
Richard Kwietniowski

Adam, A.
Sylvia and the Ghost
P
ECRAN (Fr) 1944
dir. Claude Autant-Lara

Adamovich, A.
Story of Khatyn, The
Come and See
MOSFILM (USSR) 1985
dir. Elem Klimov

Adams, C.
Dangerous Days of Kiowa Jones, The
MGM (US) 1966 dir. Alex March
TV(US)

Adams, D.
Hitch-Hiker's Guide to the Galaxy, The
BBC (GB) 1981 dir. Alan Bell
TVSe(GB)

Adams, H. D. and Mylander, M.
Gesundheit, Good Health is a Laughing Matter
Patch Adams
BLUE WOLF (US) 1998 dir. Tom Shadyac

Adams, J.
Sex and the Single Parent
TIME-LIFE (US) 1979
dir. Jackie Cooper
TV(US)

Adams, P. and Cooklin, S.
Knockback
BBC (GB) 1985
TV(GB)

Adams, R.
Girl in a Swing, The
J&M (GB/US) 1989 dir. Gordon Hessler

Adams, R.
Watership Down
CIC (GB) 1978 dir. Martin Rosen
A, Ch

Adams, R. G.
Plague Dogs, The
NEPENTHE (GB) 1982
dir. Martin Rosen
A

Adams, S. H.
Gorgeous Hussy, The
MGM (US) 1936 dir. Clarence Brown

Adams, S. H.
In Person
RKO (US) 1935 dir. William A. Seiter

Adams, S. H.
Night Bus
It Happened One Night
COL (US) 1934 dir. Frank Capra

Adamson, J.
Born Free
COL (GB) 1965 dir. James Hill

Adamson, J.
Living Free
COL (GB) 1972 dir. Jack Couffer

Adleman, R. H. and Walton, G.
Devil's Brigade, The
UA (US) 1968 dir. Andrew V. MacLaglen

Adler, P.
Amies de Ma Femme, Les
STUDIO CANAL+ (Fr) 1992 dir. Didier Van Cauwelaert

Adler, P.
House is not a Home, A
PAR (US) 1964 dir. Russell Rouse

Adler, R. and Ross, J.
Damn Yankees
P
WAR (US) 1958 dir. George Abbott,
Stanley Donen
GB title: What Lola Wants
M

Adler, W.
Random Hearts
COL (US) 1999 dir. Sydney Pollack

Adler, W.
Sunset Gang, The
AM PLAY (US) 1991 dir. Calvin Skaggs,
Tony Drazan
TVSe(US)

Adler, W.
War of the Roses, The
FOX (US) 1989 dir. Danny DeVito

Aeschylus
Oresteia Trilogy, The
Serpent Son, The
BBC (GB) 1979 dir. Bill Hays
TVSe(GB)

Agee, J.
Death in the Family, A
All the Way Home
PAR (US) 1963 dir. Alex Segal
PAR (US) 1971 dir. Fred Coe
TV (US)

Ahlberg, A.
Woof
CENTRAL (GB) 1990
dir. David Cobham
Ch, TVSe(GB)

Aiken, J.
Wolves of Willoughby Chase, The
ZENITH (GB) 1988 dir. Stuart Orme

Ainsworth, H.
Rookwood
Dick Turpin
STOLL-STAFFORD (GB) 1933
dir. Victor Hanbury, John Stafford

Akae, B.
Irezumi: The Spirit of Tattoo
DAIEI (Jap) 1983
dir. Yoichi Takabayashi

Akins, Z.
Morning Glory
P
RKO (US) 1933 dir. Lowell Sherman

Akins, Z.
Stage Struck
P
RKO (US) 1957 dir. Sidney Lumet

Aladar, L.
Honest Finder, The
Trouble in Paradise
PAR (US) 1932 dir. Ernst Lubitsch

Albaret, C.
Monsieur Proust
Celeste
PEL (W. Ger) 1981 dir. Percy Adlon

Albee, E.
Ballad of the Sad Café, The
P
MI/HOBO (US/GB)
1991 dir. Simon Callow

Albee, E.
Delicate Balance, A
P
SEVEN KEYS (US) 1975
dir. Tony Richardson

Albee, E.
Who's Afraid of Virginia Woolf?
P
WAR (US) 1966 dir. Mike Nichols

Albert, M. H.
Apache Rising
Duel at Diablo
UA (US) 1966 dir. Ralph Nelson

Albert, M. H.
Don is Dead, The
UN (US) 1973 dir. Richard Fleischer

Albert, M. H.
Lady in Cement
FOX (US) 1968 dir. Gordon Douglas

Albert, M. H.
Man in Black, The
Rough Night in Jericho
UN (US) 1967 dir. Arnold Laven

Albert, M. H.
Miami Mayhem
Tony Rome
FOX (US) 1967 dir. Gordon Douglas

Albom, M.
Tuesdays With Morrie
HARPO (US) 1999 dir. Mick Jackson
TV(US)

Albrand, M.
Desperate Moment
GFD (GB) 1953 dir. Compton Bennett

Albrand, M.
Dishonoured
Captain Carey USA
PAR (US) 1950 dir. Mitchell Leisen
GB title: After Midnight

Alcock, V.
Cuckoo Sister, The
BBC (GB) 1986 dir. Marilyn Fox
TVSe(GB)

Alcock, V.
Travellers by Night
TVS (GB) 1985
Ch, TVSe(GB)

Alcott, L. M.
Inheritance, The
ALLIANCE (US) 1997 dir. Bobby Roth
TV(US)

Alcott, L. M.
Little Men
RKO (US) 1935 dir. Philip Rosen
TELEFILM (Can) 1998 dir. Rodney Gibbons

Alcott, L. M.
Little Women
RKO (US) 1933 dir. George Cukor
MGM (US) 1948 dir. Mervyn LeRoy
BBC (GB) 1970 dir. Paddy Russell
TVSe(GB)
UN (US) 1978 dir. David Lowell Rich
TVSe(US)
COL (US) 1994 dir. Gillian Armstrong

Alcu, Y.
MacArthur's Children
ORION (Jap) 1985
dir. Masahiro Shinoda

Aldington, R.
All Men are Enemies
FOX (US) 1934 dir. George Fitzmaurice

Aldiss, B.
Frankenstein Unbound
TCF (US) 1990 dir. Roger Corman

Aldrich, B. S.
Lantern in Her Hand, A
Mother's Gift, A
RHI (US) 1995 dir. Jerry London
TV(US)

Aldrich, B. S.
Silent Stars Go By, The
Gift of Love, The: A Christmas Story
TELECOM (US) 1983
dir. Delbert Mann
TV(US)

Aldrich, Mrs B.
Miss Bishop

Cheers for Miss Bishop
PAR (US) 1941 dir. Tay Garnett

Aldridge, J.
Captive in the Land, A

GLORIA/GORKY (US/USSR) 1991
dir. John Berry

Aldridge, J.
Sporting Proposition, A

Ride a Wild Pony
DISNEY (Aust) 1976 dir. Don Chaffey

Aldrin, Jr., E. and Warga, W.
Return to Earth

KH (US) 1976 dir. Jud Taylor
TV(US)

Alexander, K.
Private Investigation, A

Missing Pieces
TTC (US) 1983 dir. Mike Hodges
TV(US)

Alexander, K. and Hayes, S.
Time After Time

WAR (US) 1979 dir. Nicholas Meyer

Alexander, L.
Chronicles of Prydain, The

Black Cauldron, The
DISNEY (US) 1985 dir. Ted Berman,
Richard Rich
A, Ch

Alexander, R.
Time Out for Ginger

P
Billie
UA (US) 1965 dir. Don Weis

Alexander, S.
Nutcracker: Money, Madness, Murder:
A Family Album

Nutcracker: Money, Madness and Murder
WAR TV (US) 1987
dir. Paul Bogart
TVSe(US)

Algren, N.
Man with the Golden Arm, The

UA (US) 1955 dir. Otto Preminger

Algren, N.
Walk on the Wild Side, A

COL (US) 1962 dir. Edward Dmytryk

Ali, J.
Dark Days and Light Nights

P
Black Joy
WINCAST/WEST ONE (GB) 1977
dir. Anthony Simmons

Ali, M.
Greatest, The

COL-WAR (US/GB) 1977 dir. Tom
Gries

Alibrandi, T. and Armani, F. H.
Privileged Information

Sworn to Silence
BLATT/SINGER (US) 1987
dir. Peter Levin
TV(US)

Allan, N.
Lies My Father Told Me

COL (Can) 1975 dir. Jan Kadar

Allan, T.
Love Streams

P
CANNON (US) 1984
dir. John Cassavetes

Allardice, J.
At War with the Army
P
PAR (US) 1951 dir. Hal Walker

Allbeury, T.
No Place to Hide
Hostage
SKOURAS (US) 1992 dir. Robert Young

Allegretto, M.
Night of Reunion
Terror in the Shadows
HEARST (US) 1995 dir. William A.
Graham
TV(US)

Allen, H.
Anthony Adverse
WAR (US) 1936 dir. Mervyn LeRoy

Allen, J.
Nu
Tumult
ATHENA (Den) 1970
dir. Hans Abramson

Allen, J. and Livingston, M.
Thanks God, I'll Take it From Here
Without Reservations
RKO (US) 1946 dir. Mervyn LeRoy

Allen, J. P.
First Wife, The
P
Wives and Lovers
PAR (US) 1963 dir. John Rich

Allen, J. P.
Just Tell Me What You Want
WAR (US) 1980 dir. Sidney Lumet

Allen, T. B.
Possessed: The True Story of an Exorcism
Possessed
SHOWTIME (US) 2000 dir. Steven E. de
Souza
TV(US)

Allen, W.
Don't Drink the Water
P
AVCO (US) 1969
dir. Howard Morris
MAGNOLIA (US) 1994 dir. Woody
Allen
TV(US)

Allen, W.
Play it Again, Sam
P
PAR (US) 1972 dir. Herbert Ross

Allende, I.
House of the Spirits, The
COSTADO (Den/Ger/US) 1993 dir.
Bille August

Allende, I.
Of Love and Shadows
MIRAMAX (Arg/Sp) 1994 dir. Betty
Kaplan

Allfrey, P. S.
Orchid House, The
BBC (GB) 1991 dir. Harold Ove
TV(GB)

Allingham, M.
Tiger in the Smoke
RANK (GB) 1956 dir. Roy Baker

Allison, D.
Bastard Out of Carolina
SHOWTIMEWORKS (US) 1996 dir.
Anjelica Huston
TV(US)

Allison, W. and Fairley, J.
Monocled Mutineer, The
BBC (GB) 1986 dir. Jim O'Brien
TVSe(GB)

Allister, R.
Friese-Greene
Magic Box, The
BL (GB) 1951 dir. John Boulting

Allman, S. and Pickett, B.
I'm Sorry the Bridge is Out, You'll Have to Spend the Night
P
Monster Mash: The Movie
PRISM (US) 1995 dir. Joel Cohen, Alec Sokolow

Almagor, G.
Etz Hadomim Tafus
Under the Domim Tree
HSA (Israel) 1995 dir. Eli Cohen

Altieri, Major J.
Darby's Rangers
WAR (US) 1957 dir. William Wellman
GB title: Young Invaders, The

Alvarez, J.
In the Time of the Butterflies
SHOWTIME (US) 2001 dir. Mariano Barroso
TV(US)

Amado, J.
Dona Flor and her Two Husbands
FD (Bra) 1977 dir. Bruno Barretto

Amado, J.
Gabriela, Clove and Cinnamon
Gabriela
MGM/UA (Port) 1984
dir. Bruno Barreto

Amado, J.
Tieta do Agreste
COL (Bra/GB) 1996 dir. Carlos Diegnes

Amateau, R. and Robinson, B.
Operator, The
Where Does it Hurt?
HEMDALE (US) 1971 dir. Rod Amateau

Ambler, E.
Care of Time, The
ANGLIA (GB) 1990 dir. John Howard Davies
TV(GB)

Ambler, E.
Epitaph for a Spy
Hotel Reserve
RKO (GB) 1944 dir. Victor Hanbury

Ambler, E.
Journey into Fear
RKO (US) 1942
dir. Norman Foster, Orson Welles

Ambler, E.
Light of Day, The
Topkapi
UA (US) 1964 dir. Jules Dassin

Ambler, E.
Mask of Dimitrios, The
WAR (US) 1944 dir. Jean Negulesco

Ambler, E.
October Man, The
GFD (GB) 1947 dir. Roy Baker

Ambler, E.
Quiet Conspiracy, A
ANGLIA (GB) 1989 dir. John Gorrie
TVSe(GB)

Ambler, E.
Uncommon Danger
Background to Danger
WAR (US) 1943 dir. Raoul Walsh

Ambrose, S. E.
Band of Brothers, A: E Company 506th Regiment, 101st Airborne From Normandy to Hitler's Nest

Band of Brothers
DREAMWORKS (US/GB) 2001 dir. David Franken, Tom Hanks, David Leland, Richard Loncraine, David Nutter, Phil Alden Robinson, Mikael Salomon, Tony To
TVSe(US/GB)

Amen, C.
Last Testament, The

Testament
PAR (US) 1983 dir. Lynne Littman

Ames, D.
She Shall Have Murder
BL (GB) 1950 dir. Daniel Birt

Amis, K.
Ending Up
THAMES (GB) 1989 dir. Peter Sasdy
TV(GB)

Amis, K.
Green Man, The
BBC (GB) 1990 dir. Elijah Moshinsky
TVSe(GB)

Amis, K.
Lucky Jim
BL (GB) 1957 dir. John Boulting

Amis, K.
Old Devils, The
BBC (GB) 1992 dir. Tristram Powell
TVSe(GB)

Amis, K.
Stanley and the Women
CENTRAL (GB) 1991 dir. David Tucker
TVSe(GB)

Amis, K.
Take a Girl Like You
COL (GB) 1969 dir. Jonathan Miller
BBC/WGBH (GB) 2000 dir. Nick Hurran
TV(GB)

Amis, K.
That Uncertain Feeling
Only Two Can Play
BL (GB) 1961 dir. Sidney Gilliat

Amis, M.
Dead Babies
OVERSEAS (US) 2001 dir. William Marsh

Amis, M.
Rachel Papers, The
UA (GB) 1989 dir. Damian Harris

Anders, P.
Summer with Monika
SVENSK (Swe) 1952
dir. Ingmar Bergman

Andersen, C.
Madonna: Unauthorized
Madonna: Innocence Lost
JAFFE/BRAUNSTEIN (US) 1994 dir. Bradford May
TV(US)

Andersen, H. C.
Emperor's New Clothes, The
CANNON (US) 1987 dir. David Irving
Ch

Andersen, H. C.
Little Match Girl, The
NBC (US) 1987
dir. Michael Lindsay-Hogg
Ch, TV(US)

Andersen, H. C.
Little Mermaid, The
DISNEY (US) 1989 dir. John Masker,
Ron Clements
A, Ch

Anderson, B.
Rendezvous
DIRECTORS' CIRCLE (US) 1999 dir.
Roy Campanella II
TV(US)

Anderson, E.
Thieves Like Us
UA (US) 1974 dir. Robert Altman

Anderson, J.
Assault and Matrimony
NBC (US) 1987 dir. James Frawley
TV(US)

Anderson, J.
Baby Dance, The
P
EGG (US) 1998 dir. Jane Anderson
TV(US)

Anderson, L.
Sky has Many Colours, The
Lili Marleen
ROXY (Ger) 1980
dir. Rainer Werner Fassbinder

Anderson, M.
Anne of the Thousand Days
P
UN (GB) 1969 dir. Charles Jarrot

Anderson, M.
Barefoot in Athens
P
COMPASS (US) 1966
dir. George Schaefer
TV(US)

Anderson, M.
Elizabeth the Queen
P
Private Lives of Elizabeth and Essex, The
WAR (US) 1939 dir. Michael Curtiz

Anderson, M.
Elizabeth the Queen
P
COMPASS (US) 1968
dir. George Schaefer
TV(US)

Anderson, M.
Eve of St. Mark, The
P
FOX (US) 1944 dir. John M. Stahl

Anderson, M.
Joan of Lorraine
P
Joan of Arc
RKO (US) 1948 dir. Victor Fleming

Anderson, M.
Key Largo
P
WAR (US) 1948 dir. John Huston

Anderson, M.
Mary of Scotland
P
RKO (US) 1936 dir. John Ford

Anderson, M.
Saturday's Children
P
WAR (US) 1940 dir. Vincent Sherman

Anderson, M.
Winterset
P
RKO (US) 1936 dir. Alfred Santell
COMPASS (US) 1959
dir. George Schaefer
TV(US)

Anderson, M. and Casella, A.
Death Takes a Holiday

P
PAR (US) 1934 dir. Mitchell Leisen
UN TV (US) 1971 dir. Robert Butler
TV(US)

Anderson, M. and Stallings, L.
What Price Glory?

P
FOX (US) 1952 dir. John Ford

Anderson, P.
High Crusade, The
CENTROPOLIS (Ger) 1994 dir. Klaus
Knoesel, Holger Neuhauser

Anderson, P.
Nurse
HALMI (US) 1980
dir. David Lowell Rich
TV(US)

Anderson, P.
President's Mistress, The
KINGS ROAD (US) 1978
dir. John Llewellyn Moxey
TV(US)

Anderson, R.
Getting Up and Going Home
POLONE/HEARST (US) 1992 dir.
Steven Schachter
TV(US)

Anderson, R.
Silent Night, Lonely Night

P
UN TV (US) 1969 dir. Daniel Petrie
TV(US)

Anderson, R.
Tea and Sympathy

P
MGM (US) 1956 dir. Vincente Minnelli

Anderson, R. W.
I Never Sang for my Father

P
COL (US) 1970 dir. Gilbert Cates

Anderson, V.
Beware of Children
No Kidding
AA (GB) 1960 dir. Gerald Thomas
US title: Beware of Children

Anderson, W. C.
Hurricane Hunters
Hurricane
METRO (US) 1974 dir. Jerry Jameson
TV(US)

Andrevan, J.-P.
Robots Against Gandahar
Light Years
MIRAMAX (Fr) 1988 dir. René Laloux
A

Andrew, R. H.
Great Day in the Morning
RKO (US) 1955 dir. Jacques Tourneur

Andrews, G.
All or Nothing At All
LWT (GB) 1993 dir. Andrew Grieve
TVSe(GB)

Andrews, M. R.
Perfect Tribute, The
P&G (US) 1991 dir. Jack Bender
TV(US)

Andrews, V. C.
Flowers in the Attic
NEW WORLD (US) 1987
dir. Jeffrey Bloom

Andrzejewski, J.
Ashes and Diamonds
POLSKI (Pol) 1958 dir. Andrzej Wajda

Anet, C.
Mayerling

NERO (Fr) 1935 dir. Anatole Litvak
WAR (Fr/GB) 1968 dir. Terence Young

Angelou, M.
I Know Why the Caged Bird Sings

TOM (US) 1979
dir. Fielder Cook
TV(US)

Angerson, W. C.
BAT 21

TRISTAR (US) 1988 dir. Peter Markle

Annixter, P.
Swift Water

Those Calloways
DISNEY (US) 1964 dir. Norman Tokar

Anon.
Sir Gawain and the Green Knight

Gawain and the Green Knight
THAMES (GB) 1990 dir. J. M. Phillips
TV(GB)

Anouilh, J.
Becket

P
PAR (GB) 1963 dir. Peter Glenville

Anouilh, J.
Lark, The

P
MILBERG (US) 1957
dir. George Schaefer
TV(US)

Anouilh, J.
Time Remembered

P
COMPASS (US) 1961
dir. George Schaefer
TV(US)

Anouilh, J.
Waltz of the Toreadors

P
RANK (GB) 1962 dir. John Guillermin

Anson, J.
Amityville Horror, The

AIP (US) 1979 dir. Stuart Rosenberg

Anson, R. A.
Best Intentions: The Education and
Killing of Edmund Perry

*Murder Without Motive: The Edmund
Perry Story*
L. HILL TV (US) 1992
dir. Kevin Hooks
TV(US)

Anstey, F.
Brass Bottle, The

RANK (US) 1964 dir. Harry Keller

Anstey, F.
Tinted Venus

Goddess of Love, The
NEW WORLD TV (US) 1988
dir. James Drake
TV(US)

Anstey, F.
Vice Versa

TC (GB) 1948 dir. Peter Ustinov

Anthelme, P.
I Confess

P
WAR (US) 1953 dir. Alfred Hitchcock

Anthony, C. L.
Autumn Crocus

P
BI (GB) 1934 dir. Basil Dearden

Anthony, C. L.
Service

P
Looking Forward
MGM (US) 1933 dir. Clarence Brown

Anthony, D.
Midnight Lady and the Mourning Man
Midnight Man, The
UN (US) 1974 dir. Roland Kibbee

Anthony, E.
Tamarind Seed, The
SCOTIA-BARBER (GB) 1974
dir. Blake Edwards

Antoine, W. P.
Ennemie, L'
P
Tendre Ennemie
WORLD (Fr) 1938 dir. Max Ophuls

Appel, B.
Fortress in the Rice
Cry of Battle
WAR (US) 1964 dir. Irving Lerner

Appel, D.
Comanche
Tonka
DISNEY (US) 1958 dir. Lewis R. Foster

Arbuzov, A.
Promise, The
P
COMM (GB) 1969 dir. Michael Hayes

Archard, M.
Alibi
CORONA (GB) 1942
dir. Brian Desmond Hirst

Archer, J.
First Among Equals
ITV (GB) 1986 dir. John Gorrie, Sarah
Harding, Brian Mills
TVSe(GB)

Archer, J.
Kane and Abel
EMBASSY (US) 1985 dir. Buzz Kulik
TVSe(US)

Archer, J.
Not a Penny More, Not a Penny Less
BBC (GB) 1990 dir. Clive Donner
TVSe(GB)

Archer, W.
Green Goddess, The
P
Adventure in Iraq
WAR (US) 1943 dir. D. Ross-Lederman

Archer, W.
Green Goddess, The
P
WAR (US) 1930 dir. Alfred E. Green

Ardies, T.
Kosygin is Coming
Russian Roulette
ITC (US) 1975 dir. Lou Lombardo

Ardrey, R.
Thunder Rock
P
MGM (GB) 1942 dir. Roy Boulting

Arent, A.
One Third of a Nation
P
PAR (US) 1939 dir. Dudley Murphy

Arianet, C.
Love in the Afternoon
AA (US) 1957 dir. Billy Wilder

Arjourni, J.
Happy Birthday, Turke!
SENATOR (Ger) 1992
dir. Dorris Dorrie

Arkell, R.
Charley Moon
BL (GB) 1956 dir. Guy Hamilton

Arlen, M.
Golden Arrow
P
WAR (US) 1936 dir. Alfred E. Green

Arlen, M.
Green Hat, The
Outcast Lady
MGM (US) 1934 dir. Robert Z. Leonard
GB title: Woman of the World, A

Arley, C.
Woman of Straw
UA (GB) 1964 dir. Basil Dearden

Arlington, A.
These, Our Strangers
Those Kids from Town
BN (GB) 1941 dir. Lance Comfort

Armandy, A.
Renegades
FOX (US) 1930 dir. Victor Fleming

Armbrister, T.
Act of Vengeance
LORIMAR (US) 1986
dir. John MacKenzie
TV(US)

Armont, P. and Gerbidon, M.
Coiffeur Pour Dames
P
HOCHE (Fr) 1952 dir. Jean Boyer
GB title: Artist with Ladies, An

Armstrong, A.
He was Found in the Road
Man in the Road, The
GN (GB) 1956 dir. Lance Comfort

Armstrong, A.
Ten Minute Alibi
P
BL (GB) 1935 dir. Bernard Vorhaus

Armstrong, C.
Case of the Three Weird Sisters, The
Three Weird Sisters, The
BN (GB) 1948 dir. Dan Birt

Armstrong, C.
Chocolate Cobweb, The
Merci Pour le Chocolat
STUDIO CANAL+ (Fr) 2000 dir. Claude
Chabrol

Armstrong, C.
Mischief
Don't Bother to Knock
FOX (US) 1952 dir. Roy Ward Baker

Armstrong, C.
Mischief
Sitter, The
FNM (US) 1991 dir. Rick Berger
TV(US)

Armstrong, C.
Talk About a Stranger
MGM (US) 1952 dir. David Bradley

Armstrong, C.
Unsuspected, The
WAR (US) 1947 dir. Michael Curtiz

Armstrong, R.
Passage Home
GFD (GB) 1955 dir. Roy Baker

Armstrong, T.
Crowthers of Bankdam, The
Master of Bankdam
ALL (GB) 1947 dir. Walter Forde

Armstrong, W. H.
Sounder
FOX (US) 1972 dir. Martin Ritt

Arnaud, G.
Wages of Fear, The

Sorcerer
UN (US) 1977 dir. William Friedkin
GB title: Wages of Fear

Arnaud, G.
Wages of Fear

FDF (Fr/It) 1953
dir. Henri-Georges Clouzot

Arnold, E.
Blood Brother

Broken Arrow
FOX (US) 1950 dir. Delmer Daves

Arnold, E.
Commandos, The

First Comes Courage
COL (US) 1943 dir. Dorothy Arzner

Arnold, E.
Deep in my Heart

MGM (US) 1954 dir. Stanley Donen
M

Arnold, E.
Flight from Ashiya

UA (US/Jap) 1963
dir. Michael Anderson

Arnow, A.
Dollmaker, The

IPC (US) 1984 dir. Daniel Petrie
TV(US)

Arpino, G.
Buio e il Miele, Il

Scent of a Woman
UN (US) 1992 dir. Martin Brest

Arrighi, M.
Alter Ego

Murder by the Book
ORION TV (US) 1987 dir. Mel Damski
TV(US)

Arsan, E.
Emmanuelle

SF (Fr) 1975 dir. Just Jacklin

Arsan, E.
Néa

NEW REALM (Fr/Ger) 1976
dir. Nelly Kaplan
US/GB title: Young Emanuelle

Arthur, R. A.
Edge of the City

P
MGM (US) 1957 dir. Martin Ritt
GB title: Man is Ten Feet Tall, A

Arundel, E.
Persistent Warrior, The

Green Fingers
BN (GB) 1946 dir. John Harlow

Asche, O. and Norton, F.
Chu Chin Chow

P
GAU (GB) 1934 dir. Walter Forde
M

Ashford, D.
Young Visitors, The

CHANNEL 4 (GB) 1984 dir. James Hill

Ashley, B.
Break in the Sun

BBC (GB) 1981 dir. Roger Singleton-Turner
TVSe(GB)

Ashman, H. and Menken, A.
Little Shop of Horrors

P
WAR (US) 1986 dir. Frank Oz
M

Ashton, H.
Yeoman's Hospital

White Corridors
GFD (GB) 1951 dir. Pat Jackson

Ashton-Warner, S.
Spinster

Two Loves
MGM (US) 1961 dir. Charles Walters
GB title: Spinster, The

Ashton-Warner, S.
Teacher, I Passed This Way

Sylvia
ENT (NZ) 1985 dir. Michael Firth

Asimov, I. and Silverberg, R.
Positronic Man, The

Bicentennial Man
COL (US) 1999 dir. Chris Columbus

Asimov, I.
Nightfall

CONCORDE (US) 1988 dir. Paul
Mayersburg
CONCORDE (US) 2000 dir. Tim Clark,
Gwyneth Gibby

Asinof, E.
Eight Men Out

ORION (US) 1988 dir. John Sayles

Asinof, E., Hinckle, W. and Turner, W.
Ten-Second Jailbreak, The

Breakout
COL (US) 1975 dir. Tom Gries

Athanas, V.
Proud Ones, The

FOX (US) 1956 dir. Robert D. Webb

Atkins, Z.
Greeks Had a Word for Them, The
P

UA (US) 1932 dir. Lowell Sherman

Atkins, Z.
Old Maid, The
P

WAR (US) 1939 dir. Edmund Goulding

Atkinson, E.
Greyfriar's Bobby

Challenge to Lassie
MGM (US) 1949 dir. Richard Thorpe

Atkinson, H.
Games, The

FOX (GB) 1969 dir. Michael Winner

Attiwill, K.
Sky Steward

Non Stop New York
GFD (GB) 1937 dir. Robert Stevenson

Atwood, M.
Handmaid's Tale, The

CINECOM (US) 1990
dir. Volker Schlondorff

Atzeni, S.
Son of Bukunin, The

MEDUSA (It) 1998 dir. Gianfranco
Cabiddu

Aubert, B.
Transfixions

Mauvais Genres
STUDIO CANAL+ (Fr/Bel) 2001 dir.
Francis Girod

Aubert, J.-M.
Kurtz

Art (delicat) de la Seduction, L'
BLUE DAHLIA (Fr) 2001 dir. Richard
Berry

Aubrac, L.
Outwitting the Gestapo

Lucie Aubrac
CNC (Fr) 1997 dir. Claude Berri

Auel, J. M.
Clan of the Cave Bear, The

WAR (US) 1986 dir. Michael Chapman

Auerbach, J.
Sleep, Baby, Sleep
CITADEL ENT (US) 1995 dir. Armand
Mastroianni
TV(US)

Auque, R. and Forestier, P.
Hors La Vie
BAC (Fr/It/Bel) 1991
dir. Maroun Bagdadi

Austen, J.
Emma
BBC (GB) 1972 dir. John Glenister
TVSe(GB)
MIRAMAX (GB/US) 1996 dir. Douglas
McGrath
A&E/MERIDIAN (GB) 1997 dir.
Diarmuid Lawrence
TV(GB)

Austen, J.
Mansfield Park
BBC (GB) 1983 dir. David Giles
TVSe(GB)
MIRAMAX (GB) 1999 dir. Patricia
Rozema

Austen, J.
Northanger Abbey
BBC (GB) 1987 dir. Giles Foster
TV(GB)

Austen, J.
Persuasion
GRANADA (GB) 1971
dir. Howard Baker
TVSe(GB)
BBC/SONY (GB/US) 1995 dir. Roger
Michell

Austen, J.
Pride and Prejudice
MGM (US) 1940 dir. Robert Z. Leonard
BBC (GB) 1980 dir. Cyril Coke
TVSe(GB)
BBC/A&E (GB) 1995 dir. Simon
Langton
TVSe(GB)

Austen, J.
Sense and Sensibility
BBC (GB) 1971 dir. David Giles
TVSe(GB)
BBC (GB) 1981 dir. Rodney Bennett
TVSe(GB)
COL (GB/US) 1995 dir. Ang Lee

Auster, P.
Music of Chance, The
IRS MEDIA (US) 1993 dir. Philip Haas

Austin, A.
Wicked Woman, A
MGM (US) 1934 dir. Charles Brabin

Axelrod, G.
Goodbye Charlie
P
FOX (US) 1964 dir. Vincente Minnelli

Axelrod, G.
Seven Year Itch, The
P
FOX (US) 1955 dir. Billy Wilder

Axelrod, G.
Will Success Spoil Rock Hunter?
P
FOX (US) 1957 dir. Frank Tashlin
GB title: Oh! For a Man!

Axelson, M. M.
Life Begins
P
WAR (US) 1932 dir. James Flood
GB title: Dream of Life

Axelson, Mrs M. M.
Child is Born, A
P
WAR (US) 1939 dir. Lloyd Bacon

Ayckbourn, A.
Chorus of Disapproval, A
P
HOBO (GB) 1989 dir. Michael Winner

Ayckbourn, A.
Intimate Exchanges
P
Smoking/No Smoking
ARENA (Fr) 1993 dir. Alain Resnais

Ayckbourn, A.
Revenger's Comedies, The
P
BBC (GB/Fr) 1998 dir. Malcolm
Mowbray

Ayres, H.
Common Touch, The
BN (GB) 1941 dir. John Baxter

B

Babe, T.
Fathers and Sons
P
Wild Bill
UA (US) 1995 dir. Walter Hill

Baber, D.
My Death is a Mockery
ADELPHI (GB) 1952 dir. Tony Young

Babson, M.
Bejewelled Death
Bejewelled
DISNEY CH (US/GB) 1991
dir. Terry Marcel
TV(GB/US)

Bacchelli, R.
Mill on the Po, The
LUX (It) 1949 dir. Alberto Lattuardo

Bach, R.
Jonathan Livingstone Seagull
PAR (US) 1973 dir. Hill Bartlett

Bache, E.
Safe Passage
NEW LINE (US) 1994 dir. Robert Allan
Ackerman

Bachman, R.
Running Man, The
TRISTAR (US) 1987
dir. Paul Michael Glaser

Bachmann, L.
Kiss of Death
Devil Makes Three, The
MGM (US) 1952 dir. Andrew Marton

Bachmann, L.
Phoenix, The
Ten Seconds to Hell
UA (US) 1959 dir. Robert Aldrich

Bacon, F. and Smith, W.
Lightnin'
P
FOX (US) 1930 dir. Henry King

Bagley, D.
Enemy, The
PROMARK (US/GB) 2001 dir. Tom
Kinninmont

Bagley, D.
Freedom Trap, The
Mackintosh Man, The
COL-WAR (GB) 1973 dir. John Huston

Bagley, D.
Landslide
GOLDWYN (US) 1992 dir. Jean-Claude
Lord

Bagley, D.
Running Blind
BBC (GB) 1979 dir. William Brayne
TVSe(GB)

Bagley, D.
Story of the Vivero Letter, The

Vivero Letter, The
PROMARK (US) 1999 dir. H. Gordon
Boos

Bagnold, E.
Chalk Garden, The

RANK (GB) 1963 dir. Ronald Neame

Bagnold, E.
National Velvet

MGM (US) 1944 dir. Clarence Brown

Baiesu, O.
Bylanta

Oak, The
STUDIO CANAL+ (Fr) 1992 dir. Lucian
Pintilie

Bailey, A.
Airport

International Airport
SPELLING (US) 1985
dir. Charles Dubin, Don Chaffey
TV(US)

Bailly, A.
Flame and the Flesh, The

MGM (US) 1954 dir. Richard Brooks

Baily, L.
Gilbert and Sullivan and Their World

Story of Gilbert and Sullivan, The
BL (GB) 1953 dir. Sidney Gilliatt

Bainbridge, B.
Awfully Big Adventure, An

BRIT SCREEN (GB) 1995 dir. Mike
Newell

Bainbridge, B.
Dressmaker, The

FILM 4 (GB) 1988 dir. Jim O'Brien

Bainbridge, B.
Sweet William

ITC (GB) 1980 dir. Claude Whatham

Baird, M. T.
Lesson in Love, A

Circle of Two
BORDEAUX (Can) 1980
dir. Jules Dassin

Baitz, J. R.
Substance of Fire, The

P
MIRAMAX (US) 1996 dir. Daniel J.
Sullivan

Bakeer, D.
Crips

South Central
MONUMENT (US) 1992 dir. Steven
Anderson

Baker, C.
Ernest Hemingway: A Life Story

Hemingway
WILSON (US) 1988 dir. Bernhard Sinkel
TVSe(US)

Baker, D.
Young Man with a Horn

WAR (US) 1950 dir. Michael Curtiz
GB title: Young Man of Music

Baker, E.
Fine Madness, A

WAR (US) 1966 dir. Irvin Kershner

Baker, F.
Lease of Life

EAL (GB) 1954 dir. Charles Frend

Baker, F.
White Trash

P
BAKER (US) 1992 dir. Fred Baker

Baker, L.
Flamingo Rising, The
HALLMARK (US) 2001 dir. Martha
Coolidge
TV(US)

Baker, L.
Her Twelve Men
MGM (US) 1954 dir. Robert Z. Leonard

Baker, S.
Finding Signs
Love Always
CINEWEST (US) 1997 dir. Jude Pauline
Eberhard

Baker, T. and Jones, R.
Coffee, Tea or Me?
CBS ENT (US) 1983
dir. Norman Panama
TV(US)

Bakos, S. C.
Appointment for Murder
Beyond Suspicion
VZ/SERTNER (US) 1993 dir. William A.
Graham
TV(US)

Balazs, J.
Hungarians
IFEX (Hun) 1981 dir. Zoltan Fabri

Balchin, N.
Mine Own Executioner
BI (GB) 1947 dir. Anthony Kimmins

Balchin, N.
Small Back Room, The
LF (GB) 1949 dir. Michael Powell,
Emeric Pressburger
US title: Hour of Glory

Balchin, N.
Sort of Traitor, A
Suspect
BL (GB) 1960 dir. Roy Boulting

Baldacci, D.
Absolute Power
COL (US) 1997 dir. Clint Eastwood

Balderston, J. L.
Berkeley Square
P
House in the Square, The
FOX (GB) 1951 dir. Roy Baker
US title: I'll Never Forget You

Balderston, J. L.
Berkeley Square
P
FOX (US) 1933 dir. Frank Lloyd
MILBERG (US) 1959
dir. George Schaefer
TV(US)

Balderston, J. and Deane, H.
Dracula
P
CIC (GB) 1979 dir. John Badham

Baldwin, F.
Beauty
Beauty for Sale
MGM (US) 1933
dir. Richard Boleslawski

Baldwin, F.
Men are Such Fools
WAR (US) 1938 dir. Busby Berkeley

Baldwin, F.
Moon's Our Home, The
PAR (US) 1936 dir. William A. Seiter

Baldwin, F.
Portia on Trial
REP (US) 1937 dir. George Nicholls, Jr.

Baldwin, F.
Skyscraper
Skyscraper Souls
MGM (US) 1932 dir. Edgar Selwyn

Baldwin, F.
Spinster Dinner
Love Before Breakfast
UN (US) 1936 dir. Walter Lang

Baldwin, F.
Wife Vs. Secretary
MGM (US) 1936 dir. Clarence Brown

Baldwin, J.
Go Tell It On The Mountain
PRICE (US) 1985 dir. Stan Latham
TV(US)

Baldwin, J.
If Beale Street Could Talk
À La Place Du Coeur
STUDIO CANAL+ (Fr) 1998 dir. Robert
Guediguian

Ball, J.
In the Heat of the Night
UA (US) 1967 dir. Norman Jewison

Balland, P.
Affaires de Gout
Matter of Taste, A
STUDIO CANAL+ (Fr) 1999 dir.
Bernard Rapp

Ballantyne, S.
Imaginary Crimes
MORGAN CREEK (US) 1994 dir.
Anthony Drazan

Ballard, J. G.
Atrocity Exhibition, The
THE BUSINESS (US) 1999 dir. Jonathan
Weiss

Ballard, J. G.
Crash
ALLIANCE (Can/Fr/GB) 1996 dir.
David Cronenberg

Ballard, J. G.
Empire of the Sun
WAR (US) 1987 dir. Steven Spielberg

Ballinger, W.
Rafferty
Pushover
COL (US) 1954 dir. Richard Quine

Balmer, E. and Wylie, P.
When Worlds Collide
PAR (US) 1951 dir. Rudolph Maté

Bancroft, G. P.
Ware Case, The
P
EAL (GB) 1938 dir. Robert Stevenson

Bando, M.
Inugami
ASMIK (Jap) 2001 dir. Masato Harada

Banks, I.
Complicity
CARLTON FILMS (GB) 2000 dir. Gavin
Millar

Banks, L. R.
Indian in the Cupboard, The
COL (US) 1995 dir. Frank Oz
Ch

Banks, L. R.
L-Shaped Room, The
BL (GB) 1962 dir. Bryan Forbes

Banks, P.
Carriage Entrance
My Forbidden Past
RKO (US) 1951 dir. Robert Stevenson

Banks, P.
January Heights
Great Lie, The
WAR (US) 1941 dir. Edmund Goulding

Banks, R.
Affliction
LARGO (US) 1997 dir. Paul Schrader

Banks, R.
Sweet Hereafter, The
ALLIANCE (Can) 1997 dir. Atom
Egoyan

Bannerjee, B. B.
Pather Panchali
SAT RAY (Ind) 1955 dir. Satyajit Ray

Bao, S.
Remembrance
Road Home, The
COL (China) 1999 dir. Yimou Zhang

Barak, M.
Enigma
EMBASSY (GB/Fr) 1983
dir. Jeannot Szwarc

Barbach, L.
Pleasures
COL TV (US) 1986 dir. Sharron Miller

Barber, A.
Ghosts, The
Amazing Mr Blunden, The
HEMDALE (GB) 1972
dir. Lionel Jeffries
Ch

Barber, E. O.
Jenny Angel
Angel Baby
ALLIED (US) 1960 dir. Paul Wendkos

Barber, N.
Other Side of Paradise, The
CENTRAL (GB) 1992 dir. Renny Rye
TVSe(GB)

Barber, R.
Night They Raided Minsky's, The
UA (US) 1968 dir. William Friedkin
GB title: Night They Invented
Striptease, The

Bard, M.
Doctor Wears Three Faces, The
Mother Didn't Tell Me
FOX (US) 1950 dir. Claude Binyon

Bardawil, G.
Do You Like Women?
FRANCORITZ (Fr/It) 1964
dir. Jean Leon

Barfoot, J.
Dancing in the Dark
CBC (Can) 1986 dir. Leon Marr

Barillet, P. and Gredy, J.-P.
Forty Carats
P
COL (US) 1973 dir. Milton Katselas

Barker, C.
Cabal
Nightbreed
FOX (US) 1990 dir. Clive Barker

Barker, C.
Hellbound Heart, The
Hellraiser
CINEMARQUE (GB) 1987
dir. Clive Barker

Barker, P.
Regeneration
BBC (GB/Can) 1997 dir. Gillies
MacKinnon

Barker, P.
Union Street
Stanley and Iris
MGM (US) 1990 dir. Martin Ritt

Barker, R.
Thousand Plan, The
1,000 Plane Raid, The
UA (GB) 1969 dir. Boris Sagal

Barkley, D.
Freeway
NEW WORLD (US) 1988
dir. Francis Delia

Barkow, N.
Song of Gloomy Sunday, The
Piano Player, The
STUDIO HAMBURG (Ger) 1999 dir.
Rolf Schubel

Barlow, J.
Burden of Proof, The
Villain
EMI (GB) 1971 dir. Michael Tuchner

Barlow, J.
Term of Trial
WAR (GB) 1962 dir. Peter Glenville

Barnes, J.
Evita: First Lady
Evita Peron
ZEPHYR (US) 1981
dir. Marvin Chomsky
TVSe(US)

Barnes, J.
Metroland
BBC (GB/Fr) 1997 dir. Philip Saville

Barnes, M. A.
Murder in Coweta County
TELECOM (US) 1983 dir. Gary Nelson
TV(US)

Barnes, M. A.
Westward Passage
RKO (US) 1932 dir. Robert Milton

Barnes, P.
Ruling Class, The
P
KEEP (GB) 1971 dir. Peter Medak

Baron, A.
Human Kind, The
Victors, The
BL (GB) 1963 dir. Carl Foreman

Barr, G.
Epitaph for an Enemy
Up From the Beach
FOX (US) 1965 dir. Robert Parrish

Barrasch, N. and Moore, C.
Send Me No Flowers
P
UN (US) 1964 dir. Norman Jewison

Barrett, M.
Appointments in Zahrein
Escape from Zahrein
PAR (US) 1962 dir. Ronald Neame

Barrett, M.
Heroes of Yucca, The
Invincible Six, The
MOULIN ROUGE (US/Iran) 1970
dir. Jean Negulesco

Barrett, M.
Reward, The
FOX (US) 1965 dir. Serge Bourgignon

Barrett, W.
Sign of the Cross, The
P
PAR (US) 1932 dir. Cecil B. De Mille

Barrett, W. E.
Left Hand of God, The
FOX (US) 1955 dir. Edward Dmytryk

Barrett, W. E.
Lilies of the Field, The
UA (US) 1963 dir. Ralph Nelson

Barrett, W. E.
Wine and the Music, The

Pieces of Dreams
UA (US) 1970 dir. Daniel Haller

Barrie, Sir J. M.
Admirable Crichton, The

P
We're Not Dressing
PAR (US) 1934 dir. Norman Taurog

Barrie, Sir J. M.
Admirable Crichton, The

P
COL (GB) 1957 dir. Lewis Gilbert
US title: Paradise Lagoon
COMPASS (US) 1968
dir. George Schaefer
TV(US)

Barrie, Sir J. M.
Alice Sit-by-the-Fire

P
Darling, How Could You
PAR (US) 1951 dir. Mitchell Leisen
GB title: Rendezvous

Barrie, Sir J. M.
Little Minister, The

P
RKO (US) 1934 dir. Richard Wallace

Barrie, Sir J. M.
Old Lady Shows Her Medals, The

P
Seven Days' Leave
PAR (US) 1930 dir. Richard Wallace
GB title: Medals

Barrie, Sir J. M.
Quality Street

P
RKO (US) 1937 dir. George Stevens

Barrie, Sir J. M.
Rosalind

P
Forever Female
PAR (US) 1953 dir. Irving Rapper

Barrie, Sir J. M.
What Every Woman Knows

P
MGM (US) 1934 dir. Gregory La Cava

Barringer, E. D.
Bowery to Bellevue

Girl in White, The
MGM (US) 1952 dir. John Sturges
GB title: So Bright the Flame

Barringer, M.
Inquest

P
CHARTER (GB) 1939 dir. Roy Boulting

Barrington, P.
Account Rendered

RANK (GB) 1957
dir. Peter Graham Scott

Barry, D.
Whales of August, The

P
ALIVE (US) 1987 dir. Lindsay Anderson

Barry, J.
Lenny

P
UA (US) 1974 dir. Bob Fosse

Barry, J.
Moi, Ma Soeur

Invitation au Voyage
TRIUMPH (Fr) 1983
dir. Peter Del Monte

Barry, P.
Animal Kingdom, The

P
One More Tomorrow
WAR (US) 1946 dir. Peter Godfrey

Barry, P.
Animal Kingdom, The

P
RKO (US) 1932 dir. Edward H. Griffith
GB title: Woman in His House, The

Barry, P.
Holiday

P
PATHE (US) 1930
dir. Edward H. Griffith
COL (US) 1938 dir. George Cukor
GB title: Free to Live

Barry, P.
Philadelphia Story, The
P
MGM (US) 1940 dir. George Cukor

Barry, P.
Philadelphia Story, The
P
High Society
MGM (US) 1956 dir. Charles Walters
M

Barry, P.
Tomorrow and Tomorrow
P
PAR (US) 1932 dir. Richard Wallace

Barry, P.
Without Love
P
MGM (US) 1945 dir. Harold S. Bucquet

Barrymore, D. and Frank, G.
Too Much, Too Soon

WAR (US) 1958 dir. Art Napoleon

Barstow, S.
Brother's Tale, A
GRANADA (GB) 1983 dir. Les Chatfield
TVSe(GB)

Barstow, S.
Kind of Loving, A

AA (GB) 1962 dir. John Schlesinger
GRANADA (GB) 1982 dir. Oliver
Horsburgh, Gerry Mill,
Jeremy Summers
TVSe(GB)

Barstow, S.
Raging Calm, A

GRANADA (GB) 1974 dir. June
Howson, Gerry Mill
TVSe(GB)

Barstow, S.
Watchers on the Shore, The; Rigid True End, The

(TVSe only)
Kind of Loving, A
AA (GB) 1962 dir. John Schlesinger
GRANADA (GB) 1982 dir. Oliver
Horsburgh, Gerry Mill,
Jeremy Summers

Barth, J.
End of the Road

ALLIED (US) 1970 dir. Aram Avakian

Barth, R.
Rag Bag Clan, The

Small Killing, A
MOTOWN (US) 1981
dir. Steven Hilliard Stern
TV(US)

Barthel, J.
Death in California, A

LORIMAR (US) 1985 dir. Delbert Mann
TVSe(US)

Barthel, J.
Death in Canaan, A

WAR (US) 1978 dir. Tony Richardson
TV(US)

Bartlett, L. V. S.
Adios
Lash, The
IN (US) 1930 dir. Frank Lloyd

Bartolini, L.
Bicycle Thief, The
MGM (It) 1949 dir. Vittorio de Sica

Bartolomeo, C.
Cupid and Diana
Cupid & Cate
HALLMARK (US) 2000 dir. Brent
Shields
TV(US)

Bass, M. R.
Jory
AVCO (US) 1973 dir. Jorge Fons

Bass, R.
Emerald Illusion, The
Code Name: Emerald
MGM/UA (US) 1985
dir. Jonathan Sanger

Bassani, G.
Garden of the Finzi-Continis, The
DOCUMENTO (It/Ger) 1970
dir. Vittorio de Sica

Bassett, J.
Harm's Way
In Harm's Way
PAR (US) 1965 dir. Otto Preminger

Bassett, R.
Witchfinder General
TIGON (GB) 1968 dir. Michael Reeves

Bassing, E.
Home Before Dark
WAR (US) 1958 dir. Mervyn LeRoy

Basso, H.
View from Pompey's Head, The
FOX (US) 1955 dir. Philip Donne
GB title: Secret Interlude

Bataille, H.
Private Life of Don Juan, The
P
LF (GB) 1934
dir. Alexander Korda

Bataille, M.
Christmas Tree, The
FOX (Fr/It) 1969 dir. Terence Young

Bateman, C.
Cycle of Violence
Crossmaheart
LEX (GB) 1998 dir. Henry Herbert

Bateman, C.
Divorcing Jack
SCALA (GB) 1998 dir. David Caffrey

Bates, H. E.
Breath of French Air, A
YTV (GB) 1991 dir. Robert Tronson
TV(GB)

Bates, H. E.
Darling Buds of May, The
Mating Game, The
MGM (US) 1959 dir. George Marshall

Bates, H. E.
Darling Buds of May, The
YTV (GB) 1991 dir. Robert Tronson
TV(GB)

Bates, H. E.
Dulcima
EMI (GB) 1971 dir. Frank Nesbitt

Bates, H. E.
Fair Stood the Wind For France
BBC (GB) 1980 dir. Martyn Friend
TVSe(GB)

Bates, H. E.
Feast of July
MI (GB) 1995 dir. Christopher Menaul

Bates, H. E.
Little Farm, The
GRANADA (GB) 1973 dir. Silvio
Narizzano
TV(GB)

Bates, H. E.
Love for Lydia
LWT (GB) 1977 dir. John Glenister, Piers
Haggard, Christopher Hodson, Simon
Langton, Michael Simpson, Tony
Wharmby
TVSe(GB)

Bates, H. E.
Moment in Time, A
BBC (GB) 1979 dir. Renny Rye
TVSe(GB)

Bates, H. E.
Month by the Lake, A
MIRAMAX (GB/US) 1995 dir. John
Irvin

Bates, H. E.
Purple Plain, The
GFD (GB) 1954 dir. Robert Parrish

Bates, H. E.
Triple Echo
HEMDALE (GB) 1972
dir. Michael Apted

Bates, H. E.
When the Green Woods Laugh
YTV (GB) 1991 dir. Robert Tronson
TV(GB)

Battin, B. W.
Smithereens
Hell Hath No Fury
BAR-GENE (US) 1991
dir. Thomas J. Wright
TV(US)

Baugh, J. W. and Morgan, J.
Why Have They Taken Our Children?
*They've Taken Our Children: The
Chowchilla Kidnapping*
L. HILL (US) 1993 d. Vern Gillum
TV(US)

Baulenas, L.-A.
Bones Obres
Anita no Perd el Tren
CANAL+ ESPANA (Sp) 2001 dir.
Ventura Pons

Baum, L. F.
Marvellous Land of Oz, The; Ozma of
Oz
Return to Oz
DISNEY (US) 1985 dir. Walter Murch

Baum, L. F.
Wonderful Wizard of Oz, The
Wizard of Oz, The
MGM (US) 1939 dir. Victor Fleming
M

Baum, L. F.
Wonderful Wizard of Oz, The
P
Wiz, The
DISNEY (US) 1978 dir. Sidney Lumet
M

Baum, V.
Berlin Hotel
Hotel Berlin
WAR (US) 1945 dir. Peter Godfrey

Baum, V.
Grand Hotel
Weekend at the Waldorf
MGM (US) 1945 dir. Robert Z. Leonard
M

Baum, V.
Grand Hotel
MGM (US) 1932 dir. Edmund Goulding

Baum, V.
Hotel Shanghai
DURNIOK (Aust) 1997 dir. Peter Patzak

Baum, V.
Mortgage on Life
Woman's Secret, A
RKO (US) 1949 dir. Nicholas Ray

Baumer, M.
Penny Arcade
P
Sinner's Holiday
WAR (US) 1930 dir. John G. Adolfi

Bausch, R.
Last Good Time, The
GOLDWYN (US) 1994 dir. Bob Balaban

Bawden, N.
Carrie's War
BBC (GB) 1974 dir. Paul Stone
TVSe(GB)

Bawden, N.
On The Run
CFF (GB) 1969 dir. Pat Jackson
Ch

Bawden, N.
Peppermint Pig, The
BBC (GB) 1977 dir. Paul Stone
TVSe(GB)

Bawden, N.
Runaway Summer, The
BBC (GB) 1971 dir. Mary Ridge
TVSe(GB)

Bawden, N.
Solitary Child, The
BL (GB) 1958 dir. Gerald Thomas

Bawden, N.
Witch's Daughter, The
BBC (GB) 1971 dir. David Maloney ·
TVSe(GB)
HALLMARK (GB) 1996 dir. Alan Macmillan
TV(GB)

Bax, R.
Came the Dawn
Never Let Me Go
MGM (GB) 1953 dir. Delmer Daves

Bayer, W.
Switch
Doubletake
TITUS (US) 1985 dir. Jud Taylor
TVSe(US)

Bayer, W.
Wallflower
Forget-Me-Not Murders, The
SPELLING TV (US) 1994 dir. Robert Iscove
TV(US)

Bayley, J.
Iris, a Memoir of Iris Murdoch; Elegy for Iris
Iris
MIRAMAX (GB/US) 2001 dir. Richard Eyre

Beach, E. L.
Run Silent, Run Deep
UA (US) 1958 dir. Robert Wise

Beach, L.
Merry Andrew
P
Handy Andy
FOX (US) 1934 dir. David Butler

Beach, R.
Spoilers, The
PAR (US) 1930 dir. Edward Carew
UN (US) 1942 dir. Ray Enright
UN (US) 1955 dir. Jesse Hibbs

Beach, R.
World in His Arms, The
UN (US) 1952 dir. Raoul Walsh

Beach, R. E.
Don Careless

Avengers, The
REP (US) 1950 dir. John Auer

Beagle, P. S.
Last Unicorn, The
SCHICK SUNN (US) 1982
dir. Jules Bass, Arthur Rankin, Jr.
A

Beattie, A.
Chilly Scenes of Winter (*also known
as* Head Over Heels)
UA (US) 1979 dir. Joan Micklin Silver

Beatty, D.
Cone of Silence
BL (GB) 1960 dir. Charles Frend
US title: Trouble in the Sky

Beaumarchais, P. A. C. de
Marriage of Figaro, The
P
BBC (GB) 1990 dir. D. Bailey
M, TV(GB)

Beaumont, C.
Intruder, The
FILMGROUP (US) 1961
dir. Roger Corman
GB title: Stranger, The

Beaussant, P.
Lully ou le Musicien du Soleil
Roi Danse, Le
FRANCE 2 (Bel/Fr) 2000 dir. Gerard
Corbiau

Beck, B.
Léon Morin, Priest
ROME-PARIS (Fr/It) 1961
dir. Jean-Pierre Melville

Beck, K. K.
Unwanted Attentions
Shadow of Obsession
SABAN ENT (US) 1994 dir. Kevin
Connor
TV(US)

Beck, P. and Massman, P.
Rich Men, Single Women
SPELLING (US) 1990
dir. Elliot Silverstein
TV(US)

Becker, J.
Jakob der Lugner
Jakob the Liar
TRISTAR (US/Fr) 1999 dir. Peter
Kassovitz

Becker, S.
Covenant with Death, A
WAR (US) 1966 dir. Lamont Johnson

Beckhardt, I. and Brown, W.
Violators, The
RKO (US) 1957 dir. John Newland

Beckles, G.
East of Piccadilly
ABPC (GB) 1940 dir. Harold Huth

Beckwith R.
Boys in Brown
P
GFD (GB) 1949 dir. Montgomery Tully

Beckwith, R.
Soldier for Christmas, A
This Man is Mine
COL (GB) 1946 dir. Marcel Varnel

Bedford, S.
Legacy, A
BBC (GB) 1975 dir. Derek Martinus
TVSe(GB)

Beeding, F.
House of Dr. Edwards, The

Spellbound
UA (US) 1945 dir. Alfred Hitchcock

Beeding, F.
Norwich Victims, The

Dead Men Tell No Tales
ALL (GB) 1938 dir. David MacDonald

Begag, A.
Gone du Chaaba, Le

ORLY (Fr) 1998 dir. Christophe Ruggia

Behan, B.
Borstal Boy

BRIT SCREEN (GB/Ire) 2000 dir. Peter
Sheridan

Behan, B.
Quare Fellow, The

P
BL (GB) 1962 dir. Arthur Dreifuss

Behm, M.
Eye of the Beholder

FILMLINE (GB/Can/US) 1999 dir.
Stephan Elliott

Behn, N.
Kremlin Letter, The

FOX (US) 1970 dir. John Huston

Behrenberg, B.
My Little Brother is Coming
Tomorrow

Grambling's White Tiger
INTERPLAN (US) 1981
dir. Georg Stanford Brown
TV(US)

Behrman, S. N.
Biography

P
Biography (of a Bachelor Girl)
MGM (US) 1935 dir. Edward H. Griffith

Behrman, S. N.
No Time for Comedy

P
WAR (US) 1940 dir. William Keighley

Behrman, S. N.
Pirate, The

P
MGM (US) 1948 dir. Vincente Minnelli
M

Behrman, S. N. and Logan, J.
Fanny

P
WAR (US) 1960 dir. Joshua Logan

Beinhart, L.
American Hero

Wag the Dog
NEW LINE (US) 1997 dir. Barry
Levinson

Belasco, D.
Return of Peter Grimm, The

P
RKO (US) 1935 dir. George Nicholls

Belasco, D. and Long, J. L.
Madame Butterfly

P
PAR (US) 1932 dir. Marion Gering

Belbel, S.
Caresses

P
TVE (Sp) 1997 dir. Ventura Pons

Belber, S.
Tape

P
IFC (US) 2001 dir. Richard Linklater

Belden, C. S.
Mystery of the Wax Museum

P
WAR (US) 1933 dir. Michael Curtiz

Bell, C.
Perez Family, The
GOLDWYN (US) 1995 dir. Mira Nair

Bell, D.
Shot, The
P
B&W (US) 1994 dir. Dan Bell

Bell, M. H.
Whistle Down the Wind
RANK (GB) 1961 dir. Bryan Forbes

Bell, N.
Raw Youth
P
Undertow
CAPSTONE (US) 1991
dir. Thomas Mazziotti

Bell, N.
Two Small Bodies
P
ZETA FILM (Ger) 1993 dir. Beth B.

Bell, R.
This Same Garden
P
While I Live
DRYHURST (GB) 1947 dir. John Harlow

Bell, T.
All Brides are Beautiful
From This Day Forward
RKO (US) 1946 dir. John Berry

Bell, V.
Swamp Water
FOX (US) 1941 dir. Jean Renoir
GB title: Man Who Came Back, The

Bellah, J. W.
Command, The
WAR (US) 1954 dir. David Butler

Bellah, J. W.
Dancing Lady
MGM (US) 1933 dir. Robert Z. Leonard
M

Bellah, J. W.
Massacre
Fort Apache
RKO (US) 1948 dir. John Ford

Bellamann, H.
King's Row
WAR (US) 1941 dir. Sam Wood

Belletto, R.
Machine, The
FRANCE 2 (Fr) 1994 dir. François
Dupeyron

Belletto, R.
Sur la Terre Comme au Ciel
Peril
TRIUMPH (Fr) 1985 dir. Michel DeVille

Bello, S.
Doing Life
PHOENIX (US) 1986
dir. Gene Reynolds
TV(US)

Bembenek, L.
Woman on Trial, A
*Woman on the Run: The Lawrencia
Bembenek Story*
NBC (US) 1993 dir. Sandor Stern
TVSe(US)

Bemelmans, L.
Borrowed Christmas, A
Christmas Festival, A
COMPASS (US) 1959
dir. Albert McCleery
TV(US)

Ben Amitz, D.
I Don't Give a Damn
ROLL (Israel) 1988
dir. Shmuel Imberman

Ben Jelloun, T.
Nuit Sacrée, La; Enfant Des Sables, L'

Sacred Night, The
FRANCE 3 (Fr) 1993 dir. Nicolas Klotz

Benacquista, T.
Morsures de l'aube, Les

Love Bites
STUDIO CANAL+ (Fr) 2001 dir.
Antoine de Caunes

Benchley, N.
Off-Islanders, The Russians are
Coming, The Russians are Coming,
The

UA (US) 1966 dir. Norman Jewison

Benchley, N.
Sail a Crooked Ship

COL (US) 1961 dir. Irving Brecher

Benchley, N.
Visitors, The

Spirit is Willing, The
PAR (US) 1967 dir. William Castle

Benchley, N.
Welcome to Xanadu

Sweet Hostage
BRUT (US) 1975 dir. Lee Phillips
TV(US)

Benchley, P.
Beast, The

M. R. JOYCE (US) 1996 dir. Jeff
Bleckner
TVSe(US)

Benchley, P.
Deep, The

COL-WAR (US) 1977 dir. Peter Yates

Benchley, P.
Island, The

UN (US) 1980 dir. Michael Ritchie

Benchley, P.
Jaws

UN (US) 1975 dir. Steven Spielberg

Benchley, P.
White Shark

Creature
MGM TV (US) 1998 dir. Stuart Gillard
TVSe(US)

Benedictus, D.
You're a Big Boy Now

WAR (US) 1967
dir. Francis Ford Coppola

Benefield, B.
Chicken-Wagon Family

FOX (US) 1939 dir. Herbert I. Leeds

Benefield, B.
Valiant is the Word for Carrie

RKO (US) 1936 dir. Wesley Ruggles

Benes, K. J.
Stolen Life, A

PAR (GB) 1939 dir. Paul Czinner
WAR (US) 1946 dir. Curtis Bernhardt

Benet I. and Jornet, J. M.
Testament

Beloved/Friend
CANAL+ ESPANA (Sp) 1999 dir.
Ventura Pons

Benet, S. V.
Famous

Just for You
PAR (US) 1952 dir. Elliot Nugent

Benet, S. V.
Sobbin' Women, The

Seven Brides for Seven Brothers
MGM (US) 1954 dir. Stanley Donen
M

Benet, S.V.
Devil and Daniel Webster, The

All that Money can Buy
RKO (US) 1941 dir. William Dieterle

Benet, T.
One Game, The

CENTRAL (GB) 1988 dir. Mike Vardy
TVSe(GB)

Benford, T.
Hitler's Daughter

WIL COURT (US) 1990
dir. James A. Contner
TV(US)

Bengtsson, F.
Long Ships, The

BL (GB/Yugo) 1963 dir. Jack Cardiff

Benjamin, P.
Quick, Before it Melts

MGM (US) 1964 dir. Delbert Mann

Benjamin, W.
Aaron Slick from Punkin Crick

P
PAR (US) 1952 dir. Claude Binyon
GB title: Marshmallow Moon

Bennett, A.
Anna of the Five Towns

BBC (GB) 1985 dir. Martyn Friend
TVSe(GB)

Bennett, A.
Buried Alive

AIRTIME (GB) 1983
TVSe(GB)

Bennett, A.
Buried Alive

His Double Life
PAR (US) 1933 dir. Arthur Hopkins

Bennett, A.
Buried Alive

Holy Matrimony
PAR (US) 1943 dir. John Stahl

Bennett, A.
Card, The

GFD (GB) 1952 dir. Ronald Neame
US title: Promoter, The

Bennett, A.
Clayhanger

ATV (GB) 1976 dir. John Davies, David
Reid
TVSe(GB)

Bennett, A.
Insurance Man, The

P
BBC (GB) 1986 dir. Richard Eyre
TV(GB)

Bennett, A.
Madness of George III, The

P
Madness of King George, The
CHANNEL 4 FILMS (GB) 1994 dir.
Nicholas Hytner

Bennett, A.
Mr Prohack

Dear Mr Prohack
GFD (GB) 1949 dir. Thornton Freeland

Bennett, A.
Old Wives' Tale, The

Sophia and Constance
BBC (GB) 1988 dir. Rodney Allison,
Hugh David
TVSe(GB)

Bennett, A.
Question of Attribution, A

P
BBC (GB) 1992 dir. John Schlesinger
TV(GB)

Bennett, C.
Blackmail

P
BI (GB) 1929 dir. Alfred Hitchcock

Bennett, D.
Fly Away Home

P
Daughters Courageous
WAR (US) 1939 dir. Michael Curtiz

Bennett, D.
Jigsaw Man, The

J&M (GB) 1984
dir. Terence Young

Bennett D. and White, I.
Fly Away Home

P
Always in My Heart
WAR (US) 1942 dir. Joe Graham

Bennett, J.
Catacombs

BL (GB) 1964 dir. Gordon Hessler
US title: Woman Who Wouldn't Die,
The

Benoit, P.
Atlantide

STUDIO CANAL+ (Fr/It) 1992 dir. Bob
Swain

Benoit, P.
Moscow Nights

LF (GB) 1935 dir. Anthony Asquith

Benson, E. F.
Mapp and Lucia

P
CHANNEL 4 (GB) 1985
dir. Donald McWhinnie
TVSe(GB)

Benson, Mrs. S.
Meet Me in St Louis

MGM (US) 1944 dir. Vincente Minnelli
M

Benson, R.
Necromancers, The

Spellbound
PYRAMID (GB) 1940 dir. John Harlow
US title: Spell of Amy Nugent, The

Benson, S.
Junior Miss

FOX (US) 1945 dir. George Seaton

Bentham, J. and Williams, H. V.
Janie

P
WAR (US) 1944 dir. Michael Curtiz

Bentley, E. C.
Trent's Last Case

BL (GB) 1952 dir. Herbert Wilcox

Bentley, N.
Floating Dutchman, The

AA (GB) 1953 dir. Vernon Sewell

Bentley, N.
Third Party Risk

EXCL (GB) 1955 dir. Daniel Birt

Bentley, P.
Inheritance

GRANADA (GB) 1967
TV(GB)

Berberova, N.
Accompanist, The

STUDIO CANAL+ (Fr) 1992 dir. Claude
Miller

Bercovici, E.
So Little Cause for Caroline

One Shoe Makes it Murder
LORIMAR TV (US) 1982
dir. William Hale
TV(US)

Berendt, J.
Midnight in the Garden of Good and
Evil
WAR (US) 1997 dir. Clint Eastwood

Berg, E.
Range of Motion
HEARST (US) 2000 dir. Donald Wrye
TV(US)

Berger, P.
Price of Glory
NEW LINE (US) 2000 dir. Carlos Avila

Berger, T.
Feud, The
CASTLE HILL (US) 1990 dir. Bill D'Elia

Berger, T.
Little Big Man
CIN CEN (US) 1970 dir. Arthur Penn

Berger, T.
Neighbors
COL (US) 1981 dir. John G. Avildsen

Berkeley, A.
Flight from Destiny
P
WAR (US) 1941 dir. Vincent Sherman

Berkeley, R.
Dawn
Nurse Edith Cavell
RKO (US) 1939 dir. Herbert Wilcox

Berkeley, R.
French Leave
P
AB (GB) 1930 dir. Jack Raymond

Berkeley, R.
Lady with a Lamp, The
P
BL (GB) 1951 dir. Herbert Wilcox

Berkey, B. F.
Keys to Tulsa
POLYGRAM (US) 1997 dir. Leslie Grief

Berkman, T.
Cast a Giant Shadow
UA (US) 1966 dir. Melville Shavelson

Berkoff, S.
Decadence
P
VENDETTA (GB/Ger) 1993 dir. Steven
Berkoff

Berman, J. G.
Misbegotten
AM WORLD (US) dir. Mark L. Lester

Berman, J. G.
Uninvited: He Followed a Dark Path
to Obsession
Uninvited
MEDIASET (US/It) 1999 dir. Carlo
Gabriel Nero

Berna, P.
Hundred Million Frames, A
Horse Without a Head, The
DISNEY (GB) 1963 dir. Don Chaffey
Ch

Bernanos, G.
Diary of a Country Priest, The
GGT (Fr) 1950 dir. Robert Bresson

Bernanos, G.
Under Satan's Sun
ERATO (Fr) 1987 dir. Maurice Pialat

Bernstein, H.
Claw, The
P
Washington Masquerade
MGM (US) 1932 dir. Charles Brabin
GB title: Mad Masquerade

Bernstein, H.
Death is Part of the Process
BBC (GB) 1986 dir. Bill Hays
TV(GB)

Bernstein, H.
Dreaming Lips
P
TRAFALGAR (GB) 1936
dir. Paul Czinner, Lee Garmes

Bernstein, H.
Mélo
P
MK2 (Fr) 1986 dir. Alain Resnais

Bernstein, M.
Body and Soul
CARLTON (GB) 1993 dir. Moira
Armstrong
TVSe(GB)

Bernstein, M.
Search for Bridey Murphy, The
PAR (US) 1956 dir. Noel Langley

Berteaut, S.
Piaf
Piaf—The Early Years
FOX (Fr) 1982 dir. Guy Casaril

Berton, P. and Simon, C.
Zaza
P
PAR (US) 1938 dir. George Cukor

Besier, R.
Barretts of Wimpole Street, The
P
MGM (US) 1934 dir. Sidney Franklin
MGM (US) 1956 dir. Sidney Franklin

Bessa-Luis, A.
Vale Abraao
Valley of Abraham, The
GEMINI (Fr/Port) 1993 dir. Manoel de
Oliveira

Bessie, A.
Bread and a Stone
Hard Travelling
NEW WORLD (US) 1986
dir. Dan Bessie

Bessie, A.
Symbol, The
Sex Symbol, The
COL (US) 1974 dir. David Lowell Rich
TV(US)

Bevan, A. C.
Story of Zarak Khan, The
Zarak
COL (GB) 1956 dir. Terence Young

Bevan, D. and Trzcinski, E.
Stalag 17
P
PAR (US) 1953 dir. Billy Wilder

Bezzerides, A. I.
Long Haul
They Drive by Night
WAR (US) 1940 dir. Raoul Walsh
GB title: Road to Frisco, The

Bezzerides, A. I.
Thieves' Market
Thieves' Highway
FOX (US) 1949 dir. Jules Dassin

Bible
Samuel I & II; Chronicles I; Psalms of
David
King David
PAR (US/GB) 1985
dir. Bruce Beresford

Bickerton, D.
Payroll
AA (GB) 1960 dir. Sidney Hayers

Bickham, J. M.
Apple Dumpling Gang, The
DISNEY (US) 1974 dir. Norman Tokar
Ch

Biddle, C. D. and Crichton, K.
Happiest Millionaire, The
P
DISNEY (US) 1967 dir. Norman Tokar
M

Bielenberg, C.
Past is Myself, The
Christabel
BBC (GB) 1988 dir. Adrian Shergold
TVSe(GB)

Biggers, E. D.
Agony Column
Passage from Hong Kong
WAR (US) 1941 dir. D. Ross Lederman

Biggers, E. D.
Behind that Curtain
FOX (US) 1929 dir. Irving Cummings

Biggers, E. D.
Black Camel
FOX (US) 1931
dir. Hamilton-MacFadden

Biggers, E. D.
Charlie Chan Carries On
FOX (US) 1931 dir. Hamilton McFadden

Biggers, E. D.
Seven Keys to Baldpate
House of the Long Shadows, The
CANNON (GB) 1983 dir. Pete Walker

Biggers, E. D.
Seven Keys to Baldpate
RKO (US) 1930 dir. Reginald Parker
RKO (US) 1935 dir. William Hamilton
RKO (US) 1947 dir. Lew Landers

Billetdoux, F.
Tchin-Tchin
P
Fine Romance, A
PC (It) 1992 dir. Gene Saks

Billing, G.
Mr. Forbush and the Penguins
BL (GB) 1971 dir. Roy Bantling, Arne
Sacksdorff

Binchy, M.
Circle of Friends
RANK (Ire/GB) 1995 dir. Pat O'Connor

Binchy, M.
Echoes
WORKING TITLE (GB) 1988 dir.
Barbara Rennie
TVSe(GB)

Bingham, J.
Fragment of Fear
COL (GB) 1969 dir. Richard C. Sarafian

Bingham, S.
Charters and Caldicott
BBC (GB) 1985 dir. Julian Amyes
TVSe(GB)

Binosi, R.
Rosa e Cornelia
P
FILMTRE (It) 2000 dir. Giorgio Treves

Bird, J.
Percy Grainger
Passion
BEYOND (Aust) 1999 dir. Peter Duncan

Bird, S.
Boyfriend School, The
Don't Tell Her It's Me
HEMDALE (US) 1990
dir. Malcolm Mowbray

Birmingham, J.
He Died With a Felafel in His Hand
VILLAGE ROADSHOW (Aust/It) 2001
dir. Richard Lowenstein

Birney, H.
Dice of God, The

Glory Guys
UA (US) 1965 dir. Arnold Laven

Biro, L.
Dark Journey

P
LF GBN (US) 1937
dir. Victor Saville

Biro, L.
Five Graves to Cairo

P
PAR (US) 1943 dir. Billy Wilder

Biro, L.
Hotel Imperial

P
PAR (US) 1939 dir. Robert Florey

Biro, L. and Lengyel, M.
Royal Scandal, A

P
FOX (US) 1945 dir. Otto Preminger
GB title: Czarina

Bishop, C.
Shadow Range

Cow Country
ABP (US) 1953 dir. Lesley Selander

Bishop, J.
Day Lincoln Was Shot, The

GREENWALD (US) 1998 dir. John Gray
TV(US)

Bishop, J.
FDR's Last Year

FDR – The Last Year
TITUS (US) 1980
dir. Anthony Page
TV(US)

Bishop, L.
Against Heaven's Hand

Seven in Darkness
PAR TV (US) 1969 dir. Michael Caffey
TV(US)

Bissell, R. P.
7½ Cents

Pajama Game, The
WAR (US) 1957 dir. Stanley Donen
M

Bisson, A.
Madame X

P
MGM (US) 1929 dir. John Barrymore
MGM (US) 1937
dir. James K. McGuiness
UN (US) 1965 dir. David Lowell Rich
UN (US) 1981 dir. Robert Ellis Miller
TV(US)

Bizet, G.
Carmen

TRIUMPH (Fr) 1984 dir. Francesco Rosi

Black, B. and Bishop, C.
Sisterhood

Ladies Club, The
NEW LINE (US) 1986 dir. A. K. Allen

Black, I. S.
High Bright Sun, The

RANK (GB) 1965 dir. Ralph Thomas
US title: McGuire Go Home

Black, I. S.
In the Wake of a Stranger

BUTCHER (GB) 1959 dir. David Eady

Black, J. R.
Shadow Zone: The Undead Express

SHOWTIME (US) 1996 dir. Stephen
Williams
TV(US)

Blackburn, J.
Nothing but the Night
FOX-RANK (GB) 1972 dir. Peter Sasdy

Blackburn, W. J.
Gaunt Women, The
Destiny of a Spy
UN TV (US) 1969 dir. Boris Sagal
TV(US)

Blackman, M.
Operation Gadgetman
Gadgetman
HALLMARK (US/GB) 1996 dir. Jim Goddard
TV(US/GB)

Blackmore, P.
Miranda
P
GFD (GB) 1947 dir. Ken Annakin

Blackmore, R. D.
Lorna Doone
ATP (GB) 1934 dir. Basil Dean
COL (US) 1951 dir. Phil Karlson
BBC (GB) 1976 dir. Barry Letts
TVSe(GB)
THAMES (GB) 1990 dir. Alistair Grieve
TV(GB)
BBC/A&E (GB/US) 2000 dir. Mike Barker
TV(GB/US)

Blair, C.
Survive
STIGWOOD (Mex) 1976
dir. Rene Cardona

Blair, G.
Almost Golden
Almost Golden: The Jessica Savitch Story
ABC PROD (US) 1995 dir. Peter Werner
TV(US)

Blair, J. and Blair, C.
Return from the River Kwai
RANK (GB) 1987
dir. Andrew V. McLaglen

Blaisdell, A.
Nightmare
Fanatic
COL (GB) 1965 dir. Silvio Narizzano
US title: Die! Die! My Darling

Blake, G.
Shipbuilders, The
BN (GB) 1944 dir. John Baxter

Blake, M.
Dances with Wolves
ORION (US) 1990 dir. Kevin Costner

Blake, N.
This Man Must Die
AA (Fr) 1970 dir. Claude Chabrol

Blanc, H.-F.
Combat de Fauves au Crepuscule
Wild Games
INTEGRAL (Bel/Ger/Fr) 1997 dir. Benoît Lamy

Blankenship, W. D.
Brotherly Love
CBS (US) 1985 dir. Jeff Bleckner
TV(US)

Blankfort, M.
Juggler, The
COL (US) 1953 dir. Edward Dmytryk

Blankfort, M.
Widow Makers, The
See How They Run
UN TV (US) 1964 dir. David Lowell Rich
TV(US)

Blasco-Ibanez, V.
Four Horsemen of the Apocalypse,
The
MGM (US) 1961 dir. Vincente Minnelli

Blatty, W. P.
Exorcist, The
WAR (US) 1973 dir. William Friedkin

Blatty, W. P.
Legion
Exorcist III, The
TCP (US) 1990 dir. William Peter Blatty

Blatty, W. P.
Ninth Configuration, The
LORIMAR (US) 1980
dir. William P. Blatty

Blatty, W. P.
Twinkle, Twinkle, 'Killer' Kane
UFD (US) 1980 dir. William Peter Blatty

Bledsoe, J.
Before He Wakes
CBS (US) 1998 dir. Michael Scott
TV(US)

Bledsoe, J.
Bitter Blood
In the Best of Families: Marriage, Pride and Madness
AMBROCO (US) 1994 dir. Jeff Bleckner
TVSe(US)

Bledsoe, J.
Blood Games
Honor Thy Mother
POV (US) 1992 dir. David Greene
TV(US)

Bleeck, O.
Procane Chronicle, The
St. Ives
WAR (US) 1976 dir. J. Lee Thompson

Bleier, R. and O'Neil, T.
Fighting Back
MTM (US) 1980 dir. Robert Lieberman
TV(US)

**Blinkoff, S., Bernhard, M.,
Borrus J. and Green K.**
Belly Fruit
P
STANDARD (US) 1999 dir. Kerri Green

Bliss, M.
Discovery of Insulin, The; Banting: A
Biography
Glory Enough for All
THAMES (GB) 1989 dir. Eric Till
TV(GB)

Blixen, K.
Immortal Story
ORTF (Fr) 1968 dir. Orson Welles

Blixen, K. aka Dinesen, I.
Babette's Feast
DAN FI (Den) 1987 dir. Gabriel Axel

Bloch, R.
Psycho
Bates Motel
UN TV (US) 1987 dir. Richard Rothstein
TV(US)

Bloch, R.
Psycho
UN (US) 1960 dir. Alfred Hitchcock
UN (US) 1998 dir. Gus Van Sant

Blochman, L. G.
Bombay Mail
UN (US) 1933 dir. Edwin L. Martin

Block, L.
Burglar
WAR (US) 1987 dir. Hugh Wilson

Block, L.
Stab in the Dark

8 Million Ways to Die
TRISTAR (US) 1986 dir. Hal Ashby

Block, L.
Wild Calendar

Caught
MGM (US) 1948 dir. Max Ophuls

Blodgett, M.
Hero and the Terror

CANNON (US) 1988
dir. William Tanner

Blodgett, M.
White Raven, The

HERMES (US) 1998 dir. Andrew
Stevens
TV(US)

Blondin, A.
Monkey in Winter, A

CIPRA (Fr) 1962 dir. Henri Verneuil

Bloom, J. and Atkinson, J.
Evidence of Love

Killing in a Small Town
INDIEPROD (US) 1990
dir. Stephen Gyllenhaal
TV(US)

Bloom, M. T.
13th Man, The

Last Embrace
UA (US) 1979 dir. Jonathan Demme

Blum, H.
I Pledge Allegiance ... The True Story
of an American Spy Family

Family of Spies
KING PHOENIX (US) 1990 dir. Stephen
Gyllenhaal
TVSe(US)

Blume, J.
Forever

EMI (US) 1978 dir. John Korty
TV(US)

Blythe, R.
Akenfield

ANGLIA (GB) 1975 dir. Peter Hall

Blyton, E.
Castle of Adventure

TVS (GB) 1990
Ch, TV(GB)

Blyton, E.
Five Have A Mystery to Solve

CFF (GB) 1964 dir. Ernest Morris
Ch

Blyton, E.
Five on a Treasure Island

BI (GB) 1957 dir. Gerald Landau
Ch

Boccaccio, G.
Decameron, The

Decameron Nights
EROS (GB) 1952 dir. Hugo Fregonese

Boccaccio, G.
Decameron, The

UA (It/Fr/W. Ger) 1970
dir. Pier Paolo Pasolini

Bockoven, G.
Marriage of Convenience, A

CATFISH (US) 1998 dir. James Keach
TV(US)

Bodelsen, A.
Hit, and Run, Run, Run

One of Those Things
RANK (Den) 1971 dir. Erik Balling

Bodelsen, A.
Think of a Number

Silent Partner, The
CAROLCO (Can) 1978 dir. Daryl Duke

Boehm, D.
Employee's Entrance

P
WAR (US) 1933 dir. Roy del Ruth

Bogner, N.
Seventh Avenue

UN TV (US) 1977 dir. Richard Irving,
Russ Mayberry
TVSe(US)

Bogosian, E.
subUrbia

P
CASTLE ROCK (US) 1996 dir. Richard
Linklater

Bogosian, E.
Talk Radio

P
UN (US) 1988 dir. Oliver Stone

Bohjalian, C.
Midwives

C. ANDERSON (US) 2001 dir. Glenn
Jordan
TV(US)

Bohjalian, C. A.
Past the Bleachers

SIGNBOARD HILL (US) 1995 dir.
Michael Switzer
TV(US)

Boileau, P and Narcejac, T.
Choice Cuts

Body Parts
PAR (US) 1991 dir. Eric Red

Boileau, P. and Narcejac, T.
Celle qui n'etait pas

Diabolique
WAR (US) 1996 dir. Jeremiah C.
Chechik

Boileau, P. and Narcejac, T.
Celle qui n'etait pas

Diaboliques, Les
FILMSONOR (Fr) 1954
dir. Henri-Georges Clouzot

Boileau, P. and Narcejac, T.
Celle qui n'etait Plus

House of Secrets
MULTIMEDIA (US) 1993 dir. Mimi
Leder
TV(US)

Boileau, P. and Narcejac, T.
Celle qui n'etait Plus

Reflections of Murder
ABC (US) 1974 dir. John Badham
TV(US)

Boileau, P. and Narcejac, T.
Faces in the Dark

RANK (GB) 1960 dir. David Eady

Boileau, P. and Narcejac, T.
Living and the Dead, The

Vertigo
PAR (US) 1958 dir. Alfred Hitchcock

Boileau, P. and Narcejac, T.
Veufs, Les

Entangled
TELEFILM (Can/Fr) 1993 dir. Max
Fischer

Boland, B.
Cockpit

P
Lost People, The
GFD (GB) 1949 dir. Bernard Knowles

Boland, B.
Prisoner, The
P
COL (GB) 1955 dir. Peter Glenville

Boland, J.
League of Gentlemen, The
RANK (GB) 1960 dir. Basil Dearden

Boland, T.
In the Name of the People
P
CBS (US) 2000 dir. Peter Levin
TV(US)

Boldrewood, R.
Robbery Under Arms
RANK (GB) 1957 dir. Jack Lee

Boll, H.
Lost Honor of Katharina Blum, The
Lost Honor of Kathryn Beck, The
COMWORLD (US) 1984
dir. Simon Langton
TV(US)

Bolnick, J. P.
Winnie: My Life in the Institution
Winnie
NBC (US) 1988 dir. John Korty
TV(US)

Bolt, R.
Man for all Seasons, A
P
COL (GB) 1966 dir. Fred Zinnemann
AGAMEMNON (US) 1988
dir. Charlton Heston
TV(US)

Bolton, G.
Dark Angel, The
P
GOLDWYN (US) 1935
dir. Sidney Franklin

Bolton, G.
Waltzes from Vienna
P
GFD (GB) 1933 dir. Alfred Hitchcock
US title: Strauss's Great Waltz

Bolton, G., Kern, J. and Grey, C.
Sally
P
WAR (US) 1930 dir. John Francis Dillon
M

Bolton, G. and McGowan, J.
Girl Crazy
P
MGM (US) 1943 dir. Norman Taurog
M

Bolton, G. and McGowan, J.
Girl Crazy
P
When the Boys Meet the Girls
MGM (US) 1965 dir. Alvin Ganzer

Bolton, G., Wodehouse, P. G., Lindsay, H. and Crouse, R.
Anything Goes
P
PAR (US) 1936 dir. Lewis Milestone
M
PAR (US) 1956 dir. Robert Lewis
M

Bombeck, E.
Grass is Always Greener over the Septic Tank, The
J. HAMILTON (US) 1978
dir. Robert Day
TV(US)

Bonacci, A.
Oro della Fantasia, L'
P
Kiss Me Stupid
UA (US) 1964 dir. Billy Wilder

Bonanno, B.
Bound by Honor

Bonanno: A Godfather's Story
PAULSON (US) 1999 dir. Michael
Poulette
TVSe(US)

Bonanno, J. and Lalli, S.
Man of Honor, A

Bonanno: A Godfather's Story
PAULSON (US) 1999 dir. Michael
Poulette
TVSe(US)

Bonassi, F.
Starry Sky, A

RIOFILMES (Bra) 1996 dir. Tata Amaral

Bond, E.
Bingo

BBC (GB) 1990 dir. Don Taylor
TV(GB)

Bonestell, C. and Ley, W.
Conquest of Space

P
PAR (US) 1955 dir. Byron Haskin

Bonett, E.
Girl Must Live, A

UN (GB) 1939 dir. Carol Reed

Bonett, E.
High Pavement

My Sister and I
GFD (GB) 1948 dir. Harold Huth

Bonilla, J.
Nadie Conoce a Nadie

DMVB (Sp) 1999 dir. Mateo Gil

Bonnano, R.
Mafia Marriage

*Love, Honor & Obey: The Last Mafia
Marriage*
CBS ENT (US) 1993 dir. John Patterson
TVSe(US)

Bonnell, R.
Grand Vacance

Return to Algiers
STUDIO CANAL+ (Fr) 2000 dir.
Alexandre Arcady

Bonner, C.
Legacy

Adam had Four Sons
COL (US) 1941 dir. Gregory Ratoff

Bonnet, T.
Mudlark, The

FOX (GB) 1950 dir. Jean Negulesco

Bono, S.
And the Beat Goes On

*And the Beat Goes On: The Sonny and
Cher Story*
L THOMPSON (US) 1999 dir. David
Burton Morris
TV(US)

Bontempelli, M.
Boy With Two Mothers, The

Comedie de L'innocence
STUDIO CANAL+ (Fr) 2000 dir. Raoul
Ruiz

Boo, S.
Servant's Entrance

FOX (US) 1934 dir. Frank Lloyd

Boom, C. T.
Hiding Place, The

WORLD WIDE (US) 1974
dir. James F. Collier

Booth, C. G.
General Died at Dawn, The

PAR (US) 1936 dir. Lewis Milestone

Booth, C. G.
Mr. Angel Comes Aboard

Johnny Angel
RKO (US) 1945 dir. Edwin L. Marin

Booth, M.
Toys of Glass

Evolution's Child
FOXTAIL (US) 1999 dir. Jeffrey Reiner
TV(US)

Boothe, C.
Kiss the Boys Goodbye
P
PAR (US) 1941 dir. Victor Schertzinger

Boothe, C.
Margin for Error
P
FOX (US) 1943 dir. Otto Preminger

Boothe, C.
Women, The
P
MGM (US) 1939 dir. George Cukor

Boothe, C.
Women, The
P
Opposite Sex, The
MGM (US) 1956 dir. David Miller

Boothe, E.
Ladies of the Mob
City Streets
PAR (US) 1931 dir. Rouben Mamoulian

Boothroyd, D.
Value for Money
RANK (GB) 1955 dir. Ken Annakin

Borden, M.
Action for Slander
UA (GB) 1938 dir. Tim Whelan

Borden, W.
Last Prostitute who took Pride in her Work, The
P
Last Prostitute, The
BBK (US) 1991 dir. Lou Antonio
TV(US)

Bordewijk, F.
Karakter

Character
ALMERICA (Bel/Neth) 1997 dir. Mike van Diem

Borenstein, T.
Kofiko

Going Bananas
CANNON (US) 1988 dir. Boat Davidson

Borges, J. L.
Theme of the Traitor and the Hero, The

Spider's Stratagem, The
RED FILM (It) 1970
dir. Bernardo Bertolucci

Borland, H.
When the Legends Die
FOX (US) 1972 dir. Stuart Millar

Born, N.
Circle of Deceit
BIOSKOP/ARTEMIS (Fr/W. Ger) 1981 dir. Volker Schlondorff

Bosley, J.
Fun
P
GREYCAT (Can) 1994 dir. Rafal Zielinsky

Bosse, M.
Ordinary Magic
FILMWORKS (Can) 1993 dir. Giles Walker

Bost, P.
Monsieur L'Admiral va Bientôt Mourir

Sunday in the Country, A
MGM/UA (Fr) 1984
dir. Bertrand Tavernier

Boston, L. M.
Children of Green Knowe, The
BBC (GB) 1986 dir. Colin Cant
TVSe(GB)

Bosworth, A. R.
Crows of Edwina Hill, The
Nobody's Perfect
UN (US) 1978 dir. Alan Rafkin

Bottome, P.
Danger Signal
WAR (US) 1945 dir. Robert Florey

Bottome, P.
Heart of a Child
RANK (GB) 1958 dir. Clive Donner

Bottome, P.
Mortal Storm, The
MGM (US) 1940 dir. Frank Borzage

Bottome, P.
Private Worlds
PAR (US) 1935 dir. Gregory La Cava

Bottrell, D. D. and Jones, J.
Dearly Departed
P
Kingdom Come
FOX (US) 2001 dir. Doug McHenry

Bouchard, M. M.
Feuillets ou la Répétition d'un Drame
Romantique, Les
P
Lilies
ALLIANCE (Can) 1996 dir. John
Greyson

Bouchard, M. M.
Muses Orphelines, Les
P
LYLA (Can) 2000 dir. Robert Favreau

Boulle, P.
Bridge on the River Kwai, The
COL (GB) 1957 dir. David Lean

Boulle, P.
Monkey Planet
Planet of the Apes
FOX (US) 1968 dir. Franklin Schaffner
FOX (US) 2001 dir. Tim Burton

Bovell, A.
Speaking in Tongues
P
Lantana
LIONS GATE (Aust) 2000 dir. Ray
Lawrence

Bowden, M.
Black Hawk Down: A Story of Modern
War
Black Hawk Down
COL (US) 2001 dir. Ridley Scott

Bowen, C. D. and von Meek, B.
Beloved Friend
Music Lovers, The
UA (GB) 1970 dir. Ken Russell

Bowen, E.
Death of the Heart, The
GRANADA (GB) 1985 dir. Peter
Hammond
TV(GB)

Bowen, E.
Heat of the Day, The
GRANADA (GB) 1989 dir. Christopher
Morahan
TV(GB)

Bowen, E.
Last September, The
BRIT SCREEN (GB/Fr/Ire) 1999 dir.
Deborah Warner

Bowen, G.
Colder Kind of Death, A
CTV (Can) 2001 dir. Brad Turner
TV(Can)

Bowen, G.
Deadly Appearances
SHAFTESBURY (Can) 2000 dir. George Bloomfield
TV(Can)

Bowen, G.
Murder at the Mendel
Love and Murder
SHAFTESBURY (Can) 2000 dir. George Bloomfield
TV(Can)

Bowen, G.
Wandering Soul Murders, The
CTV (Can) 2001 dir. Brad Turner
TV(Can)

Bowen, J.
McGuffin, The
BBC (GB) 1986 dir. Colin Bucksey
TV(GB)

Bowles, P.
Sheltering Sky, The
WAR (US) 1990
dir. Bernardo Bertolucci

Boyd, W.
Good Man in Africa, A
CAPITOL (US) 1994 dir. Bruce Beresford

Boyd, W.
Stars and Bars
COL (US) 1988 dir. Pat O'Connor

Boyer, D.
Sidelong Glances of a Pigeon Kicker, The
MGM (US) 1970 dir. John Dexter

Boyer, F.
Jeux Interdits
R. DORFMANN (Fr) 1952
dir. René Clément

Boylan, G. D.
Thy Son Liveth, Messages from a Soldier to His Mother
Rumor of Angels, A
MPCA (US) 2000 dir. Peter O'Fallon

Boyle, K.
Maiden Maiden
Five Days One Summer
WAR (US) 1982 dir. Fred Zinnemann

Boyle, T. C.
Road to Wellville, The
COL (US) 1994 dir. Alan Parker

Brackett, L.
Tiger Amongst Us, The
13 West Street
COL (US) 1962 dir. Philip Leacock

Bradbury, M.
History Man, The
BBC (GB) 1981 dir. Robert Knights
TVSe(GB)

Bradbury, R.
Fahrenheit 451
UI (GB) 1966 dir. François Truffaut

Bradbury, R.
Foghorn, The
Beast From 20,000 Fathoms, The
WAR (US) 1953 dir. Eugene Lourie

Bradbury, R.
Illustrated Man, The
WAR (US) 1969 dir. Jack Smight

Bradbury, R.
Magic White Suit, The
P
Wonderful Ice Cream Suit, The
DISNEY (US) 1998 dir. Stuart Gordon

Bradbury, R.
Martian Chronicles, The
NBC ENT (US/GB) 1980
dir. Michael Anderson
TVSe(GB/US)

Bradbury, R.
Screaming Woman, The
UN TV (US) 1972 dir. Jack Smight
TV(US)

Bradbury, R.
Something Wicked This Way Comes
DISNEY (US) 1983 dir. Jack Clayton
Ch

Braddon, R.
Year of the Angry Rabbit, The
Night of the Lepus
MGM (US) 1972 dir. William F. Claxton

Bradfield, S.
History of Luminous Motion, The
Luminous Motion
GOOD MACHINE (US) 1998 dir. Bette
Gordon

Bradford, B. T.
Act of Will
PORTMAN (GB) 1989 dir. Don Sharp
TVSe(GB)

Bradford, B. T.
Everything to Gain
ADELSON (US) 1996 dir. Michael L.
Miller
TV(US)

Bradford, B. T.
Her Own Rules
ADELSON (US) 1998 dir. Bobby Roth
TV(US)

Bradford, B. T.
Hold the Dream
TAFT (GB) 1986 dir. Don Sharp
TVSe(GB)

Bradford, B. T.
Love in Another Town
ADELSON (US) 1997 dir. Lorraine
Senna
TV(US)

Bradford, B. T.
Remember
NBC (US) 1993 dir. John Herzfeld
TVSe(US)

Bradford, B. T.
Secret Affair, A
ADELSON (US) 1999 dir. Bobby Roth
TV(US)

Bradford, B. T.
To Be the Best
GEMMY (US/GB) 1992 dir. Tony
Wharmby
TVSe(US/GB)

Bradford, B. T.
Voice of the Heart
PORTMAN (GB) 1989
dir. Tony Wharmby
TVSe(GB)

Bradford, B. T.
Woman of Substance, A
OPT (US) 1984 dir. Don Sharp
TVSe(US)

Bradford, R.
Red Sky at Morning
UN (US) 1971 dir. James Goldstone

Bradlee, Jr., B.
Ambush Murders, The
FRIES (US) 1982
dir. Steven Hilliard Stern
TV(US)

Bradlee, Jr., B.
Guts and Glory: The Rise and Fall of Oliver North

Guts and Glory: The Oliver North Story
PAPAZIAN-HIRSCH (US) 1989
dir. Mike Robe
TVSe(US)

Bradley, M. H.
I Passed for White
WAR (US) 1960 dir. Fred M. Wilcox

Brady, L.
Edge of Doom
RKO (US) 1950 dir. Mark Robson
GB title: Stronger than Fear

Brady, M.
To Gillian on her 37th Birthday
P
RASTAR (US) 1996 dir. Michael Pressman

Bragg, M.
Time to Dance, A
BBC (GB) 1992 dir. Melvyn Bragg
TVSe(GB)

Brahms, C. and Sherrin, N.
Beecham
YTV (GB) 1990 dir. Vernon Lawrence
TV(GB)

Brahms, C. and Simon, S. J.
Elephant is White, The
Give Us the Moon
GFD (GB) 1944 dir. Val Guest

Brahms, C. and Simon, S. J.
No Nightingales
Ghosts of Berkeley Square, The
BN (GB) 1947 dir. Vernon Sewell

Brahms, C. and Simon, S. J.
Trottie True
TC (GB) 1949 dir. Brian Desmond Hurst
US title: Gay Lady, The

Braine, J.
Room at the Top
BI (GB) 1958 dir. Jack Clayton

Braine, J.
Stay With Me Till Morning
YTV (GB) 1981 dir. David Reynolds
TVSe(GB)

Braithwaite, E. R.
To Sir, With Love
COL (GB) 1966 dir. James Clavell

Braithwaite, M.
Why Shoot the Teacher?
QUARTET (Can) 1976
dir. Silvio Narizzano

Bram, C.
Father of Frankenstein
Gods and Monsters
LIONS GATE (US/GB) 1998 dir. Bill Condon

Bramly, S.
Terror in the Bedroom
Sade
STUDIO CANAL+ (Fr) 2000 dir. Jacques Benoit

Brancati, V.
Bell'Antonio, Il
CINA (It/Fr) 1960 dir. Piero Piccioni

Brancato, R. F.
Blinded by the Light
TIME-LIFE (US) 1980
dir. John A. Alonzo
TV(US)

Branch, H.
River Lady
UI (US) 1948 dir. George Sherman

Brand, C.
Green for Danger
INDIVIDUAL (GB) 1946
dir. Sidney Gilliat

Brand, M.
Destry Rides Again
Destry
UI (US) 1954 dir. George Marshall

Brand, M.
Destry Rides Again
UN (US) 1939 dir. George Marshall

Brand, M.
Young Dr. Kildare
MGM (US) 1938 dir. Harold S. Bucquet

Brande, D.
Wake up and Live
FOX (US) 1937 dir. Sidney Lanfield

Brandel, M.
Lizard's Tail, The
Hand, The
ORION/WAR (US) 1981
dir. Oliver Stone

Branden, B.
Passion of Ayn Rand, The
PEG (US) 1999 dir. Christopher Menaul
TV(US)

Brandner, G.
Cameron's Closet
SVS (US) 1989 dir. Armand Mastroianni

Brandner, G.
Howling III
SQUARE (Aust) 1987 dir. Philippe
Mora

Brandner, G.
Howling, The
AVCO (US) 1981 dir. Joe Dante

Brandner, G.
Walkers
From the Dead of Night
PHOENIX (US) 1989 dir. Paul Wendkos
TVSe(US)

Brandon, D.
Outsider, The
P
MGM (GB) 1931 dir. Harry Lachtman
ABPC (GB) 1939 dir. Paul Stein

Brashler, W.
Bingo Long Travelling All-Stars and Motor Kings, The
UN (US) 1976 dir. John Badham

Braun, M.
Black Fox
RHI (US) 1995 dir. Steven H. Stern
TV(US)

Brawley, E.
Rap, The
Fast-Walking
PICKMAN (US) 1982
dir. James B. Harris

Brecht, B.
Galileo
P
CINEVISION (GB) 1975
dir. Joseph Losey

Brecht, B.
Herr Puntila and his Servant Matti
P
BAUERFILM (Austria) 1955
dir. Alberto Cavalcanti

Brecht, B.
Mother Courage
P
ITV (GB) 1959
TV(GB)

Brecht, B. and Weill, K.
Threepenny Opera, The
P
Mack the Knife
21st CENTURY (US) 1989
dir. Menahem Golan
M

Brelis, N.
Mummy Market, The
Trading Mom
FOX (US) 1994 dir. Tia Brelis

Brennan, P.
Razorback
WAR (Aust) 1984 dir. Russell Mulcahy

Brent, J.
Few Days in Weasel Creek, A
WAR TV (US) 1981 dir. Dick Lowry
TV(US)

Brentano, L.
Melody Lingers On, The
IN (US) 1935 dir. David Burton

Breslin, H.
Bad Time at Honda
Bad Day at Black Rock
MGM (US) 1954 dir. John Sturges

Breslin, J.
Gang That Couldn't Shoot Straight, The
MGM (US) 1971
dir. James Goldstone

Brett, S.
Shock to the System, A
MEDUSA (US) 1990 dir. Jan Egleson

Brewer, B.
Memory of Love
In Name Only
RKO (US) 1939 dir. John Cromwell

Brewer, G. E. and Bloch, B.
Dark Victory
P
WAR (US) 1939 dir. Edmund Goulding
UN (US) 1976 dir. Robert Butler
TV(US)

Brewer, G.
K-PAX
UN (US) 2001 dir. Iain Softley

Brickhill, P.
Dam Busters, The
ABP (GB) 1954 dir. Michael Anderson

Brickhill, P.
Great Escape, The
UA (US) 1963 dir. John Sturges

Brickhill, P.
Reach for the Sky
COL (GB) 1956 dir. Lewis Gilbert

Bridie, J.
It Depends What You Mean
P
Folly to be Wise
BL (GB) 1952 dir. Frank Launden

Bridie, J.
Sleeping Clergyman, A
P
Flesh and Blood
BL (GB) 1951 dir. Anthony Kimmins

Bridie, J.
What Say They
P
You're Only Young Twice
ABP (GB) 1952 dir. Terry Gilbert

Briggs, R.
When the Wind Blows
MELTDOWN (GB) 1987
dir. J. T. Murakami
A

Brighouse, H.
Hobson's Choice

P
BL (GB) 1931 dir. Thomas Bentley
BL (GB) 1953 dir. David Lean
CBS ENT (US) 1983 dir. Gilbert Cates
TV(US)

Brin, D.
Postman, The
WAR (US) 1997 dir. Kevin Costner

Brinig, M.
Sisters, The
WAR (US) 1938 dir. Anatole Litvak

Brink, A.
Dry White Season, A
MGM (US) 1989 dir. Euzhan Palcy

Brink, C. R.
Caddie Woodlawn

Caddie
HEMDALE (Aust) 1976
dir. Donald Crombie

Brinkley, D. and Perry, P.
Saved by the Light
FOUR POINT (US) 1995 dir. Lewis
Teague
TV(US)

Brinkley, W.
Don't Go Near the Water
MGM (US) 1957 dir. Charles Walters

Brinkman, B.
Ice House Heat Waves

P
Ice House
UPFRONT/CACTUS (US) 1989
dir. Eagle Pennell

Bristow, G.
Jubilee Trail
REP (US) 1954 dir. Joseph Kane

Bristow, G.
Ninth Guest, The
COL (US) 1934 dir. Roy William Neill

Bristow, G.
Tomorrow is Forever
RKO (US) 1946 dir. Irving Pichel

Brisville, J.-C.
Souper, Le

P
Supper, The
FRANCE 2 (Fr) 1993 dir. Edouard
Molinaro

Brittain, V.
Testament of Youth
BBC (GB) 1979 dir. Moira Armstrong
TVSe(GB)

Britten, B.
War Requiem
BBC (GB) 1989 dir. Derek Jarman
TV(GB)

Brodeur, P.
Stunt Man, The
FOX (US) 1980 dir. Richard Rush

Bromfield, L.
Better Than Life

It All Came True
WAR (US) 1940 dir. Lewis Seiler

Bromfield, L.
McLeod's Folly

Johnny Come Lately
CAGNEY (US) 1943
dir. William K. Howard
GB title: Johnny Vagabond

Bromfield, L.
Modern Hero, A
WAR (US) 1934 dir. G. W. Pabst

Bromfield, L.
Mrs. Parkington
MGM (US) 1944 dir. Tay Garnett

Bromfield, L.
Rains Came, The
FOX (US) 1939 dir. Clarence Brown

Bromfield, L.
Rains Came, The
Rains of Ranchipur, The
FOX (US) 1955 dir. Jean Negulesco

Bromfield, L.
Single Night
Night After Night
PAR (US) 1932 dir. Archie Mayo

Bronder, L.
Rockabye
P
RADIO (US) 1932 dir. George Cukor

Bronson, H.
Hey Hey We're the Monkees
Daydream Believers: The Monkees Story
PEBBLEHUT (US) 2000 dir. Neil
Fearnley
TV(US)

Bronte, C.
Jane Eyre
MON (US) 1934 dir. Christy Cabanne
FOX (US) 1943 dir. Robert Stevenson
OMNIBUS (GB) 1971
dir. Delbert Mann
BBC (GB) 1973 dir. Joan Craft
TVSe(GB)
BBC (GB) 1984 dir. Julian Amyes
TV(GB)
MIRAMAX (Fr/It/GB) 1996 dir. Franco
Zeffirelli

Bronte, C.
Villette
BBC (GB) 1970 dir. Moira Armstrong
TVSe(GB)

Bronte, E.
Wuthering Heights
UA (US) 1939 dir. William Wyler
BBC (GB) 1978 dir. Peter Hammond
TVSe(GB)
MGM-EMI (GB) 1970 dir. Robert Fuest
PLEXUS (Sp) 1983 dir. Luis Bunuel
PAR (GB/US) 1992 dir. Peter
Kosminsky

Brooke, H.
Saturday Island
RKO (GB) 1951 dir. Stuart Heisler
US title: Island of Desire

Brooke, H. and Bannerman, K.
All for Mary
P
RANK (GB) 1955 dir. Wendy Toye

Brooke, H. and Bannerman, K.
Handful of Tansy, A
P
No, My Darling Daughter
RANK (GB) 1961 dir. Ralph Thomas

Brooke, H. and Bannerman, K.
How Say You?
P
Pair of Briefs
RANK (GB) 1961 dir. Ralph Thomas

Brookner, A.
Hotel du Lac
BBC (GB) 1986 dir. Giles Foster
TV(GB)

Brooks, J. Y.
Guests of the Emperor
Silent Cries
YTV/TRISTAR TV (GB) 1993 dir.
Anthony Page
TV(GB)

Brooks, N.
Fragile Fox
P
Attack
UA (US) 1956 dir. Robert Aldrich

Brooks, R.
Brick Foxhole, The
Crossfire
RKO (US) 1947 dir. Edward Dmytryk

Brophy, J.
Day They Robbed the Bank of England, The
MGM (GB) 1959 dir. John Guillermin

Brophy, J.
Immortal Sergeant, The
FOX (US) 1943 dir. John Stahl

Brophy, J.
Turn the Key Softly
GFD (GB) 1953 dir. Jack Lee

Brophy, J.
Waterfront
GFD (GB) 1950 dir. Michael Anderson
US title: Waterfront Women

Broster, D. K.
Flight of the Heron, The
BBC (GB) 1976 dir. Alastair Reid
TVSe(GB)

Brown, A.
Legally Blond
MGM (US) 2001 dir. Robert Luketic

Brown, C.
My Left Foot
PALACE (GB) 1989 dir. Jim Sheridan

Brown, F. Y.
Bengal Lancer
Lives of a Bengal Lancer
PAR (US) 1935 dir. Henry Hathaway

Brown, F.
His Name Was Death
Veille Canaille
FRANCE 3 (Fr) 1992 dir. Gerard Jourd'hui

Brown, F.
Martians Go Home
TAURUS (US) 1990 dir. David Odell

Brown, F.
Screaming Mimi
COL (US) 1958 dir. Gerd Oswald

Brown, G.
I Want What I Want
CINERAMA (GB) 1972 dir. John Dexter

Brown, H.
Sound of Hunting, A
P
Eight Iron Men
COL (US) 1952 dir. Edward Dmytryk

Brown, H.
Stars in their Courses, The
El Dorado
PAR (US) 1966 dir. Howard Hawks

Brown, H. G.
Sex and the Single Girl
WAR (US) 1964 dir. Richard Quine

Brown, H. P. M.
Walk in the Sun, A
FOX (US) 1945 dir. Lewis Milestone

Brown, J. D.
Addie Pray
Paper Moon
PAR (US) 1973 dir. Peter Bogdanovich

Brown, J. D.
Kings Go Forth
UA (US) 1958 dir. Delmer Daves

Brown, J. D.
Stars in My Crown
MGM (US) 1950 dir. Jacques Tourneur

Brown, J. E.
Incident at 125th Street
Incident in San Francisco
ABC TV (US) 1971 dir. Don Medford
TV(US)

Brown, J. P. S.
Jim Kane
Pocket Money
FIRST (US) 1972 dir. Stuart Rosenberg

Brown, K.
Vanquished, The
PAR (US) 1953 dir. Edward Ludwig

Brown, M.
Idol, The
P
Mad Genius, The
WAR (US) 1931 dir. Michael Curtiz

Brown, P. E.
Bad Man, The
P
MGM (US) 1940 dir. Richard Thorpe
GB title: Two Gun Cupid

Brown, R.
Before and After
HOLLYWOOD (US) 1996 dir. Barbet
Schroeder

Brown, R.
Tintype, The
Timestalkers
FRIES (US) 1987 dir. Michael Schultz
TV(US)

Brown, S.
French Silk
VZ/SERTNER (US) 1994 dir. Noel
Nosseck
TV(US)

Brown, W.
Monkey on my Back
UA (US) 1957 dir. André de Toth

Brown, W.
Wiz, The
P
DISNEY (US) 1978 dir. Sidney Lumet
M

Brown, W. C.
Border Jumpers, The
Man of the West
UA (US) 1958 dir. Anthony Mann

Browne, A.
Beirut
P
Daybreak
HBO SHOW (US) 1993 dir. Steven
Tolkin
TV(US)

Browne, G. A.
11 Harrowhouse
FOX (GB) 1974 dir. Aram Avakian

Browne, G. A.
Green Ice
ITC (GB) 1981 dir. Ernest Day

Browne, W.
Holly and the Ivy, The
P
BL (GB) 1952
dir. George More O'Ferrall

Browning, R.
Pied Piper, The
SAG (GB) 1971 dir. Jacques Demy

Bruce, J. C.
Escape from Alcatraz
PAR (US) 1979 dir. Don Siegel

Bruckner, P.
Lunes de Fiel
Bitter Moon
COL (Fr/GB) 1992. dir. Roman Polanski

Brumpton, J.
Containment
P
Life
ROUGH TRADE (Aust) 1996 dir.
Lawrence Johnston

Brush, K.
Red Headed Woman
MGM (US) 1932 dir. Jack Conway

Bryan, C. D. B.
Friendly Fire
M. ARCH (US) 1979 dir. David Greene
TV(US)

Bryan, M.
Intent to Kill
FOX (GB) 1958 dir. Jack Cardiff

Bryson, J.
Evil Angels
Cry in the Dark, A
CANNON (US) 1988 dir. Fred Schepisi

Buarque, C.
Opera do Malandro
P
AUSTRA/TFl (Bra/Fr) 1986
dir. Ruy Guerra

Bucatinsky, D.
I Know You Are, But What Am I?
P
All Over the Guy
LIONS GATE (US) 2001 dir. Julie Davis

Buch, B.
Kleine Blonde Dood, De
Little Blond Death
VER NED (Neth) 1994 dir. Jean van de
Velde

Buchan, J.
Huntingtower
BBC (GB) 1978 dir. Bob Hird
TVSe(GB)

Buchan, J.
John Macnab
BBC (GB) 1976 dir. Donald McWhinnie
TVSe(GB)

Buchan, J.
Thirty-Nine Steps, The
GB (GB) 1935 dir. Alfred Hitchcock
RANK (GB) 1959 dir. Ralph Thomas
RANK (GB) 1978 dir. Don Sharp

Buchanan, E.
Nobody Lives Forever
O'HARA-HORO (US) 1998 dir. Paul
Wendkos
TV(US)

Buchanan, J. D.
Prince of Malta, The
Curacao
SHOWTIME (US) 1993 dir. Carl Schultz
TV(US)

Buchanan, T.
Easy to Love
P
WAR (US) 1933 dir. William Keighley

Buchanan, W.
Shining Season, A
COL TV (US) 1979 dir. Stuart Margolin
TV(US)

Buchheim, L.-G.
Boat, The
COL (Ger) 1981 dir. Wolfgang Petersen

Buchwald, A.
Gift From the Boys, A
Surprise Package
COL (GB) 1960 dir. Stanley Donen

Buck, P.
China Sky
RKO (US) 1945 dir. Ray Enright

Buck, P.
Devil Never Sleeps, The
FOX (GB) 1962 dir. Leo McCarey

Buck, P.
Dragon Seed
MGM (US) 1944 dir. Jack Conway

Buck, P.
Good Earth, The
MGM (US) 1937 dir. Sidney Franklin

Buck, P. S.
Pavilion of Women
BEIJING (China/US) 2001 dir. Ho Yim

Budd, J.
Convict has Escaped, A
They Made Me a Fugitive
WAR (GB) 1947 dir. Alberto Cavalcanti
US title: I Became a Criminal

Budrys, A.
Who?
BL (GB) 1974 dir. Jack Gold
US title: Man Without a Face

Buel, J. D. and Buel, Jr., R.
Way of Duty, The
Mary Silliman's War
CITADEL FILMS (Can) 1994 dir.
Stephen Surjik
TV(Can)

Buffie, M.
My Mother's Ghost
FOX FAMILY (Can) 1997 dir. Elise
Swerhone
TV(Can)

Buffington, S.
Three on a Date
ABC (US) 1978 dir. Bill Bixby
TV(US)

Bugliosi, V.
Till Death Us Do Part
SABAN/SCHERICK 1992
dir. Yves Simoneau
TV(US)

Bugliosi, V. and Gentry, C.
Helter Skelter
LORIMAR (US) 1976 dir. Tom Gries
TVSe(US)

Bugliosi, V. and Henderson, B. B.
And the Sea will Tell
COL (US) 1991 dir. Tommy L. Wallace
TVSe(US)

Buhet, G.
Honey Siege, The
HTV (GB) 1987 dir. John Jacobs
Ch, TVSe(GB)

Bukowski, C.
Copulating Mermaid of Venice;
Trouble with the Battery
Cold Moon
GAU (Fr) 1991 dir. Luc Besson, Andrée
Martinez

Bukowski, C.
Erections, Ejaculations, Exhibitions
and Tales of Ordinary Madness
Tales of Ordinary Madness
GINIS (It) 1981 dir. Marco Ferri

Bullett, G.
Jury, The
Last Man to Hang?, The
COL (GB) 1956 dir. Terence Fisher

Bunker, E.
Animal Factory
FRANCHISE (US) 2000 dir. Steve
Buscemi

Bunker, E.
No Beast so Fierce
Straight Time
WAR (US) 1978 dir. Ulu Grosbard

Bunyan, J.
Pilgrim's Progress, The
Dangerous Journey
CHANNEL 4 (GB) 1985
TVSe (GB)

Burdick, E. and Wheeler, H.
Fail Safe
COL (US) 1963 dir. Sidney Lumet
WAR (US) 2000 dir. Stephen Frears
TV(US)

Burehard, P.
One Gallant Rush
Glory
TRISTAR (US) 1989 dir. Edward Zwick

Burger, G.
Baron Munchhausen
CESK (Czech) 1962 dir. Karel Zeman

Burgess, A.
Clockwork Orange, A
WAR (GB) 1971 dir. Stanley Kubrick

Burgess, A.
Seven Men at Daybreak
Operation Daybreak
WAR (US) 1975 dir. Lewis Gilbert

Burgess, A.
Small Woman, The
Inn of the Sixth Happiness, The
FOX (GB) 1958 dir. Mark Robson

Burgess, G.
Two in the Dark
RKO (US) 1936 dir. Ben Stoloff

Burke, J.
Echo of Barbara
RANK (GB) 1961 dir. Sidney Hayers

Burke, J. L.
Heaven's Prisoners
NEW LINE (US) 1996 dir. Phil Joanou

Burke, S.
Guilty
J&M ENT (GB/US) 2000 dir. Anthony
Waller

Burman, B. L.
Steamboat Round the Bend
FOX (US) 1935 dir. John Ford

Burmeister, J.
Running Scared
Tigers Don't Cry
RANK (SA) 1978
dir. Peter Collinson

Burnet, D.
Private Pettigrew's Girl
P
Shopworn Angel
MGM (US) 1938 dir. H. C. Potter

Burnett, F. H.
Little Lord Fauntleroy
UA (US) 1936 dir. John Cromwell
BBC (GB) 1976 dir. Paul Annett
TVSe(GB)
ROSEMONT (GB) 1980 dir. Jack Gold
TV(GB)
BBC (GB) 1995 dir. Andrew Morgan
TVSe(GB)

Burnett, F. H.
Little Princess, The
FOX (US) 1939 dir. Walter Lang
BBC (GB) 1973 dir. Derek Martinus
TVSe(GB)
LWT (GB) 1987 dir. Carol Wiseman
TVSe(GB)
WAR (US) 1995 dir. Alfonso Cuaron

Burnett, F. H.
Secret Garden, The
MGM (US) 1949 dir. Fred M. Wilcox
Ch
BBC (GB) 1975 dir. Katrina Murray
TVSe(GB)
ROSEMONT (US) 1987 dir. Alan Grint
Ch, TV(US)
WAR (US/GB) 1993 dir. Agnieszka
Holland

Burnett, M. and Alison, J.
Everybody Comes to Rick's
P
Casablanca
WAR (US) 1943 dir. Michael Curtiz

Burnett, W. R.
Adobe Walls
Arrowhead
PAR (US) 1953
dir. Charles Marquis Warren

Burnett, W. R.
Asphalt Jungle, The
Cairo
MGM (GB) 1963 dir. Wolf Rilla

Burnett, W. R.
Asphalt Jungle, The
Cool Breeze
MGM (US) 1972 dir. Barry Pollack

Burnett, W. R.
Asphalt Jungle, The
MGM (US) 1950 dir. John Huston

Burnett, W. R.
Captain Lightfoot
UI (US) 1955 dir. Douglas Sirk

Burnett, W. R.
Dance Hall
FOX (US) 1941 dir. Irving Pichel

Burnett, W. R.
Dark Command
REP (US) 1940 dir. Raoul Walsh

Burnett, W. R.
Dr. Socrates
WAR (US) 1935 dir. William Dieterle

Burnett, W. R.
High Sierra
I Died a Thousand Times
WAR (US) 1955 dir. Stuart Heisler

Burnett, W. R.
High Sierra
WAR (US) 1941 dir. Raoul Walsh

Burnett, W. R.
Iron Man
UN (US) 1931 dir. Tod Browning
UI (US) 1951 dir. Joseph Pevney

Burnett, W. R.
Little Caesar
WAR (US) 1930 dir. Mervyn LeRoy

Burnett, W. R.
Saint Johnson
Law and Order
UN (US) 1932 dir. Edward L. Cahn

Burnett, W. R.
Vanity Row
Accused of Murder
REP (US) 1956 dir. Joe Kane

Burnett, W. R.
Whole Town's Talking, The
COL (US) 1935 dir. John Ford
GB title: Passport to Fame

Burnford, S.
Incredible Journey, The
Homeward Bound: The Incredible Journey
DISNEY (US) 1993 dir. Duwayne
Dunham
Ch

Burnford, S.
Incredible Journey, The
DISNEY (US) 1963 dir. Fletcher Markle
A, Ch

Burns, O. A.
Cold Sassy Tree
TNT (US) 1989 dir. Joan Tewkesbury
TV(US)

Burns, R.
Avenging Angels, The
Messenger of Death
CANNON (US) 1988
dir. J. Lee Thompson

Burns, R. E.
I am a Fugitive from a Chain Gang
WAR (US) 1932 dir. Mervyn LeRoy

Burns, S.
Daybreak of Freedom
Boycott
N. TWAIN (US) 2001 dir. Clark Johnson
TV(US)

Burns, V. G.
Man Who Broke 1,000 Chains, The
JOURNEY (US) 1987 dir. Daniel Mann
TV(US)

Burns, W. N.
Saga of Billy the Kid, The
Billy the Kid
MGM (US) 1930 dir. King Vidor
MGM (US) 1941 dir. David Millar

Burrough, B. and Helyar, J.
Barbarians at the Gate: The Fall of RJR Nabisco
Barbarians at the Gate
COL/HBO (US) 1993 dir. Glenn Jordan
TV(US)

Burroughs, E. R.
At the Earth's Core
BL (GB) 1976 dir. Kevin Connor

Burroughs, E. R.
Land that Time Forgot, The
BL (GB) 1974 dir. Kevin Connor

Burroughs, E. R.
People That Time Forgot, The
BW (GB) 1977 dir. Kevin Connor

Burroughs, E. R.
Tarzan of the Apes
Greystoke: The Legend of Tarzan, Lord of the Apes
WAR (GB) 1984 dir. Hugh Hudson

Burroughs, E. R.
Tarzan of the Apes
Tarzan
DISNEY (US) 1999 dir. Chris Buck,
Kevin Lima
A, Ch

Burroughs, E. R.
Tarzan of the Apes
Tarzan, The Ape Man
MGM (US) 1932 dir. W. S. Van Dyke

Burroughs, W.
Naked Lunch
FOX (US) 1991 dir. David Cronenberg

Burrows, A.
Cactus Flower
P
COL (US) 1969 dir. Gene Saks

Burrows, A.
Can Can
P
TCF (US) 1960 dir. Walter Lang
M

Burrows, A., Loesser, F. and Swerling, J.
Guys and Dolls
P
MGM (US) 1955
dir. Joseph L. Mankiewicz
M

Burt, G.
After the Hole
Hole, The
PATHE (GB) 2001 dir. Nick Hamm

Burt, K. and Leasor, J.
One That Got Away, The
RANK (GB) 1957 dir. Roy Baker

Burtis, T.
New Guinea Gold
Crosswinds
PAR (US) 1951 dir. Lewis R. Foster

Burton, J. G.
Pentagon Wars, The
JERSEY (US) 1998 dir. Richard
Benjamin
TV(US)

Busch, C.
Psycho Beach Party
P
STRAND (US) 2000 dir. Robert Lee
King

Busch, N.
Duel in the Sun
MGM (US) 1946 dir. King Vidor

Busch, N.
Furies, The
PAR (US) 1950 dir. Anthony Mann

Busch, N.
They Dream of Home
Till the End of Time
RKO (US) 1946 dir. Edward Dmytryk

Busch, N.
We the O'Leary's
In Old Chicago
FOX (US) 1937 dir. Henry King

Bus-Fekete, L.
Birthday
P
Heaven Can Wait
FOX (US) 1943 dir. Ernst Lubitsch

Bus-Fekete, L.
Ladies in Love
P
FOX (US) 1936 dir. Edward H. Griffith

Bus-Fekete, L.
Lady Has a Heart, A
P
Baroness and the Butler, The
FOX (US) 1938 dir. Walter Lang

Butler, G.
Kiss the Blood Off My Hands
UN (US) 1948 dir. Norman Foster
GB title: Blood on my Hands

Butler, G.
On Dangerous Ground
RKO (US) 1951 dir. Nicholas Ray

Butler, W.
Butterfly Revolution, The
Summer Camp Nightmare
CONCORDE (US) 1987
dir. Bert C. Dragin

Butterfield, R. P.
Al Schmid, Marine
Pride of the Marines
WAR (US) 1945 dir. Delmer Daves
GB title: Forever in Love

Butterworth, J.
Mojo

P
BBC (GB) 1997 dir. Jez Butterworth

Buzzati, D.
Barnabo of the Mountains
NAUTILUS (It/Fr) 1994 dir. Mario Brenta

Byatt, A. S.
Morpho Eugenia

Angels and Insects
GOLDWYN (GB) 1995 dir. Philip Haas

Byrd, D. and D'Orso, M.
Rise & Walk: The Trial & Triumph of Dennis Byrd

Rise & Walk: The Dennis Byrd Story
FOX WEST (US) 1994 dir. Michael Dinner
TV(US)

Byrne, J.
Slab Boys, The

P
SKREBA (GB) 1997 dir. John Byrne

Byrne, R.
Thrill
NBC STUDIOS (US) 1996 dir. Sam Pillsbury
TV(US)

C

Cabot, M.
Princess Diaries, The
DISNEY (US) 2001 dir. Garry Marhsall

Cacucci, P.
Puerto Escondido
PENRAFILM (It) 1992 dir. Gabriele Salvatores

Cacucci, P.
San Isidro Futbol
Viva San Isidro!
CECCHI (It) 1995 dir. Dante Cappelletti

Cadwell, L. L.
Bruce Lee: The Man Only I Knew
Dragon: The Bruce Lee Story
UN (US) 1993 dir. Rob Cohen

Cahen, A.
Yekl
Hester Street
CONN (US) 1975
dir. Joan Micklin Silver

Cahill, B.
Butterbox Babies
SULLIVAN ENT (Can) 1995 dir. Don McBrearty
TV(Can)

Caidin, M.
Cyborg
Bionic Ever After?
GALLANT (US) 1994 dir. Steve Stafford
TV(US)

Caidin, M.
Cyborg
Six Million Dollar Man, The
UN TV (US) 1973 dir. Richard Irving
TV(US)

Caidin, M.
Marooned
COL (US) 1969 dir. John Sturges

Caillou, A.
Cheetahs, The
Cheetah
DISNEY (US) 1989 dir. Jeff Blyth
Ch

Caillou, A.
Khartoum
UA (GB) 1966 dir. Basil Dearden

Caillou, A.
Rampage
WAR (US) 1963 dir. Philip Carlson

Cain, B.
Stand-Up Tragedy
P
Thicker Than Blood
TNT PICT (US) 1998 dir. Richard Pearce
TV(US)

Cain, J. A.
Slightly Scarlet
RKO (US) 1956 dir. Allan Dwan

Cain, J. A.
When Tomorrow Comes
UN (US) 1939 dir. John M. Stahl

Cain, J. M.
Butterfly
J&M (US) 1982 dir. Matt Cimber

Cain, J. M.
Double Indemnity
PAR (US) 1944 dir. Billy Wilder
UN (US) 1973 dir. Jack Smight
TV(US)

Cain, J. M.
Enchanted Isle, The
Girl in the Cadillac
OVERSEAS (US) 1995 dir. Lucas Platt

Cain, J. M.
Mildred Pierce
WAR (US) 1945 dir. Michael Curtiz

Cain, J. M.
Postman Always Rings Twice, The
Dernier Tournant, Le
LUX (Fr) 1939 dir. Pierre Garnett

Cain, J. M.
Postman Always Rings Twice, The
MGM (US) 1946 dir. Tay Garnets
PAR (US) 1981 dir. Bob Rafaelson

Cain, J. M.
Serenade
WAR (US) 1956 dir. Anthony Mann

Caine, J.
Cold Room, The
HBO PREM (US) 1984
dir. James Dearden
TV(US)

Caine, L.
Widow
LORIMAR (US) 1976
dir. J. Lee Thompson
TV(US)

Cairn, J.
Guy Named Joe, A
MGM (US) 1943 dir. Victor Fleming

Calaferte, L.
Mecanique des Femmes, La
CNC (Fr) 2000 dir. Jerome de Missolz

Calderoni, P.
Avventura di un Uomo Tranquillo, L'
Testimone a Rischio
MEDIASET (It) 1997 dir. Pasqualte
Pozzessere

Caldwell, A.
Flying Down to Rio
P
RKO (US) 1933 dir. Thornton Freeland

Caldwell, E.
Claudelle Inglish
WAR (US) 1961 dir. Gordon Douglas
GB title: Young and Eager

Caldwell, E.
God's Little Acre
UA (US) 1958 dir. Anthony Mann

Caldwell, E.
Tobacco Road
FOX (US) 1941 dir. John Ford

Caldwell, T.
Captains and the Kings
UN TV (US) 1976 dir. Douglas Heyes,
Allen Reisner
TVSe(US)

Caldwell, T.
Testimony of Two Men
UN TV (US) 1977 dir. Leo Penn, Larry
Yust
TVSe(US)

Calef, N.
Lift to the Scaffold
NEF (Fr) 1957 dir. Louis Malle

Callwood, J.
Sleepwalker, The
Sleepwalker Killing
COS-MEU (US) 1997 dir. John Cosgrove
TV(US)

Cameron, I.
Lost Ones, The
Island at the Top of the World, The
DISNEY (US) 1974
dir. Robert Stevenson

Cameron, J.
It was an Accident
PATHE (GB) 2000 dir. Metin Huseyin

Cameron, P.
Weekend, The
GRANADA (GB/US) 2000 dir. Brian
Skeet

Camoletti, M.
Boeing-Boeing
P
PAR (US) 1965 dir. John Rich

Camp, W.
Idle on Parade
COL (GB) 1959 dir. John Gilling

Campanella, R.
It's Good to be Alive
METRO (US) 1974 dir. Michael Landon
TV(US)

Campbell, G.
Cry for Happy
COL (US) 1961 dir. George Marshall

Campbell, J. W.
Who Goes There?
Thing, The
RKO (US) 1951 dir. Christian Nyby
GB title: Thing from Another World,
The
UN (US) 1982 dir. John Carpenter

Campbell, R. W.
Where Pigeons Go To Die
WORLD (US) 1990 dir. Michael Landon
TV(US)

Campbell, Sir M.
Salute to the Gods
Burn 'em up O'Connor
MGM (US) 1938
dir. Edward Sedgwick

Camus, A.
Plague, The
ARABA (Fr/Arg) 1992 dir. Luis Puenzo

Camus, A.
Stranger, The
PAR (Fr/It) 1967 dir. Luchino Visconti

Canada, L.
To Elvis with Love
Touched by Love
COL (US) 1980 dir. Gus Trikonis

Canaway, W. H.
Sammy Going South
BL (GB) 1963
dir. Alexander Mackendrick
US title: Boy Ten Feet Tall, A

Canin, E.
Blue River
HALLMARK (US) 1995 dir. Larry
Elikann
TV(US)

Canning, V.
Castle Minerva
Masquerade
UA (GB) 1965 dir. Basil Dearden

Canning, V.
Golden Salamander, The
GFD (GB) 1949 dir. Ronald Neame

Canning, V.
House of the Seven Flies, The
House of the Seven Hawks, The
MGM (GB) 1959 dir. Richard Thorpe

Canning, V.
Limbo Line, The
MONARCH (GB) 1968
dir. Samuel Gallen

Canning, V.
Panther's Moon
Spy Hunt
UN (US) 1950 dir. George Sherman
GB title: Panther's Moon

Canning, V.
Rainbird Pattern, The
Family Plot
UN (US) 1976 dir. Alfred Hitchcock

Canning, V.
Runaways, The
LORIMAR (US) 1974 dir. Harry Harris
TV(US)

Canning, V.
Scorpio Letters, The
MGM (US) 1967 dir. Richard Thorpe

Canning, V.
Venetian Bird
GFD (GB) 1952 dir. Ralph Thomas
US title: Assassin, The

Cantor, E.
Nest, The
CONCORDE (US) 1988
dir. Terence Winkless

Capeci, J. and Mustain, G.
Gotti: Rise and Fall
Gotti
LUCCHESI (US) 1996 dir. Robert
Harmon
TV(US)

Capon, P.
Murder at Shinglestrand
Hidden Homicide
RANK (US) 1959 dir. Tony Young

Capote, T.
Breakfast at Tiffany's
PAR (US) 1961 dir. Blake Edwards

Capote, T.
Grass Harp, The
FINE LINE (US) 1995 dir. Charles
Matthau

Capote, T.
In Cold Blood
COL (US) 1967 dir. Richard Brooks
HALLMARK (US) 1996 dir. Jonathan
Kaplan
TVSe(US)

Capote, T.
Other Voices, Other Rooms
GOLDEN EYE (US) 1995 dir. David
Rocksavage

Capote, T. and Cooper, W.
Glass House, The
TOM (US) 1972 dir. Tom Gries
TV(US)

Capra, F.
Turning Point, The
Mindwalk
ATLAS (US) 1991 dir. Bernt Capra

Caputo, P.
Rumor of War, A
FRIES (US) 1980 dir. Richard T. Heffron
TVSe(US)

Carcaterra, L.
Sleepers
POLYGRAM (US) 1996 dir. Barry
Levinson

Carey, J.
Mr. Johnson
AVENUE (Aust) 1990
dir. Bruce Beresford

Carey, P.
Bliss
NSW (Aust) 1984 dir. Ray Lawrence

Carey, P.
Oscar and Lucinda
FOX (Aust/US) 1997 dir. Gillian
Armstrong

Cargill, P. and Beale, J.
Ring for Catty
P
Twice Round the Daffodils
AA (GB) 1962 dir. Gerald Thomas

Carleton, Mrs M. C.
Cry Wolf
WAR (US) 1947 dir. Peter Godfrey

Carlile, C.
Children of the Dust
KONIGSBERG (US) 1995 dir. David
Greene
TVSe(US)

Carlile, C.
Honkytonk Man
WAR (US) 1982 dir. Clint Eastwood

Carlucci, A. and Rossetti, P.
Io il Tabano
Altri Uomini
DEAN (It) 1997 dir. Claudio Bonivento

Carney, D.
Square Circle, The
Wild Geese II
UN (GB) 1985 dir. Peter Hunt

Carney, D.
Wild Geese, The
RANK (GB) 1978
dir. Andrew V. McLaglen

Carney, J.
Playboy and the Yellow Lady, The
Love and Rage
SCHLEMMER (Ger/Ire) 1999 dir.
Cathal Black

Carpenter E. C.
One New York Night
P
MGM (US) 1935 dir. Jack Conway
GB title: Trunk Mystery, The

Carpenter, M.
Experiment Perilous
RKO (US) 1944 dir. Jacques Tourneur

Carpenter, T.
Death of a Playmate
Star 80
WAR (US) 1983 dir. Bob Fosse

Carr, A. H. Z.
Finding Maubee
Mighty Quinn, The
MGM (US) 1989 dir. Carl Schenkel

Carr, J. D.
Emperor's Snuffbox, The
That Woman Opposite
MON (GB) 1957 dir. Compton Bennett

Carr, J. L.
Month in the Country, A
EUSTON (GB) 1987 dir. Pat O'Connor

Carrere, E.
Classe de Neige, La
STUDIO CANAL+ (Fr) 1998 dir. Claude
Miller
US title: Class Trip

Carrière, J.-P.
Mahabharata, The
P
CHANNEL 4 (GB) 1990
dir. Peter Brook

Carroll, C.
Golden Herd
San Antone
REP (US) 1952 dir. Joe Kane

Carroll, G.
As the Earth Turns
WAR (US) 1934 dir. Alfred E. Green

Carroll, J.
Basketball Diaries, The
NEW LINE (US) 1995 dir. Scott Kalvert

Carroll, L.
Alice's Adventures in Wonderland
FOX (GB) 1972 dir. William Sterling
A, Ch

Carroll, L.
Alice's Adventures in Wonderland
Alice
HEMDALE (Bel/Pol/GB) 1980
dir. Jerry Gruza

Carroll, L.
Alice's Adventures in Wonderland
Alice in Wonderland
PAR (US) 1933 dir. Norman Z. McLeod
Ch
DISNEY (US) 1951
dir. Clyde Geronomi, Hamilton Luske,
Wilfred Jackson
A, Ch
M. EVANS (US) 1955
dir. George Schaefer
Ch, TV(US)
COL TV (US) 1985 dir. Harry Harris
Ch, TV(US)
BBC (GB) 1986 dir. Barry Letts
TVSe(GB)
HALLMARK (US) 1999 dir. Nick
Willing
Ch, TV(US)

Carroll, L.
**Through the Looking Glass and What
Alice Found There**
Alice Through the Looking Glass
PROJECTOR (GB) 1998 dir. John
Henderson
TV(GB)

Carroll, S.
Big Hand for the Little Lady, A
P
WAR (US) 1966 dir. Fielder Cook
GB title: Big Deal at Dodge City

Carson, R.
Come Be My Love
Once More My Darling
UI (US) 1949 dir. Robert Montgomery

Carstairs, J. P.
Solid! Said the Earl
Yank in Ermine, A
MON (GB) 1955 dir. Gordon Parry

Carter, A.
Company of Wolves, The
PALACE (GB) 1984 dir. Neil Jordan

Carter, A.
Magic Toyshop, The
GRANADA (GB) 1987
dir. David Wheatley
TV(GB)

Carter, A.
Operation Mad Ball
P
COL (US) 1957 dir. Richard Quine

Carter, B.
Late Shift, The
HBO (US) 1996 dir. Betty Thomas
TV(US)

Carter, D. T.
Scottsboro: A Tragedy of the American South
Judge Horton and the Scottsboro Boys
TOM (US) 1976 dir. Fielder Cook
TV(US)

Carter, F.
Education of Little Tree, The
ALLIED FILMS (Can) 1997 dir. Richard Friedenberg

Carter, F.
Gone to Texas
Outlaw Josey Wales, The
WAR (US) 1976 dir. Clint Eastwood

Carter, M.
Tell Me My Name
TALENT (US) 1977 dir. Delbert Mann
TV(US)

Carter, R.
Sixteenth Round, The
Hurricane, The
UN (US) 1999 dir. Norman Jewison

Carter, R.
Sugar Factory, The
IMAGINE (Aust) 1998 dir. Robert Carter

Carter, S. F.
Sudie
Sudie & Simpson
HEARST (US) 1990
dir. Joan Tewkesbury
TV(US)

Carter, T. and Rimes, L.
Holiday in Your Heart
VZ/SERTNER (US) 1997 dir. Michael Switzer
TV(US)

Cartland, B.
Cupid Rides Phillion
Lady and the Highwayman, The
GRADE (GB) 1989 dir. John Hough
TV(GB)

Cartland, B.
Duel of Hearts
TNT (US/GB) 1992 dir. John Hough
TV(US/GB)

Cartland, B.
Flame is Love, The
NBC ENT (US) 1979
dir. Michael O'Herlihy
TV(US)

Cartland, B.
Ghost in Monte Carlo, A
GRADE (GB) 1990 dir. John Hough
TV(GB)

Cartland, B.
Hazard of Hearts, A
MGM (GB) 1987 dir. John Hough
TV(GB)

Cartwright, G.
Blood Will Tell
Texas Justice
CBS TV (US) 1995 dir. Dick Lawry
TV(US)

Cartwright, J.
Look at it this Way
BBC (GB) 1992 dir. Gavin Millar
TVSe(GB)

Cartwright, J.
Rise and Fall of Little Voice, The
P
Little Voice
SCALA (GB) 1998 dir. Mark Herman

Cary, F. L. and King, P.
Watch it Sailor!
P
COL (GB) 1961 dir. Wolf Rilla

Cary, J.
Horse's Mouth, The
UA (GB) 1958 dir. Ronald Neame

Casariego, M.
Chico que imitaba a Roberto Carlos, El
Tu Que Harias Por Amor
FANDANGO (Sp/It) 2000 dir. Carlos
Saura Medrano

Case, D.
Fengriffen
And Now the Screaming Starts
AMICUS (GB) 1973
dir. Roy Ward Baker

Casella, A.
Death Takes a Holiday
P
Meet Joe Black
UN (US) 1998 dir. Martin Brest

Caspary, V.
Bachelor in Paradise
MGM (US) 1961 dir. Jack Arnold

Caspary, V.
Bedelia
GFD (GB) 1946 dir. Lance Comfort

Caspary, V.
Easy Living
PAR (US) 1937 dir. Mitchell Leisen

Caspary, V.
Girls, Les
MGM (US) 1957 dir. George Cukor
M

Caspary, V.
Laura
FOX (US) 1944 dir. Otto Preminger

Cassady, C.
Heart Beat
WAR (US) 1979 dir. John Byrum

Castle, J.
Password is Courage, The
MGM (GB) 1962 dir. Andrew L. Stone

Castleton, P. A.
Son of Robin Hood
Bandit of Sherwood Forest, The
COL (US) 1946
dir. George Sherman, Henry Levin

Cather, W.
Lost Lady, A
WAR (US) 1934 dir. Alfred E. Green

Cather, W.
My Antonia
GIDEON (US) 1995 dir. Joseph Sargent
TV(US)

Cather, W.
O Pioneers!
LORIMAR (US) 1992 dir. Glenn Jordan
TV(US)

Cato, N.
All the Rivers Run
Crawford (Aust) 1983 dir. George
Miller, Pino Amenta
TV(Aust)

Catto, M.
Devil at 4 O'Clock, The
COL (US) 1961 dir. Mervyn LeRoy

Catto, M.
Ferry to Hong Kong
RANK (GB) 1959 dir. Lewis Gilbert

Catto, M.
Fire Down Below
COL (GB) 1957 dir. Robert Parrish

Catto, M.
Hill in Korea, A
BL (GB) 1956 dir. Julian Aymes
US title: Hell in Korea

Catto, M.
Killing Frost, The

Trapeze
UA (US) 1956 dir. Carol Reed

Catto, M.
Lions at the Kill

Seven Thieves
FOX (US) 1960 dir. Henry Hathaway

Catto, M.
Mister Moses

Mr. Moses
UA (GB) 1965 dir. Ronald Neame

Catto, M.
Murphy's War

PAR (GB) 1971 dir. Peter Yates

Catto, M.
Prize of Gold, A

COL (GB) 1955 dir. Mark Robson

Catton, B.
Blue and the Gray, The

COL TV (US) 1982
dir. Andrew McLaglen
TVSe(US)

Caunitz, W. J.
One Police Plaza

CBS ENT (US) 1986 dir. Jerry Jameson
TV(US)

Caute, D.
Comrade Jacob

Winstanley
OTHER (GB) 1977
dir. Kevin Brownlow, Andrew Mollo

Cauvin, P.
Blind Love

Little Romance, A
WAR (US) 1979 dir. George Roy Hill

Cauvin, P.
Theatre Dans la Nuit

Lisa
STUDIO CANAL+ (Fr) 2001 dir. Pierre
Grimblat

Cavanaugh, A.
Children are Gone, The

Deadly Trap, The
NG (Fr/It) 1971
dir. René Clément

Cavazzini, E.
Poem of the Lunatics, The

Voce Delle Lune, La
PENTA (It) 1990 dir. Federico Fellini

Cecil, H.
Brothers in Law

BL (GB) 1957 dir. Ray Boulting

Cellini, B.
Infamous Life, An

LC/CINEMAX (It/Fr/Ger) 1990
dir. Giacomo Battiato

Ceraso, C.
Home Fires Burning

P
Turning, The
PHAEDRA (US) 1992 dir. L. A. Puopolo

Cervantes, M. de
Don Quixote

VANDOR (Fr) 1933 dir. G. W. Pabst
LENFILM (USSR) 1957
dir. Grigori Kozintsev
EUSTON (GB) 1985
TV(GB)
HALLMARK (US) 2000 dir. Peter Yates
TV(US)

Cervantes, M. de
Don Quixote

P
Man of La Mancha
UA (US) 1972 dir. Arthur Hiller
M

Cha, L.
Eagle Shooting Heroes, The

Ashes of Time
SCHOLAR (HK) 1994 dir. Kar-Wai
Wong

Cha, L.
Eagle Shooting Heroes, The: Dong
Cheng Xi Jiu

JET TONE (HK) 1994 dir. Jeffrey Lau

Chabon, M.
Wonder Boys

PAR (US) 2000 dir. Curtis Hanson

Chaikin, A.
Man on the Moon, A

From the Earth to the Moon
HBO (US) 1998 dir. Tom Hanks, David
Frankel, Lili Fini Zanuck, Graham Yost,
Frank Marshall, Jon Turtletaub, Gary
Fleder, David Carson, Sally Field,
Jonathan Mostow
TVSe(US)

Chais, P. H.
Six Weeks in August

Guess Who's Sleeping in my Bed?
ABC (US) 1973 dir. Theodore J. Flicker
TV(US)

Chaiton, S. and Swinton, T.
Lazarus and the Hurricane

Hurricane, The
UN (US) 1999 dir. Norman Jewison

Chamales, T.
Go Naked in the World

MGM (US) 1960
dir. Ronald MacDougall

Chamales, T.
Never so Few

MGM (US) 1959 dir. John Sturges

Chamberlain, G. A.
April Love

TCF (US) 1957 dir. Henry Levin

Chamberlain, G. A.
Phantom Filly, The

Home in Indiana
TCF (US) 1944 dir. Henry Hathaway

Chamberlain, G. A.
Red House, The

UA (US) 1947 dir. Delmer Daves

Chamberlain, G. A.
Scudda Hoo! Scudda Hay!

FOX (US) 1948 dir. F. Hugh Herbert
GB title: Summer Lightning

Chamberlain, W.
Company of Cowards, The

Advance to the Rear
MGM (US) 1964 dir. George Marshall

Chamberlain, W.
Trumpets of Company K

Imitation General
MGM (US) 1958 dir. George Marshall

Chambers, W.
Murder of a Wanton

Sinner Take All
MGM (US) 1937 dir. Errol Taggart

Champion, B. and Powell, J.
Champion's Story: A Great Human
Triumph

Champions
EMBASSY (GB) 1983 dir. John Irvin

Chancellor, J.
King of the Damned

P
GAU (BG) 1935 dir. Walter Forde

Chandler, J. G.
Fire and Rain

WIL COURT (US) 1989
dir. Jerry Jameson
TV(US)

Chandler, R.
Big Sleep, The
WAR (US) 1946 dir. Howard Hawks
ITC (GB) 1977 dir. Michael Winner

Chandler, R.
Farewell, My Lovely
Murder, My Sweet
RKO (US) 1944 dir. Edward Dmytryk

Chandler, R.
Farewell, My Lovely
RKO (US) 1944 dir. Edward Dmytryk
AVCO (US) 1975 dir. Dick Richards

Chandler, R.
High Window, The
Brasher Doubloon, The
FOX (US) 1946 dir. John Brahm
GB title: High Window, The

Chandler, R.
Lady in the Lake
MGM (US) 1946
dir. Robert Montgomery

Chandler, R.
Little Sister, The
Marlowe
MGM (US) 1969 dir. Paul Bogart

Chandler, R.
Long Goodbye, The
UA (US) 1973 dir. Robert Altman

Chang, E.
Eighteen Springs
MANDARIN (China) 1997 dir. Ann Hui

Chang Rehyer, E.
Golden Horse
Red Rose, White Rose
GOLDEN FLARE (HK) 1994 dir.
Stanley Kwan

Chanslor, R.
Ballad of Cat Ballou, The
Cat Ballou
COL (US) 1965 dir. Eliot Silverstein

Chanslor, R.
Hazard
PAR (US) 1948 dir. George Marshall

Chanslor, R.
Johnny Guitar
REP (US) 1953 dir. Nicholas Ray

Chaplin, P.
Siesta
LORIMAR (US) 1987 dir. Mary Lambert

Chapman, E.
Joey Boy
BL (GB) 1965 dir. Frank Launder

Chapman, J.
Dry Rot
P
BL (GB) 1956 dir. Maurice Elvey

Chapman, R.
Behind the Headlines
RANK (GB) 1956 dir. Charles Saunders

Chapman, R.
Murder for the Million
Murder Reported
COL (GB) 1957 dir. Charles Saunders

Chapman, R.
Winter Wears a Shroud
Delavine Affair, The
MON (GB) 1954 dir. Douglas Pierce

Chapman, V.
King's Damsel, The
Quest for Camelot
WAR (US) 1998 dir. Frederik Du Chau
A, Ch, M

Chardonne, J.
Sentimental Destinies
STUDIO CANAL+ (Fr) 2000 dir. Olivier Assayas

Charef, M.
Thé au harem d'Archi Ahmen, Le
Tea in the Harem
M&R (Fr) 1986
dir. Mehdi Charef

Charles, T.
Happy Now I Go
Woman With No Name, The
ABP (GB) 1950 dir. Ladislas Vajda

Charles-Roux, E.
Dimenticare Palermo
PENTA (It/Fr) 1990 dir. Francesco Rosi

Charrière, H.
Papillon
COL (US) 1973 dir. Franklin Schaffner

Charteris, L.
Lady on a Train
UN (US) 1945 dir. Charles David

Charteris, L.
Saint in New York
RKO (US) 1938 dir. Ben Holmes

Charters, S.
Louisiana Black
White Lie
MCA TV (US) 1991 dir. Bill Condon
TV(US)

Chase, B.
Chisolm Trail, The
Red River
UA (US) 1948 dir. Howard Hawks

Chase, J. H.
Eve
GALA (Fr/It) 1963 dir. Joseph Losey

Chase, J. H.
High Stakes
I'll Get You For This
BL (GB) 1950 dir. Joseph M. Newman
US title: Lucky Nick Cain

Chase, J. H.
Just Another Sucker
Palmetto
COL (Ger/US) 1997 dir. Volker Schlondorff

Chase, J. H.
Last Page, The
P
EXCL (GB) 1952 dir. Terence Fisher

Chase, J. H.
Miss Shumley Waves a Wand
Rough Magic
RPC (GB/US) 1995 dir. Clare Peploe

Chase, J. H.
My Laugh Comes Last
Set Up, The
MGM/SHOWTIME (US) 1995 dir. Strathford Hamilton
TV(US)

Chase, J. H.
No Orchids for Miss Blandish
ALL (GB) 1948 dir. St. John L. Clowes

Chase, J. H.
No Orchids for Miss Blandish
Grissom Gang, The
CINERAMA (US) 1971
dir. Robert Aldrich

Chase, J. H.
World In My Pocket, The
On Friday at 11
BL (Ger/Fr/It) 1961 dir. Alvin Rakoff

Chase, M.
Bernardine
P
FOX (US) 1957 dir. Henry Levin

Chase, M.
Harvey

P
UN (US) 1950 dir. Henry Koster
TALENT (US)
1972 dir. Fielder Cook
TV(US)
HALLMARK (US) 1999 dir. George
Schaefer
TV(US)

Chase, T.
When Rabbit Howls

Voices Within: The Lives of Truddi Chase
NEW WORLD TV (US) 1990
dir. Lamont Johnson
TVSe(US)

Chastain, T.
Death Stalk

D. WOLPER (US) 1975 dir. Robert Day
TV(US)

Chatterjee, U.
English, August

TROPIC (Ind) 1994 dir. Dev Benegal

Chatwin, B.
On the Black Hill

CHANNEL 4 (GB) 1989
dir. Andrew Grieve
TV(GB)

Chatwin, B.
Utz

BBC (GB/It/Ger) 1992
dir. George Sluizer

Chaucer, G.
Canterbury Tales, The

UA (It/Fr) 1972 dir Pier Paolo Pasolini

Chayefsky, P.
Altered States

WAR (US) 1980 dir. Ken Russell

Chayefsky, P.
Bachelor Party, The

P
UA (US) 1957 dir. Delbert Mann

Chayefsky, P.
Catered Affair, The

P
MGM (US) 1956 dir. Richard Brooks

Chayefsky, P.
Marty

P
COL (US) 1955 dir. Delbert Mann

Chayefsky, P.
Middle of the Night

P
COL (US) 1959 dir. Delbert Mann

Cheever, J.
Swimmer, The

COL (US) 1968 dir. Frank Perry, Sydney
Pollack

Chekhov, A.
Cherry Orchard, The

P
MELANDA (Gre/Fr) 1999 dir. Michael
Cacoyannis

Chekhov, A.
Peasant Women, The

Lover's Prayer
OVERSEAS (US/GB) 2001 dir. Reverge
Anselmo

Chekhov, A.
Platonov

P
Unfinished Piece for Player Piano, An
MOSFILM (USSR) 1977
dir. Nikita Mikhalkov

Chekhov, A.
Seagull, The

P
WAR (GB) 1969 dir. Sidney Lumet

Chekhov, A.
Shooting Party, The
MOSFILM (USSR) 1981
dir. Emil Loteanu

Chekhov, A.
Shooting Party, The
Summer Storm
UA (US) 1944 dir. Douglas Sirk

Chekhov, A.
Stories
Dark Eyes
EXCELSIOR (It) 1987
dir. Nikita Mikhalkov

Chekhov, A.
Three Sisters
P
BL (GB) 1970 dir. Laurence Olivier

Chekhov, A.
Uncle Vanya
P
August
GOLDWYN (US) 1996 dir. Anthony
Hopkins

Chekhov, A.
Uncle Vanya
P
Country Life
MIRAMAX (Aust) 1994 dir. Michael
Blakemore

Chekhov, A.
Uncle Vanya
P
Vanya on 42nd Street
CHANNEL 4 FILMS (GB/US) 1994 dir.
Louis Malle

Chen, Y. B.
Wan Family's Lawsuit, The
Story of Qiu Ju, The
SIL-METROPOLE (China) 1992 dir.
Yimou Zhang

Cheng-en, W.
Journey to the West
Lost Empire, The
HALLMARK (US/Ger) 2001 dir. Peter
MacDonald
TVSe(US/Ger)

Cherman, Y.
My Friend Ivan Lapshin
LENFILM (USSR) 1986
dir. Alexei Cherman

Chertas, J.
Zoo 2000
BBC (GB) 1984
TV(GB)

Chessman, C.
Cell 2455, Death Row
COL (US) 1955 dir. Fred F. Sears

Chesterton, G. K.
Blue Cross, The
Father Brown
COL (GB) 1954 dir. Robert Hamer

Chesterton, G. K.
Father Brown, Detective
Sanctuary of Fear
M. ARCH (US) 1979
dir. John Llewellyn Moxey
TV(US)

Chesterton, G. K.
Wisdom of Father Brown, The
Father Brown, Detective
PAR (US) 1935 dir. Edward Sedgwick
ATV (GB) 1974 dir. Robert Tronson
TVSe(GB)

Chetham-Strode, W.
Background
P
ABP (GB) 1953 dir. Daniel Birt
US title: Edge of Divorce

Chetwynd-Hayes, R.
Elemental, The; Gate Crasher, The; Act of Kindness, An; Door, The

From Beyond the Grave
EMI (GB) 1973 dir. Kevin Connor

Chevallier, G.
Clochemerle

BLUE RIBBON (Fr) 1948
dir. Pierre Chénal
BBC (GB) 1972 dir. Spencer Chapman
TVSe(GB)

Cheyney, P.
Sinister Errand

Diplomatic Courier
FOX (US) 1952 dir. Henry Hathaway

Cheyney, P.
Uneasy Terms

BN (GB) 1948 dir. Vernon Sewell

Cheyney, P.
Urgent Hangman, The

Meet Mr Callaghan
EROS (GB) 1954 dir. Charles Saunders

Childers, E.
Riddle of the Sands, The

RANK (GB) 1979 dir. Tony Maylam

Childress, A.
Hero Ain't Nothing But a Sandwich, A

NEW WORLD (US) 1977
dir. Ralph Nelson

Childress, M.
Crazy in Alabama

TRISTAR (US) 1999 dir. Antonio
Banderas

Childs, H.
Gaucho

Way of a Gaucho
FOX (US) 1952 dir. Jacques Tourneur

Chilton, C. and Littlewood, J.
Long, Long Trail, The

P
Oh! What a Lovely War
PAR (GB) 1969
dir. Richard Attenborough

Chittenden, F.
Uninvited, The

Stranger in Town
EROS (GB) 1957 dir. George Pollock

Chodorov, E.
Kind Lady

P
MGM (US) 1935 dir. George B. Seitz
MGM (US) 1951 dir. John Sturges

Chodorov, E.
Oh! Men! Oh! Women!

P
FOX (US) 1957 dir. Nunnally Johnson

Chonkadze, D.
Legend of Suram Fortress, The

GRUZIA (USSR) 1985
dir. Sergei Paradjanov

Chopin, K.
Awakening, The

End of August, The
QUARTET (US) 1981 dir. Bob Graham

Chopin, K.
Awakening, The

Grand Isle
TURNER (US) 1992 dir. Mary Lambert
TV(US)

Christensen, J. C.
Voyage of the Basset, The

Voyage of the Unicorn
HALLMARK (US) 2000 dir. Philip
Spink
TVSe(US)

Christensen, M.
Her I Naerheden
NORDISK (Den) 2000 dir. Kaspar
Rostrup

Christian, T. C.
Baby Love
AVCO (GB) 1969 dir. Alistair Reid

Christie, A.
ABC Murders, The
Alphabet Murders, The
MGM (GB) 1966 dir. Frank Tashlin

Christie, A.
After the Funeral
Murder at the Gallop
MGM (GB) 1963 dir. George Pollock

Christie, A.
Appointment with Death
CANNON (US) 1989
dir. Michael Winner

Christie, A.
At Bertram's Hotel
BBC (GB) 1986 dir. Mary McMurray
TV(GB)

Christie, A.
Body in the Library, The
BBC (GB) 1984 dir. George Gallaccio
TV(GB)

Christie, A.
Caribbean Mystery, A
WAR (US) 1983 dir. Robert Lewis
TV(US)
BBC (GB) 1988 dir. Christopher Pettit
TV(GB)

Christie, A.
Dead Man's Folly
WAR (US) 1986 dir. Clive Donner
TV(US)

Christie, A.
Death on the Nile
EMI (GB) 1978 dir. John Guillermin

Christie, A.
Endless Night
BL (GB) 1971 dir. Sidney Gilliat

Christie, A.
Evil Under the Sun
UN (GB) 1982 dir. Guy Hamilton

Christie, A.
4.50 from Paddington
Murder She Said
MGM (GB) 1961 dir. George Pollock

Christie, A.
Hound of Hell, The
Last Seance, The
GRANADA (GB) 1987 dir. June
Wyndham-Davies
TV(GB)

Christie, A.
Lord Edgware Dies
Thirteen at Dinner
WAR (US) 1985 dir. Lou Antonio
TV(US)

Christie, A.
Lord Edgware Dies
TWICKENHAM (GB) 1934
dir. Henry Edwards
BBC (GB) 2000 dir. Brian Farnham
TV(GB)

Christie, A.
Man in the Brown Suit, The
WAR TV (US) 1989 dir. Alan Grint
TV(US)

Christie, A.
Mirror Crack'd from Side to Side, The
Mirror Crack'd, The
EMI (GB) 1980 dir. Guy Hamilton

Christie, A.
Moving Finger, The
BBC (GB) 1984 dir. Roy Boulting
TV(GB)

Christie, A.
Mrs. McGinty's Dead
Murder Most Foul
MGM (GB) 1964 dir. George Pollock

Christie, A.
Murder at the Vicarage
BBC (GB) 1986 dir. Julian Amyes
TV(GB)

Christie, A.
Murder in Three Acts
WAR TV (US) 1986 dir. Gary Nelson
TV(US)

Christie, A.
Murder is Announced, A
BBC (GB) 1985 dir. George Gallaccio
TV(GB)
BBC (GB) 1987 dir. David Giles
TVSe(GB)

Christie, A.
Murder is Easy
WAR (US) 1982 dir. Claude Whatham
TV(US)

Christie, A.
Murder of Roger Ackroyd, The
BBC (GB) 2000 dir. Andrew Grieve
TV(GB)

Christie, A.
Murder on the Orient Express
EMI (GB) 1974 dir. Sidney Lumet
BLATT (US) 2001 dir. Cark Schenkel
TV(US)

Christie, A.
Mysterious Affair at Styles
LWT (GB) 1990 dir. Roy Devenish
TV(GB)

Christie, A.
Nemesis
BBC (GB) 1986 dir. David Tucker
TV(GB)

Christie, A.
Ordeal by Innocence
CANNON (GB) 1985
dir. Desmond Davis

Christie, A.
Pale Horse, The
ANGLIA/A&E (GB) 1997 dir. Charles Beeson
TV(GB)

Christie, A.
Peril at End House
LWT (GB) 1991 dir. Renny Rye
TV(GB)

Christie, A.
Pocketful of Rye, A
BBC (GB) 1985 dir. Guy Slater
TV(GB)

Christie, A.
Secret Adversary, The
LWT (GB) 1986 dir. Tony Wharmby
TV(GB)

Christie, A.
Sparkling Cyanide
WAR (US) 1983 dir. Robert Lewis
TV(US)

Christie, A.
Spider's Web, The
P
UA (GB) 1960 dir. Godfrey Grayson
BBC (GB) 1982 dir. Basil Coleman
TV(GB)

Christie, A.
Ten Little Niggers

And Then There Were None
ABP (US) 1945 dir. René Clair
GB title: Ten Little Niggers
EMI (GB) 1974 dir. Peter Collinson

Christie, A.
Ten Little Niggers

Ten Little Indians
ABP (GB) 1965 dir. George Pollock
CANNON (US) 1989
dir. Alan Birkinshaw

Christie, A.
They do it with Mirrors

Murder with Mirrors
WAR (US) 1985 dir. Dick Lowry
TV(US)

Christie, A.
Why Didn't They Ask Evans?

LWT (GB) 1980 dir. John Davies, Tony
Wharmby
TVSe(GB)

Christie, A.
Witness for the Prosecution

P
UA (US) 1957 dir. Billy Wilder
UA TV (US) 1982 dir. Alan Gibson
TV(US)

Christie, D. and Christie, C.
Carrington, V. C.

P
BL (GB) 1954 dir. Anthony Asquith
US title: Court Martial

Christie, D. and Christie, C.
Grand National Night

P
REN (GB) 1953 dir. Bob McNaught
US title: Wicked Wife, The

Christie, D. and Christie, C.
Someone at the Door

P
BIP (GB) 1936 dir. Herbert Brenon

Christie, D. and Christie, P.
His Excellency

P
GFD (GB) 1951 dir. Robert Hamer

Christman, E.
Nice Italian Girl, A

Black Market Baby
BRUT (US) 1977 dir. Robert Day
GB title: Don't Steal My Baby
TV(US)

Christopher, J.
Death of Grass

No Blade of Grass
MGM (GB) 1970 dir. Cornel Wilde

Christopher, J.
White Mountains, The

Tripods, The
BBC (GB/US/Aust) 1981
dir. Graham Theakston, Christopher
Barry
TVSe(GB/US/Aust)

Chu, L.
Eat a Bowl of Tea

COL (US) 1989 dir. Wayne Wang

Chubin, B.
Feet of the Snake, The

WELLER/MYERS (GB) 1985
TV(GB)

Churchill, Sir W. S.
My Early Life

Young Winston
COL-WAR (GB) 1972
dir. Richard Attenborough

Churchill, Sir W.
Gathering Storm, The

BBC (GB/US) 1974 dir. Herbert Wise
TV(GB/US)

Chute, C.
Beans of Egypt, Maine, The
AM PLAY (US) 1994 dir. Jennifer
Warren

Clancy, T.
Clear and Present Danger
PAR (US) 1994 dir. Phillip Noyce

Clancy, T.
Hunt for Red October, The
PAR (US) 1990 dir. John McTiernan

Clancy, T.
Patriot Games
PAR (US) 1992 dir. Phillip Noyce

Clark, B.
Whose Life is it Anyway?
P
MGM (US) 1981 John Badham

Clark, M. H.
Cradle will Fall, The
P&G (US) 1983
dir. John Llewellyn Moxey
TV(US)

Clark, M. H.
Cry in the Night, A
TELESCENE (Can/Fr) 1993 dir. Robin
Spry
TV(Can/Fr)

Clark, M. H.
Let Me Call You Sweetheart
GROSSO-JACOB (US) 1997 dir. Bill
Corcoran
TV(US)

Clark, M. H.
Loves Music, Loves to Dance
ALLTIME (US) 2001 dir. Mario
Azzopardi
TV(US)

Clark, M. H.
Moonlight Becomes You
GROSSO-JACOB (US) 1998 dir. Bill
Corcoran
TV(US)

Clark, M. H.
Remember Me
HALLMARK (US) 1995 dir. Michael
Switzer
TV(US)

Clark, M. H.
Stillwatch
INTERSCOPE (US) 1987
dir. Rod Holcomb
TV(US)

Clark, M. H.
Stranger is Watching, A
MGM/UA (US) 1982
dir. Sean Cunningham

Clark, M. H.
Weep No More My Lady
STUDIO CANAL+/RYSHER
(US/Fr) 1992 dir. Michael Andrieu
TV(US/Fr)

Clark, M. H.
Where are the Children?
COL (US) 1986 dir. Bruce Malmuth

Clark, M. H.
While My Pretty One Sleeps
GROSSO-JACOB (US) 1997 dir. Jorge
Montesi
TV(US)

Clark, R. and Bobrick, S.
Norman, Is That You?
P
MGM (US) 1976 dir. George Schlatter

Clarke, A. C.
2010
MGM (US) 1984 dir. Peter Hyams

Clarke, A. C.
Sentinel, The

2001, A Space Odyssey
MGM (GB) 1968 dir. Stanley Kubrick

Clarke, D. H.
Housekeeper's Daughter, The
UA (US) 1939 dir. Hal Roach

Clarke, D. H.
Impatient Virgin, The
Impatient Maiden
UN (US) 1932 dir. James Whale

Clarke, D. H.
Louis Beretti
Born Reckless
FOX (US) 1930 dir. John Ford

Clarke, M.
For the Term of his Natural Life
FILMO (Aust) 1985 dir. Rob Stewart
TVSe(Aust)

Clauser, S.
Girl Named Sooner, A
FOX TV (US) 1975 dir. Delbert Mann
TV(US)

Clavell, J.
King Rat
COL (US) 1965 dir. Bryan Forbes

Clavell, J.
Noble House
DELAUR (US) 1988 dir. Gary Nelson
TVSe(US)

Clavell, J.
Shogun
PAR (Jap/US) 1981 dir. Jerry London
TVSe(Jap/US)

Clavell, J.
Tai-Pan
ORION (US) 1986 dir. Daryl Duke

Clay, S. B.
Ritual
P
GOTHAM (US) 1999 dir. Stanley
Bennett Clay

Cleary, J.
Green Helmet, The
MGM (GB) 1960 dir. Michael Forlong

Cleary, J.
High Commissioner, The
Nobody Runs Forever
RANK (GB) 1968 dir. Ralph Thomas
US title: High Commissioner, The

Cleary, J.
High Road to China
WAR (US) 1983 dir. Brian G. Hutton

Cleary, J.
Spearfield's Daughter
FILMLINE (US) 1986
dir. Gilbert Shelton
TVSe(US)

Cleary, J.
Sundowners, The
WAR (GB/Aust) 1960
dir. Fred Zinnemann

Cleary, J.
You Can't See Round Corners
UI (Aust) 1969 dir. David Cahill

Cleaver, V. and Cleaver, B.
Where the Lilies Bloom
UA (US) 1974 dir. William A. Graham

Clebert, J. P.
Blockhaus, Le
Blockhouse, The
GALACTUS (GB) 1973 dir. Clive Rees

Cleland, J.
Fanny Hill
GALA (Ger) 1965 dir. Russ Meyer
BW (GB) 1983 dir. Gerry O'Hare

Clemente, G. W and Stevens, K.
Cops are Robbers, The
Good Cops, Bad Cops
KUSHNER-LOCKE (US) 1990 dir. Paul
Wendkos
TV(US)

Cleveland, R.
Jerry and Tom
P
LIONS GATE (US) 1998 dir. Saul
Rubinek

Clewes, H.
Green Grow the Rushes
BL (GB) 1951 dir. Derek Twist

Clewes, H.
Long Memory, The
GFD (GB) 1953 dir. Robert Hamer

Clewlow, C.
Woman's Guide to Adultery, A
CARLTON (GB) 1993 dir. David
Hayman
TVSe(GB)

Clifford, C. L.
Real Glory, The
UA (US) 1939 dir. Henry Hathaway

Clifford, F.
Act of Mercy
Guns of Darkness
WAR (GB) 1962 dir. Anthony Asquith

Clifford, F.
Naked Runner, The
WAR (GB) 1967 dir. Sidney J. Furie

Clift, D.
Man About Town
FOX (US) 1932 dir. John Francis Dillon

Clift, D.
Scotland Yard
P
FOX (US) 1941 dir. Norman Foster

Clift, D.
Warn London
BL (GB) 1934 dir. T. Hayes Hunter

Cloete, S.
Fiercest Heart, The
FOX (US) 1961 dir. George Sherman

Clooney, R. and Strait, R.
This For Remembrance
Rosie: The Rosemary Clooney Story
FRIES (US) 1982 dir. Jackie Cooper
TV(US)

Clouston, J. S.
Spy in Black, The
COL (GB) 1939 dir. Michael Powell
US title: U-Boat 29

Clowes, St. J. L.
Dear Murderer
P
GFD (GB) 1947 dir. Arthur Crabtree

Coates, J.
True as a Turtle
RANK (GB) 1957 dir. Wendy Toye

Coates, R. M.
Wisteria Cottage
Edge of Fury
UA (US) 1958 dir. Robert Gurney, Irving
Lerner

Cobb, H.
Paths of Glory
UA (US) 1957 dir. Stanley Kubrick

Cobb, I. S.
Sun Shines Bright, The; Mob From
Massac, The; Lord Provides, The

Sun Shines Bright, The
REP (US) 1953 dir. John Ford

Coburn, A.
Sweetheart

Toutes Peines Confondues
FRANCE 3 (Fr) 1992 dir. Michael
Deville

Cochran, E.
Climax, The

P
UN (US) 1944 dir George Waggner

Cochran, M.
And Deliver Us From Evil

Fugitive Among Us
ABC PROD (US) 1992 dir. Michael
Toshiyuki Uno
TV(US)

Cockell, J.
Yesterday's Children

COS/MEU (US) 2000 dir. Marcus Cole
TV(US)

Cockrell, F. M. and Cockrell, M.
Dark Waters

UA (US) 1944 dir. André de Toth

Cocteau, J.
Amore, L'

P
TEVERE (It) 1948
dir. Roberto Rossellini

Cocteau, J.
Enfants Terribles, Les

MELVILLE (Fr) 1950
dir. Jean-Pierre Melville

Cocteau, J.
Orphée

P
A. PAULVÉÉ (Fr) 1949
dir. Jean Cocteau

Cocteau, J.
Parents Terribles, Les

P
SIRIUS (Fr) 1948 dir. Jean Cocteau

Cody, R.
Ricochet River

DEEGEE (US) 1998 dir. Deborah Del
Prete

Coe, C. F.
Nancy Steele is Missing

FOX (US) 1937 dir. George Marshall

Coen, F.
Vinegar Hill

Deadly Family Secrets
FILERMAN (US) 1995 dir. Richard T.
Heffron
TV(US)

Coetzee, J. M.
In the Heart of the Country

Dust
DASKA (Bel/Fr) 1985
dir. Marion Hansel

Coffee, L.
Weep No More

Another Time, Another Place
PAR (GB) 1958 dir. Lewis Allen

Cohan, G. M.
Little Nellie Kelly

P
MGM (US) 1940 dir. Norman Taurog
M

Cohan, G. M.
Meanest Man in the World, The

P
FOX (US) 1943 dir. Sidney Lanfield

Cohen, E. A. and Shapiro, M. J.
Dangerous Evidence

*Dangerous Evidence: The Lori Jackson
Story*
HEARST (US) 1999 dir. Sturla
Gunnarsson
TV(US)

Cohn, A.
Joker is Wild, The
PAR (US) 1957 dir. Charles Vidor

Coke, P.
Breath of Spring
P
Make Mine Mink
RANK (GB) 1960 dir. Robert Asher

Cole, B.
Illuminata
P
OVERSEAS (US/Sp) 1998 dir. John
Turturro

Cole, B.
Olimpia
Bobo, The
WAR (US) 1978 dir. Robert Parrish

Colegate, I.
Shooting Party, The
REEVE (GB) 1984 dir. Alan Bridges

Coleman, G. and Garrick, D.
Clandestine Marriage, The
P
BRIT SCREEN (GB) 1999 dir.
Christopher Miles

Coleman, J.
At Mother's Request
VISTA (US) 1987 dir. Michael Tuchner
TVSe(US)

Coleman, J. R.
Blue Collar Journal

Secret Life of John Chapman, The
JOZAK (US) 1976 dir. David Lowell
Rich
TV(US)

Coleman, L.
Beulah Land
COL TV (US) 1980 dir. Virgil Vogel,
Harry Falk
TVSe(US)

Coleman, L.
Next of Kin
P
Hot Spell
PAR (US) 1958 dir. Daniel Mann

Coleman, T.
Southern Cross
G. REEVES (GB) 1983
TV(GB)

Colette
Cheri
BBC (GB) 1973 dir. Claude Whatham
TVSe(GB)

Colette
Gigi
CODO (Fr) 1948 dir. Jacqueline Audry
MGM (US) 1958 dir. Vincente Minnelli
M

Colette
Ingenue Libertine, L'
CODO (Fr) 1950 dir. Jacqueline Audry

Collard, C.
Nuits Fauves, Les
Savage Nights
STUDIO CANAL+ (Fr/It) 1992 dir.
Cyril Collard

Colley, P.
I'll Be Back Before Midnight
P
Illusions
PRISM ENT (US) 1992 dir. Victor Kulle
TV(US)

Collier, J. L.
Fires of Youth
Danny Jones
CINERAMA (GB) 1972
dir. Jules Bricken

Collier, Z.
Cooler Climate, A
PAR (US) 1999 dir. Susan Seidelman
TV(US)

Collins, A.
In the Sleep Room: The Story of the CIA Brainwashing Experiments in Canada
Sleep Room, The
CBC (Can) 1998 dir. Anne Wheeler
TV(Can)

Collins, D.
Rich and Strange
BIP (GB) 1931 dir. Alfred Hitchcock
US title: East of Shanghai

Collins, D.
Sentimentalists, The
His Woman
PAR (US) 1931 dir. Edward Sloman

Collins, J.
Bitch, The
BW (GB) 1979 dir. Gerry O'Hara

Collins, J.
Hollywood Wives
WAR (US) 1985 dir. Robert Day
TVSe(US)

Collins, J.
Lady Boss
VZ/SERTNER (US) 1992 dir. Charles Jarrott
TVSe(US)

Collins, J.
Lucky; Chances
Lucky/Chances
NBC (US) 1990 dir. Buzz Kulik
TVSe(US)

Collins, J.
Stud, The
BW (GB) 1978 dir. Quentin Masters

Collins, J.
World is Full of Married Men, The
NEW REALM (GB) 1979
dir. Robert Young

Collins, L.
Fall From Grace
RYSHER (US) 1994 dir. Waris Hussein
TVSe(US)

Collins, L. and Lapierre, D.
Is Paris Burning?
PAR (Fr/US) 1965 dir. René Clément

Collins, N.
London Belongs to Me
UN (GB) 1948 dir. Sydney Gilliatt
US title: Dulcimer Street
THAMES (GB) 1977
dir. Raymond Menmuir, Bill Hays
TVSe(GB)

Collins, W.
Basil
SHOWCAREER (GB) 1998 dir. Radha Bharadwaj

Collins, W.
Moonstone, The
BBC (GB) 1972 dir. Paddy Russell
TVSe(GB)

Collins, W.
Woman in White, The
WAR (US) 1948 dir. Peter Godfrey
BBC (GB) 1982 dir. John Bruce
TVSe(GB)

Collison, W.
Farewell to Women
P
Mogambo
MGM (US) 1953 dir. John Ford

Collison, W.
Farewell to Women
P
Red Dust
MGM (US) 1932 dir. Victor Fleming

Collodi, C.
Adventures of Pinocchio, The
NEW LINE (US/GB) 1996 dir. Steve Barron
Ch

Collodi, C.
Pinocchio
DISNEY (US) 1940 dir. Ben Sharpsteen
A, Ch
CANTO (US) 1968 dir. Sid Smith
TV(US)
BBC (GB) 1978 dir. Barry Letts
Ch, TVSe(GB)

Collura, M. L.
Winners
Spirit Rider
CREDO (Can) 1994 dir. Michael J. F. Scott
TV(Can)

Colson, C.
Born Again,
AVCO (US) 1978 dir. Irving Rapper

Colton, J.
Shanghai Gesture, The
P
IN (US) 1941 dir. Josef von Sternberg

Comden, B. and Green, A.
Bells are Ringing
P
MGM (US) 1960 dir. Vincente Minnelli
M

Comden, B., Green, A. and Leigh, C.
Peter Pan
P
MBC (US) dir. Michael Kidd
M, TV(US)

Compton, D.
Unsleeping Eye, The
Deathwatch
CONTEM (Fr/Ger) 1979 dir. Bertrand Tavernier

Comstock, H. W.
Dr. X
P
WAR (US) 1932 dir. Michael Curtiz

Conchon, G.
Etat Sauvage, L'
FILMS 1966 (Fr) 1990 dir. Francis Girod

Conde, N.
In the Deep of the Woods
In the Deep Woods
GOLCHAN/HILL (US) 1992 dir. Charles Correll
TV(US)

Conde, N.
Religion, The
Believers, The
ORION (US) 1987 dir. John Schlesinger

Condon, R.
Manchurian Candidate, The
UA (US) 1962 dir. John Frankenheimer

Condon, R.
Oldest Confession, The
Happy Thieves, The
UA (US) 1962 dir. George Marshall

Condon, R.
Prizzi's Honor
FOX (US) 1985 dir. John Huston

Condon, R.
Winter Kills
AVCO (US) 1979 dir. William Richert

Congwen, S.
Xiao, Xiao
Girl from Hunan, The
CHINA (China) 1986 dir. Xie Fei, U Lan

Conlon, K.
My Father's House
GRANADA (GB) 1981 dir. Alan Grint
TVSe(GB)

Connaughton, S.
Run of the Country, The
COL (Ire/US) 1995 dir. Peter Yates

Connell, E. S.
Mr Bridge; Mrs. Bridge
Mr. and Mrs. Bridge
MIRAMAX (US) 1990 dir. James Ivory

Connell, E. S.
Son of the Morningstar: Custer and
the Little Big Horn
Son of the Morning Star
REP (US) 1991 dir. Mike Robe
TVSe(US)

Connell, R. E.
Brother Orchid
WAR (US) 1940 dir. Lloyd Bacon

Connelly, J.
Bringing Out the Dead
PAR (US) 1999 dir. Martin Scorsese

Connelly, M.
Green Pastures, The
P
WAR (US) 1936
dir. William Keighley, Marc Connelly
MILBERG (US) 1957
dir. George Schaefer
TV(US)

Conner, R.
Shake Hands with the Devil
UA (Ire) 1959 dir. Michael Anderson

Conners, B.
Applesauce
P
Brides are Like That
WAR (US) 1936 dir. William McGann

Conrad, J.
Heart of Darkness
TURNER (US) 1994 dir. Nicolas Roeg
TV(US)

Conrad, J.
Lord Jim
COL (GB) 1964 dir. Richard Brooks

Conrad, J.
Nostromo
BBC (GB) 1997 dir. Alastair Reid
TVSe(GB)

Conrad, J.
Outcast of the Islands, An
LF (GB) 1951 dir. Carol Reed

Conrad, J.
Point of Honour, The
Duellists, The
CIC (GB) 1977 dir. Ridley Scott

Conrad, J.
Secret Agent, The
Sabotage
GB (GB) 1936 dir. Alfred Hitchcock
US title: Woman Alone, A

Conrad, J.
Secret Agent, The

BBC (GB) 1992 dir. David Drury
TVSe(GB)
FOX (US) 1996 dir. Christopher
Hampton

Conrad, J.
Secret Sharer, The

Face to Face
RKO (US) 1952
dir. John Brahm, Bretaigne Windust

Conrad, J.
Victory

PAR (US) 1940 dir. John Cromwell
BRIT SCREEN (GB/Fr) 1997 dir. Mark
Peploe

Conrad, J.
Within the Tides

Laughing Anne
REP (GB) 1953 dir. Herbert Wilcox

Conrad, P.
My Daniel

Dinosaur Hunter, The
IMP (Can) 2000 dir. Rick Stevenson

Conran, S.
Lace

LORIMAR (US) 1984 dir. Billy Hale
TVSe(US)

Conroy, P.
Great Santini, The

ORION (US) 1979 dir. Lewis John
Carlino

Conroy, P.
Lords of Discipline, The

PAR (US) 1983 dir. Franc Roddam

Conroy, P.
Prince of Tides, The

COL (US) 1991 dir. Barbra Streisand

Conroy, P.
Water is Wide, The

Conrack
FOX (US) 1974 dir. Martin Ritt

Constanduros, M. and Constanduros, D.
Acacia Avenue

P
29 Acacia Avenue
COL (GB) 1945 dir. Henry Cass
US title: Facts of Love, The

Cook, D.
Second Best

REGENCY (GB/US) 1994 dir. Chris
Menges

Cook, D.
Winter Doves

Loving Walter
FF (GB) 1986 dir. Stephen Frears

Cook, K.
Wake in Fright

Outback
NIT (Aust) 1970 dir. Ted Kotcheff

Cook, K.
What Girls Learn

SHOWTIME (US) 2001 dir. Lee Rose
TV(US)

Cook, R.
Acceptable Risk

V Z/SERTNER (US/Can) 2001 dir.
William A. Graham
TV(US/Can)

Cook, R.
Coma

MGM (US) 1978 dir. Michael Crichton

Cook, R.
Harmful Intent

ROSEMONT (US) 1993 dir. John
Patterson
TV(US)

Cook, R.
Mortal Fear

VZ/SERTNER (US) 1994 dir. Larry Shaw
TV(US)

Cook, R.
Sphinx

WAR (US) 1981
dir. Franklin D. Schaffner

Cook, R.
Virus

VZ/SERTNER (US) 1995 dir. Armand Mastroianni
TV(US)

Cook, T. H.
Evidence of Blood

MGM TV (US) 1998 dir. Andrew Mondshein
TV(US)

Cooke, W. E.
Two Rode Together

COL (US) 1961 dir. John Ford

Cookson, C.
Black Candle, The

TYNE-TEES (GB) 1991
dir. Roy Battersby
TV(GB)

Cookson, C.
Black Velvet Gown, The

TYNE-TEES (GB) 1991
dir. Norman Stone
TV(GB)

Cookson, C.
Cinder Path, The

TYNE TEES (GB) 1994 dir. Simon Langton
TVSe(GB)

Cookson, C.
Dwelling Place, The

TYNE TEES (GB) 1994 dir. Gavin Millar
TVSe(GB)

Cookson, C.
Fifteen Streets, The

TYNE-TEES (GB) 1991
dir. David Wheatley
TV(GB)

Cookson, C.
Gambling Man, The

TYNE-TEES (GB) 1995 dir. Norman Stone
TVSe(GB)

Cookson, C.
Glass Virgin, The

TYNE-TEES (GB) 1995 dir. Sarah Hellings
TVSe(GB)

Cookson, C.
Joe and the Gladiator

BBC (GB) 1971 dir. Anna Home
TVSe(GB)

Cookson, C.
Mallen Streak, The

Mallens, The
GRANADA (GB) 1979 dir. Richard Martin, Mary McMurray, Brian Mills
TVSe(GB)

Cookson, C.
Our John Willie

BBC (GB) 1980 dir. Marilyn Fox
TVSe(GB)

Cookson, C.
Rooney

RANK (GB) 1958 dir. George Pollock

Coolen, A.
Doctor in the Village

NFM (Neth) 1958 dir. Fons Rademakers

Coolidge, S.
What Katy Did; What Katy Did at School

Katy
BBC (GB) 1976 dir. Julia Smith
TVSe(GB)

Cooney, C. B.
Face on the Milk Carton, The

FAMILY (US) 1995 dir. Waris Hussein
TV(US)

Cooney, C. B.
Rearview Mirror

SCHICK SUNN (US) 1984 dir. Lou Antonio
TV(US)

Cooney, C. B.
Whatever Happened to Janie?

Face on the Milk Carton, The
FAMILY (US) 1995 dir. Waris Hussein
TV(US)

Cooney, M.
Murder in Mind

P
CBS (US) 1997 dir. Robert Iscove
TV(US)

Cooney, R.
Not Now Darling

P
MGM (GB) 1973 dir. Ray Cooney, David Croft

Cooney, R.
Out of Order

P
Miniszter Felrelep, A
INTERCOM (Hun) 1997 dir. Andras Kern, Robert Koltai

Cooney, R.
There Goes the Bride

P
ENT (GB) 1980 dir. Terence Marcel

Coonts, S.
Flight of the Intruder

PAR (US) 1991 dir. John Milius

Cooper, D.
Frisk

STRAND (US) 1995 dir. Todd Verow

Cooper, J. F.
Deerslayer, The

FOX (US) 1957 dir. Kurt Neumann
SCHICK SUNN (US) 1978
dir. Dick Friedenberg
TV(US)

Cooper, J. F.
Last of the Mohicans, The

Last of the Redmen
COL (US) 1947 dir. George Sherman

Cooper, J. F.
Last of the Mohicans, The

UA (US) 1936 dir. George B. Seitz
BBC (GB) 1971 dir. David Maloney
TVSe(GB)
SCHICK SUNN (US) 1977
dir. James L. Conway
MORGAN CREEK (US) 1992 dir. Michael Mann
TV(US)

Cooper, J. F.
Pathfinder, The

Hawkeye, The Pathfinder
BBC (GB) 1973 dir. David Maloney
TVSe(GB)

Cooper, J. F.
Pathfinder, The

HALLMARK (US) 1996 dir. Donald Shebib
TV(US)

Cooper, R. R.
Last To Go, The

INTERSCOPE (US) 1991
dir. John Erman
TV(US)

Cooper, S. and Cronyn, H.
Foxfire

P

M. REES (US) 1987 dir. Jod Taylor
TV(US)

Cope, T. F.
Shift, The

Last Dance, The
POLSON (US) 2000 dir. Kevin Dowling
TV(US)

Coppel, A.
Gazebo, The

MGM (US) 1959 dir. George Marshall

Coppel, A.
I Killed The Count

P

GN (GB) 1939 dir Fred Zelnik

Coppel, A.
Man About a Dog, A

P

Obsession
GFD (GB) 1949 dir. Edward Dmytryk
US title: Hidden Room, The

Coppel, A.
Mr. Denning Drives North

BL (GB) 1951 dir. Anthony Kimmins

Corbett, J. J.
Roar of the Crowd, The

Gentleman Jim
WAR (US) 1942 dir. Raoul Walsh

Corbett, S.
Love Nest

FOX (US) 1951 dir. Joseph Newman

Corbin, W.
Smoke

DISNEY (US) 1970
dir. Vincent McEveety

Corcoran, J.
Bitter Harvest: Murder in the Heartland

In the Line of Duty: Manhunt in the Dakotas
PATCHETT-KAUFMAN (US) 1991 dir. Dick Lowry
TV(US)

Cordelier, J.
Life, The

Memoirs of a French Whore
AIDART (Fr) 1982 dir. Daniel Duval

Corliss, A.
Summer Lightning

I Met My Love Again
WANGER (US) 1937 dir. Joshua Logan, Arthur Ripley

Cormack, B.
Racket, The

P

RKO (US) 1951 dir. John Cromwell

Corman, A.
Kramer vs Kramer

COL (US) 1979 dir. Robert Benton

Corman, A.
Oh! God!

WAR (US) 1977 dir. Carl Reiner

Cormier, R.
Bumblebee Flies Anyway, The

SHOOTING GALLERY (US) 2000 dir. Martin Duffy
TV(US)

Cormier, R.
Chocolate War, The

MCEG (US) 1988 dir. Keith Gordon

Cormier, R.
I am the Cheese

ALMI (US) 1983 dir. Robert Jiras

Cormier, R.
I Am the Cheese

Lapse of Memory
MAX (Can/Fr) 1992 dir. Patrick Dewolf

Cornwell, B.
Sharpe's Battle
PICTURE PALACE (GB) 1995 dir. Tom Clegg
TV(GB)

Cornwell, B.
Sharpe's Company
PICTURE PALACE (GB) 1994 dir. Tom Clegg
TV(GB)

Cornwell, B.
Sharpe's Eagle
PICTURE PALACE (GB) 1993 dir. Tom Clegg
TV(GB)

Cornwell, B.
Sharpe's Enemy
PICTURE PALACE (GB) 1994 dir. Tom Clegg
TV(GB)

Cornwell, B.
Sharpe's Gold
PICTURE PALACE (GB) 1995 dir. Tom Clegg
TV(GB)

Cornwell, B.
Sharpe's Honour
PICTURE PALACE (GB) 1994 dir. Tom Clegg
TV(GB)

Cornwell, B.
Sharpe's Regiment
CELTIC/PICTURE PALACE (GB) 1996 dir. Tom Clegg
TV(GB)

Cornwell, B.
Sharpe's Revenge
PICTURE PALACE (GB) 1997 dir. Tom Clegg
TV(GB)

Cornwell, B.
Sharpe's Rifles
PICTURE PALACE (GB) 1993 dir. Tom Clegg
TV(GB)

Cornwell, B.
Sharpe's Siege
CELTIC/PICTURE PALACE (GB) 1996 dir. Tom Clegg
TV(GB)

Cornwell, B.
Sharpe's Sword
PICTURE PALACE (GB) 1995 dir. Tom Clegg
TV(GB)

Cornwell, B.
Sharpe's Waterloo
PICTURE PALACE (GB) 1997 dir. Tom Clegg
TV(GB)

Corrente, M.
Federal Hill
P
TRIMARK (US) 1993 dir. Michael Corrente

Corrington, J. W.
Decoration Day
M. REES (US) 1990
dir. Robert Markowitz
TV(US)

Corwin, N.
Rivalry, The
P
DEFARIA (US) 1975 dir. Fielder Cook
TV(US)

Cory, D.
Deadfall
FOX (GB) 1968 dir. Bryan Forbes

Cosby, V.
Mind Reader, The
WAR (US) 1933 dir. Roy del Ruth

Costain, T. B.
Black Rose, The
FOX (US) 1950 dir. Henry Hathaway

Costain, T. B.
Silver Chalice, The
WAR (US) 1954 dir. Victor Saville

Costello, M.
Titanic Town
BRIT SCREEN (Ire/GB) 1998 dir. Roger Michell

Cotler, G.
Bottletop Affair, The
Horizontal Lieutenant, The
MGM (US) 1962 dir. Richard Thorpe

Cotterell, G.
Tiara Tahiti
RANK (GB) 1962
dir. William T Kotcheff

Coughlin, P.
Awakening, The
ALLIANCE (Can) 1995 dir. George Bloomfield
TV(Can)

Coughlin, W. J.
Shadow of a Doubt
SCRIPPS HOWARD (US) 1995 dir. Brian Dennehy
TV(US)

Coulter, S.
Embassy
HEMDALE (GB) 1972
dir. Gordon Hessler

Coupon, H.
Verdict
CCC (Fr/It) 1974 dir. André Cayatte

Courtenay, B.
Power of One, The
VILLAGE ROADSHOW (Aust/Fr/US) 1992 dir. John G. Avildsen

Cousins, M.
Life of Lucy Gallant, The
Lucy Gallant
PAR (US) 1955 dir. Robert Parrish

Cousins, N.
Anatomy of an Illness
CBS ENT (US) 1984
dir. Richard Heffron
TV(US)

Coward, N.
Astonished Heart, The
P
GFD (GB) 1949 dir. Terence Fisher, Anthony Darnborough

Coward, N.
Bitter Sweet
P
UA (GB) 1933 dir. Herbert Wilcox
MGM (US) 1940 dir. W. S. Van Dyke
M

Coward, N.
Blithe Spirit
P
CIN (GB) 1945 dir. David Lean
COMPASS (US) 1966
dir. George Schaefer
TV(US)

Coward, N.
Bon Voyage
BBC (GB) 1985 dir. Mike Vardy
TV(GB)

Coward, N.
Cavalcade
P
FOX (US) 1932 dir. Frank Lloyd

Coward, N.
Design for Living
P
PAR (US) 1933 dir. Ernst Lubitsch

Coward, N.
Me and the Girls
BBC (GB) 1985 dir. Jack Gold
TV(GB)

Coward, N.
Mr. and Mrs. Edgehill
BBC (GB) 1985 dir. Gavin Miller
TV(GB)

Coward, N.
Mrs. Capper's Birthday
BBC (GB) 1985 dir. Mike Ockrent
TV(GB)

Coward, N.
Pretty Polly Barlow
Pretty Polly
RANK (GB) 1967 dir. Guy Green
US title: Matter of Innocence, A

Coward, N.
Private Lives
P
MGM (US) 1931 dir. Sidney Franklin

Coward, N.
Queen was in the Parlour, The
P
Tonight is Ours
PAR (US) 1933 dir. Stuart Walker

Coward, N.
Red Peppers; Fumed Oak; Ways &
Means
P
Meet Me Tonight
GFD (GB) 1952 dir. Anthony Pelissier

Coward, N.
Relative Values
P
OVERSEAS (GB) 1999 dir. Eric Styles

Coward, N.
Star Quality
BBC (GB) 1985 dir. Alan Dosser
TVSe(GB)

Coward, N.
Still Life
P
Brief Encounter
CIN (GB) 1945 dir. David Lean
ITC (US) 1974 dir. Alan Bridges
TV(US)

Coward, N.
This Happy Breed
P
TC (GB) 1944 dir. David Lean

Coward, N.
Tonight at 8.30
P
We Were Dancing
MGM (GB) 1942 dir. Robert Z. Leonard

Coward, N.
Tonight at 8.30
P
BBC (GB) 1991 dir. Joan Collins, Paul
Annett
TV(GB)

Coward, N.
What Mad Pursuit
BBC (GB) 1985 dir. Tony Smith
TV(GB)

Cowell, A.
Decade of Destruction
Burning Season, The
HBO (US) 1994 dir. John
Frankenheimer
TV(US)

Cowen, R.
Summertree
P
WAR (US) 1971 dir. Anthony Newley

Cowen, W. J.
They Gave Him a Gun
MGM (US) 1937 dir. W. S. Van Dyke

Cowl, J. and Murfin, J.
Smilin' Through
P
MGM (US) 1932 dir. Sidney Franklin
MGM (US) 1941 dir. Frank Borzage

Cowley, J.
Nest in a Falling Tree
Night Digger, The
MGM (GB) 1971 dir. Alistair Reid

Coxhead, E.
Friend in Need, The
Cry from the Streets, A
EROS (GB) 1958 dir. Lewis Gilbert

Coyle, D.
Hardball: A Season in the Projects
Hardball
PAR (US) 2001 dir. Brian Robbins

Cozzens, J. G.
By Love Possessed
UA (US) 1961 dir. John Sturges

Cozzens, J. G.
Last Adam, The
Dr. Bull
FOX (US) 1933 dir. John Ford

Craig, D.
Squeeze, The
WAR (GB) 1977 dir. Michael Apted

Craig, J.
If You Want to See Your Wife Again
Your Money or Your Wife
BRENTWOOD (US) 1972
dir. Allen Reisner
TV(US)

Craig, R.
Storm and Sorrow in the High High Pamirs
Storm and Sorrow
HEARST (US) 1990 dir. Richard Colla
TV(US)

Craik, D.
John Halifax, Gentleman
BBC (GB) 1974 dir. Tristan de Vere Cole
TVSe(GB)

Cram, M.
Tinfoil
Faithless
MGM (US) 1932 dir. Harry Beaumont

Cramer, R. W.
Babe: The Legend Comes to Life
Babe Ruth
LYTTLE (US) 1991 dir. Mark Tinker
TV(US)

Crane, C.
Summer Girl
LORIMAR (US) 1983
dir. Robert Michael Lewis
TV(US)

Crane, R.
Hero's Walk
Voices, The
BBC (GB) 1965 dir. Dennis Vance
TV(GB)

Crane, S.
Bride Comes to Yellow Sky, The
Face to Face
RKO (US) 1952
dir. John Brahm, Bretaigne Windust

Crane, S.
Red Badge of Courage, The
MGM (US) 1951 dir. John Huston
M. ARCH (US) 1981 dir. Don Taylor
TV(US)

Craven, F.
First Year, The
P
FOX (US) 1932 dir. William K. Howard

Craven, M.
I Heard the Owl Call My Name
TOM (US) 1973
dir. Daryl Duke
TV(US)

Cravens, G. and Marr, J. S.
Black Death, The
Quiet Killer
SABAN/SCHERICK (US) 1992 dir.
Sheldon Larry
TV(US)

Crawford, C.
Mommie Dearest
PAR (US) 1981 dir. Frank Perry

Crawford, E. M. and Hackett, W.
White Sister
P
MGM (US) 1933 dir. Victor Fleming

Crawford, J.
Birch Interval
GAMMA III (US) 1976
dir. Delbert Mann

Crawford, O.
Execution, The
COMWORLD (US) 1985
dir. Paul Wendkos
TV(US)

Creasey, J.
Gideon's Day
COL (GB) 1958 dir. John Ford
US title: Gideon of Scotland Yard

Creasey, J.
Hammer the Toff
BUTCHER (GB) 1952
dir. Maclean Rogers

Creasey, J.
Salute the Toff
BUTCHER (GB) 1952
dir. Maclean Rogers

Creighton, K.
Christmas Love, A
Holiday to Remember, A
JAFFE BRAUNSTEIN (US) 1995 dir. Jud
Taylor
TV(US)

Cresswell, H.
Moondial
BBC (GB) 1988 dir. Colin Cant
Ch, TVSe(GB)

Cresswell, H.
Secret World of Polly Flint
CENTRAL (GB) 1987 dir. David
Cobham
Ch, TVSe(GB)

Crichton, M.
Andromeda Strain, The
UN (US) 1971 dir. Robert Wise

Crichton, M.
Binary
Pursuit
ABC (US) 1972 dir. Michael Crichton
TV(US)

Crichton, M.
Congo
PAR (US) 1995 dir. Frank Marshall

Crichton, M.
Disclosure

WAR (US) 1994 dir. Barry Levinson

Crichton, M.
Eaters of the Dead

13th Warrior, The
TOUCHSTONE (US) 1999 dir. John
McTiernan

Crichton, M.
Great Train Robbery, The

First Great Train Robbery, The
UA (GB) 1978 dir. Michael Crichton

Crichton, M.
Jurassic Park

UN (US) 1993 dir. Steven Spielberg

Crichton, M.
Lost World, The

Lost World, The: Jurassic Park
UN (US) 1997 dir. Steven Spielberg

Crichton, M.
Rising Son

FOX (US) 1993 dir. Philip Kaufman

Crichton, M.
Sphere

PUNCH (US) 1997 dir. Barry Levinson

Crichton, R.
Camerons, The

BBC (GB) 1979 dir. Peter Moffatt
TVSe(GB)

Crichton, R.
Great Imposter, The

UI (US) 1961 dir. Robert Mulligan

Crichton, R.
Secret of Santa Vittoria, The

UA (US) 1969 dir. Stanley Kramer

Crisp, N. J.
Darkness Falls

P
LIONS GATE (GB) 1998 dir. Gerry
Lively

Crisp, Q.
Naked Civil Servant, The

THAMES (GB) 1975 dir. Jack Gold
TV(GB)

Cristofer, M.
Breaking Up

P
WAR (US) 1997 dir. Robert Greenwald

Cristofer, M.
Shadow Box, The

P
SHADOW BOX (US) 1980
dir. Paul Newman
TV(US)

Crockett, L. H.
Magnificent Devils

Proud and Profane, The
PAR (US) 1956 dir. George Seaton

Croft, M.
Spare the Rod

BL (GB) 1961 dir. Leslie Norman

Croft-Cooke, R.
Seven Thunders

RANK (GB) 1957 dir. Hugo Fregonese
US title: Beasts of Marseilles, The

Crompton, R.
Just William

AB (GB) 1939 dir. Graham Cutts

Cronin, A. J.
Beyond this Place

REN (GB) 1959 dir. Jack Cardiff

Cronin, A. J.
Citadel, The
MGM (GB) 1938 dir. King Vidor
BBC (GB) 1983 dir. Peter Jefferies
TVSe(GB)

Cronin, A. J.
Grand Canary
FOX (US) 1934 dir. Irving Cummings

Cronin, A. J.
Green Years, The
MGM (US) 1946 dir. Victor Saville

Cronin, A. J.
Hatter's Castle
PAR (GB) 1941 dir. Lance Comfort

Cronin, A. J.
Jupiter Laughs
P
Shining Victory
WAR (US) 1941 dir. Irving Rapper

Cronin, A. J.
Keys of the Kingdom, The
FOX (US) 1944 dir. John M. Stahl

Cronin, A. J.
Spanish Gardener, The
RANK (GB) 1956 dir. Philip Leacock

Cronin, A. J.
Stars Look Down, The
GN (GB) 1939 dir. Carol Reed

Cronin, A. J.
Stars Look Down, The
GRANADA (GB) 1974 dir. Roland Joffe,
Alan Grint, Howard Baker
TVSe(GB)

Cronin, A. J.
Vigil in the Night
RKO (US) 1940 dir. George Stevens

Cronin, M.
Paid in Full
Johnny on the Spot
FANCEY (GB) 1954
dir. Maclean Rogers

Cronley, J.
Funny Farm
WAR (US) 1988 dir. George Roy Hill

Cronley, J.
Good Vibes
Let It Ride
PAR (US) 1989 dir. Joe Pytka

Cronley, J.
Quick Change
WAR (US) 1990 dir. Howard Franklin,
Bill Murray

Cross, B.
Half a Sixpence
P
PAR (GB) 1967 dir. George Sidney
M

Crossley, R. and McDonald, A.
Annie's Coming Out
ENT (Aust) 1984 dir. Gil Brealey
US title: Test of Love, A

Crothers, R.
As Husbands Go
P
FOX (US) 1934 dir. Hamilton McFadden

Crothers, R.
Old Lady 31
P
Captain is a Lady, The
MGM (US) 1940 dir. Robert Sinclair

Crothers, R.
Splendor
P
GOLDWYN (US) 1935
dir. Elliott Nugent

Crothers, R.
Susan and God

P

MGM (US) 1940 dir. George Cukor
GB title: Gay Mrs. Trexel, The

Crothers, R.
When Ladies Meet

P

MGM (US) 1933 dir. Harry Beaumont
MGM (US) 1941 dir. Robert Z. Leonard

Crowe, C.
Fast Times at Ridgemont High

UN (US) 1982 dir. Amy Heckerling

Crowe, E.
So Hard to Forget

Hard To Forget
ALLIANCE (Can) 1998 dir. Victor Sarin
TV(Can)

Crowley, M.
Boys in the Band, The

P

WAR (US) 1970 dir. William Friedkin

Croy, H.
Family Honeymoon

UN (US) 1948 dir. Claude Binyon

Croy, H.
Sixteen Hands

I'm From Missouri
PAR (US) 1939 dir. Theodore Reed

Cullen, R.
Killer Department, The

Citizen X
HBO (US) 1995 dir. Chris Gerolmo
TV(US)

Cullinan, T.
Bedeviled, The

Beguiled, The
UN (US) 1971 dir. Don Siegel

Culotta, N.
They're a Weird Mob

RANK (GB) 1966 dir. Michael Powell

Cunningham, E. V.
Penelope

MGM (US) 1966 dir. Arthur Hiller

Cunningham, E. V.
Sally

Face of Fear, The
Q. MARTIN (US) 1971
dir. George McCowan
TV(US)

Cunningham, E. V.
Shirley

What's a Nice Girl Like You …?
UN TV (US) 1971 dir. Jerry Paris
TV(US)

Cunningham, E. V.
Sylvia

PAR (US) 1965 dir. Gordon Douglas

Cunningham, J. M.
Tin Star, The

High Noon
UA (US) 1952 dir. Fred Zinnemann

Cunningham, J.
Hunter's Blood

CONCORDE (US) 1987
dir. Robert C. Hughes

Curie, E.
Madame Curie

MGM (US) 1943 dir. Mervyn LeRoy

Curran, R.
Haunted, The

FOX TV (US) 1991 dir. Robert Mandel
TV(US)

Curtis, J.
Christmas in Calico

Secret of Giving
JAFFE/BRAUNSTEIN (US) 1999 dir.
Sam Pillsbury
TV(US)

Curtis, J.
They Drive by Night
WAR (GB) 1938 dir. Arthur Woods

Curtis, P.
Devil's Own, The

Witches, The
HAMMER (GB) 1966 dir. Cyril Frankel
US title: Devil's Own, The

Curtis, P.
You're Best Alone

Guilt is my Shadow
ABP (GB) 1950 dir. Roy Kellino

Curtiss, U.
Forbidden Garden, The

Whatever Happened to Aunt Alice?
PALOMAR (US) 1969 dir. Lee H. Katzin

Curtiss, U.
I Saw What You Did
UN (US) 1965 dir. William Castle
UN (US) 1988 dir. Fred Walton
TV(US)

Curwood, J. O.
Back to God's Country
UN (US) 1953 dir. Joseph Pevney

Curwood, J. O.
Baree, Son of Kazan

Northern Passage
GAU TV (Fr/Can) 1994 dir. Arnaud
Selignac
TV(Fr/Can)

Curwood, J. O.
God's Country and the Woman
WAR (US) 1936 dir. William Keighley

Curwood, J. O.
Grizzly King, The

Bear, The
TRISTAR (Fr) 1989
dir. Jean-Jacques Annaud

Curwood, J. O.
Kazan
COL (US) 1949 dir. Will Jason

Curwood, J. O.
Nomads of the North

Nikki, Wild Dog of the North
DISNEY (US) 1961 dir. Jack Couffer

Curwood, J. O.
River's End
WAR (US) 1930 dir. Michael Curtiz

Curwood, J. O.
Warrior Spirit
CINEVIDEO (Can) 1994 dir. René
Manzor
TV(Can)

Cusack, D.
Come in Spinner
BBC (GB) 1991 dir. Ray Marchand
TV(GB)

Cushman, C. F.
Young Widow, The
UA (US) 1946 dir. Edwin L. Marin

Cushman, D.
Ripper from Rawhide

Timberjack
REP (US) 1954 dir. Joe Kane

Cushman, D.
Stay Away, Joe
MGM (US) 1968 dir. Peter Tewkesbury

Cushman, K.
Ballad of Lucy Whipple, The

C. ANDERSON (US) 2001 dir. Jeremy
Paul Kagan
TV(US)

Cussler, C.
Raise the Titanic

ITC (US) 1980 dir. Jerry Jameson

Czeszko, B.
Generation

POLSKI (Pol) 1954 dir. Andrzej Wajda

D

Daeninckx, D.
Lumière Noire

Black Light
MH FILMS (GB) 1994 dir. Med Hondo

Daeninckx, D.
Playback

Heroines
NTV-PROFIT (Fr) 1997 dir. Gerard Krawczyk

Dahl, R.
Charlie and the Chocolate Factory

Willy Wonka and the Chocolate Factory
PAR (US) 1971 dir. Mel Stuart
Ch

Dahl, R.
Danny the Champion of the World

COL (GB) 1989 dir. Gavin Millar
Ch

Dahl, R.
James and the Giant Peach

DISNEY (US) 1996 dir. Henry Selick
Ch

Dahl, R.
Matilda

TRISTAR (US) 1996 dir. Danny DeVito
Ch

Dahl, R.
Witches, The

WAR (US) 1990 dir. Nicolas Roeg

Dalby, L.
Geisha

American Geisha
INTERSCOPE (US) 1986
dir. Lee Philips
TV(US)

Dale, C.
Spring of Love, A

Mr. Right
BBC (GB) 1983 dir. Peter Smith
TVSe(GB)

Daley, R.
Hands of a Stranger

TAFT (US) 1987 dir. Larry Elikann
TV(US)

Daley, R.
Prince of the City

ORION (US) 1981 dir. Sidney Lumet

Daley, R.
Tainted Evidence

Night Falls on Manhattan
PAR (US) 1997 dir. Sidney Lumet

Daley, R.
To Kill A Cop

COL TV (US) 1978 dir. Gary Nelson
TVSe(US)

Daley, R.
Year of the Dragon

MGM/UA (US) 1985
dir. Michael Cimino

D'Alpuget, B.
Turtle Beach

VILLAGE ROADSHOW (Aust) 1992
dir. Stephen Wallace

Dalton, M.
Another Woman

ALLIANCE (Can) 1994 dir. Alan
Smythe
TV(Can)

Daly, B.
Big and Hairy

NEW CITY (US) 1998 dir. Philip Spink
TV(US)

Dan, O.
Futai no Kisetsu

BONOBO (Jap) 2000 dir. Ryuichi Hiroki

Dan, U., Eisenberg, D. and Landau, E.
Meyer Lansky: Mogul of the Mob

Lansky
HBO (US) 1999 dir. John McNaughton
TV(US)

Dana, R. H.
Two Years Before the Mast

PAR (US) 1946 dir. John Farrow

Dane, C.
Bill of Divorcement, A

P
RKO (US) 1932 dir. George Cukor
RKO (US) 1940 dir. John Farrow
GB title: Never to Love

Dane, C. and Simpson, H.
Enter, Sir John

Murder
BI (GB) 1930 dir. Alfred Hitchcock

Daneman, M.
Chance to Sit Down, A

BBC (GB) 1981 dir. Paul Ciappessoni
TVSe(GB)

Dangerfield, Y.
Maison d'Esther, La

Saint-Cyr
STUDIO CANAL+ (Fr/Bel) 2000 dir.
Patricia Mazuy

Dangerfield, Y.
Petite Sirène, La

WA (Fr) 1984 dir. Roger Andrieux

Daniels, J.
Escanaba in da Moonlight

P
PURPLE ROSE (US) 2001 dir. Jeff
Daniels

Daninos, P.
Notebooks of Major Thompson, The

Diary of Major Thompson, The
GALA (Fr) 1955 dir. Preston Sturges
US title: French They are a Funny Race,
The

Dann, P.
Mermaids

ORION (US) 1990
dir. Richard Benjamin

Dante Alighieri
Divina Commedia, La

TV Dante, A: The Inferno Cantos
CHANNEL 4 (GB) 1990
dir. Tom Phillips, Peter Greenaway
TV(GB)

Dante, N., Kirkwood, J. and Hamlisch, M.
Chorus Line, A

P
COL (US) 1985
dir. Richard Attenborough
M

Dard, F.
Lady who Wades in the Sea, The

PRESIDENT (Fr) 1991
dir. Laurent Heynemann

Darlington, W.A.
Alf's Button

Alf's Button Afloat
GAINS (GB) 1938 dir. Marcel Varnel

Dart, I. R.
Beaches

TOUCHSTONE (US) 1988 dir. Garry Marshall

d'Ashelbe, R.
Pépé le Moko

PARIS (Fr) 1936 dir. Julian Duvivier

d'Ashelbe, R.
Pépé le Moko

Algiers
WANGER (US) 1938 dir. John Cromwell

Dataller, R.
Steel Saraband

Hard Steel
GFD (GB) 1942 dir. Norman Walker

Davenport, G.
Belvedere

Sitting Pretty
FOX (US) 1948 dir. Walter Lang

Davenport, M.
East Side, West Side

MGM (US) 1949 dir. Mervyn LeRoy

Davenport, M.
Valley of Decision, The

MGM (US) 1945 dir. Tay Garnett

Davidsen, L.
Russian Singer, The

NORDISK (Den) 1994 dir. Morten Arnfred

Davidson, A.
Out of the Shadows

KUSHNER-LOCKE/YTV (US/GB) 1988 dir. Willi Patterson
TV(GB/US)

Davidson, B.
Indict and Convict

UN TV (US) 1974 dir. Boris Sagal
TV(US)

Davidson, L.
Night Before Wenceslas, The

Hot Enough for June
RANK (GB) 1963 dir. Ralph Thomas

Davidson, M.
Thursday Woman, The

Wednesday Woman, The
CBP (US) 2000 dir. Christopher Leitch
TV(US)

Davidson, S.
Loose Change

UN TV (US) 1978 dir. Jules Irving
TVSe(US)

Davies, A.
B. Monkey

MIRAMAX (GB/It) 1998 dir. Michael Radford

Davies, H.
Here we go Round the Mulberry Bush

UA (GB) 1967 dir. Clive Donner

Davies, H. H.
Girl from Tenth Avenue, The
P

WAR (US) 1935 dir. Alfred E. Green
GB title: Men on her Mind

Davies, J.
Esther, Ruth and Jennifer

North Sea Hijack
CIC (GB) 1980 dir. Andrew V. McLaglen
US title: Ffolkes

Davies, J. E.
Mission to Moscow

WAR (US) 1943 dir. Michael Curtiz

Davies, L. P.
Alien, The
Groundstar Conspiracy, The
UN (US) 1972 dir. Lamont Johnson

Davies, L. P.
Project X
PAR (US) 1968 dir. William Castle

Davies, V.
Miracle on 34th Street
FOX (US) 1947 dir. George Seaton
GB title: Big Heart, The
TCF (US) 1973 dir. Fielder Cook
TV(US)

Davila, J. G.
De la Calle
P
TIEMPE (Mex) 2001 dir. Gerardo Tort

Davis, B.
Full Fathom Fire
CONCORDE (US) 1990
dir. Carl Franklin

Davis, B. C.
Mass Appeal
P
UN (US) 1984 dir. Glenn Jordan

Davis, C. B.
Anointed, The
Adventure
MGM (US) 1945 dir. Victor Fleming

Davis, D.
Jezebel
P
WAR (US) 1938 dir. William Wyler

Davis, D. S.
Where the Dark Streets Go
Broken Vows
HALMI (US) 1987 dir. Jud Taylor
TV(US)

Davis, E.
Me Two
All of Me
UN (US) 1984 dir. Carl Reiner

Davis, E.
Revenge
CARLINER (US) 1971 dir. Jud Taylor
TV(US)

Davis, M.
Christmas Romance, A
JAFFE/BRAUNSTEIN (US) 1994 dir.
Sheldon Larry
TV(US)

Davis, O.
Mr. and Mrs. North
P
MGM (US) 1941 dir. Robert B. Sinclair

Davis, R. P.
Glass Cockpit, The
Final Descent
COL TRISTAR (US) 1997 dir. Mike Robe
TV(US)

Davis, R. P.
Pilot, The
SUMMIT (Can) 1981
dir. Cliff Robertson

Davis, S.
Love Field
P
Ruby
POLYGRAM (US) 1992 dir. John
MacKenzie

Davis, T.
Vision Quest
WAR (US) 1985 dir. Harold Becker

Day, C.
Life with Father
WAR (US) 1947 dir. Michael Curtiz

Day, L.
Youngest Profession, The
MGM (US) 1943 dir. Edward Buzzell

Dayub, M.
Amateur, El
ALEPH (Arg) 2000 dir. Juan Bautista
Stagnaro

de Assis, M.
Posthumous Memories of Bras Cubas
Memorias Postumas
SUPERFILMES (Bra/Port) 2001 dir.
Andre Klotzel

de Balzac, H.
Belle Noiseuse, La
FRANCE 3 (Fr) 1991 dir. Jacques
Rivette

de Balzac, H.
Colonel Chabert, Le
CCFC (Fr) 1943 dir. Réne Le Hénaff
STUDIO CANAL+ (Fr) 1994 dir. Yves
Angelo

de Balzac, H.
Cousin Bette
BBC (GB) 1971 dir. Gareth Davies
TVSe(GB)
FOX (GB/US) 1998 dir. Des McAnuff

de Balzac, H.
Passion in the Desert
FINE LINE (US) 1997 dir. Lavinia
Currier

De Beauvoir, S.
All Men are Mortal
WAR (GB/Neth) 1995 dir. Até de Jong

De Beauvoir, S.
Blood of Others, The
HBO PREM (Can/Fr) 1984
dir. Claude Chabrol
TV(Can/Fr)

de Bernières, L.
Corelli's Mandolin
Captain Corelli's Mandolin
WORKING TITLE (GB/Fr) 2001 dir.
John Madden

de Bri, L.
Moulin Rouge
P
FOX (US) 1934 dir. Sidney Lanfield

de Brunhoff, J.
Babar: King of the Elephants
NELVANA (Can/Fr) 1999 dir. Raymond
Jafelice
A, Ch

de Croisset, F.
Il était une fois
P
Woman's Face, A
MGM (US) 1941 dir. George Cukor

de Erauso, C.
Memorias
Monja Alferez, La
GOYA (Sp) 1992 dir. Javier Aguirre

De Felitta, F.
Audrey Rose
UA (US) 1977 dir. Robert Wise

De Felitta, F.
Entity, The
FOX (US) 1982 dir. Sidney J. Furie

De Frece, Lady
Recollections of Vesta Tilly
After the Ball
BL (GB) 1957 dir. Compton Bennett

de Gouriadec, L.
Morte en fuite, La
Break the News
GFD (GB) 1938 dir. René Clair

de Hartog, J.
Four-Poster, The
P
COL (GB) 1952 dir. Irving Reis

de Hartog, J.
Inspector, The
FOX (GB) 1962 dir. Philip Dunne
US title: Lisa

de Hartog, J.
Little Ark, The
FOX (US) 1971 dir. James B. Clark

de Hartog, J.
Spiral Road, The
UI (US) 1962 dir. Robert Mulligan

de Hartog, J.
Stella
Key, The
COL (GB) 1958 dir. Carol Reed

de Hennezel, M. and Bottaro, C.
Morte Intime, La
C'est La Vie
FRANCE 3 (Fr) 2001 dir. Jean-Pierre
Ameris

de Jolyot Crebillon, C.-P.
Nuit et le Moment, La
P
Night and the Moment, The
CECCHI (It/Fr) 1994 dir. Anna Maria
Tato

de la Fayette, Mme.
Princesse de Cleves, La
Fidelité, La
STUDIO CANAL+ (Fr) 2000 dir.
Andrzej Zulawski

de la Fouchardière, G.
Chienne, La
P
Scarlet Street
UN (US) 1945 dir. Fritz Lang

de la Fouchardière, G.
Chienne, La
BRAU (Fr) 1931 dir. Jean Renoir

de la Roche, M.
Jalna
RKO (US) 1935 dir. John Cromwell

de Laclos, P.
Liaisons Dangéreuses, Les
Dangerous Liaisons
WAR (US) 1988 dir. Stephen Frears

de Laclos, P.
Liaisons Dangéreuses, Les
Valmont
ORION (GB) 1989 dir. Milos Forman

de Laclos, P.
Liaisons Dangereuses, Les
MARCEAU (Fr) 1959 dir. Roger Vadim

de Lampedusa, G.
Leopard, The
FOX (US/It) 1963 dir. Luchino Visconti

de Ligneris, F.
Psyche 63
Psyche 59
BL (GB) 1964 dir. Alexander Singer

de Mandiargues, A. P.
Motocyclette, La
Girl on a Motorcycle
BL (GB/Fr) 1968 dir. Jack Cardiff
US title: Naked Under Leather

de Maupassant, G.
Bel Ami
Private Affairs of Bel Ami, The
UA (US) 1947 dir. Albert Lewin

de Maupassant, G.
Bel Ami
BBC (GB) 1971 dir. John Davies
TVSe(GB)

De Qunicey, T.
Spanish Military Nun, The
Monja Alferez, La
GOYA (Sp) 1992 dir. Javier Aguirre

de Rojas, R.
Celestina, La
LOLAFILMS (Sp) 1996 dir. Gerardo Vera

De Sade, Marquis
Justine
Cruel Passion
TARGET (GB) 1977 dir. Chris Boger

de Soto, J. M. V.
Infierno y la Brisa, El
Hail Hazana
STILLMAN (Sp) 1978
dir. Jose Maria Guttierez

de Villeneuve, Mme.
Beauty and the Beast
LOPERT (Fr) 1947 dir. Jean Cocteau
PALM (US) 1976 dir. Fielder Cook
TV(US)
CANNON (US) 1987
dir. Eugene Marner
DISNEY (US) 1991
dir. Gary Trousdale, Kirk Wise
A, Ch, M

de Vilmorin, L.
Madame De
FRANCO-LF (Fr/It) 1953
dir. Max Ophuls
US title: The Earrings of Madame De

De Voto, B.
Across the Wide Missouri
MGM (US) 1951 dir. William Wellman

De Vries, P.
Let Me Count the Ways
How Do I Love Thee?
ABC (US) 1970 dir. Michael Gordon

De Vries, P.
Reuben, Reuben
FOX (US) 1983 dir. Robert Ellis Miller

De Vries, P.
Tunnel of Love, The
MGM (US) 1958 dir. Gene Kelly

De Vries, P.
Witch's Milk
Pete 'n Tillie
UN (US) 1972 dir. Martin Ritt

Deal, B.
Dunbar's Cove
Wild River
FOX (US) 1960 dir. Elia Kazan

Deal, B.
Bluegrass
LAN (US) 1988 dir. Simon Wincer
TVSe(US)

Deal, B. H.
Walls Came Tumbling Down, The
Friendships, Secrets and Lies
WAR TV (US) 1979
dir. Ann Zane Shanks, Marlena Laird
TV(US)

Dean, B. and Munro, G.
Murder Gang
P
Sensation
BIP (GB) 1936
dir. Brian Desmond Hurst

Dean, J.
Blind Ambition
TIME-LIFE (US) 1979
dir. George Schaefer
TVSe(US)

Dean, M.
Mo: A Woman's View of Watergate
Blind Ambition
TIME-LIFE (US) 1979
dir. George Schaefer
TVSe(US)

Dearsley, A. P.
Fly Away Peter
P
GFD (GB) 1948 dir. Charles Saunders

Deaver, J.
Bone Collector, The
COL (US) 1999 dir. Phillip Noyce

Deaver, J.
Maiden's Grave, A
Dead Silence
HBO (US) 1996 dir. Daniel Petrie, Jr.
TV(US)

DeCapite, R.
Lost King, A
Harry and Son
ORION (US) 1984 dir. Paul Newman

Decca, D.
Roman de Lulu, Le
P
LAMBERT (Fr) 2001 dir. Pierre-Olivier
Scotto

Decoin, D.
Femme de Chambre du Titanic, La
Chambermaid on the Titanic, The
FRANCE 2 (Fr) 1997 dir. J. J. Bigas Luna

Deeping, W.
Sorrell and Son
UA (GB) 1933 dir. Jack Raymond
YTV (GB) 1984 dir. Derek Bennett
TVSe(GB)

Defoe, D.
Fortunes and Misfortunes of the Famous Moll Flanders, The
Amorous Adventures of Moll Flanders, The
PAR (GB) 1965 dir. Terence Young

Defoe, D.
Fortunes and Misfortunes of the Famous Moll Flanders, The
Fortunes and Misfortunes of Moll Flanders, The
GRANADA (GB) 1996 dir. David Attwood
TVSe(GB)

Defoe, D.
Fortunes and Misfortunes of the Famous Moll Flanders, The
Moll Flanders
MGM (US) 1996 dir. Pen Densham
BBC (GB) 1975 dir. Donald McWhinnie
TVSe(GB)

Defoe, D.
Robinson Crusoe
Adventures of Robinson Crusoe, The
UA (Mex/US) 1954 dir. Luis Bunuel

Defoe, D.
Robinson Crusoe
BBC (GB) 1974 dir. James MacTaggart
TV(GB)
MIRAMAX (UK/Gre) 1996 dir. Rod Hardy, George Miller

Defoe, D.
Robinson Crusoe
Crusoe
ISLAND (US) 1989 dir. Caleb Deschanel

Deford, F.
Alex: The Life of a Child
MANDY (US) 1986
dir. Robert Markowitz
TV (US)

Deford, F.
Everybody's All-American
WAR (US) 1988 dir. Taylor Hackford

Deforges, R.
Cahier Volé, La
PROVIDENCE (Fr) 1992 dir. Christine Lipinska

Deighton, L.
Berlin Game; Mexico Set, London Match
Game, Set and Match
GRANADA (GB) 1987 dir. Ken Grieve, Patrick Lau
TVSe(GB)

Deighton, L.
Berlin Memorandum, The
Funeral in Berlin
PAR (GB) 1966 dir. Guy Hamilton

Deighton, L.
Billion Dollar Brain
UA (GB) 1967 dir. Ken Russell

Deighton, L.
Ipcress File, The
RANK (GB) 1965 dir. Sidney J. Furie

Deighton, L.
Only When I Larf
PAR (GB) 1968 dir. Basil Dearden

Deighton, L.
Spy Story
GALA (GB) 1976 dir. Lindsay Shonteff

Dekobra, M.
Hell is Sold Out
EROS (GB) 1951 dir. Michael Anderson

Dekobra, M.
Sphinx has Spoken, The
Friends and Lovers
RKO (US) 1931 dir. Victor Schertzinger

del Moral, I.
Mirada del Hombre, La
P
Bwana
AURUM (Sp) 1996 dir. Imanol Uribe

Del Rivo, L.
Furnished Room, The
West Eleven
WAR (GB) 1963 dir. Michael Winner

Del Valle-Inclan, R.
Tirano Banderas
ION (Sp) 1993 dir. Jose Luis Garcia Sanchez

Delacorta
Diva
GALAXIE (Fr) 1981
dir. Jean-Jacques Beineix

Delaney, S.
Taste of Honey, A
P
BRYANSTON (GB) 1961
dir. Tony Richardson

Delany, S. L., Delany, A. E. and Hearth, A. H.
Having Our Say
Having Our Say: The Delany Sisters' First 100 Years
COL TRISTAR (US) 1999 dir. Lynne Littman
TV(US)

Delderfield, R. F.
All Over the Town
P
RANK (GB) 1948 dir. Derek Twist

Delderfield, R. F.
Bull Boys, The
P
Carry on Sergeant
AAM (GB) 1958 dir. Gerald Thomas

Delderfield, R. F.
Come Home Charlie and Face Them
LWT (GB) 1990 dir. Roger Bamford
TVSe(GB)

Delderfield, R. F.
Glad Tidings
P
EROS (GB) 1953 dir. Wolf Rilla

Delderfield, R. F.
Horseman Riding By, A
BBC (GB) 1978 dir. Paul Ciappessoni,
Philip Dudley, Alan Grint
TVSe(GB)

Delderfield, R. F.
Orchard Walls, The
P
Now and Forever
ABP (GB) 1955 dir. Mario Zampi

Delderfield, R. F.
Stop at a Winner
On the Fiddle
AA (GB) 1961 dir. Cyril Frankel
US title: Operation Snafu

Delderfield, R. F.
There was a Fair Maid Dwelling;
The Unjust Skies
Diana
BBC (GB) 1983 dir. David Tucker
TVSe(GB)

Delderfield, R. F.
To Serve Them All My Days
BBC (GB) 1980 dir. Ronald Wilson
TVSe(GB)

Delderfield, R. F.
Where There's A Will
P
EROS (GB) 1955 dir. Vernon Sewell

Delderfield, R. F.
Worm's Eye View
P
ABP (GB) 1951 dir. Jack Raymond

Delgado, F. G.
Naked Eye, The
LOLAFILMS (Sp) 1998 dir. Vicente
Aranda

Delibes, M.
Holy Innocents, The
GANESH (Sp) 1985 dir. Mario Camus
Spanish title: Los Santos Inocentes

Delinsky, B.
Woman's Place, A
Custody of the Heart
HEARST (US) 2000 dir. David Jones
TV(US)

Dell, F.
Bachelor Father
P
Casanova Brown
INTERNATIONAL (US) 1944 dir. Sam
Wood

Dell, J.
Payment Deferred
P
MGM (US) 1932 dir. Lothar Mendel

Dell. G.
Earth Abideth, The
Seasons of Love
SULLIVAN ENT (US) 1999 dir. Daniel
Petrie
TVSe(US)

Delman, D.
Conspiracy of Terror
LORIMAR (US) 1975
dir. John Llewellyn Moxey
TV(US)

Delmar, V.
About Mrs. Leslie
PAR (US) 1954 dir. Daniel Mann

DeMille, N.
General's Daughter, The
PAR (US/Ger) 1999 dir. Simon West

Deming, R.
Careful Man, The
Drop Dead Darling
SEVEN ARTS (GB) 1966
dir. Ken Hughes
US title: Arrivederci Baby

Dempsey, J. and Dempsey, B. P.
Dempsey
FRIES (US) 1983 dir. Gus Trikonis
TV(US)

Denham, R. and Percy, E.
Ladies in Retirement
P
Mad Room, The
COL (US) 1969 dir. Bernard Girard

Deniau, J.-F.
Self-Made Hero, A
LUMIERE (Fr) 1996 dir. Jacques
Audiard

Denker, H.
Outrage!
COL TV (US) 1986 dir. Walter Grauman
TV(US)

Denker, H. and Berkey, R.
Time Limit
P
UA (US) 1967 dir. Karl Malden

Dennis, C.
Next-to-Last Train Ride, The
Finders Keepers
RANK (US) 1984 dir. Richard Lester

Dennis, P.
Auntie Mame
WAR (US) 1958 dir. Morton da Costa

Dennis, P.
Auntie Mame
Mame
WAR (US) 1974 dir. Gene Saks
M

Denton, Jr., J. A. and Brandt, E.
When Hell was in Session
AUBREY-HAMNER (US) 1979 dir. Paul
Krasny
TV(US)

Denuzière, M.
Louisiane; Fausse-Rivière
Louisiana
CINEMAX (US) 1984
dir. Philippe de Broca
TVSe(US)

Denver, J. and Tobier, A.
Take Me Home
Take Me Home: The John Denver Story
GRANADA (US) 2000 dir. Jerry London
TV(US)

Dershowitz, A.
Advocate's Devil, The
COL TRISTAR (US) 1997 dir. Jeff
Bleckner
TV(US)

Dershowitz, A.
Reversal of Fortune
WAR (US) 1990 dir. Barbet Schroeder

des Cars, G.
Brute, The
Green Scarf, The
BL (GB) 1954
dir. George More O'Ferrall

des Cars, G.
Brute, La
CAPRICORNE (Fr) 1987 dir. Claude Guillemot

Desai, A.
In Custody
MI (GB/Ind) 1994 dir. Ismail Merchant

Despentes, V.
Baise-moi
STUDIO CANAL+ (Fr) 2000 dir. Coralie Trinh Thi, Virginie Despentes

Despentes, V.
Jolies Choses, Les
M6 (Fr) 2001 dir. Gilles Paquet-Brenner

Deval, J.
Her Cardboard Lover
P
MGM (US) 1942 dir. George Cukor

Deval, J.
Tovarich
P
WAR (US) 1937 dir. Anatole Litvak

deVere Stacpoole, H. D.
Truth About Spring, The
UI (GB) 1964 dir. Richard Thorpe

DeVries, T.
Girl with the Red Hair, The
UA (Neth) 1983 dir. Ben Verbong

Dewar, I.
Women Talking Dirty
ROCKET (US) 1999 dir. Corky Giedroyc

DeWinter, L.
Hoffman's Hunger
KASSENDER (Neth) 1993 dir. Leon DeWinter

Dewlen, A.
Night of the Tiger, The
Ride Beyond Vengeance
COL (US) 1966 dir. Bernard McEveety

Dewlen, A.
Twilight of Honor
MGM (US) 1963 dir. Boris Sagal
GB title: Charge is Murder, The

Dexter, C.
Dead of Jericho, The
CENTRAL (GB) 1989
dir. Edward Bennett
TV(GB)

Dexter, C.
Last Seen Wearing
CENTRAL (GB) 1989
dir. Edward Bennett
TV(GB)

Dexter, C.
Service of all the Dead
CENTRAL (GB) 1989
dir. Edward Bennett
TV(GB)

Dexter, C.
Silent World of Nicholas Quinn
CENTRAL (GB) 1989
dir. Edward Bennett

Dexter, P.
Deadwood
Wild Bill
UA (US) 1995 dir. Walter Hill

Dexter, P.
Paris Trout
VIACOM (US) 1991
dir. Stephen Gyllenhaal
TV(US)

Di Donata, P.
Christ in Concrete

Give Us This Day
GFD (GB) 1949 dir. Edward Dmytryk
US title: Salt to the Devil

di Meana, M. R.
My First Forty Years

TRISTAR/COL (It) 1989
dir. Carlo Vanzina

Di Pego, G.
Keeper of the City

VIACOM (US) 1992 dir. Bobby Roth
TV(US)

Diamond, P.
Chicken Chronicles, The

AVCO (US) 1977 dir. Francis Simon

Dibdin-Pitt, G.
Sweeney Todd, the Demon Barber of Fleet Street

P
KING (GB) 1936 dir. George King

Dibdin-Pitt, G.
Sweeny Todd, the Demon Barber of Fleet Street

P
Sweeney Todd
THAMES (GB) 1982 dir. Reginald Collin
TV(GB)

Dibner, M.
Deep Six, The

WAR (US) 1958 dir. Rudolph Maté

Dick, P. K.
Confessions of a Crap Artist

Barjo
CENTRE EURO (Fr) 1992 dir. Jerome Boivin

Dick, P. K.
Do Androids Dream of Electric Sheep?

Blade Runner
WAR (US) 1982 dir. Ridley Scott

Dick, P. K.
We can Remember it for you Wholesale

Total Recall
CAROLCO (US) 1990
dir. Paul Verhoeven

Dick, R. A.
Ghost and Mrs Muir, The

FOX (US) 1947
dir. Joseph L. Mankiewicz

Dickens, C.
Bleak House

BBC (GB) 1985 dir. Ross Devenish
TVSe(GB)

Dickens, C.
Christmas Carol, A

MGM (US) 1938 dir. Edwin L. Marin
ENT PART (US)
1984 dir. Clive Donner
TV(US)
HALLMARK (US) 1999 dir. David Jones
TV(US)

Dickens, C.
Christmas Carol, A

American Christmas Carol, An
SM-HEM (US) 1979 dir. Eric Till
TV(US)

Dickens, C.
Christmas Carol, A

Christmas Carol: The Movie
CHANNEL 4 FILMS (GB/Ger) 2001 dir. Jimmy T. Murakami

Dickens, C.
Christmas Carol, A

Ebbie
CRESCENT (US) 1995 dir. George
Kaczender
TV(US)

Dickens, C.
Christmas Carol, A

Scrooge
PAR (GB) 1935 dir. Henry Edwards
REN (GB) 1951
dir. Brian Desmond Hurst
FOX (GB) 1970 dir. Ronald Neame
M

Dickens, C.
Christmas Carol, A

Scrooged
PAR (US) 1988 dir. Richard Donner

Dickens, C.
David Copperfield

MGM (US) 1935 dir. George Cukor
OMNIBUS (GB) 1970
dir. Delbert Mann
TV(GB)
BBC (GB) 1974 dir. Joan Crift
TVSe(GB)
BBC (GB) 1986 dir. Barry Letts
TVSe(GB)
BBC (GB) 2000 dir. Simon Curtis
TVSe(GB)
HALLMARK (US) 2000 dir. Peter
Medak
TVSe(US)

Dickens, C.
Dombey and Son

BBC (GB) 1983 dir. Rodney Bennett
TVSe(GB)

Dickens, C.
Dombey and Son

Rich Man's Folly
PAR (US) 1931 dir. John Cromwell

Dickens, C.
Great Expectations

UN (US) 1934 dir. Stuart Walker
RANK/CIN (GB) 1946
dir. David Lean
SCOTIA-BARBER/ITC (GB) 1974
dir. Joseph Hardy
TV(GB/US)
BBC (GB) 1981 dir. Julian Amyes
TVSe(GB)
PRIMETIME/HTV (GB/US) 1991
dir. Kevin Connor
TVSe(GB/US)
FOX (US) 1998 dir. Alfonso Cuaron

Dickens, C.
Hard Times

GRANADA (GB) 1977 dir. John Irvin
TVSe(GB)
BBC (GB) 1994 dir. Peter Barnes
TV(GB)

Dickens, C.
Little Dorrit

CANNON (GB) 1988
dir. Christine Edzard

Dickens, C.
Martin Chuzzlewit

BBC (GB) 1994 dir. Pedr James
TVSe(GB)

Dickens, C.
Mystery of Edwin Drood, The

UN (US) 1935 dir. Stuart Walker
FIRST STANDARD (GB) 1993 dir.
Timothy Forder

Dickens, C.
Nicholas Nickleby

EAL (GB) 1947 dir. Alberto Cavalcanti
BBC (GB) 1977 dir. Christopher Barry
TVSe(GB)

Dickens, C.
Nicholas Nickleby

Life and Adventures of Nicholas Nickleby, The
PRIMETIME (GB) 1984
dir. Jim Goddard
TVSe(GB)
COMPANY TV (GB) 2001 dir. Stephen Whittaker
TV(GB)

Dickens, C.
Old Curiosity Shop, The

BIP (GB) 1934 dir. Thomas Bentley
BBC (GB) 1979 dir. Julian Amyes
TVSe(GB)
RHI (US) 1995 dir. Kevin Connor
TVSe(US)

Dickens, C.
Old Curiosity Shop, The

Mister Quilp
EMI (GB) 1975 dir. Elliot Scott

Dickens, C.
Oliver Twist

CINEGUILD (GB) 1948 dir. David Lean
TRIDENT (US/GB) 1982
dir. Clive Donner
TV(US/GB)
BBC (GB) 1985 dir. Gareth Davies
TVSe(GB)
DISNEY (US) 1997 dir. Tony Bill
TV(US)

Dickens, C.
Oliver Twist

Oliver!
COL (GB) 1968 dir. Carol Reed
M

Dickens, C.
Our Mutual Friend

BBC (GB) 1976 dir. Peter Hammond
TVSe(GB)
BBC (GB) 1998 dir. Julian Farino
TVSe(GB)

Dickens, C.
Pickwick Papers, The

REN (GB) 1952 dir. Noel Langley
BBC (GB) 1985 dir. Brian Lighthill
TVSe(GB)

Dickens, C.
Tale of Two Cities, A

MGM (US) 1935 dir. Jack Conway
RANK (GB) 1958 dir. Ralph Thomas
ROSEMONT (US/GB) 1980
dir. Jim Goddard
TV(GB/US)
BBC (GB) 1980 dir. Michael E. Briant
TVSe(GB)
GRANADA (GB) 1989 dir. Philippe Monnier
TVSe(GB)

Dickens, M.
One Pair of Feet

Lamp Still Burns, The
TC (GB) 1943 dir. Maurice Elvey

Dickenson, M.
Thumbs Up: The Life and Courageous Comeback of White House Press Secretary Jim Brady

Without Warning: The James Brady Story
HBO (US) 1991
dir. Michael Toshiyuki Uno
TV(US)

Dickey, J.
Deliverance

WAR (US) 1973 dir. John Boorman

Dickey, P.
Ghost Breakers, The

P
PAR (US) 1940 dir. George Marshall

Dickinson, P.
Changes, The

BBC (GB) 1975 dir. John Prowse
Ch, TVSe(GB)

Dickinson, P.
Gift, The
BBC (GB) 1990 dir. Marc Evans, Red
Saunders
TVSe(GB)

Didion, J.
Play it as it Lays
UN (US) 1972 dir. Frank Perry

Diehl, M.
Men
SHONDEROSA (US) 1997 dir. Zoe
Clarke-Williams

Diehl, W.
Sharky's Machine
WAR (US) 1981 dir. Burt Reynolds

Dietl, B. and Gross, K.
One Tough Cop: The Bo Dietl Story
One Tough Cop
PATRIOT (US) 1998 dir. Bruno Barreto

Dietrich, W. and Thomas, B.
Howard: The Amazing Mr. Hughes
Amazing Howard Hughes, The
EMI TV (US) 1977
dir. William A. Graham
TVSe(US)

Dietz, L.
Year of the Big Cat, The
Return of the Big Cat
DISNEY (US) 1974 dir. Tom Leetch

Dighton, J.
Happiest Days of Your Life, The
P
BL (GB) 1950 dir. Frank Launder

Dighton, J.
Who Goes There?
P
BL (GB) 1952 dir. Anthony Kimmins
US title: Passionate Sentry, The

Dijan, P.
372 Le Matin
Betty Blue
GAU (Fr) 1986 dir. Jean-Jacques Beineix

Dillman, J.
Unholy Matrimony
TAFT (US) 1988 dir. Jerrold Freedman
TV(US)

Dillon, B.
Mom by Magic, A
Mom for Christmas, A
DISNEY (US) 1990 dir. George Miller
TV(US)

Dineli, M.
Man, The
P
Beware My Lovely
RKO (US) 1952 dir. Harry Horner

Dinesen, I.
Out of Africa
UN (US) 1985 dir. Sydney Pollack

Dingwall, J.
House in the Timberwoods, The
Winds of Jarrah, The
FILMCORP (Aust) 1983
dir. Mark Egerton

Dinneen, J. F.
They Stole $2.5 Million and Got Away
with It
Six Bridges to Cross
UN (US) 1955 dir. Joseph Pevney

Dinner, W. and Morum, W.
Late Edwina Black, The
P
GFD (GB) 1951 dir. Maurice Elvey

Disch, T. M.
Brave Little Toaster, The
HYP (US) 1989 dir. Jerry Rees
A, Ch

Disch, T. M.
Brave Little Toaster Goes to Mars, The
HYP (US) 1999 dir. Robert C. Ramirez
A, Ch, TV(US)

Disney, D. M.
Do Not Fold, Spindle or Mutilate
LEE RICH (US) 1971 dir. Ted Post
TV(US)

Disney, D. M.
Night of Clear Choice
Yesterday's Child
PAR TV (US) 1977 dir. Corey Allen, Bob Rosenbaum
TV(US)

Disney, D. M.
Only Couples Need Apply
Betrayal
METRO (US) 1974 dir. Gordon Hessler
TV(US)

Divine, D.
Boy on a Dolphin, The
FOX (US) 1957 dir. Jean Negulesco

Dixon, R.
Confessions of a Night Nurse
Rosie Dixon–Night Nurse
COL (GB) 1978 dir. Justin Cartwright

Dobbs, M.
Final Cut, The
BBC (GB) 1995 dir. Mike Vardy
TVSe(GB)

Dobbs, M.
House of Cards
BBC (GB) 1991 dir. Paul Seed
TVSe(GB)

Dobbs, M.
To Play the King
BBC (GB) 1993 dir. Paul Seed
TVSe(GB)

Dobie, L. and Sloman, R.
Tinker, The
P
Wild and the Willing, The
RANK (GB) 1962 dir. Ralph Thomas
US title: Young and Willing

Doblin, A.
Berlin Alexanderplatz
TELECUL/CH 4 (Fr/GB) 1985 dir. Rainer Werner Fassbinder
TVSe(Fr/GB)

Doctorow, E. L.
Billy Bathgate
TOUCHSTONE (US) 1991 dir. Robert Benton

Doctorow, E. L.
Book of Daniel, The
Daniel
PAR (GB) 1983 dir. Sidney Lumet

Doctorow, E. L.
Ragtime
PAR (US) 1981 dir. Milos Forman

Doctorow, E. L.
Welcome to Hard Times
MGM (US) 1967 dir. Burt Kennedy
GB title: Killer on a Horse

Dodge, D.
Plunder of the Sun
WAR (US) 1953 dir. John Farrow

Dodge, D.
To Catch a Thief
PAR (US) 1955 dir. Alfred Hitchcock

Dodge, M. M.
Hans Brinker, or the Silver Skates
MILBERG (US) 1957 dir. Sidney Lumet
TV(US)

Dodson, J.
Faithful Travelers: A Father, A Daughter, A Fly-Fishing Journey of the Heart
Dodson's Journey
CBS TV (US) 2001 dir. Gregg Champion
TV(US)

Dodson, K.
Away All Boats
UI (US) 1956 dir. Joseph Pevney

Doerr, H.
Stones for Ibarra
TITUS (US) 1988 dir. Jack Gold
TV(US)

Doherty, B.
White Peak Farm
BBC (GB) 1988 dir. Andrew Morgan
Ch, TVSe(GB)

Donald, S.
Life of Stuff, The
P
PRAIRIE (GB) 1997 dir. Simon Donald

Donaldson, F.
Edward VIII
Edward & Mrs. Simpson
THAMES (GB) 1978 dir. Waris Hussein
TVSe(GB)

Donnelly, D.
Poppy
P
PAR (US) 1936
dir. A. Edward Sutherland

Donofrio, B.
Riding in Cars With Boys
COL (US) 2001 dir. Penny Marshall

Donohue, C. and Hall, S.
Deadly Relations: A True Story of Murder in a Suburban Family
Deadly Relations
WIL COURT (US) 1993 dir. Bill Condon
TV(US)

Donoso, J.
Hell Without Limits
AZTECA (Mex) 1978
dir. Arturo Ripstein

Donovan, P.
Paint Cans
SALTER ST (Can) 1994 dir. Paul Donovan

Donovan, R. J.
PT109—John F. Kennedy in World War II
PT 109
WAR (US) 1963 dir. Leslie H. Martinson

Dooling, R.
Critical Care
VILLAGE ROADSHOW (Aust/US) 1997 dir. Sidney Lumet

Dorfman, A.
Death and the Maiden
P
FINE LINE (US/GB) 1994 dir. Roman Polanski

Dorner, M.
Nightmare
Don't Touch My Daughter
PATCHETT-KAUFMAN (US) 1991 dir. John Pasquin
TV(US)

Dorris, M.
Broken Cord, The
UN TV (US) 1992 dir. Ken Olin
TV(US)

D'Orta, M.
Io Speriamo Che Me Lo Cavo

Ciao, Professore
CECCHI (It) 1992 dir. Lina Wertmuller

Doss, H.
Family Nobody Wanted, The

UN TV (US) 1975 dir. Ralph Senensky
TV(US)

Dossick, P.
Transplant

TIME-LIFE (US) 1979
dir. William A. Graham
TV(US)

Dostoevsky, F.
Brothers Karamazov, The

MGM (US) 1957 dir. Richard Brooks
MOSFILM (USSR) 1968 dir. Ivan Pyriev

Dostoevsky, F. M.
Crime and Punishment

COL (US) 1935 dir. Josef von Sternberg
GAU (Fr) 1935 dir. Pierre Chenal
AA (US) 1958 dir. Denis Sanders
BBC (GB) 1979 dir. Michael Darlow
TVSe(GB)
HALLMARK (US) 1998 dir. Joseph
Sargent
TV(US)

Dostoevsky, F.
Crime and Punishment

Crime + Punishment in Suburbia
KILLER (US) 2000 dir. Rob Schmidt

Dostoevsky, F.
Eternal Husband, The

Homme au Chapeau Rond, L'
ALCINA (Fr) 1946 dir. Pierre Billon

Dostoevsky, F.
Gambler, The

LENFILM (USSR) 1982 dir. Alexei
Batalov
BBC (GB) 1968 dir. Michael Ferguson
TVSe(GB)

Dostoevsky, F.
Great Gambler

Great Sinner, The
MGM (US) 1949 dir. Robert Siodmak

Dostoevsky, F.
Idiot, The

Nastasja
HIT (Pol) 1994 dir. Andrzej Wajda

Dostoevsky, F.
Notes From Underground

RENEGADE (US) 1995 dir. Gary
Walkow

Dostoevsky, F.
Possessed, The

BBC (GB) 1969 dir. Naomi Capon
TVSe(GB)

Dougherty, R.
Commissioner, The

Madigan
UI (US) 1968 dir. Don Siegel

Douglas, C.
Houseman's Tale, A

BBC (GB) 1987 dir. Alastair Reid
TVSe(GB)

Douglas, F.
It's Never too Late

P
ABP (GB) 1956 dir. Michael McCarthy

Douglas, L. C.
Big Fisherman, The

CENT (US) 1959 dir. Frank Borzage

Douglas, L. C.
Disputed Passage

PAR (US) 1939 dir. Frank Borzage

Douglas, L. C.
Green Light, The

WAR (US) 1937 dir. Frank Borzage

Douglas, L. C.
Magnificent Obsession
UN (US) 1935 dir. John M. Stahl
UI (US) 1954 dir. Douglas Sirk

Douglas, L. C.
Robe, The
FOX (US) 1953 dir. Henry Koster

Douglas, L. C.
White Banners
WAR (US) 1938 dir. Edmund Goulding

Douglas, M.
Dealing: or The Berkeley-to-Boston-Forty-Brick-Lost-Bag-Blues
WAR (US) 1972 dir. Paul Williams

Downes, D.
Easter Dinner, The
Pigeon That Took Rome, The
PAR (US) 1962 dir. Melville Shavelson

Downs, R. C. S.
Peoples
Billy: Portrait of a Street Kid
CARLINER (US) 1977
dir. Steven Gethers
TV(US)

Doyle, M.
Signpost to Murder
P
MGM (US) 1964 dir. George Englund

Doyle, R.
Commitments, The
Fox (GB/US) 1991 dir. Alan Parker

Doyle, R.
Snapper, The
BBC (GB) 1993 dir. Stephen Frears
TV(GB)

Doyle, R.
Van, The
BBC (GB) 1996 dir. Stephen Frears

Doyle, Sir A. C.
Adventure of the Five Orange Pips
House of Fear
UN (US) 1945 dir. Roy William Neill

Doyle, Sir A. C.
Adventures of Sherlock Holmes, The
FOX (US) 1939 dir. Alfred Werker
GB title: Sherlock Holmes
GRANADA (GB) 1984 dir. Paul Annett
TVSe(GB)

Doyle, Sir A. C.
Exploits of Brigadier Gerard, The
Adventures of Gerard, The
UA (GB) 1970 dir. Jerzy Skolimowski

Doyle, Sir A. C.
Hound of the Baskervilles, The
ID (GB) 1932 dir. V. G. Gundrey
FOX (US) 1939 dir. Sidney Lawfield
UA (GB) 1959 dir. Terence Fisher
UN (US) 1972 dir. Barry Crane
TV(US)
HEMDALE (GB) 1977
dir. Paul Morrissey
BBC (GB) 1982 dir. Peter Duguid
TVSe(GB)
EMBASSY (GB) 1983
dir. Douglas Hickox
MUSE ENT (Can) 2000 dir. Rodney Gibbons
TV(Can)

Doyle, Sir A. C.
His Last Bow
Sherlock Holmes and the Voice of Terror
UN (US) 1942 dir. John Rawlins

Doyle, Sir A. C.
Lot 27a
Tales from the Darkside: the Movie
PAR (US) 1990 dir. John Harrison

Doyle, Sir A. C.
Lost World, The
FOX (US) 1960 dir. Irwin Allen

Doyle, Sir A. C.
Man with the Twisted Lip, The
GN (GB) 1951 dir. Richard M. Grey

Doyle, Sir A. C.
Return of Sherlock Holmes
GRANADA (GB) 1988 dir. Michael Cox
TV(GB)

Doyle, Sir A. C.
Sign of Four, The
WW (GB) 1932 dir. Rowland V. Lee
EMBASSY (GB) 1983
dir. Desmond Davis
GRANADA (GB) 1988 dir. Michael Cox
TV(GB)
MUSE ENT (US) 2001 dir. Rodney
Gibbons
TV(US)

Doyle, Sir A. C.
Six Napoleons, The
Pearl of Death, The
UN (US) 1944 dir. Roy William Neill

Doyle, Sir A. C.
Study in Scarlet, The
WW (US) 1933 dir. Edward L. Marin

Doyle, Sir A. C.
Valley of Fear, The
Triumph of Sherlock Holmes, The
TWICKENHAM (GB) 1935
dir. Leslie Hiscott

Drabble, M.
Millstone, The
Touch of Love, A
BL (GB) 1969 dir. Waris Hussein
US title: Thank You All Very Much

Drabble, M.
Waterfall, The
BBC (GB) 1980 dir. Peter Duffell
TVSe(GB)

Drake, D.
Night Larry Kramer Kissed Me, The
P
MONTROSE (US) 2000 dir. Tim
Kirkman

Dratler, J.
Pitfall
UA (US) 1948 dir. André de Toth

Drawbell, J. W.
Love and Forget
Love Story
GFD (GB) 1944 dir. Leslie Arliss
US title: Lady Surrenders, A

Dreiser, T.
American Tragedy, An
PAR (US) 1931 dir. Josef von Sternberg

Dreiser, T.
American Tragedy, An
Place in the Sun, A
PAR (US) 1951 dir. George Stevens

Dreiser, T.
Jennie Gerhardt
PAR (US) 1933 dir. Marion Gering

Dreiser, T.
My Brother Paul
My Gal Sal
FOX (US) 1942 dir. Irving Cummings

Dreiser, T.
Prince Who Was a Thief, The
UN (US) 1951 dir. Rudolph Maté

Dreiser, T.
Sister Carrie
Carrie
PAR (US) 1952 dir. William Wyler

Drexler, R.
To Smithereens

Below the Belt
ATLANTIC (US) 1982
dir. Robert Fowler

Drilling, E.
River Red

P
CASTLE HILL (US) 1997 dir. Eric
Drilling

Driscoll, P.
Wilby Conspiracy, The

UA (GB) 1975 dir. Ralph Nelson

Drought, J.
Gypsy Moths, The

MGM (US) 1969
dir. John Frankenheimer

Drucker, M. and Block, G.
Rescuers: Portraits of Moral Courage
in the Holocaust

Rescuers: Stories of Courage
SHOWTIME (US) 1997 dir. Peter
Bogdanovich, Tim Hunter,
Lynne Littman, Tony Bill
TVSe(US)

Drummond, J. D.
But for These Men

Heroes of the Telemark
RANK (GB) 1965 dir Anthony Mann

Druon, M.
Film of Memory, The

Matter of Time, A
AIP (US/It) 1976 dir. Vincente Minnelli

Drury, A.
Advise and Consent

COL (US) 1962 dir. Otto Preminger

Du Maurier, D.
Birds, The

UN (US) 1963 dir. Alfred Hitchcock

Du Maurier, D.
Breakthrough, The

Lifeforce Experiment, The
FILMLINE (UK/Can) 1994 dir. Piers
Haggard
TV(UK/Can)

Du Maurier, D.
Don't Look Now

BL (GB) 1973 dir. Nicolas Roeg

Du Maurier, D.
Frenchman's Creek

PAR (US) 1944 dir. Mitchell Leisen

Du Maurier, D.
Hungry Hill

TC (GB) 1947 dir. Brian Desmond Hurst

Du Maurier, D.
Jamaica Inn

PAR (GB) 1939 dir. Alfred Hitchcock
HTV (GB) 1983
dir. Lawrence Gordon Clark
TV(GB)

Du Maurier, D.
My Cousin Rachel

FOX (US) 1952 dir. Henry Koster
BBC (GB) 1983 dir. Brian Farnham
TVSe(GB)

Du Maurier, D.
Rebecca

UA (US) 1940 dir. Alfred Hitchcock
BBC (GB) 1979 dir. Simon Langton
TVSe(GB)
CARLTON TV (GB) 1997 dir. Jim
O'Brien
TVSe(GB)

Du Maurier, D.
Scapegoat, The

MGM (GB) 1959 dir. Robert Hamer

Du Maurier, D.
Years Between, The
P
FOX (GB) 1946 dir. Compton Bennett

Du Maurier, G.
Peter Ibbetson
PAR (US) 1935 dir. Henry Hathaway

Du Maurier, G.
Trilby
Svengali
WAR (US) 1931 dir. Archie Mayo
REN (GB) 1954 dir. William Alwyn
HALMI (US) 1983 dir. Anthony Harvey
TV(US)

Duberman, M.
Stonewall
BBC (GB) 1995 dir. Nigel Finch

Dubois, R. D.
Being at Home With Claude
P
NFB (Can) 1992 dir. Jean Beaudin

Dubyns, S.
Two Deaths of Senora Puccini, The
Two Deaths
BRIT SCREEN (GB) 1995 dir. Nicolas
Roeg

Duck, C. and Thomas, M.
Whose Baby?
7 NETWORK-CRAWFORDS (Aust)
1990 dir. Ian Barry
TVSe(Aust)

Duder, T.
Alex
NZ FILM (Aust/NZ) 1992 dir. Megan
Simpson Huberman

Duerrenmatt, F.
Justiz
BR (Ger) 1993 dir. Hans W.
Geissendorfer

Duerrenmatt, F.
Versprechen, Das
Pledge, The
WAR (US) 2001 dir. Sean Penn

Duff, A.
Once Were Warriors
FINE LINE (NZ) 1994 dir. Lee Tamahori

Duff, A.
What Becomes of the Broken Hearted?
POLYGRAM (NZ) 1999 dir. Ian Mune

Duff, J.
Homefront
P
War at Home, The
TOUCHSTONE (US) 1996 dir. Emilio
Estevez

Duffy, C. T. and Jennings, D.
San Quentin Story, The
Duffy of San Quentin
WAR (US) 1954 dir. Walter Doniger

Duffy, M.
Gor Saga, The
First Born
BBC (GB) 1988 dir. Philip Saville
TVSe(GB)

Dugain, M.
Chambre des Officiers, La
FRANCE 2 (Fr) 2001 dir. François
Dupeyron

Duke, P. and Thomas, J.
Too Rich
Too Rich: The Secret Life of Doris Duke
VZ/SERTNER (US) 1999 dir. John
Erman
TVSe(US)

Duke, P. and Turan, K.
My Name is Anna: The Autobiography of Patty Duke

Call me Anna
FINNEGAN (US) 1990
dir. Gilbert Cates
TV(US)

Dulay, C.
Chanel Solitaire

GARDENIA (Fr/GB) 1981
dir. George Kaczender

Dumas, A.
Black Tulip, The

CINERAMA (Fr) 1963
dir. Christian-Jaque
BBC (GB) 1970 dir. Derek Martinus
TVSe(GB)

Dumas, A.
Companions of Jehu, The

Fighting Guardsman, The
COL (US) 1945 dir. Henry Levin

Dumas, A.
Count of Monte Cristo, The

UA (US) 1934 dir. Rowland V. Lee
ROSEMONT (GB) 1975
dir. David Greene
TV(GB)
(Fr/GB) 1987 dir. Denys de la Patellière
TV(Fr/GB)
CITE (Fr) 1998 dir. Josee Dayan
TVSe(Fr)
TOUCHSTONE (US) 2002 dir. Kevin Reynolds

Dumas, A.
Deux Frères

Corsican Brothers, The
UA (US) 1942 dir. Gregory Ratoff
ROSEMONT (US) 1985 dir. Ian Sharp
TV(US)

Dumas, A.
Man in the Iron Mask, The

UA (US) 1939 dir. James Whale
ITC (US/GB) 1976 dir. Mike Newell
TV(GB/US)
UA (US/GB) 1998 dir. Randall Wallace
INVISIBLE (US) 1998 dir. William Richert

Dumas, A.
Man in the Iron Mask, The

Fifth Musketeer, The
SASCH WIEN (Austria) 1978
dir. Ken Annakin

Dumas, A.
Memoirs of a Physician

Black Magic
UA (US) 1949 dir. Gregory Ratoff

Dumas, A.
Queen Margot

STUDIO CANAL+ (Fr) 1994 dir. Patrice Chereau

Dumas, A.
Three Musketeers, The

RKO (US) 1935 dir. Rowland V. Lee
FOX (US) 1939 dir. Allan Dwan
GB title: Singing Musketeer, The
MGM (US) 1948 dir. George Sidney
FOX-RANK (Pan) 1973
dir. Richard Lester
DISNEY (US/GB) 1993 dir. Stephen Herek

Dumas, A.
Three Musketeers, The

Four Musketeers, The
FOX-RANK (Pan/Sp) 1974
dir. Richard Lester

Dumas, A.
Three Musketeers, The

Musketeer, The
MIRAMAX (US/Ger) 2001 dir. Peter Hyams

Dumas, A. fils
Dame aux Camélias, La
Camille
MGM (US) 1936 dir. George Cukor
ROSEMONT (US/GB) 1984
dir. Desmond Davis
TV(GB/US)

Dumas fils, A.
Lady of the Camellias, The
BBC (GB) 1976 dir. Robert Knights
TVSe(GB)

Dunbar, A.
Rita, Sue and Bob Too
P
ORION (GB) 1987 dir. Alan Clarke

Duncan, A.
It's a Vet's Life
In the Doghouse
RANK (GB) 1961 dir. Darcy Conyers

Duncan, I.
My Life
Isadora
UI (GB) 1969 dir. Karel Reisz
US title: Loves of Isadora, The

Duncan, L.
Don't Look Behind You
FOX FAMILY (US) 1999 dir. David
Winning
TV(US)

Duncan, L.
Gallows Hill
I've Been Waiting For You
NBC (US) 1998 dir. Christopher Leitch
TV(US)

Duncan, L.
I Know What You Did Last Summer
COL (US) 1997 dir. Jim Gillespie

Duncan, L.
Killing Mr. Griffin
NBC STUDIOS (US) 1997 dir. Jack
Bender
TV(US)

Duncan, L.
Summer of Fear
INTERPLAN (US) 1978 dir. Wes Craven

Duncan, L.
Summer of Fear
Stranger in our House
INTERPLAN (US) 1978 dir. Wes Craven
TV(US)

Dunn, N.
Poor Cow
WAR (GB) 1967 dir. Ken Loach

Dunn, N.
Steaming
P
NEW WORLD (GB) 1985
dir. Joseph Losey

Dunn, N.
Up the Junction
PAR (GB) 1967 dir. Peter Collinson

Dunne, D.
Inconvenient Woman, An
ABC (US) 1991 dir. Larry Elikann
TVSe(US)

Dunne, D.
People Like Us
ITC (US) 1990 dir. Billy Hale
TVSe(US)

Dunne, D.
Season in Purgatory, A
D. BROWN (US) 1996 dir. David
Greene
TVSe(US)

Dunne, D.
Two Mrs. Grenvilles, The
LORIMAR (US) 1989 dir. John Erman
TVSe(US)

Dunne, J. G.
True Confessions
UA (US) 1981 dir. Ulu Grosbard

Dunne, L.
Goodbye to the Hill
Paddy
FOX (Ireland) 1969 dir. Daniel Haller

Dunning, P. and Abbott, G.
Broadway
P
UN (US) 1942 dir. W. A. Seiter

DuPre, H. and DuPre, P.
Genius in the Family, A
Hilary and Jackie
BRIT SCREEN (GB) 1998 dir. Anand
Tucker

Duprez, F., Stephens, H. and Linton, H. B.
My Wife's Family
P
GB (GB) 1931 dir. Monty Banks
ABPC (GB) 1941 dir. Walter C. Mycroft
ABP (GB) 1956 dir. Gilbert Gunn

Duran, M.
Liberté Provisoire
P
He Stayed for Breakfast
COL (US) 1940 dir. Alexander Hall

Durang, C.
Beyond Therapy
P
NEW WORLD (US) 1987
dir. Robert Altman

Durang, C.
Sister Mary Ignatius Explains It All For You
P
Sister Mary Explains It All
TENNANT/STAMBLER (US) 2001 dir.
Marshall Brickman
TV(US)

Durant, T.
Marble Forest
Macabre
ABP (US) 1958 dir. William Castle

Duras, M.
Barrage contre le Pacifique, Un
This Angry Age
DELAUR (It) 1957 dir. René Clément

Duras, M.
Lover, The
FILMS A2 (Fr/GB) 1992 dir. Jean-
Jacques Annaud

Duras, M.
Moderato Cantabile
R. J. LEVY (Fr/It) 1960 dir. Peter Brook

Duras, M.
Sailor from Gibraltar, The
WOODFALL (GB) 1967
dir. Tony Richardson

Duras, M.
10.30 p.m. on a Summer Night
10.30 p.m. Summer
UA (US/Sp) 1966 dir. Jules Dassin

Durham, M.
Man Who Loved Cat Dancing, The
MGM (US) 1973 dir. Richard Sarafian

Duroy, L.
Pray For Us
FRANCE 3 (Fr) 1994 dir. Jean-Pierre
Vergne

Durrell, L.
Alexandria Quartet, The

Justine
FOX (US) 1969 dir. George Cukor

Durrenmatt, F.
Judge and his Hangman, The
P
End of the Game
TCF (US/Ger) 1976
dir. Maximilian Schell

Durrenmatt, F.
Visit, The
P
FOX (US) 1964 dir. Bernhard Wicki

D'Usseau, A. and Gow, J.
Deep are the Roots
P
Tomorrow the World
UA (US) 1944 dir. Leslie Fenton

Dutton, G.
Queen Emma of the South Seas

Emma: Queen of the South Seas
FRIES (US) 1988 dir. Bryan Forbes
TVSe(US)

Dwyer, K. R.
Shattered

Passengers, The
COL-WAR (Fr) 1977 dir. Serge LeRoy

Dyer, B. V.
Port Afrique
COL (GB) 1956 dir. Rudolph Maté

Dyer, C.
Rattle of a Simple Man
P
WAR (GB) 1964 dir. Muriel Box

Dyer, C.
Staircase
P
FOX (US/Fr) 1969 dir. Stanley Donen

Dyer, G.
Fog Over Frisco
WAR (US) 1934 dir. William Dieterle

E

Eareckson, J.
Joni
WORLD WIDE (US) 1980
dir. James F. Collier

Earl, L.
Yangtse Incident
BL (GB) 1957 dir. Michael Anderson
US title: Battle Hell

Early, J.
Donato and Daughter
MULTIMEDIA (US) 1993 dir. Rod
Holcomb
TV(US)

Early, P.
Family of Spies, A: Inside the John
Walker Spy Ring
Family of Spies
KING PHOENIX (US) 1990 dir. Stephen
Gyllenhaal
TVSe(US)

Eastlake, W.
Castle Keep
COL (US) 1969 dir. Sydney Pollack

Easton Ellis, B.
American Psycho
MUSE (US) 2000 dir. Mary Harron

Eastwood, J.
Mark of the Leopard
Beyond Mombasa
COL (GB) 1955 dir. George Marshall

Eberhart, M. G.
From this Dark Stairway
Murder of Dr. Harrigan
WAR (US) 1936 dir. Frank McDonald

Eberhart, M. G.
While the Patient Slept
IN (US) 1935 dir. Ray Enright

Eberhart, M. G.
White Cockatoo
WAR (US) 1935 dir. Alan Crosland

Echard, M.
Dark Fantastic
Lightning Strikes Twice
WAR (US) 1951 dir. King Vidor

Echasseriaux, B.
Sundays and Cybèle
TERRA (Fr) 1962 dir. Serge Bourgignon

Eco, U.
Name of the Rose, The
FOX (US/Ger/It/Fr) 1987
dir. Jean-Jacques Annaud

Ede, H. S.
Savage Messiah
MGM-EMI (GB) 1972 dir. Ken Russell

Edens, O.
Heart & Hand
House Divided, A
UN (US) 1932 dir. William Wyler

Edgerton, C.
Walking Across Egypt
MITCHUM (US) 2001 dir. Arthur Allan
Seidelman
TV(US)

Edmonds, A.
Hot Toddy
*White Hot: The Mysterious Murder of
Thelma Todd*
NEWFELD-KEATING (US) 1991
dir. Paul Wendkos
TV(US)

Edmonds, W. D.
Chad Hanna
FOX (US) 1940 dir. Henry King

Edmonds, W. D.
Drums Along the Mohawk
FOX (US) 1939 dir. John Ford

Edmonds, W. D.
Rome Haul
Farmer Takes a Wife, The
FOX (US) 1935 dir. Victor Fleming
FOX (US) 1953 dir. Henry Levin
M

Edson, M.
Wit
P
HBO FILMS (US) 2001 dir. Mike
Nichols
TV(US)

Edwards, A.
Haunted Summer
CANNON (US) 1988 dir. Ivan Passer

Eells, G.
Hedda and Louella
Malice in Wonderland
ITC (US) 1985 dir. Gus Trikonis
TV(US)

Eftimiades, M.
Amy Fisher: My Story
SPECTACOR/JAFFE (US) 1992 dir:
Bradford May
TVSe(US)

Egan, J.
Invisible Circus, The
FINELINE (US) 2001 dir. Adam Brooks

Egan, M.
Dominant Sex, The
P
AB (GB) 1937 dir. Herbert Brenon

Egbers, T.
Zwart Meteoor, De
SIGMA (Neth) 2001 dir. Guido Pieters

Egleton, C.
Seven Days to a Killing
Black Windmill, The
PAR (GB) 1974 dir. Don Siegel

Ehle, J.
Journey of August King, The
MIRAMAX (US) 1995 dir. John Duigan

Ehle, J.
Winter People
COL (US) 1989 dir. Ted Kotcheff

Ehrlich, J.
Gun and the Pulpit, The
CINETV (US) 1974 dir. Daniel Petrie
TV(US)

Ehrlich, M.
First Train to Babylon
Naked Edge, The
UA (GB) 1961 dir. Michael Anderson

Ehrlich, M.
Reincarnation of Peter Proud, The
AVCO (US) 1975 dir. J. Lee Thompson

Ehrlichman, J.
Company, The
Washington: Behind Closed Doors
PAR (US) 1977 dir. Gary Nelson
TVSe(US)

Einstein, C.
Blackjack Hijack, The
Nowhere to Run
MTM (US) 1978 dir. Richard Lang
TV(US)

Einstein, C.
Bloody Spur The
While the City Sleeps
RKO (US) 1956 dir. Fritz Lang

Eisner, J. P.
Survivor, The
War and Love
CANNON (US/Israel) 1985
dir. Moshe Mizrahi

Elder, L. and Streshinsky, S.
And I Alone Survived
OSL (US) 1978 dir. William Graham
TV(US)

Elder, R. and Elder, S.
Crash
FRIES (US) 1978 dir. Barry Shear
TV(US)

Elfman, B.
Girls of Huntington House, The
LORIMAR (US) 1973 dir. Alf Kjellin
TV(US)

Eliot, G.
Adam Bede
BBC (GB) 1991 dir. Giles Foster
TV(GB)

Eliot, G.
Daniel Deronda
BBC (GB) 1970 dir. Joan Croft
TVSe(GB)

Eliot, G.
Middlemarch
BBC (GB) 1994 dir. Anthony Page
TVSe(GB)

Eliot, G.
Mill on the Floss, The
STANDARD (GB) 1937 dir. Tim Whelan
BBC (GB) 1978 dir. Ronald Wilson
TVSe(GB)

Eliot, G.
Silas Marner
BBC (GB) 1985 dir. Giles Foster
TV(GB)

Eliot, T. S.
Murder in the Cathedral
P
FILM TRADERS (GB) 1951
dir. George Hoellering

Elkin, S.
Bailbondsman, The
Alex and the Gypsy
TCF (US) 1976 dir. John Korty

Elkind, M.
Internecine Project, The
MACLEAN (GB) 1974 dir. Ken Hughes

Elli, F.
Riot
PAR (US) 1968 dir. Buzz Kulik

Ellin, S.
Bind, The
Sunburn
HEMDALE (GB/US) 1979
dir. Richard C. Sarafian

Ellin, S.
Dreadful Summit
Big Night, The
UA (US) 1951 dir. Joseph Losey

Ellin, S.
House of Cards
UN (US) 1968 dir. John Guillerman

Ellin, S.
Stronghold
Prayer in the Dark, A
WIL COURT (US) 1997 dir. Jerry
Ciccoritti
TV(US)

Elliot, J.
Buttercup Chain, The
COL (GB) 1969 dir. Robert Ellis Miller

Elliott, J.
Secret Places
RANK (GB) 1983 dir. Zelda Barron

Elliott, S.
Signs of Life
Careful, He Might Hear You
SYME (Aust) 1983 dir. Carl Schultz

Ellis, A. T.
Clothes in the Wardrobe, The
BBC (GB) 1992 dir. Waris Hussein
TV(GB)

Ellis, B. E.
Less than Zero
FOX (US) 1987 dir. Marek Kanievska

Ellis, E.
White Collars
P
Rich Man, Poor Girl
MGM (US) 1938 dir. Reinbold Schunzel

Ellis, K. M.
Trial of Vivienne Ware, The
FOX (US) 1932 dir. William K. Howard

Ellison, J. W.
Double Standard
FRIES (US) 1988 dir. Louis Rudolph
TV (US)

Ellroy, J.
Blood on the Moon
Cop
ATLANTIC (US) 1988
dir. James B. Harris

Ellroy, J.
Brown's Requiem
J&T (US) 1998 dir. Jason Freeland

Ellroy, J.
L.A. Confidential
WAR (US) 1997 dir. Curtis Hanson

Ellsberg, E.
Pigboats
Hell Below
MGM (US) 1933 dir. Jack Conway

Elton, B.
Inconceivable
Maybe Baby
BBC (GB) 2000 dir. Ben Elton

Elton, B.
Stark
BBC (GB) 1993 dir. Nadia Tass
TVSe(GB)

Ely, D.
Seconds
PAR (US) 1966 dir. John Frankenheimer

Emerson, C.
Treacherous Beauties
ALLIANCE (Can) 1994 dir. Charles
Jarrott
TV(Can)

Emery, L.
After All
DIRECTOR'S CIRCLE (US) 1999 dir.
Helaine Head
TV(US)

Emery, R.
Gilded Rooster, The
Savage Wilderness
COL. (US) 1956 dir. Anthony Mann
GB title: The Last Frontier

Emmons, D. G.
Sacajawea of the Shoshones
Far Horizons, The
PAR (US) 1955 dir. Rudolph Maté

Ende, M.
Momo
CECCHI (It) 2001 dir. Enzo D'Alo

Ende, M.
Neverending Story, The
Neverending Story II, The: The Next Chapter
WAR (Ger) 1989 dir. George Miller
Ch

Ende, M.
Neverending Story, The
WAR (Ger/GB) 1984
dir. Wolfgang Petersen
Ch

Endo, S.
Woman I Abandoned, The
Aisuru
NIKKATSU (Jap) 1997 dir. Kei Kumai

Endore, G.
Methinks the Lady
Whirlpool
FOX (US) 1949 dir. Otto Preminger

Endore, G.
Werewolf of Paris, The
Curse of the Werewolf, The
RANK (GB) 1961 dir. Terence Fisher

England, B.
Conduct Unbecoming
P
BL (GB) 1975 dir. Michael Anderson

England, B.
Figures in a Landscape
CINECREST (GB) 1970
dir. Joseph Losey

Englehard, J.
Indecent Proposal
PAR (US) 1993 dir. Adrian Lyne

Engstrandt, S. D.
Beyond the Forest
WAR (US) 1949 dir. King Vidor

Ephron, D.
Hanging Up
COL (US) 2000 dir. Diane Keaton

Ephron, N.
Heartburn
PAR (US) 1986 dir. Mike Nichols

Ephron, P. and Ephron, H.
Take Her, She's Mine
P
MGM (US) 1963 dir. Henry Koster

Ephron, P. and Ephron, H.
Three is a Family
P
UA (US) 1944 dir. Edward Ludwig

Epstein, E. Z. and Morella, J.
Mia: The Life of Mia Farrow
Love and Betrayal: The Mia Farrow Story
FOX CIRCLE (US) 1995 dir. Karen Arthur
TVSe(US)

Epstein, S.
Eye of the Beholder
Comeback, The
CBS ENT (US) 1989
dir. Jerrold Freedman
TV(US)

Erdman, P.
Silver Bears
EMI (GB) 1978 dir. Ivan Passer

Ericson, W.
Mirage
UI (US) 1965 dir. Edward Dmytryk

Erskine, C.
Sailor Takes a Wife, The
P
MGM (US) 1945 dir. Richard Whorf

Erskine, J.
Sincerity
Lady Surrenders, A
UN (US) 1930 dir. John Stahl

Erskine, L. Y.
Renfrew's Long Trail
Danger Ahead
MON (GB) 1940 dir. Ralph Staub

Ertz, S.
In the Cool of the Day
MGM (US) 1962 dir. Robert Stevens

Ervine, St. J. G.
Boyd's Shop
P
RANK (GB) 1960 dir. Henry Cass

Esquivel, L.
Like Water For Chocolate
CINEVISTA (Mex) 1992 dir. Alfonso Arau

Esstman, B.
Night Ride Home
HALLMARK (US) 1999 dir. Glenn Jordan
TV(US)

Esstman, B.
Other Anna, The
Secrets
RHI (US) 1995 dir. Jud Taylor
TV(US)

Etons, U.
Angel Dusted
NRW (US) 1981 dir. Dick Lowry
TV(US)

Eugenides, J.
Virgin Suicides, The
AM ZOETROPE (US) 1999 dir. Sofia Coppola

Euripides
Iphighenia
P
UA (Gre) 1978
dir. Michael Cacoyannis

Euripides
Medea
P
JANUS (It/Fr/Ger) 1970
dir. Pier Paolo Pasolini

Euripides
Trojan Women, The
P
CINERAMA (US) 1971
dir. Michael Cacoyannis

Evans, E.
Branded
PAR (US) 1950 dir. Rudolph Maté

Evans, E.
Wishing Well
P
Happiness of Three Women, The
ADELPHI (GB) 1954 dir. Maurice Elvey

Evans, M.
Hi-Lo Country, The
POLYGRAM (GB/US) 1998 dir. Stephen Frears

Evans, M.
Rounders, The
MGM (US) 1965 dir. Burt Kennedy

Evans, N.
Horse Whisperer, The
TOUCHSTONE (US) 1998 dir. Robert Redford

Evans, P.
Ari: The Life and Time of Aristotle Onassis
Richest Man in the World, The: The Story of Aristotle Onassis
KON-SAN (US) 1988 dir. Waris Hussein
TVSe(US)

Evans, R. M.
Childhood's Thief
Secret Path, The
GREENWALD (US) 1999 dir. Bruce Pittman
TV(US)

Evans, R. P.
Christmas Box, The
BPG (US) 1995 dir. Marcus Cole
TV(US)

Evans, R. P.
Timepiece
SIGNBOARD HILL (US) dir. Marcus Cole
TV(US)

Everett, P.
Negatives
CRISPIN (GB) 1968 dir. Peter Medak

Everett, P.
Walk Me to the Distance
Follow Your Heart
NBC (US) 1990 dir. Noel Nosseck
TV(US)

Evers, M. and Peters, B.
For Us The Living
Ghosts of Mississippi
COL (US) 1996 dir. Rob Reiner

F

Fabian, R.
Fabian of the Yard
EROS (GB) 1954
dir. Edward Thommen, Anthony
Beauchamp

Fairchild, W.
Do Not Disturb
P
FOX (US) 1965 dir. Ralph Levy

Fairchild, W.
Sound of Murder, The
P
Last Shot you Hear, The
FOX (GB) 1970 dir. Gordon Hessler

Fairstein, L.
Final Jeopardy
SANITSKY (US) 2001 dir. Nick Gomez
TV(US)

Fallada, H.
Little Man, What Now?
UN (US) 1934 dir. Frank Borzage

Fallet, R.
Grande Ceinture, La
Porte des Lilas
FILMSONOR (Fr/It) 1957
dir. René Clair

Fantazzini, H.
Outlaw!
HERA (It) 1999 dir. Enzo Monteleone

Fante, J.
Full of Life
COL (US) 1956 dir. Richard Quine

Farago, L.
Last Days of Patton, The
ENT PAR (US) 1986 dir. Delbert Mann
TV(US)

Farago, L.
Patton: Ordeal & Triumph
Patton
FOX (US) 1970 dir. Franklin Schaffner
GB title: Patton: Lust for Glory

Farjeon, J. J.
Number Seventeen
P
BIP (GB) 1932 dir. Alfred Hitchcock

Farley, W.
Black Stallion, The
UA (US) 1979 dir. Carroll Ballard
Ch

Farley, W.
Black Stallion Returns, The
MGM (US) 1983 dir. Robert Dalva
Ch

Farmer, F.
Will There Really Be A Morning?
ORION (US) 1983 dir. Fielder Cook
TV(US)

Farnol, J.
Amateur Gentlemen, The
UA (GB) 1936 dir. Thornton Freeland

Farrar, R.
Watch That Man

Man Who Knew Too Little, The
WAR (US) 1997 dir. Jon Amiel

Farre, R.
Seal Morning
ITV (GB) 1986 dir. Jim Goddard
TV(GB)

Farrell, B.
Pat & Roald

Patricia Neal Story, The
SCHILLER (US) 1981
dir. Antony Harvey, Anthony Page
TV(US)

Farrell, H.
Baby Jane

What Ever Happened to Baby Jane?
WAR (US) 1962 dir. Robert Aldrich
SPECTACOR (US) 1991
dir. David Greene
TV(US)

Farrell, H.
How Awful About Allan

SPELLING (US) 1970
dir. Curtis Harrington
TV(US)

Farrell, J. G.
Troubles

LWT (GB) 1988
dir. Christopher Morahan
TVSe(GB)

Farrell, J. T.
Young Manhood of Studs Lonigan, The

Studs Lonigan
UA (US) 1960 dir. Irving Lerner
LORIMAR (US) 1979
dir. James Goldstone
TVSe(US)

Farrell, M. J. and Perry, J.
Spring Meeting

P
ABPC (GB) 1940 dir. Walter C. Mycroft

Farrell, M. J. and Perry, J.
Treasure Hunt

P
BL (GB) 1952 dir. John Paddy Carstairs

Farrelly, P.
Outside Providence

MIRAMAX (US) 1999 dir. Michael
Corrente

Farrere, C.
Battle, The

GAU (Fr) 1934 dir. Nicolas Farkas

Farrimond, J.
Hills of Heaven, The

BBC (GB) 1978 dir. Eric Davidson
TVSe(GB)

Farrington, F.
Little Game, A

UN TV (US) 1971 dir. Paul Wendkos
TV(US)

Farrington, F.
Strangers in 7a, The

PALOMAR (US) 1972 dir. Paul
Wendkos
TV(US)

Farris, J.
Fury, The

FOX (US) 1978 dir. Brian De Palma

Farris, J.
Harrison High

Because They're Young
COL (US) 1960 dir. Paul Wendkos

Farris, J.
Ramey
Greatest Gift, The
UN TV (US) 1974 dir. Boris Sagal
TV(US)

Farris, J.
When Michael Calls
FOX (US) 1972 dir. Philip Lcacock
TV(US)

Fassbinder, R. W.
Tropfen auf Heisse Steine
P
Water Drops on Burning Rocks
STUDIO IMAGES 6 (Fr) 2000 dir.
François Ozon

Fassbinder, R. W.
Shadow of Angels
P
ALB/ARTCO (Ger) 1983
dir. Daniel Schmid

Fast, H.
April Morning
GOLDWYN TV (US) 1988
dir. Delbert Mann
TV(US)

Fast, H.
Crossing, The
A&E/COL TRISTAR (US) 2000 dir.
Robert Harmon
TV(US)

Fast, H.
Freedom Road
BRAUN (US) 1980 dir. Jan Kadar
TVSe(US)

Fast, H.
Immigrants, The
UN (US) 1978 dir. Alan J. Levi
TVSe(US)

Fast, H.
Rachel
Rachel and the Stranger
RKO (US) 1948 dir. Norman Foster

Fast, H.
Spartacus
UN (US) 1960 dir. Stanley Kubrick

Fast, H.
Winston Affair, The
Man in the Middle
FOX (GB) 1963 dir. Guy Hamilton

Fauchois, R.
Boudu Sauvé des Eaux
P
Down and Out in Beverly Hills
TOUCHSTONE (US) 1986 dir. Paul
Mazursky

Fauchois, R.
Boudu Sauvé des Eaux
P
M. SIMON (Fr) 1932 dir. Jean Renoir

Faulk, J. H.
Fear on Trial
LAN (US) 1975 dir. Lamont Johnson
TV(US)

Faulkner, J. M.
Moonfleet
MGM (US) 1955 dir. Fritz Lang
BBC (GB) 1984 dir. Colin Cant
TVSe(GB)

Faulkner, W.
Hamlet, The
Long, Hot Summer, The
FOX (US) 1958 dir. Martin Ritt
L. HILL (US) 1985 dir. Stuart Cooper
TVSe(US)

Faulkner, W.
Intruder in the Dust
MGM (US) 1949 dir. Clarence Brown

Faulkner, W.
Pylon
Tarnished Angels, The
UI (US) 1957 dir. Douglas Sirk

Faulkner, W.
Reivers, The
WAR (US) 1969 dir. Mark Rydell

Faulkner, W.
Sanctuary
FOX (US) 1960 dir. Tony Richardson

Faulkner, W.
Sanctuary
Story of Temple Drake, The
PAR (US) 1933 dir. Stephen Roberts

Faulkner, W.
Sound and the Fury, The
FOX (US) 1959 dir. Martin Ritt

Faulkner, W.
Turnabout
Today We Live
MGM (US) 1933 dir. Howard Hawks

Faulks, S.
Charlotte Gray
CHANNEL 4 FILMS (GB/Aust/Ger)
2001 dir. Gillian Armstrong

Fearing, K.
Big Clock, The
PAR (US) 1947 dir. John Farrow

Fearing, K.
Big Clock, The
No Way Out
ORION (US) 1987 dir. Roger Donaldson

Fedders, C. and Elliot, L.
Shattered Dreams
CAROLCO (US) 1990 dir. Robert Iscove
TV(US)

Feiden, D.
Ten Million Dollar Getaway, The
WIL COURT (US) 1991
dir. James A. Contner
TV(US)

Feifer, G.
Girl from Petrovka, The
UN (US) 1974 dir. Robert Ellis Miller

Feiffer, J.
Little Murders
P
FOX (US) 1971 dir. Alan Arkin

Feiner, R.
Three Cups of Coffee
Woman's Angle, A
ABP (GB) 1952 dir. Leslie Arliss

Feinman, J. P.
Last Days of the Victim
Two to Tango
CONCORDE (US/Arg) 1989
dir. Hector Olivera

Feinmann, J. P.
Ni el Tiro del Final
Love Walked In
TRIUMPH (Arg/US) 1997 dir. Juan Jose
Campanella

Feirstein, B.
Nice Guys Sleep Alone: Dating in the
Difficult Eighties
Nice Guys Sleep Alone
LUNACY (US) 1999 dir. Stu Pollard

Feldshuh, D.
Miss Evers' Boys
P
HBO (US) 1997 dir. Joseph Sargent
TV(US)

Fenady, A. J.
Man with Bogart's Face, The
FOX (US) 1980 dir. Robert Day

Fenelon, F.
Playing for Time

SYZYGY (US) 1980 dir. Daniel Mann
TV(US)

Fenoglio, B.
Partigiano Johnny, Il

FANDANGO (It) 2000 dir. Guido
Chiesa

Fenton, E.
Golden Doors, The

Escapade in Florence
DISNEY (US) 1962 dir. Steve Previn
Ch

Fenwick, J.-N.
Palmes de M. Schutz, Les

P
STUDIO CANAL+ (Fr) 1997 dir. Claude
Pinoteau

Ferber, E.
Cimarron

RKO (US) 1930 dir. Wesley Ruggles
MGM (US) 1960 dir. Anthony Mann

Ferber, E.
Come and Get It

UA (US) 1936
dir. Howard Hawks, William Wyler

Ferber, E.
Giant

WAR (US) 1956 dir. George Stevens

Ferber, E.
Ice Palace

WAR (US) 1960 dir. Vincent Sherman

Ferber, E.
Saratoga Trunk

WAR (US) 1945 dir. Sam Wood

Ferber, E.
Show Boat

UN (US) 1936 dir. James Whale
MGM (US) 1951 dir. George Sidney
M

Ferber, E.
So Big

WAR (US) 1932 dir. William Wellman
WAR (US) 1953 dir. Robert Wise

Ferguson, A.
Jet Stream

Mayday at 40,000 Feet
WAR (US) 1976 dir. Robert Butler
TV(US)

Ferguson, M.
Sign of the Ram, The

COL (US) 1948 dir. John Sturges

Fernandez, G.
Vietnam Trilogy

P
Cease Fire
CINEWORLD (US) 1985
dir. David Nutter

Ferrante, E.
Amore Molesto, L'

LUCKY RED (It) 1995 dir. Mario
Martone

Ferrari, M.
Alla Rivoluzione Sulla Due Cavalli

PANTER (It) 2001 dir. Maurizio Sciarra

Ferris, P.
Detective, The

BBC (GB) 1985 dir. Don Leaver
TVSe(GB)

Ferris, W.
Across 110th Street

UA (US) 1972 dir. Barry Shear

Ferro, M.
Petain
FRANCE 2 (Fr) 1992 dir. Jean Marboeuf

Fest, J.
Hitler: A Career
GTO (Ger) 1987
dir. Christian Herrendoerfer,
Joachim C. Fest

Fetcher, L.
Blindfold
UI (US) 1965 dir. Philip Dunne

Fetherstonhaugh, R. C.
Royal Canadian Mounted Police
Northwest Mounted Police
PAR (US) 1940 dir. Cecil B. De Mille

Feutchwangler, L.
Jew Süss
GAU (GB) 1934 dir. Lothar Mendes
US title: Power
TERRA (Ger) 1940 dir. Veit Harlan

Feval, P.
Bossu, Le
On Guard!
STUDIO CANAL+ (Fr) 1997 dir.
Philippe de Broca

Feydeau, G.
Flea in Her Ear, A
P
FOX (US/Fr) 1968 dir. Jacques Charon

Feydeau, G.
Occupe-toi d'Amélie
P
LUX (Fr) 1949 dir. Claude Autant-Lara

Feydeau, G. and Desvallieres, M.
Hotel Paradiso
P
MGM (US) 1966 dir. Peter Glenville

Feynman, R.
**Surely You're Joking, Mr Feynman;
What Do You Care What Other People
Think**
Infinity
OVERSEAS (US) 1996 dir. Matthew
Broderick

Fidler, K.
Flash the Sheepdog
CFF (US) 1967 dir. Laurence Henson
Ch

Fiechter, J.-J.
Tiré a Part
Limited Edition
FRANCE 3 (Fr) 1996 dir. Bernard Rapp

Field, H. and Mierzenski, S.
Angry Harvest
CCC (Ger) 1986 dir. Agnieszka Holland

Field, R.
All This and Heaven Too
WAR (US) 1940 dir. Anatole Litvak

Field, R.
And Now Tomorrow
PAR (US) 1944 dir. Irving Pichel

Field, R.
Time Out of Mind
UN (US) 1947 dir. Robert Siodmak

Fielding, H.
Bridget Jones's Diary
WORKING TITLE (GB) 2001 dir.
Sharon Maguire

Fielding, H.
History of Tom Jones, A Foundling, The
Tom Jones
UA (GB) 1963 dir. Tony Richardson
BBC/A&E (GB) 1997 dir. Metin
Huseyin
TVSe(GB)

Fielding, H.
History of Tom Jones, a, Foundling,
The

Bawdy Adventures of Tom Jones, The
UN (GB) 1976 dir. Cliff Owen
M

Fielding, H.
Joseph Andrews

UA (GB) 1977 dir. Tony Richardson

Fielding, J.
See Jane Run

HEARST (US) 1995 dir. John Patterson
TV(US)

Fielding, J.
Tell Me No Secrets

AVE PICT (US) 1997 dir. Bobby Roth
TV(US)

Fields, D.
Linda McCartney: A Portrait

Linda McCartney Story, The
COL TRISTAR (US) 2000 dir. Armand
Mastroianni
TV(US)

Fields, H.
Dubarry was a Lady
P
MGM (US) 1943 dir. Roy del Ruth
M

Fields, H.
Hit the Deck
P
MGM (US) 1955 dir. Roy Rowland
M

Fields, H. and Fields, D.
Annie Get Your Gun
P
MGM (US) 1950 dir. George Sidney
M

Fields, H. and Fields, D.
Mexican Hayride
P
UN (US) 1948 dir. Charles Barton

**Fields, H., Rodgers, R. and
Hart, L.**
Present Arms
P
Leathernecking
RKO (US) 1930 dir. Edward Cline
GB title: Present Arms
M

Fields, J.
Doughgirls, The
P
WAR (US) 1944 dir. James V. Kern

Fields, J. and Chodorov, J.
Anniversary Waltz
P
Happy Anniversary
UA (US) 1959 dir. David Miller

Fields, J. and Chodorov, J.
My Sister Eileen
P
COL (US) 1955 dir. Richard Quine
M

Fienburgh, W.
No Love for Johnnie

RANK (GB) 1960 dir. Ralph Thomas

Fierstein, H.
Torch Song Trilogy
P
NEW LINE (US) 1988 dir. Paul Bogart

Finch, C.
Rainbow

TEN-FOUR (US) 1978 dir. Jackie
Cooper
TV(US)

Finch, M.
Dentist in the Chair
REN (GB) 1960 dir. Don Chaffey

Fine, A.
Alias Madame Doubtfire
Mrs. Doubtfire
FOX (US) 1993 dir. Chris Columbus

Fine, A.
Goggle Eyes
BBC (GB) 1993 dir. Carol Wiseman
TVSe(GB)

Finney, C. G.
Seven Faces of Dr. Lao, The
MGM (US) 1964 dir. George Pal

Finney, J.
Assault on a Queen
PAR (US) 1966 dir. Jack Donohue

Finney, J.
Body Snatchers, The
Invasion of the Body Snatchers, The
ALLIED (US) 1956 dir. Don Siegel
UA (US) 1978 dir. Philip Kaufman

Finney, J.
Five Against the House
COL (US) 1955 dir. Phil Karlson

Finney, J.
Good Neighbour Sam
COL (US) 1964 dir. David Swift

Finney, J.
House of Numbers
MGM (US) 1957 dir. Russell Rouse

Finney, J.
Invasion of the Body Snatchers
Body Snatchers
WAR (US) 1993 dir. Abel Ferrara

Finney, J.
Marion's Wall
Maxie
ORION (US) 1985 dir. Paul Aaron

Finstad, S.
Sleeping with the Devil
NBC (US) 1997 dir. William A. Graham
TV(US)

Fischer, E.
Aimee & Jaguar
SENATOR (Ger) 1997 dir. Max
Farberbock

Fish, R. L.
Pursuit
Twist of Fate
COL TV/HTV (US/GB) 1989
dir. Ian Sharp
TVSe(GB/US)

Fishburne, L.
Riff Raff
P
Once in the Life
SHOOTING GALLERY (US) 2000 dir.
Laurence Fishburne

Fisher, B. and Marx, A.
Impossible Years, The
P
MGM (US) 1968 dir. Michael Gordon

Fisher, C.
Postcards from the Edge
COL (US) 1990 dir. Mike Nichols

Fisher, C.
Tall Men, The
FOX (US) 1955 dir. Raoul Walsh

Fisher, C.
Yellowstone Kelly
WAR (US) 1959 dir. Gordon Douglas

Fisher, D.
Pack, The
WAR (US) 1977 dir. Robert Clouse

Fisher, M.
Bethnal Green
Place To Go, A
BL (GB) 1963 dir. Basil Dearden

Fisher, S.
I Wake up Screaming
FOX (US) 1941
dir. H. Bruce Humberstone
GB title: Hot Spot

Fisher, S.
I Wake Up Screaming
Vicki
FOX (US) 1953 dir. Harry Horner

Fisher, S. G.
Destination Tokyo
WAR (US) 1943 dir. Delmer Daves

Fisher, V.
Jeremiah Johnson
WAR (US) 1972 dir. Sidney Pollack

Fitch, C.
Beau Brummell
P
MGM (GB) 1954 dir. Curtis Bernhardt

Fitzgerald, F. S.
Babylon Revisited
Last Time I Saw Paris, The
MGM (US) 1954 dir. Richard Brooks

Fitzgerald, F. S.
Great Gatsby, The
PAR (US) 1949 dir. Elliot Nugent
PAR (US) 1974 dir. Jack Clayton
A&E/BBC (US/GB) 2001 dir. Robert
Markowitz
TV(US/GB)

Fitzgerald, F. S.
Last of the Belles
TITUS (US) 1974 dir. George Schlatter
TV(US)

Fitzgerald, F. S.
Last Tycoon, The
PAR (US) 1976 dir. Elia Kazan

Fitzgerald, F. S.
Tender is the Night
FOX (US) 1962 dir. Henry King
BBC/SHOWTIME (US/GB) 1985
dir. Robert Knights
TVSe(US/GB)

Fitzhugh, L.
Harriet the Spy
PAR (US) 1996 dir. Bronwen Hughes

Fitzpatrick, J.
Major Taylor Down Under
Tracks of Glory: The Major Taylor Story
BARRON (Aust) 1992 dir. Marcus Cole
TVSe(Aust)

Fitz-Simons, F.
Bright Leaf
WAR (US) 1950 dir. Michael Curtiz

Flagg, F.
Fried Green Tomatoes at the Whistle
Stop Cafe
Fried Green Tomatoes
UN (US) 1991 dir. Jon Avnet

Flaherty, J.
Tin Wife
My Husband's Secret Life
USA NETWORK (US) 1998 dir. Graeme
Clifford
TV(US)

Flanagan, R.
Sound of One Hand Clapping, The
S. AUST (Aust) 1998 dir. Richard
Flanagan

Flanigan, S.
Alice

Wildflower
HEARST (US) 1991 dir. Diane Keaton
TV(US)

Flaubert, G.
Madame Bovary

MGM (US) 1949 dir. Vincente Minnelli
BBC (GB) 1975 dir. Rodney Bennett
TVSe(GB)
GOLDWYN (Fr) 1991
dir. Claude Chabrol

Flaubert, G.
Première Education Sentimentale, La

Toutes les Nuits
TPS CINEMA (Fr) 2001 dir. Eugene
Green

Flaubert, G.
Sentimental Education

BBC (GB) 1970 dir. David Maloney
TVSe(GB)

Flavin, M.
One Way Out

P
Convicted
COL (US) 1950 dir. Henry Levin

Fleetwood, H.
Order of Death, The

Corrupt
NEW LINE (It) 1983 dir. Robert Faenza

Fleischman, A. S.
Blood Alley

WAR (US) 1955 dir. William Wellman

Fleischman, A. S.
Whipping Boy, The

COL TV (US/GB) 1994 dir. Sydney
Macartney
TV(US/GB)

Fleischman, A. S.
Yellowleg

Deadly Companions, The
WAR (US) 1961 dir. Sam Peckinpah

Fleischman, S.
By the Great Horn Spoon

Adventures of Bullwhip Griffin, The
DISNEY (US) 1965 dir. James Neilson

Fleming, B.
Colonel Effingham's Raid

FOX (US) 1945 dir. Irving Pichel
GB title: Man of the Hour

Fleming, I.
Casino Royale

COL (GB) 1967 dir. John Huston

Fleming, I.
Chitty, Chitty Bang Bang

UA (GB) 1968 dir. Ken Hughes
Ch

Fleming, I.
Diamonds are Forever

UA (GB) 1971 dir. Guy Hamilton

Fleming, I.
Dr No

UA (GB) 1962 dir. Terence Young

Fleming, I.
From Russia With Love

UA (GB) 1963 dir. Terence Young

Fleming, I.
Goldfinger

UA (GB) 1964 dir. Guy Hamilton

Fleming, I.
Live and Let Die

UA (GB) 1973 dir. Guy Hamilton

Fleming, I.
Living Daylights, The
MGM (GB) 1987 dir. John Glen

Fleming, I.
Man with the Golden Gun, The
UA (GB) 1974 dir. Guy Hamilton

Fleming, I.
Moonraker
UA (GB) 1979 dir. Lewis Gilbert

Fleming, I.
On Her Majesty's Secret Service
UA (GB) 1969 dir. Peter Hunt

Fleming, I.
Spy Who Loved Me, The
UA (GB) 1977 dir. Lewis Gilbert

Fleming, I.
Thunderball
UA (GB) 1965 dir. Terence Young

Fleming, I.
You Only Live Twice
UA (GB) 1966 dir. Lewis Gilbert

Fleming, M.
From Amalgamated Morons to American Icons: The Three Stooges
Three Stooges, The
ICON (US) 2000 dir. James Frawley
TV(US)

Flender, H.
Paris Blues
UA (US) 1961 dir. Martin Ritt

Fletcher, G.
London Nobody Knows, The
BL (GB) 1969 dir. Norman Cohen

Fletcher, L.
Night Watch
P
AVCO (GB) 1973 dir. Brian G. Hutton

Fletcher, L.
Sorry, Wrong Number
P
PAR (US) 1948 dir. Anatole Litvak
WIL COURT (US) 1989
dir. Tony Wharmby
TV(US)

Flexner, J. T.
George Washington
MGM TV (US) 1984 dir. Buzz Kulik
TVSe(US)

Flexner, J. T.
George Washington II: The Forging of a Nation
MGM/UA TV (US) 1986 dir. William A. Graham
TVSe(US)

Flynn, E.
My Wicked, Wicked Ways ... The Legend of Errol Flynn
CBS ENT (US) 1985 dir. Don Taylor
TV(US)

Fo, D.
Mistero Buffo
P
BBC (GB) 1990 dir. Don Coutts
TV(GB)

Fodor, L.
Birthday Gift
P
North to Alaska
FOX (US) 1960 dir. Henry Hathaway

Fodor, L.
Blondie White
P
Footsteps in the Dark
WAR (US) 1941 dir. Lloyd Bacon

Fodor, L.
Jewel Robbery
P
Peterville Diamond, The
WAR (GB) 1942 dir. Walter Forde

Fodor, L.
Jewel Robbery
P
WAR (US) 1932 dir. William Dieterle

Fodor, L.
Unguarded Hour, The
P
MGM (US) 1936 dir. Sam Wood

Fodor, L.
Woman Lies, A
P
Thunder in the Night
FOX (US) 1935 dir. George Archainbaud

Fogle, J.
Drugstore Cowboy
AVENUE (US) 1989 dir. Gus van Sant

Folco, M.
Dieu et Nous Seuls Pouvons
Justinien Trouvé
SOLO (Fr) 1993 dir. Christian Fechner

Foldes, Y.
Golden Ear-Rings
PAR (US) 1947 dir. Mitchell Leisen

Foldes, Y.
Make You a Fine Wife
My Own True Love
PAR (US) 1948 dir. Compton Bennett

Follett, K.
Eye of the Needle
UA (GB) 1981 dir. Richard Marquand

Follett, K.
Key to Rebecca, The
TAFT (US) 1985 dir. David Hemmings
TVSe(US)

Follett, K.
Lie Down With Lions
HANNIBAL (US) 1994 dir. Jim
Goddard
TV(US)

Follett, K.
On Wings of Eagles
TAFT (US) 1986
dir. Andrew V. McLaglen
TVSe(US)

Follett, K.
Third Twin, The
JAFFE/BRAUNSTEIN (US) 1997 dir.
Tom McLoughlin
TV(US)

Fonseca, R.
Exposure
MIRAMAX (Bra) 1991 dir. Walter Salles,
Jr.

Fontaine, R. L.
Happy Time, The
Happy Time, The
COL (US) 1952 dir. Richard Fleischer

Fontane, T.
Fontane Effi Briest
TANGO (W. Ger) 1974
dir. Rainer Werner Fassbinder

Foote, H.
Chase, The
COL (US) 1966 dir. Arthur Penn

Foote, H.
Convicts
P
STERLING (US) 1991 dir. Peter
Masterson

Foote, H.
Habitation of Dragons, The
P
AMBLIN (US) 1992 dir. Michael
Lindsay-Hogg
TV(US)

Foote, H.
Lily Dale
P
HALLMARK (US) 1996 dir. Peter
Masterson
TV(US)

Foote, H.
Travelling Lady, The
P
Baby, The Rain Must Fall
COL (US) 1965 dir. Robert Mulligan

Foote, H.
Trip to Bountiful, The
P
ISLAND (US) 1985 dir. Peter Masterson

Foote, H.
Valentine's Day
P
On Valentine's Day
ANGELIKA (US) 1986 dir. Ken
Harrison

Foote, J. T.
Look of Eagles, The
Kentucky
FOX (US) 1938 dir. David Butler

Foote, S.
September, September
Memphis
PROPAGANDA (US) 1992
dir. Yves Simoneau
TV(US)

Forbes, B.
Endless Game, The
TELSO (GB) 1990 dir. Bryan Forbes
TV(GB)

Forbes, C.
Avalanche Express
FOX (Eire) 1979 dir. Mark Robson

Forbes, E.
Johnny Tremain
DISNEY (US) 1957
dir. Robert Stevenson
Ch

Forbes, J. S.
Meter Man, The
P
Penthouse, The
PAR (GB) 1967 dir. Peter Collinson

Forbes, M.
Hollow Triumph
EL (US) 1948 dir. Steve Sekely

Forbes, R.
Fourth Brother, The
China
PAR (US) 1943 dir. John Farrow

Forbes, S.
Go to thy Deathbed
Reflection of Fear
COL (US) 1973 dir. William A. Fraker

Ford, B. and Chase, C.
Times Of My Life, The
Betty Ford Story, The
WAR TV (US) 1987 dir. David Greene
TV(US)

Ford, J. H.
Liberation of Lord Byron Jones, The
COL (US) 1970 dir. William Wyler

Foreman, L. L.
Don Desperado
Savage, The
PAR (US) 1952 dir. George Marshall

Foreman, L. L.
Road to San Jacinto
Arrow in the Dust
ABP (US) 1954 dir. Lesley Selander

Forest, J.-C.
Barbarella
PAR (Fr/It) 1967 dir. Roger Vadim

Forester, C. S.
African Queen, The
ROMULUS (US/GB) 1951
dir. John Huston

Forester, C. S.
Brown on 'Resolution'
GB (GB) 1935 dir. Walter Forde
US title: Born for Glory

Forester, C. S.
Captain Hornblower, R. N.
Captain Horatio Hornblower, R. N.
WAR (GB) 1951 dir. Raoul Walsh

Forester, C. S.
Gun, The
Pride and the Passion, The
UA (US) 1957 dir. Stanley Kramer

Forester, C. S.
Mr. Midshipman Hornblower;
Lieutenant Hornblower
Horatio Hornblower
A&E/PICTURE PALACE (GB) 1999 dir.
Andrew Grieve
TVSe(GB)
A&E/PICTURE PALACE (GB) 2001 dir.
Andrew Grieve
TVSe(GB)

Forester, C. S.
Hunting the Bismarck
Sink the Bismarck
FOX (GB) 1960 dir. Lewis Gilbert

Forman, Sir D.
Son of Adam
My Life So Far
MIRAMAX (GB) 1999 dir. Hugh
Hudson

Forrest, A. J.
Interpol
COL (GB) 1957 dir. John Gilling
US title: Pickup Alley

Forrest, D.
Great Dinosaur Robbery, The
One of our Dinosaurs is Missing
DISNEY (US) 1975
dir. Robert Stevenson
Ch

Forrester, L.
Girl Called Fathom, A
Fathom
FOX (GB) 1967 dir. Leslie Martinson

Forster, E. M.
Howards End
MI (GB) 1992
dir. James Ivory

Forster, E. M.
Maurice
MI (GB) 1987 dir. James Ivory

Forster, E. M.
Passage to India, A
COL-EMI (GB) 1984 dir. David Lean

Forster, E. M.
Room With a View, A
GOLD (GB) 1985 dir. James Ivory

Forster, M.
Georgy Girl
COL (GB) 1966 dir. Silvio Narizzano

Forsyth, F.
Casualty of War, A
BLAIR (US) 1990 dir. Tom Clegg
TV(GB/US)

Forsyth, F.
Day of the Jackal, The
UN (Fr/GB) 1973 dir. Fred Zinnemann

Forsyth, F.
Dogs of War, The
UA (GB) 1980 dir. John Irvin

Forsyth, F.
Fourth Protocol, The
RANK (GB) 1987
dir. John MacKenzie

Forsyth, F.
In No Comebacks
Cry of the Innocent
NBC ENT (US) 1980
dir. Michael O'Herlihy

Forsyth, F.
Just Another Secret
BLAIR (US/GB) 1989
dir. Lawrence Gordon Clark
TV(GB/US)

Forsyth, F.
Odessa File, The
COL (GB) 1974 dir. Ronald Neame

Forsyth, F.
Pride and Extreme Prejudice
USA NETWORK (US) 1990 dir. Ian
Sharp
TV(US)

Forte, V.
Trailmakers, The
Wild Women
SPELLING (US) 1970 dir. Don Taylor
TV(US)

Fossey, D.
Gorillas in the Mist
WAR/UN (US) 1988 dir. Michael Apted

Foster, L. R.
Gentleman From Montana, The
Mr. Smith Goes To Washington
COL (US) 1939 dir. Frank Capra

Fowler, C.
Before Women Had Wings
HARPO (US) 1997 dir. Lloyd Kramer
TV(US)

Fowler, G.
Beau James
PAR (US) 1957 dir. Melville Shavelson

Fowler, G. and Meredyth, B.
Mighty Barnum, The
P
FOX (US) 1934 dir. Walter Lang

Fowler, H. M.
Shades Will Not Vanish
Strange Intruder
ABP (US) 1956 dir. Irving Rapper

Fowles, J.
Collector, The
BL (US) 1965 dir. William Wyler

Fowles, J.
Ebony Tower, The
GRANADA (GB) 1984
dir. Robert Knights
TV(GB)

Fowles, J.
French Lieutenant's Woman, The
UA (GB) 1981 dir. Karel Reisz

Fowles, J.
Magus, The
FOX (GB) 1968 dir. Guy Green

Fox, J.
Little Shepherd of Kingdom Come, The
FOX (US) 1961
dir. Andrew V. McLaglen

Fox, J.
White Mischief
BBC/COL (GB) 1988
dir. Michael Radford

Fox, Jr., J.
Trail of the Lonesome Pine, The
PAR (US) 1936 dir. Henry Hathaway

Fox, N. A.
Roughshod
Gunsmoke
UN (US) 1953 dir. Nathan Juran

Fox, N. A.
Tall Man Riding
WAR (US) 1955 dir. Lesley Selander

Fox, P.
Desperate Characters
ITC (US) 1971 dir. Frank D. Gilroy

Foxman, S.
Classified Love
CBS ENT (US) 1986 dir. Don Taylor
TV(US)

Frady, M.
Wallace
George Wallace
TNT (US) 1997 dir. John Frankenheimer
TVSe(US)

Frame, J.
Angel at My Table, An
FINE LINE (Aust) 1991
dir. Jane Campion

France, A.
Crime of Sylvester Bonnard, The
Chasing Yesterday
RKO (US) 1935 dir. George Nicholls, Jr.

Francis, C.
Deceit
BBC (GB) 2000 dir. Stuart Orme
TV(GB)

Francis, D.
Blood Sport
DLT (US) 1989 dir. Harvey Hart
TV(US)

Francis, D.
Dead Cert
UA (GB) 1974 dir. Tony Richardson

Francis, D.
In the Frame
DLT (US) 1989 dir. Wigbert Wicker
TV(US)

Francis, D.
Twice Shy
DLT (US) 1989 dir. Deirdre Friel
TV(US)

Franck, D.
Separation, La
STUDIO CANAL+ (Fr) 1994 dir.
Christian Vincent

Frank, A.
Anne Frank: The Diary of a Young Girl
Diary of Anne Frank, The
FOX (US) 1959 dir. George Stevens
FOX (US) 1980 dir. Boris Sagal
TV(US)
BBC (GB) 1987 dir. Gareth Davies
TVSe(GB)

Frank, B.
Cervantes
PRISMA (Sp/It/Fr) 1968
dir. Vincent Sherman

Frank, B.
Sturm in Wasserglass
P
Storm in a Teacup
LF (GB) 1937 dir. Ian Dalrymple, Victor Saville

Frank, C.
Année des Meduses, L'
AT (Fr) 1987 dir. Christopher Frank

Frank, C.
Dream of the Mad Monkey, The
Twisted Obsession
IVE (US) 1990 dir. Fernando Trueba

Frank, C.
Josepha
TRIUMPH (Fr) 1982
dir. Christopher Frank

Frank, G.
Boston Strangler, The
FOX (US) 1968 dir. Richard Fleischer

Frank, L.
Carl and Anna
Desire Me
MGM (US) 1947 dir. George Cukor

Frank, M.
F. Est un Salaud
ARENA (Fr/Swe) 1997 dir. Marcel Gisler

Frank, M. and Clark, B.
First Lady of the Seeing Eye
Love Leads the Way
DISNEY CH (US) 1984
dir. Delbert Mann
TV(US)

Frank, P.
Hold Back The Night
ABP (US) 1956 dir. Allan Dwan

Frankau, G.
Christopher Strong
RKO (US) 1933 dir. Dorothy Arzner

Franke, C. and Crane, M.
Bombshell
P
MGM (US) 1933 dir. Victor Fleming
GB title: Blonde Bombshell

Franken, A.
Stuart Saves His Family
PAR (US) 1995 dir. Harold Ramis

Franken, R.
Another Language
P
MGM (US) 1933 dir. Edward H. Griffith

Franken, R.
Claudia
FOX (US) 1943 dir. Edmund Goulding

Franken, R.
Claudia and David
FOX (US) 1946 dir. Walter Lang

Franklin, E.
Working Man, The
WAR (US) 1933 dir. John Adolf

Franklin, J.
Last of Philip Banter, The
CINEVISITA (Sp) 1988
dir. Herve Hachuel

Franklin, J. and Doelp, A.
Shock Trauma
TELECOM (Can) 1982 dir. Eric Till
TV(Can)

Franklin, M.
My Brilliant Career
GUO (Aust) 1979 dir. Gillian Armstrong

Franzero, C. M.
Life and Times of Cleopatra, The
Cleopatra
FOX (US) 1963
dir. Joseph L. Manciewicz

Fraser, A.
Quiet as a Nun
THAMES (GB) 1982 dir. Moira
Armstrong
TVSe(GB)

Fraser, B.
**Unidentified Human Remains and the
True Nature of Love**
P
Love and Human Remains
TELEFILM (Can) 1993 dir. Denys
Arcand

Fraser, G. M.
Royal Flash
FOX RANK (GB) 1975
dir. Richard Lester

Fraser, N.
Eva Peron
Evita Peron
ZEPHYR (US) 1981
dir. Marvin Chomsky
TVSe(US)

Frayn, M.
Noises Off
P
TOUCHSTONE (US) 1992 dir. Peter
Bogdanovich

Frazee, S.
Desert Guns
Gold of the Seven Saints
WAR (US) 1961 dir. Gordon Douglas

Fredd, C.
Fire and Ice
ARABESQUE FILMS (US) 2001 dir.
Bryan Goeres
TV(US)

Frede, R.
Interns, The
COL (US) 1962 dir. David Swift

Fredrickson, O. and East, B.
Silence of the North
UN (Can) 1981 dir. Allan Winton King

Freed, J.
Moonwebs
Ticket to Heaven
UA (US) 1981 dir. R. L. Thomas

Freedman, B. and Freedman, N.
Mrs. Mike
UA (US) 1950 dir. Louis King

Freedman, D.
Mendel Inc.
P
Heart of New York
WAR (US) 1932 dir. Mervyn LeRoy

Freedman, M.
Playing Mona Lisa
P
BUBBLE FACTORY (US) 2000 dir.
Matthew Huffman

Freeling, N.
Because of the Cats
Rape, The
MIRACLE (Bel/Neth) 1973
dir. Fons Rademakers

Freeling, N.
Love in Amsterdam
Amsterdam Affair
LIP/TRIO/GROUP W (GB) 1968
dir. Gerry O'Hara

Freeman, D.
Father Sky
Taps
FOX (US) 1981 dir. Harold Becker

Freeman, J.
Set For Life
Gift of Love, The
M. REES (US) 1994 dir. Paul Bogart
TV(US)

Freeman, L. and Roy, J.
Betrayal
EMI TV (US) 1978 dir. Paul Wendkos
TV(US)

Freemantle, B.
Charlie, M
Charlie Muffin
EUSTON (GB) 1979 dir. Jack Gold

Freiberger, P. and Swaine, M.
Fire in the Valley
Pirates of Silicon Valley
TNT (US) 1999 dir. Martyn Burke
TV(US)

French, M.
Women's Room, The
WAR (US) 1980 dir. Glenn Jordan
TVSe(US)

Freud, E.
Hideous Kinky
BBC (GB/Fr) 1998 dir. Gillies
MacKinnon

Frick, R. M.
Where's My Mommy Now?
Perfect Alibi
RYSHER (US) 1995 dir. Kevin Meyer

Friedman, B. J.
Change of Plan, A
Heartbreak Kid, The
FOX (US) 1972 dir. Elaine May

Friedman, B. J.
Lonely Guy's Book of Life, The
Lonely Guy, The
UN (US) 1984 dir. Arthur Hiller

Friedman, C.
Shovel and the Loom, The
Left Luggage
GREYSTONE (Bel/Neth/US) 1997 dir.
Jeroen Krabbe

Friel, B.
Dancing at Lughnasa
P
CAPITOL (Ire/GB/US) 1998 dir. Pat
O'Connor

**Friml, R., Post, W. H. and
Hooker, B.**
Vagabond King, The
P
PAR (US) 1956 dir. Michael Curtiz
M

Frings, Mrs. K.
Hold Back The Dawn
PAR (US) 1941 dir. Mitchell Leisen

Frisby, T.
There's a Girl in my Soup
P
COL (GB) 1970 dir. Roy Boulting

Froment, P.
Je te tue: Histoire Vraie de Roberto
Succo
Roberto Succo
STUDIO CANAL+ (Fr) 2001 dir. Cedric
Kahn

Fry, R. K.
Secret of Ron Mor Skerry, The
Secret of Roah Inish, The
JONES (US) 1994 dir. John Sayles

Fuentes, C.
Gringo Viejo
Old Gringo
COL (US) 1989 dir. Luis Puenzo

Fugard, A.
Boesman & Lena
P
PATHE (Fr/SA) 2000 dir. John Berry

Fugard, A.
Road to Mecca, The
P
VIDEOVISION (US) 1992
dir. Athol Fugard
TV(US)

Fuguet, A.
Tinta Roja
TORNASOL (Sp) 2000 dir. Francisco J.
Lombardi

Fuhmann, F.
Kamaraden
Duped Till Doomsday
DEFA (Ger) 1957 dir. Kurt Jung-Alsen

Fujitani, A.
Touhimu
Shiki-Jitsu
STUDIO KAJINO (Jap) 2000 dir.
Hideaki Anno

Fukazawa, S.
Ballad of Narayama
ROEI (Jap) 1983 dir. Shohei Imamura

Fulda, L.
Two-Faced Woman
P
MGM (US) 1941 dir. George Cuker

Fuller, C.
Soldier's Play, A
P
Soldier's Story, A
COL (US) 1984 dir. Norman Jewison

Fuller, C.
Zooman and the Sign
P
Zooman
SHOWTIMEWORKS (US) 1995 dir.
Leon Ichaso
TV(US)

Fuller, J. G.
Ghost of Flight 401, The
PAR TV (US) 1978
dir. Steven Hilliard Stern
TV(US)

Fuller, J. G.
Interrupted Journey, The
UFO Incident, The
UN TV (US) 1975 dir. Richard Colla
TV(US)

Fuller, S.
Scandal Sheet
COL (US) 1952 dir. Phil Karlson
GB title: Dark Page, The

Fullerton, A.
Lionheart
CFF (GB) 1968 dir. Michael Forlong

Fulop-Miller, R.
Triumph
Great Moment, The
PAR (US) 1944. dir. Preston Sturges

Gaarder, J.
Sophie's World: A Novel About the History of Philosophy

Sofies Verden
NFK (Nor) 1999 dir. Eric Gustavson

Gabeira, F.
O Que I Isso, Companheiro?

Four Days in September
COL (US/Bra) 1997 dir. Bruno Barreto

Gabriel, G. W.
I, James Lewis

This Woman is Mine
UN (US) 1941 dir. Frank Lloyd

Gaddis, T. E.
Birdman of Alcatraz

UA (US) 1961 dir. John Frankenheimer

Gaddis, T. E.
Killer: A Journal of Murder

IXTLAN (US) 1996 dir. Tim Metcalfe

Gage, N.
Eleni

WAR (US) 1985 dir. Peter Yates

Gagnol, A.
M'sieur; Lumieres du Frigo, Les

HS (hors service)
PARADIS (Bel/Fr) 2001 dir. Jean-Paul
Lilienfeld

Gaines, C. and Butler, G.
Pumping Iron

CINEMA 51 (US) 1977
dir. George Butler

Gaines, C. and Butler, G.
Pumping Iron II: The Unprecedented Woman

Pumping Iron II
BLUE DOLPHIN (US) 1984
dir. George Butler

Gaines, C.
Stay Hungry

UA (US) 1976 dir. Bob Rafaelson

Gaines, E. J.
Autobiography of Miss Jane Pittman, The

TOM (US) 1974 dir. John Korty
TV(US)

Gaines, E. J.
Gathering of Old Men, A

CONSOL (US) 1987
dir. Volker Schlondorff
TV(US)

Gaines, E. J.
Lesson Before Dying, A

HBO (US) 1999 dir. Joseph Sargent
TV(US)

Gaines, R.
Final Night

Front Page Story
BL (GB) 1953 dir. Gordon Parry

Gaines, S.
Heroes and Villains: The True Story of the Beach Boys

Story of the Beach Boys, The: Summer Dreams
L. HILL (USTV) 1990
dir. Michael Switzer
TV(US)

Gala, A.
Mas Alla del Jardin
LOLAFILMS (Sp) 1997 dir. Pedro Olea

Gala, A.
Turkish Passion
LOLAFILMS (Sp) 1994 dir. Vicente Aranda

Galante, P.
Berlin Wall, The

Freedom Fighter
COL TV (US/GB) 1987
dir. Desmond Davis
TV(GB/US)

Galbally, F. and Macklin, R.
Juryman

Storyville
DAVIS (US) 1992 dir. Mark Frost

Galdos, B. P.
Nazarin

BAR PON (Mex) 1958 dir. Luis Bunuel

Gale, R. P. and Hauser, T.
Final Warning: The Legacy of Chernobyl

Chernobyl: The Final Warning
CAROLCO (US/USSR) 1991
dir. Anthony Page
TV(US/USSR)

Galgut, D.
Quarry, The
WANDA (Fr/Bel/Sp) 1998 dir. Marion Hansel

Gall, I.
Stud Farm, The
HUN (Hun) 1978 dir. Andras Kovacs

Gallagher, J. P.
Scarlet Pimpernel of the Vatican, The

Scarlet and the Black, The
ITC (It/US) 1983 dir. Jerry London
TVSe(It/US)

Gallagher, S.
Chimera

ANGLIA (GB) 1991 dir. Nicholas Gillott
TV(GB)

Gallagher, T.
Monogamist, The

Family Man, The
TIME-LIFE (US) 1979 dir. Glenn Jordan
TV(US)

Gallico, P.
Hand of Mary Constable, The

Daughter of the Mind
FOX (US) 1969 dir. Walter Grauman
TV(US)

Gallico, P.
Lili

MGM (US) 1952 dir. Charles Walters

Gallico, P.
Matilda

AIP (US) 1978 dir. Daniel Mann

Gallico, P.
Miracle in the Wilderness

TNT (US) 1991 dir. Kevin James Dobson
TV(US)

Gallico, P.
Mrs. 'arris Goes to Paris

ACCENT (US) 1992 dir. Anthony Shaw
TV(US)

Gallico, P.
Poseidon Adventure, The
FOX (US) 1972 dir. Ronald Neame

Gallico, P.
Small Miracle, The
LAN (US) 1983 dir. Jeannot Szwarc
TV(US)

Gallico, P.
Small Miracle, The
Never Take No for an Answer
INDEPENDENT (GB) 1951
dir. Maurice Cloche, Ralph Smart

Gallico, P.
Snow Goose, The
UN/BBC (US/GB) 1971
dir. Patrick Garland
TV(US/GB)

Gallico, P.
Thomasina
Three Lives of Thomasina, The
DISNEY (GB) 1963 dir. Don Chaffey
Ch

Gallico, P.
Trial by Terror
Assignment Paris
COL (US) 1952 dir. Robert Parrish

Galouye, D.
Simulacron 3
Thirteenth Floor, The
CENTROPOLIS (US/Ger) 1999 dir.
Josef Rusnak

Galsworthy, J.
Apple Tree, The
Summer Story, A
ITC/ATLANTIC (GB) 1988
dir. Piers Haggard

Galsworthy, J.
Escape
P
RKO (GB) 1930 dir. Basil Dean
FOX (US) 1948
dir. Joseph L. Mankiewicz

Galsworthy, J.
First and the Last, The
P
Twenty-One Days
LF (GB) 1937 dir. Basil Dean

Galsworthy, J.
Forsyte Saga, The
BBC (GB) 1967 dir. David Giles, James
Cellan Jones
TVSe(GB)

Galsworthy, J.
Loyalties
P
AUT (GB) 1933 dir. Basil Dean

Galsworthy, J.
Man of Property, A
That Forsyte Woman
MGM (US) 1949 dir. Compton Bennett
GB title: Forsyte Saga, The

Galsworthy, J.
Old English
P
WAR (US) 1930 dir. Alfred E. Green

Galsworthy, J.
Over the River
One More River
UN (US) 1934 dir. James Whale
GB title: Over the River

Galsworthy, J.
Skin Game, The
P
BI (GB) 1931 dir. Alfred Hitchcock

Gambino, R.
Vendetta
HBO (US) 1999 dir. Nicholas Meyer
TV(US)

Gann, E.
Aviator, The
MGM/UA (US) 1985 dir. George Miller

Gann, E. K.
Antagonists, The
Masada
UN TV (US) 1981 dir. Boris Sagal
GB title: Antagonists, The
TVSe(US)

Gann, E. K.
Blaze of Noon
PAR (US) 1947 dir. John Farrow

Gann, E. K.
Fate is the Hunter
FOX (US) 1964 dir. Ralph Nelson

Gann, E. K.
Fiddler's Green
Raging Tide, The
UI (US) 1951 dir. George Sherman

Gann, E. K.
High and the Mighty, The
WAR (US) 1954 dir. William Wellman

Gann, E. K.
Island in the Sky
WAR (US) 1953 dir. William Wellman

Gann, E. K.
Soldier of Fortune
FOX (US) 1955 dir. Edward Dmytryk

Gann, E. K.
Twilight for the Gods
UN (US) 1958 dir. Joseph Pevney

Garbo, N.
Spy
WIL COURT (US) 1989
dir. Philip E Messina
TV(US)

Garcia Lorca, F.
Yerma
ARTIMAGEN (Sp) 1998 dir. Pilar
Tavora

Garden, J.
All on a Summer's Day
Double Confession
ABP (GB) 1950 dir. Ken Annakin

Gardiner, J. R.
Stone Fox
TAFT (US) 1987 dir. Harvey Hart
TV(US)

Gardner, E. S.
Case of the Caretaker's Cat, The
Case of the Black Cat, The
WAR (US) 1936 dir. William McGann

Gardner, E. S.
Case of the Curious Bride, The
WAR (US) 1935 dir. Michael Curtiz

Gardner, E. S.
Case of the Howling Dog, The
WAR (US) 1934 dir. Alan Crosland

Gardner, E. S.
Case of the Lucky Legs, The
WAR (US) 1935 dir. Archie Mayo

Gardner, E. S.
Case of the Stuttering Bishop, The
WAR (US) 1937 dir. William Clemens

Gardner, E. S.
Case of the Velvet Claws, The
WAR (US) 1936 dir. William Clemens

Gardner, E. S.
D.A. Draws a Circle, The
They Call it Murder
FOX (US) 1971 dir. Walter Grauman
TV(US)

Gardner, H.
Goodbye People, The
P
EMBASSY (US) 1984 dir. Herb Gardner

Gardner, H.
I'm Not Rappaport
P
GRAMERCY (US) 1996 dir. Herb
Gardner

Gardner, H.
Thousand Clowns, A
P
UA (US) 1965 dir. Fred Coe

Gardner, J.
Complete State of Death, A
Stone Killer, The
COL (US) 1973 dir. Michael Winner

Gardner, J.
Liquidator, The
MGM (GB) 1965 dir. Jack Cardiff

Gardner, L.
**Christ has Returned to Earth and
Preaches Here Nightly**
Valentino Returns
VIDMARK/SKOURAS (US) 1989
dir. Paul Hoffman

Gardner, L.
Fat City
COL (US) 1972 dir. John Huston

Gardner, R. M.
Scandalous John
DISNEY (US) 1971 dir. Robert Butler

Gare, N.
Fringe Dwellers, The
OZFILMS (Aust) 1986
dir. Bruce Beresford

Garfield, B.
Death Wish
CANNON (US) 1974
dir. Michael Winner

Garfield, B.
Fear in a Handful of Dust
Fleshburn
CROWN (US) 1984 dir. George Gage

Garfield, B.
Gun Down
Last Hard Man, The
FOX (US) 1976
dir. Andrew V. McLaglen

Garfield, B.
Hopscotch
AVCO (US) 1980 dir. Ronald Neame

Garfield, B.
Necessity
B&E (US) 1988 dir. Michael Miller
TV(US)

Garfield, B.
Relentless
CBS ENT (US) 1977 dir. Lee H. Katzin
TV(US)

Garfield, B.
Wild Times
METRO (US) 1980
dir. Richard Compton
TVSe(US)

Garfield, L.
Black Jack
ENT (GB) 1979 dir. Kenneth Loach

Garfield, L.
Strange Affair of Adelaide Harris, The
BBC (GB) 1979 dir. Paul Stone
TVSe(GB)

Garland, A.
Beach, The
FOX (US) 2000 dir. Danny Boyle

Garner, A.
Elidor
BBC (GB) 1995 dir. John Reardon
TVSe(GB)

Garner, H.
Monkey Grip
PAV (Aust) 1982 dir. Ken Cameron

Garnett, D.
Sailor's Return, The
ARIEL (GB) 1978 dir. Jack Gold

Garrett, W.
Man in the Mirror, The
WARDOUR (GB) 1936
dir. Maurice Elvey

Garrison, J.
On the Trail of the Assassins: My
Investigation and Prosecution of the
Murder of President Kennedy
JFK
WAR (US) 1991 dir. Oliver Stone

Garstin, C.
China Seas
MGM (US) 1935 dir. Tay Garnett

Garth, D.
Four Men and a Prayer
FOX (US) 1938 dir. John Ford

Garve, A.
Death and the Sky Above
Two-Letter Alibi
BL (GB) 1962 dir. Robert Lynn

Garve, A.
Megstone Plot, The
Touch of Larceny, A
PAR (GB) 1959 dir. Guy Hamilton

Garwood, J.
For the Roses
Rose Hill
HALLMARK (US) 1997 dir. Christopher
Cain
TV(US)

Gary, R.
Clair de Femme
GAU (Fr/It/Ger) 1979 dir. Costa-
Gavras

Gary, R.
Colours of the Day, The
Man Who Understood Women
FOX (US) 1959 dir. Nunnally Johnson

Gary, R.
Dance of Genghis Cohn, The
Genghis Cohn
BBC/A&E (GB) 1994 dir. Elijah
Moshinsky
TV(GB)

Gary, R.
Lady L
MGM (Fr/It/US) 1965
dir. Peter Ustinov

Gary, R.
Promisse de l'aube, La
Promise at Dawn
AVCO (US/Fr) 1970 dir. Jules Dassin

Gary, R.
Roots of Heaven, The
FOX (US) 1958 dir. John Huston

Gary, R.
Tête Coupable, La
Impostors, The
STUDIO CANAL+ (Fr) 1994 dir.
Frederic Blum

Gary, R.
White Dog
PAR (US) 1982 dir. Samuel Fuller

Gary, R.
Your Ticket is No Longer Valid
CAROLCO (Can) 1980
dir. George Kaczender

Gash, J.
Lovejoy
BBC (GB) 1990 dir. Ken Hannam, David
Reynolds
TV(GB)

Gaskell, E.
Cousin Phillis
BBC (GB) 1982 dir. Mike Healey
TVSe(GB)

Gaskell, E.
Cranford
BBC (GB) 1972 dir. Hugh David
TVSe(GB)

Gaskell, E.
North and South
BBC (GB) 1975 dir. Rodney Bennett
TVSe(GB)

Gaskell, E.
Wives and Daughters
BBC (GB) 1971 dir. Hugh David
TVSe(GB)

Gaskell, J.
All Neat in Black Stockings
WAR (GB) 1968
dir. Christopher Morahan

Gaskin, C.
File on Devlin, The
COMPASS (US) 1969
dir. George Schaefer
TV(US)

Gates, P.
My Husband, Rock Hudson
Rock Hudson
KON-SAN (US) 1990 dir. John Nicolella
TV(US)

Gates, T.
Cloud Waltzing
AVV/YTV (US/GB) 1987
dir. Gordon Flemyng
TV(GB/US)

Gattegno, J.-P.
Neutralité Malveillante
Passage à L'acte
ARENA (Fr) 1996 dir. Francis Girod

Gaulden, R.
Five Card Stud
PAR (US) 1968 dir. Henry Hathaway

Gay, J.
Beggar's Opera, The
P
BL (GB) 1952 dir. Peter Brook
M

Gay, J.
Beggar's Opera, The
P
BARRANDOV (Czech) 1991
dir. Jiri Menzel

Gazzo, M. V.
Hatful of Rain, A
P
FOX (US) 1957 dir. Fred Zinnemann

Gearino, G. D.
What the Deaf-Mute Heard
What the Deaf Man Heard
HALLMARK (US) 1997 dir. John Kent
Harrison
TV(US)

Gebler, E.
Plymouth Adventure, The
MGM (US) 1952 dir. Clarence Brown

Gebler, E.
Shall I Eat You Now?

P
Hoffman
ABP (GB) 1970 dir. Alvin Rackoff

Geer, A.
Sea Chase, The

WAR (US) 1955 dir. John Farrow

Gegauff, P.
Clé de la Rue Saint Nicolas, La

À Double Tour
PARIS/PANI (Fr/It) 1959
dir. Claude Chabrol

Gehrig, E. and Durso, J.
My Luke and I

Love Affair, A: The Eleanor and Lou Gehrig Story
FRIES (US) 1978 dir. Fielder Cook
TV(US)

Gelbart, L.
Mastergate

P
SHOWTIME (US) 1992 dir. Michael Engler
TV(US)

Gelber, J.
Connection, The

P
CONT (US) 1961 dir. Shirley Clarke

Geller, S.
She Let Him Continue

Pretty Poison
FOX (US) 1968 dir. Noel Black
WESTGATE (US) 1996 dir. David Burton Morris
TV(US)

Genet, J.
Balcony, The

P
BL (US) 1963 dir. Joseph Strick

Genet, J.
Maids, The

P
ELY LANDAU (GB) 1974
dir. Christopher Miles

Genet, J.
Querelle de Brest

Querelle
TRIUMPH (Fr/Ger) 1983
dir. Rainer Werner Fassbinder

Gent, P.
North Dallas Forty

PAR (US) 1979 dir. Ted Kotcheff

Geoffrey, W. and Mitchell, B.
Perfect Woman, The

P
GFD (GB) 1949 dir. Bernard Knowles

George, E.
Leather Boys, The

BL (GB) 1963 dir. Sidney J. Furie

George, J.
My Side of the Mountain

PAR (US/Can) 1969 dir. James B. Clark

George, M.
Memoirs of Cleopatra, The

Cleopatra
HALLMARK (US) 1999 dir. Franc Roddam
TVSe(US)

George, P.
Red Alert

Dr Strangelove; Or How I Learned to Stop Worrying and Love the Bomb
COL (GB) 1963 dir. Stanley Kubrick

George, R.
Percy and Rose

P
Passion
BEYOND (Aust) 1999 dir. Peter Duncan

German, Y.
Trial on the Road/Checkpoint
LENFILM (USSR) 1971 dir. Alexei German

Gershe, L.
Butterflies are Free
P
COL (US) 1972 dir. Milton Katselas

Gershwin, G., Gershwin, I. and Heyward, D.
Porgy and Bess
P
GOLDWYN (US) 1959
dir. Otto Preminger
M

Gerstner, H.
Die Bruder Grimm
Wonderful World of the Brothers Grimm, The
MGM (US) 1962 dir. Henry Levin, George Pal
Ch

Geyer, S.
By Candlelight
P
UN (US) 1933 dir. James Whale

Giancana, A. and Renner, T. C.
Mafia Princess
P
GROUP W (US) 1986 dir. Robert Collins
TV(US)

Giannunzio, M.
Last Tag
P
Falling for You
BBS (US) 1995 dir. Eric Till
TV(US)

Gibbon, L. G.
Cloud Howe
BBC (GB) 1982 dir. Tom Cotter
TVSe(GB)

Gibbon, L. G.
Grey Granite
BBC (GB) 1983 dir. Tom Cotter
TVSe(GB)

Gibbon, L. G.
Sunset Song
BBC (GB) 1971 dir. Moira Armstrong
TVSe(GB)

Gibbons, K.
Ellen Foster
HALLMARK (US) 1997 dir. John Erman
TV(US)

Gibbons, S.
Cold Comfort Farm
BBC (GB) 1971 dir. Peter Hammond
TV(GB)
BBC (GB) 1995 dir. John Schlesinger
TV(GB)

Gibbs, A. H.
Young Apollo
P
Men of Tomorrow
PAR (GB) 1932 dir. Leontine Sagan

Gibbs, G. and Dudley, E. L.
Voltaire
WAR (US) 1933 dir. John Adolfi

Gibson, I.
Assassination of Federico Garcia Lorca, The; Federico Garcia Lorca: A Life
Disappearance of Garcia Lorca, The
STUDIO CANAL+ (Fr/Sp/US) 1997
dir. Marcos Zurinaga

Gibson, W.
Cobweb, The
MGM (US) 1955 dir. Vincente Minnelli

Gibson, W.
Miracle Worker, The

P
UA (US) 1962 dir. Arthur Penn
KATZ-GALLIN (US) 1979
dir. Paul Aaron
TV(US)
DISNEY (US) 2000 dir. Nadia Tass
TV(US)

Gibson, W.
Monday After the Miracle

P
CBS (US) 1998 dir. Daniel Petrie
TV(US)

Gibson, W.
Two for the Seesaw

P
UA (US) 1962 dir. Robert Wise

Gide, A.
Symphonie Pastorale, La

GIBE (Fr) 1946 dir. Jean Delannoy

Gielgud, V. H.
Death at Broadcasting House

PHOENIX (GB) 1934
dir. Reginald Denham

Gies, M. and Gold, A. L.
Anne Frank Remembered: The Story of the Woman Who Helped to Hide the Frank Family

Attic, The: The Hiding of Anne Frank
TELECOM/YTV (US/GB) 1988
dir. John Erman
TV(GB/US)

Gifford, B.
59 Degrees and Raining: The Story of Perdita Durango

Perdita Durange
LOLAFILMS (Mex/US/Sp) 1997 dir.
Alex de la Iglesia

Gifford, B.
Wild at Heart

GOLDWYN (US) 1990 dir. David Lynch

Gifford, T.
Glendower Legacy, The

Dirty Tricks
FILMPLAN (Can) 1980 dir. Alvin
Rakoff

Gignoux, R.
Le Fruit Vert

P
Between Us Girls
UN (US) 1942 dir. Henry Koster

Gilbert, A.
Vanishing Corpse, The

They Met in the Dark
RANK (GB) 1943 dir. Karel Lamac

Gilbert, A.
Woman in Red, The

My Name is Julia Ross
COL (US) 1945 dir. Joseph H. Lewis

Gilbert, E.
Hot Nocturne

P
Blues in the Night
WAR (US) 1941 dir. Anatole Litvak

Gilbert, M.
Death has Deep Roots

Guilty?
GN (GB) 1956 dir. Edmund Greville

Gilbert, M.
Death in Captivity

Danger Within
BL (GB) 1958 dir. Don Chaffey
US title: Breakout

Gilbert, M.
Winston Churchill—The Wilderness Years
SOUTHERN TV (GB) 1981 dir.
Ferdinand Fairfax
TVSe(GB)

Gilbert, S.
Ratman's Notebook
Willard
CINERAMA (US) 1971 dir. Daniel Mann

Gilbert, Sir W. S. and Sullivan, Sir A.
Mikado, The
P
UN (GB) 1939 dir. Victor Scheitzinger
M

Gilbert, Sir W. S. and Sullivan, Sir A.
Ruddigore
P
GALA (GB) 1967 dir. Joy Batchelor
A, M

Gilbreth, Jr., F. B. and Carey, E.
Belles on Their Toes
FOX (US) 1952 dir. Henry Levin

Gilbreth, Jr., F. B. and Carey, E. G.
Cheaper by the Dozen
FOX (US) 1950 dir. Walter Lang

Gilden, K. B.
Hurry Sundown
PAR (US) 1967 dir. Otto Preminger

Gill, T.
Gentlemen of the Jungle
Tropic Zone
PAR (US) 1952 dir. Lewis R. Foster

Gillham, B.
Place to Hide, A
Break Out
CFTF (GB) 1983 dir. Frank Godwin
US title: Breakout
Ch

Gillies, J.
Cash on Demand
P
COL (GB) 1963 dir. Quentin Lawrence

Gilman, D.
Ghost in the Machine
P
Bad Manners
DAVIS (US) 1997 dir. Jonathan Kaufer

Gilman, D.
Palm for Mrs. Pollifax, A
Unexpected Mrs. Pollifax, The
WORLD 2000 (US) 1999 dir. Anthony Shaw
TV(US)

Gilman, D.
Unexpected Mrs. Pollifax, The
Mrs. Pollifax—Spy
UA (US) 1971 dir. Leslie Martinson

Gilman, P.
Diamond Head
COL (US) 1962 dir. Guy Green

Gilmore, J.
Rattlers
Rattled
GT FALLS (US) 1996 dir. Tony Randel
TV(US)

Gilmore, M.
Shot in the Heart
HBO (US) 2001 dir. Agnieszka Holland
TV(US)

Gilpatric, G.
Action in the North Atlantic
WAR (US) 1943 dir. Lloyd Bacon

Gilroy, F. D.
From Noon Till Three
UA (US) 1976 dir. Frank D. Gilroy

Gilroy, F. D.
Only Game in Town, The
P
FOX (US) 1969 dir. George Stevens

Gilroy, F. D.
Subject was Roses, The
P
MGM (US) 1968 dir. Ulu Grosbard

Gingher, M.
Bobby Rex's Greatest Hit
Just My Imagination
LORIMAR TV (US) 1992 dir. Jonathan
Sanger
TV(US)

Ginsbury, N.
First Gentleman, The
P
COL (GB) 1948 dir. Alberto Cavalcanti
US title: Affairs of a Rogue

Giono, J.
Ames Fortes, Les
STUDIO CANAL+ (Fr/Bel) 2001 dir.
Raoul Ruiz

Giono, J.
Angele
INTERAMA (Fr) 1934
dir. Marcel Pagnol

Giono, J.
Harvest
PAGNOL (Fr) 1937
dir. Marcel Pagnol

Giono, J.
Hussard Sur le Toit, Le
Horseman on the Roof, The
STUDIO CANAL+ (Fr) 1995 dir. Jean-
Paul Rappeneau

Giono, J.
Jean le Bleu
Femme du Boulanger, La
PAGNOL (Fr) 1938 dir. Marcel Pagnol

Giordano, M.
Black Box
Experiment, Das
FANES (Ger) 2001 dir. Oliver
Hirschbiegel

Giovanni, J.
Hole, The
PLAY ART (Fr/It) 1959
dir. Jacques Becker

Giovanni, J.
**Secret Gardens in My Father's Heart,
The**
Mon Père ... Il m'a Sauvé la Vie
STUDIO CANAL+ (Fr) 2001 dir. Jose
Giovanni

Giovanni, P.
Crucifer of Blood
P
AGAMEMNON (US) 1991
dir. Fraser Heston
TV(US)

Gipson, F. B.
Circles Round the Wagon
Hound-Dog Man
FOX (US) 1959 dir. Don Siegel

Gipson, F. B.
Old Yeller
DISNEY (US) 1957
dir. Robert Stevenson

Gipson, F. B.
Savage Sam
DISNEY (US) 1963 dir. Norman Tokar

Girardoux, J.
Madwoman of Chaillot, The
P
WAR (GB) 1969 dir. Bryan Forbes

Gittelson, C.
Saving Grace
EMBASSY (US) 1986
dir. Robert M. Young

Glasgow, E.
In This Our Life
WAR (US) 1942 dir. John Huston

Glaspell, S.
Brook Adams
Right to Love, The
PAR (US) 1930 dir. Richard Wallace

Glass, F.
Marvin and Tige
CASTLE HILL (US) 1985
dir. Eric Weston

Glass, J. M.
Woman Wanted
MOTION (Can/US) 1999 dir. Kiefer
Sutherland

Glatzle, M. and Fiore, E.
Muggable Mary
Muggable Mary: Street Cop
CBS ENT (US) 1982 dir. Sandor Stern
TV(US)

Glemser, B.
Girl on a Wing
Come Fly with Me
MGM (US) 1963 dir. Henry Levin

Glickman, W. and Stein, J.
Mrs. Gibbons' Boys
P
BL (GB) 1962 dir. Max Varnel

Glitman, R. M.
Ruling Passion, The
High Price of Passion, The
TAFT (US) 1986 dir. Larry Elikann
TV(US)

Gloag, J.
Our Mother's House
MGM (GB) 1967 dir. Jack Clayton

Godber, J.
Bouncers
P
Ritz, The
BBC (GB) 1978 dir. John Godber, Martin
Shardlow
TVSe(GB)

Godber, J.
Up 'n' Under
P
TOUCHDOWN (GB) 1998 dir. John
Godber

Goddard, R.
Into the Blue
CARLTON (GB) 1997 dir. Jack Gold
TV(GB)

Godden, R.
Battle of Villa Fiorita, The
WAR (GB) 1964 dir. Delmer Daves
US title: Affair at the Villa Morita

Godden, R.
Black Narcissus
ARC (GB) 1946 dir. Michael Powell

Godden, R.
Episode of Sparrows, An
Innocent Sinners
RANK (US) 1957 dir. Philip Leacock

Godden, R.
Fugue in Time, A
Enchantment
RKO (US) 1948 dir. Irving Reis

Godden, R.
Greengage Summer, The
RANK (GB) 1961 dir. Lewis Gilbert
US title: Loss of Innocence

Godden, R.
In this House of Brede
TOM (US) 1975
dir. George Schaefer
TV(US)
CHANNEL 4 (GB) 1984
TV(GB)

Godden, R.
Peacock Spring
BBC (GB) 1995 dir. Christopher
Morahan
TV(GB)

Godden, R.
River, The
UA (Ind) 1951 dir. Jean Renoir

Godey, J.
Never a Dull Moment
DISNEY (US) 1967 dir. Jerry Paris

Godey, J.
Taking of Pelham 123, The
UA (US) 1974 dir. Joseph Sargent
MGM TV (US) 1998 dir. Felix E. Alcara
TV(US)

Godey, J.
Three Worlds of Johnny Handsome,
The
Johnny Handsome
TRISTAR (US) 1989 dir. Walter Hill

Godwin, W.
Adventures of Caleb Williams (Or
Things As They Are), The
Caleb Williams
TYNE-TEES (GB) 1983 dir. Herbert
Wise
TVSe(GB)

Goehre, F.
St. Pauli Nacht
HAGER MOSS (Ger) 1999 dir.
Sonke Wortmann

Goethe, J. W.
Faust
CNC/BBC (Czech/GB/Fr) 1994 dir.
Ernst Gossner, Jan Svankmajer

Goetz, C.
Dr. Praetorius
P
People Will Talk
FOX (US) 1951
dir. Joseph L. Mankiewicz

Gogol, N. V.
Inspector General, The
P
WAR (US) 1949 dir. Henry Koster

Gogol, N. V.
Taras Bulba
UA (US) 1962 dir. J. Lee Thompson

Gold, H.
Salt
Threesome
CBS ENT (US) 1984 dir. Lou Antonio
TV(US)

Goldberg, Dr. M.
Critical List, The
MTM INC (US) 1978 dir. Lou Antonio
TVSe(US)

Goldberg, V.
Margaret Bourke-White
TNT (US) 1989 dir. Lawrence Schiller
TV(US)

Golden, J. and Strange, H.
After Tomorrow
P
FOX (US) 1932 dir. Frank Borzage

Golding, L.
Mr. Emmanuel
TC (GB) 1944 dir. Harold French

Golding, W.
Lord of the Flies

BL (GB) 1963 dir. Peter Brooke
COL/PALACE (GB/US) 1990
dir. Harry Hook

Goldman, J.
Lion in Winter, The

P
AVCO (GB) 1968 dir. Anthony Harvey

Goldman, J.
They Might be Giants

P
UN (US) 1972 dir. Anthony Harvey

Goldman, W.
Casual Sex

P
Casual Sex?
UN (US) 1988 dir. Genevieve Robert

Goldman, W.
Heat

NEW CENTURY (US) 1987
dir. Dick Richards

Goldman, W.
Magic

FOX (US) 1978
dir. Richard Attenborough

Goldman, W.
Marathon Man

PAR (US) 1976 dir. John Schlesinger

Goldman, W.
No Way to Treat a Lady

PAR (US) 1968 dir. Jack Smight

Goldman, W.
Princess Bride, The

FOX (US) 1987 dir. Rob Reiner

Goldman, W.
Soldier in the Rain

WAR (US) 1963 dir. Ralph Nelson

Goldsmith, B.
Little Gloria ... Happy at Last

METRO (US) 1983 dir. Waris Hussein
TVSe(US)

Goldsmith, C.
Father was a Fullback

P
FOX (US) 1949 dir. John M. Stahl

Goldsmith, C.
What a Life

P
PAR (US) 1939 dir. Theodore Reed

Goldsmith, M. M.
Detour

PRC (US) 1946 dir. Edgar G. Ulmer
ENGLEWOOD (US) 1992. dir. Wade
Williams

Goldsmith, O.
First Wives Club, The

PAR (US) 1996 dir. Hugh Wilson

Golon, S.
Angelique

FRANCOS (Fr/W. Ger/It) 1964
dir. Bernard Borderie

Goncharov, I.
Oblomov

MOSFILM (USSR) 1981
dir. Nikita Milchalkov

Goodchild, G. and Witty, F.
No Exit

P
No Escape
PATHE (GB) 1936 dir. Norman Lee

Goodhart, W.
Generation

P
AVCO (US) 1969 dir. George Schaefer
GB title: Time for Giving, A

Goodin, P.
Take Care of My Little Girl
FOX (US) 1951 dir. Jean Negulesco

Goodis, D.
Burglar, The
COL (US) 1957 dir. Paul Wendkos

Goodis, D.
Burglar, The
Burglars, The
COL (Fr/It) 1971 dir. Henri Verneuill

Goodis, D.
Dark Passage
WAR (US) 1947 dir. Delmer Daves

Goodis, D.
Down There
Shoot the Piano Player
PLEIADE (Fr) 1960
dir. François Truffaut

Goodis, D.
Nightfall
COL (US) 1956 dir. Jacques Tourneur

Goodman, G. J. W.
Wheeler-Dealers, The
Wheeler-Dealers
MGM (US) 1963 dir. Arthur Hiller
GB title: Separate Beds

Goodman, J. E.
Man Who Came Back, The
P
FOX (US) 1930 dir. Raoul Walsh

Goodman, J. E.
Silent Voice, The
P
Man Who Played God, The
WAR (US) 1932 dir. John G. Adolfi
GB title: Silent Voice, The

Goodrich, F. and Hackett, A.
Up Pops the Devil
P
Thanks for the Memory
PAR (US) 1938 dir. George Archainbaud

Goodridge, H. and Dietz, L.
Seal Called Andre, A
Andre
PAR (US) 1994 dir. George Miller

Goodschild, G.
Splendid Crime, The
Public Defender
RKO (US) 1931 dir. J. Walter Ruben

Goodwin, D. K.
Fitzgeralds and the Kennedys, The
Kennedys of Massachusetts, The
ORION TV (US) 1990
dir. Lamont Johnson
TVSe(US)

Goodwin, R.
Leontyne
LEONTYNE/ITV (GB) 1990
dir. Richard Goodwin
TV(GB)

Goodwin, R.
Remembering America: A Voice From the Sixties
Quiz Show
HOLLYWOOD (US) 1994 dir. Robert Redford

Gopegui, B.
Conquista del Aire, La
Razones de Mis Amigos, Las
TORNASOL (Sp) 2000 dir. Gerardo Herrero

Gordon, A.
Minister to Millions
One Man's Way
UA (US) 1964 dir. Denis Sanders

Gordon, A.
Reprisal
COL (US) 1956 dir. George Sherman

Gordon, B.
I'm Dancing as Fast as I Can
PAR (US) 1982 dir. Jack Hofsiss

Gordon, L.
White Cargo
P
BI (GB) 1930 dir. J. D. Williams, A. W. Barnes
MGM (US) 1942 dir. Richard Thorpe

Gordon, M. and Gordon, G.
Case File F.B.I.
Down 3 Dark Streets
UA (US) 1954 dir. Arnold Laven

Gordon, M. and Gordon, G.
Make Haste to Live
REP (US) 1954 dir. William A. Seiter

Gordon, M. and Gordon, G.
Operation Terror
Experiment in Terror
COL (US) 1962 dir. Blake Edwards
GB title: The Grip of Fear

Gordon, M. and Gordon, G.
Undercover Cat
That Darn Cat!
DISNEY (US) 1965
dir. Robert Stevenson
DISNEY (US) 1997 dir. Bob Spiers

Gordon, R.
Captain's Table, The
RANK (GB) 1958 dir. Jack Lee

Gordon, R.
Doctor in the House
GFD (GB) 1954 dir. Ralph Thomas

Gordon, R.
Over 21
P
COL (US) 1945 dir. Alexander Hall

Gordon, R.
Rosie
P
UN (US) 1967 dir. David Lowell Rich

Gordon, R.
Years Ago
P
Actress, The
MGM (US) 1953 dir. George Cukor

Gore-Brown, R.
Key, The
P
WAR (US) 1934 dir. Michael Curtiz

Gores, J.
Hammett
WAR (US) 1982 dir. Wim Wenders

Gorky, M.
Bas-Fonds, Les
P
ALB (Fr) 1936 dir. Jean Renoir

Gorky, M.
Vassa
P
IFEX (USSR) 1983 dir. Gleb Panfilov

Gorman, H.
Suzy
MGM (US) 1936
dir. George Fitzmaurice

Gosling, P.
Fair Game
WAR (US) 1995 dir. Andrew Sipes

Gosling, P.
Fair Game
Cobra
WAR (US) 1986 dir. G. P. Cosmatos

Gottlieb, P.
Agency
CAROLCO (Can) 1981
dir. George Kaczender

Gottlieb, S.
Love Bite
Deadly Love
POWER (US) 1995 dir. Jorge Montesi
TV(US)

Goudge, E.
Green Dolphin Street
MGM (US) 1947 dir. Victor Saville

Gould, H.
Cocktail
TOUCHSTONE (US) 1988
dir. Roger Donaldson

Gould, H.
Double Bang
NEW CITY (US) 2001 dir. Heywood
Gould

Gould, J.
Sins
NEW WORLD (US) 1986
dir. Douglas Hickox
TVSe(US)

Gould, L.
Such Good Friends
PAR (US) 1972 dir. Otto Preminger

Gouzenko, I.
This was my Choice
Iron Curtain
FOX (US) 1948 dir. William Wellman

Grabbe, C. D.
Faust
CNC/BBC (Czech/GB/Fr) 1994 dir.
Ernst Gossner, Jan Svankmajer

Graber, M. E.
Man Inside, The
COL (GB) 1958 dir. John Gilling

Graczyk, E.
Come Back to the Five and Dime,
Jimmy Dean, Jimmy Dean
P
SANDCASTLE (US) 1982
dir. Robert Altman

Grady, J.
Six Days of the Condor
Three Days of the Condor
PAR (US) 1975 dir. Sydney Pollack

Graeme, B.
Suspense
Face in the Night
GN (GB) 1956 dir. Lance Comfort

Graf, O. M.
Stationmaster's Wife, The
TELECUL (Ger) 1983
dir. Rainer Werner Fassbinder

Graff, T.
Grandmother Plays, The
P
Used People
LARGO (US) 1992 dir. Beeban Kidron

Grafton, S.
Lolly Madonna XXX
MGM (US) 1973 dir. Richard C. Sarafian
GB title: Lolly-Madonna War, The

Graham, C.
Bordertown
WAR (US) 1934 dir. Archie Mayo

Graham, C.
Electric Vendetta, The
YTV/A&E (GB) 2001 dir. Peter Smith
TV(GB)

Graham, C.
Faithful Unto Death
YTV/A&E (GB) 1998 dir. Baz Taylor
TV(GB)

Graham, C.
Killings at Badger's Drift, The
YTV/A&E (GB) 1997 dir. Jeremy
Silberston
TV(GB)

Graham, C.
Strangler's Wood
YTV/A&E (GB) 1999 dir. Jeremy
Silberston
TV(GB)

Graham. C.
Written in Blood
YTV/A&E (GB) 1998 dir. Jeremy
Silberston
TV(GB)

Graham, D.
Susan Lenox, Her Fall and Rise
MGM (US) 1931 dir. Robert Z. Leonard
GB title: Rise of Helga, The

Graham, G.
Boys, The
P
ARENAFILM (Aust) 1999 dir. Rowan
Woods

Graham, J.
Wrath of God, The
MGM (US) 1972 dir. Ralph Nelson

Graham, M.
Just Like the Pom Pom Girls
P
Sinful Life, A
NEW LINE (US) 1989
dir. William Schreiner

Graham, R. L. and Gill, D.
Dove, The
EMI (US) 1974 dir. Charles Jarrot

Graham, S. and Frank, G.
Beloved Infidel
FOX (US) 1959 dir. Henry King

Graham, W.
Forgotten Story, The
HTV (GB) 1983 dir. John Jacobs
TV(GB)

Graham, W.
Fortune is a Woman
COL (GB) 1956 dir. Sidney Gilliatt
US title: She Played with Fire

Graham, W.
Marnie
UI (US) 1964 dir. Alfred Hitchcock

Graham, W.
Night Without Stars
GFD (GB) 1951 dir. Anthony Pelissier

Graham, W.
Walking Stick, The
MGM (GB) 1970 dir. Eric Till

Graham, W. and Taylor, V.
Take My Life
EL (GB) 1947 dir. Ronald Neame

Graham, W. R.
Poldark; Demelza; Jeremy Poldark; Warleggan

Poldark
BBC (GB) 1975 dir. Paul Annett,
Christopher Barry, Kenneth Ives
TVSe(GB)

Grahame, K.
Wind in the Willows, The
ALLIED FILMMAKERS (GB) 1995 dir.
Terry Jones
Ch

Grammaticus, S.
Denmark Chronicle

Prince of Jutland
MIRAMAX (Neth/GB) 1994 dir. Gabriel
Axel

Grange, J.-C.
Rivieres Pourpres

Crimson Rivers, The
STUDIO CANAL+ (Fr) 2000 dir.
Mathieu Kassavitz

Granger, K. R. G.
Ten Against Caesar
Gun Fury
COL (US) 1953 dir. Raoul Walsh

Grant, N.
Dusty Ermine
P
TWICKENHAM (GB) 1938
dir. Bernard Vorhaus

Grant, N.
Nelson Touch, The
P
Man of Affairs
GAU (GB) 1937 dir. Herbert Mason
US title: His Lordship

Grass, G.
Tin Drum, The
UA (Ger/Fr) 1979
dir. Volker Schlöndorff

Graves, R.
I, Claudius
BBC (GB) 1976 dir. Herbert Wise
TVSe(GB)

Gray, D. and McCarty-Baker, A.
Florentine, The
P
BCB (US) 1999 dir. Nick Stagliano

Gray, M. and Gallo, M.
For Those I Loved
GALA (Can/Fr) 1983 dir. Robert Enrico
BBC (GB) 1991 dir. Robert R. Enrico
TV(GB)

Gray, S.
Butley
P
SEVEN KINGS (GB/US) 1973
dir. Harold Pinter

Gray, S. E. and Milton, P. R.
Search for Beauty
P
PAR (US) 1934 dir. Erle C. Kenton

Graziano, R.
Somebody Up There Likes Me
MGM (US) 1956 dir. Robert Wise

Green, B.
Soldier of Fortune Murders, The
When Love Kills: The Seducation of John Hearn
ALEXANDER-ENRIGHT (US) 1993 dir.
Larry Elikann
TVSe(US)

Green, C.
Commitments
ARABESQUE FILMS (US) 2001 dir.
Carol Mayes
TV(US)

Green, F. L.
Lost Man, The
UN (US) 1969 dir. Robert Alan Arthur

Green, F. L.
Odd Man Out
TC (GB) 1947 dir. Carol Reed
US title: Gang War

Green, F. L.
On the Night of the Fire
GFD (GB) 1939
dir. Brian Desmond Hurst
US title: Fugitive, The

Green, G.
Hostage Heart, The
MGM (US) 1977 dir. Bernard McEverty
TV(US)

Green, G.
Last Angry Man, The
COL (US) 1959 dir. Daniel Mann
COL (US) 1974 dir. Jerrold Freedman
TV(US)

Green, G.
Tourist
FOX (US) 1980 dir. Jeremy Summers
TV(US)

Green, G. D.
Caveman's Valentine, The
UN (US) 2001 dir. Kasi Lemmons

Green, G. D.
Juror, The
COL (US) 1996 dir. Brian Gibson

Green, H.
Loving
SAMSON (GB) 1995 dir. Diarmuid
Lawrence
TV(GB)

Green, J.
Life for Ruth
P
RANK (GB) 1962 dir. Basil Dearden
US title: Condemned to Life

Green, J.
Murder Mistaken
P
Cast a Dark Shadow
EROS (GB) 1955 dir. Lewis Gilbert

Green, L.
Mathilda Shouted Fire
P
Midnight Lace
UN (US) 1960 dir. David Miller
UN TV (US) 1981 dir. Ivan Nagy
TV(US)

Green, P.
House of Connelly, The
P
Carolina
FOX (US) 1934 dir. Henry King
GB title: House of Connelly

Greenan, R. H.
Secret Life of Algernon Pendleton, The
Secret Life of Algernon, The
MARANO (Can/GB) 1997 dir. Charles Jarrot

Greenberg, J.
I Never Promised You a Rose Garden
NEW WORLD (US) 1977
dir. Anthony Page

Greenberg, J.
In This Sign
Love is Never Silent
M. REES (US) 1985 dir. Joseph Sargent
TV(US)

Greenburg, D.
Love Kills
Deadly Vision, A
HILL-FIELDS (US) 1997 dir. Bill Norton
TV(US)

Greenburg, D.
Nanny, The
Guardian, The
UN (US) 1990 dir. William Friedkin

Greenburg, D.
Philly
Private Lessons
J. FARLEY (US) 1981 dir. Alan Myerson

Greene, B.
Summer of My German Soldier
HIGHGATE (US) 1978
dir. Michael Tuchner
TV(US)

Greene, G.
Across the Bridge
RANK (GB) 1957 dir. Ken Annakin

Greene, G.
Across the Bridge
Double Take
TOUCHSTONE (US) 2001 dir. George
Gallo

Greene, G.
Basement Room, The
Fallen Idol, The
FOX (GB) 1948 dir. Carol Reed
US title: Lost Illusion, The

Greene, G.
Brighton Rock
AB (GB) 1947 dir. John Boulting
US title: Young Scarface

Greene, G.
Comedians, The
MGM (US/Fr) 1967 dir. Peter Glenville

Greene, G.
Confidential Agent
WAR (US) 1945 dir. Herman Shumlin

Greene, G.
Doctor Fisher of Geneva
BBC (GB) 1984
dir. Michael Lindsay-Hogg
TV(GB)

Greene, G.
End of the Affair, The
COL (GB) 1954 dir. Edward Dmytryk
COL (GB/US) 1999 dir. Neil Jordan

Greene, G.
England Made Me
HEMDALE (GB) 1972 dir. Peter Duffell

Greene, G.
Gun For Sale, A
Short Cut to Hell
PAR (US) 1957 dir. James Cagney

Greene, G.
Gun for Sale, A
This Gun for Hire
PAR (US) 1942 dir. Frank Tuttle
BBK (US) 1991 dir. Lou Antonio
TV(US)

Greene, G.
Heart of the Matter
BL (GB) 1953
dir. George More O'Ferrall

Greene, G.
Honorary Consul, The
PAR (GB) 1983 dir. John Mackenzie
US title: Beyond the Limit

Greene, G.
Human Factor, The
RANK (GB) 1979 dir. Otto Preminger

Greene, G.
Loser Takes All
BL (GB) 1956 dir. Ken Annakin

Greene, G.
Loser Takes All

Strike It Rich
BRIT SCREEN (GB) 1990
dir. James Scott

Greene, G.
Man Within, The

GFD (GB) 1947 dir. Bernard Knowles
US title: Smugglers, The

Greene, G.
May We Borrow Your Husband?

ITV (GB) 1986 dir. Bob Mahoney
TV(GB)

Greene, G.
Ministry of Fear

PAR (US) 1944 dir. Fritz Lang

Greene, G.
Our Man in Havana

COL (GB) 1959 dir. Carol Reed

Greene, G.
Power and the Glory, The

Fugitive, The
RKO (US) 1947 dir. John Ford

Greene, G.
Quiet American, The

UA (US) 1957 dir. Joseph L. Mankiewicz

Greene, G.
Stamboul Train

Orient Express
FOX (US) 1934 dir. Paul Martin

Greene, G.
Tenth Man, The

ROSEMONT (US/GB) 1988
dir. Jack Gold
TV(GB/US)

Greene, G.
Third Man, The

GFD (GB) 1949 dir. Carol Reed

Greene, G.
Travels with my Aunt

MGM (US) 1972 dir. George Cukor

Greene, G.
Went the Day Well?

EAL (GB) 1942 dir. Alberto Cavalcanti
US title: Forty-Eight Hours

Greene, S.
Boy who Drank Too Much, The

MTM (US) 1980 dir. Jerrold Freedman
TV(US)

Greene, W.
Death in the Deep South

They Won't Forget
WAR (US) 1937 dir. Mervyn LeRoy

Greene, W.
Lady and the Tramp

DISNEY (US) 1955 dir. Hamilton Luske
A, Ch

Greenfield, I. A.
Tagget

MCA TV (US) 1991 dir. Richard T.
Heffron
TV(US)

Greenwald, H.
Call Girl, The

Girl of the Night
WAR (US) 1960 dir. Joseph Cates

Greenwood, R.
Mr. Bunting at War

Salute John Citizen
BN (GB) 1942 dir. Maurice Elvey

Greenwood, W.
Cure for Love, The

P
BL (GB) 1949 dir. Robert Donat

Greenwood, W.
Love on the Dole
BL (GB) 1941 dir. John Baxter

Greenya, J.
Calendar Girl, Cop, Killer? The Bambi Bembenek Story
VZ SERTNER (US) 1992 dir. Jerry London
TV(US)

Gregor, M.
Bridge, The
FONO (W. Ger) 1959
dir. Bernhard Wicki

Gregor, M.
Verdict, The
Town Without Pity
UA (US/Switz) 1961
dir. Gottfried Reinhardt

Gregory, Lady I. A.
Rising of the Moon, The
WAR (Ire) 1957 dir. John Ford

Gregory, S.
Cormorant, The
BBC (GB) 1993 dir. Peter Markham
TV(GB)

Grendel, F.
Ceremony, The
UA (US/Sp) 1963 dir. Laurence Harvey

Grenville, K.
Dreamhouse
Traps
FILMOPOLIS (Aust) 1994 dir. Pauline Chan

Grenville, K.
Lilian's Story
MOVIECO (Aust) 1996 dir. Jerzy Domaradzki

Gresham, W.
Nightmare Alley
FOX (GB) 1947 dir. Edmund Goulding

Grey, R.
Nightmare of Ecstasy
Ed Wood
TOUCHSTONE (US) 1994 dir. Tim Burton

Grey, Z.
Desert Gold
PAR (US) 1936 dir. James Hogan

Grey, Z.
Fighting Caravans
PAR (US) 1931 dir. Otto Brower, David Burton

Grey, Z.
Forlorn River
PAR (US) 1937 dir. Charles Barton

Grey, Z.
Maverick Queen, The
REP (US) 1956 dir. Joe Kane

Grey, Z.
Riders of the Purple Sage
FOX (US) 1931
dir. Hamilton MacFadden
FOX (US) 1941 dir. James Tinling
ROSEMONT (US) dir. Charles Haid
TV(US)

Grey, Z.
Twin Sombreros
Gunfighters
COL (US) 1947 dir. George Waggner

Grey, Z.
Vanishing American, The
PAR (US) 1925 dir. George B. Seitz

Grey, Z.
West of the Pecos
RKO (US) 1934 dir. Phil Rosen
RKO (US) 1945 dir. Edward Killy

Grey, Z.
Western Union
FOX (US) 1941 dir. Fritz Lang

Grey, Z.
Wildfire
Red Canyon
UN (US) 1949 dir. George Sherman

Grierson, E.
Reputation for a Song
My Lover, My Son
MGM (US/GB) 1970 dir. John Newland

Griffin, T.
Boys Next Door, The
P
HALLMARK (US) 1996 dir. John Erman
TV(US)

Griffith, C.
Papa's Delicate Condition
PAR (US) 1963 dir. George Marshall

Grimaldi, A.
Storia di Enza, La
Ribelle, Lo
RETEITALIA (It) 1993 dir. Aurelio
Grimaldi

Grimble, Sir A.
Pattern of Islands
Pacific Destiny
BL (GB) 1956 dir. Wolf Rilla

Grimm, J. L. K. and Grimm, W. K.
Dancing Princess, The; Cobbler & the Elves, The; Singing Bone, The
Wonderful World of the Brothers Grimm, The
MGM (US) 1962 dir. Henry Levin, George Pal
Ch

Grimm, J. L. K. and Grimm, W. K.
Hansel and Gretel
CANNON (US) 1987 dir. Len Talan
Ch

Grimm, J. L. K. and Grimm, W. K.
Red Riding Hood
CANNON (US) 1987 dir. Adam Brooks
Ch

Grimm, J. L. K. and Grimm, W. K.
Rumpelstiltskin
CANNON (US) 1987 dir. David Irving
Ch

Grimm, J. L. K. and Grimm, W. K.
Snow White
CANNON (US) 1987 dir. Michael Berz
Ch

Grimm, J. L. K. and Grimm, W. K.
Snow White and the Seven Dwarfs
DISNEY (US) 1937 dir. David Hand
A, Ch

Grimm, J. L. K. and Grimm, W. K.
Tom Thumb
MGM (GB) 1958 dir. George Pal

Gripe, M.
Glassblower's Children, The
EURIMAGES (Swe) 1998 dir. Anders
Gronkos

Grisham, J.
Chamber, The
UN (US) 1996 dir. James Foley

Grisham, J.
Client, The
WAR (US) 1994 dir. Joel Schumacher

Grisham, J.
Firm, The
PAR (US) 1993 dir. Sydney Pollack

Grisham, J.
Pelican Brief, The
WAR (US) 1993 dir. Alan J. Pakula

Grisham, J.
Rainmaker, The
AM ZOETROPE (US) 1997 dir. Francis
Ford Coppola

Grisham, J.
Time to Kill, A
WAR (US) 1996 dir. Joel Schumacher

Gronin, Y.
Karleks Pris
Rusar I Hans Famn
GOTAFILM (Swe) 1996 dir. Lennart
Hjulstrom

Groom, W.
As Summers Die
TELEPIC (US) 1986
dir. Jean-Claude Tramont
TV(US)

Groom, W.
Forrest Gump
PAR (US) 1994 dir. Robert Zemeckis

Gross, L.
Last Jews in Berlin, The
Forbidden
ENT (GB/Ger) 1984 dir. Anthony Page
TV(GB)

Gross, L. and Carpenter, E. C.
Whistling in the Dark
P
MGM (US) 1941 dir. S. Sylvan Simon

Grossbach, R.
Easy and Hard Ways Out
Best Defense
PAR (US) 1984 dir. Willard Huyck

Grossman, B.
Bachelor Flat
P
TCF (US) 1961 dir. Frank Tashlin

Grossman, V.
City of Bardish, A
Commissar
GORKY (USSR) 1988
dir. Alexander Askoldov

Grosso, N.
Peaches
P
STONERIDGE (Ire) 2000 dir. Nick
Grosso

Grosso, S. and Rosenberg, P.
Point Blank
Question of Honor, A
EMI (US) 1982 dir. Jud Taylor
TV(US)

Groteke, K. and Rosen, M.
Mia & Woody: Love and Betrayal
Love and Betrayal: The Mia Farrow Story
FOX CIRCLE (US) 1995 dir. Karen
Arthur
TVSe(US)

Groult, B.
Vaisseaux de Coeur, Les

Salt on Our Skin
VCL (Ger/Can/Fr) 1992 dir. Andrew Birkin

Groussard, S.
Blood of Israel, The

21 Hours at Munich
FILMWAYS (US) 1976
dir. William A. Graham
TV(US)

Grow, J. W.
Last Contract, The

EURIMAGES (Nor/Swe) 1998 dir. Kjell Sundvall

Grubb, D.
Fools Paradise

Fools Parade
COL (US) 1971 dir. Andrew V. McLaglen
GB title: Dynamite Man from Glory Jail

Grubb, D.
Night of the Hunter, The

UA (US) 1955 dir. Charles Laughton
KON/SAN (US) 1991
dir. David Greene
TV(US)

Gruber, F.
Buffalo Grass

Big Land, The
WAR (US) 1957 dir. Gordon Douglas
GB title: Stampeded

Gruber, F.
Town Tamer

PAR (US) 1965 dir. Lesley Selander

Gruber, F.
Twenty Plus Two

AA (US) 1962 dir. Joseph M. Newman

Gruber, G.
Bitter Sage

Tension at Table Rock
RKO (US) 1956
dir. Charles Marquis Warren

Gruber, R.
Haven: The Dramatic Story of 1,000 World War II Refugees and How They Came to America

Haven
ALLIANCE (US/Can) 2001 dir. John Gray
TVSe(US/Can)

Guare, J.
Six Degrees of Separation

P
MGM (US) 1993 dir. Fred Schepisi

Guareschi, G.
Don Camillo and the Prodigal Son

Return of Don Camillo, The
MIRACLE (Fr/It) 1953
dir. Julien Duvivier

Guareschi, G.
Don Camillo's Last Round

Rizzoli (It) 1955
dir. Carmine Guareschi

Guareschi, G.
Little World of Don Camillo, The

LF (Fr/It) 1952 dir. Julien Duvivier

Guest, J.
Ordinary People

PAR (US) 1980 dir. Robert Redford

Guido, B.
Fall, The

ARG SONO (Arg) 1958
dir. Leopoldo Torre Nilsson

Guido, B.
House of the Angel, The

ARG SONO (Arg) 1957
dir. Leopoldo Torre Nilsson

Guillot, R.
Elephant Master, The
STUDIO CANAL+ (Fr) 1995 dir. Patrick Grandperret

Guillot, R.
Sirga la Lionne
Enfant Lion, L'
STUDIO CANAL+ (Fr) 1993 dir. Patrick Grandperret

Guillou, J.
Den Demokratiske Terroristen
FILMFONDS (Ger/Swe) 1992 dir. Per Berglund

Guillou, J.
Ingen Mans Land; Enda Segern, Den
Hamilton
TV4SWE (Swe/Nor) 1998 dir. Harald Zwart

Guillou, J.
Vendetta
RAI (Swe) 1995 dir. Mikael Hafstrom

Guimard, P.
Choses de la Vie, Les
Intersection
PAR (US) 1994 dir. Mark Rydell

Guimard, P.
Choses de la Vie, Les
LIRA/FIDA (Fr/It) 1969 dir. Claude Sautet

Guitry, S.
Desire
P
FRANCE (Fr) 1995 dir. Bernard Murat

Gulick, B.
Hallelujah Trail, The
UA (US) 1965 dir. John Sturges

Gulick, W.
Bend of the Snake
Bend of the River
UI (US) 1952 dir. Anthony Mann
GB title: Where the River Bends

Gundy, E.
Bliss
Seduction of Miss Leona, The
SCHERICK (US) 1980 dir. Joseph Hardy
TV(US)

Gunn, A.
We of the Never Never
AP (Aust) 1982 dir. Igor Auzins

Gunn, J. E.
Deadlier than the Male
Born to Kill
RKO (US) 1947 dir. Robert Wise
GB title: Lady of Deceit

Gunn, K.
Rain
NZ FILMS (NZ/US) 2001 dir. Christine Jeffs

Gunn, N.
Blood Hunt
BBC (GB) 1986 dir. Peter Barber-Fleming
TV(GB)

Gunn, N. M.
Silver Darlings, The
ALL (GB) 1947 dir. Clarence Elder, Clifford Evans

Gunther, J.
Death Be Not Proud
WESTFALL (US) 1975 dir. Donald Wrye
TV(US)

Gurdjieff, G. I.
Meetings with Remarkable Men
ENT (GB) 1979 dir. Peter Brook

Gurganus, A.
Blessed Assurance: A Moral Tale

Price of Heaven, The
KONIGSBERG (US) 1997 dir. Peter
Bogdanovich
TV(US)

Gurganus, A.
**Oldest Living Confederate Widow
Tells All**

RHI (US) 1994 dir. Ken Cameron
TVSe(US)

Gurney, A. R.
Love Letters

P
MARSTAR (US) 1999 dir. Stanley
Donen
TV(US)

Gurney, A. R.
Middle Ages, The

P
My Brother's Wife
ADAM (US) 1989 dir. Jack Bender
TV(US)

Gutcheon, B.
Still Missing

Without a Trace
FOX (US) 1983 dir. Stanley R. Jaffe

Guterson, D.
Snow Falling on Cedars

UN (US) 1999 dir. Scott Hicks

Guthrie, Jr., A. B.
Big Sky, The

RKO (US) 1952 dir. Howard Hawks

Guthrie, Jr., A. B.
These Thousand Hills

FOX (US) 1958 dir. Richard Fleischer

Guthrie, Jr., A. B.
Way West, The

UA (US) 1967 dir. Andrew V. McLaglen

Guthrie, W.
Bound for Glory

UA (US) 1976 dir. Hal Ashby

Gwaltney, F. I.
Day the Century Ended, The

Between Heaven and Hell
FOX (US) 1956 dir. Richard Fleischer

Haase, J.
Erasmus with Freckles

Dear Brigitte
FOX (US) 1965 dir. Henry Koster

Haase, J.
Me and the Arch Kook Petulia

Petulia
WAR (US) 1968 dir. Richard Lester

Haber, J.
Users, The

SPELLING (US) 1978
dir. Joseph Hardy
TV(US)

Hackett, W.
Espionage

P
MGM (US) 1937 dir. Kurt Neumann

Hackett, W.
It Pays to Advertise

P
PAR (US) 1931 dir. Frank Tuttle

Hackett, W.
Love Under Fire

P
FOX (US) 1937 dir. George Marshall

Hackett, W.
Road House

P
GAU (GB) 1934 dir. Maurice Elvey

Hackney, A.
Private Life

I'm All Right, Jack
BL (GB) 1959 dir. John Boulting

Hackney, A.
Private's Progress, A

BL (GB) 1956 dir. John Boulting

Hadfield, J.
Love on a Branch Line

BBC (GB) 1994 dir. Martyn Friend
TVSe(GB)

Haedrich, M.
Crack in the Mirror

FOX (US) 1960 dir. Richard Fleischer

Hagan, J.
One Sunday Afternoon

P
Strawberry Blonde, The
WAR (US) 1941 dir. Raoul Walsh

Hagan, J.
One Sunday Afternoon

P
PAR (US) 1933 dir. Stephen Roberts
WAR (US) 1948 dir. Raoul Walsh

Hagerup, K.
Markus Og Diana

NORSK (Nor) 1997 dir. Svein
Scharffenberg

Haggard, Sir H. R.
Allan Quatermain

Allan Quatermain and the Lost City of Gold
CANNON (US) 1987 dir. Gary Nelson

Haggard, Sir H. R.
Alan Quatermain

King Solomon's Treasure
BARBER ROSE (Can/GB) 1979
dir. Alvin Rakoff

Haggard, Sir H. R.
King Solomon's Mines

GB (GB) 1937 dir. Robert Stevenson
MGM (US) 1950 dir. Compton Bennett
CANNON (US) 1985
dir. J. Lee Thompson

Haggard, Sir H. R.
King Solomon's Mines

Watusi
MGM (US) 1959 dir. Kurt Neumann

Haggard, Sir H. R.
She

RKO (US) 1935 dir. Irving Pichel
WAR (GB) 1965 dir. Robert Day
CONT (It) 1985 dir. Avi Nesher

Haggart, D.
Life of David Haggart, The

Sinful Davey
UA (GB) 1969 dir. John Huston

Hahakigi, H.
Inochi No Umi

YEE-HA (Jap) 2000 dir. Susumi
Fukuhara

Hailey, A.
Airport

UN (US) 1970 dir. George Seaton

Hailey, A.
Final Diagnosis, The

Young Doctors, The
UA (US) 1961 dir. Phil Karlson

Hailey, A.
Hotel

WAR (US) 1967 dir. Richard Quine

Hailey, A.
Moneychangers, The

PAR TV (US) 1976 dir. Boris Sagal
TVSe(US)

Hailey, A.
Wheels

UN TV (US) 1978 dir. Jerry London
TVSe(US)

Hailey, A. and Castle, J.
Runway Zero-Eight

Terror in the Sky
PAR TV (US) 1971
dir. Bernard L. Kowalski
TV(US)

Hailey, E. F.
Woman of Independent Means, A

FOGWOOD (US) 1995 dir. Robert
Greenwald
TVSe(US)

Haines, W. W.
Command Decision

MGM (US) 1948 dir. Sam Wood

Halbert, F. and Halbert, S.
Bitter Harvest

FRIES (US) 1981 dir. Roger Young
TV(US)

Hale, E. E.
Man Without a Country, The

ROSEMONT (US) 1973
dir. Delbert Mann
TV(US)

Hale, J.
Whistle Blower, The

HEMDALE (GB) 1987
dir. Simon Langton

Halevy, J.
Young Lovers, The
MGM (US) 1964 dir. Samuel Goldwyn, Jr.

Haley, A. and Malcolm X
Autobiography of Malcolm X, The
Malcolm X
40 ACRES (US) 1992 dir. Spike Lee

Haley, A.
Mama Flora's Family
AVNET/KERNER (US) 1998 dir. Peter Werner
TVSe(US)

Haley, A.
Roots
WOLPER (US) 1977
dir. David Greene, Marvin J. Chomsky, John Erman, Gilbert Moses
TVSe(US)

Haley, A.
Roots: The Next Generation
WAR TV (US) 1979 dir. John Erman, Charles Dubin, Georg Stanford Brown, Lloyd Richards
TVSe(US)

Hall, A.
Devilday-Madhouse
Madhouse
EMI (GB) 1974 dir. Jim Clark

Hall, A.
Late Boy Wonder, The
Three in the Cellar
AIP (US) 1970 dir. Theodore J. Flicker

Hall, J.
Ask Agamemnon
Goodbye Gemini
CINDERAMA (GB) 1970 dir. Alan Gibson

Hall, O.
Downhill Racers
Downhill Racer
PAR (US) 1969 dir. Michael Ritchie

Hall, O.
Warlock
FOX (US) 1959 dir. Edward Dmytryk

Hall, P.
Harp That Once, The
Reckoning, The
COL (GB) 1969 dir. Jack Gold

Hall, W.
Long and the Short and the Tall, The
P
WAR (GB) 1960 dir. Leslie Norman
US title: Jungle Fighters

Hall, W.
Return of the Antelope, The
GRANADA (GB) 1985 dir. Eugene Ferguson
Ch, TVSe(GB)

Halley, A.
Strong Medicine
TELEPIC (US) 1986 dir. Guy Green
TVSe(US)

Halliday, M.
Cat and Mouse
EROS (GB) 1958 dir. Paul Rotha

Hambledon, P.
No Difference to Me
No Place for Jennifer
ABP (GB) 1949 dir. Henry Cass

Hamill, P.
Flesh and Blood
PAR TV (US) 1979 dir. Jud Taylor
TVSe(US)

Hamill, P.
Gift, The
PAR TV (US) 1979 dir. Don Taylor
TV(US)

Hamill, P.
Snow in August
TAURUS 7 (US/Can) 2001 dir. Richard
Friedenberg
TV(US/Can)

Hamilton, C.
His Majesty the King
Exile, The
UN (US) 1948 dir. Max Ophuls

Hamilton, D.
Ambushers, The
COL (US) 1967 dir. Harry Levin

Hamilton, D.
Big Country, The
UA (US) 1958 dir. William Wyler

Hamilton, D.
Five Steps to Danger
UA (US) 1956 dir. Henry S. Kesler

Hamilton, D.
Matt Helm
COL TV (US) 1975 dir. Buzz Kulik
TV(US)

Hamilton, D.
Murderer's Row
BL (US) 1966 dir. Henry Levin

Hamilton, D.
Silencers, The
COL (US) 1966 dir. Phil Karlson

Hamilton, D.
Violent Men, The
COL (US) 1955 dir. Rudolph Maté
GB title: Rough Company

Hamilton, D.
Wrecking Crew, The
COL (US) 1968 dir. Phil Karlson

Hamilton, H.
Banjo on my Knee
TCF (US) 1936 dir. John Cromwell

Hamilton, J.
Map of the World, A
OVERSEAS (US) 1999 dir. Scott Elliott

Hamilton, N., Casey, R. and Shute, J.
Return Engagement
P
Fools for Scandal
WAR (US) 1938 dir. Mervyn LeRoy

Hamilton, N.
JFK: Reckless Youth
HEARST (US) 1993 dir. Harry Winer
TVSe(US)

Hamilton, P.
Angel Street
P
Gaslight
BN (GB) 1939 dir. Thorold Dickinson
US title: Angel Street
MGM (US) 1944 dir. George Cukor
GB title: Murder in Thornton Square,
The

Hamilton, P.
Hangover Square
FOX (US) 1945 dir. John Brahm

Hamilton, P.
Rope
P
WAR (US) 1948 dir. Alfred Hitchcock

Hamilton, P.
Street Has a Thousand Eyes, The
Bitter Harvest
RANK (GB) 1963
dir. Peter Graham Scott

Hamilton, V.
Planet of Junior Brown, The
SHOWTIME (US) 1999 dir. Clement
Virgo
TV(US)

Hamilton, W.
All the Little Animals
BRIT SCREEN (GB) 1998 dir. Jeremy
Thomas

Hammer, R.
Beyond Obsession
WAR (US) 1994 dir. David Greene
TV(US)

Hammerstein II, O. and Kern, J.
Music in the Air
P
FOX (US) 1934 dir. Joe May
M

Hammett, D.
Dain Curse, The
POLL (US) 1978 dir. E. W. Swackhamer
TVSe(US)

Hammett, D.
Glass Key, The
PAR (US) 1935 dir. Frank Tuttle
PAR (US) 1942 dir. Stuart Heisler

Hammett, D.
Maltese Falcon, The
Satan Met a Lady
WAR (US) 1936 dir. William Dieterle

Hammett, D.
Maltese Falcon, The
WAR (US) 1941 dir. John Huston

Hammett, D.
Thin Man, The
MGM (US) 1934 dir. W. S. Van Dyke

Hammond, P. J.
Hole in the Wall, The
BBC (GB) 1972 dir. Joan Craft
TVSe(GB)

Hammond, W.
Julie Johnson
P
SHOOTING GALLERY (US) 2001 dir.
Bob Gosse

Hamner, E.
Spencer's Mountain
WAR (US) 1963 dir. Delmer Daves

Hamner, Jr., E.
Homecoming, The—A Christmas
Story
LORIMAR (US) 1974 dir. Fielder Cook
TV(US)

Hampton, C.
Liaisons Dangereuses, Les
P
Dangerous Liaisons
WAR (US) 1988 dir. Stephen Frears

Hampton, C.
Total Eclipse
P
PORTMAN (GB/Fr) 1995 dir.
Agnieszka Holland

Hamsun, K.
Dreamers
Telegraphist, The
NORSK (Den/Nor) 1993 dir. Erik
Gustavson

Hamsun, K.
Hunger
MKT ST (US) 2001 dir. Maria Giese

Hamsun, K.
Last Chapter
Air Si Pur, Un
FRANCE 2 (Fr) 1997 dir. Yves Angelo

Hamsun, K.
Pan
NORDISK (Nor/Den/Ger) 1995 dir.
Henning Carlsen

Hamsun, M.
Regnbuen
Hamsun
NORDISK (Ger/Nor/Den) 1996 dir. Jan
Troell

Han Suyin
Many Splendoured Thing, A
Love is a Many Splendoured Thing
FOX (US) 1955 dir. Henry King

Hanamura, M.
Minazuki
NIKKATSU (Jap) 1999 dir. Rokuro
Mochizuki

Hancock, M. A.
Menace on the Mountain
DISNEY (US) 1970
dir. Vincent McEveety

Handley, M.
Idioglossia
P
Nell
FOX (US) 1994 dir. Michael Apted

Hanes, K.
Fixing Frank
P
MAXIMUM (US) 2001 dir. Michael
Selditch

Hanff, H.
84 Charing Cross Road
COL (US/GB) 1987 dir. David Jones

Hanley, C.
Love From Everybody
Don't Bother to Knock
WAR (GB) 1961 dir. Cyril Frankel
US title: Why Bother to Knock

Hanley, G.
Gilligan's Last Elephant
Last Safari, The
PAR (GB) 1967 dir. Henry Hathaway

Hannay, A.
Love and Other Natural Disasters
Tiger's Tale, A
ATLANTIC (US) 1988
dir. Peter Douglas

Hannum, A.
Roseanna McCoy
RKO (US) 1949 dir. Irving Reis

Hansberry, L.
Raisin in the Sun, A
P
COL (US) 1961 dir. Daniel Petrie

Hansen, R.
Atticus
Missing Pieces
HALMARK (US) 2000 dir. Richard
Kletter
TV(US)

Hansen, T.
Processen mod Hamsun
Hamsun
NORDISK (Ger/Nor/Den) 1996 dir. Jan
Troell

Hapenny, P.
Vig
P
LIONS GATE (US) 1998 dir. Graham
Theakston
TV(US)

Harbach, O. and Hammerstein, II, O.
Rose Marie

P

MGM (US) 1936 dir. W. S. Van Dyke
MGM (US) 1954 dir. Mervyn LeRoy
M

Harbach, O. and Mandel, F.
No No Nanette

P

WAR (US) 1930 dir. Clarence Badger
M
RKO (US) 1940 dir. Herbert Wilcox
M

Harbach, O., Schwab, L. and Mandel, F.
Desert Song

P

WAR (US) 1943 dir. Robert Florey
M
WAR (US) 1953
dir. Bruce Humberstone
M

Harburg, E. Y. and Saidy, F.
Finian's Rainbow

P

WAR (US) 1968 dir. Francis Ford
Coppola
M

Harding, B.
Magic Fire

REP (US) 1956 dir. William Dieterle

Harding, B.
Phantom Crown, The

Juarez
WAR (US) 1939 dir. William Dieterle

Harding, G.
North of Bushman's Rock

Ride the High Wind
BUTCHER (SA) 1966
dir. David Millin

Hardy, J. B.
Everything is Thunder

GB (GB) 1936 dir. Milton Rosmer

Hardy, L.
Grand Duke and Mr. Pimm, The

Love is a Ball
UA (US) 1963 dir. David Swift
GB title: All This and Money Too

Hardy, S.
Forbidden Valley

UN (US) 1938 dir. Wyndham Gittens

Hardy, T.
Far from the Madding Crowd

WAR (GB) 1967 dir. John Schlesinger
GRANADA (GB) 1998 dir. Nicholas
Renton
TVSe(GB)

Hardy, T.
Jude the Obscure

BBC (GB) 1971 dir. Hugh David
TVSe(GB)

Hardy, T.
Jude the Obscure

Jude
BBC (GB) 1996 dir. Michael
Winterbottom

Hardy, T.
Mayor of Casterbridge, The

BBC (GB) 1978 dir. David Giles
TVSe(GB)

Hardy, T.
Mayor of Casterbridge, The

Claim, The
BBC (GB/Fr) 2000 dir. Michael
Winterbottom

Hardy, T.
Return of the Native, The

SIGNBOARD HILL (US) 1994 dir. Jack
Gold
TV(US)

Hardy, T.
Tess of the d'Urbervilles
Tess
COL (Fr/GB) 1981 dir. Roman Polanski

Hardy, T.
Tess of the d'Urbervilles
LWT/A&E (GB) 1998 dir. Ian Sharp
TVSe(GB)

Hardy, T.
Woodlanders, The
BBC (GB) 1970 dir. John Davies
TVSe(GB)
CHANNEL 4 FILMS (GB) 1997 dir. Phil
Agland

Hare, D.
Plenty
P
FOX (US) 1985 dir. Fred Schepisi

Hare, D.
Secret Rapture, The
P
BRIT SCREEN (GB) 1993 dir. Howard
Davies

Harel, I.
House on Garibaldi Street, The
ITC (US) 1979 dir. Peter Collinson
TV(US)

Hargreaves, Sir G.
Atlantis, The Lost Continent
P
MGM (US) 1961 dir. George Pal

Hargrove, M.
Girl He Left Behind, The
WAR (US) 1956 dir. David Butler

Hargrove, M.
See Here, Private Hargrove
MGM (US) 1944 dir. Wesley Ruggles

Harker, H.
Goldenrod
TALENT (US) 1977 dir. Harvey Hart
TV(US)

Harkins, P.
Blackburn's Headhunters
Surrender-Hell
AA (US) 1959 dir. John Barnwell

Harling, R.
Steel Magnolias
P
TRISTAR (US) 1989 dir. Herbert Ross

Harmon, L. M.
Why Me?
LORIMAR (US) 1984 dir. Fielder Cook
TV(US)

Harper, D.
Hijacked
Skyjacked
MGM (US) 1972 dir. John Guillermin

Harr, J.
Civil Action, A
PAR (US) 1998 dir. Steven Zaillian

Harragan, B. L.
Games Mother Never Taught You
CBS ENT (US) 1982 dir. Lee Philips
TV(US)

Harrer, H.
Seven Years in Tibet
TRISTAR (US/Arg) 1997 dir. Jean-
Jacques Annaud

Harris, A.
Follow the Widower
Heads or Tails
CASTLE HILL (Fr) 1983
dir. Robert Enrico

Harris, B. S.
Who is Julia?
CBS ENT (US) 1986
dir. Walter Grauman
TV(US)

Harris, C.
I'd Climb the Highest Mountain
FOX (US) 1951 dir. Henry King

Harris, E.
Johnny Belinda
P
WAR (US) 1948 dir. Jean Negulesco
MILBERG (US) 1958
dir. George Schaefer
TV(US)
LORIMAR (US) 1982 dir. Anthony Page
TV(US)

Harris, F.
On the Trail: My Reminiscences as a Cowboy
Cowboy
COL (US) 1957 dir. Delmer Daves

Harris, J.
Chocolat
MIRAMAX (GB/US) 2000 dir. Lasse Hallstrom

Harris, J.
Sea Shall Not Have Them, The
EROS (GB) 1954 dir. Lewis Gilbert

Harris, M.
Bang the Drum Slowly
PAR (US) 1973 dir. John Hancock

Harris, M.
Hatter Fox
Girl Called Hatter Fox, The
EMI (US) 1977 dir. George Schaefer
TV (US)

Harris, M.
Judas Kiss, The: The Undercover Life of Paul Kelly
Murder Most Likely
ALLIANCE (Can) 1999 dir. Alex Chapple
TV(Can)

Harris, R.
Enigma
JAGGED (GB) 2001 dir. Michael Apted

Harris, R.
Fatherland
HBO (US) 1994 dir. Christopher Menaul
TV(US)

Harris, R.
Selling Hitler
BBC (GB) 1991 dir. Alastair Reid
TVSe(GB)

Harris, R.
Stepping Out
P
PAR (US) 1991 dir. Lewis Gilbert

Harris, T.
Black Sunday
PAR (US) 1977 dir. John Frankenheimer

Harris, T.
Good Night and Good Bye
Street of Dreams
PHOENIX (US) 1988
dir. William A. Graham
TV(US)

Harris, T.
Hannibal
MGM (US/GB) 2001 dir. Ridley Scott

Harris, T.
Red Dragon
Manhunter
CANNON (US) 1986 dir. Michael Mann

Harris, T.
Silence of the Lambs, The
ORION (US) 1991 dir. Jonathan Demme

Harrison, H.
Make Room, Make Room!
Soylent Green
MGM (US) 1973 dir. Richard Fleischer

Harrison, J.
Dalva
GOLDSMITH (US) 1996 dir. Ken
Cameron
TV(US)

Harrison, J.
Farmer
Carried Away
FINE LINE (US) 1996 dir. Bruno Barreto

Harrison, J.
Legends of the Fall
TRISTAR (US) 1994 dir. Edward Zwick

Harrison, J.
Revenge
COL (US) 1990 dir. Tony Scott

Harrison, W.
Burton and Speke
Mountains of the Moon
TRISTAR (US) 1990 dir. Bob Rafaelson

Hart, C.
Dead Man's Island
PAPAZIAN-HIRSCH (US) 1996 dir.
Peter Hunt
TV(US)

Hart, J.
Damage
CHANNEL 4 FILMS (Fr/GB) 1992 dir.
Louis Malle

Hart, M.
Act One
WAR (US) 1963 dir. Dore Schary

Hart, M.
Christopher Blake
P
Decision of Christopher Blake, The
WAR (US) 1948 dir. Peter Godfrey

Hart, M.
Lady in the Dark, The
P
PAR (US) 1944 dir. Mitchell Leisen

Hart, M.
Cellist, The
P
Connecting Rooms
TELSTAR (GB) 1969
dir. Franklin Gollings

Hart, M.
Winged Victory
P
FOX (US) 1944 dir. George Cukor

Harte, B.
Luck of Roaring Camp, The; Outcasts
of Poker Flat, The
California Gold Rush
TAFT (US) 1981 dir. Jack Hively
TV(US)

Harte, B.
Outcasts of Poker Flat, The
RKO (US) 1937 dir. Christy Cabanne
FOX (US) 1952 dir. Joseph M. Newman

Harte, B.
Tennessee's Partner
RKO (US) 1955 dir. Allan Dwan

Hartley, L. P.
Go-Between, The
EMI (GB) 1970 dir. Joseph Losey

Hartley, L. P.
Hireling, The
COL (GB) 1973 dir. Alan Bridges

Hartman, J.
Winter Visitor, A
P
One Special Night
GREEN/EPSTEIN (US) 1999 dir. Roger Young
TV(US)

Hartmann, N. M.
Game for Vultures
NEW LINE (GB) 1979 dir. James Fargo

Hartov, S.
Heat of Ramadan, The
Point Man, The
CAROUSEL (GB/Fr) 2001 dir. John Glen
TV(GB/Fr)

Harvey, F.
Saloon Bar
P
EAL (GB) 1940 dir. Walter Forde

Harvey, J.
Beautiful Thing
CHANNEL 4 FILMS (GB) 1996 dir. Hettie MacDonald

Harvey, W. F.
Beast with Five Fingers, The
WAR (US) 1946 dir. Robert Florey

Harwood, H. M.
Cynara
P
GOLDWYN (US) 1933 dir. King Vidor

Harwood, H. M.
Iron Duke, The
P
GAU BR (GB) 1935 dir. Victor Saville

Harwood, H. M.
Man in Possession, The
P
MGM (US) 1931 dir. Sam Wood

Harwood, H. M.
Man in Possession, The
P
Personal Property
MGM (US) 1937 dir. W. S. Van Dyke
GB title: Man in Possession, The

Harwood, R.
Dresser, The
P
COL (GB) 1983 dir. Peter Yates

Hasford, G.
Short Timers, The
Full Metal Jacket
WB (US) 1987 dir. Stanley Kubrick

Haskins, J. and Mitgang, N. R.
Mr. Bojangles—The Biogaphy of Bill Robinson
Bojangles
MGM TV (US) 2001 dir. Joseph Sargent
TV(US)

Hassel, S.
Wheels of Terror
Misfit Brigade, The
TRANSWORLD (US) 1988 dir. Gordon Hessler

Hassler, J.
Green Journey
Love She Sought, The
ORION TV (US) 1990 dir. Joseph Sargent
TV(US)

Hastings, C.
Bonaventure
P
Thunder on the Hill
UI (US) 1951 dir. Douglas Sirk
GB title: Bonaventure

Hastings, H.
Seagulls over Sorrento

P

MGM (GB) 1954 dir. John Boulting,
Roy Boulting
US title: Crest of the Wave

Hastings, M.
Tom & Viv

P

BRIT SCREEN (GB/US) 1994 dir. Brian
Gilbert

Hastings, P.
Rapture in my Rags

Rapture
FOX (US/Fr) 1965 dir. John Guillermin

Hastings, Sir P.
Blind Goddess, The

P

FOX (GB) 1947 dir. Harold French

Hatch, E.
Road Show

H. ROACH (US) 1941
dir. Gordon Douglas

Hatch, E.
Unexpected Uncle

RKO (US) 1941 dir. Peter Godfrey

Hatch, E.
Year of the Horse, The

Horse in the Grey Flannel Suit, The
DISNEY (US) 1968 dir. Norman Tokar
Ch

Hathorn, L.
Thunderwith

Echo of Thunder, The
HALLMARK (US) 1998 dir. Simon
Wincer
TV(US)

Hatvany, L.
Tonight or Never

P

GOLDWYN (US) 1931
dir. Mervyn LeRoy

Hauser, T.
Execution of Charles Horman, The

Missing
UN (US) 1982 dir. Costa-Gavras

Havel, V.
Beggar's Opera, The

P

BARRANDOV (Czech) 1991
dir. Jiri Menzel

Haviland-Taylor, K.
Failure

Man to Remember, A
RKO (US) 1938 dir. Garson Kanin

Havill, A.
Mother, the Son and the Socialite, The

*Like Mother, Like Son: The Strange Story
of Sante and Kenny Kimes*
CBS TV (US) 2001 dir. Arthur Allan
Seidelman
TV(US)

Havlicek, J.
Helimadoe

KF (Czech) 1994 dir. Jaromil Jires

Hawkes, J.
Blood Oranges, The

KARDANA (US) 1998 dir. Philip Haas

Hawkins, J. and Hawkins, W.
Floods of Fear

RANK (GB) 1958 dir. Charles Crichton

Hawksworth, H. and Schwarz, T.
Five of Me, The

FARREN (US) 1981 dir. Paul Wendkos
TV(US)

Hawley, C.
Cash McCall
WAR (US) 1960 dir. Joseph Pevney

Hawley, C.
Executive Suite
MGM (US) 1954 dir. Robert Wise

Hawthorne, N.
House of the Seven Gables
UN (US) 1940 dir. Joe May

Hawthorne, N.
Scarlet Letter, The
MAJ (US) 1934 dir. Robert G. Rignola
PBS (US) 1979 dir. Rick Hauser
TVSe(US)
CINERGI (US) 1995 dir. Roland Joffe

Hay, I.
Bachelor Born
P
Housemaster
ABPC (GB) 1938 dir. Herbert Brenon

Hay, I.
Sport of Kings, The
P
GAINS (GB) 1931 dir. Victor Saville

Hay, I. and Armstrong, A.
Orders is Orders
P
GAU (GB) 1933 dir. Walter Forde

Hay, I. and Armstrong, A.
Orders is Orders
P
Orders are Orders
BL (GB) 1954 dir. David Paltenghi

Hay, I. and Hall, S. K.
Middle Watch
P
BI (GB) 1930 dir. Norman Walker
AB (GB) 1940 dir. Thomas Bentley

Hay, I. and Hall, S. K.
Midshipmaid, The
P
GB (GB) 1932 dir. Albert de Courville

Hay, I. and Hall, S. K.
Off the Record
P
Carry on, Admiral
REN (GB) 1957 dir. Val Guest

Haycox, E.
Bugles in the Afternoon
WAR (US) 1952 dir. Roy Rowland

Haycox, E.
Canyon Passage
UN (US) 1946 dir. Jacques Tourneur

Haycox, E.
Stage to Lordsburg
Stagecoach
UA (US) 1939 dir. John Ford
FOX (US) 1966 dir. Gordon Douglas
HERITAGE (US) 1986 dir. Ted Post
TV(US)

Hayden T.
One Child
Untamed Love
HEARST (US) 1994 dir. Paul Aaron
TV(US)

Hayden, T.
Murphy's Boy
Trapped in Silence
READER'S DIG (US) 1986
dir. Michael Tuchner
TV(US)

Hayes, A.
Girl on the Via Flaminia, The
Act of Love
UA (US) 1954 dir. Anatole Litvak

Hayes, B. and Hoffer, W.
Midnight Express
COL (GB) 1978 dir. Alan Parker

Hayes, D.
Comedy Man, The
BL (GB) 1964 dir. Alvin Rakoff

Hayes, J.
Desperate Hours, The
PAR (US) 1955 dir. William Wyler
MGM (US) 1990 dir. Michael Cimino

Hayes, J.
Third Day, The
WAR (US) 1965 dir. Jack Smight

Hayes, K. and Lazzarino, A.
Broken Promise
EMI TV (US) 1981 dir. Don Taylor
TV(US)

Hayes, M. and Hayes, J. A.
Bon Voyage
DISNEY (US) 1962 dir. James Neilson

Hayes, N.
Dildo Cay
Bahama Passage
PAR (US) 1941 dir. Edward H. Griffith

Haynes, B.
Great Mom Swap, The
SIGNBOARD HILL (US) 1995 dir.
Jonathan Prince
TV(US)

Haynes, B. and Keene, T.
Spyship
BBC (GB) 1983 dir. Michael Custance
TVSe(GB)

Hayslip, J. and Hayslip, L.
Child of War, Woman of Peace
Heaven and Earth
WAR (US) 1993 dir. Oliver Stone

Hayward, B.
Haywire
WAR (US) 1980 dir. Michael Tuchner
TV(US)

Hazard, L.
Man's Castle
P
COL (US) 1933 dir. Frank Borzage

Head, A.
Mr. and Mrs. Bo Jo Jones
FOX TV (US) 1971 dir. Robert Day
TV(US)

Healey, B.
Waiting for a Tiger
Taste of Excitement, A
MONARCH (GB) 1969 dir. Don Sharp

Hearn, M. P.
Dreamer of Oz, The: The L. Frank Baum Story
ADAM (US) 1990 dir. Jack Bender
TV(US)

Hearon, S.
Life Estates
Best Friends for Life
HALLMARK (US) 1998 dir. Michael Switzer
TV(US)

Hearst, P.
Every Secret Thing
Patty Hearst
ATLANTIC (US) 1988
dir. Paul Schrader

Heath, C.
Behaving Badly
CHANNEL 4 (GB) 1989 dir. David Tucker
TVSe(GB)

Heath, W. L.
Violent Saturday
FOX (US) 1955 dir. Richard Fleischer

Hebden, M.
Eye-witness

Eyewitness
MGM (GB) 1970 dir. John Hough
US title: Sudden Terror

Hebert, J.
Ruby's Bucket of Blood

P
SHOWTIME (US) 2001 dir. Peter
Werner
TV(US)

Hechler, K.
Bridge at Remagen, The

UA (US) 1969 dir. John Guillermin

Hecht, B.
Florentine Dagger, The

WAR (US) 1935 dir. Robert Florey

Hecht, B.
Gaily, Gaily

UA (US) 1969 dir. Norman Jewison
GB title: Chicago, Chicago

Hecht, B.
I Hate Actors!

GALAXY (Fr) 1988
dir. Gerald Krawczyk

Hecht, B.
Miracle in the Rain

WAR (US) 1956 dir. Rudolph Maté

Hecht, B. and MacArthur, C.
Front Page, The

P
His Girl Friday
COL (US) 1940 dir. Howard Hawks

Hecht, B. and MacArthur, C.
Front Page, The

P
Switching Channels
TRISTAR (US) 1988 dir. Ted Kotcheff

Hecht, B. and MacArthur, C.
Front Page, The

P
UA (US) 1931 dir. Lewis Miles
U-I (US) 1974 dir. Billy Wilder

Hecht, B. and MacArthur, C.
Ladies and Gentlemen

P
Perfect Strangers
WAR (US) 1950 dir. Bretaigne Windust
GB title: Too Dangerous to Love

Heckler, J.
Circumstances Unknown

WIL COURT (US) 1995 dir. Robert
Lewis
TV(US)

Hedden, R.
Bodies, Rest and Motion

P
FINE LINE (US) 1993 dir. Michael
Steinberg

Hedges, P.
What's Eating Gilbert Grape

PAR (US) 1993 dir. Lasse Hallstrom

Heggen, T.
Mister Roberts

WAR (US) 1955 dir. John Ford, Mervyn
LeRoy

Heidish, M.
Woman Called Moses, A

H. JAFFE (US) 1978 dir. Paul Wendkos
TVSe(US)

Heilbroner, D.
Death Benefit

CHRIS/ROSE (US) 1996 dir. Mark
Piznarski
TV(US)

Heinlein, R. A.
Puppet Masters, The
HOLLYWOOD (US) 1994 dir. Stuart Orme

Heinlein, R. A.
Starship Troopers
TOUCHSTONE (US) 1997 dir. Paul Verhoeven

Helgason, H.
101 Reykjavik
FILMHUSET (Ice/Den) 2000 dir. Baltasar Kormakur

Helias, P.-J.
Horse of Pride, The
FF (Fr) 1980
dir. Claude Chabrol

Heller, J.
Catch-22
PAR (US) 1970 dir. Mike Nichols

Hellman, G. S.
Peacock's Feather
Night in Paradise, A
UN (US) 1946 dir. Arthur Lubin

Hellman, L. F.
Another Part of the Forest
P
UN (US) 1948 dir. Michael Gordon

Hellman, L. F.
Children's Hour, The
P
These Three
UA (US) 1936 dir. William Wyler

Hellman, L. F.
Children's Hour, The
P
UA (US) 1961 dir. William Wyler
GB title: Loudest Whispers, The

Hellman, L. F.
Little Foxes, The
P
RKO (US) 1941 dir. William Wyler
MILBERG (US) 1956
dir. George Schaefer
TV(US)

Hellman, L. F.
Pentimento
Julia
FOX (US) 1977 dir. Fred Zinnemann

Hellman, L. F.
Searching Wind, The
P
PAR (US) 1946 dir. William Dieterle

Hellman, L. F.
Toys in the Attic
P
UA (US) 1963 dir. George Roy Hill

Hellman, L. F.
Watch on the Rhine
P
WAR (US) 1943 dir. Herman Shumlin

Helseth, H. E.
Chair for Martin Rome, The
Cry of the City
FOX (US) 1948 dir. Robert Siodmak

Helvick, J.
Beat the Devil
ROMULUS (GB) 1953 dir. John Huston

Hely, E.
Smugglers, The
UN TV (US) 1968 dir. Norman Lloyd
TV(US)

Hembert, G.
House of Rothschild, The
P
FOX (US) 1934 dir. Alfred Werker

Hemingway, E.
Farewell to Arms, A

PAR (US) 1932 dir. Frank Borzage
FOX (US) 1957 dir. Charles Vidor

Hemingway, E.
For Whom the Bell Tolls

PAR (US) 1943 dir. Sam Wood

Hemingway, E.
Islands in the Stream

PAR (US) 1977 dir. Franklin Schaffner

Hemingway, E.
Killers, The

UN (US) 1946 dir. Robert Siodmak
UN (US) 1964 dir. Don Siegel

Hemingway, E.
My Old Man

CBS ENT (US) 1979 dir. John Erman
TV(US)

Hemingway, E.
My Old Man

Under My Skin
FOX (US) 1950 dir. Jean Negulesco

Hemingway, E.
Old Man and the Sea, The

WAR (US) 1958 dir. John Sturges
STORKE (US) 1990
dir. Jud Taylor
TV(US)

Hemingway, E.
Short Happy Life of Francis
Macomber, The

Macomber Affair, The
UA (US) 1947 dir. Zoltan Korda

Hemingway, E.
Snows of Kilimanjaro, The

FOX (US) 1952 dir. Henry King

Hemingway, E.
Sun also Rises, The

FOX (US) 1957 dir. Henry King
FOX (US) 1984 dir. James Goldstone
TVSe(US)

Hemingway, E.
To Have and Have Not

Breaking Point, The
WAR (US) 1950 dir. Michael Curtiz

Hemingway, E.
To Have and Have Not

Gun Runners, The
UA (US) 1958 dir. Don Siegel

Hemingway, E.
To Have and Have Not

WAR (US) 1944 dir. Howard Hawks

**Hemingway, J. and
Bonnecarrere, P.**
Rosebud

UA (US) 1975 dir. Otto Preminger

Hemingway, M.
Bridge, The

CHANNEL 4 (GB) 1992 dir. Sydney
Macartney

Hemon, L.
M. Ripois and his Nemesis

Knave of Hearts
ABP (GB) 1954 dir. René Clément
US title: Lover Boy

Hemon, L.
Maria Chapdelaine

SNC (Fr) 1934 dir. Julien Duvivier
ASTRAL (Can/Fr) 1983 dir. Gilles Carle

Hen, J.
Boxer and Death, The

PRAHA (Czech/Ger) 1962 dir. Peter
Solan

Henderson, L.
Sitting Target
MGM (GB) 1972 dir. Douglas Hickox

Henderson, Z.
Pilgrimage
People, The
METRO (US) 1972 dir. John Korty
US(TV)

Hendryx, S.
Last of Jane Austen, The
P
Ladies and the Champ
DISNEY (US) 2001 dir. Jeff Berry

Henley, B.
Crimes of the Heart
P
DELAUR (US) 1986
dir. Bruce Beresford

Henley, B.
Miss Firecracker Contest
P
Miss Firecracker
CORSAIR (US) 1989
dir. Thomas Schlamme

Henmi, Y.
Warm Water Under a Red Bridge
BAP (Jap/Fr) 2001 dir. Shohei Imamura

Henrich, W.
Cross of Iron
AVCO (GB/Ger) 1977
dir. Sam Peckinpah

Henry, H.
Jackdaws Strut
Bought
WAR (US) 1931 dir. Archie Mayo

Henry, J.
Who Lie in Gaol
Weak and the Wicked, The
APB (GB) 1953 dir. J. Lee Thompson

Henry, J.
Yield to the Night
ABP (GB) 1956 dir. J. Lee Thompson
US title: Blonde Sinner

Henry, M.
Misty of Chincoteague
Misty
FOX (US) 1961 dir. James B. Clark

Henry, M.
San Domingo, The Medicine Hat Stallion
Peter Lundy and the Medicine Hat Stallion
FRIENDLY (US) 1977
dir. Michael O'Herlihy
TV(US)

Henry, S.
Murder on the Iditarod Trail
Cold Heart of a Killer, The
HAMDON (US) 1996 dir. Paul
Schneider
TV(US)

Henry, W.
Journey to Shiloh
UI (US) 1966 dir. William Hale

Henry, W.
Mackenna's Gold
COL (US) 1969 dir. J. Lee Thompson

Henry, W.
North Star
WAR (Fr/It/GB) 1996 dir. Nils Gaup

Henry, W.
Who Rides with Wyatt?
Young Billy Young
UA (US) 1969 dir. Burt Kennedy

Henstell, D.
Friend
Deadly Friend
WAR (US) 1986 dir. Wes Craven

Herbert, B.
No Names . . . No Pack Drills
P
Rebel
MIRACLE (Aust) 1986
dir. Michael Jenkins

Herbert, F.
Dune
UN (US) 1984 dir. David Lynch
NEW AMSTERDAM (US/Can) dir.
John Harrison
TVSe(US/Can)

Herbert, F. H.
For Love or Money
P
This Happy Feeling
UN (US) 1958 dir. Blake Edwards

Herbert, F. H.
Kiss and Tell
P
COL (US) 1945 dir. Richard Wallace

Herbert, F. H.
Moon is Blue, The
P
UA (US) 1953 dir. Otto Preminger

Herbert, J.
Deadly Eyes
WAR (US) 1983 dir. Robert Clouse

Herbert, J.
Fluke
MGM (US) 1995 dir. Carlo Carlei

Herbert, J.
Fortune and Men's Eyes
P
MGM (US/Can) 1971 dir. Harvey Hart

Herbert, J.
Haunted
OCTOBER (US/GB) 1995 dir. Lewis
Gilbert

Herbert, J.
Survivor, The
HEMDALE (Aust) 1981
dir. David Hemmings

Herbert, Sir A. P.
House by the River
REP (US) 1950 dir. Fritz Lang

Herbert, Sir A. P.
Water Gypsies, The
SDC (GB) 1932 dir. Maurice Elvey

Herczeg, G., Farkas, K. and Katscher, R.
Wonder Bar
P
WAR (US) 1934 dir. Lloyd Bacon
M

Hergesheimer, J.
Java Head
ATP (GB) 1934 dir. J. Walter Ruben

Herley, R.
Penal Colony, The
No Escape
COL (US) 1994 dir. Martin Campbell

Herlihy, J. L. and Noble, W.
Blue Denim
P
TCF (US) 1959 dir. Philip Dunne
GB title: Blue Jeans

Herlihy, J. L.
All Fall Down
MGM (US) 1961
dir. John Frankenheimer

Herlihy, J. L.
Midnight Cowboy
UA (US) 1969 dir. John Schlesinger

Herman, V.
Coming Out of the Ice
KONIGSBERG (US) 1982
dir. Waris Hussein
TV(US)

Hermann, K. and Rieck, H.
Christiane F
FOX (Ger) 1981 dir. Ulrich Edel

Herrin, L.
Lies Boys Tell, The
Take Me Home Again
VZ/SERTNER (US) 1994 dir. Tom
McLaughlin
TV(US)

Herriot, J.
All Things Bright and Beautiful
It Shouldn't Happen to a Vet
EMI (GB) 1976 dir. Eric Till

Herriot, J.
If Only They Could Talk; It Shouldn't
Happen to a Vet; Lord God Made
Them All, The
All Creatures Great and Small
EMI (GB) 1974 dir. Claude Whatham

Hersey, J.
Bell for Adano, A
FOX (US) 1945 dir. Henry King
Hayward (US) 1967 dir. Mel Ferber
TV(US)

Hersey, J.
Wall, The
TIME-LIFE (US) 1982
dir. Robert Markowitz

Hersey, J.
War Lover, The
COL (GB) 1962 dir. Philip Leacock

Herts, B. R.
Grand Slam
WAR (US) 1933 dir. William Dieterle

Hervey, H.
Lips of Steel
Prestige
RKO (US) 1932 dir. Tay Garnett

Herzog, A.
Swarm, The
WAR (US) 1978 dir. Irwin Allen

Hesse, H.
Siddhartha
LOTUS (US) 1972 dir. Conrad Rooks

Hesse, H.
Steppenwolf
CONTEM (US) 1974 dir. Fred Haines

Heth, E. H.
Any Number Can Play
MGM (US) 1949 dir. Mervyn LeRoy

Heyer, G.
Reluctant Widow, The
GFD (GB) 1950 dir. Bernard Knowles

Heyes, D.
Twelfth of Never, The
Lonely Profession, The
UN TV (US) 1979 dir. Douglas Heyes
TV(US)

Heym, S.
Hostages
PAR (US) 1943 dir. Frank Tuttle

Heymann, C. D.
Poor Little Rich Girl
*Poor Little Rich Girl: The Barbara Hutton
Story*
ITC (US) 1987 dir. Charles Jarrot
TVSe(US)

Heymann, C. D.
Woman Named Jackie, A
L. PERSKY (US) 1991 dir. Larry Peerce
TVSe(US)

Heyward, D. and Heyward, D.
Porgy

P

Porgy and Bess
GOLDWYN (US) 1959
dir. Otto Preminger
M

Hiassen, C.
Strip Tease

Striptease
CASTLE ROCK (US) 1996 dir. Andrew
Bergman

Hichens, R.
Bella Donna

Temptation
UN (US) 1935 dir. Irving Pichel

Hichens, R.
Belladonna

OLY (GB) 1934 dir. Robert Milton

Hichens, R.
Garden of Allah, The

UA (US) 1936 dir. Richard Boleslawski

Hichens, R.
Paradine Case, The

SELZNICK (US) 1947
dir. Alfred Hitchcock

Higgins, G. V.
Friends of Eddie Coyle, The

PAR (US) 1973 dir. Peter Yates

Higgins, J.
Confessional

GRANADA (GB) 1989
dir. Gordon Flemyng
TVSe(GB)

Higgins, J.
Eagle has Landed, The

ITC (GB) 1976 dir. John Sturges

Higgins, J.
Midnight Man

SHOWTIME (US) 1995 dir. Lawrence
Gordon Clark
TV(US)

Higgins, J.
Night of the Fox

DOVE/ITC (US/GB) 1990
dir. Charles Jarrot
TVSe(GB/US)

Higgins, J.
On Dangerous Ground

TELESCENE PROD (Can/GB) 1996 dir.
Lawrence Gordon Clark
TV(Can/GB)

Higgins, J.
Prayer for the Dying, A

GOLDWYN (GB) 1987 dir. Mike
Hodges

Highsmith, P.
Dites-Lui Que Je L'Aime

ART EYE (Fr) 1977 dir. Claude Miller
GB title: This Sweet Sickness
US title: Tell Her I Love Her

Highsmith, P.
Edith's Diary

ZDF (W. Ger) 1986
dir. Hans W. Geissendoerfer

Highsmith, P.
Glass Cell, The

SOLARIS (Ger) 1981 dir. Hans C.
Geissendoerfer

Highsmith, P.
Ripley's Game

American Friend, The
CINEGATE (W. Ger) 1977
dir. Wim Wenders

Highsmith, P.
Strangers on a Train

Once You Meet a Stranger
WAR (US) 1996 dir. Tommy Lee Wallace
TV(US)

Highsmith, P.
Strangers on a Train

WAR (US) 1951 dir. Alfred Hitchcock

Highsmith, P.
Talented Mr. Ripley, The

Purple Noon
HILLCREST (Fr) 1960
dir. René Clément

Highsmith, P.
Talented Mr. Ripley, The

MIRAMAX (US) 1999 dir. Anthony
Minghella

Hijeulo, O.
Mambo Kings Play Songs of Love, The

Mambo Kings, The
WAR (US) 1992 dir. Arne Glimcher

Hill, D.
Intimate Betrayal

DIRECTORS' CIRCLE (US) 1999 dir.
Diane Wynter
TV(US)

Hill, D.
Masquerade

ARABESQUE (US) 2000 dir. Roy
Campanella II
TV(US)

Hill, D.
Private Affair, A

ARABESQUE (US) 2000 dir. Michael
Toshiyuki Uno
TV(US)

Hill, J.
Victor's Big Score

MUSHIKUKI (US) 1992 dir. Brian
Anthony

Hill, R.
Advancement of Learning, An

BBC/A&E (GB) 1996 dir. Maurice
Phillips
TV(GB)

Hill, R.
April Shroud, An

Autumn Shroud, An
BBC/A&E (GB) 1996 dir. Richard
Standeven
TV(GB)

Hill, R.
Bones and Silence

BBC/A&E (GB) 1998 dir. Maurice
Phillips
TV(GB)

Hill, R.
Child's Play

BBC/A&E (GB) 1998 dir. David
Wheatley
TV(GB)

Hill, R.
Clubbable Woman, A

BBC (GB) 1996 dir. Ross Devenish
TV(GB)

Hill, R.
Deadheads

BBC/A&E (GB) 1997 dir. Edward
Bennett
TV(GB)

Hill, R.
Exit Lines

BBC/A&E (GB) 1997 dir. Ross Devenish
TV(GB)

Hill, R.
Killing Kindness, A
BBC/A&E (GB) 1997 dir. Edward
Bennett
TV(GB)

Hill, R.
On Beulah Height
BBC/A&E (GB) 1999 dir. Maurice
Phillips
TV(GB)

Hill, R.
Pinch of Snuff, A
YTV (GB) 1994 dir. Sandy Johnson
TVSe(GB)

Hill, R.
Recalled to Life
BBC/A&E (GB) 1999 dir. Suri
Krishnamma
TV(GB)

Hill, R.
Ruling Passion
BBC/A&E (GB) 1997 dir. Gareth Davies
TV(GB)

Hill, R.
Under World
BBC/A&E (GB) 1998 dir. Edward
Bennett
TV(GB)

Hill, R.
Wood Beyond, The
BBC/A&E (GB) 1998 dir. Edward
Bennett
TV(GB)

Hill, R. B.
Hanta Yo
Mystic Warrior, The
WAR (US) 1984 dir. Richard T. Heffron
TVSe(US)

Hill, R. L.
Evil That Men Do, The
TRISTAR (US) 1984
dir. J. Lee Thompson

Hill, Rev. A. F.
North Avenue Irregulars, The
DISNEY (US) 1978 dir. Bruce Bilson
GB title: Hill's Angels

Hill, S.
Woman in Black, The
CENTRAL FILMS (GB) 1989 dir.
Herbert Wise
TV(GB)

Hill, W.
Long Summer of George Adams, The
WAR TV (US) 1982 dir. Stuart Margolin
TV(US)

Hill, W.
Onionhead
WAR (US) 1958 dir. Norman Taurog

Hillerman, T.
Dark Wind, The
SEVEN ARTS (US) 1991 dir. Errol
Morris

Hilton, J.
Dawn of Reckoning
Rage in Heaven
MGM (US) 1941 dir. W. S. Van Dyke

Hilton, J.
Goodbye Mr Chips
MGM (GB) 1939 dir. Sam Wood
BBC (GB) 1984 dir. Gareth Davies
TVSe(GB)

Hilton, J.
Knight Without Armour
UA (GB) 1937 dir. Jacques Feyder

Hilton, J.
Lost Horizon

Shangri-La
COMPASS (US) 1960
dir. George Schaefer
TV(US)

Hilton, J.
Lost Horizon

COL (US) 1937 dir. Frank Capra
COL (US) 1972 dir. Charles Jarrot
M

Hilton, J.
Random Harvest

MGM (US) 1942 dir. Mervyn LeRoy

Hilton, J.
So Well Remembered

RKO (GB) 1947 dir. Edward Dmytryk

Hilton, J.
Story of Dr. Wassell, The

PAR (US) 1944 dir. Cecil B. De Mille

Hilton, J.
We Are Not Alone

WAR (US) 1939 dir. Edmund Goulding

Hilton, J. and Burnham, B.
Goodbye Mr Chips

P
MGM (GB) 1969 dir. Herbert Ross
M

Himes, C.
Cotton Comes to Harlem

UA (US) 1969 dir. Ossie Davis

Himes, C.
Heat's On, The

Come Back Charleston Blue
WAR (US) 1972 dir. Mark Warren

Himes, C.
Rage in Harlem, A

MIRAMAX (US) 1991 dir. Bill Duke

Hine, A.
Lord Love A Duck

UA (US) 1966 dir. George Axelrod

Hines, A.
Square Dance

ISLAND (US) 1987 dir. Daniel Petrie

Hines, B.
Kestrel for a Knave, A

Kes
UA (GB) 1969 dir. Ken Loach

Hines, D.
Bondage

P
Whore
TRIMARK (GB) 1991 dir. Ken Russell

Hinton, S. E.
Outsiders, The

WAR (US) 1983
dir. Francis Ford Coppola

Hinton, S. E.
Rumble Fish

UN (US) 1983 dir. Francis Ford Coppola

Hinton, S. E.
Tex

DISNEY (US) 1982 dir. Tim Hunter

Hinton, S. E.
That Was Then … This is Now

PAR (US) 1985 dir. Christopher Cain

Hintze, N. A.
You'll Like My Mother

UN (US) 1972 dir. Lamont Johnson

Hintze, N.
Aloha Means Goodbye

UN TV (US) 1974 dir. David Lowell
Rich
TV(US)

Hirschfeld, B.
Aspen
UN TV (US) 1977 dir. Douglas Heyes
TVSe(US)

Hirst, H. H.
Night of the Generals, The
COL/BL (GB) 1966 dir. Anatole Litvak

Hitchcock, J. S.
Trick of the Eye
SIGNBOARD HILL (US) 1994 dir. Ed
Kaplan
TV(US)

Hitchcock, R.
Percy
MGM-EMI (GB) 1971
dir. Ralph Thomas

Hitchens, D. and Hitchens, B.
Fool's Gold
Bande à Part
ANOUCHKA/ORSAY (Fr) 1964
dir. Jean-Luc Godard

Hjortsberg, W.
Falling Angel
Angel Heart
TRISTAR (US) 1987 dir. Alan Parker

Hoag, T.
Night Sins
SCRIPPS HOWARD (US) 1997 dir.
Robert Allan Ackerman
TVSe(US)

Hoban, R.
Mouse and the Child, The
SANRIO (US) 1978 dir. Fred Wolf,
Chuck Swenson
GB title: Extraordinary Adventures of
the Mouse and the Child, The
A, Ch

Hoban, R.
Turtle Diary
RANK (GB) 1985 dir. John Irvin

Hobart, A. T.
Cup and the Sword, The
This Earth is Mine
UI (US) 1959 dir. Henry King

Hobart, A. T.
Oil for the Lamps of China
Law of the Tropics
WAR (US) 1941 dir. Ray Enright

Hobart, A. T.
Oil for the Lamps of China
WAR (US) 1935 dir. Mervyn LeRoy

Hobbs Birnie, L.
Such a Good Boy
Scorn
KINETIC (Can) 2000 dir. Sturla
Gunnarsson
TV(Can)

Hobhouse, A.
Hangover Murders, The
Remember Last Night?
UN (US) 1936 dir. James Whale

Hobson, Jr.. R. P.
Nothing Too Good For a Cowboy
ALLIANCE (Can) 1999 dir. Kari
Skogland
TV(Can)

Hobson, L. Z.
Consenting Adult
STARGER (US) 1985 dir. Gilbert Cates
TV(US)

Hobson, L. Z.
Gentleman's Agreement
FOX (US) 1947 dir. Elia Kazan

Hobson, L. Z.
Tenth Month, The
HAMILTON (US) 1979
dir. Joan Tewkesbury
TV(US)

Hoch, D.
Jails, Hospitals and Hip Hip
P
ARTHOUSE (US) 2000 dir. Mark
Benjamin, Danny Hoch

Hochhuth, R.
Eine Liebe in Deutschland
Love in Germany, A
TRIUMPH (Ger) 1984
dir. Andrzej Wajda

Hocken, S.
Emma and I
Second Sight: A Love Story
TTC (US) 1984 dir. John Korty
TV(US)

Hodges, H.
Fabricator, The
Why Would I Lie?
UA (US) 1980 dir. Larry Peerce

Hodgins, E.
Mr. Blandings Builds his Dream
House
RKO (US) 1948 dir. H. C. Potter

Hodson, J. L.
Return to the Woods
King and Country
WAR (GB) 1964 dir. Joseph Losey

Hoeg, P.
Miss Smilla's Feeling for Snow
Smilla's Sense of Snow
NORDISK (Den/Ger/Swe) 1997 dir.
Bille August

Hoffe, M.
Daybreak
GFD (GB) 1946 dir. Compton Bennett

Hoffe, M.
Lady Eve, The
P
PAR (US) 1941 dir. Preston Sturges

Hoffer, W. and Hoffer, M.
Freefall
Falling From the Sky! Flight 174
HILL-FIELDS (US/Can) 1995 dir. Jorge
Montesi
TV(US/Can)

Hoffman, A.
Practical Magic
WAR (US) 1998 dir. Griffin Dunne

Hoffman, A. and Hoffman, A.
To America with Love: Letters From
the Underground
Steal This Movie
GREENLIGHT (US) 2000 dir. Robert
Greenwald

Hoffman, E. T. A.
Nutcracker and the Mouseking, The
Nutcracker Prince, The
WAR (US) 1990 dir. Paul Schibli
A

Hoffman, E. T. A.
Nutcracker
ATLANTIC (US) 1986 dir. Carroll
Ballard
M

Hoffman, J.
Northern Lights
ALLIANCE (US/Can) 1997 dir. Linda
Yellen
TV(US/Can)

Hoffman, L.
Bar Girls
P
ORION (US) 1994 dir. Marita Giovanni

Hoffman, W. H.
As Is
P
BRANDMAN (US) 1986
dir. Michael Lindsay-Hogg
TV(US)

Hofmann, G.
Kinoerzaehler, Der
BIOSKOPFILM (Ger) 1993 dir.
Bernhard Sinkel

Hohimer F.
Home Invaders, The
Thief
UA (US) 1981 dir. Michael Mann
GB title: Violent Street

Holden, A.
Witness, The
Bedroom Window, The
DELAUR (US) 1987 dir. Curtis Hanson

Holden, E.
Country Diary of an Edwardian Lady,
The
CENTRAL (GB) 1984 dir. Dirk
Campbell
TVSe(GB)

Holder, M.
Give Sorrow Words
Winter Tan, A
TELEFILM (Can) 1987 dir. Louise Clark

Holding, E. S.
Blank Wall, The
Deep End, The
FOX (US) 2001 dir. Scott McGehee,
David Siegel

Holding, E. S.
Blank Wall, The
Reckless Moment, The
COL (US) 1949 dir. Max Ophuls

Holdridge, D.
Death of a Common Man
End of the River, The
GFD (GB) 1947 dir. Derek Twist

Holiday, B.
Lady Sings the Blues
PAR (US) 1972 dir. Sidney J. Furie

Holland, I.
Bump in the Night
RHI (US) 1991 dir. Karen Arthur
TV(US)

Holland, I.
Man Without a Face, The
ICON (US) 1993 dir. Mel Gibson

Holland, M.
Fallen Angel
FOX (US) 1945 dir. Otto Preminger

Hollander, X.
Happy Hooker, The
SCOTIA-BARBER (US) 1975
dir. Nicholas Sgarro

Holles, R.
Siege of Battersea, The
Guns at Batasi
FOX (GB) 1964 dir. John Guillermin

Hollingsworth, J.
Unspeakable Acts
LAN (US) 1990 dir. Linda Otto
TV(US)

Holmes, J. C.
Best Foot Forward
P
MGM (US) 1943 dir. Edward Buzzell
M

Holroyd, M.
Lytton Strachey: A Biography
Carrington
FREEWAY (GB/Fr) 1995 dir.
Christopher Hampton

Holt, F.
Gabriel Horn, The
Kentuckian, The
UA (US) 1955 dir. Burt Lancaster

Holtby, W.
South Riding
UA (GB) 1938 dir. Victor Saville
YTV (GB) 1974 dir. James Ormerod,
Alastair Reid
TVSe(GB)

Holzer, E.
Eye for an Eye
PAR (US) 1996 dir. John Schlesinger

Holzer, H.
Murder in Amityville
Amityville II: The Possession
ORION (US) 1982
dir. Damiano Damiani

Home, W. D.
Chiltern Hundreds, The
P
TC (GB) 1949 dir. John Paddy Carstairs

Home, W. D.
Now Barrabas
Now Barrabas was a Robber
WAR (GB) 1949 dir. Gordon Parry

Home, W. D.
Reluctant Debutante, The
P
MGM (US) 1958 dir. Vincente Minnelli

Homer
Odyssey, The
Ulysses
ARCHWAY (It) 1954
dir. Mario Camerini

Homes, G.
Build My Gallows High
Against all Odds
COL (US) 1984 dir. Taylor Hackford

Homes, G.
Build My Gallows High
Out of the Past
RKO (US) 1947 dir. Jacques Tourneur
GB title: Build My Gallows High

Homes, G.
Forty Whacks
Crime by Night
WAR (US) 1944 dir. William Clemens

Homes, G.
No Hands on the Clock
PAR (US) 1941 dir. Frank McDonald

Honeycombe, G.
Neither the Sea Nor the Sand
TIGON (GB) 1972 dir. Fred Burnley

Honma, Y.
Family Game, The
TOHO (Jap) 1983
dir. Yoshimitsu Morita

Hooke, N. W.
Darkness I Leave You
Gypsy and the Gentleman, The
RANK (GB) 1957 dir. Joseph Losey

Hooke, N. W.
Deadly Record
AA (GB) 1959 dir. Lawrence
Huntington

Hooker, R.
M*A*S*H
FOX (US) 1970 dir. Robert Altman
TVSe(US)

Hoover, J. E.
Persons in Hiding
Illegal Traffic
PAR (US) 1938 dir. Louis King

Hoover, J. E.
Persons in Hiding
Queen of the Mob
PAR (US) 1940 dir. James Hogan

Hoover, J. E.
Persons in Hiding
PAR (US) 1939 dir. Louis King

Hopcraft, A.
Nearly Man, The

P
GRANADA (GB) 1974 dir. John Irvin,
Alan Grint
TVSe(GB)

Hope, A.
Prisoner of Zenda

UA (US) 1937 dir. John Cromwell
MGM (US) 1952 dir. Richard Thorpe
UN (US) 1979 dir. Richard Quine
BBC (GB) 1984 dir. Leonard Lewis
TVSe(GB)

Hope, A.
Prisoner of Zenda, Inc.

SHOWTIMEWORKS (US) 1996 dir.
Stefan Scaini
TV(US)

Hope, E.
Marry the Girl

WAR (US) 1937 dir. William McGann

Hopkins, B.
Intruders

CBS ENT (US) 1992 dir. Dan Curtis
TVSe(US)

Hopkins, J.
This Story of Yours

P
Offence, The
UA (GB) 1972 dir. Sidney Lumet

Hopkins, R.
Cross Currents

Lifeline
USA NETWORK (US) 1996 dir. Fred
Gerber
TV(US)

Hopwood, A.
Gold Diggers, The

P
Gold Diggers of Broadway
WAR (US) 1939 dir. Roy del Ruth

Horgan, P.
Distant Trumpet, A

WAR (US) 1964 dir. Raoul Walsh

Horn, T.
**Life of Tom Horn, Government Scout
& Interpreter**

Tom Horn
WAR (US) 1980 dir. William Wiard

Hornburg, M.
Bongwater

ALLIANCE IND (US) 1998 dir. Richard
Sears

Hornby, N.
High Fidelity

TOUCHSTONE (GB/US) 2000 dir.
Stephen Frears

Horne, K.
Fools Rush In

P
RANK (GB) 1949
dir. John Paddy Carstairs

Horne, K.
Lady Mislaid, A

P
ABP (GB) 1958 dir. David Macdonald

Horniman, R.
Bellamy the Magnificent

Bedtime Story, A
PAR (US) 1933 dir. Norman Taurog

Horniman, R.
Noblesse Oblige

Kind Hearts and Coronets
EAL (GB) 1949 dir. Robert Hamer

Hornung, E. W.
Raffles the Amateur Cracksman

Raffles
UA (US) 1939 dir. Sam Wood

Horovitz, I.
North Shore Fish
P
SHOWTIMEWORKS (US) 1997 dir.
Steve Zuckerman
TV(US)

Horowitz, A.
Falcon's Malteser, The
Just Ask for Diamond
FOX (GB) 1977 dir. Stephen Bayly
US title: Diamond's Edge

Horowitz, S.
Calling Dr. Horowitz
Bad Medicine
TCF (US) 1985 dir. Harvey Miller

Horton, S.
Billionaire Boys Club, The
ITC (US) 1987 dir. Marvin Chomsky
TVSe(US)

Hossein, R. and Dard, F.
Caviar Rouge, Le
GALAXY (Fr/Switz) 1988
dir. Robert Hossein

Hotchner, A. E.
Looking for Miracles
DISNEY (US/Can) 1989
dir. Kevin Sullivan

Hotchner, A. E.
Man Who Lived at The Ritz, The
HG (US) 1988 dir. Desmond Davis
TVSe(US)

Hotchner, A. E.
Sophia Living and Loving: Her Own
Story
Sophia Loren—Her Own Story
EMI (US) 1980 dir. Mel Stuart
TV(US)

Houdyer, P.
Affaire Papin, L'
Murderous Maids
STUDIO CANAL+ (Fr) 2000 dir. Jean-
Pierre Denis

Houellebecq, M.
Extension du Domaine de la Lutte
STUDIO CANAL+ (Fr) 1999 dir.
Philippe Harel

Hough, E.
North of 36
Conquering Horde
PAR (US) 1931 dir. Edward Sloman

Hough, R.
Captain Bligh and Mr Christian
Bounty, The
ORION (GB) 1984 dir. Roger Donaldson

Houghton, S.
Hindle Wakes
P
GB (GB) 1931 dir. Victor Saville
MON (GB) 1952 dir. Arthur Crabtree

Household, G.
Brandy for the Parson
MGM (GB) 1952 dir. John Eldridge

Household, G.
Dance of the Dwarfs
DOVE (Phil/US) 1982 dir. Gus Trikonis

Household, G.
Rogue Male
Man Hunt
FOX (US) 1941 dir. Fritz Lang

Household, G.
Rough Shoot
UA (GB) 1952 dir. Robert Parrish
US title: Shoot First

Household, G.
Watcher in the Shadows
Deadly Harvest
CBS ENT (US) 1972
dir. Michael O'Herlihy
TV(US)

Housman, L.
Consider Your Verdict
P
CHARTER (GB) 1938 dir. Roy Boulting

Housman, L.
Victoria Regina
P
COMPASS (US) 1961
dir. George Schaefer
TV(US)

Housman, L.
Victoria Regina
P
Victoria the Great
RKO (GB) 1937 dir. Herbert Wilcox

Houston, J.
White Dawn, The
PAR (US) 1974 dir. Philip Kaufman

Houston, R.
Monday, Tuesday, Wednesday
Killing Affair, A
HEMDALE (US) 1988
dir. David Saperstein

Howard, C.
Six Against the Rock
GAYLORD (US) 1987 dir. Paul Wendkos
TV(US)

Howard, C.
Arm, The
Big Town, The
COL (US) 1987 dir. Ben Bolt

Howard, E. J.
After Julius
YTV (GB) 1979 dir. John Glenister
TV(GB)

Howard, E. J.
Getting it Right
MEDUSA (US) 1989 dir. Randal Kleiser

Howard, E. J.
Light Years, The; Marking Time
Cazalets, The
BBC (GB) 2001 dir. Suri Krishnamma
TVSe(GB)

Howard, E. J.
Something in Disguise
THAMES (GB) 1982 dir. Moira
Armstrong
TVSe(GB)

Howard, H.
Assignment 'K'
COL (GB) 1968 dir. Val Guest

Howard, L.
Blind Date
RANK (GB) 1959 dir. Joseph Losey
US title: Chance Meeting

Howard, L.
Loving Evangeline
CTV (Can) 1998 dir. Timothy Bond
TV(Can)

Howard, S.
Late Christopher Bean, The
P
Christopher Bean
MGM (US) 1933 dir. Sam Wood

Howard, S.
They Knew What They Wanted
P
Lady to Love, A
MGM (US) 1930 dir. Victor Seastrom

Howard, S.
They Knew What They Wanted
P
RKO (US) 1940 dir. Garson Kanin

Howard, S.
Yellow Jack
P
MGM (US) 1938 dir. George B. Seitz

Howarth, D.
We Die Alone
Nine Lives
NORDS (Nor) 1959 dir. Arne Skouen

Howatch, S.
Penmarric
BBC (GB) 1979 dir. Derek Martinus,
Tina Wakerell
TVSe(GB)

Howe, G. L.
Call it Treason
Decision Before Dawn
FOX (US) 1951 dir. Anatole Litvak

Howe, T.
Painting Churches
P
Portrait, The
GREENWALD (US) 1993 dir. Arthur
Penn
TV(US)

Howker, J.
Nature of the Beast, The
FILM 4 (GB) 1988 dir. Franco Rosso

Howlett, J.
Murder of a Moderate Man
BBC (GB/It) 1985 dir. Robert Tronson
TVSe(GB)

Hoyland, J.
Ivy Garland, The
Out of the Darkness
CFF (GB) 1985 dir. John Krish
Ch

Hoyt, V. J.
Malibu, A Nature Story
Sequoia
MGM (US) 1935 dir. Chester Lyons

Hrabal, B.
Closely Watched Trains
CESK (Czech) 1966 dir. Jiri Menzel

Hubbard, E. and Rowan, A. S.
Message to Garcia, A
FOX (US) 1936 dir. George Marshall

Hubbard, L. R.
Battlefield Earth
FRANCHISE (US) 2000 dir. Roger
Christian

Hubler, R. G.
I've Got Mine
Beachhead
UA (US) 1954 dir. Stuart Heisler

Huch, R.
Der Letste Sommer
Guardian Angel, The
SANDREW (Swe) 1990
dir. Suzanne Osten

Huckaby, E. P.
Crisis at Central High
TIME-LIFE (US) 1981
dir. Lamont Johnson
TV(US)

Hudson, J.
Case of Need, A
Carey Treatment, The
MGM (US) 1972 dir. Blake Edwards

Hudson, J. C. and Abbott, G.
Three Men on a Horse
P
WAR (US) 1936 dir. Mervyn LeRoy

697

Hudson, W. H.
Green Mansions
MGM (US) 1959 dir. Mel Ferrer

Hudson, W. H.
Shepherd's Life, A
Bread or Blood
BBC (GB) 1981 dir. Peter Smith
TVSe(GB)

Huelle, P.
Weiser Dawidek
Weiser
EURIMAGES (Pol) 2001 dir. Wojciech
Marczewski

Huffaker, C.
Badman
War Wagon, The
UI (US) 1967 dir. Burt Kennedy

Huffaker, C.
Flaming Lance
Flaming Star
FOX (US) 1960 dir. Don Siegel

Huffaker, C.
Guns of Rio Conchos
Rio Conchos
FOX (US) 1964 dir. Gordon Douglas

Huffaker, C.
Nobody Loves a Drunken Indian
Flap
WAR (US) 1970 dir. Carol Reed
GB title: Last Warrior, The

Huffaker, C.
Seven Ways from Sundown
UI (US) 1960 dir. Harry Keller

Huggins, R.
Appointment with Fear
State Secret, The
BL (GB) 1950 dir. Sidney Gilliat
US title: Great Manhunt, The

Huggins, R.
Double Take, The
I Love Trouble
COL (US) 1948 dir. S. Sylvan Simon

Hughes, D.
Pork Butcher, The
Souvenir
CIC (GB) 1987 dir. Geoffrey Reeve

Hughes D. B.
In a Lonely Place
COL (US) 1950 dir. Nicholas Ray

Hughes, D. B.
Fallen Sparrow, The
RKO (US) 1943 dir. Richard Wallace

Hughes, D. B.
Ride the Pink Horse
Hanged Man, The
UN (US) 1964 dir. Don Siegel
TV(US)

Hughes, D. B.
Ride the Pink Horse
UI (US) 1947 dir. Robert Montgomery

Hughes, R.
High Wind in Jamaica, A
FOX (GB) 1965
dir. Alexander Mackendrick

Hughes, T.
Tom Brown's Schooldays
RKO (US) 1940 dir. Robert Stevenson
REN (GB) 1951 dir. Gordon Parry
BBC (GB) 1971 dir. Gareth Davies
TVSe(GB)

Hugo, V.
Hunchback of Notre Dame, The

RKO (US) 1939 dir. William Dieterle
RANK (Fr/It) 1956 dir. Jean Delannoy
BBC (GB) 1977 dir. Alan Cooke
TV(GB)
COL (US/GB) 1982
dir. Michael Tuchner
TV(GB/US)
DISNEY (US) 1996 dir. Gary Trousdale,
Kirk Wise
A, Ch, M

Hugo, V.
Hunchback of Notre Dame, The

Hunchback, The
ALLIANCE (US) 1997 dir. Peter Medak
TV(US)

Hugo, V.
Les Misérables

UA (US) 1935 dir. Richard Boleslawski
FOX (US) 1952 dir. Lewis Milestone
ITC (GB) 1978 dir. Glenn Jordan
TRISTAR (US/GB/Ger) 1998 dir. Bille
August
DD/FOX FAMILY (Fr/US) 2000 dir.
Josee Dayan
TVSe(Fr/US)

Huie, W. B.
Americanization of Emily, The

MGM (US) 1964 dir. Arthur Hiller

Huie, W. B.
Execution of Private Slovik, The

UN TV (US) 1974 dir. Lamont Johnson
TV(US)

Huie, W. B.
Klansman, The

PAR (US) 1974 dir. Terence Young

Huie, W. B.
Mud on the Streets

Wild River
FOX (US) 1960 dir. Elia Kazan

Huie, W. B.
Revolt of Mamie Stover, The

FOX (US) 1956 dir. Raoul Walsh

Hulme, K.
Nun's Story, The

WAR (US) 1959 dir. Fred Zinnemann

Hulse, J.
Jody

Family of Strangers, A
ALLIANCE (US) 1993 dir. Sheldon
Larry
TV(US)

Hume, D.
Sin of Susan Slade, The

Susan Slade
WAR (US) 1962 dir. Delmer Daves

Hume, D.
They Called Him Death

This Man is Dangerous
RIALTO (GB) 1941
dir. Lawrence Huntington

Humphrey, W.
Home from the Hill

MGM (US) 1959 dir. Vincente Minnelli

Humphreys, J.
Rich in Love

MGM (US) 1993 dir. Bruce Beresford

Hunt, I.
Across Five Aprils

LCA (US) 1990 dir. Kevin Meyer
TV(US)

Hunter, E.
Blackboard Jungle, The

MGM (US) 1955 dir. Richard Brooks

Hunter, E.
Buddwing

Mister Buddwing
MGM (US) 1966 dir. Delbert Mann
GB title: Woman Without a Face

Hunter, E.
Chisholms, The

LAN (US) 1979 dir. Mel Stuart
TVSe(US)

Hunter, E.
Every Little Crook and Nanny

MGM (US) 1972 dir. Cy Howard

Hunter, E.
Last Summer

FOX (US) 1969 dir. Frank Perry

Hunter, E.
Matter of Conviction, A

Young Savages, The
UA (US) 1960 dir. John Frankenheimer

Hunter, E.
Strangers When We Meet

COL (US) 1959 dir. Richard Quine

Hunter, E.
Three Blind Mice

VIACOM (US) 2001 dir. Christopher
Leitch
TV(US)

Hunter, H.
Bengal Tiger

Bengal Brigade
UI (US) 1954 dir. Laslo Benedek
GB title: Bengal Rifles

Hunter, J. A. and Mannix, D. P.
Tales of the African Frontier

Killers of Kilimanjaro, The
COL (GB) 1959 dir. Richard Thorpe

Hunter, J. D.
Blue Max, The

FOX (US) 1966 dir. John Guillermin

Hunter, K.
Landlord, The

UA (US) 1970 dir. Hal Ashby

Hunter, R.
Fourth Angel, The

RAFFORD (Can/GB) 2001 dir. John
Irwin

Huntford, R.
Scott and Amundsen

Last Place on Earth, The
CENTRAL (GB) 1985
dir. Ferdinand Fairfax
TVSe(GB)

Hunyady, S.
House with the Red Light, The

Very Moral Night, A
HUNG (Hun) 1977 dir. Karoly Makk

Hurd, D. and Osmond, A.
Scotch on the Rocks

BBC (GB) 1973 dir. Bob Hird
TVSe(GB)

Hurlbut, G. and Logan, J.
Higher and Higher

P
RKO (US) 1943 dir. Tim Whelan
M

Hurok, S. and Goode, R.
Impressario

Tonight We Sing
FOX (US) 1953 dir. Mitchell Leisen
M

Hurst, F.
Anatomy of Me

Imitation of Life
UN (US) 1934 dir. John Stahl
UN (US) 1959 dir. Douglas Sirk

Hurst, F.
Back Street

UN (US) 1932 dir. John M. Stahl
UN (US) 1941 dir. Robert Stevenson
UN (US) 1961 dir. David Miller

Hurst, F.
Five and Ten

MGM (US) 1931 dir. Robert Z. Leonard
GB title: Daughter of Luxury

Hurst, F.
Humoresque

WAR (US) 1946 dir. Jean Negulesco

Hurst, F.
Sister Act

Four Daughters
WAR (US) 1938 dir. Michael Curtiz

Hurst, F.
Symphony of Six Million

RKO (US) 1932 dir. Gregory LaCava
GB title: Melody of Life

Hurst, F.
Young at Heart

WAR (US) 1954 dir. Gordon Douglas

Hussein, A.
Return Journey

Brothers in Trouble
RENEGADE (GB) 1995 dir. Udayan
Prasad

Husson, A.
My Three Angels

P
We're No Angels
PAR (US) 1955 dir. Michael Curtiz
PAR (US) 1989 dir. Neil Jordan

Hutchinson, A. S. M.
If Winter Comes

MGM (US) 1948 dir. Victor Saville

Huth, A.
Land Girls

CHANNEL 4 FILMS (GB) 1998 dir.
David Leland

Huth, A.
Sun Child

YTV (GB) 1988 dir. Lawrence Gordon
Clark
TV(GB)

Hutson, S.
Eff Off

Class of Miss MacMichael, The
GALA (GB) 1978 dir. Silvio Narizzano

Hutson, S.
Slugs, The Movie

NEW WORLD (Sp) 1988 dir. J. P. Simon

Hutton, M. G.
Happy Family, The

P
APEX (GB) 1952 dir. Muriel Box
US title: Mr. Lord Says No

Huxley, A.
Brave New World

UN (US) 1980 dir. D. B. Brinckerhoff
TV(US)
USA NETWORK (US) 1998 dir. Leslie
Libman, Larry Williams
TV(US)

Huxley, A.
Ape and Essence

BBC (GB) 1966 dir. David Benedictus
TV(GB)

Huxley, A.
Devils of Loudon, The

Devils, The
WAR (GB) 1971 dir. Ken Russell

Huxley, A.
Eyeless in Gaza

BBC (GB) 1971 dir. James Cellan Jones
TVSe(GB)

Huxley, A.
Gioconda Smile, The

P

Woman's Vengeance, A
UN (US) 1947 dir. Zoltan Korda

Huxley, A.
Point Counter Point

BBC (GB) 1968 dir. Rex Tucker
TVSe(GB)

Huxley, A.
Young Archimedes

Prelude to Fame
GFD (GB) 1950 dir. Fergus McDonnell

Huxley, E.
Flame Trees of Thika, The

THAMES (GB) 1981 dir. Roy Ward
Baker
TVSe(GB)

Hwang, D. H.
M. Butterfly

P

GEFFEN (US) 1993 dir. David
Cronenberg

Hyams, J.
Bogie

FRIES (US) 1980 dir. Vincent Sherman
TV(US)

Hyde, H. M.
Trials of Oscar Wilde, The

EROS (GB) 1960 dir. Ken Hughes
US title: Man with the Green Carnation,
The

Hyman, M.
No Time for Sergeants

WAR (US) 1958 dir. Mervyn LeRoy

Hynd, A.
Betrayal from the East

RKO (US) 1945 dir. William Beake

Ibanez, V. B.
Blood and Sand
FOX (US) 1941 dir. Rouben Mamoulian

Ibarguangoitia, J.
Two Crimes
CUEVANO (Mex) 1994 dir. Roberto Sneider

Ibsen, H.
Doll's House, A
P
COMPASS (US) 1959
dir. George Schaefer
TV(US)
BL (GB) 1973 dir. Patrick Garland
BBC (GB) 1992 dir. David Thacker
TV(GB)

Ibsen, H.
Doll's House, A
P
Sara
FARABI CINEMA (Iran) 1994 dir. Dariush Mehrjui

Ibsen, H.
Enemy of the People, An
P
ENT (US) 1978 dir. George Schaefer

Ibsen, H.
Enemy of the People, An
P
Ganashatru
ELECTRIC (Ind) 1989 dir. Satyajit Ray

Ibsen, H.
Ghosts
P
BBC (GB) 1986 dir. Elijah Moshinsky
TV(GB)

Ibsen, H.
Hedda Gabler
P
BBC (GB) 1993 dir. Deborah Warner
TV(GB)

Ibsen, H.
Hedda Gabler
P
Hedda
SCOTIA-BARBER (GB) 1977
dir. Trevor Nunn

Ibsen, H.
Wild Duck, The
P
ORION (GB) 1983 dir. Henri Safran

Ibuse, M.
Black Rain
ART EYE (Jap) 1988
dir. Shohei Imamura

Ide, L.
Concealment
P
Secret Bride, The
WAR (US) 1935 dir. William Dieterle
GB title: Concealment

Idell, A. E.
Centennial Summer
FOX (GB) 1946 dir. Otto Preminger

Iles, F.
Before the Fact

Suspicion
RKO (US) 1941 dir. Alfred Hitchcock

Iles, F.
Malice Aforethought

BBC (GB) 1979 dir. Cyril Coke
TVSe(GB)

Ilf, E. and Petrov, E.
Twelve Chairs, The

P
UMC (US) 1970 dir. Mel Brooks

Ilf, E. and Petrov, E.
Twelve Chairs, The

P
Keep Your Seats Please
ATP (GB) 1936 dir. Monty Banks

Ingalls, R.
End of Tragedy, The

Dead on the Money
INDIEPROD (US) 1991
dir. Mark Cullingham
TV(US)

Inge, W.
Bus Stop

P
FOX (US) 1956 dir. Joshua Logan

Inge, W.
Come Back, Little Sheba

P
PAR (US) 1952 dir. Daniel Mann
GRANADA (US) 1977
dir. Silvio Narizzano
TV(GB/US)

Inge, W.
Loss of Roses, A

P
Stripper, The
FOX (US) 1963 dir. Franklin Schaffner
GB title: Woman of Summer

Inge, W.
Picnic

P
COL (US) 1955 dir. Joshua Logan
COL TRISTAR (US) 2000 dir. Ivan
Passer
TV(US)

Inge, W. M.
Dark at the Top of the Stairs, The

P
WAR (US) 1960 dir. Delbert Mann

Inman, R.
Home Fires Burning

M. REES (US) 1989 dir. Glenn Jordan
TV(US)

Innaurato, A.
Gemini

P
Happy Birthday, Gemini
UA (US) 1980 dir. Richard Benner

Innes, H.
Campbell's Kingdom

RANK (GB) 1957 dir. Ralph Thomas

Innes, H.
Lonely Skier, The

Snowbound
RKO (GB) 1948 dir. David MacDonald

Innes, H.
White South, The

Hell Below Zero
COL (GB) 1954 dir. Mark Robson

Innes, H.
Wreck of the Mary Deare, The

MGM (US) 1959 dir. Michael Anderson

Innes, M.
Christmas at Candleshoe

Candleshoe
DISNEY (GB) 1977 dir. Norman Tokar

Ireland, A.
Certain Mr. Takahasi, A
Pianist, The
ASKA (Can) 1992 dir. Claude Gagnon

Ireland, J.
Life Lines
Reason for Living: The Jill Ireland Story
TEN-FOUR (US) 1991
dir. Michael Rhodes
TV(US)

Irish, W.
Bride Wore Black, The
UA (Fr/It) 1967 dir. François Truffaut

Irish, W.
Deadline at Dawn
RKO (US) 1946 dir. Harold Clurman

Irish, W.
I Married A Dead Man
I Married A Shadow
IS (Fr) 1983 dir. Robin Davis

Irish, W.
Phantom Lady
UN (US) 1944 dir. Robert Siodmak

Irvine, L.
Castaway
VIRGIN (GB) 1986 dir. Nicolas Roeg

Irving, C.
Spring, The
NBC STUDIOS (US) 2000 dir. David S.
Jackson
TV(US)

Irving, C.
Trial
Trial: The Price of Passion
TRISTAR TV (US) 1992 dir. Paul
Wendkos
TVSe(US)

Irving, H. R.
Bohunk
P
Black Fury
WAR (US) 1935 dir. Michael Curtiz

Irving, J.
Cider House Rules, The
MIRAMAX (US) 1999 dir. Lasse
Hallstrom

Irving, J.
Hotel New Hampshire, The
ORION (US) 1984 dir. Tony Richardson

Irving, J.
Prayer for Owen Meany, A
Simon Birch
HOLLYWOOD (US) 1998 dir. Mark
Steven Johnson

Irving, J.
World According to Garp, The
WAR (US) 1982 dir. George Roy Hill

Irving, W.
Father Knickerbocker's History of
New York
Knickerbocker Holiday
UN (US) 1944 dir. Harry Joe Brown

Irving, W.
Legend of Sleepy Hollow, The
SCHICK SUNN (US) 1980
dir. Henning Schellerup
TV(US)

Irwin, M.
Young Bess
MGM (US) 1953 dir. George Sidney

Isaacs, S.
Compromising Positions
PAR (US) 1985 dir. Frank Perry

Isaacs, S.
Shining Through
FOX (US) 1992 dir. David Selzer

Isaacson, W.
Kissinger: A Biography
Kissinger and Nixon
PARAGON (US) 1995 dir. Daniel Petrie
TV(US)

Isaksson, U.
Boken om E
Song for Martin, A
MOONLIGHT (Den/Ger) 2001 dir. Bille
August

Isham, F. S.
Nothin' But The Truth
PAR (US) 1941 dir. Elliott Nugent

Ishiguro, K.
Remains of the Day, The
COL (GB/US) 1993 dir. James Ivory

Isitt, D.
Nasty Neighbours
P
FIRST HAND (GB) 1999 dir. Debbie
Isitt

Israel, C. E.
Mark, The
FOX (GB) 1961 dir. Guy Green

Ito, S.
No Life King
NEW CENTURY (Jap) 1991
dir. Jun Ichikawa

Iwaszkiewicz, J.
Devil and the Nun, The
KADR (Pol) 1960
dir. Jerzy Kawalerowicz

Izzi, E.
Take, The
MCA TV (US) 1990 dir. Leon Ichaso
TV(US)

Jacks, J.
Murder on the Wild Side

Black Eye
WAR (US) 1974 dir. Jack Arnold

Jackson, B.
One Special Moment

ARABESQUE FILMS (US) 2001 dir.
Nelson George
TV(US)

Jackson, C.
Lost Weekend, The

PAR (US) 1945 dir. Billy Wilder

Jackson, F.
Bishop Misbehaves, The

P
MGM (US) 1935 dir. E. A. Dupont
GB title: Bishop's Misadventures, The

Jackson, H. M.
Ramona

FOX (US) 1936 dir. Henry King

Jackson, J. A.
Big Beat Heat: Alan Freed and the Early Years of Rock & Roll

Mr. Rock 'n' Roll: The Alan Freed Story
VZ/SERTNER (US) 1999 dir. Andy
Wolk
TV(US)

Jackson, M.
Midnight Blue

DIRECTORS' CIRCLE (US) 2000 dir.
Bobby Mardis
TV(US)

Jackson, S.
Bird's Nest, The

Lizzie
MGM (US) 1957 dir. Hugo Haas

Jackson, S.
Haunting of Hill House, The

Haunting, The
MGM (GB) 1963 dir. Robert Wise
DREAMWORKS (US) 1999 dir. Jan de
Bont

Jacob, N.
Under New Management

BUTCHER (GB) 1946
dir. John E. Blakeley

Jacobs, C. R.
There Was a Little Boy

LORIMAR TV (US) 1993 dir. Mimi
Leder
TV(US)

Jacobs, C. R.
Mother, May I Sleep With Danger?

TRISTAR (US) 1996 dir. Jorge Montesi
TV(US)

Jacobs, J. and Casey, W.
Grease

P
PAR (US) 1978 dir. Randal Kleiser
M

Jacobs, W. W.
Interruption, The

Footsteps in the Fog
COL (GB) 1955 dir. Arthur Lubin

Jacobsen, J.-F.
Barbara
PER HOLST (Den) 1997 dir. Nils
Malmros

Jaffe, M. G.
Dance Real Slow
Cool, Dry Place, A
FOX (US) 1999 dir. John N. Smith

Jaffe, R.
Best of Everything, The
FOX (US) 1959 dir. Jean Negulesco

Jaffe, R.
Mazes and Monsters
P&G (US) 1982
dir. Steven Hilliard Stern
TV(US)

Jakes, J.
Bastard, The
UN TV (US) 1978 dir. Lee Katzin
TVSe(US)

Jakes, J.
Heaven and Hell
Heaven and Hell: North and South, Part III
ABC PRODS. (US) 1994 dir. Larry
Peerce
TVSe(US)

Jakes, J.
Love and War
North and South, Book II
WAR TV (US) 1986 dir. Kevin Connor
TVSe(US)

Jakes, J.
North and South
WAR (US) 1985 dir. Richard T. Heffron
TVSe(US)

Jakes, J.
Rebels, The
UN TV (US) 1979 dir. Russ Mayberry
TVSe(US)

Jakes, J.
Seekers, The
UN TV (US) 1979 dir. Sidney Hayers
TVSe(US)

James, D.
Spy at Evening, A
BBC (GB) 1981 dir. Ben Rea
TVSe(GB)

James, H.
Aspern Papers, The
Aspern
CONN (Port) 1981
dir. Eduardo de Gregorion

James, H.
Aspern Papers, The
Lost Moment, The
UN (US) 1947 dir. Martin Gabel

James, H.
Bostonians, The
RANK (GB) 1984 dir. James Ivory

James, H.
Daisy Miller
PAR (US) 1974 dir. Peter Bogdanovich

James, H.
Europeans, The
GB (GB) 1979 dir. James Ivory

James, H.
Golden Bowl, The
BBC (GB) 1972 dir. James Cellan Jones
TVSe(GB)
MI (GB/US) 1999 dir. James Ivory

James, H.
Portrait of a Lady, The
POLYGRAM (US/GB) 1996 dir. Jane
Campion

James, H.
Spoils of Poynton, The
BBC (GB) 1970 dir. Peter Sasdy
TVSe(GB)

James, H.
Turn of the Screw
CURTIS (US) 1974 dir. Dan Curtis
TVSe(US)
UNITED (GB) 1999 dir. Ben Bolt
TV(GB)

James, H.
Turn of the Screw, The
Haunting of Helen Walker, The
ROSEMONT (US) 1995 dir. Tom
McLoughlin
TV(US)

James, H.
Turn of the Screw, The
Innocents, The
FOX (GB) 1961 dir. Jack Clayton

James, H.
Turn of the Screw, The
Nightcomers, The
AVCO (GB) 1972
dir. Michael Winner

James, H.
Washington Square
Heiress, The
PAR (US) 1949 dir. William Wyler

James, H.
Washington Square
HOLLYWOOD (US) 1997 dir.
Agnieszka Holland

James, H.
Wings of a Dove, The
Under Heaven
BANNER ENT (US) 1998 dir. Meg
Richman

James, H.
Wings of the Dove, The
MIRAMAX (GB/US) 1997 dir. Iain
Softley

James, M. E. C.
I Was Monty's Double
ABP (GB) 1958 dir. John Guillermin
US title: Hell, Heaven and Hoboken

James, M. R.
Casting the Runes
Night of the Demon
COL (GB) 1957 dir. Jacques Tourneur

James, P.
Host
Virtual Obsession
VZ/SERTNER (US) 1998 dir. Mick
Garris
TV(US)

James, P. D.
Black Tower, The
ANGLIA (GB) 1985 dir. Ronald Humble
TVSe(GB)

James, P. D.
Cover Her Face
ANGLIA (GB) 1985 dir. John Davies
TVSe(GB)

James, P. D.
Death of an Expert Witness
ANGLIA (GB) 1983 dir. Herbert Wise
TVSe(GB)

James, P. D.
Devices and Desires
ANGLIA (GB) 1991 dir. John Davies
TVSe(GB)

James, P. D.
Mind to Murder, A
ANGLIA (GB) 1996 dir. Gareth Davies
TV(GB)

James, P. D.
Original Sin
ANGLIA (GB) 1996 dir. Andrew Grieve
TVSe(GB)

James, P. D.
Shroud for a Nightingale
YTV (GB) 1984 dir. John Gorrie
TVSe(GB)

James, P. D.
Taste for Death, A
YTV (GB) 1987 dir. John Davies
TVSe(GB)

James, P. D.
Unnatural Causes
ANGLIA (GB) 1994 dir. John Davies
TV(GB)

James, P. D.
Unsuitable Job for a Woman, An
BOYD (GB) 1982 dir. Christopher Petit

James, W.
Lone Cowboy: My Life Story
Shootout
UN (US) 1971 dir. Henry Hathaway

James, W.
Smoky
FOX (US) 1946 dir. Louis King

Jameson, S.
Early Life of Stephen Hind, The
BBC (GB) 1974 dir. Timothy Combe
TVSe(GB)

Janeway, Mrs E.
Daisy Kenyon
FOX (US) 1947 dir. Otto Preminger

Janney, R.
Miracle of the Bells
PAR (US) 1948 dir. Irving Rapper

Janos, V.
I Married an Angel
P
MGM (US) 1942 dir. W. S. Van Dyke
M

Janowitz, T.
Slaves of New York
TRISTAR (US) 1989 dir. James Ivory

Janus, C. G.
Miss 4th of July, Goodbye
Goodbye, Miss 4th of July
FINNEGAN/PINCHUK (US) 1988
dir. George Miller
TV(US)

Jaoui, A. and Bacri, J.-P.
Air de Famille, Un
P
STUDIO CANAL+ (Fr) 1996 dir. Cedric
Klapisch

Jaoui, A. and Bacri, J.-P
Cuisine et Dependances
P
STUDIO CANAL+ (Fr) 1993 dir.
Philippe Muyl

Japrisot, S.
Lady in the Car with Glasses and a
Gun, The
COL (Fr/US) 1969 dir. Anatole Litvak

Japrisot, S.
One Deadly Summer
SNC (Fr) 1983 dir. Jean Becker

Japrisot, S.
Sleeping Car Murders, The
PECF (Fr) 1965 dir. Costa-Gavras

Jarchovsky, P.
Divided We Fall
BIOSCOP (Czech) 2000 dir. Jan Hrebejk

Jardin, A.
Fanfan
STUDIO CANAL+ (Fr) 1993 dir.
Alexandre Jardin

Jardin, A.
Petit Sauvage, Le
Prof, Le
STUDIO CANAL+ (Fr) 2000 dir.
Alexandre Jardin

Jardin, A.
Zebre, Le
LAMBART (Fr) 1992 dir. Jean Poiret

Jasmin, C.
Pleure pas Germaine
RTBF (Bel/Sp/Fr) 2000 dir. Alain de
Halleux

Jaynes, C.
Instruct my Sorrows
My Reputation
WAR (US) 1946 dir. Curtis Bernhardt

Jean, R.
Lectrice, La
ORION (Fr) 1989 dir. Michel Deville

Jeans, R.
Young Wives' Tale
P
ABP (GB) 1951 dir. Henry Cass

Jela, D.
Après-Midi d'un Tortionnaire, L'
YMC (Fr) 2001 dir. Lucian Pintilie

Jelinek, E.
Pianiste, La
MK2 (Fr) 2001 dir. Michael Haneke

Jellicoe, A.
Knack, The
P
UA (GB) 1965 dir. Richard Lester

Jenkins, D.
Baja Oklahoma
HBO (US) 1988 dir. Bobby Roth
TV(US)

Jenkins, D.
Dead Solid Perfect
HBO (US) 1988 dir. Bobby Roth
TV(US)

Jenkins, D.
Semi-Tough
UA (US) 1977 dir. Michael Ritchie

Jenkins, G.
Twist of Sand, A
UA (GB) 1968 dir. Don Chaffey

Jennings, S.
Tooth of the Lion
P
Summer My Father Grew Up, The
SHAPIRO (US) 1991
dir. Michael Tuchner
TV(US)

Jennings, W. D.
Cowboys, The
WAR (US) 1972 dir. Mark Rydell

Jeorg, W.
Saboteur, The
FOX (US) 1965 dir. Bernhard Wicki

Jepson, S.
Man Running
Stage Fright
WAR (GB) 1950 dir. Alfred Hitchcock

Jerome, H.
Conquest
P
MGM (US) 1937 dir. Clarence Brown
GB title: Marie Walewska

Jerome, J. K.
Passing of the Third Floor Back, The
P
GB (GB) 1935 dir. Berthold Viertel

Jerome, J. K.
Three Men in a Boat
BL (GB) 1956 dir. Ken Annakin

Jesse, F. T.
Pin To See the Peepshow, A
BBC (GB) 1973 dir. Raymond Menmuir
TVSe(GB)

Jeser, M.
Abbie Hoffman: American Rebel
Steal This Movie
GREENLIGHT (US) 2000 dir. Robert
Greenwald

Jessup, R.
Chuka
PAR (US) 1967 dir. Gordon Douglas

Jessup, R.
Cincinnati Kid, The
MGM (US) 1965 dir. Norman Jewison

Jessup, R.
Deadly Duo
UA (US) 1962 dir. Reginald LeBorg

Jhabvala, R. P.
Heat and Dust
UN/ENT (GB) 1983
dir. James Ivory

Jicai, F.
Red Firecracker, Green Firecracker
BEIJING SALON (China) 1994 dir. Ping
He

Jirotka, Z.
Saturnin
JUPITER (Czech) 1994 dir. Jiri Vercak

Job, T.
Uncle Harry
P
Strange Affair of Uncle Harry, The
UN (US) 1945 dir. Robert Siodmak

Johansson, E.
Kattbreven
CO FILM AB (Swe) 2001 dir. Christina
Olofson

Johnson, A. F.
Little Colonel
FOX (US) 1935 dir. David Butler

Johnson, D.
Jesus' Son
ALLIANCE (Can/US) 1999 dir. Alison
Maclean

Johnson, D. M.
Hanging Tree, The
WAR (US) 1958 dir. Delmer Daves

Johnson, D. M.
Man Called Horse, A
CIN CEN (US) 1970
dir. Elliot Silverstein

Johnson, E. R.
Mongo's Back in Town
CBS ENT (US) 1971
dir. Marvin J. Chomsky
TV(US)

Johnson, L.
My Posse Don't Do Homework
Dangerous Minds
HOLLYWOOD (US) 1995 dir. John N.
Smith

Johnson, N.
World of Henry Orient, The
UA (US) 1964 dir. George Roy Hill

Johnson, R. and McCormick, M.
Too Dangerous To Be at Large
Dangerous Company
FINNEGAN (US) 1982
dir. Lamont Johnson
TV(US)

Johnson, R. W.
Shootdown
L. HILL (US) 1988
dir. Michael Pressman
TV(US)

Johnson, S.
Commissioner, The
NEW ERA VISION (US/GB) 1998 dir.
George Sluizer

Johnston, J.
Old Jest, The
Dawning, The
TVS (GB) 1988 dir. Robert Knights
TVSe(GB)

Johnston, J.
Railway Station Man, The
TNT/BBC (US/GB) 1992 dir. Michael
Whyte
TV(US/GB)

Johnston, V.
Howling in the Woods, A
UN (US) 1971 dir. Daniel Petrie
TV(US)

Jolley, E.
Last Crop, The
CHANNEL 4 (GB) 1991
dir. Stephen Clayton
TV(GB)

Jolley, E.
Well, The
NSW (Aust) 1997 dir. Samantha Lang

Jones, A.
FBI Killer, The
Betrayed by Love
E. J. SCHERICK (US) 1994 dir. John
Power
TV(US)

Jones, C. A.
Little Sir Nicholas
BBC (GB) 1989 dir. Andrew Morgan
TVSe(GB)

Jones, D.
Thicker Than Water
BBC (GB) 1994 dir. Marc Evans
TV(GB)

Jones, D. C.
Court Martial of George Amstrong Custer, The
HALLMARK (US) 1977
dir. Glenn Jordan
TV(US)

Jones, D. F.
Colossus
Forbin Project, The
UN (US) 1970 dir. Joseph Sargent
GB title: Colossus, the Forbin Project

Jones, G.
Vengeance
Sword of Gideon
HBO (US/Can) 1986
dir. Michael Anderson
TV(US/Can)

Jones, G. P. and Jones, C. B.
Peabody's Mermaid
Mr. Peabody and the Mermaid
UN (US) 1948 dir. Irving Pichel

Jones, G. P and Jones, C. B.
There was a Little Man
Luck of the Irish, The
FOX (US) 1948 dir. Henry Koster

Jones, J.
From Here to Eternity
COL (US) 1953 dir. Fred Zinnemann
COL (US) 1979 dir. Buzz Kulik
TVSe(US)

Jones, J.
Nurse is a Neighbour
Nurse on Wheels
WAR (GB) 1963 dir. Gerald Thomas

Jones, J.
Off to Philadelphia in the Morning
BBC (GB) 1978 dir. Julian Williams
TVSe(GB)

Jones, J.
Some Came Running
MGM (US) 1959 dir. Vincente Minnelli

Jones, J.
Thin Red Line, The
PLANET (US) 1964 dir. Andrew Marton
FOX (US) 1998 dir. Terrence Malick

Jones, K.
Soldier's Daughter Never Cries, A
MI (Fr/GB/US) 1998 dir. James Ivory

Jones, M.
Exile, An
I Walk the Line
COL (US) 1970
dir. John Frankenheimer

Jones, M.
Holding On
LWT (GB) 1977 dir. Raymond Menmuir,
Gerry Mill
TVSe(GB)

Jones, M.
John and Mary
FOX (US) 1969 dir. Peter Yates

Jones, R.
Acorn People, The
NBC ENT (US) 1981
dir. Joan Tewkesbury
TV(US)

Jones, R.
B-Ball: The Team That Never Lost a Game
One Special Victory
NBC (US) 1991 dir. Stuart Cooper
TV(US)

Jones, R. F.
This Island Earth
UI (US) 1955 dir. Joseph Newman

Jones, T. and Schmidt, H.
Fantasticks, The
P
COMPASS (US) 1964
dir. George Schaefer
M, TV(US)

Jonson, B.
Volpone
P
SIRITZKY (Fr) 1947
dir. Maurice Tourneur

Jonsson, R.
My Life as a Dog
SVENSK (Swe) 1984
dir. Lasse Hallstrom

Jordan, E. G.
Daddy and I
Make Way for a Lady
RKO (US) 1936 dir. David Burton

Jordan, L.
Lost in the Pershing Point Hotel
P
NORTHERN (US) 2001 dir. Julia Jay
Pierrepont III

Jorgensen, C.
Christine Jorgensen Story, The
UA (US) 1970 dir. Irving Rapper

Josselin, J. F.
Few Days With Me, A
GALAXY (Fr) 1989 dir. Claude Sautet

Joyce, J.
Dead, The
VESTRON (US) 1987 dir. John Huston

Joyce, J.
Portrait of the Artist as a Young Man
ULYSSES (GB) 1977 dir. Joseph Strick

Joyce, J.
Ulysses
BL (GB) 1967 dir. Joseph Strick

Judson, W.
Cold River
PACIFIC (US) 1982 dir. Fred G. Sullivan

Juergensen, H. and Westfeldt, J.
Lipschtick

P
Kissing Jessica Stein
FOX (US) 2001 dir. Charles Herman-Wurmfeld

Junger, S.
Perfect Storm, The: A True Story of Men Against the Sea

Perfect Storm, The
WAR (US) 1999 dir. Wolfgang Petersen

Juster, N.
Phantom Tollbooth, The
MGM (US) 1969 dir. Chuck Jones
A

Kadare, I.
Broken April

Behind the Sun
VIDEO (Bra/Fr) 2001 dir. Walter Salles

Kaestner, E.
Puenktchen und Anton

BAVARIA (Ger) 1999 dir. Caroline Link

Kafka, F.
Amerika

Class Relations
ART EYE (Ger/Fr) 1983
dir. Jean Marie Straub, Daniele Huillet

Kafka, F.
Amerika

FILMOVE (Czech) 1994 dir. Vladimir
Michalek

Kafka, F.
Castle, The

BR (Ger) 1997 dir. Michael Haneke

Kafka, F.
Trial, The

BL (Fr/It/Ger) 1963 dir. Orson Welles
BBC (GB) 1993 dir. David Hugh Jones

Kaler, J. O.
Toby Tyler

DISNEY (US) 1959 dir. Charles Barton
Ch

Kalpakian, L.
Graced Land

Woman Who Loved Elvis, The
GROSS/BAR (US) 1993 dir. Bill Bixby
TV(US)

Kaminsky, S.
Exercise in Terror

Hidden Fears
KEY (US) 1993 dir. Jean Bodon

Kaminsky, S.
When the Dark Man Calls

WIL COURT (US) 1995 dir. Nathaniel
Gutman
TV(US)

Kammeraad-Campbell, S.
**Doc—The Story of Dennis Littky and
His Fight for a Better School**

Town Torn Apart, A
PARAGON (US) 1992 dir. Daniel Petrie
TV(US)

Kandel, A.
City for Conquest

WAR (US) 1940 dir. Anatole Litvak

Kandel, A.
Hot Money

P
High Pressure
WAR (US) 1932 dir. Mervyn LeRoy

Kane, J.
Best Actress

E! (US) 2000 dir. Harvey Frost
TV(US)

Kane, K.
Pocketful of Paradise, A

Soul Collector, The
HEARST (US) 1999 dir. Michael M.
Scott
TV(US)

Kanga, F.
Trying to Grow

Sixth Happiness, The
DREAMFACTORY (GB) 1997 dir. Waris
Hussein

Kanin, F.
Goodbye, My Fancy

P
WAR (US) 1951 dir. Vincent Sherman

Kanin, G.
Born Yesterday

P
COL (US) 1950 dir. George Cukor
MILBERG (US) 1956 dir. Garson Kanin
TV(US)
HOLLYWOOD (US) 1993 dir. Luis
Mandoki

Kanin, G.
Moviola

Moviola: The Scarlett O'Hara Wars
WAR TV (US) 1980 dir. John Erman
TV(US)

Kanin, G.
Moviola

Moviola: The Silent Lovers
WAR TV (US) 1980 dir. John Erman
TV(US)

Kanin, G.
Moviola

Moviola: This Year's Blonde
WAR TV (US) 1980 dir. John Erman
TV(US)

Kanin, G.
Rat Race, The

P
PAR (US) 1960 dir. Robert Mulligan

Kanin, G.
Right Approach, The

P
FOX (US) 1961 dir. David Butler

Kaniuk, Y.
Last Jew, The

Vulture, The
YOSHA (Israel) 1981 dir. Yaky Yosba

Kantor, L.
Dead Pigeon

P
Tight Spot
COL (US) 1955 dir. Phil Karlson

Kantor, M.
Arouse and Beware

Man from Dakota, The
MGM (US) 1940 dir. Leslie Fenton
GB title: Arouse and Beware

Kantor, M.
Gentle Annie

MGM (US) 1944 dir. Andrew Marton

Kantor, M.
Glory for Me

Best Years of Our Lives, The
GOLDWYN (US) 1946
dir. William Wyler

Kantor, M.
God and My Country

Follow Me Boys!
DISNEY (US) 1966 dir. Norman Tokar

Kantor, M.
Gun Crazy

Deadly is the Female
UA (US) 1949 dir. Joseph Lewis

Kantor, M.
Happy Land

FOX (US) 1943 dir. Irving Pichel

Kantor, M.
Romance of Rosy Ridge, The
MGM (US) 1947 dir. Roy Rowland

Kantor, M.
Voice of Bugle Ann, The
MGM (US) 1936 dir. Richard Thorpe

Kaplan, J., Papajohn, G. and Zorn, E.
Murder of Innocence
HEARST (US) 1993 dir. Tom McLoughlin
TV(US)

Kaplan, L. J.
Female Perversions: The Temptations of Emma Bovary
Female Perversions
TRANSATLANTIC (US/Ger) 1996 dir. Susan Streitfeld

Karmel, A.
Mary Ann
Something Wild
UA (US) 1961 dir. Jack Garfein

Karr, J.
Something Borrowed, Something Blue
CBS (US) 1997 dir. Gwen Arner
TV(US)

Kasischke, L.
Suspicious River
BEYOND (Can) 2000 dir. Lynne Stopkewich

Kastle, H.
Cross Country
NEW WORLD (Can) 1983
dir. Paul Lynch

Kastner, E.
Emil and the Detectives
UFA (Ger) 1931 dir. Gerhard Lamprecht
DISNEY (US) 1964
dir. Peter Tewkesbury
Ch

Kastner, E.
Fabian
UA (Ger) 1982 dir. Wolf Gremm

Kastner, E.
Lottie and Lisa
Parent Trap, The
DISNEY (US) 1961 dir. David Swift
DISNEY (US) 1998 dir. Nancy Myers
Ch

Kastner, E.
Three Men in the Snow
Paradise for Three
MGM (US) 1938 dir. Edward Buzzell

Kata, E.
Be Ready With Bells and Drums
Patch of Blue, A
MGM (US) 1965 dir. Guy Green

Katcha, V.
Eye for an Eye, An
UGC (Fr/It) 1956 dir. André Cayatte

Katcham, V.
Hameçon, The
Hook, The
MGM (US) 1962 dir. George Seaton

Katkov, N.
Blood and Orchids
LORIMAR (US) 1986 dir. Jerry Thorpe
TVSe(US)

Katz, R.
Death in Rome
Massacre in Rome
GN (Fr/It) 1973
dir. George Pan Cosmatos

Katz, W.
Death Dreams
D. CLARK (US) 1991 dir. Martin Donovan
TV(US)

Katzenbach, J.
In the Heat of the Summer

Mean Season, The
ORION (US) 1985 dir. Philip Borsos

Katzenbach, J.
Just Cause
WAR (US) 1995 dir. Arne Glimcher

Kaufelt, D.
Six Months With an Older Woman

In Love With an Older Woman
FRIES (US) 1982 dir. Jack Bender
TV(US)

Kaufman, B.
Up the Down Staircase
WAR (US) 1967 dir. Robert Mulligan

Kaufman, B. N.
Son-Rise

Son-Rise: A Miracle of Love
FILMWAYS (US) 1979 dir. Glenn Jordan
TV(US)

Kaufman, G. S.
Butter and Egg Man, The

Angel from Texas, An
WAR (US) 1940 dir. Ray Enright

Kaufman, G. S.
Butter and Egg Man, The

P
Three Sailors and a Girl
WAR (US) 1953 dir. Roy del Ruth
M

Kaufman, G. S. and Connelly, M.
Dulcy

P
MGM (US) 1940 dir. S. Sylvan Simon

Kaufman, G. S. and Dayton, K.
First Lady

P
WAR (US) 1937 dir. Stanley Logan

Kaufman, G. S. and Ferber, E.
Dinner at Eight

P
MGM (US) 1933 dir. George Cukor
TNT (US) 1989 dir. Ron Lagomarsino
TV(US)

Kaufman, G. S. and Ferber, E.
Royal Family, The

P
Royal Family of Broadway, The
PAR (US) 1930 dir. George Cukor
GB title: Theatre Royal

Kaufman, G. S. and Ferber, E.
Stage Door

P
RKO (US) 1937 dir. Gregory La Cava

Kaufman, G. S. and Hart, M.
George Washington Slept Here

P
WAR (US) 1942 dir. William Keighley

Kaufman, G. S. and Hart, M.
Man Who Came to Dinner, The

P
WAR (US) 1941 dir. William Keighley
UN (US) 1972 dir. Buzz Kulik
TV(US)

Kaufman, G. S. and Hart, M.
Once in a Lifetime

P
UN (US) 1933 dir. Russell Mack

Kaufman, G. S. and Hart, M.
You Can't Take it With You

P
COL (US) 1938 dir. Frank Capra

Kaufman, G. S. and Woollcott, A.
Dark Tower, The

P
Man with Two Faces, The
WAR (US) 1934 dir. Archie Mayo

Kaufman, G. S., Dietz, H. and Schwarz, A.
Bandwagon, The
P
Dancing in the Dark
FOX (US) 1949 dir. Irving Reis

Kaufman, G. S., McGrath, L. and Burrows, A.
Silk Stockings
P
MGM (US) 1957
dir. Rouben Mamoulian
M

Kaufman, L.
Color of Green
Love, Hate, Love
SPELLING (US) 1971
dir. George McCowan
TV(US)

Kaufman, S.
Diary of a Mad Housewife
UI (US) 1970 dir. Frank Perry

Kaus, G.
Dark Angel
Her Sister's Secret
PRC (US) 1946 dir. Edgar G. Ulmer

Kaus, G.
Luxury Liner
PAR (US) 1933 dir. Lothar Mendes

Kawabata, Y.
Sounds from the Mountains
CORINTH (Jap) 1980 dir. Mikio Naruse

Kawata, T.
Solar Crisis
SHOCHIKU (Jap) 1990
dir. Richard C. Sarafian

Kay, T.
Runaway
HALLMARK (US) 2000 dir. Brandon Thomas
TV(US)

Kay, T.
To Dance With the White Dog
P. CLIFFORD (US) 1993 dir. Glenn Jordan
TV(US)

Kaye, M. M.
Far Pavilions, The
GOLDCREST (GB) 1983 dir. Peter Duffell
TVSe(GB)

Kaysen, S.
Girl, Interrupted
COL (US) 1999 dir. James Mangold

Kazan, E.
America, America
WAR (US) 1964 dir. Elia Kazan
GB title: Anatolian Smile, The

Kazan, E.
Arrangement, The
WAR (US) 1969 dir. Elia Kazan

Kazantzakis, N.
Greek Passion, The
He Who Must Die
KASSLER (Fr/It) 1957 dir. Jules Dassin

Kazantzakis, N.
Last Temptation of Christ, The
UN (US) 1988 dir. Martin Scorsese

Kazantzakis, N.
Zorba the Greek
FOX (GB) 1964 dir. Michael Cacoyannis

Ke Lan
Echo in the Valley
Yellow Earth
GUANGXI (China) 1985 dir. Chen Kaige

Keane, C.
Hunter, The
PAR (US) 1980 dir. Buzz Kulik

Keane, C.
Huntress, The
OFFLINE (US) 2000 dir. Jeffrey Reiner
TV(US)

Keane, J. B.
Durango
HALLMARK (US) 1999 dir. Brent Shields
TV(US)

Keane, J. B.
Field, The
P
AVENUE (GB) 1990 dir. Jim Sheridan

Keane, M.
Good Behaviour
BBC (GB) 1983 dir. Bill Hays
TVSe(GB)

Keating, H. R. F.
Perfect Murder, The
MI (Ind) 1990 dir. Zafar Hai

Keating, W. J. and Carter, R.
Man Who Rocked the Boat, The
Slaughter on 10th Avenue
UI (US) 1957 dir. Arnold Laven

Keefe, F. L.
Interpreter, The
Before Winter Comes
COL (GB) 1968 dir. J. Lee Thompson

Keene, D. and Babcock, D.
Chautauqua
Trouble With Girls, The
MGM (US) 1969 dir. Peter Tewkesbury

Keene, D.
Silent Partner
P
RESCUED (Aust) 2000 dir. Alkinos Tsilimidos

Keillor, G. and Nilsson, J. L.
Sandy Bottom Orchestra, The
SHOWTIME (US) 2000 dir. Bradley Wigor
TV(US)

Keir, U.
Vintage, The
MGM (US) 1957 dir. Jeffrey Hayden

Keith, A.
Three Came Home
FOX (US) 1950 dir. Jean Negulesco

Kelland, C. B.
Arizona
COL (US) 1940 dir. Wesley Ruggles

Kelland, C. B.
Dreamland
Strike Me Pink
UA (US) 1936 dir. Norman Taurog

Kelland, C. B.
Footlights
Speak Easily
MGM (US) 1932 dir. Edward Sedgwick

Kelland, C. B.
Opera Hat
Mr. Deeds Goes to Town
COL (US) 1936 dir. Frank Capra

Kelland, C. B.
Scattergood Baines
RKO (US) 1941 dir. Christy Cabanne

Kelland, C. B.
Sugarfoot
WAR (US) 1951 dir. Edward L. Marin

Kelland, C. B.
Thirty Day Princess
PAR (US) 1934 dir. Marion Gering

Kelland, C. B.
Valley of the Sun
RKO (US) 1942 dir. George Marshall

Kellerman, B.
Tunnel, The
GAU (GB) 1935 dir. Maurice Elvey
US title: Transatlantic Tunnel

Kellerman, J.
When the Bough Breaks
TAFT (US) 1986 dir. Waris Hussein
TV(US)

Kellino, P.
Del Palma
Lady Possessed
REP (US) 1952 dir. William Spier, Roy
Kellino

Kellock, H.
Houdini
PAR (US) 1953 dir. George Marshall

Kellogg, M.
**Tell Me That You Love Me, Junie
Moon**
PAR (US) 1970 dir. Otto Preminger

Kelly, A. P.
British Intelligence
P
WAR (US) 1940 dir. Terry Morse
GB title: Enemy Agent

Kelly, A. P.
Three Faces East
P
WAR (US) 1930 dir. Roy del Ruth

Kelly, G.
Craig's Wife
P
COL (US) 1936 dir. Dorothy Arzner

Kelly, G.
Craig's Wife
P
Harriet Craig
COL (US) 1950 dir. Vincent Sherman

Kelly, G.
Show-Off, The
P
MGM (US) 1934 dir. Charles Riesner

Kelly, G.
Show-off, The
P
Men Are Like That
PAR (US) 1930 dir. Frank Tuttle

Kelly, G.
Torch Bearers, The
P
Doubting Thomas
FOX (US) 1935 dir. David Butler

Kelly, J.
Marriage is a Private Affair
MGM (US) 1944 dir. Robert Z. Leonard

Kelly, M. T.
Dream Like Mine, A
Clearcut
TELEFILM (Can) 1991
dir. Richard Bugajski

Kelman, J.
Someone's Watching
In the Shadows, Someone's Watching
SABAN ENT (US) 1993 dir. Richard
Friedman
TV(US)

Kelton, E.
Good Old Boys, The
E. J. SCHERICK (US) 1995 dir. Tommy
Lee Jones
TV(US)

Kemal, Y.
Memed my Hawk
EMI (GB) 1984 dir. Peter Ustinov

Kember, P.
Not Quite Jerusalem
P
RANK (GB) 1985 dir. Lewis Gilbert

Kemelman, H.
Friday the Rabbi Slept Late
Lanigan's Rabbi
UN TV (US) 1976 dir. Lou Antonio
TV(US)

Kempinski, T.
Duet for One
P
CANNON (GB) 1987
dir. Andrei Konchalovsky

Kenaz, Y.
On the Edge
SCREEN ENT (Israel) 1994 dir. Amnon
Rubinstein

Kendall, D.
Lazaro
Where the River Runs Black
MGM (US) 1986 dir. Christopher Cain

Kendrick, B. H.
Odour of Violets
Eyes in the Night
MGM (US) 1942 dir. Fred Zinnemann

Kendrick, B. H. and Allen, W. H.
Bright Victory
UI (US) 1951 dir. Mark Robson
GB title: Lights Out

Keneally, T.
Chant of Jimmie Blacksmith, The
FOX (Aust) 1979 dir. Fred Schepisi

Keneally, T.
Schindler's Ark
Schindler's List
UN (US) 1993 dir. Steven Spielberg

Kennaway, J.
Household Ghosts
Country Dance
MGM (GB) 1969 dir. J. Lee Thompson

Kennaway, J.
Tunes of Glory
UA (GB) 1960 dir. Ronald Neame

Kennedy, A.
Domino Principle, The
ITC (US) 1977 dir. Stanley Kramer

Kennedy, D.
Dead Heart, The
Welcome to Woop Woop
SCALA (Aust/GB) 1997 dir. Stephan
Elliott

Kennedy, J. R.
Chairman, The
Most Dangerous Man in the World, The
RANK (GB) 1969 dir. J. Lee Thompson
US title: Chairman, The

Kennedy, L.
Airman and the Carpenter, The
Crime of the Century
HBO (US) 1996 dir. Mark Rydell
TV(US)

Kennedy, L.
10 Rillington Place
COL (GB) 1970 dir. Richard Fleischer

Kennedy, M.
Constant Nymph, The
GAU (GB) 1933 dir. Basil Dean
WAR (US) 1943 dir. Edmund Goulding

Kennedy, M.
Escape Me Never
P
UA (GB) 1935 dir. Paul Czinner
WAR (US) 1947 dir. Peter Godfrey

Kennedy, M. and Surgutchoff, I.
Autumn
P
That Dangerous Age
LF (GB) 1948 dir. Gregory Ratoff
US title: If This Be Sin

Kennedy, W.
Ironweed
TRISTAR (US) 1987
dir. Hector Babenco

Kennedy, W. P.
Toy Soldiers
TRISTAR (US) 1991 dir. Daniel Petrie, Jr.

Kennerly, D. H.
Shooter
PAR TV (US) 1988 dir. Gary Nelson
TV(US)

Kennington, A.
Night Has Eyes, The
PATHE (GB) 1942 dir. Leslie Arliss

Kenny, E. and Ostenso, M.
And They Shall Walk
Sister Kenny
RKO (US) 1946 dir. Dudley Nichols

Kenrick, T.
Faraday's Flowers
Shanghai Surprise
MGM (US) 1986 dir. Jim Goddard

Kenrick, T.
Two for the Price of One
Nobody's Perfekt
COL (US) 1981 dir. Peter Bonerz

Kenward, A. R.
Proof Thru' the Night
P
Cry Havoc
MGM (US) 1943 dir. Richard Thorpe

Kenyon, C.
Lloyd's of London
FOX (US) 1936 dir. Henry King

Keon, M.
Durian Tree, The
7th Dawn, The
UA (GB) 1964 dir. Lewis Gilbert

Kern, J. and Hammerstein II, O.
Show Boat
P
UN (US) 1936 dir. James Whale
MGM (US) 1951 dir. George Sidney
M

Kern, W.
Hellcab
P
Chicago Cab
CASTLE HILL (US) dir. Mary Cybulski, John Tintori

Kerouac, J.
Subterraneans, The
MGM (US) 1960
dir. Ronald MacDougall

Kerr, G.
Cottage to Let
P
GFD (GB) 1941 dir. Anthony Asquith
US title: Bombsight Stolen

Kerr, J.
Mary, Mary
P
WAR (US) 1963 dir. Mervyn LeRoy

Kerr, J.
Please Don't Eat the Daisies
MGM (US) 1960 dir. Charles Walters

Kerr, J. and Brooke, E.
King of Hearts
P
That Certain Feeling
PAR (US) 1956 dir. Norman Panama,
Melvin Frank

Kerrvish, J. D.
Undying Monster, The
FOX (US) 1943 dir. John Brahm
GB title: Hammond Mystery, The

Kersh, G.
Night and the City
FOX (GB) 1950 dir. Jules Dassin
TRIBECA (US) 1992 dir. Irwin Winkler

Kesey, K.
One Flew Over the Cuckoo's Nest
UA (US) 1975 dir. Milos Forman

Kesey, K.
Sometimes a Great Notion
UN (US) 1974 dir. Paul Newman
GB title: Never Give an Inch

Kessel, J.
Belle de Jour
CURZON (Fr/It) 1967 dir. Luis Bunuel

Kessel, J.
Coup de Grâce
Sirocco
COL (US) 1951 dir. Curtis Bernhardt

Kessel, J.
Equippage, L'
Woman I Love, The
RKO (US) 1937 dir. Anatole Litvak
GB title: Woman Between, The

Kessel, J.
Horsemen, The
COL (US) 1970
dir. John Frankenheimer

Kessel, J.
Lion, The
FOX (GB) 1962 dir. Jack Cardiff

Kessel, J.
Lovers of Lisbon, The
EGC (Fr) 1954 dir. Henri Verneuil

Kesselman, W.
I Love You, I Love You Not
P
STUDIO CANAL+ (Fr/Ger/GB) 1997
dir. Billy Hopkins

Kesselman, W.
My Sister in This House
P
Sister My Sister
BRIT SCREEN (GB/US) 1994 dir.
Nancy Meckler

Kesselring, J. O.
Arsenic and Old Lace
P
WAR (US) 1944 dir. Frank Capra
COMPASS (US) 1962
dir. George Schaefer
TV(US)

Kessler, L.
Orphans
P
LORIMAR (US) 1987 dir. Alan J. Pakula

Kesson, J.
Another Time, Another Place
CINEGATE (GB) 1983
dir. Michael Radford

Ketron, L.
Fresh Horses
P
WEINTRAUB (US) 1988
dir. David Anspaugh

Ketron, L.
Hitching Post, The
P
Only Thrill, The
MOONSTONE (US) 1997 dir. Peter
Masterson

Key, A.
Escape to Witch Mountain
DISNEY (US) 1974 dir. John Hough
DISNEY FAMILY (US) 1995 dir. Peter
Rader
Ch, TV(US)

Key, T.
Digby – The Biggest Dog in the World
RANK (GB) 1973 dir. Joseph McGrath
Ch

Keyes, D.
Flowers for Algernon
Charly
CINERAMA (US) 1968
dir. Ralph Nelson

Keyes, D.
Flowers for Algernon
CITADEL (US) 2000 dir. Jeff Bleckner
TV(US)

Keyhoe, D. E.
Flying Saucers from Outer Space
Earth v. The Flying Saucers
COL (US) 1956 dir. Fred F. Sears

Khan-Din, A.
East is East
P
CHANNEL 4 FILMS (GB) 1999 dir.
Damian O'Donnell

Kienzle, W. X.
Rosary Murders, The
NEW LINE (US) 1987 dir. Fred Walton

Kikuchi, H.
D—Demon Deathchase
Vampire Hunter D: Bloodlust
FILMLINK (Jap/US) 2000 dir. Yoshiaki
Kawajiri

Kikuchi, K.
Gate of Hell
DAIEI (Jap) 1953
dir. Teinosuke Kinugasa

Kikuta, K.
Quiet Duel, The
P
DAIEI (Jap) 1983 dir. Akira Kurosawa

Kimmins, A.
Amorous Prawn, The
P
BL (GB) 1962 dir. Anthony Kimmins
US title: Playgirl and the War Minister,
The

Kinder, G.
Victim: The Other Side of Murder
Aftermath: A Test of Love
COL (US) 1991 dir. Glenn Jordan
TV (US)

King, F.
Ghoul, The
GAU (GB) 1933 dir. T. Hayes Hunter

King, G. S.
Slave Ship
FOX (US) 1937 dir. Tay Garnett

King, H.
Paradigm Red
Red Alert
PAR (US) 1977 dir. William Hale
TV(US)

King, L. L. and Masterson, P.
Best Little Whorehouse in Texas
P
UN (US) 1982 dir. Colin Higgins
M

King, P.
On Monday Next
P
Curtain Up
GFD (GB) 1952 dir. Ralph Smart

King, P.
See How They Run
P
BL (GB) 1955 dir. Leslie Arliss
CHANNEL 4 (GB) 1984 dir. Les
Chatfield, Ray Cooney
TV(GB)

King, P.
Serious Charge
P
EROS (GB) 1959 dir. Terence Young

King, P. and Cary, F. L.
Sailor Beware!
P
BL (GB) 1956 dir. Gordon Parry
US title: Panic in the Parlor

King, R.
Case of the Constant God, The
Love Letters of a Star
UN (US) 1936 dir. Lewis R. Foster

King, R.
Secret Beyond the Door, The
UI (US) 1948 dir. Fritz Lang

King, S.
Apt Pupil
TRISTAR (US) 1998 dir. Bryan Singer

King, S.
Body, The
Stand by Me
COL (US) 1986 dir. Rob Reiner

King, S.
Carrie
UA (US) 1976 dir. Brian De Palma

King, S.
Cat From Hell
Tales from the Darkside: the Movie
PAR (US) 1990 dir. John Harrison

King, S.
Children of the Corn
NEW WORLD (US) 1984
dir. Fritz Kiersch

King, S.
Christine
COL (US) 1983 dir. John Carpenter

King, S.
Cujo
WAR (US) 1982 dir. Lewis Teague

King, S.
Cycle of the Werewolf
Silver Bullet
PAR (US) 1985 dir. Daniel Attias

King, S.
Dark Half, The
ORION (US) 1993 dir. George A.
Romero

King, S.
Dead Zone, The
PAR (US) 1983 dir. David Cronenberg

King, S.
Dolores Claiborne
COL (US) 1995 dir. Taylor Hackford

King, S.
Firestarter
UN (US) 1984 dir. Mark L. Lester

King, S.
Graveyard Shift
PAR (US) 1990 dir. Ralph S. Singleton

King, S.
Green Mile, The
WAR (US) 1999 dir. Frank Darabont

King, S.
Hearts in Atlantis
CASTLE ROCK (US) 2001 dir. Scott
Hicks

King, S.
If Die Before I Wake
Lady from Shanghai, The
COL (US) 1948 dir. Orson Welles

King, S.
It
LORIMAR (US) 1989
dir. Tommy Lee Wallace
TVSe(US)

King, S.
Langoliers, The
LAUREL-KING (US) 1995 dir. Tom
Holland
TVSe(US)

King, S.
Misery
COL (US) 1990 dir. Rob Reiner

King, S.
Needful Things
COL (US) 1993 dir. Fraser Clarke
Heston

King, S.
Night Flier
NEW LINE (It/US) 1997 dir. Mark
Pavia

King, S.
Pet Sematary
PAR (US) 1989 dir. Mary Lambert

King, S.
Rita Hayworth and the Shawshank
Redemption
Shawshank Redemption, The
COL (US) 1994 dir. Frank Darabont

King, S.
Salem's Lot
WAR (US) 1979 dir. Tobe Hooper
TVSe(US)

King, S.
Shining, The
WAR (GB) 1980 dir. Stanley Kubrick
WAR (US) 1997 dir. Mick Garris
TVSe(US)

King, S.
Sometimes They Come Back
DELAUR (US) 1991
dir. Tom McLaughlin
TV(US)

King, S.
Stand, The
LAUREL ENT (US) 1994 dir. Mick
Garris
TVSe(US)

King, S.
Thinner
PAR (US) 1996 dir. Tom Holland

King, S.
Tommyknockers, The
KON/SAN (US) 1993 dir. John Power
TVSe(US)

King-Hall, M.
Life and Death of the Wicked Lady Skelton, The

Wicked Lady, The
GFD (GB) 1946 dir. Leslie Arliss
CANNON (GB) 1983
dir. Michael Winner

King-Smith, D.
Babe, the Gallant Pig (US); The Sheep-Pig (GB)

Babe
UN (Aust) 1995 dir. Chris Noonan
A, Ch

Kingman, L. and Green, G.
His Majesty O'Keefe

WAR (GB) 1954 dir. Byron Haskin

Kingsbury, K.
Deadly Pretender

Every Woman's Dream
KUSHNER-LOCKE (US) 1996 dir.
Steven Schachter
TV(US)

Kingsley, C.
Water Babies, The

PA (GB/Pol) 1978 dir. Lionel Jeffries
A

Kingsley, M.
Shadow Over Elveron

UN TV (US) 1968 dir. James Goldstone
TV(US)

Kingsley, S.
Dead End

P
UA (US) 1937 dir. William Wyler

Kingsley, S.
Detective Story

P
PAR (US) 1951 dir. William Wyler

Kingsley, S.
Men in White

P
MGM (US) 1934
dir. Richard Boleslawsky

Kingsley, S.
Patriots, The

P
COMPASS (US) 1963
dir. George Schaefer
TV(US)

Kinsella, W. P.
Dance Me Outside

YORKTOWN (Can) 1994 dir. Bruce
McDonald

Kinsella, W. P.
Shoeless Joe

Field of Dreams
UN (US) 1989 dir. Phil A. Robinson

Kipling, R.
Captains Courageous

MGM (US/GB) 1937
dir. Victor Fleming
ROSEMONT (US) 1977
dir. Harvey Hart
TV(GB/US)
HALLMARK (US) 1996 dir. Michael
Anderson
TV(US)

Kipling, R.
Jungle Book, The

KORDA (US) 1942 dir. Zoltan Korda,
André de Toth
DISNEY (US) 1967
dir. Wolfgang Reitherman
A, Ch, M
DISNEY (US) 1994 dir. Stephen
Sommers
Ch

Kipling, R.
Jungle Book, The

Second Jungle Book, The—Mowgli and Baloo
TRISTAR (US) 1997 dir. Duncan McLachlan
Ch

Kipling, R.
Kim

MGM (US) 1950 dir. Victor Saville
LF (GB) 1984 dir. John Davies
TVSe(GB)

Kipling, R.
Light That Failed, The

PAR (US) 1939 dir. William Wellman

Kipling, R.
Man Who Would Be King, The

COL (US) 1975 dir. John Huston

Kipling, R.
Soldiers Three

MGM (US) 1951 dir. Tay Garnett

Kipling, R.
Stalky & Co.

BBC (GB) 1982 dir. Rodney Bennett
TVSe(GB)

Kipling, R.
Toomai of the Elephants

Elephant Boy
UA (GB) 1937 dir. Robert Flaherty, Zoltan Korda

Kipling, R.
Wee Willie Winkie

FOX (US) 1937 dir. John Ford

Kippax, F.
Underbelly

BBC (GB) 1992 dir. Nicholas Renton
TVSe(GB)

Kirk, J.
Build-up Boys, The

Madison Avenue
FOX (US) 1962 dir. Bruce Humberstone

Kirkbride, R.
Girl Named Tamiko, A

PAR (US) 1962 dir. John Sturges

Kirkland, J.
Tobacco Road

P
FOX (US) 1941 dir. John Ford

Kirkwood, J.
Some Kind of Hero

PAR (US) 1981 dir. Michael Pressman

Kirkwood, J.
There Must be a Pony

COL TV (US) 1986 dir. Joseph Sargent
TV(US)

Kirstein, L.
Lay this Laurel

Glory
TRISTAR (US) 1989 dir. Edward Zwick

Kjaerstad, J.
Homo Falsus

Perfect Murder, The
NORSK (Nor) 1993 dir. Eva Isaksen

Kjelgaard, J. A.
Big Red

DISNEY (US) 1962 dir. Norman Tokar
A, Ch

Klaben, H. and Day, B.
Hey, I'm Alive!

FRIES (US) 1975 dir. Lawrence Schiller
TV(US)

Klane, R.
Fire Sale

FOX (US) 1977 dir. Alan Arkin

Klane, R.
Where's Poppa?
UA (US) 1970 dir. Carl Reiner

Klass, P.
Other Women's Children
LIFETIME TV (US) 1993 dir. Anne Wheeler
TV(US)

Klavan, A.
Don't Say a Word
FOX (US) 2001 dir. Gary Fleder

Klavan, A.
True Crime
ZANUCK (US) 1999 dir. Clint Eastwood

Kleiman, D.
Deadly Silence, A
GREENWALD (US) 1989 dir. John Patterson
TV(US)

Klein, A.
Counterfeit Traitor, The
PAR (US) 1962 dir. George Seaton

Klein, J.
Primary Colors
UN (US) 1998 dir. Mike Nichols

Klein, J.
T Bone N Weasel
P
TNT (US) 1992 dir. Lewis Teague
TV(US)

Klein, N.
Mom, the Wolfman, and Me
TIME-LIFE (US) 1980 dir. Edmond A. Levy
TV(US)

Klempner, J.
Letter to Five Wives
Letter to Three Wives, A
FOX (US) 1948 dir. Joseph L. Mankiewicz
FOX (US) 1985 dir. Larry Elikann
TV(US)

Kluge, P. F.
Eddie and the Cruisers
EMBASSY (US) 1983 dir. Martin Davidson

Kluger, R.
Simple Justice
NEW IMAGES (US) 1993 dir. Helaine Head
TV(US)

Klurfeld, H.
Walter Winchell: His Life and Times
Winchell
HBO (US) 1998 dir. Paul Mazursky
TV(US)

Knebel, F.
Vanished
UN (US) 1971 dir. Buzz Kulik
TVSe(US)

Knebel, F. and Bailey II, C. W.
Seven Days in May
PAR (US) 1964 dir. John Frankenheimer

Knebel, F. and Bailey II, C. W.
Enemy Within, The
HBO (US) 1994 Jonathan Darby
TV(US)

Kniepple, E.
That Hagen Girl
WAR (US) 1947 dir. Peter Godfrey

Knight, E. M.
Lassie Come Home
MGM (US) 1943 dir. Fred M. Wilcox

Knight, E. M.
This Above All

FOX (US) 1942 dir. Anatole Litvak

Knight, H. A.
Beyond Bedlam

METRODOME (GB) 1993 dir. Vadim Jean

Knight, H. A.
Carnosaur

NEW HORIZON (US) 1993 dir. Adam Simon

Knight, H. A.
Slimer

Proteus
METRODOME (GB) 1996 dir. Bob Keen

Knoblock, E.
Kismet

P
WAR (US) 1930 dir. John Francis Dillon
MGM (US) 1944 dir. William Dieterle
MGM (US) 1955 dir. Vincente Minnelli
M

Knoblock, E.
Lullaby, The

P
Sin of Madelon Claudet
MGM (US) 1931 dir. Edgar Selwyn

Knoll, H. H.
Cabin in the Cotton

WAR (US) 1932 dir. Michael Curtiz

Knott, F.
Dial 'M' for Murder

P
WAR (US) 1954 dir. Alfred Hitchcock
MILBERG (US) 1958
dir. George Schaefer
TIME-LIFE (US) 1981
dir. Boris Sagal
TV(US)

Knott, F.
Dial M For Murder

P
Perfect Murder, A
WAR (US) 1998 dir. Andrew Davis

Knott, F.
Wait Until Dark

P
WAR (US) 1967 dir. Terence Young

Knowles, J.
Separate Peace, A

PAR (US) 1972 dir. Larry Peerce

Knutsen, P.
Svart Cayal

Sebastian
NORDISK (Nor/Swe) 1996 dir. Svend Wam

Kobal, J.
Rita Hayworth: The Time, the Place, and the Woman

Rita Hayworth: The Love Goddess
SUSSKIND (US) 1983
dir. James Goldstone
TV(US)

Kober, A.
Having Wonderful Time

P
RKO (US) 1938 dir. Alfred Santell

Koch, C. J.
Year of Living Dangerously, The

MGM/UA (Aust) 1982 dir. Peter Weir

Koda, A.
Flowing

EAST-WEST (Jap) 1956 dir. Mikio Naruse

Koenig, L.
Little Girl Who Lives Down The Lane, The

RANK (US/Fr/Can) 1976
dir. Nicolas Gessner

Koenig, J.
Little Odessa
FINE LINE (US) 1994 dir. James Gray

Koenig, L.
Rockabye
PEREGRINE (US) 1986
dir. Richard Michael
TV(US)

Kohn, B. G.
Best Man Wins, The
COL (US) 1934 dir. Erle C. Kenton

Kohn, C.
Jude und das Madchen, Der
Leo und Claire
ODEON (Ger) 2001 dir. Joseph
Vilsmaier

Kohn, R. S.
Pillar to Post
P
Pillow to Post
WAR (US) 1945 dir. Vincent Sherman

Kohner, F.
Gidget
COL (US) 1959 dir. Paul Wendkos

Kohner, F.
Gidget Goes to New York
Gidget Grows Up
COL TV (US) 1969 dir. James Sheldon
TV(US)

Kolb, K.
Couch Trip, The
ORION (US) 1988 dir. Michael Ritchie

Kolb, K.
Getting Straight
COL (US) 1970 dir. Richard Rush

Kollek, A.
Don't Ask Me If I Love
Worlds Apart
SCANLON (Israel) 1980
dir. Barbara Noble

Kolpacoff, V.
Prisoners of Quai Dong, The
Physical Assault
TITAN (US) 1973
dir. William M. Bushnell

Komroff, M.
Magic Bow, The
GFD (GB) 1946 dir. Bernard Knowles

Konig, H.
Death of a Schoolboy
NEUE STUDIO (Austria) 1991
dir. Peter Patzak

Konig, J.
David
KINO (W. Ger) 1982 dir. Peter Lilienthal

Konigsburg, E. L.
Father's Arcane Daughter
Caroline?
B&E (US) 1990 dir. Joseph Sargent
TV(US)

Konigsburg, E. L.
**From the Mixed-up Files of Mrs Basil
E. Frankweiler**
Hideaways, The
UA (US) 1973 dir. Fielder Cook

Konigsburg, E. L.
**From the Mixed-Up Files of Mrs. Basil
E. Frankweiler**
ROSEMONT (US) 1995 dir. Marcus
Cole
TV(US)

Koningsberger, H.
Revolutionary, The
UA (US) 1970 dir. Paul Williams

Koningsberger, H.
Walk with Love and Death, A
FOX (US) 1969 dir. John Huston

Konvitz, J.
Sentinel, The
UN (US) 1977 dir. Michael Winner

Konwicki, T.
Little Apocalypse, The
K.G. (Fr) 1993 dir. Costa-Gavras

Koontz, D.
Black River
FOX TV (US) 2001 dir. Jeff Bleckner
TV(US)

Koontz, D.
Demon Seed
MGM (US) 1977 dir. Donald Cammell

Koontz, D.
Face of Fear, The
WAR TV (US) 1990 dir. Farhad Mann
TV(US)

Koontz, D.
Hideaway
TRISTAR (US) 1995 dir. Brett Leonard

Koontz, D.
Intensity
TRISTAR (US) 1997 dir. Yves Simoneau
TVSe(US)

Koontz, D.
Mr. Murder
PATCHETT-KAUFMAN (US) 1999 dir.
Dick Lowry
TVSe(US)

Koontz, D.
Phantoms
MIRAMAX (US) 1998 dir. Joe Chappelle

Koontz, D.
Sole Survivor
COL TRISTAR (US/Can) 2000 dir.
Mikael Salomon
TVSe(US/Can)

Koontz, D.
Twilight
Servants of Twilight, The
TRIMARK (US) 1991 dir. Jeffrey Obrow
TV(US)

Koontz, D.
Watchers
UN (US) 1988 dir. Jon Hess

Koontz, D.
Watchers
Watchers Reborn
CONCORDE (US) 1998 dir. John Carl
Buechler

Kopit, A.
Indians
P
Buffalo Bill and the Indians
UA (US) 1976 dir. Robert Altman

Kopit, A.
Oh Dad, Poor Dad ... Mama's Hung You In The Closet and I'm Feeling So Sad
P
PAR (US) 1966 dir. Richard Quine

Korda, M.
Queenie
NEW WORLD (US) 1987
dir. Larry Peerce
TVSe(US)

Korder, H.
Search and Destroy
P
OCTOBER (US) 1995 dir. David Salle

Kosinski, J.
Being There
LORIMAR (US) 1979 dir. Hal Ashby

Kotlowitz, A.
There Are No Children Here
HARPO (US) 1993 dir. Anita Addison
TV(US)

Kovic, R.
Born on the Fourth of July
UN (US) 1989 dir. Oliver Stone

Kozniewski, K.
Five Boys from Barska Street
POLSKI (Pol) 1953 dir. Aleksander Ford

Krabbe, T.
Golden Egg, The
Vanishing, The
INGRID (Swe) 1990 dir. George Sluizer
FOX (US) 1993 dir. George Sluizer

Krabbe, T.
Grot, De
LIVING (Neth) 2001 dir. Martin
Koolhoven

Kraft, D. and Kraft, R.
Touch of Hope, A
NBC (US) 1999 dir. Craig R. Baxley
TV(US)

Krakauer, J.
Into Thin Air
Into Thin Air: Death on Everest
COL TRISTAR (US) 1997 dir. Robert
Markowitz
TV(US)

Kramm, J.
Shrike, The
P
UI (US) 1955 dir. José Ferrer

Krantz, J.
Dazzle
MULTIMEDIA PROD (US) 1995 dir.
Richard Colla
TVSe(US)

Krantz, J.
I'll Take Manhattan
KRANTZ (US) 1987
dir. Douglas Hickox, Richard Michaels
TVSe(US)

Krantz, J.
Mistral's Daughter
KRANTZ (Fr/Lux/US) 1986
dir. David Hickox, Kevin Connor
TVSe(Fr/Lux/US)

Krantz, J.
Princess Daisy
NBC ENT (US) 1984 dir. Waris Hussein
TVSe(US)

Krantz, J.
Scruples
WAR (US) 1980 dir. Alan J. Levi
TVSe(US)

Krantz, J.
Till We Meet Again
KRANTZ/YTV (US/GB) 1989
dir. Charles Jarrot
TVSe(GB/US)

Krantz, J.
Torch Song
MULTIMEDIA (US) 1993 dir. Michael
Miller
TV(US)

Krasna, N.
Dear Ruth
P
PAR (US) 1947 dir. William D. Russell

Krasna, N.
John Loves Mary

P
WAR (US) 1948 dir. David Butler

Krasna, N.
Kind Sir

P
Indiscreet
WAR (GB) 1958 dir. Stanley Donen
REP (US) 1988
dir. Richard Michaels
TV(US)

Krasna, N.
Small Miracle

P
Four Hours to Kill
PAR (US) 1935 dir. Mitchell Leisen

Krasna, N.
Sunday in New York

P
MGM (US) 1963 dir. Peter Tewkesbury

Krasna, N.
Who Was That Lady I Saw You With?

P
Who Was That Lady?
COL (US) 1960 dir. George Sidney

Krasznahorkai, L.
Melancholy of Resistance, The

Werckmeister Harmoniak
BABELSBERG (Ger/It/Fr) 2000 dir.
Agnes Hranitzki, Bela Tarr

Krause, C. A.
Guyana Massacre: The Eyewitness Account

Guyana Tragedy: The Story of Jim Jones
KÖNIGSBERG (US) 1980
dir. William A. Graham
TVSe(US)

Krausser, H.
Grosse Bagarozy, Der

CONSTANTIN (Ger) 1999 dir. Bernd
Eichinger

Krents, H.
To Race the Wind

GRAUMAN (US) 1980
dir. Walter Grauman
TV(US)

Krentz, J. A.
Waiting Game, The

ALLIANCE (Can) 1998 dir. Victor Sarin
TV(Can)

Kressing, H.
Cook, The

Something for Everyone
NG (US) 1970 dir. Harold Prince
GB title: Black Flowers for the Bride

Krumgold, J.
And Now Miguel

UI (US) 1965 dir. James B. Clark

Kuchler-Silberman, L.
One Hundred Children

Lena: My 100 Children
GREENWALD (US) 1987 dir. Ed Sherin
TV(US)

Kummer, C.
Good Gracious Annabelle

P
Annabelle's Affairs
FOX (US) 1931 dir. Alfred Werker

Kundera, M.
Unbearable Lightness of Being, The

ORION (US) 1988 dir. Philip Kaufman

Kunen, J. S.
Strawberry Statement, The

MGM (US) 1970 dir. Stuart Hagmann

Kunhardt, Jr., P.
My Father's House
FILMWAYS (US) 1975 dir. Alex Segal
TV(US)

Kurbjuweit, D.
Einsamkeit der Krokodile, Die
Loneliness of the Crocodile, The
OLGA (Ger) 2000 dir. Jobst Oetzmann

Kureishi, H.
Buddha of Suburbia, The
BBC (GB) 1993 dir. Roger Michell
TVSe(GB)

Kureishi, H.
Intimacy
FRANCE 2 (Fr/GB) 2000 dir. Patrice
Chereau

Kurnitz, H.
Once More, With Feeling
P
COL (GB) 1960 dir. Stanley Donen

Kurth, A.
Prescription: Murder
Murder in Texas
D. CLARK (US) 1981 dir. Billy Hale
TVSe(US)

Kurth, P.
**Anastasia: The Riddle of Anna
Anderson**
Anastasia: The Mystery of Anna
TELECOM (US) 1986
dir. Marvin Chomsky
TVSe(US)

Kutagawa, R. A.
In the Grove
Iron Maze
TRANS-TOKYO (US/Jap) 1991
dir. Hiroaki Yoshida

Kuttner, H. and Moore, C. L.
Vintage Seasons
Disaster in Time
WILDSTREET (US) 1992 dir. David N.
Twohy
TV(US)

Kyne, P. B.
Never the Twain Shall Meet
MGM (US) 1931 dir. W. S. Van Dyke

Kyne, P. B.
Parson of Panamint, The
PAR (US) 1941 dir. William McGann

Kyne, P. B.
Three Godfathers, The
Hell's Heroes
UN (US) 1930 dir. William Wyler

Kyne, P. B.
Three Godfathers, The
MGM (US) 1936
dir. Richard Boleslawski
MGM (US) 1948 dir. John Ford

Kyne, P. B.
Valley of the Giants
WAR (US) 1938 dir. William Keighley

Kytle, R.
Last Voyage of the Valhalla
Desperate Voyage
WIZAN (US) 1980
dir. Michael O'Herlihy
TV(US)

L

La Bern, A. J.
Goodbye Piccadilly, Farewell Leicester Square
Frenzy
RANK (GB) 1971 dir. Alfred Hitchcock

La Bern, A. J.
It Always Rains on Sundays
EAL (GB) 1947 dir. Robert Hamer

La Bern, A. J.
Night Darkens the Streets
Good-Time Girl
GFD (GB) 1948 dir. David MacDonald

La Bern, A. J.
Paper Orchid
COL (GB) 1949 dir. Roy Baker

La Fontaine, G.
Flashpoint
TRISTAR (US) 1984
dir. William Tannen

La Fontaine, G.
Two Minute Warning
UN (US) 1976 dir. Larry Peerce

La Motta, J.
Raging Bull
UA (US) 1980 dir. Martin Scorsese

La Mure, P.
Moulin Rouge
UA (GB) 1952 dir. John Huston

La Rochhelle, P. D.
Feu Follet, Le
ARCO (Fr/It) 1963 dir. Louis Malle

Laborde, J.
Lesser of Two Evils, The
Investigation
QUARTET (Fr) 1978 dir. Etienne Perier

Labro, P.
Foreign Student
BERL (Fr/GB/US) 1994 dir. Eva Sereny

Lacey, R.
Ford: The Man and the Machine
LANTANA (US) 1987 dir. Allan
Eastman
TVSe(US)

LaFarge, O.
Laughing Boy
MGM (US) 1934 dir. W. S. Van Dyke

Laferrière, D.
Comment faire l'amour avec un nègre sans se fatiguer
How to Make Love to a Negro Without Getting Tired
ANGELIKA (Fr) 1990
dir. Jacques Benoit

Laffan, K.
It's a 2 ft 6 inch above the Ground World
P
Love Ban, The
BL (GB) 1973 dir. Ralph Thomas

Lagerkvist, P.
Barabbas
COL (It) 1962 dir. Richard Fleischer

Lagerlof, S.
Jerusalem
NORDISK (Swe/Den/Nor) 1996 dir.
Bille August

Lahr, J.
Prick up your Ears
ZENITH (GB) 1986 dir. Stephen Frears

Laine, P.
Lacemaker, The
FRANCE 3 (Fr/It/Ger) 1977
dir. Claude Goretta

Laing, R. D.
Knots
CINEGATE (GB) 1975
dir. David I. Munro

Lake, S.
Wyatt Earp, Frontier Marshall
Frontier Marshall
FOX (US) 1933 dir. Lew Seiler
FOX (US) 1939 dir. Allan Dwan

Lake, S.
Wyatt Earp, Frontier Marshal
My Darling Clementine
FOX (US) 1946 dir. John Ford

Lam, N. and Burke, I.
China Cry
PENLAND (US) 1990
dir. James E. Collier

Lambert, B.
Jennie's Story
P
Heart of the Sun
MAK (Can) 1998 dir. Francis
Damberger

Lambert, C.
Wolves of Kromer, The
P
FIRST RUN (US) 1998 dir. Will Gould

Lambert, D.
Touch the Lion's Paw
Rough Cut
PAR (US) 1980 dir. Don Siegel

Lambert, G.
Inside Daisy Clover
WAR (US) 1965 dir. Robert Mulligan

L'Amour, L.
Broken Gun, The
Cancel My Reservation
MGM-EMI (US) 1972 dir. Paul Bogart

L'Amour, L.
Burning Hills, The
WAR (US) 1956 dir. Stuart Heisler
GB title: Apache Territory

L'Amour, L.
Cadow
MGM (GB) 1971 dir. Sam Wanamaker

L'Amour, L.
Conagher
IMAGINE TV (US) 1991
dir. Reynaldo Villalobos
TV(US)

L'Amour, L.
Crossfire Trail
TNT (US) 2001 dir. Simon Wincer
TV(US)

L'Amour, L.
Diamond of Jeru, The
USA NETWORK (US/Aust) 2001 dir.
Ian Barry, Dick Lowry
TV(US/Aust)

L'Amour, L.
Down the Long Hills
DISNEY CH (US) 1986
dir. Burt Kennedy
TV(US)

L'Amour, L.
East of Sumatra
UI (US) 1953 dir. Budd Boetticher

L'Amour, L.
Guns of the Timberland
WAR (US) 1960 dir. Robert D. Webb

L'Amour, L.
Heller With A Gun
Heller in Pink Tights
PAR (US) 1960 dir. George Cukor

L'Amour, L.
Hondo
WAR (US) 1953 dir. John Farrow

L'Amour, L.
Man Called Noon, The
SCOTIA-BARBER (GB/Sp/It)
1973 dir. Peter Collinson

L'Amour, L.
Quick and the Dead, The
HBO (US) 1987 dir. Robert Day
TV(US)

L'Amour, L.
Sackett; Daybreakers, The
Sacketts, The
SHALAKO (US) 1979 dir. Robert Totten
TVSe(US)

L'Amour, L.
Shadow Riders, The
COL TV (US) 1982
dir. Andrew V. McLaglen
TV(US)

L'Amour, L.
Shalako
WAR (GB) 1968 dir. Edward Dmytryk

L'Amour, L.
Taggart
UI (US) 1965 dir. R. G. Springsteen

Lampell, M.
Hero, The
Saturday's Hero
COL (US) 1950 dir. David Miller
GB title: Idols in the Dust

Lamplugh, L.
Rockets in the Dunes
RANK (GB) 1960
dir. William Hammond
Ch

Landon, C.
Ice Cold in Alex
ABP (GB) 1958 dir. J. Lee Thompson
US title: Desert Attack

Landon, M.
Anna and the King of Siam
FOX (US) 1946 dir. John Cromwell

Landon, M.
Anna and the King of Siam
King and I, The
FOX (US) 1956 dir. Walter Lang
M

Lane, K.
Gambit
UI (US) 1966 dir. Ronald Neame

Lane, R. W.
Young Pioneers
ABC (US) 1976 dir. Michael O'Herlihy
TV(US)

Lang, D.
Casualties of War
COL (US) 1989 dir. Brian De Palma

Langelaan, G.
Fly, The
FOX (US) 1958 dir. Kurt Neumann
FOX (US) 1986 dir. David Cronenberg

Langer, A.
Blank Page, The
P
COVERT (US) 1997 dir. Adam Langer

Langley, A. L.
Lion is in the Streets, A
WAR (US) 1953 dir. Raoul Walsh

Langley, N.
Little Lambs Eat Ivy
P
Father's Doing Fine
ABP (GB) 1952 dir. Henry Cass

Langner, L. and Marshall, A.
Pursuit of Happiness, The
P
PAR (US) 1934 dir. Alexander Hall

Lansburg, O.
Dear John
SANDREW (Swe) 1964
dir. Lars Magnus Lindgren

Lantz, F. L.
Stepsister From Planet Weird
VILLAGE ROADSHOW (US) 2000 dir.
Steve Boyum
TV(US)

LaPierre, D.
City of Joy
TRISTAR (US) 1992 dir. Roland Joffe

LaPlante, L.
Bella Mafia
KONIGSBERG (US) 1997 dir. David
Greene
TV(US)

Lardner, R.
Alibi Ike
WAR (US) 1935 dir. Ray Enright

Lardner, R.
Big Town, The
So this is New York
UA (US) 1948 dir. Richard Fleischer

Lardner, R.
Champion
UA (US) 1949 dir. Mark Robson

Larner, J.
Drive, He Said
COL (US) 1970 dir. Jack Nicholson

Larreta, A.
Volaverunt
COLIFILMS (Fr/Sp) 1999 dir. J. J. Bigas
Luna

Larsen, R. W.
Bundy: The Deliberate Stranger
Deliberate Stranger, The
LORIMAR (US) 1986
dir. Marvin Chomsky
TVSe(US)

Larteguy, J.
Centurions, The
Lost Command
COL (US) 1966 dir. Mark Robson

Larusso, II, L.
Wheelbarrow Closers
P
Closer, The
ION (US) 1990 dir. Dimitri Logothetis

Lash, J. P.
Eleanor and Franklin
TALENT (US) 1976 dir. Daniel Petrie
TVSe(US)

Lash, J. P.
Eleanor and Franklin

Eleanor and Franklin: The White House Years
TALENT (US) 1977 dir. Daniel Petrie
TV(US)

Lash, J. P.
Helen and Teacher

Helen Keller—The Miracle Continues
FOX TV (US) 1984 dir. Alan Gibson
TV(US)

Laski, M.
Little Boy Lost
PAR (US) 1953 dir. George Seaton

Laszlo, M.
Parfumerie

P
You've Got Mail
WAR (US) 1998 dir. Nora Ephron

Laszlo, M.
Parfumerie

P
MGM (US) 1940 dir. Ernst Lubitsch

Laszlo, N.
Shop Around the Corner, The

P
In the Good Old Summertime
MGM (US) 1949 dir. Robert Z. Leonard
M

Latimer, J.
Dead Don't Care, The

Last Warning, The
UN (US) 1938 dir. Albert S. Rogell

Latimer, J.
Lady in the Morgue

UN (US) 1938 dir. Otis Garrett
GB title: Case of the Missing Blonde, The

Laumer, K.
Deadfall

Peeper
FOX (US) 1975 dir. Peter Hyams

Launder, F. and Gilliat, S.
Meet a Body

P
Green Man, The
BL (GB) 1956 dir. Robert Day

Laurence, M.
Diviners, The
ATLANTIS (Can) 1993 dir. Anne Wheeler
TV(Can)

Laurence, M.
Jest of God, A

Rachel, Rachel
WAR (US) 1968 dir. Paul Newman

Laurents, A.
Home of the Brave

P
UA (US) 1949 dir. Mark Robson

Laurents, A.
Time of the Cuckoo, The

P
Summertime
UA (US) 1955 dir. David Lean
GB title: Summer Madness

Laurents, A.
Way We Were, The
COL (US) 1973 dir. Sydney Pollack

Laurents, A., Sondheim, S. and Bernstein, L.
West Side Story

P
UA (US) 1961
dir. Robert Wise, Jerome Robbins
M

Laurents, A., Sondheim, S. and Styne, J.
Gypsy
P
WAR (US) 1962 dir. Mervyn LeRoy
RHI (US) 1993 dir. Emile Ardolino
TV(US)
M

Laurey, J.
Joy
UGC (Can/Fr) 1983 dir. Serge Bergon

Lauritzen, J.
Rose and the Flame, The
Kiss of Fire
UN (US) 1955 dir. Joseph M. Newman

Lauro, S.
Open Admissions
P
VIACOM (US) 1988 dir. Gus Trikonis
TV(US)

Lauzier, G.
Souvenirs d'un jeune Homme
Petit Con
GOLDWYN (Fr) 1985
dir. Gerard Lauzier

Lavallee, D.
Event One Thousand
Gray Lady Down
UN (US) 1978 dir. David Greene

Lavery, E.
First Legion, The
P
UA (US) 1951 dir. Douglas Sirk

Lavery, E.
Magnificent Yankee, The
P
MGM (US) 1950 dir. John Sturges
COMPASS (US) 1965
dir. George Schaefer
TV(US)

Lavin, N. and Thorp, M.
Hop Dog, The
Adventure in the Hopfields
ABP (GB) 1954 dir. John Guillermin

Lawes, L. and Finn, J.
Chalked Out
P
You Can't Get Away with Murder
WAR (US) 1939 dir. Lewis Seiler

Lawes, L. E.
Invisible Stripes
WAR (US) 1939 dir. Lloyd Bacon

Lawes, L. E.
20,000 Leagues Under the Sea
20,000 Years in Sing Sing
WAR (US) 1932 dir. Michael Curtiz

Lawler, R.
Summer of the Seventeenth Doll, The
P
UA (US/Aust) 1959 dir. Leslie Norman

Lawlor, H.
What Beckoning Ghost
Dominique
GRAND PRIZE (GB) 1978
dir. Michael Anderson

Lawrence, D. H.
Captain's Doll, The
BBC (GB) 1982 dir. Claude Whatham
TV(GB)

Lawrence, D. H.
Fox, The
WAR (US/Can) 1967 dir. Mark Rydell

Lawrence, D. H.
Kangaroo
WORLD FILM (Aust) 1986
dir. Tim Burstall

Lawrence, D. H.
Lady Chatterley's Lover

COL (Fr) 1956 dir. Marc Allégret
CANNON (GB/Fr) 1981
dir. Just Jaeckin

Lawrence, D. H.
Lady Chatterley

BBC (GB) 1992 dir. Ken Russell
TVSe(GB)

Lawrence, D. H.
Rainbow, The

BBC (GB) 1988 dir. Stuart Burge
TVSe(GB)
VESTRON (GB) 1989 dir. Ken Russell

Lawrence, D. H.
Rocking Horse Winner, The

TC (GB) 1949 dir. Anthony Pelissier

Lawrence, D. H.
Sons and Lovers

FOX (GB) 1960 dir. Jack Cardiff
BBC (GB) 1981 dir. Stuart Burge
TVSe(GB)

Lawrence, D. H.
Trespasser, The

C. GREGG (GB) 1981 dir. Colin Gregg

Lawrence, D. H.
Virgin and the Gypsy, The

LONDON SCR (GB) 1970
dir. Christopher Miles

Lawrence, D. H.
Women in Love

UA (GB) 1969 dir. Ken Russell

Lawrence, D. H. and Skinner, M. L.
Boy in the Bush, The

CHANNEL 4 (GB) 1984
dir. Rob Stewart
TVSe(GB)

Lawrence, H. L.
Children of the Light, The

Damned, The
BL (GB) 1961 dir. Joseph Losey
US title: These Are The Damned

Lawrence, J.
Years Are So Long, The

Make Way for Tomorrow
PAR (US) 1937 dir. Leo McCarey

Lawrence, J. and Lee, R. E.
First Monday in October

P
PAR (US) 1981 dir. Ronald Neame

Lawrence, J. and Lee, R. E.
Inherit the Wind

P
UA (US) 1960 dir. Stanley Kramer
COMPASS (US) 1965
dir. George Schaefer
TV(US)
VINCENT (US) 1988 dir. David Greene
TV(US)
MGM TV (US) 1999 dir. Daniel Petrie
TV(US)

Lawrence, J., Lee, R. E. and Herman, J.
Mame

P
WAR (US) 1974 dir. Gene Saks
M

Lawrence, M.
Madonna of the Seven Moons

GFD (GB) 1944 dir. Arthur Crabtree

Lawrence, T. E.
Seven Pillars of Wisdom

Lawrence of Arabia
COL/BL (GB/US) 1962 dir. David Lean

Lawson, J.
Roses are for the Rich

PHOENIX (US) 1987 dir. Michael Miller
TVSe(US)

Lawson, T. and Considine, R.
Thirty Seconds Over Tokyo
MGM (US) 1944 dir. Mervyn LeRoy

Lawton, H.
Willie Boy
Tell them Willie Boy is Here
UN (US) 1969 dir. Abraham Polonsky

Lay, B. and Bartlett, S.
Twelve O'Clock High
FOX (US) 1949 dir. Henry King

Laye, C.
Enfant Noir, L'
RHEA (Fr) 1995 dir. Laurent Chevallier

Le Breton, A.
Monsieur Rififi
Rififi
PATHS (Fr) 1955 dir. Jules Dassin

Le Carré, J.
Call for the Dead
Deadly Affair, The
COL (GB) 1966 dir. Sidney Lumet

Le Carré, J.
Little Drummer Girl, The
WAR (US) 1984 dir. George Roy Hill

Le Carré, J.
Looking Glass War, The
COL (GB) 1969 dir. Frank R. Pierson

Le Carré, J.
Murder of Quality, A
THAMES (GB) 1991 dir. Gavin Millar
TV(GB)

Le Carré, J.
Perfect Spy, A
BBC (GB) 1987 dir. Peter Smith
TVSe(GB)

Le Carré, J.
Russia House, The
MGM (US) 1990 dir. Fred Schepisi

Le Carré, J.
Smiley's People
BBC (GB) 1982 dir. Simon Langton
TVSe(GB)

Le Carré, J.
Spy Who Came in From the Cold, The
PAR (GB) 1966 dir. Martin Ritt

Le Carré, J.
Tailor of Panama, The
COL (US/Ire) 2001 dir. John Boorman

Le Carré, J.
Tinker, Tailor, Soldier, Spy
BBC (GB) 1979 dir. John Irvin
TVSe(GB)

Le Fanu, S.
Uncle Silas
TC (GB) 1947 dir. Charles Frank
US title: Inheritance, The

Le Fanu, S.
Uncle Silas
Dark Angel, The
BBC (GB) 1989 dir. Peter Hammond
TVSe(GB)

Lea, F. H.
Four Marys, The
Manproof
MGM (US) 1937 dir. Richard Thorpe

Lea, T.
Brave Bulls, The
COL (US) 1951 dir. Robert Rossen

Lea, T.
Confessions from a Holiday Camp
COL (GB) 1977 dir. Norman Cohen

Lea, T.
Confessions of a Driving Instructor
COL (GB) 1976 dir. Norman Cohen

Lea, T.
Confessions of a Pop Performer
COL (GB) 1975 dir. Norman Cohen

Lea, T.
Confessions of a Window Cleaner
COL (GB) 1974 dir. Val Guest

Lea, T.
Wonderful Country, The
UA (US) 1959 dir. Robert Parrish

Lear, M. W.
Heartsounds
EMBASSY (US) 1984 dir. Glenn Jordan
TV(US)

Lear, P.
Goldengirl
AVCO (US) 1979 dir. Joseph Sargent

Leasor, J.
Boarding Party
Sea Wolves, The
RANK (GB/US/Switz) 1980
dir. Andrew McLaglen

Leasor, J.
Passport to Oblivion
Where the Spies Are
MGM (GB) 1965 dir. Val Guest

Leasor, J.
Who Killed Sir Harry Oakes?
Eureka!
MGM/UA (GB/US) 1982
dir. Nicolas Roeg

Leavitt, D.
Lost Language of the Cranes, The
BBC (GB) 1991 dir. Nigel Finch
TV(GB)

LeBel, P.
Song Spinner, The
SHOWTIME (US/Can) 1995 dir. Randy
Bradshaw
TV(US/Can)

Lebert, B.
Crazy
CONSTANTIN (Ger) 2000 dir. Hans-
Christian Schmid

LeBlanc. M. and de Croisset, F.
Arsène Lupin
P
MGM (US) 1932 dir. Jack Conway

Lebow, B.
Shayna Maidel, A
P
Miss Rose White
LORIMAR TV (US) 1992 dir. Joseph
Sargent
TV(US)

Ledda, G.
Padre Padrone
RAI (It) 1977 dir. Paolo Taviani, Vittorio
Taviani

Lederer, W. J. and Burdick, E. L.
Ugly American, The
UI (US) 1962 dir. George England

Lee, B.
Paganini Strikes Again
CFF (GB) 1973 dir. Gordon Gilbert
Ch

Lee, C. Y.
Flower Drum Song
UI (US) 1961 dir. Henry Koster
M

Lee, E.
Queen Bee
COL (US) 1955 dir. Ronald MacDougall

Lee, G. R.
G-String Murders, The

Lady of Burlesque
STROMBERG (US) 1943
dir. William Wellman
GB title: Striptease Lady

Lee, G. R.
Gypsy

WAR (US) 1962 dir. Mervyn LeRoy
RHI (US) 1993 dir. Emile Ardolino
TV(US)
M

Lee, H.
To Kill a Mockingbird

UI (US) 1962 dir. Robert Mulligan

Lee, J.
Career

P
PAR (US) 1959 dir. Joseph Anthony

Lee, J.
Wanderer Never Sleeps, Even on the Road, A

Man with Three Coffins, The
MWL (S. Kor) 1987 dir. Chang Ho Lee

Lee, L.
Farewell My Concubine

BEIJING (China) 1993 dir. Kaige Chen

Lee, L.
Sweet Poison

Along Came a Spider
FOX TV (US) 1970 dir. Lee H. Katzin
TV(US)

Lee, L.
Walking Through the Fire

TIME-LIFE (US) 1979 dir. Robert Day
TV(US)

Lee, R.
Right of Way

P
HBO PREM (US) 1983
dir. George Schaefer
TV(US)

Lee, R. M.
Death and Deliverance

Ordeal in the Arctic
ALLIANCE (US) 1993 dir. Mark Sobel
TV(US)

Leech, M.
Reveille in Washington

Rose and the Jackal, The
WHITE (US) 1990 dir. Jack Gold
TV(US)

Leeson, N. and Whitley, E.
Rogue Trader: How I Brought Down Barings Bank and Shook the Financial World

Rogue Trader
GRANADA (GB) 1999 dir. James Dearden
TV(GB)

Leffland, E.
Mrs. Munck

VIACOM PICT (US) 1996 dir. Diane Ladd
TV(US)

Lefkowitz, B.
Our Guys

Our Guys: Outrage in Glen Rigde
GREENWALD (US) 1999 dir. Guy Ferland
TV(US)

LeFlore, R. and Hawkins, J.
Breakout

One in a Million: The Ron LeFlore Story
EMI (US) 1978 dir. William A. Graham
TV(US)

Leger, J. A.
Monsignore

Monsignor
FOX (US) 1982 dir. Frank Perry

Leguina, J.
Tu Nombre Envenena Mis Suenos

Your Name Poisons My Dreams
CDP(Sp) 1996 dir. Pilar Miro

Lehar, F., Leon, V. and Stein, L.
Merry Widow, The

MGM (US) 1934 dir. Ernst Lubitsch
M
MGM (US) 1952 dir. Curtis Bernhardt
M

Lehman, E.
French Atlantic Affair, The

MGM TV (US) 1979 dir. Douglas Heyes
TVSe(US)

Lehman, R.
Weather in the Streets, The

BBC (GB) 1984 dir. Gavin Millar
TV(GB)

Lehrer, J.
Last Debate, The

SHOWTIME (US) 2000 dir. John
Badham
TV(US)

Leiber, F.
Conjure Wife

Night of the Eagle
IA (GB) 1961 dir. Sidney Hayers
US title: Burn, Witch, Burn

Leigh, J.
What Can You Do?

Making It
FOX (US) 1971 dir. John Erman

Leimas, B.
Intruder, The

WIC (Can/GB) 1999 dir. David Bailey

Leimbach, M.
Dying Young

TCF (US) 1991 dir. Joel Schumacher

Leinster, C.
Heritage of Michael Flaherty, The

Outsider, The
PAR (US) 1980 dir. Tony Luraschi

Leinster, M.
Wailing Asteroid, The

Terronauts, The
EMBASSY (GB) 1967
dir. Montgomery Tully

LeMay, A.
Searchers, The

WAR (US) 1956 dir. John Ford

LeMay, A.
Siege at Dancing Bird, The

Unforgiven, The
UA (US) 1960 dir. John Huston

LeMay, A.
Useless Cowboy, The

Along Came Jones
UA (US) 1945 dir. Stuart Heisler

Lengyel, M.
Angel

P
PAR (US) 1937 dir. Ernest Lubitsch

Lengyel, M.
Czarina, The

P
Catherine the Great
KORDA (GB) 1934 dir. Paul Czinner

Lennart, I.
Funny Girl

P
COL (US) 1968 dir. William Wyler
M

Lennon, G.
Blackout
P
Drunks
BMG (US) 1996 dir. Peter Cohn
TV(US)

Lenz, S.
Das Feuerschiff
Lightship, The
WAR (US) 1985 dir. Jerzy Skolimowski

Leonard, E.
Big Bounce, The
WAR (US) 1969 dir. Alex March

Leonard, E.
Cat Chaser
VESTRON (US) 1989 dir. Abel Ferrara

Leonard, E.
52 Pick-Up
Ambassador, The
CANNON (US) 1984
dir. J. Lee Thompson

Leonard, E.
52 Pick-Up
CANNON (US) 1986
dir. John Frankenheimer

Leonard, E.
Get Shorty
MGM (US) 1995 dir. Barry Sonnenfeld

Leonard, E.
Glitz
LORIMAR (US) 1988 dir. Sandor Stern
TV(US)

Leonard, E.
Gold Coast
PAR (US) 1997 dir. Peter Weller
TV(US)

Leonard, E.
Hombre
FOX (US) 1967 dir. Martin Ritt

Leonard, E.
Last Stand at Saber River
TURNER/BRANDMAN (US) 1997 dir.
Dick Lowry
TV(US)

Leonard, E.
Moonshine War, The
MGM (US) 1970 dir. Richard Quine

Leonard, E.
Out of Sight
JERSEY (US) 1998 dir. Steven
Soderbergh

Leonard, E.
Pronto
SHOWTIMEWORKS (US) 1996 dir. Jim
McBride
TV(US)

Leonard, E.
Rum Punch
Jackie Brown
MIRAMAX (US) 1997 dir. Quentin
Tarantino

Leonard, E.
Stick
UN (US) 1985 dir. Burt Reynolds

Leonard, E.
Touch
INITIAL (US) 1997 dir. Paul Schrader

Leonard, E.
Valdez is Coming
UA (US) 1971 dir. Edwin Sherin

Leonard, H.
Big Birthday, The
P
Broth of a Boy
E. DALTON (Eire) 1958
dir. George Pollack

Leonard, H.
Da
P
FILM DALLAS (US) 1988
dir. Matt Clarke

Leopold, K.
When we Ran
Moving Targets
ACADEMY (Aust) 1987
dir. Chris Langman

LePecheur, D.
News From the Good Lord
CNC (Fr) 1996 dir. Didier LePecheur

LePere, G.
Never Pass This Way Again
Dark Holiday
ORION TV (US) 1989 dir. Lou Antonio
TV(US)

Lerner, A. J.
On a Clear Day You Can See Forever
P
PAR (US) 1970 dir. Vincente Minnelli
M

Lerner, A. J. and Loewe, F.
Brigadoon
P
MGM (US) 1954 dir. Vincente Minnelli
M

Lerner, A. J. and Loewe, F.
Camelot
P
WAR (US) 1967 dir. Joshua Logan
M

Lerner, A. J. and Loewe, F.
Paint Your Wagon
P
PAR (US) 1969 dir. Joshua Logan
M

Leroux, G.
Phantom of the Opera, The
UN (US) 1943 dir. Arthur Lubin
UI (GB) 1962 dir. Terence Fisher
HALMI (US) 1983
dir. Robert Markowitz
TV(US)
21ST CENTURY (US) 1989 dir. Dwight
H. Little
SABAN/SCHERICK (US/Fr) 1990 dir.
Tony Richardson
TV(US/Fr)
RETEITALIA (It) 1999 dir. Dario
Argento

Leroy, F.
Wonder Boy
STUDIO CANAL+ (Fr) 1994 dir. Paul
Vecchiali

Leslie, D.
Polonaise
Song to Remember, A
COL (US) 1944 dir. Charles Vidor

Leslie, D. S.
In My Solitude
Two Left Feet
BL (GB) 1963 dir. Roy Baker

Leslie, D. S.
Two Gentlemen Sharing
PAR (GB) 1969 dir. Ted Kotcheff

Leslie, K. A.
Woman of Color, Daughter of
Privilege: Amanda Dickson
House Divided, A
AVNET/KERNER (US) 2000 dir. John
Kent Harrison
TV(US)

Leslie, R. F.
Bears and I, The
DISNEY (US) 1974
dir. Bernard McEveety
Ch

Leslie-Melville, J. and Leslie-Melville, B.
Raising Daisy Rothschild
Last Giraffe, The
WESTFALL (US) 1979
dir. Jack Couffer
TV(US)

Lessing, D.
Diary of a Good Neighbour, The
Rue du Retrait
JML (Fr) 2001 dir. René Féret

Lessing, D.
Grass is Singing, The
MAINLINE (Zam/Swe) 1981
dir. Michael Raeburn

Lessing, D.
Memoirs of a Survivor
EMI (GB) 1981 dir. David Gladwell

Lester, E.
Two Seconds
WAR (US) 1932 dir. Mervyn LeRoy

Lette, K.
Mad Cows
CAPITOL (GB) 1999 dir. Sara Sugarman

Letts, B.
Where the Heart Is
FOX (US) 2000 dir. Matt Williams

Leven, J.
Creator
UN (US) 1985 dir. Ivan Passer

Levenkron, S.
Best Little Girl in the World, The
SPELLING (US) 1981
dir. Sam O'Steen
TV(US)

Levenkron, S.
Luckiest Girl in the World, The
Secret Cutting
USA NETWORKS (US) 2000 dir. Norma
Bailey
TV(US)

Levi, C.
Christ Stopped At Eboli
ART EYE (It/Fr) 1979
dir. Francesco Rosi

Levi, P.
Truce, The
DAZU (It/Fr/Ger) 1997 dir. Francesco
Rosi

Levin, I.
Boys from Brazil, The
ITC (US/GB) 1978
dir. Franklin Shaffner

Levin, I.
Critic's Choice
P
WAR (US) 1963 dir. Don Weis

Levin, I.
Deathtrap
P
WAR (US) 1982 dir. Sidney Lumet

Levin, I.
Dr. Cook's Garden
P
PAR TV (US) 1971 dir. Ted Post
TV(US)

Levin, I.
Kiss Before Dying, A
UA (US) 1956 dir. Gerd Oswald
UN (US) 1991 dir. James Dearden

Levin, I.
Rosemary's Baby
PAR (US) 1968 dir. Roman Polanski

Levin, I.
Stepford Wives, The
CONTEM (US) 1975 dir. Bryan Forbes

Levin, M.
Compulsion
FOX (US) 1959 dir. Richard Fleischer

Levin, M.
Janine and Alex, Alex and Janine
Model Behavior
DISNEY (US) 2000 dir. Mark Rosman

Levine, P.
To Speak For the Dead
Jake Lassiter: Justice on the Bayou
CANNELL (US) 1995 dir. Peter Markle
TV(US)

Levinson, N.
Room Upstairs, The
M. REES (US) 1987 dir. Stuart Margolin
TV(US)

Levinson, R. and Link, W.
Prescription: Murder
P
UN (US) 1968 dir. Richard Irving
TV(US)

Levoy, M.
Alan and Naomi
TRITON (US) 1992
dir. Sterling van Wagenen

Levy, B. W.
Evergreen
P
GAU (GB) 1934 dir. Victor Saville
M

Levy, E.
Beast Within, The
MGM/UA (US) 1982 dir. Philippe Mora

Levy, S.
Unicorn's Secret, The
Hunt For the Unicorn Killer, The
REGENCY TV (US) 1999 dir. William A. Graham
TVSe(US)

Lewandowski, D.
Worth Winning
FOX (US) 1989 dir. Will Mackenzie

Lewis, A. H.
Lament for Molly Maguires
Molly Maguires, The
PAR (US) 1970 dir. Martin Ritt

Lewis, A.
Gideon's Trumpet
WORLDVISION (US) 1980
dir. Robert Collins
TV(US)

Lewis, C. S.
Lion, the Witch and the Wardrobe, The
ITV (US/GB) 1978 dir. Bill Melendez
A, Ch, TV(GB/US)

Lewis, C. S.
Lion, The Witch and the Wardrobe, The; Prince Caspian; Voyage of the Dawn Treader, The; Silver Chair, The
Chronicles of Narnia, The
BBC (GB) 1989 dir. Marilyn Fox, Alex Kirby
TVSe(GB)

Lewis, C. S.
Prince Caspian and The Silver Chair
Silver Chair, The
BBC (GB) 1990 dir. Alex Kirby
Ch, TVSe(GB)

Lewis, D.
Sexpionage: The Exploitation of Sex
by Soviet Intelligence
Secret Weapons
ITC (US) 1985 dir. Don Taylor
TV(US)

Lewis, E.
Trader Horn
MGM (US) 1931 dir. W. S. Van Dyke
MGM (US) 1973 dir. Reza Badiyi

Lewis, H.
Day is Ours, This
Mandy
GFD (GB) 1952
dir. Alexander Mackendrick
US title: Crash of Silence, The

Lewis, I.
Chinese Coffee
P
SHOOTING GALLERY (US) 2000 dir.
Al Pacino

Lewis, M.
Great Balls of Fire
ORION (US) 1989 dir. Jim McBride

Lewis, O.
Children of Sanchez, The
HALL BARTLETT (US/Mex) 1978
dir. Hall Bartlett

Lewis, S.
Ann Vickers
RKO (US) 1933 dir. John Cromwell

Lewis, S.
Arrowsmith
UA (US) 1931 dir. John Ford

Lewis, S.
Babbit
WAR (US) 1934 dir. William Keighley

Lewis, S.
Cass Timberlane
MGM (US) 1947 dir. George Sidney

Lewis, S.
Dodsworth
UA (US) 1936 dir. William Wyler

Lewis, S.
Elmer Gantry
UA (US) 1960 dir. Richard Brooks

Lewis, S.
Main Street
I Married a Doctor
WAR (US) 1936 dir. Archie Mayo

Lewis, S.
Mantrap
Untamed
PAR (US) 1940 dir. George Archainbaud

Lewis, S.
Sparrers Can't Sing
P
Sparrows Can't Sing
WAR (GB) 1962 dir. Joan Littlewood

Lewis, T.
Jack's Return Home
Get Carter
MGM (GB) 1971 dir. Mike Hodges
WAR (US) 2000 dir. Stephen T. Kay

Li Shu Xian
Pu Yi and I; Pu Yi's Later Life; Pu Yi's
Former Life
Last Emperor, The
NKL (China) 1988 dir. Li Han Hsiang

Li-Eng, S.
Dark Night
GOODYEAR (Tai/HK) 1986
dir. Fred Tan

Liddy, G. G.
Will

Will: G. Gordon Liddy
SHAYNE (US) 1982
dir. Robert Lieberman
TV(US)

Lidz, F.
Unstrung Heroes

HOLLYWOOD (US) 1995 dir. Diane
Keaton

Lieber, J.
Move

FOX (US) 1970 dir. Stuart Rosenberg

Lieberman, H.
Crawlspace

TITUS (US) 1972 dir. Joan Newland
TV(US)

Lieberson, G.
3 for Bedroom C

INT (US) 1952 dir. Milton H. Bren

Lilar, S.
Confession Anonyme, La

Benvenuta
NI (Bel/Fr) 1982 dir. André Delvaux

Lily, P. and Glass, D.
Beg!

P
ARTS MAGIC (GB) 1994 dir. Robert
Golden

Limb, S.
Up the Garden Path

GRANADA (GB) 1990 dir. David Askey
TVSe(GB)

Lincoln, V.
February Hill

Primrose Path, The
RKO (US) 1940 dir. Gregory La Cava

Lind, H.
Super-Wife, The

CONSTANTIN (Ger) 1996 dir. Sonke
Wortmann

Lindbergh, C. A.
We

Spirit of St. Louis, The
WAR (US) 1957 dir. Billy Wilder

Lindgren, A.
Mio, My Son

Land of Faraway, The
NORD/GORKY (Swe/USSR/Nor) 1988
dir. Vladimir Grammatikov

Lindgren, A.
New Adventures of Pippi
Longstocking, The

COL (US) 1988 dir. Ken Annakin
Ch

Lindgren, A.
Pippi Longstocking

TELEFILM (Can/Ger/Swe) 1997 dir.
Bill Giggie, Michael Schaack, Clive A.
Smith
A, Ch

Lindner, R.
Fifty Minute Hour, The

Pressure Point
UA (US) 1962 dir. Hubert Cornfield

Lindo, E.
Otro Barrio, El

TORNASOL (Sp) 2000 dir. Salvador
Garcia Ruiz

Lindop, A. E.
I Start Counting

UA (GB) 1969 dir. David Greene

Lindop, A. E.
I Thank A Fool

MGM (GB) 1962 dir. Robert Stevens

Lindop, A. E.
Singer Not the Song, The
RANK (GB) 1960 dir. Roy Baker

Lindop, A. E.
Tall Headlines, The
GN (GB) 1952 dir. Terence Young

Lindquist, D.
Berlin, Tunnel 21
FILMWAYS (US) 1981
dir. Richard Michaels
TV(US)

Lindsay, F.
Tied Up
FRANCHISE (US) 2000 dir. Anthony
Hickox

Lindsay, H.
She Loves Me Not
P
PAR (US) 1934 dir. Elliott Nugent

Lindsay, H. and Carlson, C. C.
Late Great Planet Earth, The
ENT (US) 1979 dir. Robert Amram

Lindsay, H. and Crouse, R.
Call me Madam
P
TCF (US) 1953 dir. Walter Lang
M

Lindsay, H. and Crouse, R.
Life with Father
P
WAR (US) 1947 dir. Michael Curtiz

Lindsay, H. and Crouse, R.
Remains to be Seen
P
MGM (US) 1953 dir. Don Weis

Lindsay, H. and Crouse, R.
Sound of Music, The
P
FOX (US) 1965 dir. Robert Wise
M

Lindsay, H. and Crouse, R.
State of the Union
P
MGM (US) 1948 dir. Frank Capra
GB title: World and His Wife, The

Lindsay, J.
All on the Never-Never
Live Now, Pay Later
REGAL (GB) 1962 dir. Jay Lewis

Lindsay, J.
Picnic at Hanging Rock
AFC (Aust) 1975 dir. Peter Weir

Lindsay, N.
Age of Consent
COL (Aust) 1969 dir. Michael Powell

Lindsey, D. L.
Mercy
FRANCHISE (US) 2000 dir. Damian
Harris

Lindsey, R.
Falcon and the Snowman, The
ORION (US) 1985 dir. John Schlesinger

Linford, D.
Man Without a Star, The
UI (US) 1955 dir. King Vidor

Ling, P. S.
Strange Tales of Liao Zhai
Chinese Ghost Story II
GORDON (China) 1990
dir. Ching Siu-Tung

Linklater, E.
Husband of Delilah

Samson and Delilah
COMWORLD (US) 1984 dir. Lee Philips
TV(US)

Linklater, E.
Laxdale Hall

ABP (GB) 1952 dir. John Eldridge
US title: Scotch on the Rocks

Linklater, E.
Poet's Pub

AQUILA (GB) 1949
dir. Frederick Wilson

Linklater, E.
Private Angelo

ABP (GB) 1949 dir. Peter Ustinov

Lintz, G.
Animals Are My Hobby

Buddy
COL (US) 1997 dir. Caroline Thompson

Linur, I.
Song of the Siren

TALISMA (Israel) 1994 dir. Eitan Fuchs

Lippold, E.
House with the Heavy Doors, The

Fiancée, The
DEFA (Ger) 1984 dir. Gunter Reisch,
Gunther Rucker

Lipscombe, W. P. and Minney, R. J.
Clive of India

P
FOX (US) 1935 dir. Richard Boleslawski

Lipsky, E.
People Against O'Hara, The

MGM (US) 1951 dir. John Sturges

Lipton, J.
Mirrors

L. HILL (US) 1985 dir. Harry Winer
TV(US)

Lispector, C.
Hour of the Star, The

RAIZ (Bra) 1987 dir. Suzana Amaral

List, J. A.
Day the Loving Stopped, The

MONASH-ZEIT (US) 1981
dir. Delbert Mann
TV(US)

List, S.
Nobody Makes Me Cry

Between Friends
HBO (US) 1983 dir. Lou Antonio

Littell, R.
Amateur, The

FOX (Can) 1982 dir. Charles Jarrot

Little, E.
Another Day in Paradise

TRIMARK (US) 1998 dir. Larry Clark

Livings, H.
Eh?

P
Work is a Four Letter Word
UI (GB) 1968 dir. Peter Hall

Llewellyn, R.
How Green Was My Valley

FOX (US) 1941 dir. John Ford
BBC (GB) 1975 dir. Donald Wilson
TVSe(GB)

Llewellyn, R.
None but the Lonely Heart

RKO (US) 1944 dir. Clifford Odets

Llewellyn, R.
Noose
P
ABPC (GB) 1948
dir. Edmond T. Greville

Llewellyn, R.
Poison Pen
P
AB (GB) 1939 dir. Paul Stein

Llosa, M. V.
Aunt Julia and the Scriptwriter
Tune in Tomorrow ...
CINECOM (US) 1990 dir. Jon Amiel

Llosa, M. V.
City and the Dogs, The
INCA (Peru) 1985
dir. Francisco J. Lombardi

Llosa, M. V.
Pantaleon y Las Visitadoras
TORNASOL (Peru) 1999 dir. Francisco
J. Lombardi

Locke, W. J.
Beloved Vagabond, The
COL (GB) 1936 dir. Curtis Bernhardt

Locke, W. J.
Morals of Marcus Ordeyne, The
Morals of Marcus, The
GB (GB) 1935 dir. Miles Mander

Locke, W. J.
Shorn Lamb, The
Strangers in Love
PAR (US) 1932 dir. Lothar Mendes

Lockhart, R. B.
Reilly, Ace of Spies
EUSTON (GB) 1983 dir. Jim Goddard
TVSe(GB)

Lockhart, Sir R. H. B.
Memoirs of a British Agent
British Agent
WAR (US) 1934 dir. Michael Curtiz

Lockridge, R.
Raintree County
MGM (US) 1957 dir. Edward Dmytryk

Lockwood, C. A. and Adamson, H. C.
Hellcats of the Sea
Hellcats of the Navy
COL (US) 1957 dir. Nathan Juran

Lodge, D.
Nice Work
BBC (GB) 1989 dir. Christopher Menaul
TVSe(GB)

Lodge, D.
Small World
GRANADA (GB) 1988 dir. Robert
Chetwyn
TVSe(GB)

Loffler, H.
Silence Under the Sea, The
Farewell to Agnes
MUNCHEN (Ger) 1994 dir. Michael
Gwisdek

Lofting, H.
Doctor Dolittle
FOX (US) 1967 dir. Richard Fleischer
Ch, M

Lofts, N.
Jassy
GFD (GB) 1947 dir. Bernard Knowles

Loftus, J.
Belarus Secret, The
Kojak: The Belarus File
UN TV (US) 1985 dir. Robert
Markowitz
TV(US)

Logan, J. and Heggen, T.
Mister Roberts

P

Ensign Pulver
WAR (US) 1964 dir. Joshua Logan

Lombard, C.
Disappearance of Rory Brophy, The

Disappearance of Finbar, The
VICTORIA (Ire/Swe/GB) 1996 dir. Sue Clayton

London, A. and London, L.
On Trial

L'Aveu
CORONA (Fr) 1970 dir. Costa-Gavras

London, J.
Call of the Wild

UA (US) 1935 dir. William Wellman
MASSFILMS (GB/Fr/It/Ger) 1972 dir. Ken Annakin
FRIES (US) 1976 dir. Jerry Jameson
TV(US)
RHI (US) 1993 dir. Michael Toshiyuki Uno
TV(US)

London, J.
Call of the Wild

Call of the Wild: Dog of the Yukon
KING GREENLIGHT (Can) 1996 dir. Peter Svatek
TV(Can)

London, J.
Martin Eden

Adventures of Martin Eden, The
COL (US) 1942 dir. Sidney Salkow

London, J.
Mexican, The

Fighter, The
UA (US) 1952 dir. Herbert Fine

London, J.
Mutiny of the Elsinore

ARGYLE (GB) 1937 dir. Roy Lockwood

London, J.
Sea Wolf, The

FOX (US) 1930 dir. Alfred Santell
WAR (US) 1941 dir. Michael Curtiz
PRIMEDIA (US) 1993 dir. Michael Anderson
TV(US)
CONCORDE (US) 1997 dir. Gary T. McDonald

London, J.
Sea Wolf, The

Wolf Larsen
ABP (US) 1958 dir. Harman Jones

London, J.
White Fang

FOX (US) 1936 dir. David Butler
FOX (It/Sp/Fr) 1974 dir. Lucio Fulci
DISNEY (US) 1991 dir. Randal Kleiser

London, J. and Fish, R.
Assassination Bureau, The

PAR (GB) 1969 dir. Basil Dearden

Long, J.
Outlaw: The True Story of Claude Dallas

Manhunt for Claude Dallas
LONDON (US) 1986 dir. Jerry London
TV(US)

Long, S. A.
Never Too Late

P

WAR (US) 1965 dir. Bud Yorkin

Longden, D.
Diana's Story; Lost for Words

Wide-Eyed and Legless
BBC (GB) 1993 dir. Richard Loncraine
TV(GB)

Longstreet, S.
Gay Sisters, The

WAR (US) 1942 dir. Irving Rapper

Longstreet, S.
Stallion Road
WAR (US) 1947 dir. James V. Kern

Longstreet, S.
Wild Harvest
GN (US) 1961 dir. Jerry Baerwitz

Longyear, B.
Enemy Mine
FOX (US) 1986 dir. Wolfgang Petersen

Lonsdale, F.
Aren't We All?
P
PAR (GB) 1932
dir. Harry Lachman, Rudolf Maté

Lonsdale, F.
High Road, The
P
Lady of Scandal
MGM (US) 1930 dir. Sidney Franklin

Lonsdale, F.
Last of Mrs Cheyney, The
P
MGM (US) 1929 dir. Sidney Franklin
MGM (US) 1937
dir. Richard Boleslawski

Lonsdale, F.
Last of Mrs. Cheyney, The
P
Law and the Lady, The
MGM (US) 1951 dir. Edwin H. Knopf

Lonsdale, F.
On Approval
P
FOX (GB) 1944 dir. Clive Brook

Lonzeiro, J.
Injancia dos Martos
Pixote
UNIFILM (Port) 1981
dir. Hector Babenco

Loos, A.
But Gentlemen Marry Brunettes
Gentlemen Marry Brunettes
UA (US) 1955 dir. Richard Sale

Loos, A.
Gentlemen Prefer Blondes
FOX (US) 1953 dir. Howard Hawks

Loraine, P.
Break in the Circle
EXC (GB) 1955 dir. Val Guest

Loraine, P.
Day of the Arrow
Eye of the Devil
MGM (GB) 1967 dir. J. Lee Thompson

Loraine, P.
Dublin Nightmare
RANK (GB) 1957 dir. John Pomeroy

Lorca, F. G.
Blood Wedding
P
LIBRA (Sp) 1981 dir. Carlos Saura

Lorca, F. G.
House of Bernarda Alba, The
P
GALA (Sp) 1990 dir. Mario Camus
CHANNEL 4 (GB) 1992
dir. Nuria Espert, Stuart Burge
TV(GB)

Lord, G.
Fortress
HBO PREM (US) 1985
dir. Arch Nicholson
TV(US)

Lord, W.
Night to Remember, A
RANK (GB) 1957 dir. Roy Ward Baker

Loriot, N.
Cri, Un
No Time for Breakfast
BOURLA (Fr) 1980
dir. Jean-Louis Bertucelli

Lortz, R.
Children of the Night
P
Voices
HEMDALE (GB) 1973
dir. Kevin Billington

Loss, L. B.
Stranger, The
Zandy's Bride
WAR (US) 1974 dir. Jan Troell

Lothar, E.
Angel with the Trumpet, The
BL (GB) 1949 dir. Anthony Bushell

Lothar, E.
Clairvoyant, The
GB (GB) 1935 dir. Maurice Elvey

Lothar, E.
Mills of God, The
Act of Murder, An
UN (US) 1948 dir. Michael Gordon

Lothar, R. and Adler, H.
Red Cat, The
Folies Bergère
FOX (US) 1935 dir. Roy del Ruth
GB title: Man from the Folies Bergère,
The
P

Lott, B.
Jewel
ALLIANCE (Can/GB/US) 2001 dir.
Paul Shapiro
TV(Can/GB/US)

Lott, M.
Last Hunt, The
MGM (US) 1956 dir. Richard Brooks

Louganis, G. and Marcus, E.
Breaking the Surface: The Greg
Louganis Story
GREEN-EPSTEIN (US) 1997 dir. Steven
Hilliard Stern
TV(US)

Louys, P.
Femme et le Pantin, La
Devil is a Woman, The
PAR (US) 1935 dir. Josef von Sternberg

Louys, P.
Femme et le Pantin, La
That Obscure Object of Desire
GALAXIE (Fr/Sp) 1978 dir. Luis Bunuel

Lovecraft, H. P.
Case of Charles Dexter Ward, The
Haunted Palace, The
AIP (US) 1963
dir. Roger Corman

Lovecraft, H. P.
Case of Charles Dexter Ward, The
Resurrected, The
SCOTTI (US) 1992 dir. Dan O'Bannon

Lovecraft, H. P.
Color Out of Space, The
Die, Monster, Die!
AIP (US/GB) 1965 dir. Daniel Haller

Lovecraft, H. P.
From Beyond
EMPIRE (US) 1986 dir. Stuart Gordon

Lovecraft, H. P.
Herbert West—The Re-Animator
Bride of Re-Animator
WILDSTREET (US) 1991
dir. Brian Yuzna

Lovecraft, H. P.
Herbert West—The Re-Animator
Re-Animator
EMPIRE (US) 1985 dir. Stuart Gordon

Lovecraft, H. P.
Necronomicon
NEW LINE (US) 1994 dir. Christophe
Gans, Shusuke Kaneko, Brian Yuzna

Lovecraft, H. P.
Shuttered Room, The
Dunwich Horror, The
AIP (US) 1970
dir. Daniel Haller

Lovecraft, H. P.
Shuttered Room, The
WAR (GB) 1967 dir. David Greene

Lovell, Jr., J. A. and Kluger, J.
Lost Moon
Apollo 13
UN (US) 1995 dir. Ron Howard

Lovell, M.
Apple Pie in the Sky
Trouble With Spies, The
HBO (US) 1987 dir. Burt Kennedy

Lowden, D.
Bellman and True
HANDMADE (GB) 1987
dir. Richard Loncraine

Lowndes, M. B.
Letty Lynton
MGM (US) 1932 dir. Clarence Brown

Lowndes, M. B.
Lodger, The
TWICKENHAM (GB) 1932
dir. Maurice Elvey
US title: Phantom Fiend, The
FOX (US) 1944 dir. John Brahm

Lowndes, M. B.
Lodger, The
Man in the Attic, The
FOX (US) 1953 dir. Hugo Fregonese

Lowndes, M. B.
Story of Ivy
Ivy
UI (US) 1947 dir. Sam Wood

Lowry, M.
Under the Volcano
UN (US) 1984 dir. John Huston

Lucarelli, C.
Almost Blue
CECCHI (It) 2000 dir. Alex Infascelli

Lucas, C.
Prelude to a Kiss
P
FOX (US) 1992 dir. Norman Rene

Lucas, C.
Reckless
P
GOLDWYN (US) 1995 dir. Norman
Rene

Ludlum, R.
Apocalypse Watch, The
RHI (US) 1997 dir. Kevin Connor
TVSe(US)

Ludlum, R.
Bourne Identity, The
WAR TV (US) 1988 dir. Roger Young
TVSe(US)

Ludlum, R.
Holcroft Covenant, The
UN (GB) 1985 dir. John Frankenheimer

Ludlum, R.
Osterman Weekend, The
FOX (US) 1983 dir. Sam Peckinpah

Ludlum, R.
Rhineman Exchange, The
UN TV (US) 1977 dir. Burt Kennedy
TVSe(US)

Luft, L.
Me and My Shadows: A Memoir

Life with Judy Garland: Me and My Shadows
ALLIANCE (US/Can) 2001 dir. Robert
Allan Ackerman
TVSe(US/Can)

Lukas, J. A.
Common Ground

LORIMAR TV (US) 1990
dir. Michael Newell
TVSe(US)

Lukezic, J. and Schwarz, T.
False Arrest: The Joyce Lukezic Story

False Arrest
GIL/HILL (US) 1991 dir. Bill L. Norton
TVSe(US)

Lund, D.
Eric

LORIMAR (US) 1975
dir. James Goldstone
TV(US)

Lupica, M.
Dead Air

Money, Power, Murder
CBS ENT (US) 1989 dir. Lee Philips
TV(US)

Lurie, A.
Foreign Affairs

INTERSCOPE (US) 1993 dir. Jim
O'Brien
TV(US)

Lurie, A.
Imaginary Friends

THAMES (GB) 1987 dir. Peter Sasdy
TVSe(GB)

Lurie, A.
War Between the Tates, The

TALENT (US) 1977 dir. Lee Philips
TV(US)

Lutz, J.
Ex, The

LIONS GATE (US/Can) 1996 dir. Mark
L. Lester

Lutz, J.
SWF Seeks Same

Single White Female
COL (US) 1992 dir. Barbet Schroeder

Lyall, G.
Secret Servant, The

BBC (GB) 1985 dir. Alastair Reid
TVSe(GB)

Lymington, J.
Night of the Big Heat

PLANET (GB) 1967 dir. Terence Fisher

Lynch, P.
Carriers

ROSEMONT (US) 1998 dir. Alan
Metzger
TV(US)

Lyndon, B.
Amazing Dr. Clitterhouse, The

P
WAR (US) 1938 dir. Anatole Litvak

Lyndon, B.
Man in Half-Moon Street, The

P
Man Who Could Cheat Death, The
PAR (GB) 1959 dir. Terence Fisher

Lyndon, B.
Man in Half-Moon Street, The

P
PAR (US) 1944 dir. Ralph Murphy

Lyndon, B.
Sundown

UA (US) 1941 dir. Henry Hathaway

Lynn, L. and Vecsey, G.
Coal Miner's Daughter

UN (US) 1980 dir. Michael Apted

Lynn, M.
Mrs. Maitland's Affair

Other Man, The
UN TV (US) 1970 dir. Richard Colla
TV(US)

Lyon, D.
Tentacles

House on Telegraph Hill, The
FOX (US) 1951 dir. Robert Wise

Lyons, A.
Castles Burning

Slow Burn
UN TV (US) 1986
dir. Matthew Chapman
TV(US)

Lyons, N. and Lyons, I.
Someone is Killing the Great Chefs of Europe

Who is Killing the Great Chefs of Europe?
WAR (US) 1978 dir. Ted Kotcheff
GB title: Too Many Chefs

Lytton, B.
Haunted and the Haunters, The

P
Night Comes too Soon
BUTCHER (GB) 1948 dir. Denis
Kavanagh

Lytton, 1st Baron
Last Days of Pompeii, The

RKO (US) 1935 dir. Merian C. Cooper,
Ernest Schoedsack
COL (US) 1984 dir. Peter Hunt
TVSe(US)

Maas, P.
In a Child's Name
NEW WORLD (US) 1991 dir. Tom
McLoughlin
TVSe(US)

Maas, P.
King of the Gypsies
PAR (US) 1978 dir. Frank Pierson

Maas, P.
Marie: A True Story
Marie
MGM/UA (US) 1985
dir. Roger Donaldson

Maas, P.
Serpico
PAR (US) 1973 dir. Sidney Lumet

Maas, P.
Terrible Hours, The
Submerged
NBC (US) 2001 dir. James Keach
TV(US)

Maas, P.
Valachi Papers, The
CIN INT (Fr/It) 1972
dir. Terence Young

MacAnna, F.
Last of the High Kings
PARALLEL (Ire/UK) 1996 dir. David
Keating

Macardle, D.
Thursday's Child
ABPC (GB) 1942 dir. Rodney Ackland

Macardle, D.
Uneasy Freehold
Uninvited, The
PAR (US) 1944 dir. Lewis Allen

McBain, E.
Blood Relatives
FILMCORD (Can/Fr) 1981
dir. Claude Chabrol

McBain, E.
Fuzz
UA (US) 1972 dir. Richard A. Colla

McBain, E.
Ice
Ed McBain's 87th Precinct: Ice
HEARST (1996) dir. Bradford May
TV(US)

McBain, E.
King's Ransom, The
High and Low
TOHO (Jap) 1963 dir. Akira Kurosawa

McBain, E.
Lady, Lady, I Did It!
Lonely Hearts
TOHO (Jap) 1982 dir. Kon Ichikawa

McBain, E.
Lightning
Ed McBain's 87th Precinct: Lightning
HEARST (1995) dir. Bruce Paltrow
TV(US)

McBain, E.
Ten Plus One
Without Apparent Motive
VALORIA (Fr) 1971 dir. Philippe Labro

McCabe, P.
Butcher Boy, The
WAR (Ire/US) 1997 dir. Neil Jordan

McCall, D.
Jack the Bear
FOX (US) 1993 dir. Marshall Herskovitz

McCall, M.
Goldfish Bowl, The
It's Tough to be Famous
IN (US) 1932 dir. Alfred E. Green

McCall, M.
Revolt
Scarlet Dawn
WAR (US) 1932 dir. William Dieterle

McCarry, C.
Deadly Angels, The
Wrong is Right
COL (US) 1982 dir. Richard Brooks
GB title: Man with the Deadly Lens,
The

McCarthy, C.
All the Pretty Horses
COL (US) 2000 dir. Billy Bob Thornton

McCarthy, J. H.
Fighting O'Flynn, The
UN (US) 1949 dir. Arthur Pierson

McCarthy, J. H.
If I Were King
PAR (US) 1938 dir. Frank Lloyd

McCarthy, J. H.
Vagabond King, The
PAR (US) 1956 dir. Michael Curtiz
M

McCarthy, M.
Group, The
UA (US) 1966 dir. Sidney Lumet

McCauley, S.
Object of My Affection, The
FOX (US) 1998 dir. Nicholas Hytner

McCauley, S.
Other Halves
OVINGHAM (GB) 1985 dir. John Laing

McCourt, F.
Angela's Ashes
UN (US/Ire) 1999 dir. Alan Parker

McCoy, H.
Bad for Each Other
COL (US) 1954 dir. Irving Rapper

McCoy, H.
Kiss Tomorrow Goodbye
WAR (US) 1950 dir. Gordon Douglas

McCoy, H.
They Shoot Horses, Don't They?
CINERAMA (US) 1969
dir. Sydney Pollack

McCracken, E.
No Medals
P
Weaker Sex, The
TC (GB) 1948 dir. Roy Baker

McCracken, E.
Quiet Wedding
P
Happy is the Bride
BL (GB) 1957 dir. Roy Boulting

McCracken, E.
Quiet Wedding
P
PAR (GB) 1941 dir. Anthony Asquith

McCracken, E.
Quiet Weekend
P
AB (GB) 1946 dir. Harold French

MacCracken, M.
Circle of Children, A
FOX (US) 1977 dir. Don Taylor
TV(US)

MacCracken, M.
Lovey, A Very Special Child
Lovey: A Circle of Children, Part II
TIME-LIFE (US) 1978 dir. Jud Taylor
TV(US)

McCreary, L.
Minus Man, The
SHOOTING GALLERY (US) 1999 dir.
Hampton Fancher

McCrum, R.
In the Secret State
BBC (GB) 1985 dir. Christopher
Morahan
TV(GB)

McCullers, C.
Ballad of the Sad Café, The
MI/HOBO (US/GB)
1991 dir. Simon Callow

McCullers, C.
Heart is a Lonely Hunter, The
WAR (US) 1968 dir. Robert Ellis Miller

McCullers, C.
Member of the Wedding, The
COL (US) 1952 dir. Fred Zinnemann
HALLMARK (US) 1997 dir. Fielder
Cook
TV(US)

McCullers, C.
Reflections in a Golden Eye
WAR (US) 1967 dir. John Huston

McCulley, J.
Curse of Capistrano, The
Mark of the Renegade
UI (US) 1951 dir. Hugo Fregonese
FOX (US) 1974 dir. Don McDougall
TV(US)

McCulley, J.
Curse of Capistrano, The
Mark of Zorro, The
FOX (US) 1940 dir. Rouben Mamoulian

McCullough, C.
Indecent Obsession, An
PBL (Aust) 1985 dir. Lex Marinos

McCullough, C.
Thorn Birds, The
Thorn Birds, The: The Missing Years
WOLPER (US) 1996 dir. Kevin James
Dobson
TVSe(US)

McCullough, C.
Thorn Birds, The
WAR (US) 1979 dir. Daryl Duke
TVSe(US)

McCullough, C.
Tim
Mary & Tim
HALLMARK (US) 1996 dir. Glenn
Jordan
TV(US)

McCullough, D.
Truman
SPRING CREEK (US) 1995 dir. Frank
Pierson
TV(US)

McCumder, D.
X-Rated: The Mitchell Brothers, a True Story of Sex, Money and Death

Rated X
BERG/MARCIL (US) 2000 dir. Emilio Estevez
TV(US)

McCunn, R. L.
Thousand Pieces of Gold

AM PLAY (US) 1990 dir. Nancy Kelly

McCutcheon, E.
Smokescreen

BBC (GB) 1994 dir. Giancarlo Gemin
TVSe(GB)

McCutcheon, G. B.
Brewster's Millions

UA (US) 1945 dir. Allan Dwan
BRITISH & DOMINION (GB) 1935 dir. Thornton Freeland
UN (US) 1985 dir. Walter Hill

McCutcheon, G. B.
Brewster's Millions

Three on a Spree
UA (GB) 1961 dir. Sidney J. Furie

McCutcheon, H.
To Dusty Death

Pit of Darkness
BUTCHER (GB) 1961 dir. Lance Comfort

McDaniel, L.
Don't Die My Love

Champion's Fight, A
NBC STUDIOS (US) 1998 dir. James A. Contner
TV(US)

McDermott, A.
That Night

REGENCY (Fr/US) 1993 dir. Craig Bolotin

MacDermot, G., Ragni, G. and Rado, J.
Hair

P
UA (US) 1979 dir. Milos Forman
M

Macdonald, B.
Egg and I, The

UN (US) 1947 dir. Chester Erskine

McDonald, G.
Brave, The

MAJ (US) 1997 dir. Johnny Depp

McDonald, G.
Fletch

UIP (US) 1985 dir. Michael Ritchie

McDonald, G.
Running Scared

PAR (GB) 1972 dir. David Hemmings

McDonald, J. and Burleson, C.
Flight From Dhahran

Escape: Human Cargo
SHOWTIME (US) 1998 dir. Simon Wincer
TV(US)

MacDonald, J. D.
Condominium

UN TV (US) 1980 dir. Sidney Hayers
TVSe(US)

MacDonald, J. D.
Darker than Amber

FOX (US) 1970 dir. Robert Clouse

MacDonald, J. D.
Empty Copper Sea, The

Travis McGee
HAJENO (US) 1983 dir. Andrew V. McLaglen
TV(US)

MacDonald, J. D.
Executioners, The

Cape Fear
UI (US) 1962 dir. J. Lee Thompson
UN (US) 1991 dir. Martin Scorsese

MacDonald, J. D.
Girl, The Gold Watch and Everything, The

PAR TV (US) 1980 dir. William Wiard
TV(US)

MacDonald, J. D.
Linda

UN TV (US) 1973 dir. Jack Smight
TV(US)
WIL COURT (US) 1993 dir. Nathaniel Gutman
TV(US)

Macdonald, J. D.
Taint of the Tiger

Mantrap
PAR (US) 1961 dir. Edmond O'Brien

MacDonald, P.
Escape

Nightmare
UN (US) 1942 dir. Tim Whelan

MacDonald, P.
List of Adrian Messenger, The

UI (US) 1963 dir. John Huston

MacDonald, P.
Mother's Day

When Secrets Kill
SCRIPPS HOWARD (US) 1997 dir. Colin Bucksey
TV(US)

MacDonald, P.
Nursemaid Who Disappeared, The

WAR (GB) 1939 dir. Arthur Woods

MacDonald, P.
Patrol

Lost Patrol
RKO (US) 1934 dir. John Ford

MacDonald, P.
Twenty-Three Paces to Baker Street

FOX (US) 1956 dir. Henry Hathaway

MacDonald, P.
X vs Rex

Hour of Thirteen, The
MGM (GB) 1952 dir. Harold French

MacDonald, P.
X vs. Rex

Mystery of Mr. X, The
MGM (US) 1934 dir. Edgar Selwyn

Macdonald, R.
Blue City

PAR (US) 1986 dir. Michelle Manning

Macdonald, R.
Drowning Pool, The

WAR (US) 1975 dir. Stuart Rosenberg

Macdonald, R.
Ferguson Affair, The

Criminal Behavior
PRESTON FISCHER (US) 1992 dir. Michael Miller
TV(US)

Macdonald, R.
Moving Target, The

Harper
WAR (US) 1966 dir. Jack Smight
GB title: Moving Target, The

McDonald, R.
1915

BBC (GB/Aust) 1983
dir. Chris Thomson
TVSe (Aust/GB)

Macdonald, R.
Three Roads, The
Double Negative
QUADRANT (Can) 1980
dir. George Bloomfield

Macdonald, R.
Underground Man, The
PAR TV (US) 1974 dir. Paul Wendkos
TV(US)

MacDonald, S.
Winter Guest, The
P
CHANNEL 4 FILMS (GB) 1997 dir.
Alan Rickman

McDonough, J. R.
Platoon Leader
CANNON (US) 1988 dir. Aaron Norris

McDougall, C.
Execution
Firing Squad, The
ATLANTIS (Can/Fr) 1991 dir. Michel
Andrieu
TV(Can/Fr)

MacDougall, R.
Escapade
P
EROS (GB) 1955 dir. Philip Leacock

MacDougall, R.
Gentle Gunman, The
P
GFD (GB) 1952 dir. Basil Dearden

MacDougall, R.
To Dorothy, A Son
P
BL (GB) 1954 dir. Muriel Box
US title: Cash on Delivery

McEnroe, R. E.
Silver Whistle, The
P
Mr. Belvedere Rings the Bell
FOX (US) 1951 dir. Henry Koster

McEvoy, C.
Likes of 'er, The
Sally in our Alley
ABP (GB) 1931 dir. Maurice Elvey

McEwan, I.
Cement Garden, The
LAURENTIC (Fr/Ger/GB) 1993 dir.
Andrew Birkin

McEwan, I.
Comfort of Strangers, The
SOVEREIGN (US/It) 1990
dir. Paul Schrader

McEwan, I.
Innocent, The
MIRAMAX (GB/Ger) 1993 dir. John
Schlesinger

McFadden, C.
Serial
PAR (US) 1980 dir. Bill Persky

McGahan, A.
Praise
EMCEE (Aust) 1998 dir. John Curran

McGill, A.
Yea, Yea, Yea
Press for Time
RANK (GB) 1966 dir. Robert Asher

McGinley, P.
Bogmail
Murder in Eden
BBC (GB) 1991 dir. Nicholas Renton
TVSe(GB)

McGinley, P.
Goosefoot

Fantasist, The
BLUE DOLPHIN (Ire) 1987
dir. Robin Hardy

McGinniss, J.
Blind Faith

NBC (US) 1990 dir. Paul Wendkos
TVSe(US)

McGinniss, J.
Cruel Doubt

NBC (US) 1992 dir. Yves Simoneau
TVSe(US)

McGinniss, J.
Fatal Vision

NBC ENT (US) 1984 dir. David Greene
TVSe(US

McGivern, W. P.
Odds Against Tomorrow

UA (US) 1959 dir. Robert Wise

McGivern, W. P.
Big Heat, The

COL (US) 1953 dir. Fritz Lang

McGivern, W. P.
Caper of the Golden Bulls, The

EMBASSY (US) 1966 dir. Russel Rouse
GB title: Carnival of Thieves

McGivern, W. P.
Darkest Hour

Hell on Frisco Bay
WAR (US) 1955 dir. Frank Tuttle

McGivern, W. P.
Night of the Juggler

COL (US) 1980 dir. Robert Butler

McGivern, W. P.
Rogue Cop

MGM (US) 1954 dir. Roy Rowland

McGovern, J.
Fraulein

FOX (US) 1957 dir. Henry Koster

McGrady, M.
Motel Tapes, The

Talking Walls
NEW WORLD (US) 1987
dir. Stephen Verona

McGrath, J.
Blood Red Roses

CHANNEL 4 (GB) 1987
TVSe(GB)

McGrath, J.
Events Whilst Guarding the Bofors Gun

P
Bofors Gun, The
RANK (GB) 1968 dir. Jack Gold

McGrath, P.
Grotesque, The

J&M ENT (GB) 1995 dir. John-Paul
Davidson

MacGrory, Y.
Secret of the Ruby Ring

Ruby Ring, The
HALLMARK (US) 1997 dir. Harley
Cokeliss
TV(US)

McGuane, T.
Keep the Change

TISCH (US) 1992 dir. Andy Tennant
TV(US)

McGuane, T.
92 in the Shade

UA (US) 1975 dir. Thomas McGuane

McGuane, T.
Sporting Club, The

AVCO (US) 1971 dir. Larry Peerce

McGuire, W. A. and Bolton, G.
Rosalie
P
MGM (US) 1937 dir. W. S. Van Dyke
M

McHugh, M. J.
Minute's Wait, A
Rising of the Moon, The
WAR (Ire) 1957 dir. John Ford

McIlvaine, J.
It Happens Every Thursday
UN (US) 1953 dir. Joseph Pevney

McIlvanney, W.
Big Man, The
PALACE (GB) 1990 dir. David Leland

MacIlwraith, W.
Anniversary, The
P
WAR (GB) 1968 dir. Roy Ward Baker

McInerney, J.
Bright Lights, Big City
MGM/UA (US) 1988 dir. James Bridges

MacInnes, C.
Absolute Beginners
VIRGIN (GB) 1985 dir. Julien Temple

MacInnes, H.
Above Suspicion
MGM (US) 1943 dir. Richard Thorpe

MacInnes, H.
Assignment in Brittany
MGM (US) 1943 dir. Jack Conway

MacInnes, H.
Salzburg Connection, The
FOX (US) 1972 dir. Lee H. Katzin

MacInnes, H.
Venetian Affair, The
MGM (US) 1966 dir. Jerry Thorpe

MacIvor, D.
House
P
HOUSEHOLD (Can) 1995 dir. Laurie Lynd

McKay, C.
Banjo
Big Fella
FORTUNE (GB) 1937 dir. J. E. Wills

Mackel, K.
Can of Worms
DISNEY (US) 1999 dir. Paul Schneider
TV(US)

Macken, W.
Flight of the Doves
COL (US) 1971 dir. Ralph Nelson

McKenna, M.
I Was a Spy
GAU (GB) 1933 dir. Victor Saville

McKenna, M.
Lancer Spy
FOX (US) 1937 dir. Gregory Ratoff

McKenna, R.
Sand Pebbles, The
FOX (US) 1966 dir. Robert Wise

McKenney, R.
My Sister Eileen
COL (US) 1942 dir. Alexander Hall

MacKenzie, D.
Moment of Danger
ABP (GB) 1960 dir. Laslo Benedek

Mackenzie, D.
Nowhere to Go
EAL (GB) 1958 dir. Seth Holt

Mackenzie, Sir C.
Carnival
Dance Pretty Lady
BI (GB) 1932 dir. Anthony Asquith

MacKenzie, Sir C.
Carnival
RANK (GB) 1946 dir. Stanley Haynes

Mackenzie, Sir C.
Rockets Galore
RANK (GB) 1958 dir. Michael Ralph
US title: Mad Little Island

Mackenzie, Sir C.
Sylvia Scarlett
RKO (US) 1935 dir. George Cukor

Mackenzie, Sir C.
Whisky Galore
EAL (GB) 1948
dir. Alexander MacKendrick
US title: Tight Little Island

Mackie, P.
Whole Truth, The
P
COL (GB) 1958 dir. John Guillermin

McKie, R.
Heroes, The
TVS FILMS (Aust) 1990
dir. Donald Crombie
TV(Aust)

Mackle, B. and Miller, G.
83 Hours 'Til Dawn
CONSOL (US) 1990 dir. Donald Wrye
TV(US)

MacLachlan, P.
Baby
TNT (US) 2000 dir. Robert Allan
Ackerman
TV(US)

MacLachlan, P.
Journey
HALLMARK (US) 1995 dir. Tom
McLoughlin
TV(US)

MacLachlan, P.
Sarah, Plain and Tall
SELF (US) 1991 dir. Glenn Jordan
TV(US)

MacLaine, S.
Out on a Limb
ABC (US) 1987 dir. Robert Butler
TVSe(US)

MacLaverty, B.
Cal
WAR (GB) 1984 dir. Pat O'Connor

MacLaverty, B.
Lamb
CANNON (GB) 1985 dir. Colin Gregg

MacLean, A.
Bear Island
COL (Can/GB) 1979 dir. Don Sharp

MacLean, A.
Breakheart Pass
UA (US) 1975 dir. Tom Gries

MacLean, A.
Caravan to Vaccares
RANK (GB/Fr) 1974
dir. Geoffrey Reeve

MacLean, A.
Death Train
YTV (GB) 1993 dir. David S. Jackson
TV(GB)

MacLean, A.
Fear is the Key
EMI (GB) 1972 dir. Michael Tuchner

MacLean, A.
Force 10 from Navarone
COL (GB) 1978 dir. Guy Hamilton

MacLean, A.
Golden Rendezvous
RANK (US) 1977 dir. Ashley Lazarus

MacLean, A.
Guns of Navarone, The
COL (GB) 1961 dir. J. Lee Thompson

MacLean, A.
Ice Station Zebra
MGM (US) 1968 dir. John Sturges

MacLean, A.
Last Frontier
Secret Ways, The
RANK (US) 1961 dir. Phil Karlson

MacLean, A.
Night Watch
BL (US/GB) 1995 dir. David S. Jackson
TV(US/GB)

MacLean, A.
Puppet on a Chain
SCOTIA-BARBER (GB) 1970
dir. Geoffrey Reeve, Don Sharp

MacLean, A.
River of Death
CANNON (US) 1988 dir. Steve Carver

MacLean, A.
When Eight Bells Toll
RANK (GB) 1971 dir. Etienne Perier

MacLean, A.
Where Eagles Dare
MGM (GB) 1969 dir. Brian G. Hutton

McLean, A. C.
Hill of the Red Fox, The
BBC (GB) 1975 dir. Bob McIntosh
TVSe(GB)

MacLean, H.
In Broad Daylight
NEW WORLD (US) 1991
dir. James Steven Sadwith
TV(US)

McLellan, C. M. S. and Morton, H.
Belle of New York, The
P
MGM (US) 1952 dir. Charles Walters
M

McLendon, J.
Eddie Macon's Run
UN (US) 1983 dir. Jeff Kane

MacLeod, R.
Appaloosa, The
UN (US) 1968 dir. Sidney J. Furie
GB title: Southwest to Sonora

MacLeod, R.
Californio, The
100 Rifles
FOX (US) 1969 dir. Tom Gries

MacLeod, W.
House of Yes, The
P
BANDEIRA (US) 1997 dir. Mark S. Waters

McMahon, T. P.
Issue of the Bishop's Blood, The
Abduction of St. Anne
Q. MARTIN (US) 1975 dir. Harry Falk
TV(US)

McMillan, T.
Disappearing Acts
HBO (US) 2000 dir. Gina Prince-Bythewood
TV(US)

McMillan, T.
How Stella Got Her Groove Back
FOX (US) 1998 dir. Kevin Rodney Sullivan

McMillan, T.
Waiting to Exhale
FOX (US) 1995 dir. Forest Whitaker

McMinnies, M.
Visitors, The
BBC (GB) 1972 dir. Donald Wilson
TVSe(GB)

McMurtry, L.
Buffalo Girls
TRILOGY (US) 1995 dir. Charles Haid
TVSe(US)

McMurtry, L.
Dead Man's Walk
HALLMARK (US) 1996 dir. Yves Simoneau
TVSe(US)

McMurtry, L.
Evening Star, The
RYSHER (US) 1996 dir. Robert Harling

McMurtry, L.
Horseman, Pass By
Hud
PAR (US) 1963 dir. Martin Ritt

McMurtry, L.
Last Picture Show, The
COL (US) 1971 dir. Peter Bogdanovich

McMurtry, L.
Leaving Cheyenne
Lovin' Molly
GALA (US) 1974. dir. Sidney Lumet

McMurtry, L.
Lonesome Dove
MOTOWN (US) 1989 dir. Simon Wincer
TVSe (US)

McMurtry, L.
Streets of Laredo
RHI (US) 1995 dir. Joseph Sargent
TVSe(US)

McMurtry, L.
Terms of Endearment
PAR (US) 1983 dir. James L. Brooks

McMurtry, L.
Texasville
COL (US) 1990 dir. Peter Bogdanovich

McNab, A.
Bravo Two Zero
MIRAMAX (SA) 2001 dir. Tom Clegg

McNally, T.
Frankie and Johnny in the Clair de Lune
P
Frankie and Johnny
PAR (US) 1991 dir. Garry Marshall

McNally, T.
Love! Valour! Compassion!
P
FINE LINE (US) 1997 dir. Joe Mantello

McNally, T.
Ritz, The
P
WAR (US) 1976 dir. Richard Lester

McNamee, E.
Resurrection Man
POLYGRAM (GB) 1997 dir. Marc Evans

McNamee, Father J.
Diary of a City Priest
ITVS (US) 2000 dir. Eugene Martin

McNeil, J.
Consultant, The
BBC (GB) 1983 dir. Cyril Coke
TVSe(GB)

McNeile, H. C.
Sapper
Bulldog Drummond
GOLDWYN (US) 1929
dir. F. Richard Jones

McNeill, E.
9½ Weeks
MGM/UA (US) 1986 dir. Adrian Lyne

McNeill, J.
Child in the House
EROS (GB) 1956 dir. C. Baker Endfleld

MacNicholas, J.
Moving of Lilla Barton, The
P
Moving of Sophia Myles, The
PEARSON TV (Can/US) 2000 dir.
Michael Switzer
TV(Can/US)

McNulty, F.
Burning Bed, The
TA (US) 1984 dir. Robert Greenwald
TV(US)

McNulty, J. L.
Third Avenue, New York
Easy Come, Easy Go
PAR (US) 1947 dir. John Farrow

Macomber, D.
This Matter of Marriage
ALLIANCE (Can) dir. Brad Turner
TV(Can)

MacOrlan, P.
Quai Des Brumes
RAB (Fr) 1938 dir. Marcel Carné

McPartland, J.
Kingdom of Johnny Cool, The
Johnny Cool
UA (US) 1963 dir. William Asher

McPartland, J.
No Down Payment
FOX (US) 1957 dir. Martin Ritt

McPherson, C.
This Lime Tree Bower
Saltwater
ART EYE (Ire) 1999 dir. Conor
McPherson

McPherson, S.
Marvin's Room
P
TRIBECA (US) 1996 dir. Jerry Zaks

McQueen, Dr. R.
Larry: Case History of a Mistake
Larry
TOM (US) 1974 dir. William A. Graham
TV(US)

Macrae, A.
Traveller's Joy
P
GFD (GB) 1949 dir. Ralph Thomas

McShane, M.
Passing of Evil, The
Grasshopper, The
NGL (US) 1969 dir. Jerry Paris

McShane, M.
Seance on a Wet Afternoon
RANK (GB) 1964 dir. Bryan Forbes

McShane, M.
Séance on a Wet Afternoon

Korei
DAIEI STUDIOS (Jap) 2000 dir. Kiyoshi
Kurosawa
TV(Jap)

McSwigan, M.
All Aboard for Freedom

Snow Treasure
TIGON (US) 1968 dir. Irving Jacoby

McTaggart, L.
Baby Brokers, The

Born to be Sold
SAMUELS (US) 1981
dir. Burt Brinckerhoff
TV(US)

McVeigh, S.
Grand Central Murder

MGM (US) 1942 dir. S. Sylvan Simon

McVicar, J.
McVicar, by Himself

P
McVicar
BW (GB) 1980 dir. Tom Clegg

Macy, D.
Night Nurse

WAR (US) 1931 dir. William Wellman

Madden, D.
Suicide's Wife, The

FAC-NEW (US) 1979 dir. John Newland
TV(US)

Maddox, R.
Orchard Children, The

Who'll Save Our Children?
TIME-LIFE (US) 1978
dir. George Schaefer
TV(US), V

Maddux, R.
Walk in the Spring Rain, A

COL (US) 1969 dir. Guy Green

Madison, C.
Quiet Earth, The

YEL (NZ) 1985 dir. Greg Murphy
TV(NZ)

Madox Ford, F.
Good Soldier, The

GRANADA (GB) 1981 dir. Kevin
Billington
TV(GB)

Madrid, J.
Running Out of Time

ARIANE (Sp) 1994 dir. Imanol Uribe

Maeterlinck, M.
Blue Bird, The

P
FOX (US) 1940 dir. Walter Lane
FOX (US/Rus) 1976 dir. George Cukor

Magni, L.
Nemici D'Infanzia

RAI (It) 1995 dir. Luigi Magni

Magnier, C.
Oscar

P
TOUCHSTONE (US) 1991 dir. John
Landis

Magnier, C.
Where Were You When the Lights
Went Out?

P
MGM (US) 1968 dir. Hy Averback

Magorian, M.
Back Home

DISNEY (US) 1990 dir. Piers Haggard
TV(US)

Mahan, P. W.
Doctor, You've got to be Kidding

MGM (US) 1967 dir. Peter Tewkesbury

Maher, M. and Campion, N. R.
Bringing up the Brass: My 55 Years at West Point

Long Gray Line, The
COL (US) 1955 dir. John Ford

Mahfouz, N.
Beginning and the End, The

ALAMEDA (Mex) 1993 dir. Arturo Ripstein

Mahfouz, N.
Midaq Alley

ALAMEDA (Mex) 1995 dir. Jorge Fons

Mahmoody, B. and Hoffer, W.
Not Without My Daughter

MGM (US) 1991 dir. Brian Gilbert

Mahoney, B.
Sensitive, Passionate Man, A

FAC-NEW (US) 1977 dir. John Newland
TV(US)

Mahy, M.
Aliens in the Family

BBC (GB) 1987 dir. Christine Secombe
TVSe(GB)

Maier, W.
Pleasure Island

Girls of Pleasure Island, The
PAR (US) 1953
dir. E. Hugh Herbert, Alvin Ganzer

Mailer, N.
American Dream, An

WAR (US) 1966 dir. Robert Gist
GB title: See You in Hell, Darling

Mailer, N.
Executioner's Song, The

FCI (US) 1982 dir. Lawrence Schiller
TVSe(US)

Mailer, N.
Marilyn

Marilyn: The Untold Story
SCHILLER (US) 1980 dir. Jack Arnold
TVSe(US)

Mailer, N.
Naked and the Dead, The

RKO (US) 1958 dir. Raoul Walsh

Mailer, N.
Time of Her Time, The

HARDWORK (US) 1997 dir. Francis Delia

Mailer, N.
Tough Guys Don't Dance

CANNON (US) 1987
dir. Norman Mailer

Maine, C. E.
Mind of Mr. Soames, The

COL (GB) 1970 dir. Alan Cooke

Mair, J.
Never Come Back

BBC (GB) 1990 dir. Joe Waters
TVSe(GB)

Mair, J.
Never Come Back

Tiger by the Tail
EROS (GB) 1955 dir. John Gilling

› Majerus, J.
Grandpa and Frank

Home to Stay
TIME-LIFE (US) 1978
dir. Delbert Mann
TV(US)

Major, C.
When Knighthood was in Flower

Sword and the Rose, The
DISNEY (GB) 1953 dir. Ken Annakin

Malamud, B.
Angel Levine, The
UA (US) 1970 dir. Jan Kadar

Malamud, B.
Assistant, The
MIRACLE PIC (Can/GB) 1997 dir.
Daniel Petrie

Malamud, B.
Fixer, The
MGM (US) 1969
dir. John Frankenheimer

Malamud, B.
Natural, The
TRISTAR (US) 1984 dir. Barry Levinson

Malarek, V.
Hey, Malarek
Malarek
SVS/TELESCENE (Can) 1989
dir. Roger Cardinal

Malkin, P. Z. and Stein, H.
Eichmann in My Hands
Man Who Captured Eichmann, The
MARGULIES (US) 1996 dir. William A.
Graham
TV(US)

Mallett, L.
Taffin
MGM/UA (GB) 1988
dir. Francis Megahy

Mallory, J.
Sweet Aloes
P
Give Me Your Heart
WAR (US) 1936 dir. Archie Mayo
GB title: Sweet Aloes

Malory, Sir T.
Morte d'Arthur, Le
Excalibur
ORION (US) 1981 dir. John Boorman

Malory, Sir T.
Morte d'Arthur, Le
Knights of the Round Table
MGM (GB) 1954 dir. Richard Thorpe

Mamet, D.
American Buffalo
P
GOLDWYN (US) 1996 dir. Michael
Corrente

Mamet, D.
Glengarry Glen Ross
P
NEW LINE (US) 1992 dir. James Foley

Mamet, D.
Lakeboat
P
PANORAMA ENT. (US/Can) 2000 dir.
Joe Mantegna

Mamet, D.
Life in the Theatre, A
P
BEACON (US) 1993 dir. Gregory
Mosher
TV(US)

Mamet, D.
Oleanna
P
GOLDWYN (US) 1994 dir. David
Mamet

Mamet, D.
Sexual Perversity in Chicago
P
About Last Night ...
TRISTAR (US) 1986 dir. Edward Zwick

Mamet, D.
Water Engine, The
P
TNT/AMBLIN (US)
1992 dir. Steven Schachter
TV(US)

Mamoulian, R. and Anderson, M.
Devil's Hornpipe, The
P
Never Steal Anything Small
UN (US) 1958 dir. Charles Lederer

Manas, J. A.
Mensaka
TORNASOL (Sp) 1998 dir. Salvador Garcia Ruiz

Mandrell, B.
Get to the Heart: My Story
Get to the Heart: The Barbara Mandrell Story
MANDALAY (US) 1997 dir. Jerry London
TV(US)

Manhoff, B.
Owl and the Pussycat, The
P
COL (US) 1970 dir. Herbert Ross

Mankiewicz, D. M.
Trial
MGM (US) 1955 dir. Mark Robson

Mankiewicz, H. J. and Connelly, M.
Wild Man of Borneo, The
P
MGM (US) 1941 dir. Robert B. Sinclair

Mankowitz, W.
Expresso Bongo
BL (GB) 1959 dir. Val Guest
M

Mankowitz, W.
Kid for Two Farthings, A
LF (GB) 1955 dir. Carol Reed

Mankowitz, W.
Make me an Offer
BL (GB) 1954 dir. Cyril Frankel

Manley, W. F.
Wild Waves
Big Broadcast, The
PAR (US) 1932 dir. Frank Tuttle

Manling, Z.
There was that Beautiful Place
Sacrifice of Youth
ART EYE (China) 1986 dir. Zhang Luanxin

Mann, A.
Judgment at Nuremberg
P
UA (US) 1961 dir. Stanley Kramer

Mann, E.
Execution of Justice
P
PARA TV (US) 1999 dir. Leon Ichaso
TV(US)

Mann, H.
Man of Straw
BBC (GB) 1972 dir. Herbert Wise
TVSe(GB)

Mann, H.
Professor Unrath
Blue Angel, The
PAR (Ger) 1930 dir. Josef von Sternberg
FOX (US) 1959 dir. Edward Dmytryk

Mann, K.
Mephisto
MAFILM (Hun) 1981 dir. Istvan Szabo

Mann, K.
Vulkan, Der
MACT (Ger/Fr) 1999 dir. Ottokar Runze

Mann, P.
There are Two Kinds of Terrible
Two Kinds of Love
CBS (US) 1983 dir. Jack Bender
TV(US)

Mann, R.
Foreign Body
ORION (GB) 1986 dir. Ronald Neame

Mann, T.
Confessions of Felix Krull, The
FILMAUFBAU (Ger) 1958
dir. Kurt Hoffman

Mann, T.
Death in Venice
WAR (It) 1971 dir. Luchino Visconti

Mann, T.
Doktor Faustus
SAFIR (Ger) 1982 dir. Franz Seitz

Mann, T.
Magic Mountain, The
SEITZ (Ger/Fr/It) 1982
dir. Hans Geissendoerfer

Mann, T.
Mirage, Le
MOLECULE (Can/Fr) 1992 dir. Jean-
Claude Guiguet

Manners, J. H.
Peg O' My Heart
P
MGM (US) 1933 dir. Robert Z. Leonard

Manning, O.
Balkan Trilogy, The; Levant Trilogy,
The
Fortunes of War
BBC (GB) 1987 dir. James Cellan Jones
TVSe(GB)

Mannix, D.
Fox and the Hound, The
DISNEY (US) 1981 dir. Art Stevens
A, Ch

Mannuzzu, S.
Procedura
Delitto Impossibile, Un
HERA (It) 2001 dir. Antonello Grimaldi

Mansfield, S.
Richest Girl in the World, The
Too Rich: The Secret Life of Doris Duke
VZ/SERTNER (US) 1999 dir. John
Erman
TVSe(US)

Mantley, J.
Joseph
27th Day
COL (US) 1957 dir. William Asher

Mantley, J.
Snow Birch, The
Woman Obsessed
FOX (US) 1959 dir. Henry Hathaway

Mapson, J.
Blue Rodeo
WAR (US) 1996 dir. Peter Werner
TV(US)

Marasco, R.
Burnt Offerings
UA (US) 1976 dir. Dan Curtis

Marasco, R.
Child's Play
P
PAR (US) 1972 dir. Sidney Lumet

Marceau, F.
Bonne Soupe, La
P
BELSTAR (Fr/It) 1963
dir. Robert Thomas

March, W.
Bad Seed, The
WAR (US) 1956 dir. Mervyn LeRoy
WAR (US) 1985 dir. Paul Wendkos
TV(US)

Marchand, L. and Armont, P.
Tailor in the Château

P

Love Me Tonight
PAR (US) 1932 dir. Rouben Mamoulian
M

Marchant, W.
Desk Set, The

P

TCF (US) 1957 dir. Walter Lang
GB title: His Other Woman

Marchetta, M.
Looking for Alibrandi

BEYOND DIST. (Aust) 2000 dir. Kate
Woods

Marcin, M.
Cheating Cheaters

P

UN (US) 1934 dir. Richard Thorpe

Marcus, A.
Marauders, The

MGM (US) 1955 dir. Gerald Mayer

Marcus, F.
Killing of Sister George, The

P

CINERAMA (US) 1967 dir. Robert
Aldrich

Marcus, R. T.
Higher Laws

P

Stranger in Town, A
AVE PICT (US) 1995 dir. Peter Levin
TV(US)

Margolin, P. M.
Last Innocent Man, The

HBO (US) 1987 dir. Roger Spottiswoode
TV(US)

Margolin, P. M.
Third Degree Burn

HBO (US) 1989 dir. Roger Spottiswoode
TV(US)

Margolis, S. J.
Losing Isaiah

PAR (US) 1995 dir. Stephen Gyllenhaal

Margulies, D.
Dinner With Friends

P

HBO FILMS (US) 2001 dir. Norman
Jewison
TV(US)

Mariani, D.
Marianna Ucria

CECCHI (It/Fr) 1997 dir. Roberto
Faenza

Marias, J.
All Souls

Robert Rylands' Last Journey
BUXTON (Sp/GB) 1996 dir. Gracia
Querejeta

Marino, U.
Heartless

P

DANIA (It) 1995 dir. Umberto Marino

Marivaux
Fausse Suivante, La

P

STUDIO CANAL+ (Fr) 2000 dir. Benoit
Jacquot

Marivaux
Triumph of Love, The

P

PAR (GB/It) 2001 dir. Clare Peploe

Markey, G.
Great Companions, The

Meet Me at the Fair
UN (US) 1952 dir. Douglas Sirk

Markfield, W.
To an Early Grave
Bye Bye Braverman
WAR (US) 1968 dir. Sidney Lumet

Marks, L.
Girl who Couldn't Quit, The
P
MON (GB) 1950 dir. Norman Lee

Markson, D.
Ballad of Dingus Magee, The
Dirty Dingus Magee
MGM (US) 1970 dir. Burt Kennedy

Markstein, G.
Tiptoe Boys, The
Final Option, The
MGM/UA (GB) 1983 dir. Ian Sharp

Marlowe, C.
Edward II
P
WORKING TITLE (GB) 1991
dir. Derek Jarman

Marlowe, C.
Faust
P
CNC/BBC (Czech/GB/Fr) 1994 dir.
Ernst Gossner, Jan Svankmajer

Marlowe, C.
Tragical History of Doctor Faustus
P
Doctor Faustus
COL (GB) 1967 dir. Richard Burton,
Neville Coghill

Marlowe, D.
Dandy in Aspic, A
COL (GB) 1968 dir. Anthony Mann

Marlowe, D.
Echos of Celandine
Disappearance, The
CINEGATE (GB/Can) 1977
dir. Stuart Cooper

Marlowe, H.
Candle for the Dead, A
Violent Enemy, The
MONARCH (GB) 1969 dir. Don Sharp

Marquand, J. P.
B.F.'s Daughter
MGM (US) 1948 dir. Robert Z. Leonard

Marquand, J. P.
H.M. Pulham, Esq
MGM (US) 1940 dir. King Vidor

Marquand, J. P.
Melville Goodwin, USA
Top Secret Affair
WAR (US) 1957 dir. H. C. Potter
GB title: Their Secret Affair

Marquand, J. P.
Stopover Tokyo
FOX (US) 1957 dir. Richard L. Breen

Marquand, J. P.
Thank You Mr. Moto
FOX (US) 1937 dir. Norman Foster

Marquand, J. P.
Within the Tides
Late George Apley, The
FOX (US) 1946
dir. Joseph L. Mankiewicz

Marquez, G. G.
Chronicle of a Death Foretold
ITAL/MEDIA (It/Fr) 1987
dir. Francesco Rosi

Marquez, G. G.
Love in the Time of Cholera
Letters from the Park
RTVE (Cuba) 1988
dir. Tomas Guttierez Alea

Marquez, G. G.
No One Writes to the Colonel
TORNASOL (Sp) 1999 dir. Arturo
Ripstein

Marquis, D.
Old Soak, The
P
Good Old Soak
MGM (US) 1937 dir. J. Walter Ruben

Marriott, A. and Foot, A.
No Sex Please — We're British
P
COL (GB) 1973 dir. Cliff Owen

Marrs, J.
Crossfire: The Plot that Killed Kennedy
JFK
WAR (US) 1991 dir. Oliver Stone

Marryat, Captain F.
Children of the New Forest, The
BBC (GB) 1977 dir. John Frankau
TVSe(GB)
BBC (GB 1998 dir. Andrew Morgan
TVSe (GB)

Marryat, F.
Mr. Midshipman Easy
Midshipman Easy
ATP (GB) 1935 dir. Carol Reed
US title: Men of the Sea

Marse, J.
Bilingual Lover, The
ATRIUM (Sp/It) 1993 dir. Vicente
Aranda

Marse, J.
Domenica
RAI (It) 2001 dir. Wilma Labate

Marsh, N.
Artists in Crime
BBC (GB) 1990 dir. Silvio Narizzano
TV(GB)

Marsh, N.
Died in the Wool
ITV (GB) 1978 dir. Brian McDuffie
TVSe(GB)

Marsh, N.
Opening Night
ITV (GB) 1978 dir. Brian McDuffie
TV(GB)

Marshall, B.
Vespers in Vienna
Red Danube, The
MGM (US) 1949 dir. George Sidney

Marshall, C.
Christy
Christy: Choices of the Heart
CANAN (US) 2001 dir. George
Kaczender, Don McBrearty
TVSe(US)

Marshall, C.
Christy
PAX TV (US) 2000 dir. Chuck Bowman
TV(US)

Marshall, C.
Man Called Peter, A
FOX (US) 1955 dir. Henry Koster

Marshall, E.
Benjamin Blake
Son of Fury
TCF (US) 1942 dir. John Cromwell

Marshall, E.
Jewel of Mahabar
Treasure of the Golden Condor
FOX (US) 1953 dir. Delmer Daves

Marshall, E.
Viking, The
Vikings, The
UA (US) 1958 dir. Richard Fleischer

Marshall, E.
Yankee Pasha
UI (US) 1954 dir. Joseph Pevney

Marshall, J. L.
Santa Fe
COL (US) 1951 dir. Irving Pichel

Marshall, J. V.
River Ran out of Eden, A
Golden Seal, The
GOLDWYN (US) 1983 dir. Frank Zuniga

Marshall, J. V.
Walkabout
FOX (Aust) 1971 dir. Nicholas Roeg

Marshall, Mrs. R.
Kitty
PAR (US) 1945 dir. Mitchell Leisen

Marshall, P.
Raging Moon, The
MGM (GB) 1970 dir. Bryan Forbes

Marshall, R.
Bixby Girls, The
All the Fine Young Cannibals
MGM (US) 1960 dir. Michael Anderson

Marshall, S. L. A.
Pork Chop Hill
UA (US) 1959 dir. Lewis Milestone

Marshall, W.
Yellowthread Street
YTV (GB) 1990 dir. Ronald Graham
TVSe(GB)

Marszalek, J. F.
Court-Martial of Johnson Whittaker, The
Assault at West Point
MOSAIC (US) 1994 dir. Harry Moses
TV(US)

Martin, A.
Matroni et Moi
P
MAX (Can) 1999 dir. Jean-Philippe Duval

Martin, A. M.
Baby-Sitters Club, The
COL (US) 1995 dir. Melanie Mayron

Martin, C.
I'll Be Seeing You
SELZNICK (US) 1944
dir. William Dieterle

Martin, G.
Living Arrows
Between Two Women
J. AVNET (US) 1986 dir. Jon Avnet
TV(US)

Martin, G. R. R.
Nightflyers
NEW CENTURY (US) 1987
dir. T. C. Blake

Martin, G. V.
For Our Vines Have Tender Grapes
Our Vines Have Tender Grapes
MGM (US) 1945 dir. Roy Rowland

Martin, V.
Mary Reilly
TRISTAR (US) 1996 dir. Stephen Frears

Martinez, T. and Guinther, J.
Brotherhood of Murder
SHOWTIME (US) 1999 dir. Martin Bell
TV(US)

Martini, S.
Judge, The
NBC (US) 2001 dir. Mick Garris
TV(US)

Martini, S.
Undue Influence
HALLMARK (US) 1996 dir. Bruce
Pittman
TVSe(US)

Marton, G. and Meray, T.
Catch me a Spy
RANK (GB) 1971 dir. Dick Clement

Maryk, M. and Monahan, B.
Death Bite
Spasms
PDC (Can) 1984 dir. William Fruet

Maschwitz, E.
Balalaika
P
MGM (US) 1939 dir. Reinhold Schunzel

Masefield, J.
Box of Delights, The
BBC (GB) 1984 dir. Renny Rye
Ch, TVSe(GB)

Mason, A. E. W.
At the Villa Rose
AB (GB) 1939 dir. Walter Summers
US title: House of Mystery

Mason, A. E. W.
Drum, The
UA (GB) 1938 dir. Zoltan Korda
US title: Drums

Mason, A. E. W.
Fire Over England
UA (GB) 1937 dir. William K. Howard

Mason, A. E. W.
Four Feathers, The
PAR (US) 1929 dir. Lothar Mendes
UA (GB) 1939 dir. Zoltan Korda
ROSEMONT (GB) 1978 dir. Don Sharp
TV(GB)

Mason, A. E. W.
Four Feathers, The
Storm over the Nile
GFD (GB) 1955 dir. Terence Young

Mason, A. E. W.
House of the Arrow, The
AB (GB) 1930 dir. Leslie Hiscott
AB (GB) 1940 dir. Harold French
ABP (GB) 1953 dir. Michael Anderson

Mason, B. A.
In Country
WAR (US) 1989 dir. Norman Jewison

Mason, F.
Rhapsody
DIRECTORS' CIRCLE (US) 2000 dir.
Jeffrey W. Byrd
TV(US)

Mason, H.
Photo Finish
Follow that Horse!
WAR (GB) 1959 dir. Alan Bromly

Mason, R.
Shadow and the Peak, The
Passionate Summer, The
RANK (US) 1958 dir. Rudolph Cartier

Mason, R.
Weapon
Solo
TRIUMPH (US/Mex) 1996 dir. Noberto
Barba

Mason, R.
Wind Cannot Read, The
RANK (GB) 1958 dir. Ralph Thomas

Mason, R.
World of Suzie Wong, The
PAR (GB) 1960 dir. Richard Quine

Massie, C.
Corridor of Mirrors
GFD (GB) 1948 dir. Terence Young

Massie, C.
Pity My Simplicity
Love Letters
PAR (US) 1945 dir. William Dieterle

Massie, R. K.
Nicholas and Alexandra
COL (GB) 1971 dir. Franklin Schaffner

Massie, R. K.
Peter the Great
NBC ENT (US) 1986
dir. Marvin J. Chomsky, Lawrence Schiller
TVSe(US)

Masters, J.
Bhowani Junction
MGM (GB) 1955 dir. George Cukor

Masters, J.
Deceivers, The
MI (GB/Ind) 1988
dir. Nicholas Meyer

Masterson, W.
All Through the Night
Cry in the Night, A
WAR (US) 1956 dir. Frank Tuttle

Masterson, W.
Badge of Evil
Touch of Evil
UN (US) 1958 dir. Orson Welles

Masterson, W.
Death of Me Yet, The
SPELLING (US) 1971
dir. John Llewellyn Moxey
TV(US)

Masterson, W.
Evil Come, Evil Go
Yellow Canary, The
FOX (US) 1963 dir. Buzz Kulik

Masterson, W.
711—Officer Needs Help
Warning Shot
PAR (US) 1966 dir. Buzz Kulik

Masterton, G.
Manitou
ENT (US) 1978 dir. William Girdler

Mastrosimone, W.
Extremities
P
ATLANTIC (US) 1986
dir. Robert M. Young

Mastrosimone, W.
Nanawatai
P
Beast, The
COL (US) 1988 dir. Kevin Reynolds

Matalon, R.
Tale which Begins with a Funeral of a Snake, A
Dreams of Innocence
BELFILMS (Israel) 1993 dir. Dina Zvi-Riklis

Mather, A.
Leopard in the Snow
ANGLO-CAN (GB/Can) 1977
dir. Gerry O'Hara

Matheson, R.
Beardless Warriors
Young Warriors
UN (US) 1966 dir. John Peyser

Matheson, R.
Bid Time Return
Somewhere in Time
UN (US) 1980 dir. Jeannot Szwarc

Matheson, R.
Hell House
Legend of Hell House, The
FOX (GB) 1973 dir. John Hough

Matheson, R.
I Am Legend
Last Man on Earth, The
AIP (US/It) 1964 dir. Sidney Salkow

Matheson, R.
I Am Legend
Omega Man, The
WAR (US) 1971 dir. Boris Sagal

Matheson, R.
Ride the Nightmare
Cold Sweat
CORONA/FAIRFILM (It/Fr) 1974
dir. Terence Young

Matheson, R.
Shrinking Man, The
Incredible Shrinking Man, The
UN (US) 1957 dir. Jack Arnold

Matheson, R.
Stir of Echoes
ARTISAN (US) 1999 dir. David Koepp

Matheson, R.
What Dreams May Come
POLYGRAM (US) 1998 dir. Vincent
Ward

Matsuoka, K.
Saimin
TOHO (Jap) 1999 dir. Masayuki Ochiai

Matthew, C.
Perfect Hero, A
LWT (GB) 1991 dir. James Cellan Jones
TVSe(GB)

Matthiessen, P.
At Play in the Fields of the Lord
UN (US) 1991 dir. Hector Babenco

Maugham, R.
Line on Ginger
Intruder, The
BL (GB) 1953 dir. Guy Hamilton

Maugham, R.
Rough and the Smooth, The
MGM (GB) 1959 dir. Robert Siodmak
US title: Portrait of a Sinner

Maugham, R.
Servant, The
WAR (GB) 1963 dir. Joseph Losey

Maugham, W. S.
Adorable Julia
P
ETOILE (Austria/Fr) 1962
dir. Alfred Weidenmann
GB title: Seduction of Julia, The

Maugham, W. S.
Ant and the Grasshopper, The; Winter
Cruise; Gigolo and Gigolette
Encore
GFD (GB) 1951 dir. Harold French, Pat
Jackson, Anthony Pellissier

Maugham, W. S.
Ashenden
BBC (GB) 1992 dir. Christopher
Morahan
TVSe(GB)

Maugham, W. S.
Ashenden
Secret Agent
GAU BR (GB) 1936 dir. Alfred
Hitchcock

Maugham, W. S.
Cakes and Ale
BBC (GB) 1974 dir. Bill Hays
TVSe(GB)

Maugham, W. S.
Christmas Holiday
UN (US) 1944 dir. Robert Siodmak

Maugham, W. S.
Facts of Life, The; Alien Corn, The; Kite, The; Colonel's Lady, The

Quartet
GFD (GB) 1948
dir. Ralph Smart, Harold French, Arthur Crabtree, Ken Annakin

Maugham, W. S.
Flotsam and Jetsam

BBC (GB) 1970 dir. Claude Whatham
TV(GB)

Maugham, W. S.
Home and Beauty

P
Three for the Show
COL (US) 1955 dir. H. C. Potter
M

Maugham, W. S.
Home and Beauty

P
Too Many Husbands
COL (US) 1940 dir. Wesley Ruggles
GB title: My Two Husbands

Maugham, W. S.
Hour Before the Dawn, The

PAR (US) 1944 dir. Frank Tuttle

Maugham, W. S.
Letter, The

P
PAR (US) 1929 dir. Jean de Limur
WAR (US) 1940 dir. William Wyler
WAR (US) 1982 dir. John Erman
TV(US)

Maugham, W. S.
Letter, The

P
Unfaithful, The
WAR (US) 1947 dir. Vincent Sherman

Maugham, W. S.
Moon and Sixpence, The

UA (US) 1942 dir. Albert Lewin

Maugham, W. S.
Narrow Corner

WAR (US) 1933 dir. Alfred E. Green

Maugham, W. S.
Of Human Bondage

RKO (US) 1934 dir. John Cromwell
WAR (US) 1946 dir. Edmund Goulding
MGM (GB) 1964 dir. Henry Hathaway

Maugham, W. S.
Our Betters

P
RKO (US) 1933 dir. George Cukor

Maugham, W. S.
Painted Veil, The

MGM (US) 1934
dir. Richard Boleslawski

Maugham, W. S.
Painted Veil, The

Seventh Sin, The
MGM (US) 1957 dir. Ronald Neame

Maugham, W. S.
Rain

Miss Sadie Thompson
COL (US) 1953 dir. Curtis Bernhardt

Maugham, W. S.
Rain

P
UA (US) 1932 dir. Lewis Milestone

Maugham, W. S.
Razor's Edge, The

FOX (US) 1946 dir. Edmund Goulding
COL (US) 1984 dir. John Byrum

Maugham, W. S.
Sacred Flame, The

P
Right to Live, The
WAR (US) 1935 dir. William Keighley
GB title: Sacred Flame, The

Maugham, W. S.
Sacred Flame, The

P
WAR (US) 1929 dir. Archie Mayo

Maugham, W. S.
Up At the Villa
UN (US/GB) 2000 dir. Philip Haas

Maugham, W. S.
Verge, The; Mr Knowall; Sanitorium
Trio
GFD (GB) 1950
dir. Ken Annakin, Harold French

Maugham, W. S.
Vessel of Wrath
Beachcomber, The
GFD (GB) 1954 dir. Muriel Box

Maugham, W. S.
Vessel of Wrath
PAR (GB) 1938 dir. Erich Pommer
US title: Beachcomber, The

Maupin, A.
Further Tales of the City
SHOWTIME (US/Can) 2001 dir. Pierre Gang
TVSe(US/Can)

Maupin, A.
More Tales of the City
WORKING TITLE/SHOWTIME (US/GB) 1998 dir. Pierre Gang
TVSe(US/GB)

Maupin, A.
Tales of the City
AM PLAY/CHANNEL 4 FILMS (US/GB) 1994 dir. Alastair Reid
TVSe(US/GB)

Maurensig, P.
Canone Inverso
CECCHI (It) 2000 dir. Ricky Tognazzi

Maurette, M. and Bolton, G.
Anastasia

P
FOX (GB) 1956 dir. Anatole Litvak
COMPASS (US) 1967
dir. George Schaefer
TV(US)

Mauriac, F.
Thérèse Desqueyroux
Thérèse
GALA (Fr) 1964 dir. Georges Franju

Maurois, A.
Edward VII and his Times
Entente Cordiale
FLORA (Fr) 1939 dir. Marcel l'Herbier

Maurois, A.
Prometheus: The Life of Balzac
BBC (GB) 1975 dir. Joan Craft
TVSe(GB)

Maury, A.
Till We Meet Again

P
PAR (US) 1944 dir. Frank Borzage

Maxfield, H. S.
Legacy of a Spy
Double Man, The
WAR (GB) 1967 dir. Franklin Schaffner

Maxim, H. P.
Genius in the Family, A
So Goes My Love
UN (US) 1946 dir. Frank Ryan
GB title: Genius in the Family, A

Maxwell, G.
Ring of Bright Water
RANK (GB) 1968 dir. Jack Couffer

May, E. R. and Zelikow, P. D.
Kennedy Tapes, The: Inside the White House During the Cuban Missile Crisis
Thirteen Days
NEW LINE (US) 2000 dir. Roger Donaldson

Mayer, E. J.
Firebrand
P
Affairs of Cellini, The
FOX (US) 1934 dir. Gregory La Cava

Mayer, J. and Abramson, J.
Strange Justice
PAR (US) 1999 dir. Ernest Dickerson
TV(US)

Mayhew, D.
Playing With Fire
ARABESQUE (US) 2000 dir. Roy Campanella II
TV(US)

Mayle, P.
Year in Provence, A
BBC/A&E (GB) 1993 dir. David Tucker
TVSe(GB)

Maynard, J.
To Die For
COL (US/GB) 1995 dir. Gus Van Sant

Maynard, N.
This is My Street
WAR (GB) 1963 dir. Sidney Hayers

Mayo, J.
Hammerhead
COL (GB) 1968 dir. David Miller

Mayse, A.
Desperate Search
MGM (US) 1952 dir. Joseph Lewis

Mazzetti, L.
Cielo Cade, Il
RAI (It) 2000 dir. Andrea Frazzi and Antonio Frazzi

Mead, S., Burrows, A., Weinstock, J., Gilbert, W. and Loesser, F.
How to Succeed in Business Without Really Trying
P
UA (US) 1967 dir. David Swift
M

Meade, M.
Stealing Heaven
FILM DALLAS (GB/Yugo) 1989 dir. Clive Donner

Mearson, L.
Lillian Day
P
Our Wife
COL (US) 1941 dir. John M. Stahl

Medoff, M.
Children of a Lesser God
P
PAR (US) 1986 dir. Randa Haines

Medoff, M.
Homage That Follows, The
P
Homage
SKYLINE (US) 1995 dir. Ross Kagan Marks

Mee, Jr., C. L.
Seizure
Seizure: The Story of Kathy Morris
JOZAK (US) 1980 dir. Gerald Isenberg
TV(US)

Meehan, T.
Annie
P
COL (US) 1982 dir. John Huston
M

Megrue, R. C.
Seven Chances
P
Bachelor, The
NEW LINE (US) 1999 dir. Gary Sinyor

Mehren, E.
Born Too Soon
REP (US) 1993 dir. Noel Nosseck
TV(US)

Meins, J.
Murder in Little Rock
Seduction in Travis County, A
NEW WORLD (US) 1991
dir. George Kaczender
TV(US)

Melanson, Y. and Safran, C.
Looking for Lost Bird: A Jewish
Woman discovers her Navajo Roots
Lost Child, The
HALLMARK (US) 2000 dir. Karen
Arthur
TV(US)

Meldal-Johnson, T.
Always
Déjà Vu
CANNON (GB) 1985
dir. Anthony Richmond

Mellis, L. and Scinto, D.
Gangster No. 1
P
BRIT SCREEN (GB) 2000 dir. Paul
McGuigan

Melville, A.
Castle in the Air
P
ABP (GB) 1952 dir. Henry Cass

Melville, A.
Simon and Laura
P
RANK (GB) 1955 dir. Muriel Box

Melville, H.
Billy Budd
AAL (GB) 1962 dir. Peter Ustinov

Melville, H.
Moby Dick
WAR (US) 1930 dir. Lloyd Bacon
WAR (GB) 1956 dir. John Huston
USA PICTURES (US/GB/Aust) 1998
dir. Franc Roddam
TVSe(US/GB/Aust)

Melville, H.
Pierre, or, The Ambiguities
Pola X
STUDIO CANAL+ (Fr/Ger) 1999 dir.
Leos Carax

Melville, H.
Typee
Enchanted Island
WAR (US) 1958 dir. Allan Dwan

Menchell, I.
Cemetery Club, The
P
TOUCHSTONE (US) 1993 dir. Bill Duke

Mendoza, E.
Ciudad de los Prodigios, La
FRANCE 3 (Fr/Port/Sp) 1999 dir.
Mario Camus

Mercado, C.
Voice From the Grave
COS-MEU (US) 1996 dir. David S.
Jackson
TV(US)

Mercer, C.
Rachel Cade
Sins of Rachel Cade, The
WAR (US) 1960 dir. Gordon Douglas

Mercer, D.
In Two Minds
P
Family Life
EMI (GB) 1971 dir. Ken Loach

Mercer, D.
Morgan—A Suitable Case for Treatment
P
BL (GB) 1966 dir. Karel Reisz

Mercer, J., dePaul, G., Panama, N. and Frank, M.
L'il Abner
P
PAR (US) 1959 dir. Melvin Frank
M

Mergendahl, C.
Bramble Bush
WAR (US) 1960 dir. Daniel Petrie

Merimée, P.
Carmen
TRIUMPH (Fr) 1984 dir. Francesco Rosi

Merimée, P.
Carmen
First Name: Carmen
IS (Fr) 1984 dir. Jean-Luc Godard

Merimée, P.
Carmen
Hip Hopera: Carmen
NEW LINE TV (US) 2001 dir. Robert Townsend
M, TV(US)

Merimée, P.
Carmen
Loves of Carmen, The
COL (US) 1948 dir. Charles Vidor

Merimée, P.
Columba
Vendetta
RKO (US) 1950 dir. Mel Ferrer

Merimée, P.
Tamango
SNEG (Fr) 1958 dir. John Berry

Merle, R.
Day of the Dolphin, The
AVCO (US) 1973 dir. Mike Nichols

Merle, R.
Weekend à Zuydcoote
Weekend at Dunkirk
FOX (Fr/It) 1964 dir. Henri Verneuil

Merritt, A.
Burn, Witch, Burn
Devil Doll, The
MGM (US) 1936 dir. Tod Browning

Metalious, G.
Peyton Place
FOX (US) 1957 dir. Mark Robson

Metalious, G.
Return to Peyton Place
FOX (US) 1960 dir. Jose Ferrer

Metcalfe, S.
Strange Snow
P
Jackknife
CINEPLEX (US) 1989 dir. David Jones

Mewshaw, M.
Year of the Gun
TRIUMPH (US) 1991
dir. John Frankenheimer

Meyer, N.
Seven Percent Solution, The
UN (US) 1976 dir. Herbert Ross

Meyer-Foerster, W.
Old Heidelburg
P
Student Prince, The
MGM (US) 1954 dir. Richard Thorpe
M

Meyers, R.
Like Normal People
FOX TV (US) 1979 dir. Harvey Hart
TV(US)

Meyers, W. D.
Tales of a Dead King
Legend of the Lost Tomb
TRINITY (US) 1996 dir. Jonathan
Winfrey
TV(US)

Meynell, L.
Breaking Point, The
BUTCHER (GB) 1961
dir. Lance Comfort

Meynell, L.
House in Marsh Road, The
P
GN (GB) 1960 dir. Montgomery Tully

Meynell, L.
One Step From Murder
Price of Silence, The
GN (GB) 1959 dir. Montgomery Tully

Michael, J.
Deceptions
COL (US) 1985 dir. Robert Chenault
TVSe(US)

Michaels, B.
Ammie, Come Home
House That Would Not Die, The
SPELLING (US) 1980 dir. John
Llewellyn Moxey
TV(US)

Michaels, B.
Crying Child, The
IRISH (US) 1996 dir. Robert Michael
Lewis
TV(US)

Michaels, L.
Men's Club, The
ATLANTIC (US) 1986 dir. Peter Medak

Michaud, M.
Coyote
MOLECULE (Fr/Can) 1992 dir. Richard
Ciupka

Michener, J.
Texas
SPELLING TV (US) 1995 dir. Richard
Long
TVSe(US)

Michener, J. A.
Bridges at Toko-Ri, The
PAR (US) 1954 dir. Mark Robson

Michener, J. A.
Caravans
BORDEAUX (US/Iran) 1978
dir. James Fargo

Michener, J. A.
Centennial
UN TV (US) 1979 dir. Virgil Vogel, Paul
Krasny, Harry Falk, Bernard
McEveety
TVSe(US)

Michener, J. A.
Dynasty
PARADINE TV (US) 1976
dir. Lee Philips
TV(US)

Michener, J. A.
Hawaii
UA (US) 1966 dir. George Roy Hill

Michener, J. A.
Kent State: What Happened and Why
Kent State
INTERPLAN (US) 1981
dir. James Goldstone
TV(US)

Michener, J. A.
Return to Paradise
Until They Sail
MGM (US) 1957 dir. Robert Wise

Michener, J. A.
Return to Paradise
UA (US) 1953 dir. Mark Robson

Michener, J. A.
Sayonara
WAR (US) 1957 dir. Joshua Logan

Michener, J. A.
Space
PAR (US) 1985 dir. Joseph Sargent, Lee Phillips
TVSe(US)

Michener, J. P.
Tales from the South Pacific
South Pacific
TODD AO (US) 1958 dir. Joshua Logan
M
TOUCHSTONE (US) 2001 dir. Richard Pearce
M, TV(US)

Michima, Y.
Nikutai no Gakko
School of Flesh, The
ORSANS (Fr) 1998 dir. Benoit Jacquot

Mickle, S. F.
Replacing Dad
THOMPSON (US) 1999 dir. Joyce Chopra
TV(US)

Middleton, G. and Thomas, A. E.
Big Pond, The
P
PAR (US) 1930 dir. Hobart Henley

Middleton, T. and Rowley, W.
Changeling, The
P
Middleton's Changeling
HIGH TIMES (GB) 1998 dir. Marcus Thompson

Mighton, J.
Possible Worlds
P
ALLIANCE (Can) 2000 dir. Robert Lepage

Mignogna, E.
Fuga, La
TELEFE (Arg) 2001 dir. Eduardo Mignogna

Miles, B.
Lock up your Daughters
P
COL (GB) 1969 dir. Peter Coe

Miles, G.
Branwen
P
TELLESYN (GB) 1994 dir. Ceri Sherlock

Miles, R.
That Cold Day in the Park
COMM (Can) 1969 dir. Robert Altman

Milholland, R.
Submarine Patrol
FOX (US) 1938 dir. John Ford

Millar, R.
Frieda
P
EAL (GB) 1947 dir. Basil Dearden

Miller, A.
All My Sons
P
UI (US) 1948 dir. Irving Reis
BBC (GB) 1990 dir. Jack O'Brien
TV(GB)

Miller, A.
American Clock, The
P
AMBLIN (US) 1993 dir. Bob Clark
TV(US)

Miller, A.
Crucible, The
P
FOX (US) 1996 dir. Nicholas Hytner

Miller, A.
Crucible, The
P
Witches of Salem, The
FDF (Fr/Ger) 1957
dir. Raymond Rouleau

Miller, A.
Death of a Salesman
P
COL (US) 1951 dir. Laslo Benedek
PUNCH (US) 1985
dir. Volker Schlondorff
TV(US)

Miller, A.
Focus
PAR (US) 2001 dir. Neal Slavin

Miller, A.
Homely Girl
Eden
CINEVIA (Fr/Israel) 2001 dir. Amos
Gitai

Miller, A.
Price, The
P
TALENT (US) 1971 dir. Fielder Cook
TV(US)

Miller, A.
View from the Bridge, A
P
TRANS (Fr) 1961 dir. Sidney Lumet

Miller, A. D.
And One Was Wonderful
MGM (US) 1940 dir. Robert Sinclair

Miller, A. D.
Gowns by Roberta
Lovely to Look At
MGM (US) 1952 dir. Mervyn LeRoy
M

Miller, A. D.
Gowns by Roberta
Roberta
RKO (US) 1935 dir. William A. Seiter
M

Miller, A. D.
Manslaughter
PAR (US) 1930 dir. George Abbott

Miller, A. D. and Thomas, A. E.
Come out of the Kitchen
P
Honey
PAR (US) 1930 dir. Wesley Ruggles

Miller, G. H.
Dream Monger, The
Starlight Hotel
REP (NZ) 1988 dir. Sam Pillsbury

Miller, H.
Quiet Days in Clichy
MIRACLE (Den) 1970
dir. Jens Jorgen Thorsen

Miller, H.
Tropic of Cancer
PAR (US) 1970 dir. Joseph Strick

Miller, I.
Burning Bridges
LORIMAR TV (US) 1990
dir. Sheldon Larry
TV(US)

Miller, J.
That Championship Season
P
CANNON (US) 1982 dir. Jason Miller
MGM (US) 1999 dir. Paul Sorvino
TV(US)

Miller, S.
Family Pictures
HEARST (US) 1993 dir. Philip Saville
TVSe(US)

Miller, S.
Good Mother, The
TOUCHSTONE (US) 1988 dir. Leonard
Nimoy

Miller, W.
Cool World, The
WISEMAN (US) 1963
dir. Shirley Clarke

Miller, W.
Manhunter, The
UN (US) 1976 dir. Don Taylor
TV(US)

Millhauser, B. and Dix, B. M.
Life of Jimmy Dolan, The
P
WAR (US) 1933 dir. Archie Mayo
GB title: Kid's Last Fight, The

Millholland, C. B.
Napoleon of Broadway
P
Twentieth Century
COL (US) 1934 dir. Howard Hawks

Milligan, S.
Adolf Hitler—My Part in his
Downfall
UA (GB) 1972 dir. Norman Cohen

Milligan, S. and Antrobus, J.
Bed Sitting Room, The
P
UA (GB) 1969 dir. Richard Lester

Millin, S. G.
Rhodes
Rhodes of Africa
GAU BRI (GB) 1936
dir. Berthold Viertes
US title: Rhodes

Mills, E.
Dorothy Dandridge
Introducing Dorothy Dandridge
ESPARZA (US) 1999 dir. Martha
Coolidge
TV(US)

Mills, H.
Prudence and the Pill
P
FOX (GB) 1968 dir. Fielder Cook

Mills, J.
Panic in Needle Park, The
FOX (US) 1971 dir. Jerry Schatzberg

Mills, J.
Report to the Commissioner
UA (US) 1975 dir. Milton Katselas
GB title: Operation Undercover

Mills, M.
Long Haul, The
COL (GB) 1957 dir. Ken Hughes

Milne, A. A.
Dover Road, The
P
Where Sinners Meet
RKO (US) 1934 dir. J. Walter Ruben

Milne, A. A.
Four Days Wonder
UN (US) 1936 dir. Sidney Salkow

Milne, A. A.
Michael and Mary
P
UN (GB) 1931 dir. Victor Saville

Milne, A. A.
Perfect Alibi, The
P
RKO (GB) 1931 dir. Basil Dean

Milne, A. A.
Winnie the Pooh
Winnie the Pooh and the Honey Tree
DISNEY (US) 1965
dir. Wolfgang Reitherman
A, Ch

Minahan, J.
Great Diamond Robbery, The
Diamond Trap, The
COL TV (US) 1988 dir. Don Taylor
TV(US)

Minier, M.
Hypnotisme à la Portée de Tous, L'
Dormez, Je Le Veux
CDP (Fr) 1997 dir. Irene Jouannet

Minney, R. J.
Carve Her Name with Pride
RANK (GB) 1958 dir. Lewis Gilbert

Minney, R. J.
Nothing to Lose
Time Gentlemen, Please!
ABP (GB) 1952 dir. Lewis Gilbert

Miranda, E. J. O.
Lamarca Guerilla Captain
Lamarca
MORENA (Bra) 1994 dir. Sergio
Rezende

Mirbeau, O.
Diary of a Chambermaid, The
BOGEAUS (US) 1946
dir. Jean Renoir

Mishima, Y.
Gogo no Eiko
*Sailor Who Fell From Grace With the Sea,
The*
FOX RANK (GB) 1976
dir. Lewis John Carlino

Mishima, Y.
Runaway Horses; Temple of the
Golden Pavilion
Mishima
WAR (US) 1985 dir. Paul Schrader

Mistry, R.
Such a Long Journey
FILMWORKS (GB/Can) 1998 dir. Sturla
Gunnarsson

Mitani, K.
Radio no Jikan
P
Welcome Back, Mr. McDonald
TOHO (Jap) 1998 dir. Koki Mitani

Mitchard, J.
Deep End of the Ocean, The
COL (US) 1999 dir. Ulu Grosbard

Mitchell, D.
Thumb Tripping
AVCO (US) 1972 dir. Quentin Masters

**Mitchell, D., Mitchell, C. and
Ofshe, R.**
Light on Synanon, The
Attack on Fear
TOM (US) 1984 dir. Mel Damski
TV(US)

Mitchell, E.
Silver Brumby, The
*Silver Stallion King of the Wild Brumbies,
The*
FILM VICTORIA (Aust) 1993 dir. John
Tatoulis

Mitchell, G.
Speedy Death
BBC/WGBH (GB/US) 1998 dir. Audrey
Cooke
TV(GB/US)

Mitchell, J.
Another Country

P

GOLDCREST (GB) 1984 dir. Marek Kanievska

Mitchell, J.
August

P

GOLDWYN (US) 1996 dir. Anthony Hopkins

Mitchell, J.
Red File for Callan, A

Callan
EMI (GB) 1974 dir. Don Sharp

Mitchell, M.
Get Your Stuff

P

PEOPLES (US) 2000 dir. Max Mitchell

Mitchell, M.
Gone with the Wind

MGM (US) 1939 dir. Victor Fleming

Mitchell, M.
Warning to Wantons

AQUILA (GB) 1949
dir. Donald B. Wilson

Mitchell, N. and Medcraft, R.
Cradle Snatchers

P

Let's Face It
PAR (US) 1943 dir. Sidney Lanfield

Mitchell, P.
Act of Love

PAR TV (US) 1980 dir. Jud Taylor
TV(US)

Mitchell, W. O.
Who has Seen the Wind

CIN WORLD (Can) 1980 dir. Allan King

Mitford, N.
Blessing, The

Count Your Blessings
MGM (US) 1959 dir. Jean Negulesco

Mitford, N.
Love in a Cold Climate; Pursuit of Love, The

Love in a Cold Climate
THAMES (GB) 1980 dir. Donald McWhinnie
TVSe(GB)
BBC (GB) 2001 dir. Tom Hooper
TVSe(GB)

Mitra, N. M.
Big City, The

R. D. BANSAL (Ind) 1963
dir. Satyajit Ray

Miyabe, M. H.
Kurosufaia

TOHO (Jap) 2000 dir. Shusake Kaneko

Mo, T.
Soursweet

CIC (GB) 1988 dir. Mike Newell

Moberg, V.
Emigrants, The

SVENSK (Swe) 1970 dir. Jan Troell

Modiano, P.
Villa Triste

Yvonne's Perfume
ZOULOU (Fr) 1994 dir. Patrice Leconte

Modignani, S. C.
Donna D'Onore

Vendetta: Secrets of a Mafia Bride
TRIBUNE (US) 1991
dir. Stuart Margolin
TVSe(US)

Modignani, S. C.
Woman of Honor

Vendetta II: The New Mafia
FILMLINE (US) 1993 dir. Ralph L.
Thomas
TVSe(US)

Moggach, D.
To Have and to Hold
LWT (GB) 1986 dir. John Bruce
TVSe(GB)

Moiseiwitsch, M.
Sleeping Tiger, The
INSIGNIA (GB) 1954 dir. Joseph Losey

Moliere, J. B.
Don Juan
P
FRANCE 3 (Fr) 1998 dir. Jacques Weber

Molin, L.
Bomb, The
CHANNEL 4 (Ger) 1987
dir. H. C. Gorlitz

Molina, A. M.
Winter in Lisbon, The
JET (Sp) 1990 dir. Jose Antonio Zorrilla

Molnar, F.
Girl from Trieste, The
P
Bride Wore Red, The
MGM (US) 1937 dir. Dorothy Arzner

Molnar, F.
Good Fairy, The
P
UN (US) 1935 dir. William Wyler
HALLMARK (US) 1956
dir. George Schaefer
TV(US)

Molnar, F.
Great Love
P
Double Wedding
MGM (US) 1937 dir. Richard Thorpe

Molnar, F.
Guardsman, The
P
Chocolate Soldier, The
MGM (US) 1941 dir. Roy del Ruth
M

Molnar, F.
Guardsman, The
P
MGM (US) 1931 dir. Sidney Franklin

Molnar, F.
Liliom
P
Carousel
TCF (US) 1956 dir. Henry King
M

Molnar, F.
Liliom
P
FOX (US) 1930 dir. Frank Borzage

Molnar, F.
Olympia
P
Breath of Scandal, A
PAR (US) 1960 dir. Michael Curtiz,
Mario Russo

Molnar, F.
Olympia
P
His Glorious Night
MGM (US) 1929 dir. Lionel Barrymore
GB title: Breath of Scandal

Molnar, F.
One, Two, Three
P
UA (US) 1961 dir. Billy Wilder

Molnar, F.
Swan, The
P
MGM (US) 1956 dir. Charles Vidor

Monaghan, J.
Last of the Badmen
Bad Men of Tombstone
ABP (US) 1949 dir. Kurt Neumann

Monica, J.
Geraldine, For the Love of a
Transvestite
Just Like a Woman
BRIT SCREEN (GB) 1992 dir.
Christopher Monger

Monks, J. and Finklehoffe, F. F.
Brother Rat
P
About Face
WAR (US) 1952 dir. Roy del Ruth

Monks, J. and Finklehoffe, F. R.
Brother Rat
P
FOX (US) 1938 dir. William Keighley

Monro, R.
French Mistress, A
P
BL (GB) 1960 dir. Roy Boulting

Monsarrat, N.
Cruel Sea, The
GFD (GB) 1952 dir. Charles Frend

Monsarrat, N.
Ship That Died of Shame, The
RANK (GB) 1955 dir. Basil Dearden

Monsarrat, N.
Something to Hide
AVCO (GB) 1973 dir. Alastair Reid

Monsarrat, N.
Story of Esther Costello, The
COL (GB) 1957 dir. David Miller
US title: Golden Virgin, The

Montague, E. E. S.
Man Who Never Was, The
FOX (GB) 1955 dir. Ronald Neame

Montalban, M. V.
Laberinto Griego, El
IMPALA (Sp) 1992 dir. Rafael Alcazar

Monteilhet, H.
Mantes Religieuses, Les
Praying Mantis
PORTMAN (GB) 1984 dir. Jack Gold
TVSe(GB)

Monteilhet, H.
Return From the Ashes
UA (US) 1965 dir. J. Lee Thompson

Monteiro, P.
Blind Man's Buff
P
GEMINI (Port/Fr) 1994 dir. Manoel de
Oliveira

Montforez, G.
Enfants du Marais, Les
UCG/IMAGES (Fr) 1999 dir. Jean
Becker

Montgomery, F.
Misunderstood
MGM/UA (US) 1984
dir. Jerry Schatzberg

Montgomery, J.
Ready Money
P
Riding High
PAR (US) 1943 dir. George Marshall
GB title: Melody Inn

Montgomery, J. H.
Irene

P

RKO (US) 1940 dir. Herbert Wilcox

Montgomery, L. M.
Anne of Avonlea

BBC (GB) 1975 dir. Joan Croft
TVSe(GB)

Montgomery, L. M.
Anne of Green Gables

RKO (US) 1934 dir. George Nicholls
BBC (GB) 1972 dir. Joan Craft
TVSe(GB)
SULLIVAN (Can) 1985 dir. Kevin
Sullivan
TVSe(Can)

Montgomery, L. M.
Anne of Windy Willows

Anne of Windy Poplars
RKO (US) 1940 dir. Jack Hively

Montgomery, L. M.
Jane of Lantern Hill

Lantern Hill
DISNEY (US) 1990 dir. Kevin Sullivan
TV(US)

Monti, C. and Rice, C.
W.C. Fields and Me

UN (US) 1976 dir. Arthur Hiller

Montserrat, R. and Montserrat, R.
Ne crie pas

Sauve-Moi
STUDIO CANAL+ (Fr) 2000 dir.
Christian Vincent

Moody, L.
Ruthless Ones, The

What Became of Jack and Jill?
FOX (GB) 1971 dir. Bill Rain

Moody, R.
Ice Storm, The

FOX (US) 1997 dir. Ang Lee

Moody, R.
Little Britches

Wild Country, The
DISNEY (US) 1971 dir. Robert Totten

Moon, L.
Dark Star

Min and Bill
MGM (US) 1930 dir. George Hill

Mooney, M. M.
Hindenburg, The

UN (US) 1975 dir. Robert Wise

Mooney, W. H.
Corazon

Donor Unknown
CITADEL ENT (US) 1995 dir. John
Harrison
TV(US)

Moorcock, M.
Final Programme, The

MGM-EMI (GB) 1973 dir. Robert Fuest
US title: Last Days of Man on Earth,
The

Moore, B.
Black Robe

ALLIANCE (Can/Aust) 1991
dir. Bruce Beresford

Moore, B.
Catholics

GLAZIER (US) 1973 dir. Jack Gold
TV(US)

Moore, B.
Cold Heaven

HEMDALE (US) 1992 dir. Nicolas Roeg

Moore, B.
Lonely Passion of Judith Hearne, The
ISLAND/HANDMADE (GB) 1987
dir. Jack Clayton

Moore, B.
Luck of Ginger Coffey, The
BL (Can/US) 1964 dir. Irvin Kershner

Moore, B.
Temptation of Eileen Hughes, The
BBC (GB) 1988 dir. Trevor Powell
TV(GB)

Moore, C. and Johnson, P.
Santa and Pete
POLSON (US) 1999 dir. Duwayne
Dunham
TV(US)

Moore, D. T.
Gymkata
MGM/UA (US) 1985 dir. Robert Clouse

Moore, G.
Esther Waters
WESSEX (GB) 1948 dir. Jan Dalrymple
BBC (GB) 1977 dir. Jane Howell
TVSe(GB)

Moore, G.
You're Only Human Once
So This is Love
WAR (US) 1953 dir. Gordon Douglas
GB title: Grace Moore Story, The

Moore, H. T.
Priest of Love
ENT (GB) 1981 dir. Christopher Miles

Moore, R.
French Connection, The
FOX (US) 1971 dir. William Friedkin

Moore, R.
Green Berets, The
WAR (US) 1968
dir. John Wayne, Ray Kellogg

Moore, R.
Spoonhandle
Deep Waters
FOX (US) 1948 dir. Henry King

Moore, W. I. and Berlitz, C.
Philadelphia Experiment, The
NEW WORLD (US) 1984
dir. Stewart Raffill

Moorehead, A.
Rage of the Vulture
Thunder in the East
PAR (US) 1951 dir. Charles Vidor

Moorhouse, F.
Americans, Baby, The; Electrical
Experience, The
Coca-Cola Kid, The
CINECOM (Aust) 1985
dir. Dusan Makevejev

Moorhouse, F.
Everlasting Secret Family and Other
Secrets, The
Everlasting Secret Family, The
FGH (Aust) 1989 dir. Michael Thornhill

Morante, E.
Arturo's Island
MGM (It) 1962 dir. Damiano Damiani

Morante, E.
History
SACIS (It) 1988 dir. Luigi Comencina

Moravia, A.
Appointment at the Beach
Naked Hours, The
COMPTON (It) 1964 dir. Marco Vicario

Moravia, A.
Attention, L'
Lie, The
SELVAGGIA (It) 1985
dir. Giovanni Soldati

Moravia, A.
Conformist, The
CURZON (It/Fr/W. Ger) 1969
dir. Bernardo Bertolucci

Moravia, A.
Empty Canvas, The
CC (It/Fr) 1964 dir. Damiano Damiani

Moravia, A.
Io e Lui
Me and Him
NC/COL (Ger) 1989 dir. Doris Dorrie

Moravia, A.
Noia, La
Ennui, L'
GEMINI (Fr) 1998 dir. Cedric Kahn

Moravia, A.
Time of Indifference
CONT (It/Fr) 1965
dir. Francesco Maselli

Moravia, A.
Two Women
CHAMPION (It/Fr) 1960
dir. Vittorio de Sica
BBC (GB)1973 dir. Gareth Davies
TVSe(GB)

Moravia, A.
Woman of Rome
MINERVA (lt) 1954 dir. Luigi Zampa

Moray, H.
Untamed
FOX (US) 1955 dir. Henry King

Morell, D.
First Blood
ORION (US) 1982 dir. Ted Kotcheff

Morell, P.
Diamond Jim
UN (US) 1935 dir. A. Edward
Sutherland

Morey, W.
Kavik the Wolf Dog
Courage of Kavik, the Wolf Dog, The
PANTHEON (US) 1980 dir. Peter Carter
TV(US)

Morgan, A.
Great Man, The
UI (US) 1956 dir. Jose Ferrer

Morgan, C.
Burning Glass, The
ATV (GB) 1956 dir. Cyril Coke
TV(GB)
ATV (GB) 1960 dir. David Boisseau

Morgan, C.
Choir Practice
P
Valley of Song
ABPC (GB) 1953 dir. Gilbert Gunn

Morgan, C.
Fountain, The
RKO (US) 1934 dir. John Cromwell

Morgan, G.
Albert RN
P
DIAL (GB) 1953 dir. Lewis Gilbert
US title: Break to Freedom

Morgan, J.
This Was a Woman
P
FOX (GB) 1948 dir. Tim Whelan

Morgan, K. S.
Past Forgetting

Ike
ABC (US) 1979 dir. Melville Shavelson,
Boris Sagal
TVSe(US)

Morgieve, R.
À La Mode

FRANCE 2 (Fr) 1993 dir. Remy
Duchemin

Morier, J. J.
Adventures of Hajji Baba of Ispahan

Adventures of Hajji Baba, The
FOX (US) 1954 dir. Don Weis

Morison, E. and Lamont, F.
Adventure, The

Miss Morison's Ghosts
ANGLIA (GB) 1983 dir. John Bruce
TV(GB)

Morland, N.
Mrs. Pym of Scotland Yard

GN (GB) 1939 dir. Fred Elles

Morley, C. D.
Kitty Foyle

RKO (US) 1940 dir. Sam Wood

Morley, R. and Langley, N.
Edward, My Son

P
MGM (GB) 1949 dir. George Cukor

Morley, W.
Gentle Ben

Gentle Giant, The
PAR (US) 1967 dir. James Neilson
Ch

Mornin, D.
All Our Fault

Nothing Personal
BRIT SCREEN (GB/Ire) 1995 dir.
Thaddeus O'Sullivan

Morpurgo, M.
Friend or Foe

CFF (GB) 1982 dir. John Krish
Ch

Morpurgo, M.
My Friend Walter

GOLDHIL (US/GB) 1993 dir. Gavin
Millar
Ch, TV(US/GB)

Morpurgo, M.
Why Whales Came

When the Whales Came
FOX (GB) 1989 dir. Clive Rees

Morrell, D.
Brotherhood of the Rose

NBC (US) 1989 dir. Marvin Chomsky
TVSe(US)

Morrieson, R. H.
Scarecrow

OASIS (NZ) 1981 dir. Sam Pillsbury

Morrieson, R. H.
Came a Hot Friday

ORION (NZ) 1985 dir. Ian Mune

Morris, C.
Reluctant Heroes

P
ABP (GB) 1951 dir. Jack Raymond

Morris, D. R.
All Hands on Deck

TCF (US) 1961 dir. Norman Taurog
M

Morris, H. J.
Mr. Write

P
STAR PARTNERS (US) 1994 dir. Charlie
Loventhal

Morris, M. M.
Dangerous Woman, A
AMBLIN (US) 1993 dir. Stephen
Gyllenhaal

Morris, M. M.
Songs in Ordinary Time
COL TRISTAR (US) 2000 dir. Rob
Holcomb
TV(US)

Morris, R.
One is a Lonely Number
MGM (US) 1972 dir. Mel Stuart

Morris, R. and Willson, M.
Unsinkable Molly Brown, The
P
MGM (US) 1964 dir. Charles Walters
M

Morris, W.
Good Old Boy: A Delta Summer
Good Old Boy
DISNEY CH (US) 1988 dir. Tom G.
Robertson
TV(US)

Morris, W.
My Dog Skip
WAR (US) 2000 dir. Jay Russell

Morrison, A.
Love Flies in the Window
P
This Man is Mine
RKO (US) 1934 dir. John Cromwell

Morrison, T.
Beloved
TOUCHSTONE (US) 1998 dir. Jonathan
Demme

Morros, B.
My Ten Years as a Counter-Spy
Man on a String
COL (US) 1960 dir. André de Toth
GB title: Confessions of a Counterspy

Morrow, H.
Benefits Forgot
Of Human Hearts
MGM (US) 1938 dir. Clarence Brown

Morrow, H.
On to Oregon
Seven Alone
HEMDALE (US) 1974 dir. Earl Bellamy

Morse, L. A.
Old Dick, The
Jake Spanner, Private Eye
FENADY (US) 1989 dir. Lee H. Katzin
TV(US)

Mortimer, J.
Dock Brief, The
P
MGM (GB) 1962 dir. James Hill
US title: Trial & Error

Mortimer, J.
Paradise Postponed
THAMES (GB) 1986 dir. Alvin Rakoff
TVSe(GB)

Mortimer, J.
Summer's Lease
BBC (GB) 1989 dir. Martyn Friend
TVSe(GB)

Mortimer, J.
Titmuss Regained
ANGLIA (GB) 1991 dir. Martyn Friend
TVSe(GB)

Mortimer, P.
Pumpkin Eater, The
BL (GB) 1964 dir. Jack Clayton

Morton, A.
Diana: Her True Story
M. POLL (US) 1993 dir. Kevin Connor
TV(US)

Morton, M.
Yellow Ticket, The

P
FOX (US) 1931 dir. Raoul Walsh
GB title: Yellow Passport, The

Mosel, T.
Dear Heart
WAR (US) 1964 dir. Delbert Mann

Mosher, H. F.
Stranger in the Kingdom, A
KINGDOM (US) 1998 dir. Jay Craven

Mosher, H. F.
Where the Rivers Flow North
CALEDONIA (US) 1993 dir. Jay Craven

Mosley, L.
Cat and the Mice, The
Foxhole in Cairo
BL (GB) 1960 dir. John Llewellyn Moxey

Mosley, N.
Accident
MON (GB) 1967 dir. Joseph Losey

Mosley, W.
Always Outnumbered, Always
Outgunned
Always Outnumbered
HBO (US) 1998 dir. Michael Apted
TV(US)

Mosley, W.
Devil in a Blue Dress
TRISTAR (US) 1995 dir. Carl Franklin

Moss, W. S.
Ill Met By Moonlight
RANK (GB) 1956 dir. Michael Powell,
Emeric Pressburger
US title: Night Ambush

Motley, W.
Knock on Any Door
COL (US) 1949 dir. Nicholas Ray

Motley, W.
Let No Man Write My Epitaph
COL (US) 1960 dir. Philip Leacock

Mowat, F.
Curse of the Viking Grave
*Lost in the Barrens II: The Curse of the
Viking Grave*
ATLANTIS (Can) 1992 dir. Michael J. F.
Scott
TV(Can)

Mowat, F.
Lost in the Barrens
CBC (US/Can) 1991 dir. Michael Scott
TV(Can/US)

Mowat, F.
Never Cry Wolf
DISNEY (US) 1983 dir. Carroll Ballard

Mowat, F.
Whale for the Killing, A
PLAYBOY (US) 1981
dir. Richard T. Heffron
TV(US)

Mowra, L.
Radiance

P
ECLIPSE (Aust) 1998 dir. Rachel
Perkins

Moyzisch, L. C.
Operation Cicero
Five Fingers
FOX (US) 1952
dir. Joseph L. Mankiewicz

Mozart, W. A.
Magic Flute, The
SWE TV (Swe) 1974
dir. Ingmar Bergman
M, TV(Swe)

Mozart, W. A.
Marriage of Figaro, The
BBC (GB) 1990 dir. D. Bailey
M, TV(GB)

Mtwa, P.
Bopha!
P
TAUBMAN (US) 1993 dir. Morgan
Freeman

Mukoda, K.
Buddies
TOHO/SHOCHIKU (Jap) 1990
dir. Yasuo Furuhata

Mulally, F.
Looking for Clancy
BBC (GB) 1975 dir. Bill Hays
TVSe(GB)

Mulford, C. E.
Hopalong Cassidy
PAR (US) 1935 dir. Howard Bretherton

Mulisch, H.
Assault, The
CANNON (Neth) 1986
dir. Fons Rademakers

Muller, M.
Anne Frank: The Biography
Anne Frank
TOUCHSTONE (US) 2001 dir. Robert
Dornhelm
TVSe(US)

Mullin, C.
Error of Judgment: The Birmingham
Bombings
*Investigation, The: Inside a Terrorist
Bombing*
GRANADA (US/GB) 1990 dir. Mike
Beckham
TV(GB/US)

Mullin, C.
Very British Coup, A
SKREBA (GB) 1988 dir. Mick Jackson
TVSe(GB)

Mulvihill, W.
Sands of the Kalahari
PAR (GB) 1965 dir. Cy Endfield

Mundy, T.
King of the Khyber Rifles
FOX (US) 1954 dir. Henry King

Munoz Molina, A.
Plenilunio
CANAL+ ESPANA (Sp/Fr) 2000 dir.
Imanol Uribe

Munro, J.
Innocent Bystanders
SCOTIA-BARBER (GB) 1972
dir. Peter Collinson

Munro, N.
New Road, The
BBC (GB) 1973 dir. Moira Armstrong
TVSe(GB)

Murail, E.
Staircase C
FILMS 7 (Fr) 1985
dir. Jean-Charles Tacchella
French title: Escalier C

Murakami, R.
Audition
OMEGA (Jap) 1999 dir. Akashi Miike

Murakami, R.
Topaz
Tokyo Decadence
NORTHERN (Jap) 1992 dir. Ryu
Murakami

Murata, K.
Nabe-No-Kake

Rhapsody in August
ORION (Jap) 1991 dir. Akira Kurosawa

Murdoch, I.
Bell, The

BBC (GB) 1982 dir. Barry Davis
TV(GB)

Murdoch, I.
Severed Head, A

COL (GB) 1970 dir. Dick Clement

Murdoch, I.
Unofficial Rose, An

BBC (GB) 1974 dir. Basil Coleman
TVSe(GB)

Murger, H.
Scènes de la Vie Bohème

Bohemian Life
FILMS A2/PYRAMIDE (Fr)
1992 dir. Aki Kaurismaki

Murger, H.
Scènes de la Vie Bohème

Vie de Boheme, La
FILMS A2 (Fr) 1992 dir. Aki Kaurismaki

Murphy, A.
To Hell and Back

UI (US) 1955 dir. Jesse Hibbs

Murphy, D.
Sergeant, The

WAR (US) 1968 dir. John Flynn

Murphy, G.
Down Will Come Baby

HEARST (US) 1999 dir. Gregory
Goodell
TV(US)

Murphy, G.
Simon Says

Summer of Fear
M. ROBE (US) 1996 dir. Mike Robe
TV(US)

Murphy, R.
Mountain Lion, The

Run, Cougar, Run
DISNEY (US) 1972
dir. Michael Dmytryk

Murphy, W. and Sapir, R.
Destroyer, The

Remo Williams: The Adventure Begins
ORION (US) 1985 dir. Guy Hamilton

Murray, J. and Boretz, A.
Room Service

P
RKO (US) 1938 dir. William A. Seiter

Murray, J. and Boretz, A.
Room Service

P
Step Lively
RKO (US) 1944 dir. Tim Whelan

Murray, M.
Jamaica Run

PAR (US) 1953 dir. Lewis R. Foster

Murray, W.
Malibu

COL (US) 1983 dir. E. W. Swackhamer
TVSe(US)

Murray, W.
Sweet Ride, The

FOX (US) 1968 dir. Harvey Hart

Mus, A.
Senyora, La

ICA (Sp) 1987 dir. Jordi Cadenar

Mutis, A.
Ilona Comes With the Rain
CARACOL (Col/It/Sp) 1996 dir. Sergio
Cabrera

Myers, E.
Mrs Christopher
Blackmailed
GFD (US) 1950 dir. Marc Allegret

Myers, L. S.
Hungry Bachelors Club, The
REGENT ENT (US) 1999 dir. Gregory
Ruzzin

Myers, P.
K2
P
MIRAMAX (US) 1992 dir. Franc
Roddam

Myrer, A.
Big War, The
In Love and War
FOX (US) 1958 dir. Philip Dunne

Myrer, A.
Last Convertible, The
UN TV (US) 1979 dir. Sidney Hayers, Jo
Swerling, Jr., Gus Trikonis
TVSe(US)

Myrer, A.
Once an Eagle
UN TV (US) 1977 dir. E. W.
Swackhamer, Richard Michaels
TVSe(US)

Nabokov, V.
Defence, The

Luzhin Defence, The
FRANCE 2 (Fr/GB) 2000 dir. Marleen
Gorris

Nabokov, V.
Despair

GALA (Ger) 1978
dir. Rainer Werner Fassbinder

Nabokov, V.
King, Queen, Knave

WOLPER (US/Ger) 1972
dir. Jerzy Skolimowski

Nabokov, V.
Laughter in the Dark

UA (GB/Fr) 1969 dir. Tony Richardson

Nabokov, V.
Lolita

MGM (GB) 1962 dir. Stanley Kubrick
PATHE (US/Fr) 1997 dir. Adrian Lyne

Nabokov, V.
Maschenka

CLASART (GB) 1987
dir. John Goldschmidt
TVSe(GB)

Naipaul, V. S.
Mystic Masseur

MI (Ind) 2001 dir. Ismail Merchant

Nakamura, I.
Empire of Passion

PARIS/OSHIMA (Jap) 1980
dir. Magisa Oshima

Nan, S.
Soul of a Painter

SHANGHAI (China) 1994 dir. Shuqin
Huang

Nance, J. J.
Medusa's Child

COL TRISTAR (US) 1997 dir. Larry
Shaw
TVSe(US)

Nance, J. J.
Pandora's Clock

NBC ENT (US) 1996 dir. Eric Laneuville
TVSe(US)

Nasar, S.
Beautiful Mind, A: A Biography of
John Forbes Nash, Jr.

Beautiful Mind, A
IMAGINE ENT (US) 2001 dir. Ron
Howard

Nash, N. R.
Rainmaker, The

P
PAR (US) 1956 dir. Joseph Anthony

Nason, D. and Etchison, B.
Celebration Family

VZ/SAMUELS (US) 1987 dir. Robert
Day
TV(US)

Nassar, R.
Lavoura Arcaica
VIDEO (Bra) 2001 dir. Luiz Fernando
Carvalho

Natale, M. O.
Francesca e Nunziata
MEDIATRADE (It) 2001 dir. Lina
Wertmuller

Nathan, R.
In Barley Fields
Bishop's Wife, The
RKO (US) 1947 dir. Henry Koster

Nathan, R.
One More Spring
FOX (US) 1935 dir. Henry King

Nathan, R.
Portrait of Jennie
SELZNICK (US) 1948
dir. William Dieterle
GB title: Jennie

Nathansens, H.
Mendel Philipsen and Sons
Sofie
NORSK (Den/Nor/Swe) 1992 dir. Liv
Ullman

Nathanson, E. M.
Dirty Dozen, The
MGM (US) 1967 dir. Robert Aldrich

Natsume, S.
I am a Cat
TOHO (Jap) 1982 dir. Kenichi Kawa

Natsume, S.
Sorekara
TOEI (Jap) 1987 dir. Yoshimitsu Morita

Naughton, B.
Alfie
P
PAR (GB) 1966 dir. Lewis Gilbert

Naughton, B.
All in Good Time
P
Family Way, The
BL (GB) 1966 dir. Roy Boulting

Naughton, B.
Spring and Port Wine
P
AA (GB) 1970 dir. Peter Hammond

Naughton, E.
McCabe
McCabe and Mrs. Miller
WAR (US) 1971 dir. Robert Altman

Naughton, J.
Taking to the Air: The Rise of Michael
Jordan
Michael Jordan: An American Hero
FOX FAMILY (US) 1999 dir. Alan
Metzger
TV(US)

Naumoff, L.
Silk Hope
POLSON (US) 1999 dir. Kevin Dowling
TV(US)

Navarre, Y.
Kurwenal
Straight from the Heart
TELESCENE (Fr) 1990 dir. Lea Pool

Naylor, G.
Women of Brewster Place, The
PHOENIX (US) 1989 dir. Donna Deitch
TVSe(US)

Neely, R.
Innocents with Dirty Hands
FOX-RANK (Fr/It/Ger) 1975
dir. Claude Chabrol

Neely, R.
Shattered
MGM-PATHE (US) 1991
dir. Wolfgang Petersen

Neely, W.
Stand on It

Stroker Ace
UN/WAR (US) 1983 dir. Hal Needham

Neff, J.
Mobbed Up

Teamster Boss: The Jackie Presser Story
HBO (US) 1992 dir. Alastair Reid
TV(US)

Neider, C.
Authentic Death of Hendry Jones, The

One-Eyed Jacks
PAR (US) 1961 dir. Marlon Brando

Neiderman, A.
Devil's Advocate, The

WAR (US) 1997 dir. Taylor Hackford

Neimark, P.
She Lives

ABC (US) 1973 dir. Stuart Hagmann
TV(US)

Nelson, A.
Murder Under Two Flags

Show of Force, A
PAR (US) 1990 dir. Bruno Barreto

Nelson, B.
Girl

KUSHNER-LOCKE (US) 1999 dir.
Jonathan Kahn

Nelson, R.
Eight O'Clock in the Morning

They Live
UN (US) 1988 dir. John Carpenter

Nelson, T. B.
Eye of God

P
CYCLONE (US) 1997 dir. Tim Blake
Nelson

Nemerov, H.
Homecoming Game, The

Tall Story
WAR (US) 1960 dir. Joshua Logan

Nemirowsky, I.
David Golder

My Daughter Joy
BL (GB) 1950 dir. Gregory Ratoff
US title: Operation X

Nesbit, E.
Enchanted Castle, The

BBC (GB) 1979 dir. Dorothea Brooking
TVSe(GB)

Nesbit, E.
Five Children And It

BBC (GB) 1991 dir. Marilyn Fox
Ch, TVSe(GB)

Nesbit, E.
Phoenix and the Carpet, The

BBC (GB) 1976 dir. Clive Doig
TVSe(GB)

Nesbit, E.
Railway Children, The

BBC (GB) 1968 dir. Julia Smith
TVSe(GB)
MGM (GB) 1970 dir. Lionel Jeffries
Ch
CARLTON TV (GB) 2000 dir. Catherine
Morshead
Ch, TV(GB)

Nesbit, E.
Story of the Treasure Seekers, The

BBC (GB) 1982 dir. Roger Singleton-
Turner
TVSe(GB)

Neufeld, J.
Lisa, Bright and Dark

BANNER (US) 1973 dir. Jeannot Szwarc

Neumann, R.
Queen's Favourite, The
King in Shadow
BL (Ger) 1961 dir. Harold Braun

Neville E.
Vida en un Hilo, La
P
Mujer Bajo la Lluvia, Una
ATRIUM (Sp) 1992 dir. Gerardo Vera
US title: Woman in the Rain, A

Nevin, D.
Dream West
SCHICK SUNN (US) 1986
dir. Dick Lowry
TVSe(US)

Newby, E.
Love and War in the Apennines
In Love and War
HALLMARK (US) 2001 dir. John Kent
Harrison
TV(US)

Newfield, J.
Only in America: The Life and Crimes
of Don King
Don King: Only in America
HBO (US) dir. John Herzfeld
TV(US)

Newman, A.
Alexa
BBC (GB) 1982 dir. Laurence Moody
TVSe(GB)

Newman, A.
Bouquet of Barbed Wire
LWT (GB) 1976 dir. Tony Wharmby
TVSe(GB)

Newman, A.
Sense of Guilt, A
BBC (GB) 1990 dir. Bruce MacDonald
TVSe(GB)

Newman, A.
Three Into Two Won't Go
UI (GB) 1969 dir. Peter Hall

Newman, B.
Battle of the V1
MAY-SEW (GB) 1958 dir. Vernon Sewell
US title: Unseen Heroes

Newman, G. F.
Sir, You Bastard
Take, The
COL (US) 1974
dir. Robert Hartford-Davis

Nexo, M. A.
Pelle the Conqueror
CURZON (Den/Swe) 1988
dir. Bille August

Ngema, M.
Sarafina!
P
HOLLYWOOD (SA/US) 1992 dir.
Darrell Roodt

Niall, I.
No Resting Place
ABP (GB) 1951 dir. Paul Rother

Niall, I.
Tiger Walks, A
DISNEY (US) 1964 dir. Norman Tokar

Nichols, A.
Abie's Irish Rose
P
UA (US) 1952 dir. Edward A.
Sutherland

Nichols, A.
Give me a Sailor
P
PAR (US) 1938 dir. Elliott Nugent

Nichols, B.
Evensong
P
GAU (GB) 1934 dir. Victor Saville

Nichols, J.
Milagro Beanfield War, The
UN (US) 1988 dir. Robert Redford

Nichols, J.
Wizard of Loneliness
SKOURAS (US) 1988 dir. Jenny Bowen

Nichols, P.
Day in the Death of Joe Egg, A
P
COL (GB) 1971 dir. Peter Medak

Nichols, P.
National Health, The
P
COL (GB) 1973 dir. Jack Gold

Nichols, P.
Privates on Parade
P
HANDMADE (GB) 1982
dir. Michael Blakemore

Nicholson, J.
Sterile Cuckoo, The
PAR (US) 1969 dir. Alan J. Pakula
GB title: Pookie

Nicholson, K.
Barker, The
P
Diamond Horseshoe
FOX (US) 1945 dir. George Seaton

Nicholson, K.
Blind Spot, The
P
Taxi!
WAR (US) 1931 dir. Roy del Ruth

Nicholson, M.
Natasha's Story
Welcome to Sarajevo
CHANNEL 4 FILMS (GB/US) 1997 dir.
Michael Winterbottom

Nicholson, W.
Shadowlands
P
PRICE ENT (GB) 1993 dir. Richard
Attenborough

Nicolaysen, B.
Perilous Passage, The
Passage, The
HEMDALE (GB) 1978
dir. J. Lee Thompson

Nicolson, M.
House of a Thousand Candles, The
REP (US) 1936 dir. Arthur Lubin

Nicolson, N.
Portrait of a Marriage
BBC (GB) 1990 dir. Stephen Whittaker
TVSe(GB)

Nicolson, R.
Mrs. Ross
Whisperers, The
UA (GB) 1966 dir. Bryan Forbes

Nielson, H.
Murder by Proxy
EXCL (GB) 1955 dir. Terence Fisher
US title: Blackout

Niggli, J.
Mexican Village
Sombrero
MGM (US) 1953 dir. Norman Foster

Nigro, D.
Ravenscroft
P
Manor, The
FALCON (Czech) 1999 dir. Ken Berris

Nijinsky, R.
Nijinsky
PAR (US) 1980 dir. Herbert Ross

Niklaus, T.
Tamahine
WAR (GB) 1963 dir. Philip Leacock

Niland, D'A.
Shiralee, The
MGM (GB) 1957 dir. Leslie Norman
AUS (Aust) 1987 dir. Greg Ogilvie
TV(Aust)

Niles, B.
Condemned to Devil's Island
Condemned
UA (US) 1929 dir. Wesley Ruggles

Nimmo, J.
Emlyn's Moon
HTV (GB) 1990 dir. Pennant Roberts
Ch, TVSe(GB)

Nin, A.
Delta of Venus
NEW LINE (US) 1995 dir. Zalman King

Nin, A.
Henry and June
UN (US) 1990 dir. Philip Kaufman

Nini, S.
Ils disent que je suis une beurette
Samia
STUDIO CANAL+ (Fr) 2000 dir.
Philippe Faucon

Nishiki, M.
Snake Head
Shadow of China
NEW LINE (US/Jap) 1991
dir. Mitsuo Yanagimachi

Nissan, R.
Like a Bride
IMCINE (Mex) 1993 dir. Guita Schyfter

Nixon, J. L.
Other Side of Dark, The
Awake to Danger
NBC (US) 1995 dir. Michael Tuchner
TV(US)

Nobbs, D.
Life and Times of Henry Pratt, The
GRANADA (GB) 1992 dir. Adrian
Shergold
TVSe(GB)

Noble, H.
Woman with a Sword
Drums in the Deep South
RKO (GB) 1952
dir. William Cameron Menzies

Noble, J.
Away Alone
P
Gold in the Streets
FERNDALE (GB/Ire) 1997 dir.
Elizabeth Gill

Noel, B. and Watterson, K.
You Must be Dreaming
Betrayal of Trust
COS-MEU (US) 1994 dir. George
Kaczender
US(TV)

Noel, S.
House of Secrets
RANK (GB) 1956 dir. Guy Green
US title: Triple Deception

Nolan, F.
Algonquin Project, The
Brass Target
UN (US) 1978 dir. John Hough

Nolan, J.
Gather Rosebuds
Isn't it Romantic?
PAR (US) 1948 dir. Norman Z. McLeod

Nolan, W. and Johnson, G.
Logan's Run
MGM (US) 1976 dir. Michael Anderson

Nolen, J.
Harvey Potter's Balloon Farm
Balloon Farm
DISNEY (US) 1999 dir. William Dear
TV(US)
Ch

Noll, I.
Pharmacist, The
SENATOR (Ger) 1997 dir. Rainer Kaufmann

Noon, J.
Woundings
P
MUSE (GB) 1998 dir. Roberta Hanley

Noonan, T.
What Happened Was ...
P
GOOD MACHINE (US) 1993 dir. Tom Noonan

Noonan, T.
Wifey
P
Wife, The
ARTISTIC (US) 1995 dir. Tom Noonan

Nord, P.
Serpent, The
LA BOETIE (Fr/It/Ger) 1974 dir. Henri Verneuil

Norden, P.
Madam Kitty
FOX (It/Fr/Ger) 1977 dir. Giovanni Tinto Brass

Nordhoff, C. B. and Hall, J. N.
High Barbaree
MGM (US) 1947 dir. Jack Conway

Nordhoff, C. B. and Hall, J. N.
Hurricane, The
UA (US) 1937 dir. John Ford
ITC (US) 1979 dir. Jan Troell

Nordhoff, C. B. and Hall, J. N.
Botany Bay
PAR (US) 1952 dir. John Farrow

Nordhoff, C. B. and Hall, J. N.
Mutiny on the Bounty
MGM (US) 1935 dir. Frank Lloyd
MGM (US) 1962 dir. Lewis Milestone

Nordhoff, C. B. and Hall, J. N.
No More Gas
Tuttles of Tahiti, The
RKO (US) 1942 dir. Charles Vidor

Norman, J.
Tarnsman of Gor
Gor
CANNON (US) 1989 dir. Fritz Kiersch

Norman, M.
'Night, Mother
P
UN (US) 1986 dir. Tom Moore

Norman, M.
Getting Out
P
RHI (US) 1994 dir. John Korty
TV(US)

Norris, C. G.
Seed
UN (US) 1931 dir. John Stahl

Norris, K.
Passion Flower
MGM (US) 1930 dir. William de Mille

North, S.
Rascal, a Memoir of a Better Era

Rascal
DISNEY (US) 1969 dir. Norman Tokar
Ch

North, S.
So Dear to My Heart

DISNEY (US) 1948 dir. Harold Schuster

Norton, M.
Bed-Knob and Broomstick

Bedknobs and Broomsticks
DISNEY (US) 1971
dir. Robert Stevenson
Ch

Norton, M.
Borrowers, The; Borrowers Afield, The; Borrowers Afloat, The; Borrowers Aloft, The

Borrowers, The
FOX TV (US) 1973 dir. Walter C. Miller
Ch, TV(US)
WORKING TITLE TV/TNT (US/GB)
1992 dir. John Henderson
Ch, TVSe(US/GB)
POLYGRAM (US/GB) 1997 dir. Peter
Hewitt

Norton, M.
Return of the Borrowers, The

WORKING TITLE/TNT (GB) 1996 dir.
John Henderson
Ch, TVSe(US)

Nortvedt, R.
Sondagsengler

Other Side of Sunday, The
NRK DRAMA (Nor) 1996 dir. Berit
Nesheim

Nothomb, A.
Librement Trahi

Hygiene de L'Assassin
TSF (Fr) 1999 dir. François Ruggieri

Novello, I.
Dancing Years, The

ABPC (GB) 1949 dir. Harold French
ATV (GB) 1976
TV(GB)

Novello, I.
Glamorous Night

P
ABP (GB) 1937
dir. Brian Desmond Hurst
M

Novello, I.
I Lived With You

P
GB (GB) 1933 dir. Maurice Elvey

Novello, I.
Truth Game, The

P
But the Flesh is Weak
MGM (US) 1932 dir. Jack Conway

Novello, I. and Collier, C.
Rat, The

P
RKO (GB) 1937 dir. Jack Raymond

Nowra, L.
Cosi

P
MIRAMAX (Aust) 1996 dir. Mark Joffe

Nozawa, H.
Hasen no Marisu

FGP (Jap) 2000 dir. Satoshi Isaka

Nulberry, V.
Devil's Island

TRISTAR (Sp) 1994 dir. Juan Piquer
Simon

Nyala, H.
Point Last Seen

ALEXANDER/ENRIGHT (US) 1998
dir. Elodie Keene
TV(US)

O

Oakley, A.
Men's Room, The
BBC (GB) 1991 dir. Antonia Bird
TVSe(GB)

Oates, J. C.
Blonde
GREENWALD (US/Can/Aust) 2001
dir. Joyce Chopra
TVSe(US/Can/Aust)

Oates, J. C.
Foxfire
RYSHER (US) 1996 dir. Annette
Haywood-Carter

Oates, J. C.
Lies of the Twins
MCA TV (US) 1991 dir. Tim Hunter
TV(US)

Oates, J. C.
We Were the Mulvaneys
VZ/SERTNER (US) 2002 dir. Peter
Werner
TV(US)

Oates, J. C.
Where are you Going, Where have you Been?
Smooth Talk
NEPENTHE (US) 1985
dir. Joyce Chopra

Obersku, J.
Kinderjahren
Jonah Who Lived in the Whale
FOCUS (Fr/It) 1993 dir. Roberto Faenza

O'Brian, L.
Remarkable Mr. Pennypacker, The
P
FOX (US) 1958 dir. Henry Levin

O'Brien, D.
Two of a Kind: The Hillside Stranglers
Case of the Hillside Stranglers, The
FRIES (US) 1989 dir. Steven Gethers
TV(US)

O'Brien, E.
Country Girls, The
LF (GB) 1983
dir. Desmond Davis

O'Brien, E.
Lonely Girl, The
Girl With Green Eyes
UA (GB) 1964 dir. Desmond Davis

O'Brien, J.
Leaving Las Vegas
LUMIERE (US) 1995 dir. Mike Figgis

O'Brien, J. F., Kurins, A. and Shames, L.
Boss of Bosses—The Fall of the Godfather: The FBI and Paul Castellano
Boss of Bosses
BLEECKER (US) 1999 dir. Dwight H.
Little
TV(US)

O'Brien, K.
Mary Lavelle

Talk of Angels
POLARIS (US) 1998 dir. Nick Hamm

O'Brien, K.
That Lady

FOX (GB) 1955 dir. Terence Young

O'Brien, R. C.
Mrs Frisby and the Rats of N.I.M.H.

Secret of N.I.M.H., The
MGM/UA (US) 1982 dir. Don Bluth
A, Ch

O'Brien, T.
In the Lake of the Woods

HALLMARK (US) 1996 dir. Carl
Schenkel
TV(US)

O'Brine, M.
Passport to Treason

EROS (GB) 1956 dir. Robert S. Baker

O'Carroll, B.
Agnes Browne

OCTOBER (US) 1999 dir. Anjelica
Huston

O'Casey, S.
Juno and the Paycock

P
BI (GB) 1930 dir. Alfred Hitchcock

O'Casey, S.
Mirror in my House

Young Cassidy
MGM (GB) 1964
dir. Jack Cardiff, John Ford

O'Casey, S.
Plough and the Stars, The

P
RKO (US) 1936 dir. John Ford

O'Connell, T.
Face Behind the Mask, The

P
COL (US) 1941 dir. Robert Florey

O'Connor, E.
Irishman, The

S. AUST (Aust) 1978
dir. Donald Crombie

O'Connor, E.
Last Hurrah, The

COL (US) 1958 dir. John Ford
COL (US) 1977 dir. Vincent Sherman
TV(US)

O'Connor, F.
Majesty of the Law, The

Rising of the Moon, The
WAR (Ire) 1957 dir. John Ford

O'Connor, F.
Wise Blood

NEWLINE (US) 1980 dir. John Huston

O'Connor, G.
Darlings of the Gods

THAMES (GB) 1991
dir. Catherine Millar
TVSe(GB)

O'Dell, S.
Island of the Blue Dolphins

UN (US) 1964 dir. James B. Clark

Odets, C.
Big Knife, The

P
UA (US) 1955 dir. Robert Aldrich

Odets, C.
Clash by Night

P
RKO (US) 1952 dir. Fritz Lang

Odets, C.
Country Girl, The
P
PAR (US) 1954 dir. George Seaton
PAR (US) 1974 dir. Paul Bogart
TV(US)

Odets, C.
Golden Boy
P
COL (US) 1939 dir. Rouben Mamoulian

Odier, D.
Voie Sauvage, La
Light Years Away
NEW YORKER (Fr) 1932
dir. Alain Tanner

Odlum, J.
Each Dawn I Die
WAR (US) 1939 dir. William Keighley

O'Donnell, J. P.
Bunker, The
TIME-LIFE (US) 1981
dir. George Schaefer
TV(US)

O'Donnell, K. P, Powers, D. F. and McCarthy, J.
Johnny, We Hardly Knew Ye
TALENT (US) 1977 dir. Gilbert Cates
TV(US)

O'Donnell, L.
No Business Being a Cop
Prime Target
MGM/UA (US) 1989 dir. Robert Collins
TV(US)

O'Donnell, Jr., L.
Deadly Force: The Story of how a Badge can become a License to Kill
Case of Deadly Force, A
TELECOM (US) 1986
dir. Michael Miller
TV(US)

O'Farrell, W.
Turn Back the Clock
NBC (US) 1989 dir. Larry Elikann
TV(US)

Offenbach, J.
Tales of Hoffman, The
BL (GB) 1951 dir. Michael Powell,
Emeric Pressburger
M

O'Flaherty, L.
Informer, The
RKO (US) 1935 dir. John Ford

Ogburn, C.
Marauders, The
Merrill's Marauders
WAR (US) 1962 dir. Samuel Fuller

Ogden, B.
Virtuoso
BBC (GB) 1988 dir. Tony Smith
TV(GB)

Ogden, D.
Halfway House, The
P
EAL (GB) 1944 dir. Basil Dearden

O'Grady, R.
Let's Kill Uncle
UI (US) 1966 dir. William Castle

O'Hara, J.
Butterfield 8
MGM (US) 1960 dir. Daniel Mann

O'Hara, J.
Doctor's Son, The
Turning Point of Jim Malloy, The
COL TV (US) 1975 dir. Frank D. Gilroy
TV(US)

O'Hara, J.
From the Terrace
FOX (US) 1960 dir. Mark Robson

O'Hara, J.
Pal Joey
COL (US) 1957 dir. George Sidney
M

O'Hara, J.
Rage to Live, A
UA (US) 1965 dir. Walter Grauman

O'Hara, J.
Ten North Frederick
FOX (US) 1958 dir. Philip Dunne

O'Hara, M.
Green Grass of Wyoming
FOX (US) 1949 dir. Louis King

O'Hara, M.
My Friend Flicka
FOX (US) 1943 dir. Harold Schuster

O'Hara, M.
Thunderhead, Son of Flicka
FOX (US) 1945 dir. Louis King

O'Keefe, J.
Shimmer
P
AM PLAY (US) 1995 dir. John Hanson
TV(US)

Oliphant, R.
Piano for Mrs. Cimino, A
EMI (US) 1982 dir. George Schaefer
TV(US)

Olivant, A.
Owd Bob
BG (GB) 1938 dir. Robert Stevenson
US title: To the Victor
EVEREST (Can/GB) 1998 dir. Rodney
Gibbons

'Olivia'
Olivia
FDF (Fr) 1950 dir. Jacqueline Audry

Olsen, J.
Have You Seen My Son?
MGM TV (US) 1996 dir. Paul Schneider
TV(US)

Olsen, J.
Son
Sins of the Mother
CORAPEAKE (US) 1991
dir. John Patterson
TV(US)

Olsen, T.
Tell Me a Riddle
FILMWAYS (US) 1980 dir. Lee Grant

Olsen, T. V.
Arrow in the Sun
Soldier Blue
AVCO (US) 1970 dir. Ralph Nelson

Olsen, T. V.
Stalking Moon, The
WAR (US) 1968 dir. Robert Mulligan

Olshan, J.
Clara's Heart
WB (US) 1988 dir. Robert Mulligan

O'Malley, M.
Gross Misconduct
CBC (Can) 1993 dir. Atom Egoyan
TV(Can)

Ondaatje, M.
English Patient, The
MIRAMAX (US) 1996 dir. Anthony
Minghella

O'Neal, C.
Three Wishes for Jamie
COL TV (US) 1987
dir. Robert William Young
TV(US)

O'Neill, E.
Ah, Wilderness!

P
MGM (US) 1935 dir. Clarence Brown
M. ALBERG (US) 1959
dir. Robert Mulligan
TV(US)

O'Neill, E.
Ah Wilderness!

P
Summer Holiday
MGM (US) 1948
dir. Rouben Mamoulian
M

O'Neill, E.
Anna Christie

P
MGM (US) 1930 dir. Clarence Brown

O'Neill, E.
Emperor Jones, The

P
UA (US) 1933 dir. Dudley Murphy

O'Neill, E.
Desire Under the Elms

P
PAR (US) 1958 dir. Delbert Mann

O'Neill, E.
Hairy Ape, The

P
UA (US) 1944 dir. Alfred Santell

O'Neill, E.
Iceman Cometh, The

P
AFT (US) 1973 dir. John Frankenheimer

O'Neill, E.
Long Day's Journey into Night
P
FOX (US) 1962 dir. Sidney Lumet
RHOMBUS (Can) 1996 dir. David
Wellington

O'Neill, E.
Long Voyage Home, The

P
UA (US) 1940 dir. John Ford

O'Neill, E.
Mourning Becomes Electra

P
RKO (US) 1947 dir. Dudley Nichols

O'Neill, E.
Strange Interlude

P
MGM (US) 1932 dir. Robert Z. Leonard
GB title: Strange Interval
HTV (GB) 1988 dir. Herbert Wise
TVSe(GB)

Onstott, K.
Drum

PAR (US) 1976 dir. Steve Carver

Onstott, K.
Mandingo

PAR (US) 1975 dir. Richard Fleischer

O-Oka, S.
Fires on the Plain

DAIEI (JAP) 1959 dir. Kon Ichikawa

Opatashu, D.
Romance of a Horse Thief

ALLIED (Yugo) 1971
dir. Abraham Polonsky

Oppel, J.-H.
Six-Pack

CHRYSALIDE (Fr) 2000 dir. Alain
Berberian

Oppenheim, E. P.
Amazing Quest of Mr Ernest Bliss,
The

Amazing Quest of Ernest Bliss, The
KLEMENT (GB) 1936 dir. Alfred Zeisler
US title: Romance & Riches

Oppenheim, E. P.
Great Impersonation, The

UN (US) 1935 dir. Alan Crosland
UN (US) 1942 dir. John Rawlins

Oppenheim, E. P.
Strange Boarders of Paradise Crescent, The

Strange Boarders
GB (GB) 1938 dir. Herbert Mason

Orczy, Baroness E.
Elusive Pimpernel, The

BL (GB) 1950 dir. Michael Powell

Orczy, Baroness E.
Emperor's Candlesticks, The

MGM (US) 1937
dir. George Fitzmaurice

Orczy, Baroness E.
Scarlet Pimpernel, The

UA (GB) 1934 dir. Harold Young
LF (US/GB) 1982
dir. Clive Donner
TVSe(GB/US)
BBC/A&E (GB) 1999 dir. Patrick Lau
TVSe(GB)

Orczy, Baroness E.
Scarlet Pimpernel, The

Pimpernel Smith
BN (GB) 1941 dir. Leslie Howard

Orczy, Baroness E.
Scarlet Pimpernel, The

Purple Mask, The
UN (US) 1955 dir. Bruce Humberstone

Orczy, Baroness E.
Spy of Napoleon

TWICKENHAM (GB) 1936
dir. Maurice Elvey

O'Rear, F. and O'Rear, J.
Château Bon Vivant

Snowball Express
DISNEY (US) 1972 dir. Norman Tokar

Orgel, D.
Devil in Vienna, The

Friendship in Vienna, A
DISNEY CH (US) 1988
dir. Arthur Allan Seidelman
TV(US)

Oristrell, J.
Entre Las Piernas

AURUM (Fr/Sp) 1999 dir. Manuel
Gomez Pereira

Orlev, U.
Island on Bird Street, The

APRIL (GB/Den) 1997 dir. Soren
Kragh-Jacobsen

Ormandroyd, E.
Time at the Top

HALLMARK (US) 1999 dir. Jimmy
Kaufman
TV(US)

O'Rourke, F.
Bravados, The

FOX (US) 1958 dir. Henry King

O'Rourke, F.
Great Bank Robbery, The

WAR (US) 1969 dir. Hy Averback

O'Rourke, F.
Mule for the Marquesa, A

Professionals, The
COL (US) 1966 dir. Richard Brooks

Orton, J.
Entertaining Mr. Sloane

P
PAR (GB) 1969 dir. Douglas Hickox

Orton, J.
Loot

P
BL (GB) 1970 dir. Silvio Narizzano

Orwell, G.
Animal Farm

ABP (GB) 1955 dir. John Halas, Joy Batchelor
HALLMARK (US) 1999 dir. John Stephenson
TV(US)
A

Orwell, G.
Keep the Apidistra Flying

OVERSEAS (GB) 1997 dir. Robert Bierman
US title: Merry War, A

Orwell, G.
1984

ABP (GB) 1956 dir. Michael Anderson
BBC (GB) 1965
dir. Christopher Morahan
TV(GB)
BBC (GB) 1984 dir. Rudolph Cartier
TV(GB)
VIRGIN (GB) 1984 dir. Michael Radford

Osada, A.
Children of Hiroshima

KEL (Jap) 1952 dir. Kaneto Shindo

Osborn, J. J.
Paper Chase, The

FOX (US) 1973 dir. James Bridges

Osborne, H.
Shore Leave

Hit the Deck
MGM (US) 1955 dir. Roy Rowland
M

Osborne, H. and Scott, A.
Shore Leave

P
Follow the Fleet
RKO (US) 1936 dir. Mark Sandrich
M

Osborne, J.
Entertainer, The

P
BL (GB) 1960 dir. Tony Richardson
RSO (US) 1976 dir. Donald Wrye
TV(US)

Osborne, J.
Inadmissible Evidence

P
PAR (GB) 1968 dir. Anthony Page

Osborne, J.
Look Back in Anger

P
ABP (GB) 1959 dir. Tony Richardson

Osborne, J.
Luther

P
SEVEN KEYS (GB) 1973 dir. Guy Green

Ostenso, M.
Wild Geese

After the Harvest
ALBERTA (Can) 2001 dir. Jeremy Podeswa
TV(Can)

Otokichi, M.
Actor's Revenge, An

DAIEI (Jap) 1963 dir. Kon Ichikawa

Otto, W.
How to Make an American Quilt

UN (US) 1995 dir. Jocelyn Moorhouse

Ouida
Dog of Flanders, A

RKO (US) 1935 dir. Edward Sloman
FOX (US) 1959 dir. James B. Clark
WOODBRIDGE (Bel/US) 1999 dir. Kevin Brodie

Ouida
Under Two Flags

FOX (US) 1936 dir. Frank Lloyd

Oursler, F.
Great Jasper, The
RKO (US) 1933 dir. J. Walter Ruben

Oursler, F.
Greatest Story Ever Told, The
UA (US) 1965 dir. George Stevens

Overholser, W. D.
Cast a Long Shadow
UA (US) 1959 dir. Thomas Carr

Owen, F.
Eddie Chapman Story, The
Triple Cross
AA (GB) 1967 dir. Terence Young

Owen, G.
Ballad of the Flim-Flam Man, The
Flim-Flam Man, The
FOX (US) 1967 dir. Irvin Kershner

Owen, R. T.
Payoff
VIACOM (US) 1991 dir. Stuart Cooper
TV(US)

Pace, L.
Broken Lullaby
ALLIANCE (Can) 1994 dir. Michael
Kennedy
TV(Can)

Packard, F. L.
Miracle Man, The
P
PAR (US) 1932 dir. Norman Z. McLeod

Packer, J.
Nor the Moon by Night
RANK (GB) 1958 dir. Ken Annakin
US title: Elephant Gun

Paez, J. L.
Dona Herlinda and her Son
CLASA (Mex) 1986 dir. J. H. Hermosillo

Pagano, J.
Condemned, The
Try and Get Me
UA (US) 1951 dir. Cyril Endfield
GB title: Sound of Fury, The

Page, E.
Tree of Liberty, The
Howards of Virginia, The
COL (US) 1940 dir. Frank Lloyd
GB title: Tree of Liberty, The

Page, G.
Paddy the Next Best Thing
P
FOX (US) 1933 dir. Harry Lachman

Page, T.
Hephaestus Plague, The
Bug
PAR (US) 1975 dir. Jeannot Szwarc

Page, T.
Page After Page
Frankie's House
ANGLIA FILMS (GB/Aust) 1992 dir.
Peter Fisk
TVSe(GB/Aust)

Pagnol, M.
Château de ma Mère, Le
My Mother's Castle
GAU (Fr) 1991 dir. Yves Robert

Pagnol, M.
Eau des Collines, L'
ORION (Fr) 1987 dir. Claude Berri
French title: Manon des Sources

Pagnol, M.
Gloire de Mon Père, La
My Father's Glory
GAU (Fr) 1991 dir. Yves Robert

Pagnol, M.
Jean de Florette
ORION (Fr) 1987 dir. Claude Berri

Pagnol, M.
Marius
P
PAR (Fr) 1931 dir. Alexander Korda

Pagnol, M.
Topaze

P

Mr. Topaze
FOX (GB) 1961 dir. Peter Sellers
US title: I Like Money

Pagnol, M.
Topaze

P

RKO (US) 1933
dir. Harry d'Abbabie d'Arrast

Paige, L. and Lipman, D.
Maybe I'll Pitch Forever

Don't Look Back
TBA (US) 1981 dir. Richard Colla
TV(US)

Painter, H. W.
Mark, I Love You

AUBREY (US) 1980
dir. Gonna Hellstrom
TV(US)

Paladini, F.
Bangkwang

Vacation in Hell
METROPOLIS (It) 1997 dir. Tonina
Valerii

Palahniuk, C.
Fight Club

FOX (US) 1999 dir. David Fincher

Paley, F.
Rumble on the Docks

COL (US) 1956 dir. Fred Sears

Palgi, Y.
Great Wind Cometh, A

Hanna's War
CANNON (US) 1988
dir. Menahem Golan

Palin, M. and Jones, T.
Secrets

P

Consuming Passions
GOLDWYN (GB) 1988 dir. Giles Foster

Palmer, D.
Diamond Girl

ALLIANCE (Can) 1998 dir. Timothy
Bond
TV(Can)

Palmer, M.
Extreme Measure

COL (US) 1996 dir. Michael Apted

Palmer, S.
Penguin Pool Murder, The

RKO (US) 1932 dir. George Marshall

Palmer, S. and Flora, F.
Hildegarde Withers Makes the Scene

Very Missing Person, A
UN TV (US) 1972 dir. Russ Mayberry
TV(US)

Palminteri, C.
Bronx Tale, A

P

TRIBECA (US) 1993 dir. Robert De Niro

Palminteri, C.
Faithful

P

MIRAMAX (US) 1996 dir. Paul
Mazursky

**Papashvily, G. and Papashvily,
H.**
Anything Can Happen

PAR (US) 1952 dir. George Seaton
M

Pappano, M.
Season for Miracles, A

HALLMARK (US) 1999 dir. Michael
Pressman
TV(US)

Parades, A.
With a Pistol in His Hand

Ballad of Gregorio Cortez, The
EMBASSY (US) 1983
dir. Robert M. Young

Paradis, M.
This Side of Heaven

MGM (US) 1934 dir. William K.
Howard

Paraskevas, M. and Paraskevas, M.
Tangerine Bear, The

ARTISAN (US) 2000 dir. Bert Ring
A, Ch

Paretsky, S.
V. I. Warshawski

HOLLYWOOD (US) 1991
dir. Jeff Kanew

Paris, R.-M.
Camille Claudel

GAU BR (Fr) 1989 dir. Bruno Nuytten

Parker, B. J.
Suspicion of Innocence

Sisters and Other Strangers
FOX (US) 1997 dir. Roger Young
TV(US)

Parker, C. G.
Visitor, The

Of Unknown Origin
WAR (Can) 1983
dir. George P. Cosmatos

Parker, G.
Translation of a Savage, The

Behold my Wife
PAR (US) 1934 dir. Mitchell Leisen

Parker, L. and Tanner, D.
We Let Our Son Die

Promised a Miracle
REP (US) 1988 dir. Stephen Gyllenhaal
TV(US)

Parker, L. N.
Disraeli

P
WAR (US) 1929 dir. Alfred E. Green

Parker, R. B.
Savage Place, A

Spenser: A Savage Place
WAR (US) 1995 dir. Joseph L. Scanlan
TV(US)

Parker, R. B.
Small Vices

JAFFE/BRAUNSTEIN (US) 1999 dir.
Robert Markowitz
TV(US)

Parker, R. B.
Thin Air

JAFFE/BRAUNSTEIN (US) 2000 dir.
Robert Mandel
TV(US)

Parker, R. B.
Walking Shadow

A&E (US) 2001 dir. Po-Chih Leong
TV(US)

Parker, R. B. and Chandler, R.
Poodle Springs

HBO (US) 1998 dir. Bob Rafelson
TV(US)

Parker, T. J.
Laguna Heat

WESTON (US) 1987 dir. Simon Langton
TV(US)

Parkin, F.
Krippendorf's Tribe

TOUCHSTONE (US) 1998 dir. Todd
Holland

Parks, G.
Learning Tree, The

WAR (US) 1969 dir. Gordon Parks

Parks, L. R.
My Thirty Years Backstairs at the
White House

Backstairs at the White House
FRIENDLY (US) 1979
dir. Michael O'Herlihy
TVSe(US)

Parrish, A.
All Kneeling

Born to be Bad
RKO (US) 1950 dir. Nicholas Ray

Parrot, U.
There's Always Tomorrow

MGM (US) 1934 dir. Edward Sloman
UN (US) 1956 dir. Douglas Sirk

Parrott, U.
Ex-Wife

Divorcee, The
MGM (US) 1930 dir. Robert Z. Leonard

Parrott, U.
Strangers May Kiss

MGM (US) 1931
dir. George Fitzmaurice

Pascal, E.
Marriage Bed, The

Husband's Holiday
PAR (US) 1931 dir. Robert Milton

Pasolini, P. P.
Theorem

AETOS (It) 1968 dir. Pier Paolo Pasolini

Pasternak, A.
Princess in Love

KUSHNER-LOCKE (US) dir. David
Greene
TV(US)

Pasternak, B.
Doctor Zhivago

MGM (US) 1965 dir. David Lean

Patchett, A.
Patron Saint of Liars, The

PATCHETT-KAUFMAN
(US) 1998 dir. Stephen Gyllenhaal
TV(US)

Paterson, N.
Kidnappers, The

Little Kidnappers, The
DISNEY CH (US) 1990 dir. Don Shebib
Ch, TV(US)

Paton, A.
Cry, The Beloved Country

BL (GB) 1951 dir. Zoltan Korda
MIRAMAX (US/SA) 1995 dir. Darrell
Roodt

Patrick, J.
Hasty Heart, The

P
ABP (GB) 1949 dir. Vincent Sherman

Patrick, J.
Teahouse of the August Moon, The

P
MGM (US) 1956 dir. Daniel Mann
COMPASS (US) 1962
dir. George Schaefer
TV(US)

Patrick, V.
Family Business

TRISTAR (US) 1989 dir. Sidney Lumet

Patrick, V.
Pope of Greenwich Village, The

MGM/UA (US) 1984
dir. Stuart Rosenberg

Patten, L. B.
Death of a Gunfighter

UI (US) 1969 dir. Robert Totten, Don
Siegel

Patterson, H.
To Catch a King
GAYLORD (US) 1984 dir. Clive Donner
TV(US)

Patterson, J.
Along Came a Spider
PAR (US) 2001 dir. Lee Tamahori

Patterson, J.
Kiss the Girls
PAR (US) 1997 dir. Gary Fleder

Patterson, J.
Virgin
Child of Darkness, Child of Light
WIL COURT (US) 1991
dir. Marina Sargenti
TV(US)

Patterson, J. and de Jonge, P.
Miracle on the 17th Green, The
BLATT (US) 1999 dir. Michael Switzer
TV(US)

Patterson, R. N.
Degree of Guilt
Degree of Guilt
JAFFE/BRAUNSTEIN (US) 1995 dir.
Mike Robe
TVSe(US)

Patterson, R. N.
Eyes of a Child
Degree of Guilt
JAFFE/BRAUNSTEIN (US) 1995 dir.
Mike Robe
TVSe(US)

Patton, F. G.
Good Morning, Miss Dove
FOX (US) 1955 dir. Henry Koster

Paulsen, G.
Hatchet
Cry in the Wild, A
CONCORDE (US) 1990
dir. Mark Griffiths

Paulsen, G.
Kill Fee
Murder C.O.D.
KUSHNER-LOCKE (US) 1990
dir. Alan Metzger
TV(US)

Paulsen, G.
Nightjohn
HALLMARK (US) 1996 dir. Charles
Burnett
TV(US)

Paulton, E.
Money by Wire
P
Get Off My Foot
WAR (GB) 1935 dir. William Beaudine

Paxton, C. W. and Carden. G.
Papa's Angels: A Christmas Story
Papa's Angels
CBS TV (US) 2000 dir. Dwight H. Little
TV(US)

Payne, L.
Nose on my Face, The
Girl in the Headlines, The
BL (GB) 1963 dir. Michael Truman
US title: Model Murder Case, The

Payne, S.
Black Aces
UN (US) 1937 dir. Buck Jones

Peach, L. D.
Great Mr. Handel, The
RANK (GB) 1942 dir. Norman Walker

Peake, M.
Gormenghast
BBC/WGBH (GB) 2000 dir. Andy
Wilson
TVSe(GB)

Peake, M.
Mr. Pye
CHANNEL 4 (GB) 1986 dir. Michael
Darlow
TVSe(GB)

Pearce, D.
Cool Hand Luke
WAR (US) 1967 dir. Stuart Rosenberg

Pearce, P.
Tom's Midnight Garden
BBC (GB) 1974 dir. Myles Land
TVSe(GB)
BBC (GB) 1989 dir. Christine Secombe
TVSe(GB)
HYP (GB) 1999 dir. Willard Carroll

Pearson, J.
Life of Ian Fleming, The
Goldeneye
ANGLIA (GB) 1990 dir. Don Boyd
TV(GB)

Pearson, R. D.
Simple Simon
Mercury Rising
UN (US) 1998 dir. Harold Becker

Pearson, W.
Fever in the Blood, A
WAR (US) 1960 dir. Vincent Sherman

Peck, D.
Law of Enclosures, The
ALLIANCE (Can) 2000 dir. John
Greyson

Peck, G. W.
Peck's Bad Boy
FOX (US) 1934 dir. Edward Cline

Peck, R.
Don't Look and It Won't Hurt
Gas, Food and Lodging
IRS (US) 1992 dir. Allison Anders

Peck, R.
Father Figure
TIME-LIFE (US) 1980 dir. Jerry London
TV(US)

Peck, R. H.
Are You In The House Alone?
FRIES PROD (US) 1978
dir. Walter Grauman
TV(US)

Peditto, P.
Jane Doe
P
CASTLE HILL (US) 1996 dir. Paul
Peditto

Pendergraft, P.
Miracle Child
WHITE (US) 1993 dir. Michael
Pressman
TV(US)

Penhall, J.
Some Voices
P
DRAGON (GB) 2000 dir. Simon Cellan
Jones

Peple, E.
Littlest Rebel, The
P
FOX (US) 1935 dir. David Butler

Peple, E. H.
Beloved Bachelor, The
P
PAR (US) 1931 dir. Lloyd Corrigan

Percival, D.
Girlfriend
P
Girl/Boy
HEMDALE (GB) 1971 dir. Bob Kellett

Percy, E.
Shop at Sly Corner, The
P
BL (GB) 1946 dir. George King
US title: Code of Scotland Yard

Percy, E. and Denham, R.
Ladies in Retirement
P
COL (US) 1941 dir. Charles Vidor

Perelman, L. and Perelman, S. J.
Night Before Christmas, The
P
Larceny Inc.
WAR (US) 1942 dir. Lloyd Bacon

Perelman, S. J. and Nash, O.
One Touch of Venus
P
UN (US) 1948 dir. William A. Seiter

Perelman, S. J. and Perelman, L.
All Good Americans
Paris Interlude
MGM (US) 1934 dir. Edwin L. Marin

Perez-Reverte, A.
Club Dumas, The
Ninth Gate, The
STUDIO CANAL+ (Fr/Sp/US) 1999
dir. Roman Polanski

Perez-Reverte, A.
Fencing Master, The
ALTUBE (Sp) 1992 dir. Pedro Olea

Perez-Reverte, A.
Table de Flandes, La
Uncovered
CIBY 2000 (Sp/GB) 1994 dir. Jim
McBride

Perez-Reverte, A.
Territorio Comanche
Comanche Territory
TORNASOL (Sp/Fr) 1997 dir. Gerardo
Herrero

Pergaud, L.
Guerre des Boutons, La
War of the Buttons, The
ENIGMA (Jap/GB/Fr) 1994 dir. John
Roberts

Perkins, K.
Desert Voices
Desert Pursuit
ABP (US) 1952 dir. George Blair

Perrault, C.
Sleeping Beauty
DISNEY (US) 1959 dir. Clyde Geronomi
A, Ch
CANNON (US) 1987 dir. David Irving
Ch

Perrin, S. and Balzer, G.
Are You With It?
P
UN (US) 1948 dir. Jack Hively
M

Perrotta, T.
Election
PAR (US) 1999 dir. Alexander Payne

Perry, A.
Cater Street Hangman, The
YTV/A&E (GB/US) 1998 dir. Sarah
Hellings
TV(GB/US)

Perry, C.
Portrait of a Young Man Drowning
Six Ways to Sunday
SCOUT (US) 1997 dir. Adam Bernstein

Perry, G.
Bluebell
BBC (GB) 1986 dir. Moira Armstrong
TVSe(GB)

Perry, G. S.
Hold Autumn in your Hands
Southerner, The
UA (US) 1945 dir. Jean Renoir

Persico, J. E.
Nuremberg: Infamy on Trial
Nuremberg
ALLIANCE (US/Can) 2000 dir. Yves Simoneau
TVSe(US/Can)

Pertwee, M.
Don't Just Lie There, Say Something
P
RANK (GB) 1973 dir. Bob Kellet

Pertwee, M.
Night was our Friend
P
MONARCH (GB) 1951
dir. Michael Anderson

Pertwee, R.
Heat Wave
P
Road to Singapore
WAR (US) 1931 dir. Alfred E. Green

Pertwee, R.
Pink String and Sealing Wax
P
EAL (GB) 1945 dir. Robert Hamer

Pertwee, R. and Pertwee, M.
Paragon, The
P
Silent Dust
ABP (GB) 1947 dir. Lance Comfort

Peters, S.
Fourth War, The
CANNON (US) 1990
dir. John Frankenheimer

Peters, S.
Park is Mine, The
HBO (Can/US) 1985
dir. Steven Hilliard Stern
TV(US)

Peterson, J.
Here Come the Littles
ATLANTIC (US) 1985
dir. Bernard Deyries
A, Ch

Peterson, L. S.
Take a Giant Step
P
UA (US) 1959 dir. Philip Leacock

Peterson, R.
Square Ring, The
P
GFD (GB) 1953 dir. Basil Dearden

Petievich, G.
Money Men
Boiling Point
HEXAGON (US) 1993 dir. James B. Harris

Petievich, G.
To Live and Die in L.A.
MGM/UA (US) 1985
dir. William Friedkin

Petrakis, H. M.
Dream of Kings, A
WAR (US) 1969 dir. Daniel Mann

Petronius
Satyricon
Fellini Satyricon
UA (It) 1969 dir. Federico Fellini

Pettit, E.
Rich Are Always With Us, The
WAR (US) 1932 dir. Alfred E. Green

Pettit, W. H.
Nine Girls
P
COL (US) 1944 dir. Leigh Jason

Peyton, K. M.
Flambards
YTV (GB) 1979 dir. Lawrence Gordon
Clark, Peter Duffell,
Michael Ferguson, Leonard Lewis
TVSe(GB)

Peyton, K. M.
Right Hand Man, The
UAA (Aust) 1987 dir. Di Drew

Peyton, K. M.
Who, Sir? Me, Sir?
BBC (GB) 1986 dir. Colin Cant
TVSe(GB)

Philbrick, R.
Freak the Mighty
Mighty, The
MIRAMAX (US) 1998 dir. Peter
Chelsom

Phillips, M.
Blood Rights
BBC (GB) 1991 dir. Leslie Manning
TVSe(GB)

Phillips, M.
Pick up Sticks
Cherry Picker, The
FOX-RANK (GB) 1974 dir. Peter Curran

Phillpotts, E.
Farmer's Wife, The
P
AB (GB) 1940 dir. Norman Lee

Phillpotts, E. and Phillpotts, A.
Yellow Sands
P
AB (GB) 1938 dir. Herbert Brenon

Pick, J. B.
Last Valley, The
CINERAMA (GB) 1970
dir. James Clavell

Pielmeier, J.
Agnes of God
P
COL (US) 1985 dir. Norman Jewison

Pienciak, R. T.
Murder at 75 Birch Street
Murder at 75 Birch
NICKI (US) 1999 dir. Michael Scott
TV(US)

Pierson, L. R.
Roughly Speaking
WAR (US) 1945 dir. Michael Curtiz

Pierson, R.
Queen of Mean, The
Leona Helmsley: The Queen of Mean
FRIES (US) 1990 dir. Richard Michaels
TV(US)

Piglia, R.
Plata Quemada
Burnt Money
MANDARIN (Arg/Fr) 2000 dir.
Marcelo Pineyro

Pik-Wah, L.
Rouge
ICA (HK) 1988 dir. Stanley Kwan

Pike, C.
Fall Into Darkness
PATCHETT-KAUFMAN (US) 1996 dir.
Mark Sobel
TV(US)

Pike, R. L.
Mute Witness
Bullitt
WAR (US) 1968 dir. Peter Yates

Pilcher, R.
September
HALLMARK/BSKYB (UK/Ger) 1996
dir. Colin Bucksey
TV(UK/Ger)

Pilcher, R.
Shell Seekers, The
M. REES (US) 1989 dir. Waris Hussein
TV(US)

Pileggi, N.
Casino
UN (US) 1995 dir. Martin Scorsese

Pileggi, N.
Wiseguy: Life in A Mafia Family
Goodfellas
WAR (US) 1990 dir. Martin Scorsese

Pilkington, R.
Nepomuk of the River
Golden Head, The
CINERAMA (US/Hun) 1965
dir. Richard Thorpe

Pilling, A.
Henry's Leg
TVS (GB) 1990 dir. Michael Kerrigan
TVSe(GB)

Pinchon, E.
Zapata the Unconquerable
Viva Zapata!
FOX (US) 1952 dir. Elia Kazan

Pinero, Sir A. W.
Enchanted Cottage, The
P
RKO (US) 1945 dir. John Cromwell

Pinero, Sir A. W.
Magistrate, The
P
Those Were the Days
BIP (GB) 1934 dir. Thomas Bentley

Pinero, Sir A. W.
Second Mrs. Tanqueray, The
P
VANDYKE (GB) 1952 dir. Dallas Bower

Pingau, J.
Wooden Man's Bride, The
LONG SHONG (Tai) 1994 dir. Jia
Pingau

Pinsent, G.
John and the Missus
CINEMA (Can) 1987
dir. Gordon Pinsent

Pinter, H.
Betrayal
P
VIRGIN (GB) 1982 dir. David Jones

Pinter, H.
Birthday Party, The
P
CINERAMA (GB) 1968
dir. William Friedkin
BBC (GB) 1988 dir. Kenneth Ives
TV(GB)

Pinter, H.
Caretaker, The
P
BL (GB) 1963 dir. Clive Donner
US title: Guest, The

Pinter, H.
Homecoming, The
P
SEVEN KEYS (GB) 1973 dir. Peter Hall

Pinter, H.
Kind of Alaska, A
P
CENTRAL (GB) 1984 dir. Kenneth Ives
TV(GB)

Pinter, H.
Lover, The
P
ITV (GB) 1963 dir. Joan Kemp-Welch
TV(GB)

Pinter, H.
Old Times
P
BBC (GB) 1991 dir. Simon Curtis
TV(GB)

Pinto, M.
Pensamientos
E1
NACIONAL (Mex) 1952
dir. Luis Bunuel

Piper, A.
Marry at Leisure
Nice Girl Like Me, A
AVCO (GB) 1969 dir. Desmond Davis

Piper, A.
Yes, Giorgio
MGM/UA (US) 1982 dir. Franklin
Schaffner

Piper, E.
Bunny Lake is Missing
COL (GB) 1965 dir. Otto Preminger

Piper, E.
Nanny, The
WAR (GB) 1965 dir. Seth Holt

Pirandello, L.
As You Desire Me
P
MGM (US) 1932
dir. George Fitzmaurice

Pirandello, L.
Come Prima Meglio di Prima
P
Never Say Goodbye
UN (US) 1955 dir. Jerry Hopper

Pirandello, L.
Come Prima Meglio di Prima
P
This Love of Ours
UI (US) 1945 dir. William Deiterle

Pirandello, L.
Homme de Nulle Part, L'
CG (Fr) 1987 dir. Pierre Chenal

Pirandello, L.
Nanny, The
Balia, La
RAI (It) 1999 dir. Marco Bellocchio

Pirincci, A.
Felidae
FONTANA (Ger) 1994 dir. Michael
Schaack

Pirro, U.
Five Branded Women
PAR (It/US) 1960 dir. Martin Ritt

Pistone, J.
Donnie Brasco: My Undercover Life in the Mafia
Donnie Brasco
TRISTAR (US) 1997 dir. Mike Newell

Pitre, M.
Ennemi Que Je Connais, L'
Full Blast
ASKA (Can) 1999 dir. Rodrique Jean

Plain, B.
Evergreen
METRO (US) 1985 dir. Fielder Cook
TVSe(US)

Plater, A.
Misterioso
BBC (GB) 1991 dir. John Glenister
TV(GB)

Plath, S.
Bell Jar, The
AVCO (US) 1979 dir. Larry Peerce

Platt, K.
Boy Who Could Make Himself Disappear, The

Baxter!
EMI (GB) 1972 dir. Lionel Jeffries
Ch

Platt, R. B.
Promise the Moon

CBC (Can) 1997 dir. Ken Jubenvill
TV(Can)

Podhajsky, A.
Dancing White Horses of Vienna, The

Miracle of the White Stallions, The
DISNEY (US) 1963 dir. Arthur Hiller
GB title: Flight of the White Stallions, The

Poe, E. A.
Fall of the House of Usher, The

TAFT (US) 1982 dir. James Conway
TV(US)

Poe, E. A.
Fall of the House of Usher, The

House of Usher, The
AIP (US) 1960 dir. Roger Corman
GB title: Fall of the House of Usher, The
21st CENTURY (US) 1988
dir. Alan Birkinshaw

Poe, E. A.
Haunting of Morella, The

CONCORDE (US) 1990
dir. Jim Wynorski

Poe, E. A.
Masque of the Red Death, The

AA (GB) 1964 dir. Roger Corman
CONCORDE (US) 1989
dir. Larry Brand

Poe, E. A.
Morella; Black Cat, The; Facts of the Case of Dr. Valdemar, The

Tales of Terror
WAR (US) 1962 dir. Roger Corman

Poe, E. A.
Murders in the Rue Morgue

UN (US) 1932 dir. Robert Florey
AIP (US) 1971 dir. Gordon Hessler
HALMI (US/GB) 1986
dir. Jeannot Szwarc
TV(GB/US)

Poe, E. A.
Murders in the Rue Morgue

Phantom of the Rue Morgue
WAR (US) 1954 dir. Roy del Ruth

Poe, E. A.
Mystery of Marie Roget, The

UN (US) 1942 dir. Phil Rosen

Poe, E. A.
Pit and the Pendulum, The

AA (US) 1961 dir. Roger Corman
FULL MOON (US) 1991
dir. Stuart Gordon

Poe, E. A.
Premature Burial, The

AA (US) 1962 dir. Roger Corman

Poe, E. A.
Tell-Tale Heart, The

ADELPHI (GB) 1953 dir. J. B. Williams
ABP (GB) 1960 dir. Ernest Morris

Poe, E. A.
Tomb of Ligeia, The

AIP (GB) 1964 dir. Roger Corman

Pohl, P.
Janne, Min Van

My Friend Joe
PORTMAN ENT (Ger/Ire/GB) 1996
dir. Chris Bould

Poiret, J.
Cage Aux Folles, La

P
UA (Fr/It) 1978 dir. Edouard Molinaro

Poiret, J.
Cage Aux Folles, La
P
Birdcage, The
MGM (US) 1996 dir. Mike Nichols

Pollini, F.
Pretty Maids All In A Row
MGM (US) 1971 dir. Roger Vadim

Pollock, R.
Loophole
BW (GB) 1981 dir. John Quested

Polson, B.
Go Toward the Light
CORAPEAKE (US) 1988 dir. Mike Robe
TV(US)

Polson, B.
Not My Kid
FINNEGAN (US) 1985
dir. Michael Tuchner
TV(US)

Pomerantz, E.
Into It
Caught
CINEHAUS (US) 1996 dir. Robert M.
Young

Ponicsan, D.
Cinderella Liberty
FOX (US) 1974 dir. Mark Rydell

Ponicsan, D.
Last Detail, The
COL (US) 1973 dir. Hal Ashby

Poole, V.
Thursday's Child
VIACOM (US) 1983 dir. David Lowell
Rich
TV(US)

Popkin, Z.
Death of Innocence, A
CARLINER (US) 1971
dir. Paul Wendkos
TV(US)

Popplewell, J.
Tread Softly Stranger
P
ALDERDALE (GB) 1958
dir. Gordon Parry

Porter, B.
Blow
NEW LINE (US) 2001 dir. Ted Demme

Porter, E. H.
Pollyanna
DISNEY (US) 1960 dir. David Swift
Ch
BBC (GB) 1973 dir. June Wyndham-
Davies
TVSe(GB)

Porter, E. H.
Pollyanna
Polly
DISNEY (US) 1989 dir. Debbie Allen
Ch, TV(US)

Porter, G. S.
Freckles
City Boy
ACCENT ENT (Can) 1994 dir. John
Kent Harrison
TV(Can)

Porter, G. S.
Freckles
RKO (US) 1935 dir. Edward Killy
FOX (US) 1960 dir. Harry Spalding

Porter, G. S.
Girl of the Limberlost, A
MON (US) 1934 dir. Christy Cabanne
FREEDOM (US) 1990
dir. Burt Brinckerhoff
TV(US)

Porter, G. S.
Keeper of the Bees
MON (US) 1935 dir. Christy Cabanne

Porter, G. S.
Laddie
RKO (US) 1935 dir. George Stevens

Porter, K. A.
Ship of Fools
COL (US) 1965 dir. Stanley Kramer

Porter, R.
Chrysalis
P
All of Me
PAR (US) 1934 dir. James Flood

Portis, C.
True Grit
PAR (US) 1969 dir. Henry Hathaway

Posmysz-Piasecka, Z.
Passenger
P
KADR (Pol) 1963 dir. Andrzej Munk

Post, H.
Whorehouse Sting, The
Red-Light Sting, The
UN TV (US) 1984 dir. Rod Holcomb
TV(US)

Postell, C.
Escape of My Dead Man
Midnight Edition
SHAPIRO GLICKENHAUS (US) 1994
dir. Howard Libov

Potok, C.
Chosen, The
CONTEM (US) 1981
dir. Jeremy Paul Kagan

Potter, B.
Tale of Little Pig Robinson, The
TVS (GB) 1990 dir. Alan Bridges
TVSe(GB)

Potter, D.
Brimstone and Treacle
P
NAMARA (GB) 1982
dir. Richard Loncraine

Potter, D.
Sufficient Carbohydrate
P
Visitors
BBC (GB) 1987 dir. Piers Haggard
TV(GB)

Potter, S.
Gamesmanship, Oneupmanship, Lifemanship
School for Scoundrels
WAR (GB) 1960 dir. Robert Namer

Powell, D.
Hello Sister
FOX (US) 1933 dir. Erich von Stroheim

Powell, M.
Graf Spee
Battle of the River Plate, The
RANK (GB) 1956 dir. Michael Powell,
Emeric Pressburger
US title: Pursuit of the Graf Spee

Powell, R.
Philadelphian, The
Young Philadelphians, The
WAR (US) 1959 dir. Vincent Sherman
GB title: City Jungle, The

Powell, R.
Pioneer Go Home
Follow that Dream
UA (US) 1962 dir. Gordon Douglas

Power, M. S.
Children of the North
BBC (GB) 1991 dir. David Drury
TVSe(GB)

Powers, A. and Misenheimer, M.
Framed
PAR (US) 1975 dir. Phil Karlson

Powers, F. G. and Gentry, C.
Operation Overflight
Francis Gary Powers: The True Story of the U-2 Spy Incident
FRIES (US) 1976 dir. Delbert Mann
TV(US)

Praag, V.V.
Combat
Men in War
UA (US) 1957 dir. Anthony Mann

Pratt, C. and Lee, D.
Operation Julie
TYNE-TEES (GB) 1985 dir. Bob Mahoney
TVSe(GB)

Pratt, T.
Barefoot Mailman, The
COL (US) 1951 dir. Earl McEvoy

Pratt, T.
Incredible Mr. Limpet, The
WAR (US) 1964 dir. Arthur Lubin
A

Pratt, T.
Mr. Winkle Goes to War
COL (US) 1944 dir. Alfred E. Green
GB title: Arms and the Woman

Preedy, G.
General Crack
WAR (US) 1930 dir. Alan Crosland

Prejean, Sister H.
Dead Man Walking
POLYGRAM (US/GB) 1995 dir. Tim Robbins

Presley, P. and Harman, S.
Elvis and Me
NEW WORLD TV (US) 1988 dir. Larry Peerce
TVSe(US)

Presnell, F. G.
Send Another Coffin
Slightly Honourable
UA (US) 1940 dir. Tay Garnett

Pressburger, E.
Killing a Mouse on Sunday
Behold a Pale Horse
COL (US) 1964 dir. Fred Zinnemann

Pressfield, S.
Legend of Bagger Vance, The
FOX (US) 2000 dir. Robert Redford

Pressman, K.
Insider's Price
P
Diary of a Hit Man
VI (US) 1992 dir. Roy London

Preston, D.
Jennie
Jennie Project, The
H. ROACH (US) 2001 dir. Gary Nadeau
TV(US)

Preston, D. and Child, L.
Relic, The
BBC (GB/US) 1997 dir. Peter Hyams

Price, A.
Labyrinth Makers, The; Alamut Ambush, The; Colonel Butler's Wolf
Chessgame
GRANADA (GB) 1983 dir. William Brayne, Ken Grieve, Roger Tucker
TVSe(GB)

Price, E.
Red for Danger

Blondes for Danger
WILCOX (GB) 1938 dir. Jack Raymond

Price, E. and Attiwill, K.
Once a Crook

P
FOX (GB) 1941 dir. Herbert Mason

Price, N.
Sleeping with the Enemy

FOX (US) 1991 dir. Joseph Ruben

Price, R.
Bloodbrothers

WAR (US) 1978 dir. Robert Mulligan

Price, R.
Clockers

40 ACRES (US) 1995 dir. Spike Lee

Price, R.
Wanderers, The

ORION (US) 1979 dir. Philip Kaufman

Priest, L.
Conspiracy of Silence

CBC (Can) 1991 dir. Francis
Mankiewicz
TVSe(Can)

Priestley, J. B.
Benighted

Old Dark House, The
UN (US) 1932 dir. James Whale
BL (GB) 1963 dir. William Castle

Priestley, J. B.
Dangerous Corner

P
RKO (US) 1934 dir. Phil Rosen

Priestley, J. B.
Good Companions, The

GAU (GB) 1932 dir. Victor Saville
ABP (GB) 1956 dir. J. Lee Thompson
YTV (GB) 1980 dir. Bill Hays, Leonard
Lewis
TVSe(GB)

Priestley, J. B.
Inspector Calls, An

P
BL (GB) 1959 dir. Guy Hamilton
BBC (GB) 1982 dir. Michael Simpson
TVSe(GB)

Priestley, J. B.
Laburnum Grove

P
ABP (GB) 1936 dir. Carol Reed

Priestley, J. B.
Let the People Sing

BN (GB) 1942 dir. John Baxter

Priestley, J. B.
Lost Empires

GRANADA (GB) 1985 dir. Alan Grint
TVSe(GB)

Priestley, J. B.
They Came to a City

P
EAL (GB) 1944 dir. Basil Dearden

Priestley, J. B.
When we are Married

P
BN (GB) 1943 dir. Lance Comfort

Prieto, J.
Socio, El

Associate, The
HOLLYWOOD (US) 1996 dir. Daniel
Petrie

Prince, P.
Good Father, The

FILM 4 (GB) 1986 dir. Mike Newell

Pritchett, V. S.
Wedding, The
TYNE-TEES (GB) 1984
dir. Gordon Flemyng
TV(GB)

Prochnau, W.
Trinity's Child
By Dawn's Early Light
HBO (US) 1990 dir. Jack Sholder
TV(US)

Procter, M.
Hell is a City
WAR (GB) 1959 dir. Val Guest

Proffitt, N.
Gardens of Stone
TRISTAR (US) 1987
dir. Francis Ford Coppola

Prokosch, F.
City of Shadows
Conspirators, The
WAR (US) 1944 dir. Jean Negulesco

Prose, F.
Household Saints
FINE LINE (US) 1993 dir. Nancy Savoca

Protess, D. and Warden, R.
Gone in the Night
HILL-FIELDS (US) 1996 dir. Bill Norton
TVSe(US)

Proulx, E. A.
Shipping News, The
COL (US) 2001 dir. Lasse Hallstrom

Proust, M.
À La Recherche du Temps Perdu
Captive, The
STUDIO CANAL+ (Fr) 2000 dir.
Chantal Akerman

Proust, M.
À La Recherche du Temps Perdu
Time Regained
STUDIO CANAL+ (Fr/It/Port) 1999
dir. Raoul Ruiz

Proust, M.
Du côté de chez Swann
Swann in Love
GAU (Fr) 1984 dir. Volker Schlondorff

Prouty, O.
Now, Voyager
WAR (US) 1942 dir. Irving Rapper

Prouty, O.
Stella Dallas
UA (US) 1937 dir. King Vidor

Prouty, O.
Stella Dallas
Stella
TOUCHSTONE (US) 1990 dir. John
Erman

Prumbs, L. S. and Smith, S. B.
My Girl Tisa
P
IN (US) 1948 dir. Elliott Nugent

Przybyszewska, S.
Danton Affair, The
P
Danton
GAU/TF1 (Fr/Pol) 1982
dir. Andrzej Wajda

Puccini, G.
Bohème, La
NEW YORKER/ERATO (Fr/It) 1989
dir. Leo Conencini
M

Pudney, J.
Net, The
GFD (GB) 1953 dir. Anthony Asquith

Pudney, J.
Thursday Adventure

Stolen Airliner, The
BL (GB) 1955 dir. Don Sharp
Ch

Pugh, M.
Commander Crabb

Silent Enemy, The
ROMULUS (GB) 1958
dir. William Fairchild

Puig, M.
Kiss of the Spider Woman

ISLAND (US/Bra) 1985
dir. Hector Babenco

Pulitzer, R.
Roxanne: The Prize Pulitzer

QINTEX (US) 1989 dir. Richard Colla
TV(US)

Purcell, D.
Falling for a Dancer

BBC (GB) 1998 dir. Richard Standeven
TVSe(GB)

Purcell, H.
Glorious Days, The

P
Lilacs in The Spring
REP (GB) 1954 dir. Herbert Wilcox
US title: Let's Make Up

Purcell, H. and Parr-Davies, H.
Lisbon Story, The

P
BN (GB) 1946 dir. Paul Stein
M

Purdy, J.
In a Shallow Grave

SKOURAS (US) 1988 dir. Kenneth
Bowser

Pushkin, A.
Captain's Daughter, The

Tempest
PAR (It/Fr) 1958 dir. Alberto Lattuada

Pushkin, A.
Captain's Daughter, The; History of Pugachev, A

Russkij Bunt
GLOBUS (Rus/Fr) 2000 dir. Aleksandr
Proshkin

Pushkin, A.
Eugene Onegin

Onegin
CANWEST (GB) 1999 dir. Martha
Fiennes

Pushkin, A. S.
Queen of Spades, The

AB (GB) 1949 dir. Thorold Dickinson

Puzo, M.
Fortunate Pilgrim, The

NBC (US) 1988 dir. Stuart Cooper
TVSe(US)

Puzo, M.
Godfather, The

PAR (US) 1972
dir. Francis Ford Coppola

Puzo, M.
Godfather, The

Godfather Part II, The
PAR (US) 1974 dir. Francis Ford
Coppola

Puzo, M.
Last Don, The

KON-SAN (US) 1997 dir. Graeme
Clifford
TVSe(US)

Puzo, M.
Sicilian, The

FOX (It/US) 1987 dir. Michael Cimino

Pyle, E. T.
Story of G.I. Joe, The
UA (US) 1945 dir. William A. Wellman

Pyle, H.
Men of Iron
Black Shield of Falworth, The
UI (US) 1954 dir. Rudolph Maté

Pyszora, A.-F.
Expense of the Spirit
Winter Sleepers
PALLADIO (Ger) 1997 dir. Tom Tykwer

Quarrington, P.
Whale Music

ALLIANCE (Can) 1994 dir. Richard J. Lewis

Queen, E.
Cat of Many Tales

Ellery Queen: Don't Look Behind You
UN TV (US) 1971 dir. Barry Shear
TV(US)

Queen, E.
Fourth Side of the Triangle, The

Ellery Queen: Too Many Suspects
UN TV (US) 1975 dir. David Greene
TV(US)

Queen, E.
Study in Terror, A

COMPTON-TEKLI (GB) 1965
dir. James Hill

Queen, E.
Ten Days Wonder

HEMDALE (Fr) 1971
dir. Claude Chabrol

Quefflec, H.
Recteur de l'Ile de Sein, Un

Dieu à Besoin des Hommes
TRANS (Fr) 1950 dir. Jean Delannoy

Queneau, R.
Zazie Dans le Métro

CONN (Fr) 1960
dir. Louis Malle

Quentin, P.
Fatal Woman

Black Widow
FOX (US) 1954 dir. Nunnally Johnson

Quentin, P.
Man in the Net, The

UA (US) 1958 dir. Michael Curtiz

Quick, D.
Enchantment: A Little Girl's Friendship with Mark Twain

Mark Twain & Me
CHILMARK (US/Can) dir. Daniel Petrie
TV(US/Can)

Quigley, J.
King's Royal

BBC (GB) 1982 dir. Andrew Morgan, David Reynolds
TVSe(GB)

Quignard, P.
Every Morning of the World

BAC (Fr) 1992 dir. Alan Corneau

Quilici, F.
Danger Adrift

Only One Survived
CBS ENT (US) 1990 dir. Folco Quilici
TV(US)

Quindlen, A.
Black and Blue

EVOLVE (US) 1999 dir. Paul Shapiro
TV(US)

Quindlen, A.
One True Thing
UN (US) 1998 dir. Carl Franklin

Quinn, A.
Berg
Killing Dad
PALACE (US) 1989 dir. Michael Austin

Quinn, D.
Ishmael
Instinct
TOUCHSTONE (US) 1999 dir. Jon
Turteltaub

Quinn, D.
Limbo Connection, The
THAMES (GB) 1983 dir. Robert Tronson
TVSe(GB)

Quinn, P.
Thick as Thieves
OCTOBER (US) 1999 dir. Scott Sanders

Quinn, T. K.
Ishi in Two Worlds
Ishi: The Last of his Tribe
LEWIS (US) 1978
dir. Robert Ellis Miller
TV(US)

Quinnell, A. J.
Man on Fire
TRISTAR (It/Fr) 1987
dir. Elie Chouraqui

R

Raab, S.
Ariana
UN TV (US) 1989 dir. Paul Krasny
TV(US)

Raab, S.
It's Always Something
UN TV (US) 1990 dir. Richard Compton
TV(US)

Raab, S.
Justice in the Back Room
Marcus-Nelson Murders, The
UN TV (US) 1973 dir. Joseph Sargent
TV(US)

Rabe, D.
Hurlyburly
P
FINE LINE (US) 1998 dir. Anthony
Drazan

Rabe, D.
Streamers
P
UA (US) 1983 dir. Robert Altman

Radiguet, R.
Devil in the Flesh
TRANS (Fr) 1947
dir. Claude Autant-Lara
ORION (It/Fr) 1987
dir. Marco Bellocchio

Rae, H. C.
Marksman, The
BBC (GB) 1987 dir. Tom Clegg
TVSe(GB)

Rae, H. C.
Shroud Society, The
Man with a Gun
NORTHWOOD (Can) 1995 dir. David
Wyles

Rae, J.
Custard Boys, The
FOREST HALL (GB) 1979
dir. Colin Finbow

Rae, J.
Custard Boys, The
Reach for Glory
GALA (GB) 1962 dir. Philip Leacock

Raine, W. M.
Rawhide Justice
Man from Bitter Ridge, The
UN (US) 1955 dir. Jack Arnold

Ramati, A.
Assisi Underground, The
CANNON (GB) 1985
dir. Alexander Ramati

Ramati, A.
Beyond the Mountains
Desperate Ones, The
AIP (Sp/US) 1968
dir. Alexander Ramati

Ramos, F.
Veronico Cruz
BFI (Arg/GB) 1988 dir. Miguel Pereira

Ramos, G.
Memories of Prison
REGINA (Port) 1989
dir. Nelson Pereira Dos Santos

Rampo, E.
Soseiji
TOHO (Jap) 1999 dir. Shinya
Tsukamoto

Ramuz, C.-F.
Guerre Dans le Haut-Pays, La
War in the Highlands
ARENA (Fr/Swe) 1998 dir. Francis
Reusser

Rand, A.
Fountainhead, The
WAR (US) 1949 dir. King Vidor

Rand, A.
Night of January 16th, The
P
PAR (US) 1941 dir. William Clements

Rand, A.
We the Living
SCALERA (It) 1942
dir. Goffredo Allessandrini

Randall, B.
David's Mother
P
HEARST (US) 1994 dir. Robert Allan
Ackerman
TV(US)

Randall, B.
Fan, The
PAR (US) 1981 dir. Edward Bianchi

Randall, B.
Last Man on the List, The
Dead Husbands
WIL COURT (US) 1998 dir. Paul
Shapiro
TV(US)

Randall, F. E.
Watcher in the Woods
DISNEY (US) 1980 dir. John Hough

Randle, K. D. and Schmitt, D. R.
UFO Crash at Roswell
Roswell
SHOWTIMEWORKS (US) 1994 dir.
Jeremy Kagan
TV(US)

Raney, D.
Vow to Cherish, A
WORLDWIDE PICT (US) 1999 dir. John
Schmidt
TVSe(US)

Rankin, W. M.
South Sea Woman
WAR (US) 1953 dir. Arthur Lubin

Ransley, P.
Hawk, The
SCREEN (GB) 1993 dir. David Hayman

Ransley, P.
Price, The
CHANNEL 4 (GB) 1985 dir. Peter Smith
TVSe(GB)

Ransome, A.
Coot Club; Big Six, The
Swallows and Amazons Forever!
BBC (GB) 1984 dir. Andrew Morgan
TVSe(GB)

Ransome, A.
Swallows and Amazons
EMI (GB) 1974 dir. Claude Whatham
Ch

Raphael, F.
Oxbridge Blues
BBC (GB) 1984 dir. James Cellan Jones
TVSe(GB)

Raphael, F.
Richard's Things
SOUTHERN (GB) 1980
dir. Anthony Harvey

Raphaelson, S.
Accent on Youth
P
PAR (US) 1935 dir. Wesley Ruggles

Raphaelson, S.
Accent on Youth
P
But Not For Me
PAR (US) 1959 dir. Walter Lang

Raphaelson, S.
Day of Atonement
P
Jazz Singer, The
WAR (US) 1953 dir. Michael Curtiz
EMI (US) 1980 dir. Richard Fleischer

Raphaelson, S.
Hilda Crane
P
FOX (US) 1956 dir. Philip Dunne

Raphaelson, S.
Perfect Marriage, The
P
PAR (US) 1946 dir. Lewis Allen

Raphaelson, S.
Skylark
P
PAR (US) 1941 dir. Mark Sandrich

Rascovich, M.
Bedford Incident, The
COL (GB) 1965 dir. James B. Harris

Rashke, R.
Escape from Sobibor
ZENITH (US) 1987 dir. Jack Gold
TV(US)

Rashke, R.
Runaway Father
HEARST (US) 1991 dir. John Nicolella

Raskin, E.
Westing Game, The
SHOWTIMEWORKS (US) 1997 dir.
Terence H. Winkless
TV(US)

Raspe, R. E.
Twelve Adventures of the Celebrated
Baron Munchausen
Adventures of Baron Munchausen, The
COL (GB) 1988 dir. Terry Gilliam

Rattigan, T.
Bequest to the Nation
P
UN (GB) 1973 dir. James Cellan Jones

Rattigan, T.
Browning Version, The
P
GFD (GB) 1951 dir. Anthony Asquith
P. MAIN (GB) 1994 dir. Mike Figgis

Rattigan, T.
Cause Celebre
P
ANGLIA (GB) 1988 dir. John Gorrie
TV(GB)

Rattigan, T.
Deep Blue Sea, The
P
FOX (GB) 1955 dir. Anatole Litvak

Rattigan, T.
French Without Tears
P
PAR (GB) 1939 dir. Anthony Asquith

Rattigan, T.
Separate Tables
P
UA (US) 1958 dir. Delbert Mann

Rattigan, T.
Sleeping Prince, The
P
Prince and the Showgirl, The
WAR (GB) 1957 dir. Laurence Olivier

Rattigan, T.
While the Sun Shines
P
ABP (GB) 1947 dir. Anthony Asquith

Rattigan, T.
Who is Sylvia?
P
Man Who Loved Redheads, The
BL (GB) 1954 dir. Harold French

Rattigan, T.
Winslow Boy, The
P
IS (GB) 1945 dir. Anthony Asquith
SONY (US) 1999 dir. David Mamet

Rau, M. and Rau, N.
I'm Giving Them Up For Good
Cold Turkey
UA (US) 1970 dir. Norman Lear

Ravel A.
Mother Variations
P
Mothers and Daughters
PALAMA (Can) 1992 dir. Larry Kent

Raven, S.
Doctors Wear Scarlet
Incense for the Damned
GN (GB) 1970
dir. Robert Hartford-Davis

Rawlings, M. K.
Cross Creek
UN (US) 1983 dir. Martin Ritt

Rawlings, M. K.
Yearling, The
MGM (US) 1946 dir. Clarence Brown
RHI (US) dir. Rod Hardy
TV(US)

Rawls, W.
Where the Red Fern Grows
EMI (US) 1974 dir. Norman Tokar

Rawson, C.
Death in a Top Hat
Miracles for Sale
MGM (US) 1939 dir. Tod Browning

Ray, F.
Incognito
DIRECTORS' CIRCLE (US) 1999 dir.
Julie Dash
TV(US)

Ray, P.
Manushar Juddha
Target
CREATIVE (Ind) 1995 dir. Sandip Ray

Ray, R.
Strange World of Planet X, The
EROS (GB) 1958 dir. Gilbert Gunn
US title: Cosmic Monsters

Rayban, C.
Virtual Sexuality
TRISTAR (GB) 1999 dir. Nick Hurran

Rayman, S.
Women of Twilight
P
ROMULUS (GB) 1952
dir. Gordon Parry
US title: Twilight Women

Raymo, C.
Dork of Cork, The
Frankie Starlight
FINE LINE (Fr/Ire) 1995 dir. Michael
Lindsay-Hogg

Raymond, E.
Berg, The

P

Atlantic
BI (GB) 1929 dir. E. A. Dupont

Raymond, E.
For Them That Trespass

ABP (GB) 1949 dir. Alberto Cavalcanti

Raymond, E.
Tell England

CAPITOL (GB) 1931
dir. Anthony Asquith, Gerald Barkas
US title: Battle of Gallipoli, The

Raymond, E.
We, The Accused

BBC (GB) 1980 dir. Richard Stroud
TVSe(GB)

Raymond, M.
Smiley

FOX (GB) 1955 dir. Anthony Kimmins

Rayner, D. A.
Escort

Enemy Below, The
FOX (US) 1957 dir. Dick Powell

Rayner, R.
L.A. Without a Map

EUROAM (Fr/GB) 1999 dir. Mika
Kaurismaki

Rayson, H.
Hotel Sorrento

P

HORIZON (Aust/GB) 1995 dir. Richard
Franklin

Rea, D.
Ninfa Plebea

EUROLUX (It) 1996 dir. Lina
Wertmuller

Reachi, M.
Susana

PLEXUS (Sp) 1951 dir. Luis Bunuel

Read, M. B.
From the Inside

Chopper
AFFC (Aust) 2000 dir. Andrew Dominik

Read, P. P.
Alive

COL (US) 1993 dir. Frank Marshall

Read, P. P.
Free Frenchman, The

CENTRAL (GB) 1989 dir. Jim Goddard
TVSe(GB)

Read, P. P.
Married Man, A

LWT (GB) 1985 dir. Charles Jarrott
TVSe(GB)

Read, P. P.
Monk Dawson

DEWARR (GB) 1997 dir. Tom Waller

Reade, C. and Taylor, T.
Masks and Faces

P

Peg of Old Drury
WILCOX (GB) 1935 dir. Herbert Wilcox

Réage, P.
Return to the Château

Fruits of Passion
ARGOS (Fr/Jap) 1982 dir. Shuji
Terayama

Réage, P.
Story of O, The

NEW REALM (Fr) 1975 dir. Just Jaeckin

Rebeta-Burditt, J.
Cracker Factory, The

EMI (US) 1979 dir. Burt Brinckerhoff
TV(US)

Reddin, K.
All the Rage
P
It's the Rage
MUTUAL (US) 1999 dir. James D. Stern
TV(US)

Reddin, K.
Another Shore
EAL (GB) 1948 dir. Charles Crichton

Reddin, K.
Life During Wartime
P
Alarmist, The
KEY ENT (US) 1997 dir. Evan Dunsky

Redon, J.
Eyes Without A Face
CH ELYSEE (Fr/It) 1959
dir. George Franju

Redwood, J. H.
Old Settler, The
P
KCET (US) 2001 dir. Debbie Allen
TV(US)

Reed, B.
Verdict, The
FOX (US) 1982 dir. Sidney Lumet

Reed, J. D.
Free Fall
Pursuit of D. B. Cooper, The
UN (US) 1981 dir. Roger Spottiswoode

Reed, M.
Petticoat Fever
P
MGM (US) 1936
dir. George Fitzmaurice

Reed, M.
Yes, My Darling Daughter
P
WAR (US) 1939 dir. William Keighley

Reed, R. and Moore, K.
Deadly Medicine
MULTIMEDIA Ent/KRANTZ (US) 1991
dir. Richard A. Colla
TV(US)

Reese, J.
Looters, The
Charley Varrick
UN (US) 1973 dir. Don Siegel

Reeves, J.
Harbor, The
Society Doctor
MGM (US) 1935 dir. George B. Seitz
GB title: After Eight Hours

Reeves, T.
Beggars are Coming to Town
P
I Walk Alone
PAR (US) 1947 dir. Byron Haskin

Reid, R.
Madame Curie
BBC (GB) 1984
TV(GB)

Reid, R. P.
Colditz Story, The
BL (GB) 1954 dir. Guy Hamilton

Reilly, R. T.
Red Hugh, Prince of Donegal
Fighting Prince of Donegal, The
DISNEY (GB) 1966
dir. Michael O'Herlihy

Reiner, C.
Enter Laughing
P
COL (US) 1967 dir. Carl Reiner

Reitz, D.
Urban Folk Tales
P
Urbania
COMMOTION (US) 1999 dir. Jon Shear

Remarque, E. M.
All Quiet on the Western Front

UN (US) 1930 dir. Lewis Milestone
M. ARCH (US) 1979 dir. Delbert Mann
TV(US)

Remarque, E. M.
Arch of Triumph

UA (US) 1948 dir. Lewis Milestone
HTV (GB) 1984 dir. Waris Hussein
TV(GB)

Remarque, E. M.
Flotsam

So Ends Our Night
UA (US) 1941 dir. John Cromwell

Remarque, E. M.
Heaven has no Favourites

Bobby Deerfield
WAR (US) 1977 dir. Sydney Pollack

Remarque, E. M.
Road Back, The

UN (US) 1937 dir. James Whale

Remarque, E. M.
Three Comrades

MGM (US) 1938 dir. Frank Borzage

Remarque, E. M.
Time to Love and a Time to Die, A

U-I (US) 1958 dir. Douglas Sirk

Remnick, D.
King of the World

Muhammad Ali: King of the World
LIONS GATE (US) 2000 dir. John Sacret
Young
TV(US)

Renard, M.
Hands of Orlac, The

Mad Love
MGM (US) 1935 dir. Karl Freund
GB title: Hands of Orlac, The

Rendell, R.
Affair in Mind, An

BBC (GB) 1988 dir. Clive Luke
TV(GB)

Rendell, R.
Dark-Adapted Eye, The

BBC (GB) 1995 dir. Tim Fywell
TVSe(GB)

Rendell, R.
Demon in My View, A

VIDMARK (Ger) 1992 dir. Petra Haffter

Rendell, R.
Fatal Inversion, A

BBC (GB) 1992 dir. Tim Fywell
TVSe(GB)

Rendell, R.
Gallowglass

BBC (GB) 1993 dir. Tim Fywell
TVSe(GB)

Rendell, R.
Guilty Thing Surprised, A

TVS (GB) 1988 dir. Mary McMurray
TVSe(GB)

Rendell, R.
Judgement in Stone, A

SCHULZ (Can) 1987 dir. Ousama Rawi
US title: The Housekeeper

Rendell, R.
Judgment in Stone, A

Ceremonie, La
FRANCE 3 (Fr) 1995 dir. Claude
Chabrol

Rendell, R.
Live Flesh

FRANCE 3 (Fr/Sp) 1997 dir. Pedro
Almodovar

Rendell, R.
Master of the Moor
ITV (GB) 1994 dir. Marc Evans
TVSe(GB)

Rendell, R.
Some Lie and Some Die
TVS (GB) 1990 dir. Neil Zeiger
TVSe(GB)

Rendell, R.
Tree of Hands
GRANADA (GB) 1988 dir. Giles Foster

Rendell, R.
Tree of Hands, The
Betty Fisher et Autres Histoires
STUDIO CANAL+ (Fr/Can) 2001 dir.
Claude Miller

Rendell, R.
Unkindness of Ravens, An
TVS (GB) 1988 dir. John Gorrie
TV(GB)

Rendell, R.
Vanity Dies Hard
ITV (GB) 1995 dir. Alan Grint
TVSe(GB)

Rendell, R.
Wolf to the Slaughter
TVS (GB) 1988 dir. John Gorrie
TVSe(GB)

Rentschler, L. A.
Jitters
ABC PICT (US) 1997 dir. Bob Saget
TV(US)

Resko, J.
Reprieve
Convicts Four
ALLIED (US) 1962 dir. Millard
Kaufman
GB title: Reprieve

Resnik, M.
Any Wednesday
P
WAR (US) 1966 dir. Robert Ellis Miller
GB title: Bachelor Girl Apartment

Resnik, M.
Girl in the Turquoise Bikini, The
How Sweet It Is
WAR (US) 1968 dir. Jerry Paris

Reuben, D.
Everything You Ever Wanted to Know
about Sex but were Afraid to Ask
UA (US) 1972 dir. Woody Allen

Reuter, B.
Zappa
IS (Den) 1984 dir. Bille August

Reve, G.
Fourth Man, The
VER NED (Neth) 1984
dir. Paul Verhoeven

Revkin, A.
Burning Season, The
HBO (US) 1994 dir. John
Frankenheimer
TV(US)

Reyes, A.
Butcher, The
FREEWAY (It) 1998 dir. Aurelia
Grimaldi

Reyher, F.
Wait til the Sun Shines Nellie
FOX (US) 1952 dir. Henry King

Reynolds Naylor, P.
Shiloh
UTOPIA (US) 1996 dir. Dale
Rosenbloom

Reynolds Naylor, P.
Shiloh 2: Shiloh Season
WAR (US/GB) 1999 dir. Sandy Tung

Rhodes, E.
Prince of Central Park, The
LORIMAR (US) 1977 dir. Harvey Hart
TV(US)
SEAGAL/NASSO (US) 1999 dir. John
Leekley

Rhodes, E. M.
Paso Por Aqui
Four Faces West
UA (US) 1948 dir. Alfred E. Green

Rhys, J.
Quartet
NEW WORLD (GB/Fr) 1981
dir. James Ivory

Rhys, J.
Wide Sargasso Sea
LAUGH KOOK (Aust) 1993 dir. John
Duigan

Ricardei, M. and Dubois, W.
I Loved You Wednesday
P
TCF (US) 1933 dir. Henry King, William
Cameron Menzies

Rice, A.
Exit to Eden
SAVOY (US) 1994 dir. Garry Marshall

Rice, A.
Feast of All Saints, The
SHOWTIME (US) 2001 dir. Peter Medak
TVSe(US)

Rice, A.
Interview With the Vampire
GEFFEN (US) 1994 dir. Neil Jordan

Rice, A. H. and Flexner, A. C.
Mrs. Wiggs of the Cabbage Patch
PAR (US) 1934 dir. Norman Taurog
PAR (US) 1942 dir. Ralph Murphy

Rice, C.
Having Wonderful Crime
RKO (US) 1945 dir. Eddie Sutherland

Rice, C.
Home Sweet Homicide
FOX (US) 1946 dir. Lloyd Bacon

Rice, C.
Lucky Stiff, The
UA (US) 1948 dir. Lewis R. Foster

Rice, E.
Adding Machine, The
P
RANK (GB) 1968 dir. Jerome Epstein

Rice, E.
Counsellor at Law
P
UN (US) 1933 dir. William Wyler

Rice, E.
Dream Girl
P
PAR (US) 1947 dir. Mitchell Leisen
M. EVANS (US) 1955
dir. George Schaefer
TV(US)

Rice, E.
Street Scene
P
UA (US) 1931 dir. King Vidor

Rice, L.
Blue Moon
COL TRISTAR (US) 1999 dir. Ron
Lagomarsino
TV(US)

Rice, L.
Crazy in Love
OHYLMEYER (US) 1992 dir. Martha
Coolidge
TV(US)

Rice, L.
Follow the Stars Home
HALLMARK (US) 2001 dir. Dick Lowry
TV(US)

Rich, D. L.
Amelia Earhart: A Biography
Amelia Earhart: The Final Flight
AVE PICT (US) 1994 dir. Yves Simoneau
TV(US)

Rich, K.
Johnny's Girl
SIGNBOARD HILL (US) 1995 dir. John
Kent Harrison
TV(US)

Rich, M.
Bare Essence
WAR TV (US) 1982 dir. Walter
Grauman
TVSe(US)

Richards, C.
Sweet Country
CINEMA (US) 1987
dir. Michael Cacoyannis

Richards, D. A.
Nights Below Station Street
CBC (Can) 1998 dir. Norma Bailey
TV(Can)

Richards, L. E.
Captain January
FOX (US) 1936 dir. David Butler
Ch

Richards, R. and Ames, J.
Renee Richards Story, The: The
Second Serve
Second Serve
LORIMAR (US) 1986 dir. Anthony Page
TV(US)

Richardson, H. H.
Getting of Wisdom, The
TEDDERWICK (Aust) 1979
dir. Bruce Beresford

Richardson, H. H.
Maurice Guest
Rhapsody
MGM (US) 1954 dir. Charles Vidor

Richardson, S.
Clarissa
BBC (GB) 1991 dir. Robert Bierman
TVSe(GB)

Richardson, S.
Pamela
Mistress Pamela
MGM-EMI (GB) 1973
dir. Jim O'Connolly

Riche, E.
Rare Birds
LIONS GATE (Can) 2001 dir. Sturla
Gunnarsson

Richer, C.
Tikoyo and his Shark
Beyond the Reef
UN (US) 1981 dir. Frank C. Clark

Richert, W.
Aren't You Even Gonna Kiss Me
Goodbye
Night in the Life of Jimmy Reardon, A
FOX (US) 1988 dir. William Richert

Richler, M.
Apprenticeship of Duddy Kravitz, The
RANK (Can) 1974 dir. Ted Kotcheff

Richler, M.
Joshua Then and Now
TCF (Can) 1985 dir. Ted Kotcheff

Richman, A.
Awful Truth, The
P
COL (US) 1937 dir. Leo McCarey

Richman, A.
Not so Long Ago
P
Let's Do It Again
COL (US) 1953 dir. Alexander Hall
M

Richter, C.
Awakening Land, The
WAR TV (US) 1978 dir. Boris Sagal
TVSe(US)

Richter, C.
Light in the Forest, The
DISNEY (US) 1958
dir. Herschel Daugherty

Richter, C.
Tracy Cromwell
One Desire
UI (US) 1955 dir. Jerry Hopper

Richter, C.
Sea of Grass, The
MGM (US) 1947 dir. Elia Kazan

Rico-Godoy, C.
How to be Miserable and Enjoy It
ATRIUM (SP) 1994 dir. Enrique Urbizu

Rico-Godoy, C.
Infidelity
ATRIUM (Sp) 1995 dir. Enrique Urbizu

Ridley, A.
Beggar My Neighbour
P
Meet Mr Lucifer
GFD (GB) 1953 dir. Anthony Pelissier

Ridley, A.
Easy Money
P
GFD (GB) 1948 dir. Bernard Knowles

Ridley, A.
Ghost Train, The
P
GFD (GB) 1931 dir. Walter Forde
GFD (GB) 1941 dir. Walter Forde

Ridley, A.
Keepers of Youth
P
POWERS (GB) 1931
dir. Thomas Bentley

Ridley, A. and Borer, M.
Tabitha
P
Who Killed the Cat?
GN (GB) 1966 dir. Montgomery Tully

Ridley, A. and Merivale, B.
Wrecker, The
P
Seven Sinners
GAU (GB) 1937 dir. Albert de Courville
US title: Doomed Cargo

Ridley, J.
U-Turn
PHOENIX PICT (US) 1997 dir. Oliver Stone

Rigby, R. and Allen, R. S.
Hill, The
P
MGM (GB) 1965 dir. Sidney Lumet

857

Rigsby, H.
Showdown at Crazy Horse

Last Sunset, The
UI (US) 1961 dir. Robert Aldrich

Riggs, L.
Green Grow the Lilacs

P
Oklahoma!
MAGNA (US) 1955 dir. Fred
Zinnemann
M

Riley, L.
Personal Appearance

P
Go West Young Man
PAR (US) 1936 dir. Henry Hathaway

Riley, W.
Peter Pettinger

Agitator, The
BN (GB) 1944 dir. John Harlow

Rimmer, R. H.
Harrad Experiment, The

CINERAMA (US) 1973 dir. Ted Post

Rinehart, M. R.
Bat, The

P
ALLIED (US) 1959 dir. Crane Wilbur

Rinehart, M. R.
Bat, The

P
Bat Whispers, The
UA (US) 1930 dir. Roland West

Rinehart, M. R.
Lost Ecstasy

I Take This Woman
PAR (US) 1931 dir. Marion Gering

Rinehart, M. R.
Miss Pinkerton

Nurse's Secret, The
WAR (US) 1941 dir. Noel M. Smith

Rinehart, M. R.
Tish Marches On

Tish
MGM (US) 1942 dir. S. Sylvan Simon

Ripley, A.
Scarlett

RHI (US) 1994 dir. John Erman
TVSe(US)

Riskin, R. and Meehan, J.
Bless You Sister

P
Miracle Woman, The
COL (US) 1932 dir. Frank Capra

Riss, W.
Darker Purpose, A

P
Winner, The
VILLAGE ROADSHOW (US) 1997 dir.
Alex Cox

Ritchie, J.
Green Heart, The

New Leaf, A
PAR (US) 1970 dir. Elaine May

Rivera, T.
Y No Se Lo Trago La Tierra

... And the Earth Did Not Swallow Him
AM PLAY (US) 1995 dir. Severo Perez

Roark, G.
Fair Wind to Java

REP (US) 1952 dir. Joseph Kane

Roark, G.
Wake of the Red Witch

REP (US) 1948 dir. Edward Ludwig

Robb, J.
Punitive Action

Desert Sands
UA (US) 1955 dir. Lesley Selander

Robbins, C.
Air America
TRISTAR (US) 1990
dir. Roger Spottiswoode

Robbins, H.
Adventurers, The
PAR (US) 1970 dir. Lewis Gilbert

Robbins, H.
Betsy, The
UA (US) 1978 dir. Daniel Petrie

Robbins, H.
Carpetbaggers, The
PAR (US) 1964 dir. Edward Dmytryk

Robbins, H.
Dream Merchants, The
COL TV (US) 1980
dir. Vincent Sherman
TVSe(US)

Robbins, H.
Lonely Lady, The
UN (US) 1982 dir. Peter Sasdy

Robbins, H.
Never Love a Stranger
ABP (US) 1958 dir. Robert Stevens

Robbins, H.
Pirate, The
WAR TV (US) 1978
dir. Kenneth C. Annakin
TVSe(US)

Robbins, H.
79 Park Avenue
UN (US) 1977 dir. Paul Wendkos
TVSe(US)

Robbins, H.
Stiletto
AVCO (US) 1969 dir. Bernard Kowalski

Robbins, H.
Stone for Danny Fisher, A
King Creole
PAR (US) 1958 dir. Michael Curtiz

Robbins, H.
Where Love has Gone
PAR (US) 1964 dir. Edward Dmytryk

Robbins, T.
Even Cowgirls Get the Blues
NEW LINE (US) 1994 dir. Gus Van Sant

Robbins, T.
Spurs
Freaks
MGM (US) 1932 dir. Tod Browning

Roberts, C. E. B.
Don Chicago
BN (GB) 1945 dir. Maclean Rogers

Roberts, D.
Smuggler's Circuit
Law and Disorder
BL (GB) 1957 dir. Charles Crichton

Roberts, E. B. and Cavett, F. M.
Forsaking All Others
P
MGM (US) 1934 dir. W. S. Van Dyke

Roberts, E. M.
Great Meadow, The
MGM (US) 1931 dir. Charles Brabin

Roberts, K.
Captain Caution
UA (US) 1940 dir. Richard Wallace

Roberts, K.
Lydia Bailey
FOX (US) 1952 dir. Jean Negulesco

Roberts, K.
Northwest Passage
MGM (US) 1940 dir. King Vidor

Roberts, K.
Northwest Passage
Mission of Danger
MGM (US) 1959 dir. George Waggner,
Jacques Tourneur

Roberts, N.
Sanctuary
CBS TV (US) 2001 dir. Katt Shea
TV(US)

Roberts, N.
This Magic Moment
Magic Moments
ATLANTIC/YTV (GB/US)
dir. Lawrence Gordon Clarke
TV(GB/US)

Roberts, R. E.
Star in the West
Second Time Around, The
FOX (US) 1961 dir. Vincent Sherman

Robertson, D.
Greatest Thing That Almost Never
Happened, The
FRIES (US) 1977 dir. Gilbert Moses
TV(US)

Robertson, D.
Survive the Savage Sea
VZ/SERTNER (US) 1992 dir. Kevin
James Dobson
TV(US)

Robertson, E. A.
Four Frightened People
PAR (US) 1934 dir. Cecil B. de Mille

Robertson, W.
Moontide
FOX (US) 1942 dir. Archie Mayo

Robeson, K.
Doc Savage—Man of Bronze
WAR (US) 1975 dir. Michael Anderson

Robinson, D.
Piece of Cake
LWT (GB) 1988 dir. Ian Toynton
TVSe(GB)

Robinson, F.
Power, The
MGM (US) 1968 dir. Byron Hoskin

Robinson, H. M.
Cardinal, The
COL (US) 1963 dir. Otto Preminger

Robinson, H. M.
Perfect Round, The
Americana
CROWN (US) 1983 dir. David
Carradine

Robinson, J. S.
Bedtime Story
Cry for Love, A
FRIES/SACKS (US) 1980
dir. Paul Wendkos
TV(US)

Robinson, M.
Housekeeping
COL (US) 1987 dir. Bill Forsyth

Robison, M.
Oh!
Twister
VESTRON (US) 1990
dir. Michael Almereyda

Robles, E.
Cela S'Appelle L'Aurore
MARCEAU/LAE (Fr/It) 1955
dir. Luis Bunuel

Roche, A. S.
Case Against Mrs Ames, The
PAR (US) 1936 dir. William A. Seiter

Roche, H.-P.
Jules et Jim
SEDIF (Fr) 1962 dir. François Truffaut

Rock, P.
Extraordinary Seaman, The
MGM (US) 1969
dir. John Frankenheimer

Rodgers, M.
Freaky Friday
DISNEY (US) 1976 dir. Gary Nelson
DISNEY FAMILY (US) 1995 dir. Melanie
Mayron
Ch, TV(US)

**Rodgers, R. and Hammerstein
II, O.**
King and I, The
P
FOX (US) 1956 dir. Walter Lang
M

**Rodgers, R. and Hammerstein
II, O.**
Oklahoma!
P
MAGNA (US) 1955 dir. Fred
Zinnemann
M

**Rodgers, R., Hammerstein II,
O., Logan, J. and Osborn, P.**
South Pacific
P
TODD AO (US) 1958 dir. Joshua Logan
M
TOUCHSTONE (US) 2001 dir. Richard
Pearce
M, TV(US)

Rodman, D. and Keown, T.
Bad As I Wanna Be
*Bad As I Wanna Be: The Dennis Rodman
Story*
COL TRISTAR (US) 1998 dir. Jean De
Segonzac
TV(US)

**Rodriguez, S. and Hobbs
Birnie, L.**
Uncommon Will: The Death and Life
of Sue Rodriguez
*At the End of the Day: The Sue Rodriguez
Story*
AMW (Can) 1999 dir. Sheldon Larry
TV(Can)

Roe, V.
Golden Tide, The
Perilous Journey, A
REP (US) 1953 dir. R. G. Springsteen

Roemer, Jr., W. F.
Roemer: Man Against the Mob
Sugartime
HBO (US) 1995 dir. John N. Smith
TV(US)

Roffey, J.
Hostile Witness
P
UA (GB) 1968 dir. Ray Milland

Rogers, J.
Mr. Wroe's Virgins
BBC (GB) 1993 dir. Danny Boyle
TVSe(GB)

Rogers, M. E.
Runestone, The
HY (US) 1992
dir. Willard Carroll

Rogers, T.
Pursuit of Happiness, The
COL (US) 1971 dir. Robert Mulligan

Rogger, L. L.
Princess Comes Across, The
PAR (US) 1936 dir. William K. Howard

Rohan, C.
Delinquents, The
VILLAGE ROADSHOW (Aust) 1990
dir. Chris Thomson

Rohmer, S.
Daughter of Fu Manchu
Daughter of the Dragon
PAR (US) 1931 dir. Lloyd Corrigan

Rohmer, S.
Drums of Fu Manchu
REP (US) 1940 dir. William Witney, John
English

Rohmer, S.
Mask of Fu Manchu
MGM (US) 1932 dir. Charles Brabin,
Charles Vidor

Rohmer, S.
Mysterious Dr. Fu Manchu
PAR (US) 1929 dir. Rowland V. Lee

Roiphe, A. R.
Up the Sandbox
WAR (US) 1973 dir. Irwin Kershner

Rollin, B.
First You Cry
MTM (US) 1978 dir. George Schaefer
TV(US)

Rollin, B.
Last Wish
GROSS/BAR
(US) 1992 dir. Jeff Bleckner
TV(US)

Roman, E.
After the Trial
Death Sentence
SPEL-GOLD (US) 1974
dir. E.W. Swackhamer
TV(US)

Romberg, S.
Student Prince, The
MGM (US) 1954 dir. Richard Thorpe
M

Ronald, J.
Medal for the General, A
BN (GB) 1944 dir. Maurice Elvey

Ronald, J.
Murder in the Family
FOX (GB) 1938 dir. Al Parker

Ronald, J.
This Way Out
Suspect, The
UN (US) 1944 dir. Robert Siodmak

Rook, D.
Ballad of the Belstone Fox, The
Belstone Fox, The
RANK (GB) 1973 dir. James Hill

Rook, D.
White Colt, The
Run Wild, Run Free
COL (GB) 1989 dir. Richard C. Sarafian

Rooke, L.
Good Baby, A
KARDANA (US) 1998 dir. Katherine
Dieckmann
TV(US)

Rooney, P.
Captain Boycott
INDIVIDUAL (GB) 1947
dir. Frank Launder

Roos, K.
To Save His Life
Dead Men Tell No Tales
FOX (US) 1971 dir. Walter Grauman
TV(US)

Root, L.
Cabin in the Sky
P
MGM (US) 1943 dir. Vincente Minnelli
M

Ropes, B.
Forty-Second Street
WAR (US) 1933 dir. Lloyd Bacon
M

Rorick, I. S.
Mr and Mrs Cugat
Are Husbands Necessary?
PAR (US) 1942 dir. Norman Taurog

Rose, A.
Four Horse Players are Missing
Who's Got the Action?
PAR (US) 1963 dir. Daniel Mann

Rose, A. P.
Room for One More
WAR (US) 1952 dir. Norman Taurog

Rose, R.
Crime in the Streets
P
AA (US) 1956 dir. Don Siegel

Rose, R.
Twelve Angry Men
P
UA (US) 1957 dir. Sidney Lumet

Rosenbaum, E.
Taste of my Own Medicine, A
Doctor, The
TOUCHSTONE (US) 1991 dir. Randa
Haines

Rosenberg, H.
Atomic Soldiers
Nightbreaker
TNT (US) 1989 dir. Peter Markle
TV(US)

Rosenberg, P.
Contract on Cherry Street
COL TV (US) 1977
dir. William A. Graham
TV(US)

Rosenfeld, S. Z.
Brother's Kiss, A
P
OVERSEAS (US) 1996 dir. Seth Zvi
Rosenfeld

Rosenthall, M.
Honest Courtesan, The
Dangerous Beauty
NEW REGENCY (US) 1998 dir.
Marshall Herskovitz

Rosny, J. H.
Quest for Fire
FOX (Can/Fr) 1982
dir. Jean-Jacques Annaaud

Ross, K.
Breaker Morant
P
S. AUST (Aust) 1980
dir. Bruce Beresford

Ross, S.
He Ran All The Way
UA (US) 1951 dir. John Berry

Rossi, N.
Glass Full of Snow, A
CIN IT (It) 1988 dir. Florestano Vancini

Rossner, J.
Looking for Mr Goodbar
PAR (US) 1987 dir. Richard Brooks

Rostand, E.
Cyrano de Bergerac
P
UA (US) 1950 dir. Michael Gordon
COMPASS (US) 1962
dir. George Schaefer
TV(US)
UGC (Fr) 1990 dir. Jean-Paul
Rappeneau

Rostand, E.
Cyrano de Bergerac
P
Roxanne
COL (US) 1987 dir. Fred Schepisi

Rostand, M.
Homme que J'ai tué, L'
P
Broken Lullaby
PAR (US) 1931 dir. Ernst Lubitsch

Rostand, R.
Killer Elite, The
UA (US) 1975 dir. Sam Peckinpah

Rosten, L.
Captain Newman, M.D.
UI (US) 1963 dir. David Miller

Rosten, L.
Sleep my Love
UA (US) 1948 dir. Douglas Sirk

Roth, A.
Terrible Beauty, A
UA (GB) 1960 dir. Tay Garnett

Roth, J.
Legend of the Holy Drinker
ART EYE (It) 1989 dir. Ermanno Olnu

Roth, L. and Frank, G.
I'll Cry Tomorrow
MGM (US) 1955 dir Daniel Mann

Roth, P.
Goodbye Columbus
PAR (US) 1969 dir. Larry Peerce

Roth, P.
Portnoy's Complaint
WAR (US) 1972 dir. Ernest Lehman

Rothenberg, M. and White, M.
David
ITC (US) 1988 dir. John Erman
TV(US)

Rouland, J.-P. and Olivier, C.
Tendre Poulet
Dear Inspector
ARIANE/MONDEX (Fr) 1977
dir. Philippe de Broca

Roussin, A. and Mitford, N.
Little Hut, The
P
MGM (US) 1957 dir. Mark Robson

Rouverol, A.
Skidding
P
Family Affair, A
MGM (US) 1937 dir. George B. Seitz

Rowe, Jr., G. T.
My Years with the KKK
Undercover with the KKK
COL TV (US) 1979 dir. Barry Shear
TV(US)

Rowling, J. K.
Harry Potter and the Philosopher's
Stone
WAR (US) 2001 dir. Chris Columbus
US title: Harry Potter and the Sorcerer's
Stone

Roy, G.
Children of My Heart
TAPESTRY (Can) 2001 dir. Keith Ross
Leckie
TV(Can)

Royle, E. M.
Squaw Man, The

P

MGM (US) 1931 dir. Cecil B. De Mille
GB title: White Man, The

Ruark, R.
Something of Value

MGM (US) 1957 dir. Richard Brooks

Rubens, B.
I Sent a Letter to My Love

ATLANTIC (Fr) 1981
dir. Moshe Mizrahi

Rubens, B.
Madame Sousatzka

UN (GB) 1988 dir. John Schlesinger

Rubens, B.
Mr. Wakefield's Crusade

BBC (GB) 1992 dir. Angela Pope
TVSe(GB)

Rubin, D.
Riddle Me This

P

Guilty as Hell
PAR (US) 1932 dir. Erle C. Kenton

Rubin, D.
Riddle Me This

P

Night Club Scandal
PAR (US) 1937 dir. Ralph Murphy

Rubin, T. I.
Lisa and David

David and Lisa
BL (US) 1963 dir. Frank Perry
HARPO (US) 1998 dir. Lloyd Kramer

Ruckman, I.
Night of the Twisters, The

MTM (US) 1996 dir. Tim Bond
TV(US)

Rudnick, P.
Jeffrey

P

ORION (US) 1995 dir. Christopher
Ashley

Rueff, R.
Hospitality Suite

P

Big Kahuna, The
FRANCHISE (US) 1999 dir. John
Swanbeck

Ruell, P.
Long Kill, The

Last Hit, The
MTE UNIVERSAL (US) 1993 dir. Jan
Egelson
TV(US)

Ruesch, H.
Racer, The

Racers, The
FOX (US) 1955 dir. Henry Hathaway
GB title: Such Men are Dangerous

Ruesch, H.
Top of the World

Savage Innocents, The
RANK (Fr/It/GB) 1960
dir. Nicholas Ray

Ruggles, E.
Prince of Players

FOX (US) 1954 dir. Philip Dunne

Rule, A.
**And Never Let Her Go: Thomas
Capano: The Deadly Seducer**

And Never Let Her Go
GREENWALD (US) 2001 dir. Peter
Levin
TVSe(US)

Rule, A.
Dead by Sunset

TRISTAR TV (US) 1995 dir. Karen
Arthur
TVSe(US)

Rule, A.
Small Sacrifices

FRIES (US) 1989 dir. David Greene
TVSe(US)

Rule, J.
Desert of the Heart

Desert Hearts
MGM (US) 1986 dir. Donna Deitch

Runyon, D.
Bloodhounds of Broadway

FOX (US) 1952 dir. Harmon Jones
COL (US) 1989 dir. Howard Brookner

Runyon, D.
Idyll of Miss Sarah Brown, The

Guys and Dolls
MGM (US) 1955
dir. Joseph L. Mankiewicz
M

Runyon, D.
Johnny One-Eye

UA (US) 1950 dir. Robert Florey

Runyon, D.
Lemon Drop Kid, The

PAR (US) 1951 dir. Sidney Lanfield

Runyon, D.
Little Miss Marker

PAR (US) 1934 dir. Alexander Hall
GB title: Girl in Pawn, The
UN (US) 1980 dir. Walter Bernstein

Runyon, D.
Little Pinks

Big Street, The
RKO (US) 1942 dir. Irving Reis

Runyon, D.
Madame la Gimp

Lady for a Day
COL (US) 1933 dir. Frank Capra

Runyon, D.
Madame la Gimp

Pocketful of Miracles
UA (US) 1961 dir. Frank Capra

Runyon, D.
Money from Home

PAR (US) 1953 dir. George Marshall

Runyon, D. and Lindsay, H.
Slight Case of Murder, A

P
Stop, You're Killing Me
WAR (US) 1952 dir. Roy del Ruth

Runyon, D. and Caesar, I.
Straight, Place and Show

P
FOX (US) 1938 dir. David Butler
GB title: They're Off

Runyon, D. and Lindsay, H.
Slight Case of Murder, A

P
WAR (US) 1938 dir. Lloyd Bacon

Russell, K.
Visit, The

P
URBANWORLD (US) 2000 dir. Jordan
Walker-Pearlman

Russell, R.
Incubus, The

NEW REALM (Can) 1982
dir. John Hough

Russell, S. M.
Lamp is Heavy, A

Feminine Touch, The
RANK (GB) 1956 dir. Pat Jackson

Russell, W.
Educating Rita

P
RANK (GB) 1983 dir. Lewis Gilbert

Russell, W.
Shirley Valentine
P
PAR (GB) 1989 dir. Lewis Gilbert

Russo, E.
Martedì del Diavolo, Il
Russicum
TRISTAR/CECCHI (It) 1989
dir. Pasquale Squitieri

Russo, R.
Nobody's Fool
PAR (US) 1994 dir. Robert Benton

Ryan, C.
Bridge Too Far, A
UA (GB/US) 1977
dir. Richard Attenborough

Ryan, C.
Longest Day, The
FOX (US) 1962 dir. Ken Annakin,
Andrew Marton, Bernhard Wicki

Ryan, C. and Ryan, K. M.
Private Battle, A
P&G (US) 1980
dir. Robert Michael Lewis
TV(US)

Ryan Hyde, C.
Pay it Forward
WAR (US) 2000 dir. Mimi Leder

Ryan, J.
Little Girls in Pretty Boxes
ABC PROD (US) 1997 dir. Christopher
Leitch
TV(US)

Ryan, J. F.
Little Brothers of St. Mortimer, The
White River Kid, The
NEW CITY (US) 1999 dir. Arne
Glimcher

Ryan, J. M.
Brook Wilson Ltd
Loving
COL (US) 1970 dir. Irvin Kershner

Ryan, M. C.
Me Two
Other Me, The
H. ROACH (US) 2000 dir. Manny Coto
TV(US)

Ryan, P.
How I Won the War
UA (GB) 1967 dir. Richard Lester

Ryazanov, E.
Prediction, The
MOSFILM (Rus/Fr) 1994 dir. Eldar
Ryazanov

Ryck, F.
Family Business
EUROPEAN (Fr) 1987 dir. Costa-
Gavras

Ryskind, M.
Louisiana Purchase
P
PAR (US) 1941 dir. Irving Cummings
M

Ryskind, M. and Kaufman, G. S.
Animal Crackers
P
PAR (US) 1930 dir. Victor Heerman

Ryton, R.
Crown Matrimonial
P
TALENT (US) 1974 dir. Alan Bridges
TV(US)

S

Saba, U.
Ernesto
CLESI (It) 1978 dir. Salvatore Samperi

Sabatini, R.
Black Swan, The
FOX (US) 1942 dir. Henry King

Sabatini, R.
Captain Blood
WAR (US) 1935 dir. Michael Curtiz

Sabatini, R.
Captain Blood Returns
Captain Pirate
COL (US) 1952 dir. Ralph Murphy
GB title: Captain Blood, Fugitive

Sabatini, R.
Fortunes of Captain Blood, The
COL (US) 1950 dir. Gordon Douglas

Sabatini, R.
Scaramouche
MGM (US) 1952 dir. George Sidney

Sabatini, R.
Sea Hawk, The
WAR (US) 1940 dir. Michael Curtiz

Sacchettoni, D.
Notti di Arancia Meccanica, Le
Smell of the Night, The
SORPASSO (It) 1998 dir. Claudio
Caligari

Sackler, H.
Great White Hope, The
P
FOX (US) 1970 dir. Martin Ritt

Sacks, O.
Awakenings
COL (US) 1990 dir. Penny Marshall

Sacks, O.
Man Who Mistook His Wife for a Hat,
The
CHANNEL 4 (GB) 1988
dir. Christopher Rawlence
TV(GB)

Sackville-West, V.
All Passion Spent
BBC (GB) 1986 dir. Martyn Friend
TVSe(GB)

Sadleir, M.
Fanny by Gaslight
GFD (GB) 1944 dir. Anthony Asquith
US title: Man of Evil
BBC (GB) 1981 dir. Peter Jefferies
TVSe(GB)

Sadler, M. and Bollen, R.
Zenon: Girl of the 21st Century
DISNEY (US) 1999 dir. Kenneth
Johnson
TV(US)

Sae, S.
Rojuko Kazoku
Promise, A
KT (Jap) 1987 dir. Yoshishige Yoshida

Safdie, O.
Hyper-Allergenic
P
You Can Thank Me Later
CINEQUEST (Can) 1998 dir. Shimon Dotan

Sagan, C.
Contact
WAR (US) 1997 dir. Robert Zemeckis

Sagan, F.
Aimez-vous Brahms?
Goodbye Again
UA (US) 1961 dir. Anatole Litvak

Sagan, F.
Bonjour Tristesse
COL (GB) 1957 dir. Otto Preminger

Sagan, F.
Certain Smile, A
FOX (US) 1958 dir. Jean Negulesco

Sagan, F.
Chamade, La
ARIANE (Fr) 1969 dir. Alain Cavalier
US title: Heartkeeper, The

Saint, H. F.
Memoirs of an Invisible Man
WAR (US) 1992
dir. John Carpenter

Saint-Exupery, A. de
Little Prince, The
PAR (US) 1974 dir. Stanley Donen
M

Saint-Laurent, C.
Caroline Chérie
GAU (Fr) 1951 dir. Richard Pottier

Saint-Laurent, C.
Lola Montes
GAMMA (Fr/Ger) 1955
dir. Max Ophuls

Sakaguchi, A.
Doctor Liver
Dr. Akagi
TOEI (Jap) 1998 dir. Shohei Imamura

Sakaguchi, A.
Hakuchi
TEZUKA (Jap) 1999 dir. Makoto Tezuka

Saki, R.
Vengeance is Mine
KINO (Jap) 1979 dir. Shohei Imamura

Salamanca, J. R.
Lilith
COL (US) 1964 dir. Robert Rossen

Salamanca, J. R.
Lost Country, The
Wild in the Country
FOX (US) 1961 dir. Philip Dunne

Salamon, J. and Weber, J.
Christmas Tree, The
DISNEY TELEFILMS (US) 1996 dir. Sally Field
TV(US)

Salas, A.
Latin Boys Go To Hell
STRAND (US) 1997 dir. Ela Troyano

Sale, D.
Come to Mother
Live Again, Die Again
UN TV (US) 1974 dir. Richard Colla
TV(US)

Sale, R.
Not Too Narrow, Not Too Deep
Strange Cargo
MGM (US) 1940
dir. Joseph L. Mankiewicz

Sale, R.
Oscar, The
PAR (US) 1966 dir. Russel Rouse

Sale, R.
White Buffalo, The
EMI (US) 1977 dir. J. Lee Thompson

Salemme, V.
Amico del Cuore, L'
P
CECCHI (It) 1999 dir. Vincenzo
Salemme

Salerno, S.
Deadly Blessing
Bed of Lies
WOLPER TV(US) 1992
dir. William A. Graham

Sallenave, D.
Vie Fantome, La
MAXFILMS (Can) 1992 dir. Jacques
Leduc

Salles Gomes, P. E.
Jean Vigo
Vigo—Passion For Life
NITRATE (US) 1998 dir. Julien Temple

Salten, F.
Bambi
DISNEY (US) 1942 dir. David Hand
A, Ch

Salten, F.
Florian
MGM (US) 1940 dir. Edwin L. Marin

Salten, F.
Hound of Florence, The
Shaggy Dog, The
DISNEY (US) 1959 dir. Charles Barton
Ch

Salten, F.
Perri
DISNEY (US) 1957 dir. Ralph Wright
Ch

Salter, J.
Hunters, The
FOX (US) 1958 dir. Dick Powell

Sams, G.
Punk, The
Punk and the Princess, The
M2 (GB) 1993 dir. Michael Sarne

Sanchez, J.
Krampack
P
Nico and Dani
MESSIDOR (Sp) 2000 dir. Cesc Gay

Sanchez-Scott, M.
Roosters
P
AM PLAY (US) 1993 dir. Robert M.
Young

Sandemose, A.
Sailor Goes Ashore, A
Misery Harbour
UIP (Can/Den) 1999 dir. Nils Gaup

Sanders, D.
Clover
RHI (US) 1997 dir. Jud Taylor
TV(US)

Sanders, G.
Stranger at Home
Stranger Came Home, The
EXCL (GB) 1954 dir. Terence Fisher
US title: Unholy Four, The

Sanders, L.
Anderson Tapes, The
COL (US) 1971 dir. Sidney Lumet

Sanders, L.
First Deadly Sin, The
CIC (US) 1980 dir. Brian G. Hutton

Sandford, J.
Mind Prey
ABC (US) 1999 dir. D. J. Caruso
TV(US)

Sandier, S.
Crossing Delancey
P
WAR (US) 1988 dir. Joan Micklin Silver

Sandlin, T.
Skipped Parts
TRIMARK (US) 2001 dir. Tamra Davis

Sandlin, T.
Sorrow Floats
Floating Away
PEG (US) 1998 dir. John Badham
TV(US)

Sandoz, M.
Cheyenne Autumn
WAR (US) 1964 dir. John Ford

Sands, A.
Airspeed
AIRSPEED (US) 1998 dir. Robert Tinnell
TV(US)

Sands, L.
Deadlock
P
Another Man's Poison
EROS (GB) 1951 dir. Irving Rapper

Sandstrom, F.
Madness of the Heart
TC (GB) 1949 dir. Charles Bennett

Sandstrom, F.
Midwife of Pont Clery, The
Jessica
UA (Fr/It) 1961 dir. Jean Negulesco

Sandstrom, F.
Milk White Unicorn, The
White Unicorn, The
GFD (GB) 1947 dir. Bernard Knowles
US title: Bad Sister

Sanford, H. and Lamb, M.
Emporia
Waco
PAR (US) 1966 dir. R. G. Springsteen

Sangster, J.
Foreign Exchange
ABC (US) 1970 dir. Roy Baker
TV(US)

Sangster, J.
Private I
Spy Killer, The
ABC (US) 1969 dir. Roy Baker
TV(US)

Sansom, W.
Last Hours of Sandra Lee, The
Wild Affair, The
BL (GB) 1965 dir. John Irish

Sant'Anna, S.
Miss Simpson
Bossa Nova
COL (Bra/US) 2000 dir. Bruno Barreto

Saperstein, D.
Cocoon
FOX (US) 1985 dir. Ron Howard

Sapir, R. B.
Body, The
COMPASS (Ger/US) 2000 dir. Jonas McCord

Sardou, V.
Madame Sans-Gene
P
FOX (Fr/It/Sp) 1962
dir. Christian-Jaque
US/GB title: Madame

Saroyan, W.
Human Comedy, The
MGM (US) 1943 dir. Clarence Brown

Saroyan, W.
Time of Your Life, The
P
UA (US) 1948 dir. H. C. Potter

Sarris, G.
Grand Avenue
WILDWOOD (US) 1996 dir. Dave
Sackman
TV(US)

Sartre, J.-P.
Age of Reason, The; Reprieve, The;
Iron in the Soul
Roads to Freedom, The
BBC (GB) 1970 dir. James Cellan Jones
TVSe(GB)

Sartre, J.-P.
Condemned of Altona, The
P
FOX (Fr/It) 1962 dir. Vittorio di Sica

Sartre, J.-P.
Huis Clos
P
MARCEAU (Fr) 1954
dir. Jacqueline Audry

Sartre, J.-P.
Kean
P
BBC (GB) 1978 dir. James Cellan Jones
TV(GB)

Sartre, J.-P.
Mains Sales, Les
P
RIVERS (Fr) 1951 dir. Fernand Rivers

Sartre, J.-P.
Respectable Prostitute, The
P
MARCEAU (Fr) 1952
dir. Marcel Pagliero, Charles Brabant

Saul, J.
Cry for the Strangers
MGM (US) 1982 dir. Peter Medak
TV(US)

Saul, O.
Dark Side of Love, The
My Kidnapper, My Love
EMI (US) 1980 dir. Sam Wanamaker
TV(US)

Saunders, H. St. G.
Red Beret, The
COL (GB) 1953 dir. Terence Young
US title: Paratrooper

Saunders, J. M.
Devil Dogs of the Air
WAR (US) 1935 dir. Lloyd Bacon

Saunders, J. M.
Single Lady
Last Flight, The
WAR (US) 1931 dir. William Dieterle

Savage, G.
Slate Wyn and Blanche McBride
Slate, Wyn and Me
HEMDALE (Aust) 1987
dir. Don McLennan

Savage, M.
Parrish
WAR (US) 1961 dir. Delmer Daves

Savage, T.
Valentine
WAR (US) 2001 dir. Jamie Blanks

Savan, G.
White Palace
UN (US) 1990 dir. Luis Mandoki

Savoir, A.
Bluebeard's Eighth Wife
P
PAR (US) 1938 dir. Ernst Lubitsch

Savory, G.
George and Margaret
P
WAR (GB) 1940 dir. George King

Savoy, A. A.
I Went to the Dance
BRAZOS (US) 1989 dir. Leon Blank,
Chris Strachwitz

Saxon, L.
LaFitte the Pirate
Buccaneer, The
PAR (US) 1937 dir. Cecil B. De Mille
PAR (US) 1958 dir. Anthony Quinn

Saxon, P.
Disorientated Man, The
Scream and Scream Again
AIP (GB) 1969 dir. Gordon Hessler

Saxton, M.
Jayne Mansfield and the American Fifties
Jayne Mansfield Story, The
LAN (US) 1980 dir. Dick Lowry
TV(US)

Sayers, D. L.
Busman's Honeymoon
MGM (GB) 1940 dir. Arthur Woods
US title: Haunted Honeymoon

Sayers, D. L.
Clouds of Witness
BBC (GB) 1972 dir. Hugh David
TVSe(GB)

Sayers, D. L.
Five Red Herrings
BBC (GB) 1975 dir. Robert Tronson
TVSe(GB)

Sayers, D. L.
Gaudy Night
BBC (GB) 1987 dir. Michael Simpson
TVSe(GB)

Sayers, D. L.
Have His Carcase
BBC (GB) 1987 dir. Christopher Hodson
TVSe(GB)

Sayers, D. L.
Murder Must Advertise
BBC (GB) 1973 dir. Rodney Bennett
TVSe(GB)

Sayers, D. L.
Nine Tailors, The
BBC (GB) 1974 dir. Raymond Menmuir
TVSe(GB)

Sayers, D. L.
Strong Poison
BBC (GB) 1987 dir. Christopher Hodson
TVSe(GB)

Sayers, D. L.
Unpleasantness at the Bellona Club, The
BBC (GB) 1973 dir. Ronald Wilson
TVSe(GB)

Sayers, G. and Silverman, A.
I am Third
Brian's Song
COL TV (US) 1971 dir. Buzz Kulik
TV(US)
COL TRISTAR (US) 2001 dir. John Gray
TV(US)

Scaling-Kiley, D. and Noona, M.
Albatross
Two Came Back
VZ/SERTNER (US) 1997 dir. Dick Lowry
TV(US)

Scarborough, C.
Aftershock: Earthquake in New York
HALLMARK (US) 1999 dir. Mikael Salomon
TVSe(US)

Scepanovic, B.
Mort de Monsieur Golouja, La
Julian Po
CYPRESS (US) 1997 dir. Alan Wade

Schaefer, J.
Monte Walsh
CIN CEN (US) 1970
dir. William A. Fraker

Schaefer, J.
Shane
PAR (US) 1953 dir. George Stevens

Schary, D.
Sunrise at Campobello
P
WAR (US) 1960 dir. Vincent J. Donehue

Schauffler, E.
Parnell
P
MGM (US) 1937 dir. John M. Stahl

Scherfig, H.
Det Forsomte Forar
REGNER (Den) 1993 dir. Peter Schroder

Schiff, R.
Ladies Room, The
P
Romy and Michele's High School Reunion
TOUCHSTONE (US) 1997 dir. David Mirkin

Schiller, L.
Perfect Murder, Perfect Town
FOX TV (US) 2000 dir. Kris Kristofferson
TVSe(US)

Schiller, L. and Willwerth, J.
American Tragedy: The Uncensored Story of the Simpson Defense
American Tragedy, An
FOX TV (US) 2000 dir. Lawrence Schiller
TVSe(US)

Schine, C.
Love Letter, The
DREAMWORKS (US) 1999 dir. Peter Chan

Schine, C.
Rameau's Niece
Misadventures of Margaret, The
GRANADA (GB/Fr/US) 1998 dir. Brian Skeet

Schisgal, M.
Luv
P
COL (US) 1967 dir. Clive Donner

Schisgal, M.
Tiger, The
P
Tiger Makes Out, The
COL (US) 1967 dir. Arthur Hiller

Schlesinger, Jr., A. M.
Robert Kennedy and his Times
COL (US) 1985 dir. Marvin J. Chomsky
TVSe(US)

Schmidt, L.
Only a Dream
P
One Hour With You
PAR (US) 1932 dir. George Cukor, Ernst Lubitsch
M

Schmitt, E.-E.
Libertine, Le

P

STUDIO CANAL+ (Fr) 2000 dir. Gabriel Aghion

Schneider, R.
Schlafes Bruder

Brother Of Sleep
BA FILMPROD (Ger) 1995 dir. Joseph Vilsmaier

Schnitzler, A.
Casanovas Heimfahrt

Retour de Casanova, Le
STUDIO CANAL+ (Fr) 1992 dir. Edouard Niermans

Schnitzler, A.
Liebelei

P

ELITE (Fr) 1932 dir. Max Ophuls

Schnitzler, A.
Ronde, La

P

S. GARDINE (Fr) 1950 dir. Max Ophuls
INTEROPA (Fr) 1964 dir. Roger Vadim

Schnitzler, A.
Traumnovelle

Eyes Wide Shut
WAR (GB/US) 1999 dir. Stanley Kubrick

Schoendoerffer, P.
Crabe Tambour, Le

AMLF (Fr) 1977
dir. Pierre Schoendoerffer

Schoendoerffer, P.
Farewell to the King

ORION (US) 1989 dir. John Milius

Scholefield, A.
Venom

PAR (GB) 1982 dir. Piers Haggard

Schott, M.
Murphy's Romance

COL (US) 1985 dir. Martin Ritt

Schrank, J. and Dunning, P.
Page Miss Glory

P

PAR (US) 1935 dir. Mervyn LeRoy

Schreiber, F. R.
Sybil

LORIMAR (US) 1976 dir. Daniel Petrie
TVSe(US)

Schulberg, B. W.
Harder They Fall

COL (US) 1956 dir. Mark Robson

Schulberg, B. W.
On the Waterfront

COL (US) 1954 dir. Elia Kazan

Schulberg, B. W.
Your Arkansas Traveller

Face in the Crowd, A
WAR (US) 1957 dir. Elia Kazan

Schulman, A.
Hole in the Head, A

P

UA (US) 1959 dir. Frank Capra

Schutt, R.
Kadisbellan

Slingshot, The
NORDISK (Den/Swe) 1993 dir. Ake Sandgren

Schutze, J.
Bully: A True Story of High School Revenge

Bully
STUDIO CANAL+ (Fr/GB) 2000 dir. Larry Clark

Schutze, J.
Preacher's Girl

Black Widow Murders: The Blanche Tayor Moore Story
LORIMAR (US) 1993 dir. Alan Metzger
TV(US)

Schwanitz, D.
Campus, Der
CONSTANTIN (Ger) 1998 dir. Sonke Wortmann

Schwartz, S.
Like Mother Like Me

Like Mom, Like Me
CBS ENT (US) 1978
dir. Michael Pressman
TV(US)

Schwarz, T.
Deadly Whispers
HILL-FIELDS (US) 1995 dir. Bill Norton
TV(US)

Schweizer, R.
Last Chance, The
MGM (Switz) 1945
dir. Leopold Lindtberg

Sciascia, L.
Context, The
Illustrious Corpses
PEA/LAA (It) 1976 dir. Francesco Rosi

Sclavi, T.
Dellamorte Dellamore
DARC (It/Fr/Ger) 1994 dir. Michele Soavi

Sclavi, T.
Nero
INTERSOUND (It) 1992 dir. Giancarlo Soldi

Scortia, T. N. and Robinson, R. M.
Glass Inferno, The
Towering Inferno, The
COL-WAR (US) 1975
dir. John Gullermin, Irwin Allen

Scortia, T. N. and Robinson, R. M.
Gold Crew, The
Fifth Missile, The
MGM/UA TV (US) 1986
dir. Larry Peerce
TV(US)

Scott, A.
At the Midnight Hour
ALLIANCE (Can) 1995 dir. Charles Jarrott
TV(Can)

Scott, A.
Great Man's Whiskers, The
P
UN TV (US) 1973 dir. Philip Leacock
TV(US)

Scott, A. and Haight, G.
Goodbye Again
P
Honeymoon for Three
WAR (US) 1941 dir. Lloyd Bacon

Scott, J. M.
Sea Wyf and Biscuit
Sea-Wife
FOX (GB) 1957 dir. Bob McNaught

Scott, P.
Raj Quartet, The
Jewel in the Crown, The
GRANADA (GB) 1984
dir. Jim O'Brien, Christopher Morahan
TVSe(GB)

Scott, P.
Staying On
GRANADA (GB) 1980
dir. Silvio Narizzano, Waris Hussein
TV(GB)

Scott, R. L.
God is My Co-Pilot
WAR (US) 1945 dir. Robert Florey

Scott, Sir W.
Bride of Lammermoor, The
Lucia
LEX (GB) 1999 dir. Don Boyd

Scott, Sir W.
Fortunes of Nigel, The
BBC (GB) 1974 dir. Peter Cregeen
TVSe(GB)

Scott, Sir W.
Ivanhoe
MGM (GB) 1952 dir. Richard Thorpe
BBC (GB) 1970 dir. David Maloney
TVSe(GB)
COL (US/GB) 1982
dir. Douglas Canfield
TV(GB/US)
BBC/A&E (GB) 1997 dir. Stuart Orme
TVSe(GB)

Scott, Sir W.
Ivanhoe
Young Ivanhoe
FILMLINE (Can/Fr) 1995 dir. Ralph L.
Thomas
TV(Can/Fr)

Scott, Sir W.
Quentin Durward
Adventures of Quentin Durward, The
MGM (GB) 1955 dir. Richard Thorpe
US title: Quentin Durward

Scott, Sir W.
Rob Roy
BBC (GB) 1977 dir. Bob Hird
TVSe(GB)

Scott, Sir W.
Talisman, The
BBC (GB) 1980 dir. Richard Bramall
TVSe(GB)

Scott, Sir W.
Talisman, The
King Richard and the Crusaders
WAR (US) 1954 dir. David Butler

Scott, Sir W.
Woodstock
BBC (GB) 1973 dir. David Maloney
TVSe(GB)

Scott, W.
Umbrella Man, The
P
London by Night
MGM (US) 1937 dir. William Thiele

Scruggs, J. C. and Swerdlow, J. L.
To Heal a Nation
ORION TV (US) 1988
dir. Michael Pressman
TV(US)

Scudder, K. J.
Prisoners are People
Unchained
WAR (US) 1955 dir. Hall Bartlett

Seals, D.
Pow Wow Highway
WAR (US) 1989 dir. Jonathan Wacks

Searls, H.
Crowded Sky, The
WAR (US) 1960 dir. Joseph Pevney

Searls, H.
Lost Prince, The: Young Joe, The
Forgotten Kennedy
Young Joe, the Forgotten Kennedy
ABC (US) 1977 dir. Richard T. Heffron
TV(US)

Searls, H.
Overboard
FAC-NEW (US) 1978 dir. John Newland
TV(US)

Seaton, G.
Cockeyed Miracle, The
P
MGM (US) 1946 dir. S. Sylvan Simon

Secondari, J. H.
Coins in the Fountain
Pleasure Seekers, The
FOX (US) 1964 dir. Jean Negulesco

Secondari, J.
Coins in the Fountain
Three Coins in the Fountain
FOX (US) 1954 dir. Jean Negulesco

Seeley, C.
Storm Fear
UA (US) 1955 dir. Cornel Wilde

Sefchovich, S.
Demasiado Amor
COLIFILMS (Fr/Sp) 2001 dir. Ernesto
Rimoch

Seff, M. and Wilson, F.
Blessed Event
P
WAR (US) 1932 dir. Roy del Ruth

Segal, E.
Love Story
PAR (US) 1970 dir. Arthur Hiller

Segal, E.
Man, Woman and Child
PAR (US) 1983 dir. Dick Richards

Segal, E.
Oliver's Story
PAR (US) 1978 dir. John Korty

Segal, E.
Only Love
HALLMARK (US) 1998 dir. John Erman
TV(US)

Segall, H.
For Heaven's Sake
P
FOX (US) 1950 dir. George Seaton

Segall, H.
Halfway to Heaven
P
Heaven Can Wait
PAR (US) 1978 dir. Warren Beatty, Buck
Henry

Segall, H.
Halfway to Heaven
P
Here Comes Mr. Jordan
COL (US) 1941 dir. Alexander Hall

Seghers, A.
Seventh Cross, The
MGM (US) 1944 dir. Fred Zinnemann

Seidler, T.
Rat's Tale, A
MONTY (US) 1998 dir. Michael F. Huse
A, Ch

Selby, Jr., H.
Last Exit to Brooklyn
GUILD (Ger) 1989 dir. Ulrich Edel

Selby, Jr., H.
Requeim for a Dream
ARTISAN (US) 2000 dir. Darren
Aronofsky

Selinko, A.
Desirée
FOX (US) 1954 dir. Henry Koster

Sellers, S.
Terror on Highway 59
Terror on Highway 91
CBS (US) 1989 dir. Jerry Jameson
TV(US)

Sellier, Jr., C. E.
Capture of Grizzly Adams, The
TAFT (US) 1982 dir. Don Kessler
TV(US)

Selvin, J.
Ricky Nelson—Idol For a Generation
Ricky Nelson: Original Teen Idol
VH1 (US) 1999 dir. Sturla Gunnarsson
TV(US)

Selwyn, E.
Barbarian, The
P
MGM (US) 1933 dir. Sam Wood
GB title: Night in Cairo, A

Selwyn, E.
Mirage, The
P
Possessed
MGM (US) 1931 dir. Clarence Brown

Semple, L.
Golden Fleecing, The
P
Honeymoon Machine, The
MGM (US) 1961 dir. Richard Thorpe

Sender, R. J.
Days of Dawn
Valentina
OFELIA (Sp) 1983
dir. Antonio José Betancor

Senesh, H.
Diaries of Hannah Senesh, The
Hanna's War
CANNON (US) 1988
dir. Menahem Golan

Sepulveda, L.
Old Man Who Read Love Stories, The
KINO VISION (Fr/Aust/Neth) 2001
dir. Rolf de Heer

Sepulveda, L.
Story of a Seagull and the Cat who
Taught her to Fly
Zorba and Lucky
CECCHI (It) 1998 dir. Elzo D'Alo
A, Ch

Serling, R.
Patterns
P
UA (US) 1956 dir. Fielder Cook
GB title: Patterns of Power

Serling, R.
Requiem for a Heavyweight
P
COL (US) 1962 dir. Ralph Nelson
GB title: Blood Money

Serling, R. J.
President's Plane is Missing, The
ABC (US) 1973 dir. Daryl Duke
TV(US)

Serraillier, I.
Silver Sword, The
BBC (GB) 1971 dir. Joan Craft
TVSe(GB)

Seton, A.
Dragonwyck
FOX (US) 1946
dir. Joseph L. Mankiewicz

Seton, A.
Foxfire
UI (US) 1955 dir. Joseph Pevney

Seton, E. T.
Biography of a Grizzly, The

King of Grizzlies
DISNEY (US) 1970 dir. Ron Kelly

Seton, E. T.
Biography of a Grizzly and Other Animal Stories, The

Legend of Lobo, The
DISNEY (US) 1962 dir. James Algar
Ch

Seward, F. A.
Gold for the Caesars

MGM (US) 1964 dir. Andre de Toth

Sewell, A.
Black Beauty

FOX (US) 1946 dir. Max Nosseck
TIGON (GB) 1971 dir. James Hill
UN (US) 1978 dir. Daniel Haller
Ch, TVSe(US)
WAR (US/GB) 1994 dir. Caroline Thompson

Sexton, L. G.
Points of Light

Reunion
RHI (US) 1994 dir. Lee Grant
TV(US)

Seymour, G.
Field of Blood

Informant, The
SHOWTIME (US) 1998 dir. Jim McBride
TV(US)

Seymour, G.
Glory Boys, The

YTV (GB) 1984 dir. Michael Ferguson
TV(GB)

Seymour, G.
Harry's Game

YTV (GB) 1982
dir. Lawrence Gordon Clark
TVSe(GB)

Seymour, H.
Infernal Idol

Craze
EMI (GB) 1973 dir. Freddie Francis

Shaara, M.
For Love of the Game

UN (US) 1999 dir. Sam Raimi

Shaara, M.
Killer Angels, The

Gettysburg
TURNER (US) 1993 dir. Ronald F. Maxwell

Shabtai, Y.
Past Continuous

Devarim
AGAV (Israel) 1995 dir. Amos Gitai

Shadbolt, M.
Among the Cinders

NEW WORLD (US) 1985
dir. Rolf Haedrich

Shadbolt, M.
Chunuk Bair

P
AVALON (NZ) 1992 dir. Dale G. Bradley

Shaefer, C.
Other Mother, The

O'HARA-HORO (US) 1995 dir. Bethany Rooney
TV(US)

Shaffer, A.
Sleuth

P
FOX (GB) 1972
dir. Joseph L. Mankiewicz

Shaffer, P.
Amadeus

P
ORION (US) 1984 dir. Milos Forman

Shaffer, P.
Equus
P
UA (GB) 1977 dir. Sidney Lumet

Shaffer, P.
Five Finger Exercise
P
COL (US) 1962 dir. Delbert Mann

Shaffer, P.
Private Ear, The
P
Pad (And How to Use It), The
UI (US) 1966 dir. Brian C. Hutton

Shaffer, P.
Public Eye, The
P
Follow Me
UN (GB) 1972 dir. Carol Reed
US title: Public Eye, The

Shaffer, P.
Royal Hunt of the Sun, The
P
RANK (GB) 1969 dir. Irving Lerner

Shaffer, R. K.
Finger Man, The
Lady Killer
WAR (US) 1933 dir. Roy del Ruth

Shagan, S.
Formula, The
MGM (US) 1980 dir. John G. Avildsen

Shakespeare, W.
Antony and Cleopatra
P
RANK (GB) 1972 dir. Charlton Heston
ITV (GB) 1974 dir. Trevor Nunn, Jon
Scoffield
TV(GB)

Shakespeare, W.
As You Like It
P
FOX (GB) 1936 dir. Paul Czinner
SANDS (GB) 1992 dir. Christine Edzard

Shakespeare, W.
Comedy of Errors, The
P
Boys from Syracuse, The
UN (US) 1940 dir. E. A. Sutherland
M

Shakespeare, W.
Hamlet
P
TC (GB) 1948 dir. Laurence Olivier
M. EVANS (US) 1953 dir. Albert
McCleery
TV(US)
CLASSIC (USSR) 1964
dir. Grigori Kozintsev
COL (GB) 1969 dir. Tony Richardson
ATV/UN (GB/US) 1970 dir. Peter Wood
TV(GB/US)
WAR/GUILD (US/GB) 1990
dir. Franco Zeffirelli
COL (GB) 1996 dir. Kenneth Branagh
MIRAMAX (US) 2000 dir. Michael
Almereyda
HALLMARK (US) 2000 dir. Campbell
Scott, Eric Simonson
TV(US)

Shakespeare, W.
Henry V
P
TC (GB) 1944 dir. Laurence Olivier
RENAISSANCE (GB) 1989
dir. Kenneth Branagh

Shakespeare, W.
Julius Caesar
P
MGM (US) 1953
dir. Joseph L. Mankiewicz
MGM (GB) 1969 dir. Stuart Burge

Shakespeare, W.
King Lear

P
COL (Den/GB) 1970 dir. Peter Brook
GRANADA (GB) 1983
dir. Michael Elliott
TV(GB)
CANNON (US) 1988
dir. Jean-Luc Godard

Shakespeare, W.
King Lear

P
Ran
NIPPON HERALD (Jap) 1985 dir. Akira
Kurosawa

Shakespeare, W.
King Richard II

P
M. EVANS (US) 1954
dir. George Schaefer
TV(US)

Shakespeare, W.
Love's Labour's Lost

P
MIRAMAX (GB/Fr) 2000 dir. Kenneth
Branagh
M

Shakespeare, W.
Macbeth

P
REP (US) 1948 dir. Orson Welles
M. EVANS (US) 1954
dir. George Schaefer
TV(US)
COMPASS (US) 1960
dir. George Schaefer
TV(US)
COL-WAR (GB) 1971
dir. Roman Polanski
CROMWELL (GB) 1997 dir. Jeremy
Freeston

Shakespeare, W.
Merchant of Venice, The

P
ATV (GB) 1974 dir. Jonathan Miller
TV(GB)

Shakespeare, W.
Midsummer Night's Dream, A

P
Children's Midsummer Night's Dream, A
SANDS (GB) 2001 dir. Christine Edzard
Ch

Shakespeare, W.
Midsummer Night's Dream, A

P
WAR (US) 1935 dir. Max Reinhardt
ITV (GB) 1964 dir. Joan Kemp-Welch
TV(GB)
COL (US) 1967 dir. Dan Eriksen
EAGLE (GB) 1968 dir. Peter Hall
MAINLINE (GB/Sp) 1985
dir. Celestino Corrado
CAPITOL (GB) 1996 dir. Adrian Noble
FOX (GB) 1999 dir. Michael Hoffman

Shakespeare, W.
Much Ado About Nothing

P
GOLDWYN (GB/US) 1993 dir. Kenneth
Branagh

Shakespeare, W.
Othello

P
MERCURY (US/Fr) 1951
dir. Orson Welles
EAGLE (GB) 1965 dir. Stuart Burge
COL (US/GB) 1995 dir. Oliver Parker

Shakespeare, W.
Othello

P
O
LIONS GATE (US) 2001 dir. Tim Blake
Nelson

Shakespeare, W.
Othello

P
Othello, the Black Commando
EUROCINE (Sp/Fr) 1982 dir. Max H.
Boulois

Shakespeare, W.
Richard III

P
BL (GB) 1955 dir. Laurence Olivier
BRIT SCREEN (GB) dir. Richard
Loncraine

Shakespeare, W.
Richard III

P
Looking for Richard
FOX (US) 1996 dir. Al Pacino

Shakespeare, W.
Romeo and Juliet

P
MGM (US) 1936 dir. George Cukor
GFD (GB) 1954 dir. Renato Castellani
PAR (GB) 1968 dir. Franco Zeffirelli
FOX (US) 1996 dir. Baz Lurhmann

Shakespeare, W.
Romeo and Juliet

P
Tromeo and Juliet
TROMA (US) 1996 dir. Lloyd Kaufman

Shakespeare, W.
Taming of the Shrew, The

P
M. EVANS (US) 1956
dir. George Schaefer
TV(US)
COL (US) 1967 dir. Franco Zeffirelli

Shakespeare, W.
Taming of the Shrew, The

P
Kiss Me Kate
MGM (US) 1953 dir. George Sidney
M
MILBERG (US) 1958 dir. George
Schaefer
TV(US)

Shakespeare, W.
Taming of the Shrew, The

P
10 Things I Hate About You
TOUCHSTONE (US) 1999 dir. Gil
Junger

Shakespeare, W.
Tempest, The

P
COMPASS (US) 1960
dir. George Schaefer
TV(US)
MAINLINE (GB) 1980
dir. Derek Jarman
NBC STUDIOS (US) 1998 dir. Jack
Bender
TV(US)

Shakespeare, W.
Tempest, The

P
Prospero's Books
FILM 4 (GB/Fr) 1991
dir. Peter Greenaway

Shakespeare, W.
Titus Andronicus

P
Titus
OVERSEAS (US/It) 1999 dir. Julie
Taymor

Shakespeare, W.
Twelfth Night

P
MILBERG (US) 1957 dir. David Greene
TV(US)
RENAISSANCE (GB) 1996 dir. Trevor
Nunn

Shakespeare, W.
Winter's Tale, The
P
WAR (GB) 1968 dir. Frank Dunlop

Shankar
Company Limited
CHILRANGALI (Ind) 1971
dir. Satyajit Ray

Shannon, E.
Desperados: Latin Drug Lords, US Lawmen and the War America Can't Win

Drug Wars: The Camarena Story
ZZY (US) 1990 dir. Brian Gibson
TVSe(US)

Shannon, E.
Desperados: Latin Drug Lords, US Lawmen and the War America Can't Win

Drug Wars: The Cocaine Cartel
ZZY (US) 1992 dir. Paul Krasny
TVSe(US)

Shannon, R.
Fabulous Ann Medlock

Adventures of Captain Fabian, The
REP (US) 1951 dir. William Marshall

Shapiro, L.
Sealed Verdict
PAR (US) 1948 dir. Lewis Allen

Shapiro, L.
Sixth of June, The

D-Day the Sixth of June
FOX (US) 1956 dir. Henry Koster

Shapiro, S.
Time to Remember, A

Running Against Time
FINNEGAN-PINCHUK (US) 1990 dir.
Bruce Seth Green
TV(US)

Sharp, D.
Conflict of Wings

BL (GB) 1953 dir. John Eldridge
US title: Fuss Over Feathers

Sharp, M.
Britannia Mews

TCF (GB) 1948 dir. Jean Negulesco
US title: Forbidden Street, The

Sharp, M.
Cluny Brown

FOX (US) 1946 dir. Ernst Lubitsch

Sharp, M.
Nutmeg Tree, The

Julia Misbehaves
MGM (US) 1948 dir. Jack Conway

Sharp, M.
Rescuers, The; Miss Bianca

Rescuers, The
DISNEY (US) 1977
dir. Wolfgang Reitherman
A, Ch

Sharpe, T.
Blott on the Landscape

BBC (GB) 1985 dir. Roger Bamford
TVSe(GB)

Sharpe, T.
Porterhouse Blue

CHANNEL 4 (GB) 1987 dir. Robert
Knights
TVSe(GB)

Sharpe, T.
Wilt

RANK (GB) 1989 dir. Michael Tuchner

Sharpe, T.
Wilt

Misadventures of Mr. Wilt, The
GOLDWYN (US) 1990
dir. Michael Tuchner

Shaw, C.
Heaven Knows Mr. Allison
FOX (US) 1957 dir. John Huston

Shaw, G. B.
Androcles and the Lion
P
RKO (US) 1952 dir. Chester Erskine

Shaw, G. B.
Arms And The Man
P
WARDOUR (GB) 1932 dir. Cecil Lewis
ARGENT (GB) 1982
TV(GB)

Shaw, G. B.
Arms and the Man
P
Helden
SOKAL/GOLDBAUM (Ger) 1959
dir. Franz Peter Wirth

Shaw, G. B.
Caesar and Cleopatra
P
RANK (GB) 1945 dir. Gabriel Pascal
TALENT (US) 1976
dir. James Cellan Jones
TV(US)

Shaw, G. B.
Captain Brassbound's Conversion
P
COMPASS (US) 1960
dir. George Schaefer
TV(US)

Shaw, G. B.
Devil's Disciple, The
P
M. EVANS (US) 1955
dir. George Schaefer
TV(US)
UA (GB) 1959 dir. Guy Hamilton

Shaw, G. B.
Doctor's Dilemma, The
P
MGM (GB) 1958 dir. Anthony Asquith

Shaw, G. B.
Great Catherine
P
WAR (GB) 1968 dir. Gordon Flemyng

Shaw, G. B.
How He Lied to Her Husband
P
BI (GB) 1931 dir. Cecil Lewis

Shaw, G. B.
Love Among the Artists
GRANADA (GB) 1979 dir. Howard
Baker, Marc Miller
TVSe(GB)

Shaw, G. B.
Major Barbara
P
PASCAL (GB) 1941 dir. Gabriel Pascal

Shaw, G. B.
Man and Superman
P
MILBERG (US) 1956
dir. George Schaefer
TV(US)

Shaw, G. B.
Millionairess, The
P
FOX (GB) 1960 dir. Anthony Asquith

Shaw, G. B.
Pygmalion
P
MGM (GB) 1938 dir. Anthony Asquith
COMPASS (US) 1963
dir. George Schaefer
TV(US)

Shaw, G. B.
Pygmalion
P
My Fair Lady
WAR (US) 1964 dir. George Cukor
M

Shaw, G. B.
Saint Joan
P
UA (GB) 1957 dir. Otto Preminger
COMPASS (US) 1967
dir. George Schaefer
TV(US)

Shaw, I.
Beggarman, Thief
UN TV (US) 1979 dir. Lawrence Doheny
TVSe(US)

Shaw, I.
Evening in Byzantium
UN TV (US) 1978 dir. Jerry London
TVSe(US)

Shaw, I.
Gentle People, The
P
Out of the Fog
WAR (US) 1941 dir. Anatole Litvak

Shaw, I.
In the French Style
COL (US/Fr) 1963 dir. Robert Parrish

Shaw, I.
Rich Man, Poor Man
UN (US) 1976 dir. David Greene, Boris
Sagal
TVSe(US)

Shaw, I.
Then There Were Three
Three
UA (GB) 1969 dir. James Salter

Shaw, I.
Tip on a Dead Jockey
MGM (US) 1957 dir. Richard Thorpe
GB title: Time for Action

Shaw, I.
Two Weeks in Another Town
MGM (US) 1962 dir. Vincente Minnelli

Shaw, I.
Young Lions, The
FOX (US) 1958 dir. Edward Dmytryk

Shaw, R.
Hiding Place, The
Situation Hopeless But Not Serious
PAR (US) 1965 dir. Gottfried Reinhardt

Shawn, W.
Designated Mourner, The
P
BBC (GB) 1997 dir. David Hare

Shea, T.
Sarah and Son
PAR (US) 1930 dir. Dorothy Arzner

Shearer, A.
Greatest Store in the World, The
BBC (GB) 1999 dir. Jane Prowse
TV(GB)

Shearing, J.
Airing in a Closed Carriage
Mark of Cain, The
TC (GB) 1948 dir. Brian Desmond Hurst

Shearing, J.
Blanche Fury
CIN (GB) 1948 dir. Marc Allégret

Shearing, J.
For Her to See
So Evil My Love
PAR (GB) 1948 dir. Lewis Allen

Sheckley, R.
Game of X, The

Condorman
DISNEY (US) 1981 dir. Charles Jarrot

Sheckley, R.
Immortality, Inc.

Freejack
WAR (US) 1992 dir. Geoff Murphy

Sheckley, R.
Prize of Peril, The

UGC (Fr/Yugo) 1983 dir. Yves Boisset

Sheean, V.
Personal History

Foreign Correspondent
UA (US) 1940 dir. Alfred Hitchcock

Sheehan, N.
Bright Shining Lie, A: John Paul Vann and America in Vietnam

Bright Shining Lie, A
HBO (US) 1998 dir. Terry George
TV(US)

Sheldon, E.
Romance

P
MGM (US) 1930 dir. Clarence Brown

Sheldon, E.
Song of Songs

P
PAR (US) 1933 dir. Rouben Mamoulian

Sheldon, E. and Barnes, M. A.
Dishonoured Lady

P
MARS (US) 1947 dir. Robert Stevenson

Sheldon, S.
Bloodline

PAR (US) 1979 dir. Terence Young

Sheldon, S.
If Tomorrow Comes

CBS ENT (US) 1986 dir. Jerry London
TVSe(US)

Sheldon, S.
Master of the Game

ROSEMONT (US/GB) 1984
dir. Kevin Connor, Harvey Hart
TVSe(GB/US)

Sheldon, S.
Memories of Midnight

DOVE AUDIO (US) 1991 dir. Gary Nelson
TVSe(US)

Sheldon, S.
Naked Face, The

CANNON (US) 1984 dir. Bryan Forbes

Sheldon, S.
Nothing Lasts Forever

GERBER/ITC (US) 1995 dir. Jack Bender
TVSe(US)

Sheldon, S.
Other Side of Midnight, The

FOX (US) 1977 dir. Charles Jarrott

Sheldon, S.
Rage of Angels

NBC (US) 1983 dir. Buzz Kulik
TVSe(US)

Sheldon, S.
Sands of Time, The

WAR TV (US) 1992 dir. Gary Nelson
TV(US)

Sheldon, S.
Stranger in the Mirror, A

SPELLING TV (US) 1993 dir. Charles Jarrot
TV(US)

Sheldon, S.
Windmills of the Gods
ITC (US) 1988 dir. Lee Philips
TVSe(US)

Shellabarger, S.
Captain from Castille
FOX (US) 1947 dir. Henry King

Shellabarger, S.
Prince of Foxes
FOX (US) 1949 dir. Henry King

Shelley, E.
Pick Up Girl
P
Too Young to Go
RANK (GB) 1959 dir. Muriel Box

Shelley, M. W.
Frankenstein
UN (US) 1931 dir. James Whale
CURTIS (US) 1973
dir. Glenn Jordan
TV(US)
D. WICKES (US) 1993 dir. David
Wickes
TV(US)
TRISTAR (US/GB) 1994 dir. Kenneth
Branagh

Shelley, M. W.
Frankenstein
Curse of Frankenstein, The
WAR (GB) 1957 dir. Terence Fisher

Shelley, M. W.
Frankenstein
Frankenstein: The True Story
UN TV (US) 1973 dir. Jack Smight
TVSe(US)

Shelley, P. B.
Zastrozzi
CHANNEL 4 (GB) 1986 dir. David G.
Hopkins
TVSe(GB)

Shelley, S.
McKenzie Break, The
UA (GB) 1970 dir. Lamont Johnson

Shelton, W. R.
Stowaway to the Moon: The Camelot
Odyssey
Stowaway to the Moon
FOX (US) 1975
dir. Andrew V. McLaglen
TV(US)

Shem, S.
House of God, The
UA (US) 1984 dir. Donald Wrye

Shemin, M.
Little Riders, The
DISNEY CH (US) 1996 dir. Kevin
Connor
TV(US)

Shepard, S.
Curse of the Starving Class
P
SHOWTIME (US) 1995 dir. Michael
McClary
TV(US)

Shepard, S.
Fool for Love
P
CANNON (US) 1985 dir. Robert
Altman

Shepard, S.
Simpatico
P
FINE LINE (US/GB) 1999 dir. Matthew
Warchus

Shepherd, J.
In God We Trust, All Others Pay Cash
Christmas Story, A
MGM/UA (US) 1983 dir. Bob Clark

Shepherd, J.
In God We Trust, All Others Pay Cash; Wanda Hickey's Night of Golden Memories and Other Disasters

It Runs in the Family
MGM (US) 1994 dir. Bob Clark

Shepherd, J.
Never Tell Me Never

GOLDEN SQUARE (Aust) 1998 dir. David Elfick
TV(Aust)

Sheppard, S.
Monte Carlo

HIGHGATE (US) 1986
dir. Anthony Page
TVSe(US)

Sheppard, S. R. and Cooper, C. L.
Mockery of Justice: The True Story of the Sheppard Murder Case

My Father's Shadow: The Sam Sheppard Story
JAFFE/BRAUNSTEIN (US) 1998 dir. Peter Levin
TV(US)

Sherburne, Z.
Stranger in the House

Memories Never Die
UN TV (US) 1982 dir. Sandor Stern
TV(US)

Sherlock, J.
Ordeal of Major Grigsby, The

Last Grenade, The
CINERAMA (GB) 1969
dir. Gordon Flemyng

Sherman, M.
Bent

P
CHANNEL 4 FILMS (GB) 1997 dir. Sean Mathias

Sherriff, R. C.
Home at Seven

P
BL (GB) 1952 dir. Ralph Richardson
US title: Murder on Monday

Sherriff, R. C.
Journey's End

P
Aces High
EMI (GB/Fr) 1976 dir. Jack Gold

Sherriff, R. C.
Journey's End

P
TIFFANY (GB/US) 1930
dir. James Whale

Sherry, E.
Sudden Fear

RKO (US) 1952 dir. David Miller

Sherry, G.
Black Limelight

P
ABPC (GB) 1938 dir. Paul Stein

Sherry, S.
Liverpool Cats, The

Rocky O'Rourke
BBC (GB) 1976 dir. John Prowse
TVSe(GB)

Sherwin, D. and Howlett, J.
Crusaders

If ...
PAR (GB) 1968 dir. Lindsay Anderson

Sherwood, R. E.
Abe Lincoln of Illinois

P
Abe Lincoln in Illinois
RKO (US) 1940 dir. John Cromwell
COMPASS (US) 1964
dir. George Schaefer
TV(US)

Sherwood, R. E.
Idiot's Delight

P

MGM (US) 1939 dir. Clarence Brown

Sherwood, R. E.
Petrified Forest, The

P

WAR (US) 1936 dir. Archie Mayo

Sherwood, R. E.
Petrified Forest, The

P

Escape in the Desert
WAR (US) 1945 dir. Edward A. Blatt

Sherwood, R. E.
Queen's Husband, The

P

Royal Bed, The
RKO (US) 1931 dir. Lowell Sherman

Sherwood, R. E.
Reunion in Vienna

P

MGM (US) 1933 dir. Sidney Franklin

Sherwood, R. E.
Road to Rome, The

P

Jupiter's Darling
MGM (US) 1954 dir. George Sidney

Sherwood, R. E.
There Shall Be No Night

P

MILBERG (US) 1956
dir. George Schaefer
TV(US)

Sherwood, R. E.
This is New York

P

Two Kinds of Women
PAR (US) 1932 dir. William C. De Mille

Sherwood, R. E.
Waterloo Bridge

P

UN (US) 1931 dir. James Whale
MGM (US) 1940 dir. Mervyn LeRoy

Sherwood, R. E.
Waterloo Bridge

P

Gaby
MGM (US) 1956 dir. Curtis Bernhardt

Shevelove, B. and Gelbart, L.
Funny Thing Happened on the Way to the Forum, A

P

UA (GB) 1966 dir. Richard Lester

Shiba, R.
With a Lock of Hair Over His Forehead; Revolt of the Mountain, The; Chronicles of the Shinsengumi

Taboo
IMAGICA (Jap/Fr) 1999 dir. Nagisa Oshima

Shiber, E.
Paris Underground

UA (US) 1945 dir. Gregory Ratoff
GB title: Madame Pimpernel

Shiel, M. P.
Purple Cloud, The

World, The Flesh and the Devil, The
MGM (US) 1959
dir. Ronald MacDougall

Shields, C.
Swann

NORSTAR (Can/GB) 1996 dir. Anna Benson Gyles

Shiina, M.
My Sons

OTANI (Jap) 1992 dir. Yoji Yamada

Shilts, R.
And the Band Played On
HBO (US) 1993 dir. Roger Spottiswoode
TV(US)

Shimao, T.
Shi No Toge
SHOCHIKU (Jap) 1990 dir. Kohei Oguri

Shimomura, T. and Markoff, J.
Takedown
DIMENSION (US) 2000 dir. Joe
Chappelle

Shirer, W.
Nightmare Years, The
CONSOL (US) 1989 dir. Anthony Page
TV(US)

Shirk, A.
Ape, The
P
MON (US) 1940 dir. William Nigh

Shirreffs, G. D.
Trails End
Oregon Passage
ABP (US) 1958 dir. Paul Landres

Shisgall, O.
Swastika
Man I Married, The
TCF (US) 1940 dir. Irving Pichel

Shivers, L.
Here to get my Baby out of Jail
Summer Heat
ATLANTIC (US) 1987
dir. Michie Gleason

Sholokhov, M.
And Quiet Flows the Don
Quiet Flows the Don
GORKI (USSR) 1958
dir. Sergei Gerasimov

Shores, D.
Daddy's Dyin' ... Who's Got the Will?
P
MGM/UA (US) 1990 dir. Jack Fisk

Shores, D.
Sordid Lives
P
DAVIS (US) 2000 dir. Del Shores

Short, L.
Albuquerque
PAR (US) 1948 dir. Ray Enright

Short, L.
Ambush
MGM (US) 1949 dir. Sam Wood

Short, L.
Coroner Creek
COL (US) 1948 dir. Ray Enright

Short, L.
Gunman's Choice
Blood on the Moon
RKO (US) 1948 dir. Robert Wise

Short, L.
Ramrod
UA (US) 1947 dir. André de Toth

Short, L.
Station West
RKO (US) 1948 dir. Sidney Lanfield

Short, L.
Vengeance Valley
MGM (US) 1951 dir. Richard Thorpe

Shreve, A.
Weight of Water
STUDIO CANAL+ (Fr/US) 2000 dir.
Kathryn Bigelow

Shreve, S. R.
Daughters of the New World

Will of Their Own, A
WAR (US) 1998 dir. Karen Arthur
TVSe(US)

Shulman, I.
Amboy Dukes, The

City Across The River
UI (US) 1949 dir. Maxwell Shane

Shulman, I.
Children of the Dark

Cry Tough
UA (US) 1959 dir. Paul Stanley

Shulman, I.
Cry Tough

Ring, The
UA (US) 1952 dir. Kurt Neumann

Shulman, I.
Harlow

PAR (US) 1965 dir. Gordon Douglas

Shulman, M. and Smith, R. P.
Tender Trap, The

P
MGM (US) 1955 dir. Charles Walters

Shulman, M.
Rally Round the Flag, Boys

FOX (US) 1958 dir. Leo McCarey

Shulman, N. B.
What? ... Dead Again?

Doc Hollywood
WAR (US) 1991
dir. Michael Caton-Jones

Shute, N.
Landfall

AB (GB) 1949 dir. Ken Annakin

Shute, N.
No Highway

FOX (GB) 1951 dir. Henry Koster
US title: No Highway in the Sky

Shute, N.
On the Beach

UA (US) 1959 dir. Stanley Kramer
SHOWTIME (US/Aust) 2000 dir.
Russell Mulcahy
TV(US/Aust)

Shute, N.
Pied Piper, The

FOX (US) 1942 dir. Irving Pichel

Shute, N.
Pied Piper, The

Crossing to Freedom
TELECOM/GRANADA (GB/US) 1990
dir. Norman Stone
TV(GB/US)

Shute, N.
Town like Alice, A

RANK (GB) 1956 dir. Jack Lee
US title: Rape of Malaya, The
AFC (Aust) 1981 dir. David Stevens
TVSe(Aust)

Siddons, A. R.
Heartbreak Hotel

Heart of Dixie
ORION (US) 1989 dir. Martin Davidson

Siddoway, R.
Christmas Wish, The

POLSON (US) 1998 dir. Ian Barry
TV(US)

Sidley, M.
Five Little Peppers and How They Grew

COL (US) 1939 dir. Charles Barton

Sieminski, W.
Woman from the Provinces, A

OKO (Pol) 1987 dir. Andrzej Baranski

Sienkiewicz, H.
Deluge, The
POLSKI (Pol) 1974 dir. Jerzy Hoffman

Sienkiewicz, H.
Knights of the Troubled Order
STUDIO (Pol) 1960
dir. Aleksander Ford

Sienkiewicz, H.
Quo Vadis
MGM (US) 1951 dir. Mervyn LeRoy
RAI (It) 1985 dir. Franco Rossi
TVSe(It)

Sierra, G. M.
Cradle Song, The
P
M. EVANS (US) 1956
dir. George Schaefer
TV(US)
COMPASS (US) 1960
dir. George Schaefer
TV(US)

Siggins, M.
Canadian Tragedy, A
Love and Hate: A Marriage Made in Hell
CBC/BBC (US/Can/GB) 1991
dir. Francis Mankiewicz
TVSe(US/Can/GB)

Sigurdardottir, S.
Voleur de Vie
FRANCE 3 (Fr) 1997 dir. Yves Angelo

Silliphant, S.
Maracaibo
PAR (US) 1958 dir. Cornel Wilde

Sillitoe, A.
General, The
Counterpoint
UI (US) 1968 dir. Ralph Nelson

Sillitoe, A.
Loneliness of the Long Distance
Runner, The
BL (GB) 1962 dir. Tony Richardson

Sillitoe, A.
Ragman's Daughter, The
FOX (GB) 1972 dir. Harold Becker

Sillitoe, A.
Saturday Night and Sunday Morning
BL (GB) 1960 dir. Karel Reisz

Silver, J.
Limbo
UN (US) 1972 dir. Mark Robson

Silverman, A.
Foster and Laurie
FRIES (US) 1975
dir. John Llewellyn Moxey
TV(US)

Silvis, R.
Occasional Hell, An
GREENLIGHT (US) 1996 dir. Salome
Breziner
TV(US)

Simenon, G.
Act of Passion
Forbidden Fruit
CAMEO-POLY (Fr) 1952
dir. Henri Verneuil

Simenon, G.
Battle of Nerves, A
Man on the Eiffel Tower, The
BL (US) 1948 dir. Burgess Meredith

Simenon, G.
Betty
MK2 (Fr) 1992 dir. Claude Chabrol

Simenon, G.
Bottom of the Bottle, The

TCF (US) 1956 dir. Henry Hathaway
GB title: Beyond the River

Simenon, G.
Brothers Rico, The

COL (US) 1957 dir. Phil Karlson

Simenon, G.
Brothers Rico, The

Family Rico, The
CBS (US) 1972 dir. Paul Wendkos
TV(US)

Simenon, G.
En Cas de Malheur

UCIL (Fr/It) 1958
dir. Claude Autant-Lara

Simenon, G.
En Cas de Malheur

In All Innocence
STUDIO CANAL+ (Fr) 1998 dir. Pierre
Jolivet

Simenon, G.
Fiançailles de M. Hire, Les

Monsieur Hire
ORION (Fr) 1989 dir. Patrice Leconte

Simenon, G.
Inconnu Dans La Maison, L'

STUDIO CANAL+ (Fr) 1992 dir.
Georges Lautner

Simenon, G.
Locataire, La

Etoile du Nord, L'
UA (Fr) 1982
dir. Pierre Granier-Deferre

Simenon, G.
Maigret Sets a Trap

JOLLY (Fr) 1957 dir. Jean Delannoy

Simenon, G.
Man Who Watched Trains Go By, The

EROS (GB) 1952 dir. Harold French

Simenon, G.
Monsieur La Souris

Midnight Episode
COL (GB) 1950 dir. Gordon Parry

Simenon, G.
Newhaven-Dieppe

Temptation Harbour
AB (GB) 1947 dir. Lance Comfort

Simenon, G.
Strangers in the House

Stranger in the House
JARFID (GB) 1967 dir. Pierre Rouve

Simmons, A.
Optimists of Nine Elms, The

SCOTIA-BARBER (GB) 1973
dir. Anthony Simmons

Simon, E.
Moonlight and Valentino

P
POLYGRAM (US) 1995 dir. David
Anspaugh

Simon, N.
Barefoot in the Park

P
PAR (US) 1967 dir. Gene Saks

Simon, N.
Biloxi Blues

P
UN (US) 1988 dir. Mike Nichols

Simon, N.
Brighton Beach Memoirs

P
UN (US) 1986 dir. Gene Saks

Simon, N.
Broadway Bound

P

ABC PRODS. (US) 1992 dir. Paul Bogart
TV(US)

Simon, N.
California Suite

P

COL (US) 1975 dir. Herbert Ross

Simon, N.
Chapter Two

P

COL (US) 1979 dir. Robert Moore

Simon, N.
Come Blow Your Horn

P

PAR (US) 1963 dir. Bud Yorkin

Simon, N.
Gingerbread Lady, The

P

Only When I Laugh
COL (US) 1981 dir. Glenn Jordan
GB title: It Only Hurts When I Laugh

Simon, N.
I Ought to be in Pictures

P

TCF (US) 1982 dir. Herbert Ross

Simon, N.
Jake's Women

P

RHI (US) 1996 dir. Glenn Jordan
TV(US)

Simon, N.
Last of the Red Hot Lovers

P

PAR (US) 1972 dir. Gene Saks

Simon, N.
Laughter on the 23rd Floor

P

SHOWTIME (US) 2000 dir. Richard
Benjamin
TV(US)

Simon, N.
London Suite

P

HALLMARK (US) 1996 dir. Jay
Sandrich
TV(US)

Simon, N.
Lost in Yonkers

P

COL (US) 1993 dir. Martha Coolidge

Simon, N.
Odd Couple, The: Together Again

P

PAR TV (US) 1993 dir. Robert Klane
TV(US)

Simon, N.
Odd Couple, The

P

PAR (US) 1968 dir. Gene Saks

Simon, N.
Plaza Suite

P

PAR (US) 1971 dir. Arthur Hiller
PAR (US) 1987 dir. Roger Beatty
TV(US)

Simon, N.
Prisoner of Second Avenue, The

P

WAR (US) 1975 dir. Melvin Frank

Simon, N.
Star Spangled Girl, The

P

PAR (US) 1971 dir. Jerry Paris

Simon, N.
Sunshine Boys, The
P
MGM (US) 1975 dir. Herbert Ross
HALLMARK (US) 1997 dir. John Erman
TV(US)

Simon, N., Fields, D. and Coleman, C.
Sweet Charity
P
UN (US) 1969 dir. Robert Fosse
M

Simon, R. L.
Big Fix, The
UN (US) 1978 dir. Jeremy Paul Kagan

Simon, R. L.
Heir
Jennifer on my Mind
UA (US) 1971 dir. Noel Black

Simpson, H.
Saraband for Dead Lovers
EL (GB) 1949 dir. Basil Dearden

Simpson, H.
Under Capricorn
WAR (GB) 1949 dir. Alfred Hitchcock
S. AUST (Aust) 1983
dir. Rod Hardy

Simpson, M.
Anywhere But Here
FOX (US) 1999 dir. Wayne Wang

Simpson, N. F.
One Way Pendulum
P
UA (GB) 1964 dir. Peter Yates

Sinclair, H.
Horse Soldiers, The
UA (US) 1959 dir. John Ford

Sinclair, T.
Change of Place, A
ALLIANCE (Can) 1994 dir. Donna Deitch
TV(Can)

Sinclair, U.
Gnome-Mobile, The
DISNEY (US) 1967
dir. Robert Stevenson
Ch

Sinclair, U.
Wet Parade, The
MGM (US) 1932 dir. Victor Fleming

Singer, H.
Wake Me When It's Over
FOX (US) 1960 dir. Mervyn LeRoy

Singer, I. B.
Enemies, A Love Story
FOX (US) 1989 dir. Paul Mazursky

Singer, I. B.
Magician of Lublin, The
RANK (Israel/Ger) 1979
dir. Menahem Golan

Singer, I. B.
Yentl, the Yeshiva Boy
Yentl
MGM/UA (US) 1983
dir. Barbra Streisand
M

Singer, L.
Parallax View, The
PAR (US) 1974 dir. Alan J. Pakula

Singh, V.
Jaya Ganga
NFDC (Fr/Ind) 1996 dir. Vijay Singh

Singular, S.
Charmed to Death

Legacy of Sin: The William Coit Story
CITADEL ENT (US) 1995 dir. Steven
Schachter
TV(US)

Singular, S.
Talked to Death: The Life and Murder
of Alan Berg

P
Talk Radio
UN (US) 1988 dir. Oliver Stone

Siodmak, C.
Donovan's Brain

UA (US) 1953 dir. Felix Feist

Siodmak, C.
Donovan's Brain

Lady and the Monster, The
REP (US) 1944 dir. George Sherman
GB title: Lady and the Doctor, The

Siodmak, C.
Donovan's Brain

Vengeance
BL (GB/Ger) 1962 dir. Freddie Francis

Siodmak, C.
Hauser's Memory

UN (US) 1970 dir. Boris Sagal
TV(US)

Sitwell, Sir O.
Place of One's Own, A

GFD (GB) 1945 dir. Bernard Knowles

Sjowall, M. and Wahloo, M.
Abominable Man, The

Man on the Roof, The
SVENSK (Swe) 1976
dir. Bo Widenberg

Sjowall, M. and Wahloo, P.
Laughing Policeman, The

TCF (US) 1973 dir. Stuart Rosenberg
GB title: Investigation of Murder, An

Sjowall, M. and Wahloo, P.
Locked Room, The

Beck
FILMCASE (Neth/Bel) 1993 dir. Jacob
Bijl

Sjowall, M. and Wahloo, P.
Mannen pa Balkogen

NORDISK (Swe/Ger) 1993 dir. Daniel
Alfredson

Skarmeta, A.
Burning Patience

Postino, Il
CECCHI (It) 1994 dir. Michael Radford

Skelton, B.
Tears Before Bedtime; Weep No More

Business Affair, A
STUDIO CANAL+ (GB/Fr) 1994 dir.
Charlotte Brandstorm

**Skinner, C. O. and Kimbrough,
E.**
Our Hearts Were Young and Gay

PAR (US) 1944 dir. Lewis Allen

Skou-Hansen, T.
Nogne Traer, De

NORSK (Den) 1992 dir. Morten
Henriksen

Slade, B.
Romantic Comedy

P
MGM/UA (US) 1983 dir. Arthur Hiller

Slade, B.
Same Time, Next Year

P
UN (US) 1978
dir. Robert Mulligan

Slade, B.
Tribute

P
FOX (Can) 1980 dir. Bob Clark

Slater, H.
Conspirator
MGM (GB) 1949 dir. Victor Saville

Slater, M.
Once a Jolly Swagman
WESSEX (GB) 1948 dir. Jack Lee
US title: Maniacs on Wheels

Slater, N.
Mad Death, The
BBC (GB) 1983 dir. Robert Young
TVSe(GB)

Slaughter, F. G.
Doctor's Wives
COL (US) 1971 dir. George Schaefer

Slaughter, F. G.
Sangaree
PAR (US) 1953 dir. Edward Ludwig

Slaughter, F. G.
Warrior, The
Naked in the Sun
ALLIED (US) 1957 dir. R. John Hugh

Slaughter, F. G.
Women in White
UN TV (US) 1979 dir. Jerry London
TVSe(US)

Sloane, W.
Edge of Running Water, The
Devil Commands, The
COL (US) 1941 dir. Edward Dmytryk

Slote, A.
Finding Buck McHenry
LIN OLIVER (US) 2000 dir. Charles Burnett
TV(US)

Slowacki, J.
Mazepa
Blanche
TELEPRESSE (Fr) 1971
dir. Walerian Borowczyk

Small, G. R.
Mittelmann's Hardware
Finding the Way Home
MGM/UA TV (US) 1991
dir. Rob Holcomb
TV(US)

Smiley, J.
Thousand Acres, A
TOUCHSTONE (US) 1997 dir. Jocelyn Moorhouse

Smith, A. D.
Twilight: Los Angeles
P
OFFLINE (US) 2000 dir. Marc Levin

Smith, B.
Joy in the Morning
MGM (US) 1965 dir. Alex Segal

Smith, B.
Tree Grows in Brooklyn, A
FOX (US) 1945 dir. Elia Kazan
FOX (US) 1974 dir. Joseph Hardy
TV(US)

Smith, C.
Ladystinger
Scam
VIACOM (US) 1993 dir. John Flynn
TV(US)

Smith, D.
Call it a Day
P
WAR (US) 1937 dir. Archie Mayo

Smith, D.
Dear Octopus

P

GFD (GB) 1943 dir. Harold French
US title: Randolph Family, The

Smith, D.
Hundred and One Dalmations, The

One Hundred and One Dalmatians
DISNEY (US) 1961
dir. Wolfgang Reitherman, Clyde
Geronimi, Hamilton Luske
A, Ch

Smith, D.
Hundred and One Dalmations, The

101 Dalmations
DISNEY (US) 1996 dir. Stephen Herek
Ch

Smith, D.
Hundred and One Dalmations, The

102 Dalmations
DISNEY (US) 2000 dir. Kevin Lima
Ch

Smith, E.
Maidens' Trip

BBC (GB) 1977 dir. Moira Armstrong
TVSe(GB)

Smith, F. E.
633 Squadron

UA (GB) 1964 dir. Walter Grauman

Smith, H. A.
Rhubarb

PAR (US) 1951 dir. Allan Lubin

Smith, Lady E.
Ballerina

Men in her Life
COL (US) 1941 dir. Gregory Ratoff

Smith, Lady E.
Caravan

BL (GB) 1946 dir. Arthur Crabtree

Smith, Lady E.
Man in Grey, The

GFD (GB) 1943 dir. Leslie Arliss

Smith, Lady E.
Red Wagon

BIP (GB) 1935 dir. Paul Stein

Smith, M.
Gypsy in Amber

Art of Crime, The
UN TV (US) 1975 dir. Richard Irving
TV(US)

Smith, M.
Sacrifice

LIONS GATE (US) 2000 dir. Mark L.
Lester
TV(US)

Smith, M. C.
Gorky Park

ORION (GB) 1983 dir. Michael Apted

Smith, M. C.
Nightwing

COL (Neth) 1975 dir. Arthur Miller

Smith, P.
Angel City

FAC-NEW (US) 1980 dir. Philip Leacock
TV(US)

Smith, R. G.
Huey P. Newton Story, A

P

40 ACRES (US) 2001 dir. Spike Lee
TV(US)

Smith, R. K.
Jane's House

SPELLING TV (US) 1994 dir. Glenn
Jordan
TV(US)

Smith, S.
Ballad of the Running Man, The

Running Man, The
COL (GB) 1963 dir. Carol Reed

Smith, S.
My Mother's Early Lovers

OFF THE GRID (US) 1998 dir. Nora
Jacobson

Smith, S.
Simple Plan, A

PAR (US/GB/Fr) 1998 dir. Sam Raimi

Smith, S. K.
Joanna Godden

Loves of Joanna Godden, The
GFD (GB) 1947 dir. Charles Frend

Smith, T.
Jovial Ghosts, The

Topper
MGM (US) 1937
dir. Norman Z. MacLeod
PAPAZIAN (US) 1979
dir. Charles S. Dubin
TV(US)

Smith, T.
Night Life of the Gods, The

UN (US) 1935 dir. Lowell Sherman

Smith, T.
Passionate Witch, The

I Married a Witch
UA (US) 1942 dir. René Clair

Smith, T.
Turnabout

UA (US) 1940 dir. Hal Roach

Smith, T. L.
Thief Who Came to Dinner, The

WAR (US) 1973 dir. Bud Yorkin

Smith, W.
Dark of the Sun

Mercenaries, The
MGM (GB) 1968 dir. Jack Cardiff
US title: Dark of the Sun

Smith, W.
Gold Mine

Gold
HEMDALE (GB) 1974 dir. Peter Hunt

Smith, W.
Shout at the Devil

HEMDALE (GB) 1976 dir. Peter Hunt

Smith, W.
Thor

Bad Moon
MORGAN CREEK (US) 1996 dir. Eric
Red

Smith, W.
Wild Justice

LEE LIGHTING (GB) 1993 dir. Tony
Wharmby
TVSe(GB)

Smitter, W.
F.O.B. Detroit

Reaching for the Sun
PAR (US) 1941 dir. William Wellman

Smolla, R. A.
Deliberate Intent: A Lawyer Tells the
Story of Murder by the Book

Deliberate Intent
FOX TV (US) 2000 dir. Andy Wolk
TV(US)

Smucker, B.
Underground to Canada

*Race to Freedom: The Underground
Railroad*
XENON (Can) 1994 dir. Don McBrearty
TV(Can)

Sneider, V.
Teahouse of the August Moon, The

MGM (US) 1956 dir. Daniel Mann
COMPASS (US) 1962
dir. George Schaefer
TV(US)

Snow, C. P.
Strangers and Brothers

BBC (GB) 1984 dir. Jeremy Summers,
Ronald Wilson
TVSe(GB)

Sobel, D.
Longitude

GRANADA/A&E (GB) 2000 dir.
Charles Sturridge
TVSe(GB)

Soble, R. and Johnson, J.
Blood Brothers

*Honor Thy Father and Mother—The True
Story of the Menendez Brothers*
SABAN ENT (US) dir. Paul Schneider
TV(US)

Sod, T.
Satan and Simon DeSoto

P
Crocodile Tears
ARIZTICAL (US) 1997 dir. Ann Coppel

Soderberg, H.
Gertrud

P
PATHE (Den) 1966 dir. C. T. Dreyer

Sohl, J.
Night Slaves

B. CROSBY (US) 1970 dir. Ted Post
TV(US)

Sohmer, S.
Favorite Son

NBC (US) 1988 dir. Jeff Bleckner
TVSe(US)

Solomon, L. and Buchman, H.
Snafu

P
COL (US) 1945 dir. Jack Moss
GB title: Welcome Home

Solzhenitsyn, A.
**One Day in the Life of Ivan
Denizovich**

CINERAMA (GB) 1971
dir. Caspar Wrede

Somers, P.
Beginner's Luck

Desperate Man, The
AA (GB) 1959 dir. Peter Maxwell

Somers, S.
Keeping Secrets

FINNEGAN/PINCHUCK (US) 1991
dir. John Korty
TV(US)

Somerville, E. and Ross, M.
Irish RM, The

CHANNEL 4 (GB) 1982 dir. Roy Ward
Baker, Robert Chetwyn
TVSe(GB)

Somerville, E. and Ross, M.
Real Charlotte, The

YTV (GB) 1991 dir. Timothy Barry
TVSe(GB)

Sommer, E.
Teenage Rebel

P
FOX (US) 1956 dir. Edmund Goulding

Sommer, S.
CrissCross

MGM (US) 1992 dir. Chris Menges

Sophocles
Electra

P
UA (Gre) 1962
dir. Michael Cacoyannis

Sophocles
Oedipus the King

P

Edipo Alcalde
IMCINE (Mex/Sp) 1996 dir. Jorge Ali Triana

Sophocles
Oedipus the King

P

UI (GB) 1968 dir. Philip Saville

Sophocles
Oedipus the King

P

Oedipus Rex
HORIZON (It) 1947
dir. Pier Paolo Pasolini

Sorensen, V.
On This Star

Loss of Innocence, A
KONIGSBERG (US) 1996 dir. Graeme Clifford
TV(US)

Sorino, O.
Funny Dirty Little War

CINEVISTA (Sp) 1986
dir. Hector Olivera

Sorkin, A.
Few Good Men, A

P

CASTLE ROCK (US) 1992 dir. Rob Reiner

Soutar, A.
Devil's Triangle

Almost Married
FOX (US) 1932
dir. W. Cameron Menzies

Southard, R.
No Sad Songs for Me

COL (US) 1950 dir. Rudolph Maté

Southern, T.
Magic Christian, The

COMM (GB) 1969 dir. Joseph McGrath

Southern, T. and Hoffenberg, M.
Candy

CINERAMA (US) 1968
dir. Christian Marquand

Spaak, C.
Kermesse Heroique, La

TOBIS (Fr) 1935 dir. Jacques Feyder

Spark, M.
Abbess of Crewe, The

Nasty Habits
SCOTIA-BARBER (GB) 1976
dir. Michael Lindsay-Hogg
US title: Abbess, The

Spark, M.
Girls of Slender Means, The

BBC (GB) 1975 dir. Moira Armstrong
TVSe(GB)

Spark, M.
Memento Mori

BBC (GB) 1992 dir. Jack Clayton
TV(GB)

Spark, M.
Prime of Miss Jean Brodie, The

FOX (GB) 1969 dir. Ronald Neame
STV (GB) 1978 dir. John Bruce, Mark Cullingham, Christopher Hodson, Tina Wakerell
TVSe(GB)

Sparks, N.
Message in a Bottle

WAR (US) 1999 dir. Luis Mandoki

Speare, E. G.
Sign of the Beaver, The

Keeping the Promise
ATLANTIS (US) 1997 dir. Sheldon
Larry
TV(US)

Spearman, F. H.
Whispering Smith

PAR (US) 1948 dir. Leslie Fenton

Speer, A.
Inside the Third Reich

ABC (US) 1982 dir. Marvin J. Chomsky
TVSe(US)

Speight, R.
Desperate Justice

Mother's Revenge, A
MARTINES (US) 1993 dir. Armand
Mastroianni
TV(US)

Spellman, C. C.
Bless the Child

PAR (US/Ger) 2000 dir. Chuck Russell

Spence, H.
One Foot in Heaven

WAR (US) 1941 dir. Irving Rapper

Spence, R.
Gorilla, The

P
FOX (US) 1939 dir. Allan Dwan

Spencer, E.
Light in the Piazza, The

MGM (GB) 1962 dir. Guy Green

Spencer, L.
Family Blessings

DOVE ENT (US/Can) 1996 dir. Nina
Foch, Deborah Raffin
TV(US/Can)

Spencer, L.
Fulfillment, The

Fulfillment of Mary Gray, The
INDIAN NECK (US) 1989
dir. Piers Haggard
TV(US)

Spencer, L.
Home Song

DOVE ENT (US) 1996 dir. Nancy
Malone
TV(US)

Spencer, L.
Morning Glory

DOVE (US) 1993 dir. Steven Hilliard
Stern
TV(US)

Spencer, S.
Endless Love

UN (US) 1981 dir. Franco Zeffirelli

Spencer, S.
Waking the Dead

POLYGRAM (US) 1999 dir. Keith
Gordon

Spewack, B. and Spewack, S.
Boy Meets Girl

P
WAR (US) 1938 dir. Lloyd Bacon

Spewack, S. and Spewack, B.
Kiss Me Kate

P
MGM (US) 1953 dir. George Sidney
M
MILBERG (US) 1958 dir. George
Schaefer
TV(US)

Spewack, B. and Spewack, S.
Solitaire Man, The

P
MGM (US) 1933 dir. Jack Conway

Spiegelgass, L.
Majority of One, A

P

WAR (US) 1961 dir. Mervyn LeRoy

Spillane, M.
Girl Hunters, The

FOX (GB) 1963 dir. Roy Rowland

Spillane, M.
I, The Jury

UA (US) 1953 dir. Harry Essex
FOX (US) 1982 dir. Richard T. Heffron

Spillane, M.
Kiss Me Deadly

UA (US) 1955 dir. Robert Aldrich

Spillane, M.
Long Wait, The

UA (US) 1954 dir. Victor Saville

Spillane, M.
My Gun is Quick

UA (US) 1957 dir. George A. White

Spiridakis, T. and Bitterman, S.
Self Storage

P

Tinseltown
GOLDWYN (US) 1998 dir. Tony
Spiridakis

Sportes, M.
Fresh Bait

FRANCE 2 (Fr) 1995 dir. Bertrand
Tavernier

Sprecht, R.
Soul of Betty Fairchild, The

Nightscream
VZ/SERTNER (US) 1997 dir. Noel
Nosseck
TV(US)

Spring, H.
Fame is the Spur

TC (GB) 1947 dir. Roy Boulting
BBC (GB) 1982 dir. David Giles
TVSe(GB)

Spring, H.
My Son, My Son

UA (US) 1940 dir. Charles Vidor
BBC (GB) 1979 dir. Peter Cregeen
TVSe(GB)

Spring, H.
Shabby Tiger

GRANADA TV (GB) 1977 dir. Baz
Taylor
TVSe(GB)

Spyri, J.
Heidi

FOX (US) 1937 dir. Allan Dwan
NBC (US) 1968 dir. Delbert Mann
TV(US)
BBC (GB) 1974
dir. June Wyndham-Davies
TVSe(GB)
DISNEY CH (US) 1993 dir. Michael
Rhodes
TVSe(US)
Ch

Spyri, J.
Heidi

Heidi's Song
HANNA-BARBERA (US) 1982
dir. Robert Taylor
A

St. John, A. R.
Final Verdict

Final Verdict, The
TURNER (US) 1991 dir. Jack Fisk
TV(US)

St. John, A. R.
Free Soul, A

MGM (US) 1931 dir. Clarence Brown

St. John, A. R.
Girl Who Had Everything, The
MGM (US) 1953 dir. Richard Thorpe

Stacpoole, H. D.
Blue Lagoon, The
GFD ((1B) 1949 dir. Frank Launder
COL (US) 1980 dir. Randal Kleiser

Stacpoole, H. D.
Garden of God, The
Return to the Blue Lagoon
COL (US) 1991 dir. William A. Graham

Stadley, P.
Autumn of a Hunter
Deadly Hunt, The
FOUR STAR (US) 1971
dir. John Newland
TV(US)

Stahl, B.
Blackbeard's Ghost
DISNEY (US) 1968
dir. Robert Stevenson
Ch

Stahl, J.
Permanent Midnight
JD (US) 1998 dir. David Veloz

Stajano, C.
Ordinary Hero, An
INSTITUTO LUCE (It) 1995 dir. Michele
Placido

Standish, R.
Elephant Walk
PAR (US) 1954 dir. William Dieterle

Stanford, S.
Lady of the House
METRO (US) 1978 dir. Ralph Norton,
Vincent Sherman
TV(US)

Stanton, W.
Golden Evenings of Summer, The
Charley and the Angel
DISNEY (US) 1974
dir. Vincent McEveety

Stanush, C.
**Newton Boys, The: Portrait of an
Outlaw Gang**
Newton Boys, The
FOX (US) 1998 dir. Richard Linklater

Stanwood, D. A.
Memory of Eva Ryker, The
IRWIN ALLEN (US) 1980
dir. Walter Grauman
TV(US)

Stark, R.
Outfit, The
MGM (US) 1973 dir. John Flynn

Stark, R.
Point Blank
MGM (US) 1967 dir. John Boorman

Stark, R.
Seventh, The
Split, The
MGM (US) 1968 dir. Gordon Flemyng

Stark, R.
Slayground
UN/EMI (GB) 1983 dir. Terry Bedford

Stark, U.
Sixten
SVENSK (Swe) 1994 dir. Catti Edfeldt

Starnone, D.
Denti
CECCHI (It) 2000 dir. Gabriele
Salvatores

Starnone, D.
Scuola, La
CECCHI (It) 1995 dir. Daniele Luchetti

Starr, B. and Perry, H.
Blaze Starr: My Life as Told to Huey
Perry
Blaze
TOUCHSTONE (US) 1989
dir. Ron Shelton

Starr, J.
Corpse Came C.O.D., The
COL (US) 1947 dir. Henry Levin

Stassinopoulos, A. H.
Picasso: Creator and Destroyer
Surviving Picasso
WAR (US) 1996 dir. James Ivory

Stater, B. and Leighton, F. S.
Stranger in my Bed
TAFT (US) 1987 dir. Larry Elikann
TV(US)

Stawinski, J.
Kloakerne
Kanal
POLSKI (Pol) 1956 dir. Andrzej Wajda

Stawinski, J. S.
Eroica
KADR (Pol) 1957 dir. Andrzej Munk

Stead, C.
For Love Alone
WARRANTY (Aust) 1986
dir. Stephen Wallace

Steakley, J.
Vampire$
LARGO (US) 1998 dir. John Carpenter

Steel, D.
Changes
NBC (US) 1991 dir. Charles Jarrot
TV(US)

Steel, D.
Crossings
SPELLING (US) 1986
dir. Karen Arthur
TVSe(US)

Steel, D.
Daddy
NBC (US) 1991 dir. Michael Miller

Steel, D.
Family Album
NBC (US) 1994 dir. Jack Bender
TVSe(US)

Steel, D.
Fine Things
NBC (US) 1990 dir. Tom Moore
TV(US)

Steel, D.
Full Circle
NBC (US) 1996 dir. Bethany Rooney
TV(US)

Steel, D.
Heartbeat
NBC (US) 1993 dir. Michael Miller
TV(US)

Steel, D.
Jewels
NBC (US) 1992 dir. Roger Young
TVSe(US)

Steel, D.
Kaleidoscope
NBC (US) 1990 dir. Jud Taylor
TV(US)

Steel, D.
Message From 'Nam
NBC (US) 1993 dir. Paul Wendkos
TV(US)

Steel, D.
Mixed Blessings
NBC (US) 1995 dir. Bethany Rooney
TV(US)

Steel, D.
No Greater Love
NBC (US) 1996 dir. Richard T. Heffron
TV(US)

Steel, D.
Once in a Lifetime
NBC (US) 1994 dir. Michael Miller
TV(US)

Steel, D.
Palomino
NBC (US) 1991 dir. Michael Miller
TV(US)

Steel, D.
Perfect Stranger, A
NBC (US) 1994 dir. Michael Miller
TV(US)

Steel, D.
Remembrance
NBC (US) 1996 dir. Bethany Rooney
TV(US)

Steel, D.
Ring, The
NBC (US) 1996 dir. Armand
Mastroianni
TV(US)

Steel, D.
Secrets
NBC (US) 1992 dir. Peter H. Hunt
TV(US)

Steel, D.
Star
SCHOOLFIELD (US) 1993 dir. Michael
Miller
TV(US)

Steel, D.
Vanished
NBC (US) 1995 dir. George Kaczender
TV(US)

Steel, D.
Zoya
NBC (US) 1995 dir. Richard Colla
TVSe(US)

Steele, K.
Murder Goes to College
PAR (US) 1937 dir. Charles Reisner

Steele, W. D.
Way to the Gold, The
FOX (US) 1957 dir. Robert D. Webb

Steeman, S.-A.
Legitime Defense
Quai des Orfèvres
MAJ (Fr) 1947
dir. Henri-Georges Clouzot

Steiger, B. and Mank, C.
Valentino
UA (GB) 1977 dir. Ken Russell

Stein, B.
Ludes
Boost, The
HEMDALE (US) 1988
dir. Harold Becker

Stein, D. M.
Wall of Noise
WAR (US) 1963 dir. Richard Wilson

Stein, J.
Fiddler on the Roof
P
UA (US) 1971 dir. Norman Jewison
M

Steinbeck, J.
Cannery Row
MGM (US) 1982 dir. David S. Ward

Steinbeck, J.
East of Eden

WAR (US) 1954 dir. Elia Kazan
NEUFELD (US) 1980
dir. Harvey Hart
TVSe(US)

Steinbeck, J.
Grapes of Wrath, The

FOX (US) 1940 dir. John Ford

Steinbeck, J.
Moon is Down, The

FOX (US) 1943 dir. Irving Pichel

Steinbeck, J.
Of Mice and Men

UA (US) 1939 dir. Lewis Milestone
METROMEDIA (US) 1981
dir. Reza Badiyi
TV(US)
MGM (US) 1992 dir. Gary Sinese

Steinbeck, J.
Pearl, The

RKO (US/Mex) 1948
dir. Emilio Fernandez

Steinbeck, J.
Red Pony, The

BL (US) 1949 dir. Lewis Milestone
UN (US) 1973 dir. Robert Totten
TV(US)

Steinbeck, J.
Tortilla Flat

MGM (US) 1942 dir. Victor Fleming

Steinbeck, J.
Wayward Bus, The

FOX (US) 1957 dir. Victor Vicas

Steinbeck, J.
Winter of our Discontent, The

LORIMAR (US) 1983 dir. Waris Hussein
TV(US)

Stendahl, M. H. B.
Rouge et le Noir, Le

Red and the Black, The
TELFRANCE (Fr/It) 1997 dir. Jean-
Daniel Verhaeghe
TVSe(Fr/It)

Stendahl, M. H. B.
Rouge et le Noir, Le

Scarlet and the Black, The
BBC (GB) 1993 dir. Ben Bolt
TVSe(GB)

Stendahl, M. H. B.
Rouge et le Noir, Le

FRANCO-LF (Fr/It) 1954
dir. Claude Autant-Lara

Stephenson, C.
Leiningen Versus the Ants

Naked Jungle, The
PAR (US) 1954 dir. Byron Haskin

Sterling, T.
Evil of the Day, The

Honey Pot, The
UA (US) 1966 dir. Joseph L. Mankiewicz

Stern, B.
How to Shoot a Feature Under $10,000 and Not Go to Jail

R2PC: Road to Park City
PHAEDRA (US) 1999 dir. Bret Stern

Stern, D.
Francis

UI (US) 1949 dir. Arthur Lubin

Stern, G. B.
Long Lost Father

RICO (US) 1934
dir. Ernest B. Schoedsack

Stern, G. B.
Ugly Dachshund, The

DISNEY (US) 1965 dir. Norman Tokar

Stern, G. B.
Woman in the Hall, The
GFD (GB) 1947 dir. Jack Lee

Stern, H. J.
Judgment in Berlin
NEW LINE (US) 1988 dir. Leo Penn

Stern, P. V. D.
Greatest Gift, The
It Happened One Christmas
UN TV (US) 1977 dir. Donald Wrye
TV(US)

Stern, R. M.
Tower, The
Towering Inferno, The
COL-WAR (US) 1975
dir. John Gullermin, Irwin Allen

Sterner, J.
Other People's Money
P
WAR (US) 1991 dir. Norman Jewison

Stevens, D.
Sum of Us, The
P
SOUTHERN STAR (Aust) 1994 dir.
Geoff Burton, Kevin Dowling

Stevens, L.
Lovers, The
P
War Lord, The
UN (US) 1965 dir. Franklin Schaffner

Stevens, W. R.
Deadly Intentions
GREEN-EPSTEIN (US) 1985
dir. Noel Black
TVSe(US)

Stevenson, J. and Stevenson, P.
Counterattack
P
COL (US) 1945 dir. Zoltan Korda
GB title: One Against Seven

Stevenson, R. L.
Black Arrow
COL (US) 1948 dir. Gordon Douglas
GB title: Black Arrow Strikes, The
SOUTHERN TV (GB) 1972
TVSe(GB)
TOWER (US) 1985 dir. John Hough
TV(US/GB)

Stevenson, R. L.
Body Snatcher, The
RKO (US) 1945 dir. Robert Wise

Stevenson, R. L.
Dr Jekyll and Mr Hyde
PAR (US) 1931 dir. Rouben Mamoulian
MGM (US) 1941 dir. Victor Fleming
BBC (GB) 1980 dir. Alastair Reid
TV(GB)
TELESCENE FG (Can/Aust) 1999 dir.
Colin Budds
TV(Can/Aust)

Stevenson, R. L.
Dr. Jekyll and Mr. Hyde
Jekyll & Hyde
KING PHOENIX (US/GB) 1990
dir. David Wickes
TV(GB/US)

Stevenson, R. L.
Dr. Jekyll and Mr. Hyde
Two Faces of Dr. Jekyll, The
HAMMER (GB) 1960
dir. Terence Fisher
US title: House of Fright

Stevenson, R. L.
Ebb Tide
Adventure Island
PAR (US) 1947 dir. Peter Stewart

Stevenson, R. L.
Kidnapped

FOX (US) 1938 dir. Alfred L. Werker
DISNEY (GB) 1959
dir. Robert Stevenson
RANK (GB) 1971 dir. Delbert Mann
HTV (GB) 1979 dir. Jean Pierre Decourt,
Bob Fuest
TVSe(GB)
HALLMARK (US) 1995 dir. Ivan Passer
TVSe(US)
Ch

Stevenson, R. L.
Master of Ballantrae, The

WAR (US) 1953 dir. William Keighley
BBC (GB) 1975 dir. Fiona Cumming
TVSe(GB)
COL (US/GB) 1983 dir. Douglas Hickox
TVSe(GB/US)

Stevenson, R. L.
Sire of Maletroit's Door, The

Strange Door, The
UI (US) 1951 dir. Joseph Pevney

Stevenson, R. L.
St. Ives

Secret of St. Ives, The
COL (US) 1949 dir. Phil Rosen

Stevenson, R. L.
St. Ives

BBC (GB) 1998 dir. Harry Hook

Stevenson, R. L.
Suicide Club, The

ANGELIKA (US) 1988 dir. James Bruce

Stevenson, R. L.
Suicide Club, The

Trouble for Two
MGM (US) 1936 dir. J. Walter Rubin
GB title: Suicide Club, The

Stevenson, R. L.
Treasure Island

MGM (US) 1934 dir. Victor Fleming
DISNEY (GB) 1950 dir. Byron Haskin
MGM-EMI (GB/Fr/Ger) 1971
dir. John Hough
BBC (GB) 1977 dir. Michael E. Briant
TVSe(GB)
AGAMEMNON (US) 1990
dir. Fraser Heston
TV(US)

Stevenson, R. L.
Treasure of Franchard

Treasure of Lost Canyon, The
UI (US) 1952 dir. Ted Tetzlaff

Stevenson, R. L.
Weir of Hermiston

BBC (GB) 1973 dir. Tina Wakerell
TVSe(GB)

Stevenson, R. L. and Osbourne, L.
Ebb-Tide, The

Ebb Tide
PAR (US) 1937 dir. James Hogan

Stevenson, R. L. and Osbourne, L.
Ebb-Tide, The

GRANADA/A&E (GB) 1998 dir.
Nicholas Renton
TV(GB)

Stevenson, R. L. and Osbourne, L.
Wrong Box, The

COL (GB) 1966 dir. Bryan Forbes

Stevenson, W.
Man Called Intrepid, A

LORIMAR (GB) 1979 dir. Peter Carter
TVSe(GB)

Stewart, D. O.
Mr and Mrs Haddock Abroad
Finn and Hattie
PAR (US) 1930 dir. Norman Taurog,
Norman McLeod

Stewart, F.
Mephisto Waltz, The
FOX (US) 1971 dir. Paul Wendkos

Stewart, F. M.
Ellis Island
TELEPIC (US) 1984 dir. Jerry London
TVSe(US)

Stewart, F. M.
Six Weeks
UN (US) 1982 dir. Tony Bill

Stewart, G.
Avenging Angel, The
CURTIS LOWE (US) 1995 dir. Craig R.
Baxley
TV(US)

Stewart, M.
Bye Bye Birdie
P
COL (US) 1963 dir. George Sidney
M

Stewart, M.
Monkey Shines
ORION (US) 1988
dir. George A. Romero

Stewart, M.
Moon-Spinners, The
DISNEY (GB) 1964 dir. James Neilson

Stewart, M. and Herman, J.
Hello, Dolly!
P
FOX (US) 1969 dir. Gene Kelly
M

Stewart, R.
Desert Town
Desert Fury
PAR (US) 1947 dir. Lewis Allen

Stewart, R.
Possession of Joel Delaney, The
SCOTIA-BARBER (US) 1971
dir. Waris Hussein

Still, J.
Velocity of Gary, The
P
CINEVILLE (US) 1999 dir. Dan Ireland

Stille, A.
Excellent Cadavers
HBO (US) 1999 dir. Ricky Tognazzi
TV(US)

Stine, H.
Season of the Witch
Memory Run
MERIDIAN ENT (US) 1995 dir. Allan A.
Goldstein

Stine, R. L.
When Good Ghouls Go Bad
FOX (Aust/US) 2001 dir. Patrick Read
Johnson
TV(Aust/US)

Stinetorf, L. A.
White Witch Doctor
FOX (US) 1953 dir. Henry Hathaway

Stitt, M.
Runner Stumbles, The
P
SIMON (US) 1979 dir. Stanley Kramer

Stockdale, J. and Stockdale, S.
In Love and War
TA (US) 1987 dir. Paul Aaron
TV(US)

Stoddart, D.
Prelude to Night

Ruthless
EL (US) 1948 dir. Edgar G. Ulmer

Stoker, B.
Dracula

UN (US) 1931 dir. Tod Browning
UI (GB) 1958 dir. Terence Fisher
US title: House of Dracula
EMI (It) 1973 dir. Paul Morrissey
UN (US) 1974 dir. Dan Curtis
TV (US)
AM ZOETROPE (US) 1992 dir. Francis
Ford Coppola

Stoker B.
Dracula

CIC (GB) 1979 dir. John Badham

Stoker, B.
Dracula's Guest

Dracula's Daughter
UN (US) 1936 dir. Lambert Hillyer

Stoker, B.
Jewel of the Seven Stars, The

Awakening, The
EMI (GB) 1980 dir. Mike Newell

Stoker, B.
Jewel of the Seven Stars, The

Blood from the Mummy's Tomb
MGM-EMI (GB) 1971 dir. Seth Holt

Stoker, B.
Jewel of the Seven Stars, The

Legend of the Mummy
UNAPIX (US) 1997 dir. Jeffrey Obrow

Stoker, B.
Lair of the White Worm, The

VESTRON (GB) 1988 dir. Ken Russell

Stokes, S.
Court Circular

I Believe in You
EAL (GB) 1952 dir. Basil Dearden

Stokes, S.
Isadora Duncan, An Intimate Portrait

Isadora
UI (GB) 1969 dir. Karel Reisz
US title: Loves of Isadora, The

Stone, G.
Little Girl Fly Away

LONGBOW (US) 1998 dir. Peter Levin
TV(US)

Stone, G. and Cooney, R.
Why Not Stay for Breakfast?

P
ENT (GB) 1979 dir. Terence Martel

Stone, I.
Agony and the Ecstacy, The

FOX (US) 1965 dir. Carol Reed

Stone, I.
Immortal Wife

President's Lady, The
FOX (US) 1953 dir. Henry Levin

Stone, I.
Lust for Life

MGM (US) 1956 dir. Vincente Minnelli

Stone, Mrs G.
Bitter Tea of General Yen, The

COL (US) 1932 dir. Frank Capra

Stone, P.
1776

P
COL (US) 1972 dir. Peter Hunt
M

Stone, R.
Dog Soldiers

Who'll Stop the Rain?
UA (US) 1978 dir. Karel Reisz
GB title: Dog Soldiers

Stone, R.
Hall of Mirrors
WUSA
PAR (US) 1970 dir. Stuart Rosenberg

Stoneley, J.
Jenny's War
HTV (US/GB) 1985 dir. Steven Gethers
Ch, TVSe(GB/US)

Stong, P. D.
Career
RKO (US) 1939 dir. Leigh Jason

Stong, P. D.
State Fair
FOX (US) 1933 dir. Henry King
FOX (US) 1945 dir. Walter Lang
M
FOX (US) 1962 dir. José Ferrer
M

Stong, P. D.
Strangers Return
MGM (US) 1933 dir. King Vidor

Stoppard, T.
Rosencrantz and Guildenstern are Dead
P
HOBO/CINECOM (US/GB) 1991
dir. Tom Stoppard

Storey, D.
In Celebration
P
SEVEN KEYS (GB) 1974
dir. Lindsay Anderson

Storey, D.
This Sporting Life
RANK (GB) 1963 dir. Lindsay Anderson

Storey, R.
Touch it Light
P
Light up the Sky
BL (GB) 1960 dir. Lewis Gilbert

Storm, B.
Thunder God's Gold
Lust for Gold
COL (US) 1949 dir. S. Sylvan Simon

Storm, L.
Great Day
RKO (GB) 1945 dir. Lance Comfort

Storm, L.
Personal Affair
P
RANK (GB) 1953 dir. Anthony Pelissier

Storm, L.
Tony Draws a Horse
P
GFD (GB) 1950
dir. John Paddy Carstairs

Storr, C.
Marianne Dreams
Paperhouse
VESTRON (GB) 1988 dir. Bernard Rose

Story, J. T.
Mix me a Person
BL (GB) 1962 dir. Leslie Norman

Story, J. T.
Trouble with Harry, The
PAR (US) 1955 dir. Alfred Hitchcock

Stout, D.
Carolina Skeletons
KUSHNER-LOCKE (US) 1991
dir. John Erman
TV (US)

Stout, D.
Dog Hermit, The
Child is Missing, A
MOORE-WEISS (US) 1995 dir. John Power
TV(US)

Stout, R.
Doorbell Rang, The

Nero Wolfe
PAR TV (US) 1979 dir. Frank D. Gilroy
TV(US)

Stout, R.
Fer de Lance

Meet Nero Wolfe
COL (US) 1936 dir. Herbert Biberman

Stout, R.
Golden Spiders, The

JAFFE/BRAUNSTEIN (US) 2000 dir.
Bill Duke
TV(US)

Stout, R.
Hand in the Glove

Lady Against the Odds
MGM/UA (US) 1992 dir. Bradford May
TV(US)

Stout, R.
League of Frightened Men, The

COL (US) 1937 dir. Alfred E. Green

Stowe, H. B.
Uncle Tom's Cabin

TAFT (US) 1989 dir. Stan Lathan
TV(US)

Strabel, T.
Reap the Wild Wind

PAR (US) 1942 dir. Cecil B. De Mille

Straker, J. F.
Hell is Empty

RANK (Czech/GB) 1967
dir. John Ainsworth and Bernard
Knowles

Strasser, T.
How I Created My Perfect Prom Date

Drive Me Crazy
FOX (US) 1999 dir. John Schultz

Straub, P.
Ghost Story

UN (US) 1981 dir. John Irvin

Straub, P.
Julia

Full Circle
PAR (GB/Can) 1976
dir. Richard Loncraine

Straub, P.
Shadowlands

BBC (Neth/GB) 1985
dir. Norman Stone
TV(GB)

Streatfeild, N.
Aunt Clara

BL (GB) 1954 dir. Anthony Kimmins

Streatfeild, N.
Ballet Shoes

BBC (GB) 1975 dir. Timothy Combe
TVSe(GB)

Streatfeild, N.
Thursday's Child

BBC (GB) 1972 dir. Antony Thorpe
TVSe(GB)

Street, A. G.
Strawberry Roan

BN (GB) 1944 dir. Maurice Elvey

Street, J. H.
Goodbye, My Lady

WAR (US) 1956 dir. William Wellman

Street, J. H.
Letter to the Editor

Nothing Sacred
SELZNICK (US) 1937
dir. William Wellman

Street, J. H.
Tap Roots

UI (US) 1948 dir. George Marshall

Streeter, E.
Father of the Bride

MGM (US) 1950 dir. Vincente Minnelli
DISNEY (US) 1991 dir. Charles Shyer

Streeter, E.
Hobbs' Vacation

Mr. Hobbs takes a Vacation
FOX (US) 1962 dir. Henry Koster

Strege, J.
Tiger

Tiger Woods Story, The
SHOWTIME (US) 1998 dir. LeVar
Burton
TV(US)

Streiber, W.
Communion

NEW LINE (US) 1989
dir. Philippe Mora

Streuvels, S.
Flaxfield, The

COURIER (Bel/Neth) 1983
dir. Jan Gruyaert

Strieber, W.
Hunger, The

MGM/UA (US) 1983 dir. Tony Scott

Strieber, W.
Wolfen

WAR (US) 1981 dir. Michael Wadleigh

Strindberg, A.
Dance of Death, The

P
PAR (GB) 1968 dir. David Giles

Strindberg, A.
Father, The

P
BBC (GB) 1985
TV(GB)

Strindberg, J. A.
Miss Julie

P
LF (Swe) 1950 dir. Alf Sjoberg
TIGON (GB) 1972
dir. Robin Phillips, John Glenister
MOONSTONE (US) 1999 dir. Mike
Figgis

Stringer, D.
Touch Wood

P
Nearly a Nasty Accident
BL (GB) 1961 dir. Don Chaffey

Strode, W. S.
Guinea Pig, The

P
PILGRIM-PATHE (GB) 1948
dir. Roy Boulting
US title: Outsider, The

Strong, A.
Seventh Heaven

P
FOX (US) 1937 dir. Henry King

Strong, A.
Three Wise Fools

P
MGM (US) 1946 dir. Edward Buzzell

Strong, L. A. G.
Brothers, The

GFD (GB) 1947 dir. David MacDonald

Strong, P.
Village Tale, A

RKO (US) 1935 dir. John Cromwell

Strout, E.
Amy and Isabelle

HARPO (US) 2001 dir. Lloyd Kramer
TV(US)

Strueby, K.
General Goes Too Far, The

High Command, The
ABFD (GB) 1936 dir. Thorold Dickinson

Strugatsky, B. and Strugatsky, A.
Picnic by the Roadside

Stalker
MOSFILM (USSR) 1979 dir. Andrei Tarkovsky

Struther, J.
Mrs. Miniver

MGM (US) 1942 dir. William Wyler

Stryzkowski, J.
Austeria

POLSKI (Pol) 1988
dir. Jerzy Kawaterowicz

Stuart, A.
Jeannie

P
TANSA (GB) 1941 dir. Harold French
US title: Girl in Distress

Stuart, A.
Jeannie

P
Let's Be Happy
ABP (GB) 1957 dir. Henry Levin
M

Stuart, A.
War Zone, The

CHANNEL 4 FILMS (GB) 1999 dir. Tim Roth

Stuart, C.
Walks Far Woman

Legend of Walks Far Woman, The
EMI (US) 1982 dir. Mel Damski
TV(US)

Stuart, I.
Satan Bug, The

UA (US) 1965 dir. John Sturges

Stuart, M. A.
Double Jeopardy

Voices From a Locked Room
SONY (US/GB) 1995 dir. Malcolm Clarke

Stuart, W. L.
Night Cry

Where the Sidewalk Ends
FOX (US) 1960 dir. Otto Preminger

Stump, A.
Cobb: A Biography

Cobb
WAR (US) 1994 dir. Ron Shelton

Sturgeon, T.
Killdozer

UN TV (US) 1974 dir. Jerry London
TV(US)

Sturges, P.
Strictly Dishonourable

P
UN (US) 1931 dir. John Stahl
MGM (US) 1951 dir. Norman Panama, Melvin Frank

Styron, W.
Sophie's Choice

UN/ITC (US) 1982 dir. Alan J. Pakula

Suassuna, A.
Auto da Compadecida, O

P
GLOBO (Bra) 2000 dir. Guel Arraes

Sudermann, H.
Song of Songs, The

BBC (GB) 1973 dir. Peter Wood
TVSe(GB)

Sullivan, R., Wolfe, G. and Porter, J.
Flight of the Reindeer

Christmas Secret, The
CBS TV (US) 2000 dir. Ian Barry
TV(US)

Sullivan, Sir A. and Gilbert, Sir W.
Pirates of Penzance, The
P
UN (GB) 1982 dir. Wilford Leach
M

Sullivan, Sir A. and Gilbert, Sir W.
Pirates of Penzance, The
P
Pirate Movie, The
FOX (Aust) 1982 dir. Ken Annakin

Sullivan, T. and Gill, D.
If You Could See What I Can Hear
SCHICK SUNN (US) 1982 dir. Eric Till

Sullivan, W. G. and Brown, W. S.
My 30 Years in Hoover's FBI
J. Edgar Hoover
RLC (US) 1987 dir. Robert Collins
TV(US)

Sulzberger, C.
My Brother Death
Playground, The
JERAND (US) 1965 dir. Richard Hilliard

Summers, R. A.
Vigilante
San Francisco Story, The
WAR (US) 1952 dir. Robert Parrish

Sumner, C. R.
Quality
Pinky
FOX (US) 1949 dir. Elia Kazan

Sumner, C. R.
Tammy and the Bachelor
UN (US) 1957 dir. Joseph Pevney
GB title: Tammy

Sundman, P.O.
Flight of the Eagle
SUMMIT (Swe) 1983 dir. Jan Troell

Susann, J.
Love Machine, The
COL (US) 1971 dir. Jack Haley, Jr.

Susann, J.
Once is not Enough
PAR (US) 1975 dir. Guy Green

Susann, J.
Valley of the Dolls
FOX (US) 1967 dir. Mark Robson

Susann, J.
Valley of the Dolls
Valley of the Dolls 1981
FOX TV (US) 1981 dir. Walter Grauman
TVSe(US)

Sutcliff, R.
Eagle of the Ninth
BBC (GB) 1977 dir. Michael Simpson
TVSe(GB)

Suzuki, K.
Ringu
OMEGA (Jap) 1998 dir. Hideo Nakata, Chisiri Takigawa

Svevo, I.
Conscience of Zeno, The
Parole di Mio Padre, Le
RAI (Fr/It) 2001 dir. Francesca Comencini

Svoray, Y. and Taylor, N.
In Hitler's Shadow: An Israeli's Amazing Journey Inside Germany's Neo-Nazi Movement
Infiltrator, The
HBO SHOW (US) 1995 dir. Jud Taylor
TV(US)

Swan, S.
Wives of Bath, The
Lost and Delirious
LIONS GATE (Can) 2001 dir. Lea Pool

Swann, F.
Out of the Frying Pan
P
Young and Willing
UA (US) 1942 dir. Edward H. Griffith

Swanson, N. H.
First Rebel, The
Allegheny Uprising
RKO (US) 1939 dir. William A. Seiter
GB title: First Rebel, The

Swanson, N. H.
Unconquered
PAR (US) 1947 dir. Cecil B. De Mille

Swarthout, G.
Bless the Beasts and Children
COL (US) 1971 dir. Stanley Kramer

Swarthout, G.
Melodeon, The
Christmas to Remember, A
ENGLUND (US) 1978
dir. George Englund
TV(US)

Swarthout, G.
Shootist, The
PAR (US) 1976 dir. Don Siegel

Swarthout, G.
They Came to Cordura
COL (US) 1959 dir. Robert Rossen

Swarthout, G.
Where the Boys Are
MGM (US) 1960 dir. Henry Levin
ITC (US) 1980 dir. Hy Averback

Sweeney, J.
God Said, Ha!
P
MIRAMAX (US) 1998 dir. Julia
Sweeney

Swift, G.
Last Orders
SCALA (GB/Ger) 2001 dir. Fred
Schepisi

Swift, G.
Shuttlecock
KM (Fr/GB) 1992 dir. Andrew
Piddington

Swift, G.
Waterland
CHANNEL 4 (GB) 1992 dir. Stephen
Gyllenhaal

Swift, J.
Gulliver's Travels
PAR (US) 1939 dir. Dave Fleischer
EMI (GB) 1976 dir. Peter Hunt
A
HALLMARK (US/GB) dir. Charles
Sturridge
TVSe(US/GB)

Swift, J.
Gulliver's Travels
Three Worlds of Gulliver, The
COL (US/Sp) 1959 dir. Jack Sher

Swift, K.
Who Could Ask For Anything More
Never a Dull Moment
RKO (US) 1950 dir. George Marshall

Swiggett, H.
Power and the Prize, The
MGM (US) 1956 dir. Henry Koster

Sylvaine, V.
Aren't Men Beasts!
P
AB (GB) 1937 dir. Graham Cutts

Sylvaine, V.
As Long As They're Happy
P
GFD (GB) 1955 dir. J. Lee Thompson

Sylvaine, V.
One Wild Oat
P
EROS (GB) 1951 dir. Charles Saunders

Sylvaine, V.
Warn That Man
P
AB (GB) 1942 dir. Laurence Huntington

Sylvaine, V.
Will Any Gentleman
P
ABP (GB) 1953 dir. Michael Anderson

Sylvester, R.
Big Boodle, The
UA (US) 1957 dir. Richard Wilson
GB title: Night in Havana

Sylvester, R.
Rough Sketch
We Were Strangers
COL (US) 1949 dir. John Huston

Symons, J.
Blackheath Poisonings, The
CENTRAL (GB) 1992 dir. Stuart Orme
TVSe(GB)

Symons, J.
Narrowing Circle, The
EROS (GB) 1955 dir. Charles Saunders

Synge, J. M.
Playboy of the Western World, The
P
FOUR PROVINCES (GB) 1962
dir. Brian Desmond Hurst

Syrett, N.
Portrait of a Rebel
Woman Rebels, A
RKO (US) 1936 dir. Mark Sandrich

Szekely, H.
School of Drama
P
Dramatic School
MGM (US) 1938 dir. Robert B. Sinclair,
Jr.

Szekely, H. and Stemmple, R. A.
Desire
P
PAR (US) 1936 dir. Frank Borzage

Szilagyi, S.
Photographing Fairies
BRIT SCREEN (GB) 1997 dir. Nick
Willing

Szpiner, F.
Affaire de Femmes, Une
Story of Women
NEW YORKER (Fr) 1989
dir. Claude Chabrol

Tabor, M.
Nightmare Street
LONGBOW (US) 1998 dir. Colin
Bucksey
TV(US)

Tabori, G.
My Mother's Courage
BBS FILMS (Ger/Ire) 1995 dir. Michael
Verhoeven

Tabucchi, A.
Requiem
GEMINI (Fr) 1998 dir. Alain Tanner

Tabucci, A.
Sostiene Pereira
Pereira Declares
KG (Port/It) 1995 dir. Roberto Faenza

Tagore, R.
Home and the World, The
NFC (Ind) 1985 dir. Satyajit Ray

Takami, K.
Battle Royale
TOEI (Jap) 2000 dir. Kinji Fukasaku

Takeoa, T.
Violence at Noon
KINO (Jap) 1966 dir. Nagisa Oshima

Takeyama, M.
Burmese Harp, The
NIKKATSU (Jap) 1956
dir. Kon Ichikawa

Talese, G.
Honor Thy Father
METRO (US) 1973 dir. Paul Wendkos
TVSe(US)

Tamaro, S.
Va' Dove ti Porta il Cuore
Follow Your Heart
GMT (Fr/Ger/It) 1996 dir. Cristina
Comencini

Tammuz, B.
Minotaur
CINEMA PARDES (US) 1997 dir.
Jonathan Tammuz

Tan A.
Joy Luck Club, The
HOLLYWOOD (US) 1993 dir. Wayne
Wang

Tanaka, H.
Moving
HERALD ACE (Jap) 1993 dir. Shinji
Soomai

Tani, T.
Kimura Family, The
Yen Family, The
FUJI (Jap) 1990 dir. Yojiro Takita

Tanizaki, J.
Buddhist Cross, The
Berlin Affair, The
CANNON (It/Ger) 1985
dir. Liliana Cavani

Tanizaki, J.
Key, The
ENT (It) 1983 dir. Giovanni Tinto Brass

Tanizaki, J.
Makioka Sisters, The
R5/S8 (Jap) 1985 dir. Kon Ichikawa

**Tannenbaum, R. K. and
Rosenberg, P.**
Badge of the Assassin
BLATT/SINGER (US) 1985
dir. Mel Damski
TV(US)

Taraborrelli, J. R.
Jackie, Ethel, Joan: Women of Camelot
JUST SINGER (US) 2000 dir. Larry
Shaw
TVSe(US)

Tarkington, B.
Alice Adams
RKO (US) 1933 dir. George Stevens

Tarkington, B.
Magnificent Ambersons, The
RKO (US) 1942 dir. Orson Welles

Tarkington, B.
Monsieur Beaucaire
PAR (US) 1946 dir. George Marshall

Tarkington, B.
Monsieur Beaucaire
Monte Carlo
PAR (US) 1930 dir. Ernst Lubitsch

Tarkington, B.
Penrod
By the Light of the Silvery Moon
WAR (US) 1953 dir. David Butler

Tarkington, B.
Penrod
On Moonlight Bay
WAR (US) 1951 dir. Roy del Ruth
M

Tarkington, B.
Presenting Lily Mars
MGM (US) 1943 dir. Norman Taurog
M

Tarkington, B.
Seventeen
PAR (US) 1940 dir. Louis King

Tarloff, F.
Guide for the Married Man, The
FOX (US) 1967 dir. Gene Kelly

Tate, S.
Fuzzy Pink Nightgown, The
UA (US) 1957 dir. Norman Taurog

Taulbert, C. L.
Once Upon a Time ... When We Were
Colored
BET (US) 1995 dir. Tim Reid

Taylor, B.
Godsend, The
CANNON (US) 1980
dir. Gabrielle Beaumont

Taylor, B.
Mother's Boys
MIRAMAX (US) 1994 dir. Yves
Simoneau

Taylor, C.
Heaven
MIRAMAX (US) 1999 dir. Scott
Reynolds

Taylor, C. P.
And a Nightingale Sang

P

PORTMAN (GB) 1989 dir. Robert
Knights
TV(GB)

Taylor, D.
Mother Love

BBC (GB) 1989 dir. Simon Langton
TVSe(GB)

Taylor, D.
Paris in Spring

P

PAR (US) 1935 dir. Lewis Milestone

Taylor, E.
Wreath of Roses, A

GRANADA (GB) 1987) dir. John
Madden
TV(GB)

Taylor, G.
Alone in the Australian Wilderness

Over the Hill
VILLAGE ROADSHOW (Aust) 1992
dir. George Miller

Taylor, J.
Asking for It

Invasion of Privacy, An
EMBASSY TV (US) 1983
dir. Mel Damski
TV(US)

Taylor, J. D. and Bross, D. G.
Murder on Shadow Mountain, A

VZ/SERTNER (US) 1999 dir. Dick
Lowry
TV(US)

Taylor, K.
Address Unknown

COL (US) 1944
dir. William Cameron Menzies

Taylor, R.
Chicken Every Sunday

FOX (US) 1948 dir. George Seaton

Taylor, R. B.
Long Road Home

ROSEMONT (US) 1991 dir. John Korty

Taylor, R. L.
Journey to Matecumbe, A

Treasure of Matecumbe
DISNEY (US) 1976
dir. Vincent McEveety

Taylor, R. L.
Travels of Jaimie McPheeters, The

Guns of Diablo
MGM (US) 1964 dir. Boris Sagal

Taylor, S.
Avanti!

P

UA (US) 1972 dir. Billy Wilder

Taylor, S.
First Love

P

Promise at Dawn
AVCO (US/Fr) 1970 dir. Jules Dassin

Taylor, S.
Happy Time, The

P

COL (US) 1952 dir. Richard Fleischer

Taylor, S.
Sabrina Fair

P

Sabrina
PAR (US) 1954 dir. Billy Wilder
GB title: Sabrina Fair
PAR (US) 1995 dir. Sydney Pollack

Taylor, S. and Skinner, C. O.
Pleasure of his Company, The

P

PAR (US) 1961 dir. George Seaton

Taylor, S. W.
Man with my Face, The
UA (US) 1951 dir. Edward J. Montague

Tazewell, C.
Littlest Angel, The
OSTERMAN (US) 1969
dir. Walter C. Miller
TV(US)

Tebelak, J. M.
Godspell
P
COL (US) 1973 dir. David Greene
M

Teichman, H. and Kaufman, G. S.
Solid Gold Cadillac, The
P
COL (US) 1956 dir. Richard Quine

Teilhet, D.
Fearmakers, The
PACEMAKER (US) 1958
dir. Jacques Tourneur

Teilhet, D. L.
My True Love
No Room for the Groom
UI (US) 1952 dir. Douglas Sirk

Telander, R.
Heaven is a Playground
NEW LINE (US) 1991 dir. Randall Fried

Telfer, D.
Caretakers, The
UA (US) 1963 dir. Hall Bartlett
GB title: Borderlines

Tellado, C.
Mi Bodo Contigo
Our Marriage
PASSAGE (Fr) 1985 dir. Valeria
Sarimento

Temple Black, S.
Child Star
Child Star: The Shirley Temple Story
DISNEY (US/Aust) 2001 dir. Nadia
Tass

Temple, J.
No Room at the Inn
P
BN (GB) 1948 dir. Dan Birt

Temple, W. F.
Four-Sided Triangle
HAMMER (GB) 1952
dir. Terence Fisher

Templeton, C.
Kidnapping of the President, The
CROWN (US) 1980
dir. George Mendelink

Tengroth, B.
Three Strange Lives
FF (Swe) 1980
dir. Ingmar Bergman

Terasaki, G.
Bridge to the Sun
MGM (Fr/US) 1961 dir. Etienne Périer

Terrot, C.
Alligator Named Daisy, An
RANK (GB) 1955 dir. J. Lee Thompson

Terrot, C.
Angel Who Pawned Her Harp, The
BL (GB) 1954 dir. Alan Bromly

Tessier, T.
Rapture
TRISTAR (US) 1993 dir. Timothy Bond
TV(US)

Tevis, J. H.
Arizona in the 50's
Tenderfoot, The
DISNEY (US) 1964 dir. Byron Paul

Tevis, W.
Color of Money, The

DISNEY (US) 1986 dir. Martin Scorsese

Tevis, W.
Hustler, The

FOX (US) 1961 dir. Robert Rossen

Tevis, W.
Man Who Fell to Earth, The

BL (GB) 1976 dir. Nicholas Roeg
MGM/UA (US) 1987 dir. Robert J. Roth
TV(US)

Tey, J.
Brat Farrar

PHILCO (US) 1950 dir. Gordon Duff
TV(US)
BBC (GB) 1986 dir. Leonard Lewis
TVSe(GB)

Tey, J.
Franchise Affair, The

ABP (GB) 1951
dir. Lawrence Huntington
BBC (GB) 1988 dir. Leonard Lewis
TVSe(GB)

Tey, J.
Shilling for Candles, A

Young and Innocent
GFD (GB) 1937 dir. Alfred Hitchcock
US title: Girl was Young, A

Thackeray, W. M.
Barry Lyndon

WAR/HAWK (GB) 1975
dir. Stanley Kubrick

Thackeray, W. M.
Vanity Fair

HOL (US) 1932 dir. Chester M. Franklin
BBC (GB) 1967 dir. David Giles
TVSe(GB)
BBC (GB) 1987 dir. Diarmuid Lawrence,
Michael Owen Morris
TVSe(GB)
BBC/A&E (GB) 1999 dir. Marc Munden
TVSe(GB)

Thackeray, W. M.
Vanity Fair

Becky Sharp
RKO (US) 1935 dir. Rouben Mamoulian

Thackrey, Jr., T.
Preacher

Wild Card
DAVIS (US) 1992 dir. Mel Damski
TV(US)

Tharoor, S.
Show Business

Bollywood
SONI-KAHN (Ind) 1994 dir. B. J. Kahn
M

Thayer, N.
Spirit Lost

BET (US) 1997 dir. Neema Barnette

Thayer, T.
Call Her Savage

PAR (US) 1932 dir. John Francis Dillon

Thayer, T.
One Woman

Fame is the Name of the Game
UN TV (US) 1966 dir. Stuart Rosenberg
TV(US)

Theriault, Y.
Agaguk

Shadow of the Wolf
STUDIO CANAL+ (Fr/Can) 1992 dir.
Jacques Dorfmann, Pierre Magny

Theroux, P.
Half Moon Street

RKO (US) 1986 dir. Bob Swaim

Theroux, P.
London Embassy, The

THAMES (GB) 1988 dir. David Giles,
Roland Wilson
TVSe(GB)

Theroux, P.
Mosquito Coast, The
WAR (US) 1986 dir. Peter Weir

Theroux, P.
Saint Jack
NEW WORLD (US) 1979
dir. Peter Bogdanovich

Thiele, C.
Blue Fin
S. AUST (Aust) 1978 dir. Carl Schultz

Thigpen, C. H. and Cleckley, H. M.
Three Faces of Eve, The
FOX (US) 1957 dir. Nunnally Johnson

Thom, J. A.
Follow the River
SIGNBOARD HILL (US) 1995 dir.
Martin Davidson
TV(US)

Thom, J. A.
Panther in the Sky
Tecumseh: The Last Warrior
AM ZOETROPE (US) 1995 dir. Larry
Elikann
TV(US)

Thomas, A. E. and Miller, A. D.
Come Out of the Kitchen
P
Spring in Park Lane
BL (GB) 1948 dir. Herbert Wilcox

Thomas, A. E.
No More Ladies
P
MGM (US) 1935
dir. Edward H. Griffith, George Cukor

Thomas, A. E.
Witching Hour, The
P
PAR (US) 1934 dir. Henry Hathaway

Thomas, B.
Book of the Month
P
Please Turn Over
AA (GB) 1959 dir. Gerald Thomas

Thomas, B.
Bud and Lou
BANNER (US) 1978
dir. Robert C. Thompson
TV(US)

Thomas, B.
Charley's Aunt
P
FOX (US) 1941 dir. Archie Mayo
GB title: Charley's American Aunt

Thomas, B.
Charley's Aunt
P
Where's Charley?
WAR (US) 1952 dir. David Butler

Thomas, B.
Shooting Star
P
Great Game, The
ADELPHI (GB) 1952 dir. Maurice Elvey

Thomas, C.
Firefox
WAR (US) 1982 dir. Clint Eastwood

Thomas, D.
Mouse and the Woman, The
FACELIFT (GB) 1981 dir. Karl Francis

Thomas, D.
Under Milk Wood
P
RANK (GB) 1971 dir. Andrew Sinclair

Thomas, G. and Witts, M. M.
Day the Bubble Burst, The
FOX (US) 1982 dir. Joseph Hardy
TV(US)

Thomas, G. and Witts, M. M.
Day the World Ended, The

When Time Ran Out
WAR (US) 1980 dir. James Goldstone

Thomas, G. and Witts, M. M.
Enola Gay

VIACOM (US) 1980
dir. David Lowell Rich
TV(US)

Thomas, G. and Witts, M. M.
Voyage of the Damned

ITC (GB) 1976 dir. Stuart Rosenberg

Thomas, H.
John Perkins

Paddy
ARTE FRANCE (Fr) 1999 dir. Gerard
Mordillat

Thomas, J.
Hidden Blessings

ARABESQUE FILMS (US) 2000 dir.
Timothy Folsome
TV(US)

Thomas, L.
**Dangerous Davies – The Last
Detective**

INNER CIRCLE (GB) 1980
dir. Val Guest

Thomas, L.
Stand up Virgin Soldiers

WAR (GB) 1977 dir. Norman Cohen

Thomas, L.
Tropic of Ruislip, The

Tropic
ATV (GB) 1979 dir. Matthew Robinson
TVSe(GB)

Thomas, L.
Virgin Soldiers, The

COL (GB) 1969 dir. John Dexter

Thomas, P.
Spy, The

Defector, The
PECF (Fr/W. Ger) 1966 dir. Raoul Levy

Thomas, R.
Piège pour un Homme Seul

P
Honeymoon with a Stranger
TCF (US) 1969 dir. John Peyser
TV(US)

Thomas, R.
Piège pour un homme seul

P
Vanishing Act
LEVINSON-LINK (US) 1986
dir. David Greene
TV(US)

Thomas, R.
Trap for a Single Man

P
One of my Wives is Missing
SPEL-GOLD (US) 1976
dir. Glenn Jordan

Thomas, W. V.
Anzio

PAN (It) 1968 dir. Edward Dmytryk
GB title: Battle for Anzio, The

Thompson, C.
**A Glimpse of Hell: Explosion on the
USS Iowa and Its Cover-Up**

Glimpse of Hell, A
FOX TV (US/Can) 2001 dir. Mikael
Salomon
TV(US/Can)

Thompson, E.
On Golden Pond

P
UN (US) 1981 dir. Mark Rydell
CBS TV (US) 2001 dir. Ernest Thompson
TV(US)

Thompson, E.
West Side Waltz, The

P

VZ/SERTNER (US) 1995 dir. Ernest
Thompson
TV(US)

Thompson, H. S.
Fear and Loathing in Las Vegas

UN (US) 1998 dir. Terry Gilliam

Thompson, J.
After Dark, My Sweet

AVENUE (US) 1990 dir. James Foley

Thompson, J.
Getaway, The

CINERAMA (US) 1972
dir. Sam Peckinpah
UN (US) 1994 dir. Roger Donaldson

Thompson, J.
Grifters, The

MIRAMAX (US) 1990
dir. Stephen Frears

Thompson, J.
Kill Off, The

CABRIOLET (US) 1990
dir. Maggie Greenwald

Thompson, J.
One Hell of a Woman

Serie Noire
GAU (Fr) 1979 dir. Alain Corneau

Thompson, J.
POP: 1280

Coup de Torchon
FT (Fr) 1981 dir. Bertrand Tavernier
GB title: Clean Slate

Thompson, J.
Swell Looking Babe, A

Hit Me
CASTLE HILL (US) 1996 dir. Steven
Shainberg

Thompson, J. Lee
Double Error

P

Murder Without Crime
ABP (GB) 1950 dir. J. Lee Thompson

Thompson, M.
Not as a Stranger

UA (US) 1955 dir. Stanley Kramer

Thompson, T.
Celebrity

NBC (US) 1984 dir. Paul Wendkos
TVSe(US)

Thompson, T.
Death of Richie, The

H. JAFFE (US) 1977 dir. Paul Wendkos
TV(US)

Thorn, R. S.
Full Treatment, The

COL (GB) 1960 dir. Val Guest
US title: Stop Me Before I Kill

Thorn, R. S.
Upstairs and Downstairs

RANK (GB) 1959 dir. Ralph Thomas

Thornburg, N.
Cutter and Bone

UA (US) 1981 dir. Ivan Passer
GB title: Cutter's Way

Thorndike, R.
Christopher Syn

Dr Syn
GAU (GB) 1937 dir. Roy William Neill

Thorndike, R.
Christopher Syn

Dr. Syn, Alias the Scarecrow
DISNEY (US) 1962 dir. James Neilson

Thorne, A.
Baby and the Battleship, The

BL (GB) 1956 dir. Jay Lewis

Thorne, A.
So Long at the Fair
GFD (GB) 1950 dir. Terence Fisher

Thorp, R.
Detective, The
FOX (US) 1968 dir. Gordon Douglas

Thorp, R.
Devlin
VIACOM PICT (US) 1992 dir. Rick
Rosenthal
TV(US)

Thorp, R.
Die Hard
FOX (US) 1988 dir. John McTiernan

Thorpe, R.
Rainbow Drive
VIACOM (US) 1990 dir. Bobby Roth
TV(US)

Thorton, Y. and Coudert, J.
Ditchdiggers, Daughters, The
MTM (US) 1997 dir. Johnny Jensen
TV(US)

Thurber, J.
Catbird Seat, The
Battle of the Sexes, The
PROM (GB) 1960 dir. Charles Crichton

Thurber, J.
My Life and Hard Times
Rise and Shine
FOX (US) 1941 dir. Allan Dwan

Thurber, J.
Secret Life of Walter Mitty, The
RKO (US) 1947 dir. Norman Z. Macleod

Thurber, J. and Nugent, E.
Male Animal, The
P
WAR (US) 1942 dir. Elliot Nugent

Thurber, J. and Nugent, E.
Male Animal, The
P
She's Working Her Way Through College
WAR (US) 1952
dir. Bruce Humberstone

Thurman, J.
Isak Dinesen
Out of Africa
UN (US) 1985 dir. Sidney Pollack

Thurston, E. T.
Wandering Jew, The
P
OLY (GB) 1933 dir. Maurice Elvey

Thurston, K. C.
Masquerader, The
GOLDWYN (US) 1933
dir. Richard Wallace

Thynne, A.
Carry Cot, The
Blue Blood
MIQ (GB) 1973 dir. Andrew Sinclair

Tickell, J.
Appointment with Venus
GFD (GB) 1951 dir. Ralph Thomas
US title: Island Rescue

Tickell, J.
Hand and the Flower, The
Day to Remember, A
GFD (GB) 1953 dir. Ralph Thomas

Tickell, J.
Odette
BL (GB) 1950 dir. Herbert Wilcox

Tidmarsh, E. V.
Is Your Honeymoon Really Necessary?
P
ADELPHI (GB) 1953 dir. Maurice Elvey

Tidyman, E.
Dummy

WAR TV (US) 1979 dir. Frank Perry
TV(US)

Tidyman, E.
Shaft

MGM (US) 1971 dir. Gordon Parks
PAR (US/Ger) 2000 dir. John Singleton

Tierney, H.
Valkyrie's Armour

P

One Brief Summer
FOX (GB) 1969 dir. John MacKenzie

Tiesheng, S.
Life on a String

PBC (Ger/GB/China) 1991
dir. Chen Kaige

Tilsley, F.
Mutiny

H.M.S. Defiant
COL (GB) 1962 dir. Lewis Gilbert
US title: Damn the Defiant

Timerman, J.
**Prisoner Without a Name, Cell
Without a Number**

*Jacobo Timerman: Prisoner Without a
Name, Cell Without a Number*
CHRYS-YELL (US) 1983
dir. Linda Yellen
TV(US)

Timm, U.
Rennschwein Rudi Russel

Rudy, The Racing Pig
ROYAL (Ger) 1995 dir. Peter Timm

Tinkle, J. L.
**Thirteen Days to Glory: The Seige of
the Alamo**

Alamo: 13 Days to Glory, The
FRIES (US) 1987 dir. Burt Kennedy
TV(US)

Tinniswood, P.
Mog

LWT (GB) 1985 dir. Nic Phillips
TVSe(GB)

Tippette, G.
Bank Robber, The

Spikes Gang, The
UA (US) 1974 dir. Richard Fleischer

Titus, E.
Basil of Baker Street

Great Mouse Detective, The
DISNEY (US) 1986
dir. Burny Mattinson
A, Ch

Tobias, M.
Fatal Exposure

Sky's on Fire, The
ALL AM TV (US) 1998 dir. Dan Lerner
TV(US)

Toby, M.
Courtship of Eddie's Father, The

MGM (US) 1963 dir. Vincente Minnelli

Toffler, L.
Death Benefits

P

Settlement, The
CINETEL (US) 1999 dir. Mark Steilen

Tolins, J.
Twilight of the Golds, The

P

HALLMARK (US) 1996 dir. Ross Marks
TV(US)

Tolkien, J. R. R.
**Fellowship of the Ring, The; Two
Towers, The**

Lord of the Rings, The
UA (US) 1978 dir. Ralph Bakshi
A

Tolkien, J. R. R.
Lord of the Rings, The: The Fellowship of the Ring

NEW LINE (NZ/US) 2001 dir. Peter Jackson

Tolkin, M.
Player, The

AVE PICT (US) 1992 dir. Robert Altman

Toller, E.
Pastor Hall

P
UA (GB) 1940 dir. Roy Boulting

Tolstoy, L.
Anna Karenina

MGM (US) 1935 dir. Clarence Brown
BL (GB) 1947 dir. Julien Duvivier
BBC (GB) 1977 dir. Basil Coleman
TVSe(GB)
RASTAR (US) 1985 dir. Simon Langton
TV(GB/US)
CHANNEL 4/WGBH (GB/US) 2000
dir. David Blair
TVSe(GB/US)
WAR (US) 1997 dir. Bernard Rose

Tolstoy, L.
False Note, The

Argent, L'
EOS (Switz/Fr) 1983
dir. Robert Bresson

Tolstoy, L.
Father Sergius

MOSFILM (USSR) 1978
dir. Igor Talankin

Tolstoy, L.
Kreutzer Sonata, The

FOR (Fr) 1938 dir. Charles Guichard
MOSFILM (USSR) 1987
dir. Mikhail Schweitzer and Sofiya Milkina

Tolstoy, L.
Resurrection

UN (US) 1931 dir. Edwin Carewe
BBC (GB) 1968 dir. David Giles
TVSe(GB)

Tolstoy, L.
Resurrection

We Live Again
UA (US) 1934 dir. Rouben Mamoulian

Tolstoy, L.
War and Peace

PAR (US/It) 1956 dir. King Vidor
MOSFILM (Rus) 1967
dir. Sergei Bondarchuk
BBC (GB) 1972 dir. John Davies
TVSe(GB)

Toms, B.
Strange Affair, The

PAR (GB) 1968 dir. David Greene

Tong, S.
Blush

BEIJING (China) 1994 dir. Shaohong Li

Tong, S.
Wives and Concubines

Raise the Red Lantern
ORION (China) 1991 dir. Zhang Yimov

Tonkonogy, G.
Three Cornered Moon

P
PAR (US) 1933 dir. Elliott Nugent

Toole, B. A.
Ada, the Enchantress of Numbers, A Selections from the Letters of Lord Byron's Daughter and Her Description of the First Computer

Conceiving Ada
HOTWIRE (Ger/US) 1997 dir. Lynn Hershman-Leeson

Toole, J. K.
Neon Bible, The
CHANNEL 4 FILMS (GB/Sp) 1995 dir..
Terence Davies

Toombs, A.
Raising a Riot
BL (GB) 1955 dir. Wendy Toye

Topkins, K.
Kotch
CINERAMA (US) 1971
dir. Jack Lemmon

Topolski, D. and Robinson, P.
True Blue
CHANNEL 4 FILMS (GB) 1996 dir.
Ferdinand Fairfax

Topor, R.
Tenant, The
PAR (Fr) 1976 dir. Roman Polanski

Topor, T.
Nuts
P
WAR (US) 1987 dir. Martin Ritt

Torberg, F.
Auch das war Wein
38: Vienna Before the Fall
SATEL/ALMARO (Ger) 1988
dir. Wolfgang Gluck

Torres, E.
Carlito's Way; After Hours
Carlito's Way
UN (US) 1993 dir. Brian De Palma

Torres, E.
Q&A
TRISTAR (US) 1990 dir. Sidney Lumet

Totheroh, D.
Deep Valley
WAR (US) 1947 dir. Jean Negulesco

Tourner, M.
Roi Des Aulnes, Le
Ogre, The
STUDIO CANAL+ (Fr/Ger) 1996 dir.
Volker Schlondorff

Tournier, J.
Jeanne de Luynes, Comtesse de Verne
King's Whore, The
J&M (GB) 1990 dir. Axel Corti

Townsend, J. R.
Intruder, The
GRANADA (GB) 1972 dir. Peter
Caldwell
TVSe(GB)

Townsend, S.
Secret Diary of Adrian Mole, Aged 13¾, The
THAMES (GB) 1985 dir. Peter Sasdy
TVSe(GB)

Toyama, T.
Visas and Virtue
P
CEDAR GROVE (US) 1997 dir. Chris
Tashima

Tozzi, F.
With Closed Eyes
PARADIS (It/Fr/Sp) 1994 dir.
Francesca Archibugi

Tracy, D.
Criss Cross
UI (US) 1949 dir. Robert Siodmak

Tracy, D.
Criss Cross
Underneath
POPULIST (US) 1995 dir. Steven
Soderbergh

Tracy, M.
Mrs. White

White of the Eye
CANNON (GB) 1987
dir. Donald Cammell

Trahey, J.
Life with Mother Superior

Trouble with Angels, The
COL (US) 1966 dir. Ida Lupino

Traili, A.
Scarface

UA (US) 1932 dir. Howard Hawks

Tranter, F.
Courtneys of Curzon Street, The

BL (GB) 1947 dir. Herbert Wilcox
US title: Courtney Affair, The

Tranter, N.
Bridal Path, The

BL (GB) 1959 dir. Frank Launder

Trapp, M. A.
Story of the Trapp Family Singers, The

Sound of Music, The
FOX (US) 1965 dir. Robert Wise
M

Traven, B.
Bridge in the Jungle, The

UA (US/Mex) 1970
dir. Pancho Kohner

Traven, B.
Treasure of the Sierra Madre, The

WAR (US) 1948 dir. John Huston

Traver, R.
Anatomy of a Murder

COL (US) 1959 dir. Otto Preminger

Travers, B.
Banana Ridge

P
ABP (GB) 1941 dir. Walter C. Mycroft

Travers, B.
Cuckoo in the Nest, A

P
GB (GB) 1938 dir. Tom Walls

Travers, B.
Cuckoo in the Nest, A

P
Fast and Loose
GFD (GB) 1954 dir. Gordon Parry

Travers, B.
Dirty Work

P
GAU (GB) 1934 dir. Tom Walls

Travers, B.
Plunder

P
WILCOX (GB) 1931 dir. Tom Walls

Travers, B.
Rookery Nook

P
MGM (GB) 1930 dir. Tom Walls

Travers, B.
Thark

P
GB (GB) 1932 dir. Tom Walls

Travers, P. L.
Mary Poppins

DISNEY (US) 1964
dir. Robert Stevenson
Ch, M

Tregaskis, R. W.
Guadalcanal Diary

FOX (US) 1943 dir. Lewis Seiler

Tremaine, R.
Restoration

MIRAMAX (US/Arg) 1995 dir. Michael
Hoffman

Trenhaile, J.
Man Called Kyril, A

Codename: Kyril
INCITO/HTV (US/GB) 1988
dir. Ian Sharp
TV(GB/US)

Trevanian
Eiger Sanction, The

UN (US) 1975 dir. Clint Eastwood

Treves, Sir F.
**Elephant Man and Other
Reminiscences, The**

Elephant Man, The
PAR (GB) 1980 dir. David Lynch

Trevor, E.
Big Pick-Up, The

Dunkirk
MGM (GB) 1958 dir. Leslie Norman

Trevor, E.
Expressway

Smash-up on Interstate 5
FILMWAYS (US) 1976
dir. John Llewellyn Moxey
TV(US)

Trevor, E.
Flight of the Phoenix, The

FOX (US) 1965 dir. Robert Aldrich

Trevor, E.
Penthouse, The

GREEN-WHITE (US) 1989
dir. David Greene
TV(US)

Trevor, E.
Pillars of Midnight, The

80,000 Suspects
RANK (GB) 1963 dir. Val Guest

Trevor, E.
Quiller Memorandum, The

RANK (GB) 1966 dir. Michael Anderson

Trevor, W.
Ballroom of Romance, The

BBC (GB) 1980 dir. Patrick O'Connor
TV(GB)

Trevor, W.
Children of Dynmouth, The

BBC (GB) 1987 dir. Peter Hammond
TV(GB)

Trevor, W.
Felicia's Journey

ALLIANCE (Can/GB) 1999 dir. Atom
Egoyan

Trevor, W.
Fools of Fortune

PALACE (GB) 1990 dir. Pat O'Connor

Trollope, A.
Barchester Towers; Warden, The

Barchester Chronicles, The
BBC (GB) 1982 dir. David Giles
TVSe(GB)

Trollope, A.
**Can You Forgive Her?; Phineas Finn
The Irish Member; Eustace Diamonds,
The; Phineas Redux; Prime Minister,
The; Duke's Children, The**

Pallisers, The
BBC (GB) 1974 dir. Hugh David, Ronald
Wilson
TVSe(GB)

Trollope, A.
Malachi's Cove

PENRITH (GB) 1973
dir. Henry Herbert
US title: Seaweed Children, The

Trollope, A.
Way We Live Now, The

BBC (GB) 2001 dir. David Yates
TVSe(GB)

Trollope, J.
Choir, The
BBC (GB) 1995 dir. Ferdinand Fairfax
TVSe(GB)

Trollope, J.
Rector's Wife, The
CHANNEL 4 (GB) 1994 dir. Giles Foster
TVSe(GB)

Troy, U.
We Are Seven
She Didn't Say No!
ABP (GB) 1958 dir. Cyril Frankel

Troyat, H.
Mountain, The
PAR (US) 1956 dir. Edward Dmytryk

Truesdell, J.
Be Still My Love
Accused, The
PAR (US) 1948 dir. William Dieterle

Trumbo, D.
Johnny Got His Gun
CINEMATION (US) 1971
dir. Dalton Trumbo

Trump, I.
For Love Alone
RHI (US) 1996 dir. Michael Lindsay-Hogg
TV(US)

Truscott IV, L. K.
Dress Gray
WAR TV (US) 1986 dir. Glenn Jordan
TVSe(US)

Tryon, T.
Crowned Heads
Fedora
MAINLINE (Ger/Fr) 1978
dir. Billy Wilder

Tryon, T.
Harvest Home
Dark Secret of Harvest Home, The
UN TV (US) 1978 dir. Leo Penn
TVSe(US)

Tryon, T.
Other, The
FOX (US) 1972 dir. Robert Mulligan

Tryzna, T.
Panna Nikt
Miss Nobody
ZESPOL (Pol) 1997 dir. Andrzej Wajda

Tsiolkas, C.
Loaded
Head On
Gt SCOTT (Aust) 1998 dir. Ana Kokkinos

Tsuzuki, C.
Life of Eleanor Marx 1855–1899, The: A Socialist Tragedy
Eleanor Marx
BBC (GB) 1977 dir. Jane Howell
TVSe(GB)

Tucholsky, K.
Schloss Gripsholm
Gripsholm
BABELSBERG (Ger) 2000 dir. Xavier Koller

Tucker, A.
Miss Susie Slagle's
PAR (US) 1946 dir. John Berry

Tucker, P.
Last Yellow, The
P
SCALA (GB) 1999 dir. Julian Farino

Tulloch, J.
Season Ticket, The
Purely Belter
CHANNEL 4 FILMS (GB) 2000 dir. Mark Herman

Tully, J.
Beggars of Life
PAR (US) 1928 dir. William Wellman

Tunis, J. R.
Hard, Fast and Beautiful
RKO (US) 1951 dir. Ida Lupino

Tunstrom, G.
Juloratoriet
SANDREWS (Den/Nor/Swe) 1996 dir.
Kjell-Ake Andersson

Turgenev, A.
Month in the Country, A
P
ITV (GB) 1955 dir. Robert Hamer
TV(GB)
BBC (GB) 1955 dir. Bill Hays
TV(GB)
PAR (US) 1985 dir. Quentin Lawrence

Turgenev, I.
Fathers and Sons
BBC (GB) 1971 dir. Paddy Russell
TVSe(GB)

Turgenev, I.
First Love
Lover's Prayer
OVERSEAS (US/GB) 2001 dir. Reverge
Anselmo

Turgenev, I.
First Love
Summer Lightning
CHANNEL 4 (GB) 1984 dir. Paul Joyce
TV(GB)

Turgenev, I.
House of the Gentle Folk
Nest of Gentry
CORINTH (USSR) 1970
dir. Andrei Konchalovski

Turgenev, I.
Torrents of Spring
MILLIMETER (US) 1990
dir. Jerzy Skolimowski

Turkus, B. and Feder, S.
Murder, Inc.
FOX (US) 1960 dir. Burt Balaban, Stuart
Rosenberg

Turnbull, M.
Looking After Sandy
Bad Little Angel
MGM (US) 1939 dir. William Thiele

Turner, D.
Semi Detached
P
All the Way Up
GRANADA/EMI (GB) 1970
dir. James MacTaggart

Turner, E.
One-Way Ticket
COL (US) 1935 dir. Herbert Biberman

Turner, M.
Hard Core Logo
MIRAMAX (Can) 1996 dir. Bruce
McDonald

Turner, T. and Loder, K.
I, Tina
What's Love Got to Do With It?
TOUCHSTONE (US) 1993 dir. Brian
Gibson

Turney, C.
Other One, The
Back from the Dead
FOX (US) 1957
dir. Charles Marquis Warren

Turow, S.
Burden of Proof, The
ABC PROD (US) 1992
dir. Mike Robe
TVSe(US)

Turow, S.
Presumed Innocent
WAR (US) 1990 dir. Alan J. Pakula

Tutein, P.
Larsen
Zero Kelvin
NORSK (Nor/Swe) 1995 dir. Hans
Petter Moland

Tuttle Villegas, A. and Hugo, L.
Swimming Lessons
Another Woman's Husband
HEARST (US) 2000 dir. Noel Nosseck
TV(US)

Tuuri, A.
Talvisota
FINN (Fin) 1989 dir. Pekka Parikka

Twain, M.
Adventures of Huckleberry Finn, The
MGM (US) 1960 dir. Michael Curtiz
TAFT (US) 1981 dir. Jack B. Hively
TV(US)

Twain, M.
Adventures of Huckleberry Finn, The
Adventures of Huck Finn, The
DISNEY (US) 1993 dir. Stephen
Sommers

Twain, M.
Adventures of Huckleberry Finn, The
Huck and the King of Hearts
TRIMARK (US) 1994 dir. Michael
Keusch

Twain, M.
Adventures of Huckleberry Finn, The
Huckleberry Finn
PAR (US) 1931 dir. Norman Taurog
MGM (US) 1939 dir. Richard Thorpe
UA (US) 1974 dir. J. Lee Thompson
M
ABC (US) 1975 dir. Robert Totten
TV(US)

Twain, M.
Adventures of Tom Sawyer, The
UA (US) 1938 dir. Norman Taurog

Twain, M.
Adventures of Tom Sawyer, The
Tom and Huck
DISNEY (US) 1995 dir. Peter Hewitt
Ch

Twain, M.
Adventures of Tom Sawyer, The
Tom Sawyer
UA (US) 1973 dir. Don Taylor
M
UN (US) 1973 dir. James Neilson
TV(US)
STONE CANYON (US) 2000 dir. Phil
Mendez, Paul Sabella
A, M

Twain, M.
Connecticut Yankee in King Arthur's
Court, A
Connecticut Yankee, A
FOX (US) 1931 dir. David Butler

Twain, M.
Connecticut Yankee in King Arthur's
Court, A
*Connecticut Yankee in King Arthur's
Court, A*
PAR (US) 1948 dir. Tay Garnett
GB title: Yankee in King Arthur's
Court, A
M
CONSOL (US) 1989 dir. Mel Damski
TV(US)

Twain, M.
Connecticut Yankee in King Arthur's
Court, A
Knight in Camelot, A
ROSEMONT (US) 1998 dir. Roger
Young
TV(US)

Twain, M.
Connecticut Yankee in King Arthur's Court, A

Spaceman and King Arthur, The
DISNEY (GB) 1979 dir. Russ Mayberry
US title: Unidentified Flying Oddball

Twain, M.
Million Pound Note, The

GFD (GB) 1954 dir. Ronald Neame
US title: Man with a Million

Twain, M.
Prince and the Pauper, The

WAR (US) 1937 dir. William Keighley
DISNEY (US) 1961 dir. Don Chaffey
TV(US)
BBC (GB) 1976 dir. Barry Letts
TVSe(GB)
WAR (PAN) 1977 dir. Richard Fleischer
US title: Crossed Swords
HALLMARK (US) 2000 dir. Giles Foster
TV(US)

Twain, M.
Prince and the Pauper, The

Prince For a Day
NBC (US) 1995 dir. Corey Blechman
TV(US)

Tweed, T. F.
Rinehard

Gabriel Over the White House
MGM (US) 1933 dir. Gregory LaCava

Twiss, C.
Long, Long Trailer, The
MGM (US) 1954 dir. Vincente Minnelli

Tyler, A.
Accidental Tourist, The
WAR (US) 1988 dir. Lawrence Kasdan

Tyler, A.
Breathing Lessons
SIGNBOARD HILL (US) 1994 dir. Jorn Erman
TV(US)

Tyler, A.
Earthly Possessions
RASTAR (US) 1999 dir. James Lapine
TV(US)

Tyler, A.
Saint Maybe
HALLMARK (US) 1998 dir. Michael Pressman
TV(US)

Tyler, A.
Slipping Down Life, A
DVC (US) 1999 dir. Toni Kalem

Tyler, P.
Garden of Cucumbers, A
Fitzwilly
UA (US) 1967 dir. Delbert Mann
GB title: Fitzwilly Strikes Back

Uchida, Y.
Noh Mask Murders
TOEI (Jap) 1991 dir. Kon Ichikawa

Ueno, J.
New York Undercover Cop
New York Cop
STP (US) 1995 dir. Toru Murakawa

Uhlman, F.
Reunion
RANK (US/Fr/Ger) 1989
dir. Jerry Schatzberg

Uhnak, D.
Bait, The
ABC (US) 1973 dir. Leonard Horn
TV(US)

Uhnak, D.
False Witness
NEW WORLD TV (US) 1989
dir. Arthur Allan Seidelman
TV(US)

Uhnak, D.
Investigation, The
Kojak: The Price of Justice
MCA/UN (US) 1987 dir. Alan Metzger
TV(US)

Uhnak, D.
Law and Order
PAR (US) 1976 dir. Marvin J. Chomsky
TV(US)

Uhnak, D.
Ledger, The
Get Christy Love!
WOLPER (US) 1974 dir.
William A. Graham
TV(US)

Uhry, A.
Driving Miss Daisy
P
WAR (US) 1989 dir. Bruce Beresford

Ullman, J. R.
Banner in the Sky
Third Man on the Mountain
DISNEY (GB) 1959 dir. Ken Annakin
Ch

Ullman, J. R.
White Tower, The
RKO (US) 1950 dir. Ted Tetzlaff

Ullman, J. R.
Windom's Way
RANK (GB) 1957 dir. Ronald Neame

Undset, S.
Kristin Lavransdatter
NORSK (Nor/Swe/Ger) 1995 dir. Liv
Ullman

Unekis, R.
Chase, The
Dirty Mary, Crazy Larry
FOX (US) 1974 dir. John Hough

Unsworth, B.
Idol Hunter, The
Pascali's Island
AVENUE (GB) 1988 dir. James Dearden

Updike, J.
Rabbit, Run
WAR (US) 1970 dir. Jack Smight

Updike, J.
Too Far to Go
ZOETROPE (US) 1982 dir. Fielder Cook

Updike, J.
Witches of Eastwick, The
WAR (US) 1987 dir. George Miller

Uris, L.
Angry Hills, The
MGM (GB) 1959 dir. Robert Aldrich

Uris, L.
Battle Cry
WAR (US) 1954 dir. Raoul Walsh

Uris, L.
Exodus
UA (US) 1960 dir. Otto Preminger

Uris, L.
QB VII
COL (US) 1974 dir. Tom Gries
TVSe(US)

Uris, L.
Topaz
UI (US) 1969 dir. Alfred Hitchcock

Ustinov, P.
Romanoff and Juliet
P
UN (US) 1961 dir. Peter Ustinov

Uttley, A.
Traveller in Time, A
BBC (GB) 1978 dir. Dorothea Brooking
TVSe(GB)

Vaccaro, R.
And the Home of the Brave

P
Run the Wild Fields
SHOWTIME (US) 2000 dir. Paul A.
Kaufman
TV(US)

Vachell, H. A.
Case of Lady Camber, The

P
Lord Camber's Ladies
BI (GB) 1932 dir. Benn W. Levy

Vailland, R.
Truite, La

Trout, The
TRIUMPH (Fr) 1982 dir. Joseph Losey

Vailland, R.
Where the Hot Wind Blows

MGM (Fr/It) 1958 dir. Jules Dassin

Valdes, D.
Bailame el Agua

PLOT (Sp) 2000 dir. Josecho San Mateo

Valdez, L.
Zoot Suit

P
UN (US) 1982 dir. Luis Valdez

Vale, M.
Two Mrs. Carrolls, The

P
WAR (US) 1947 dir. Peter Godfrey

Valens, E. G.
Long Way Up, A

Other Side of the Mountain, The
UN (US) 1975 dir. Larry Peerce
GB title: Window to the Sky, A

Valin, J.
Final Notice

SHARMHILL (US) 1989
dir. Steven Hilliard Stern
TV(US)

Vallejo, F.
Virgin de Los Sicarios, La

Our Lady of the Assassins
STUDIO CANAL+ (Fr) 2000 dir. Barbet
Schroeder

Valme and Terzolli
Bankers Also Have Souls

P
Gift, The
GOLDWYN (Fr) 1983 dir. Michel Lang

Valtos, W.
Resurrection

Almost Dead
DELTA (US) 1996 dir. Ruben Preuss
TV(US)

Van Allsburg, C.
Jumanji

INTERSCOPE (US) 1995 dir. Joe
Johnston

Van Atta, W.
Shock Treatment

WAR (US) 1964 dir. Denis Sanders

van Daalen, J.
Sans Rancune

Lek
RCV (Neth) 2000 dir. Jean van de Velde

van Dantzig, R.
For a Lost Soldier

SIGMA (Neth) 1992 dir. Roeland
Kerbosch

van der Laan, H.
Waar Blijft Het Licht

When the Light Comes
ADDED (Ger/Neth) 1999 dir. Stijn
Coninx

van der Meersch, M.
Bodies and Souls

Doctor and the Girl, The
MGM (US) 1949 dir. Curtis Bernhardt

Van Der Post, Sir L.
Far Off Place, A; Story Like The Wind, A

Far Off Place, A
DISNEY (US) 1993 dir. Mikael Salomon

van der Post, Sir L.
Seed and the Sower The

Merry Christmas, Mr. Lawrence
UN (GB) 1983 dir. Nagisa Oshima

van Dine, S. S.
Bishop Murder Case, The

MGM (US) 1930 dir. Nick Grinde,
David Burton

van Dine, S. S.
Casino Murder Case, The

MGM (US) 1935 dir. Edwin Marin

van Dine, S. S.
Gracie Allen Murder Case, The

PAR (US) 1939 dir. Alfred E. Green

van Dine, S. S.
Kennel Murder Case, The

Calling Philco Vance
WAR (US) 1939 dir. William Clemens

van Dine, S. S.
Kennel Murder Case, The

WAR (US) 1933 din Michael Curtiz

van Druten, J.
After All

P
New Morals for Old
MGM (US) 1932 dir. Charles Brabin

van Druten, J.
Behold We Live

P
If I Were Free
RKO (US) 1933 dir. Elliot Nugent

van Druten, J.
Bell, Book and Candle

P
COL (US) 1958 dir. Richard Quine

van Druten, J.
I am a Camera

P
BI (GB) 1955 dir. Henry Cornelius

van Druten, J.
I am a Camera

P
Cabaret
CINERAMA (US) 1972 dir. Bob Fosse
M

van Druten, J.
I Remember Mama

P
RKO (US) 1948 dir. George Stevens

van Druten, J.
London Wall

P
After Office Hours
BI (GB) 1935 dir. Thomas Bentley

van Druten, J.
Old Acquaintance

P
WAR (US) 1943 dir. Vincent Sherman

van Druten, J.
Old Acquaintance

P
Rich and Famous
MGM (US) 1981 dir. George Cukor

van Druten, J.
There's Always Juliet

P
One Night in Lisbon
PAR (US) 1941 dir. Edward H. Griffith

van Druten, J.
Voice of the Turtle

P
WAR (US) 1947 dir. Irving Rapper

van Druten, J.
Young Woodley

P
BI (GB) 1929 dir. Thomas Bentley

Van Greenaway, P.
Medusa Touch, The

ITC (GB/Fr) 1978 dir. Jack Gold

Van Gulik, R.
Haunted Monastery, The

Judge Dee and the Monastery Murders
ABC (US) 1974 dir. Jeremy Paul Kagan
TV(US)

Van Loon, H. W.
Story of Mankind, The

WAR (US) 1957 dir. Irwin Allen

Van Peebles, M.
Bellyful

STUDIO CANAL+ (Fr) 2000 dir. Melvin
Van Peebles

Van Peebles, M.
Blowing in the Wind

Panther
POLYGRAM (US/GB) 1995 dir. Mario
Van Peebles

van Slyke, H.
Best Place To Be, The

R. HUNTER (US) 1979 dir. David Miller
TVSe(US)

Van Tilburg Clark, W.
Ox-Bow Incident, The

FOX (US) 1943 dir. William Wellman
US title: Strange Incident

Van Tilburg Clark, W.
Track of the Cat

WAR (US) 1954 dir. William A. Wellman

Vance, E.
Escape

MGM (US) 1940 dir. Mervyn LeRoy

Vance, E.
Winter Meeting

WAR (US) 1948 dir. Bretaigne Windust

Vance, J. H.
Bad Ronald

LORIMAR (US) 1974 dir. Buzz Kulik
TV(US)

Vance, L. J.
Lone Wolf Returns, The

COL (US) 1936
dir. Roy William McNeill

Vandercook, J. W.
Murder in Trinidad

FOX (US) 1934 dir. Louis King

Vane, S.
Outward Bound

P
WAR (US) 1930 dir. Robert Milton

Vane, S.
Outward Bound
P
Between Two Worlds
WAR (US) 1944 dir. Edward A. Blatt

Varley, J.
Air Raid
Millenium
FOX (US) 1989 dir. Michael Anderson

Vasquez-Figueroa, A.
Ebano
Ashanti
COL (Switz) 1979 dir. Richard Fleischer

Vassilikos, V.
Z
WAR (Fr/Alg) 1968 dir. Costa-Gavras

Veber, F.
Buddy Buddy
P
MGM (US) 1981 dir. Billy Wilder

Veber, F.
Diner de Cons, Le
P
Dinner Game, The
GAU (Fr) 1998 dir. Francis Veber

Vegliani, F.
Frontiera, La
CORRIDORI (It) 1996 dir. Franco Giraldi

Veiller, B.
Within the Law
P
MGM (US) 1939 dir. Gustav Machaty

Veiller, B.
Within the Law
P
Paid
MGM (US) 1930 dir. Sam Wood
GB title: Within the Law

Vercel, R.
Captain Conan
STUDIO CANAL+ (Fr) 1996 dir. Bertrand Tavernier

Verdi, G.
Otello
CANNON (It) 1986 dir. Franco Zeffirelli
M

Verghese, A.
My Own Country
SHOWTIME (US) 1998 dir. Mira Nair
TV(US)

Verne, J.
Around the World in Eighty Days
UA (US) 1956 dir. Michael Anderson, Kevin McClory
HARMONY (US) 1989
dir. Buzz Kulik
TVSe(US)

Verne, J.
Captain Grant's Children
In Search of the Castaways
DISNEY (GB) 1961 dir. Robert Stevenson
Ch

Verne, J.
800 Leagues Down the Amazon
IGUANA (US/Peru) 1993 dir. Luis Llosa

Verne, J.
Five Weeks in a Balloon
FOX (US) 1962 dir. Irwin Allen

Verne, J.
From the Earth to the Moon
WAR (US) 1958 dir. Byron Haskin

Verne, J.
Journey to the Centre of the Earth

FOX (US) 1959 dir. Henry Levin
CANNON (US) 1989
dir. Rusty Lemorande
HIGH (US) 1993 dir. William Dear
TV(US)
HALLMARK (US) 1999 dir. George
Miller
TVSe(US)

Verne, J.
Lighthouse at the End of the World

Light at the Edge of the World, The
MGM (US/Sp) 1971
dir. Kevin Billington

Verne, J.
Master of the World

AA (US) 1961 dir. William Witney

Verne, J.
Michael Strogoff

Soldier and the Lady, The
RKO (US) 1937 dir. George Nicholls, Jr.
GB title: Michael Strogoff

Verne, J.
Mysterious Island

COL (GB) 1962 dir. Cy Endfield

Verne, J.
Southern Star Mystery, The

Southern Star, The
COL (GB/Fr) 1969 dir. Sidney Hayers

Verne, J.
20,000 Leagues Under the Sea

DISNEY (US) 1954
dir. Richard Fleischer
HALLMARK (US) 1997 dir. Michael
Anderson
TV(US)
VILLAGE ROADSHOW (US) dir. Rod
Hardy
TVSe(US)

Verneuil, L.
Jealousy

P
Deception
WAR (US) 1946 dir. Irving Rapper

Verneuil, L. and Berr, G.
Mon Crime

P
True Confession
PAR (US) 1937 dir. Wesley Ruggles

Very, P.
Goupi Mains Rouges

MINERVA (Fr) 1943
dir. Jacques Becker
US title: It Happened at the Inn

Vetere, R.
Marriage Fool, The

P
GROSS/BAR (US) 1998 dir. Charles
Matthau
TV(US)

Vetere, R.
Rage of the Blue Moon

P
Touched By a Killer
WI (Can) 2001 dir. Gilbert M. Shilton
TV(Can)

Vetere, R.
Third Miracle, The

AM ZOETROPE (US) 1999 dir.
Agnieszka Holland

Vian, B.
Ecume des Jours, L'

Chloe
DENTSU (Jap) 2001 dir. Go Riju

Vicent, M.
Son de Mar

LOLAFILMS (Sp) 2001 dir. J. J. Bigas
Luna

Vickers, R.
Girl in the News, The
FOX (GB) 1940 dir. Carol Reed

Vidal, G.
Best Man, The
P
UA (US) 1964 dir. Franklin Schaffner

Vidal, G.
Lincoln
Gore Vidal's Lincoln
FINNEGAN/PINCHUK (US) 1988
dir. Lamont Johnson
TVSe(US)

Vidal, G.
Myra Breckenridge
FOX (US) 1970 dir. Mike Sarne

Vidal, G.
Visit to a Small Planet
P
PAR (US) 1960 dir. Norman Taurog

Vidalie, A.
Heaven Fell That Night
IENA (Fr/It) 1958 dir. Roger Vadim

Viertel, P.
White Hunter, Black Heart
WAR (US) 1990 dir. Clint Eastwood

Vigny, B.
Amy Jolly
P
Morocco
PAR (US) 1930 dir. Josef von Sternberg

Villard, H. S. and Nagel, J.
Hemingway in Love and War
In Love and War
NEW LINE (US) 1996 dir. Richard
Attenborough

Vincent, M.
Trenvia a la Malvarrosa
LOLAFILMS (Sp) 1996 dir. Jose Luis
Garcia Sanchez

Vinje, K.
Kamilla and the Thief
PENELOPE (Nor/GB) 1988
dir. Grete Salamonsen

Vinton, I.
Flying Ebony
Mooncussers, The
DISNEY (US) 1971 dir. James Neilson

Viola, C. G.
Prico
Children Are Watching Us, The
MAGLI (It) 1942 dir. Vittorio de Sica

Vitoux, F.
Comedie de Terracina, Le
Dolce Far Niente
EURIMAGES (Bel/Fr) 1999 dir. Nae
Caranfil

Vittorini, E.
Conversation in Sicily
Sicilia!
ALIA (It/Fr) 1999 dir. Daniele Huillet,
Jean-Marie Straub

Vivant, D.
Point de Lendemain
Amants, Les
NEF (Fr) 1958 dir. Louis Malle

Vizinczey, S.
In Praise of Older Women
ASTRAL (Can) 1977
dir. George Kaczender
CANAL+ ESPANA (Sp) 1997 dir.
Manuel Lombadero

Vogel, K.
Virgin Witch
TIGON (GB) 1970 dir. Ray Austin

Voight, C.
Homecoming
HALLMARK (US) 1996 dir. Mark Jean
TV(US)

Voinovich, V.
Life and Extraordinary Adventures of Private Ivan Chonkin, The
PORTOBELLO (Czech/GB/Fr) 1995 dir. Jiri Menzel

Volkman, E. and Cummings, J.
Heist, The: How a Gang Stole $8,000,000 at Kennedy Airport and Lived to Regret It
Big Heist, The
ALLIANCE/A&E (US/Can) 2001 dir. Robert Markowitz
TV(US/Can)

Vollmer, L.
Trigger
P
Spitfire
RKO (US) 1934 dir. John Cromwell

Vollmoeller, K.
Miracle, The
P
WAR (US) 1959 dir. Irving Rapper

Voltaire
Candide
Cultivating Charlie
GMS (US) 1993 dir. Alex Georges

von Arnim, E.
Enchanted April, The
Enchanted April
RKO (US) 1935 dir. Harry Beaumont
BBC (GB) 1992 dir. Mike Newell

von Arnim, E.
Mr. Skeffington
WAR (US) 1944 dir. Vincent Sherman

Von Hoffman, N.
Citizen Cohn
HBO (US) 1992 dir. Frank Pierson
TV(US)

von Horvath, O.
Tales from the Vienna Woods
P
CINEMA 5 (Austria/Ger) 1981 dir. Maximilian Schell

von Kleist, H.
Michael Kohlhaas
COL (Ger) 1980 dir. Volker Schlondorff

von Kleist, H.
Michael Kohlhaas
Jack Bull, The
NEW CRIME (US) 1999 dir. John Badham
TV(US)

von Kleist, H.
Prinz Friedrich von Homburg
P
Prince of Homburg, The
PBS (US) 1997 dir. Kirk Browning
TV(US)

von Krusenstjerna, A.
Froknarna von Pahlen
Loving Couples
SANDREW (Swe) 1964 dir. Mai Zetterling

von Sacher-Masoch, L.
Venus im Pelz
Venus in Furs
COMM (GB/It/Ger) 1970 dir. Jess Franco
K FILMS (Neth) 1994 dir. Victor Nieuwenhuijs, Maarte Seyferth

Vonnegut, K.
Breakfast of Champions
SUMMIT (US) 1999 dir. Alan Rudolph

Vonnegut, K.
Happy Birthday, Wanda Jane
P
COL (US) 1971 dir. Mark Robson

Vonnegut, K.
Mother Night
FINE LINE (US) 1996 dir. Keith Gordon

Vonnegut, K.
Next Door; Euphio Question, The; All the King's Men
Monkey House
ATLANTIS (US) 1991 dir. Paul Shapiro, Gilbert Shilton, Allan King
TV(US)

Vonnegut, K.
Slapstick
Slapstick of Another Kind
LORIMAR (US) 1984 dir. Steven Paul

Vonnegut, K.
Slaughterhouse Five
UN (US) 1972 dir. George Roy Hill

Vosper, F.
Love from a Stranger
P
UA (GB) 1937 dir. Rowland V. Lee
EL (US) 1947
dir. Richard Whorf
GB title: Stranger Walked In, A

Votler, G.
Cipher, The
Arabesque
UN (US) 1966 dir. Stanley Donen

Vreeland, S.
What Love Sees
ROSEMONT (US) 1996 dir. Michael Switzer
TV(US)

Vulliamy, C. E.
Don Among the Dead Men
Jolly Bad Fellow, A
BL (GB) 1964 dir. Robert Hamer

Vulliamy, C. E.
William Penn
Penn of Pennsylvania
BN (GB) 1941 dir. Lance Comfort
US title: Courageous Mr. Penn, The

Vulpuis, P.
Youth at the Helm
P
Jack of all Trades
GAINS (GB) 1936 dir. Jack Hubert, Robert Stevenson

Waddell, M.
Otley
COL (GB) 1968 dir. Dick Clement

Wade, K.
Key Exchange
P
FOX (US) 1985 dir. Barnet Kellman

Wadler, J.
My Breast
HEARST (US) 1994 dir. Betty Thomas
TV(US)

Wagenheim, K.
Babe Ruth, His Life and Legend
Babe Ruth
LYTTLE (US) 1991 dir. Mark Tinker
TV(US)

Wager, W.
58 Minutes
Die Hard 2
FOX (US) 1990 dir. Renny Harlin

Wager, W.
Telefon
MGM (US) 1977 dir. Don Siegel

Wager, W.
Viper Three
Twilight's Last Gleaming
HEMDALE (US/Ger) 1977
dir. Robert Aldrich

Wagner, B.
I'm Losing You
LIONS GATE (US) 1999 dir. Bruce
Wagner

Wagoner, D.
Escape Artist, The
ORION (US) 1982 dir. Caleb Deschanel

Wahloo, P.
Murder on the 31st Floor
Kamikaze '89
TELECUL (Ger) 1983 dir. Wolf Gremm

Wainwright, J.
Brainwash
Inquisitor, The
GALA (Fr) 1981 dir. Claude Miller

Wainwright, J.
Brainwash
Under Suspicion
LIONS GATE (US/Fr) 2000 dir. Stephen
Hopkins

Waitzkin, F.
Waiting for Bobby Fischer
MIRAGE (US) 1993 dir. Steven Zaillian

Wakatsuki, J. and Houston, J. D.
Farewell to Manzanar
UN TV (US) 1976 dir. John Korty
TV(US)

Wakefield, D.
Going All the Way
POLYGRAM (US) 1997 dir. Mark Pellington

Wakefield, D.
James at 15
FOX TV (US) 1977 dir. Joseph Hardy
TV(US)

Wakefield, D.
Starting Over
PAR (US) 1979 dir. Alan J. Pakula

Wakefield, G.
Counsel's Opinion
P
KORDA (GB) 1933 dir. Allan Dwan

Wakefield, G.
Counsel's Opinion
P
Divorce of Lady X, The
LONDON (GB) 1938 dir. Tim Whelan

Wakeman, F.
Hucksters, The
MGM (US) 1947 dir. Jack Conway

Wakeman, F.
Saxon Charm, The
UI (US) 1948 dir. Claude Binyon

Wakeman, F.
Shore Leave
Kiss Them for Me
FOX (US) 1957 dir. Stanley Donen

Walker, A.
Color Purple, The
WAR (US) 1986 dir. Steven Spielberg

Walker, D.
Geordie
BL (GB) 1955 dir. Frank Launder
US title: Wee Geordie

Walker, D.
Harry Black and the Tiger
FOX (GB) 1958 dir. Hugo Fregonese
US title: Harry Black

Walker, D. E.
Adventure in Diamonds
Operation Amsterdam
RANK (GB) 1958
dir. Michael McCarthy

Walker, D. E.
Diamonds are Danger
Man Could Get Killed, A
UN (US) 1966 dir. Ronald Neame

Walker, G.
Case History
Damned Don't Cry, The
WAR (US) 1950 dir. Vincent Sherman

Walker, G.
Cruising
LORIMAR (US) 1980
dir. William Friedkin

Walker, G. F.
Better Living
P
GOLDHEART (US) 1998 dir. Max Meyer

Walker, L.
Sudden Fury
Family Torn Apart, A
HALMI (US) 1993 dir. Craig Baxley
TV(US)

Wall, J. H.
Mother Love
Family Divided, A
CITADEL ENT (US) 1995 dir. Donald Wrye
TV(US)

Wall, M.
Amongst Barbarians
BBC (GB) 1990 dir. Jane Howell
TV(GB)

Wallace, E.
Calendar, The
GFD (GB) 1948 dir. Arthur Crabtree

Wallace, E.
Case of the Frightened Lady, The
Frightened Lady, The
BL (GB) 1932 dir. T. Hayes Hunter

Wallace, E.
Case of the Frightened Lady, The
BL (GB) 1940 dir. George King
US title: Frightened Lady, The

Wallace, E.
Crimson Circle, The
NEW ERA (GB) 1929 dir. Fred Zelnick
WAINRIGHT (GB) 1936
dir. Reginald Denham

Wallace, E.
Daffodil Mystery, The
Devil's Daffodil, The
BL (GB) 1962 dir. Akos Rathonyi

Wallace, E.
Feathered Serpent
Menace, The
COL (US) 1932 dir. Roy William Neill

Wallace, E.
Fellowship of the Frog, The
Frog, The
WILCOX (GB) 1937 dir. Jack Raymond

Wallace, E.
Four Just Men, The
EAL (GB) 1939 dir. Walter Forde
US title: Secret Four, The

Wallace, E.
Ghost of John Holling, The
Mystery Liner
MON (US) 1934 dir. William Nigh

Wallace, E.
Jack O'Judgement
Share Out, The
AA (GB) 1962 dir. Gerald Glaister

Wallace, E.
Kate Plus Ten
WAINWRIGHT (GB) 1938
dir. Reginald Denham

Wallace, E.
Lone House Mystery, The
Attempt to Kill
AA (GB) 1961 dir. Royston Murray

Wallace, E.
Man At The Carlton
Man at the Carlton Tower
AA (GB) 1961 dir. Robert Tronson

Wallace, E.
Man Who Knew, The
Partners in Crime
AA (GB) 1961 dir. Peter Duffell

Wallace, E.
Mind of Mr J. G. Reeder, The
Mind of Mr. Reeder, The
RAYMOND (GB) 1936
dir. Jack Raymond

Wallace, E.
On The Spot
P
Dangerous to Know
PAR (US) 1938 dir. Robert Florey

Wallace, E.
Ringer, The
REGENT (GB) 1952 dir. Guy Hamilton

Wallace, E.
Ringer, The
Gaunt Stranger, The
NORTHWOOD (GB) 1938
dir. Walter Forde
US title: Phantom Strikes, The

Wallace, E.
Sanders of the River
UA (GB) 1935 dir. Zoltan Korda
US title: Bosambo

Wallace, E.
Squeaker, The
GAU BR (GB) 1937
dir. William K. Howard
US title: Murder on Diamond Row

Wallace, E.
Terror, The
ALL (GB) 1938 dir. Richard Bird

Wallace, E.
Traitor's Gate
COL (GB) 1965 dir. Freddie Francis

Wallace, F.
Kid Galahad
WAR (US) 1937 dir. Michael Curtiz
UA (US) 1962 dir. Phil Karlson
M

Wallace, I.
Chapman Report, The
WAR (US) 1962 dir. George Cukor

Wallace, I.
Man, The
PAR (US) 1972 dir. Joseph Sargent

Wallace, I.
Prize, The
MGM (US) 1963 dir. Mark Robson

Wallace, I.
Seven Minutes, The
FOX (US) 1971 dir. Russ Meyer

Wallace, I.
Word, The
FRIES (US) 1978 dir. Richard Lang
TVSe(US)

Wallace, L.
Ben Hur
MGM (US) 1926 dir. Fred Niblo
MGM (US) 1959 dir. William Wyler

Wallace, P.
Dreams Lost, Dreams Found
ATLANTIC/YTV (US/GB) 1987
dir. Willi Patterson
TV(GB/US)

Wallace, P.
Love with a Perfect Stranger
ATLANTIC/YTV (US/GB) 1988 dir.
Desmond Davis
TV(GB/US)

Wallace, P.
Tears in the Rain
ATLANTIC/BL (US/GB) 1988
dir. Don Sharpe
TV(GB/US)

Wallach, I.
Muscle Beach
Don't Make Waves
MGM (US) 1967 dir. Alexander
Mackendrick

Wallant, E. L.
Pawnbroker, The
PAR (US) 1964 dir. Sidney Lunnet

Waller, L.
Hide in Plain Sight
UA (US) 1980 dir. James Caan

Waller, R. J.
Bridges of Madison County, The
WAR (US) 1995 dir. Clint Eastwood

Wallington, M.
Happy Birthday Shakespeare
BBC (GB) 2000 dir. Nick Hurran
TV(GB)

Wallis, A. J. and Blair, C. E.
Thunder Above
Beyond the Curtain
RANK (GB) 1960 dir. Compton Bennett

Wallis, J. H.
Once Off Guard
Woman in the Window, The
RKO (US) 1944 dir. Fritz Lang

Wallop, D.
Year the Yankees Lost the Pennant,
The
Damn Yankees
WAR (US) 1958 dir. George Abbott,
Stanley Donen
GB title: What Lola Wants
M

Walmsley, L.
Three Fevers
Turn of the Tide
BN (GB) 1935 dir. Norman Walker

Walmsley, T.
Paris, France
ALLIANCE (Can) 1993 dir. Jerry
Ciccoritti

Walpole, H.
Mr. Perrin and Mr. Traill
TC (GB) 1948 dir. Lawrence
Huntington

Walpole, H.
Vanessa, Her Love Story
MGM (US) 1935 dir. William K.
Howard

Walser, R.
Jakob von Gunten
Institute Benjamenta
IMAGE (GB) 1995 dir. Stephen Quay,
Timothy Quay

Walsh, E.
Disco Pigs
P
TEMPLE (Ire) 2001 dir. Kirsten
Sheridan

Walsh, M.
Green Rushes
Quiet Man, The
REP (US) 1952 dir. John Ford

Walsh, M.
Trouble in the Glen
REP (GB) 1954 dir. Herbert Wilcox

Walsh, T.
Nightmare in Manhattan
Union Station
PAR (US) 1950 dir. Rudolph Maté

Walsh, T.
Night Watch, The
Pushover
COL (US) 1954 dir. Richard Quine

Waltari, M.
Egyptian, The
FOX (US) 1954 dir. Michael Curtiz

Walter, E.
Easiest Way, The
P
MGM (US) 1931 dir. Jack Conway

Walter, J.
Every Knee Shall Bow
Ruby Ridge: An American Tragedy
SCHERICK (US) 1996 dir. Roger Young
TVSe(US)

Walters, G. M. and Hopkins, A.
Burlesque

P

Swing High, Swing Low
PAR (US) 1937 dir. Mitchell Leisen

Walters, G. M. and Hopkins, A.
Burlesque

P

When my Baby Smiles at Me
FOX (US) 1948 dir. Walter Lang

Walters, M.
Scold's Bridle, The

BBC (GB) 1998 dir. David Thacker
TV(GB)

Walton, T.
Inside Moves

BARBER (US) 1980 dir. Richard Donner

Walton, T.
Walton Experience, The

Fire in the Sky
PAR (US) 1993 dir. Robert Lieberman

Wambaugh, J.
Black Marble, The

AVCO (US) 1980
dir. Harold Becker

Wambaugh, J.
Blue Knight, The

LORIMAR (US) 1973 dir. Robert Butler
TVSe(US)

Wambaugh, J.
Choirboys, The

LORIMAR (US) 1977 dir. Robert
Aldrich

Wambaugh, J.
Echoes in the Darkness

NEW WORLD TV (US) 1987
dir. Glenn Jordan
TVSe(US)

Wambaugh, J.
From the Files of Joseph Wambaugh:
A Jury of One

TRISTAR TV (US) 1992 dir. Alan
Metzger
TV(US)

Wambaugh, J.
Fugitive Nights: Danger in the Desert

TRISTAR TV (US) 1993 dir. Gary
Nelson
TV(US)

Wambaugh, J.
Glitter Dome, The

HBO (US) 1984 dir. Stuart Margolin
TV(US)

Wambaugh, J.
New Centurions, The

COL (US) 1972 dir. Richard Fleischer
GB title: Precinct 45: Los Angeles Police

Wambaugh, J.
Onion Field, The

AVCO (US) 1979 dir. Harold Becker

Wanderer, Dr. Z. and Cabot, T.
Letting Go

ITC (US) 1985 dir. Jack Bender
TV(US)

Wang, D.-L.
Crouching Tiger, Hidden Dragon

SONY (China/US) 2000 dir. Ang Lee

Wang, S.
I Am Your Dad

Baba
BEIJING (China) 2000 dir. Shou Wang

Ward, B.
Marshal of Medicine Bend, The

Lawless Street, A
COL (US) 1955 dir. Joseph H. Lewis

Ward, C.
Love's a Revolution

P

Vigo—Passion For Life
NITRATE (US) 1998 dir. Julien Temple

Ward, M. J.
Snake Pit, The
FOX (US) 1948 dir. Anatole Litvak

Ward, R.
Cattle Annie and Little Britches
UN (US) 1981 dir. Lamont Johnson

Ware, H.
Come Fill the Cup
WAR (US) 1951 dir. Gordon Douglas

Warner, D.
Death of a Snout

Informers, The
RANK (GB) 1963 dir. Ken Annakin
US title: Underworld Informers

Warner, R.
Aerodrome, The
BBC (GB) 1983 dir. Giles Foster
TV(GB)

Warren, C. E. T. and Benson, J.
Above us the Waves
GFD (GB) 1955 dir. Ralph Thomas

Warren, C. M.
Only the Valiant
WAR (US) 1950 dir. Gordon Douglas

Warren, F. B.
Face at the Window

P
PENNANT (GB) 1939 dir. George King

Warren, R. P.
All the King's Men
COL (US) 1949 dir. Robert Rossen

Warren, R. P.
Band of Angels
WAR (US) 1957 dir. Raoul Walsh

Warwick, J.
Blind Alley

P
COL (US) 1939 dir. Charles Vidor

Wasserman, D.
Man of La Mancha
UA (US) 1972 dir. Arthur Hiller
M

Wasserstein, W.
American Daughter, An

P
HEARST (US) 2000 dir. Sheldon Larry
TV(US)

Wasserstein, W.
Heidi Chronicles, The

P
TNT (US) 1995 dir. Paul Bogart
TV(US)

Waterhouse, K.
Billy Liar
WAR (GB) 1963 dir. John Schlesinger

Watkins, L. E.
On Borrowed Time
MGM (US) 1939 dir. Harold S. Bucquet
MILBERG (US) 1957
dir. George Schaefer
TV(US)

Watkins, M.
Chicago

P
Roxie Hart
FOX (US) 1942 dir. William A. Wellman

Watkins, P.
Calm at Sunset, Calm at Dawn

Calm at Sunset
HALLMARK (US) 1996 dir. Daniel
Petrie
TV(US)

Watkyn, A.
For Better, For Worse

P
ABP (GB) 1954 dir. J. Lee Thompson

Watkyn, A.
Moonraker, The

P
ABP (GB) 1958 dir. David MacDonald

Watson, C.
Flaxborough Chronicles, The

Murder Most Easy
BBC (GB) 1977 dir. Ronald Wilson
TVSe(GB)

Watson, C.
Miss Lonelyhearts 4122

Crooked Hearts, The
LORIMAR (US) 1972 dir. Jay Sandrich
TV(US)

Watson, E. L. G.
Priest Island

Exile
ILLUMINATION (Aust) 1994 dir. Paul
Cox

Waugh, A.
Guy Renton, A London Story

Circle of Deception
FOX (GB) 1960 dir. Jack Lee

Waugh, A.
Island in the Sun

FOX (GB) 1957 dir. Robert Rossen

Waugh, E.
Brideshead Revisited

GRANADA (GB) 1981
dir. Charles Sturridge
TVSe(GB)

Waugh, E.
Decline and Fall

Decline and Fall … of a Birdwatcher
FOX (GB) 1968 dir. John Karsh

Waugh, E.
Handful of Dust, A

NEW LINE (GB) 1988
dir. Charles Sturridge

Waugh, E.
Loved One, The

MGM (US) 1965 dir. Tony Richardson

Waugh, E.
Scoop

BBC (GB) 1972 dir. Roger Murray-Leach
TVSe(GB)
LWT (GB) 1987 dir. Gavin Millar
TV(GB)

Waugh, H.
Sleep Long My Love

Jigsaw
BL (GB) 1962 dir. Val Guest

Wawrzyn, L.
Blaue, Der

BR (Ger) 1994 dir. Lienhard Wawrzyn

Wead, F.
Ceiling Zero

P
WAR (US) 1935 dir. Howard Hawks

Weaver, G.
Count a Lonely Cadence

Cadence
NEW LINE (US) 1990 dir. Martin Sheen

Weaver, W.
Red Earth, White Earth

VIACOM (US) 1989 dir. David Greene
TV(US)

Webb, C.
Graduate, The

UA (US) 1967 dir. Mike Nichols

Webb, C.
Marriage of a Young Stockbroker, The

FOX (US) 1971 dir. Laurence Turman

Webb, M.
Gone to Earth

BL (GB) 1950
dir. Michael Powell, Emeril Pressburger
US title: Wild Heart, The

Webb, M.
Precious Bane

BBC (GB) 1989 dir. Christopher Menaul
TV(GB)

Webb, S., West, R. and Sikora, F.
Selma, Lord, Selma

DISNEY (US) 1999 dir. Charles Burnett
TV(US)

Webber, A. L. and Rice, T.
Jesus Christ Superstar

P
UN (US) 1973 dir. Norman Jewison
M

Weber, D. W. and Bosworth, Jr., C.
Precious Victims

LAUREL (US) 1993 dir. Peter Levin
TV(US)

Webster, J.
Daddy Long Legs

FOX (US) 1931 dir. Alfred Santell
FOX (US) 1955 dir. Jean Negulesco
M

Weibe, R.
Temptations of Big Bear, The

Big Bear
TELEFILM (Can) 1999 dir. Gil Cardinal
TVSe(Can)

Weidman, J.
House of Strangers

FOX (US) 1949
dir. Joseph L. Mankiewicz

Weidman, J.
I Can Get It For You Wholesale

FOX (US) 1951 dir. Michael Gordon
GB title: This is My Affair

Weil, B. E. and Winter, R.
Adultery, The Forgivable Sin

Silence of Adultery, The
HEARST (US) 1995 dir. Steven H. Stern
TV(US)

Weiman, R.
One Man's Secret

Possessed
WAR (US) 1947 dir. Curtis Bernhardt

Weiner, J. B.
Morning After, The

WOLPER (US) 1974
dir. Richard T. Heffron
TV(US)

Weisman, M.-L.
Intensive Care

Time to Live, A
ITC (US) 1985 dir. Rick Wallace
TV(US)

Weiss, E. and Friedman, M.
Poof Point, The

H. ROACH (US) 2001 dir. Neal Israel
TV(US)

Weiss, P.
Marat/Sade

P
UA (GB) 1966 dir. Peter Brook

Weitz, P.
Captive
P
Sex and the Other Man
RIVER ONE (US) 1995 dir. Karl Slovin

Weitzenkorn, L.
Five Star Final
P
WAR (US) 1931 dir. Mervyn LeRoy

Weitzenkorn, L.
Five-Star Final
P
Two Against the World
WAR (US) 1936 dir. William McGann
GB title: Case of Mrs. Pembroke, The

Weldon, F.
Cloning of Joanna May, The
GRANADA (GB) 1992 dir. Philip Saville
TVSe(GB)

Weldon, F.
Life and Loves of a She-Devil, The
She-Devil
ORION (US) 1989 dir. Susan Seidelman

Weldon, F.
Life and Loves of a She-Devil, The
BBC (GB) 1986 dir. Philip Saville
TVSe(GB)

Weldon, F.
President's Child, The
LAUREN (US) 1992 dir. Sam Pillsbury
TV(US)

Wellard, J.
Action of the Tiger
MGM (GB) 1957 dir. Terence Young

Weller, A.
Day of the Dog
BANON (Aust) 1993 dir. James
Ricketson

Weller, M.
Spoils of War
P
EVOLUTION (US) 1994 dir. Richard
Lowry
TV(US)

Wellesley, G.
Report on a Fugitive
Night Train to Munich
TCF (GB) 1940 dir. Carol Reed

Wellman, A.
S.F.W.
POLYGRAM (US) 1994 dir. Jefery Levy

Wellman, P. I.
Bronco Apache
Apache
UA (US) 1954 dir. Robert Aldrich

Wellman, P. I.
Comancheros, The
FOX (US) 1961 dir. Michael Curtiz

Wellman, P. I.
Iron Mistress, The
WAR (US) 1952 dir. Gordon Douglas

Wellman, P. I.
Jubal Troop
Jubal
COL (US) 1956 dir. Delmer Daves

Wellman, P. I.
Walls of Jericho, The
FOX (US) 1948 dir. John M. Stahl

Wells, H. G.
Door in the Wall, The
ABP (GB) 1956 dir. Glenn H. Alvey, Jr.

Wells, H. G.
First Men in the Moon
COL (GB) 1963 dir. Nathan Juran

Wells, H. G.
History of Mr. Polly, The

GFD (GB) 1949 dir. Anthony Pelissier
BBC (GB) 1980 dir. Lovett Bickford
TVSe(GB)

Wells, H. G.
Invisible Man, The

UN (US) 1933 dir. James Whale
UN (US) 1975 dir. Robert Michael Lewis
BBC (GB) 1984 dir. Brian Lighthill
TVSe(GB)

Wells, H. G.
Invisible Man, The

Gemini Man
UN TV (US) 1976 dir. Alan J. Levi
TV(US)

Wells, H. G.
Island of Dr. Moreau, The

AIP (US) 1977 dir. Don Taylor
NEW LINE (US) 1996 dir. John
Frankenheimer

Wells, H. G.
Island of Dr Moreau, The

Island of Lost Souls
PAR (US) 1932 dir. Erle C. Kenton

Wells, H. G.
Kipps

FOX (GB) 1941 dir. Carol Reed
US title: Remarkable Mr Kipps, The
GRANADA (GB) 1960 dir. Stuart
Latham
TVSe(GB)

Wells, H. G.
Kipps

Half a Sixpence
PAR (GB) 1967 dir. George Sidney
M

Wells, H. G.
Love and Mr. Lewisham

BBC (GB) 1972 dir. Christopher Barry
TVSe(GB)

Wells, H. G.
Man Who Could Work Miracles, The

UA (GB) 1936 dir. Lothar Mendes

Wells, H. G.
Passionate Friends, The

CIN (GB) 1949 dir. David Lean
GB title: One Woman's Story

Wells, H. G.
Shape of Things to Come, The

BARBER DANN (Can) 1979
dir. George McGowan

Wells, H. G.
Shape of Things to Come, The

Things to Come
UA (GB) 1936
dir. William Cameron Menzies

Wells, H. G.
Time Machine, The

MGM (US) 1960 dir. George Pal
SCHICK SUNN (US) 1978
dir. Henning Schellerup
TV(US)

Wells, H. G.
Valley of the Ants, The

Empire of the Ants
AIP (US) 1977 dir. Bert I. Gordon

Wells, H. G.
War of the Worlds

PAR (US) 1953 dir. Byron Haskin

Wells, L.
Night of the Running Man

AM WORLD (US) 1995 dir. Mark L.
Lester

Wells, L. E.
Day of the Outlaw, The

UA (US) 1958 dir. André de Toth

Welsh, I.
Trainspotting

CHANNEL 4 FILMS (GB) 1996 dir.
Danny Boyle

Welty, E.
Ponder Heart, The

PBS (US) 2001 dir. Martha Coolidge
TV(US)

Werbell, F. and Clarke, T.
**Lost Hero: The Mystery of Raoul
Wallenberg**

Wallenberg: A Hero's Story
PAR (US) 1985 dir. Lamont Johnson
TVSe(US)

Werfel, F.
Forty Days of Musa Dagh

HIGH INV (US/Tur) 1987
dir. Sarky Mouradia

Werfel, F.
Jacobowsky and the Colonel

P
Me and The Colonel
COL (US) 1958 dir. Peter Glenville

Werfel, F.
Song of Bernadette, The

FOX (US) 1943 dir. Henry King

Werlin, M. and Werlin, M.
Face to Die For, A

KONIGSBERG (US) 1996 dir. Jack
Bender
TV(US)

Wersba, B.
Country of the Heart, The

Matters of the Heart
MCA TV (US) 1990 dir. Michael Rhodes
TV(US)

Wesker, A.
Kitchen, The

P
BL (GB) 1961 dir. James Hill

Wesley, M.
Camomile Lawn, The

CHANNEL 4 (GB) 1992 dir. Peter Hall
TVSe(GB)

Wesley, M.
Harnessing Peacocks

MERIDIAN (GB) 1993 dir. James Cellan
Jones
TV(GB)

Wesley, M.
Jumping the Queue

BBC (GB) 1989 dir. Clade Whatham
TVSe(GB)

West, C. L.
Holiday Heart

P
MGM TV (US) 2000 dir. Robert
Townsend
TV(US)

West, D.
Wedding, The

HARPO (US) 1998 dir. Charles Burnett
TVSe(US)

West, J.
Friendly Persuasion

MGM (US) 1956 dir. William Wyler
AA (US) 1975 dir. Joseph Sargent
TV(US)

West, M. L.
Big Story, The

Crooked Road, The
GALA (GB/Yugo) 1964 dir. Don
Chaffey

West, M. L.
Devil's Advocate, The

RANK (Ger) 1977 dir. Guy Green

West, M. L.
Diamond Lil
P
She Done Him Wrong
PAR (US) 1933 dir. Lowell Sherman

West, M. L.
Naked Country, The
FILMWAYS (Aust) 1984
dir. Tim Burstall

West, M. L.
Salamander, The
ITC (It/GB/US) 1981 dir. Peter Zinner

West, M. L.
Shoes of the Fisherman, The
MGM (US) 1968 dir. Michael Anderson

West, N.
Day of the Locust, The
PAR (US) 1975 dir. John Schlesinger

West, N.
Miss Lonelyhearts
Lonelyhearts
UA (US) 1958 dir. Vincent J. Donehue

West, R.
Birds Fall Down, The
BBC (GB) 1978 dir. John Glenister
TVSe(GB)

West, R.
Return of the Soldier, The
BW (GB) 1983 dir. Alan Bridges

West, S.
Amos
BRYNA (US) 1985 dir. Michael Tuchner
TV(US)

Westall, R.
Machine Gunners, The
BBC (GB) 1983 dir. Colin Cant
TVSe(GB)

Westall, R.
Watch House, The
BBC (GB) 1988 dir. Ian Keill
TVSe(GB)

Westerby, R.
Small Voice, The
BL (GB) 1948 dir. Fergus McDonell
US title: Hideout

Westermann, J.
Exit Wounds
WAR (US) 2001 dir. Andrzej Bartkowiak

Westheimer, D.
My Sweet Charlie
P
UN TV (US) 1970 dir. Lamont Johnson
TV(US)

Westheimer, D.
Von Ryan's Express
FOX (US) 1965 dir. Mark Robson

Westlake, D. E.
Bank Shot, The
UA (US) 1974 dir. Gower Champion

Westlake, D. E.
Busy Body, The
PAR (US) 1967 dir. William Castle

Westlake, D. E.
Dancing Aztec
Divine Poursuite, La
STUDIO CANAL+ (Fr) 1997 dir. Michel
Deville

Westlake, D. E.
Hot Rock, The
TCF (US) 1972 dir. Peter Yates
GB title: How to Steal a Diamond in
Four Uneasy Lessons

Westlake, D. E.
Hunter, The

Payback
PAR (US) 1999 dir. Brian Helgeland

Westlake, D. E.
Jimmy the Kid

NEW WORLD (US) 1982
dir. Gary Nelson

Westlake, D. E.
Travesty, A

Slight Case of Murder, A
TNT (US) 1999 dir. Steven Schachter
TV(US)

Westlake, D. E.
Two Much

POLYGRAM (Sp/US) 1995 dir.
Fernando Trueba

Westlake, D. E.
What's the Worst That Could Happen?

MGM (US) 2001 dir. Sam Weisman

Westlake, D. E.
Why Me?

TRIUMPH (US) 1990
dir. Gene Quintano

Weston, C.
Poor, Poor Ophelia

Streets of San Francisco, The
WAR TV (US) 1972 dir. Walter
Grauman
TV(US)

Weston, J.
Hail, Hero!

CIN CEN (US) 1969 dir. David Miller

Wetjen, A. R.
Way for a Sailor

MGM (US) 1930 dir. Sam Wood

Weverka, R. and Sellier, Jr., C.
Hangar 18

SCHICK SUNN (US) 1980
dir. James L. Conway

Weyman, S.
Under the Red Robe

FOX (GB) 1937 dir. Victor Sjostrom

Wharton, E.
Age of Innocence, The

RKO (US) 1934 dir. Philip Moeller
COL (US) 1993 dir. Martin Scorsese

Wharton, E.
Buccaneers, The

BBC (GB) 1995 dir. Philip Saville
TVSe(GB)

Wharton, E.
Children, The

Marriage Playground, The
PAR (US) 1929 dir. Lothar Mendes

Wharton, E.
Ethan Frome

AM PLAY (US) 1993 dir. John Madden

Wharton, E.
House of Mirth, The

PBS (US) 1981 dir. Adrian Hall
TV(US)
CHANNEL 4 FILMS (GB/US) 2000 dir.
Terence Davies

Wharton, E.
Old Maid, The

WAR (US) 1939 dir. Edmund Goulding

Wharton, E.
Reef, The

Passion's Way
HEARST (US) 1999 dir. Robert Allan
Ackerman
TV(US)

Wharton, W.
Birdy
TRISTAR (US) 1984 dir. Alan Parker

Wharton, W.
Dad
UN (US) 1989 dir. Gary D. Goldberg

Wharton, W.
Midnight Clear, A
A&M (US) 1992 dir. Keith Gordon

Wheatley, D.
Devil Rides Out, The
ABP (GB) 1971 dir. Terence Fisher
US title: Devil's Bride, The

Wheatley, D.
Eunuch of Stamboul, The
Secret of Stamboul, The
GENERAL (GB) 1936 dir. Andrew
Marton

Wheatley, D.
Forbidden Territory
GAU (GB) 1934 dir. Phil Rosen

Wheatley, D.
To the Devil, a Daughter
EMI (GB/Ger) 1976 dir. Peter Sykes

Wheatley, D.
Uncharted Seas
Lost Continent, The
WAR (GB) 1968 dir. Michael Carreras

Wheeler, H. and Sondheim, S.
Little Night Music, A
P
S&T (Austria/Ger) 1977
dir. Harold Prince
M

Whipple, D.
They Knew Mr. Knight
GFD (GB) 1945 dir. Norman Walker

Whipple, D.
They Were Sisters
GFD (GB) 1945 dir. Arthur Crabtree

Whisnant, S.
Innocent Victims
KUSHNER-LOCKE (US) 1996 dir.
Gilbert Cates
TV(US)

White, A.
**Frost in May; Lost Traveller, The;
Sugar House, The; Beyond the Glass**
Frost in May
BBC (GB) 1982 dir. Ronald Wilson
TVSe(GB)

White, A.
Long Day's Dying, The
PAR (GB) 1968 dir. Peter Collinson

White, E. B.
Charlotte's Web
SCOTIA-BARBER (US) 1972
dir. Charles A. Nichols
A, Ch

White, E. B.
Stuart Little
COL (US) 1999 dir. Rob Minkoff
Ch

White, E. L.
Her Heart in Her Throat
Unseen, The
PAR (US) 1945 dir. Lewis Allen

White, E. L.
Some Must Watch
Spiral Staircase, The
RKO (US) 1946 dir. Robert Siodmak
WAR (GB) 1975 dir. Peter Collinson
SABAN (US) 2000 dir. James Head

White, E. L.
Wheel Spins, The

Lady Vanishes, The
MGM (GB) 1938 dir. Alfred Hitchcock
RANK (GB) 1979 dir. Anthony Page

White, G. M.
Tess of the Storm Country

FOX (US) 1932 dir. Alfred Santell
FOX (US) 1961 dir. Paul Guilfoyle

White, G.
Mothertime

BBC (GB) 1997 dir. Matthew Jacobs
TV(GB)

White, L.
Clean Break

Killing, The
UA (US) 1956 dir. Stanley Kubrick

White, L.
Money Trap, The

MGM (US) 1966 dir. Burt Kennedy

White, L.
Snatchers, The

Night of the Following Day, The
UN (US) 1969 dir. Hubert Cornfield

White, L. T.
Harness Bull

Vice Squad
UA (US) 1953 dir. Arnold Laven
GB title: Girl in Room 17, The

White, R.
Death Watch

Savages
SPEL-GOLD (US) 1974 dir. Lee Katzin
TV(US)

White, R.
Our Virgin Island

Virgin Island
BL (GB) 1958 dir. Pat Jackson

White, R.
Up Periscope

WAR (US) 1959 dir. Gordon Douglas

White, S. E.
Wild Geese Calling

FOX (US) 1991 dir. John Brahm

White, T.
Max Trueblood and the Jersey Desperado

Max et Jeremie
TF1 (Fr) 1992 dir. Claire Devers

White, T.
Triangle

See How They Fall
FRANCE 3 (Fr) 1994 dir. Jacques
Audiard

White, T. H.
Mountain Road, The

COL (US) 1960 dir. Delbert Mann

White, T. H.
Once and Future King, The

Camelot
WAR (US) 1967 dir. Joshua Logan
M

White, T. H.
Once and Future King, The

Sword in the Stone, The
DISNEY (US) 1963
dir. Wolfgang Reitherman
A, Ch

White, W. L.
Journey for Margaret

MGM (US) 1942 dir. W. S. Van Dyke

White, W. L.
They Were Expendable

MGM (US) 1945 dir. John Ford

Whitehead, D.
Attack on Terror: The FBI Against The Ku Klux Klan in Mississippi

Attack on Terror: The FBI Versus The Ku Klux Klan
WAR TV (US) 1975
dir. Marvin Chomsky
TVSe(US)

Whitehead, D.
FBI Story, The
WAR (US) 1959 dir. Mervyn LeRoy

Whitemore, H.
Best of Friends, The
LONDON (GB) 1994 dir. Alvin Rakoff
TV(GB)

Whitemore, H.
Pack of Lies
P
HALMI (US) 1987 dir. Anthony Page
TV(US)

Whitemore, H.
Stevie
P
FIRST (US/(GB) 1978
dir. Robert Enders

Whitman, S. E.
Captain Apache
BENMAR (US/Sp) 1971
dir. Alexander Singer

Whittemore, L. H.
Super Cops, The
MGM (US) 1974 dir. Gordon Parks

Whitten, L. H.
Moon of the Wolf
FILMWAYS (US) 1972 dir. Daniel Petrie
TV(US)

Whittington, H.
Desire in the Dust
TCF (US) 1960 dir. William F. Claxton

Whittington, H.
Web of Murder
Dead in the Water
K. BRIGHT/MTE (US) 1991 dir. Bill Condon
TV(US)

Wibberley, L.
Hands of Cormac Joyce, The
CRAWFORD (US) 1972
dir. Fielder Cook
TV(US)

Wibberley, L.
Mouse that Roared, The
COL (GB) 1959 dir. Jack Arnold

Wicker, T.
Time to Die, A
Attica
ABC (US) 1980 dir. Marvin J. Chomsky
TV(US)

Wiesenthal, S.
Max and Helen: A Remarkable True Love Story
Max and Helen
TNT (US) 1990 dir. Philip Saville
TV(US)

Wiggin, K. D.
Mother Carey's Chickens
Summer Magic
DISNEY (US) 1963 dir. James Neilson

Wiggin, K. D.
Mother Carey's Chickens
RKO (US) 1938 dir. Rowland V. Lee

Wiggin, K. D.
Rebecca of Sunnybrook Farm
FOX (US) 1932 dir. Alfred Santell
FOX (US) 1938 dir. Allan Dwan
BBC (GB) 1978 dir. Rodney Bennett
TVSe(GB)

Wilbur, C.
Solomon and Sheba

UA (US) 1959 dir. King Vidor

Wilde, H. and Eunson, D.
Guest in the House

P

UA (US) 1944 dir. John Brahm

Wilde, O.
Canterville Ghost, The

MGM (US) 1943 dir. Jules Dassin
HTV (GB/US) 1986 dir. Paul Bogart
TV(GB/US)
SIGNBOARD HILL (US) 1996 dir. Syd
Macartney
TV(US)

Wilde, O.
Ideal Husband, An

P

BL (GB) 1948 dir. Alexander Korda
BBC (GB) 1999 dir. Rudolph Cartier
TV(GB)
MIRAMAX (GB/US) 1999 dir. Oliver
Parker

Wilde, O.
Importance of Being Earnest, The

P

RANK/GFD (GB) 1952
dir. Anthony Asquith
BBC (GB) 1986 dir. Stuart Burge
TV(GB)
ELEC CON (US) 1992 dir. Kurt Baker
MIRAMAX (GB/US) 2002 dir. Oliver
Parker

Wilde, O.
Lady Windemere's Fan

P

Fan, The
FOX (US) 1949 dir. Otto Preminger
GB title: Lady Windemere's Fan

Wilde, O.
Lord Arthur Savile's Crime

Flesh and Fantasy
UN (US) 1943 dir. Julien Duvivier

Wilde, O.
Picture of Dorian Gray, The

MGM (US) 1945 dir. Albert Lewin
CURTIS (US) 1973 dir. Glenn Jordan
TV(US)

Wilde, O.
Picture of Dorian Gray, The

Dorian Gray
AIP (It/Ger) 1970
dir. Massimo Dallamano

Wilde, O.
Picture of Dorian Gray, The

Sins of Dorian Gray, The
RANKIN-BASS (US) 1983
dir. Tony Maylam
TV(US)

Wilde, O.
Salome

P

CANNON (Fr/It) 1987
dir. Claude d'Anna

Wilde, O.
Salome

P

Salome's Last Dance
VESTRON (GB) 1988 dir. Ken Russell

Wilde, P.
What's Wrong With Angry?

P

Get Real
BRIT SCREEN (GB) 1998 dir. Simon
Shore

Wilder, L. I.
Little House on the Prairie

NBC ENT (US) 1974
dir. Michael Landon
TV(US)

Wilder, M. B.
Since You Went Away

UA (US) 1944 dir. John Cromwell

Wilder, R.
And Ride a Tiger

Stranger in my Arms, A
UI (US) 1958 dir. Helmut Kautner

Wilder, R.
Flamingo Road

WAR (US) 1949 dir. Michael Curtiz

Wilder, R.
Written on the Wind

UN (US) 1956 dir. Douglas Sirk

Wilder, T.
Bridge of San Luis Rey, The

UA (US) 1944 dir. Rowland V. Lee

Wilder, T.
Matchmaker, The

P
PAR (US) 1958 dir. Joseph Anthony

Wilder, T.
Matchmaker, The

P
Hello Dolly
FOX (US) 1969 dir. Gene Kelly
M

Wilder, T.
Our Town

P
UA (US) 1940 dir. Sam Wood

Wilder, T.
Skin of our Teeth, The

P
GRANADA TV (GB) 1959
TV(GB)

Wilder, T.
Theophilus North

Mr. North
GOLDWYN (US) 1988
dir. Danny Huston

Wilk, M.
Don't Raise the Bridge, Lower the River

BL (GB) 1967 dir. Jerry Paris

Wilkerson, D.
Cross and the Switchblade, The

FOX (US) 1970 dir. Don Murray

Wilkins, V.
King Reluctant, A

Dangerous Exile
RANK (GB) 1957
dir. Brian Desmond Hurst

Wilkinson, G. R.
Monkeys, The

Monkeys, Go Home!
DISNEY (US) 1967
dir. Andrew V. McLaglen

Willard, J.
Cat and the Canary, The

P
PAR (US) 1939 dir. Elliot Nugent
GALA (GB) 1978 dir. Radley Metzger

Willard, J.
Cat and the Canary, The

P
Cat Creeps, The
UN (US) 1930 dir. Rupert Julian

Willeford, C.
Cockfighter

EMI (US) 1974 dir. Monte Hellman

Willeford, C.
Miami Blues

ORION (US) 1990 dir. George Armitage

Willeford, C.
Woman Chaser, The

DEFINITIVE (US) 1999 dir. Robinson Devor

Williams, A.
Snake Water

Pink Jungle, The
UI (US) 1968 dir. Delbert Mann

Williams, B.
Earl of Chicago

MGM (US) 1940 dir. Richard Thorpe

Williams, B.
In This Fallen City

P

Night of Courage
TITUS (US) 1987 dir. Elliot Silverstein
TV(US)

Williams, B. A.
All the Brothers were Valiant

MGM (US) 1953 dir. Richard Thorpe

Williams, B. A.
Leave Her to Heaven

FOX (US) 1945 dir. John M. Stahl

Williams, B. A.
Leave Her to Heaven

Too Good to be True
NEWLAND-RAYNOR (US) 1988
dir. Christian I. Nyby II
TV(US)

Williams, B. A.
Small Town Girl

MGM (US) 1936
dir. William A. Wellmen

Williams, B. A.
Strange Woman, The

UA (US) 1946 dir. Edgar G. Ulmer

Williams, B. and Kreski, C.
Growing Up Brady ... I Was a Teenage Greg

Growing Up Brady
PAR TV (US) 2000 dir. Richard Colla
TV(US)

Williams, B., Williams, J. and Shoemaker, J. B.
Black Hope Horror, The: The True Story of a Haunting

Grave Secrets: The Legacy of Hilltop Drive
HEARST (US) 1992 dir. John Patterson
TV(US)

Williams, C.
All the Way

Third Voice, The
FOX (US) 1959 dir. Hubert Cornfield

Williams, C.
Dead Calm

WAR (Aust) 1989 dir. Phillip Noyce

Williams, C.
Hell Hath no Fury

Hot Spot, The
ORION (US) 1990 dir. Dennis Hopper

Williams, C.
Long Saturday Night, The

Confidentially Yours
IS (Fr) 1984 dir. François Truffaut

Williams, C.
Long Saturday Night, The

Finally, Sunday
FILMS A2 (Fr) 1983
dir. François Truffaut

Williams, C.
Wrong Venus, The

Don't Just Stand There
UN (US) 1967 dir. Ron Winston

Williams, D.
Second Sight

Two Worlds of Jennie Logan, The
FRIES (US) 1979 dir. Frank DeFelitta
TV(US)

Williams, E.
Corn is Green, The

P
WAR (US) 1945 dir. Irving Rapper
M. EVANS (US) 1956
dir. George Schaefer
TV(US)
WAR (US) 1979 dir. George Cukor
TV(US)

Williams, E.
Headlong

King Ralph
UN (US) 1991 dir. David S. Ward

Williams, E.
Light of Heart, The

P
Life Begins at Eight Thirty
FOX (US) 1942 dir. Irving Pichel
GB title: Light of Heart, The

Williams, E.
Night Must Fall

P
MGM (US) 1937 dir. Richard Thorpe
MGM (GB) 1964 dir. Karel Reisz

Williams, E.
Someone Waiting

P
Time Without Pity
HARLEQUIN (GB) 1957
dir. Joseph Losey

Williams, E.
Wooden Horse, The

BL (GB) 1950 dir. Jack Lee

Williams, G.
Man Who Had Power over Women, The

AVCO (GB) 1970 dir. John Krish

Williams, G.
Weak at Denise

GUERILLA (GB) 1999 dir. Julian Nott

Williams, G. M.
Siege at Trencher's Farm, The

Straw Dogs
CINERAMA (GB) 1971
dir. Sam Peckinpah

Williams, H. and Williams, M.
Grass is Greener, The

P
UI (GB) 1960 dir. Stanley Donen

Williams, J.
Night Song

Sweet Love, Bitter
FILM 2 (US) 1967 dir. Herbert Danska

Williams, J. A.
Junior Bachelor Society, The

Sophisticated Gents, The
D. WILSON (US) 1981 dir. Harry Falk
TVSe(US),

Williams, Jr., H. and Bane, M.
Living Proof

Living Proof: The Hank Williams, Jr. Story
TELECOM (US) 1983 dir. Dick Lowry
TV(US)

Williams, Mrs. R.
Father was a Handful

Vanishing Virginian, The
MGM (US) 1941 dir. Frank Borzage

Williams, N.
Class Enemy

P
SFB (Ger) 1984 dir. Peter Stein

Williams, N.
Wimbledon Prisoner, The

BBC (GB) 1994 dir. Robert Young
TVSe(GB)

Williams, O. and Romanowski, P.
Temptations, The

DE PASSE (US) 1998 dir. Allan Arkush
TVSe(US)

Williams, P.
General, The: Godfather of Crime
General, The
J&M (Ire/GB) 1998 dir. John Boorman

Williams, T.
Baby Doll
P
WAR (US) 1956 dir. Elia Kazan

Williams, T.
Cat on a Hot Tin Roof
P
MGM (US) 1958 dir. Richard Brooks
GRANADA (GB) 1976
dir. Robert Moore
TV(GB/US)

Williams, T.
Cocaine Kids, The
illtown
SHOOTING GALLERY (US) 1996 dir.
Nick Gomez

Williams, T.
Glass Menagerie, The
P
WAR (US) 1950 dir. Irving Rapper
TALENT (US) 1973
dir. Anthony Harvey
TV(US)
CINEPLEX (US) 1987 dir. Paul
Newman

Williams, T.
**Milk Train Doesn't Stop Here
Anymore, The**
P
Boom!
UI (GB) 1968 dir. Joseph Losey

Williams, T.
Night of the Iguana, The
P
MGM (US) 1964 dir. John Huston

Williams, T.
Orpheus Descending
P
NED (US) 1990 dir. Peter Hall
TV(US)

Williams, T.
Orpheus Descending
P
Fugitive Kind, The
UA (US) 1960 dir. Sidney Lumet

Williams, T.
Period of Adjustment
P
MGM (US) 1962 dir. George Roy Hill

Williams, T.
Roman Spring of Mrs. Stone, The
WAR (GB/US) 1961 dir. José Quintero

Williams, T.
Rose Tattoo, The
P
PAR (US) 1955 dir. Daniel Mann

Williams, T.
Streetcar Named Desire, A
P
WAR (US) 1951 dir. Elia Kazan
PSO (US) 1984 dir. John Erman
TV(US)
CBS (US) 1995 dir. Glenn Jordan
TV(US)

Williams, T.
Suddenly, Last Summer
P
COL (GB) 1959
dir. Joseph I. Mankiewicz

Williams, T.
Summer and Smoke
P
PAR (US) 1961 dir. Peter Glenville

Williams, T.
Sweet Bird of Youth

P
MGM (US) 1962 dir. Richard Brooks
KUSHNER-LOCK (US) 1989
dir. Nicolas Roeg
TV(US)

Williams, T.
This Property is Condemned

P
PAR (US) 1966 din Sydney Pollack

Williams, V.
Clubfoot

Crouching Beast, The
OLY (GB) 1935 dir. Victor Hanbury

Williams, W.
Ada Dallas

Ada
MGM (US) 1961 dir. Daniel Mann

Williamson, D.
Brilliant Lies

P
BAYSIDE (Aust) 1996 dir. Richard
Franklin

Williamson, D.
Don's Party

DOUBLE HEAD (Aust) 1976
dir. Bruce Beresford

Williamson, D.
Travelling North

P
VIEW PIC (Aust) 1986 dir. Carl Schultz

Williamson, H.
Tarka the Otter

RANK (GB) 1979 dir. David Cobham

Willingham, C.
End as a Man

Strange One, The
COL (US) 1957 dir. Jack Garfein
GB title: End as a Man

Willingham, C.
Rambling Rose

NEW LINE (US) 1991
dir. Martha Coolidge

Willis Holt, K.
My Louisiana Sky

HYP PICTURES (US) 2001 dir. Adam
Arkin
TV(US)

Willis, M. P. and Willis, J.
But There are Always Miracles

Some Kind of Miracle
LORIMAR (US) 1979
dir. Jerrold Freedman
TV(US)

Willis, T.
Hot Summer Night

P
Flame in the Streets
RANK (GB) 1961 dir. Roy Baker

Willis, T.
Man-eater

Maneaters are Loose!
MONA BBC (GB) 1984
dir. Timothy Galfos
TV(GB)

Willis, T.
No Trees in the Street

P
ABP (US) 1958 dir. J. Lee Thompson

Willis, T.
Woman in a Dressing Gown

P
GODWIN (GB) 1957
dir. J. Lee Thompson

Willmott, K.
Ninth Street

P
HODCARRIER (US) 1999 dir. Tim
Rebman, Kevin Willmott

Willocks, T.
Bad City Blues
SHOWCASE (US) 1999 dir. Michael Stevens

Willson, M.
Music Man, The
WAR (US) 1962 dir. Morton da Costa
M

Wilmot, C.
Price She Paid, The
P
WI (US) 1992 dir. Fred Walton
TV(US)

Wilson, A.
Anglo-Saxon Attitudes
EUSTON (GB) 1992 dir. Diarmuid Lawrence
TVSe(GB)

Wilson, A.
Late Call
BBC (GB) 1975 dir. Philip Dudley
TVSe(GB)

Wilson, A.
Old Men at the Zoo, The
BBC (GB) 1982 dir. Stuart Burge
TVSe(GB)

Wilson, A.
Piano Lesson, The
P
HALLMARK (US) 1995 dir. Lloyd Richards
TV(US)

Wilson, B.
Gaudi Afternoon
LOLAFILMS (Sp) 2001 dir. Susan Seidelman

Wilson, C.
Empty Saddles
UN (US) 1937 dir. Les Selander

Wilson, C.
Space Vampires
Lifeforce
CANNON (US) 1985 dir. Tobe Hooper

Wilson, D. P.
My Six Convicts
COL (US) 1952 dir. Hugo Fregonese

Wilson, F. P.
Keep, The
PAR (GB) 1983 dir. Michael Mann

Wilson, H. L.
Bunker Bean
RKO (US) 1936
dir. William Hamilton, Edward Kelly

Wilson, H. L.
Merton of the Movies
MGM (US) 1947 dir. Robert Alton

Wilson, H. L.
Merton of the Movies
Make me a Star
PAR (US) 1932 dir. William Beaudine

Wilson, H. L.
Ruggles of Red Gap
PAR (US) 1935 dir. Leo McCarey

Wilson, H. L.
Ruggles of Red Gap
Fancy Pants
PAR (US) 1950 dir. George Marshall

Wilson, J.
Hamp
P
King and Country
WAR (GB) 1964 dir. Joseph Losey

Wilson, J. R.
Pack, The
Behind the Mask
BL (GB) 1958 dir. Brian Desmond Hurst

Wilson, L.
Redwood Curtain
P
HALLMARK (US) 1995 dir. John Korty
TV(US)

Wilson, M.
None so Blind
Woman on the Beach, The
RKO (US) 1947 dir. Jean Renoir

Wilson, R. M.
Eureka Street
BBC (GB) 1999 dir. Adrien Shergold
TV(GB)

Wilson, S.
Beauty
GRAND (US) 1998 dir. Jerry London
TV(US)

Wilson, S.
Boy Friend, The
P
MGM (GB) 1971 dir. Ken Russell
M

Wilson, S.
Man in the Grey Flannel Suit, The
FOX (US) 1956 dir. Nunnally Johnson

Wilson, S.
Summer Place, A
WAR (US) 1959 dir. Delmer Daves

Wilson, S. J.
To Find a Man
COL (US) 1971 dir. Buzz Kulik

Wilstach, F.
Wild Bill Hickok
Plainsman, The
PAR (US) 1937 dir. Cecil B. De Mille

Wiltshire, D.
Child of Vodyanoi
Nightmare Man, The
BBC (US) 1981 dir. Douglas Camfield
TVSe(GB)

Winckler, M.
Maladie de Sachs, La
STUDIO CANAL+ (Fr) 1999 dir.
Michael Deville

Windle, J. W.
True Women
HALLMARK (US) 1997 dir. Karen
Arthur
TVSe(US)

Wing, A.
Angie, I Says
Angie
HOLLYWOOD (US) 1994 dir. Martha
Coolidge

Wingate, W.
Shotgun
Malone
ORION (US) 1987 dir. Harley Kokliss

Winkler, A. C.
Lunatic, The
ISLAND PICT (Fr) 1992
dir. Lol Creme

Winski, N.
Sex and the Criminal Mind
Man in the Attic, The
ATLANTIS (US) 1995 dir. Graeme
Campbell
TV(US)

Winski, N.
Shadowhunter
REP (US) 1993 dir. J. S. Cardone
TV(US)

Winsor, K.
Forever Amber
FOX (US) 1947 dir. Otto Preminger

Winter, K.
Shining Hour, The
P
MGM (US) 1938 dir. Frank Borzage

Winterson, J.
Oranges are not the only Fruit
A&E/BBC (US/GB) 1990
dir. Beeban Kidron
TVSe(GB/US)

Winton, J.
We Joined the Navy
WAR (GB) 1962 dir. Wendy Toye

Winton, T.
In the Winter Dark
RB (Aust) 1998 dir. James Boyle

Winton, T.
That Eye, The Sky
WORKING TITLE (Aust) 1994 dir. John Ruane

Wise, L.
Diggstown Ringers, The
Diggstown
MGM (US) 1992 dir. Michael Ritchie

Wiseman, T.
Romantic Englishwoman, The
DIAL (GB) 1975 dir. Joseph Losey

Wister, O.
Virginian, The
PAR (US) 1929 dir. Victor Fleming
PAR (US) 1946 dir. Stuart Gilmore
WAR (US) 2000 dir. Bill Pullman
TV(US)

Wittig, M.
Girl, The
METHOD (Fr) 2000 dir. Sande Zeig

Wixom, H. and Wixom, J.
When Angels Intervene
To Save the Children
WESTCOM (US) 1994 dir. Steven Hilliard Stern
TV(US)

Wodehouse, P. G.
Code of the Woosters
CENTRAL (GB) 1991 dir. Simon Langton
TV(GB)

Wodehouse, P. G.
Damsel in Distress, A
RKO (US) 1937 dir. George Stevens
M

Wodehouse, P. G.
Girl on the Boat, The
UA (GB) 1962 dir. Henry Kaplan

Wodehouse, P. G.
Piccadilly Jim
MGM (US) 1936 dir. Robert Z. Leonard

Wodehouse, P. G.
Thank You, Jeeves
FOX (US) 1936
dir. Arthur Greville Collins

Wohl, B.
Cold Wind in August
UA (US) 1961 dir. Alexander Singer

Wojnarowicz, D.
Close to the Knives; Memories That Smell Like Gasoline
Postcards from America
CHANNEL 4 FILMS (GB/US) 1994 dir. Steve McLean

Wolaston, N.
Eclipse
GALA (GB) 1976 dir. Simon Perry

Wolcott, J.A.
Brujo

Seduced by Evil
WIL COURT (US) 1994 dir. Tony
Wharmby
TV(US)

Wolf, G. K.
Who Censored Roger Rabbit?

Who Framed Roger Rabbit?
TOUCHSTONE (US) 1988 dir. Robert
Zemeckis
A, Ch

Wolfe, T.
Bonfire of the Vanities, The
WAR (US) 1990 dir. Brian De Palma

Wolfe, T.
Right Stuff, The
WAR (US) 1983 dir. Philip Kaufman

Wolfe, T.
You Can't Go Home Again
CBS ENT (US) 1979 dir. Ralph Nelson
TV(US)

Wolfe, W.
Ask Any Girl
MGM (US) 1959 dir. Charles Walters

Wolfe, W.
If a Man Answers
UN (US) 1962 dir. Henry Levin

Wolfert, I.
**American Guerilla in the Philippines,
An**
TCF (US) 1950 dir. Fritz Lang
GB title: I Shall Return

Wolfert, I.
Tucker's People
Force of Evil
MGM (US) 1948 dir. Abraham Polonsky

Wolff, M. M.
Whistle Stop
UA (US) 1946 dir. Leonide Moguy

Wolff, R.
Abdication, The
P
WAR (GB) 1974 dir. Anthony Harvey

Wolford, N. and Wolford, S.
Southern Blade
Time for Killing, A
COL (US) 1967 dir. Phil Karlson
GB title: Long Ride Home, The

Wolitzer, M.
This is Your Life
This is My Life
FOX (US) 1992 dir. Nora Ephron

Wolpert, S.
Nine Hours to Rama
FOX (GB) 1962 dir. Mark Robson

Wolzien, V.
Menu for Murder
VZ/SERTNER (US) 1990
dir. Larry Peerce
TV(US)

Wong, Dr. M. G.
Nun: A Memoir
Shattered Vows
RIVER CITY (US) 1984 dir. Jack Bender
TV(US)

Wood, B.
Doll's Eyes
In Dreams
DREAMWORKS (US) 1999 dir. Neil
Jordan

Wood, B. and Geasland, J.
Twins
Dead Ringers
FOX (Can) 1988 dir. David Cronenberg

Wood, C.
My Family and Other Animals
BBC (GB) 1987 dir. Peter Barber-Fleming
TVSe(GB)

Wood, C. B.
Welcome to the Club
COL (US) 1970 dir. Walter Shenson

Wood, D. and Dempster, D.
Narrow Margin, The
Battle of Britain
UA (GB) 1969 dir. Guy Hamilton

Wood, Mrs H.
East Lynne
Ex-Flame
TIFFANY (US) 1930 dir. Victor Halperin

Wood, Mrs. H.
East Lynne
FOX (US) 1931 dir. Frank Lloyd

Wood, W. P.
Court of Honor
Broken Trust
FONDA (US) 1995 dir. Geoffrey Sax
TV(US)

Woodrell, D.
Woe To Live On
Ride With the Devil
UN (US) 1999 dir. Ang Lee

Woods, D.
Biko
Cry Freedom
UN (GB) 1987
dir. Richard Attenborough

Woods, S.
Chiefs
HIGHGATE (US) 1983
dir. Jerry London
TVSe(US)

Woods, S.
Grass Roots
JBS (US) 1992 dir. Jerry London
TVSe(US)

Woods, W.
Manuela
BL (GB) 1957 dir. Guy Hamilton
US title: Stowaway Girl

Woods, W. H.
Edge of Darkness
WAR (US) 1943 dir. Lewis Milestone

Woodward, B.
Wired
TAURUS (US) 1989 dir. Larry Peerce

Woodward, R. and Bernstein, C.
All the President's Men
WAR (US) 1976 dir. Alan J. Pakula

Woodward, R. and Bernstein, C.
Final Days, The
SAMUELS (US) 1989
dir. Richard Pearce
TV(US)

Woodward, W. E.
Evelyn Prentice
MGM (US) 1934 dir.William K. Howard

Woolcott, A. and Kaufman, G. S.
Dark Tower, The
P
WAR (GB) 1943 dir. John Harlow

Woolf, V.
Mrs. Dalloway
BBC (GB) 1997 dir. Marleen Gorris

Woolf, V.
Orlando
BRIT SCREEN (GB) 1992 dir. Sally Potter

Woolf, V.
To the Lighthouse
BBC (GB) 1983 dir. Colin Gregg
TV(GB)

Wooll, E.
Libel
P
MGM (GB) 1959 dir. Anthony Asquith

Woollard, K.
Morning Departure
P
GFD (GB) 1950 dir. Roy Baker
US title: Operation Disaster

Woolley, P.
Guinevere
LIFETIME (US) 1994 dir. Jud Taylor
TV(US)

Woolrich, C.
Black Alibi
Leopard Man, The
RKO (US) 1943 dir. Jacques Tourneur

Woolrich, C.
Black Angel
UN (US) 1946 dir. Roy William Neill

Woolrich, C.
Black Curtain, The
Lady Forgets, The
HILL (US) 1989 dir. Bradford May
TV(US)

Woolrich, C.
Black Curtain, The
Street of Chance
PAR (US) 1942 dir. Jack Hively

Woolrich, C.
Black Path of Fear, The
Chase, The
NERO (US) 1947 dir. Arthur Ripley

Woolrich, C.
Bride in Black, The
NEW WORLD (US) 1990 dir. James Goldstone,
TV(US)

Woolrich, C.
I Married a Dead Man
Mrs. Winterbourne
TRISTAR (US) 1996 dir. Richard Benjamin

Woolrich, C.
I'm Dangerous Tonight
MCA TV (US) 1990 dir. Tobe Hooper
TV(US)

Woolrich, C.
Night Has a Thousand Eyes
PAR (US) 1948 dir. John Farrow

Woolrich, C.
Nightmare
UA (US) 1956 dir. Maxwell Shane

Woolrich, C.
Rear Window
PAR (US) 1954 dir. Alfred Hitchcock

Woolrich, C.
Waltz Into Darkness
Original Sin
MGM (US/Fr) 2001 dir. Michael Cristofer

Woolrich, C.
You'll Never See Me Again
UN (US) 1973 dir. Jeannot Szwarc
TV(US)

Worker, D. and Worker, B.
Escape
H. JAFFE (US) 1980
dir. Robert Michael Lewis
TV(US)

Wortman, E.
Almost Too Late

Anything to Survive
SABAN/SCHERICK (US) 1990
dir. Zale Dalen
TV(US)

Woudstra, K.
Total Loss

MAJADE (Neth) 2000 dir. Dana
Nechushtan

Wouk, H.
Caine Mutiny Court-Martial, The

P
MALTESE (US) 1988
dir. Robert Altman
TV(US)

Wouk, H.
Caine Mutiny, The

COL (US) 1954 dir. Edward Dmytryk

Wouk, H.
Marjorie Morningstar

WAR (US) 1958 dir. Irving Rapper

Wouk, H.
Slattery's Hurricane

FOX (US) 1949 dir. André de Toth

Wouk, H.
War and Remembrance

LWT (US/GB) 1989 dir. Dan Curtis
TVSe(US/GB)

Wouk, H.
Winds of War, The

PAR (US) 1983 dir. Dan Curtis
TVSe(US)

Wouk, H.
Youngblood Hawke

WAR (US) 1963 dir. Delmer Daves

Wozencraft, K.
Rush

MGM (US) 1991 dir. Lili Fini Zanuck

Wray, R. and Lewis, S.
Angela is 22

P
This is the Life
UN (US) 1943 dir. Felix Feist
M

Wren, P. C.
Beau Geste

PAR (US) 1939 dir. William A. Wellman
UI (US) 1966 dir. Douglas Heyes
BBC (GB) 1982 dir. Douglas Camfield
TVSe(GB)

Wren, P. C.
Beau Ideal

RKO (US) 1931 dir. Herbert Brenon

Wright, B. R.
Dollhouse Murders, The

AMIS (US) 1994 dir. Dianne Haak
TV(US)

Wright, D.
Quills

P
FOX (US/Ger) 2000 dir. Philip
Kaufman

Wright, H. B.
Shepherd of the Hills, The

PAR (US) 1941 dir. Henry Hathaway

Wright, R.
Native Son

CLASSIC (Arg) 1951 dir. Pierre Chenal
CINECOM (US) 1986
dir. Jerrold Freedman

Wurts, J.
When Heaven and Earth Changed Places

Heaven and Earth
WAR (US) 1993 dir. Oliver Stone

Wyden, P.
Day One: Before Hiroshima and After

Day One
SPELLING (US) 1989
dir. Joseph Sargent
TV(US)

Wyka, F.
Wishful Thinking

Implicated
COL TRISTAR (US) 1998 dir. Irving
Belatche

Wylie, I. A. R.
Gay Banditti, The

Young in Heart, The
SELZNICK (US) 1938
dir. Richard Wallace

Wylie, I. A. R.
Keeper of the Flame

MGM (US) 1942 dir. George Cukor

Wylie, I. A. R.
Pilgrimage

FOX (US) 1933 dir. John Ford

Wylie, P.
Night unto Night

WAR (US) 1949 dir. Don Siegel

Wynd, O.
Ginger Tree, The

BBC (GB) 1989 dir. Anthony Garner
TVSe(GB)

Wyndham, J.
Chocky

THAMES (GB) 1984 dir. Chris Hodson
Ch, TVSe(GB)

Wyndham, J.
Day of the Triffids, The

RANK (GB) 1962 dir. Steve Sekely
BBC (GB) 1981 dir. Ken Hannam
TVSe (GB)

Wyndham, J.
Midwich Cuckoos, The

Village of the Damned
MGM (GB) 1960 dir. Wolf Rilla
UN (US) 1995 dir. John Carpenter

Wynette, T. and Dew, J.
Stand by Your Man

GUBER-PETERS (US) 1981
dir. Jerry Jameson
TV(US)

Wynne, G.
Man from Moscow, A

Wynne and Penkovsky
BBC (GB/US) 1985 dir. Paul Seed
TVSe(GB/US)

Wynne, P.
Little Flat in the Temple, A

Devotion
RKO (US) 1931 dir. Robert Milton

Wyse, L.
Kiss, Inc.

Million Dollar Face, The
NEPHI-HAMNER (US) 1981
dir. Michael O'Herlihy
TV(US)

Wyss, J. D.
Swiss Family Robinson

RKO (US) 1940 dir. Edward Ludwig
DISNEY (GB) 1960 dir. Ken Annakin
FOX (US) 1975 dir. Harry Harris
TV(US)

Wyss, J. D.
Swiss Family Robinson

New Swiss Family Robinson, The
TOTAL (US) 1999 dir. Stewart Raffill
TV(US)

Xaurof, L. and Chancel, J.
Prince Consort, The

P

Love Parade, The
PAR (US) 1929 dir. Ernst Lubitsch
M

Yafa, S.
Paxton Quigley's had the Course

Three in the Attic
WAR (US) 1968 dir. Richard Wilson

Yallop, D.
Beyond Reasonable Doubt

J&M (NZ) 1980 dir. John Laing

Yamada, T.
Discarnates, The

SHOCHIKU (Jap) 1989
dir. Nobuhiko Obayashi

Yamamoto
Redbeard

TOHO (Jap) 1965 dir. Akira Kurosawa

Yamazaki, T.
Family, The

PUBLIC (Jap) 1974
dir. Karei Naru Ichikozo

Yan, G.
Siao Yu

CENTRAL MOTION (Tai) 1995 dir.
Sylvia Chang

Yan, G.
Tian Yu

Xiu Xiu: The Sent-Down Girl
GOOD MACHINE (China/HK) 1998
dir. Joan Chen

Yardley, H. O.
American Black Chamber, The

Rendezvous
MGM (US) 1935 dir. William K.
Howard

Yarmolinsky, J.
Angels Without Wings

Promise to Keep, A
WAR TV (US) 1990 dir. Rod Holcomb
TV(US)

Yates, D.
She Fell Among Thieves
BBC (GB) 1979 dir. Clive Donner
TV(GB)

Yates, E.
Skeezer: Dog With a Mission
Skeezer
M. ARCH (US) 1982 dir. Peter H. Hunt
TV(US)

Yeats, W. B.
Words Upon the Window Pane
P
PEMBRIDGE (Ire) 1994 dir. Mary
McGuckian

Yerby, F.
Foxes of Harrow, The
FOX (US) 1947 dir. John M. Stahl

Yerby, F.
Golden Hawk, The
COL (US) 1952 dir. Sidney Salkow

Yerby, F.
Saracen Blade, The
COL (US) 1954 dir. William Castle

Yglesias, R.
Fearless
WAR (US) 1993 dir. Peter Weir

Yolen, J.
Devil's Arithmetic, The
PUNCH 21 (US) 1999 dir. Donna Deitch
TV(US)

Yordan, P.
Anna Lucasta
P
COL UA (US) 1949 dir. Irving Rapper
UA (US) 1958 dir. Arnold Laven

Yordan, P.
Man of the West
Gun Glory
MGM (US) 1957 dir. Roy Rowland

Yorgason, B.
Windwalker
PACIFIC (US) 1981 dir. Keith Merrill

Yorgason, B. and Yorgason, B.
Chester, I Love You
Thanksgiving Promise, The
DISNEY (US) 1986 dir. Beau Bridges
TV(US)

York, A.
Eliminator, The
Danger Route
UA (GB) 1967 dir. Seth Holt

Yorke, M.
Point of Murder, The
Kiss of a Killer
ABC PROD (US) 1993 dir. Larry
Elikann
TV(US)

Yoshimoto, B.
Kitchen
HARVEST CROWN (HK/Jap) 1996 dir.
Ho Yim

Yoshimura, A.
Sparkles in the Darkness
Eel, The
KSS (Jap) 1997 dir. Shohei Imamura

Young, C. U.
Gun Shy
Showdown at Abilene
UN (US) 1956 dir. Charles Haas

Young, D.
Rommel, The Desert Fox
Desert Fox, The
FOX (US) 1951 dir. Henry Hathaway
GB title: Rommel, Desert Fox

Young, E. H.
Miss Mole

Hannah
BBC (GB) 1980 dir. Peter Jefferies
TVSe(GB)

Young, F. B.
My Brother Jonathan

AB (GB) 1947 dir. Harold French
BBC (GB) 1985 dir. Anthony Garner
TVSe(GB)

Young, F. B.
Portrait of Clare

ABP (GB) 1950 dir. Lance Comfort

Young, F. B. and Perry, J.
Man About the House, A
P
LF (GB) 1947 dir. Leslie Arliss

Young, J. R.
Behind the Rising Sun

RKO (US) 1943 dir. Edward Dmytryk

Young, K.
Ravine, The

Assault
RANK (GB) 1971 dir. Sidney Hayers

Young, M.
Mother Wore Tights

FOX (US) 1947 dir. Walter Lang

Young, R. J.
Checkers

P
FOX (US) 1937
dir. H. Bruce Humberstone

Young, R. J.
Little Old New York

P
FOX (US) 1940 dir. Henry King

Young, S.
So Red the Rose

PAR (US) 1935 dir. King Vidor

Yurick, S.
Fertig

Confession, The
EL DORADO (US) 1999 dir. David
Hugh Jones

Zacha, Sr., W. T.
Capricorn Man, The

Ultimate Imposter, The
UN TV (US) 1979 dir. Paul Stanley
TV(US)

Zackel, F.
Cocaine and Blue Eyes

COL TV (US) 1983
dir. E.W. Swackhamer
TV(US)

Zaharias, B. D. and Paxton, H.
This Life I've Led: My Autobiography

Babe
MGM TV (US) 1975 dir. Buzz Kulik
TV(US)

Zahavi, H.
Dirty Weekend

SCIMITAR (GB) 1993 dir. Michael
Winner

Zalazny, R.
Damnation Alley

FOX (US) 1977 dir. Jack Smight

Zangwill, I.
Big Bow Mystery, The

Verdict, The
WAR (US) 1946 dir. Don Siegel

Zavada, P.
Jadviga Parnaja

MAFILM (Hun) 2000 dir. Krisztina
Deak

Zavattini, C.
Toto il Buono

Miracle in Milan
PDS (It) 1951 dir. Vittorio de Sica

Zeldis, C.
Forbidden Love, A

Torn Apart
CASTLE HILL (US) 1990
dir. Jack Fisher

Zetterling, M.
Night Games

GALA (Swe) 1966 dir. Mai Zetterling

Zhaxidawa
Ming

Yixizhuoma
BEIJING (China) 2000 dir. Fei Xie

Ziao, L.
Shanghai Triad

SHANGHAI (China) 1995 dir. Yimou
Zhang

Ziegler, I. G.
Nine Days of Father Serra

Seven Cities of Gold
FOX (US) 1955 dir. Robert D. Webb

Ziegler, T.
Grace & Glorie

P
HALLMARK (US) 1998 dir. Arthur
Allan Seidelman
TV(US)

Ziemer, G.
Education for Death

Hitler's Children
RKO (US) 1943 dir. Edward Dmytryk

Zigman, L.
Animal Husbandry

Someone Like You
FOX (US) 2000 dir. Tony Goldwyn

Zimmer Bradley, M.
Mists of Avalon, The

TNT (US) 2001 dir. Uli Edel
TVSe(US)

Zindel, P.
Effect of Gamma Rays on Man-in-the-Moon Marigolds,The

P
FOX-RANK (US) 1972 dir. Paul
Newman

Zindel, P.
Undertaker's Gone Bananas, The

*New Adventures of Spin & Marty, The:
Suspect Behavior*
DISNEY (US) 2000 dir. Rusty Cundieff
Ch, TV(US)

Zinik, Z.
Mushroom Picker, The

BBC (GB) 1993 dir. Andy Wilson
TVSe(GB)

Zobel, J.
Rue Cases Negres, La

Sugar Cane Alley
ORION (Fr) 1984 dir. Euzhan Palcy

Zola, E.
Assommoir, L'

Gervaise
CLCC (Fr) 1956 dir. René Clément

Zola, E.
Bête Humaine, La

Human Desire
COL (US) 1954 dir. Fritz Lang

Zola, E.
Bête Humaine, La

PARIS (Fr) 1938 dir. Jean Renoir

Zola, E.
Bête Humaine, La

Cruel Train
BBC (GB) 1995 dir. Malcolm McKay
TV(GB)

Zola, E.
For a Night of Love

Manifesto
CANNON (Yugo) 1988
dir. Dusan Makajevev

Zola, E.
Germinal

BBC (GB) 1970 dir. John Davies
TVSe(GB)
STUDIO CANAL+ (Fr/Bel) 1993 dir.
Claude Berri

Zola, E.
Kill, The

Game is Over, The
COL (Fr/It) 1967 dir. Roger Vadim

Zola, E.
Nana

MGM (US) 1934 dir. Dorothy Arzner
GB title: Lady of the Boulevards
GALA (Fr/1t) 1955 dir. Christian Jacque
MINERVA (Swe) 1971 dir. Mac Ahlberg
CANNON (It) 1982 dir. Dan Wolman

Zola, E.
Therese Raquin

BBC (GB) 1980 dir. Simon Langton
TVSe(GB)

Zuckmayer, C.
Devil's General, The

P
RYAL (W. Ger) 1955 dir. Helmut
Kautner

Zumwalt, Jr., Admiral, E. and Zumwalt III, E. R.
My Father, My Son
WEINTRAUB (US) 1988
dir. Jeff Bleckner
TV(US)

Zweibel, A.
North
COL (US) 1994 dir. Rob Reiner

Zweig, A.
Case of Sergeant Grischa, The
RKO (US) 1930 dir. Herbert Brenon

Zweig, S.
Beware of Pity
TC (GB) 1946 dir. Maurice Elvey

Zweig, S.
Brennendes Geheimnis
Burning Secret
VESTRON (GB/Ger) 1988
dir. Andrew Birkin

Zweig, S.
Letter from an Unknown Woman
UI (US) 1948 dir. Max Ophuls

Zweig, S.
Marie Antoinette
MGM (US) 1938 dir. W. S. Van Dyke

Zweig, S.
Twenty-Four Hours of a Woman's Life
ABPC (GB) 1952 dir. Victor Saville
US title: Affair in Monte Carlo

CHANGE OF ORIGINAL
TITLE INDEX

Book or play title —— **Taming of the Shrew, The**

Author's name ——— Shakespeare, W.

Kiss Me Kate ———————————————— Film title

Studio name, ———— MGM (US) 1953 dir. George Sidney ——— Director's name
location and MILBERG (US) 1958 dir. George Schaefer
release date GB title:

British, etc. title
(if different)

À La Recherche du Temps Perdu
Proust, M.

Captive, The
STUDIO CANAL+ (Fr) 2000 dir.
Chantal Akerman

À la Recherche du Temps Perdu
Proust, M.

Time Regained
STUDIO CANAL+ (Fr/It/Port) 1999
dir. Raoul Ruiz

Abbess of Crewe, The
Spark, M.

Nasty Habits
SCOTIA-BARBER (GB) 1976
dir. Michael Lindsay-Hogg
US title: The Abbess

Abbie Hoffman: American Rebel
Jeser, M.

Steal This Movie
GREENLIGHT (US) 2000 dir. Robert
Greenwald

ABC Murders, The
Christie, A.

Alphabet Murders, The
MGM (GB) 1966 dir. Frank Tashlin

Abe Lincoln of Illinois
Sherwood, R. E.

Abe Lincoln in Illinois
RKO (US) 1940 dir. John Cromwell
COMPASS (US) 1964 dir. George
Schaefer

Abominable Man, The
Sjowall, M. and Wahloo, M.

Man on the Roof, The
SVENSK (Swe) 1976
dir. Bo Widenberg

Acacia Avenue
Constanduros, M. and Constanduros,
D.

29 Acacia Avenue
COL (GB) 1945 dir. Henry Cass
US title: Facts of Love, The

Accent on Youth
Raphaelson, S.

But Not For Me
PAR (US) 1959 dir. Walter Lang

Across the Bridge
Greene, G.

Double Take
TOUCHSTONE (US) 2001 dir. George
Gallo

Act of Mercy
Clifford, F.

Guns of Darkness
WAR (GB) 1962 dir. Anthony Asquith

Act of Passion
Simenon, G.

Forbidden Fruit
CAMEO-POLY (Fr) 1952
dir. Henri Verneuil

Ada Dallas
Williams, W.
Ada
MGM (US) 1961 dir. Daniel Mann

Ada, the Enchantress of Numbers, A Selections from the Letters of Lord Byron's Daughter and Her Description of the First Computer
Toole, B. A.
Conceiving Ada
HOTWIRE (Ger/US) 1997 dir. Lynn Hershman-Leeson

Addie Pray
Brown, J. D.
Paper Moon
PAR (US) 1973 dir. Peter Bogdanovich

Adios
Bartlett, L. V. S.
Lash, The
IN (US) 1930 dir. Frank Lloyd

Admirable Crichton, The
Barrie, Sir J. M.
We're Not Dressing
PAR (US) 1934 dir. Norman Taurog

Adobe Walls
Burnett, W. R.
Arrowhead
PAR (US) 1953 dir. Charles Marquis Warren

Adultery, The Forgivable Sin
Weil, B. E. and Winter, R.
Silence of Adultery, The
HEARST (US) 1995 dir. Steven H. Stern

Adventure, The
Morison, E. and Lamont, F.
Miss Morison's Ghosts
ANGLIA (GB) 1983 dir. John Bruce

Adventure in Diamonds
Walker, D. E.
Operation Amsterdam
RANK (GB) 1958 dir. Michael McCarthy

Adventure of the Five Orange Pips
Doyle, Sir A. C.
House of Fear
UN (US) 1945 dir. Roy William Neill

Adventures of Caleb Williams (Or Things As They Are), The
Godwin, W.
Caleb Williams
TYNE-TEES (GB) 1983 dir. Herbert Wise

Adventures of Hajji Baba of Ispahan
Morier, J. J.
Adventures of Hajji Baba, The
FOX (US) 1954 dir. Don Weis

Adventures of Huckleberry Finn, The
Twain, M.
Adventures of Huck Finn, The
DISNEY (US) 1993 dir. Stephen Sommers

Adventures of Huckleberry Finn, The
Twain, M.
Huck and the King of Hearts
TRIMARK (US) 1994 dir. Michael Keusch

Adventures of Huckleberry Finn, The
Twain, M.
Huckleberry Finn
PAR (US) 1931 dir. Norman Taurog
MGM (US) 1939 dir. Richard Thorpe
UA (US) 1974 dir. J. Lee Thompson
ABC (US) 1975 dir. Robert Totten

Adventures of Tom Sawyer, The
Twain, M.

Tom and Huck
DISNEY (US) 1995 dir. Peter Hewitt

Adventures of Tom Sawyer, The
Twain, M.

Tom Sawyer
UA (US) 1973 dir. Don Taylor
UN (US) 1973 dir. James Neilson
STONE CANYON (US) 2000 dir. Phil
Mendez, Paul Sabella

Affaire de Femmes, Une
Szpiner, F.

Story of Women
NEW YORKER (Fr) 1989 dir. Claude
Chabrol

Affaire Papin, L'
Houdyer, P.

Murderous Maids
STUDIO CANAL+ (Fr) 2000 dir. Jean-
Pierre Denis

Affaires de Gout
Balland, P.

Matter of Taste, A
STUDIO CANAL+ (Fr) 1999 dir.
Bernard Rapp

After All
van Druten, J.

New Morals for Old
MGM (US) 1932 dir. Charles Brabin

After the Funeral
Christie, A.

Murder at the Gallop
MGM (GB) 1963 dir. George Pollock

After the Hole
Burt, G.

Hole, The
PATHE (GB) 2001 dir. Nick Hamm

After the Trial
Roman, E.

Death Sentence
SPEL-GOLD (US) 1974
dir. E.W. Swackhamer

Agaguk
Theriault, Y.

Shadow of the Wolf
STUDIO CANAL+ (Fr/Can) 1992 dir.
Jacques Dorfmann, Pierre Magny

Against Heaven's Hand
Bishop, L.

Seven in Darkness
PAR TV (US) 1969 dir. Michael Caffey

**Age of Reason, The; Reprieve,
The; Iron in the Soul**
Sartre, J.-P.

Roads to Freedom, The
BBC (GB) 1970 dir. James Cellan Jones

Agony Column
Biggers, E. D.

Passage from Hong Kong
WAR (US) 1941 dir. D. Ross Lederman

Ah Wilderness!
O'Neill, E. G.

Summer Holiday
MGM (US) 1948 dir. Rouben
Mamoulian

Aimez-vous Brahms?
Sagan, F.

Goodbye Again
UA (US) 1961 dir. Anatole Litvak

Air Raid
Varley, J.

Millenium
FOX (US) 1989 dir. Michael Anderson

Airing in a Closed Carriage
Shearing, J.

Mark of Cain, The
TC (GB) 1948 dir. Brian Desmond Hurst

Airman and the Carpenter, The
Kennedy, L.
Crime of the Century
HBO (US) 1996 dir. Mark Rydell

Airport
Bailey, A.
International Airport
SPELLING (US) 1985 dir. Charles
Dubin, Don Chaffey

Al Schmid, Marine
Butterfield, R. P.
Pride of the Marines
WAR (US) 1945 dir. Delmer Daves
GB title: Forever in Love

Alan Quatermain
Haggard, Sir H. R.
King Solomon's Treasure
BARBER ROSE (Can/GB) 1979
dir. Alvin Rakoff

Albatross
Scaling-Kiley, D. and Noona, M.
Two Came Back
VZ/SERTNER (US) 1997 dir. Dick
Lowry

Alexandria Quartet, The
Durrell, L.
Justine
FOX (US) 1969 dir. George Cukor

Alf's Button
Darlington, W.A.
Alf's Button Afloat
GAINS (GB) 1938 dir. Marcel Varnel

Algonquin Project, The
Nolan, F.
Brass Target
UN (US) 1978 dir. John Hough

Alias Madame Doubtfire
Fine, A.
Mrs. Doubtfire
FOX (US) 1993 dir. Chris Columbus

Alice
Flanigan, S.
Wildflower
HEARST (US) 1991 dir. Diane Keaton

Alice Sit-by-the-Fire
Barrie, Sir J. M.
Darling, How Could You
PAR (US) 1951 dir. Mitchell Leisen
GB title: Rendezvous

Alice's Adventures in Wonderland
Carroll, L.
Alice
HEMDALE (Bel/Pol/GB) 1980 dir.
Jerry Gruza

Alice's Adventures in Wonderland
Carroll, L.
Alice in Wonderland
PAR (US) 1933 dir. Norman Z. McLeod
DISNEY (US) 1951
dir. Clyde Geronomi, Hamilton Luske,
Wilfred Jackson
M. EVANS (US) 1955
dir. George Schaefer
COL TV (US) 1985 dir. Harry Harris
BBC (GB) 1986 dir. Barry Letts
HALLMARK (US) 1999 dir. Nick
Willing

Alien, The
Davies, L. P.
Groundstar Conspiracy, The
UN (US) 1972 dir. Lamont Johnson

All Aboard for Freedom
McSwigan, M.
Snow Treasure
TIGON (US) 1968 dir. Irving Jacoby

All Brides are Beautiful
Bell, T.
From This Day Forward
RKO (US) 1946 dir. John Berry

All Good Americans
Perelman, S. J. and Perelman, L.
Paris Interlude
MGM (US) 1934 dir. Edwin L. Marin

All in Good Time
Naughton, B.
Family Way, The
BL (GB) 1966 dir. Roy Boulting

All Kneeling
Parrish, A.
Born to be Bad
RKO (US) 1950 dir. Nicholas Ray

All on a Summer's Day
Garden, J.
Double Confession
ABP (GB) 1950 dir. Ken Annakin

All on the Never-Never
Lindsay, J.
Live Now, Pay Later
REGAL (GB) 1962 dir. Jay Lewis

All Our Fault
Mornin, D.
Nothing Personal
BRIT SCREEN (GB/Ire) 1995 dir. Thaddeus O'Sullivan

All Souls
Marias, J.
Robert Rylands' Last Journey
BUXTON (Sp/GB) 1996 dir. Gracia Querejeta

All the Rage
Reddin, K.
It's the Rage
MUTUAL (US) 1999 dir. James D. Stern

All the Way
Williams, C.
Third Voice, The
FOX (US) 1959 dir. Hubert Cornfield

All Things Bright and Beautiful
Herriot, J.
It Shouldn't Happen to a Vet
EMI (GB) 1976 dir. Eric Till

All Through the Night
Masterson, W.
Cry in the Night, A
WAR (US) 1956 dir. Frank Tuttle

Allan Quatermain
Haggard, H. R.
Allan Quatermain and the Lost City of Gold
CANNON (US) 1987 dir. Gary Nelson

Almost Golden
Blair, G.
Almost Golden: The Jessica Savitch Story
ABC PROD (US) 1995 dir. Peter Werner

Almost Too Late
Wortman, E.
Anything to Survive
SABAN/SCHERICK (US) 1990 dir. Zale Dalen

Alone in the Australian Wilderness
Taylor, G.
Over the Hill
VILLAGE ROADSHOW (Aust) 1992 dir. George Miller

Alter Ego
Arrighi, M.
Murder by the Book
ORION TV (US) 1987 dir. Mel Damski

Always
Meldal-Johnson, T.
Déjà Vu
CANNON (GB) 1985 dir. Anthony Richmond

Always Outnumbered, Always Outgunned
Mosley, W.

Always Outnumbered
HBO (US) 1998 dir. Michael Apted

Amazing Quest of Mr Ernest Bliss, The
Oppenheim, E. P.

Amazing Quest of Ernest Bliss, The
KLEMENT (GB) 1936 dir. Alfred Zeisler
US title: Romance & Riches

Amboy Dukes, The
Shulman, I.

City Across The River
UI (US) 1949 dir. Maxwell Shane

Amelia Earhart: A Biography
Rich, D. L.

Amelia Earhart: The Final Flight
AVE PICT (US) 1994 dir. Yves Simoneau

American Black Chamber, The
Yardley, H. O.

Rendezvous
MGM (US) 1935 dir. William K. Howard

American Hero
Beinhart, L.

Wag the Dog
NEW LINE (US) 1997 dir. Barry Levinson

American Tragedy, An
Dreiser, T.

Place in the Sun, A
PAR (US) 1951 dir. George Stevens

American Tragedy: The Uncensored Story of the Simpson Defense
Schiller, L. and Willwerth, J.

American Tragedy, An
FOX TV (US) 2000 dir. Lawrence Schiller

Americans, Baby, The; Electrical Experience, The
Moorhouse, F.

Coca-Cola Kid, The
CINECOM (Aust) 1985 dir. Dusan Makevejev

Amerika
Kafka, F.

Class Relations
ART EYE (Ger/Fr) 1983 dir. Jean Marie Straub, Daniele Huillet

Ammie, Come Home
Michaels, B.

House That Would Not Die, The
SPELLING (US) 1980 dir. J. L. Moxey

Amy Jolly
Vigny, B.

Morocco
PAR (US) 1930 dir. Josef von Sternberg

Anastasia: The Riddle of Anna Anderson
Kurth, P.

Anastasia: The Mystery of Anna
TELECOM (US) 1986 dir. Marvin Chomsky

Anatomy of Me
Hurst, F.

Imitation of Life
UN (US) 1934 dir. John Stahl
UN (US) 1959 dir. Douglas Sirk

And Deliver Us From Evil
Cochran, M.

Fugitive Among Us
ABC PROD (US) 1992 dir. Michael Toshiyuki Uno

And Never Let Her Go: Thomas Capano: The Deadly Seducer
Rule, A.

And Never Let Her Go
GREENWALD (US) 2001 dir. Peter Levin

And Quiet Flows the Don
Sholokhov, M.

Quiet Flows the Don
GORKI (USSR) 1958 dir. Sergei
Gerasimov

And Ride a Tiger
Wilder, R.

Stranger in my Arms, A
UI (US) 1958 dir. Helmut Kautner

And the Beat Goes On
Bono, S.

*And the Beat Goes On: The Sonny and
Cher Story*
L THOMPSON (US) 1999 dir. David
Burton Morris

And the Home of the Brave
Vaccaro, R.

Run the Wild Fields
SHOWTIME (US) 2000 dir. Paul A.
Kaufman

And They Shall Walk
Kenny, E. and Ostenso, M.

Sister Kenny
RKO (US) 1946 dir. Dudley Nichols

Angel Street
Hamilton, P.

Gaslight
BN (GB) 1939 dir. Thorold Dickinson
US title: Angel Street
MGM (US) 1944 dir. George Cukor
GB title: Murder in Thornton Square,
The

Angela is 22
Wray, R. and Lewis, S.

This is the Life
UN (US) 1943 dir. Felix Feist

Angels Without Wings
Yarmolinsky, J.

Promise to Keep, A
WAR TV (US) 1990 dir. Rod Holcomb

Angie, I Says
Wing, A.

Angie
HOLLYWOOD (US) 1994 dir. Martha
Coolidge

Animal Husbandry
Zigman, L.

Someone Like You
FOX (US) 2000 dir. Tony Goldwyn

Animal Kingdom, The
Barry, P.

One More Tomorrow
WAR (US) 1946 dir. Peter Godfrey

Animals Are My Hobby
Lintz, G.

Buddy
COL (US) 1997 dir. Caroline Thompson

Anna and the King of Siam
Landon, M.

King and I, The
FOX (US) 1956 dir. Walter Lang

Anne Frank: The Biography
Muller, M.

Anne Frank
TOUCHSTONE (US) 2001 dir. Robert
Dornhelm

Anne Frank: The Diary of a Young Girl
Frank, A.

Diary of Anne Frank, The
FOX (US) 1959 dir. George Stevens
FOX (US) 1980 dir. Boris Sagal
BBC (GB) 1987 dir. Gareth Davies

Anne Frank Remembered: The Story of the Woman Who Helped to Hide the Frank Family
Gies, M. and Gold, A. L.

Attic, The: The Hiding of Anne Frank
TELECOM/YTV (US/GB) 1988
dir. John Erman

Anne of Windy Willows
Montgomery, L. M.

Anne of Windy Poplars
RKO (US) 1940 dir. Jack Hively

Annie's Coming Out
Crossley, R. and McDonald, A.

Test of Love, A
UN (US) 1985 dir. Gil Brealey

Anniversary Waltz
Fields, J. and Chodorov, J.

Happy Anniversary
UA (US) 1959 dir. David Miller

Anointed, The
Davis, C. B.

Adventure
MGM (US) 1945 dir. Victor Fleming

Ant and the Grasshopper, The; Winter Cruise; Gigolo and Gigolette
Maugham, W. S.

Encore
GFD (GB) 1951 dir. Harold French, Pat Jackson, Anthony Pellissier

Antagonists, The
Gann, E. K.

Masada
UN TV (US) 1981 dir. Boris Sagal
GB title: Antagonists, The

Apache Rising
Albert, M. H.

Duel at Diablo
UA (US) 1966 dir. Ralph Nelson

Apple Pie in the Sky
Lovell, M.

Trouble With Spies, The
HBO (US) 1987 dir. Burt Kennedy

Apple Tree, The
Galsworthy, J.

Summer Story, A
ITC / ATLANTIC (GB) 1988 dir. Piers Haggard

Applesauce
Conners, B.

Brides are Like That
WAR (US) 1936 dir. William McGann

Appointment at the Beach
Moravia, A.

Naked Hours, The
COMPTON (It) 1964 dir. Marco Vicario

Appointment for Murder
Bakos, S. C.

Beyond Suspicion
VZ / SERTNER (US) 1993 dir. William A. Graham

Appointment with Fear
Huggins, R.

State Secret, The
BL (GB) 1950 dir. Sidney Gilliat
US title: Great Manhunt, The

Appointments in Zahrein
Barrett, M.

Escape from Zahrein
PAR (US) 1962 dir. Ronald Neame

April Shroud, An
Hill, R.

Autumn Shroud, An
BBC / A&E (GB) 1996 dir. Richard Standeven

Aren't You Even Gonna Kiss Me Goodbye
Richert, W.

Night in the Life of Jimmy Reardon, A
FOX (US) 1988 dir. William Richert

Ari: The Life and Time of Aristotle Onassis
Evans, P.

Richest Man in the World, The: The Story of Aristotle Onassis
KON-SAN (US) 1988 dir. Waris Hussein

Arizona in the 50's
Tevis, J. H.

Tenderfoot, The
DISNEY (US) 1964 dir. Byron Paul

Arm, The
Howard, C.

Big Town, The
COL (US) 1987 dir. Ben Bolt

Arms and the Man
Shaw, G. B.

Helden
SOKAL/GOLDBAUM (Ger) 1959 dir. Franz Peter Wirth

Arouse and Beware
Kantor, M.

Man from Dakota, The
MGM (US) 1940 dir. Leslie Fenton
GB title: Arouse and Beware

Arrow in the Sun
Olsen, T. V.

Soldier Blue
AVCO (US) 1970 dir. Ralph Nelson

Ashenden
Maugham, W. S.

Secret Agent
GAU BR (GB) 1936 dir. Alfred Hitchcock

Ask Agamemnon
Hall, J.

Goodbye Gemini
CINDERAMA (GB) 1970 dir. Alan Gibson

Asking for It
Taylor, J.

Invasion of Privacy, An
EMBASSY TV (US) 1983 dir. Mel Damski

Aspern Papers, The
James, H.

Aspern
CONN (Port) 1981 dir. Eduardo de Gregorion

Aspern Papers, The
James, H.

Lost Moment, The
UN (US) 1947 dir. Martin Gabel

Asphalt Jungle, The
Burnett, W. R.

Cairo
MGM (GB) 1963 dir. Wolf Rilla

Asphalt Jungle, The
Burnett, W. R.

Cool Breeze
MGM (US) 1972 dir. Barry Pollack

Assassination of Federico Garcia Lorca, The; Federico Garcia Lorca: A Life
Gibson, I.

Disappearance of Garcia Lorca, The
STUDIO CANAL+ (Fr/Sp/US) 1997 dir. Marcos Zurinaga

Assommoir, L'
Zola, E.

Gervaise
CLCC (Fr) 1956 dir. René Clément

Atomic Soldiers
Rosenberg, H.

Nightbreaker
TNT (US) 1989 dir. Peter Markle

Attack on Terror: The FBI Against The Ku Klux Klan in Mississippi
Whitehead, D.

Attack on Terror: The FBI Versus The Ku Klux Klan
WAR TV (US) 1975 dir. Marvin Chomsky

Attention, L'
Moravia, A.

Lie, The
SELVAGGIA (It) 1985 dir. Giovanni Soldati

Atticus
Hansen, R.

Missing Pieces
HALMARK (US) 2000 dir. Richard Kletter

Auch das war Wein
Torberg, F.

38: Vienna Before the Fall
SATEL/ALMARO (Ger) 1988 dir. Wolfgang Gluck

Aunt Julia and the Scriptwriter
Llosa, M. V.

Tune in Tomorrow ...
CINECOM (US) 1990 dir. Jon Amiel

Auntie Mame
Dennis, P.

Mame
WAR (US) 1974 dir. Gene Saks

Authentic Death of Hendry Jones, The
Neider, C.

One-Eyed Jacks
PAR (US) 1961 dir. Marlon Brando

Autobiography of Malcolm X, The
Haley, A. and Malcolm X

Malcolm X
40 ACRES (US) 1992 dir. Spike Lee

Autumn of a Hunter
Stadley, P.

Deadly Hunt, The
FOUR STAR (US) 1971 dir. John Newland

Autumn
Kennedy, M. and Surgutchoff, I.

That Dangerous Age
LF (GB) 1948 dir. Gregory Ratoff
US title: If This Be Sin

Avenging Angels, The
Burns, R.

Messenger of Death
CANNON (US) 1988 dir. J. Lee Thompson

Avventura di un Uomo Tranqillo, L'
Calderoni, P.

Testimone a Rischio
MEDIASET (It) 1997 dir. Pasqualte Pozzessere

Awakening, The
Chopin, K.

End of August, The
QUARTET (US) 1981 dir. Bob Graham

Awakening, The
Chopin, K.

Grand Isle
TURNER (US) 1992 dir. Mary Lambert

Away Alone
Noble, J.

Gold in the Streets
FERNDALE (GB/Ire) 1997 dir. Elizabeth Gill

B

B-Ball: The Team That Never Lost a Game
Jones, R.

One Special Victory
NBC (US) 1991 dir. Stuart Cooper

Babe, the Gallant Pig (US); The Sheep-Pig (GB)
King-Smith, D.

Babe
UN (Aust) 1995 dir. Chris Noonan

Babe: The Legend Comes to Life
Cramer, R. W.

Babe Ruth
LYTTLE (US) 1991 dir. Mark Tinker

Babe Ruth, His Life and Legend
Wagenheim, K.

Babe Ruth
LYTTLE (US) 1991 dir. Mark Tinker

Baby Brokers, The
MeTaggart, L.

Born to be Sold
SAMUELS (US) 1981 dir. Burt Brinckerhoff

Baby Jane
Farrell, H.

What Ever Happened to Baby Jane?
WAR (US) 1962 dir. Robert Aldrich
SPECTACOR (US) 1991 dir. David Greene

Babylon Revisited
Fitzgerald, F. S.

Last Time I Saw Paris, The
MGM (US) 1954 dir. Richard Brooks

Bachelor Born
Hay, I.

Housemaster
ABPC (GB) 1938 dir. Herbert Brenon

Bachelor Father
Dell, F.

Casanova Brown
INTERNATIONAL (US) 1944 dir. Sam Wood

Bad As I Wanna Be
Rodman, D. and Keown, T.

Bad As I Wanna Be: The Dennis Rodman Story
COL TRISTAR (US) 1998 dir. Jean De Segonzac

Bad Time at Honda
Breslin, H.

Bad Day at Black Rock
MGM (US) 1954 dir. John Sturges

Badge of Evil
Masterson, W.

Touch of Evil
UN (US) 1958 dir. Orson Welles

Badman
Huffaker, C.

War Wagon, The
UI (US) 1967 dir. Burt Kennedy

Balkan Trilogy, The; Levant Trilogy, The
Manning, O.
Fortunes of War
BBC (GB) 1987, dir. James Cellan Jones

Bailbondsman, The
Elkin, S.
Alex and the Gypsy
TCF (US) 1976 dir. John Korty

Ballad of Cat Ballou, The
Chanslor, R.
Cat Ballou
COL (US) 1965 dir. Eliot Silverstein

Ballad of Dingus Magee, The
Markson, D.
Dirty Dingus Magee
MGM (US) 1970 dir. Burt Kennedy

Ballad of the Belstone Fox, The
Rook, D.
Belstone Fox, The
RANK (GB) 1973 dir. James Hill

Ballad of the Flim-Flam Man, The
Owen, G.
Flim-Flam Man, The
FOX (US) 1967 dir. Irvin Kershner

Ballad of the Running Man, The
Smith, S.
Running Man, The
COL (GB) 1963 dir. Carol Reed

Ballerina
Smith, Lady E.
Men in her Life
COL (US) 1941 dir. Gregory Ratoff

Band of Brothers, A: E Company 506th Regiment, 101st Airborne From Normandy to Hitler's Nest
Ambrose, S. E.
Band of Brothers
DREAMWORKS (US/GB) 2001 dir. David Franken, Tom Hanks, David Leland, Richard Loncraine, David Nutter, Phil Alden Robinson, Mikael Salomon, Tony To

Bandwagon, The
Kaufman, G. S., Dietz, H. and Schwarz, A.
Dancing in the Dark
FOX (US) 1949 dir. Irving Reis

Bangkwang
Paladini, F.
Vacation in Hell
METROPOLIS (It) 1997 dir. Tonina Valerii

Banjo
McKay, C.
Big Fella
FORTUNE (GB) 1937 dir. J. E. Wills

Bank Robber, The
Tippette, G.
Spikes Gang, The
UA (US) 1974 dir. Richard Fleischer

Bankers Also Have Souls
Valme and Terzolli
Gift, The
GOLDWYN (Fr) 1983 dir. Michel Lang

Banner in the Sky
Ullman, J. R.
Third Man on the Mountain
DISNEY (GB) 1959 dir. Ken Annakin

Barbarians at the Gate: The Fall of RJR Nabisco
Burrough, B. and Helyar, J.
Barbarians at the Gate
COL/HBO (US) 1993 dir. Glenn Jordan

Barchester Towers; Warden, The
Trollope, A.

Barchester Chronicles, The
BBC (GB) 1982 dir. David Giles

Baree, Son of Kazan
Curwood, J. O.

Northern Passage
GAU TV (Fr/Can) 1994 dir. Arnaud Selignac

Barker, The
Nicholson, K.

Diamond Horseshoe
FOX (US) 1945 dir. George Seaton

Barrage contre le Pacifique, Un
Duras, M.

This Angry Age
DELAUR (It) 1957 dir. René Clément

Basement Room, The
Greene, G.

Fallen Idol, The
FOX (GB) 1948 dir. Carol Reed
US title: Lost Illusion, The

Basil of Baker Street
Titus, E.

Great Mouse Detective, The
DISNEY (US) 1986
dir. Burny Mattinson

Bat, The
Rinehart, M. R.

Bat Whispers, The
UA (US) 1930 dir. Roland West

Battle of Nerves, A
Simenon, G.

Man on the Eiffel Tower, The
BL (US) 1948 dir. Burgess Meredith

Be Ready With Bells and Drums
Kata, E.

Patch of Blue, A
MGM (US) 1965 dir. Guy Green

Be Still My Love
Truesdell, J.

Accused, The
PAR (US) 1948 dir. William Dieterle

Beardless Warriors
Matheson, R.

Young Warriors
UN (US) 1966 dir. John Peyser

Beautiful Mind, A: A Biography of John Forbes Nash, Jr.
Nasar, S.

Beautiful Mind, A
IMAGINE ENT (US) 2001 dir. Ron Howard

Beauty
Baldwin, F.

Beauty for Sale
MGM (US) 1933 dir. Richard Boleslawski

Because of the Cats
Freeling, N.

Rape, The
MIRACLE (Bel/Neth) 1973 dir. Fons Rademakers

Bed-Knob and Broomstick
Norton, M.

Bedknobs and Broomsticks
DISNEY (US) 1971 dir. Robert Stevenson

Bedeviled, The
Cullinan, T.

Beguiled, The
UN (US) 1971 dir. Don Siegel

Bedtime Story
Robinson, J. S.

Cry for Love, A
FRIES/SACKS (US) 1980 dir. Paul Wendkos

Before the Fact
Iles, F.

Suspicion
RKO (US) 1941 dir. Alfred Hitchcock

Beggar My Neighbour
Ridley, A.

Meet Mr Lucifer
GFD (GB) 1953 dir. Anthony Pelissier

Beggars are Coming to Town
Reeves, T.

I Walk Alone
PAR (US) 1947 dir. Byron Haskin

Beginner's Luck
Somers, P.

Desperate Man, The
AA (GB) 1959 dir. Peter Maxwell

Behold We Live
van Druten, J.

If I Were Free
RKO (US) 1933 dir. Elliot Nugent

Beirut
Browne, A.

Daybreak
HBO SHOW (US) 1993 dir. Steven Tolkin

Bejewelled Death
Babson, M.

Bejewelled
DISNEY CH (US/GB) 1991 dir. Terry Marcel

Bel Ami
De Maupassant, G.

Private Affairs of Bel Ami, The
UA (US) 1947 dir. Albert Lewin

Belarus Secret, The
Loftus, J.

Kojak: The Belarus File
UN TV (US) 1985 dir. Robert Markowitz

Bella Donna
Hichens, R.

Temptation
UN (US) 1935 dir. Irving Pichel

Bellamy the Magnificent
Horniman, R.

Bedtime Story, A
PAR (US) 1933 dir. Norman Taurog

Beloved Friend
Bowen, C. D. and von Meek, B.

Music Lovers, The
UA (GB) 1970 dir. Ken Russell

Belvedere
Davenport, G.

Sitting Pretty
FOX (US) 1948 dir. Walter Lang

Bend of the Snake
Gulick, W.

Bend of the River
UI (US) 1952 dir. Anthony Mann
GB title: Where the River Bends

Benefits Forgot
Morrow, H.

Of Human Hearts
MGM (US) 1938 dir. Clarence Brown

Bengal Lancer
Brown, F. Y.

Lives of a Bengal Lancer
PAR (US) 1935 dir. Henry Hathaway

Bengal Tiger
Hunter, H.

Bengal Brigade
UI (US) 1954 dir. Laslo Benedek
GB title: Bengal Rifles

Benighted
Priestley, J. B.

Old Dark House, The
UN (US) 1932 dir. James Whale
BL (GB) 1963 dir. William Castle

Benjamin Blake
Marshall, E.

Son of Fury
TCF (US) 1942 dir. John Cromwell

Berg, The
Raymond, E.

Atlantic
BI (GB) 1929 dir. E. A. Dupont

Berg
Quinn, A.

Killing Dad
PALACE (US) 1989 dir. Michael Austin

Berkeley Square
Balderston, J. L.

House in the Square, The
FOX (GB) 1951 dir. Roy Baker
US title: I'll Never Forget You

Berlin Game; Mexico Set, London Match
Deighton, L.

Game, Set and Match
GRANADA (GB) 1987 dir. Ken Grieve,
Patrick Lau

Berlin Hotel
Baum, V.

Hotel Berlin
WAR (US) 1945 dir. Peter Godfrey

Berlin Memorandum, The
Deighton, L.

Funeral in Berlin
PAR (GB) 1966 dir. Guy Hamilton

Berlin Wall, The
Galante, P.

Freedom Fighter
COL TV (US/GB) 1987 dir. Desmond
Davis

Best Intentions: The Education and Killing of Edmund Perry
Anson, R. A.

Murder Without Motive: The Edmund Perry Story
L. HILL TV (US) 1992 dir. Kevin Hooks

Bête Humaine, La
Zola, E.

Cruel Train
BBC (GB) 1995 dir. Malcolm McKay

Bête Humaine, La
Zola, E.

Human Desire
COL (US) 1954 dir. Fritz Lang

Bethnal Green
Fisher, M.

Place To Go, A
BL (GB) 1963 dir. Basil Dearden

Better Than Life
Bromfield, L.

It All Came True
WAR (US) 1940 dir. Lewis Seiler

Beware of Children
Anderson, V.

No Kidding
AA (GB) 1960 dir. Gerald Thomas
US title: Beware of Children

Beyond the Mountains
Ramati, A.

Desperate Ones, The
AIP (Sp/US) 1968 dir. Alexander
Ramati

Bid Time Return
Matheson, R.

Somewhere in Time
UN (US) 1980 dir. Jeannot Szwarc

Big Beat Heat: Alan Freed and the Early Years of Rock & Roll
Jackson, J. A.

Mr. Rock 'n' Roll: The Alan Freed Story
VZ/SERTNER (US) 1999 dir. Andy
Wolk

Big Birthday, The
Leonard, H.

Broth of a Boy
E. DALTON (Eire) 1958
dir. George Pollack

Big Bow Mystery, The
Zangwill, I.

Verdict, The
WAR (US) 1946 dir. Don Siegel

Big Clock, The
Fearing, K.

No Way Out
ORION (US) 1987 dir. Roger Donaldson

Big Pick-Up, The
Trevor, E.

Dunkirk
MGM (GB) 1958 dir. Leslie Norman

Big Story, The
West, M. L.

Crooked Road, The
GALA (GB/Yugo) 1964 dir. Don
Chaffey

Big Town, The
Lardner, R. W.

So this is New York
UA (US) 1948 dir. Richard Fleischer

Big War, The
Myrer, A.

In Love and War
FOX (US) 1958 dir. Philip Dunne

Biko
Woods, D.

Cry Freedom
UN (GB) 1987 dir. Richard
Attenborough

Binary
Crichton, M.

Pursuit
ABC (US) 1972 dir. Michael Crichton

Bind, The
Ellin, S.

Sunburn
HEMDALE (GB/US) 1979
dir. Richard C. Sarafian

Biography
Behrman, S. N.

Biography (of a Bachelor Girl)
MGM (US) 1935 dir. Edward H. Griffith

Biography of a Grizzly and Other Animal Stories, The
Seton, E. T.

Legend of Lobo, The
DISNEY (US) 1962 dir. James Algar

Biography of a Grizzly, The
Seton, E. T.

King of Grizzlies
DISNEY (US) 1970 dir. Ron Kelly

Bird's Nest, The
Jackson, S.

Lizzie
MGM (US) 1957 dir. Hugo Haas

Birthday
Bus-Fekete, L.

Heaven Can Wait
FOX (US) 1943 dir. Ernst Lubitsch

Birthday Gift
Fodor, L.

North to Alaska
FOX (US) 1960 dir. Henry Hathaway

Bitter Blood
Bledsoe, J.

In the Best of Families: Marriage, Pride and Madness
AMBROCO (US) 1994 dir. Jeff Bleckner

Bitter Harvest: Murder in the Heartland
Corcoran, J.

In the Line of Duty: Manhunt in the Dakotas
PATCHETT-KAUFMAN (US) 1991 dir. Dick Lowry

Bitter Sage
Gruber, G.

Tension at Table Rock
RKO (US) 1956 dir. Charles Marquis Warren

Bixby Girls, The
Marshall, R.

All the Fine Young Cannibals
MGM (US) 1960 dir. Michael Anderson

Black Alibi
Woolrich, C.

Leopard Man, The
RKO (US) 1943 dir. Jacques Tourneur

Black Box
Giordano, M.

Experiment, Das
FANES (Ger) 2001 dir. Oliver Hirschbiegel

Black Curtain, The
Woolrich, C.

Lady Forgets, The
HILL (US) 1989 dir. Bradford May

Black Curtain, The
Woolrich, C.

Street of Chance
PAR (US) 1942 dir. Jack Hively

Black Death, The
Cravens, G. and Marr, J. S.

Quiet Killer
SABAN/SCHERICK (US) 1992 dir. Sheldon Larry

Black Hawk Down: A Story of Modern War
Bowden, M.

Black Hawk Down
COL (US) 2001 dir. Ridley Scott

Black Hope Horror, The: The True Story of a Haunting
Williams, B., Williams, J. and Shoemaker, J. B.

Grave Secrets: The Legacy of Hilltop Drive
HEARST (US) 1992 dir. John Patterson

Black Path of Fear, The
Woolrich, C.

Chase, The
NERO (US) 1947 dir. Arthur Ripley

Blackburn's Headhunters
Harkins, P.

Surrender-Hell
AA (US) 1959 dir. John Barnwell

Blackjack Hijack, The
Einstein, C.

Nowhere to Run
MTM (US) 1978 dir. Richard Lang

Blackout
Lennon, G.

Drunks
BMG (US) 1996 dir. Peter Cohn

Blank Wall, The
Holding, E. S.

Deep End, The
FOX (US) 2001 dir. Scott McGehee, David Siegel

Blank Wall, The
Holding, E. S.
Reckless Moment, The
COL (US) 1949 dir. Max Ophuls

Blaze Starr: My Life as Told to Huey Perry
Starr, B. and Perry, H.
Blaze
TOUCHSTONE (US) 1989 dir. Ron Shelton

Bless You Sister
Riskin, R. and Meehan, J.
Miracle Woman, The
COL (US) 1932 dir. Frank Capra

Blessed Assurance: A Moral Tale
Gurganus, A.
Price of Heaven, The
KONIGSBERG (US) 1997 dir. Peter Bogdanovich

Blessing, The
Mitford, N.
Count Your Blessings
MGM (US) 1959 dir. Jean Negulesco

Blind Love
Cauvin, P.
Little Romance, A
WAR (US) 1979 dir. George Roy Hill

Blind Spot, The
Nicholson, K.
Taxi!
WAR (US) 1931 dir. Roy del Ruth

Bliss
Gundy, E.
Seduction of Miss Leona, The
SCHERICK (US) 1980 dir. Joseph Hardy

Blockhaus, Le
Clebert, J. P.
Blockhouse, The
GALACTUS (GB) 1973 dir. Clive Rees

Blondie White
Fodor, L.
Footsteps in the Dark
WAR (US) 1941 dir. Lloyd Bacon

Blood Brother
Arnold, E.
Broken Arrow
FOX (US) 1950 dir. Delmer Daves

Blood Brothers
Soble, R. and Johnson, J.
Honor Thy Father and Mother—The True Story of the Menendez Brothers
SABAN ENT (US) dir. Paul Schneider

Blood Games
Bledsoe, J.
Honor Thy Mother
POV (US) 1992 dir. David Greene

Blood of Israel, The
Groussard, S.
21 Hours at Munich
FILMWAYS (US) 1976 dir. William A. Graham

Blood on the Moon
Ellroy, J.
Cop
ATLANTIC (US) 1988 dir. James B. Harris

Blood Will Tell
Cartwright, G.
Texas Justice
CBS TV (US) 1995 dir. Dick Lowry

Bloody Spur, The
Einstein, C.
While the City Sleeps
RKO (US) 1956 dir. Fritz Lang

Blowing in the Wind
Van Peebles, M.

Panther
POLYGRAM (US/GB) 1995 dir. Mario
Van Peebles

Blue Collar Journal
Coleman, J. R.

Secret Life of John Chapman, The
JOZAK (US) 1976 dir. David Lowell
Rich

Blue Cross, The
Chesterton, G. K.

Father Brown
COL (GB) 1954 dir. Robert Hamer

Boarding Party
Leasor, J.

Sea Wolves, The
RANK (GB/US/Switz) 1980
dir. Andrew McLaglen

Bobby Rex's Greatest Hit
Gingher, M.

Just My Imagination
LORIMAR TV (US) 1992 dir. Jonathan
Sanger

Bodies and Souls
van der Meersch, M.

Doctor and the Girl, The
MGM (US) 1949 dir. Curtis Bernhardt

Body Snatchers, The
Finney, J.

Invasion of the Body Snatchers, The
ALLIED (US) 1956 dir. Don Siegel
UA (US) 1978 dir. Philip Kaufman

Body, The
King, S.

Stand by Me
COL (US) 1986 dir. Rob Reiner

Bogmail
McGinley, P.

Murder in Eden
BBC (GB) 1991 dir. Nicholas Renton

Bohunk
Irving, H. R.

Black Fury
WAR (US) 1935 dir. Michael Curtiz

Boken om E
Isaksson, U.

Song for Martin, A
MOONLIGHT (Den/Ger) 2001 dir. Bille
August

Bonaventure
Hastings, C.

Thunder on the Hill
UI (US) 1951 dir. Douglas Sirk
GB title: Bonaventure

Bondage
Hines, D.

Whore
TRIMARK (GB) 1991 dir. Ken Russell

Bones Obres
Baulenas, L.-A.

Anita no Perd el Tren
CANAL+ ESPANA (Sp) 2001 dir.
Ventura Pons

Book of Daniel, The
Doctorow, E. L.

Daniel
PAR (GB) 1983 dir. Sidney Lumet

Book of the Month
Thomas, B.

Please Turn Over
AA (GB) 1959 dir. Gerald Thomas

Border Jumpers, The
Brown, W. C.

Man of the West
UA (US) 1958 dir. Anthony Mann

Borrowed Christmas, A
Bemelmans, L.

Christmas Festival, A
COMPASS (US) 1959 dir. Albert
McCleery

Borrowers, The; Borrowers Afield, The; Borrowers Afloat, The; Borrowers Aloft, The
Norton, M.

Borrowers, The
FOX TV (US) 1973 dir. Walter C. Miller
WORKING TITLE TV/TNT (US/GB)
1992 dir. John Henderson
POLYGRAM (US/GB) 1997 dir. Peter
Hewitt

Boss of Bosses—The Fall of the Godfather: The FBI and Paul Castellano
O'Brien, J. F., Kurins, A. and Shames, L.

Boss of Bosses
BLEECKER (US) 1999 dir. Dwight H.
Little

Bossu, Le
Feval, P.

On Guard!
STUDIO CANAL+ (Fr) 1997 dir.
Philippe de Broca

Bottletop Affair, The
Cotler, G.

Horizontal Lieutenant, The
MGM (US) 1962 dir. Richard Thorpe

Boudu Sauvé des Eaux
Fauchois, R.

Down and Out in Beverly Hills
TOUCHSTONE (US) 1986 dir. Paul
Mazursky

Bouncers
Godber, J.

Ritz, The
BBC (GB) 1978 dir. John Godber, Martin
Shardlow

Bound by Honor
Bonanno, B.

Bonanno: A Godfather's Story
PAULSON (US) 1999 dir. Michael
Poulette

Bowery to Bellevue
Barringer, E. D.

Girl in White, The
MGM (US) 1952 dir. John Sturges
GB title: So Bright the Flame

Boy Who Could Make Himself Disappear, The
Platt, K.

Baxter!
EMI (GB) 1972 dir. Lionel Jeffries

Boy With Two Mothers, The
Bontempelli, M.

Comedie de L'innocence
STUDIO CANAL+ (Fr) 2000 dir. Raoul
Ruiz

Boyfriend School, The
Bird, S.

Don't Tell Her It's Me
HEMDALE (US) 1990 dir. Malcolm
Mowbray

Brainwash
Wainwright, J.

Inquisitor, The
GALA (Fr) 1981 dir. Claude Miller

Brainwash
Wainwright, J.

Under Suspicion
LIONS GATE (US/Fr) 2000 dir. Stephen
Hopkins

Brave Cowboy
Abbey, E.

Lonely are the Brave
UI (US) 1962 dir. David Miller

Bread and a Stone
Bessie, A.
Hard Travelling
NEW WORLD (US) 1986 dir. Dan
Bessie

Breakout
LeFlore, R. and Hawkins, J.
One in a Million: The Ron LeFlore Story
EMI (US) 1978 dir. William A. Graham

Breakthrough, The
Du Maurier, D.
Lifeforce Experiment, The
FILMLINE (UK/Can) 1994 dir. Piers
Haggard

Breath of Spring
Coke, P.
Make Mine Mink
RANK (GB) 1960 dir. Robert Asher

Brennendes Geheimnis
Zweig, S.
Burning Secret
VESTRON (GB/Ger) 1988 dir. Andrew
Birkin

Brewster's Millions
McCutcheon, G. B.
Three on a Spree
UA (GB) 1961 dir. Sidney J. Furie

Brick Foxhole, The
Brooks, R.
Crossfire
RKO (US) 1947 dir. Edward Dmytryk

Bride Comes to Yellow Sky, The
Crane, S.
Face to Face
RKO (US) 1952 dir. John Brahm,
Bretaigne Windust

Bride of Lammermoor, The
Scott, Sir W.
Lucia
LEX (GB) 1999 dir. Don Boyd

Bright Shining Lie, A: John Paul Vann and America in Vietnam
Sheehan, N.
Bright Shining Lie, A
HBO (US) 1998 dir. Terry George

Bringing up the Brass: My 55 Years at West Point
Maher, M. and Campion, N. R.
Long Gray Line, The
COL (US) 1955 dir. John Ford

Broken April
Kadare, I.
Behind the Sun
VIDEO (Bra/Fr) 2001 dir. Walter Salles

Broken Gun, The
L'Amour, L.
Cancel My Reservation
MGM-EMI (US) 1972 dir. Paul Bogart

Bronco Apache
Wellman, P. I.
Apache
UA (US) 1954 dir. Robert Aldrich

Brook Adams
Glaspell, S.
Right to Love, The
PAR (US) 1930 dir. Richard Wallace

Brook Wilson Ltd
Ryan, J. M.
Loving
COL (US) 1970 dir. Irvin Kershner

Brother Rat
Monks, J. and Finklehoffe, F. F.
About Face
WAR (US) 1952 dir. Roy del Ruth

Brothers Rico, The
Simenon, G.
Family Rico, The
CBS (US) 1972 dir. Paul Wendkos

Bruce Lee: The Man Only I Knew
Cadwell, L. L.
Dragon: The Bruce Lee Story
UN (US) 1993 dir. Rob Cohen

Brujo
Wolcott, J.A.
Seduced by Evil
WIL COURT (US) 1994 dir. Tony Wharmby

Brute, The
des Cars, G.
Green Scarf, The
BL (GB) 1954 dir. George More O'Ferrall

Buddhist Cross, The
Tanizaki, J.
Berlin Affair, The
CANNON (It/Ger) 1985 dir. Liliana Cavani

Buddwing
Hunter, E.
Mister Buddwing
MGM (US) 1966 dir. Delbert Mann
GB title: Woman Without a Face

Buffalo Grass
Gruber, F.
Big Land, The
WAR (US) 1957 dir. Gordon Douglas
GB title: Stampeded

Build My Gallows High
Homes, G.
Against all Odds
COL (US) 1984 dir. Taylor Hackford

Build My Gallows High
Homes, G.
Out of the Past
RKO (US) 1947 dir. Jacques Tourneur
GB title: Build My Gallows High

Build-up Boys, The
Kirk, J.
Madison Avenue
FOX (US) 1962 dir. Bruce Humberstone

Buio e il Miele, Il
Arpino, G.
Scent of a Woman
UN (US) 1992 dir. Martin Brest

Bull Boys, The
Delderfield, R. F.
Carry on Sergeant
AAM (GB) 1958 dir. Gerald Thomas

Bully: A True Story of High School Revenge
Schutze, J.
Bully
STUDIO CANAL+ (Fr/GB) 2000 dir. Larry Clark

Bundy: The Deliberate Stranger
Larsen, R. W.
Deliberate Stranger, The
LORIMAR (US) 1986
dir. Marvin Chomsky

Burden of Proof The
Barlow, J.
Villain
EMI (GB) 1971 dir. Michael Tuchner

Burglar, The
Goodis, D.
Burglars, The
COL (Fr/It) 1971 dir. Henri Verneuill

Buried Alive
Bennett, A.
His Double Life
PAR (US) 1933 dir. Arthur Hopkins

Buried Alive
Bennett, A.
Holy Matrimony
PAR (US) 1943 dir. John Stahl

Burlesque
Walters, G. M. and Hopkins, A.

Swing High, Swing Low
PAR (US) 1937 dir. Mitchell Leisen

Burlesque
Walters, G. M. and Hopkins, A.

When my Baby Smiles at Me
FOX (US) 1948 dir. Walter Lang

Burn, Witch, Burn
Merritt, A.

Devil Doll, The
MGM (US) 1936 dir. Tod Browning

Burning Patience
Skarmeta, A.

Postino, Il
CECCHI (It) 1994 dir. Michael Radford

Burton and Speke
Harrison, W.

Mountains of the Moon
TRISTAR (US) 1990 dir. Bob Rafaelson

But for These Men
Drummond, J. D.

Heroes of the Telemark
RANK (GB) 1965 dir. Anthony Mann

But Gentlemen Marry Brunettes
Loos, A.

Gentlemen Marry Brunettes
UA (US) 1955 dir. Richard Sale

But There are Always Miracles
Willis, M. P. and Willis, J.

Some Kind of Miracle
LORIMAR (US) 1979 dir. Jerrold Freedman

Butter and Egg Man, The
Kaufman, G. S.

Angel from Texas, An
WAR (US) 1940 dir. Ray Enright

Butter and Egg Man, The
Kaufman, G. S.

Three Sailors and a Girl
WAR (US) 1953 dir. Roy del Ruth

Butterfly Revolution, The
Butler, W.

Summer Camp Nightmare
CONCORDE (US) 1987 dir. Bert C. Dragin

By the Great Horn Spoon
Fleischman, S.

Adventures of Bullwhip Griffin, The
DISNEY (US) 1965 dir. James Neilson

Bylanta
Baiesu, O.

Oak, The
STUDIO CANAL+ (Fr) 1992 dir. Lucian Pintilie

Cabal
Barker, C.

Nightbreed
FOX (US) 1990 dir. Clive Barker

Caddie Woodlawn
Brink, C. R.

Caddie
HEMDALE (Aust) 1976 dir. Donald Crombie

Cage Aux Folles, The
Poiret, J.

Birdcage, The
MGM (US) 1996 dir. Mike Nichols

Californio, The
MaeLeod, R.

100 Rifles
FOX (US) 1969 dir. Tom Gries

Call for the Dead
Le Carré, J.

Deadly Affair, The
COL (GB) 1966 dir. Sidney Lumet

Call Girl, The
Greenwald, H.

Girl of the Night
WAR (US) 1960 dir. Joseph Cates

Call it Treason
Howe, G. L.

Decision Before Dawn
FOX (US) 1951 dir. Anatole Litvak

Call of the Wild
London, J.

Call of the Wild: Dog of the Yukon
KING GREENLIGHT (Can) 1996 dir. Peter Svatek

Calling Dr. Horowitz
Horowitz, S.

Bad Medicine
TCF (US) 1985 dir. Harvey Miller

Calm at Sunset, Calm at Dawn
Watkins, P.

Calm at Sunset
HALLMARK (US) 1996 dir. Daniel Petrie

Came the Dawn
Bax, R.

Never Let Me Go
MGM (GB) 1953 dir. Delmer Daves

Can You Forgive Her?; Phineas Finn The Irish Member; Eustace Diamonds, The; Phineas Redux; Prime Minister, The; Duke's Children, The
Trollope, A.

Pallisers, The
BBC (GB) 1974 dir. Hugh David, Ronald Wilson

Canadian Tragedy, A
Siggins, M.

Love and Hate: A Marriage Made in Hell
CBC/BBC (US/Can/GB) 1991 dir. Francis Mankiewicz

Candide
Voltaire

Cultivating Charlie
GMS (US) 1993 dir. Alex Georges

Candle for the Dead, A
Marlowe, H.

Violent Enemy, The
MONARCH (GB) 1969 dir. Don Sharp

Capricorn Man, The
Zacha, Sr., W. T.

Ultimate Imposter, The
UN TV (US) 1979 dir. Paul Stanley

Captain Bligh and Mr Christian
Hough, R.

Bounty, The
ORION (GB) 1984 dir. Roger Donaldson

Captain Blood Returns
Sabatini, R.

Captain Pirate
COL (US) 1952 dir. Ralph Murphy
GB title: Captain Blood, Fugitive

Captain Grant's Children
Verne, J.

In Search of the Castaways
DISNEY (GB) 1961 dir. Robert
Stevenson

Captain Hornblower, R. N.
Forester, C. S.

Captain Horatio Hornblower, R. N.
WAR (GB) 1951 dir. Raoul Walsh

Captain's Daughter, The
Pushkin, A.

Tempest
PAR (It/Fr) 1958 dir. Alberto Lattuada

Captain's Daughter, The; History of Pugachev, A
Pushkin, A.

Russkij Bunt
GLOBUS (Rus/Fr) 2000 dir. Aleksandr
Proshkin

Captive
Weitz, P.

Sex and the Other Man
RIVER ONE (US) 1995 dir. Karl Slovin

Careful Man, The
Deming, R.

Drop Dead Darling
SEVEN ARTS (GB) 1966 dir. Ken
Hughes
US title: Arrivederci Baby

Carl and Anna
Frank, L.

Desire Me
MGM (US) 1947 dir. George Cukor

Carlito's Way; After Hours
Torres, E.

Carlito's Way
UN (US) 1993 dir. Brian De Palma

Carmen
Merimée, P.

First Name: Carmen
IS (Fr) 1984 dir. Jean-Luc Godard

Carmen
Merimée, P.

Hip Hopera: Carmen
NEW LINE TV (US) 2001 dir. Robert
Townsend

Carmen
Merimée, P.

Loves of Carmen, The
COL (US) 1948 dir. Charles Vidor

Carnival
Mackenzie, Sir C.

Dance Pretty Lady
BI (GB) 1932 dir. Anthony Asquith

Carriage Entrance
Banks, P.

My Forbidden Past
RKO (US) 1951 dir. Robert Stevenson

Carry Cot, The
Thynne, A.

Blue Blood
MIQ (GB) 1973 dir. Andrew Sinclair

Casanovas Heimfahrt
Schnitzler, A.

Retour de Casanova, Le
STUDIO CANAL+ (Fr) 1992 dir.
Edouard Niermans

Case File F.B.I.
Gordon, M. and Gordon G.

Down 3 Dark Streets
UA (US) 1954 dir. Arnold Laven

Case History
Walker, G.

Damned Don't Cry, The
WAR (US) 1950 dir. Vincent Sherman

Case of Charles Dexter Ward, The
Lovecraft, H. P.

Resurrected, The
SCOTTI (US) 1992 dir. Dan O'Bannon

Case of Charles Dexter Ward, The
Lovecraft, H. P.

Haunted Palace, The
AIP (US) 1963 dir. Roger Corman

Case of Lady Camber, The
Vachell, H. A.

Lord Camber's Ladies
BI (GB) 1932 dir. Benn W. Levy

Case of Need, A
Hudson, J.

Carey Treatment, The
MGM (US) 1972 dir. Blake Edwards

Case of the Caretaker's Cat, The
Gardner, E. S.

Case of the Black Cat, The
WAR (US) 1936 dir. William McGann

Case of the Constant God, The
King, R.

Love Letters of a Star
UN (US) 1936 dir. Lewis R. Foster

Case of the Frightened Lady, The
Wallace, E.

Frightened Lady, The
BL (GB) 1932 dir. T. Hayes Hunter

Case of the Three Weird Sisters, The
Armstrong, C.

Three Weird Sisters, The
BN (GB) 1948 dir. Dan Birt

Casting the Runes
James, M. R.

Night of the Demon
COL (GB) 1957 dir. Jacques Tourneur

Castle Minerva
Canning, V.

Masquerade
UA (GB) 1965 dir. Basil Dearden

Castles Burning
Lyons, A.

Slow Burn
UN TV (US) 1986 dir. Matthew Chapman

Casual Sex
Goldman, W.

Casual Sex?
UN (US) 1988 dir. Genevieve Robert

Cat and the Canary, The
Willard, J.

Cat Creeps, The
UN (US) 1930 dir. Rupert Julian

Cat and the Mice, The
Mosley L.

Foxhole in Cairo
BL (GB) 1960 dir. John Moxey

Cat From Hell
King, S.

Tales from the Darkside: the Movie
PAR (US) 1990 dir. John Harrison

Cat of Many Tales
Queen, E.

Ellery Queen: Don't Look Behind You
UN TV (US) 1971 dir. Barry Shear

Catbird Seat, The
Thurber, J.

Battle of the Sexes, The
PROM (GB) 1960 dir. Charles Crichton

Celle qui n'etait pas
Boileau, P. and Narcejac, T.

Diabolique
WAR (US) 1996 dir. Jeremiah C.
Chechik

Celle qui n'etait pas
Boileau, P. and Narcejac, T.

Diaboliques, Les
FILMSONOR (Fr) 1954 dir. Henri-
Georges Clouzot

Celle qui n'etait Plus
Boileau, P. and Narcejac, T.

House of Secrets
MULTIMEDIA (US) 1993 dir. Mimi
Leder

Celle qui n'etait Plus
Boileau, P. and Narcejac, T.

Reflections of Murder
ABC (US) 1974 dir. John Badham

Cellist, The
Hart, M.

Connecting Rooms
TELSTAR (GB) 1969
dir. Franklin Gollings

Centurions, The
Larteguy, J.

Lost Command
COL (US) 1966 dir. Mark Robson

Certain Mr. Takahasi, A
Ireland, A.

Pianist, The
ASKA (Can) 1992 dir. Claude Gagnon

Chair for Martin Rome, The
Helseth, H. E.

Cry of the City
FOX (US) 1948 dir. Robert Siodmak

Chairman, The
Kennedy, J. R.

Most Dangerous Man in the World, The
RANK (GB) 1969 dir. J. Lee Thompson
US title: Chairman, The

Chalked Out
Lawes, L. and Finn, J.

You Can't Get Away with Murder
WAR (US) 1939 dir. Lewis Seiler

Champion's Story: A Great Human Triumph
Champion, B. and Powell, J.

Champions
EMBASSY (GB) 1983 dir. John Irvin

Change of Plan, A
Friedman, B. J.

Heartbreak Kid, The
FOX (US) 1972 dir. Elaine May

Changeling, The
Middleton, T. and Rowley, W.

Middleton's Changeling
HIGH TIMES (GB) 1998 dir. Marcus
Thompson

Charley's Aunt
Thomas, B.

Where's Charley?
WAR (US) 1952 dir. David Butler

Charlie and the Chocolate Factory
Dahl, R.

Willy Wonka and the Chocolate Factory
PAR (US) 1971 dir. Mel Stuart

Charlie, M
Freemantle, B.
Charlie Muffin
EUSTON (GB) 1979 dir. Jack Gold

Charmed to Death
Singular, S.
Legacy of Sin: The William Coit Story
CITADEL ENT (US) 1995 dir. Steven
Schachter

Chase, The
Unekis, R.
Dirty Mary, Crazy Larry
FOX (US) 1974 dir. John Hough

Château Bon Vivant
O'Rear, F. and O'Rear, J.
Snowball Express
DISNEY (US) 1972 dir. Norman Tokar

Château de ma Mère, Le
Pagnol, M.
My Mother's Castle
GAU (Fr) 1991 dir. Yves Robert

Chautauqua
Keene, D. and Babcock, D.
Trouble With Girls, The
MGM (US) 1969 dir. Peter Tewkesbury

Cheetahs, The
Caillou, A.
Cheetah
DISNEY (US) 1989 dir. Jeff Blyth

Chester, I Love You
Yorgason, B. and Yorgason, B.
Thanksgiving Promise, The
DISNEY (US) 1986 dir. Beau Bridges

Chicago
Watkins, M.
Roxie Hart
FOX (US) 1942 dir. William A. Wellman

Chico que imitaba a Roberto Carlos, El
Casariego, M.
Tu Que Harias Por Amor
FANDANGO (Sp/It) 2000 dir. Carlos
Saura Medrano

Chienne, La
de la Fouchardière, G.
Scarlet Street
UN (US) 1945 dir. Fritz Lang

Child of Vodyanoi
Wiltshire, D.
Nightmare Man, The
BBC (US) 1981 dir. Douglas Camfield

Child of War, Woman of Peace
Hayslip, J. and Hayslip, L.
Heaven and Earth
WAR (US) 1993 dir. Oliver Stone

Child Star
Temple Black, S.
Child Star: The Shirley Temple Story
DISNEY (US/Aust) 2001 dir. Nadia
Tass

Childhood's Thief
Evans, R. M.
Secret Path, The
GREENWALD (US) 1999 dir. Bruce
Pittman

Children, The
Wharton, E.
Marriage Playground, The
PAR (US) 1929 dir. Lothar Mendes

Children are Gone, The
Cavanaugh, A.
Deadly Trap, The
NG (Fr/It) 1971 dir. René Clément

Children of the Dark
Shulman, I.
Cry Tough
UA (US) 1959 dir. Paul Stanley

Children of the Light, The
Lawrence, H. L.

Damned, The
BL (GB) 1961 dir. Joseph Losey
US title: These Are The Damned

Children of the Night
Lortz, R.

Voices
HEMDALE (GB) 1973 dir. Kevin Billington

Children's Hour, The
Hellman, L. F.

These Three
UA (US) 1936 dir. William Wyler

Chisolm Trail, The
Chase, B.

Red River
UA (US) 1948 dir. Howard Hawks

Chocolate Cobweb, The
Armstrong, C.

Merci Pour le Chocolat
STUDIO CANAL+ (Fr) 2000 dir. Claude Chabrol

Choice Cuts
Boileau, P and Narcejac, T.

Body Parts
PAR (US) 1991 dir. Eric Red

Choir Practice
Morgan, C.

Valley of Song
ABPC (GB) 1953 dir. Gilbert Gunn

Choses de la Vie, Les
Guimard, P.

Intersection
PAR (US) 1994 dir. Mark Rydell

Christ has Returned to Earth and Preaches Here Nightly
Gardner, L.

Valentino Returns
VIDMARK/SKOURAS (US) 1989 dir. Paul Hoffman

Christ in Concrete
Di Donata, P.

Give Us This Day
GFD (GB) 1949 dir. Edward Dmytryk
US title: Salt to the Devil

Christmas at Candleshoe
Innes, M.

Candleshoe
DISNEY (GB) 1977 dir. Norman Tokar

Christmas Carol, A
Dickens, C.

American Christmas Carol, An
SM-HEM (US) 1979 dir. Eric Till

Christmas Carol, A
Dickens, C.

Christmas Carol: The Movie
CHANNEL 4 FILMS (GB/Ger) 2001 dir. Jimmy T. Murakami

Christmas Carol, A
Dickens, C.

Ebbie
CRESCENT (US) 1995 dir. George Kaczender

Christmas Carol, A
Dickens, C.

Scrooge
PAR (GB) 1935 dir. Henry Edwards
REN (GB) 1951
dir. Brian Desmond Hurst
FOX (GB) 1970 dir. Ronald Neame

Christmas Carol, A
Dickens, C.

Scrooged
PAR (US) 1988 dir. Richard Donner

Christmas in Calico
Curtis, J.
Secret of Giving
JAFFE/BRAUNSTEIN (US) 1999 dir.
Sam Pillsbury

Christmas Love, A
Creighton, K.
Holiday to Remember, A
JAFFE BRAUNSTEIN (US) 1995 dir. Jud
Taylor

Christopher Blake
Hart, M.
Decision of Christopher Blake, The
WAR (US) 1948 dir. Peter Godfrey

Christopher Syn
Thorndike, R.
Dr Syn
GAU (GB) 1937 dir. Roy. William Neill

Christopher Syn
Thorndike, R.
Dr. Syn, Alias the Scarecrow
DISNEY (US) 1962 dir. James Neilson

Christy
Marshall, C.
Christy: Choices of the Heart
CANAN (US) 2001 dir. George
Kaczender and Don McBrearty

Chronicles of Prydain, The
Alexander, L.
Black Cauldron, The
DISNEY (US) 1985 dir. Ted Berman,
Richard Rich

Chrysalis
Porter, R.
All of Me
PAR (US) 1934 dir. James Flood

Cipher, The
Votler, G.
Arabesque
UN (US) 1966 dir. Stanley Donen

Circles Round the Wagon
Gipson, F. B.
Hound-Dog Man
FOX (US) 1959 dir. Don Siegel

City of Bardish, A
Grossman, V.
Commissar
GORKY (USSR) 1988
dir. Alexander Askoldov

City of Shadows
Prokosch, F.
Conspirators, The
WAR (US) 1944 dir. Jean Negulesco

Claw, The
Bernstein, H.
Washington Masquerade
MGM (US) 1932 dir. Charles Brabin
GB title: Mad Masquerade

Clé de la Rue Saint Nicolas, La
Gegauff, P.
À Double Tour
PARIS/PANI (Fr/It) 1959
dir. Claude Chabrol

Clean Break
White, L.
Killing, The
UA (US) 1956 dir. Stanley Kubrick

**Close to the Knives; Memories
That Smell Like Gasoline**
Wojnarowicz, D.
Postcards from America
CHANNEL 4 FILMS (GB/US) 1994 dir.
Steve McLean

Club Dumas, The
Perez-Reverte, A.
Ninth Gate, The
STUDIO CANAL+ (Fr/Sp/US) 1999
dir. Roman Polanski

Clubfoot
Williams, V.

Crouching Beast, The
OLY (GB) 1935 dir. Victor Hanbury

Cobb: A Biography
Stump, A.

Cobb
WAR (US) 1994 dir. Ron Shelton

Cocaine Kids, The
Williams, T.

illtown
SHOOTING GALLERY (US) 1996 dir.
Nick Gomez

Cockpit
Boland, B.

Lost People, The
GFD (GB) 1949 dir. Bernard Knowles

Coins in the Fountain
Secondari, J. H.

Pleasure Seekers, The
FOX (US) 1964 dir. Jean Negulesco

Coins in the Fountain
Secondari, J.

Three Coins in the Fountain
FOX (US) 1954 dir. Jean Negulesco

Color of Green
Kaufman, L.

Love, Hate, Love
SPELLING (US) 1971 dir. George
McCowan

Color Out of Space, The
Lovecraft, H. P.

Die, Monster, Die!
AIP (US/GB) 1965 dir. Daniel Haller

Colossus
Jones, D. F.

Forbin Project, The
UN (US) 1970 dir. Joseph Sargent
GB title: Colossus, the Forbin Project

Colours of the Day, The
Gary, R.

Man Who Understood Women
FOX (US) 1959 dir. Nunnally Johnson

Columba
Merimée, P.

Vendetta
RKO (US) 1950 dir. Mel Ferrer

Comanche
Appel, D.

Tonka
DISNEY (US) 1958 dir. Lewis R. Foster

Combat
Praag, V.V.

Men in War
UA (US) 1957 dir. Anthony Mann

Combat de Fauves au Crepuscule
Blanc, H.-F.

Wild Games
INTEGRAL (Bel/Ger/Fr) 1997 dir.
Benoit Lamy

Come Be My Love
Carson, R.

Once More My Darling
UI (US) 1949 dir. Robert Montgomery

Come out of the Kitchen
Miller, A. D. and Thomas, A. E.

Honey
PAR (US) 1930 dir. Wesley Ruggles

Come Out of the Kitchen
Thomas, A. E. and Miller, A. D.

Spring in Park Lane
BL (GB) 1948 dir. Herbert Wilcox

Come Prima Meglio di Prima
Pirandello, L.

Never Say Goodbye
UN (US) 1955 dir. Jerry Hopper

Come Prima Meglio di Prima
Pirandello, L.

This Love of Ours
UI (US) 1945 dir. William Deiterle

Come to Mother
Sale, D.

Live Again, Die Again
UN TV (US) 1974 dir. Richard Colla

Comedie de Terracina, Le
Vitoux, F.

Dolce Farniente
EURIMAGES (Bel/Fr) 1999 dir. Nae
Caranfil

Comedy of Errors, The
Shakespeare, W.

Boys from Syracuse, The
UN (US) 1940 dir. E. A. Sutherland

Commander Crabb
Pugh, M.

Silent Enemy, The
ROMULUS (GB) 1958 dir. William
Fairchild

Commandos, The
Arnold, E.

First Comes Courage
COL (US) 1943 dir. Dorothy Arzner

Comment faire l'amour avec un nègre sans se fatiguer
Laferrière, D.

How to Make Love to a Negro Without Getting Tired
ANGELIKA (Fr) 1990 dir. Jacques
Benoit

Commissioner, The
Dougherty, R.

Madigan
UI (US) 1968 dir. Don Siegel

Companions of Jehu, The
Dumas, A.

Fighting Guardsman, The
COL (US) 1945 dir. Henry Levin

Company, The
Ehrlichman, J.

Washington: Behind Closed Doors
PAR (US) 1977 dir. Gary Nelson

Company of Cowards, The
Chamberlain, W.

Advance to the Rear
MGM (US) 1964 dir. George Marshall

Complete State of Death, A
Gardner, J.

Stone Killer, The
COL (US) 1973 dir. Michael Winner

Comrade Jacob
Caute, D.

Winstanley
OTHER (GB) 1977
dir. Kevin Brownlow, Andrew Mollo

Concealment
Ide, L.

Secret Bride, The
WAR (US) 1935 dir. William Dieterle
GB title: Concealment

Condemned, The
Pagano, J.

Try and Get Me
UA (US) 1951 dir. Cyril Endfield
GB title: Sound of Fury, The

Condemned to Devil's Island
Niles, B.

Condemned
UA (US) 1929 dir. Wesley Ruggles

Confession Anonyme, La
Lilar, S.

Benvenuta
NI (Bel/Fr) 1982 dir. André Delvaux

Confessions of a Crap Artist
Dick, P. K.

Barjo
CENTRE EURO (Fr) 1992 dir. Jerome
Boivin

Confessions of a Night Nurse
Dixon, R.

Rosie Dixon-Night Nurse
COL (GB) 1978 dir. Justin Cartwright

Conjure Wife
Leiber, F.

Night of the Eagle
IA (GB) 1961 dir. Sidney Hayers
US title: Burn, Witch, Burn

Connecticut Yankee in King Arthur's Court, A
Twain, M.

Connecticut Yankee, A
FOX (US) 1931 dir. David Butler

Connecticut Yankee in King Arthur's Court, A
Twain, M.

Knight in Camelot, A
ROSEMONT (US) 1998 dir. Roger
Young

Connecticut Yankee in the Court of King Arthur, A
Twain, M.

Spaceman and King Arthur, The
DISNEY (GB) 1979 dir. Russ Mayberry
US title: Unidentified Flying Oddball

Conquista del Aire, La
Gopegui, B.

Razones de Mis Amigos, Las
TORNASOL (Sp) 2000 dir. Gerardo
Herrero

Conscience of Zeno, The
Svevo, I.

Parole di Mio Padre, Le
RAI (Fr/It) 2001 dir. Francesca
Comencini

Containment
Brumpton, J.

Life
ROUGH TRADE (Aust) 1996 dir.
Lawrence Johnston

Context, The
Sciascia, L.

Illustrious Corpses
PEA/LAA (It) 1976 dir. Francesco Rosi

Conversation in Sicily
Vittorini, E.

Sicilia!
ALIA (It/Fr) 1999 dir. Daniele Huillet,
Jean-Marie Straub

Convict has Escaped, A
Budd, J.

They Made Me a Fugitive
WAR (GB) 1947 dir. Alberto Cavalcanti
US title: I Became a Criminal

Cook, The
Kressing, H.

Something for Everyone
NG (US) 1970 dir. Harold Prince
GB title: Black Flowers for the Bride

Coot Club; Big Six, The
Ransome, A.

Swallows and Amazons Forever!
BBC (GB) 1984 dir. Andrew Morgan

Cops are Robbers, The
Clemente, G. W and Stevens, K.

Good Cops, Bad Cops
KUSHNER-LOCKE (US) 1990 dir. Paul
Wendkos

Copulating Mermaid of Venice; Trouble with the Battery
Bukowski, C.

Cold Moon
GAU (Fr) 1991 dir. Luc Besson, Andrée
Martinez
French title: Lune Froide

Corazon
Mooney, W. H.
Donor Unknown
CITADEL ENT (US) dir. John Harrison

Corelli's Mandolin
de Bernieres, L.
Captain Corelli's Mandolin
WORKING TITLE (GB/Fr) 2001 dir.
John Madden

Counsel's Opinion
Wakefield, G.
Divorce of Lady X, The
LONDON (GB) 1938 dir. Tim Whelan

Count a Lonely Cadence
Weaver, G.
Cadence
NEW LINE (US) 1990 dir. Martin Sheen

Country of the Heart, The
Wersba, B.
Matters of the Heart
MCA TV (US) 1990 dir. Michael Rhodes

Coup de Grâce
Kessel, J.
Sirocco
COL (US) 1951 dir. Curtis Bernhardt

Court Circular
Stokes, S.
I Believe in You
EAL (GB) 1952 dir. Basil Dearden

Court of Honor
Wood, W. P.
Broken Trust
FONDA (US) 1995 dir. Geoffrey Sax

Court-Martial of Johnson Whittaker, The
Marszalek, J. F.
Assault at West Point
MOSAIC (US) 1994 dir. Harry Moses

Cradle Snatchers
Mitchell, N. and Medcraft, R.
Let's Face It
PAR (US) 1943 dir. Sidney Lanfield

Craig's Wife
Kelly, G.
Harriet Craig
COL (US) 1950 dir. Vincent Sherman

Cri, Un
Loriot, N.
No Time for Breakfast
BOURLA (Fr) 1980 dir. Jean-Louis
Bertucelli

Crime and Punishment
Dostoevsky, F.
Crime + Punishment in Suburbia
KILLER (US) 2000 dir. Rob Schmidt

Crime of Sylvester Bonnard, The
France, A.
Chasing Yesterday
RKO (US) 1935 dir. George Nicholls, Jr.

Crips
Bakeer, D.
South Central
MONUMENT (US) 1992 dir. Steven
Anderson

Criss Cross
Tracy, D.
Underneath
POPULIST (US) 1995 dir. Steven
Soderbergh

Cross Currents
Hopkins, R.
Lifeline
USA NETWORK (US) 1996 dir. Fred
Gerber

Crossfire: The Plot that Killed Kennedy
Marrs, J.
JFK
WAR (US) 1991 dir. Oliver Stone

Crowned Heads
Tryon, T.
Fedora
MAINLINE (Ger/Fr) 1978 dir. Billy
Wilder

Crows of Edwina Hill, The
Bosworth, A. R.
Nobody's Perfect
UN (US) 1978 dir. Alan Rafkin

Crowthers of Bankdam, The
Armstrong, T.
Master of Bankdam
ALL (GB) 1947 dir. Walter Forde

Crucible, The
Miller, A.
Witches of Salem, The
FDF (Fr/Ger) 1957 dir. Raymond
Rouleau

Crusaders
Sherwin, D. and Howlett, J.
If ...
PAR (GB) 1968 dir. Lindsay Anderson

Cry Tough
Shulman, I.
Ring, The
UA (US) 1952 dir. Kurt Neumann

Cuckoo in the Nest, A
Travers, B.
Fast and Loose
GFD (GB) 1954 dir. Gordon Parry

Cup and the Sword, The
Hobart, A. T.
This Earth is Mine
UI (US) 1959 dir. Henry King

Cupid and Diana
Bartolomeo, C.
Cupid & Cate
HALLMARK (US) 2000 dir. Brent
Shields

Cupid Rides Phillion
Cartland, B.
Lady and the Highwayman, The
GRADE (GB) 1989 dir. John Hough

Curse of Capistrano, The
McCulley, J.
Mark of the Renegade
UI (US) 1951 dir. Hugo Fregonese
FOX (US) 1974 dir. Don McDougall

Curse of Capistrano, The
McCulley, J.
Mark of Zorro, The
FOX (US) 1940 dir. Rouben Mamoulian

Curse of the Viking Grave
Mowat, F.
*Lost in the Barrens II: The Curse of the
Viking Grave*
ATLANTIS (Can) 1992 dir. Michael J. F.
Scott

Custard Boys, The
Rae, J.
Reach for Glory
GALA (GB) 1962 dir. Philip Leacock

Cyborg
Caidin, M.
Bionic Ever After?
GALLANT (US) 1994 dir. Steve Stafford

Cyborg
Caidin, M.
Six Million Dollar Man, The
UN TV (US) 1973 dir. Richard Irving

Cycle of the Werewolf
King, S.
Silver Bullet
PAR (US) 1985 dir. Daniel Attias

Cycle of Violence
Bateman, C.

Crossmaheart
LEX (GB) 1998 dir. Henry Herbert

Cyrano de Bergerac
Rostand, E.

Roxanne
COL (US) 1987 dir. Fred Schepisi

Czarina, The
Lengyel, M.

Catherine the Great
KORDA (GB) 1934 dir. Paul Czinner

D

D.A. Draws a Circle, The
Gardner, E. S.

They Call it Murder
FOX (US) 1971 dir. Walter Grauman

Daddy and I
Jordan, E. G.

Make Way for a Lady
RKO (US) 1936 dir. David Burton

Daffodil Mystery, The
Wallace, E.

Devil's Daffodil, The
BL (GB) 1962 dir. Akos Rathonyi

Dame aux Camélias, La
Dumas, A. fils

Camille
MGM (US) 1936 dir. George Cukor
ROSEMONT (US/GB) 1984
dir. Desmond Davis

Dance of Genghis Cohn, The
Gary, R.

Genghis Cohn
BBC/A&E (GB) 1994 dir. Elijah
Moshinsky

Dance Real Slow
Jaffe, M. G.

Cool, Dry Place, A
FOX (US) 1999 dir. John N. Smith

Dancing Aztec
Westlake, D. E.

Divine Poursuite, La
STUDIO CANAL+ (Fr) 1997 dir. Michel
Deville

Dancing Princess, The; Cobbler & the Elves, The; Singing Bone, The
Grimm, J. L. K. and Grimm, W. K.

Wonderful World of the Brothers Grimm, The
MGM (US) 1962 dir. Henry Levin,
George Pal

Dancing White Horses of Vienna, The
Podhajsky, A.

Miracle of the White Stallions, The
DISNEY (US) 1963 dir. Arthur Hiller
GB title: Flight of the White Stallions, The

Danger Adrift
Quilici, F.

Only One Survived
CBS ENT (US) 1990 dir. Folco Quilici

Dangerous Evidence
Cohen, E. A. and Shapiro, M. J.

Dangerous Evidence: The Lori Jackson Story
HEARST (US) 1999 dir. Sturla
Gunnarsson

Danton Affair, The
Przybyszewska, S.

Danton
GAU/TF1 (Fr/Pol) 1982 dir. Andrzej
Wajda

Dark Angel
Kaus, G.

Her Sister's Secret
PRC (US) 1946 dir. Edgar G. Ulmer

Dark Days and Light Nights
Ali, J.

Black Joy
WINCAST/WEST ONE (GB) 1977
dir. Anthony Simmons

Dark Fantastic
Echard, M.

Lightning Strikes Twice
WAR (US) 1951 dir. King Vidor

Dark of the Sun
Smith, W.

Mercenaries, The
MGM (GB) 1968 dir. Jack Cardiff
US title: Dark of the Sun

Dark Side of Love, The
Saul, O.

My Kidnapper, My Love
EMI (US) 1980 dir. Sam Wanamaker

Dark Star
Moon, L.

Min and Bill
MGM (US) 1930 dir. George Hill

Dark Tower, The
Kaufman, G. S. and Woollcott, A.

Man with Two Faces, The
WAR (US) 1934 dir. Archie Mayo

Darker Purpose, A
Riss, W.

Winner, The
VILLAGE ROADSHOW (US) 1997 dir.
Alex Cox

Darkest Hour
McGivern, W. P.

Hell on Frisco Bay
WAR (US) 1955 dir. Frank Tuttle

Darkness I Leave You
Hooke, N. W.

Gypsy and the Gentleman, The
RANK (GB) 1957 dir. Joseph Losey

Darling Buds of May, The
Bates, H. E.

Mating Game, The
MGM (US) 1959 dir. George Marshall

Das Feuerschiff
Lenz, S.

Lightship, The
WAR (US) 1985 dir. Jerzy Skolimowski

Daughter of Fu Manchu
Rohmer, S.

Daughter of the Dragon
PAR (US) 1931 dir. Lloyd Corrigan

Daughters of the New World
Shreve, S. R.

Will of Their Own, A
WAR (US) 1998 dir. Karen Arthur

David Golder
Nemirowsky, I.

My Daughter Joy
BL (GB) 1950 dir. Gregory Ratoff
US title: Operation X

Dawn
Berkeley, R.

Nurse Edith Cavell
RKO (US) 1939 dir. Herbert Wilcox

Dawn of Reckoning
Hilton, J.

Rage in Heaven
MGM (US) 1941 dir. W. S. Van Dyke

Day is Ours, This
Lewis, H.

Mandy
GFD (GB) 1952 dir. Alexander
Mackendrick
US title: Crash of Silence, The

Day of Atonement
Raphaelson, S.

Jazz Singer, The
WAR (US) 1953 dir. Michael Curtiz
EMI (US) 1980 dir. Richard Fleischer

Day of the Arrow
Loraine, P.

Eye of the Devil
MGM (GB) 1967 dir. J. Lee-Thompson

Day One: Before Hiroshima and After
Wyden, P.

Day One
SPELLING (US) 1989 dir. Joseph Sargent

Day the Century Ended, The
Gwaltney, F. I.

Between Heaven and Hell
FOX (US) 1956 dir. Richard Fleischer

Day the World Ended, The
Thomas, G. and Witts, M. M.

When Time Ran Out
WAR (US) 1980 dir. James Goldstone

Daybreak of Freedom
Burns, S.

Boycott
N. TWAIN (US) 2001 dir. Clark Johnson

Days of Dawn
Sender, R. J.

Valentina
OFELIA (Sp) 1983
dir. Antonio José Betancor

Dead Air
Lupica, M.

Money, Power, Murder
CBS ENT (US) 1989 dir. Lee Philips

Dead Don't Care, The
Latimer, J.

Last Warning, The
UN (US) 1938 dir. Albert S. Rogell

Dead Heart, The
Kennedy, D.

Welcome to Woop Woop
SCALA (Aust/GB) 1997 dir. Stephan Elliott

Dead Pigeon
Kantor, L.

Tight Spot
COL (US) 1955 dir. Phil Karlson

Deadfall
Laumer, K.

Peeper
FOX (US) 1975 dir. Peter Hyams

Deadlier than the Male
Gunn, J. E.

Born to Kill
RKO (US) 1947 dir. Robert Wise
GB title: Lady of Deceit

Deadlock
Sands, L.

Another Man's Poison
EROS (GB) 1951 dir. Irving Rapper

Deadly Angels, The
McCarry, C.

Wrong is Right
COL (US) 1982 dir. Richard Brooks
GB title: Man with the Deadly Lens, The

Deadly Blessing
Salerno, S.

Bed of Lies
WOLPER TV(US) 1992 dir. William A. Graham

Deadly Force: The Story of how a Badge can become a License to Kill
O'Donnell, Jr., L.

Case of Deadly Force, A
TELECOM (US) 1986 dir. Michael Miller

Deadly Pretender
Kingsbury, K.

Every Woman's Dream
KUSHNER-LOCKE (US) 1996 dir. Steven Schachter

Deadly Relations: A True Story of Murder in a Suburban Family
Donohue, C. and Hall, S.
Deadly Relations
WIL COURT (US) 1993 dir. Bill Condon

Deadwood
Dexter, P.
Wild Bill
UA (US) 1995 dir. Walter Hill

Dearly Departed
Bottrell, D. D. and Jones, J.
Kingdom Come
FOX (US) 2001 dir. Doug McHenry

Death and Deliverance
Lee, R. M.
Ordeal in the Arctic
ALLIANCE (US) 1993 dir. Mark Sobel

Death and the Sky Above
Garve, A.
Two-Letter Alibi
BL (GB) 1962 dir. Robert Lynn

Death Benefits
Toffler, L.
Settlement, The
CINETEL (US) 1999 dir. Mark Steilen

Death Bite
Maryk, M. and Monahan, B.
Spasms
PDC (Can) 1984 dir. William Fruet

Death has Deep Roots
Gilbert, M.
Guilty?
GN (GB) 1956 dir. Edmund Greville

Death in a Top Hat
Rawson, C.
Miracles for Sale
MGM (US) 1939 dir. Tod Browning

Death in Captivity
Gilbert, M.
Danger Within
BL (GB) 1958 dir. Don Chaffey
US title: Breakout

Death in Rome
Katz, R.
Massacre in Rome
GN (Fr/It) 1973 dir. George Pan Cosmatos

Death in the Deep South
Greene, W.
They Won't Forget
WAR (US) 1937 dir. Mervyn LeRoy

Death in the Family, A
Agee, J.
All the Way Home
PAR (US) 1963 dir. Alex Segal
PAR (US) 1971 dir. Fred Coe

Death of a Common Man
Holdridge, D.
End of the River, The
GFD (GB) 1947 dir. Derek Twist

Death of a Playmate
Carpenter, T.
Star 80
WAR (US) 1983 dir. Bob Fosse

Death of a Snout
Warner, D.
Informers, The
RANK (GB) 1963 dir. Ken Annakin
US title: Underworld Informers

Death of Grass
Christopher, J.
No Blade of Grass
MGM (GB) 1970 dir. Cornel Wilde

Death Takes a Holiday
Casella, A.
Meet Joe Black
UN (US) 1998 dir. Martin Brest

Death Watch

White, R.

Savages
SPEL-GOLD (US) 1974 dir. Lee Katzin

Decade of Destruction

Cowell, A.

Burning Season, The
HBO (US) 1994 dir. John Frankenheimer

Decameron, The

Boccaccio, G.

Decameron Nights
EROS (GB) 1952 dir. Hugo Fregonese

Decline and Fall

Waugh, E.

Decline and Fall ... of a Birdwatcher
FOX (GB) 1968 dir. John Karsh

Deep are the Roots

D'Usseau, A. and Gow, J.

Tomorrow the World
UA (US) 1944 dir. Leslie Fenton

Defence, The

Nabokov, V.

Luzhin Defence, The
FRANCE 2 (Fr/GB) 2000 dir. Marleen Gorris

Degree of Guilt

Patterson, R. N.

Degree of Guilt
JAFFE/BRAUNSTEIN (US) 1995 dir. Mike Robe

Del Palma

Kellino, P.

Lady Possessed
REP (US) 1952 dir. William Spier, Roy Kellino

Deliberate Intent: A Lawyer Tells the Story of Murder by the Book

Smolla, R. A.

Deliberate Intent
FOX TV (US) 2000 dir. Andy Wolk

Denmark Chronicle

Grammaticus, S.

Prince of Jutland
MIRAMAX (Neth/GB) 1994 dir. Gabriel Axel

Der Letste Sommer

Huch, R.

Guardian Angel, The
SANDREW (Swe) 1990 dir. Suzanne Osten

Desert Guns

Frazee, S.

Gold of the Seven Saints
WAR (US) 1961 dir. Gordon Douglas

Desert of the Heart

Rule, J.

Desert Hearts
MGM (US) 1986 dir. Donna Deitch

Desert Town

Stewart, R.

Desert Fury
PAR (US) 1947 dir. Lewis Allen

Desert Voices

Perkins, K.

Desert Pursuit
ABP (US) 1952 dir. George Blair

Desperados: Latin Drug Lords, US Lawmen and the War America Can't Win

Shannon, E.

Drug Wars: The Camarena Story
ZZY (US) 1990 dir. Brian Gibson

Desperados: Latin Drug Lords, US Lawmen and the War America Can't Win
Shannon, E.

Drug Wars: The Cocaine Cartel
ZZY (US) 1992 dir. Paul Krasny

Desperate Justice
Speight, R.

Mother's Revenge, A
MARTINES (US) 1993 dir. Armand Mastroianni

Destroyer, The
Murphy, W. and Sapir, R.

Remo Williams: The Adventure Begins
ORION (US) 1985 dir. Guy Hamilton

Destry Rides Again
Brand, M.

Destry
UI (US) 1954 dir. George Marshall

Deux Frères
Dumas, A.

Corsican Brothers, The
UA (US) 1942 dir. Gregory Ratoff
ROSEMONT (US) 1985 dir. Ian Sharp

Devil and Daniel Webster, The
Benet, S.V.

All that Money can Buy
RKO (US) 1941 dir. William Dieterle

Devil in Vienna, The
Orgel, D.

Friendship in Vienna, A
DISNEY CH (US) 1988
dir. Arthur Allan Seidelman

Devilday-Madhouse
Hall, A.

Madhouse
EMI (GB) 1974 dir. Jim Clark

Devil's Hornpipe, The
Mamoulian, R. and Anderson, M.

Never Steal Anything Small
UN (US) 1958 dir. Charles Lederer

Devils of Loudon, The
Huxley, A.

Devils, The
WAR (GB) 1971 dir. Ken Russell

Devil's Own, The
Curtis, P.

Witches, The
HAMMER (GB) 1966 dir. Cyril Frankel

Devil's Triangle
Soutar, A.

Almost Married
FOX (US) 1932
dir. W. Cameron Menzies

Dial M For Murder
Knott, F.

Perfect Murder, A
WAR (US) 1998 dir. Andrew Davis

Diamond Lil
West, M.

She Done Him Wrong
PAR (US) 1933 dir. Lowell Sherman

Diamonds are Danger
Walker, D. E.

Man Could Get Killed, A
UN (US) 1966 dir. Ronald Neame

Diana's Story; Lost for Words
Longden, D.

Wide-Eyed and Legless
BBC (GB) 1993 dir. Richard Loncraine

Diaries of Hannah Senesh, The
Senesh, H.

Hanna's War
CANNON (US) 1988 dir. Menahem Golan

Diary of a Good Neighbour, The
Lessing, D.

Rue du Retrait
JML (Fr) 2001 dir. Rene Feret

Dice of God, The
Birney, H.

Glory Guys
UA (US) 1965 dir. Arnold Laven

Die Bruder Grimm
Gerstner, H.

Wonderful World of the Brothers Grimm, The
MGM (US) 1962 dir. Henry Levin, George Pal

Dieu et Nous Seuls Pouvons
Folco, M.

Justinien Trouvé
SOLO (Fr) 1993 dir. Christian Fechner

Diggstown Ringers, The
Wise, L.

Diggstown
MGM (US) 1992 dir. Michael Ritchie

Dildo Cay
Hayes, N.

Bahama Passage
PAR (US) 1941 dir. Edward H. Griffith

Diner de Cons, Le
Veber, F.

Dinner Game, The
GAU (Fr) 1998 dir. Francis Veber

Disappearance of Rory Brophy, The
Lombard, C.

Disappearance of Finbar, The
VICTORIA (Ire/Swe/GB) 1996 dir. Sue Clayton

Discovery of Insulin, The; Banting: A Biography
Bliss, M.

Glory Enough for All
THAMES (GB) 1989 dir. Eric Till

Dishonoured
Albrand, M.

Captain Carey USA
PAR (US) 1950 dir. Mitchell Leisen
GB title: After Midnight

Disorientated Man, The
Saxon, P.

Scream and Scream Again
AIP (GB) 1969 dir. Gordon Hessler

Divina Commedia, La
Dante Alighieri

TV Dante, A: The Inferno Cantos
CHANNEL 4 (GB) 1990
dir. Tom Phillips, Peter Greenaway

Do Androids Dream of Electric Sheep?
Dick, P. K.

Blade Runner
WAR (US) 1982 dir. Ridley Scott

Doc—The Story of Dennis Littky and His Fight for a Better School
Kammeraad-Campbell, S.

Town Torn Apart, A
PARAGON (US) 1992 dir. Daniel Petrie

Doctor Liver
Sakaguchi, A.

Dr. Akagi
TOEI (Jap) 1998 dir. Shohei Imamura

Doctor Wears Three Faces, The
Bard, M.

Mother Didn't Tell Me
FOX (US) 1950 dir. Claude Binyon

Doctor's Son, The
O'Hara, J.

Turning Point of Jim Malloy, The
COL TV (US) 1975 dir. Frank D. Gilroy

Doctors Wear Scarlet
Raven, S.

Incense for the Damned
GN (GB) 1970 dir. Robert Hartford-Davis

Dog Hermit, The
Stout, D.

Child is Missing, A
MOORE-WEISS (US) 1995 dir. John Power

Dog Soldiers
Stone, R.

Who'll Stop the Rain?
UA (US) 1978 dir. Karel Reisz
GB title: Dog Soldiers

Doll's Eyes
Wood, B.

In Dreams
DREAMWORKS (US) 1999 dir. Neil Jordan

Doll's House, A
Ibsen, H.

Sara
FARABI CINEMA (Iran) 1994 dir. Dariush Mehrjui

Dombey and Son
Dickens, C.

Rich Man's Folly
PAR (US) 1931 dir. John Cromwell

Don Among the Dead Men
Vulliamy, C. E.

Jolly Bad Fellow, A
BL (GB) 1964 dir. Robert Hamer

Don Camillo and the Prodigal Son
Guareschi, G.

Return of Don Camillo, The
MIRACLE (Fr/It) 1953 dir. Julien Duvivier

Don Careless
Beach, R. E.

Avengers, The
REP (US) 1950 dir. John Auer

Don Desperado
Foreman, L. L.

Savage, The
PAR (US) 1952 dir. George Marshall

Don Quixote
Cervantes, M. de

Man of La Mancha
UA (US) 1972 dir. Arthur Hiller

Donna D'Onore
Modignani, S. C.

Vendetta: Secrets of a Mafia Bride
TRIBUNE (US) 1991
dir. Stuart Margolin

Donnie Brasco: My Undercover Life in the Mafia
Pistone, J.

Donnie Brasco
TRISTAR (US) 1997 dir. Mike Newell

Donovan's Brain
Siodmak, C.

Lady and the Monster, The
REP (US) 1944 dir. George Sherman
GB title: Lady and the Doctor, The

Donovan's Brain
Siodmak, C.

Vengeance
BL (GB/Ger) 1962 dir. Freddie Francis

Don't Ask Me If I Love
Kollek, A.

Worlds Apart
SCANLON (Israel) 1980
dir. Barbara Noble

Don't Die My Love
McDaniel, L.

Champion's Fight, A
NBC STUDIOS (US) 1998 dir. James A.
Contner

Don't Look and It Won't Hurt
Peck, R.

Gas, Food and Lodging
IRS (US) 1992 dir. Allison Anders

Doorbell Rang, The
Stout, R.

Nero Wolfe
PAR TV (US) 1979 dir. Frank D. Gilroy

Dork of Cork, The
Raymo, C.

Frankie Starlight
FINE LINE (Fr/Ire) 1995 dir. Michael
Lindsay-Hogg

Dorothy Dandridge
Mills, E.

Introducing Dorothy Dandridge
ESPARZA (US) 1999 dir. Martha
Coolidge

Double Error
Thompson, J. L.

Murder Without Crime
ABP (GB) 1950 dir. J. Lee-Thompson

Double Jeopardy
Stuart, M. A.

Voices From a Locked Room
SONY (US/GB) 1995 dir. Malcolm
Clarke

Double Take, The
Huggins, R.

I Love Trouble
COL (US) 1948 dir. S. Sylvan Simon

Dover Road, The
Milne, A. A.

Where Sinners Meet
RKO (US) 1934 dir. J. Walter Ruben

Down There
Goodis, D.

Shoot the Piano Player
PLEIADE (Fr) 1960 dir. François
Truffaut

Downhill Racers
Hall, O.

Downhill Racer
PAR (US) 1969 dir. Michael Ritchie

Dr. Jekyll and Mr. Hyde
Stevenson, R. L.

Jekyll & Hyde
KING PHOENIX (US/GB) 1990
dir. David Wickes

Dr. Jekyll and Mr. Hyde
Stevenson, R. L.

Two Faces of Dr. Jekyll, The
HAMMER (GB) 1960 dir. Terence Fisher
US title: House of Fright

Dr. Praetorius
Goetz, C.

People Will Talk
FOX (US) 1951 dir. Joseph L.
Mankiewicz

Dracula's Guest
Stoker, B.

Dracula's Daughter
UN (US) 1936 dir. Lambert Hillyer

Dreadful Summit
Ellin, S.

Big Night, The
UA (US) 1951 dir. Joseph Losey

Dream Like Mine, A
Kelly, M. T.

Clearcut
TELEFILM (Can) 1991 dir. Richard Bugajski

Dream Monger, The
Miller, G. H.

Starlight Hotel
REP (NZ) 1988 dir. Sam Pillsbury

Dream of the Mad Monkey, The
Frank, C.

Twisted Obsession
IVE (US) 1990 dir. Fernando Trueba

Dreamers
Hamsun, K.

Telegraphist, The
NORSK (Den/Nor) 1993 dir. Erik Gustavson

Dreamhouse
Grenville, K.

Traps
FILMOPOLIS (Aust) 1994 dir. Pauline Chan

Dreamland
Kelland, C. B.

Strike Me Pink
UA (US) 1936 dir. Norman Taurog

Du côté de chez Swann
Proust, M.

Swann in Love
GAU (Fr) 1984 dir. Volker Schlondorff

Dumbo, the Flying Elephant
Aberson, H. and Pearl, H.

Dumbo
DISNEY (US) 1941 dir. Ben Sharpsteen

Dunbar's Cove
Deal, B.

Wild River
FOX (US) 1960 dir. Elia Kazan

Durian Tree, The
Keon, M.

7th Dawn, The
UA (GB) 1964 dir. Lewis Gilbert

D—Demon Deathchase
Kikuchi, H.

Vampire Hunter D: Bloodlust
FILMLINK (Jap/US) 2000 dir. Yoshiaki Kawajiri

E

Eagle Shooting Heroes, The
Cha, L.

Ashes of Time
SCHOLAR (HK) 1994 dir. Kar-Wai
Wong

Earth Abideth, The
Dell. G.

Seasons of Love
SULLIVAN ENT (US) 1999 dir. Daniel
Petrie

East Lynne
Wood, Mrs H.

Ex-Flame
TIFFANY (US) 1930 dir. Victor Halperin

Easter Dinner, The
Downes, D.

Pigeon That Took Rome, The
PAR (US) 1962 dir. Melville Shavelson

Easy and Hard Ways Out
Grossbach, R.

Best Defense
PAR (US) 1984 dir. Willard Huyck

Eaters of the Dead
Crichton, M.

13th Warrior, The
TOUCHSTONE (US) 1999 dir. John
McTiernan

Eau des Collines, L'
Pagnol, M.

Manon of the Spring
ORION (Fr) 1987 dir. Claude Berri
French title: Manon des Sources

Ebano
Vasquez-Figueroa, A.

Ashanti
COL (Switz) 1979 dir. Richard Fleischer

Ebb Tide
Stevenson, R. L.

Adventure Island
PAR (US) 1947 dir. Peter Stewart

Ebb-Tide, The
Stevenson, R. L. and Osbourne, L.

Ebb Tide
PAR (US) 1937 dir. James Hogan

Echo in the Valley
Ke Lan

Yellow Earth
GUANGXI (China) 1985 dir. Chen
Kaige

Echos of Celandine
Marlowe, D.

Disappearance, The
CINEGATE (GB/Can) 1977
dir. Stuart Cooper

Écume des Jours, L'
Vian, B.

Chloe
DENTSU (Jap) 2001 dir. Go Riju

Eddie Chapman Story, The
Owen, F.

Triple Cross
AA (GB) 1967 dir. Terence Young

Edge of Running Water, The
Sloane, W.

Devil Commands, The
COL (US) 1941 dir. Edward Dmytryk

Education for Death
Ziemer, G.

Hitler's Children
RKO (US) 1943 dir. Edward Dmytryk

Edward VII and his Times
Maurois, A.

Entente Cordiale
FLORA (Fr) 1939 dir. Marcel l'Herbier

Edward VIII
Donaldson, F.

Edward & Mrs. Simpson
THAMES (GB) 1978 dir. Waris Hussein

Eff Off
Hutson, S.

Class of Miss MacMichael, The
GALA (GB) 1978 dir. Silvio Narizzano

Eh?
Livings, H.

Work is a Four Letter Word
UI (GB) 1968 dir. Peter Hall

Eichmann in My Hands
Malkin, P. Z. and Stein, H.

Man Who Captured Eichmann, The
MARGULIES (US) 1996 dir. William A.
Graham

Eight O'Clock in the Morning
Nelson, R.

They Live
UN (US) 1988 dir. John Carpenter

Eine Liebe in Deutschland
Hochhuth, R.

Love in Germany, A
TRIUMPH (Ger) 1984 dir. Andrzej
Wajda

Einsamkeit der Krokodile, Die
Kurbjuweit, D.

Loneliness of the Crocodile, The
OLGA (Ger) 2000 dir. Jobst Oetzmann

Eleanor and Franklin
Lash, J. P.

*Eleanor and Franklin: The White House
Years*
TALENT (US) 1977 dir. Daniel Petrie

Elemental, The; Gate Crasher, The; Act of Kindness, An; Door, The
Chetwynd-Hayes, R.

From Beyond the Grave
EMI (GB) 1973 dir. Kevin Connor

Elephant is White, The
Brahms, C. and Simon, S. J.

Give Us the Moon
GFD (GB) 1944 dir. Val Guest

Elephant Man and Other Reminiscences, The
Treves, Sir F.

Elephant Man, The
PAR (GB) 1980 dir. David Lynch

Eliminator, The
York, A.

Danger Route
UA (GB) 1967 dir. Seth Holt

Elizabeth the Queen
Anderson, M.

Private Lives of Elizabeth and Essex, The
WAR (US) 1939 dir. Michael Curtiz

Emerald Illusion, The
Bass, R.

Code Name: Emerald
MGM/UA (US) 1985 dir. Jonathan
Sanger

Emma and I
Hocken, S.

Second Sight: A Love Story
TTC (US) 1984 dir. John Korty

Emperor's Snuffbox, The
Carr, J. D.

That Woman Opposite
MON (GB) 1957 dir. Compton Bennett

Emporia
Sanford, H. and Lamb, M.

Waco
PAR (US) 1966 dir. R. G. Springsteen

Empty Copper Sea, The
MacDonald, J. D.

Travis McGee
HAJENO (US) 1983
dir. Andrew V. McLaglen

En Cas de Malheur
Simenon, G.

In All Innocence
STUDIO CANAL+ (Fr) 1998 dir. Pierre
Jolivet

Enchanted April, The
von Arnim, E.

Enchanted April
RKO (US) 1935 dir. Harry Beaumont
BBC (GB) 1992 dir. Mike Newell

Enchanted Isle, The
Cain, J. M.

Girl in the Cadillac
OVERSEAS (US) 1995 dir. Lucas Platt

Enchantment: A Little Girl's Friendship with Mark Twain
Quick, D.

Mark Twain & Me
CHILMARK (US/Can) dir. Daniel
Petrie

End as a Man
Willingham, C.

Strange One, The
COL (US) 1957 dir. Jack Garfein
GB title: End as a Man

End of Tragedy, The
Ingalls, R.

Dead on the Money
INDIEPROD (US) 1991
dir. Mark Cullingham

Enemy of the People, An
Ibsen, H.

Ganashatru
ELECTRIC (Ind) 1989 dir. Satyajit Ray

Ennemi Que Je Connais, L'
Pitre, M.

Full Blast
ASKA (Can) 1999 dir. Rodrique Jean

Ennemie, L'
Antoine, W. P.

Tendre Ennemie
WORLD (Fr) 1938 dir. Max Ophuls

Enter, Sir John
Dane, C. and Simpson, H.

Murder
BI (GB) 1930 dir. Alfred Hitchcock

Episode of Sparrows, An
Godden, R.

Innocent Sinners
RANK (US) 1957 dir. Philip Leacock

Epitaph for a Spy
Ambler, E.

Hotel Reserve
RKO (GB) 1944 dir. Victor Hanbury

Epitaph for an Enemy
Barr, G.

Up From the Beach
FOX (US) 1965 dir. Robert Parrish

Equippage, L'
Kessel, J.

Woman I Love, The
RKO (US) 1937 dir. Anatole Litvak
GB title: Woman Between, The

Erasmus with Freckles
Haase, J.

Dear Brigitte
FOX (US) 1965 dir. Henry Koster

Erections, Ejaculations, Exhibitions and Tales of Ordinary Madness
Bukowski, C.

Tales of Ordinary Madness
GINIS (It) 1981 dir. Marco Ferri

Ernest Hemingway: A Life Story
Baker, C.

Hemingway
WILSON (US) 1988 dir. Bernhard Sinkel

Error of Judgment: The Birmingham Bombings
Mullin, C.

Investigation, The: Inside a Terrorist Bombing
GRANADA (US/GB) 1990 dir. Mike Beckham

Escape
MacDonald, P.

Nightmare
UN (US) 1942 dir. Tim Whelan

Escape of My Dead Man
Postell, C.

Midnight Edition
SHAPIRO GLICKENHAUS (US) 1994 dir. Howard Libov

Escort
Rayner, D. A.

Enemy Below, The
FOX (US) 1957 dir. Dick Powell

Esther, Ruth and Jennifer
Davies, J.

North Sea Hijack
CIC (GB) 1980 dir. Andrew V. McLaglen
US title: Ffolkes

Eternal Husband, The
Dostoevsky, F.

Homme au Chapeau Rond, L'
ALCINA (Fr) 1946 dir. Pierre Billon

Etz Hadomim Tafus
Almagor, G.

Under the Domim Tree
HSA (Israel) 1995 dir. Eli Cohen

Eugene Onegin
Pushkin, A.

Onegin
CANWEST (GB) 1999 dir. Martha Fiennes

Eunuch of Stamboul, The
Wheatley, D.

Secret of Stamboul, The
GENERAL (GB) 1936 dir. Andrew Marton

Eva Peron
Fraser, N.

Evita Peron
ZEPHYR (US) 1981 dir. Marvin Chomsky

Event One Thousand
Lavallee, D.

Gray Lady Down
UN (US) 1978 dir. David Greene

Events Whilst Guarding the Bofors Gun
McGrath, J.

Bofors Gun, The
RANK (GB) 1968 dir. Jack Gold

Everlasting Secret Family and Other Secrets, The
Moorhouse, F.

Everlasting Secret Family, The
FGH (Aust) 1989 dir. Michael Thornhill

Every Knee Shall Bow
Walter, J.

Ruby Ridge: An American Tragedy
SCHERICK (US) 1996 dir. Roger Young

Every Secret Thing
Hearst, P.

Patty Hearst
ATLANTIC (US) 1988 dir. Paul
Schrader

Everybody Comes to Rick's
Burnett, M. and Alison, J.

Casablanca
WAR (US) 1943 dir. Michael Curtiz

Evidence of Love
Bloom, J. and Atkinson, J.

Killing in a Small Town
INDIEPROD (US) 1990
dir. Stephen Gyllenhaal

Evil Angels
Bryson, J.

Cry in the Dark, A
CANNON (US) 1988 dir. Fred Schepisi

Evil Come, Evil Go
Masterson, W.

Yellow Canary, The
FOX (US) 1963 dir. Buzz Kulik

Evil of the Day, The
Sterling, T.

Honey Pot, The
UA (US) 1966 dir. Joseph L.
Mankiewicz

Evita: First Lady
Barnes, J.

Evita Peron
ZEPHYR (US) 1981 dir. Marvin
Chomsky

Execution
McDougall, C.

Firing Squad, The
ATLANTIS (Can/Fr) 1991 dir. Michel
Andrieu

Execution of Charles Horman, The
Hauser, T.

Missing
UN (US) 1982 dir. Costa-Gavras

Executioners, The
MacDonald, J. D.

Cape Fear
UI (US) 1962 dir. J. Lee Thompson
UN (US) 1991 dir. Martin Scorsese

Exercise in Terror
Kaminsky, S.

Hidden Fears
KEY (US) 1993 dir. Jean Bodon

Exile, An
Jones, M.

I Walk the Line
COL (US) 1970 dir. John Frankenheimer

Expense of the Spirit
Pyszora, A.-F.

Winter Sleepers
PALLADIO (Ger) 1997 dir. Tom Tykwer

Exploits of Brigadier Gerard, The
Doyle, Sir A. C.

Adventures of Gerard, The
UA (GB) 1970 dir. Jerzy Skolimowski

Expressway
Trevor, E.

Smash-up on Interstate 5
FILMWAYS (US) 1976 dir. John
Llewellyn Moxey

Ex-Wife
Parrott, U.

Divorcee, The
MGM (US) 1930 dir. Robert Z. Leonard

Eye of the Beholder
Epstein, S.

Comeback, The
CBS ENT (US) 1989 dir. Jerrold
Freedman

Eyes of a Child
Patterson, R. N.

Degree of Guilt
JAFFE/BRAUNSTEIN (US) 1995 dir.
Mike Robe

Eye-witness
Hebden, M.

Eyewitness
MGM (GB) 1970 dir. John Hough
US title: Sudden Terror

F

F.O.B. Detroit
Smitter, W.

Reaching for the Sun
PAR (US) 1941 dir. William Wellman

Fabricator, The
Hodges, H.

Why Would I Lie?
UA (US) 1980 dir. Larry Peerce

Fabulous Ann Medlock
Shannon, R.

Adventures of Captain Fabian, The
REP (US) 1951 dir. William Marshall

Face on the Milk Carton, The
Cooney, C. B.

Face on the Milk Carton, The
FAMILY (US) 1995 dir. Waris Hussein

Facts of Life, The; Alien Corn, The; Kite, The; Colonel's Lady, The
Maugham, W. S.

Quartet
GFD (GB) 1948 dir. Ralph Smart,
Harold French, Arthur Crabtree, Ken
Annakin

Failure
Haviland-Taylor, K.

Man to Remember, A
RKO (US) 1938 dir. Garson Kanin

Fair Game
Gosling, P.

Cobra
WAR (US) 1986 dir. G. P Cosmatos

Faithful Travelers: A Father, A Daughter, A Fly-Fishing Journey of the Heart
Dodson, J.

Dodson's Journey
CBS TV (US) 2001 dir. Gregg Champion

Falcon's Malteser The
Horowitz, A.

Diamond's Edge
KINGS (US) 1990 dir. Stephen Bayly

Falcon's Malteser, The
Horowitz, A.

Just Ask for Diamond
FOX (GB) 1988 dir. Stephen Bayly

Fall of the House of Usher, The
Poe, E. A.

House of Usher, The
AIP (US) 1960 dir. Roger Corman
GB title: Fall of the House of Usher, The
21st CENTURY (US) 1988 dir. Alan
Birkinshaw

Falling Angel
Hjortsberg, W.

Angel Heart
TRISTAR (US) 1987 dir. Alan Parker

False Arrest: The Joyce Lukezic Story
Lukezic, J. and Schwarz, T.

False Arrest
GIL/HILL (US) 1991 dir. Bill L. Norton

False Note, The
Tolstoy, L.
Argent, L'
EOS (Switz/Fr) 1983 dir. Robert
Bresson

Family of Spies, A: Inside the John Walker Spy Ring
Early, P.
Family of Spies
KING PHOENIX (US) 1990 dir. Stephen
Gyllenhaal

Famous
Benet, S. V.
Just for You
PAR (US) 1952 dir. Elliot Nugent

Far Off Place, A; Story Like The Wind, A
Van Der Post, L.
Far Off Place, A
DISNEY (US) 1993 dir. Mikael Salomon

Faraday's Flowers
Kenrick, T.
Shanghai Surprise
MGM (US) 1986 dir. Jim Goddard

Farewell to Women
Collison, W.
Mogambo
MGM (US) 1953 dir. John Ford

Farewell to Women
Collison, W.
Red Dust
MGM (US) 1932 dir. Victor Fleming

Farewell, My Lovely
Chandler, R.
Murder, My Sweet
RKO (US) 1944 dir. Edward Dmytryk

Farmer
Harrison, J.
Carried Away
FINE LINE (US) 1996 dir. Bruno Barreto

Fatal Exposure
Tobias, M.
Sky's on Fire, The
ALL AM TV (US) 1998 dir. Dan Lerner

Fatal Woman
Quentin, P.
Black Widow
FOX (US) 1954 dir. Nunnally Johnson

Father Brown, Detective
Chesterton, G. K.
Sanctuary of Fear
M. ARCH (US) 1979 dir. John Llewellyn
Moxey

Father Knickerbocker's History of New York
Irving, W.
Knickerbocker Holiday
UN (US) 1944 dir. Harry Joe Brown

Father of Frankenstein
Bram, C.
Gods and Monsters
LIONS GATE (US/GB) 1998 dir. Bill
Condon

Father Sky
Freeman, D.
Taps
FOX (US) 1981 dir. Harold Becker

Father was a Handful
Williams, Mrs. R.
Vanishing Virginian, The
MGM (US) 1941 dir. Frank Borzage

Father's Arcane Daughter
Konigsburg, E. L.
Caroline?
B&E (US) 1990 dir. Joseph Sargent

Fathers and Sons
Babe, T.

Wild Bill
UA (US) 1995 dir. Walter Hill

FBI Killer, The
Jones, A.

Betrayed by Love
E. J. SCHERICK (US) 1994 dir. John Power

FDR's Last Year
Bishop, J.

FDR – The Last Year
TITUS (US) 1980 dir. Anthony Page

Fear in a Handful of Dust
Garfield, B.

Fleshburn
CROWN (US) 1984 dir. George Gage

Feathered Serpent
Wallace, E.

Menace, The
COL (US) 1932 dir. Roy William Neill

February Hill
Lincoln, V.

Primrose Path, The
RKO (US) 1940 dir. Gregory La Cava

Fellowship of the Frog, The
Wallace, E.

Frog, The
WILCOX (GB) 1937 dir. Jack Raymond

Fellowship of the Ring, The; Two Towers, The
Tolkien, J. R. R.

Lord of the Rings, The
UA (US) 1978 dir. Ralph Bakshi

Feuillets ou la Répétition d'un Drame Romantique, Les
Bouchard, M. M.

Lilies
ALLIANCE (Can) 1996 dir. John Greyson

Female Perversions: The Temptations of Emma Bovary
Kaplan, L. J.

Female Perversions
TRANSATLANTIC (US/Ger) 1996 dir. Susan Streitfeld

Femme de Chambre du Titanic, La
Decoin, D.

Chambermaid on the Titanic, The
FRANCE 2 (Fr) 1997 dir. J. J. Bigas Luna

Femme et le Pantin, La
Louys, P.

Devil is a Woman, The
PAR (US) 1935 dir. Josef von Sternberg

Femme et le Pantin, La
Louys, P.

That Obscure Object of Desire
GALAXIE (Fr/Sp) 1978 dir. Luis Bunuel

Fengriffen
Case, D.

And Now the Screaming Starts
AMICUS (GB) 1973 dir. Roy Ward Baker

Fer de Lance
Stout, R.

Meet Nero Wolfe
COL (US) 1936 dir. Herbert Biberman

Ferguson Affair, The
MacDonald, R.

Criminal Behavior
PRESTON FISCHER (US) 1992 dir. Michael Miller

Fertig
Yurick, S.

Confession, The
EL DORADO (US) 1999 dir. David
Hugh Jones

Fiancailles de M. Hire, Les
Simenon, G.

Monsieur Hire
ORION (Fr) 1989 dir. Patrice Leconte

Fiddler's Green
Gann, E. K.

Raging Tide, The
UI (US) 1951 dir. George Sherman

Field of Blood
Seymour, G.

Informant, The
SHOWTIME (US) 1998 dir. Jim McBride

Fifty Minute Hour, The
Lindner, R.

Pressure Point
UA (US) 1962 dir. Hubert Cornfield

52 Pick-Up
Leonard, E.

Ambassador, The
CANNON (US) 1984 dir. J. Lee
Thompson

58 Minutes
Wager, W.

Die Hard 2
FOX (US) 1990 dir. Renny Harlin

59 Degrees and Raining: The Story of Perdita Durango
Gifford, B.

Perdita Durange
LOLAFILMS (Mex/US/Sp) 1997 dir.
Alex de la Iglesia

Film of Memory, The
Druon, M.

Matter of Time, A
AIP (US/It) 1976 dir. Vincente Minnelli

Final Diagnosis, The
Hailey, A.

Young Doctors, The
UA (US) 1961 dir. Phil Karlson

Final Night
Gaines, R.

Front Page Story
BL (GB) 1953 dir. Gordon Parry

Final Verdict
St. John, A. R.

Final Verdict, The
TURNER (US) 1991 dir. Jack Fisk

Final Warning: The Legacy of Chernobyl
Gale, R. P. and Hauser, T.

Chernobyl: The Final Warning
CAROLCO (US/USSR) 1991 dir.
Anthony Page

Finding Maubee
Carr, A. H. Z.

Mighty Quinn, The
MGM (US) 1989 dir. Carl Schenkel

Finding Signs
Baker, S.

Love Always
CINEWEST (US) 1997 dir. Jude Pauline
Eberhard

Finger Man, The
Shaffer, R. K.

Lady Killer
WAR (US) 1933 dir. Roy del Ruth

Fire in the Valley
Freiberger, P. and Swaine, M.

Pirates of Silicon Valley
TNT (US) 1999 dir. Martyn Burke

Firebrand
Mayer, E. J.

Affairs of Cellini, The
FOX (US) 1934 dir. Gregory La Cava

Fires of Youth
Collier, J. L.

Danny Jones
CINERAMA (GB) 1972 dir. Jules Bricken

First and the Last, The
Galsworthy, J.

Twenty-One Days
LF (GB) 1937 dir. Basil Dean

First Lady of the Seeing Eye
Frank, M. and Clark, B.

Love Leads the Way
DISNEY CH (US) 1984 dir. Delbert Mann

First Love
Taylor, S.

Promise at Dawn
AVCO (US/Fr) 1970 dir. Jules Dassin

First Love
Turgenev, I.

Lover's Prayer
OVERSEAS (US/GB) 2001 dir. Reverge Anselmo

First Love
Turgenev, I.

Summer Lightning
CHANNEL 4 (GB) 1984 dir. Paul Joyce

First Rebel, The
Swanson, N. H.

Allegheny Uprising
RKO (US) 1939 dir. William A. Seiter
GB title: First Rebel, The

First Train to Babylon
Ehrlich, M.

Naked Edge, The
UA (GB) 1961 dir. Michael Anderson

First Wife, The
Allen, J. P.

Wives and Lovers
PAR (US) 1963 dir. John Rich

Fitzgeralds and the Kennedys, The
Goodwin, D. K.

Kennedys of Massachusetts, The
ORION TV (US) 1990 dir. Lamont Johnson

Five-Star Final
Weitzenkorn, L.

Two Against the World
WAR (US) 1936 dir. William McGann
GB title: Case of Mrs. Pembroke, The

Flaming Lance
Huffaker, C.

Flaming Star
FOX (US) 1960 dir. Don Siegel

Flaxborough Chronicles, The
Watson, C.

Murder Most Easy
BBC (GB) 1977 dir. Ronald Wilson

Flight From Dhahran
McDonald, J. and Burleson, C.

Escape: Human Cargo
SHOWTIME (US) 1998 dir. Simon Wincer

Flight of the Reindeer
Sullivan, R., Wolfe, G. and Porter, J.

Christmas Secret, The
CBS TV (US) 2000 dir. Ian Barry

Flotsam
Remarque, E. M.

So Ends Our Night
UA (US) 1941 dir. John Cromwell

Flowers for Algernon
Keyes, D.

Charly
CINERAMA (US) 1968 dir. Ralph Nelson

Fly Away Home
Bennett D. and White, I.

Always in My Heart
WAR (US) 1942 dir. Joe Graham

Fly Away Home
Bennett, D.

Daughters Courageous
WAR (US) 1939 dir. Michael Curtiz

Flying Ebony
Vinton, I.

Mooncussers, The
DISNEY (US) 1971 dir. James Neilson

Flying Saucers from Outer Space
Keyhoe, D. E.

Earth v. The Flying Saucers
COL (US) 1956 dir. Fred F. Sears

Foghorn, The
Bradbury, R.

Beast From 20,000 Fathoms, The
WAR (US) 1953 dir. Eugene Lourie

Follow the Widower
Harris, A.

Heads or Tails
CASTLE HILL (Fr) 1983
dir. Robert Enrico

Fool's Gold
Hitchens, D. and Hitchens, B.

Bande à Part
ANOUCHKA/ORSAY (Fr) 1964
dir. Jean-Luc Godard

Fools Paradise
Grubb, D.

Fools Parade
COL (US) 1971 dir. Andrew V.
McLaglen
GB title: Dynamite Man from Glory Jail

Footlights
Kelland, C. B.

Speak Easily
MGM (US) 1932 dir. Edward Sedgwick

For a Night of Love
Zola, E.

Manifesto
CANNON (Yugo) 1988 dir. Dusan
Makajevev

For Her to See
Shearing, J.

So Evil My Love
PAR (GB) 1948 dir. Lewis Allen

For Love or Money
Herbert, F. H.

This Happy Feeling
UN (US) 1958 dir. Blake Edwards

For Our Vines Have Tender Grapes
Martin, G. V.

Our Vines Have Tender Grapes
MGM (US) 1945 dir. Roy Rowland

For the Roses
Garwood, J.

Rose Hill
HALLMARK (US) 1997 dir. Christopher
Cain

For Us The Living
Evers, M. and Peters, B.

Ghosts of Mississippi
COL (US) 1996 dir. Rob Reiner

Forbidden Garden, The
Curtiss, U.

Whatever Happened to Aunt Alice?
PALOMAR (US) 1969 dir. Lee H. Katzin

Forbidden Love, A
Zeldis, C.

Torn Apart
CASTLE HILL (US) 1990 dir. Jack Fisher

Fortress in the Rice
Appel, B.
Cry of Battle
WAR (US) 1964 dir. Irving Lerner

Fortunes and Misfortunes of the Famous Moll Flanders, The
Defoe, D.
Amorous Adventures of Moll Flanders, The
PAR (GB) 1965 dir. Terence Young

Fortunes and Misfortunes of the Famous Moll Flanders, The
Defoe, D.
Fortunes and Misfortunes of Moll Flanders, The
GRANADA (GB) 1996 dir. David Attwood

Fortunes and Misfortunes of the Famous Moll Flanders, The
Defoe, D.
Moll Flanders
MGM (US) 1996 dir. Pen Densham
BBC (GB) 1975 dir. Donald McWhinnie

Forty Whacks
Homes, G.
Crime by Night
WAR (US) 1944 dir. William Clemens

Four Feathers, The
Mason, A. E. W.
Storm over the Nile
GFD (GB) 1955 dir. Terence Young

4.50 from Paddington
Christie, A.
Murder She Said
MGM (GB) 1961 dir. George Pollock

Four Horse Players are Missing
Rose, A.
Who's Got the Action?
PAR (US) 1963 dir. Daniel Mann

Four Marys, The
Lea, F. H.
Manproof
MGM (US) 1937 dir. Richard Thorpe

Fourth Brother, The
Forbes, R.
China
PAR (US) 1943 dir. John Farrow

Fourth Side of the Triangle, The
Queen, E.
Ellery Queen: Too Many Suspects
UN TV (US) 1975 dir. David Greene

Fragile Fox
Brooks, N.
Attack
UA (US) 1956 dir. Robert Aldrich

Frankenstein
Shelley, M. W.
Curse of Frankenstein, The
WAR (GB) 1957 dir. Terence Fisher

Frankenstein
Shelley, M. W.
Frankenstein: The True Story
UN TV (US) 1973 dir. Jack Smight

Frankie and Johnny in the Clair de Lune
McNally, T.
Frankie and Johnny
PAR (US) 1991 dir. Garry Marshall

Freak the Mighty
Philbrick, R.
Mighty, The
MIRAMAX (US) 1998 dir. Peter Chelsom

Freckles
Porter, G. S.
City Boy
ACCENT ENT (Can) 1994 dir. John Kent Harrison

Free Fall
Reed, J. D.
Pursuit of D. B. Cooper, The
UN (US) 1981 dir. Roger Spottiswoode

Freedom Trap, The
Bagley, D.
Mackintosh Man, The
COL-WAR (GB) 1973 dir. John Huston

Freefall
Hoffer, W. and Hoffer, M.
Falling From the Sky! Flight 174
HILL-FIELDS (US/Can) 1995 dir. Jorge
Montesi

Friday the Rabbi Slept Late
Kemelman, H.
Lanigan's Rabbi
UN TV (US) 1976 dir. Lou Antonio

Fried Green Tomatoes at the Whistle Stop Cafe
Flagg, F.
Fried Green Tomatoes
UN (US) 1991 dir. Jon Avnet

Friend
Henstell, D.
Deadly Friend
WAR (US) 1986 dir. Wes Craven

Friend in Need, The
Coxhead, E.
Cry from the Streets, A
EROS (GB) 1958 dir. Lewis Gilbert

Friese-Greene
Allister, R.
Magic Box, The
BL (GB) 1951 dir. John Boulting

Froknarna von Pahlen
von Krusenstjerna, A.
Loving Couples
SANDREW (Swe) 1964 dir. Mai
Zetterling

From Amalgamated Morons to American Icons: The Three Stooges
Fleming, M.
Three Stooges, The
ICON (US) 2000 dir. James Frawley

From the Inside
Read, M. B.
Chopper
AFFC (Aust) 2000 dir. Andrew
Dominik

From the Mixed-up Files of Mrs Basil E. Frankwester
Konigsburg, E. L.
Hideaways, The
UA (US) 1973 dir. Fielder Cook

From this Dark Stairway
Eberhart, M. G.
Murder of Dr. Harrigan
WAR (US) 1936 dir. Frank McDonald

Front Page, The
Hecht, B. and MacArthur, C.
His Girl Friday
COL (US) 1940 dir. Howard Hawks

Front Page, The
Hecht, B. and MacArthur, C.
Switching Channels
TRISTAR (US) 1988 dir. Ted Kotcheff
Frost in May; Lost Traveller, The; Sugar
House, The; Beyond the Glass
White, A.
Frost in May
BBC (GB) 1982 dir. Ronald Wilson

Fugue in Time, A
Godden, R.
Enchantment
RKO (US) 1948 dir. Irving Reis

Fulfillment, The
Spencer, L.

Fulfillment of Mary Gray, The
INDIAN NECK (US) 1989
dir. Piers Haggard

Furnished Room, The
Del Rivo, L.

West Eleven
WAR (GB) 1963 dir. Michael Winner

G-String Murders, The
Lee, G. R.

Lady of Burlesque
STROMBERG (US) 1943
dir. William Wellman
GB title: Striptease Lady

Gabriel Horn, The
Holt, F.

Kentuckian, The
UA (US) 1955 dir. Burt Lancaster

Gabriela, Clove and Cinnamon
Amado, J.

Gabriela
MGM/UA (Port) 1984
dir. Bruno Barreto

Gallows Hill
Duncan, L.

I've Been Waiting For You
NBC (US) 1998 dir. Christopher Leitch

Game of X, The
Sheckley, R.

Condorman
DISNEY (US) 1981 dir. Charles Jarrot

Gamesmanship, Oneupmanship, Lifemanship
Potter, S.

School for Scoundrels
WAR (GB) 1960 dir. Robert Namer

Garden of Cucumbers, A
Tyler, P.

Fitzwilly
UA (US) 1967 dir. Delbert Mann
GB title: Fitzwilly Strikes Back

Garden of God, The
Stacpoole, H. D.

Return to the Blue Lagoon
COL (US) 1991 dir. William A. Graham

Gather Rosebuds
Nolan, J.

Isn't it Romantic?
PAR (US) 1948 dir. Norman Z. McLeod

Gaucho
Childs, H.

Way of a Gaucho
FOX (US) 1952 dir. Jacques Tourneur

Gaunt Women, The
Blackburn, W. J.

Destiny of a Spy
UN TV (US) 1969 dir. Boris Sagal

Gay Banditti, The
Wylie, I. A. R.

Young in Heart, The
SELZNICK (US) 1938 dir. Richard Wallace

Geisha
Dalby, L.

American Geisha
INTERSCOPE (US) 1986 dir. Lee Philips

Gemini
Innaurato, A.

Happy Birthday, Gemini
UA (US) 1980 dir. Richard Benner

General, The
Sillitoe, A.

Counterpoint
UI (US) 1968 dir. Ralph Nelson

General Goes Too Far, The
Strueby, K.

High Command, The
ABFD (GB) 1936 dir. Thorold Dickinson

General, The: Godfather of Crime
Williams, P.

General, The
J&M (Ire/GB) 1998 dir. John Boorman

Genius in the Family, A
DuPre, H. and DuPre, P.

Hilary and Jackie
BRIT SCREEN (GB) 1998 dir. Anand Tucker

Genius in the Family, A
Maxim, H. P.

So Goes My Love
UN (US) 1946 dir. Frank Ryan
GB title: Genius in the Family, A

Gentle Ben
Morley, W.

Gentle Giant, The
PAR (US) 1967 dir. James Neilson

Gentle People, The
Shaw, I.

Out of the Fog
WAR (US) 1941 dir. Anatole Litvak

Gentleman From Montana, The
Foster, L. R.

Mr. Smith Goes To Washington
COL (US) 1939 dir. Frank Capra

Gentlemen of the Jungle
Gill, T.

Tropic Zone
PAR (US) 1952 dir. Lewis R. Foster

Geraldine, For the Love of a Transvestite
Monica, J.

Just Like a Woman
BRIT SCREEN (GB) 1992 dir. Christopher Monger

Gesundheit, Good Health is a Laughing Matter
Adams, H. D. and Mylander, M.

Patch Adams
BLUE WOLF (US) 1998 dir. Tom Shadyac

Get to the Heart: My Story
Mandrell, B.

Get to the Heart: The Barbara Mandrell Story
MANDALAY (US) 1997 dir. Jerry London

Ghost in the Machine
Gilman, D.

Bad Manners
DAVIS (US) 1997 dir. Jonathan Kaufer

Ghost of John Holling, The
Wallace, E.

Mystery Liner
MON (US) 1934 dir. William Nigh

Ghosts, The
Barber, A.

Amazing Mr Blunden, The
HEMDALE (GB) 1972 dir. Lionel Jeffries

Gidget Goes to New York
Kohner, F.

Gidget Grows Up
COL TV (US) 1969 dir. James Sheldon

Gift From the Boys, A
Buchwald, A.
Surprise Package
COL (GB) 1960 dir. Stanley Donen

Gilbert and Sullivan and Their World
Baily, L.
Story of Gilbert and Sullivan, The
BL (GB) 1953 dir. Sidney Gilliatt

Gilded Rooster, The
Emery, R.
Savage Wilderness
COL. (US) 1956 dir. Anthony Mann
GB title: The Last Frontier

Gilligan's Last Elephant
Hanley, G.
Last Safari, The
PAR (GB) 1967 dir. Henry Hathaway

Gingerbread Lady, The
Simon, N.
Only When I Laugh
COL (US) 1981 dir. Glenn Jordan
GB title: It Only Hurts When I Laugh

Gioconda Smile, The
Huxley, A. L.
Woman's Vengeance, A
UN (US) 1947 dir. Zoltan Korder

Girl Called Fathom, A
Forrester, L.
Fathom
FOX (GB) 1967 dir. Leslie Martinson

Girl Crazy
Bolton, G. and McGowan, J.
When the Boys Meet the Girls
MGM (US) 1965 dir. Alvin Ganzer

Girl from Trieste, The
Molnar, F.
Bride Wore Red, The
MGM (US) 1937 dir. Dorothy Arzner

Girl in the Turquoise Bikini, The
Resnik, M.
How Sweet It Is
WAR (US) 1968 dir. Jerry Paris

Girl on a Wing
Glemser, B.
Come Fly with Me
MGM (US) 1963 dir. Henry Levin

Girl on the Via Flaminia, The
Hayes, A.
Act of Love
UA (US) 1954 dir. Anatole Litvak

Girlfriend
Percival, D.
Girl/Boy
HEMDALE (GB) 1971 dir. Bob Kellett

Give Sorrow Words
Holder, M.
Winter Tan, A
TELEFILM (Can) 1987 dir. Louise Clark

Glass Cockpit, The
Davis, R. P.
Final Descent
COL TRISTAR (US) 1997 dir. Mike Robe

Glass Inferno, The
Scortia, T. N. and Robinson, F. M.
Towering Inferno, The
COL-WAR (US) 1975 dir. John Gullermin, Irwin Allen

Glendower Legacy, The
Gifford, T.
Dirty Tricks
FILMPLAN (Can) 1980 dir. Alvin Rakoff

Glimpse of Hell, A: Explosion on the USS Iowa and Its Cover-Up
Thompson, C.

Glimpse of Hell, A
FOX TV (US/Can) 2001 dir. Mikael Salomon

Gloire de Mon Père, La
Pagnol, M.

My Father's Glory
GAU (Fr) 1991 dir. Yves Robert

Glorious Days, The
Purcell, H.

Lilacs in The Spring
REP (GB) 1954 dir. Herbert Wilcox
US title: Let's Make Up

Glory for Me
Kantor, M.

Best Years of Our Lives, The
GOLDWYN (US) 1946 dir. William Wyler

Go to thy Deathbed
Forbes, S.

Reflection of Fear
COL (US) 1973 dir. William A. Fraker

God and My Country
Kantor, M.

Follow Me Boys!
DISNEY (US) 1966 dir. Norman Tokar

Godfather, The
Puzo, M.

Godfather Part II, The
PAR (US) 1974 dir. Francis Ford Coppola

Gogo no Eiko
Mishima, Y.

Sailor Who Fell From Grace With the Sea, The
FOX RANK (GB) 1976 dir. Lewis John Carlino

Gold Crew, The
Scortia, T. N. and Robinson, R. M.

Fifth Missile, The
MGM/UA TV (US) 1986 dir. Larry Peerce

Gold Diggers, The
Hopwood, A.

Gold Diggers of Broadway
WAR (US) 1939 dir. Roy del Ruth

Gold Mine
Smith, W.

Gold
HEMDALE (GB) 1974 dir. Peter Hunt

Golden Doors, The
Fenton, E.

Escapade in Florence
DISNEY (US) 1962 dir. Steve Previn

Golden Egg, The
Krabbe, T.

Vanishing, The
INGRID (Swe) 1990 dir. George Sluizer
FOX (US) 1993 dir. George Sluizer

Golden Evenings of Summer, The
Stanton, W.

Charley and the Angel
DISNEY (US) 1974 dir. Vincent McEveety

Golden Fleecing, The
Semple, L.

Honeymoon Machine, The
MGM (US) 1961 dir. Richard Thorpe

Golden Herd
Carroll, C.

San Antone
REP (US) 1952 dir. Joe Kane

Golden Horse
Chang Rehyer, E.

Red Rose, White Rose
GOLDEN FLARE (HK) 1994 dir.
Stanley Kwan

Golden Tide, The
Roe, V.

Perilous Journey, A
REP (US) 1953 dir. R. G. Springsteen

Goldfish Bowl, The
McCall, M.

It's Tough to be Famous
IN (US) 1932 dir. Alfred E. Green

Gone to Texas
Carter, F.

Outlaw Josey Wales, The
WAR (US) 1976 dir. Clint Eastwood

Good Gracious Annabelle
Kummer, C.

Annabelle's Affairs
FOX (US) 1931 dir. Alfred Werker

Good Night and Good Bye
Harris, T.

Street of Dreams
PHOENIX (US) 1988 dir. William A.
Graham

Good Old Boy: A Delta Summer
Morris, W.

Good Old Boy
DISNEY CH (US) 1988 dir. Tom G.
Robertson

Good Vibes
Cronley, J.

Let It Ride
PAR (US) 1989 dir. Joe Pytka

Goodbye Again
Scott, A. and Haight, G.

Honeymoon for Three
WAR (US) 1941 dir. Lloyd Bacon

Goodbye Piccadilly, Farewell Leicester Square
La Bern, A. J.

Frenzy
RANK (GB) 1971 dir. Alfred Hitchcock

Goodbye to the Hill
Dunne, L.

Paddy
FOX (Ireland) 1969 dir. Daniel Haller

Goosefoot
McGinley, P.

Fantasist, The
BLUE DOLPHIN (Ire) 1987 dir. Robin
Hardy

Gor Saga, The
Duffy, M.

First Born
BBC (GB) 1988 dir. Philip Saville

Gotti: Rise and Fall
Capeci, J. and Mustain, G.

Gotti
LUCCHESI (US) 1996 dir. Robert
Harmon

Gowns by Roberta
Miller, A. D.

Lovely to Look At
MGM (US) 1952 dir. Mervyn LeRoy

Gowns by Roberta
Miller, A. D.

Roberta
RKO (US) 1935 dir. William A. Seiter

Graced Land
Kalpakian, L.

Woman Who Loved Elvis, The
GROSS/BAR (US) 1993 dir. Bill Bixby

Graf Spee
Powell, M.

Battle of the River Plate, The
RANK (GB) 1956 dir. Michael Powell,
Emeric Pressburger
US title: Pursuit of the Graf Spee

Grand Duke and Mr. Pimm, The
Hardy, L.

Love is a Ball
UA (US) 1963 dir. David Swift
GB title: All This and Money Too

Grand Hotel
Baum, V.

Weekend at the Waldorf
MGM (US) 1945 dir. Robert Z. Leonard

Grand Vacance
Bonnell, R.

Return to Algiers
STUDIO CANAL+ (Fr) 2000 dir.
Alexandre Arcady

Grande Ceinture, La
Fallet, R.

Porte des Lilas
FILMSONOR (Fr/It) 1957
dir. René Clair

Grandmother Plays, The
Graff, T.

Used People
LARGO (US) 1992 dir. Beeban Kidron

Grandpa and Frank
Majerus, J.

Home to Stay
TIME-LIFE (US) 1978 dir. Delbert Mann

Great Companions, The
Markey, G.

Meet Me at the Fair
UN (US) 1952 dir. Douglas Sirk

Great Diamond Robbery, The
Minahan, J.

Diamond Trap, The
COL TV (US) 1988 dir. Don Taylor

Great Dinosaur Robbery, The
Forrest, D.

One of our Dinosaurs is Missing
DISNEY (US) 1975 dir. Robert
Stevenson

Great Gambler
Dostoevsky, F.

Great Sinner, The
MGM (US) 1949 dir. Robert Siodmak

Great Love
Molnar, F.

Double Wedding
MGM (US) 1937 dir. Richard Thorpe

Great Train Robbery, The
Crichton, M.

First Great Train Robbery, The
UA (GB) 1978 dir. Michael Crichton

Great Wind Cometh, A
Palgi, Y.

Hanna's War
CANNON (US) 1988 dir. Menahem
Golan

Greatest Gift, The
Stern, P. V. D.

It Happened One Christmas
UN TV (US) 1977 dir. Donald Wrye

Greek Passion, The
Kazantzakis, N.

He Who Must Die
KASSLER (Fr/It) 1957 dir. Jules Dassin

Green Goddess, The
Archer, W.

Adventure in Iraq
WAR (US) 1943 dir. D. Ross-Lederman

Green Grow the Lilacs
Riggs, L.
Oklahoma!
MAGNA (US) 1955 dir. Fred
Zinnemann

Green Hat, The
Arlen, M.
Outcast Lady
MGM (US) 1934 dir. Robert Z. Leonard
GB title: Woman of the World, A

Green Heart, The
Ritchie, J.
New Leaf, A
PAR (US) 1970 dir. Elaine May

Green Journey
Hassler, J.
Love She Sought, The
ORION TV (US) 1990 dir. Joseph
Sargent

Green Rushes
Walsh, M.
Quiet Man, The
REP (US) 1952 dir. John Ford

Greyfriar's Bobby
Atkinson, E.
Challenge to Lassie
MGM (US) 1949 dir. Richard Thorpe

Gringo Viejo
Fuentes, C.
Old Gringo
COL (US) 1989 dir. Luis Puenzo

Grizzly King, The
Curwood, J. O.
Bear, The
TRISTAR (Fr) 1989
dir. Jean-Jacques Annaud

Growing Up Brady ... I Was a Teenage Greg
Williams, B. and Kreski, C.
Growing Up Brady
PAR TV (US) 2000 dir. Richard Colla

Guardsman, The
Molnar, F.
Chocolate Soldier, The
MGM (US) 1941 dir. Roy del Ruth

Guerre Dans le Haut-Pays, La
Ramuz, C.-F.
War in the Highlands
ARENA (Fr/Swe) 1998 dir. Francis
Reusser

Guerre des Boutons, La
Pergaud, L.
War of the Buttons, The
ENIGMA (Jap/GB/Fr) 1994 dir. John
Roberts

Guests of the Emperor
Brooks, J. Y.
Silent Cries
YTV/TRISTAR TV (GB) 1993 dir.
Anthony Page

Gulliver's Travels
Swift, J.
Three Worlds of Gulliver, The
COL (US/Sp) 1959 dir. Jack Sher

Gun Crazy
Kantor, M.
Deadly is the Female
UA (US) 1949 dir. Joseph Lewis

Gun Down
Garfield, B.
Last Hard Man, The
FOX (US) 1976
dir. Andrew V. McLaglen

Gun For Sale, A
Greene, G.

Short Cut to Hell
PAR (US) 1957 dir. James Cagney

Gun for Sale, A
Greene, G.

This Gun for Hire
PAR (US) 1942 dir. Frank Tuttle
BBK (US) 1991 dir. Lou Antonio

Gun Shy
Young, C.U.

Showdown at Abilene
UN (US) 1956 dir. Charles Haas

Gun, The
Forester, C. S.

Pride and the Passion, The
UA (US) 1957 dir. Stanley Kramer

Gunman's Choice
Short, L.

Blood on the Moon
RKO (US) 1948 dir. Robert Wise

Guns of Rio Conchos
Huffaker, C.

Rio Conchos
FOX (US) 1964 dir. Gordon Douglas

Guts and Glory: The Rise and Fall of Oliver North
Bradlee, Jr., B.

Guts and Glory: The Oliver North Story
PAPAZIAN-HIRSCH (US) 1989
dir. Mike Robe

Guy Renton, A London Story
Waugh, A.

Circle of Deception
FOX (GB) 1960 dir. Jack Lee

Guyana Massacre: The Eyewitness Account
Krause, C. A.

Guyana Tragedy: The Story of Jim Jones
KONIGSBERG (US) 1980
dir. William A. Graham

Gypsy in Amber
Smith, M.

Art of Crime, The
UN TV (US) 1975 dir. Richard Irving

Halfway to Heaven
Segall, H.

Heaven Can Wait
PAR (US) 1978 dir. Warren Beatty, Buck Henry

Halfway to Heaven
Segall, H.

Here Comes Mr. Jordan
COL (US) 1941 dir. Alexander Hall

Hall of Mirrors
Stone, R.

WUSA
PAR (US) 1970 dir. Stuart Rosenberg

Hameçon, The
Katcham, V.

Hook, The
MGM (US) 1962 dir. George Seaton

Hamlet, The
Faulkner, W.

Long, Hot Summer, The
FOX (US) 1958 dir. Martin Ritt
L. HILL (US) 1985 dir. Stuart Cooper

Hamp
Wilson, J.

King and Country
WAR (GB) 1964 dir. Joseph Losey

Hand and the Flower, The
Tickell, J.

Day to Remember, A
GFD (GB) 1953 dir. Ralph Thomas

Hand in the Glove
Stout, R.

Lady Against the Odds
MGM/UA (US) 1992 dir. Bradford May

Hand of Mary Constable, The
Gallico, P.

Daughter of the Mind
FOX (US) 1969 dir. Walter Grauman

Handful of Tansy, A.
Brooke, H. and Bannerman, K.

No, My Darling Daughter
RANK (GB) 1961 dir. Ralph Thomas

Hands of Orlac, The
Renard, M.

Mad Love
MGM (US) 1935 dir. Karl Freund
GB title: Hands of Orlac, The

Hangover Murders, The
Hobhouse, A.

Remember Last Night?
UN (US) 1936 dir. James Whale

Hanta Yo
Hill, R.B.

Mystic Warrior, The
WAR (US) 1984 dir. Richard T. Heffron

Happy Now I Go
Charles, T.

Woman With No Name, The
ABP (GB) 1950 dir. Ladislas Vajda

Happy Time, The (*both book and play*)

Fontaine, R. L.; Taylor, S. A.

Happy Time, The
COL (US) 1952 dir. Richard Fleischer

Harbor, The

Reeves, J.

Society Doctor
MGM (US) 1935 dir. George B. Seitz
GB title: After Eight Hours

Hardball: A Season in the Projects

Coyle, D.

Hardball
PAR (US) 2001 dir. Brian Robbins

Harm's Way

Bassett, J.

In Harm's Way
PAR (US) 1965 dir. Otto Preminger

Harness Bull

White, L. T.

Vice Squad
UA (US) 1953 dir. Arnold Laven
GB title: Girl in Room 17, The

Harp That Once, The

Hall, P.

Reckoning, The
COL (GB) 1969 dir. Jack Gold

Harrison High

Farris, J.

Because They're Young
COL (US) 1960 dir. Paul Wendkos

Harvest Home

Tryon, T.

Dark Secret of Harvest Home, The
UN TV (US) 1978 dir. Leo Penn

Harvey Potter's Balloon Farm

Nolen, J.

Balloon Farm
DISNEY (US) 1999 dir. William Dear

Hatchet

Paulsen, G.

Cry in the Wild, A
CONCORDE (US) 1990 dir. Mark Griffiths

Hatter Fox

Harris, M.

Girl Called Hatter Fox, The
EMI (US) 1977 dir. George Schaefer

Haunted and the Haunters, The

Lytton, B.

Night Comes too Soon
BUTCHER (GB) 1948 dir. Denis Kavanagh

Haunted Monastery, The

Van Gulik, R.

Judge Dee and the Monastery Murders
ABC (US) 1974 dir. Jeremy Paul Kagan

Haunting of Hill House, The

Jackson, S.

Haunting, The
MGM (GB) 1963 dir. Robert Wise
DREAMWORKS (US) 1999 dir. Jan de Bont

Haven: The Dramatic Story of 1,000 World War II Refugees and How They Came to America

Gruber, R.

Haven
ALLIANCE (US/Can) 2001 dir. John Gray

Having Our Say
Delany, S. L., Delany, A. E. and Hearth, A. H.
Having Our Say: The Delany Sisters' First 100 Years
COL TRISTAR (US) 1999 dir. Lynne Littman

He was Found in the Road
Armstrong, A.
Man in the Road, The
GN (GB) 1956 dir. Lance Comfort

Headlong
Williams, E.
King Ralph
UN (US) 1991 dir. David S. Ward

Heart & Hand
Edens, O.
House Divided, A
UN (US) 1932 dir. William Wyler

Heartbreak Hotel
Siddons, A. R.
Heart of Dixie
ORION (US) 1989 dir. Martin Davidson

Heat of Ramadan, The
Hartov, S.
Point Man, The
CAROUSEL (GB/Fr) 2001 dir. John Glen

Heat Wave
Pertwee, R.
Road to Singapore
WAR (US) 1931 dir. Alfred E. Green

Heat's On, The
Himes, C.
Come Back Charleston Blue
WAR (US) 1972 dir. Mark Warren

Heaven and Hell
Jakes, J.
Heaven and Hell: North and South, Part III
ABC PRODS. (US) 1994 dir. Larry Peerce

Heaven has no Favourites
Remarque, E. M.
Bobby Deerfield
WAR (US) 1977 dir. Sydney Pollack

Hedda and Louella
Eells, G.
Malice in Wonderland
ITC (US) 1985 dir. Gus Trikonis

Hedda Gabler
Ibsen, H.
Hedda
SCOTIA-BARBER (GB) 1977 dir. Trevor Nunn

Heidi
Spyri, J.
Heidi's Song
HANNA-BARBERA (US) 1982 dir. Robert Taylor

Heir
Simon, R. L.
Jennifer on my Mind
UA (US) 1971 dir. Noel Black

Heist, The: How a Gang Stole $8,000,000 at Kennedy Airport and Lived to Regret It
Volkman, E. and Cummings, J.
Big Heist, The
ALLIANCE/A&E (US/Can) 2001 dir. Robert Markowitz

Helen and Teacher
Lash, J. P.
Helen Keller—The Miracle Continues
FOX TV (US) 1984 dir. Alan Gibson

Hell Hath no Fury
Williams, C.

Hot Spot, The
ORION (US) 1990 dir. Dennis Hopper

Hell House
Matheson, R.

Legend of Hell House, The
FOX (GB) 1973 dir. John Hough

Hellbound Heart, The
Barker, C.

Hellraiser
CINEMARQUE (GB) 1987
dir. Clive Barker

Hellcab
Kern, W.

Chicago Cab
CASTLE HILL (US) dir. Mary Cybulski,
John Tintori

Hellcats of the Sea
Lockwood, C. A. and Adamson, H. C.

Hellcats of the Navy
COL (US) 1957 dir. Nathan Juran

Heller With A Gun
L'Amour, L.

Heller in Pink Tights
PAR (US) 1960 dir. George Cukor

Hemingway in Love and War
Villard, H. S. and Nagel, J.

In Love and War
NEW LINE (US) 1996 dir. Richard
Attenborough

Hephaestus Plague, The
Page, T.

Bug
PAR (US) 1975 dir. Jeannot Szwarc

Her Heart in Her Throat
White, E. L.

Unseen, The
PAR (US) 1945 dir. Lewis Allen

Herbert West—The Re-Animator
Lovecraft, H. P.

Bride of Re-Animator
WILDSTREET (US) 1991
dir. Brian Yuzna

Herbert West—The Re-Animator
Lovecraft, H. P.

Re-Animator
EMPIRE (US) 1985 dir. Stuart Gordon

Here to get my Baby out of Jail
Shivers, L.

Summer Heat
ATLANTIC (US) 1987
dir. Michie Gleason

Heritage of Michael Flaherty, The
Leinster, C.

Outsider, The
PAR (US) 1980 dir. Tony Luraschi

Hero, The
Lampell, M.

Saturday's Hero
COL (US) 1950 dir. David Miller
GB title: Idols in the Dust

Heroes and Villains: The True Story of the Beach Boys
Gaines, S.

Story of the Beach Boys, The: Summer Dreams
L. HILL (USTV) 1990
dir. Michael Switzer

Heroes of Yucca, The
Barrett, M.

Invincible Six, The
MOULIN ROUGE (US/Iran) 1970
dir. Jean Negulesco

Hero's Walk
Crane, R.

Voices, The
BBC (GB) 1965 dir. Dennis Vance

Hey Hey We're the Monkees
Bronson, H.

Daydream Believers: The Monkees Story
PEBBLEHUT (US) 2000 dir. Neil
Fearnley

Hey, Malarek
Malarek, V.

Malarek
SVS/TELESCENE (Can) 1989
dir. Roger Cardinal

Hiding Place, The
Shaw, R.

Situation Hopeless But Not Serious
PAR (US) 1965 dir. Gottfried Reinhardt

High Commissioner, The
Cleary, J.

Nobody Runs Forever
RANK (GB) 1968 dir. Ralph Thomas
US title: High Commissioner, The

High Pavement
Bonett, E.

My Sister and I
GFD (GB) 1948 dir. Harold Huth

High Road, The
Lonsdale, F.

Lady of Scandal
MGM (US) 1930 dir. Sidney Franklin

High Sierra
Burnett, W. R.

I Died a Thousand Times
WAR (US) 1955 dir. Stuart Heisler

High Stakes
Chase, J. H.

I'll Get You For This
BL (GB) 1950 dir. Joseph M. Newman
US title: Lucky Nick Cain

High Window, The
Chandler, R.

Brasher Doubloon, The
FOX (US) 1946 dir. John Brahm
GB title: High Window, The

Higher Laws
Marcus, R. T.

Stranger in Town, A
AVE PICT (US) 1995 dir. Peter Levin

Hijacked
Harper, D.

Skyjacked
MGM (US) 1972 dir. John Guillermin

Hildegarde Withers Makes the Scene
Palmer, S. and Flora, F.

Very Missing Person, A
UN TV (US) 1972 dir. Russ Mayberry

His Last Bow
Doyle, Sir A. C.

Sherlock Holmes and the Voice of Terror
UN (US) 1942 dir. John Rawlins

His Majesty the King
Hamilton, C.

Exile, The
UN (US) 1948 dir. Max Ophuls

His Name Was Death
Brown, F.

Veille Canaille
FRANCE 3 (Fr) 1992 dir. Gerard
Jourd'hui

History of Luminous Motion, The
Bradfield, S.

Luminous Motion
GOOD MACHINE (US) 1998 dir. Bette
Gordon

History of Tom Jones, A Foundling, The
Fielding, H.

Tom Jones
UA (GB) 1963 dir. Tony Richardson
BBC/A&E (GB) 1997 dir. Metin Huseyin

History of Tom Jones, A Foundling, The
Fielding, H.

Bawdy Adventures of Tom Jones, The
UN (GB) 1976 dir. Cliff Owen

Hit, and Run, Run, Run
Bodelsen, A.

One of Those Things
RANK (Den) 1971 dir. Erik Balling

Hitching Post, The
Ketron, L.

Only Thrill, The
MOONSTONE (US) 1997 dir. Peter Masterson

Hobbs' Vacation
Streeter, E.

Mr. Hobbs takes a Vacation
FOX (US) 1962 dir. Henry Koster

Hold Autumn in your Hands
Perry, G. S.

Southerner, The
UA (US) 1945 dir. Jean Renoir

Homage That Follows, The
Medoff

Homage
SKYLINE (US) 1995 dir. Ross Kagan Marks

Home and Beauty
Maugham, W. S.

Three for the Show
COL (US) 1955 dir. H. C. Potter

Home and Beauty
Maugham, W. S.

Too Many Husbands
COL (US) 1940 dir. Wesley Ruggles
GB title: My Two Husbands

Home Fires Burning
Ceraso, C.

Turning, The
PHAEDRA (US) 1992 dir. L. A. Puopolo

Home Invaders, The
Hohimer F.

Thief
UA (US) 1981 dir. Michael Mann
GB title: Violent Street

Homecoming Game, The
Nemerov, H.

Tall Story
WAR (US) 1960 dir. Joshua Logan

Homefront
Duff, J.

War at Home, The
TOUCHSTONE (US) 1996 dir. Emilio Estevez

Homely Girl
Miller, A.

Eden
CINEVIA (Fr/Israel) 2001 dir. Amos Gitai

Homme que J'ai tué, L'
Rostand, M.

Broken Lullaby
PAR (US) 1931 dir. Ernst Lubitsch

Homo Falsus
Kjaerstad, J.

Perfect Murder, The
NORSK (Nor) 1993 dir. Eva Isaksen

Honest Courtesan, The
Rosenthall, M.

Dangerous Beauty
NEW REGENCY (US) 1998 dir.
Marshall Herskovitz

Honest Finder, The
Aladar, L.

Trouble in Paradise
PAR (US) 1932 dir. Ernst Lubitsch

Hoods, The
Aaronson, D.

Once Upon a Time in America
WAR (US) 1984 dir. Sergio Leone

Hop Dog, The
Lavin, N. and Thorp, M.

Adventure in the Hopfields
ABP (GB) 1954 dir. John Guillermin

Horseman, Pass By
McMurtry, L.

Hud
PAR (US) 1963 dir. Martin Ritt

Hospitality Suite
Rueff, R.

Big Kahuna, The
FRANCHISE (US) 1999 dir. John
Swanbeck

Host
James. P.

Virtual Obsession
VZ/SERTNER (US) 1998 dir. Mick
Garris

Hot Money
Kandel, A.

High Pressure
WAR (US) 1932 dir. Mervyn LeRoy

Hot Nocturne
Gilbert, E.

Blues in the Night
WAR (US) 1941 dir. Anatole Litvak

Hot Summer Night
Willis, T.

Flame in the Streets
RANK (GB) 1961 dir. Roy Baker

Hot Toddy
Edmonds, A.

*White Hot: The Mysterious Murder of
Thelma Todd*
NEWFELD-KEATING (US) 1991
dir. Paul Wendkos

Hound of Florence, The
Salten, F.

Shaggy Dog, The
DISNEY (US) 1959 dir. Charles Barton

Hound of Hell, The
Christie, A.

Last Seance, The
GRANADA (GB) 1987 dir. June
Wyndham-Davies

House in the Timberwoods, The
Dingwall, J.

Winds of Jarrah, The
FILMCORP (Aust) 1983
dir. Mark Egerton

House of Connelly, The
Green, P.

Carolina
FOX (US) 1934 dir. Henry King
GB title: House of Connelly

House of Dr. Edwards, The
Beeding, F.

Spellbound
UA (US) 1945 dir. Alfred Hitchcock

House of the Gentle Folk
Turgenev, I.

Nest of Gentry
CORINTH (USSR) 1970
dir. Andrei Konchalovski

House of the Seven Flies, The
Canning, V.

House of the Seven Hawks, The
MGM (GB) 1959 dir. Richard Thorpe

House with the Heavy Doors, The
Lippold, E.

Fiancée, The
DEFA (Ger) 1984 dir. Gunter Reisch, Gunther Rucker

House with the Red Light, The
Hunyady, S.

Very Moral Night, A
HUNG (Hun) 1977 dir. Karoly Makk

Household Ghosts
Kennaway, J.

Country Dance
MGM (GB) 1969 dir. J. Lee Thompson

How I Created My Perfect Prom Date
Strasser, T.

Drive Me Crazy
FOX (US) 1999 dir. John Schultz

How Say You?
Brooke, H. and Bannerman, K.

Pair of Briefs
RANK (GB) 1961 dir. Ralph Thomas

How to Shoot a Feature Under $10,000 and Not Go to Jail
Stern, B.

R2PC: Road to Park City
PHAEDRA (US) 1999 dir. Bret Stern

Howard: The Amazing Mr. Hughes
Dietrich, W. and Thomas, B.

Amazing Howard Hughes, The
EMI TV (US) 1977
dir. William A. Graham

Human Kind, The
Baron, A.

Victors, The
BL (GB) 1963 dir. Carl Foreman

Hunchback of Notre Dame, The
Hugo, V.

Hunchback, The
ALLIANCE (US) 1997 dir. Peter Medak

Hundred and One Dalmations, The
Smith, D.

One Hundred and One Dalmatians
DISNEY (US) 1961
dir. Wolfgang Reitherman, Clyde Geronimi, Hamilton Luske

Hundred and One Dalmations, The
Smith, D.

101 Dalmations
DISNEY (US) 1996 dir. Stephen Herek

Hundred and One Dalmations, The
Smith, D.

102 Dalmations
DISNEY (US) 2000 dir. Kevin Lima

Hundred Million Frames, A
Berna, P.

Horse Without a Head, The
DISNEY (GB) 1963 dir. Don Chaffey

Hunter, The
Westlake, D. E.

Payback
PAR (US) 1999 dir. Brian Helgeland

Hunting the Bismarck
Forester, C. S.

Sink the Bismarck
FOX (GB) 1960 dir. Lewis Gilbert

Hurricane Hunters
Anderson, W. C.

Hurricane
METRO (US) 1974 dir. Jerry Jameson

Husband of Delilah
Linklater, E.

Samson and Delilah
COMWORLD (US) 1984 dir. Lee Philips

Hussard Sur le Toit, Le
Giono, J.

Horseman on the Roof, The
STUDIO CANAL+ (Fr) 1995 dir. Jean-Paul Rappeneau

Hyper-Allergenic
Safdie, O.

You Can Thank Me Later
CINEQUEST (Can) 1998 dir. Shimon Dotan

Hypnotisme à la Portée de Tous, L'
Minier, M.

Dormez, Je Le Veux
CDP (Fr) 1997 dir. Irene Jouannet

I

I am a Camera
van Druten, J.

Cabaret
CINERAMA (US) 1972 dir. Bob Fosse

I Am Legend
Matheson, R.

Last Man on Earth, The
AIP (US/It) 1964 dir. Sidney Salkow

I Am Legend
Matheson, R.

Omega Man, The
WAR (US) 1971 dir. Boris Sagar

I Am the Cheese
Cormer, R.

Lapse of Memory
MAX (Can/Fr) 1992 dir. Patrick Dewolf

I am Third
Sayers, G. and Silverman, A.

Brian's Song
COL TV (US) 1971 dir. Buzz Kulik
COL TRISTAR (US) 2001 dir. John Gray

I Am Your Dad
Wang, S.

Baba
BEIJING (China) 2000 dir. Shou Wang

I, James Lewis
Gabriel, G. W.

This Woman is Mine
UN (US) 1941 dir. Frank Lloyd

I Know You Are, But What Am I?
Bucatinsky, D.

All Over the Guy
LIONS GATE (US) 2001 dir. Julie Davis

I Married A Dead Man
Irish, W.

I Married A Shadow
IS (Fr) 1983 dir. Robin Davis

I Married a Dead Man
Woolrich, C.

Mrs. Winterbourne
TRISTAR (US) 1996 dir. Richard Benjamin

I Pledge Allegiance ... The True Story of an American Spy Family
Blum, H.

Family of Spies
KING PHOENIX (US) 1990 dir. Stephen Gyllenhaal

I, Tina
Turner, T. and Loder, K.

What's Love Got to Do With It?
TOUCHSTONE (US) 1993 dir. Brian Gibson

I Wake Up Screaming
Fisher, S.

Vicki
FOX (US) 1953 dir. Harry Horner

Ice
McBain, E.

Ed McBain's 87th Precinct: Ice
HEARST (1996) dir. Bradford May

Ice House Heat Waves
Brinkman, B.

Ice House
UPFRONT/CACTUS (US) 1989
dir. Eagle Pennell

Idioglossia
Handley, M.

Nell
FOX (US) 1994 dir. Michael Apted

Idiot, The
Dostoevsky, F.

Nastasja
HIT (Pol) 1994 dir. Andrzej Wajda

Idol, The
Brown, M.

Mad Genius, The
WAR (US) 1931 dir. Michael Curtiz

Idol Hunter, The
Unsworth, B.

Pascali's Island
AVENUE (GB) 1988 dir. James Dearden

Idyll of Miss Sarah Brown, The
Runyon, D.

Guys and Dolls
MGM (US) 1955
dir. Joseph L. Mankiewicz

If Beale Street Could Talk
Baldwin, J.

A La Place Du Coeur
STUDIO CANAL+ (Fr) 1998 dir. Robert
Guediguian

If Die Before I Wake
King, S.

Lady from Shanghai, The
COL (US) 1948 dir. Orson Welles

If Only They Could Talk; It Shouldn't Happen to a Vet; Lord God Made Them All, The
Herriot, J.

All Creatures Great and Small
EMI (GB) 1974 dir. Claude Whatham

If You Want to See Your Wife Again
Craig, J.

Your Money or Your Wife
BRENTWOOD (US) 1972
dir. Allen Reisner

Il était une fois
de Croisset, F.

Woman's Face, A
MGM (US) 1941 dir. George Cukor

I'll Be Back Before Midnight
Colley, P.

Illusions
PRISM ENT (US) 1992 dir. Victor Kulle

Ils disent que je suis une beurette
Nini, S.

Samia
STUDIO CANAL+ (Fr) 2000 dir.
Philippe Faucon

I'm Giving Them Up For Good
Rau, M. and Rau, N.

Cold Turkey
UA (US) 1970 dir. Norman Lear

I'm Sorry the Bridge is Out, You'll Have to Spend the Night
Allman, S. and Pickett, B.

Monster Mash: The Movie
PRISM (US) 1995 dir. Joel Cohen, Alec
Sokolow

Immortal Wife
Stone, I.

President's Lady, The
FOX (US) 1953 dir. Henry Levin

Immortality, Inc.
Sheckley, R.

Freejack
WAR (US) 1992 dir. Geoff Murphy

Impatient Virgin, The
Clarke, D. H.

Impatient Maiden
UN (US) 1932 dir. James Whale

Impressario
Hurok, S. and Goode, R.

Tonight We Sing
FOX (US) 1953 dir. Mitchell Leisen

In Barley Fields
Nathan, R.

Bishop's Wife, The
RKO (US) 1947 dir. Henry Koster

In God We Trust, All Others Pay Cash
Shepherd, J.

Christmas Story, A
MGM/UA (US) 1983 dir. Bob Clark

In God We Trust, All Others Pay Cash; Wanda Hickey's Night of Golden Memories and Other Disasters
Shepherd, J.

It Runs in the Family
MGM (US) 1994 dir. Bob Clark

In Hitler's Shadow: An Israeli's Amazing Journey Inside Germany's Neo-Nazi Movement
Svoray, Y. and Taylor, N.

Infiltrator, The
HBO SHOW (US) 1995 dir. Jud Taylor

In My Solitude
Leslie, D. S.

Two Left Feet
BL (GB) 1963 dir. Roy Baker

In No Comebacks
Forsyth, F.

Cry of the Innocent
NBC ENT (US) 1980
dir. Michael O'Herlihy

In the Deep of the Woods
Conde, N.

In the Deep Woods
GOLCHAN/HILL (US) 1992 dir.
Charles Correll

In the Grove
Kutagawa, R. A.

Iron Maze
TRANS-TOKYO (US/Jap) 1991
dir. Hiroaki Yoshida

In the Heart of the Country
Coetzee, J. M.

Dust
DASKA (Bel/Fr) 1985
dir. Marion Hansel

In the Heat of the Summer
Katzenbach, J.

Mean Season, The
ORION (US) 1985 dir. Philip Borsos

In the Sleep Room: The Story of the CIA Brainwashing Experiments in Canada
Collins, A.

Sleep Room, The
CBC (Can) 1998 dir. Anne Wheeler

In This Fallen City
Williams, B.

Night of Courage
TITUS (US) 1987 dir. Elliot Silverstein

In This Sign
Greenberg, J.

Love is Never Silent
M. REES (US) 1985 dir. Joseph Sargent

In Two Minds
Mercer, D.
Family Life
EMI (GB) 1971 dir. Ken Loach

Incident at 125th Street
Brown, J. E.
Incident in San Francisco
ABC TV (US) 1971 dir. Don Medford

Inconceivable
Elton, B.
Maybe Baby
BBC (GB) 2000 dir. Ben Elton

Incredible Journey, The
Burnford, S.
Homeward Bound: The Incredible Journey
DISNEY (US) 1993 dir. Duwayne Dunham

Indians
Kopit, A.
Buffalo Bill and the Indians
UA (US) 1976 dir. Robert Altman

Infernal Idol
Seymour, H.
Craze
EMI (GB) 1973 dir. Freddie Francis

Infierno y la Brisa, El
de Soto, J. M. V.
Hail Hazana
STILLMAN (Sp) 1978
dir. Jose Maria Guttierez

Ingen Mans Land; Enda Segern, Den
Guillou, J.
Hamilton
TV4SWE (Swe/Nor) 1998 dir. Harald Zwart

Injancia dos Martos
Lonzeiro, J.
Pixote
UNIFILM (Port) 1981
dir. Hector Babenco

Insider's Price
Pressman, K.
Diary of a Hit Man
VI (US) 1992 dir. Roy London

Instruct my Sorrows
Jaynes, C.
My Reputation
WAR (US) 1946 dir. Curtis Bernhardt

Intensive Care
Weisman, M.-L.
Time to Live, A
ITC (US) 1985 dir. Rick Wallace

Interpreter, The
Keefe, F. L.
Before Winter Comes
COL (GB) 1968 dir. J. Lee Thompson

Interrupted Journey, The
Fuller, J. G.
UFO Incident, The
UN TV (US) 1975 dir. Richard Colla

Interruption, The
Jacobs, W. W.
Footsteps in the Fog
COL (GB) 1955 dir. Arthur Lubin

Intimate Exchanges
Ayckbourn, A.
Smoking/No Smoking
ARENA (Fr) 1993 dir. Alain Resnais

Into It
Pomerantz, E.
Caught
CINEHAUS (US) 1996 dir. Robert M. Young

Into Thin Air
Krakauer, J.
Into Thin Air: Death on Everest
COL TRISTAR (US) 1997 dir. Robert Markowitz

Invasion of the Body Snatchers
Finney, J.
Body Snatchers
WAR (US) 1993 dir. Abel Ferrara

Investigation, The
Uhnak, D.
Kojak: The Price of Justice
MCA/UN (US) 1987 dir. Alan Metzger

Invisible Man, The
Wells, H. G.
Gemini Man
UN TV (US) 1976 dir. Alan J. Levi

Io e Lui
Moravia, A.
Me and Him
NC/COL (Ger) 1989 dir. Doris Dorrie

Io il Tabano
Carlucci, A. and Rossetti, P.
Altri Uomini
DEAN (It) 1997 dir. Claudio Bonivento

Io Speriamo Che Me Lo Cavo
D'Orta, M.
Ciao, Professore
CECCHI (It) 1992 dir. Lina Wertmuller

Iris, a Memoir of Iris Murdoch; Elegy for Iris
Bayley, J.
Iris
MIRAMAX (GB/US) 2001 dir. Richard Eyre

Isadora Duncan, An Intimate Portrait
Stokes, S.
Isadora
UI (GB) 1969 dir. Karel Reisz
US title: Loves of Isadora, The

Isak Dinesen
Thurman, J.
Out of Africa
UN (US) 1985 dir. Sidney Pollack

Ishi in Two Worlds
Quinn, T. K.
Ishi: The Last of his Tribe
LEWIS (US) 1978
dir. Robert Ellis Miller

Ishmael
Quinn, D.
Instinct
TOUCHSTONE (US) 1999 dir. Jon Turteltaub

Island of Dr Moreau, The
Wells, H. G.
Island of Lost Souls
PAR (US) 1932 dir. Erle C. Kenton

Issue of the Bishop's Blood, The
McMahon, T. P.
Abduction of St. Anne
Q. MARTIN (US) 1975 dir. Harry Falk

It Depends What You Mean
Bridie, J.
Folly to be Wise
BL (GB) 1952 dir. Frank Launden

It's a 2 ft 6 inch above the Ground World
Laffan, K.
Love Ban, The
BL (GB) 1973 dir. Ralph Thomas

It's a Vet's Life
Duncan, A.
In the Doghouse
RANK (GB) 1961 dir. Darcy Conyers

Ivanhoe
Scott, Sir W.
Young Ivanhoe
FILMLINE (Can/Fr) 1995 dir. Ralph L. Thomas

I've Got Mine
Hubler, R. G.
Beachhead
UA (US) 1954 dir. Stuart Heisler

Ivy Garland, The
Hoyland, J.
Out of the Darkness
CFF (GB) 1985 dir. John Krish

J

Jack O'Judgement
Wallace, E.
Share Out, The
AA (GB) 1962 dir. Gerald Glaister

Jackdaws Strut
Henry, H.
Bought
WAR (US) 1931 dir. Archie Mayo

Jack's Return Home
Lewis, T.
Get Carter
MGM (GB) 1971 dir. Mike Hodges
WAR (US) 2000 dir. Stephen T. Kay

Jacobowsky and the Colonel
Werfel, F.
Me and The Colonel
COL (US) 1958 dir. Peter Glenville

Jakob der Lugner
Becker, J.
Jakob the Liar
TRISTAR (US/Fr) 1999 dir. Peter Kassovitz

Jakob von Gunten
Walser, R.
Institute Benjamenta
IMAGE (GB) 1995 dir. Stephen Quay, Timothy Quay

Jane of Lantern Hill
Montgomery, L. M.
Lantern Hill
DISNEY (US) 1990 dir. Kevin Sullivan

Janine and Alex, Alex and Janine
Levin, M.
Model Behavior
DISNEY (US) 2000 dir. Mark Rosman

Janne, Min Van
Pohl, P.
My Friend Joe
PORTMAN ENT (Ger/Ire/GB) 1996 dir. Chris Bould

January Heights
Banks, P.
Great Lie, The
WAR (US) 1941 dir. Edmund Goulding

Jayne Mansfield and the American Fifties
Saxton, M.
Jayne Mansfield Story, The
LAN (US) 1980 dir. Dick Lowry

Je te tue: Histoire Vraie de Roberto Succo
Froment, P.
Roberto Succo
STUDIO CANAL+ (Fr) 2001 dir. Cedric Kahn

Jealousy
Verneuil, L.
Deception
WAR (US) 1946 dir. Irving Rapper

Jean le Bleu
Giono, J.
Femme du Boulanger, La
PAGNOL (Fr) 1938 dir. Marcel Pagnol

Jean Vigo
Salles Gomes, P. E.
Vigo—Passion For Life
NITRATE (US) 1998 dir. Julien Temple

Jeanne de Luynes, Comtesse de Verne
Tournier, J.
King's Whore, The
J&M (GB) 1990 dir. Axel Corti

Jeannie
Stuart, A.
Let's Be Happy
ABP (GB) 1957 dir. Henry Levin

Jennie
Preston, D.
Jennie Project, The
H. ROACH (US) 2001 dir. Gary Nadeau

Jennie's Story
Lambert, B.
Heart of the Sun
MAK (Can) 1998 dir. Francis Damberger

Jenny Angel
Barber, E. O.
Angel Baby
ALLIED (US) 1960 dir. Paul Wendkos

Jest of God, A
Laurence, M.
Rachel, Rachel
WAR (US) 1968 dir. Paul Newman

Jet Stream
Ferguson, A.
Mayday at 40,000 Feet
WAR (US) 1976 dir. Robert Butler

Jewel of Mahabar
Marshall, E.
Treasure of the Golden Condor
FOX (US) 1953 dir. Delmer Daves

Jewel of the Seven Stars
Stoker, B.
Awakening, The
EMI (GB) 1980 dir. Mike Newell

Jewel of the Seven Stars
Stoker, B.
Blood from the Mummy's Tomb
MGM-EMI (GB) 1971 dir. Seth Holt

Jewel of the Seven Stars, The
Stoker, B.
Legend of the Mummy
UNAPIX (US) 1997 dir. Jeffrey Obrow

Jewel Robbery
Fodor, L.
Peterville Diamond, The
WAR (GB) 1942 dir. Walter Forde

Jim Kane
Brown, J. P. S.
Pocket Money
FIRST (US) 1972 dir. Stuart Rosenberg

Joan of Lorraine
Anderson, M.
Joan of Arc
RKO (US) 1948 dir. Victor Fleming

Joanna Godden
Smith, S. K.
Loves of Joanna Godden, The
GFD (GB) 1947 dir. Charles Frend

Jody
Hulse, J.
Family of Strangers, A
ALLIANCE (US) 1993 dir. Sheldon Larry

John Perkins
Thomas, H.

Paddy
ARTE FRANCE (Fr) 1999 dir. Gerard Mordillat

Joseph
Mantley, J.

27th Day
COL (US) 1957 dir. William Asher

Journey to Matecumbe, A
Taylor, R. L.

Treasure of Matecumbe
DISNEY (US) 1976
dir. Vincent McEveety

Journey to the West
Cheng-en, W.

Lost Empire, The
HALLMARK (US/Ger) 2001 dir. Peter MacDonald

Journey's End
Sherriff, R. C.

Aces High
EMI (GB/Fr) 1976 dir. Jack Gold

Jovial Ghosts, The
Smith, T.

Topper
MGM (US) 1937
dir. Norman Z. MacLeod
PAPAZIAN (US) 1979
dir. Charles S. Dubin

Jubal Troop
Wellman, P. I.

Jubal
COL (US) 1956 dir. Delmer Daves

Judas Kiss, The: The Undercover Life of Paul Kelly
Harris, M.

Murder Most Likely
ALLIANCE (Can) 1999 dir. Alex Chapple

Jude the Obscure
Hardy, T.

Jude
BBC (GB) 1996 dir. Michael Winterbottom

Jude und das Madchen, Der
Kohn, C.

Leo und Claire
ODEON (Ger) 2001 dir. Joseph Vilsmaier

Judge and his Hangman, The
Durrenmatt, F.

End of the Game
TCF (US/Ger) 1976
dir. Maximilian Schell

Judgment in Stone, A
Rendell, R.

Ceremonie, La
FRANCE 3 (Fr) 1995 dir. Claude Chabrol

Julia
Straub, P.

Full Circle
PAR (GB/Can) 1976
dir. Richard Loncraine

Jungle Book, The
Kipling, R.

Second Jungle Book, The—Mowgli and Baloo
TRISTAR (US) 1997 dir. Duncan McLachlan

Junior Bachelor Society, The
Williams, J. A.

Sophisticated Gents, The
D. WILSON (US) 1981 dir. Harry Falk

Jupiter Laughs
Cronin, A. J.

Shining Victory
WAR (US) 1941 dir. Irving Rapper

Jury, The
Bullett, G.
Last Man to Hang?, The
COL (GB) 1956 dir. Terence Fisher

Juryman
Galbally, F. and Macklin, R.
Storyville
DAVIS (US) 1992 dir. Mark Frost

Just Another Sucker
Chase, J. H.
Palmetto
COL (Ger/US) 1997 dir. Volker
Schlondorff

Just Like the Pom Pom Girls
Graham, M.
Sinful life, A
NEW LINE (US) 1989
dir. William Schreiner

Justice in the Back Room
Raab, S.
Marcus-Nelson Murders, The
UN TV (US) 1973 dir. Joseph Sargent

Justine
De Sade, Marquis
Cruel Passion
TARGET (GB) 1977 dir. Chris Boger

Kadisbellan
Schutt, R.

Slingshot, The
NORDISK (Den/Swe) 1993 dir. Ake Sandgren

Kamaraden
Fuhmann, F.

Duped Till Doomsday
DEFA (Ger) 1957 dir. Kurt Jung-Alsen

Karakter
Bordewijk, F.

Character
ALMERICA (Bel/Neth) 1997 dir. Mike van Diem

Karleks Pris
Gronin, Y.

Rusar I Hans Famn
GOTAFILM (Swe) 1996 dir. Lennart Hjulstrom

Kavik the Wolf Dog
Morey, W.

Courage of Kavik, the Wolf Dog, The
PANTHEON (US) 1980 dir. Peter Carter

Kennedy Tapes, The: Inside the White House During the Cuban Missile Crisis
May, E. R. and Zelikow, P. D.

Thirteen Days
NEW LINE (US) 2000 dir. Roger Donaldson

Kennel Murder Case, The
van Dine, S. S.

Calling Philco Vance
WAR (US) 1939 dir. William Clemens

Kent State: What Happened and Why
Michener, J. A.

Kent State
INTERPLAN (US) 1981
dir. James Goldstone

Kestrel for a Knave, A
Hines, B.

Kes
UA (GB) 1969 dir. Ken Loach

Kidnappers, The
Paterson, N.

Little Kidnappers, The
DISNEY CH (US) 1990 dir. Don Shebib

Kill, The
Zola, E.

Game is Over, The
COL (Fr/It) 1967 dir. Roger Vadim

Kill Fee
Paulsen, G.

Murder C.O.D.
KUSHNER-LOCKE (US) 1990
dir. Alan Metzger

Killer Angels, The
Shaara, M.

Gettysburg
TURNER (US) 1993 dir. Ronald F. Maxwell

Killer Department, The
Cullen, R.

Citizen X
HBO (US) 1995 dir. Chris Gerolmo

Killing a Mouse on Sunday
Pressburger, E.

Behold a Pale Horse
COL (US) 1964 dir. Fred Zinnemann

Killing Frost, The
Catto, M.

Trapeze
UA (US) 1956 dir. Carol Reed

Kimura Family, The
Tani, T.

Yen Family, The
FUJI (Jap) 1990 dir. Yojiro Takita

Kind Sir
Krasna, N.

Indiscreet
WAR (GB) 1958 dir. Stanley Donen
REP (US) 1988
dir. Richard Michaels

Kinderjahren
Obersku, J.

Jonah Who Lived in the Whale
FOCUS (Fr/It) 1993 dir. Roberto Faenza

King Lear
Shakespeare, W.

Ran
NIPPON HERALD (Jap) 1985 dir. Akira Kurosawa

King of Hearts
Kerr, J. and Brooke, E.

That Certain Feeling
PAR (US) 1956 dir. Norman Panama, Melvin Frank

King of the World
Remnick, D.

Muhammad Ali: King of the World
LIONS GATE (US) 2000 dir. John Sacret Young

King Reluctant, A
Wilkins, V.

Dangerous Exile
RANK (GB) 1957
dir. Brian Desmond Hurst

King Solomon's Mines
Haggard, Sir H. R.

Watusi
MGM (US) 1959 dir. Kurt Neumann

Kingdom of Johnny Cool, The
McPartland, J.

Johnny Cool
UA (US) 1963 dir. William Asher

King's Damsel, The
Chapman, V.

Quest for Camelot
WAR (US) 1998 dir. Frederik Du Chau

King's Ransom, The
McBain, E.

High and Low
TOHO (Jap) 1963 dir. Akira Kurosawa

Kipps
Wells, H. G.

Half a Sixpence
PAR (GB) 1967 dir. George Sidney

Kiss, Inc.
Wyse, L.

Million Dollar Face, The
NEPHI-HAMNER (US) 1981
dir. Michael O'Herlihy

Kiss of Death
Bachmann, L.

Devil Makes Three, The
MGM (US) 1952 dir. Andrew Marton

Kissinger: A Biography
Isaacson, W.

Kissinger and Nixon
PARAGON (US) 1995 dir. Daniel Petrie

Klinkevals
Aamund, J.

Juliane
PER HOLST (Den) 1999 dir. Hans
Kristensen

Kloakerne
Stawinski, J.

Kanal
POLSKI (Pol) 1956 dir. Andrzej Wajda

Kofiko
Borenstein, T.

Going Bananas
CANNON (US) 1988 dir. Boat Davidson

Kosygin is Coming
Ardies, T.

Russian Roulette
ITC (US) 1975 dir. Lou Lombardo

Krampack
Sanchez, J.

Nico and Dani
MESSIDOR (Sp) 2000 dir. Cesc Gay

Kurtz
Aubert, J.-M.

Art (delicat) de la Seduction, L'
BLUE DAHLIA (Fr) 2001 dir. Richard
Berry

Kurwenal
Navarre, Y.

Straight from the Heart
TELESCENE (Fr) 1990 dir. Lea Pool

L

Labyrinth Makers, The; Alamut Ambush, The; Colonel Butler's Wolf
Price, A.

Chessgame
GRANADA (GB) 1983 dir. William Brayne, Ken Grieve, Roger Tucker

Ladies and Gentlemen
Hecht, B. and MacArthur, C.

Perfect Strangers
WAR (US) 1950 dir. Bretaigne Windust
GB title: Too Dangerous to Love

Ladies in Retirement
Denham, R. and Percy, E.

Mad Room, The
COL (US) 1969 dir. Bernard Girard

Ladies of the Mob
Boothe, E.

City Streets
PAR (US) 1931 dir. Rouben Mamoulian

Ladies Room, The
Schiff, R.

Romy and Michele's High School Reunion
TOUCHSTONE (US) 1997 dir. David Mirkin

Lady Has a Heart, A
Bus-Fekete, L.

Baroness and the Butler, The
FOX (US) 1938 dir. Walter Lang

Lady, Lady, I Did It!
McBain, E.

Lonely Hearts
TOHO (Jap) 1982 dir. Kon Ichikawa

Lady Windemere's Fan
Wilde, O.

Fan, The
FOX (US) 1949 dir. Otto Preminger
GB title: Lady Windemere's Fan

Ladystinger
Smith, C.

Scam
VIACOM (US) 1993 dir. John Flynn

LaFitte the Pirate
Saxon, L.

Buccaneer, The
PAR (US) 1937 dir. Cecil B. de Mille
PAR (US) 1958 dir. Anthony Quinn

Lamarca Guerilla Captain
Miranda, E. J. O.

Lamarca
MORENA (Bra) 1994 dir. Sergio Rezende

Lament for Molly Maguires
Lewis, A. H.

Molly Maguires, The
PAR (US) 1970 dir. Martin Ritt

Lamp is Heavy, A
Russell, S. M.

Feminine Touch, The
RANK (GB) 1956 dir. Pat Jackson

Lantern in Her Hand, A
Aldrich, B. S.
Mother's Gift, A
RHI (US) 1995 dir. Jerry London

Larry: Case History of a Mistake
McQueen, Dr. R.
Larry
TOM (US) 1974 dir. William A. Graham

Larsen
Tutein, P.
Zero Kelvin
NORSK (Nor/Swe) 1995 dir. Hans Petter Moland

Last Adam, The
Cozzens, J. G.
Dr. Bull
FOX (US) 1933 dir. John Ford

Last Chapter
Hamsun, K.
Air Si Pur, Un
FRANCE 2 (Fr) 1997 dir. Yves Angelo

Last Days of the Victim
Feinman, J. P.
Two to Tango
CONCORDE (US/Arg) 1989 dir. Hector Olivera

Last Frontier
MacLean, A.
Secret Ways, The
RANK (US) 1961 dir. Phil Karlson

Last Hours of Sandra Lee, The
Sansom, W.
Wild Affair, The
BL (GB) 1965 dir. John Irish

Last Jew, The
Kaniuk, Y.
Vulture, The
YOSHA (Israel) 1981 dir. Yaky Yosba

Last Jews in Berlin, The
Gross, L.
Forbidden
ENT (GB/Ger) 1984 dir. Anthony Page

Last Man on the List, The
Randall, B.
Dead Husbands
WIL COURT (US) 1998 dir. Paul Shapiro

Last of Jane Austen, The
Hendryx, S.
Ladies and the Champ
DISNEY (US) 2001 dir. Jeff Berry

Last of Mrs. Cheyney, The
Lonsdale, F.
Law and the Lady, The
MGM (US) 1951 dir. Edwin H. Knopf

Last of the Badmen
Monaghan, J.
Bad Men of Tombstone
ABP (US) 1949 dir. Kurt Neumann

Last of the Mohicans, The
Cooper, J. F.
Last of the Redmen
COL (US) 1947 dir. George Sherman

Last Prostitute who took Pride in her Work, The
Borden, W.
Last Prostitute, The
BBK (US) 1991 dir. Lou Antonio

Last Tag
Giannunzio, M.
Falling for You
BBS (US) 1995 dir. Eric Till

Last Testament, The
Amen, C.
Testament
PAR (US) 1983 dir. Lynne Littman

Last Voyage of the Valhalla
Kytle, R.

Desperate Voyage
WIZAN (US) 1980
dir. Michael O'Herlihy

Late Boy Wonder, The
Hall, A.

Three in the Cellar
AIP (US) 1970 dir. Theodore J. Flicker

Late Christopher Bean, The
Howard, S.

Christopher Bean
MGM (US) 1933 dir. Sam Wood

Lay this Laurel
Kirstein, L.

Glory
TRISTAR (US) 1989 dir. Edward Zwick

Lazaro
Kendall, D.

Where the River Runs Black
MGM (US) 1986 dir. Christopher Cain

Lazarus and the Hurricane
Chaiton, S. and Swinton, T.

Hurricane, The
UN (US) 1999 dir. Norman Jewison

Le Fruit Vert
Gignoux, R.

Between Us Girls
UN (US) 1942 dir. Henry Koster

Leave Her to Heaven
Williams, B. A.

Too Good to be True
NEWLAND-RAYNOR (US) 1988
dir. Christian I. Nyby II

Leaving Cheyenne
McMurtry, L.

Lovin' Molly
GALA (US) 1974. dir. Sidney Lumet

Ledger, The
Uhnak, D.

Get Christy Love!
WOLPER (US) 1974 dir.
William A. Graham

Legacy
Bonner, C.

Adam had Four Sons
COL (US) 1941 dir. Gregory Ratoff

Legacy of a Spy
Maxfield, H. S.

Double Man, The
WAR (GB) 1967 dir. Franklin Schaffner

Legion
Blatty, W. P.

Exorcist III, The
TCP (US) 1990 dir. William Peter Blatty

Legitime Defense
Steeman, S.-A.

Quai des Orfèvres
MAJ (Fr) 1947
dir. Henri-Georges Clouzot

Leiningen Versus the Ants
Stephenson, C.

Naked Jungle, The
PAR (US) 1954 dir. Byron Haskin

Lesser of Two Evils, The
Laborde, J.

Investigation
QUARTET (Fr) 1978 dir. Etienne Perier

Lesson in Love, A
Baird, M. T.

Circle of Two
BORDEAUX (Can) 1980
dir. Jules Dassin

Let Me Count the Ways
De Vries, P.

How Do I Love Thee?
ABC (US) 1970 dir. Michael Gordon

Letter to Five Wives
Klempner, J.

Letter to Three Wives, A
FOX (US) 1948
dir. Joseph L. Mankiewicz
FOX (US) 1985 dir. Larry Elikann

Letter to the Editor
Street, James H.

Nothing Sacred
SELZNICK (US) 1937
dir. William Wellman

Letter, The
Maugham, W. S.

Unfaithful, The
WAR (US) 1947 dir. Vincent Sherman

Liaisons Dangéreuses, Les
Hampton, C.

Dangerous Liaisons
WAR (US) 1988 dir. Stephen Frears

Liaisons Dangéreuses, Les
de Laclos, P.

Dangerous Liaisons
WAR (US) 1988 dir. Stephen Frears

Liaisons dangéreuses, Les
Laclos, P. de

Valmont
ORION (GB) 1989 dir. Milos Forman

Liberté Provisoire
Duran, M.

He Stayed for Breakfast
COL (US) 1940 dir. Alexander Hall

Librement Trahi
Nothomb, A.

Hygiene de L'Assassin
TSF (Fr) 1999 dir. François Ruggieri

Lies Boys Tell, The
Herrin, L.

Take Me Home Again
VZ/SERTNER (US) 1994 dir. Tom
McLaughlin

Life, The
Cordelier, J.

Memoirs of a French Whore
AIDART (Fr) 1982 dir. Daniel Duval

Life and Death of the Wicked Lady Skelton, The
King-Hall, M.

Wicked Lady, The
GFD (GB) 1946 dir. Leslie Arliss
CANNON (GB) 1983 dir. Michael
Winner

Life and Loves of a She-Devil, The
Weldon, F.

She-Devil
ORION (US) 1989 dir. Susan Seidelman

Life and Times of Cleopatra, The
Franzero, C. M.

Cleopatra
FOX (US) 1963
dir. Joseph L. Manciewicz

Life During Wartime
Reddin, K.

Alarmist, The
KEY ENT (US) 1997 dir. Evan Dunsky

Life Estates
Hearon, S.

Best Friends for Life
HALLMARK (US) 1998 dir. Michael
Switzer

Life Lines
Ireland, J.

Reason for Living: The Jill Ireland Story
TEN-FOUR (US) 1991 dir. Michael
Rhodes

Life of David Haggart, The
Haggart, D.

Sinful Davey
UA (GB) 1969 dir. John Huston

Life of Eleanor Marx 1855–1899, The: A Socialist Tragedy
Tsuzuki, C.

Eleanor Marx
BBC (GB) 1977 dir. Jane Howell

Life of Ian Fleming, The
Pearson, J.

Goldeneye
ANGLIA (GB) 1990 dir. Don Boyd

Life of Lucy Gallant, The
Cousins, M.

Lucy Gallant
PAR (US) 1955 dir. Robert Parrish

Life of Tom Horn, Government Scout & Interpreter
Horn, T.

Tom Horn
WAR (US) 1980 dir. William Wiard

Life with Mother Superior
Trahey, J.

Trouble with Angels, The
COL (US) 1966 dir. Ida Lupino

Light of Day, The
Ambler, E.

Topkapi
UA (US) 1964 dir. Jules Dassin

Light of Heart, The
Williams, E.

Life Begins at Eight Thirty
FOX (US) 1942 dir. Irving Pichel
GB title: Light of Heart, The

Light on Synanon, The
Mitchell, D., Mitchell, C. and Ofshe, R.

Attack on Fear
TOM (US) 1984 dir. Mel Damski

Light Years, The; Marking Time
Howard, E. J.

Cazalets, The
BBC (GB) 2001 dir. Suri Krishnamma

Lighthouse at the End of the World
Verne, J.

Light at the Edge of the World, The
MGM (US/Sp) 1971
dir. Kevin Billington

Lightning
McBain, E.

Ed McBain's 87th Precinct: Lightning
HEARST (1995) dir. Bruce Paltrow

Like Mother Like Me
Schwartz, S.

Like Mom, Like Me
CBS ENT (US) 1978
dir. Michael Pressman

Likes of 'er, The
McEvoy, C.

Sally in our Alley
ABP (GB) 1931 dir. Maurice Elvey

Liliom
Molnar, F.

Carousel
TCF (US) 1956 dir. Henry King

Lillian Day
Mearson, L.

Our Wife
COL (US) 1941 dir. John M. Stahl

Lincoln
Vidal, G.

Gore Vidal's Lincoln
FINNEGAN/PINCHUK (US) 1988
dir. Lamont Johnson

Linda McCartney: A Portrait
Fields, D.

Linda McCartney Story, The
COL TRISTAR (US) 2000 dir. Armand Mastroianni

Line on Ginger
Maugham, R.

Intruder, The
BL (GB) 1953 dir. Guy Hamilton

Lion, The Witch and the Wardrobe, The; Prince Caspian; Voyage of the Dawn Treader, The; Silver Chair, The
Lewis, C. S.

Chronicles of Narnia, The
BBC (GB) 1989 dir. Marilyn Fox, Alex Kirby

Lions at the Kill
Catto, M.

Seven Thieves
FOX (US) 1960 dir. Henry Hathaway

Lips of Steel
Hervey, H.

Prestige
RKO (US) 1932 dir. Tay Garnett

Lipschtick
Juergensen, H. and Westfeldt, J.

Kissing Jessica Stein
FOX (US) 2001 dir. Charles Herman-Wurmfeld

Lisa and David
Rubin, T. I.

David and Lisa
BL (US) 1963 dir. Frank Perry
HARPO (US) 1998 dir. Lloyd Kramer

Little Britches
Moody, R.

Wild Country, The
DISNEY (US) 1971 dir. Robert Totten

Little Brothers of St. Mortimer, The
Ryan, J. F.

White River Kid, The
NEW CITY (US) 1999 dir. Arne Glimcher

Little Flat in the Temple, A
Wynne, P.

Devotion
RKO (US) 1931 dir. Robert Milton

Little Lambs Eat Ivy
Langley, N.

Father's Doing Fine
ABP (GB) 1952 dir. Henry Cass

Little Pinks
Runyon, D.

Big Street, The
RKO (US) 1942 dir. Irving Reis

Little Sister, The
Chandler, R.

Marlowe
MGM (US) 1969 dir. Paul Bogart

Liverpool Cats, The
Sherry, S.

Rocky O'Rourke
BBC (GB) 1976 dir. John Prowse

Living and the Dead, The
Boileau, P. and Narcejac, T.

Vertigo
PAR (US) 1958 dir. Alfred Hitchcock

Living Arrows
Martin, G.

Between Two Women
J. AVNET (US) 1986 dir. Jon Avnet

Living Proof
Williams, Jr., H. and Bane, M.

Living Proof: The Hank Williams, Jr. Story
TELECOM (US) 1983 dir. Dick Lowry

Lizard's Tail, The
Brandel, M.

Hand, The
ORION/WAR (US) 1981
dir. Oliver Stone

Loaded
Tsiolkas, C.

Head On
Gt SCOTT (Aust) 1998 dir. Ana Kokkinos

Locataire, La
Simenon, G.

Etoile du Nord, L'
UA (Fr) 1982
dir. Pierre Granier-Deferre

Locked Room, The
Sjowall, M. and Wahloo, P.

Beck
FILMCASE (Neth/Bel) 1993 dir. Jacob Bijl

Lodger, The
Lowndes, Mrs. B.

Man in the Attic, The
FOX (US) 1953 dir. Hugo Fregonese

London Wall
van Druten, J.

After Office Hours
BI (GB) 1935 dir. Thomas Bentley

Lone Cowboy: My Life Story
James, W.

Shootout
UN (US) 1971 dir. Henry Hathaway

Lone House Mystery, The
Wallace, E.

Attempt to Kill
AA (GB) 1961 dir. Royston Murray

Lonely Girl, The
O'Brien, E.

Girl With Green Eyes
UA (GB) 1964 dir. Desmond Davis

Lonely Guy's Book of Life, The
Friedman, B. J.

Lonely Guy, The
UN (US) 1984 dir. Arthur Hiller

Lonely Skier, The
Innes, H.

Snowbound
RKO (GB) 1948 dir. David MacDonald

Long Haul
Bezzerides, A. I.

They Drive by Night
WAR (US) 1940 dir. Raoul Walsh
GB title: Road to Frisco, The

Long Kill, The
Ruell, P.

Last Hit, The
MTE UNIVERSAL (US) 1993 dir. Jan Egelson

Long, Long Trail, The
Chilton, C. and Littlewood, J.

Oh! What a Lovely War
PAR (GB) 1969
dir. Richard Attenborough

Long Saturday Night, The
Williams, C.

Confidentially Yours
IS (Fr) 1984 dir. François Truffaut

Long Saturday Night, The
Williams, C.

Finally, Sunday
FILMS A2 (Fr) 1983
dir. François Truffaut

Long Way Up, A
Valens, E. G.

Other Side of the Mountain, The
UN (US) 1975 dir. Larry Peerce
GB title: Window to the Sky, A

Look of Eagles, The
Foote, J. T.

Kentucky
FOX (US) 1938 dir. David Butler

Looking After Sandy
Turnbull, M.

Bad Little Angel
MGM (US) 1939 dir. William Thiele

Looking for Lost Bird: A Jewish Woman discovers her Navajo Roots
Melanson, Y. and Safran, C.

Lost Child, The
HALLMARK (US) 2000 dir. Karen Arthur

Looters, The
Reese, J.

Charley Varrick
UN (US) 1973 dir. Don Siegel

Lord Arthur Savile's Crime
Wilde, O.

Flesh and Fantasy
UN (US) 1943 dir. Julien Duvivier

Lord Edgware Dies
Christie, A.

Thirteen at Dinner
WAR (US) 1985 dir. Lou Antonio

Loser Takes All
Greene, G.

Strike It Rich
BRIT SCREEN (GB) 1990
dir. James Scott

Loss of Roses, A
Inge, W.

Stripper, The
FOX (US) 1963 dir. Franklin Schaffner
GB title: Woman of Summer

Lost Country, The
Salamanca, J. R.

Wild in the Country
FOX (US) 1961 dir. Philip Dunne

Lost Ecstasy
Rinehart, M. R.

I Take This Woman
PAR (US) 1931 dir. Marion Gering

Lost Hero: The Mystery of Raoul Wallenberg
Werbell, F. and Clarke, T.

Wallenberg: A Hero's Story
PAR (US) 1985 dir. Lamont Johnson

Lost Honor of Katharina Blum, The
Boll, H.

Lost Honor of Kathryn Beck, The
COMWORLD (US) 1984
dir. Simon Langton

Lost Horizon
Hilton, J.

Shangri-La
COMPASS (US) 1960
dir. George Schaefer

Lost King, A
DeCapite, R.

Harry and Son
ORION (US) 1984 dir. Paul Newman

Lost Moon
Lovell, Jr., J. A. and Kluger, J.

Apollo 13
UN (US) 1995 dir. Ron Howard

Lost Ones, The
Cameron, I.

Island at the Top of the World, The
DISNEY (US) 1974
dir. Robert Stevenson

Lost Prince, The: Young Joe, The Forgotten Kennedy
Searls, H.

Young Joe, the Forgotten Kennedy
ABC (US) 1977 dir. Richard T. Heffron

Lost World, The
Crichton, M.

Lost World, The: Jurassic Park
UN (US) 1997 dir. Steven Spielberg

Lot 27a
Conan Doyle, Sir A.

Tales from the Darkside: the Movie
PAR (US) 1990 dir. John Harrison

Lottie and Lisa
Kastner, E.

Parent Trap, The
DISNEY (US) 1961 dir. David Swift
DISNEY (US) 1998 dir. Nancy Myers

Louis Beretti
Clarke, D. H.

Born Reckless
FOX (US) 1930 dir. John Ford

Louisiana Black
Charters, S.

White Lie
MCA TV (US) 1991 dir. Bill Condon

Louisiane; Fausse-Rivière
Denuzière, M.

Louisiana
CINEMAX (US) 1984
dir. Philippe de Broca

Love and Forget
Drawbell, J. W.

Love Story
GFD (GB) 1944 dir. Leslie Arliss
US title: Lady Surrenders, A

Love and Other Natural Disasters
Hannay, A.

Tiger's Tale, A
ATLANTIC (US) 1988
dir. Peter Douglas

Love and War
Jakes, J.

North and South, Book II
WAR TV (US) 1986 dir. Kevin Connor

Love and War in the Apennines
Newby, E.

In Love and War
HALLMARK (US) 2001 dir. John Kent
Harrison

Love Bite
Gottlieb, S.

Deadly Love
POWER (US) 1995 dir. Jorge Montesi

Love Field
Davis, S.

Ruby
POLYGRAM (US) 1992 dir. John
MacKenzie

Love Flies in the Window
Morrison, A.

This Man is Mine
RKO (US) 1934 dir. John Cromwell

Love From Everybody
Hanley, C.

Don't Bother to Knock
WAR (GB) 1961 dir. Cyril Frankel
US title: Why Bother to Knock

Love in Amsterdam
Freeling, N.

Amsterdam Affair
LIP/TRIO/GROUP W (GB) 1968
dir. Gerry O'Hara

Love in a Cold Climate; Pursuit of Love, The
Mitford, N.

Love in a Cold Climate
THAMES (GB) 1980 dir. Donald
McWhinnie
BBC (GB) 2001 dir. Tom Hooper

Love in the Time of Cholera
Marquez, G. G.

Letters from the Park
RTVE (Cuba) 1988
dir. Tomas Guttierez Alea

Love Kills
Greenburg, D.

Deadly Vision, A
HILL-FIELDS (US) 1997 dir. Bill Norton

Lovers, The
Stevens, L.

War Lord, The
UN (US) 1965 dir. Franklin Schaffner

Love's a Revolution
Ward, C.

Vigo—Passion For Life
NITRATE (US) 1998 dir. Julien Temple

Lovey, A Very Special Child
MacCracken, M.

Lovey: A Circle of Children, Part II
TIME-LIFE (US) 1978 dir. Jud Taylor

**Luck of Roaring Camp, The;
Outcasts of Poker Flat, The**
Harte, B.

California Gold Rush
TAFT (US) 1981 dir. Jack Hively

Luckiest Girl in the World, The
Levenkron, S.

Secret Cutting
USA NETWORKS (US) 2000 dir. Norma
Bailey

Lucky; Chances
Collins, J.

Lucky/Chances
NBC (US) 1990 dir. Buzz Kulik

Ludes
Stein, B.

Boost, The
HEMDALE (US) 1988 dir. Harold
Becker

Lullaby, The
Knoblock, E.

Sin of Madelon Claudet
MGM (US) 1931 dir. Edgar Selwyn

Lully ou le Musicien du Soleil
Beaussant, P.

Roi Danse, Le
FRANCE 2 (Bel/Fr) 2000 dir. Gerard
Corbiau

Lumiere Noire
Daeninckx, D.

Black Light
MH FILMS (GB) 1994 dir. Med Hondo

Lunes de Fiel
Bruckner, P.

Bitter Moon
COL (Fr/GB) 1992. dir. Roman Polanski

Lytton Strachey: A Biography
Holroyd, M.

Carrington
FREEWAY (GB/Fr) 1995 dir.
Christopher Hampton

M

M. Ripois and his Nemesis
Hemon, L.

Knave of Hearts
ABP (GB) 1954 dir. René Clément
US title: Lover Boy

McCabe
Naughton, E.

McCabe and Mrs. Miller
WAR (US) 1971 dir. Robert Altman

McLeod's Folly
Bromfield, L.

Johnny Come Lately
CAGNEY (US) 1943
dir. William K. Howard
GB title: Johnny Vagabond

McVicar, by Himself
McVicar, J.

McVicar
BW (GB) 1980 dir. Tom Clegg

Madame la Gimp
Runyon, D.

Lady for a Day
COL (US) 1933 dir. Frank Capra

Madame la Gimp
Runyon, D.

Pocketful of Miracles
UA (US) 1961 dir. Frank Capra

Madness of George III, The
Bennett, A.

Madness of King George, The
CHANNEL 4 FILMS (GB) 1994 dir.
Nicholas Hytner

Madonna: Unauthorized
Andersen, C.

Madonna: Innocence Lost
JAFFE/BRAUNSTEIN (US) 1994 dir.
Bradford May

Mafia Marriage
Bonnano, R.

Love, Honor & Obey: The Last Mafia Marriage
CBS ENT (US) 1993 dir. John Patterson

Magic White Suit, The
Bradbury, R.

Wonderful Ice Cream Suit, The
DISNEY (US) 1998 dir. Stuart Gordon

Magistrate, The
Pinero, Sir A. W.

Those Were the Days
BIP (GB) 1934 dir. Thomas Bentley

Magnificent Devils
Crockett, L. H.

Proud and Profane, The
PAR (US) 1956 dir. George Seaton

Maiden Maiden
Boyle, K.

Five Days One Summer
WAR (US) 1982 dir. Fred Zinnemann

Maiden's Grave, A
Deaver, J.

Dead Silence
HBO (US) 1996 dir. Daniel Petrie, Jr.

Main Street
Lewis, S.

I Married a Doctor
WAR (US) 1936 dir. Archie Mayo

Maison d'Esther, La
Dangerfield, Y.

Saint-Cyr
STUDIO CANAL+ (Fr/Bel) 2000 dir.
Patricia Mazuy

Majesty of the Law, The
O'Connor, F.

Rising of the Moon, The
WAR (Ire) 1957 dir. John Ford

Major Taylor Down Under
Fitzpatrick, J.

Tracks of Glory: The Major Taylor Story
BARRON (Aust) 1992 dir. Marcus Cole

Make Room, Make Room!
Harrison, H.

Soylent Green
MGM (US) 1973 dir. Richard Fleischer

Make You a Fine Wife
Foldes, Y.

My Own True Love
PAR (US) 1948 dir. Compton Bennett

Male Animal, The
Thurber, J. and Nugent, E.

She's Working Her Way Through College
WAR (US) 1952
dir. Bruce Humberstone

Malibu, A Nature Story
Hoyt, V. J.

Sequoia
MGM (US) 1935 dir. Chester Lyons

Mallen Streak, The
Cookson, C.

Mallens, The
GRANADA (GB) 1979 dir. Richard
Martin, Mary McMurray, Brian Mills

Maltese Falcon, The
Hammett, D.

Satan Met a Lady
WAR (US) 1936 dir. William Dieterle

Mambo Kings Play Songs of Love, The
Hijeulo, O.

Mambo Kings, The
WAR (US) 1992 dir. Arne Glimcher

Man, The
Dineli, M.

Beware My Lovely
RKO (US) 1952 dir. Harry Horner

Man About a Dog, A
Coppel, A.

Obsession
GFD (GB) 1949 dir. Edward Dmytryk
US title: Hidden Room, The

Man At The Carlton
Wallace, E.

Man at the Carlton Tower
AA (GB) 1961 dir. Robert Tronson

Man Called Kyril, A
Trenhaile, J.

Codename: Kyril
INCITO/HTV (US/GB) 1988
dir. Ian Sharp

Man from Moscow, A
Wynne, G.

Wynne and Penkovsky
BBC (GB/US) 1985 dir. Paul Seed

Man in Black, The
Albert, M. H.

Rough Night in Jericho
UN (US) 1967 dir. Arnold Laven

Man in Half-Moon Street, The
Lyndon, B.

Man Who Could Cheat Death, The
PAR (GB) 1959 dir. Terence Fisher

Man in Possession, The
Harwood, H. M.

Personal Property
MGM (US) 1937 dir. W. S. Van Dyke
GB title: Man in Possession, The

Man in the Iron Mask, The
Dumas, A.

Fifth Musketeer, The
SASCH WIEN (Austria) 1978
dir. Ken Annakin

Man of Honor, A
Bonanno, J. and Lalli, S.

Bonanno: A Godfather's Story
PAULSON (US) 1999 dir. Michael
Poulette

Man of Property, A
Galsworthy, J.

That Forsyte Woman
MGM (US) 1949 dir. Compton Bennett
GB title: Forsyte Saga, The

Man of the West
Yordan, P.

Gun Glory
MGM (US) 1957 dir. Roy Rowland

Man on the Moon, A
Chaikin, A.

From the Earth to the Moon
HBO (US) 1998 dir. Tom Hanks, David
Frankel,
Lili Finni Zanuck, Graham Yost, Frank
Marshall,
Jon Turtletaub, Gary Fleder, David
Carson, Sally Field,
Jonathan Mostow

Man Running
Jepson, S.

Stage Fright
WAR (GB) 1950 dir. Alfred Hitchcock

Man Who Knew, The
Wallace, E.

Partners in Crime
AA (GB) 1961 dir. Peter Duffell

Man Who Rocked the Boat, The
Keating, W. J. and Carter, R.

Slaughter on 10th Avenue
UI (US) 1957 dir. Arnold Laven

Man-eater
Willis, T.

Maneaters are Loose!
MONA BBC (GB) 1984
dir. Timothy Galfos

Mantes Religieuses, Les
Monteilhet, H.

Praying Mantis
PORTMAN (GB) 1984 dir. Jack Gold

Mantrap
Lewis, S.

Untamed
PAR (US) 1940 dir. George Archainbaud

Manushar Juddha
Ray, P.

Target
CREATIVE (Ind) 1995 dir. Sandip Ray

Many Splendoured Thing, A
Han Suyin

Love is a Many Splendoured Thing
FOX (US) 1955 dir. Henry King

Marauders, The
Ogburn, C.

Merrill's Marauders
WAR (US) 1962 dir. Samuel Fuller

Marble Forest
Durant, T.

Macabre
ABP (US) 1958 dir. William Castle

Marianne Dreams
Storr, C.
Paperhouse
VESTRON (GB) 1988 dir. Bernard Rose

Marie: A True Story
Maas, P.
Marie
MGM/UA (US) 1985
dir. Roger Donaldson

Marilyn
Mailer, N.
Marilyn: The Untold Story
SCHILLER (US) 1980 dir. Jack Arnold

Marion's Wall
Finney, J.
Maxie
ORION (US) 1985 dir. Paul Aaron

Mark of the Leopard
Eastwood, J.
Beyond Mombasa
COL (GB) 1955 dir. George Marshall

Marriage Bed, The
Pascal, E.
Husband's Holiday
PAR (US) 1931 dir. Robert Milton

Marry at Leisure
Piper, A.
Nice Girl Like Me, A
AVCO (GB) 1969 dir. Desmond Davis

Marshal of Medicine Bend, The
Ward, B.
Lawless Street, A
COL (US) 1955 dir. Joseph H. Lewis

Martedì del Diavolo, Il
Russo, E.
Russicum
TRISTAR/CECCHI (It) 1989
dir. Pasquale Squitieri

Martin Eden
London, J.
Adventures of Martin Eden, The
COL (US) 1942 dir. Sidney Salkow

Marvellous Land of Oz, The; Ozma of Oz
Baum, L. F.
Return to Oz
DISNEY (US) 1985 dir. Walter Murch

Mary Ann
Karmel, A.
Something Wild
UA (US) 1961 dir. Jack Garfein

Mary Lavelle
O'Brien, K.
Talk of Angels
POLARIS (US) 1998 dir. Nick Hamm

Masks and Faces
Reade, C. and Taylor, T.
Peg of Old Drury
WILCOX (GB) 1935 dir. Herbert Wilcox

Massacre
Bellah, J. W.
Fort Apache
RKO (US) 1948 dir. John Ford

Matchmaker, The
Wilder, T.
Hello Dolly
FOX (US) 1969 dir. Gene Kelly

Mathilda Shouted Fire
Green, L.
Midnight Lace
UN (US) 1960 dir. David Miller
UN TV (US) 1981 dir. Ivan Nagy

Matter of Conviction, A
Hunter, E.
Young Savages, The
UA (US) 1960 dir. John Frankenheimer

Maurice Guest
Richardson, H. H.
Rhapsody
MGM (US) 1954 dir. Charles Vidor

Max and Helen: A Remarkable True Love Story
Wiesenthal, S.
Max and Helen
TNT (US) 1990 dir. Philip Saville

Max Trueblood and the Jersey Desperado
White, T.
Max et Jeremie
TF1 (Fr) 1992 dir. Claire Devers

Maybe I'll Pitch Forever
Paige, L. and Lipman, D.
Don't Look Back
TBA (US) 1981 dir. Richard Colla

Mayor of Casterbridge, The
Hardy, T.
Claim, The
BBC (GB/Fr) 2000 dir. Michael Winterbottom

Mazepa
Slowacki, J.
Blanche
TELEPRESSE (Fr) 1971
dir. Walerian Borowczyk

Me and My Shadows: A Memoir
Luft, L.
Life with Judy Garland: Me and My Shadows
ALLIANCE (US/Can) 2001 dir. Robert Allan Ackerman

Me and the Arch Kook Petulia
Haase, J.
Petulia
WAR (US) 1968 dir. Richard Lester

Me Two
Davis, E.
All of Me
UN (US) 1984 dir. Carl Reiner

Me Two
Ryan, M. C.
Other Me, The
H. ROACH (US) 2000 dir. Manny Coto

Meet a Body
Launder, F. and Gilliat, S.
Green Man, The
BL (GB) 1956 dir. Robert Day

Megstone Plot, The
Garve, A.
Touch of Larceny, A
PAR (GB) 1959 dir. Guy Hamilton

Melancholy of Resistance, The
Krasznahorkai, L.
Werckmeister Harmoniak
BABELSBERG (Ger/It/Fr) 2000 dir. Agnes Hranitzki, Bela Tarr

Melodeon, The
Swarthout, G.
Christmas to Remember, A
ENGLUND (US) 1978
dir. George Englund

Melville Goodwin, USA
Marquand, J. P.
Top Secret Affair
WAR (US) 1957 dir. H. C. Potter
GB title: Their Secret Affair

Memoirs of a British Agent
Lockhart, Sir R. H. B.
British Agent
WAR (US) 1934 dir. Michael Curtiz

Memoirs of a Physician
Dumas, A.
Black Magic
UA (US) 1949 dir. Gregory Ratoff

Memoirs of Cleopatra, The
George, M.

Cleopatra
HALLMARK (US) 1999 dir. Franc
Roddam

Memorias
de Erauso, C.

Monja Alferez, La
GOYA (Sp) 1992 dir. Javier Aguirre

Memory of Love
Brewer, B.

In Name Only
RKO (US) 1939 dir. John Cromwell

Men of Iron
Pyle, H.

Black Shield of Falworth, The
UI (US) 1954 dir. Rudolph Maté

Mendel Inc.
Freedman, D.

Heart of New York
WAR (US) 1932 dir. Mervyn LeRoy

Mendel Philipsen and Sons
Nathansens, H.

Sofie
NORSK (Den/Nor/Swe) 1992 dir. Liv
Ullman

Merry Andrew
Beach, L.

Handy Andy
FOX (US) 1934 dir. David Butler

Merton of the Movies
Wilson, H. L.

Make me a Star
PAR (US) 1932 dir. William Beaudine

Meter Man, The
Forbes, J. S.

Penthouse, The
PAR (GB) 1967 dir. Peter Collinson

Methinks the Lady
Endore, G.

Whirlpool
FOX (US) 1949 dir. Otto Preminger

Mexican, The
London, J.

Fighter, The
UA (US) 1952 dir. Herbert Fine

Mexican Village
Niggli, J.

Sombrero
MGM (US) 1953 dir. Norman Foster

Meyer Lansky: Mogul of the Mob
Dan, U., Eisenberg, D. and Landau, E.

Lansky
HBO (US) 1999 dir. John McNaughton

Mi Bodo Contigo
Tellado, C.

Our Marriage
PASSAGE (Fr) 1985 dir. Valeria
Sarimento

Mia: The Life of Mia Farrow
Epstein, E. Z. and Morella, J.

Love and Betrayal: The Mia Farrow Story
FOX CIRCLE (US) 1995 dir. Karen
Arthur

Mia & Woody: Love and Betrayal
Groteke, K. and Rosen, M.

Love and Betrayal: The Mia Farrow Story
FOX CIRCLE (US) 1995 dir. Karen
Arthur

Miami Mayhem
Albert, M. H.

Tony Rome
FOX (US) 1967 dir. Gordon Douglas

Michael Kohlhaas
von Kleist, H.

Jack Bull, The
NEW CRIME (US) 1999 dir. John
Badham

Michael Strogoff
Verne, J.

Soldier and the Lady, The
RKO (US) 1937 dir. George Nicholls, Jr.
GB title: Michael Strogoff

Middle Ages, The
Gurney, A. R.

My Brother's Wife
ADAM (US) 1989 dir. Jack Bender

Midnight Lady and the Mourning Man
Anthony, D.

Midnight Man, The
UN (US) 1974 dir. Roland Kibbee

Midsummer Night's Dream, A
Shakespeare, W.

Children's Midsummer Night's Dream, A
SANDS (GB) 2001 dir. Christine Edzard

Midwich Cuckoos, The
Wyndham, J.

Village of the Damned
MGM (GB) 1960 dir. Wolf Rilla
UN (US) 1995 dir. John Carpenter

Midwife of Pont Clery, The
Sandstrom, F.

Jessica
UA (Fr/It) 1961 dir. Jean Negulesco

Milk Train Doesn't Stop Here Anymore, The
Williams, T.

Boom!
UI (GB) 1968 dir. Joseph Losey

Milk White Unicorn, The
Sandstrom, F.

White Unicorn, The
GFD (GB) 1947 dir. Bernard Knowles
US title: Bad Sister

Mills of God, The
Lothar, E.

Act of Murder, An
UN (US) 1948 dir. Michael Gordon

Millstone, The
Drabble, M.

Touch of Love, A
BL (GB) 1969 dir. Waris Hussein
US title: Thank You All Very Much

Mind of Mr J. G. Reeder, The
Wallace, E.

Mind of Mr. Reeder, The
RAYMOND (GB) 1936
dir. Jack Raymond

Ming
Zhaxidawa

Yixizhuoma
BEIJING (China) 2000 dir. Fei Xie

Minister to Millions
Gordon, A.

One Man's Way
UA (US) 1964 dir. Denis Sanders

Minute's Wait, A
McHugh, M. J.

Rising of the Moon, The
WAR (Ire) 1957 dir. John Ford

Mio, My Son
Lindgren, A.

Land of Faraway, The
NORD/GORKY (Swe/USSR/Nor) 1988
dir. Vladimir Grammatikov

Mirada del Hombre, La
del Moral, I.

Bwana
AURUM (Sp) 1996 dir. Imanol Uribe

Mirage, The
Selwyn, E.
Possessed
MGM (US) 1931 dir. Clarence Brown

Mirror Crack'd from Side to Side, The
Christie, A.
Mirror Crack'd, The
EMI (GB) 1980 dir. Guy Hamilton

Mirror in my House
O'Casey, S.
Young Cassidy
MGM (GB) 1964
dir. Jack Cardiff, John Ford

Mischief
Armstrong, C.
Don't Bother to Knock
FOX (US) 1952 dir. Roy Ward Baker

Mischief
Armstrong, C.
Sitter, The
FNM (US) 1991 dir. Rick Berger

Miss Bishop
Aldrich, Mrs B.
Cheers for Miss Bishop
PAR (US) 1941 dir. Tom Garnett

Miss Firecracker Contest
Henley, B.
Miss Firecracker
CORSAIR (US) 1989
dir. Thomas Schlamme

Miss 4th of July, Goodbye
Janus, C. G.
Goodbye, Miss 4th of July
FINNEGAN/PINCHUK (US) 1988
dir. George Miller

Miss Lonelyhearts
West, N.
Lonelyhearts
UA (US) 1958 dir. Vincent J. Donehue

Miss Lonelyhearts 4122
Watson, C.
Crooked Hearts, The
LORIMAR (US) 1972 dir. Jay Sandrich

Miss Mole
Young, E. H.
Hannah
BBC (GB) 1980 dir. Peter Jefferies

Miss Pinkerton
Rinehart, M. R.
Nurse's Secret, The
WAR (US) 1941 dir. Noel M. Smith

Miss Shumley Waves a Wand
Chase, J. H.
Rough Magic
RPC (GB/US) 1995 dir. Clare Peploe

Miss Simpson
Sant'Anna, S.
Bossa Nova
COL (Bra/US) 2000 dir. Bruno Barreto

Miss Smilla's Feeling for Snow
Hoeg, P.
Smilla's Sense of Snow
NORDISK (Den/Ger/Swe) 1997 dir.
Bille August

Mister Moses
Catto, M.
Mr. Moses
UA (GB) 1965 dir. Ronald Neame

Mister Roberts
Logan, J. and Heggen, T.
Ensign Pulver
WAR (US) 1964 dir. Joshua Logan

Misty of Chincoteague
Henry, M.
Misty
FOX (US) 1961 dir. James B. Clark

Mittelmann's Hardware
Small, G. R.
Finding the Way Home
MGM/UA TV (US) 1991
dir. Rob Holcomb

Mo: A Woman's View of Watergate
Dean, M.
Blind Ambition
TIME-LIFE (US) 1979
dir. George Schaefer

Mobbed Up
Neff, J.
Teamster Boss: The Jackie Presser Story
HBO (US) 1992 dir. Alastair Reid

Mockery of Justice: The True Story of the Sheppard Murder Case
Sheppard, S. R. and Cooper, C. L.
My Father's Shadow: The Sam Sheppard Story
JAFFE/BRAUNSTEIN (US) 1998 dir. Peter Levin

Moi, Ma Soeur
Barry, J.
Invitation au Voyage
TRIUMPH (Fr) 1983
dir. Peter Del Monte

Mom by Magic, A
Dillon, B.
Mom for Christmas, A
DISNEY (US) 1990 dir. George Miller

Mon Crime
Verneuil, L. and Berr, G.
True Confession
PAR (US) 1937 dir. Wesley Ruggles

Monday, Tuesday, Wednesday
Houston, R.
Killing Affair, A
HEMDALE (US) 1988
dir David Saperstein

Money by Wire
Paulton, E.
Get Off My Foot
WAR (GB) 1935 dir. William Beaudine

Money Men
Petievich, G.
Boiling Point
HEXAGON (US) 1993 dir. James B. Harris

Monkey Planet
Boulle, P.
Planet of the Apes
FOX (US) 1968 dir. Franklin Schaffner
FOX (US) 2001 dir. Tim Burton

Monkeys, The
Wilkinson, G. R.
Monkeys, Go Home!
DISNEY (US) 1967
dir. Andrew V. McLaglen

Monogamist, The
Gallagher, T.
Family Man, The
TIME-LIFE (US) 1979 dir. Glenn Jordan

Monsieur Beaucaire
Tarkington, B.
Monte Carlo
PAR (US) 1930 dir. Ernst Lubitsch

Monsieur L'Admiral va Bientôt Mourir
Bost, P.
Sunday in the Country, A
MGM/UA (Fr) 1984
dir. Bertrand Tavernier

Monsieur La Souris
Simenon, G.
Midnight Episode
COL (GB) 1950 dir. Gordon Parry

Monsieur Proust
Albaret, C.

Celeste
PEL (W. Ger) 1981 dir. Percy Adlon

Monsieur Rififi
Le Breton, A.

Rififi
PATHS (Fr) 1955 dir. Jules Dassin

Monsignore
Leger, J. A.

Monsignor
FOX (US) 1982 dir. Frank Perry

Moonwebs
Freed, J.

Ticket to Heaven
UA (US) 1981 dir. R. L. Thomas

Morals of Marcus Ordeyne, The
Locke, W. J.

Morals of Marcus, The
GB (GB) 1935 dir. Miles Mander

Morella; Black Cat, The; Facts of the Case of Dr. Valdemar, The
Poe, E. A.

Tales of Terror
WAR (US) 1962 dir. Roger Corman

Morpho Eugenia
Byatt, A. S.

Angels and Insects
GOLDWYN (GB) 1995 dir. Philip Haas

Morsures de l'aube, Les
Benacquista, T.

Love Bites
STUDIO CANAL+ (Fr) 2001 dir. Antoine de Caunes

Mort de Monsieur Golouja, La
Scepanovic, B.

Julian Po
CYPRESS (US) 1997 dir. Alan Wade

Morte en fuite, La
de Gouriadec, L.

Break the News
GFD (GB) 1938 dir. Rene Clair

Morte Intime, La
de Hennezel, M. Bottaro, C.

C'est La Vie
FRANCE 3 (Fr) 2001 dir. Jean-Pierre Ameris

Morte d'Arthur, La
Malory, Sir T.

Excalibur
ORION (US) 1981 dir. John Boorman

Morte d'Arthur, La
Malory, Sir T.

Knights of the Round Table
MGM (GB) 1954 dir. Richard Thorpe

Mortgage on Life
Baum, V.

Woman's Secret, A
RKO (US) 1949 dir. Nicholas Ray

Motel Tapes, The
McGrady, M.

Talking Walls
NEW WORLD (US) 1987 dir. Stephen Verona

Mother Carey's Chickens
Wiggin, K. D.

Summer Magic
DISNEY (US) 1963 dir. James Neilson

Mother Love
Wall, J. H.

Family Divided, A
CITADEL ENT (US) 1995 dir. Donald Wrye

Mother Variations
Ravel A.

Mothers and Daughters
PALAMA (Can) 1992 dir. Larry Kent

Mother, the Son and the Socialite, The
Havill, A.

Like Mother, Like Son: The Strange Story of Sante and Kenny Kimes
CBS TV (US) 2001 dir. Arthur Allan Seidelman

Mother's Day
MacDonald, P.

When Secrets Kill
SCRIPPS HOWARD (US) 1997 dir. Colin Bucksey

Motocyclette, La
de Mandiargues, A. P.

Girl on a Motorcycle
BL (GB/Fr) 1968 dir. Jack Cardiff
US title: Naked Under Leather

Mountain Lion, The
Murphy, R.

Run, Cougar, Run
DISNEY (US) 1972 dir. Michael Dmytryk

Moving of Lilla Barton, The
MacNicholas, J.

Moving of Sophia Myles, The
PEARSON TV (Can/US) 2000 dir. Michael Switzer

Moving Target, The
Macdonald, R.

Harper
WAR (US) 1966 dir. Jack Smight
GB title: Moving Target, The

Moviola
Kanin, G.

Moviola: The Scarlett O'Hara Wars
WAR TV (US) 1980 dir. John Erman

Moviola
Kanin, G.

Moviola: The Silent Lovers
WAR TV (US) 1980 dir. John Erman

Moviola
Kanin, G.

Moviola: This Year's Blonde
WAR TV (US) 1980 dir. John Erman

Mr and Mrs Cugat
Rorick, I. S.

Are Husbands Necessary?
PAR (US) 1942 dir. Norman Taurog

Mr and Mrs Haddock Abroad
Stewart, D. O.

Finn and Hattie
PAR (US) 1930 dir. Norman Taurog, Norman McLeod

Mr. Angel Comes Aboard
Booth, C. G.

Johnny Angel
RKO (US) 1945 dir. Edwin L. Marin

Mr. Bojangles—The Biogaphy of Bill Robinson
Haskins, J. and Mitgang, N. R.

Bojangles
MGM TV (US) 2001 dir. Joseph Sargent

Mr Bridge; Mrs. Bridge
Connell, E. S.

Mr. and Mrs. Bridge
MIRAMAX (US) 1990 dir. James Ivory

Mr. Bunting at War
Greenwood, R.

Salute John Citizen
BN (GB) 1942 dir. Maurice Elvey

Mr. Midshipman Easy
Marryat, F.

Midshipman Easy
ATP (GB) 1935 dir. Carol Reed
US title: Men of the Sea

Mr. Midshipman Hornblower; Lieutenant Hornblower
Forester, C. S.

Horatio Hornblower
A&E/PICTURE PALACE (GB) 1999 dir. Andrew Grieve
A&E/PICTURE PALACE (GB) 2001 dir. Andrew Grieve

Mr Prohack
Bennett, A.

Dear Mr Prohack
GFD (GB) 1949 dir. Thornton Freeland

Mrs Christopher
Myers, E.

Blackmailed
GFD (US) 1950 dir. Marc Allegret

Mrs Frisby and the Rats of N.I.M.H.
O'Brien, R. C.

Secret of N.I.M.H., The
MGM/UA (US) 1982 dir. Don Bluth

Mrs. McGinty's Dead
Christie, A.

Murder Most Foul
MGM (GB) 1964 dir. George Pollock

Mrs. Maitland's Affair
Lynn, M.

Other Man, The
UN TV (US) 1970 dir. Richard Colla

Mrs. Ross
Nicolson, R.

Whisperers, The
UA (GB) 1966 dir. Bryan Forbes

Mrs. White
Tracy, M.

White of the Eye
CANNON (GB) 1987
dir. Donald Cammell

M'sieur; Lumières du Frigo, Les
Gagnol, A.

HS (hors service)
PARADIS (Bel/Fr) 2001 dir. Jean-Paul Lilienfeld

Mud on the Streets
Huie, W. B.

Wild River
FOX (US) 1960 dir. Elia Kazan

Muggable Mary
Glatzle, M. and Fiore, E.

Muggable Mary: Street Cop
CBS ENT (US) 1982 dir. Sander Stern

Mule for the Marquesa, A
O'Rourke, F.

Professionals, The
COL (US) 1966 dir. Richard Brooks

Mummy Market, The
Brelis, N.

Trading Mom
FOX (US) 1994 dir. Tia Brelis

Murder at 75 Birch Street
Pienciak, R. T.

Murder at 75 Birch
NICKI (US) 1999 dir. Michael Scott

Murder at Shinglestrand
Capon, P.

Hidden Homicide
RANK (US) 1959 dir. Tony Yound

Murder at the Mendel
Bowen, G.

Love and Murder
SHAFTESBURY (Can) 2000 dir. George Bloomfield

Murder for the Million
Chapman, R.

Murder Reported
COL (GB) 1957 dir. Charles Saunders

Murder Gang
Dean, B. and Munro, G.

Sensation
BIP (GB) 1936
dir. Brian Desmond Hurst

Murder in Amityville
Holzer, H.

Amityville II: The Possession
ORION (US) 1982
dir. Damiano Damiani

Murder in Little Rock
Meins, J.

Seduction in Travis County, A
NEW WORLD (US) 1991
dir. George Kaczender

Murder Mistaken
Green, J.

Cast a Dark Shadow
EROS (GB) 1955 dir. Lewis Gilbert

Murder of a Wanton
Chambers, W.

Sinner Take All
MGM (US) 1937 dir. Errol Taggart

Murder of the Circus Queen, The
Abbot, A.

Circus Queen Murder
COL (US) 1933 dir. Roy William Neill

Murder on the Iditarod Trail
Henry, S.

Cold Heart of a Killer, The
HAMDON (US) 1996 dir. Paul
Schneider

Murder on the 31st Floor
Wahloo, P.

Kamikaze '89
TELECUL (Ger) 1983 dir. Wolf Gremm

Murder on the Wild Side
Jacks, J.

Black Eye
WAR (US) 1974 dir. Jack Arnold

Murder Under Two Flags
Nelson, A.

Show of Force, A
PAR (US) 1990 dir. Bruno Barreto

Murders in the Rue Morgue
Poe, E. A.

Phantom of the Rue Morgue
WAR (US) 1954 dir. Roy del Ruth

Murphy's Boy
Hayden, T.

Trapped in Silence
READER'S DIG (US) 1986
dir. Michael Tuchner

Muscle Beach
Wallach, I.

Don't Make Waves
MGM (US) 1967 dir. Alexander
Mackendrick

Mute Witness
Pike, R. L.

Bullitt
WAR (US) 1968 dir. Peter Yates

Mutiny
Tilsley, F.

H.M.S. Defiant
COL (GB) 1962 dir. Lewis Gilbert
US title: Damn the Defiant

My Brother Death
Sulzberger, C.

Playground, The
JERAND (US) 1965 dir. Richard Hilliard

My Brother Paul
Dreiser, T.

My Gal Sal
FOX (US) 1942 dir. Irving Cummings

My Daniel
Conrad, P.

Dinosaur Hunter, The
IMP (Can) 2000 dir. Rick Stevenson

My Early Life
Churchill, Sir W. S.

Young Winston
COL-WAR (GB) 1972
dir. Richard Attenborough

My Husband, Rock Hudson
Gates, P.

Rock Hudson
KON-SAN (US) 1990 dir. John Nicolella

My Laugh Comes Last
Chase, J. H.

Set Up, The
MGM/SHOWTIME (US) 1995 dir.
Strathford Hamilton

My Life
Duncan, I.

Isadora
UI (GB) 1969 dir. Karel Reisz
US title: Loves of Isadora, The

My Life and Hard Times
Thurber, J.

Rise and Shine
FOX (US) 1941 dir. Allan Dwan

My Little Brother is Coming Tomorrow
Behrenberg, B.

Grambling's White Tiger
INTERPLAN (US) 1981
dir. Georg Stanford Brown

My Luke and I
Gehrig, E. and Durso, J.

Love Affair, A: The Eleanor and Lou Gehrig Story
FRIES (US) 1978 dir. Fielder Cook

My Name is Anna: The Autobiography of Patty Duke
Duke, P. and Turan, K.

Call me Anna
FINNEGAN (US) 1990
dir. Gilbert Cates

My Old Man
Hemingway, E.

Under My Skin
FOX (US) 1950 dir. Jean Negulesco

My Posse Don't Do Homework
Johnson, L.

Dangerous Minds
HOLLYWOOD (US) 1995 dir. John N. Smith

My Sister in This House
Kesselman, W.

Sister My Sister
BRIT SCREEN (GB/US) 1994 dir.
Nancy Meckler

My Ten Years as a Counter-Spy
Morros, B.

Man on a String
COL (US) 1960 dir. André de Toth
GB title: Confessions of a Counterspy

My Thirty Years Backstairs at the White House
Parks, L. R.

Backstairs at the White House
FRIENDLY (US) 1979
dir. Michael O'Herlihy

My 30 Years in Hoover's FBI
Sullivan, W. G. and Brown, W. S.

J. Edgar Hoover
RLC (US) 1987 dir. Robert Collins

My Three Angels
Husson, A.

We're No Angels
PAR (US) 1955 dir. Michael Curtiz
PAR (US) 1989 dir. Neil Jordan

My True Love
Teilhet, D. L.

No Room for the Groom
UI (US) 1952 dir. Douglas Sirk

My Years with the KKK
Rowe, Jr., G. T.

Undercover with the KKK
COL TV (US) 1979 dir. Barry Shear

Nabe-No-Kake
Murata, K.

Rhapsody in August
ORION (Jap) 1991 dir. Akira Kurosawa

Nanawatai
Mastrosimone, W.

Beast, The
COL (US) 1988 dir. Kevin Reynolds

Nanny, The
Pirandello, L.

Balia, La
RAI (It) 1999 dir. Marco Bellocchio

Nanny, The
Greenburg, D.

Guardian, The
UN (US) 1990 dir. William Friedkin

Napoleon of Broadway
Millholland, C. B.

Twentieth Century
COL (US) 1934 dir. Howard Hawks

Narrow Margin, The
Wood, D. and Dempster, D.

Battle of Britain
UA (GB) 1969 dir. Guy Hamilton

Natasha's Story
Nicholson, M.

Welcome to Sarajevo
CHANNEL 4 FILMS (GB/US) 1997 dir.
Michael Winterbottom

Ne crie pas
Montserrat, R. and Montserrat, R.

Sauve-Moi
STUDIO CANAL+ (Fr) 2000 dir.
Christian Vincent

Necromancers, The
Benson, R.

Spellbound
PYRAMID (GB) 1940 dir. John Harlow
US title: Spell of Amy Nugent, The

Nelson Touch, The
Grant, N.

Man of Affairs
GAU (GB) 1937 dir. Herbert Mason
US title: His Lordship

Nepomuk of the River
Pilkington, R.

Golden Head, The
CINERAMA (US/Hun) 1965
dir. Richard Thorpe

Nest in a Falling Tree
Cowley, J.

Night Digger, The
MGM (GB) 1971 dir. Alistair Reid

Neutralité Malveillante
Gattegno, J.-P.

Passage a L'acte
ARENA (Fr) 1996 dir. Francis Girod

Never Come Back
Mair, J.

Tiger by the Tail
EROS (GB) 1955 dir. John Gilling

Never Pass This Way Again
LePere, G.
Dark Holiday
ORION TV (US) 1989 dir. Lou Antonio

Neverending Story, The
Ende, M.
Neverending Story II, The: The Next Chapter
WAR (Ger) 1989 dir. George Miller

New Guinea Gold
Burtis, T.
Crosswinds
PAR (US) 1951 dir. Lewis R. Foster

New York Undercover Cop
Ueno, J.
New York Cop
STP (US) 1995 dir. Toru Murakawa

Newhaven-Dieppe
Simenon, G.
Temptation Harbour
AB (GB) 1947 dir. Lance Comfort

Newton Boys, The: Portrait of an Outlaw Gang
Stanush, C.
Newton Boys, The
FOX (US) 1998 dir. Richard Linklater

Next Door; Euphio Question, The; All the King's Men
Vonnegut, K.
Monkey House
ATLANTIS (US) 1991 dir. Paul Shapiro, Gilbert Shilton, Allan King

Next of Kin
Coleman, L.
Hot Spell
PAR (US) 1958 dir. Daniel Mann

Next-to-Last Train Ride, The
Dennis, C.
Finders Keepers
RANK (US) 1984 dir. Richard Lester

Ni el Tiro del Final
Feinmann, J. P.
Love Walked In
TRIUMPH (Arg/US) 1997 dir. Juan Jose Campanella

Nice Guys Sleep Alone: Dating in the Difficult Eighties
Feirstein, B.
Nice Guys Sleep Alone
LUNACY (US) 1999 dir. Stu Pollard

Nice Italian Girl, A
Christman, E.
Black Market Baby
BRUT (US) 1977 dir. Robert Day
GB title: Don't Steal My Baby

Nicholas Nickleby
Dickens, C.
Life and Adventures of Nicholas Nickleby, The
PRIMETIME (GB) 1984
dir. Jim Goddard
COMPANY TV (GB) 2001 dir. Stephen Whittaker

Night Before Christmas, The
Perelman, L. and Perelman, S. J.
Larceny Inc.
WAR (US) 1942 dir. Lloyd Bacon

Night Before Wenceslas, The
Davidson, L.
Hot Enough for June
RANK (GB) 1963 dir. Ralph Thomas

Night Bus
Adams, S. H.
It Happened One Night
COL (US) 1934 dir. Frank Capra

Night Cry
Stuart, W. L.

Where the Sidewalk Ends
FOX (US) 1960 dir. Otto Preminger

Night Darkens the Streets
La Bern, A. J.

Good-Time Girl
GFD (GB) 1948 dir. David MacDonald

Night of Clear Choice
Disney, D. M.

Yesterday's Child
PAR TV (US) 1977 dir. Corey Allen, Bob Rosenbaum

Night of Reunion
Allegretto, M.

Terror in the Shadows
HEARST (US) 1995 dir. William A. Graham

Night of the Tiger, The
Dewlen, A.

Ride Beyond Vengeance
COL (US) 1966 dir. Bernard McEveety

Night Song
Williams, J.

Sweet Love, Bitter
FILM 2 (US) 1967 dir. Herbert Danska

Night Watch, The
Walsh, T.

Pushover
COL (US) 1954 dir. Richard Quine

Nightmare
Dorner, M.

Don't Touch My Daughter
PATCHETT-KAUFMAN (US) 1991 dir. John Pasquin

Nightmare
Blaisdell, A.

Fanatic
COL (GB) 1965 dir. Silvio Narizzano
US title: Die! Die! My Darling

Nightmare in Manhattan
Walsh, T.

Union Station
PAR (US) 1950 dir. Rudolph Mate

Nightmare of Ecstasy
Grey, R.

Ed Wood
TOUCHSTONE (US) 1994 dir. Tim Burton

Nikutai no Gakko
Michima, Y.

School of Flesh, The
ORSANS (Fr) 1998 dir. Benoit Jacquot

Nine Days of Father Serra
Ziegler, I. G.

Seven Cities of Gold
FOX (US) 1955 dir. Robert D. Webb

No Beast so Fierce
Bunker, E.

Straight Time
WAR (US) 1978 dir. Ulu Grosbard

No Business Being a Cop
O'Donnell, L.

Prime Target
MGM/UA (US) 1989 dir. Robert Collins

No Difference to Me
Hambledon, P.

No Place for Jennifer
ABP (GB) 1949 dir. Henry Cass

No Exit
Goodchild, G. and Witty, F.

No Escape
PATHE (GB) 1936 dir. Norman Lee

No Medals
McCracken, E.

Weaker Sex, The
TC (GB) 1948 dir. Roy Baker

No More Gas
Nordhoff, C. B. and Hall, J. N.
Tuttles of Tahiti, The
RKO (US) 1942 dir. Charles Vidor

No Names . . . No Pack Drills
Herbert, B.
Rebel
MIRACLE (Aust) 1986
dir. Michael Jenkins

No Nightingales
Brahms, C. and Simon, S. J.
Ghosts of Berkeley Square, The
BN (GB) 1947 dir. Vernon Sewell

No Orchids for Miss Blandish
Chase, J. H.
Grissom Gang, The
CINERAMA (US) 1971
dir. Robert Aldrich

No Place to Hide
Allbeury, T.
Hostage
SKOURAS (US) 1992 dir. Robert Young

Noblesse Oblige
Horniman, R.
Kind Hearts and Coronets
EAL (GB) 1949 dir. Robert Hamer

Nobody Loves a Drunken Indian
Huffaker, C.
Flap
WAR (US) 1970 dir. Carol Reed
GB title: Last Warrior, The

Nobody Makes Me Cry
List, S.
Between Friends
HBO (US) 1983 dir. Lou Antonio

Noia, La
Moravia, A.
Ennui, L'
GEMINI (Fr) 1998 dir. Cedric Kahn

Nomads of the North
Curwood, J. O.
Nikki, Wild Dog of the North
DISNEY (US) 1961 dir. Jack Couffer

None so Blind
Wilson, M.
Woman on the Beach, The
RKO (US) 1947 dir. Jean Renoir

North of Bushman's Rock
Harding, G.
Ride the High Wind
BUTCHER (SA) 1966
dir. David Millin

North of 36
Hough, E.
Conquering Horde
PAR (US) 1931 dir. Edward Sloman

Northwest Passage
Roberts, K.
Mission of Danger
MGM (US) 1959 dir. George Waggner,
Jacques Tourneur

Norwich Victims, The
Beeding, F.
Dead Men Tell No Tales
ALL (GB) 1938 dir. David MacDonald

Nose on my Face, The
Payne, L.
Girl in the Headlines, The
BL (GB) 1963 dir. Michael Truman
US title: Model Murder Case, The

Not so Long Ago
Richman, A.
Let's Do It Again
COL (US) 1953 dir. Alexander Hall

Not Too Narrow, Not Too Deep
Sale, R.
Strange Cargo
MGM (US) 1940
dir. Joseph L. Mankiewicz

Notebooks of Major Thompson, The
Daninos, P.

Diary of Major Thompson, The
GALA (Fr) 1955 dir. Preston Sturges
US title: French They are a Funny Race, The

Nothing to Lose
Minney, R. J.

Time Gentlemen, Please!
ABP (GB) 1952 dir. Lewis Gilbert

Notti di Arancia Meccanica, Le
Sacchettoni, D.

Smell of the Night, The
SORPASSO (It) 1998 dir. Claudio Caligari

Now Barrabas
Home, W. D.

Now Barrabas was a Robber
WAR (GB) 1949 dir. Gordon Parry

Nuit et le Moment, La
de Jolyot Crebillon, C.-P.

Night and the Moment, The
CECCHI (It/Fr) 1994 dir. Anna Maria Tato

Nuit Sacrée, La; Enfant Des Sables, L'
Ben Jelloun, T.

Sacred Night, The
FRANCE 3 (Fr) 1993 dir. Nicolas Klotz

Nuits Fauves, Les
Collard, C.

Savage Nights
STUDIO CANAL+ (Fr/It) 1992 dir. Cyril Collard

Nun: A Memoir
Wong, Dr. M. G.

Shattered Vows
RIVER CITY (US) 1984 dir. Jack Bender

Nuremberg: Infamy on Trial
Persico, J. E.

Nuremberg
ALLIANCE (US/Can) 2000 dir. Yves Simoneau

Nurse is a Neighbour
Jones, J.

Nurse on Wheels
WAR (GB) 1963 dir. Gerald Thomas

Nutcracker and the Mouseking, The
Hoffman, E. T. A.

Nutcracker Prince, The
WAR (US) 1990 dir. Paul Schibli

Nutcracker: Money, Madness, Murder: A Family Album
Alexander, S.

Nutcracker: Money, Madness and Murder
WAR TV (US) 1987
dir. Paul Bogart

Nutmeg Tree, The
Sharp, M.

Julia Misbehaves
MGM (US) 1948 dir. Jack Conway

Nu
Allen, J.

Tumult
ATHENA (Den) 1970
dir. Hans Abramson

O Que I Isso, Companheiro?
Gabeira, F.
Four Days in September
COL (US/Bra) 1997 dir. Bruno Barreto

Odour of Violets
Kendrick, B. H.
Eyes in the Night
MGM (US) 1942 dir. Fred Zinnemann

Odyssey, The
Homer
Ulysses
ARCHWAY (It) 1954
dir. Mario Camerini

Oedipus Rex
Sophocles
Edipo Alcalde
IMCINE (Mex/Sp) 1996 dir. Jorge Ali
Triana

Oedipus the King
Sophocles
Oedipus Rex
HORIZON (It) 1947
dir. Pier Paolo Pasolini

Off the Record
Hay, I. and King-Hall, S.
Carry on, Admiral
REN (GB) 1957 dir. Val Guest

Off-Islanders, The
Benchley, N.
Russians are Coming, The Russians are Coming, The
UA (US) 1966 dir. Norman Jewison

Oh!
Robison, M.
Twister
VESTRON (US) 1990
dir. Michael Almereyda

Oil for the Lamps of China
Hobart, A. T.
Law of the Tropics
WAR (US) 1941 dir. Ray Enright

Old Acquaintance
van Druten, J.
Rich and Famous
MGM (US) 1981 dir. George Cukor

Old Curiosity Shop, The
Dickens, C.
Mister Quilp
EMI (GB) 1975 dir. Elliot Scott

Old Dick, The
Morse, L. A.
Jake Spanner, Private Eye
FENADY (US) 1989 dir. Lee H. Katzin

Old Heidelburg
Meyer-Foerster, W.
Student Prince, The
MGM (US) 1954 dir. Richard Thorpe

Old Jest, The
Johnston, J.
Dawning, The
TVS (GB) 1988 dir. Robert Knights

Old Lady Shows Her Medals, The

Barrie, Sir J. M.

Seven Days' Leave
PAR (US) 1930 dir. Richard Wallace
GB title: Medals

Old Lady 31

Crothers, R.

Captain is a Lady, The
MGM (US) 1940 dir. Robert Sinclair

Old Soak, The

Marquis, D.

Good Old Soak
MGM (US) 1937 dir. J. Walter Ruben

Old Wives' Tale, The

Bennett, A.

Sophia and Constance
BBC (GB) 1988 dir. Rodney Allison,
Hugh David

Oldest Confession, The

Condon, R.

Happy Thieves, The
UA (US) 1962 dir. George Marshall

Olimpia

Cole, B.

Bobo, The
WAR (US) 1978 dir. Robert Parrish

Oliver Twist

Dickens, C.

Oliver!
COL (GB) 1968 dir. Carol Reed

Olympia

Molnar, F.

Breath of Scandal, A.
PAR (US) 1960 dir. Michael Curtiz,
Mario Russo

Olympia

Molnar, F.

His Glorious Night
MGM (US) 1929 dir. Lionel Barrymore
GB title: Breath of Scandal

On Monday Next

King, P.

Curtain Up
GFD (GB) 1952 dir. Ralph Smart

On The Spot

Wallace, E.

Dangerous to Know
PAR (US) 1938 dir. Robert Florey

On the Trail: My Reminiscences as a Cowboy

Harris, F.

Cowboy
COL (US) 1957 dir. Delmer Daves

On the Trail of the Assassins: My Investigation and Prosecution of the Murder of President Kennedy

Garrison, J.

JFK
WAR (US) 1991 dir. Oliver Stone

On This Star

Sorensen, V.

Loss of Innocence, A
KONIGSBERG (US) 1996 dir. Graeme
Clifford

On to Oregon

Morrow, H.

Seven Alone
HEMDALE (US) 1974 dir. Earl Bellamy

On Trial

London, A. and London, L.

L'Aveu
CORONA (Fr) 1970 dir. Costa-Gavras

Once and Future King, The
White, T. H.

Camelot
WAR (US) 1967 dir. Joshua Logan

Once and Future King, The
White, T. H.

Sword in the Stone, The
DISNEY (US) 1963
dir. Wolfgang Reitherman

Once Off Guard
Wallis, J. H.

Woman in the Window, The
RKO (US) 1944 dir. Fritz Lang

One Child
Hayden T.

Untamed Love
HEARST (US) 1994 dir. Paul Aaron

One Gallant Rush
Burehard, P.

Glory
TRISTAR (US) 1989 dir. Edward Zwick

One Hell of a Woman
Thompson, J.

Serie Noire
GAU (Fr) 1979 dir. Alain Corneau

One Hundred Children
Kuchler-Silberman, L.

Lena: My 100 Children
GREENWALD (US) 1987 dir. Ed Sherin

One Man's Secret
Weiman, R.

Possessed
WAR (US) 1947 dir. Curtis Bernhardt

One Pair of Feet
Dickens, M.

Lamp Still Burns, The
TC (GB) 1943 dir. Maurice Elvey

One Step From Murder
Meynell, L.

Price of Silence, The
GN (GB) 1959 dir. Montgomery Tully

One Sunday Afternoon
Hagan, J.

Strawberry Blonde, The
WAR (US) 1941 dir. Raoul Walsh

One Tough Cop: The Bo Dietl Story
Dietl, B. and Gross, K.

One Tough Cop
PATRIOT (US) 1998 dir. Bruno Barreto

One Way Out
Flavin, M.

Convicted
COL (US) 1950 dir. Henry Levin

One Woman
Thayer, T.

Fame is the Name of the Game
UN TV (US) 1966 dir. Stuart Rosenberg

Only a Dream
Schmidt, L.

One Hour With You
PAR (US) 1932 dir. George Cukor, Ernst Lubitsch

Only Couples Need Apply
Disney, D. M.

Betrayal
METRO (US) 1974 dir. Gordon Hessler

Only in America: The Life and Crimes of Don King
Newfield, J.

Don King: Only in America
HBO (US) dir. John Herzfeld

Opera Hat
Kelland, C. B.

Mr. Deeds Goes to Town
COL (US) 1936 dir. Frank Capra

Operation Cicero
Moyzisch, L. C.

Five Fingers
FOX (US) 1952
dir. Joseph L. Mankiewicz

Operation Gadgetman
Blackman, M.

Gadgetman
HALLMARK (US/GB) dir. Jim
Goddard

Operation Overflight
Powers, F. G. and Gentry, C.

*Francis Gary Powers: The True Story of the
U-2 Spy Incident*
FRIES (US) 1976 dir. Delbert Mann

Operation Terror
Gordon, M. and Gordon, G.

Experiment in Terror
COL (US) 1962 dir. Blake Edwards
GB title: The Grip of Fear

Operator, The
Amateau, R. and Robinson, B.

Where Does it Hurt?
HEMDALE (US) 1971 dir. Rod Amateau

Orchard Children, The
Maddox, R.

Who'll Save Our Children?
TIME-LIFE (US) 1978
dir. George Schaefer

Orchard Walls, The
Delderfield, R. F.

Now and Forever
ABP (GB) 1955 dir. Mario Zampi

Ordeal of Major Grigsby, The
Sherlock, J.

Last Grenade, The
CINERAMA (GB) 1969
dir. Gordon Flemyng

Order of Death, The
Fleetwood, H.

Corrupt
NEW LINE (It) 1983 dir. Robert Faenza

Orders is Orders
Hay, I. and Armstrong, A.

Orders are Orders
BL (GB) 1954 dir. David Paltenghi

Oresteia Trilogy, The
Aeschylus

Serpent Son, The
BBC (GB) 1979 dir. Bill Hays

Oro della Fantasia, L'
Bonacci, A.

Kiss Me Stupid
UA (US) 1964 dir. Billy Wilder

Orpheus Descending
Williams, T.

Fugitive Kind, The
UA (US) 1960 dir. Sidney Lunnet

Othello
Shakespeare, W.

O
LIONS GATE (US) 2001 dir. Tim Blake
Nelson

Othello
Shakespeare, W.

Othello, the Black Commando
EUROCINE (Sp/Fr) 1982 dir. Max H.
Boulois

Other Anna, The
Esstman, Barbara

Secrets
RHI (US) 1995 dir. Jud Taylor

Other One, The
Turney, C.

Back from the Dead
FOX (US) 1957
dir. Charles Marquis Warren

Other Side of Dark, The
Nixon, J. L.

Awake to Danger
NBC (US) 1995 dir. Michael Tuchner

Our Guys
Lefkowitz, B.

Our Guys: Outrage in Glen Rigde
GREENWALD (US) 1999 dir. Guy
Ferland

Our Virgin Island
White, R.

Virgin Island
BL (GB) 1958 dir. Pat Jackson

Out of Order
Cooney, R.

Miniszter Felrelep, A
INTERCOM (Hun) 1997 dir. Andras
Kern, Robert Koltai

Out of the Frying Pan
Swann, F.

Young and Willing
UA (US) 1942 dir. Edward H. Griffith

Outlaw: The True Story of Claude Dallas
Long, J.

Manhunt for Claude Dallas
LONDON (US) 1986 dir. Jerry London

Outward Bound
Vane, S.

Between Two Worlds
WAR (US) 1944 dir. Edward A. Blatt

Outwitting the Gestapo
Aubrac, L.

Lucie Aubrac
CNC (Fr) 1997 dir. Claude Berri

Over the River
Galsworthy, J.

One More River
UN (US) 1934 dir. James Whale
GB title: Over the River

P

Pack, The
Wilson, J. R.

Behind the Mask
BL (GB) 1958 dir. Brian Desmond Hurst

Page After Page
Page, T.

Frankie's House
ANGLIA FILMS (GB/Aust) 1992 dir. Peter Fisk

Paid in Full
Cronin, M.

Johnny on the Spot
FANCEY (GB) 1954 dir. Maclean Rogers

Painted Veil, The
Maugham, W. S.

Seventh Sin, The
MGM (US) 1957 dir. Ronald Neame

Painting Churches
Howe, T.

Portrait, The
GREENWALD (US) 1993 dir. Arthur Penn

Palm for Mrs. Pollifax, A
Gilman, D.

Unexpected Mrs. Pollifax, The
WORLD 2000 (US) 1999 dir. Anthony Shaw

Pamela
Richardson, S.

Mistress Pamela
MGM-EMI (GB) 1973 dir. Jim O'Connolly

Panna Nikt
Tryzna, T.

Miss Nobody
ZESPOL (Pol) 1997 dir. Andrzej Wajda

Panther in the Sky
Thom, J. A.

Tecumseh: The Last Warrior
AM ZOETROPE (US) 1995 dir. Larry Elikann

Panther's Moon
Canning, V.

Spy Hunt
UN (US) 1950 dir. George Sherman
GB title: Panther's Moon

Papa's Angels: A Christmas Story
Paxton, C. W. and Carden. G.

Papa's Angels
CBS TV (US) 2000 dir. Dwight H. Little

Paradigm Red
King, H.

Red Alert
PAR (US) 1977 dir. William Hale

Paragon, The
Pertwee, R. and Pertwee, M.

Silent Dust
ABP (GB) 1947 dir. Lance Comfort

Parfumerie
Laszlo, N.

Shop Around the Corner, The
MGM (US) 1940 dir. Ernst Lubitsch

Parfumerie
Laszlo, N.
You've Got Mail
WAR (US) 1998 dir. Nora Ephron

Paso Por Aqui
Rhodes, E. M.
Four Faces West
UA (US) 1948 dir. Alfred E. Green

Passing of Evil, The
McShane, M.
Grasshopper, The
NGL (US) 1969 dir. Jerry Paris

Passionate Witch, The
Smith, T.
I Married a Witch
UA (US) 1942 dir. René Clair

Passport to Oblivion
Leasor, J.
Where the Spies Are
MGM (GB) 1965 dir. Val Guest

Past Continuous
Shabtai, Y.
Devarim
AGAV (Israel) 1995 dir. Amos Gitai

Past Forgetting
Morgan, K. S.
Ike
ABC (US) 1979 dir. Melville Shavelson,
Boris Sagal

Past is Myself, The
Bielenberg, C.
Christabel
BBC (GB) 1988 dir. Adrian Shergold

Pat & Roald
Farrell, B.
Patricia Neal Story, The
SCHILLER (US) 1981
dir. Antony Harvey, Anthony Page

Pathfinder, The
Cooper, J. F.
Hawkeye, The Pathfinder
BBC (GB) 1973 dir. David Maloney

Patrol
MacDonald, P.
Lost Patrol
RKO (US) 1934 dir. John Ford

Pattern of Islands
Grimble, Sir A.
Pacific Destiny
BL (GB) 1956 dir. Wolf Rilla

Patton: Ordeal & Triumph
Farago, L.
Patton
FOX (US) 1970 dir. Franklin Schaffner
GB title: Patton: Lust for Glory

Paxton Quigley's had the Course
Yafa, S.
Three in the Attic
WAR (US) 1968 dir. Richard Wilson

Peabody's Mermaid
Jones, G. P. and Jones, C. B.
Mr. Peabody and the Mermaid
UN (US) 1948 dir. Irving Pichel

Peacock's Feather
Hellman, G. S.
Night in Paradise, A
UN (US) 1946 dir. Arthur Lubin

Peasant Women, The
Chekhov, A.
Lover's Prayer
OVERSEAS (US/GB) 2001 dir. Reverge
Anselmo

Penal Colony, The
Herley, R.
No Escape
COL (US) 1994 dir. Martin Campbell

Penny Arcade
Baumer, M.
Sinner's Holiday
WAR (US) 1930 dir. John G. Adolfi

Penrod
Tarkington, B.
By the Light of the Silvery Moon
WAR (US) 1953 dir. David Butler

Penrod
Tarkington, B.
On Moonlight Bay
WAR (US) 1951 dir. Roy del Ruth

Pensamientos
Pinto, M.
E1
NACIONAL (Mex) 1952
dir. Luis Bunuel

Pentimento
Hellman, L.
Julia
FOX (US) 1977 dir. Fred Zinnemann

Peoples
Downs, R. C. S.
Billy: Portrait of a Street Kid
CARLINER (US) 1977
dir. Steven Gethers

Pépé le Moko
d'Ashelbe, R.
Algiers
WANGER (US) 1938 dir. John Cromwell

Percy and Rose
George, R.
Passion
BEYOND (Aust) 1999 dir. Peter Duncan

Percy Grainger
Bird, J.
Passion
BEYOND (Aust) 1999 dir. Peter Duncan

Perfect Round, The
Robinson, H. M.
Americana
CROWN (US) 1983 dir. David
Carradine

Perfect Storm, The: A True Story of Men Against the Sea
Junger, S.
Perfect Storm, The
WAR (US) 1999 dir. Wolfgang Petersen

Perilous Passage, The
Nicolaysen, B.
Passage, The
HEMDALE (GB) 1978
dir. J. Lee Thompson

Persistent Warrior, The
Arundel, E.
Green Fingers
BN (GB) 1946 dir. John Harlow

Personal Appearance
Riley, L.
Go West Young Man
PAR (US) 1936 dir. Henry Hathaway

Personal History
Sheean, V.
Foreign Correspondent
UA (US) 1940 dir. Alfred Hitchcock

Persons in Hiding
Hoover, J. E.
Illegal Traffic
PAR (US) 1938 dir. Louis King

Persons in Hiding
Hoover, J. E.
Queen of the Mob
PAR (US) 1940 dir. James Hogan

Peter Pettinger
Riley, W.
Agitator, The
BN (GB) 1944 dir. John Harlow

Petit Sauvage, Le
Jardin, A.
Prof, Le
STUDIO CANAL+ (Fr) 2000 dir.
Alexandre Jardin

Petrified Forest, The
Sherwood, R. E.
Escape in the Desert
WAR (US) 1945 dir. Edward A. Blatt

Phantom Crown, The
Harding, B.
Juarez
WAR (US) 1939 dir. William Dieterle

Phantom Filly, The
Chamberlain, G. A.
Home in Indiana
TCF (US) 1944 dir. Henry Hathaway

Philadelphia Story, The
Barry, P.
High Society
MGM (US) 1956 dir. Charles Walters

Philadelphian, The
Powell, R.
Young Philadelphians, The
WAR (US) 1959 dir. Vincent Sherman
GB title: City Jungle, The

Philly
Greenburg, D.
Private Lessons
J. FARLEY (US) 1981 dir. Alan Myerson

Phoenix, The
Bachmann, L.
Ten Seconds to Hell
UA (US) 1959 dir. Robert Aldrich

Photo Finish
Mason, H.
Follow that Horse!
WAR (GB) 1959 dir. Alan Bromly

Piaf
Berteaut, S.
Piaf—The Early Years
FOX (Fr) 1982 dir. Guy Casaril

Picasso: Creator and Destroyer
Stassinopoulos, A. H.
Surviving Picasso
WAR (US) 1996 dir. James Ivory

Pick Up Girl
Shelley, E.
Too Young to Go
RANK (GB) 1959 dir. Muriel Box

Pick up Sticks
Phillips, M.
Cherry Picker, The
FOX-RANK (GB) 1974 dir. Peter Curran

Picnic by the Roadside
Strugatsky, B. and Strugatsky, A.
Stalker
MOSFILM (USSR) 1979 dir. Andrei
Tarkovsky

Picture of Dorian Gray, The
Wilde, O.
Dorian Gray
AIP (It/Ger) 1970
dir. Massimo Dallamano

Picture of Dorian Gray, The
Wilde, O.
Sins of Dorian Gray, The
RANKIN-BASS (US) 1983
dir. Tony Maylam

Pied Piper, The
Shute, N.
Crossing to Freedom
TELECOM/GRANADA (GB/US) 1990
dir. Norman Stone

Piège pour un Homme Seul
Thomas, R.
Honeymoon with a Stranger
TCF (US) 1969 dir. John Peyser

Piège pour un homme seul
Thomas, R.
Vanishing Act
LEVINSON-LINK (US) 1986
dir. David Greene

Pierre, or, The Ambiguities
Melville, H.
Pola X
STUDIO CANAL+ (Fr/Ger) 1999 dir.
Leos Carax

Pigboats
Ellsberg, E.
Hell Below
MGM (US) 1933 dir. Jack Conway

Pilgrimage
Henderson, Z.
People, The
METRO (US) 1972 dir. John Korty

Pilgrim's Progress, The
Banyan, J.
Dangerous Journey
CHANNEL 4 (GB) 1985

Pillar to Post
Kohn, R. S.
Pillow to Post
WAR (US) 1945 dir. Vincent Sherman

Pillars of Midnight, The
Trevor, E.
80,000 Suspects
RANK (GB) 1963 dir. Val Guest

Pink Room, The
Ackland, R.
Absolute Hell
BBC (GB) 1991 dir. Anthony Page

Pioneer Go Home
Powell, R.
Follow that Dream
UA (US) 1962 dir. Gordon Douglas

Pirates of Penzance, The
Sullivan, Sir A. and Gilbert, Sir W.
Pirate Movie, The
FOX (Aust) 1982 dir. Ken Annakin

Pity My Simplicity
Massie, C.
Love Letters
PAR (US) 1945 dir. William Dieterle

Place to Hide, A
Gillham, B.
Break Out
CFTF (GB) 1983 dir. Frank Godwin
US title: Breakout

Plata Quemada
Piglia, R.
Burnt Money
MANDARIN (Arg/Fr) 2000 dir.
Marcelo Pineyro

Platonov
Chekhov, A.
Unfinished Piece for Player Piano, An
MOSFILM (USSR) 1977
dir. Nikita Mikhalkov

Playback
Daeninckx, D.
Heroines
NTV-PROFIT (Fr) 1997 dir. Gerard
Krawczyk

Playboy and the Yellow Lady, The
Carney, J.
Love and Rage
SCHLEMMER (Ger/Ire) 1999 dir.
Cathal Black

Pleasure Island
Maier, W.
Girls of Pleasure Island, The
PAR (US) 1953
dir. E. Hugh Herbert, Alvin Ganzer

Pocketful of Paradise, A
Kane, K.

Soul Collector, The
HEARST (US) 1999 dir. Michael M.
Scott

Poem of the Lunatics, The
Cavazzini, E.

Voce Delle Lune, La
PENTA (It) 1990 dir. Federico Fellini

Point Blank
Grosso, S. and Rosenberg, P.

Question of Honor, A
EMI (US) 1982 dir. Jud Taylor

Point de Lendemain
Vivant, D.

Amants, Les
NEF (Fr) 1958 dir. Louis Malle

Point of Honour, The
Conrad, J.

Duellists, The
CIC (GB) 1977 dir. Ridley Scott

Point of Murder, The
Yorke, M.

Kiss of a Killer
ABC PROD (US) 1993 dir. Larry
Elikann

Points of Light
Sexton, L. G.

Reunion
RHI (US) 1994 dir. Lee Grant

Poldark; Demelza; Jeremy Poldark; Warleggan
Graham, W. Ross

Poldark
BBC (GB) 1975 dir. Paul Annett,
Christopher Barry, Kenneth Ives

Pollyanna
Porter, E. H.

Polly
DISNEY (US) 1989 dir. Debbie Allen

Polonaise
Leslie, D.

Song to Remember, A
COL (US) 1944 dir. Charles Vidor

Poor Little Rich Girl
Heymann, C. D.

*Poor Little Rich Girl: The Barbara Hutton
Story*
ITC (US) 1987 dir. Charles Jarrot

Poor, Poor Ophelia
Weston, C.

Streets of San Francisco, The
WAR TV (US) 1972 dir. Walter
Grauman

POP: 1280
Thompson, J.

Coup de Torchon
FT (Fr) 1981 dir. Bertrand Tavernier
GB title: Clean Slate

Porgy
Heyward, D. and Heyward, D.

Porgy and Bess
GOLDWYN (US) 1959
dir. Otto Preminger

Pork Butcher, The
Hughes, D.

Souvenir
CIC (GB) 1987 dir. Geoffrey Reeve

Portrait of a Rebel
Syrett, N.

Woman Rebels, A
RKO (US) 1936 dir. Mark Sandrich

Portrait of a Young Man Drowning
Perry, C.

Six Ways to Sunday
SCOUT (US) 1997 dir. Adam Bernstein

Positronic Man, The
Asimov, I. and Silverberg, R.

Bicentennial Man
COL (US) 1999 dir. Chris Columbus

Possessed: The True Story of an Exorcism
Allen, T. B.

Possessed
SHOWTIME (US) 2000 dir. Steven E. de Souza

Posthumous Memories of Bras Cubas
de Assis, M.

Memorias Postumas
SUPERFILMES (Bra/Port) 2001 dir. Andre Klotzel

Postman Always Rings Twice, The
Cain, J. M.

Dernier Tournant, Le
LUX (Fr) 1939 dir. Pierre Chenal

Power and the Glory, The
Greene, G.

Fugitive, The
RKO (US) 1947 dir. John Ford

Prayer for Owen Meany, A
Irving, J.

Simon Birch
HOLLYWOOD (US) 1998 dir. Mark Steven Johnson

Preacher
Thackrey, Jr., T.

Wild Card
DAVIS (US) 1992 dir. Mel Damski

Preacher's Girl
Schutze, J.

Black Widow Murders: The Blanche Tayor Moore Story
LORIMAR (US) 1993 dir. Alan Metzger

Prelude to Night
Stoddart, D.

Ruthless
EL (US) 1948 dir. Edgar G. Ulmer

Première Education Sentimentale, La
Flaubert, G.

Toutes les Nuits
TPS CINEMA (Fr) 2001 dir. Eugene Green

Prescription: Murder
Kurth, A.

Murder in Texas
D. CLARK (US) 1981 dir. Billy Hale

Present Arms
Fields, H., Rodgers, R. and Hart, L.

Leathernecking
RKO (US) 1930 dir. Edward Cline
GB title: Present Arms

Pretty Polly Barlow
Coward, N.

Pretty Polly
RANK (GB) 1967 dir. Guy Green
US title: Matter of Innocence, A

Prico
Viola, C. G.

Children Are Watching Us, The
MAGLI (It) 1942 dir. Vittorio de Sica

Priest Island
Watson, E. L. G.

Exile
ILLUMINATION (Aust) 1994 dir. Paul Cox

Prince and the Pauper, The
Twain, M.

Prince For a Day
NBC (US) 1995 dir. Corey Blechman

Prince Caspian and The Silver Chair
Lewis, C. S.

Silver Chair, The
BBC (GB) 1990 dir. A. Kirby

Prince Consort, The
Xaurof, L. and Chancel, J.

Love Parade, The
PAR (US) 1929 dir. Ernst Lubitsch

Prince of Malta, The
Buchanan, J. D.

Curacao
SHOWTIME (US) 1993 dir. Carl Schultz

Princesse de Cleves, La
de la Fayette, Mme.

Fidelité, La
STUDIO CANAL+ (Fr) 2000 dir.
Andrzej Zulawski

Prinz Friedrich von Homburg
von Kleist, H.

Prince of Homburg, The
PBS (US) 1997 dir. Kirk Browning

Prisoner Without a Name, Cell Without a Number
Timerman, J.

Jacobo Timerman: Prisoner Without a Name, Cell Without a Number
CHRYS-YELL (US) 1983
dir. Linda Yellen

Prisoners are People
Scudder, K. J.

Unchained
WAR (US) 1955 dir. Hall Bartlett

Prisoners of Quai Dong, The
Kolpacoff, V.

Physical Assault
TITAN (US) 1973
dir. William M. Bushnell

Private Ear, The
Shaffer, R.

Pad (And How to Use It), The
UI (US) 1966 dir. Brian C. Hutton

Private Investigation, A
Alexander, K.

Missing Pieces
TTC (US) 1983 dir. Mike Hodges

Private I
Sangster, J.

Spy Killer, The
ABC (US) 1969 dir. Roy Baker

Private Life
Hackney, A.

I'm All Right, Jack
BL (GB) 1959 dir. John Boulting

Private Pettigrew's Girl
Burnet, D.

Shopworn Angel
MGM (US) 1938 dir. H. C. Potter

Privileged Information
Alibrandi, T. and Armani, F. H.

Sworn to Silence
BLATT/SINGER (US) 1987
dir. Peter Levin

Procane Chronicle, The
Bleeck, O.

St. Ives
WAR (US) 1976 dir. J. Lee Thompson

Procedura
Mannuzzu, S.

Delitto Impossibile, Un
HERA (It) 2001 dir. Antonello Grimaldi

Processen mod Hamsun
Hansen, T.

Hamsun
NORDISK (Ger/Nor/Den) 1996 dir. Jan Troell

Professor Unrath
Mann, H.
Blue Angel, The
PAR (Ger) 1930 dir. Josef von Sternberg
FOX (US) 1959 dir. Edward Dmytryk

Promisse de l'aube, La
Gary, R.
Promise at Dawn
AVCO (US/Fr) 1970 dir. Jules Dassin

Proof Thru' the Night
Kenward, A. R.
Cry Havoc
MGM (US) 1943 dir. Richard Thorpe

Psyche 63
de Ligneris, F.
Psyche 59
BL (GB) 1964 dir. Alexander Singer

Psycho
Bloch, R.
Bates Motel
UN TV (US) 1987 dir. Richard Rothstein

PT109—John F. Kennedy in World War II
Donovan, R. J.
PT 109
WAR (US) 1963 dir. Leslie H. Martinson

Pu Yi and I; Pu Yi's Later Life; Pu Yi's Former Life
Li Shu Xian
Last Emperor, The
NKL (China) 1988 dir. Li Han Hsiang

Public Eye, The
Shaffer, P.
Follow Me
UN (GB) 1972 dir. Carol Reed
US title: Public Eye, The

Pumping Iron II: The Unprecedented Woman
Gaines, C. and Butler, G.
Pumping Iron II
BLUE DOLPHIN (US) 1984
dir. George Butler

Punitive Action
Robb, J.
Desert Sands
UA (US) 1955 dir. Lesley Selander

Punk, The
Sams, G.
Punk and the Princess, The
M2 (GB) 1993 dir. Michael Sarne

Purple Cloud, The
Shiel, M. P.
World, The Flesh and the Devil, The
MGM (US) 1959
dir. Ronald MacDougall

Pursuit
Fish, R. L.
Twist of Fate
COL TV/HTV (US/GB) 1989
dir. Ian Sharp

Pygmalion
Shaw, G. B.
My Fair Lady
WAR (US) 1964 dir. George Cukor

Pylon
Faulkner, W.
Tarnished Angels, The
UI (US) 1957 dir. Douglas Sirk

Q

Quality
Sumner, C. R.

Pinky
FOX (US) 1949 dir. Elia Kazan

Queen Emma of the South Seas
Dutton, G.

Emma: Queen of the South Seas
FRIES (US) 1988 dir. Bryan Forbes

Queen of Mean, The
Pierson, R.

Leona Helmsley: The Queen of Mean
FRIES (US) 1990 dir. Richard Michaels

Queen was in the Parlour, The
Coward, N.

Tonight is Ours
PAR (US) 1933 dir. Stuart Walker

Queen's Favourite, The
Neumann, R.

King in Shadow
BL (Ger) 1961 dir. Harold Braun

Queen's Husband, The
Sherwood, R. E.

Royal Bed, The
RKO (US) 1931 dir. Lowell Sherman

Quentin Durward
Scott, Sir W.

Adventures of Quentin Durward, The
MGM (GB) 1955 dir. Richard Thorpe
US title: Quentin Durward

Querelle de Brest
Genet, J.

Querelle
TRIUMPH (Fr/Ger) 1983
dir. Rainer Werner Fassbinder

Quiet Wedding
McCracken, E.

Happy is the Bride
BL (GB) 1957 dir. Roy Boulting

R

Racer, The
Ruesch, H.

Racers, The
FOX (US) 1955 dir. Henry Hathaway
GB title: Such Men are Dangerous

Rachel
Fast, H.

Rachel and the Stranger
RKO (US) 1948 dir. Norman Foster

Rachel Cade
Mercer, C.

Sins of Rachel Cade, The
WAR (US) 1960 dir. Gordon Douglas

Radio no Jikan
Mitani, K.

Welcome Back, Mr. McDonald
TOHO (Jap) 1998 dir. Koki Mitani

Rafferty
Ballinger, W.

Pushover
COL (US) 1954 dir. Richard Quine

Raffles the Amateur Cracksman
Hornung, E. W.

Raffles
UA (US) 1939 dir. Sam Wood

Rag Bag Clan, The
Barth, R.

Small Killing, A
MOTOWN (US) 1981
dir. Steven Hilliard Stern

Rage of the Blue Moon
Vetere, R.

Touched By a Killer
WI (Can) 2001 dir. Gilbert M. Shilton

Rage of the Vulture
Moorehead, A.

Thunder in the East
PAR (US) 1951 dir. Charles Vidor

Rain
Maugham, W. S.

Miss Sadie Thompson
COL (US) 1953 dir. Curtis Bernhardt

Rainbird Pattern, The
Canning, V.

Family Plot
UN (US) 1976 dir. Alfred Hitchcock

Rains Came, The
Bromfield, L.

Rains of Ranchipur, The
FOX (US) 1955 dir. Jean Negulesco

Raising Daisy Rothschild
Leslie-Melville, J. and Leslie-Melville, B.

Last Giraffe, The
WESTFALL (US) 1979
dir. Jack Couffer

Raj Quartet, The
Scott, P.

Jewel in the Crown, The
GRANADA (GB) 1984
dir. Jim O'Brien, Christopher Morahan

Rameau's Niece
Schine, C.
Misadventures of Margaret, The
GRANADA (GB/Fr/US) 1998 dir. Brian
Skeet

Ramey
Farris, J.
Greatest Gift, The
UN TV (US) 1974 dir. Boris Sagal

Rap, The
Brawley, E.
Fast-Walking
PICKMAN (US) 1982
dir. James B. Harris

Rapture in my Rags
Hastings, P.
Rapture
FOX (US/Fr) 1965 dir. John Guillermin

Rascal, a Memoir of a Better Era
North, S.
Rascal
DISNEY (US) 1969 dir. Norman Tokar

Ratman's Notebook
Gilbert, S.
Willard
CINERAMA (US) 1971 dir. Daniel
Mann

Rattlers
Gilmore, J.
Rattled
GT FALLS (US) 1996 dir. Tony Randel

Ravenscroft
Nigro, D.
Manor, The
FALCON (Czech) 1999 dir. Ken Berris

Ravine, The
Young, K.
Assault
RANK (GB) 1971 dir. Sidney Hayers

Raw Youth
Bell, N.
Undertow
CAPSTONE (US) 1991
dir. Thomas Mazziotti

Rawhide Justice
Raine, W. M.
Man from Bitter Ridge, The
UN (US) 1955 dir. Jack Arnold

Ready Money
Montgomery, J.
Riding High
PAR (US) 1943 dir. George Marshall
GB title: Melody Inn

Recollections of Vesta Tilly
De Frece, Lady
After the Ball
BL (GB) 1957 dir. Compton Bennett

Recteur de l'Ile de Sein, Un
Quefflec, H.
Dieu à Besoin des Hommes
TRANS (Fr) 1950 dir. Jean Delannoy

Red Alert
George, P.
*Dr Strangelove; Or How I Learned to Stop
Worrying and Love the Bomb*
COL (GB) 1963 dir. Stanley Kubrick

Red Cat, The
Lothar, R. and Adler, H.
Folies Bergère
FOX (US) 1935 dir. Roy del Ruth
GB title: Man from the Folies Bergère,
The

Red Dragon
Harris, T.
Manhunter
CANNON (US) 1986 dir. Michael Mann

Red File for Callan, A
Mitchell, J.
Callan
EMI (GB) 1974 dir. Don Sharp

Red for Danger
Price, E.
Blondes for Danger
WILCOX (GB) 1938 dir. Jack Raymond

Red Hugh, Prince of Donegal
Reilly, R. T.
Fighting Prince of Donegal, The
DISNEY (GB) 1966
dir. Michael O'Herlihy

Red Peppers; Fumed Oak; Ways & Means
Coward, N.
Meet Me Tonight
GFD (GB) 1952 dir. Anthony Pelissier

Reef, The
Wharton, E.
Passion's Way
HEARST (US) 1999 dir. Robert Allan Ackerman

Regnbuen
Hamsun, M.
Hamsun
NORDISK (Ger/Nor/Den) 1996 dir. Jan Troell

Religion, The
Conde, N.
Believers, The
ORION (US) 1987 dir. John Schlesinger

Remembering America: A Voice From the Sixties
Goodwin, R.
Quiz Show
HOLLYWOOD (US) 1994 dir. Robert Redford

Remembrance
Bao, S.
Road Home, The
COL (China) 1999 dir. Yimou Zhang

Renée Richards Story, The: The Second Serve
Richards, R. and Ames, J.
Second Serve
LORIMAR (US) 1986 dir. Anthony Page

Renfrew's Long Trail
Erskine, L. Y.
Danger Ahead
MON (GB) 1940 dir. Ralph Staub

Rennschwein Rudi Russel
Timm, U.
Rudy, The Racing Pig
ROYAL (Ger) 1995 dir. Peter Timm

Report on a Fugitive
Wellesley, G.
Night Train to Munich
TCF (GB) 1940 dir. Carol Reed

Reprieve
Resko, J.
Convicts Four
ALLIED (US) 1962 dir. Millard Kaufman
GB title: Reprieve

Reputation for a Song
Grierson, E.
My Lover, My Son
MGM (US/GB) 1970 dir. John Newland

Rescuers, The; Miss Bianca
Sharp, M.
Rescuers, The
DISNEY (US) 1977
dir. Wolfgang Reitherman

Rescuers: Portraits of Moral Courage in the Holocaust

Drucker, M. and Block, G.

Rescuers: Stories of Courage
SHOWTIME (US) 1997 dir. Peter
Bogdanovich, Tim Hunter,
Lynne Littman, Tony Bill

Resurrection

Valtos, W.

Almost Dead
DELTA (US) 1996 dir. Ruben Preuss

Resurrection

Tolstoy, L.

We Live Again
UA (US) 1934 dir. Rouben Mamoulian

Return Engagement

Hamilton, N., Casey, R. and Shute, J.

Fools for Scandal
WAR (US) 1938 dir. Mervyn LeRoy

Return Journey

Hussein, A.

Brothers in Trouble
RENEGADE (GB) 1995 dir. Udayan
Prasad

Return to Paradise

Michener, J. A.

Until They Sail
MGM (US) 1957 dir. Robert Wise

Return to the Château

Réage, P.

Fruits of Passion
ARGOS (Fr/Jap) 1982 dir. Shuji
Terayama

Return to the Woods

Hodson, J. L.

King and Country
WAR (GB) 1964 dir. Joseph Losey

Reveille in Washington

Leech, M.

Rose and the Jackal, The
WHITE (US) 1990 dir. Jack Gold

Revolt

McCall, M.

Scarlet Dawn
WAR (US) 1932 dir. William Dieterle

Rhodes

Millin, S. G.

Rhodes of Africa
GAU BRI (GB) 1936
dir. Berthold Viertes
US title: Rhodes

Richard III

Shakespeare, W.

Looking for Richard
FOX (US) 1996 dir. Al Pacino

Richest Girl in the World, The

Mansfield, S.

Too Rich: The Secret Life of Doris Duke
VZ/SERTNER (US) 1999 dir. John
Erman

Ricky Nelson—Idol For a Generation

Selvin, J.

Ricky Nelson: Original Teen Idol
VH1 (US) 1999 dir. Sturla Gunnarsson

Riddle Me This

Rubin, D.

Guilty as Hell
PAR (US) 1932 dir. Erle C. Kenton

Riddle Me This

Rubin, D.

Night Club Scandal
PAR (US) 1937 dir. Ralph Murphy

Ride the Nightmare
Matheson, R.

Cold Sweat
CORONA/FAIRFILM (It/Fr) 1974
dir. Terence Young

Ride the Pink Horse
Hughes, D. B.

Hanged Man, The
UN (US) 1964 dir. Don Siegel

Riff Raff
Fishburne, L.

Once in the Life
SHOOTING GALLERY (US) 2000 dir.
Laurence Fishburne

Rinehard
Tweed, T. F.

Gabriel Over the White House
MGM (US) 1933 dir. Gregory LaCava

Ring for Catty
Cargill, P. and Beale, J.

Twice Round the Daffodils
AA (GB) 1962 dir. Gerald Thomas

Ringer, The
Wallace, E.

Gaunt Stranger, The
NORTHWOOD (GB) 1938
dir. Walter Forde
US title: Phantom Strikes, The

Ripley's Game
Highsmith, P.

American Friend, The
CINEGATE (W. Ger) 1977
dir. Wim Wenders

Ripper from Rawhide
Cushman, D.

Timberjack
REP (US) 1954 dir. Joe Kane

Rise and Fall of Little Voice, The
Cartwright, J.

Little Voice
SCALA (GB) 1998 dir. Mark Herman

Rise & Walk: The Trial & Triumph of Dennis Byrd
Byrd, D. and D'Orso, M.

Rise & Walk: The Dennis Byrd Story
FOX WEST (US) 1994 dir. Michael
Dinner

Rita Hayworth and the Shawshank Redemption
King, S.

Shawshank Redemption, The
COL (US) 1994 dir. Frank Darabont

Rita Hayworth: The Time, the Place, and the Woman
Kobal, J.

Rita Hayworth: The Love Goddess
SUSSKIND (US) 1983
dir. James Goldstone

River Ran out of Eden, A
Marshall, J. V.

Golden Seal, The
GOLDWYN (US) 1983 dir. Frank
Zuniga

Rivières Pourpres
Grange, J.-C.

Crimson Rivers, The
STUDIO CANAL+ (Fr) 2000 dir.
Mathieu Kassavitz

Road to Rome, The
Sherwood, R. E.

Jupiter's Darling
MGM (US) 1954 dir. George Sidney

Road to San Jacinto
Foreman, L. L.

Arrow in the Dust
ABP (US) 1954 dir. Lesley Selander

Roar of the Crowd, The
Corbett, J. J.

Gentleman Jim
WAR (US) 1942 dir. Raoul Walsh

Robinson Crusoe
Defoe, D.

Adventures of Robinson Crusoe, The
UA (Mex/US) 1954 dir. Luis Bunuel

Robinson Crusoe
Defoe, D.

Crusoe
ISLAND (US) 1989 dir. Caleb Deschanel

Robots Against Gandahar
Andrevan, J.-P.

Light Years
MIRAMAX (Fr) 1988 dir. René Laloux

Roemer: Man Against the Mob
Roemer, Jr., W. F.

Sugartime
HBO (US) 1995 dir. John N. Smith

Rogue Male
Household, G.

Man Hunt
FOX (US) 1941 dir. Fritz Lang

Rogue Trader: How I Brought Down Barings Bank and Shook the Financial World
Leeson, N. and Whitley, E.

Rogue Trader
GRANADA (GB) 1999 dir. James Dearden

Roi Des Aulnes, Le
Tourner, M.

Ogre, The
STUDIO CANAL+ (Fr/Ger) 1996 dir. Volker Schlondorff

Rojuko Kazoku
Sae, S.

Promise, A
KT (Jap) 1987 dir. Yoshishige Yoshida

Rome Haul
Edmonds, W. D.

Farmer Takes a Wife, The
FOX (US) 1935 dir. Victor Fleming
FOX (US) 1953 dir. Henry Levin

Romeo and Juliet
Shakespeare, W.

Tromeo and Juliet
TROMA (US) 1996 dir. Lloyd Kaufman

Rommel, The Desert Fox
Young, D.

Desert Fox, The
FOX (US) 1951 dir. Henry Hathaway
GB title: Rommel, Desert Fox

Rookwood
Ainsworth, H.

Dick Turpin
STOLL-STAFFORD (GB) 1933
dir. Victor Hanbury, John Stafford

Room Service
Murray, J. and Boretz, A.

Step Lively
RKO (US) 1944 dir. Tim Whelan

Rosalind
Barrie, Sir J. M.

Forever Female
PAR (US) 1953 dir. Irving Rapper

Rose and the Flame, The
Lauritzen, J.

Kiss of Fire
UN (US) 1955 dir. Joseph M. Newman

Rouge et le Noir, Le
Stendahl, M. H. B.

Red and the Black, The
TELFRANCE (Fr/It) 1997 dir. Jean-Daniel Verhaeghe

Rouge et le Noir, Le
Stendahl, M. H. B.
Scarlet and the Black, The
BBC (GB) 1993 dir. Ben Bolt

Rough Sketch
Sylvester, R.
We Were Strangers
COL (US) 1949 dir. John Huston

Roughshod
Fox, N. A.
Gunsmoke
UN (US) 1953 dir. Nathan Juran

Royal Canadian Mounted Police
Fetherstonhaugh, R. C.
Northwest Mounted Police
PAR (US) 1940 dir. Cecil B. De Mille

Royal Family, The
Kaufman, G. S. and Ferber, E.
Royal Family of Broadway, The
PAR (US) 1930 dir. George Cukor
GB title: Theatre Royal

Rue Cases Negres, La
Zobel, J.
Sugar Cane Alley
ORION (Fr) 1984 dir. Euzhan Palcy

Ruggles of Red Gap
Wilson, H. L.
Fancy Pants
PAR (US) 1950 dir. George Marshall

Ruling Passion, The
Glitman, R. M.
High Price of Passion, The
TAFT (US) 1986 dir. Larry Elikann

Rum Punch
Leonard, E.
Jackie Brown
MIRAMAX (US) 1997 dir. Quentin Tarantino

Runaway Horses; Temple of the Golden Pavilion
Mishima, Y.
Mishima
WAR (US) 1985 dir. Paul Schrader

Running Scared
Burmeister, J.
Tigers Don't Cry
RANK (SA) 1978
dir. Peter Collinson

Runway Zero-Eight
Hailey, A. and Castle, J.
Terror in the Sky
PAR TV (US) 1971 dir. Bernard L. Kowalski

Ruthless Ones, The
Moody, L.
What Became of Jack and Jill?
FOX (GB) 1971 dir. Bill Rain

S

Sabrina Fair
Taylor, S.

Sabrina
PAR (US) 1954 dir. Billy Wilder
GB title: Sabrina Fair
PAR (US) 1995 dir. Sydney Pollack

Sacajawea of the Shoshones
Emmons, D. G.

Far Horizons, The
PAR (US) 1955 dir. Rudolph Maté

Sackett; Daybreakers, The
L'Amour, L.

Sacketts, The
SHALAKO (US) 1979 dir. Robert Totten

Sacred Flame, The
Maugham, W. S.

Right to Live, The
WAR (US) 1935 dir. William Keighley
GB title: Sacred Flame, The

Saga of Billy the Kid, The
Burns, W. N.

Billy the Kid
MGM (US) 1930 dir. King Vidor
MGM (US) 1941 dir. David Millar

Sailor Goes Ashore, A
Sandemose, A.

Misery Harbour
UIP (Can/Den) 1999 dir. Nils Gaup

Saint Johnson
Burnett, W. R.

Law and Order
UN (US) 1932 dir. Edward L. Cahn

Sally
Cunningham, E. V.

Face of Fear, The
Q. MARTIN (US) 1971
dir. George McCowan

Salome
Wilde, O.

Salome's Last Dance
VESTRON (GB) 1988 dir. Ken Russell

Salt
Gold, H.

Threesome
CBS ENT (US) 1984 dir. Lou Antonio

Salute to the Gods
Campbell, Sir M.

Burn 'em up O'Connor
MGM (US) 1938
dir. Edward Sedgwick

Samuel I & II; Chronicles I; Psalms of David
Bible

King David
PAR (US/GB) 1985
dir. Bruce Beresford

San Domingo, The Medicine Hat Stallion
Henry, M.

Peter Lundy and the Medicine Hat Stallion
FRIENDLY (US) 1977
dir. Michael O'Herlihy

San Isidro Futbol
Cacucci, P.

Viva San Isidro!
CECCHI (It) 1995 dir. Dante Cappelletti

San Quentin Story, The
Duffy, C. T. and Jennings, D.

Duffy of San Quentin
WAR (US) 1954 dir. Walter Doniger

Sanctuary
Faulkner, W.

Story of Temple Drake, The
PAR (US) 1933 dir. Stephen Roberts

Sans Rancune
van Daalen, J.

Lek
RCV (Neth) 2000 dir. Jean van de Velde

Sapper
McNeile, H. C.

Bulldog Drummond
GOLDWYN (US) 1929
dir. F. Richard Jones

Satan and Simon DeSoto
Sod, T.

Crocodile Tears
ARIZTICAL (US) 1997 dir. Ann Coppel

Satyricon
Petronius

Fellini Satyricon
UA (It) 1969 dir. Federico Fellini

Savage Place, A
Parker, R. B.

Spenser: A Savage Place
WAR (US) 1995 dir. Joseph L. Scanlan

Scarlet Pimpernel, The
Orczy, Baroness E.

Pimpernel Smith
BN (GB) 1941 dir. Leslie Howard

Scarlet Pimpernel, The
Orczy, Baroness E.

Purple Mask, The
UN (US) 1955 dir. Bruce Humberstone

Scarlet Pimpernel of the Vatican, The
Gallagher, J. P.

Scarlet and the Black, The
ITC (It/US) 1983 dir. Jerry London

Scènes de la Vie Bohème
Murger, H.

Bohemian Life
FILMS A2/PYRAMIDE (Fr)
1992 dir. Aki Kaurismaki

Scènes de la Vie de Boheme
Murger, H.

Vie de Boheme, La
FILMS A2 (Fr) 1992 dir. Aki Kaurismaki

Schindler's Ark
Keneally, T.

Schindler's List
UN (US) 1993 dir. Steven Spielberg

Schlafes Bruder
Schneider, R.

Brother Of Sleep
BA FILMPROD (Ger) 1995 dir. Joseph Vilsmaier

Schloss Gripsholm
Tucholsky, K.

Gripsholm
BABELSBERG (Ger) 2000 dir. Xavier Koller

School of Drama
Szekely, H.

Dramatic School
MGM (US) 1938 dir. Robert B. Sinclair, Jr.

Scott and Amundsen
Huntford, R.

Last Place on Earth, The
CENTRAL (GB) 1985
dir. Ferdinand Fairfax

Scottsboro: A Tragedy of the American South
Carter, D. T.

Judge Horton and the Scottsboro Boys
TOM (US) 1976 dir. Fielder Cook

Sea Wolf, The
London, J.

Wolf Larsen
ABP (US) 1958 dir. Harman Jones

Sea Wyf and Biscuit
Scott, J. M.

Sea-Wife
FOX (GB) 1957 dir. Bob McNaught

Seal Called Andre, A
Goodridge, H. and Dietz, L.

Andre
PAR (US) 1994 dir. George Miller

Séance on a Wet Afternoon
McShane, M.

Korei
DAIEI STUDIOS (Jap) 2000 dir. Kiyoshi Kurosawa

Season of the Witch
Stine, H.

Memory Run
MERIDIAN ENT (US) 1995 dir. Allan A. Goldstein

Season Ticket, The
Tulloch, J.

Purely Belter
CHANNEL 4 FILMS (GB) 2000 dir. Mark Herman

Second Sight
Williams, D.

Two Worlds of Jennie Logan, The
FRIES (US) 1979 dir. Frank DeFelitta

Secret Agent, The
Conrad, J.

Sabotage
GB (GB) 1936 dir. Alfred Hitchcock
US title: Woman Alone, A

Secret Gardens in My Father's Heart, The
Giovanni, J.

Mon Pere ... Il m'a Sauve la Vie
STUDIO CANAL+ (Fr) 2001 dir. Jose Giovanni

Secret Life of Algernon Pendleton, The
Greenan, R. H.

Secret Life of Algernon, The
MARANO (Can/GB) 1997 dir. Charles Jarrot

Secret of Ron Mor Skerry, The
Fry, R. K.

Secret of Roah Inish, The
JONES (US) 1994 dir. John Sayles

Secret of the Ruby Ring
MacGrory, Y.

Ruby Ring, The
HALLMARK (US) 1997 dir. Harley Cokeliss

Secret Sharer, The
Conrad, J.

Face to Face
RKO (US) 1952
dir. John Brahm, Bretaigne Windust

Secrets
Palin, M. and Jones, T.

Consuming Passions
GOLDWYN (GB) 1988 dir. Giles Foster

Seed and the Sower The
van der Post, Sir L.
Merry Christmas, Mr. Lawrence
UN (GB) 1983 dir. Nagisa Oshima

Seizure
Mee, Jr., C. L.
Seizure: The Story of Kathy Morris
JOZAK (US) 1980 dir. Gerald Isenberg

Self Storage
Spiridakis, T. and Bitterman, S.
Tinseltown
GOLDWYN (US) 1998 dir. Tony
Spiridakis

Semi Detached
Turner, D.
All the Way Up
GRANADA/EMI (GB) 1970
dir. James MacTaggart

Send Another Coffin
Presnell, F. G.
Slightly Honourable
UA (US) 1940 dir. Tay Garnett

Sentimentalists, The
Collins, D.
His Woman
PAR (US) 1931 dir. Edward Sloman

Sentinel, The
Clarke, A. C.
2001, A Space Odyssey
MGM (GB) 1968 dir. Stanley Kubrick

September, September
Foote, S.
Memphis
PROPAGANDA (US) 1992
dir. Yves Simoneau

Service
Anthony, C. L.
Looking Forward
MGM (US) 1933 dir. Clarence Brown

Set For Life
Freeman, J.
Gift of Love, The
M. REES (US) 1994 dir. Paul Bogart

7½ Cents
Bissell, R. P.
Pajama Game, The
WAR (US) 1957 dir. Stanley Donen

Seven Chances
Megrue, R. C.
Bachelor, The
NEW LINE (US) 1999 dir. Gary Sinyor

Seven Days to a Killing
Egleton, C.
Black Windmill, The
PAR (GB) 1974 dir. Don Siegel

Seven Keys to Baldpate
Biggers, E. D.
House of the Long Shadows, The
CANNON (GB) 1983 dir. Pete Walker

Seven Men at Daybreak
Burgess, A.
Operation Daybreak
WAR (US) 1975 dir. Lewis Gilbert

711—Officer Needs Help
Masterson, W.
Warning Shot
PAR (US) 1966 dir. Buzz Kulik

Seven Pillars of Wisdom
Lawrence, T. E.
Lawrence of Arabia
COL/BL (GB/US) 1962 dir. David Lean

Seventh, The
Stark, R.
Split, The
MGM (US) 1968 dir. Gordon Flemyng

Sex and the Criminal Mind
Winski, N.

Man in the Attic, The
ATLANTIS (US) 1995 dir. Graeme
Campbell

Sexpionage: The Exploitation of Sex by Soviet Intelligence
Lewis, D.

Secret Weapons
ITC (US) 1985 dir. Don Taylor

Sexual Perversity in Chicago
Mamet, D.

About Last Night ...
TRISTAR (US) 1986 dir. Edward Zwick

Shades Will Not Vanish
Fowler, H. M.

Strange Intruder
ABP (US) 1956 dir. Irving Rapper

Shadow and the Peak, The
Mason, R.

Passionate Summer, The
RANK (US) 1958 dir. Rudolph Cartier

Shadow Range
Bishop, C.

Cow Country
ABP (US) 1953 dir. Lesley Selander

Shall I Eat You Now?
Gebler, E.

Hoffman
ABP (GB) 1970 dir. Alvin Rackoff

Shape of Things to Come, The
Wells, H. G.

Things to Come
UA (GB) 1936
dir. William Cameron Menzies

Shattered
Dwyer, K. R.

Passengers, The
COL-WAR (Fr) 1977 dir. Serge LeRoy

Shayna Maidel, A
Lebow, B.

Miss Rose White
LORIMAR TV (US) 1992 dir. Joseph
Sargent

She Let Him Continue
Geller, S.

Pretty Poison
FOX (US) 1968 dir. Noel Black
WESTGATE (US) 1996 dir. David
Burton Morris

Shepherd's Life, A
Hudson, W. H.

Bread or Blood
BBC (GB) 1981 dir. Peter Smith

Shift, The
Cope, T. F.

Last Dance, The
POLSON (US) 2000 dir. Kevin Dowling

Shilling for Candles, A
Tey, J.

Young and Innocent
GFD (GB) 1937 dir. Alfred Hitchcock
US title: Girl was Young, A

Shirley
Cunningham, E. V.

What's a Nice Girl Like You ...?
UN TV (US) 1971 dir. Jerry Paris

Shoeless Joe
Kinsella, W. P.

Field of Dreams
UN (US) 1989 dir. Phil A. Robinson

Shooting Party, The
Chekhov, A.

Summer Storm
UA (US) 1944 dir. Douglas Sirk

Shooting Star
Thomas, B.

Great Game, The
ADELPHI (GB) 1952 dir. Maurice Elvey

Shop Around the Corner, The
Laszlo, N.

In the Good Old Summertime
MGM (US) 1949 dir. Robert Z. Leonard

Shore Leave
Osborne, H. and Scott, A.

Follow the Fleet
RKO (US) 1936 dir. Mark Sandrich

Shore Leave
Osborne, H.

Hit the Deck
MGM (US) 1955 dir. Roy Rowland

Shore Leave
Wakeman, F.

Kiss Them for Me
FOX (US) 1957 dir. Stanley Donen

Shorn Lamb, The
Locke, W. J.

Strangers in Love
PAR (US) 1932 dir. Lothar Mendes

Short Happy Life of Francis Macomber, The
Hemingway, E.

Macomber Affair, The
UA (US) 1947 dir. Zoltan Korda

Short Timers, The
Hasford, G.

Full Metal Jacket
WB (US) 1987 dir. Stanley Kubrick

Shotgun
Wingate, W.

Malone
ORION (US) 1987 dir. Harley Kokliss

Shovel and the Loom, The
Friedman, C.

Left Luggage
GREYSTONE (Bel/Neth/US) 1997 dir. Jeroen Krabbe

Show Business
Tharoor, S.

Bollywood
SONI-KAHN (Ind) 1994 dir. B. J. Kahn

Showdown at Crazy Horse
Rigsby, H.

Last Sunset, The
UI (US) 1961 dir. Robert Aldrich

Show-off, The
Kelly, G.

Men Are Like That
PAR (US) 1930 dir. Frank Tuttle

Shrinking Man, The
Matheson, R.

Incredible Shrinking Man, The
UN (US) 1957 dir. Jack Arnold

Shroud Society, The
Rae, H. C.

Man with a Gun
NORTHWOOD (Can) 1995 dir. David Wyles

Shuttered Room, The
Lovecraft, H. P.

Dunwich Horror, The
AIP (US) 1970
dir. Daniel Haller

Siege at Dancing Bird, The
LeMay, A.

Unforgiven, The
UA (US) 1960 dir. John Huston

Siege at Trencher's Farm, The
Williams, G. M.

Straw Dogs
CINERAMA (GB) 1971
dir. Sam Peckinpah

Siege of Battersea, The
Holles, R.

Guns at Batasi
FOX (GB) 1964 dir. John Guillermin

Sign of the Beaver, The
Speare, E. G.

Keeping the Promise
ATLANTIS (US) 1997 dir. Sheldon
Larry

Signs of Life
Elliott, S.

Careful, He Might Hear You
SYME (Aust) 1983 dir. Carl Schultz

Silence Under the Sea, The
Loffler, H.

Farewell to Agnes
MUNCHEN (Ger) 1994 dir. Michael
Gwisdek

Silent Stars Go By, The
Aldrich, B. S.

Gift of Love, The: A Christmas Story
TELECOM (US) 1983
dir. Delbert Mann

Silent Voice, The
Goodman, J. E.

Man Who Played God, The
WAR (US) 1932 dir. John G. Adolfi
GB title: Silent Voice, The

Silver Brumby, The
Mitchell, E.

*Silver Stallion King of the Wild Brumbies,
The*
FILM VICTORIA (Aust) 1993 dir. John
Tatoulis

Silver Whistle, The
McEnroe, R. E.

Mr. Belvedere Rings the Bell
FOX (US) 1951 dir. Henry Koster

Simon Says
Murphy, G.

Summer of Fear
M. ROBE (US) 1996 dir. Mike Robe

Simple Simon
Pearson, R. D.

Mercury Rising
UN (US) 1998 dir. Harold Becker

Simulacron 3
Galouye, D.

Thirteenth Floor, The
CENTROPOLIS (US/Ger) 1999 dir.
Josef Rusnak

Sin of Susan Slade, The
Hume, D.

Susan Slade
WAR (US) 1962 dir. Delmer Daves

Sincerity
Erskine, J.

Lady Surrenders, A
UN (US) 1930 dir. John Stahl

Single Lady
Saunders, J. M.

Last Flight, The
WAR (US) 1931 dir. William Dieterle

Single Night
Bromfield, L.

Night After Night
PAR (US) 1932 dir. Archie Mayo

Sinister Errand
Cheyney, P.

Diplomatic Courier
FOX (US) 1952 dir. Henry Hathaway

Sir Gawain and the Green Knight
Anon.

Gawain and the Green Knight
THAMES (GB) 1990 dir. J. M. Phillips

Sir, You Bastard
Newman, G. F.

Take, The
COL (US) 1974
dir. Robert Hartford-Davis

Sire of Maletroit's Door, The
Stevenson, R. L.
Strange Door, The
UI (US) 1951 dir. Joseph Pevney

Sirga la Lionne
Guillot, R.
Enfant Lion, L'
STUDIO CANAL+ (Fr) 1993 dir. Patrick Grandperret

Sister Act
Hurst, F.
Four Daughters
WAR (US) 1938 dir. Michael Curtiz

Sister Carrie
Dreiser, T.
Carrie
PAR (US) 1952 dir. William Wyler

Sister Mary Ignatius Explains It All For You
Durang, C.
Sister Mary Explains It All
TENNANT/STAMBLER (US) 2001 dir. Marshall Brickman

Sisterhood
Black, B. and Bishop, C.
Ladies Club, The
NEW LINE (US) 1986 dir. A. K. Allen

Six Days of the Condor
Grady, J.
Three Days of the Condor
PAR (US) 1975 dir. Sydney Pollack

Six Months With an Older Woman
Kaufelt, D.
In Love With an Older Woman
FRIES (US) 1982 dir. Jack Bender

Six Napoleons, The
Doyle, Sir A. C.
Pearl of Death, The
UN (US) 1944 dir. Roy William Neill

Six Weeks in August
Chais, P. H.
Guess Who's Sleeping in my Bed?
ABC (US) 1973 dir. Theodore J. Flicker

Sixteen Hands
Croy, H.
I'm From Missouri
PAR (US) 1939 dir. Theodore Reed

Sixteenth Round, The
Carter, R.
Hurricane, The
UN (US) 1999 dir. Norman Jewison

Sixth of June, The
Shapiro, L.
D-Day the Sixth of June
FOX (US) 1956 dir. Henry Koster

Skeezer: Dog With a Mission
Yates, E.
Skeezer
M. ARCH (US) 1982 dir. Peter H. Hunt

Skidding
Rouverol, A.
Family Affair, A
MGM (US) 1937 dir. George B. Seitz

Sky has Many Colours, The
Anderson, L.
Lili Marleen
ROXY (Ger) 1980
dir. Rainer Werner Fassbinder

Sky Steward
Attiwill, K.
Non Stop New York
GFD (GB) 1937 dir. Robert Stevenson

Skyscraper
Baldwin, F.
Skyscraper Souls
MGM (US) 1932 dir. Edgar Selwyn

Slapstick
Vonnegut, K.
Slapstick of Another Kind
LORIMAR (US) 1984 dir. Steven Paul

Slate Wyn and Blanche McBride
Savage, G.
Slate, Wyn and Me
HEMDALE (Aust) 1987
dir. Don McLennan

Sleep Long My Love
Waugh, H.
Jigsaw
BL (GB) 1962 dir. Val Guest

Sleeping Clergyman, A
Bridie, J.
Flesh and Blood
BL (GB) 1951 dir. Anthony Kimmins

Sleeping Prince, The
Rattigan, T.
Prince and the Showgirl, The
WAR (GB) 1957 dir. Laurence Olivier

Sleepwalker, The
Callwood, J.
Sleepwalker Killing
COS-MEU (US) 1997 dir. John Cosgrove

Slight Case of Murder, A
Runyon, D. and Lindsay, H.
Stop, You're Killing Me
WAR (US) 1952 dir. Roy del Ruth

Slimer
Knight, H. A.
Proteus
METRODOME (GB) 1996 dir. Bob Keen

Small Miracle, The
Gallico, P.
Never Take No for an Answer
INDEPENDENT (GB) 1951
dir. Maurice Cloche, Ralph Smart

Small Miracle
Krasna, N.
Four Hours to Kill
PAR (US) 1935 dir. Mitchell Leisen

Small Woman, The
Burgess, A.
Inn of the Sixth Happiness, The
FOX (GB) 1958 dir. Mark Robson

Smithereens
Battin, B. W.
Hell Hath No Fury
BAR-GENE (US) 1991
dir. Thomas J. Wright

Smuggler's Circuit
Roberts, D.
Law and Disorder
BL (GB) 1957 dir. Charles Crichton

Snake Head
Nishiki, M.
Shadow of China
NEW LINE (US/Jap) 1991
dir. Mitsuo Yanagimachi

Snake Water
Williams, A.
Pink Jungle, The
UI (US) 1968 dir. Delbert Mann

Snatchers, The
White, L.
Night of the Following Day, The
UN (US) 1969 dir. Hubert Cornfield

Snow Birch, The
Mantley, J.
Woman Obsessed
FOX (US) 1959 dir. Henry Hathaway

So Hard to Forget
Crowe, E.

Hard To Forget
ALLIANCE (Can) 1998 dir. Victor Sarin

So Little Cause for Caroline
Bercovici, E.

One Shoe Makes it Murder
LORIMAR TV (US) 1982
dir. William Hale

Sobbin' Women, The
Benet, S. V.

Seven Brides for Seven Brothers
MGM (US) 1954 dir. Stanley Donen

Socio, El
Prieto, J.

Associate, The
HOLLYWOOD (US) 1996 dir. Daniel
Petrie

Soldier for Christmas, A
Beckwith, R.

This Man is Mine
COL (GB) 1946 dir. Marcel Varnel

Soldier of Fortune Murders, The
Green, B.

When Love Kills: The Seducation of John Hearn
ALEXANDER-ENRIGHT (US) 1993 dir.
Larry Elikann

Soldier's Play, A
Fuller, C.

Soldier's Story, A
COL (US) 1984 dir. Norman Jewison

Solid! Said the Earl
Carstairs, J. P.

Yank in Ermine, A
MON (GB) 1955 dir. Gordon Parry

Some Must Watch
White, E. L.

Spiral Staircase, The
RKO (US) 1946 dir. Robert Siodmak
WAR (GB) 1975 dir. Peter Collinson
SABAN (US) 2000 dir. James Head

Someone is Killing the Great Chefs of Europe
Lyons, N. and Lyons, I.

Who is Killing the Great Chefs of Europe?
WAR (US) 1978 dir. Ted Kotcheff
GB title: Too Many Chefs

Someone Waiting
Williams, E.

Time Without Pity
HARLEQUIN (GB) 1957
dir. Joseph Losey

Someone's Watching
Kelman, J.

In the Shadows, Someone's Watching
SABAN ENT (US) 1993 dir. Richard
Friedman

Son
Olsen, J.

Sins of the Mother
CORAPEAKE (US) 1991
dir. John Patterson

Son of Adam
Forman, Sir D.

My Life So Far
MIRAMAX (GB) 1999 dir. Hugh
Hudson

Son of Robin Hood
Castleton, P. A.

Bandit of Sherwood Forest, The
COL (US) 1946
dir. George Sherman, Henry Levin

Son of the Morningstar: Custer and the Little Big Horn
Connell, E. S.

Son of the Morning Star
REP (US) 1991 dir. Mike Robe

Son-Rise
Kaufman, B. N.

Son-Rise: A Miracle of Love
FILMWAYS (US) 1979 dir. Glenn Jordan

Sondagsengler
Nortvedt, R.

Other Side of Sunday, The
NRK DRAMA (Nor) 1996 dir. Berit Nesheim

Song of Gloomy Sunday, The
Barkow, N.

Piano Player, The
STUDIO HAMBURG (Ger) 1999 dir. Rolf Schubel

Sophia Living and Loving: Her Own Story
Hotchner, A. E.

Sophia Loren—Her Own Story
EMI (US) 1980 dir. Mel Stuart

Sophie's World: A Novel About the History of Philosophy
Gaarder, J.

Sofies Verden
NFK (Nor) 1999 dir. Eric Gustavson

Sorrow Floats
Sandlin, T.

Floating Away
PEG (US) 1998 dir. John Badham

Sort of Traitor, A
Balchin, N.

Suspect
BL (GB) 1960 dir. Roy Boulting

Sostiene Pereira
Tabucci, A.

Pereira Declares
KG (Port/It) 1995 dir. Roberto Faenza

Soul of Betty Fairchild, The
Sprecht, R.

Nightscream
VZ/SERTNER (US) 1997 dir. Noel Nosseck

Sound of Hunting, A
Brown, H.

Eight Iron Men
COL (US) 1952 dir. Edward Dmytryk

Sound of Murder, The
Fairchild, W.

Last Shot you Hear, The
FOX (GB) 1970 dir. Gordon Hessler

Souper, Le
Brisville, J.-C.

Supper, The
FRANCE 2 (Fr) 1993 dir. Edouard Molinaro

Southern Blade
Wolford, N. and Wolford, S.

Time for Killing, A
COL (US) 1967 dir. Phil Karlson
GB title: Long Ride Home, The

Southern Star Mystery, The
Verne, J.

Southern Star, The
COL (GB/Fr) 1969 dir. Sidney Hayers

Souvenirs d'un jeune Homme
Lauzier, G.

Petit Con
GOLDWYN (Fr) 1985
dir. Gerard Lauzier

Space Vampires
Wilson, C.

Lifeforce
CANNON (US) 1985 dir. Tobe Hooper

Spanish Military Nun, The
De Qunicey, T.

Monja Alferez, La
GOYA (Sp) 1992 dir. Javier Aguirre

Sparkles in the Darkness
Yoshimura, A.

Eel, The
KSS (Jap) 1997 dir. Shohei Imamura

Sparrers Can't Sing
Lewis, S.

Sparrows Can't Sing
WAR (GB) 1962 dir. Joan Littlewood

Speaking in Tongues
Bovell, A.

Lantana
LIONS GATE (Aust) 2000 dir. Ray Lawrence

Sphinx has Spoken, The
Dekobra, M.

Friends and Lovers
RKO (US) 1931 dir. Victor Schertzinger

Spinster
Ashton-Warner, S.

Two Loves
MGM (US) 1961 dir. Charles Walters
GB title: Spinster, The

Spinster Dinner
Baldwin, F.

Love Before Breakfast
UN (US) 1936 dir. Walter Lang

Splendid Crime, The
Goodschild, G.

Public Defender
RKO (US) 1931 dir. J. Walter Ruben

Spoonhandle
Moore, R.

Deep Waters
FOX (US) 1948 dir. Henry King

Sporting Proposition, A
Aldridge, J.

Ride a Wild Pony
DISNEY (Aust) 1976 dir. Don Chaffey

Spring of Love, A
Dale, C.

Mr. Right
BBC (GB) 1983 dir. Peter Smith

Spurs
Robbins, T.

Freaks
MGM (US) 1932 dir. Tod Browning

Spy, The
Thomas, P.

Defector, The
PECF (Fr/W. Ger) 1966 dir. Raoul Levy

Square Circle, The
Carney, D.

Wild Geese II
UN (GB) 1985 dir. Peter Hunt

St. Ives
Stevenson, R. L.

Secret of St. Ives, The
COL (US) 1949 dir. Phil Rosen

Stab in the Dark
Block, L.

8 Million Ways to Die
TRISTAR (US) 1986 dir. Hal Ashby

Stage to Lordsburg
Haycox, E.

Stagecoach
UA (US) 1939 dir. John Ford
FOX (US) 1966 dir. Gordon Douglas
HERITAGE (US) 1986 dir. Ted Post

Stamboul Train
Greene, G.

Orient Express
FOX (US) 1934 dir. Paul Martin

Stand on It
Neely, W.

Stroker Ace
UN/WAR (US) 1983 dir. Hal Needham

Stand-Up Tragedy
Cain, B.

Thicker Than Blood
TNT PICT (US) 1998 dir. Richard Pearce

Star in the West
Roberts, R. E.

Second Time Around, The
FOX (US) 1961 dir. Vincent Sherman

Stars in their Courses, The
Brown, H.

El Dorado
PAR (US) 1966 dir. Howard Hawks

Steel Saraband
Dataller, R.

Hard Steel
GFD (GB) 1942 dir. Norman Walker

Stella
de Hartog, J.

Key, The
COL (GB) 1958 dir. Carol Reed

Stella Dallas
Prouty, O.

Stella
TOUCHSTONE (US) 1990 dir. John
Erman

Still Life
Coward, N.

Brief Encounter
CIN (GB) 1945 dir. David Lean
ITC (US) 1974 dir. Alan Bridges

Still Missing
Gutcheon, B.

Without a Trace
FOX (US) 1983 dir. Stanley R. Jaffe

Stone for Danny Fisher, A
Robbins, H.

King Creole
PAR (US) 1958 dir. Michael Curtiz

Stop at a Winner
Delderfield, R. F.

On the Fiddle
AA (GB) 1961 dir. Cyril Frankel
US title: Operation Snafu

Storia di Enza, La
Grimaldi, A.

Ribelle, La
RETEITALIA (It) 1993 dir. Aurelio
Grimaldi

Stories
Chekhov, A.

Dark Eyes
EXCELSIOR (It) 1987 dir. Nikita
Mikhalkov

Storm and Sorrow in the High High Pamirs
Craig, R.

Storm and Sorrow
HEARST (US) 1990 dir. Richard Colla

Story of a Seagull and the Cat who Taught her to Fly
Sepulveda, L.

Zorba and Lucky
CECCHI (It) 1998 dir. Elzo D'Alo

Story of Ivy
Lowndes, Mrs M. B.

Ivy
UI (US) 1947 dir. Sam Wood

Story of Khatyn, The
Adamovich, A.

Come and See
MOSFILM (USSR) 1985
dir. Elem Klimov

Story of the Trapp Family Singers, The
Trapp, M. A.
Sound of Music, The
FOX (US) 1965 dir. Robert Wise

Story of the Vivero Letter, The
Bagley, D.
Vivero Letter, The
PROMARK (US) 1999 dir. H. Gordon Boos

Story of Zarak Khan, The
Bevan, A. C.
Zarak
COL (GB) 1956 dir. Terence Young

Stowaway to the Moon: The Camelot Odyssey
Shelton, W. R.
Stowaway to the Moon
FOX (US) 1975
dir. Andrew V. McLaglen

Strange Boarders of Paradise Crescent, The
Oppenheim, E. P.
Strange Boarders
GB (GB) 1938 dir. Herbert Mason

Strange Snow
Metcalfe, S.
Jackknife
CINEPLEX (US) 1989 dir. David Jones

Strange Tales of Liao Zhai
Ling, P. S.
Chinese Ghost Story II
GORDON (China) 1990
dir. Ching Siu-Tung

Stranger, The
Loss, L. B.
Zandy's Bride
WAR (US) 1974 dir. Jan Troell

Stranger at Home
Sanders, G.
Stranger Came Home, The
EXCL (GB) 1954 dir. Terence Fisher
US title: Unholy Four, The

Stranger in the House
Sherburne, Z.
Memories Never Die
UN TV (US) 1982 dir. Sandor Stern

Strangers in the House
Simenon, G.
Stranger in the House
JARFID (GB) 1967 dir. Pierre Rouve

Strangers on a Train
Highsmith, P.
Once You Meet a Stranger
WAR (US) 1996 dir. Tommy Lee Wallace

Street Has a Thousand Eyes, The
Hamilton, P.
Bitter Harvest
RANK (GB) 1963
dir. Peter Graham Scott

Strip Tease
Hiassen, C.
Striptease
CASTLE ROCK (US) 1996 dir. Andrew Bergman

Stronghold
Ellin, S.
Prayer in the Dark, A
WIL COURT (US) 1997 dir. Jerry Ciccoritti

Sturm in Wasserglass
Frank, B.
Storm in a Teacup
LF (GB) 1937 dir. Ian Dalrymple, Victor Saville

Such a Good Boy
Hobbs Birnie, L.

Scorn
KINETIC (Can) 2000 dir. Sturla
Gunnarsson

Sudden Fury
Walker, L.

Family Torn Apart, A
HALMI (US) 1993 dir. Craig Baxley

Sudie
Carter, S. F.

Sudie & Simpson
HEARST (US) 1990
dir. Joan Tewkesbury

Sufficient Carbohydrate
Potter, D.

Visitors
BBC (GB) 1987 dir. Piers Haggard

Suicide Club, The
Stevenson, R. L.

Trouble for Two
MGM (US) 1936 dir. J. Walter Rubin
GB title: Suicide Club, The

Summer Lightning
Corliss, A.

I Met My Love Again
WANGER (US) 1937 dir. Joshua Logan,
Arthur Ripley

Summer of Fear
Duncan, L.

Stranger in our House
INTERPLAN (US) 1978 dir. Wes Craven

Sun Shines Bright, The; Mob From Massac, The; Lord Provides, The
Cobb, I. S.

Sun Shines Bright, The
REP (US) 1953 dir. John Ford

Sur la Terre Comme au Ciel
Belletto, R.

Peril
TRIUMPH (Fr) 1985 dir. Michel DeVille

Surely You're Joking, Mr Feynman; What Do You Care What Other People Think
Feynman, R.

Infinity
OVERSEAS (US) 1996 dir. Matthew
Broderick

Survivor, The
Eisner, J. P.

War and Love
CANNON (US/Israel) 1985
dir. Moshe Mizrahi

Suspense
Graeme, B.

Face in the Night
GN (GB) 1956 dir. Lance Comfort

Suspicion of Innocence
Parker, B. J.

Sisters and Other Strangers
FOX (US) 1997 dir. Roger Young

Svart Cayal
Knutsen, P.

Sebastian
NORDISK (Nor/Swe) 1996 dir. Svend
Wam

Swastika
Shisgall, O.

Man I Married, The
TCF (US) 1940 dir. Irving Pichel

Sweeny Todd, the Demon Barber of Fleet Street
Dibdin-Pitt, G.

Sweeney Todd
THAMES (GB) 1982 dir. Reginald
Collin

Sweet Aloes
Mallory, J.

Give Me Your Heart
WAR (US) 1936 dir. Archie Mayo
GB title: Sweet Aloes

Sweet Poison
Lee, L.

Along Came a Spider
FOX TV (US) 1970 dir. Lee H. Katzin

Sweetheart
Coburn, A.

Toutes Peines Confondues
FRANCE 3 (Fr) 1992 dir. Michael
Deville

Swell Looking Babe, A
Thompson, J.

Hit Me
CASTLE HILL (US) 1996 dir. Steven
Shainberg

SWF Seeks Same
Lutz, J.

Single White Female
COL (US) 1992 dir. Barbet Schroeder

Swift Water
Annixter, P.

Those Calloways
DISNEY (US) 1964 dir. Norman Tokar

Swimming Lessons
Tuttle Villegas, A. and Hugo, L.

Another Woman's Husband
HEARST (US) 2000 dir. Noel Nosseck

Swiss Family Robinson, The
Wyss, J. D.

New Swiss Family Robinson, The
TOTAL (US) 1999 dir. Stewart Raffill

Switch
Bayer, W.

Doubletake
TITUS (US) 1985 dir. Jud Taylor

Symbol, The
Bessie, A.

Sex Symbol, The
COL (US) 1974 dir. David Lowell Rich

T

Tabitha
Ridley, A. and Borer, M.
Who Killed the Cat?
GN (GB) 1966 dir. Montgomery Tully

Table de Flandes, La
Perez-Reverte, A.
Uncovered
CIBY 2000 (Sp/GB) 1994 dir. Jim
McBride

Tailor in the Château
Marchand, L. and Armont, P.
Love Me Tonight
PAR (US) 1932 dir. Rouben Mamoulian

Taint of the Tiger
Macdonald, J. P.
Mantrap
PAR (US) 1961 dir. Edmond O'Brien

Tainted Evidence
Daley, R.
Night Falls on Manhattan
PAR (US) 1997 dir. Sidney Lumet

Take Me Home
Denver, J. and Tobier, A.
Take Me Home: The John Denver Story
GRANADA (US) 2000 dir. Jerry London

Taking to the Air: The Rise of Michael Jordan
Naughton, J.
Michael Jordan: An American Hero
FOX FAMILY (US) 1999 dir. Alan
Metzger

Tale which Begins with a Funeral of a Snake, A
Matalon, R.
Dreams of Innocence
BELFILMS (Israel) 1993 dir. Dina Zvi-
Riklis

Talented Mr. Ripley, The
Highsmith, P.
Purple Noon
HILLCREST (Fr) 1960
dir. René Clément

Tales of a Dead King
Meyers, W. D.
Legend of the Lost Tomb
TRINITY (US) 1996 dir. Jonathan
Winfrey

Tales from the South Pacific
Michener, J. P.
South Pacific
TODD AO (US) 1958 dir. Joshua Logan
TOUCHSTONE (US) 2001 dir. Richard
Pearce

Tales of the African Frontier
Hunter, J. A. and Mannix, D. P.
Killers of Kilimanjaro, The
COL (GB) 1959 dir. Richard Thorpe

Talisman, The
Scott, Sir W.
King Richard and the Crusaders
WAR (US) 1954 dir. David Butler

Talked to Death: The Life and Murder of Alan Berg
Singular, S.
Talk Radio
UN (US) 1988 dir. Oliver Stone

Taming of the Shrew, The
Shakespeare, W.
Kiss Me Kate
MGM (US) 1953 dir. George Sidney
MILBERG (US) 1958 dir. George Schaefer

Taming of the Shrew, The
Shakespeare, W.
10 Things I Hate About You
TOUCHSTONE (US) 1999 dir. Gil Junger

Tarnsman of Gor
Norman, J.
Gor
CANNON (US) 1989 dir. Fritz Kiersch

Tarzan of the Apes
Burroughs, E. R.
Greystoke: The Legend of Tarzan, Lord of the Apes
WAR (GB) 1984 dir. Hugh Hudson

Tarzan of the Apes
Burroughs, E. R.
Tarzan
DISNEY (US) 1999 dir. Chris Buck, Kevin Lima

Tarzan of the Apes
Burroughs, E. R.
Tarzan, The Ape Man
MGM (US) 1932 dir. W. S. Van Dyke

Taste of my Own Medicine, A
Rosenbaum, E.
Doctor, The
TOUCHSTONE (US) 1991 dir. Randa Haines

Tchin-Tchin
Billetdoux, F.
Fine Romance, A
PC (It) 1992 dir. Gene Saks

Teacher, I Passed This Way
Ashton-Warner, S.
Sylvia
ENT (NZ) 1985 dir. Michael Firth

Tears Before Bedtime; Weep No More
Skelton, B.
Business Affair, A
STUDIO CANAL+ (GB/Fr) 1994 dir. Charlotte Brandstorm

Tempest, The
Shakespeare, W.
Prospero's Books
FILM 4 (GB/Fr) 1991
dir. Peter Greenaway

Temptations of Big Bear, The
Weibe, R.
Big Bear
TELEFILM (Can) 1999 dir. Gil Cardinal

Ten Against Caesar
Granger, K. R. G.
Gun Fury
COL (US) 1953 dir. Raoul Walsh

Ten Little Niggers
Christie, A.
And Then There Were None
ABP (US) 1945 dir. Rene Clair
GB title: Ten Little Niggers
EMI (GB) 1974 dir. Peter Collinson

Ten Little Niggers
Christie, A.
Ten Little Indians
ABP (GB) 1965 dir. George Pollock
CANNON (US) 1989
dir. Alan Birkinshaw

Ten Plus One
McBain, E.

Without Apparent Motive
VALORIA (Fr) 1971 dir. Philippe Labro

Ten-Second Jailbreak, The
Asinof, E., Hinckle, W. and Turner, W.

Breakout
COL (US) 1975 dir. Tom Gries

10.30 p.m. on a Summer Night
Duras, M.

10.30 p.m. Summer
UA (US/Sp) 1966 dir. Jules Dassin

Tendre Poulet
Rouland, J.-P. and Olivier, C.

Dear Inspector
ARIANE/MONDEX (Fr) 1977
dir. Philippe de Broca

Tentacles
Lyon, D.

House on Telegraph Hill, The
FOX (US) 1951 dir. Robert Wise

Terrible Hours, The
Maas, P.

Submerged
NBC (US) 2001 dir. James Keach

Territorio Comanche
Perez-Reverte, A.

Comanche Territory
TORNASOL (Sp/Fr) 1997 dir. Gerardo
Herrero

Terror in the Bedroom
Bramly, S.

Sade
STUDIO CANAL+ (Fr) 2000 dir. Benoit
Jacques

Terror on Highway 59
Sellers, S.

Terror on Highway 91
CBS (US) 1989 dir. Jerry Jameson

Tess of the d'Urbervilles
Hardy, T.

Tess
COL (Fr/GB) 1981 dir. Roman Polanski

Testament
Benet I. and Jornet, J. M.

Beloved/Friend
CANAL+ ESPANA (Sp) 1999 dir.
Ventura Pons

Tête Coupable, La
Gary, R.

Impostors, The
STUDIO CANAL+ (Fr) 1994 dir.
Frederic Blum

Thanks God, I'll Take it From Here
Allen, J. and Livingston, M.

Without Reservations
RKO (US) 1946 dir. Mervyn LeRoy

That Uncertain Feeling
Amis, K.

Only Two Can Play
BL (GB) 1961 dir. Sidney Gilliat

Thé au harem d'Archi Ahmen, Le
Charef, M.

Tea in the Harem
M&R (Fr) 1986 dir. Mehdi Charef

Théâtre Dans la Nuit
Cauvin, P.

Lisa
STUDIO CANAL+ (Fr) 2001 dir. Pierre
Grimblat

Theme of the Traitor and the Hero, The
Borges, J. L.

Spider's Stratagem, The
RED FILM (It) 1970
dir. Bernardo Bertolucci

Then There Were Three
Shaw, I.
Three
UA (GB) 1969 dir. James Salter

Theophilus North
Wilder, T.
Mr. North
GOLDWYN (US) 1988
dir. Danny Huston

There are Two Kinds of Terrible
Mann, P.
Two Kinds of Love
CBS (US) 1983 dir. Jack Bender

There was a Fair Maid Dwelling; The Unjust Skies
Delderfield, R. F.
Diana
BBC (GB) 1983 dir. David Tucker

There was a Little Man
Jones, G. P and Jones, C. B.
Luck of the Irish, The
FOX (US) 1948 dir. Henry Koster

There was that Beautiful Place
Manling, Z.
Sacrifice of Youth
ART EYE (China) 1986
dir. Zhang Luanxin

There's Always Juliet
van Druten, J.
One Night in Lisbon
PAR (US) 1941 dir. Edward H. Griffith

Thérèse Desqueyroux
Mauriac, F.
Thérèse
GALA (Fr) 1964 dir. Georges Franju

These, Our Strangers
Arlington, A.
Those Kids from Town
BN (GB) 1941 dir. Lance Comfort

They Called Him Death
Hume, D.
This Man is Dangerous
RIALTO (GB) 1941
dir. Lawrence Huntington

They do it with Mirrors
Christie, A.
Murder with Mirrors
WAR (US) 1985 dir. Dick Lowry

They Dream of Home
Busch, N.
Till the End of Time
RKO (US) 1946 dir. Edward Dmytryk

They Knew What They Wanted
Howard, S.
Lady to Love, A
MGM (US) 1930 dir. Victor Seastrom

They Stole $2.5 Million and Got Away with It
Dinneen, J. F.
Six Bridges to Cross
UN (US) 1955 dir. Joseph Pevney

Thieves' Market
Bezzerides, A. I.
Thieves' Highway
FOX (US) 1949 dir. Jules Dassin

Think of a Number
Bodelsen, A.
Silent Partner, The
CAROLCO (Can) 1978 dir. Daryl Duke

Third Avenue, New York
McNulty, J. L.
Easy Come, Easy Go
PAR (US) 1947 dir. John Farrow

Thirteen Days to Glory: The Seige of the Alamo
Tinkle, J. L.
Alamo: 13 Days to Glory, The
FRIES (US) 1987 dir. Burt Kennedy

13th Man, The
Bloom, M. T.

Last Embrace
UA (US) 1979 dir. Jonathan Demme

This For Remembrance
Clooney, R. and Strait, R.

Rosie: The Rosemary Clooney Story
FRIES (US) 1982 dir. Jackie Cooper

This is New York
Sherwood, R. E.

Two Kinds of Women
PAR (US) 1932 dir. William C. De Mille

This is Your Life
Wolitzer, M.

This is My Life
FOX (US) 1992 dir. Nora Ephron

This Life I've Led: My Autobiography
Zaharias, B. D. and Paxton, H.

Babe
MGM TV (US) 1975 dir. Buzz Kulik

This Lime Tree Bower
McPherson, C.

Saltwater
ART EYE (Ire) 1999 dir. Conor McPherson

This Magic Moment
Roberts, N.

Magic Moments
ATLANTIC/YTV (GB/US)
dir. Lawrence Gordon Clarke

This Same Garden
Bell, R.

While I Live
DRYHURST (GB) 1947 dir. John Harlow

This Story of Yours
Hopkins, J.

Offence, The
UA (GB) 1972 dir. Sidney Lumet

This was my Choice
Gouzenko, I.

Iron Curtain
FOX (US) 1948 dir. William Wellman

This Way Out
Ronald, J.

Suspect, The
UN (US) 1944 dir. Robert Siodmak

Thomasina
Gallico, P.

Three Lives of Thomasina, The
DISNEY (GB) 1963 dir. Don Chaffey

Thorn Birds, The
McCullough, C.

Thorn Birds, The: The Missing Years
WOLPER (US) 1996 dir. Kevin James Dobson

Thor
Smith, W.

Bad Moon
MORGAN CREEK (US) 1996 dir. Eric Red

Thousand Plan, The
Barker, R.

1,000 Plane Raid, The
UA (GB) 1969 dir. Boris Sagal

Three Cups of Coffee
Feiner, R.

Woman's Angle, A
ABP (GB) 1952 dir. Leslie Arliss

Three Fevers
Walmsley, L.

Turn of the Tide
BN (GB) 1935 dir. Norman Walker

Three Godfathers, The
Kyne, P. B.

Hell's Heroes
UN (US) 1930 dir. William Wyler

Three Men in the Snow
Kastner, E.
Paradise for Three
MGM (US) 1938 dir. Edward Buzzell

Three Musketeers, The
Dumas, A.
Four Musketeers, The
FOX-RANK (Pan/Sp) 1974
dir. Richard Lester

Three Musketeers, The
Dumas, A.
Musketeer, The
MIRAMAX (US/Ger) 2001 dir. Peter
Hyams

Three Roads, The
Macdonald, R.
Double Negative
QUADRANT (Can) 1980 dir. George
Bloomfield

372 Le Matin
Dijan, P.
Betty Blue
GAU (Fr) 1986 dir. Jean-Jacques Beineix

**Three Worlds of Johnny
Handsome, The**
Godey, J.
Johnny Handsome
TRISTAR (US) 1989 dir. Walter Hill

Threepenny Opera, The
Brecht, B. and Weill, K.
Mack the Knife
21st CENTURY (US) 1989 dir. Menahem
Golan

**Through the Looking Glass and
What Alice Found There**
Carroll, L.
Alice Through the Looking Glass
PROJECTOR (GB) 1998 dir. John
Henderson

**Thumbs Up: The Life and
Courageous Comeback of
White House Press Secretary
Jim Brady**
Dickenson, M.
Without Warning: The James Brady Story
HBO (US) 1991
dir. Michael Toshiyuki Uno

Thunder Above
Wallis, A. J. and Blair, C. E.
Beyond the Curtain
RANK (GB) 1960 dir. Compton Bennett

Thunder God's Gold
Storm, B.
Lust for Gold
COL (US) 1949 dir. S. Sylvan Simon

Thunderwith
Hathorn, L.
Echo of Thunder, The
HALLMARK (US) 1998 dir. Simon
Wincer

Thursday Adventure
Pudney, J.
Stolen Airliner, The
BL (GB) 1955 dir. Don Sharp

Thursday Woman, The
Davidson, M.
Wednesday Woman, The
CBP (US) 2000 dir. Christopher Leitch

**Thy Son Liveth, Messages from
a Soldier to His Mother**
Boylan, G. D.
Rumor of Angels, A
MPCA (US) 2000 dir. Peter O'Fallon

Tian Yu
Yan, G.
Xiu Xiu: The Sent-Down Girl
GOOD MACHINE (China/HK) 1998
dir. Joan Chen

Tiger
Strege, J.
Tiger Woods Story, The
SHOWTIME (US) 1998 dir. LeVar
Burton

Tiger, The
Schisgal, M.
Tiger Makes Out, The
COL (US) 1967 dir. Arthur Hiller

Tiger Amongst Us, The
Brackett, L.
13 West Street
COL (US) 1962 dir. Philip Leacock

Tikoyo and his Shark
Richer, C.
Beyond the Reef
UN (US) 1981 dir. Frank C. Clark

Time of the Cuckoo, The
Laurents, A.
Summertime
UA (US) 1955 dir. David Lean
GB title: Summer Madness

Time Out for Ginger
Alexander, R.
Billie
UA (US) 1965 dir. Don Weis

Time to Die, A
Wicker, T.
Attica
ABC (US) 1980 dir. Marvin J. Chomsky

Time to Remember, A
Shapiro, S.
Running Against Time
FINNEGAN-PINCHUK (US) 1990 dir.
Bruce Seth Green

Times Of My Life, The
Ford, B. and Chase, C.
Betty Ford Story, The
WAR TV (US) 1987 dir. David Greene

Tim
McCullough, C.
Mary & Tim
HALLMARK (US) 1996 dir. Glenn
Jordan

Tin Star, The
Cunningham, J. M.
High Noon
UA (US) 1952 dir. Fred Zinnemann

Tin Wife
Flaherty, J.
My Husband's Secret Life
USA NETWORK (US) 1998 dir. Graeme
Clifford

Tinfoil
Cram, M.
Faithless
MGM (US) 1932 dir. Harry Beaumont

Tinker, The
Dobie, L. and Sloman, R.
Wild and the Willing, The
RANK (GB) 1962 dir. Ralph Thomas
US title: Young and Willing

Tinted Venus
Antley, F.
Goddess of Love, The
NEW WORLD TV (US) 1988
dir. James Drake

Tintype, The
Brown, R.
Timestalkers
FRIES (US) 1987 dir. Michael Schultz

Tiptoe Boys, The
Markstein, G.
Final Option, The
MGM/UA (GB) 1983 dir. Ian Sharp

Tiré a Part
Fiechter, J.-J.
Limited Edition
FRANCE 3 (Fr) 1996 dir. Bernard Rapp

Tish Marches On
Rinehart, M. R.
Tish
MGM (US) 1942 dir. S. Sylvan Simon

Titus Andronicus
Shakespeare, W.
Titus
OVERSEAS (US/It) 1999 dir. Julie Taymor

To America with Love: Letters From the Underground
Hoffman, A. and Hoffman, A.
Steal This Movie
GREENLIGHT (US) 2000 dir. Robert Greenwald

To an Early Grave
Markfield, W.
Bye Bye Braverman
WAR (US) 1968 dir. Sidney Lumet

To Dusty Death
McCutcheon, H.
Pit of Darkness
BUTCHER (GB) 1961
dir. Lance Comfort

To Elvis with Love
Canada, L.
Touched by Love
COL (US) 1980 dir. Gus Trikonis

To Have and Have Not
Hemingway, E.
Breaking Point, The
WAR (US) 1950 dir. Michael Curtiz

To Have and Have Not
Hemingway, E.
Gun Runners, The
UA (US) 1958 dir. Don Siegel

To Save His Life
Roos, K.
Dead Men Tell No Tales
FOX (US) 1971 dir. Walter Grauman

To Smithereens
Drexler, R.
Below the Belt
ATLANTIC (US) 1982
dir. Robert Fowler

To Speak For the Dead
Levine, P.
Jake Lassiter: Justice on the Bayou
CANNELL (US) 1995 dir. Peter Markle

Tonight at 8.30
Coward, N.
We Were Dancing
MGM (GB) 1942 dir. Robert Z. Leonard

Too Dangerous To Be at Large
Johnson, R. and McCormick, M.
Dangerous Company
FINNEGAN (US) 1982
dir. Lamont Johnson

Too Rich
Duke, P. and Thomas, J.
Too Rich: The Secret Life of Doris Duke
VZ/SERTNER (US) 1999 dir. John Erman

Toomai of the Elephants
Kipling, R.
Elephant Boy
UA (GB) 1937 dir. Robert Flaherty, Zoltan Korda

Tooth of the Lion
Jennings, S.
Summer My Father Grew Up, The
SHAPIRO (US) 1991
dir. Michael Tuchner

Top of the World
Ruesch, H.
Savage Innocents, The
RANK (Fr/It/GB) 1960
dir. Nicholas Ray

Topaz
Murakami, R.
Tokyo Decadence
NORTHERN (Jap) 1992 dir. Ryu
Murakami

Topaze
Pagnol, M.
Mr. Topaze
FOX (GB) 1961 dir. Peter Sellers
US title: I Like Money

Torch Bearers, The
Kelly, G.
Doubting Thomas
FOX (US) 1935 dir. David Butler

Toto il Buono
Zavattini, C.
Miracle in Milan
PDS (It) 1951 dir. Vittorio de Sica

Touch it Light
Storey, R.
Light up the Sky
BL (GB) 1960 dir. Lewis Gilbert

Touch the Lion's Paw
Lambert, D.
Rough Cut
PAR (US) 1980 dir. Don Siegel

Touch Wood
Stringer, D.
Nearly a Nasty Accident
BL (GB) 1961 dir. Don Chaffey

Touhimu
Fujitani, A.
Shiki-Jitsu
STUDIO KAJINO (Jap) 2000 dir.
Hideaki Anno

Tower, The
Stern, R. M.
Towering Inferno, The
COL-WAR (US) 1975
dir. John Gullermin, Irwin Allen

Toys of Glass
Booth, M.
Evolution's Child
FOXTAIL (US) 1999 dir. Jeffrey Reiner

Tracy Cromwell
Richter, C.
One Desire
UI (US) 1955 dir. Jerry Hopper

Tragical History of Doctor Faustus
Marlowe, C.
Doctor Faustus
COL (GB) 1967 dir. Richard Burton,
Neville Coghill

Trailmakers, The
Forte, V.
Wild Women
SPELLING (US) 1970 dir. Don Taylor

Trails End
Shirreffs, G. D.
Oregon Passage
ABP (US) 1958 dir. Paul Landres

Transfixions
Aubert, B.
Mauvais Genres
STUDIO CANAL+ (Fr/Bel) 2001 dir.
Francis Girod

Translation of a Savage, The
Parker, G.
Behold my Wife
PAR (US) 1934 dir. Mitchell Leisen

Trap for a Single Man
Thomas, R.
One of my Wives is Missing
SPEL-GOLD (US) 1976
dir. Glenn Jordan

Traumnovelle
Schnitzler, A.
Eyes Wide Shut
WAR (GB/US) 1999 dir. Stanley
Kubrick

Travelling Lady, The
Foote, H.
Baby, The Rain Must Fall
COL (US) 1965 dir. Robert Mulligan

Travels of Jaimie McPheeters, The
Taylor, R. L.
Guns of Diablo
MGM (US) 1964 dir. Boris Sagal

Travesty, A
Westake, D. E.
Slight Case of Murder, A
TNT (US) 1999 dir. Steven Schachter

Treasure of Franchard
Stevenson, R. L.
Treasure of Lost Canyon, The
UI (US) 1952 dir. Ted Tetzlaff

Tree of Hands, The
Rendell, R.
Betty Fisher et Autres Histoires
STUDIO CANAL+ (Fr/Can) 2001 dir.
Claude Miller

Tree of Liberty, The
Page, E.
Howards of Virginia, The
COL (US) 1940 dir. Frank Lloyd
GB title: Tree of Liberty, The

Trial
Irving, C.
Trial: The Price of Passion
TRISTAR TV (US) 1992 dir. Paul
Wendkos

Trial by Terror
Gallico, P.
Assignment Paris
COL (US) 1952 dir. Robert Parrish

Triangle
White, T.
See How They Fall
FRANCE 3 (Fr) 1994 dir. Jacques
Audiard

Trigger
Vollmer, L.
Spitfire
RKO (US) 1934 dir. John Cromwell

Trilby
Du Maurier, G.
Svengali
WAR (US) 1931 dir. Archie Mayo
REN (GB) 1954 dir. William Alwyn
HALMI (US) 1983 dir. Anthony Harvey

Trinity's Child
Prochnau, W.
By Dawn's Early Light
HBO (US) 1990 dir. Jack Sholder

Triumph
Fulop-Miller, R.
Great Moment, The
PAR (US) 1944. dir. Preston Sturges

Tropfen auf Heisse Steine
Fassbinder, R. W.
Water Drops on Burning Rocks
STUDIO IMAGES 6 (Fr) 2000 dir.
François Ozon

Tropic of Ruislip, The
Thomas, L.
Tropic
ATV (GB) 1979 dir. Matthew Robinson

Truite, La
Vailland, R.
Trout, The
TRIUMPH (Fr) 1982 dir. Joseph Losey

Trumpets of Company K
Chamberlain, W.

Imitation General
MGM (US) 1958 dir. George Marshall

Truth Game, The
Novello, I.

But the Flesh is Weak
MGM (US) 1932 dir. Jack Conway

Trying to Grow
Kanga, F.

Sixth Happiness, The
DREAMFACTORY (GB) 1997 dir. Waris
Hussein

Tu Nombre Envenena Mis Suenos
Leguina, J.

Your Name Poisons My Dreams
CDP(Sp) 1996 dir. Pilar Miro

Tucker's People
Wolfert, I.

Force of Evil
MGM (US) 1948 dir. Abraham Polonsky

Turn of the Screw, The
James, H.

Haunting of Helen Walker, The
ROSEMONT (US) 1995 dir. Tom
McLoughlin

Turn of the Screw, The
James, H.

Innocents, The
FOX (GB) 1961 dir. Jack Clayton

Turn of the Screw, The
James, H.

Nightcomers, The
AVCO (GB) 1972
dir. Michael Winner

Turnabout
Faulkner, W.

Today We Live
MGM (US) 1933 dir. Howard Hawks

Turning Point, The
Capra, F.

Mindwalk
ATLAS (US) 1991 dir. Bernt Capra

Twelfth of Never, The
Heyes, D.

Lonely Profession, The
UN TV (US) 1979 dir. Douglas Heyes

Twelve Adventures of the Celebrated Baron Munchausen
Raspe, R. E.

Adventures of Baron Munchausen, The
COL (GB) 1988 dir. Terry Gilliam

Twelve Chairs
Ilf, E. and Petrov, E.

Keep Your Seats Please
ATP (GB) 1936 dir. Monty Banks

Twilight
Koontz, D.

Servants of Twilight, The
TRIMARK (US) 1991 dir. Jeffrey Obrow

Twin Sombreros
Grey, Z.

Gunfighters
COL (US) 1947 dir. George Waggner

Twins
Wood, B. and Geasland, J.

Dead Ringers
FOX (Can) 1988 dir. David Cronenberg

Two Deaths of Senora Puccini, The
Dubyns, S.

Two Deaths
BRIT SCREEN (GB) 1995 dir. Nicolas
Roeg

Two for the Price of One
Kenrick, T.

Nobody's Perfekt
COL (US) 1981 dir. Peter Bonerz

Two of a Kind: The Hillside Stranglers
O'Brien, D.
Case of the Hillside Stranglers, The
FRIES (US) 1989 dir. Steven Gethers

Typee
Melville, H.
Enchanted Island
WAR (US) 1958 dir. Allan Dwan

UFO Crash at Roswell
Randle, K. D. and Schmitt, D. R.

Roswell
SHOWTIMEWORKS (US) 1994 dir.
Jeremy Kagan

Umbrella Man, The
Scott, W.

London by Night
MGM (US) 1937 dir. William Thiele

Uncharted Seas
Wheatley, D.

Lost Continent, The
WAR (GB) 1968 dir. Michael Carreras

Uncle Harry
Job, T.

Strange Affair of Uncle Harry, The
UN (US) 1945 dir. Robert Siodmak

Uncle Silas
le Fanu, S.

Dark Angel, The
BBC (GB) 1989 dir. Peter Hammond

Uncle Vanya
Chekhov, A.

August
GOLDWYN (US) 1996 dir. Anthony
Hopkins

Uncle Vanya
Chekhov, A.

Country Life
MIRAMAX (Aust) 1994 dir. Michael
Blakemore

Uncle Vanya
Chekhov, A.

Vanya on 42nd Street
CHANNEL 4 FILMS (GB/US) 1994 dir.
Louis Malle

Uncommon Danger
Ambler, E.

Background to Danger
WAR (US) 1943 dir. Raoul Walsh

Uncommon Will: The Death
and Life of Sue Rodriguez
Rodriguez, S. and Hobbs Birnie, L.

*At the End of the Day: The Sue Rodriguez
Story*
AMW (Can) 1999 dir. Sheldon Larry

Undercover Cat
Gordon, M. and Gordon, G.

That Darn Cat!
DISNEY (US) 1965
dir. Robert Stevenson
DISNEY (US) 1997 dir. Bob Spiers

Underground to Canada
Smucker, B.

*Race to Freedom: The Underground
Railroad*
XENON (Can) 1994 dir. Don McBrearty

Undertaker's Gone Bananas,
The
Zindel, P.

*New Adventures of Spin & Marty, The:
Suspect Behavior*
DISNEY (US) 2000 dir. Rusty Cundieff

Uneasy Freehold
Macardle, D.

Uninvited, The
PAR (US) 1944 dir. Lewis Allen

Unexpected Mrs. Pollifax, The
Gilman, D.

Mrs. Pollifax—Spy
UA (US) 1971 dir. Leslie Martinson

Unicorn's Secret, The
Levy, S.

Hunt For the Unicorn Killer, The
REGENCY TV (US) 1999 dir. William A.
Graham

Unidentified Human Remains and the True Nature of Love
Fraser, B.

Love and Human Remains
TELEFILM (Can) 1993 dir. Denys
Arcand

Uninvited, The
Chittenden, F.

Stranger in Town
EROS (GB) 1957 dir. George Pollock

Uninvited: He Followed a Dark Path to Obsession
Berman, J. G.

Uninvited
MEDIASET (US/It) 1999 dir. Carlo
Gabriel Nero

Union Street
Barker, P.

Stanley and Iris
MGM (US) 1990 dir. Martin Ritt

Unsleeping Eye, The
Compton, D.

Deathwatch
CONTEM (Fr/Ger) 1979
dir. Bertrand Tavernier

Unwanted Attentions
Beck, K. K.

Shadow of Obsession
SABAN ENT (US) 1994 dir. Kevin
Connor

Up Pops the Devil
Goodrich, F. and Hackett, A.

Thanks for the Memory
PAR (US) 1938 dir. George Archainbaud

Urban Folk Tales
Reitz, D.

Urbania
COMMOTION (US) 1999 dir. Jon Shear

Urgent Hangman, The
Cheyney, P.

Meet Mr Callaghan
EROS (GB) 1954 dir. Charles Saunders

Useless Cowboy, The
LeMay, A.

Along Came Jones
UA (US) 1945 dir. Stuart Heisler

V

Va' Dove ti Porta il Cuore
Tamaro, S.
Follow Your Heart
GMT (Fr/Ger/It) 1996 dir. Cristina
Comencini

Vaisseaux de Coeur, Les
Groult, B.
Salt on Our Skin
VCL (Ger/Can/Fr) 1992 dir. Andrew
Birkin

Vale Abraao
Bessa-Luis, A.
Valley of Abraham, The
GEMINI (Fr/Port) 1993 dir. Manoel de
Oliveira

Valentine's Day
Foote, H.
On Valentine's Day
ANGELIKA (US) 1986 dir. Ken
Harrison

Valkyrie's Armour
Tierney, H.
One Brief Summer
FOX (GB) 1969 dir. John MacKenzie

Valley of Fear, The
Conan Doyle, Sir A.
Triumph of Sherlock Holmes, The
TWICKENHAM (GB) 1935
dir. Leslie Hiscott

Valley of the Ants, The
Wells, H. G.
Empire of the Ants
AIP (US) 1977 dir. Bert I. Gordon

Valley of the Dolls
Susann, J.
Valley of the Dolls 1981
FOX TV (US) 1981 dir. Walter Grauman

Vanishing Corpse, The
Gilbert, A.
They Met in the Dark
RANK (GB) 1943 dir. Karel Lamac

Vanity Fair
Thackeray, W. M.
Becky Sharp
RKO (US) 1935 dir. Rouben Mamoulian

Vanity Row
Burnett, W. R.
Accused of Murder
REP (US) 1956 dir. Joe Kane

Vengeance
Jones, G.
Sword of Gideon
HBO (US/Can) 1986
dir. Michael Anderson

Venus im Pelz
von Sacher-Masoch, L.
Venus in Furs
COMM (GB/It/Ger) 1970
dir. Jess Franco
K FILMS (Neth) 1994 dir. Victor
Nieuwenhuijs, Maarte Seyferth

Verdict, The
Gregor, M.
Town Without Pity
UA (US/Switz) 1961
dir. Gottfried Reinhardt

**Verge, The; Mr Knowall;
Sanitorium**
Maugham, W. S.
Trio
GFD (GB) 1950
dir. Ken Annakin, Harold French

Versprechen, Das
Duerrenmatt, F.
Pledge, The
WAR (US) 2001 dir. Sean Penn

Vespers in Vienna
Marshall, B.
Red Danube, The
MGM (US) 1949 dir. George Sidney

Vessel of Wrath
Maugham, W. S.
Beachcomber, The
GFD (GB) 1954 dir. Muriel Box

Veufs, Les
Boileau, P. and Narcejac, T.
Entangled
TELEFILM (Can/Fr) 1993 dir. Max
Fischer

**Victim: The Other Side of
Murder**
Kinder, G.
Aftermath: A Test of Love
COL (US) 1991 dir. Glenn Jordan

Victoria Regina
Housman, L.
Victoria the Great
RKO (GB) 1937 dir. Herbert Wilcox

Vida en un Hilo, La
Neville E.
Mujer Bajo la Lluvia, Una
ATRIUM (Sp) 1992 dir. Gerardo Vera
US title: Woman in the Rain, A

Vietnam Trilogy
Fernandez, G.
Cease Fire
CINEWORLD (US) 1985
dir. David Nutter

Vigilante
Summers, R. A.
San Francisco Story, The
WAR (US) 1952 dir. Robert Parrish

Viking, The
Marshall, E.
Vikings, The
UA (US) 1958 dir. Richard Fleischer

Villa Triste
Modiano, P.
Yvonne's Perfume
ZOULOU (Fr) 1994 dir. Patrice Leconte

Vinegar Hill
Coen, F.
Deadly Family Secrets
FILERMAN (US) 1995 dir. Richard T.
Heffron

Vintage Seasons
Kuttner, H. and Moore, C. L.
Disaster in Time
WILDSTREET (US) 1992 dir. David N.
Twohy

Viper Three
Wager, W.
Twilight's Last Gleaming
HEMDALE (US/Ger) 1977
dir. Robert Aldrich

Virgin
Patterson, J.

Child of Darkness, Child of Light
WIL COURT (US) 1991
dir. Marina Sargenti

Virgin de Los Sicarios, La
Vallejo, F.

Our Lady of the Assassins
STUDIO CANAL+ (Fr) 2000 dir. Barbet
Schroeder

Visitor, The
Parker, C. G.

Of Unknown Origin
WAR (Can) 1983
dir. George P. Cosmatos

Visitors, The
Benchley, N.

Spirit is Willing, The
PAR (US) 1967 dir. William Castle

Voie Sauvage, La
Odier, D.

Light Years Away
NEW YORKER (Fr) 1932
dir. Alain Tanner

Voyage of the Basset, The
Christensen, J. C.

Voyage of the Unicorn
HALLMARK (US) 2000 dir. Philip
Spink

Waar Blijft Het Licht
van der Laan, H.

When the Light Comes
ADDED (Ger/Neth) 1999 dir. Stijn
Coninx

Wages of Fear, The
Arnaud, G.

Sorcerer
UN (US) 1977 dir. William Friedkin
GB title: Wages of Fear

Wailing Asteroid, The
Leinster, M.

Terronauts, The
EMBASSY (GB) 1967
dir. Montgomery Tully

Waiting for a Tiger
Healey, B.

Taste of Excitement, A
MONARCH (GB) 1969 dir. Don Sharp

Wake in Fright
Cook, K.

Outback
NIT (Aust) 1970 dir. Ted Kotcheff

Walk Me to the Distance
Everett, P.

Follow Your Heart
NBC (US) 1990 dir. Noel Nosseck

Walkers
Brandner, G.

From the Dead of Night
PHOENIX (US) 1989 dir. Paul Wendkos

Walks Far Woman
Stuart, C.

Legend of Walks Far Woman, The
EMI (US) 1982 dir. Mel Damski

Wallace
Frady, M.

George Wallace
TNT (US) 1997 dir. John Frankenheimer

Wallflower
Bayer, W.

Forget-Me-Not Murders, The
SPELLING TV (US) 1994 dir. Robert
Iscove

Walls Came Tumbling Down, The
Deal, B. H.

Friendships, Secrets and Lies
WAR TV (US) 1979
dir. Ann Zane Shanks, Marlena Laird

Walter Winchell: His Life and Times
Klurfeld, H.

Winchell
HBO (US) 1998 dir. Paul Mazursky

Walton Experience, The
Walton, T.

Fire in the Sky
PAR (US) 1993 dir. Robert Lieberman

Waltz Into Darkness
Woolrich, C.
Original Sin
MGM (US/Fr) 2001 dir. Michael
Cristofer

Wan Family's Lawsuit, The
Chen, Y. B.
Story of Qiu Ju, The
SIL-METROPOLE (China) 1992 dir.
Yimou Zhang

Wanderer Never Sleeps, Even on the Road, A
Lee, J.
Man with Three Coffins, The
MWL (S. Kor) 1987 dir. Chang Ho Lee

Warrior, The
Slaughter, F. G.
Naked in the Sun
ALLIED (US) 1957 dir. R. John Hugh

Washington Square
James, H.
Heiress, The
PAR (US) 1949 dir. William Wyler

Watch That Man
Farrar, R.
Man Who Knew Too Little, The
WAR (US) 1997 dir. Jon Amiel

Watcher in the Shadows
Household, G.
Deadly Harvest
CBS ENT (US) 1972 dir. Michael
O'Herlihy

Watchers
Koontz, D.
Watchers Reborn
CONCORDE (US) 1998 dir. John Carl
Buechler

Watchers on the Shore, The; Rigid True End, The
Barstow, S.
Kind of Loving, A
AA (GB) 1962 dir. John Schlesinger
GRANADA (GB) 1982 dir. Oliver
Horsburgh, Gerry Mill,
Jeremy Summers

Water is Wide, The
Conroy, P.
Conrack
FOX (US) 1974 dir. Martin Ritt

Waterloo Bridge
Sherwood, R. E.
Gaby
MGM (US) 1956 dir. Curbs Bernhardt

Way of Duty, The
Buel, J. D. and Buel, Jr., R.
Mary Silliman's War
CITADEL FILMS (Can) 1994 dir.
Stephen Surjik

We
Lindbergh, C. A.
Spirit of St. Louis, The
WAR (US) 1957 dir. Billy Wilder

We Are Seven
Troy, U.
She Didn't Say No!
ABP (GB) 1958 dir. Cyril Frankel

We can Remember it for you Wholesale
Dick, P.
Total Recall
CAROLCO (US) 1990 dir. Paul
Verhoeven

We Die Alone
Howarth, D.
Nine Lives
NORDS (Nor) 1959 dir. Arne Skouen

We Let Our Son Die
Parker, L. and Tanner, D.

Promised a Miracle
REP (US) 1988 dir. Stephen Gyllenhaal

We the O'Leary's
Busch, N.

In Old Chicago
FOX (US) 1937 dir. Henry King

Weapon
Mason, R.

Solo
TRIUMPH (US/Mex) 1996 dir. Noberto Barba

Web of Murder
Whittington, H.

Dead in the Water
K. BRIGHT/MTE (US) 1991 dir. Bill Condon

Weekend à Zuydcoote
Merle, R.

Weekend at Dunkirk
FOX (Fr/It) 1964 dir. Henri Verneuil

Weep No More
Coffee, L.

Another Time, Another Place
PAR (GB) 1958 dir. Lewis Allen

Weiser Dawidek
Huelle, P.

Weiser
EURIMAGES (Pol) 2001 dir. Wojciech Marczewski

Welcome to Xanadu
Benchley, N.

Sweet Hostage
BRUT (US) 1975 dir. Lee Phillips

Werewolf of Paris, The
Endore, G.

Curse of the Werewolf, The
RANK (GB) 1961 dir. Terence Fisher

What Beckoning Ghost
Lawlor, H.

Dominique
GRAND PRIZE (GB) 1978 dir. Michael Anderson

What Can You Do?
Leigh, J.

Making It
FOX (US) 1971 dir. John Erman

What Katy Did; What Katy Did at School
Coolidge, S.

Katy
BBC (GB) 1976 dir. Julia Smith

What Say They
Bridie, J.

You're Only Young Twice
ABP (GB) 1952 dir. Terry Gilbert

What the Deaf-Mute Heard
Gearino, G. D.

What the Deaf Man Heard
HALLMARK (US) 1997 dir. John Kent Harrison

What? ... Dead Again?
Shulman, N. B.

Doc Hollywood
WAR (US) 1991 dir. Michael Caton-Jones

What's Wrong With Angry?
Wilde, P.

Get Real
BRIT SCREEN (GB) 1998 dir. Simon Shore

Whatever Happened to Janie?
Cooney, C. B.

Face on the Milk Carton, The
FAMILY (US) 1995 dir. Waris Hussein

Wheel Spins, The
White, E. L.
Lady Vanishes, The
MGM (GB) 1938 dir. Alfred Hitchcock
RANK (GB) 1979 dir. Anthony Page

Wheelbarrow Closers
Larusso, II, L.
Closer, The
ION (US) 1990 dir. Dimitri Logothetis

Wheeler-Dealers, The
Goodman, G. J. W.
Wheeler-Dealers
MGM (US) 1963 dir. Arthur Hiller
GB title: Separate Beds

Wheels of Terror
Hassel, S.
Misfit Brigade, The
TRANSWORLD (US) 1988
dir. Gordon Hessler

When Angels Intervene
Wixom, H. and Wixom, J.
To Save the Children
WESTCOM (US) 1994 dir. Steven H. Stern

When Heaven and Earth Changed Places
Wurts, J.
Heaven and Earth
WAR (US) 1993 dir. Oliver Stone

When Knighthood was in Flower
Major, C.
Sword and the Rose, The
DISNEY (GB) 1953 dir. Ken Annakin

When Rabbit Howls
Chase, T.
Voices Within: The Lives of Truddi Chase
NEW WORLD TV (US) 1990
dir. Lamont Johnson

When we Ran
Leopold, K.
Moving Targets
ACADEMY (Aust) 1987
dir. Chris Langman

Where are you Going, Where have you Been?
Oates, J. C.
Smooth Talk
NEPENTHE (US) 1985
dir. Joyce Chopra

Where the Dark Streets Go
Davis, D. S.
Broken Vows
HALMI (US) 1987 dir. Jud Taylor

Where's My Mommy Now?
Frick, R. M.
Perfect Alibi
RYSHER (US) 1995 dir. Kevin Meyer

White Collars
Ellis, E.
Rich Man, Poor Girl
MGM (US) 1938 dir. Reinbold Schunzel

White Colt, The
Rook, D.
Run Wild, Run Free
COL (GB) 1989 dir. Richard C. Sarafian

White Mountains, The
Christopher, J.
Tripods, The
BBC (GB/US/Aust) 1981
dir. Graham Theakston, Christopher Barry

White Shark
Benchley, P.
Creature
MGM TV (US) 1998 dir. Stuart Gillard

White South, The
Innes, H.
Hell Below Zero
COL (GB) 1954 dir. Mark Robson

Who Censored Roger Rabbit?
Wolf, G. K.
Who Framed Roger Rabbit?
TOUCHSTONE (US) 1988 dir. Robert Zemeckis

Who Could Ask For Anything More
Swift, K.
Never a Dull Moment
RKO (US) 1950 dir. George Marshall

Who Goes There?
Campbell, J. W.
Thing, The
RKO (US) 1951 dir. Christian Nyby
GB title: Thing from Another World, The
UN (US) 1982 dir. John Carpenter

Who is Sylvia?
Rattigan, T.
Man Who Loved Redheads, The
BL (GB) 1954 dir. Harold French

Who Killed Sir Harry Oakes?
Leasor, J.
Eureka!
MGM/UA (GB/US) 1982
dir. Nicolas Roeg

Who Lie in Gaol
Henry, J.
Weak and the Wicked, The
APB (GB) 1953 dir. J. Lee Thompson

Who Rides with Wyatt?
Henry, W.
Young Billy Young
UA (US) 1969 dir. Burt Kennedy

Who Was That Lady I Saw You With?
Krasna, N.
Who Was That Lady?
COL (US) 1960 dir. George Sidney

Whorehouse Sting, The
Post, H.
Red-Light Sting, The
UN TV (US) 1984 dir. Rod Holcomb

Why Have They Taken Our Children?
Baugh, J. W. and Morgan, J.
They've Taken Our Children: The Chowchilla Kidnapping
L. HILL (US) 1993 d. Vern Gillum

Why Whales Came
Morpurgo, M.
When the Whales Came
FOX (GB) 1989 dir. Clive Rees

Widow Makers, The
Blankfort, M.
See How They Run
UN TV (US) 1964 dir. David Lowell Rich

Wifey
Noonan, T.
Wife, The
ARTISTIC (US) 1995 dir. Tom Noonan

Wild Bill Hickok
Wilstach, F.
Plainsman, The
PAR (US) 1937 dir. Cecil B. De Mille

Wild Calendar
Block, L.
Caught
MGM (US) 1948 dir. Max Ophuls

Wild Geese
Ostenso, M.

After the Harvest
ALBERTA (Can) 2001 dir. Jeremy Podeswa

Wild Waves
Manley, W. F.

Big Broadcast, The
PAR (US) 1932 dir. Frank Tuttle

Wildfire
Grey, Z.

Red Canyon
UN (US) 1949 dir. George Sherman

Will
Liddy, G. G.

Will: G. Gordon Liddy
SHAYNE (US) 1982
dir. Robert Lieberman

William Penn
Vulliamy, C. E.

Penn of Pennsylvania
BN (GB) 1941 dir. Lance Comfort
US title: The Courageous Mr. Penn

Willie Boy
Lawton, H.

Tell them Willie Boy is Here
UN (US) 1969 dir. Abraham Polonsky

Wilt
Sharpe, T.

Misadventures of Mr. Wilt, The
GOLDWYN (US) 1990
dir. Michael Tuchner

Wine and the Music, The
Barrett, W. E.

Pieces of Dreams
UA (US) 1970 dir. Daniel Haller

Wings of a Dove
James, H.

Under Heaven
BANNER ENT (US) 1998 dir. Meg Richman

Winners
Collura, M. L.

Spirit Rider
CREDO (Can) 1994 dir. Michael J. F. Scott

Winnie: My Life in the Institution
Bolnick, J. P.

Winnie
NBC (US) 1988 dir. John Korty

Winnie the Pooh
Milne, A. A.

Winnie the Pooh and the Honey Tree
DISNEY (US) 1965
dir. Wolfgang Reitherman

Winston Affair, The
Fast, H.

Man in the Middle
FOX (GB) 1963 dir. Guy Hamilton

Winter Doves
Cook, D.

Loving Walter
FF (GB) 1986 dir. Stephen Frears

Winter Visitor, A
Hartman, J.

One Special Night
GREEN/EPSTEIN (US) 1999 dir. Roger Young

Winter Wears a Shroud
Chapman, R.

Delavine Affair, The
MON (GB) 1954 dir. Douglas Pierce

Wisdom of Father Brown, The
Chesterton, G. K.

Father Brown, Detective
PAR (US) 1935 dir. Edward Sedgwick
ATV (GB) 1974 dir. Robert Tronson

Wiseguy: Life in A Mafia Family
Pileggi, N.
Goodfellas
WAR (US) 1990 dir. Martin Scorsese

Wishful Thinking
Wyka, F.
Implicated
COL TRISTAR (US) 1998 dir. Irving
Belatche

Wishing Well
Evans, E.
Happiness of Three Women, The
ADELPHI (GB) 1954 dir. Maurice Elvey

Wisteria Cottage
Coates, R. M.
Edge of Fury
UA (US) 1958 dir. Robert Gurney, Irving
Lerner

Witch's Milk
De Vries, P.
Pete 'n Tillie
UN (US) 1972 dir. Martin Ritt

With a Lock of Hair Over His Forehead; Revolt of the Mountain, The; Chronicles of the Shinsengumi
Shiba, R.
Taboo
IMAGICA (Jap/Fr) 1999 dir. Nagisa
Oshima

With a Pistol in His Hand
Parades, A.
Ballad of Gregorio Cortez, The
EMBASSY (US) 1983
dir. Robert M. Young

Within the Law
Veiller, B.
Paid
MGM (US) 1930 dir. Sam Wood
GB title: Within the Law

Within the Tides
Marquand, J. P.
Late George Apley, The
FOX (US) 1946
dir. Joseph L. Mankiewicz

Within the Tides
Conrad, J.
Laughing Anne
REP (GB) 1953 dir. Herbert Wilcox

Witness, The
Holden, A.
Bedroom Window, The
DELAUR (US) 1987 dir. Curtis Hanson

Wives and Concubines
Tong, S.
Raise the Red Lantern
ORION (China) 1991 dir. Zhang Yimov

Wives of Bath, The
Swan, S.
Lost and Delirious
LIONS GATE (Can) 2001 dir. Lea Pool

Woe To Live On
Woodrell, D.
Ride With the Devil
UN (US) 1999 dir. Ang Lee

Woman I Abandoned, The
Endo, S.
Aisuru
NIKKATSU (Jap) 1997 dir. Kei Kumai

Woman in Red, The
Gilbert, A.
My Name is Julia Ross
COL (US) 1945 dir. Joseph H. Lewis

Woman in the Dunes
Abé, K.
Woman of the Dunes, The
CONTEM (Jap) 1964
dir. Hiroshi Teshigahara

Woman Lies, A
Fodor, L.
Thunder in the Night
FOX (US) 1935 dir. George Archainbaud

Woman of Color, Daughter of Privilege: Amanda Dickson
Leslie, K. A.
House Divided, A
AVNET/KERNER (US) 2000 dir. John Kent Harrison

Woman of Honor
Modignani, S. C.
Vendetta II: The New Mafia
FILMLINE (US) 1993 dir. Ralph L. Thomas

Woman on Trial, A
Bembenek, L.
Woman on the Run: The Lawrencia Bembenek Story
NBC (US) 1993 dir. Sandor Stern

Woman with a Sword
Noble, H.
Drums in the Deep South
RKO (GB) 1952
dir. William Cameron Menzies

Woman's Place, A
Delinsky, B.
Custody of the Heart
HEARST (US) 2000 dir. David Jones

Women, The
Boothe, C.
Opposite Sex, The
MGM (US) 1956 dir. David Miller

Wonderful Wizard of Oz, The
Baum, L. F.
Wiz, The
DISNEY (US) 1978 dir. Sidney Lumet

Wonderful Wizard of Oz, The
Baum, L. F.
Wizard of Oz, The
MGM (US) 1939 dir. Victor Fleming

World In My Pocket, The
Chase, J. H.
On Friday at 11
BL (Ger/Fr/It) 1961 dir. Alvin Rakoff

Wrecker, The
Ridley, A. and Merivale, B.
Seven Sinners
GAU (GB) 1937 dir. Albert de Courville
US title: Doomed Cargo

Wrong Venus, The
Williams, C.
Don't Just Stand There
UN (US) 1967 dir. Ron Winston

Wyatt Earp, Frontier Marshall
Lake, S.
Frontier Marshall
FOX (US) 1933 dir. Lew Seiler
FOX (US) 1939 dir. Allan Dwan

Wyatt Earp, Frontier Marshal
Lake, S.
My Darling Clementine
FOX (US) 1946 dir. John Ford

X vs Rex
MacDonald, P.
Hour of Thirteen, The
MGM (GB) 1952 dir. Harold French

X vs. Rex
MacDonald, P.
Mystery of Mr. X, The
MGM (US) 1934 dir. Edgar Selwyn

X-Rated: The Mitchell Brothers, a True Story of Sex, Money and Death
McCumder, D.
Rated X
BERG/MARCIL (US) 2000 dir. Emilio Estevez

Xiao, Xiao
Congwen, S.
Girl from Hunan, The
CHINA (China) 1986 dir. Xie Fei, U Lan

... Y No Se Lo Trago La Tierra
Rivera, T.
... And the Earth Did Not Swallow Him
AM PLAY (US) 1995 dir. Severo Perez

Yea, Yea, Yea
McGill, A.
Press for Time
RANK (GB) 1966 dir. Robert Asher

Year of the Angry Rabbit, The
Braddon, R.
Night of the Lepus
MGM (US) 1972 dir. William F. Claxton

Year of the Big Cat, The
Dietz, L.
Return of the Big Cat
DISNEY (US) 1974 dir. Tom Leetch

Year of the Horse, The
Hatch, E.
Horse in the Grey Flannel Suit, The
DISNEY (US) 1968 dir. Norman Tokar

Year the Yankees Lost the Pennant, The
Wallop, D.
Damn Yankees
WAR (US) 1958 dir. George Abbott, Stanley Donen
GB title: What Lola Wants

Years Ago
Gordon, R.
Actress, The
MGM (US) 1953 dir. George Cukor

Years Are So Long, The
Lawrence, J.
Make Way for Tomorrow
PAR (US) 1937 dir. Leo McCarey

Yekl
Cahen, A.
Hester Street
CONN (US) 1975
dir. Joan Micklin Silver

Yellowleg
Fleischman, A. S.
Deadly Companions, The
WAR (US) 1961 dir. Sam Peckinpah

Yentl, the Yeshiva Boy
Singer, I. B.
Yentl
MGM/UA (US) 1983
dir. Barbra Streisand

Yeoman's Hospital
Ashton, H.
White Corridors
GFD (GB) 1951 dir. Pat Jackson

You Must be Dreaming
Noel, B. and Watterson, K.
Betrayal of Trust
COS-MEU (US) 1994 dir. George
Kaczender

Young Apollo
Gibbs, A. H.
Men of Tomorrow
PAR (GB) 1932 dir. Leontine Sagan

Young Archimedes
Huxley, A. L.
Prelude to Fame
GFD (GB) 1950 dir. Fergus McDonell

Young Manhood of Studs Lonigan, The
Farrell, J. T.
Studs Lonigan
UA (US) 1960 dir. Irving Lerner
LORIMAR (US) 1979
dir. James Goldstone

You're Best Alone
Curtis, P.
Guilt is my Shadow
ABP (GB) 1950 dir. Roy Kellino

You're Only Human Once
Moore, G.
So This is Love
WAR (US) 1953 dir. Gordon Douglas
GB title: Grace Moore Story, The

Your Arkansas Traveller
Schulberg, B. W.
Face in the Crowd, A
WAR (US) 1957 dir. Elia Kazan

Youth at the Helm
Vulpuis, P.
Jack of all Trades
GAINS (GB) 1936 dir. Jack Hubert,
Robert Stevenson

Zapata the Unconquerable
Pinchon, E.

Viva Zapata!
FOX (US) 1952 dir. Elia Kazan

Zooman and the Sign
Fuller, C.

Zooman
SHOWTIMEWORKS (US) 1995 dir.
Leon Ichaso

MUSICALS INDEX

MADE-FOR-TV INDEX:
— FILMS, MINISERIES AND SERIALS —

Dream West
Dress Gray
Drug Wars: The Camarena Story
Drug Wars: The Cocaine Cartel
Dubai
Dune
Dwelling Place, The
Eagle of the Ninth
Early Life of Stephen Hind, The
East of Eden
Echoes
Echoes in the Darkness
Edward & Mrs Simpson
Eleanor Marx
Eleanor of Franklin
Elidor
Ellis Island
Elvis and Me
Emlyn's Moon
Emma
Emma: Queen of the South Seas
Enchanted Castle, The
Esther Waters
Evening in Byzantium
Evergreen
Executioner's Song, The
Eyeless in Gaza
Fair Stood the Wind for France
Fall From Grace
Falling for a Dancer
False Arrest
Fame is the Spur
Family Album
Family Pictures
Family of Spies
Fanny by Gaslight
Far from the Madding Crowd
Far Pavilions, The
Fatal Inversion, A
Fatal Vision
Father Brown, Detective
Fathers and Sons
Favourite Son
Feast of All Saints, The
Final Cut, The

First Among Equals
First Born
Five Children And It
Five Red Herrings
Flambards
Flame Trees of Thika, The
Flesh and Blood
Flight of the Heron, The
For the Term of his Natural Life
Ford: The Man and the Machine
Forsyte Saga, The
Fortunate Pilgrim, The
Fortunes and Misfortunes of Moll
    Flanders, The
Fortunes of Nigel, The
Fortunes of War
Franchise Affair, The
Frankenstein: The True Story
Frankie's House
Free Frenchman, The
Freedom Road
French Atlantic Affair, The
From the Dead of Night
From the Earth to the Moon
From Here to Eternity
Frost in May
Further Tales of the City
Gallowglass
Gambler, The
Gambling Man, The
Game, Set and Match
Gaudy Night
George Wallace
George Washington
George Washington II: The Forging
    of a Nation
Germinal
Gift, The
Ginger Tree, The
Girls of Slender Means, The
Glass Virgin, The
Goggle Eyes
Golden Bowl, The
Gone in the Night
Good Behaviour

Lady Chatterley
Lady of the Camellias, The
Langoliers, The
Last Convertible, The
Last Days of Pompeii, The
Last Don, The
Last of the Mohicans, The
Last Place on Earth, The
Late Call
Legacy, A
Life and Adventures of Nicholas
   Nickleby, The
Life with Judy Garland: Me and My
   Shadows
Life and Loves of a She-Devil, The
Life and Times of Henry Pratt, The
Limbo Connection, The
Little Gloria … Happy at Last
Little Lord Fauntleroy
Little Princess, The
Little Sir Nicholas
Little Women
London Belongs to Me
Lonesome Dove
Long, Hot Summer, The
Longitude
Look at it this Way
Looking for Clancy
Loose Change
Lorna Doone
Lost Empire, The
Lost Empires
Louisiana
Love Among the Artists
Love and Betrayal: The Mia Farrow
   Story
Love on a Branch Line
Love in a Cold Climate
Love and Hate: A Marriage Made in
   Hell
Love, Honor & Obey: The Last
   Mafia Marriage
Love for Lydia
Love and Mr Lewisham
Lucky Chances

Machine Gunners, The
Mad Death, The
Madame Bovary
Maidens' Trip
Malibu
Malice Aforethought
Mallens, The
Mama Flora's Family
Man Called Intrepid, A
Man of Straw
Man Who Lived at The Ritz, The
Mansfield Park
Mapp and Lucia
Marilyn: The Untold Story
Marksman, The
Married Man, A
Martian Chronicles, The
Martin Chuzzlewit
Masada
Maschenka
M*A*S*H
Master of Ballantrae, The
Master of the Game
Master of the Moor
Mayor of Casterbridge, The
Medusa's Child
Memories of Midnight
Men's Room, The
Middlemarch
Mill on the Floss, The
Misérables, Les
Mistral's Daughter
Mists of Avalon, The
Moby Dick
Mog
Moll Flanders
Moment in Time, A
Moneychangers, The
Monocled Mutineer, The
Monte Carlo
Moondial
Moonfleet
Moonstone, The
More Tales of the City
Mother Love

War and Remembrance
Washington: Behind Closed Doors
Watch House, The
Water Babies, The
Waterfall, The
Way We Live Now, The
We, The Accused
Wedding, The
Weir of Hermiston
Wheels
When Love Kills: The Seduction of
    John Hearn
White Peak Farm
Who, Sir? Me, Sir?
Whose Baby?
Why Didn't They Ask Evans?
Wild Justice
Wild Times
Will of Their Own, A
Wimbledon Prisoner, The
Windmills of the Gods
Winds of War, The
Winston Churchill – The Wilderness
    Years

Witch's Daughter, The
Wives and Daughters
Wolf to the Slaughter
Woman Called Moses, A
Woman of Independent Means, A
Woman Named Jackie, A
Woman on the Run: The Lawrencia
    Bembenek Story
Woman of Substance, A
Woman in White, The
Woman's Guide to Adultery, A
Women of Brewster Place, The
Women in White
Women's Room, The
Woodlanders, The
Woodstock
Woof
Word, The
Wuthering Heights
Wynne and Penkovsky
Year in Provence, A
Yellowthread Street
Zastrozzi
Zoya

ANIMATED FILMS INDEX

ABBREVIATED PRODUCTION AND
— DISTRIBUTION COMPANY NAMES —

21ST CENTURY	21st Century Film
40 ACRES	40 Acres & a Mule
A & E	Arts & Entertainment
A & E PICT PAL	A & E Picture Palace
A & M	A & M Films
AA	Anglo-American
AAL	Anglo-Allied
AAM	Anglo Amalgamated
AB	Associated British
ABC	ABC Circle Films
ABC PICT	ABC Pictures
ABC PROD	ABC Productions
ACCENT	Accent Films
ACCENT ENT	Accent Entertainment
ACI	American Communications Industries
ADAM	Adam Productions
ADDED	Added Entertainment
ADELSON	Adelson Entertainment
AFC	Australian Film Commission
AFFC	Australian Film Finance Corporation
AFT	American Film Theatre
AGAMEMNON	Agamemnon Films
AGAV	AGAV Films
AIP	American International Productions
AIRSPEED	Airspeed Productions
ALAMEDA	Alameda Films
ALB	Albatross
ALBERTA	Alberta Filmworks
ALEPH	Aleph Productions
ALIA	Alia Film
ALIVE	Alive Films
ALL AM TV	All American TV
ALLIANCE	Alliance Communications
ALLIANCE IND	Alliance Industries
ALLIED	Allied Artists
ALLTIME	Alltime Entertainment
ALMARO	Almaro Film
ALMERICA	Almerica Film
ALTUBE	Altube Films
AM PLAY	American Playhouse
AM WORLD	American World Pictures
AM ZOETROPE	American Zoetrope
AMBLIN	Amblin Entertainment

AMBROCO	Ambroco Media Group
AMIS	Amis Media
AMW	Atlantic Media Works
ANGELIKA	Angelika Films
ANGLE	Angle Films
ANGLIA	Anglia Television
AP	Adams Packer
APRIL	April Productions
ARABA	Araba Films
ARABESQUE	Arabesque Productions
ARENA	Arena Films
ARG SONO	Argentine Sono
ARIANE	Ariane Filmes
ARIEL	Ariel Productions
ARIZTICAL	Ariztical Entertainment
ART EYE	Artificial Eye Film
ARTCO	Artcofilm
ARTE FRANCE	Arte France Cinema
ARTHOUSE	Arthouse Films
ARTISAN	Artisan Entertainment
ARTISTIC	Artistic License
ASKA	Aska Film
ASMIK	Asmik Ace Entertainment
ASTRAL	Astral Films
AT	AT Films
ATLANTIC	Atlantic Entertainment
ATLANTIS	Atlantis Films
ATLAS	Atlas Productions
ATRIUM	Atrium Productions
AUS	Australia Television
AVALON	Avalon Films
AVCO	AVCO Embassy
AVE PICT	Avenue Pictures
AVENUE	Avenue Entertainment
AVNET	Avnet/Kerner
AVV	Atlantic Video Ventures
AZTECA	Azteca Films
B & E	Barry and Enright
B & W	Bread & Water
B. CROSBY	Bing Crosby Productions
BA	BA Film Production
BABELSBERG	Studio Babelsberg
BAC	Bac Films
BAKER	Baker Film
BANDEIRA	Bandeira Entertainment
BANNER	Banner Associates
BANNER ENT	Banner Entertainment
BANON	Banon Films
BAR PON	Barbachano Ponce
BAR-GENE	Bar-Gene Productions
BARRON	Barron Films
BAVERIA	Baveria Film
BAYSIDE	Bayside Pictures
BBC	British Broadcasting Corporation

BBK	BBK Productions
BBS	BBS Productions
BCB	BCB Productions
BEACON	Beacon Pictures
BEIJING	Beijing Film Studios
BEIJING SALON	Beijing Salon Films
BERG/MARCIL	Berg/Marcil Productions
BERL	Berlusconi Communications
BET	Bet Pictures
BEYOND	Beyond Films
BEYOND DIST	Beyond Distributors
BFI	BFI Productions
BI	British International
BL	British Lion Productions
BLAIR	Blair Entertainment
BLATT	Daniel Blatt Productions
BLEECKER	Bleecker Street Film
BLUE DAHLIA	Blue Dahlia Productions
BLUE DOLPHIN	Blue Dolphin Films
BMG	BMG Independents
BN	British National
BOGEAUS	Benedict Bogeaus
BORDEAUX	Bordeaux Films
BOYD	Boyd's Co. Film Productions
BPG	Bonneville Producers Group
BR	Bayerischer Rundfunk
BRANDMAN	Brandman Productions
BRAU	Braunberger-Richebe
BRIT SCREEN	British Screen
BRUT	Brut Productions
BUXTON	Buxton Films
BW	Brent Walker Films
C. ANDERSON	Craig Anderson Productions
C. GREGG	Colin Gregg
CABRIOLET	Cabriolet Films
CAGNEY	Cagney Productions
CALEDONIA	Caledonia Pictures
CANAN	Canan Films
CANNELL	Stephen J. Cannell Productions
CANNON	Cannon Films
CAPITOL	Capitol Films
CAPRICORNE	Capricorne Productions
CAPSTONE	Capstone Films
CARLINER	Mark Carliner Productions
CAROLCO	Carolco Pictures
CAROUSEL	Carousel Pictures
CARSON	Carson Productions
CASTLE HILL	Castle Hill Productions
CATFISH	Catfish Productions
CBC	Canadian Broadcasting Corporation
CBP	CBP Productions
CBS	CBS Productions
CBS ENT	CBS Entertainment
CCC	CCC Filmkunst

CDP	Central de Producciones
CECCHI	Cecchi Gori Group
CEDAR GROVE	Cedar Grove Productions
CENT	Centurion
CENTRAL	Central Independent Television
CENTRE EURO	Centre Europeen
CESK	Ceskoslovensky Film
CH ELYSEE	Champs Elysée
CHANNEL 4	Channel Four Television
CHANNEL 4 FILMS	Channel Four Films
CHILMARK	Chilmark Productions
CHINA	China Film
CHRIS/ROSE	Chris/Rose Productions
CHRYSALIDE	Chrysalide Film
CHRYS-YELL	Chrysallis-Yellen
CIN	Cineguild
CIN CEN	Cinema Center
CIN INT	Cinema International
CIN IT	Cinema Italia
CIN WORLD	Cinema World
CINA	Cina del Duca
CINECOM	Cinecom International Films
CINEMA	Cinema Group
CINEQUEST	Cinequest Films
CINETEL	Cinetel Films
CINETV	Cinetelevision
CINEVIA	Cinevia Films
CITADEL ENT	Citadel Entertainment
CITE	Cite Films
CLASSIC	Classic Cinemas
CLESI	Clesi Cinematografica
CODO	Codo-Cinema
COL	Columbia Pictures
COMM	Commonwealth
COMMOTION	Commotion Pictures
COMPASS	Compass Film Productions
COMWORLD	Comworld Productions
CONCORDE	Concorde Pictures
CONN	Connoisseur
CONSOL	Consolidated Entertainment
CONSTANTIN	Constantin Films
CONT	Continental
CONTEM	Contemporary
CORAPEAKE	Corapeake Productions
CORONA	Films Corona
CORSAIR	Corsair Pictures
COS-MEU	Cosgrove-Meurer Productions
COSTADO	Costado Castelo Filmes
COVERT	Covert Creative
CRAWFORD	Crawford Productions
CREATIVE	Creative Entertainment Group
CREDO	Credo Entertainment
CRESCENT	Crescent Entertainment
CROMWELL	Cromwell Productions

CUEVANO	Cuevano Films
CURTIS	Curtis Productions
CURTIS LOWE	Curtis Lowe Productions
CYCLONE	Cyclone Productions
CYPRESS	Cypress Films
D. BROWN	David Brown Productions
D. CLARK	Dick Clark Productions
D. WICKES	David Wickes Productions
D. WILSON	Daniel Wilson Productions
D. WOLPER	David Wolper Productions
DAIEI	Daiei Films
DAN FI	Danish Film Institute
DANIA	Dania Film
DASKA	DASKA Films
DAVIS	Davis Entertainment
DAZU	Dazu Films
DD	DD Productions
DE PASSE	De Passe Entertainment
DEAN	Dean Film
DEE GEE	Dee Gee Entertainment
DEFINITIVE	Definitive Films
DELAUR	DeLaurentiis
DELTA	Delta Entertainment
DEWARR	Dewarrenne Pictures
DIMENSION	Dimension Films
DIRECTORS' CIRCLE	Directors' Circle Filmworks
DISNEY	Disney Productions
DISNEY CH	Disney Channel
DLT	DLT Entertainment
DMVB	DMVB Films
DOVE ENT	Dove Entertainment
DRAGON	Dragon Pictures
DURNIOK	Durniok Productions
DVC	DVC Entertainment
E!	E! Entertainment TV
E. DALTON	Emmet Dalton
E. J. SCHERICK	Edgar J. Scherick Productions
EAL	Ealing
ECLIPSE	Eclipse Films
ECRAN	Ecran Français
EGG	Egg Pictures
EL	Eagle Lion
EL DORADO	El Dorado Pictures
ELEC. CON	Electric Concepts
ELECTIRC	Electric Pictures
EMBASSY	Embassy Films
EMCEE	Emcee Films
EMI	EMI Films
ENGLEWOOD	Englewood Entertainment
ENGLUND	George Englund Entertainment
ENIGMA	Enigma Productions
ENT	Enterprise
ENT PAR	Entertainment Partners
ERATO	Erato Films

ESPARZA	Esparza/Katz Productions
EUROAM	Euroamerican Films
EUROLUX	Eurolux Productions
EUROPEAN	European Classics
EUSTON	Euston Films
EVEREST	Everest Entertainment
EVOLUTION	Evolution Entertainment
EVOLVE	Evolve Entertainment
EXCALIBUR	Excalibur Films
EXCL	Exclusive
FAC-NEW	Factor-Newland Productions
FAMILY	Family Productions
FANES	Fanes Film
FCI	Film Communication Incorporated
FDF	Films de France
FERNDALE	Ferndale Films
FF	Film Forum
FILERMAN	Filerman Productions
FILMLINE	Filmline International
FILMLINK	Filmlink International
FILMOVE	Filmove Studio
FINN	Finn Kimo
FINNEGAN	Finnegan Associates
FIRST	First Artists
FIRST HAND	First Hand Films
FIRST IND	First Independent
FIRST RUN	First Run Features
FIRST STANDARD	First Standard Media
FLORA	Flora Films
FNM	FNM Films
FOCUS	Focus film
FOGWOOD	Fogwood Films
FONDA	Fonda Film
FONTANA	Fontana Film
FOR-PAR	Forrestier-Parant
FOUR POINT	Four Point Entertainment
FOX	20th Century Fox
FOX CIRCLE	Fox Circle Productions
FOX WEST	Fox West Pictures
FOXTAIL	Foxtail Productions
FRANCE 2	France 2 Cinema
FRANCE 3	France 3 Cinema
FRANCHISE	Franchise Pictures
FREEDOM	Freedom Productions
FREEWAY	Freeway Films
FREEWAY PROD	Freeway Productions
FRIENDLY	Fred Friendly Productions
FRIES	Charles Fries Entertainment
FRIES PROD	Charles Fries Productions
FULL MOON	Full Moon Entertainment
G. REEVES	Geoff Reeves
GAINS	Gainsborough
GALAXY	Galaxy International
GALLANT	Gallant Entertainment

GAU	Gaumont
GAU BR	Gaumont British
GAYLORD	Gaylord Productions
GEFFEN	Geffen Pictures
GEMINI	Gemini Films
GEMMY	Gemmy Productions
GFD	General Film Distributors
GIBE	Films Gibe
GIDEON	Gideon Productions
GIL/HILL	Gilbert/Hill Films
GINIS	Ginis Film
GLAZIER	Glazier Productions
GLOBO	Globo Filmas
GLOBUS	Globus Film Studio
GLORIA	Gloria Productions
GMS	GMS Productions
GMT	GMT Productions
GN	Grand National
GOLCHAN/HILL	Golchan Productions/Leonard Hill Films
GOLDCREST	Goldcrest Films and Television
GOLDEN EYE	Golden Eye Films
GOLDEN FLARE	Golden Flare Films
GOLDEN SQ	Golden Square Pictures
GOLDHEART	Goldheart Pictures
GOLDHIL	Goldhil Home Media
GOLDSMITH	Goldsmith Entertainment
GOLDWYN	Samuel Goldwyn Productions
GOODYEAR	Goodyear Movie Company
GORDON	Gordon Films
GORKY	Gorky Film Studios
GOTHAM	Gotham Entertainment
GOYA	Goya Film
GRAMERCY	Gramercy Pictures
GRANADA	Granada Television
GRAND	Grand Productions
GREEN-EPSTEIN	Green-Epstein Productions
GREENLIGHT	Greenlight Productions
GREENWALD	Robert Greenwald Productions
GREEN-WHITE	Green-White Productions
GREYCAT	Greycat Films
GREYSTONE	Greystone Films
GROSS/BAR	Grossbart/Barnett Productions
GROSSO-JACOB	Grosso-Jacobson Entertainment
GRUZIA	Gruziafilm
GT FALLS	Great Falls Productions
GT SCOTT	Great Scott Productions
GT UNION	Greater Union Distributors
GUBER-PETERS	Guber-Peters Entertainment
GUERILLA	Guerilla Films
H. JAFFE	Henry Jaffe Entertainment
H. ROACH	Hal Roach Studios
HAGER MOSS	Hager Moss Film
HAJENO	Hajeno Productions
HALLMARK	Hallmark Hall of Fame

HALMI	Robert Halmi Productions
HAMDON	Hamdon Entertainment
HAMILTON	Hamilton Productions
HAMMER	Hammer Film Productions
HANDMADE	HandMade Films
HANNA-BARBERA	Hanna-Barbera Productions
HANNIBAL	Hannibal Films
HARDWORK	Hardwork Productions
HARLECH	Harlech Television
HARMONY	Harmony Gold
HARPO	Harpo Films
HBO	HBO Pictures
HBO PREM	HBO Premiere
HBO SHOW	HBO Showcase
HEARST	Hearst Entertainment
HEMDALE	Hemdale Film
HERA	Hera International
HERMES	Hermes Film Studios
HIGH	High Productions
HIGH TIMES	High Times Pictures
HIGHGATE	Highgate Pictures
HILL	Hill Films
HILL-FIELDS	Hill-Fields Entertainment
HODCARRIER	Hodcarrier Films
HOLLYWOOD	Hollywood Pictures
HORIZON	Horizon Films
HOTWIRE	Hotwire Productions
HOUSEHOLD	Household Entertainment
HUN	Hungarofilm
HYP	Hyperion
I. ALLEN	Irwin Allen Productions
IA	Independent Artists
ICON	Icon Entertainment
IFC	IFC Productions
IFEX	International Film Exchange
IGUANA	Iguana Films
ILLUMINATION	Illumination Films
IMAGE	Image Forum
IMAGINE	Imagine Films
IMAGINE ENT	Imagine Entertainment
IMP	Independent Moving Productions
INCA	Inca Films
INCITO	Incito Productions
INDEPENDENT	Independent Television
INDIAN NECK	Indian Neck Entertainment
INGRID	Ingrid Productions
INITIAL	Initial Productions
INNER CIRCLE	Inner Circle Films
INTEGRAL	Integral Films
INTERPLAN	Interplanetary Productions
INTERSCOPE	Interscope Communications
INTERSOUND	Produzioni Intersound
INVISIBLE	Invisible Studio
ION	Ion Productions

ION PICT	Ion Pictures
IPC	IPC Films
IRISH	Irish Films
IS	International Spectrafilm
ISLAND	Island Films
ISLAND PICT	Island Pictures
ITC	ITC Entertainment
IXTLAN	Ixtlan Productions
J & M	J & M Films
J & M ENT	J & M Entertainment
J. AVNET	Jon Avnet
J. FARLEY	Jensen Farley Pictures
J. HAMILTON	Joe Hamilton Productions
JAFFE/BRAU	Jaffe/Braunstein Films
JAGGED	Jagged Films
JBS	JBS Productions
JD	JD Productions
JERAND	Jerand Films
JET	Jet Films
JET TONE	Jet Tone Productions
JML	JML Productions
JOLLY	Jolly Films
JONES	Jones Entertainment Group
JOURNEY	Journey Entertainment
JUPITER	Jupiter films
JUST SINGER	Just Singer Entertainment
K. BRIGHT	Kevin Bright Productions
KARDANA	Kardana Films
KASSENDER	K. Kassender
KD	K. D. Productions
KEL	Kendai Eiga Lyokai
KEY	Key Pictures
KEY ENT	Key Entertainment
KILLER	Killer films
KINETIC	Kinetic Productions
KING GREENLIGHT	Kingsborough Greenlight
KING PHOENIX	King Phoenix Entertainment
KINGDOM	Kingdom Come Pictures
KING-HITZIG	King-Hitzig Productions
KON-SAN	Konigsberg-Sanitsky Productions
KRANTZ	Steve Krantz Productions
KUSHNER-LOCKE	Kushner-Locke Productions
L HILL	Leonard Hill Films
L. PERSKY	Lester Persky Productions
L. THOMPSON	Larry Thompson Organization
LA BOETIE	Films la Boetie
LA TOUR	Films de la Tour
LAA	Les Artistes Associés
LAE	Laetitia
LAMBART	Lambart Productions
LAMBERT	Lambert Productions
LAN	Lansburg
LANTANA	Lantana Productions
LARGO	Largo Entertainment

LAUGH KOOK	Laughing Kookaburra
LAUREL	Laurel Productions
LAUREL ENT	Laurel Entertainment
LAUREN	Lauren Film Production
LAURENTIC	Laurentic Film
LC	Leader Cinematografica
LCA	LCA Productions
LEE RICH	Lee Rich Productions
LEWIS	Lewis Productions
LEX	Lexington Films
LF	London Film Productions
LIFETIME	Lifetime Productions
LIN OLIVER	Lin Oliver Productions
LIONS GATE	Lions Gate Productions
LIVING	Living Films
LONDON SCR	London Screenplays
LONG SHONG	Long Shong Pictures
LONGBOW	Longbow Productions
LORIMAR	Lorimar Telepictures
LUCCHESI	Gary Lucchesi Productions
LUMIERE	Lumiere Pictures
LUNACY	Lunacy Productions
LWT	London Weekend Television
LYLA	Lyla Films
LYTTLE	Lyttle Productions
M & R	M & R Films
M. ARCH	Marble Arch
M. EVANS	Maurice Evans Productions
M. POLL	Martin Poll Productions
M. R. JOYCE	Michael R. Joyce Productions
M. REES	Marion Rees Associates
M. ROBE	Mike Robe Productions
M. SIMON	Michel Simon
M2	M2 Films
M6	M6 Films
MACT	Mact Productions
MAGLI	Franco Magli
MAGNOLIA	Magnolia Productions
MAINLINE	Mainline Films
MAJ	Majestic
MAJADE	Majade Film
MAK	Makara Pictures
MALTESE	Maltese Productions
MANDALEY	Mandalay Entertainment
MANDARIN	Mandarin Films
MANDY	Mandy Films
MARANO	Marano Productions
MARCEAU	Films Marceau
MARGULIES	Stan Margulies Productions
MARS	Mars Film
MARSTAR	Marstar Productions
MARTINES	Martines Productions
MAX	Max Films
MAXI MUM	Maximum Vacuum

MAY-SEW	Maynard-Sewell
MB DIFF	MB Diffusion
MEDUSA	Medusa Productions
MELANDA	Melanda Film Productions
MERIDIAN	Meridian Broadcasting
MERIDIAN ENT	Meridian Entertainment
MESSIDOR	Messidor Films
METHOD	Method Films
METRODOME	Metrodome Films
METROMEDIA	Metromedia Producers
METROPOLIS	Metropolis Film
MH	MH Film
MI	Merchant-Ivory
MINERVA	Minerva International
MIQ	Mallard-Impact-Quadrant
MIRACLE	Miracle Films
MIRACLE PICT	Miracle Pictures
MIRAGE	Mirage Entertainment
MIRAMAX	Miramax Films
MITCHUM	Mitchum Entertainment
MK2	MK2 Productions
MKT ST	Market St Productions
MON	Monogram
MONA	Mona Productions
MONASH-ZEIT	Monash-Zeitman Productions
MONTROSE	Montrose Pictures
MONTY	Monty Film
MONUMENT	Monument Pictures
MOONLIGHT	Moonlight film
MOONSTONE	Moonstone Entertainment
MOORE-WEISS	Moore-Weiss Productions
MORENA	Morena Filmes
MOSAIC	Mosaic Group
MOSFILM	Moscow Films
MOTION	Motion International
MOTOWN	Motown Productions
MTM	MTM Enterprises
MULTIMEDIA	Multimedia Motion Pictures
MULTIMEDIA ENT	Multimedia Entertainment
MULTIMEDIA PROD	Multimedia Productions
MUNCHEN	Filmhaus Munchen
MUSE	Muse Productions
MUSE ENT	Muse Entertainment
MUSHIKUKI	Mushikuki Productions
MUTUAL	Mutual Films International
MWL	Myung-Won Lee
N. TWAIN	Norman Twain Productions
NAUTILUS	Nautilus Films
NBC	NBC Productions
NBC ENT	NBC Entertainment
NC	Nieue Constantin
NED	Nederlander
NEF	Nouvelles Editions de Film
NEPHI-HAMNER	Nephi-Hamner Productions

NERO	Nero Films
NEUE STUDIO	Neue Studio Film
NEW AMSTERDAM	New Amsterdam Entertainment
NEW CITY	New City Releasing
NEW CITY PROD	New City Productions
NEW CRIME	New Crime Productions
NEW IMAGES	New Images Productions
NEW KWUN LUN	New Kwun Lun Films
NEW LINE	New Line Cinema
NEW REGENCY	New Regency
NEW YORKER	New Yorker Films
NEWFELD-KEATING	Newfeld-Keating Productions
NEWLAND-RAYNOR	Newland-Raynor Productions
NFC	National Film Corporation
NFM	Nationale Filmproductie Maatschapp
NG	National General
NGL	National General Lectures
NI	Nouvelle Imagerie
NICKI	Nicki Film Productions
NITRATE	Nitrate Film
NORD	Nordisk Tonefilm
NORDISK	Nordisk Films
NORDS	Nordsjfilm
NORSK	Norsk Film
NORSTAR	Norstar Entertainment
NORTHERN	Northern Arts Entertainment
NORTHWOOD	Northwood Pixtures
NRW	NRW Features
NSW	New South Wales Film
NZ FILM	NZ Film Group
O'HARA-HORO	O'Hara-Horowitz Productions
OCTOBER	October Films
ODEON	Odeon Films
OFELIA	Ofelia Films
OFF THE GRID	Off the Grid Productions
OFFLINE	Offline Entertainment
OHYLMEYER	Ohylmeyer Communications
OKO	Oko Film
OLGA	Olga Film
OMEGA	Omega Project
OMNIBUS	Omnibus Productions
OPT	Operation Prime Time
ORION	Orion Pictures
ORLY	Orly Films
ORSANS	Orsans Productions
OSHIMA	Oshima Productions
OTHER	The Other Cinema
OVERSEAS	Overseas Filmgroup
P & G	Procter and Gamble Productions
P. CLIFFORD	Patricia Clifford Productions
P. MAIN	Percy Main
PA	Producer Associates
PAGNOL	Marcel Pagnol
PALACE	Palace Productions

PALLADIO	Palladio Film
PALM	Palm Productions
PALOMAR	Palomar Productions
PAN	Panavision
PANORAMA	Panorama Entertainment
PANTER	Panter Film
PANTHEON	Pantheon Productions
PAPAZIAN	Papazian Productions
PAPAZIAN-HIRSCH	Papazian-Hirsch Entertainment
PAR	Paramount Pictures
PARADIS	Paradis Films
PARAGON	Paragon Entertainment
PARALLEL	Parallel Film
PARIS	Paris Films
PASSAGE	Les Films du Passage
PATCHETT-KAUFMAN	Patchett-Kaufman Entertainment
PATHE	Pathe News
PATRIOT	Patriot Pictures
PAVILION	Pavilion Films
PBC	Pandora-Beijing-China Film
PBL	PBL Australia
PC	Production Cienematografiche
PDC	Producers Distribution Company
PEARSON	Pearson TV International
PEBBLEHUT	Pebblehut Productions
PEG	Producers Entertainment Group
PEL	Pelemele
PEMBRIDGE	Pembridge Films
PENELOPE	Penelope Film
PEOPLES	Peoples Productions
PER HOLST	Per Holst Film
PEREGRINE	Peregrine Entertainment
PHAEDRA	Phaedra Cinema
PHOENIX	Phoenix Entertainment
PHOENIX PICT	Phoenix Pictures
PLAYBOY	Playboy Productions
PLEIADE	Films de la Pleiade
PLOT	Plot Films
POLARIS	Polaris Pictures
POLL	Poll Productions
POLSKI	Film Polski
POLSON	Polson Compnay
POPULIST	Populist Pictures
PORTMAN	Portman Productions
PORTMAN ENT	Portman Entertainment
PORTOBELLO	Portobello Pictures
POV	Point of View Productions
POWER	Power Pictures
PRAHA	Filmu Praha
PRAIRIE	Prairie Pictures
PRESIDENT	President Films
PRICE ENT	Price Entertainment
PRIMEDIA	Primedia Productions
PRIMETIME	Primetime Television

PRISM	Prism Pictures
PRISM ENT	Prism Entertainment
PROJECTOR	Projector Pictures
PROM	Prometheus
PROMARK	Promark Entertainment
PROPAGANDA	Propaganda Films
PROV	Providence Films
PSO	Producers Sales Organization
PUNCH	Punch Productions
PUNCH 21	Punch 21 Productions
PYRAMIDE	Pyramide Productions
Q. MARTIN	Quinn Martin
QINTEX	Qintex Entertainment
R. HUNTER	Ross Hunter Productions
RAB	Rabinovitch
RAFFORD	Rafford Films
RASTAR	Rastar Productions
RB	RB Films
RCV	RCV Film
READER'S DIG	Reader's Digest Entertainment
REEVE	Reeve and Partners Film
REGENCY	Regency Enterprises
REGENT	Regent Productions
REGENT ENT	Regent Entertainment
REGINA	Regina Films
REGNER	Regner Grasten
REN	Renown Pictures
RENAISSANCE	Renaissance Films
RENEGADE	Renegade Film
REP	Republic
RESCUED	Rescued Films
RHEA	Rhea Films
RHI	RHI Entertainment
RHOMBUS	Rhombus Media
RIVER CITY	River City Productions
RIVER ONE	River One Productions
RKO	RKO Productions International
RLC	RLC Productions
ROCKET	Rocket Pictures
ROLL	Roll Film
ROME-PARIS	Rome-Paris Films
ROSEMONT	Rosemont Productions
ROUGH TRADE	Rough Trade Pictures
ROYAL	Royal Film
RPC	Recorded Picture Company
RSO	RSO Films
RYSHER	Rysher Entertainment
S. AUST	South Australia Film Corporation
SABAN	Saban Productions
SABAN ENT	Saban Entertainment
SACKS	Alan Sacks Productions
SAG	Sagittarius
SAMSON	Samson Films
SAMUELS	Samuels Productions

SANDS	Sands Films
SASCH WIEN	Sasch Wien Films
SAVOY	Savoy pictures
SCALA	Scala Productions
SCALERA	Scalera Films
SCHERICK	Edgar Scherick Associates
SCHICK SUNN	Schick Sunn Classics
SCHLEMMER	Schlemmer Film
SCHOLAR	Scholar Productions
SCHOOLFIELD	Schoolfield Productions
SCIMITAR	Scimitar Films
SCOTTI	Scotti Brothers
SCOUT	Scout Productions
SCREEN	Screen Partners
SCREEN ENT	Screen Entertainment
SCRIPPS HOWARD	Scripps Howard Entertainment
SEGAL/NASSO	Seagal/Nasso Productions
SELF	Self Productions
SENATOR	Senator Films
SHADOW BOX	Shadow Box Films
SHAFTESBURY	Shaftesbury Film
SHALAKO	Shalako Entertainment
SHANGHAI	Shanghai Film
SHAPIRO	Shapiro Productions
SHOCHIKU	Shochiku-Fuji
SHONDEROSA	Shonderosa Productions
SHOWCASE	Showcase Entertainment
SIGMA	Sigma Film Productions
SIGNBOARD HILL	Signboard Hill Productions
SIMON	Simon Productions
SKOURAS	Skouras Pictures
SKYLINE	Skyline Entertainment
SM-HEM	Smith-Hemion
SOLO	Solo Productions
SORPASSO	Sorpasso Films
SOUTHERN	Southern Pictures
SPECTACOR/JAFFE	Spectacor/Jaffe Films
SPEL-GOLD	Spelling-Goldberg
SPELLING	Aaron Spelling Productions
SPRING CREEK	Spring Creek Productions
SQUARE	Square Pictures
STANDARD	Standard Film Trust
STERLING	Sterling Entertainment
STIGWOOD	Robert Stigwood
STILLMAN	Stillman International
STONE CANYON	Stone Canyon Entertainment
STONERIDGE	Stoneridge Entertainment
STORKE	Storke Productions
STP	STP International
STRAND	Strand Releasing
STUDIO	Studio Unit
STUDIO CANAL+	Le Studio Canal +
SULLIVAN	Sullivan Films
SULLIVAN ENT	Sullivan Entertainment

SVENSK	Svensk Film
SWE TV	Swedish TV
SYZYGY	Syzygy Productions
TAFT	Taft International
TALENT	Talent Associates
TALISMA	Talisma Productions
TAPESTRY	Tapestry Films
TAUBMAN	Taubman Entertainemnt
TAURUS	Taurus Entertainment
TAURUS 7	Taurus 7 Films
TBA	TBA Productions
TC	Two Cities
TCF	See FOX
TELECOM	Telecom Entertainment
TELECUL	Teleculture
TELEFILM	Telefilm Canada
TELEPIC	Telepictures
TELESCENE	Les Films Telescene
TELESCENE FG	Telescene Film Group
TELESCENE PROD	Telescene Productions
TELLESYN	Tellesyn Ty Helwick
TELSO	Telso International
TEMPLE	Temple Films
TEN-FOUR	Ten-Four Productions
TEVERE	Tevere Film
TEZUKA	Tezuka Productions
TF1	TF1 Films
THAMES	Thames Television
TIEMPE	Tiempe y Tono Films
TIME-LIFE	Time-Life Productions
TISCH	Steve Tisch
TISCH-AVNET	Tisch-Avnet Productions
TITUS	Titus Productions
TNT	Turner Network Television
TOKYO	Kinema Tokyo
TOM	Tomorrow Entertainment
TORNASOL	Tornasol Films
TOTAL	Total Film Group
TOUCHDOWN	Touchdown Films
TOWER	Tower Productions
TRANS	Transcontinental
TRANS WORLD	Trans World International
TRANSATLANTIC	Transatlantic Entertainment
TRILOGY	Trilogy Group
TRINITY	Trinity Pictures
TRISTAR	Tristar Pictures
TRITON	Triton Films
TRIUMPH	Triumph Enterprises
TROMA	Troma Films
TROPIC	Tropicfilm
TSF	TSF Productions
TTC	TTC Productions
TURNER	Turner Pictures
TURNER/BRANDMAN	Turner/Brandman Productions

TV4SWE	TV4Sweden
TVS	Television South
TYNE-TEES	Tyne-Tees Television
UA	United Artists
UGG	UGG/Images
UI	Universal International
ULYSSES	Ulysses Film
UN	Universal Studios
UNAPIX	Unapix Films
UPFRONT	Upfront Films
URBANWORLD	Urbanworld Films
UTOPIA	Utopia Productions
VCL	VCL Communications
VENDETTA	Vendetta Films
VER NED	Verenigde Nederlandsche
VH1	VH1 Productions
VI	Vision International
VIACOM	Viacom Productions
VIACOM PICT	Viacom Pictures
VICTORIA	Victoria Film
VIDEO	Videofilmes
VIEW	View Pictures
VILLAGE ROADSHOW	Village Roadshow Production
VINCENT	Vincent Pictures
VISTA	Vista Organization Productions
VZ/SAMUELS	Von Zerneck/Samuels Productions
VZ/SERTNER	Von Zerneck/Sertner Films
WA	World Artists
WANDA	Wanda Films
WANGER	Walter Wanger
WAR	Warner Brothers
WARDOUR	Wardour Motion Pictures
WEINTRAUB	Weintraub Productions
WESTCOM	Westcom Entertainment
WESTFALL	Westfall Productions
WESTGATE	Westgate Productions
WESTON	Weston Productions
WHITE	Steve White Productions
WI	World International Network
WIC	WIC Entertainment
WIL COURT	Wilshire Court Productions
WILDSTREET	Wildstreet Pictures
WILDWOOD	Wildwood Entertainment
WOLPER	Wolper Productions
WOODBRIDGE	Woodbridge Films
WORLD 2000	World 2000 Productions
WORLD WIDE	World Wide Films
WORLD WIDE PICT	World Wide Pictures
WORLDVISION	Worldvision Entertainment
XENON	Xenon Entertainment
YEE-HA	Yee-Ha Films
YEL	Yellowthread
YMC	YMC Productions
YORKTOWN	Yorktown Productions

YOSHA	Yosha Productions
YTV	Yorkshire Television
ZENITH	Zenith Productions
ZESPOL	Zespol Filmowy
ZOULOU	Zoulou Films